MAGIC AND WITCHCRAFT IN THE WEST

This book provides a thorough and interdisciplinary overview of the theory and practice of magic in the West in twenty chapters by experts in their fields. Its chronological scope extends from the Ancient Near East to twenty-first-century North America; its objects of analysis range from Persian curse tablets to U.S. Neopaganism. For comparative purposes, the volume includes chapters on developments in the Jewish and Muslim worlds, which are evaluated not simply for what they contributed at various points to European notions of magic but also as models of alternative development in the Mediterranean world. Similarly, the volume highlights the transformative and challenging encounters of Europeans with non-Europeans regarding the practice of magic in both early modern colonization and more recent decolonization.

DAVID J. COLLINS, S.J., is an associate professor of History at Georgetown University. His research has been supported by prestigious fellowships from the Charlotte Newcombe Foundation, the Alexander Humboldt Foundation, and the Gerda Henkel Foundation. He has published extensively on the medieval cult of the saints, Renaissance humanism, and learned magic, especially in central Europe. He is currently working on the reception of Albertus Magnus's teachings on magic in the Middle Ages and the early modern period.

THE CAMBRIDGE HISTORY OF
MAGIC AND WITCHCRAFT IN THE WEST

From Antiquity to the Present

★

Edited by

DAVID J. COLLINS, S.J.

Georgetown University

CAMBRIDGE
UNIVERSITY PRESS

CAMBRIDGE
UNIVERSITY PRESS

University Printing House, Cambridge CB2 8BS, United Kingdom

One Liberty Plaza, 20th Floor, New York, NY 10006, USA

477 Williamstown Road, Port Melbourne, VIC 3207, Australia

314-321, 3rd Floor, Plot 3, Splendor Forum, Jasola District Centre, New Delhi - 110025, India

79 Anson Road, #06-04/06, Singapore 079906

Cambridge University Press is part of the University of Cambridge.

It furthers the University's mission by disseminating knowledge in the pursuit of education, learning and research at the highest international levels of excellence.

www.cambridge.org
Information on this title: www.cambridge.org/9781108703079

First published 2015
First paperback edition 2018

A catalogue record for this publication is available from the British Library

Library of Congress Cataloging in Publication data
The Cambridge history of magic and witchcraft in the West : from antiquity to the present / edited by David J. Collins, S.J., Georgetown University, History Department.
pages   cm
Includes bibliographical references and index.
ISBN 978-0-521-19418-1 (hardback)
1. Magic – History.   2. Witchcraft – History.   I. Collins, David J., 1965–
BF1589.C28   2015
133.4′309–dc23   2014020960

ISBN 978-0-521-19418-1 Hardback
ISBN 978-1-108-70307-9 Paperback

Contents

Contents

Contents

PART VI

THE MODERN WEST

Notes on Contributors

MICHAEL D. BAILEY is a professor of History at Iowa State University in Ames. His research interests include medieval religious and cultural history; the history of magic, witchcraft, and superstition; and heresy and religious dissent. He recently published *Fearful Spirits, Reasoned Follies: The Boundaries of Superstition in Late Medieval Europe* (2013), which traces and analyzes Western thinking about superstition.

GIDEON BOHAK is an associate professor in the Departments of Hebrew Culture and Jewish Philosophy at Tel Aviv University. He has published extensively on ancient and medieval Jewish culture, literature, and myth. Cambridge University Press published his most recent scholarly volume, *Ancient Jewish Magic: A History*, in 2008.

LOUISE M. BURKHART is a professor in the Department of Anthropology at the State University of New York in Albany. Her research focuses on the religion of Nahuatl speakers in central Mexico and their appropriation of Christianity, in particular through study of Nahuatl catechistic and devotional literature written by native authors and European priests. Her most recent scholarly monograph is *Aztecs on Stage: Religious Theater in Colonial Mexico* (2011).

DAVID J. COLLINS, S.J., is an associate professor of History at Georgetown University in Washington, DC. He has published extensively on the cult of the saints, Renaissance humanism, and learned magic. His most recent scholarly monograph is *Reforming Saints* (2008), a study of humanist engagement in the cult of the saints during the Renaissance.

OWEN DAVIES is a professor in the Department of History at the University of Hertfordshire. His research interests include the Western belief in magic, witchcraft, and ghosts from antiquity to the modern era, as well as the related topics of popular medicine and folklore. His most recent scholarly monograph is *America Bewitched: The Story of Witchcraft after Salem* (2013).

KYLE A. FRASER is an associate professor in the History of Science and Technology Programme at the University of King's College in Halifax. He has published extensively on magic, alchemy, and esotericism in Roman Antiquity, including "The Contested

Boundaries of Magic and Religion in Late Pagan Monotheism" in the journal *Magic, Ritual and Witchcraft* (4 (2009): 131–151).

RICHARD GODBEER is a professor in the Department of History at Virginia Commonwealth University in Richmond. His current research project is a joint biography of Elizabeth and Henry Drinker, a Quaker couple who lived in Philadelphia during the second half of the eighteenth century. His most recent scholarly monograph is *The Overflowing of Friendship: Love between Men and the Creation of the American Republic* (2009).

DAVID ALLEN HARVEY is a professor of History at the New College of Florida in Sarasota. His primary area of interest is the intellectual and cultural history of modern France and Germany. His most recent scholarly monograph is *The French Enlightenment and Its Others: The Mandarin, the Savage, and the Invention of the Human Sciences* (2012).

YITZHAK HEN is a professor of History at the Ben Gurion University of the Negev in Be'er Sheva. His research interests include early Christian liturgy, Western Arianism, and tribal migrations in early medieval Europe and North Africa. He recently published a history of those early tribes: *Roman Barbarians: The Royal Court and Culture in the Early Medieval West* (2007).

FRIEDHELM HOFFMANN is a professor at the Institute for Egyptology at the University of Munich. He has worked extensively on the Hieratic and Demotic literature of Roman Egypt. He recently published *Die dreisprachige Stele des C. Cornelius Gallus* (Archiv für Papyrusforschung, 2009), a scholarly edition and commentary.

MAIJASTINA KAHLOS is a university researcher on the faculty of theology at the University of Helsinki. Her research interests include religion in the Roman Empire and Roman everyday life. Her most recent scholarly monograph is *Forbearance and Compulsion: Rhetoric of Tolerance and Intolerance in Late Antiquity* (2009).

SABINA MAGLIOCCO is a professor of Anthropology at the California State University in Northridge. She has published extensively on religion, folklore, foodways, festival, witchcraft, and Neopaganism in Europe and the United States. Her most recent monograph is *Witching Culture: Folklore and Neo-Paganism in America* (2004).

HELEN PARISH is a professor in the Department of History at the University of Reading. Her current research interests lie in early modern religious and cultural history, particularly the Reformation in England and Europe. Her most recent monograph is a study of clerical marriage in the era of the Reformation: *Clerical Celibacy in the West, c. 1100–1700* (2010).

CATHERINE RIDER is a senior lecturer in the Department of History at the University of Exeter. Her research interests include medieval cultural and religious history. Much of her research to date has focused on the history of magic and popular religion in the late Middle Ages. Her most recent book, *Magic and Religion in Medieval England* (2012), focuses on the church's attitude toward magic from the thirteenth century onwards.

RAQUEL ROMBERG is a professor of Anthropology at Tel Aviv University. Her most recent scholarly monograph, *Witchcraft and Welfare* (2009), examines the history and ethnography of Puerto Rican brujería.

DANIEL SCHWEMER is a professor of Ancient and Near Eastern Studies at the University of Würzburg and a research associate at the School of Oriental and African Studies in London. His research specialties include Akkadian, Ancient Near Eastern religion, magic and ritual, and Hittitology. He recently contributed the twelfth volume to *Texte aus dem Bezirk des Großen Tempels* (2011).

KIMBERLY B. STRATTON is an associate professor of the History of Religions at Carleton University in Ottawa. Her research covers the fields of early Christianity and Rabbinic Judaism, as well as Greco-Roman culture and religion. Her most recent scholarly monograph is *Naming the Witch: Magic, Ideology, and Stereotype in the Ancient World* (2007).

ALICIA WALKER is an assistant professor of Medieval Art and Architecture at Bryn Mawr College in Bryn Mawr outside of Philadelphia. Her primary fields of research include cross-cultural artistic interaction in the medieval world from the ninth to thirteenth centuries and gender issues in the art and material culture of Byzantium. Cambridge University Press published her most recent scholarly monograph, *The Emperor and the World: Exotic Elements and the Imaging of Middle Byzantine Imperial Power*, in 2012.

MARGARET J. WIENER is an associate professor in the Department of Anthropology at the University of North Carolina in Chapel Hill. Her research interests include the processes of producing shared and conflicting truths and realities at sites of inter(natural-)cultural engagement, particularly related to historical and contemporary Indonesia. Her most recent scholarly monograph is *Visible and Invisible Realms: Power, Magic, and Colonial Conquests* (1995).

TRAVIS ZADEH is an associate professor of Religion at Haverford College. His research focuses on the role of translation in the formative stages of Islamic intellectual and cultural history, particularly in the areas of geographical writings on the wonders of the world and scriptural hermeneutics concerning the transcendental nature of the Qur'ān. His most recent monograph, *The Vernacular Qur'ān: Translation and the Rise of Persian Exegesis* (2012), examines early juridical and theological debates over the translatability of the Qur'ān and the rise of vernacular cultures with the development of Persian exegetical literature and translations of the Qur'ān.

Introduction

DAVID J. COLLINS, S.J.

Edward Burnett Tylor minced no words in his seminal work *Primitive Culture* (1871) when he wrote that magic was "one of the most pernicious delusions that ever vexed mankind." Neither did his intellectual scion James George Frazer when he called magic "the bastard sister of science" in his monumental *The Golden Bough* (1890). Their rousing denunciations of magic as primitive and their placement of it between and below laudably advanced forms of religion and scientific rationalism stand at the origins of the modern scholarly approach to magic, which this volume hopes also to advance. The contributors to this volume are of course not the immediate heirs of Tylor and Frazer. Luminary figures in early twentieth-century sociology and anthropology – Emile Durkheim, Bronislaw Malinowski, Marcel Mauss (too often treated as the by-product of his accomplished uncle, but original and substantial in his contributions to the study of magic), and Lucien Lévy-Bruhl, to name but a few – stand between them and us. These researchers developed overarching theories, analytic frameworks, and definitions that redound in the scholarship to this day. The scholarly approach to magic did not just change – as Tylor and Frazer, early social evolutionists, might instinctively expect: it diversified. The developments have in large part corresponded to general trends in the humanities and social sciences toward disciplinary specialization and multi-cultural sensibilities that militate against the application of selective, contemporary characteristics of Western society as universal measures of human accomplishment. The study of magic has won much in the process: errors in the early scholarship have been corrected; subtleties missed have been captured; and the scope of the possible has been opened wide. But the gains have come with loss too, paradoxically including the siloing of scholarship within ever narrowing disciplines and sub-disciplines, on the one hand, and the insurmountable accumulation of new scholarship, on the other. No single work could likely solve this paradox, but the aim of this volume is to attenuate it. It aspires to shed light on magic as a cultural phenomenon in the West from Antiquity to the present. Its scope, "the West," places Europe at center but incorporates both cultural antecedents and global influences. It situates Western Europe, moreover, alongside related civilizations in the ancient and medieval Mediterranean world for comparative purposes. Its goal is, in twenty chapters, to present readers – specialists in the study of magic and witchcraft, scholars in related fields, and advanced students – with the current state of historical knowledge about magic in the West, to recover the rich variety of ways that magic has been understood and practiced, to embody interdisciplinary cooperation, and so to suggest directions for future scholarship.[1]

Any digital bibliographic search will speedily indicate the abundance of scholarship about magic that has been produced in the past quarter century. Its quality ranges from the most erudite and judicious to the most superficial and partisan. The challenge to the contributors of this volume has been to discern, synthesize, and build on the best of this abundance. The extent to which they have accomplished that is left to the reader, but by way of introduction, it will be helpful to introduce the reader to the important works already available, specifically in three kinds: the textbook overview; the edited, scholarly reference work; and the monograph and volume of collected essays.

There are several textbook overviews currently in print that address aspects of the history of magic in Europe in well-founded, scholarly ways. The best are R. Kieckhefer's *Magic in the Middle Ages*, M. D. Bailey's *Magic and Superstition in Europe*, and B. P. Levack's *The Witch-Hunt in Early Modern Europe*. These are commonly used textbooks for undergraduate and graduate students, and scholars in related fields looking for overviews safely rely on them, as well. All three books benefit from the research specialties of their authors, as well as the synthesizing coherence that the individual authors bring to their work. By way of comparison, a goal of this volume is to establish a larger context by bringing together a range of scholars to write in their areas of expertise, by giving substantive consideration to magic as it was understood and practiced in Mediterranean cultures in parallel to Western Europe, and by considering how Europe's encounters with non-Mediterranean, non-European cultures shaped magic in Europe and around the globe.

The scholarly work to which the proposed volume bears the greatest resemblance is B. Ankarloo and S. Clark's *Witchcraft and Magic in Europe*, which appeared in six volumes of eighteen individually authored chapters between 1999 and 2002.[2] The Ankarloo-Clark volumes are a masterful work and will long remain an essential resource for the study of witchcraft in Europe. The volumes have shaped the more recent scholarship in terms of their overarching chronological structure and thematic organization, and they include individual articles that synthesize the latest scholarship and make persuasive new arguments on central points of witchcraft's history. On three key points, however, the current volume has developed in different directions. First, like the authors of the aforementioned textbook overviews, the editors of *Witchcraft and Magic in Europe* limited their geographical and cultural focus to Europe. What this distinction excludes, however, is a potentially very enlightening comparison between magic in Europe and magic in the Mediterranean and colonial worlds. Byzantine, Islamic, and medieval Jewish societies shared with Latin Christendom associations with antiquity that offered them a shared legacy in magic. The legacy, however, was drawn on in quite distinctive ways: the other systems of magic developed in parallel to European magic and at key historical moments influenced it and were influenced by it. The increasing contact and exchange Europeans had with non-European, non-Mediterranean peoples, especially from the fifteenth century onward, likewise warrant our attention for the ways they shaped each other's appreciation of what magic was and how it worked. For these reasons, this volume has expanded its scope to "the West" and has placed a high priority on incorporating the ways that Europe was not isolated from a larger world, even in its understandings of magic.

Second, the issue of periodization has become a debated one in the study of magic, as it has in other topics in Western intellectual and cultural history. There are several important disputed moments in the overarching periodization from antiquity to the twentieth century. One example has to do with the significance of the Renaissance and the Reformation to developments in attitudes toward and the actual practice of magic in Europe. The Ankarloo-Clark volumes incorporate that debate by including contributions that fall on both sides: the third and fifth volumes explicitly presuppose a fundamental caesura around 1500 in this history of magic; the fourth volume, in contrast, makes a strong case against dividing analysis of witchcraft around 1500 or taking the sixteenth-century Reformations as a turning point in the intellectual and social history of the witch trials. On this particular question of periodization, this volume has followed a periodization that holds the eleventh to the eighteenth centuries, dubbed "Old Europe" here and in other historiographical contexts, to stand on its own as a coherent epoch in the study of magic in general and diabolic witchcraft in particular. In this volume, the significance of Christianization in late antiquity has also been carefully reconsidered, and the influence of the seventeenth-century Enlightenment on the following two centuries has been critiqued.

A third way that this volume aims to advance the overarching conversation on the practice of magic in the West is to attend, through the historical literature, to the practitioners. At points, this means highlighting their significance and at other times, attenuating it. The "Renaissance Magus," for example, is a looming figure in Western traditions of magic, and he offers the modern scholar an entrée to address the vexed relationship – theoretical and practical – of magic to science. He – and he was always male – comes naturally into the foreground in Chapter 11 on learned magic in Old Europe, and his analogs in other periods surface in several other chapters, especially with an eye to the boundaries and connections between magic and science in a historical context. In contrast, the witch – that practitioner of harmful magic whose diabolic form is so peculiar to the West – figures less prominently than common knowledge would lead one to anticipate. The "burning times" were, to be sure, a horrific episode in the legal, religious, and social history of Europe, but they are hardly emblematic of Europe's attitudes toward magic in the first and second millennia CE. Ankarloo and Clark addressed this dissonance between what is conventionally thought to be true of the period of witch hunts and what research has over the past half century found to be true when they wrote in the introduction to their volume on the witch trials, "the successful recognition of a topic's significance always runs the risk of exaggerating that significance." In response to this problem, specialized scholarship on witchcraft in the past decade generally includes a warning against or an apology for any distortive impressions it might leave. This volume takes this caveat very much to heart; it aims to examine the phenomenon of witchcraft, its late medieval diabolization, and its persecution directly; but it limits witchcraft to one chapter and therefore situates its significance appropriately within the broader framework of magic's history in the West.

Third, in the past fifteen years, a large number of noteworthy monographs and edited volumes, to say nothing of scholarly articles, have brought to light new historical phenomena and contributed to the reframing of fundamental questions. It would be impossible to list, let alone describe, all of these works; the following sampling represents directions that scholarship has moved in the past fifteen years: T. Abusch has ensured continued interest in magic in ancient Near Eastern contexts with his own research and important edited volumes. P. A. Mirecki and M. Meyer have brought together some of antiquity's most learned scholars to make new sources available and to challenge numerous conventional understandings of their subject in *Magic and Ritual in the Ancient World*. The essays in J. N. Bremmer and J. R. Veenstra's *The Metamorphosis of Magic* have also called for a reassessment of magic's relationship to religion from antiquity to the early modern period. A. Boureau's *Satan hérétique* has redefined the origins of demonology as a medieval field of study and its relationship to heresy. S. Clark's *Thinking with Demons* and W. Stephens's *Demon*

Lovers have proposed new ways of understanding how and why demonology attracted so much scholarly attention in the late medieval and early modern centuries. R. Kieckhefer's *Forbidden Rites* and M. D. Bailey's *Battling Demons* have shed new light on the demon-conjuring and demon-combating clerical cultures of the late Middle Ages. É. Pócs and G. Klaniczay's three-volume essay collection, *Demons, Spirits, Witches*, enriches the current discussion with its cooperative multidisciplinary approach, as well as its attentiveness to the Central and Eastern European dimensions of the topic. C. Gilly and C. van Heertum, A. Paravicini Bagliani, J. R. Veenstra, N. Weill-Parot, G. S. Williams and C. D. Gunnoe, P. Zambelli, and C. Zika, among many others, have turned their attention to the relationship between magic and developments in late medieval natural philosophy and early modern science. B. Copenhaver, R. Feldhay, and H. D. Rutkin addressed related topics in chapters of the recent early modern volume of the *Cambridge History of Science*. By attending to the relationship of certain kinds of magic to medieval and early modern natural philosophy, F. F. Klaassen has proposed a significantly revised approach to early modern ritual magic. He, B. Láng, and O. Davies have encouraged the closest look at the literature of magic. A. Games has drawn concepts of witchcraft into the burgeoning new field of the Atlantic World. In *Witchcraft Continued* and *Beyond the Witch Trials*, W. de Blécourt and O. Davies have pointed our attention to ways the Enlightenment should and should not be understood to mark a break in Western thought and practice concerning witchcraft; and Occultism, Neopaganism, and especially Wicca have received new scholarly attention in the past decade in critical studies of modernity and the modern disenchantment thesis, as in the works of D. A. Harvey on nineteenth-century France, A. Owen on nineteenth-century Great Britain, and S. Magliocco on the twentieth-century United States. M. D. Bailey in *Fearful Spirits* and E. Cameron in *Enchanted Europe* investigate the relationship between Western thinking on superstition and on magic. R. Styers's *Making Magic* and B. Meyer and P. Pels's *Magic and Modernity* represent new attempts – the former from a religious studies perspective, the latter from anthropology – to synthesize the latest historical scholarship and reframe magic's significance against notions of Western modernity. Lastly, it bears mentioning that scholars of witch hunting have had a helpful new resource at their disposal since 2006 in the first complete English/Latin critical edition of the *Malleus maleficarum* translated by C. Mackay. The same year saw the appearance of R. M. Golden's much-anticipated *Encyclopedia of Witchcraft*. Moreover, B. P. Levack's collection of article reprints in *New Perspectives* in 2001 and B. Copenhaver and M. D. Bailey's founding editorship of the journal *Magic, Ritual, and Witchcraft* in 2006 have created invaluable repositories for specialized scholarship on magic. These works represent a small portion of the newest scholarship that informs and inspires the contributions to this volume.[3]

This volume consists of twenty chapters. A challenge for such an edited volume is ensuring suitable coherence and consistency across the individual contributions. A number of issues are particular to the study of the history of magic. A first set of problems revolves around the much-discussed and highly contested question of how to define magic. Since the outset of scholarly reflection on magic, it has commonly been defined in relation to religion and science, sometimes as their more primitive, less rational, or incipient manifestation. Dissatisfaction with triangulating definitions as well as with simple dichotomies has several causes. For one, the terms simply enjoy no univocal definition across scholarly disciplines and subfields; and for another, their crafting and application have often entailed considerable historiographical bias, even arrogance. In consequence, some scholars have proposed rejecting the term "magic" altogether, most usually by subsuming magic into religion. The most obvious problem with erasing the distinction between magic and religion is that in all of the cultures under consideration in the proposed volume, historical actors from all walks of life discussed, debated, defined, and redefined their sense of what magic was vis-à-vis religion and acted according to that distinction. Moreover, the premise that magic had (and has) coherent, rational significance in relation to discourses of religion has so far proven itself more elucidative of the historical phenomena than has the alternate premise that magic and religion cannot be rationally distinguished at all. The contributors in this volume have largely aligned themselves in favor of the former premise, even as they acknowledge the terminological slipperiness across cultures and through time. Accordingly, contributors address within the relevant historical, cultural contexts the problem of magic's definition, its conceptual and practical relationship to religion and science, and the qualifications and characteristics of its practitioners, both self-described and authoritatively recognized as such. Contours of difference also follow disciplinary lines, and inconsistencies point toward interdisciplinary challenges and development.

A second hallmark of the volume is its analytical framework, which consists of roughly designated historical periods within which magic is organized taxonomically. The three epoch-dividing watersheds adopted in the volume are: first, the Christianization of the Mediterranean world and the barbarian north (Celtic, Germanic, and Slavic tribes); second, the legal and intellectual revolutions of the eleventh through thirteenth centuries; and finally, the Enlightenment in conjunction with the French Revolution, industrialization, and secularization around 1800. The corresponding parts of the volume address magic in antiquity (until the fourth century), early Latin Christendom (until the eleventh century), "Old Europe" (until the eighteenth century), and the modern West (up through the twentieth century). This structure diverges most markedly from a periodization of the West that sharply distinguishes the medieval from the early modern periods. To these chronological sections are added the two thematic parts: one on alternate traditions found in Greek Christianity, Islam, and Judaism; the other on Europeans' colonial encounters with magic.

For the most part, the chapters are then organized around kinds of magical practice. The chapters within the parts and the parts within the whole are held together by a series of logical and chronological questions: What were the taxonomies of magic in antiquity? How did they change with the coming of Christianity? Within Christianity, how did taxonomies differ in the East and the West? What were the taxonomies within coeval Islamic and Jewish understandings of magic, and how were they independent from or derivative of magic in antiquity? How were they imported and reinterpreted in the Latin West? Within the West, how did taxonomies change between the early and late medieval periods? Witchcraft, to take a particular issue from Part IV, can then be treated according to how it was classified within the broader contexts of magical practice and perceptions of magic rather than according to how it was persecuted: What was witchcraft in the West before its diabolization? How and why was "diabolic witchcraft" constructed? How fully did it ever supersede other kinds of magical practice? How did that particular taxonomy break down and become rejected? Such an approach will also prove enlightening in the discussion of the "end of magic," an issue that connects and distinguishes the periods of "Old Europe" and the "modern West." It is, on the one hand, axiomatic to understand that the Enlightenment precipitously furthered Europe's "disenchantment." On the other hand, the Enlightenment can also be understood as having committed itself to the Christian project of defining all magic in a univocal way, condemning it, and eradicating it. Magic might no longer be immoral, irreligious, or demonic, as it was considered by Christian lights, but magic was, to the Lumière, still a superstition in the sense of being irrational and unscientific.

Part I: Antiquity. Part I's topic is magic in ancient Near Eastern and Mediterranean societies up to Imperial Rome. Building on recent studies of the Mediterranean world's Platonization and Christianization in later antiquity, this volume proposes a noteworthy discontinuity between understandings of magic up to Imperial Antiquity and those thereafter. Part I thus functions in certain respects as an analytical prologue to the remainder of the volume.

It consists of three chapters: Chapter 1 on magic in Ancient Near Eastern societies (D. Schwemer); Chapter 2, in Egyptian society (F. Hoffmann); and Chapter 3, in pagan Greek and Roman societies (K. B. Stratton). Although the earlier of these societies may generally not be considered "Western," their ideas, social customs, and written texts surely were integral parts of the cultural legacy inherited by the West.

Part I takes as its own the following four goals: first, to address the particular difficulties of using modern categories of "magic," "science," and "religion" to organize and describe ancient understandings of magic and its practice, with special attention paid to the ambiguous and contested lines separating the healing arts, divination, and magic; second, to describe the spectrum of sacred and natural powers that various specialists, authorized and unauthorized, accessed in a range of ways in the ancient cultures that eventually converged in Western Europe from the early Middle Ages onward; third, to define and trace the development of key concepts – *mageía*, *magia*, and *superstitio* – that the early Christians adopted, but also transformed, from pagan antiquity; and fourth, to establish a reference point for later comparison with the recurrent claims in the West of a rediscovery of "ancient" magic.

Part II: The Early Latin West. Part II focuses on magic as it was understood and practiced in the northern Mediterranean world and on the Western and Central European peninsula as these regions underwent, at various levels and in various ways, both a Platonization and their first Christianization. By "Christianization" is understood the establishment of basic theological and philosophical doctrines, the shaping of common beliefs and practices, and the corresponding revision of social and political structures. Christianization included complex appropriations of and expansions on the notions of magic outlined in Part I. This process continued as Celtic, Germanic, and Slavic tribes were brought to Christianity throughout (and beyond) the period covered in Part II.

The association of late antiquity's burgeoning Neo-Platonism with changing understandings of magic is not meant to distract from the well-established thesis that the spread of Christianity led to fundamental developments in a condemning direction vis-à-vis magic but rather to broaden our understanding of developments in late antiquity to encompass a growing hostility and condescension toward magic identifiable in late antiquity among decidedly non-Christian, although sometimes monotheistic, segments of Imperial society. The analysis in this volume is thus driven by a slight revision of two stimulating, seemingly contradictory theses that have shaped recent scholarship on magic in early Latin Christendom. On the one hand, the process of Christianization is argued to have included creative appropriations of common pagan ritual practices that to a modern observer would qualify as magical, even given the various ways in which such practices were "Christianized." This thesis of hybridization between ancient Christianity and indigenous paganisms thus emphasizes a range of continuities between pre- and post-Christianized European tribes and peoples. On the other hand, Christianization indisputably disrupted beliefs in, the practice of, and judgments about magic within the Roman Empire and on the European continent, especially insofar as magic's effectiveness was reassigned from the morally ambiguous daemon to the demon, the fallen angel, appeal to whom could by Christian reckoning only be repugnant. This latter development was, however, not entirely original to Christianity, but in the moment, it tapped into a homologous hostility toward magic emerging out of a decidedly non-Christian philosophical tradition that had, of course, influence on Christianity in innumerable ways.

Part II consists of three chapters. Chapter 4 examines attitudes toward magic in Imperial Rome, especially insofar as a growing hostility toward magic emerged from centers of the new Platonist thought (K. A. Fraser). Chapter 5 considers how magic was understood and practiced within the once-pagan, Roman Mediterranean world with its cultic priests, civic piety, and private cults (M. Kahlos). And Chapter 6 examines the corresponding issues within the context of the once-heathen world of the Celts, Germans, and Slavs (Y. Hen).

Part II derives its two overarching goals from this tension: first, to sketch how magic was understood, who practiced it, and how it was practiced in late antiquity and early medieval Latin Christendom; and second, to demonstrate the length, complexity, and ambiguities of the processes of magic's appropriations and condemnations. Part II also lays the groundwork for the evaluation of certain propositions about the later history of magic in the West: for example, that a heightened association between magic and heresy (or even apostasy) drove the frenzied concern in later centuries about diabolic magic and set the stage for the witch hunts of the sixteenth and seventeenth centuries and that the Enlightenment condemnation of magic as irrational and unscientific was different in substance but parallel in form to the early Christian hostility toward it as demonic, immoral, and irreligious.

Part III: Parallel Traditions. Part III addresses magic as it was conceived and practiced in Mediterranean cultures following the disintegration of the Western Roman Empire in cultural milieus outside of the Latin West. The chapters in Part III cover magic as it was found in early Greek Christian culture and Byzantium (Chapter 7, A. Walker), in Islamic culture and the Arab world from the seventh to the thirteenth centuries (Chapter 8, T. Zadeh), and in medieval Judaism (Chapter 9, G. Bohak). Magic in these milieus are already familiar to students of European magic to the extent that they influenced European thought and practice at key historical moments: for example, the high medieval appropriation of learned texts from the Islamic world via the Castilian court of King Alphonse and the inspiration Renaissance mages derived from Kaballic mysticism. The chapters of Part III have, however, as their first task the sketching of magic as it was understood and practiced in these other cultural milieus on its own terms. Magic in these other milieus was a more significant phenomenon than what was at crucial moments adopted into Latin Christendom. Moreover, they had in common with the Latin West the shared legacy of antiquity. Part III's contribution to the volume as a whole rests on these simple but heretofore underappreciated premises, namely, that all four cultural milieu were antiquity's heirs as regards magic and that all four appropriated antiquity's understanding and practices differently. Part III's goals are consequently twofold: to enhance appreciation of the specific ways that Latin Christendom appropriated antiquity's legacy of magic by encouraging comparison between how it happened in the Latin West and in the three principal historical alternatives; and to enhance the appreciation of the medieval, Renaissance, and modern appropriations of magic from these parallel traditions by offering a vantage as much on what was not appropriated as on what was. This part of the volume arguably counts as quite experimental and, in terms of the achievement of its goals, both the most promising and the most prolegomenous.

Part IV: Old Europe. Part IV's coverage begins with the legal and intellectual revolutions of the eleventh to thirteenth centuries and ends with the secularization and cultural "disenchantment" that came about with the eighteenth-century Enlightenment. Of the four chapters in this part, the first three are organized around kinds of magic, namely, common, learned, and demonic. The fourth examines the medieval and early modern critiques of Catholic priestcraft as magic. The first three chapters address a number of common issues: Who practiced and patronized these kinds of magic? To what extent did these kinds of magic represent appropriations of classical, pagan, Islamic, or Jewish traditions of magic? Who were the practitioners and clients? To what extent did they understand what they were doing as magic? How did they understand what they were doing in terms of Christian thought and cultic norms? How did civil and ecclesiastical authorities understand these same forms of knowledge, belief, and practice? How did the authorities view their own responsibilities vis-à-vis this magic – defining, fostering, patronizing, and condemning it and its practitioners? How did the authorities cooperate and conflict in these matters? And how did such patterns of cooperation and conflict change over time?

Chapter 10 focuses on common magic (C. Rider). By "common" magic is meant the range of practices, interest in which can be found across otherwise stratified medieval society. Agents and clients included the learned and illiterate; clergy, religious, and laity; and nobility and peasantry. Their goals were to curse and bless, injure and heal, kill and protect, enchant and repulse, ascertain and befuddle, and conceive and contracept. Although few agents or beneficiaries of common magic labeled what they were doing as magic, their practices – simple rituals intended to control natural or supernatural powers – appeared to many contemporaries (no less than to us today) as magical, raising once again the question of how to define magic. The focus of Chapter 11 is on the forms of magic that attracted attention, positive and negative, in learned circles, most especially at universities and among the clergy (D. J. Collins). The material in this chapter raises the corresponding set of questions regarding the relationship of magic to science (or, by medieval reckoning, to natural philosophy), as well as the relationships between supernatural and occult powers and between black and white magic.

Chapter 12 looks to the rise of a concern in the late medieval and early modern West about demonic magic with an explanation largely found at the intersection of concerns examined in the previous two chapters on common and learned magic (M. D. Bailey). Discussion of the late medieval invocation of demons and a corresponding concern that Christendom lay under siege in Chapter 11 leads to Chapter 12's consideration of the witch, Old Europe's most infamous practitioner of harmful magic. Although in early periods the witch was considered to be "simply" a practitioner of harmful magic, by the fourteenth century, witches were understood to work in commerce with the Devil and to meet together in secret to worship him. Whereas the evil-working witch is a figure of transcultural significance, the *diabolic* witch – evil working and devil worshipping – is, by our best scholarly lights, a uniquely Western invention whose rise to and fall from prominence occurred within the history of "Old Europe." These witches' contemporaries feared them tremendously, condemned them vociferously, and prosecuted them with varying degrees of élan across Europe from the fifteenth to the eighteenth centuries. The witch trials have attracted considerable scholarly (and pseudo-scholarly) attention over the years, as have questions regarding what the witch was; why she (or, occasionally, he) became the object of such strong fear and energetic persecution; how and why she was diabolized; and how and why concerns over her, and concomitantly the persecutions, diminished as they did. The goals of Chapter 12 are to summarize the scholarly *status quaestionis* regarding witchcraft and the witch hunts in the late medieval and early modern West and, to point in directions for further research.

Chapter 13 addresses criticisms and polemics against the Catholic priest as a magician and his rites and sacramentals as magic (H. Parish). The high point of these condemnations occurred during the sixteenth-century Reformations, but the conviction that the priest exercised irreligious powers and fostered superstition rather than real Christianity has older roots in an anti-clericalism that was an integral part of both mainstream and heretical Christianity in the Middle Ages and that can be found within popular Catholicism and other forms of Christianity up to the present day. The critique had a learned dimension, as well, based on the theological rejection of *ex opere operato*, the sacramental theory according to which a priest's words and actions effected divine intervention. Insofar as a key Protestant critique of Catholic priestcraft was that popish rituals could effect nothing, we must consider anticipatory indications of the disenchantment that is taken as a characteristic development of "the modern West."

Part V: Colonial Encounters. The age of exploration exposed Europeans to new cultures and societies that had their own proper ways of dealing with extraordinary power summoned to effect in the ordinary human world. In our own day, colonial and postcolonial studies, as well as such burgeoning new fields as "Atlantic World," have heightened our appreciation of how the European arrival in these "new worlds" mutually affected the colonizing and the colonized. The goal of Part V is to offer, in three chapters, a set of complementary cases that analyze the range of ways in which Europeans reacted to and categorized as magical and/or demonic the practices and beliefs they encountered in the course of their colonial expansions beginning in the fifteenth century, on the one hand, and how this European reaction shaped that which had been discovered, on the other hand. Case studies of such encounters could fill volumes; here we offer three emblematic cases: Spaniards in Mexico in the sixteenth century (Chapter 14, L. M. Burkhart); witch hunting by English colonialists in the North American colonies at the turn of the eighteenth century (Chapter 15, R. Godbeer); and European traders and tribal witchdoctors in the Dutch East Indies (Chapter 16, M. J. Wiener).

Part VI: The Modern West. The Enlightenment of the eighteenth century was surely the revolution in Western history that most affected the belief in and the practice of magic in the West. At the same time, recent scholarship has muddied the waters separating a superstitious and enchanted early modern Europe from a rational and disenchanted modern West, principally by highlighting continuities across the divide that once seemed so self-evident. All four chapters in Part VI have as their goal the casting of light on the principal systems of magic that manifested themselves in the modern West "beyond the Enlightenment": to sketch and analyze continuities and discontinuities – real and imagined – in magical beliefs and practices across the frontier year of 1800; to evaluate the analogous nature of distinctions once made between *religion* and magic, now made between *science* and magic; and to address the complicated ways in which modern magic adapted itself to contemporary sets of needs, aspirations, and anxieties and yet still drew on the traditional forms.

Chapter 17 focuses both on the nature of magic as practiced in nineteenth-century Europe and on its treatment in the law (O. Davies). This chapter thus draws attention, first, to the practice of common magic in the modern West and its meaning for convinced practitioners and clients, second, to the intellectual, juridical, and religious developments that led to condemnations of magic as fraud, and third, to the social implications of both developments. Chapter 18 focuses on nineteenth-century magic in more learned and socially well-situated milieus (D. A. Harvey). It focuses on the rise of occultisms – from Victorian supernaturalism to Masonic lodges – that seemingly counter-indicate other trends that support an Enlightenment disenchantment thesis. Its goal is not to tilt against Max Weber but to investigate the appeal of the magical, the mysterious, and the superstitious beyond the milieus of the poor, powerless, and unlettered and to consider its inspiration in Romanticist rejections of nineteenth-century scientism and rationalism.

Chapter 19 turns to modern magical systems in postcolonial contexts (R. Romberg). On the grounds that decolonization was hardly the undoing of colonization, this chapter considers the nature of magic and its transformed cultural functions in once-colonized, now-decolonized parts of the West. Chapter 20, the final chapter of this part and of the volume, turns to current movements such as Neopaganism, Wicca, Satanism, and New Age that in varying ways appeal to older Western traditions, but at the same time it effectively redefines them, especially in their demonic modes. In these movements, self-proclaimed witches turn the witch from a practitioner of harmful magic in league with the Devil into the embodiment of the pre-patriarchalized female genius; and the Satanists reject definition of their movement as the worship of cosmic evil but rather exult in aspects of otherwise repressed human instinct. Some of these movements originated in the nineteenth century; others were founded after World War II. Their study raises the problem of understanding continuities and discontinuities with the past in another mode, given that most movements, especially Wicca, are of relatively recent founding but claim to be fostering abiding ancient and subaltern medieval traditions. These movements find in reconceived notions of magic a fullness of knowledge and deeper truth that neither rational science nor Christian religion offers. Embrace of this fullness corrects the Western tradition – be it Christian or Enlightened – of demonization, condemnation, and repression, adherents would have us believe. In this respect, at least by their reckoning, the *Cambridge History of Magic and Witchcraft in the West* comes full circle.

Notes

1. A very fine overview of the nineteenth- and twentieth-century early scholarship on magic has recently been published by a contributor to this volume: Davies, *Magic: A Very Short Introduction*. See also Michael Bailey, "The Meanings of Magic," 1–23.
2. Ankarloo and Clark, eds., *Witchcraft and Magic in Europe*.
3. Abusch, *Mesopotamian Witchcraft: Toward a History and Understanding of Babylonian Witchcraft Beliefs and Literature*; Abusch and Schwemer, eds., *Corpus of Mesopotamian Anti-Witchcraft Rituals*; Bailey, *Battling Demons: Witchcraft, Heresy, and Reform in the Late Middle Ages*; Bailey, *Fearful Spirits, Reasoned Follies: The Boundaries of Superstition in Late Medieval Europe*; de Blécourt and Davies, eds., *Witchcraft Continued*; Boureau, *Satan hérétique*; Bremmer and Veenstra, eds., *The Metamorphosis of Magic from Late Antiquity to the Early Modern Period*; Cameron, *Enchanted Europe*; Clark, *Thinking with Demons: The Idea of Witchcraft in Early Modern Europe*; Davies, *Grimoires*; Davies and de Blécourt, eds., *Beyond the Witch Trials*; Games, *Witchcraft in Early North America*; Gilly and van Heertum, eds., *Magic, Alchemy and Science, 15th–18th Centuries: The Influence of Hermes Trismegistus*; Golden, ed., *Encyclopedia of Witchcraft: The Western Tradition*; Harvey, *Beyond Enlightenment*; Kieckhefer, *Forbidden Rites*; Klaassen, *Transformations*; Kramer, *Malleus Maleficarum*; Láng, *Unlocked Books*; Levack, ed., *New Perspectives on Witchcraft, Magic, and Demonology*; Magliocco, *Witching Culture: Folklore and Neopaganism in America*; Meyer and Pels, *Magic and Modernity: Interfaces of Revelation and Concealment*; Mirecki and Meyer, eds., *Magic and Ritual in the Ancient World*; Owen, *The Place of Enchantment: British Occultism and the Culture of the Modern*; Paravicini Bagliani, *Le "Speculum astronomiae"*; Pócs and Klaniczay, *Demons, Spirits, Witches*; Rutkin, "Astrology"; Stephens, *Demon Lovers: Witchcraft, Sex, and the Crisis of Belief*; Styers, *Making Magic: Religion, Magic, and Science in the Modern World*; Veenstra, *Magic and Divination*; Weill-Parot, *Les "images astrologiques" au Moyen Age et à la Renaissance: Spéculations intellectuelles et pratiques magiques, XIIe–XVe siècle*; Williams and Gunnoe, eds., *Paracelsian Moments: Science, Medicine, and Astrology in Early Modern Europe*; Zambelli, *White Magic*; Zika, *Exorcising Our Demons*.

PART I

★

ANTIQUITY

Chapter 1

The Ancient Near East

DANIEL SCHWEMER

Magic: Origin and Meaning

The roots of magic, one could argue, lie in the ancient Near East.[1] The Greek word *mageía* owes its existence to a loanword from an ancient Near Eastern language. One might thus expect a study of ancient Near Eastern rituals and incantations to lead directly to the core of what is meant when rituals, ceremonies, or treatments are called magic. As is often the case, however, the origins of the term "magic" are specific and, in fact, hardly overlap with what we would regard as ancient Near Eastern magic. From the very beginning, *mageía* was not a word that objectively referred to ancient Near Eastern practices; rather it is a term that carries a value judgment prompted by Greek perceptions of their neighbors to the East. The origins of "magic" may well be regarded therefore as an early example of "Orientalism," reflecting a blend of fascination, contempt, and misunderstanding that has accompanied the concept of magic ever since its inception.

Already in the fifth century BC, Greek authors used the term *mágos*, a direct loan from Old Persian *maguš*, not only as a designation for Iranian experts in religious matters but also as a pejorative term for ritualists whose practices, in the author's view, lacked piety.[2] Derived from *mágos*, the term *mageía* soon ubiquitously came to carry the same polemical connotation. Although both meanings of the word continue to be attested, *mageía* is used with reference to the lore of Zoroaster only rarely; usually it serves as a derogatory label for ritualistic activities that are, by using this designation, characterized as obscure, irrational, and impious. By this token, *mageía* was understood to be a powerful form of deception performed by shrewd practitioners on immature, credulous victims. It is surely no surprise that the term was usually applied, as Jens Braarvig puts it, "to the activity of the Others."[3] Magic had become a term that was used to indicate the inferiority of religious or therapeutic practices other than one's own.

The range of meanings the Greeks imputed to *mageía* finds resonance in the present day in the word "magic" in English (and its equivalent in other languages). More importantly, based on its use in Greek sources, magic not only came to function as a key category of religious demarcation (e.g., by missionaries with regard to non-Christian beliefs and practices, as well as by Protestants with regard to the rituals of the Roman Catholic Church), but it also became, especially in anthropology and the history of religions, one of the three main paradigms of describing and classifying human interactions with the natural world. The triad of magic, science, and religion still provides a powerful heuristic framework for organizing the study of past and contemporary cultures: science is concerned with rational, empirical human investigations producing objective, verifiable knowledge, whereas the sphere of religion encompasses all phenomena associated with the worship of the divine, including theology and ethics; magic, however, is the wayward (and therefore often secret) child spawned by science and religion, combining the latter's credulous engagement with the supernatural with the former's belief in the unlimited power and effectiveness of human actions. An early elaboration of this trichotomy can be found in the Hippocratic treatise *On the Sacred Disease*, dating to the late fifth or early fourth century BC, which contains a polemic against deceptive magicians who fall short of the standards of both science and religion.[4] Its most influential exposition was formulated much later by James Frazer in *The Golden Bough*; there, of course, it was presented not in the context of a polemic against contemporaries, but as an attempt at providing an overarching concept for the ethnological study of the rituals, therapies, and beliefs of other peoples.[5]

Anthropologists have criticized this approach ever since, arguing that the three categories neither reflect the actual structure of the relevant segments of such cultures adequately nor correspond to the conceptualizations of these segments that were produced within the given cultures.[6] Students of magic in particular have argued that the term "magic," intrinsically tied to its pejorative connotations and common misconceptions (e.g., the mechanical interpretation of the *ex opere operato* principle), should be avoided altogether or, at least, be reserved for practices that were regarded with disdain within the culture under study.[7]

Although the critical reaction against the Frazerian trichotomy highlighted the substantial inadequacy of each of the three concepts and rightly drew attention to its inherent value judgments and the consequent scholarly misunderstandings, it did not provide heuristic instruments that could match the immediate associative power, cultural translatability, and productive imprecision of magic, science, and religion. The dilemma was neatly summed up by

Henk Versnel: "You cannot talk about magic without using the term magic."[8] Abandoning the use of such categories altogether would prove to be unworkable and would not do justice to the differentiated views all societies have on their rituals and therapies. Whether these differentiations agree with the presuppositions implied in our heuristic instruments is a different matter.

Against this background, it makes little sense to start a survey of magical practices in the ancient Near East with a detailed and narrow definition of what we understand magic to be. Rather, we should approach the extant sources with an initial, general, and pragmatic definition of magic that we are willing and prepared to modify through the study of the sources themselves. Only then can we hope to achieve an adequate understanding of what may be subsumed under the heading of "ancient Near Eastern magic." A provisional general definition of magic should be fit to serve as a first guide to the available sources from different cultures and periods, conveying the essential characteristics of magic activities without unduly prejudicing the interpretation of the sources (if only by way of an ill-judged selection). The association of magic with the mysterious tricks a stage conjurer performs for the entertainment of his audience may be disregarded for the present purpose; the same is true for the colloquial use of "magical" for anything wonderful and out of the ordinary. It may thus be acceptable to describe magic as an activity consisting of symbolic gestures (e.g., the burning of a substitute figurine), usually accompanied by recitations, performed by an expert (relying on transmitted knowledge) with the goal of effecting an immediate change and transformation of the object of the activity (e.g., the cure of an ill person or the removal of an agent of evil from a house). The actual techniques, texts, and symbols involved in the magic activity can vary widely and depend on the cultural context and the aim of the activity – the magic activity performed by the ritual expert may be socially acceptable or prohibited; gods may be invoked or ignored; symbolic gestures may be combined with a physical and pharmaceutical treatment of the patient or stand on their own; the expert in charge may be a high-ranking, well-educated professional or an illiterate healer relying on orally transmitted specialist knowledge – but the activity is still essentially the same and may justifiably be called magic.

The World of Cuneiform Cultures and the Nature of the Sources

Like "modern Western civilization" and other general designations for major cultural eras and areas, the term "ancient Near East" covers a vast, sometimes ill-defined, array of diverse cultures and regions whose boundaries were drawn by the academic disciplines that established themselves in the nineteenth and early twentieth centuries subsequent to the archaeological rediscovery of the pre-Hellenistic cultures of the Middle East. For all their regional diversity and historical transformations, the ancient civilizations of modern Iraq, Iran, Syria, Turkey, and some of their neighbors were linked by a long history of commerce and exchange that reaches far back into prehistoric periods. They shared the same broad stages of technological, ideological, social, and political development; more importantly, the adoption of the Babylonian cuneiform script across the whole region and, with it, the emergence of interconnected writing cultures, whose canon was heavily shaped by Babylonian traditions, further contributed to a certain cultural cohesiveness of the ancient Near East. Sumerian and Akkadian magical texts, originally composed and written down in Babylonia, were excavated as far afield as Hattusa, the Hittite capital in central Anatolia, where Babylonian rituals and incantations were housed in the royal tablet collections alongside Hittite ritual texts stemming from various Anatolian and Syrian traditions. At the same royal court, physicians and exorcists from Anatolia, Egypt, Babylonia, and Assyria could be found, a situation that was not unique to thirteenth-century Hittite Anatolia. Studying similarities between rituals and incantations from the various cuneiform traditions, it is notoriously difficult to distinguish between cross-cultural universals, long-term shared traditions, and evidence of specific adaptations of foreign texts, motifs, or practices.[9]

Clay tablets inscribed in the cuneiform script are the main (although not the only) sources that provide information on the ideas associated with magic in ancient Near Eastern societies: letters that formed part of the correspondence between kings and their officials give insight into the relationships at court and supply particulars on quarrels and conflicts that ended in witchcraft accusations. Legal texts, such as law collections, documents, loyalty oaths, and treaties, shed light on which ritual practices were prohibited and how their performance would be punished. Lexical texts give important information on the terminology for magic and witchcraft in the various ancient Near Eastern languages. Myths contribute to a better understanding of the role the gods played in magic rituals. But, and this is true for all ancient Near Eastern societies, the most significant and numerous relevant sources are ritual instructions, prescriptions, and incantations that were recorded and copied by ritual experts or other scribes, who added them to their private libraries or produced new copies for larger, usually royal, tablet collections. Many of the tablets that were found in the context of private libraries were written by younger

FIGURE I.I. *Maqlû*, tablet I, Neo-Assyrian period, 7th century BC, Ashur, library N5. İstanbul Arkeoloji Müzeleri, Istanbul, A 43 obverse. Photo by the author, with kind permission of the İstanbul Arkeoloji Müzeleri.

scribes, who copied the professional lore as part of their training. A typical example is the Neo-Assyrian library recovered in the so-called "house of the exorcist" in Neo-Assyrian Ashur (seventh century BC).[10] The tablets in the royal libraries, most famously the tablet collections of Neo-Assyrian Nineveh and of Empire-period Hattusa, were usually written by fully trained scribes who worked under supervision and often used multiple sources; the creation of these libraries involved systematic collecting, textual editing, the requisition of tablets, and the recruitment of experts.[11] Figure 1.1 shows the fragment of a Neo-Assyrian manuscript of the Babylonian anti-witchcraft ritual *Maqlû*; the name and status of the scribe are unknown, but the many intrusions of the scribe's Assyrian vernacular in the transmitted Babylonian text suggest that the tablet is the work of an apprentice scribe. Figure 1.2 shows the line drawing of another manuscript of *Maqlû*; the tablet was written for the library of Ashurbanipal and is a fine example of the high standard of copying that was typical for royal libraries.

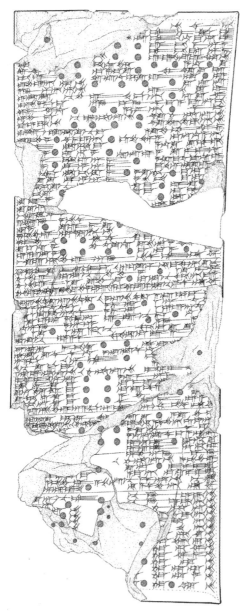

FIGURE 1.2. *Maqlû*, tablet I, Neo-Assyrian period, 7th century BC, Nineveh, library of Ashurbanipal. British Museum, London, K 43 + 142 + 2601 + Sm 1433 obverse. Author's line drawing, with kind permission of the Trustees of the British Museum.

Sumerian and Akkadian ritual and incantation texts were associated in ancient Mesopotamia (Babylonia in southern Iraq and Assyria in the north) with one specific profession, an expert called in Akkadian *āšipu*, or *mašmaššu*, conventionally translated as "exorcist"; the body of texts itself could summarily be referred to as *āšipūtu* "exorcistic lore," or simply "magic." Babylonian tradition considered this corpus of texts to be of great antiquity, originally authored by Enki-Ea himself, the god of wisdom and exorcism.[12] The earliest incantations attested in cuneiform writing date to the pre-Sargonic period (mid-third millennium BC). They are composed in Sumerian or archaic forms of Akkadian and were excavated at Babylonian sites and at Ebla in northwest Syria.[13] The sizable body of Sumerian and Akkadian incantations and rituals dating to the late third and early second millennia BC (Ur III and Old Babylonian periods) already begins to prefigure thematically, and in many cases textually, what would become the standard repertoire of *āšipūtu*, but the formation and organization of the canon of serialized texts took place mostly in the later second millennium BC.[14] Even though the body of Sumerian and Akkadian incantations and rituals in the first millennium BC had reached a certain canonical stability, which is apparent in the similar composition of the libraries of this period, the redaction and serialization of texts continued, and some text groups seem to have been organized in a comprehensive series, first by the seventh-century scholars of the Sargonid kings of Assyria (although smaller collections of these texts had certainly been compiled earlier).[15] The texts continued to be copied well into the Seleucid period until the cuneiform tradition finally came to an end during the Parthian reign over Babylonia.[16] Of course, many text series and individual texts of the *āšipūtu* corpus are only preserved in fragments or not at all. Larger cuneiform tablets rarely survive intact, and in addition to clay tablets, wooden or ivory writing boards were in widespread use, nearly all of which have perished. Parchment was used as a writing material in the first millennium in Mesopotamia but probably for writing the Aramaic alphabetic script, which would only exceptionally have been used for writing Sumerian or Akkadian magical texts.

The other sizeable body of ancient Near Eastern rituals and incantations survived as part of the libraries of the Hittite royal residence Hattusa and, to a lesser degree, of Hittite provincial centers. Although the chronological extent of the Hittite body of texts is more limited (ca. late sixteenth–thirteenth century BC) and the scribal tradition more homogeneous, the rituals themselves originate from a wide variety of Anatolian, Syrian, and Mesopotamian traditions and include recitations not only in Hittite but also in Hattic, Palaic, Luwian, and Hurrian.[17]

A few early second-millennium Hurrian incantations were found at Babylonian sites and on the Middle Euphrates. In addition, Elamite incantations are attested in Babylonia at this time, and garbled versions of Hurrian and Elamite incantations became part of the Babylonian incantation tradition. A small group of incantations in Ugaritic language are known from tablets in Ugaritic alphabetic script excavated at Ugarit and Ras Ibn Hani (thirteenth century BC), and a few first-millennium Aramaic and Phoenician magical texts should at least be mentioned here.[18]

The available sources are not restricted to the textual record. Babylonians and Assyrians used amulets and apotropaic figurines to protect their houses and themselves; apotropaic demons were depicted on the walls of palaces and protected their entrances[19]; the exorcist used weapons, drums, gongs, and bells to chase away the evil; and scenes on some cylinder seals show a patient being treated by an exorcist.[20] Apotropaic figurines could take the form of model guard dogs that were deposited in groups of five on each side of a doorway; one complete set was found next to a door of Ashurbanipal's palace at Nineveh (Figure 1.3). The dogs' names, which are also known from a ritual text, are inscribed on their sides and underline their apotropaic function: "Catcher of the enemy"; "Don't think, bite!"; "Biter of his foe"; "Expeller of evildoers"; and "Loud is his bark."[21] An exorcist's copper bell found at Neo-Assyrian Ashur is adorned with a relief depicting well-known apotropaic demons (Figure 1.4): pairs of lion-demons called *ugallu* guarding an entrance (only seemingly facing each other), a fish-garbed *apkallu* sprinkling purifying water, and the warrior-god Lulal with his arm raised ready to expel any evil attackers. On top of the bell crouch a pair of lizards and a pair of turtles. The latter symbolize the god of exorcism, Enki-Ea, whose home is the subterranean ocean. The frightening lizards repel any evil that might come near. Perhaps they represent the lizard called *ḫumbabītu* in Akkadian, a name that refers to the monstrous giant Ḫuwawa (Ḫumbaba), whose head was often used as an apotropaion.[22]

In contrast to apotropaic objects, ritual remains, which were regarded as impure and usually had to be buried in secluded places far from human habitation, are unlikely to be observed by modern archaeologists. But on rare occasions, even such discoveries are made: excavations at Yazılıkaya, a prominent Hittite rock sanctuary near Hattusa, uncovered the embryo of a pig that had been buried in the ground and fixed with nails, probably as a magic substitute and carrier of impurity.[23] The fragment of an anthropomorphic clay figurine that was pierced several times was excavated at Old Babylonian Tell ed-Dēr. This find can be connected with the rite of piercing substitute figurines of

FIGURE 1.3. Painted and inscribed clay figurines of apotropaic guard dogs, Neo-Assyrian period, 7th century BC, Nineveh, palace of Ashurbanipal. British Museum, London, WA 30001–5. © Trustees of the British Museum.

warlocks and witches with the thorn of a date palm that is well known from Babylonian anti-witchcraft rituals.[24]

Exorcists, Physicians, Snake Charmers, and Witches

The Babylonian and Assyrian exorcist (*āšipu*), a male professional, performed purification rituals for houses, stables, and fields; he participated in temple rituals and was competent in the ceremonies associated with the induction of people into office, the initiation of divine statues, and the foundation of temples.[25] But a large proportion of the *āšipūtu* corpus focuses on protective

FIGURE I.4. Apotropaic copper bell, Neo-Assyrian period, 8th–7th century BC, Ashur. Vorderasiatisches Museum, Berlin, VA 2517. © bpk – Bildagentur für Kunst, Kultur und Geschichte / Olaf M. Teßmer.

and therapeutic measures against various human illnesses, and the exorcist, who usually held his office at the royal court or within the temple hierarchy, was one of the most important healing professionals in ancient Mesopotamia, treating complex and serious illnesses by dispelling the evil force at their root, purifying the patient, and protecting him or her against similar future threats. The exorcist was not the only expert an ill person could consult. Besides him, the Mesopotamian letters and magical-medical texts often mention the *asû*, usually translated as "physician." Originally, the remit of the *asû* was concerned with ailments whose cause was evident (such as heat stroke, external injuries, fractures, common coughs and sneezes, etc.); he would set bones, perform (hit-and-miss) surgery, and employ medications whose preparation and application could include the recitation of incantations. The subdivision of the art of healing into *āšipūtu*, the lore of the exorcist, and *asûtu*, the lore of the physician, deeply influenced the organization and transmission of Babylonian magical and medical texts and is visible in many individual prescriptions that refer to the knowledge of both crafts as the two basic strategies of fighting illness. But the structure of individual rituals and therapies, a survey of the tablet collections of these experts, and, last but not least, letters written by them demonstrate that not only were these two strategies regarded as complementary but that the actual competence of an individual expert was not necessarily defined by the traditional and ideal profile of his profession.[26] Of course, it is tempting to associate *āšipūtu* with magic and *asûtu* with medicine; in many respects, the healing strategy associated with the exorcist's profession and the therapies associated with the physician's coincide with our concepts of magic and medicine respectively. But one must not forget that, even within the ideal definition of the arts of *āšipūtu* and *asûtu*, the former included physical treatment of the patient, whereas the latter, as a matter of course, involved the recitation of incantations and the use of other techniques and ideas that we would regard as magic.

The exorcist and the physician are the two professionals that are mentioned in the corpus of magical and medical texts; they participated actively in the transmission and development of this written tradition. Like the diviner (*bārû*), they were members of the urban elite holding offices at local temples or the royal court, and their patients would usually belong to or be associated with the same social stratum. Very little is known about the healers, magicians, and diviners who did not have part in the written tradition. One certainly encountered them in the streets of Babylonian and Assyrian cities. A prayer to Marduk praises the god as the divine guarantor of ritual experts: "Without you the exorcist (*āšipu*) could not treat the sick person, without you the exorcist (*āšipu*), the owlman (*eššebû*) and the snake charmer (*mušlaḫḫu*) would not walk about in the street (offering their service)."[27] Usually experts like the owlman and the snake charmer are mentioned in the incantation literature together with other low-ranking incantation experts and cultic officials. They are often drawn as shady characters and accused of having performed illegal, evil witchcraft against the patient.[28] In the following passage from an Akkadian incantation to be recited during the performance of the anti-witchcraft ritual *Maqlû*, the patient describes how he is enlisting all possible agents of witchcraft against the witch who has attacked him, thereby defeating her with her own means:

> I seek against you *kurgarrû*-hierodules and owlmen – I break your bond!
> May warlocks perform rituals against you – I break your bond!
> May witches perform rituals against you – I break your bond!
> May *kurgarrû*-hierodules perform rituals against you – I break your bond!
> May owlmen perform rituals against you – I break your bond!
> May *naršindu*-sorcerers perform rituals against you – I break your bond!
> May snake charmers perform rituals against you – I break your bond!
> May *agugillu*-sorcerers perform rituals against you – I break your bond!
> I slap your cheek, I tear out your tongue![29]

Of the magic practitioners invoked in this list, only warlock and witch (Akkadian *kaššāpu* and *kaššāptu*) are regarded as illegitimate and their "professional" activity (*kašāpu*, "to bewitch") as illegal and punishable per se. Witches are mentioned in the textual record only with reference to others who are accused of having performed illegal witchcraft, and there is, so far, no evidence that *kaššāptu* at one point served as a designation for a legitimate female healing profession that over time (or among the elites) lost its status and only then became *the* pejorative designation for the perpetrator of evil magic.[30]

It is a typical feature of Mesopotamian magic and medicine that the two professionals participating in the textual tradition – exorcist and physician – are both male, whereas female healers are restricted to the divine sphere (the healing goddess Gula), the lower rungs of society, and the stereotypes associated with the agents of harmful magic. But this pattern is by no means universal in the ancient Near East. In Hittite Anatolia, male and female physicians are attested,[31] and the main bodies of therapeutic rituals are assigned to various groups of ritual experts, the most prominent among which are the "old woman" and the "diviner."[32] It is common for Hittite rituals to be assigned to a named individual ritual expert, but the scribal tradition as it is preserved to us seems to be largely the work of (male) scribes of the royal administration.[33]

Categories of Magic, Sources of Affliction

Purity is the state of undisturbed, flawless perfection that is characteristic of the divine sphere but achieved by humans only temporarily and not without effort. Certain substances, such as urine, saliva, or sewage, are typically considered as impure, whereas others, such as water, soap, oil, or silver, are regarded as pure and possessing purifying powers. Misfortune, ill-health, and failure are experienced as conditions in which man's aspiration to god-like perfection and equilibrium is poignantly frustrated, and, consequently, people or objects suffering from such conditions are considered to have been affected by impurity. Hence, all potential causes of calamity, including moral transgressions, are at the same time sources of impurity. This impurity is usually invisible, but it can be mobilized and removed by the performance of purifying rituals whose gestures and symbols draw on the regular practice of cleaning and washing. The transition from impurity to purity is one of the basic goals and regular elements of magic rituals in all ancient Near Eastern cultures.

Ancient Near Eastern magic as a whole can be subdivided into four major categories: (a) liminal magic, by which the ritual client is transformed and taken to another status; (b) defensive magic, by which an evil that has beset (or threatened to beset) the ritual client is removed and repelled; (c) aggressive magic, by which the ritual client gains superiority, strength, and attractiveness; and (d) witchcraft, an illegal and aggressive form of magic by which the ritual client has been harmed. The last category may be called "black magic," the two categories named first "white magic," and aggressive magic falls into a gray area in between. The vast majority of the transmitted ritual texts belong to the first two categories; the transition from impurity to purity plays a central role in both of them. Ritual texts for performing illegal witchcraft were not transmitted. But information on the concepts and ideas associated with what was considered to be witchcraft can be gleaned from defensive anti-witchcraft rituals and some aggressive rituals within the lore of the exorcist.

The category of liminal magic comprises mainly rituals performed on healthy persons or intact objects that were to enter the sphere of the cult. Regarded as the realm of the gods, temples and sanctuaries required anyone entering them to be properly induced and purified. The buildings themselves, cultic objects (including divine statues), and the temple personnel all underwent induction rituals by which they were purified, transformed, and introduced into the sacred domain.[34] An incantation that was recited during the induction of Babylonian priests into office illustrates how the purification was achieved by both symbolic actions and a request for divine endorsement; in the following passage, Marduk, often called the "exorcist of the gods," is asked to validate the washing and shaving rites the new priest has to undergo:

Pouring water over the head, rubbing with soap,
giving a bath in a pure fashion with the shaving knife,
giving a bath with water, rubbing with soap,

giving a bath with water, washing his limbs –
may Marduk, son of Eridu, purify (him), clean (him and) make (him)
   sparkle!
May the evil tongue stand aside![35]

Apart from washing rites, various types of passage rites could be employed to perform the transition from impurity to purity. In Hittite rituals, passing through a gate made of a hawthorn bush was a common symbol of leaving behind the evil, which was held back by the thorns, and entering a new state of purity. Other Hittite transition rites that separated the ritual client from a past state of impurity include passing through two inseparable halves that, once passed, formed an impenetrable barrier. Two fires could be lit on each side of a path. Also, puppies, piglets, and even humans could be killed, halved, and laid out on each side of the passage.[36] The killing of animals or humans within such rites was not regarded as a sacrifice to the gods; rather it served the purpose of creating a symbolic barrier that could be overcome once and was then closed forever.

Most ancient Near Eastern magic rituals belong to the category of defensive magic. The goal of these rituals was to free the ritual client of an evil that has beset him or her. The person affected by the evil was regarded as impure, and that person's condition was interpreted as a state of being bound. By the performance of the defensive ritual, the patient was purified and set free; the calamity or illness, which had been interpreted as the manifestation of the evil, was cured, and the underlying evil removed. Thus, most defensive rituals served therapeutic purposes, although some could also be performed prophylactically or were designed for this purpose only. Moreover, various types of amulets and other apotropaic measures could be used to prevent evil forces from attacking a person.

Because the removal of the evil that had caused the suffering was considered to be of crucial importance for the recovery of the patient, the diagnosis of an illness, which would rely on examination, anamnesis, and, if required, confirmation by means of divination, very much consisted in identifying the ultimate cause of the patient's suffering (etiology). Akkadian texts often briefly refer to the maleficent force that was held responsible for an illness with the phrase "hand of ...." The body of defensive ritual texts used by the Mesopotamian exorcist is largely organized according to these etiologies, comprising of rituals against various demons, rituals for reconciling angry deities, rituals for undoing evil omens, rituals for banning ghosts of deceased persons, rituals for removing curses that resulted from the transgression of a taboo or contact with tabooed substances, and, last but not least, rituals for countering witchcraft performed by fellow humans.

Demons are envisaged as low-ranking, often monstrous creatures of the divine sphere. They roam the wilderness and mountains (both associated in some sources with the netherworld) and become dangerous to men, women, and children on their raids into human habitations. They fly with the wind, they slip into the house through windows and pivots; doors and bolts are no obstacle for them. A bilingual incantation from the series *Evil Demons* describes a gang of these fearsome predators as follows:

> They have no god, they are children of the netherworld,
> the evil Utukku, the evil Alû, the evil ghost, the evil Gallû, the Evil God, the
>   evil Rābiṣu, Lamaštu, Labāṣu and Aḫḫāzu: they descend on a man,
> they walk about stealthily in the street at night,
> they destroy the cattle pen and smash the sheepfold,
> . . .
> they slither in through the door like a serpent,
> they drift in through the door-pivot like the wind.
> They drive the wife from her husband's lap,
> they remove the child from a man's knee,
> they oust the groom from his father-in-law's house.
> They (spread) stupour and oblivion, it is they who keep chasing a man.[37]

The best-known of the demons named in this passage is Lamaštu: a lion-headed creature with the ears of a donkey, the teeth of a dog, and the talons of an eagle, she attacks infants and women before, during, and after childbirth. Rituals against Lamaštu include apotropaic measures, among them the destruction or removal of figurines representing Lamaštu, amulets showing Lamaštu herself, and, if an attack has already happened, various remedies, especially against fever. A group of amulets depicts Lamaštu being driven off by the demon Pazuzu as she crosses, surrounded by her provisions, the Ulaya River on a boat to return to the "steppe" (i.e., the netherworld).[38] The following incantation passage describes how Lamaštu is supplied with provisions and sent on her journey with no return:

> Pull up your (tent) pegs, roll up your ropes,
> go off to your mountain like a wild ass of the steppe.
> May Marduk, the incantation expert, the exorcist, give you
> a comb, a clasp, a spindle, a blanket, and a dress-pin.
> Set out to the animals of the wilderness!
> May you be anointed with fine oil,

> may you be equipped with lasting sandals,
> may you carry a waterskin for your thirst![39]

Another female demon is Ardat-lilî ("Wind-maiden"), the daughter of Lilû and Lilîtu, a pair of wind-demons. She represents the young girl that was never allowed to enjoy the pleasures of love, marriage, and family life:

> Wind-maiden who slipped with the wind into a man's house, the … maiden,
> the maiden who is like a woman who had never had sex,
> the maiden who is like a woman who was never deflowered,
> the maiden who never made love in her husband's lap …[40]

Isolated and angry, Ardat-lilî drifts along with the wind, travels through the uninhabited plains, and takes revenge by inflicting illness on people.

The demon Sāmānu ("Redness") causes various ailments that are accompanied by abnormal redness (inflammation, bleeding, etc.). Incantations against Sāmānu, which are attested already in the third millennium, describe him as a monster coming from the mountains who crosses the river and attacks humans and animals alike.[41] Incantations used to cure dog bites, scorpion stings, and snake bites are very common, notably in earlier periods, and they often demonize these animals, which, like demons, live in the wilderness but invade human habitations.[42] Here and in other cases, the distinction between magical incantations against demons and medical incantations against (sometimes personified) illnesses becomes rather blurred.

Slander and malevolent glances are widely feared; witches eye their victims, slander them, and utter evil spells. The organs of these evil actions are personified, and the evil eye in particular, but also the evil tongue or mouth, although originally bound to a human or demonic agent, are considered to be demonic forces in their own right. The evil eye can be held responsible for all kinds of calamities in a person's house, stable, and fields, but it is also regarded as a possible cause of illness.[43]

Whereas demons are creatures of the wilderness and pose a threat from the outside, other evils originate from within human society. Individuals can inflict impurity and divine anger on themselves and their relatives by transgressing a taboo. The evil that befalls them is called *māmītu* in Akkadian (Sumerian *namerim*), a word for oath that also designates the consequence of a broken oath (curse) and, in a wider sense, the evil effects on the perpetrator of any transgression, crime, or sin. But it is not only a person's own actions that can bring harm to that person and his or her family. Other people may cause illness and mishap by using rituals, prayers, and incantations, manipulated food and drink, and drugs and ointments against an innocent victim.

Several words could be used to refer to this kind of evil magic, but the most important term is Akkadian *kišpū*, or "witchcraft" (Sumerian *uš*). Significantly, these two human sources of evil, sin and witchcraft, seem to have been regarded as a complementary pair within the lore of the exorcist. The so-called *Exorcist's Manual* names rituals for undoing witchcraft (*ušburruda*) and for undoing a curse (*namerimburruda*) side by side, and the same is true for *Maqlû* (burning) and *Šurpu* (incineration), the two extensive rituals against witchcraft and curse, respectively.[44] That this arrangement is not due to chance is indicated by the fact that a number of rituals and prescriptions were regarded as effective against both *kišpū* and *māmītu* (witchcraft and curse, respectively); there also seems to be a certain complementary distribution between the symptoms that indicated witchcraft or curse as the cause of an illness.[45] The rationale underlying this pairing is nowhere explained explicitly, but it seems significant that both evils originate in human actions: in the case of *māmītu* by the patient or (living or deceased) members of the patient's family who have transgressed a taboo; in the case of *kišpū* by fellow humans who have practiced sorceries against the patient. Both ritual types also share a common typical technique that aims at a complete annihilation of the causes of the patient's sorrows: the burning of materials representing the evil or its agents.

The performance of the anti-witchcraft ritual *Maqlû* stretches over one night and includes the recitation of almost a hundred incantations.[46] The basic pattern of the ritual is that shared by most anti-witchcraft rituals and consists of a simple transition: the victim is transferred from a state of imminent death back to life, he or she is purified, and his or her bound state is undone; sorcerer and sorceress are assigned the fate they had intended for their victim because the witchcraft is sent back to them. Due to this basic pattern, anti-witchcraft rituals often consist of a mirror-image performance of the rituals that the sorcerers supposedly carried out against the patient, the only difference being that the patient – as a number of incantations emphasize – claims to have his or her ritual performed in public, whereas the alleged sorcerers acted secretly. The reversion of the patient's and the sorcerers' fate is interpreted as a legal process that ends with the acquittal of the innocent patient whose unjustified verdict had been provoked by the sorcerers' slander. The ritual *Maqlû* begins after sunset with an invocation of the stars, the astral manifestations of the gods. The patient allies himself or herself with the gods of the netherworld and asks them to imprison the witches and also with the gods of heaven and asks them to purify him or her. The exorcist protects the crucible, which plays a central role in the following proceedings, with a magic circle, and the whole cosmos is asked to pause and support the patient's cause.[47] This is followed by a long series of burning rites during which various figurines representing the warlock and the witch are burned in the crucible. The following incantation is recited at this stage of the ritual. During the recitation of the incantation, figurines of the warlock and the witch made of clay and tallow are put into the fire, where the clay bursts and the tallow melts:

> Whoever you are witch who took clay for my (figurine) from the river,
> who buried figurines of me in the "dark house,"
> who buried my water in a tomb,
> who picked up scraps (discarded by) me from the dustheaps,
> who tore off the fringe (of a garment) of mine at the fuller's house,
> who gathered dirt (touched by) my feet from a threshold –
> I sent to the gate of the quay: they bought me tallow for your (figurine).
> I sent to the canal of the city: they brought me clay for your (figurine).
> I am sending against you the burning oven, the flaring Fire-god,
> the ever alight Fire-god, the steady light of the gods,
> . . .
> She trusts in her artful witchcraft,
> but I (trust) in the steady light of the Fire-god, the judge.
> Fire-god, burn [her], Fire-god, incinerate her,
> Fire-god, overpower her![48]

After the sorcerers' death by fire has thus been enacted repeatedly, a figurine of the witch's personal fate-goddess is defiled by the pouring of a black liquid over its head. By this act, the witch's evil fate, her death, is sealed, and the patient leaves her behind in the darkness of the night.[49] In the second half of the night, destructive rites directed against the evildoers are increasingly superseded by ritual segments that focus on the purification and future protection of the patient. The incantations greet the rising sun-god as the patient's savior, and the ritual ends with the patient identifying himself or herself with his or her own reflection in a bowl of pure water shimmering in the morning light:

> You are my reflection, you are my vitality,
> you are my spirit, you are my bodily form,
> you are my bodily shape, you are my vigor,
> you are my great reflection(?), you are my self-renewing reflection.
> [Reject] witchcraft, reject sorceries!
> . . .
> You are mine, (and) I am yours.
> May nobody know you, may no evil approach you –
> by the command of Šamaš, Marduk and the princess Bēletilī![50]

Whereas the burning of the witches' figurines dominates the proceedings of *Maqlû*, the ritual *Šurpu* aims at removing the patient's impurity that has been caused by his or her own transgressions. It is not figurines representing the patient's enemies, but the consequences of his or her own actions that have to be eliminated and are destroyed by fire. Thus, the performance of *Šurpu* includes the burning of dough that is applied to and wiped off of the patient's body. The patient throws various items representing his or her crimes into the fire, among them garlic peels. The accompanying incantation explains the ritual action:

> Just as this garlic is peeled and thrown into the fire,
> (just as) the Fire-god, the burner, consumes (it),
> ...
> (so) may ... my illness, my weariness, my guilt, my crime, my sin, my
>   transgression,
> the illness that is present in my body, my flesh (and) my veins,
> be peeled off like this garlic so that
> the Fire-god, the burner, consumes (it) today!
> May the curse leave so that I may see the light![51]

Other *Šurpu* incantations give long enumerations of the possible transgressions that may have caused the patient's sorrows. The lists include ordinary crimes, such as murder, theft, perjury, and witchcraft, but also less tangible wrongdoing, such as arrogance against gods or fellow humans and mere contact with an accursed person or substances touched by such a person.

In many ways related to *Šurpu* (and other rituals for undoing curses), Babylonian prayers and rituals are designed to appease a deity's anger that has been caused by the patient's wrongdoing (*dingiršadabba*). The incantation texts recited during rituals for appeasing a god's anger were composed in Sumerian, but already in the early second millennium, they were often accompanied by an Akkadian translation. The genre became known across scribal centers of the ancient Near East, and Hittite adaptations of these incantations played a formative role in the development of Hittite prayer literature. The following extract from a Hittite prayer composed for a prince called Kantuzzili consists almost entirely of passages that can be shown to have been adapted from Sumerian-Akkadian incantations:

> Life is bound up with death for me, and death is bound up with life for me. A
> mortal does not live forever, the days of his life are counted. If a mortal were
> to live forever, (even) if also the evils befalling man, illness, were to remain, it
> would not be a grievance for him.

[Now] may my god open his innermost soul to me with all his heart, and may he [tell] me my sins so that I (can) acknowledge them. May my god either speak to me in a dream – and may my god open his heart and tell [me] my sins so that I (can) acknowledge them – or let a dream interpretess speak to me [or] let a diviner of the Sun-god speak [to me] (by reading) from a liver (in extispicy), and may my god open [his innermost soul] to me with all his heart, and may he tell me my sins so that I (can) acknowledge them.[52]

Ghosts of deceased people are considered to be another possible source of affliction. The deceased dwell in the netherworld, a dark and inhospitable place in the earth that is inaccessible to the living. Families provide their dead with food and drink that are supplied in the form of regular funerary offerings. Not all dead people receive these offerings regularly and stay in the nether-world: their family may not fulfill the obligations to care for the deceased, or the deceased themselves may have suffered a horrible death that prevented them from being properly buried and thus from entering the netherworld. The ghosts of such people are regarded as aggressive and dangerous; they wander through the land and haunt the living. The exorcist has a wide variety of rituals and remedies at his disposal, and the purpose of those rituals and remedies is to send such ghosts back to the netherworld and heal the sufferings they cause. The ghosts of a father and a mother receive a friendly treatment. The exorcist prepares figurines representing them, which are decorated and fed with hot soup, a typical provision for the dead. On the day of the funerary offerings, their fate is decided before the sun-god Šamaš. Then, the figurines and their provisions are placed in a sailing boat, sent off, and, in a common feature of anti-ghost rituals, placed under an oath not to return.[53] Evil ghosts of other peo-ple that pursue the patient are not always treated so kindly. They usually receive libations; figurines of them are ritually buried and thereby banned to the neth-erworld. For the fabrication of the figurines and the libations, less than pleasant materials, such as excrement and donkey's urine, may be used.

If a healthy person heard the cry of a ghost in his or her house, this por-tended death and calamity for that person's family, and there are a number of ghost rituals that were designed to avert such evil before it actually struck. Such preemptive ritual measures against misfortune heralded by specific events that were interpreted as indicating a bad fate are quite common in Mesopotamian magic. They are based on a dualistic concept of fate that distinguishes the eternal, unchanging destinies that rule human life (e.g., mortality) from the changeable, and therefore flexible, fate of the individual. A large body of texts labeled namburbi, or "its release," served exclusively this purpose.[54] These ritu-als had two principal goals: on the one hand, the evil sign as such (e.g., a miscarriage) had to be physically removed; on the other hand, Šamaš as the divine judge was implored with offerings and prayers to revise the evil fate that had been ordained for the patient. In exceptional cases, the removal of the evil sign could involve the killing of humans: one text advises that a person suffering from fits, whose condition is interpreted as an evil portent, should be either buried alive or burnt.[55]

Other rituals could be employed if bad dreams portended evil,[56] and even royal war rituals were stylized as defensive rituals against evil omens. An incantation that was to be recited during a war ritual informs us that the Babylonians assumed that their enemies would pray to the same deities and try to convince them to take sides with them against the Babylonian king:

> [...] [t]hey implored you to smash my weapons: do not accept [their ...], their [pra]yer (and) their pleading, [do not] listen(?) to the words of the barbar-ians, [to their ... do not] listen! Do not eat their bread offerings, [do not drink their water libations(?)], do not accept their incense offerings! [... either by] their witchcraft or their sorceries or their (evil) magic [let the weapons of(?)] my [...] not be smashed, not be bound, not be defeated![57]

If a solar eclipse portended the worst for the king (the sun of his people), a substitute king, usually a prisoner, could be installed during the time of dan-ger, whereas the king was addressed as "farmer" and underwent purification rites. The substitute king ritual and its performance are best documented in letters from the Neo-Assyrian period and in Hittite adaptations of the origi-nally Babylonian ritual.[58] These texts show that the unfortunate substitute on the throne usually did not survive the ritual, although an anecdote reports that a gardener in Old Babylonian Isin stayed on the throne after the real king had died from sipping an overly hot broth. In at least one Hittite substitute king ritual, the idea of the substitute king suffering the evil fate intended for the king is combined with the well-known rite of sending off a substitute as the carrier of an impurity. Thus, the prisoner of war on the throne is not killed but sent off to his land:

> They anoint the prisoner of war with the oil of kingship, and (the king) speaks thus: "Now this one is king. [I have given] the royal title to this one, I have invested this one with the royal [robe], I have crowned this one with the (royal) cap. Evil signs, short years, short days, notice [this one] and follow this substitute!" ... They lead an officer before the prisoner, and he takes him back to his land.[59]

But of course prophylactic measures did not have to wait for a bad omen indicating imminent danger. Amulets (sometimes in the form of cuneiform tablets), phylacteries, and apotropaic figurines (see Figure 1.3) could always be used to protect houses and persons. One would employ them especially in situations of obvious danger (e.g., pregnancy and childbirth),[60] but the foundation of a new house was also accompanied by apotropaic rites.

The rituals devised for the protection of the king are characterized by their complexity. A Babylonian purification ritual for the king, which was known as the ritual of the "bath-house" (*bīt rimki*), involved the ceremonial purification of the palace, the recitation of numerous Akkadian and Sumerian incantations and prayers, the ceremonial washing of the king in seven huts erected outside the city (bath-houses), various substitute rites, and the performance of rituals against evil signs, curses, witchcraft, and divine anger. In an early section of the ritual, a goat is slaughtered and the king speaks several short pleas over various parts of the animal's carcass. These pleas offer a fine example of how the principle of analogy was used in magic on various levels. On the one hand, they refer to the parts of the carcass themselves; on the other hand, they use the Akkadian designations of the parts of the carcass as reference points, thereby lending weight to the request by "linguistic" means. The last analogical spell quoted here was spoken by the king while washing over two sets of seven silver sickles, and it refers to both the purity of the metal and the function of the sickles as cutting tools:

The king [...] to the cut from which the goat's(?) blood ... and speaks thus: "Let the blood of the evil witch be poured out. May the earth not accept her blood, may the River undo [her ...], may he have [her] gnaw off her fingers, let her tongue [turn] dark, may the Fire-god burn [her]!"

The king purifies the carcass (*pagru*) of the she-goat and speaks thus: "Let the people be gathered (*paḫāru*) around me; may they heed my orders!"

The king speaks thus to the *isru*-intestine: "May the curses (*izziru*) in the mouth of the many people be driven away from my body!"

[The king] speaks thus to the (black) hide: "May 'the darkness of my face' be driven away [from m]y [body]!"

...

The king speaks thus to the intestines (*qerbū*): "May prayers for well-being be brought near (*qerēbu*) to me, and may I acquire life before Šamaš!"

The king rinses himself off over fourteen sickles of silver, seven on the right, seven on the left; then he speaks thus: "May the tablets inscribed with my sins be smashed, may my evil deeds be cleared, may my crimes and my wrongdoings be cut off, be chopped off, be scattered – the evil (about me) in the mouth of the many people. May life (for me) be present in the mouth of the people like silver!"[61]

Analogical spells are not a feature unique to Mesopotamian magic rituals, but they are very common in all ancient Near Eastern rituals. They are also used in the context of oath ceremonies, wherein the horrible consequences of breaking the oath would be shown to the participants. A Hittite oath ceremony for the army uses several analogical spells, among them one that imposes effeminacy on any soldier who should break the oath:

> They bring women's clothes, a distaff and a spindle. They break an arrow, and you speak thus to them: "What is this? Are these not women's clothes? And we have them here for the oath. Whoever transgresses these oaths and does evil to the king, the queen (or) the children of the king: let these oaths turn him from a man into a woman, let them turn his troups into women, may they dress them like women, may they put a woman's scarf on them. Let them break bows, arrows (and any other) weapons in their hands and let them put distaff and spindle into their hands!"[62]

The art of the Mesopotamian exorcist was not restricted to dispelling an evil that had befallen or threatened to befall the patient. Besides the large group of defensive rituals, the exorcist's lore comprised also of several types of aggressive rituals whose performance was intended to give the client power over other people, attractiveness, and success: a man could force a woman into loving him; a woman could equip herself with captivating charisma.[63] The incantation texts of this genre are free of prudish inhibition; often they use comparisons with animals to express wishes for sexual fulfillment and success. In the following passage from an Old Babylonian love incantation, the male suitor speaks to the object of his desire:

> May Love make love to me also,
>> so I can cast (this spell), speak, talk, flirt (with her):
> "Think of me as an *ašnugallum*-snake,
>> so your mood grows wanton as a wild cow!
> Do not wait on your father's counsel,
>> do not heed your mother's advice!"[64]

An innkeeper who suffered from slow business could be helped by means of a special ritual that would ensure that punters were attracted to his tavern.[65] A merchant could have a ritual performed that would ensure brisk trade on his business trip.[66] There are rituals for calming the anger of one's adversary and for strengthening oneself before going to the palace or appearing in a court of law. Someone who was called before the king or before a nobleman could whisper a short incantation beginning with the words "Laughing, charm, eloquence, affection, rise(?) before me!" before entering the palace; thus, he or she would gain irresistible charm and ensure a favorable treatment.[67] There were also methods to gag one's opponent ritually before one had to confront him in court. The relevant Sumerian rubrics include *kadabbeda* ("seizing the mouth"), *egalkura* ("entering the palace"), *šurḫunga* ("soothing the anger"), *šudu'a* ("loosening the (closed) hand"), *igibiḫulla* ("delighting his face"), and *dikugubba* ("standing before the judge").[68] Often these rituals prescribe anointing the ritual client with oil, thereby conferring purity, charm, and power on him.

A runaway slave could be forced to return by the performance of a ritual. The pertinent incantations use the image of the turning door that swings outward but ultimately stays in its place.[69] If slaves did not obey their owner and caused trouble, another simple ritual could be performed that would force them into submission. Figurines of the slaves were prepared and put in a position where they would be defiled and degraded by their master every day:

> A slave and a slave-girl who do not serve you with respect and do not carry out orders: You make bitumen figurines representing them. You bury them at the foot of your bed so that the wash water of your hands and feet will run over them. Then the slave (and the slave-girl) [will serve(?)] you [with respect(?)].[70]

Examples of all of the aggressive ritual types mentioned thus far are attested on cuneiform tablets from Mesopotamian libraries, but lists of ritual types – such as can be found in the *Exorcist's Almanac*, a first millennium text that indicates favorable periods of time for the performance of certain rituals – suggest that other aggressive rituals were known, for example, rituals for removing someone from an office or for depriving someone of the king's favor.[71]

The aggressive rituals occupy a peculiar place in the exorcist's lore. Tablets with instructions for their performance were found in the libraries of Mesopotamian scholars; they studied and certainly also used them if required. On the other hand, lists of various methods of (illegal) witchcraft include some of these aggressive rituals,[72] and the *Exorcist's Manual*, which claims to present a representative catalog of the exorcist's texts, silently omits them all. It is noteworthy that the remains of the royal libraries of Nineveh, whose collections primarily housed texts that were necessary for the protection of the king's person, have thus far not produced a single fragment of a ritual of this type. Did the king's scholars regard these texts as dubious, or were these rituals just irrelevant for someone in the king's all powerful position? Whatever the answer, there can be little doubt that the aggressive rituals were regarded with a certain ambivalence, situated in a gray area between the approved lore of the exorcist and illegal witchcraft.

Gods, Stars, Monsters, Nature, and Man

All ancient Near Eastern magic is performed in the context of a polytheistic worldview. Some Mesopotamian incantations, especially recitations that are to be recited over an ointment or other simple remedies whose application does not involve the performance of a ritual, do not appeal to divine authority at all. Usually, however, divine approval is sought at least by ending the requests expressed in the incantation with the formula "by the command of ... [divine name(s)]." Another way to ensure divine endorsement is the formulaic assertion at the end of a recitation that the incantation itself is of divine origin: "This incantation is not mine, it is the incantation of ... [divine name(s)]." In some text groups, the entire ritual procedure is attributed to a divine authority and only reenacted by the human ritual expert. Sumerian incantations incorporate the ritual instructions into the incantation text as actions performed by Enki himself or, more commonly, stylize them as Enki's advice to his son, the divine exorcist Asalluḫi. In Hittite mythological texts, such as the myth of Telipinu, the ritual setting of the text is included in the narrative, mainly as the action of the healing goddess Kamrusepa. Many rituals are explicitly addressed to a specific deity or group of deities; they usually include the presentation of offerings and the recitation of incantations that take the form of prayers to the divinity addressed.

The main deities invoked in Mesopotamian magic rituals are Enki-Ea, the god of wisdom and exorcism, who resides in the subterranean ocean; Asalluḫi-Marduk, his son, who too is regarded as a god of exorcistic lore; and the sun-god Utu-Šamaš, the god of justice and light. Some incantations are addressed to all three gods who, in the later tradition, were considered to be the quintessential gods of magic. Whereas Ea and Marduk are characterized as divine exorcists and purification experts, Šamaš acts as the divine judge who frees the patient, brings light into the patient's darkness, and favorably revises the divine verdict manifest in the patient's suffering. Other deities that occur regularly in the incantations include the incantation goddess Ningirima, who is in charge of the holy water vessel; the purification god Kusu, who is foremost associated with the censer; the divine fire Gibil-Girra, who represents both the destructive and purifying force of fire; and Siriš, the divine beer, "releaser of god and man." During nocturnal rituals, the moon-god, the stars, and the deified night can be addressed; also the period of the new moon, a favorable time for the performance of anti-witchcraft rituals, can be personified and invoked in incantations.[73] The opening incantation of *Maqlû* calls on "the gods of the night," that is, the stars as the manifestations of the great gods, the deified night, who was identified with the healing-goddess Gula, and the personified three watches of the night:

> I invoke you, gods of the night,
> with you I invoke the Night, the veiled bride,
> I invoke Dusk, Midnight and Dawn![74]

Often purificatory water is left outside under the stars overnight and thus exposed to the power of the astral deities. Many rituals are designed to be performed before specific stars, such as Jupiter, Scorpius, or Ursa Major. The goat star (Lyra) is, like the deified night, associated with the goddess Gula and plays a special role in magic rituals.[75]

But not only rituals of the exorcist could be performed before the stars. Evil rituals are thought to have been performed before the same stars by witches,[76] and a number of texts indicate that at least some forms of witchcraft were assumed to have been performed before the very same deities that the ritual client invoked in order to be freed of witchcraft. The gods were not by their very nature allies of the patient. They could have rendered a wrong verdict against the patient because witches had slandered him or her; they could have averted their favor in anger because of his or her failures. One of the functions of a therapeutic ritual was therefore to convince the invoked gods of the patient's innocence and to make them change their mind with regard to the patient.[77] But witchcraft and divine anger are not the only areas of Mesopotamian magic where the gods played an ambivalent role. The abode of Enki-Ea, the subterranean ocean (*apsû*), was not only the source of incantations and purification rites, but it was also considered a place from which demons, diseases, and witchcraft had emerged.[78] Also, Ekur, the seat of the god Enlil, was known to be a dwelling place of demons.[79] One demon who is regularly mentioned in lists of evil spirits was simply called "Evil God."

Not all demons and monsters of the divine sphere were evil. Defeated monsters became powerful apotropaia, and many monsters and demons were regarded as protective spirits.[80] Pazuzu, who repels and rules the evil wind-demons, was one of the popular protective monsters in the first millennium BC. Pazuzu figurines and heads were common apotropaia, and he is depicted on many amulets of that period. The figure of Pazuzu emerged from a combination of the personified west wind and Ḫuwawa, a monster living in the western mountains who was defeated by Gilgameš.[81] The four winds themselves were regarded as carriers of good and evil. Travelers especially sought protection from the many dangers they would face in the open country by invoking these forces of nature. An incantation that was recited in a ritual for the protection of travelers asks the south and east wind, as well as earth and sky, to guard the ritual client who had to pitch camp in the wilderness:

> I pick up a stone, I defy all (attackers),
> I have been caught up among the animals of the wilderness.
> . . .
> South wind, do not neglect your watch,
> east wind, do not neglect your watch,
> earth (and) sky, do not neglect your watches
> until the Sun-god is rising and has arrived![82]

At the beginning of the anti-witchcraft ritual *Maqlû*, the patient asks the cosmos to ally itself with him or her. The whole world, its regions, and the creatures populating it are requested to pause, keep still, and pay attention to the patient's plea. Thus, a protected, undisturbed period of time is established during which the ritual can be performed. Even the ever-moving wind and the buzzing traffic on the streets and roads are asked to stand still:

> You in heaven, pay attention, you in the netherworld, listen!
> You in the river, pay attention to me, you on dry land, listen to my speech!
> The howling wind is beaten: "You must not blow!"
> He who carries stick and rod is beaten: "Do not blow!"
> Let the road stand still, the daughter of the great gods![83]

Reality, Efficacy, Limitations, and Risks

Witches, ghosts, demons, and deities all formed part of the ancient Near Eastern world. For all we know, the reality of these beings was never questioned, but there can be no doubt that the people of the ancient Near East were well aware of their out-of-the-ordinary and elusive natures. The average person did not live in constant fear of evil witches; only specific situations of crisis would be interpreted as witchcraft-induced. The ghosts of one's family lived in the distant netherworld, and they would regularly be provided with funerary offerings; again, only extraordinary circumstances indicated that a ghost haunted a house or had taken hold of an individual. Demons dwelt in the netherworld or drifted through the wilderness. Apotropaia offered protection against potential attacks, especially in situations of heightened vulnerability, but one does not get the impression that fear of demons normally hindered people from going about their daily business. People expected their protective deities to accompany them constantly; proper induction and care ensured that the gods dwelt in their temples and were present in their cult images to guarantee the welfare of the land. At the same time, the great gods evidently lived at an insurmountable distance in their cosmic locations, and experience taught that a deity, powerful as it was, would usually be difficult to offend.

Counterintuitive events, like serious illness or premature death, demand counterintuitive, yet plausible and rational, explanations and causes.[84] In the world of the ancient Near East, demons, witches, angry deities, and one's own transgressions were regarded as extraordinary causes whose identification would enable the expert to appropriately and rationally react to the patient's situation. But, of course, the healers' art could not guarantee success. The Mesopotamian exorcists and physicians regarded certain syndromes or certain stages of a disease as beyond their power. Some therapeutic texts give alternative instructions in case the first treatment did not improve the patient's condition; often a false diagnosis or the insuperable power of a demon or a god was blamed for failure. The desperation of those beyond any help is reflected in letters and wisdom literature:

> I spend the night in my dung like an ox,
> I wallow in my excrements like a sheep.
> The incantation expert has been frightened by my symptoms,
> and the diviner has confused my omens.
> The exorcist has not diagnosed the nature of my illness,
> nor has the diviner established the term of my disease.[85]

Of course, prophylactic rituals are often effective per se, and the self-limiting nature of diseases ensured that an *āšipu*'s rituals and remedies also had a certain rate of success with those already affected by illness. Moreover, the herbal and mineral drugs that were used in the treatment of the patient would show certain effects, and the suggestive power of the rituals performed within their own cultural context must not be underestimated. In analogy to other cultures, we may assume that even if the objectively observable symptoms remained or worsened, the interpretation of the illness by the patient and his or her environment would often have changed. The condition that had indicated an attack of evil powers or a dramatic alienation from the gods and had presented an unsettling and unlimited threat was transformed by the performance of the ritual into a normal illness, into a situation with which one could cope. Whereas the modern bystander would observe the foreseeable failure of a superstitious endeavor, to Mesopotamian eyes, the removal of the evil restored the world's equilibrium.

This, however, did not protect the exorcist from being ridiculed by his contemporaries for pompous behavior or incompetence. An Akkadian literary parody stylized as a dialogue between a jester and his interlocutor makes fun of various professionals, among them an exorcist who expels a demon from a house by reducing it to ashes:

"Jester, what can you do?"
All of the exorcistic lore, I master it.
"Jester, how is your exorcistic lore (performed)?"
Here's how: I take over the house haunted by a demon, I put the holy water vessel in place,
I set up the scape goat,
I skin a mule and stuff (its hide) with straw;
I tie a bundle of reeds, set it on fire, and throw it inside.
I have spared the boundaries of the house and its surroundings,
but the demon of that house, the snake and the scorpion, have not been spared![86]

Jokes about the elites and the powerful are often an outlet of fear. It seems likely that the exorcist, his competence, and his powers were regarded by many with mixed feelings, even though such reservations are not expressed in any of the preserved sources from Mesopotamia. Certain misgivings against the activities of the Hittite ritual expert called "old woman" transpire from the final paragraph of the "Testament" of Hattusili I, wherein the dying king is warned by his courtiers that Hastayar (perhaps his daughter) keeps consulting the "old women."[87]

The performance of magic rituals by people who were not professional exorcists or healers could, of course, give rise to suspicions. Usually, however, witchcraft accusations against concrete persons did not arise because specific rituals had been performed, but because social or personal conflicts escalated and certain persons, especially women, became marginalized. In such exceptional circumstances, legal proceedings were initiated and actual people were brought to trial as alleged witches.[88] But the regular response to witchcraft suspicions throughout all periods of ancient Near Eastern history were anti-witchcraft rituals and remedies applied to the victim of witchcraft. Because counter-magic was never delegitimized, ancient Near Eastern societies were spared the excesses of violence that can emerge when the therapy of witchcraft focuses exclusively on the identification of alleged witches and their judicial prosecution.

Notes

1. An overview and general discussion of Mesopotamian magic by the same author was published as Schwemer, "Magic Rituals." Although overall organization, scope, and length differ, some passages in the first, third, fourth, and sixth sections of the present chapter also form part of "Magic Rituals" in the same or a similar form.

2. For the development and use of the word *mágos* in Greek, see Delling, "*Mageía, mágos, mageúein*"; cf. also Versnel, "Some Reflections," 182.

3. Braarvig, "Magic," 51.

4. For the text, see Grensemann, *Die hippokratische Schrift "Über die heilige Krankheit."* For a full discussion of the treatise and its seminal role with regard to the concept of magic, see Braarvig, "Magic," 37–40. The treatise argues that epilepsy, "the sacred disease," has natural causes and is only assigned a sacred nature by deceitful magicians who mislead their patients with their rites and incantations. The practice of the magicians is "in opposition not only to true science but also to true religion" (Braarvig, "Magic," 37).

5. See especially Frazer, *Golden Bough*, 58–72. Frazer's discussion of the relationship between magic, science, and religion is characterized by a negative judgment on magic: "[A]ll magic is necessarily false and barren; for were it ever to become true and fruitful, it would no longer be magic but science" (Ibid., 59–60). On the relationship between magic and religion, Frazer states that there is "a radical conflict of principle" between the two, which "explains the relentless hostility with which in history the priest has often pursued the magician" (Ibid., 62); whereas the magician's doing is guided by "haughty self-sufficiency" and "arrogant demeanour towards the higher powers," the priest has an "awful sense of the divine majesty" and rejects magic as impious (Ibid., 62).

6. For an overview of the reaction to Frazer, see Versnel, "Some Reflections," 177–181. Important stages of the discussion are marked, among others, by the works of Edward E. Evans-Pritchard, Mary Douglas, Claude Lévi-Strauss, Robert R. Marett, Marcel Mauss, Stanley J. Tambiah, and, most recently, Pascal Boyer; for a primer on these various approaches to magic, see Cunningham, *Religion and Magic.*

7. Among them are Clyde Kluckhohn, David F. Pocock, and Alfred R. Radcliffe-Brown; see Versnel, "Some Reflections," 193 n. 9, for relevant passages from their works.

8. Versnel, "Some Reflections," 181.

9. For a discussion of the influence of Babylonian ritual literature on Hittite magic and the methodological problems involved, see Schwemer, *Abwehrzauber*, 255–276, and Schwemer, "Gauging the Influence."

46

10. For the reconstruction of this library, an analysis of its composition, and a discussion of the family of exorcists who owned it, see Pedersén, *Archives and Libraries*, part II, 41–76, and Maul, "Die Tontafelbibliothek."

11. For the library of Ashurbanipal, see Frame and George, "The Royal Libraries of Nineveh," as well as Parpola, "Assyrian Library Records." For the collecting of ritual tablets at the Hittite court, see Otten, *Puduḫepa*, 16; Haas, *Materia Magica*, 26; and Miller, *Kizzuwatna Rituals*, 469–532.

12. See Lambert, "A Catalogue of Texts and Authors," 64–65, 68–69.

13. For the pre-Sargonic incantations, see Krebernik, *Die Beschwörungen aus Fara und Ebla*. Cunningham, "*Deliver Me from Evil*," gives an overview and catalog of Mesopotamian incantation literature from the pre-Sargonic to the Old Babylonian periods. For a recent edition of Ur III-incantations and a discussion of their relationship to the earlier third-millennium texts and the later tradition, see van Dijk and Geller, *Ur III Incantations*.

14. Obviously, the literary history of individual compositions and series varies; an important reorganization and expansion of the corpus of *āšipūtu* was ascribed to the eleventh-century Babylonian scholar Esangil-kīn-apli (see Finkel, "Adad-apla-iddina," 150; Beaulieu, "Late Babylonian Intellectual Life," 477; and, differently, Jean, *La magie néo-assyrienne*, 62–82; cf. also Heeßel, "Neues von Esagil-kīn-apli").

15. See Maul, *Zukunftsbewältigung*, 216–222 (*namburbi* rituals for counteracting bad omens) and Schwemer, *Abwehrzauber*, 56–61 (*ušburruda* rituals against witchcraft).

16. For the latest phase of cuneiform writing in Babylonia, see Westenholz, "The Graeco-Babyloniaca Once Again," 294–309.

17. Haas, *Materia Magica*, 32–48, gives a general overview of the ritual traditions attested in the texts from Hattusa and other Hittite libraries. For rituals from Kizzuwatna, see Miller, *Kizzuwatna Rituals*; for Luwian rituals, see Hutter, "Aspects of Luwian Religion," 232–254; for the presence of Babylonian ritual traditions at the Hittite royal court, see Schwemer, "Gauging the Influence."

18. For the Hurrian incantations of the Old Babylonian period, see Prechel and Richter, "Abrakadabra oder Althurritisch"; for the Elamite incantations of the same period, see Koch, "Texte aus Iran," 387–390. An overview of Ugaritic incantations was given by Spronk, "The Incantations"; for recent translations of selected texts, see Pardee, *Ritual and Cult*, 157–166, and Niehr, "Texte aus Ugarit," 253–257. For the incantations on a pair of amulets from Arslan Tash, see most recently Pardee, "Les documents d'Arslan Tash"; for the Aramaic incantation in cuneiform script, see Geller, "The Aramaic Incantation in Cuneiform Script."

19. For a comprehensive study of apotropaic demons in both the textual and the archaeological record, see Wiggermann, *Mesopotamian Protective Spirits*.

20. See Salje, "Siegelverwendung," 126–129. Seals of this type were probably designed to protect the wearer of the seal from evil.

21. See George, "Model Dogs."

22. According to the Gilgameš epic, Ḫuwawa was defeated and beheaded by Gilgameš.

23. See Hauptmann, "Die Felsspalte D," 64–70, and Haas, *Materia Magica*, 422.

24. See Schwemer, *Abwehrzauber*, 209–214.

25. The so-called *Exorcist's Manual*, a catalog-like list of texts, gives an overview of the "series of *āšipūtu*," i.e., the canonical knowledge an exorcist was expected to master (Geller, "Incipits and Rubrics," 242–254; Jean, *La magie néo-assyrienne*, 62–72; cf. also Schwemer, "Magic Rituals," 421–423).

26. For discussions of the professions of the exorcist and physician in Mesopotamia, see Ritter, "Magical-Expert (= *āšipu*) and Physician (= *asû*)"; Stol, "Diagnosis and Therapy in Babylonian Medicine"; Biggs, "Medicine, Surgery, and Public Health"; Scurlock, "Physician, Exorcist, Conjurer, Magician"; and Schwemer, *Abwehrzauber*, 188–193.

27. *KAR* 26 = KAL 2, 21 obverse 24–25 (Mayer, "Das Ritual *KAR* 26"). Note that *āšipu* is written with the logogram ^{lú}KA.PÌRIG in line 24 but syllabically in line 25; no difference in meaning seems to be intended.

28. See Schwemer, *Abwehrzauber*, 76–79, with the relevant attestations.

29. *Maqlû* VII 88–96.

30. Schwemer, *Abwehrzauber*, 139–146; differently, Abusch, *Mesopotamian Witchcraft*, 3–25, 65–66, 84–87.

31. Rarely, female physicians are also attested in the Old Babylonian period (see Ziegler, *Le harem de Zimrî-Lîm*, 29, for the royal harem at Mari; for Larsa, see Oppenheim, *Ancient Mesopotamia*, 385 n. 14).

32. The physician is always written with the Sumerian logogram in Hittite texts, the gender being indicated by the determinative (^{lú}A.ZU, ^{munus}A.ZU). The designation "old woman" is a literal translation of the logogram ^{munus}ŠU.GI; the underlying Hittite word is *ḫašawa-*, which has rightly been connected with *ḫaš-*, "to give birth." "Diviner," too, is the literal translation of a logogram (^{lú}AZU); the functions of this "diviner" in the Hittite culture are largely those of an exorcist.

33. See Haas, *Materia Magica*, 6–25, and Miller, *Kizzuwatna Rituals*, 472–481.

34. For the Babylonian mouth-washing ritual that was used for the induction of cult images and the mouth-washing rite more generally, see Walker and Dick, *The Induction of the Cultic Image*. The prime example for the induction of cult objects is the kettledrum ritual (see Linssen, *The Cults of Uruk and Babylon*, 92–100, 252–282). For temple foundation rituals, see Ambos, *Mesopotamische Baurituale*.

35. Borger, "Die Weihe eines Enlil-Priesters," 165–166, column i, lines 47–56; for the induction of Babylonian priests, see also Waerzeggers and Jursa, "On the Initiation of Babylonian Priests." Although the exorcist participated in many

of the liminal rites that were performed to introduce people and objects into the divine realm of the temple cult, rituals of this type were considered first of all the remit of another official called *kalû* in Akkadian. The *kalû* also performed many of the liturgies of the temple cult, and the title is therefore translated as "lamentation singer" or "lamentation priest" (for the office of the *kalû*, see Shehata, *Musiker und ihr vokales Repertoire*, 55–93).

36. See Haas, *Materia Magica*, 77, 784–785, with further literature.

37. *Utukkū lemnūtu* IV 67–71, 74–79, edited by Geller in ed., *Evil Demons*, 112–113, 205.

38. See Wiggermann, "Lamaštu, Daughter of Anu," with previous literature; for Pazuzu, see Heeßel, *Pazuzu*, and Wiggermann, "Four Winds."

39. Lamaštu I 193–200, edited by Myhrman, in "Die Labartu-Texte," 162–163; for the items that are given to Lamaštu, see Farber, "Tamarisken, Fibeln, Skolopender."

40. Beginning of a bilingual incantation against Ardat-lilî; see Geller, "New Duplicates," 12–14, lines 28–31.

41. For incantations against Sāmānu, see Finkel, "A Study in Scarlet."

42. A large group of incantations of this type was edited by Finkel, "On Some Dog, Snake and Scorpion Incantations"; for a comprehensive overview of early incantations, see Cunningham, "*Deliver Me from Evil.*"

43. For the evil eye, see most recently Geller, "Akkadian Evil Eye Incantations," 67–68.

44. See n. 25.

45. See Schwemer, *Abwehrzauber*, 66, 195–196.

46. A new edition of *Maqlû* is being prepared by Tzvi Abusch; for the time being, see Meier, *Die assyrische Beschwörungssammlung Maqlû*, and Abusch and Schwemer, "Das Abwehrzauber-Ritual *Maqlû*." For discussions of various aspects of *Maqlû*, see Abusch, *Mesopotamian Witchcraft*, and Schwemer, *Abwehrzauber*, 37–55. For editions of other anti-witchcraft rituals and a general introduction to this body of texts, see Abusch and Schwemer, *Corpus of Mesopotamian Anti-Witchcraft Rituals*, vol. 1.

47. For the opening section of the ritual, see Schwemer, "Empowering the Patient."

48. *Maqlû* II 183–192, 200–203.

49. See Schwemer, *Abwehrzauber*, 226–228.

50. *Maqlû* VIII 127–131, 137–139; for the interpretation of the text, see Schwemer, *Abwehrzauber*, 228–230.

51. *Šurpu* V–VI 60–61, 68–72, edited by Reiner, in *Šurpu*, 31.

52. KUB 30.10 obverse 20′–28′. For the Babylonian *dingiršadabba*-texts, see Lambert, "DINGIR.ŠÀ.DIB.BA Incantations," and Jaques, "'Mon dieu, qu'ai-je donc fait?'"; for the quoted Hittite passage and its Babylonian parallels, see Metcalf, "New Parallels."

53. See *BAM* 323, lines 79–88 with duplicate, edited by Scurlock, in *Magico-Medical Means of Treating Ghost-Induced Illnesses*, 537–538.
54. For a comprehensive edition with a discussion of this ritual genre, see Maul, *Zukunftsbewältigung* (cf. also Caplice, *The Akkadian Namburbi Texts*).
55. *STT* 89 reverse iv 174–186, edited by Stol, in *Epilepsy in Babylonia*, 96.
56. For comprehensive editions with discussions of this ritual genre, see Oppenheim, *The Interpretation of Dreams*, and Butler, *Mesopotamian Conceptions of Dreams*.
57. See Schwemer, "Witchcraft and War," 35–37 obverse 6′–12′; see ibid., 29–35, for a general overview and discussion of Babylonian war rituals.
58. See Kümmel, *Ersatzrituale*, 169–187, and Parpola, *Letters*, vol. II, xxii–xxxii.
59. KUB 24.5 + 9.13 + FHL 125 obverse 19′–26′, edited by Kümmel, in *Ersatzrituale*, 10–11.
60. For Mesopotamian rituals associated with pregnancy and childbirth, see Stol, *Birth in Babylonia*; for Hittite rituals of this type, see Beckman, *Hittite Birth Rituals*.
61. *BBR* 26 + obverse ii 10′–20′, iii 1–9 with duplicates; see Farber, "Rituale und Beschwörungen," 245–255 (specifically 247–248); for the first paragraph, see Schwemer, "Entrusting the Witches," 65.
62. KBo 6.34 + obverse ii 42 – reverse iii 1 with duplicate, edited by Oettinger, in *Die Militärischen Eide*, 10–13.
63. For Babylonian love magic, see Biggs, "Liebeszauber"; Wilcke, "Lie-bes-be-schwö-run-gen"; Scurlock, "Was There a 'Love-Hungry' Ēntu-Priestess Named Eṭirtum?"; Schwemer, *Abwehrzauber*, 159–160; Wasserman, "From the Notebook"; and George, *Babylonian Literary Texts*, 50–70.
64. George, *Babylonian Literary Texts*, 69, no. 11 obverse 6–11 (translation by George).
65. See Farber, "Rituale und Beschwörungen," 277–281, and Maul, "Der Kneipenbesuch als Heilverfahren."
66. A 522 obverse ii 10–27 (other parts of the tablet were published as *BAM* 318). The rubric of the incantation describes the ritual's purpose as "for going on a business trip and achieving your objective" (obverse ii 19: *ḫarrāna alāku ṣibûtka k[ašādi]*).
67. See BM 47457 reverse 8–12.
68. See Schwemer, *Abwehrzauber*, 127–130, 159–160, with further literature.
69. See *LKA* 135 obverse 11–16, cf. also BM 40482.
70. BM 36330 left edge 27–30.
71. For a brief discussion of the relevant passages, see Schwemer, *Abwehrzauber*, 160; for a different overall interpretation of the text, see Scurlock, "Sorcery in the Stars."
72. See Schwemer, *Abwehrzauber*, 67, with the relevant references.

73. For the role of the day of the new moon in anti-witchcraft rituals, see Schwemer, "Washing, Defiling and Burning," and Schwemer, "Evil Witches."

74. *Maqlû* I 1–3; see Schwemer, "Empowering the Patient," 313–318.

75. For the role of Lyra in magic rituals, see Reiner, *Astral Magic*, 54–56, as well as Abusch and Schwemer, "Chicago *Maqlû* Fragment," 71–72; for the role of stars in Mesopotamian magic in general, see Reiner, *Astral Magic*.

76. For the role of stars in witchcraft beliefs and anti-witchcraft rituals, see Schwemer, *Abwehrzauber*, 102–105, as well as Abusch and Schwemer, "Chicago *Maqlû* Fragment," 71–72. For editions of relevant rituals, see also Abusch and Schwemer, *Corpus of Mesopotamian Anti-Witchcraft Rituals*, vol. 1, text 7.8, 4: 1′–24′ and texts 10.1–10.3; cf. also text 12.1.

77. For a discussion of the relationship between the theistic worldview and witchcraft beliefs in ancient Mesopotamia, see Schwemer, *Abwehrzauber*, 149–157; for a different view, see van Bimsbergen and Wiggermann, "Magic in History."

78. Reiner, *Astral Magic*, 81–82, argues convincingly that this ambivalence is succinctly expressed in the Akkadian incantation incipit *Īpuš Ea ipšur Ea*: "Ea has wrought (*scil.* the evil), Ea has undone (*scil.* the evil)." For witchcraft emerging from the subterranean ocean, see BM 47451 obverse 10, edited by Schwemer, "Washing, Defiling and Burning," 46–58; attestations for the association of demons and illnesses with the subterranean ocean can be found in *PSD* A II 196b and *CAD* A II 195b.

79. See Schwemer, "Empowering the Patient," 321 n. 42.

80. For a comprehensive study of Mesopotamian protective spirits, see Wiggermann, *Mesopotamian Protective Spirits*; for defeated enemies of the gods turned into apotropaia, see ibid., 145–164.

81. See Wiggermann, "Four Winds," 125–136; for Pazuzu, see also Heeßel, *Pazuzu*.

82. Th 1905–4–9, 67 = BM 98561 obverse 9–10, 14–17.

83. *Maqlû* I 63–67; see Schwemer, "Empowering the Patient," 325–327.

84. The interpretation of religious and magic concepts as founded in rational causal judgments in reaction to counterintuitive events follows Boyer, *The Naturalness of Religious Ideas*, 125–154.

85. *Ludlul bēl nēmeqi* II 106–111, edited by Lambert, in *Babylonian Wisdom Literature*, 44–45.

86. The interpretation of the passage follows the edition of the text by Foster ("Humor and Cuneiform Literature," 77; *Before the Muses*, 940).

87. KUB 1.16+ reverse iii // iv 66–70 (full bibliography at S. Košak, http://hethiter.net/: hetkonk (v. 1.81) s.v.); cf. Schwemer, *Abwehrzauber*, 259–260.

88. For an overview of actual witchcraft accusations in Mesopotamia and Hittite Anatolia, see Schwemer, *Abwehrzauber*, 118–127, 258–263.

Chapter 2

Ancient Egypt

FRIEDHELM HOFFMANN

Introduction

This chapter on ancient Egyptian magic consists of two sections.[1] The first deals with the question of whether magic is an appropriate or useful term for scholars to use in the context of ancient Egypt. As will be shown, it should primarily be understood emically as the rendering of the Egyptian term *heka*, which refers to a special power created by the gods as a means of warding off evil effects, of influencing gods, demons or humans and of "charging" things with a special efficacy. The transmission of Egyptian magical texts is then briefly considered: magic and its uses were a matter of learned knowledge.

The second section provides a historical overview of the development of Egyptian magic from the third millennium BC until the end of paganism during the first centuries AD. The primary sources for each of the six epochs are highlighted to give a clear impression of the Egyptian material and to make the specific research more accessible to a wider audience. The selected material includes not only magical texts, such as spells against demons and people(s), spells for healing and protection or divination and explanatory texts, but also stories that show "magicians" in action.

General

The question has been asked as to whether magic is a useful category in modern research.[2] One could and perhaps should abandon the term and incorporate it simply within the field of religion, for both are concerned with the relationship between humans and the divine. But magic can be taken in the emic sense as a concept that was understood by the ancient Egyptians themselves. The following comments, therefore, cover mainly these phenomena of ancient Egyptian magic and seek to give an overview of the different sources available.

What Egyptians meant by the term *heka* (*ḥkȝ*), which is best translated as "magic", can be deduced from the following two Egyptian papyri. The first, *Papyrus Ebers* (second millennium BC), is mainly a collection of recipes against different diseases. In a spell accompanying the drinking of a medicament (*pekheret* [*pḥr.t*]), we read: "Strong is the *heka* because of the *pekheret* – (and) vice versa" (*Papyrus Ebers* 2.2–2.3).[3] The other one, *Papyrus Brooklyn* 47.218.48+85 (sixth century BC), is a compilation of texts against snake-bites. In 2.3–2.4 it reads: "[One] (can) rescue (the patient) from it (= the snake) by *heka* (and) by *pekheret*".[4]

Pekheret is a substance and action intended to fight or keep away a disease. Many medical recipes are titled *"pekheret* for healing (a malady)." A list of drugs and an instruction for their preparation and use typically follow. Thus *pekheret* signifies something along the lines of "prescription."

The efficacy of the drugs can be increased by charging them with magic. Here is an example taken from the snake papyrus:

PRESCRIPTION (*PEKHERET*) FOR HEALING SOMEONE BITTEN BY ANY SNAKE:

itju-plant – it grows in Hibis ... Then one has to grind it with sweet beer. (It) has to be drunk by the bitten one. He will be healthy at once.

To be spoken over it as magic:

(Oh) this *itju*-plant which grows under the side of Osiris as efflux which comes out from those in their Netherworld: kill the poison ...! (*Papyrus Brooklyn* 47.218.48+85 5.22–5.25)

More often the words to be spoken are explicitly called spells (singular *ra* [*rȝ*]) in the heading. These are the typical Egyptian magical texts. Substances can be used together with them, and, if they are to be used, they are mentioned in the instructions after the spell.

For the Egyptians, magic is a constituent part of the world as it was divinely created. The *Teaching for King Merikare* (second millennium BC) highlights the origin of magic with the creation:

"[The Creator] has made for them *heka* as weapons in order to ward off (the) effects of what happens (= the events), over which one keeps watch night (and) day" (*Merikare* E 136–137).[5]

Thus magic is natural in the sense of being associated with forces in nature. Any internal disease, any enemy one could not reach physically, any desire, any dangerous animal and any possible divine intervention could be treated by magic. This is not intrinsically morally good or wicked: it is only through its use that the practice of magic can be morally evaluated. The origins of magic in the creation and its preservation in medical papyri further associate

Egyptian magic with learnedness (Egyptian *rekh* [*rḫ*]). Performing magic was made easier by having access to texts and following their instructions; and conversely, one only needed to be able to read the texts to perform magical rites. In a well-known narrative, *The First Tale of Setne Khaemwase* (third or second century BC), a story about the adventures of an Egyptian sorcerer, we are told how Naneferkaptah was able to steal a magical book written by Thoth, the god of wisdom. And:

> He (= Naneferkaptah) recited a spell from it; [he charmed the sky, the earth, the netherworld, the] mountains, the waters. He discovered what all the birds of the sky and the fish of the deep and the beasts of the desert were saying. He recited another spell; he saw [Pre (= the sun-god) appearing in the sky with his Ennead], and the Moon rising, and the stars in their forms. He saw the fish of the deep, though there were twenty-one divine cubits of water over them. He recited a spell to the [water; he made it resume its form]. (*I Khaemwase* 3.35–3.38)[6]

Naneferkaptah's wife is curious and tries out the same spells. And, indeed, they work simply by reading them! In short, no special supernatural inspiration was necessary for the successful performance of magical acts. It was enough to follow the written instructions.

Naneferkaptah is able to learn the texts very quickly by a special technique: "He had a sheet of new papyrus brought to him. He wrote on it every word that was in the book before him. He burnt it with fire, he dissolved it in water. He realized that it was dissolved. He drank it. (Now) he knew what had been on it" (*I Khaemwase* 4.3–4.4).[7] This incorporation of the spells prevents Naneferkaptah from ever forgetting them.

As a special form of written knowledge, magic could become dangerous, in that the texts could fall into the wrong hands. The so-called *Admonitions of an Egyptian Sage* (written ca. 1800 BC?), a literary composition dealing with the motif of losing order in state and society, describes exactly such a situation: "LO, the private chamber, its books are stolen, the secrets in it are laid bare. LO, magic (spells) are divulged, spells are made worthless through being repeated by people" (*Admonitions* 6.5–6.7).[8]

Measures could be taken to restrict access to magical texts. The learned priests could decide not to record the instructions and formulae in writing, like, for example, when one finds admonitions such as: "His (= of a god) matters shall not be specified in gods words (= in writing)" in a cult-topographical text[9]; or "Do not let the eye of any man whatsoever look upon it with the exception of yourself, or your father or your son".[10] Even though such passages are sometimes found as appendices to magical texts, they suggest that the magical formulae and instructions nonetheless circulated. These exhortations to keep a text secret seem to be nothing more than a hint at the exclusive character and thus at the efficacy of the spell in question. But it is conceivable that there was also a real secret oral tradition which only sporadically or much later found its way into writing.

Another method of preventing a magical ritual or spell from being recited by anybody who could read was to deploy an uncommon writing system. For example, Greek characters could be used for writing whole Egyptian texts, or a special cipher system could be used for key words.[11]

To say that magic was used by everybody regardless of their social position would not be an exaggeration. Even the actual performance of magic was not restricted to learned people. Of course, the lector priests, the masters of the secrets, and the ritualists were the "magicians" par excellence because they had access to a great number of magical texts. But even shepherds knew some spells and performed magic for protecting their cattle.

In narratives, the abilities of magicians are without limits. These stories are extremely rich in fantastic motifs, and we can be fairly sure that they were greatly enjoyed and that the magicians acting in them were much admired.

One final point should be addressed: Where and how were magical texts transmitted? Of course, texts that were exclusively transmitted orally are lost to us. Our main source today is papyri, the ancient books. These comprise both large collections of magical texts and sheets with only a single spell. Other relevant material can be found on ostraca (potsherds and limestone flakes). On papyri and ostraca, typically the Hieratic and Demotic cursive scripts were used. Hieroglyphs are normally restricted to texts on tomb or temple walls or on stelae. In the Late Period, however, even statues are found totally covered with magical compositions.[12]

In Egypt there was no formally sanctioned canon of magical texts. Each set of formulae and instructions, and sometimes even separate spells, could exist as independent units. When common spells are recorded in different collections, the actual wording can vary. This is a frequent phenomenon in Egyptian literature: texts rarely took invariable, stable forms. Rather, they were continuously reshaped over time. They could be dissembled into separate parts, which in turn could be reassembled and recombined with other textual material, resulting in new compositions.

Manuscripts extant today were generally composed either for a specific individual, who is named in the text, or for general use, in which case the Egyptian word for "NN" (Egyptian *men* [*mn*]) served as a placeholder for the name. In both cases it is clear that the personal object of the magic needed to be named, just as knowledge of a name implied power over someone. In religious texts, for example, gods were often unwilling to reveal their real, most secret name. In one story, we are told how the goddess Isis, well versed in magic, tortured the sun-god to gain his real name.[13]

Quite often pictures accompanied the magical texts.[14] One common form of illustration displayed helpful gods overcoming pestering demons; sometimes the divine helpers are depicted alone. Such illustrations are generally crudely drawn, a result of the papyri having been copied by individuals for their own use or that of others rather than by artisans for the official temple cult. Consequently, the magical papyri document the private use of religious knowledge by individuals. Sometimes three-dimensional depictions, that is, statuettes of the enemy or the bewitched person, were also used.

The iconography of the enemies against whom magic was deployed shows how the Egyptians imagined them: sometimes they appear as ordinary humans, but at other times such enemies appear monstrously disfigured. For example, a demon called *sehekek* (*shqq*) is drawn naked with one arm folded before his face and his tongue at his anus. Other demonic beings are depicted with animal heads (cf. the quite customary type of anthropomorphic gods with animal heads). Very common is the notion of animals as the incarnation of evil gods and their entourages.

At this point, we are in a position to offer a summary description of Egyptian magic (Egyptian *heka*) as it was understood within ancient Egyptian society:

- Magic is a form of knowledge that could be used to manipulate the natural and human world.
- The powers manipulated through magic are intrinsic to the world as it was divinely created.
- Magical power and knowledge were not intrinsically moralized; their use, however, could be morally evaluated.
- Magic's learnedness is incorporated in papyri, and that made magic accessible in the first instance only to the literate.
- Magical knowledge was also imbued with a certain exclusiveness through admonitions in the texts to keep the knowledge out of the wrong hands.
- The crude illustrations decorating magical texts give limited evidence of magical formulae being disseminated beyond temple precincts.

Historical Overview

Magical texts and objects are known from Egypt from the third millennium BC until well into the first millennium AD. But the material is unevenly distributed. The earliest texts we have are spells against dangerous animals. This sort of text shows a remarkable continuity across the epochs.

During the second millennium BC, the sources increase in number and diversity. We now also have spells against other people and peoples, divinatory texts, stories about sorcerers and even objects related to magical rites.

When early in the first millennium BC Egypt was governed by pharaohs from several foreign dynasties, magic was still very much present. However, new forms like the Oracular Amuletic Decrees emerged alongside traditional techniques.

After Alexander's conquest of Egypt (332 BC), the Greek language began to play an important role in Egypt. The late Egyptian magical papyri show also signs of contact with Greek magic, which in turn was influenced by Egyptian magic. When Egypt was Christianized, the Greek alphabet was regularly used for writing the Egyptian language (Coptic script). The church authorities condemned magic, but in spite of this it was still much in use.

The more than 3,000 years of Egyptian magic call for a short summary of the most important continuities and discontinuities. Right up until Egypt was Christianized, magic was considered to be a quite natural phenomenon. It was widely accepted to look for divine help in cases of disease or other problems that were supposed to be of divine origin. Magic was always a sort of practical application of religious knowledge. This knowledge could also be used to do harm.

Not every type of magic is attested for every epoch, and sometimes practices could change. But at all times the principal way of performing magic remained the same: the combination of (1) a substance or substances used, (2) an act performed and (3) words (a spell) spoken was essential. Egyptian magic was always open to the reception of foreign material. The explicit inclusion of spells in foreign languages attests to this in a very obvious way.

The most important discontinuity was caused by the Christianization of Egypt. It was not only responsible for the end of the pagan temple cult; it also meant the abandonment of the pagan religion and that religion's magic. Suddenly not only black magic but any form of magic was demonized. Before this time, magic had also been used officially by the highest representatives of the Egyptian state. But now magic was only used privately and secretly.

Old Kingdom

The earliest period of Egyptian history from which texts have survived is the Old Kingdom (ca. 2740–2140 BC). Writing had been invented in the early dynastic period, but only from the third dynasty onwards are coherent texts extant. The earliest magic texts are concerned with dangerous animals. In several tombs one finds the following or a similar threat formula:

> The crocodile (be) against him in the water,
> the snake (be) against him on land,
> against him who will act against this (tomb)![15]

People wished to ward off the attacks of these animals. In Old Kingdom private (i.e. non-royal) tombs, there is quite often a scene of herdsmen crossing a ford with their cattle. Crocodiles are shown lurking for prey. But some of the men are stretching out an arm against the crocodiles in what is likely a magical gesture. The scene is sometimes captioned: "Warding off the crocodile by the shepherd".[16] A suitable spell was probably recited at the same time.

Elaborate spells against snakes are found in the corpus of the so-called *Pyramid Texts*. These texts – or rather many of them – were first incised on the walls of the burial chamber and the adjacent rooms of the pyramid of Wenis (twenty-fourth century BC), the last king of the fifth dynasty. The *Pyramid Texts* were originally royal funerary texts for the kings of the Old and Middle Kingdoms and were later adapted for private use in the Middle Kingdom (called *Coffin Texts*). Such texts include magical and religious injunctions, such as, for example, the following:

> One snake is enveloped by another.
> A toothless calf which came forth from the pasture is enveloped.
> O earth, swallow up what went forth from you!
> O monster, lie down, stumble!
> The pelican (*ḥm-psḏ.t*) has fallen into the water.
> O snake, turn round, for Re sees you. (*Pyramid Texts* spell 226)[17]

The language is cryptic and terse, and it is thus not easily interpreted. The method of making allusions through single words is very typical for these early magical and also religious spells in the *Pyramid Texts*. Are the two snakes fighting each other? Does this result in a mutual neutralisation? Why is the calf mentioned? Could it be the victim of the snakes instead of Wenis? The earth is addressed and summoned to swallow the snake. Because snakes live on the surface of the earth or dig holes in it, the earth was considered to be an obvious helper against snakes. The snake is then addressed directly and ordered to be paralysed. The significance of the pelican is even more difficult to determine. Noisily landing in the water, it is certainly not acting directly against the snake. Is the attention of the snake diverted to the splashing bird simply to get the dangerous animal away from Wenis? The warning that the sun-god Re, the Lord of Maat (= the Right Order), has already detected the snake might indirectly threaten punishment for the snake should it attack. Threatening the enemy by having recourse to somebody still mightier is a general feature of Egyptian magical texts of all periods.

Middle Kingdom and Second Intermediate Period

Several types of material related to magic are attested from the Middle Kingdom. First of all, several execration figures are known. These are roughly shaped statuettes of bound captives. Inscribed with the names of Egyptian and foreign enemies of the Egyptian king, these figures were accoutrements for official practices by the highest officials of the Egyptian state. Although corresponding and explanatory ritual texts have been lost, we can assume that the figures were probably used in voodoo-like rituals. Moreover, the figures themselves are inscribed with a more or less standard text:

Ruler of Ta[. . .] (called) Kemek, born by his mother, over whom it is said "Are you a rebel?", (and) his army;

ruler of [. . .]wa (called) Iny, born by his mother, over whom it is said "Are you a [. . .] there?", (and) his army;

(female) ruler of Yamnaes (called) Satjit, born by her mother, over whom it is said "[. . .] does not kill(?)", (and) her army;

ruler of Rukit (called) Saktui, born by his mother, over whom it is said "Is there anybody who adheres to him?", (and) his army;

ruler of Makja (called) Wai, born by his mother, over whom it is said "Calf!" (and) his army;

. . .

all people;

all nobles;

all commoners;

all men;

all eunuchs;

all women;

Fountain of Horus (= region of the First Cataract?);

Wawat (= region south of the First Cataract);

[…]

Upper Egypt;

Lower Egypt;

…

(Now the text mentions their possible crimes:)

who might rebel;

who might conspire;

who might make a rebellion;

who might fight;

…

(The text starts again with the enumeration of dangerous people in Nubia and their allies:)

[their] champions;

their messengers;

all people (i.e. Egyptians), who are with them;

all Nubians, who are with them;

all Asiatics, who are with them;

…

(Next the Libyans are enumerated. Finally, the text mentions the names of two Egyptian individuals.)[18]

Another important find is the library of a healer and magician dating to the thirteenth dynasty. Altogether twenty-three papyrus rolls were found together in a box in a shaft below the Ramesseum at Thebes. This collection of books contained inter alia: an onomasticon, the tale of the Eloquent Peasant, the tale of Sinuhe, the teaching of Sisobek and other wisdom texts, a hymn to the crocodile god Sobek, rituals and no fewer than fifteen magical and medical papyri. In addition, there were many objects used for performing magic, for example, amulets (cf. Figure 2.1, a *djed* pillar, and Figure 2.2, a composite *wedjat*-eye).[19]

All of these texts belonged to the same man. He was a lector priest (*kheri-hebet* [*ḫry-ḥb.t*]). It is clear that reciting religious compositions like hymns to gods, using magical texts like spells for warding off demons and preparing and

FIGURE 2.1. A *djed*-pillar, Late Period. British Museum, London, BM/Big no. 2100. Image AN00881443_001.jpg of the British Museum.

FIGURE 2.2. A composite *wedjat*-eye. British Museum, London, BM/Big no. 7378. Image AN00948666_001.jpg of the British Museum.

applying medicine were the functions of one and the same man, and these functions were associated with each other in ancient Egypt.

The Egyptians were particularly afraid that magical texts might be used by the wrong people. The passage from the so-called Admonitions quoted in the second section of this chapter shows this clearly. It becomes obvious that according to Egyptian belief the papyri alone contain whatever is necessary for enacting magic.

From the Second Intermediate Period comes *Papyrus Westcar*, a well-known manuscript containing stories about Old Kingdom kings and chief lector priests (*kheri-hebet heri-dep* [*ḥry-ḥb.t ḥry-dp*]) acting as magicians.[20] This gives a vivid picture of what magicians were able to perform in fictional literature. In one of these stories, a magician forms a little crocodile out of wax and transforms it into a large living crocodile in order to catch an adulterous man. In another story, a magician folds up the water of a pool and thus gets back a piece of jewellery that has fallen into the water and sunk to the bottom. In the final story, a magician is able to reattach the heads of beheaded animals and make them alive again. Interestingly, the man is first summoned to perform this feat with a human being, but he refuses to do so. The same magician also knows the number of the very secret chambers of Thot. Here again the important role of knowledge and its association with magic and magicians becomes apparent.

New Kingdom

The amount of written evidence for magical practice in the New Kingdom is significantly greater than that from the previous epochs. Although this increasing trend continues through later periods, it cannot be concluded that magic itself was more common in the New Kingdom and later. It is simply the result of preservation: the more recent a text copy, the better its chances of survival.

Spells for a mother and child are quite illustrative of magic more generally in the early New Kingdom. Pregnancy, labour and birth were dangerous and important at the same time. But the reasons for miscarriage, sudden bleedings, death of a child and so on were not transparent for the ancients. It is no wonder that people thought of demons as the agents and that they sought magical help.

ANOTHER SPELL FOR ACCELERATING (?) (*sḥȝḥ*) LABOUR:

Open for me!
I am the one whose favour(?) is large,
the builder who built the pylon of/for Hathor, the lady of Dendera,
who lifts up in order that she may give (birth).
Hathor, the lady of Dendera, is <the> one who is giving birth.
[THIS SPELL IS TO BE SAID] FOR A WOMAN. (*Papyrus Leiden I 348* recto 13.9–13.11)[21]

Although the meaning of the word *sḥȝḥ* is not entirely certain, the general drift of the spell makes it clear that some sort of help during birth was the aim of these sentences. The text begins directly by addressing someone who remains unnamed. But "Open for me!" is an order that is perfectly understandable in this context. The speaker next identifies himself as a god who is described as a builder. This is Khnum, who is known from other texts as the one who fashions the children. Here he is considered as a god who has erected a high building for the goddess Hathor, who is responsible for love and motherhood. He has thus built for her a place for giving birth. It is then asserted that the woman who is giving birth is actually Hathor herself. In this way, both the speaking healer and the woman are transferred to the divine sphere. This should help, and the spell ends here. Only a very brief instruction for its use is appended.

The close association between Egyptian magic and medicine becomes explicitly clear in the famous *Edwin Smith Papyrus* of about 1550 BC. This manuscript is, however, certainly a copy of an older text. On the front, there is a long sequence of chapters dealing with wounds. The text is arranged from the head downwards, but when it reaches the shoulders, the papyrus breaks off. What is important for us here is that these texts are completely free of magic. But the back of the papyrus contains a series of spells against demons that were thought to cause infectious diseases. The normal procedures against them are applied: an address to the demons that refers back to a mythological precedent, magical spells and ritual performances. Both sides of the *Edwin Smith Papyrus* belong together. Wounds have an obvious cause, such as a blow from a weapon. This was perfectly clear to the Egyptians. But what about fevers, infections, parasites? The Egyptians had no chance of detecting the real cause of all these diseases and therefore considered harmful supernatural forces. It was logical that there could only be one way of getting rid of them: the gods had to help. Magic is the practical application of religious knowledge, that is, the knowledge about the gods, their cults, their myths, etc., just as Egyptian astrology could in principle be understood to be the practical side of astronomy. Thus, like the Ramesseum library to which magical, religious and medical papyri belonged, the *Edwin Smith Papyrus*, which contains medical and magical texts, shows that for the Egyptians these groups of texts formed a unit and should be taken together as healing texts.

The search for help and protection from demons must have led to the question of what would happen if a demon comes from a foreign country and does not understand the Egyptian language. During the New Kingdom, when Egypt had extended its territory far into the Near East and into Nubia, contacts with other cultures were most intense. No doubt the Egyptians must have noticed that other peoples used magical spells in their own languages. Why not try to be on the safe side by using at least some of them, too? Here is a good example:

> Conjuration of the Asiatic disease IN THE SPEECH OF CRETE:
>
> *sntkppwyiymntrkr.*
>
> THIS INCANTATION IS TO BE SPOKEN OVER FERMENTED BARM(?), URINE . . . TO BE APPLIED TO IT. (*Papyrus BM EA 10059 7.4–7.6* [old numbering 11.4–11.6])[22]

The Asiatic disease is possibly leprosy. Because of its foreign origin, a spell in a foreign language likely seemed especially helpful. The short spell was to be recited over the medicine, which was to be applied to the infected parts of the skin.

From the New Kingdom, there exists a long papyrus, the *Magical Papyrus Harris* = *Papyrus BM EA 10042*, with hymns and spells against dangerous animals. Interestingly, most of the hymns do not show any sign of their intended use. But the heading to them is clear: "THE PERFECT INCANTATIONS TO BE SUNG which drive off the 'immersed' (= the crocodiles)" (*Papyrus BM EA 10042* 1.1).[23]

Later on, another heading introduces spells and instructions against these animals. The first section runs as follows:

FIRST INCANTATION OF ALL CONJURATIONS ON WATER OF WHICH THE MAGI-
CIANS SAY: DO NOT REVEAL IT TO OTHERS! A TRUE SECRET OF THE HOUSE OF
LIFE (= THE TEMPLE SCRIPTORIUM)!
O egg of the water, spit of the earth,
seed of the Ogdoad,
Great one in heaven, prince in the underworld,
he who is in the nest before the Lake of Knives (i.e. the sun-god)!
I came with you out of the water,
I penetrate with you from your nest.
I am Min of Coptos.
THIS INCANTATION IS TO BE SPOKEN <OVER> AN EGG OF CLAY,
PLACED IN THE HAND OF A MAN AT THE FORE OF A BOAT.
IF THERE APPEARS THE ONE WHO IS ON THE WATER (= THE CROCODILE),
IT IS TO BE THROWN INTO THE WATER. (*Papyrus BM EA 10042* 6.10–7.1)[24]

First the reader is urged to keep the spell secret. Then the sun-god, who rises in the morning from the water and his abode in the swamps (like a crocodile!), is addressed. The magician says he is with the sun-god all the time, because he is the fertility god Min himself. The spell is to be recited over a lump of clay and can be thrown against a crocodile in case of an encounter with this dangerous animal.

Also relevant to a chapter on magic in ancient Egypt is the phenomenon of divination.[25] Two types can be distinguished for the New Kingdom: hemerology, that is, the determination of lucky and unlucky days, and dream divination, by which the fate of an individual is foretold according to his or her dreams. The beginning of *Papyrus Cairo JE 86637* and its parallels give an idea of what a text on lucky and unlucky days looks like:

BEGINNING OF THE EPIPHANY FESTIVALS OF all gods (and) all goddesses
<ON> THIS DAY IN HIS TIME, FOUND IN OLD BOOKS:

FIRST MONTH OF THE INUNDATION SEASON DAY 1 – THIS IS THE SECOND OPENING OF THE YEAR: half good, half dangerous. (The god) Nehebkaw (*nḥb-kꜣ*) came into being on this day. FESTIVAL OF Osiris, FESTIVAL OF Isis, FESTIVAL OF every god, FESTIVAL OF (the crocodile god) Sobek, lord of Iwneferu (*iw-nfrw*). This means, you shall not travel with ships which are on the water on this day.

FIRST MONTH OF THE INUNDATION SEASON DAY 2: good, good. FESTIVAL OF (the god of the air) Shu, the son of Re, FESTIVAL OF (the divine sistrum player) Ihi, the son of Hathor, FESTIVAL OF (the hunter- and fighter-god) Onuris in Heliopolis, FESTIVAL OF (the lion-god) Miysis. This is the festival of victory which Re celebrated for Onuris, when (he) took the Horus eye for him. You shall not eat the *'fꜣ*-plant (nor) cross the water on this day.

...

FIRST MONTH OF THE INUNDATION SEASON DAY 4: DANGEROUS. Festival of Hathor, the lady of Byblos. FESTIVAL OF Nekhbet, the White One of (the city of) Nekhen, FESTIVAL OF (the sky-goddess) Nut. Beginning a work <is> an offense. It is dangerous to join people. As for anybody who suffers from his heart on this [day], he will not (sur)vive. (*Papyrus Cairo JE 86637* 1.1–1.5)[26]

With column 3, the papyrus continues with a second and more elaborate calendar. We are not told why a certain day is considered to be good or bad. Egyptologists have worked hard to find the reasons behind the verdicts.[27]

Another type of divinatory text is *Papyrus Chester Beatty III*, which contained at least 230 dreams and their explanations (Figure 2.3). It is the longest Egyptian dream text. Many sentences are lost; others are incomprehensible as far as the way of reaching the prognosis is concerned. From those which we are able to understand, it becomes apparent that a similarity between the things dreamt and the dreaming person's situation is supposed to exist:

> If a man sees himself in a dream
> > burying an old man,
> > good; it means prosperity.
> > cultivating herbs,
> > good; it means finding victuals.
> > bringing in the cattle,
> > good; the assembly of people for him by his god.
> > working stone in his house,
> > good; the establishment of a man in his home.
> > ...
> > towing a boat,
> > good; his landing happily in his home. (*Papyrus Chester Beatty III* 6.1–6.6)[28]

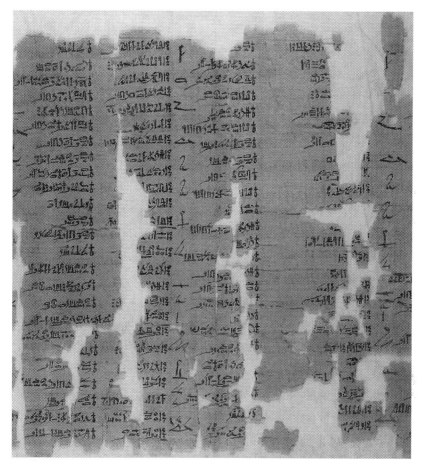

FIGURE 2.3. Dream Book (*Papyrus Chester Beatty III*), detail of sheet 2, New Kingdom, 19th dynasty. British Museum, London, BM / Big no. 10683. Image AN00423176_001.jpg of the British Museum.

Or, by means of word play, a connection between a dream and fate is found (it is simply by chance that only bad interpretations occur in the following selection):

> If a man sees himself in a dream
>> seeing his penis stiff (*nḫt.w*),
>> BAD; victory (*nḫt.w*) to his enemies.
>> ...
>> being given a harp (*bin.t*),

BAD; it means something through which he fares ill (*bin*).

. . .

removing (*iṯ.t*) the nails of his fingers, BAD;
removal (*iṯ.t*) of the work of his hands.

. . .

entering into a room with his clothes wet (*iwḥ*), BAD; it means
fighting (*ꜥḥꜣ*). (*Papyrus Chester Beatty III* 8.2–8.16)[29]

The Egyptians were not content with discovering what fate might bring in
the future. They also tried to fight against it. The idea is simple: if the gods
were to forbid animals to kill men, organs to die, demons to act badly and
so on, everything would be fine. People tried to ensure that they were fully
protected against these and other dangers with the so-called Divine Decrees.
These often quite long texts were styled as decrees issued by great gods. They
could be written on a piece of papyrus, put into a little box and worn as an
amulet around the neck for protection. These writings often contained an
enumeration of any possible dangers, as well as threats against the animals,
demons and gods who were viewed as adversaries, should they neglect the following command issued by Osiris:

Royal decree of Osiris, First One [of the Westerners (= of the dead
people)] . . .

Driving away a male dead (= a restless ghost), a female dead and so on . . . any
god, the (bad) influence of a god, the influence of a goddess . . . as death of
his head, death of his eyes, death of his belly, death of his backbone . . . death
by a crocodile, death by a lion . . . death by a snake, death by a scorpion . . .
death of being killed by a bronze (weapon), death of being buried, death of
not being buried, death of falling off a wall, death of drowning . . . death of
his loins, death of the lung(s) . . . death of his teeth . . . death of a (falling[?])
sycamore . . . death of any herbs . . . death of the bone of a bird (in the throat),
death of the bone of any fish . . . death of starving, death of thirsting . . . death
of going<-to>-one's ka (= dying), any death which comes about by men and
gods . . .

If the removal of any (demonic) enemy, fiend, male dead, female dead, and
so on is delayed:

Then the enemy of the heaven will split it asunder, then the enemy of the
earth will turn it over forcibly, then Apophis (i.e. the enemy of the sun-god)
<will be> in the Bark of Millions (= the bark of the sun-god), no water will
be given to the One who is in the coffin, the One who is in Abydos (i.e. Osiris)
will not be buried, the One who is in Busiris (i.e. Osiris) will not be covered
up, no offerings will be made to the One in Heliopolis (i.e. the sun-god) . . .

the people will not offer on all their festivals to any gods. (*Papyrus Turin 1993* verso 7.6–10.1)[30]

Such threats, promising as they do the destruction of world order, it was hoped, would force Osiris enforce his command and protect the man or woman who was using such a text.

Although it commended protective magic, Egyptian society took the harmful uses of magic seriously as well and criminalized it. The most famous case stems from an assassination attempt against Ramesses III. As the trial acts recount, one conspirator made voodoo-like figures and brought them into the palace:

When Penhuibin who was overseer of the cattle said to him, "Give me a text in order to lend me terror and might!", he gave him one text from the papyrus box of Usimaremiamun (= Ramesses III), the great god, his lord. And he began (to cause) (magical) excitement among the people during the god's arrival (= procession). He reached the side of the harim (and) also this great, deep place (i.e. the royal tomb which was under construction?). And he began to make inscribed men of wax, in order to have them taken inside by the agent Idrem, entangling one gang, bewitching the other one, taking some words (= messages) inside, bringing the others out. (*Papyrus Lee* 1.2–1.5 = *KRI* V 361,15–362,8)[31]

The Egyptians were well aware of the dangers of black magic. Because the use or the fear of magic was not a phenomenon linked to any specific social strata, it is no surprise that king Amenhotep II (1428–1397 BC) warned his viceroy in Nubia in an official letter, which was later incised on a stela, "Beware of their (= the Nubians) people and their magicians!" (*Urk.* IV 1344,12).[32]

Illness, misfortune and even death were sometimes blamed on bad demons or malevolent magic.[33] As treatment could only be properly applied if the agent of the misfortune was known, it was essential for the Egyptians to ascertain which god had been provoked to do harm. A so-called "wise woman" (*remtjet rekhet* [*rmt̠.t rḫ.t*]) was regarded as a proper source for this information. She remains a quite shadowy figure in the extant texts, but she must have played an important role. From Deir el-Medine there are some New Kingdom texts that give us at least an impression of when and how the "wise woman" was consulted:

I went to the wise woman (and) [she] said to me: 'A manifestation (*baw* [*bꜣw*]) of (the god) Ptah is with you because of (the man) Pashu because of an oath on behalf of his wife. Not at all a manifestation of (the god) Seth' (*Ostracon Gardiner* 149).[34]

In this instance, someone was seeking to identify the god who had caused his or her problems. Only when it was revealed to that person could he or she act against it. We do not know what the education of a "wise woman" was or what her qualifications were, nor whether there was one in each town or village. But we know that even the goddess Isis, the great sorceress among the gods, could act in the role of the "wise woman".

A charming story from the New Kingdom tells us about necromantia, the calling of dead people who have become spirits (singular *akh* [*ȝḥ*]). The First Prophet[35] of (the god) Amunre Khensemhab encounters a spirit whose tomb and funerary equipment are decaying and who has ceased receiving offerings. Such ghosts could become dangerous, as they might haunt living people in order to get their share or to do harm to them; in this instance, however, the ghost does not seem to be particularly evil. Because the text is incompletely preserved, one cannot tell why Khensemhab tries to win the favour of the ghost:

> And he (= Khensemhab) climbed on the roof [of his house. And he said to th]e gods of the sky, the gods of the earth, (the gods) of south, north, west (and) east ... "Cause this noble spirit to come to me!" And he (= the spirit) came [... THEN] the First Prophet of Amunre, the king of gods, Khens[emhab, said to him: "Tell me your wishes!] I will have it done for you".... [... THEN this noble spirit said to him:] "The one who is naked <in> the wind in wintertime [cannot feel warm]; hungry, without fo[od ..." THEN the First Prophet of Amunre, the king of gods,] Khensemhab, sat down weeping: "What a terrible state of existence: not eating, not drinking, not g[etting old, not becoming] young, not seeing the rays of the sun disk, not smelling the north wind!"[36]

The ghost seems to be sceptical about the High Priest's promises to renew the funeral of the spirit, because it is not for the first time that he was told this. One can only guess that now he gets what he wants but that Khensemhab is pursuing his own interests.

Third Intermediate Period and Late Period

About six centuries of mostly foreign rule over Egypt followed the era of the New Kingdom: the Libyans (946/945–ca. 735 BC), the Nubians (ca. 746–ca. 655 BC) and the Persians (525–401 and 342–332 BC). In between, native Egyptian dynasties could establish themselves, but sometimes Egypt was divided among several local rulers. Times of disorder and times of restoration followed each other. Magic continued to be of the greatest importance, and some new forms emerged alongside older ones.

One Oracular Amuletic Decree in particular exemplifies the great efforts in this period to enumerate more and more possible dangers (*Papyrus London BM 10083*, from the ninth or eighth century BC):

> We (= the protective gods) will protect her from a female demon of a canal, from a female demon of a well, from a female demon of the Nile, from a female demon of a lake, from a female demon of a pool which (the inundation) has left behind, from a male demon, from a female demon of her father and of her mother, from a female demon of her family of her father, from a female demon of her family of her mother.
>
> We will appease them (= the demons) for her.
>
> We will cause her to be sound during all of her life time.
>
> We will protect her from the magic of a Syrian, from the magic of a Nubian, from the magic of a Libyan, from the magic of an Egyptian, from the magic of a sorcerer (or) a sorceress, from any magic of any kind. (*Papyrus London BM 10083* verso 21–40)[37]

This section is followed with an enumeration of diseases and then with promises such as these: "We will provide her estate with cattle, with goats, with servants (and) female servants, with barley, with emmer, with copper, with clothing" (*Papyrus London BM 10083* verso 64–67).[38]

During the Late Period, a new type of magical device appears quite regularly – the so-called Horus cippi or Horus stelae. An example is illustrated in Figure 2.4. The god Horus, depicted as a naked child, is standing in the centre. He is grasping dangerous animals of the desert (snakes, a gazelle, a lion and a scorpion) and is thus annihilating them. Over his head, there is the face of the god Bes, a protective deity. To the left and to the right respectively, there are a papyrus-stem with a falcon and the symbol of the god Nefertem. Under Horus, there are two crocodiles, which again symbolize the victory over the powers of chaos and danger. On the back of these stelae, there is often a long spell against dangerous animals and sometimes other spells accompanied by illustrations depicting demonic beings being overpowered. Although some of the Horus stelae are very small and could possibly have been worn as a kind of amulet, others are really large and bear an extensive collection of spells and illustrations. The normal use of these stelae was to pour water over them, collect the water and then deploy it as a kind of holy water. To accomplish this, the more elaborate Horus stelae stood on block-like bases which contained basins for receiving the water. Even a human statue could be combined with a stela on the same base. A famous example is the statue of Djedher, dated to the fourth century BC. Djedher

FIGURE 2.4. Horus stela, front side, Late Period. British Museum, London, EA 36250, BM/ Big no. 60958. Image AN00179099_001.jpg of the British Museum.

is squatting on a large base block and is holding a Horus stela in front of him. The figure and the base are entirely covered with inscriptions. Only the skin is left free. Most of the texts are spells against poisonous animals, but we are also informed about Djedher's reasons for having the statue made. In one passage Djedher addresses the reader: "O every priest, every scribe, every wise (man) who will see this 'reciter' (i.e. a statue which recites), who will recite its [writing]s, who will know its formulae: You should protect its spells!" (lines 123–124).[39]

After the request for a funerary offering for Djedher, the text continues with the reasons why Djedher should be respected:

> ... since I have done good things to all people (and) to all the inhabitants of the nome of Athribis, in order to rescue everybody, who comes on the way, from the poison of any male serpent, any female serpent, and reptile. I have done likewise to everybody, who is in the house of the necropolis, in order to make alive the one who is dead (and) to rescue them from any biting mouth (i.e. snake). (lines 127–131)[40]

A famous papyrus of about 600 BC, *Papyrus Brooklyn 47.218.48+85*, could be called a handbook on snakes (cf. p. 53). It consists of two parts. The first treats all of the snakes known to the Egyptians; the second gives many magico-medical spells and treatments against snake-bites. Interestingly, the first part includes not only zoological features of the snakes but also the key information for magically treating them, namely, which god or goddess they represent, for example:

> AS FOR THE MALE ASIATIC (SNAKE) (= *Vipera ammodytes*): It is (coloured) like a quail, its head is large, its neck is short, its tail is like the tail of a mouse.... It is the manifestation of (the god) Sobek – VARIANT: (the goddess) Neith. (*Papyrus Brooklyn 47.218.48+85* § 18)[41]

As one can see, in this case, there existed conflicting views about the god or goddess of whom the snake was a manifestation.

Just as in the earlier epochs, in the Late Period, there are narratives which demonstrate how marvellous the abilities of magicians were imagined to be in Egyptian literature. One story is preserved in the *Papyrus Vandier* from about 600 BC. The main character is Merire, an extremely good magician. But the wicked lector priests at the royal court have prevented him from becoming known to Pharaoh and even tried to kill Merire. They poison Pharaoh. Merire is called in order to save Pharaoh, who is predicted to have only seven more days to live. The only way to save his life is to send Merire into the netherworld in place of Pharaoh. Once Pharaoh has sworn to Merire that he would touch neither Merire's property nor his wife, Merire prepares himself and goes to the dead ones. Osiris grants Pharaoh seventy-five additional years of life.

After some time, the goddess Hathor tells Merire that Pharaoh has broken the oath, that he has taken Merire's wife and has killed his son. Because Merire cannot leave the netherworld, he forms a golem-like man out of clay and sends him to the world of the living. The golem has Pharaoh punish and burn all of the evil magicians in Heliopolis, returns to Merire and brings him a bouquet. This, however, makes Osiris angry, because he thinks that Merire had left the netherworld. The rest of the story becomes very fragmentary and then breaks off completely.

A Greek story belonging to the so-called *Alexander Romance* tells us about Nectanebos (II), the last native king of Egypt (360–342 BC). Whenever Egypt is attacked, he uses magic in order to fight the enemy. Later on he comes to the royal court in Macedonia and begets Alexander the Great.

Graeco-Roman Period

After Alexander's conquest in 332 BC, a fundamental change took place in Egypt. Unlike the earlier foreign dynasties that ruled Egypt, the new Greek overlords used their own language and writing to an unprecedented extent. True, the Persians had already made use of Aramaic for administrative purposes in Egypt, but Greek became much more prominent and visible, because it was also used for official inscriptions by the king.

When Egypt lost its independence and fell to the Romans in 30 BC, the state administration used Greek nearly exclusively and Egyptian survived only in the temples. During the Graeco-Roman period, therefore, Egyptian scripts were almost exclusively retained in texts of priestly scholarship. Very long compilations have survived, especially from the Roman period, a very productive epoch.

During Graeco-Roman times, the Hellenistic and the Egyptian worlds saw a scholarly exchange of ideas and knowledge, although in other respects each culture adhered to its own traditions. More difficult to grasp is their relationship with Jewish and Mesopotamian elements. An extreme case is seen in the following section of a late Roman magical spell from a lamp divination:

HERE IS the copy of the summons itself which you should recite:

"O, speak to me, speak to me, *thes* (= Greek *theós* 'god'?),[42] *tēnor* (= Hebrew 'Give light!'?),[43] the father of eternity and everlastingness, the god who is over the entire land, *salgmo, balkmo brak* (= Hebrew 'flash of lightning'?) *nephro-banpre* (= Egyptian 'beautiful of face, soul of [the sun-god] Pre') *brias* (= Greek 'you are strong'?) *sari* (= Egyptian 'lord'?) of gods, *melikhriphs* (= Greek 'honey …') *larnknanes herephes* (= Greek *euryphyēs* 'broad-grown'?) *mephro-brias* (= Egyptian 'beautiful of face' [i.e. *nephro*] + Greek 'you are strong'?) *phrga-phekse ntsiwpshia marmareke* (= Greek *marmarygē* 'flashing'?) *laore-grepshie* (= … + Greek *kryphie* '(o) hidden one'?)! Let me see the answer to the inquiry on account of which I am here. Let an answer be made to me concerning everything about which I am asking here today, truly, without falsehood. *O atael apthe gho-gho-mole hesen-minga-nton-rotho-boubo*[44] *noere* (= Greek *noeré* '(o) intellectual one'?) *seresere* (= Greek *sýre sýre* '(o) Syrian, (o) Syrian'?) *san* (= Egyptian 'brother') *gathara eresgshingal* (= Ereshkigal) *sakgiste ntote-gagiste* (= Greek *dodeka-kistai?* = 'twelve baskets'?) *akruro-bore* (= Greek *akrourobóre* 'swallowing the tip of her tail', i.e. the moon) *gontere!*" (*Magical Papyrus London/Leiden* 7.19–7.26)[45]

In the long sequences of *voces magicae*, that is, magical names, which were often impossible to understand,[46] not only is a beneficent Egyptian god like the sun-god Pre (= Re) invoked but so are many Greek ones, whereas others are Hebrew and Mesopotamian, including Ereshkigal, the Sumerian goddess of the netherworld.

This text has a feature in common with the other Demotic magical texts, but it differs from the older Egyptian corpus. Whereas in the earlier epochs the sequence was heading – spell – instruction, it is now heading – instruction – spell, as in the Greek magical papyri.

There is even a spell in a foreign language (cf. p. 64 for a similar case in the New Kingdom): "SPELL OF GIVING PRAISE [and] love in Nubian: '*symyth kesyth hrbaba brasakhs lat*, son of(?) *bakha*'. Say these; put gum on your hand; and kiss your shoulder twice, and go before the man whom you desire" (*PDM* lxi 95–99).[47]

In another instance, a Greek and an Egyptian version of one and the same spell can be found next to each other:

> (Demotic:) [A spell] for going before a superior if he fights with you and he will not speak with you:

> (Greek:) Do not pursue me, you, so-and-so, (Old Coptic:) I am (Greek:) *papipetou metoubanes*. I am carrying the mummy of Osiris, and I go to take it to Abydos, to take it to Tastai, and to bury it at [Al]khas (= the necropolis of Abydos). If he, NN, causes me trouble, I will throw the mummy at him.

> (Demotic:) Its invocation in Egyptian again is that which is below:

> (Demotic:) Do not run after me, NN. I am *papipety metybanes*, carrying the mummy of Osiris, going to take it to Abydos to let it rest in Alkhah (*'lgh'h*). If NN fights with me today, I shall cast it out. (*PDM* xiv. 451–458 = *PGM* XIVb. 12–15 = *Magical Papyrus London/Leiden* 15.24–15.31)[48]

Very often glosses indicating the pronunciation of a word were added. Their use shows that a knowledge of Greek and Egyptian was required if someone wished to consult the papyrus. Interestingly, the Demotic written passages also show signs of being transformations of a Greek original. But matters can be complicated: the Demotic written word *'lgh'h* clearly represents the Greek *alkhai* [αλχαι]. This in turn, however, is a phonetic rendering of the Egyptian *'rq-ḥḥ*, the name of the necropolis of Abydos. All three forms of the word occur in the same London/Leiden papyrus, which gives us some idea of the transformation processes from one language and script to the other and back again underlying the extant text. It also shows how easily the etymological understanding was lost. Did those who wrote *'lgh'h* not know that the Greek *alkhai* in their *Vorlage* was a way of writing *'rq-ḥḥ*? If they did not, how much of what they wrote did they understand? If they were aware of it, why then did they choose a purely phonetic rendering? Were just the sounds important or was it for encrypting the text? One might point to the Egyptian cipher system for disguising certain words – only single words, never whole sentences.

The Demotic magical papyri do not contain only magical and medical instructions. One also finds short explanations of Greek mineral and plant names in Demotic, like the following:

> (Greek:) *thithymalos* (= *tithýmallos* = "spurge"),
>
> (Demotic:) which is this small herb which is in the gardens and which exudes milk. If you put its milk on a man's skin, it eats. (*Magical Papyrus London/ Leiden* verso 1.7–1.11)[49]

First the Greek name of the plant is given in Greek. Then the characteristics of the plant are given in Demotic.

Many similar Demotic magical texts are still extant, including three further manuals.[50] The types of matters covered in these texts include the following: lamp divinations, vessel divinations, rituals for seeing a god in a vision ("god's arrival") and other divinatory inquiries, spells for causing favour, love charms, instructions on how to separate a man from a woman, spells against bites and stings, spells against bones in the throat, rituals for performing harm to others, explanations of plants and minerals, and medical and other prescriptions, even including one for a donkey that is not moving.

Just as in the earlier periods, there are also extant in the Graeco-Roman epoch manuscripts of narratives on magicians. The best-preserved and best-known stories are centred around Setne Khaemwase, the fourth son of Ramesses II (1279–1213 BC). During his father's long reign, he developed a strong interest in Egyptian antiquities and several restoration inscriptions he left on older monuments bear witness to this. Setne Khaemwase's reputation as a great sorcerer likely derived from his preoccupation with antique buildings and tombs. Although the longest Demotic manuscripts we have are from the Ptolemaic Period (First Setne Story) and the Roman Period (Second Setne Story), the narratives are much older. An Aramaic papyrus from Egypt of the fifth century BC contains a story on Horus-son-of-Paneshe (i.e. "Horus, son of the wolf"), a character who is later known from the Second Setne Story.

In this narrative, we are told how Setne and his son Siosiris descend into the netherworld, where they discover the fate of people who have been just or unjust during their lifetime on earth. Later on, a Nubian magician comes to Pharaoh asking the Egyptian to read a sealed papyrus roll he has brought with him without opening it. For Siosiris, this is a trifling request, and he is easily able to read what is written. This story within the story takes us back into far distant times and tells how the Nubian king had one of his sorcerers – the Nubian title *ate* is used – bring Pharaoh to Nubia in the night, beat him before the Nubian king and return him to his palace within six hours. Pharaoh understandably disliked the idea of having to suffer the same treatment again. His magician, Horus-son-of-Paneshe, realized who was using magic against Pharaoh, protected him with amulets and succeeded in preventing the Nubian magic from being effective during the following night. Horus-son-of-Paneshe then started his magical counter-attack against the Nubian king. For three nights, the Nubian king was taken magically to Egypt, severely beaten before Pharaoh and returned to Nubia. The Nubian sorcerer was unable to protect his lord. To seek help for him, the sorcerer went to Egypt to look for the one who was acting against him. He identified Horus-son-of-Paneshe and began a magical contest with him. This fantastic showdown deserves to be quoted in full:

> The sorcerer then did a feat of magic: he made a fire break out in the court. Pharaoh and the nobles of Egypt cried out aloud, saying: "Hasten to us, you lector priest, Horus-son-of-Paneshe!" Horus-son-of-Paneshe made a magic formula and made the sky pour a heavy rain on top of the fire. It was extinguished at once.

> The Nubian did another feat of sorcery: he cast a big cloud on the court, so that no man could see his brother or his companion. Horus-son-of-Paneshe recited a spell to the sky and made it vanish and be stilled from the evil wind in which it had been.

> Horus-son-of-the-Nubian-woman did another feat of sorcery: he made a great vault of stone, 200 cubits long and 50 cubits wide, above Pharaoh and his nobles, so that Egypt would be separated from its king and the land deprived of its lord. When Pharaoh looked up at the sky and saw the vault of stone above him, he opened his mouth in a great cry, together with the people who were in the court. Horus-son-of-Paneshe recited a magical spell: he created a boat of papyrus and made it carry away the vault of stone. It sailed with it to the Great Lake, the big water of Egypt.

> Then the sorcerer of Nubia knew that he could not contend with the Egyptian. He did a feat of sorcery so as to become invisible in the court, in order to escape to the land of Nubia, his home. Horus-son-of-Paneshe recited a spell against him, revealed the sorceries of the Nubian, and let him be seen by Pharaoh and the people of Egypt who stood in the court: he had assumed the

shape of a bad bird and was about to depart. Horus-son-of-Paneshe recited a spell against him and made him turn on his back, while a fowler stood over him, his sharp knife in his hand, and about to do him harm. (*II Khaemwase* 6.13–6.24)[51]

Very shortly after this final defeat of the Nubian sorcerer, the story takes an unanticipated turn: this very sorcerer of this old story is the same Nubian who has brought the papyrus roll to Pharaoh's court 1,500 years later, and Siosiris is identified as the reincarnation of the excellent ancient magician Horus-son-of-Paneshe!

The First Setne Story shows also a remarkably fantastic and complex plot. Setne is looking for a book written by the god of wisdom, Thoth. He finds it in the tomb of Naneferkaptah and steals it.

Later on, he sees a beautiful woman called Tabubu and wants to have sex with her. But she asks him first to donate all his possessions to her, to have his children agree to this formally and to have them killed. Setne does all of this, but then when he goes to touch Tabubu, he finds himself in the street. He and the reader realize that the whole Tabubu episode was nothing but a phantasmagoria effected by the dead but still magically powerful tomb owner, who forces Setne to return the book.

These Setne Stories are not the only narratives on magicians in the Graeco-Roman period. There are other fragmentary Setne texts and a still unpublished story about king Zoser (twenty-seventh century BC) and his famous vizier Imhotep, who, among other things, has to fight a magical duel with an Assyrian sorceress.

Coptic Period

Egypt was Christianized during the first centuries AD. Having in Roman Egypt become exclusively used by a diminishing priestly elite, the scripts that had hitherto been used for writing Egyptian were gradually abandoned. The Copts, that is, the Egyptian Christians, considered these writings to be heathen and wrote their language, the latest form of Egyptian, with Greek letters, including some additional signs taken from the Demotic script for sounds not represented in the Greek alphabet.

Despite the changing scripts and the new religious prohibitions, magical practice remained ensconced in Egyptian society. As in other parts of the newly Christianized world, many magical texts were altered rather than abandoned, as is exemplified in the following prayer, written in Coptic but shaped by vestigial magical notions from Egyptian antiquity:

Move yourself, father, in the seventh heaven and the fourteenth firmament! Send me Jesus Christ, your only-begotten son, in order that he seals my body and this bowl – since what you bless will be full of blessing – (and) in order that he dispels every unclean spirit of the dirty aggressor, from 100 years downward and for 21 miles round, be it a male demon, be it a female demon, be it a male poison, be it a female poison, be it a vain, ill-bred, dirty demon![52]

Apart from the inclusion of Jesus as the supernatural helper, the text is not really different from much older Egyptian texts. One gets the impression that those practising magic simply used Christianity as a new source of divine helpers.[53]

It seems possible that at least some of the Coptic magical texts originate in older Egyptian ones. Others, however, are probably translations of Greek versions, but those in turn may also be translations of Egyptian texts.

The Coptic authorities considered pagan religion, as well as its magical practices, demonic. Therefore, they fought against the use of magic at the same time as they were attempting to destroy the pagan temples and books.[54]

A personal view of conversion can be found in the *Confession of Cyprianus*. The author admits to having acquired secret and magical knowledge in several countries, including Egypt, and to having performed many kinds of black magic before he was baptized. Cyprianus eventually became a bishop and was martyred during the persecutions that occurred under Diocletian (284–305 AD). Cyprianus writes:

Then I began confessing my sins ... I cut open the womb of women for the demons.... I have buried for him (= the devil) children who drink milk from their mother in the earth, I have suffocated others, I have cut off their head for the dragon, since he promised me "I will effect your matters by this".... I took the head of children for Hekate's sake who is said to be a virgin. I offered the blood of unmarried girls to Pallas (Athena).... I have persuaded numerous other demons by such offerings in order to go my way to the devil.[55]

Cyprianus also confesses to practising alchemy and forging gold, killing friends, conjuring illusions, empowering others to fly and walk on water, summoning the winds and so on. He also admits teaching and training many magicians (the Greek word *magos* is used).

In sum, the attempt to suppress magic within the campaign of Christianizing Egypt was not very successful. Still long after the Arab conquest of Egypt (642 AD), Coptic magical documents are found, including, for example, this spell from the tenth or eleventh century AD:

To bring a man to death: About three (times) daily borax and *al-mumiya* (= asphalt) (and) sweat of a black ass. Anoint his head (with it) (*Papyrus Cairo 42573*).[56]

In this Coptic prescription, we find the Arabic word *al-mumiya*. The occurrence of this foreign word shows that one fundamental feature of Egyptian magic remained unaltered during throughout millennia: whatever was considered to be helpful was incorporated into the magical practice.

Perspectives for Future Research

Apart from the necessity of publishing new material – a general need in Egyptology which cannot keep up with the many new discoveries – four points can be singled out:

Because magical texts are no longer considered to be garbled phantasms that do not deserve serious scholarly treatment, one must try to understand the magical texts within their cultural framework as purposely worded and intentionally written. Texts against diseases must therefore reflect in some way the illnesses against which they were designed. Thus it should be possible to get an idea of which disease a spell was meant to counteract. Such a medical reading of Egyptian magical texts is still in its infancy. This approach could possibly lead to an understanding of how the Egyptians thought about internal ailments, psychosomatic diseases and even mental illnesses, as well as how they grouped and categorized them.

A better understanding must also be sought of the religious and mythological concepts underlying each individual spell. How could this or that god help in a particular situation? Why just this god and not another one? Why in this special mythical constellation or at this particular locality? A careful comparison of magical texts to other religious texts can certainly be rewarding for a better understanding of both corpora.

It could be interesting to unravel the textual connections and transmissions. How are cultic texts transformed into magical ones? How are parts of them transplanted into magical spells? How are these in turn reworked? What does it mean when we find a spell in one case alone on a piece of papyrus but in another case embedded in a long magical manual? Although these are questions of details, they can possibly also help in detecting general patterns.

Finally, a fundamental point still deserves more thought, namely the long-debated question of the relationship between religion and magic. It is true that in Egypt, magic was a part of religion. But a phenomenon like the explicit inclusion of spells in foreign languages is found only in magical texts and not, for example, in temple cult texts. Magic was not, therefore, simply a part of Egyptian religion; at the same time, it was actually something more.

Notes

1. I would like to thank Cary Martin for correcting my English. Please note that small capitals are used in quotations for indicating red ink in the original manuscripts. The texts summarised on p. 73 and p. 78 can be found in Hoffmann, Friedhelm, and Joachim Friedrich Quack, *Anthologie der demotischen Literatur*. Münster: Lit, 2007.
2. Otto, *Magie*.
3. Cf. Westendorf, *Handbuch*, vol. II, 548.
4. Cf. Sauneron, *Traité d'ophiologie*, 23–24.
5. Cf. Quack, *Merikare*, 78–79.
6. Cf. Lichtheim, *Ancient Egyptian Literature*, vol. III, 130.
7. Ibid., 131.
8. Cf. Lichtheim, *Ancient Egyptian Literature*, vol. I, 155.
9. Quack, "Explizite Aufzeichnungsmeidung", 340.
10. Book of the Dead, rubric to chapter 133.
11. Dieleman, *Priests, Tongues, and Rites*.
12. E.g. Jelínková-Reymond, *Djed-her*.
13. Borghouts, *Magical Texts*, 51–55.
14. Eschweiler, *Bildzauber*.
15. Cf. Sethe, *Urkunden des Alten Reichs*, 23, 12ff. Cf. also 226, 13ff. Hawass, in *Egypt, Israel, and the Ancient Mediterranean World*, 30, publishes an extended version.
16. Cf. Erman, *Reden, Rufe und Lieder*, 29.
17. Cf. Leitz, "Die Schlangensprüche in den Pyramidentexten", 392–396, and Fischer-Elfert, *Zaubersprüche*, 53.
18. Posener, *Cinq Figurines d'envoûtement*. Cf. Fischer-Elfert, *Zaubersprüche*, 79–81.
19. Gnirs, "Nilpferdstoßzähne und Schlangenstäbe", 128–156. For amulets in general, see Andrews, *Amulets*; Müller-Winkler, *Objekt-Amulette*; and Petrie, *Amulets*.
20. Lichtheim, *Ancient Egyptian Literature*, vol. I, 215–222; Parkinson, *Poems*, 102–127.
21. Cf. Fischer-Elfert, *Zaubersprüche*, 72–73.
22. This and other sentences in foreign languages contained in the same papyrus are collected in Deines and Westendorf, *Wörterbuch der medizinischen Texte*, vol. II, 1032. Cf. Leitz, *Magical and Medical Papyri*, 63.
23. Cf. Leitz, *Magical and Medical Papyri*, 31.
24. Cf. Ibid., 39–40.
25. Lieven, "Divination in Ägypten", 77–126.
26. Cf. Leitz, *Tagewählerei*, 428–432.
27. Cf. Ibid., 452–479.
28. Cf. Gardiner, *Chester Beatty Gift*, vol. I, 15.
29. Cf. Ibid., 17.

30. Cf. Borghouts, *Magical Texts*, 4–6, and Fischer-Elfert, *Zaubersprüche*, 104–107.

31. Cf. Fischer-Elfert, *Zaubersprüche*, 91.

32. Cf. Helck, *Urkunden der 18. Dynastie*, 50

33. Cf. Zandee, *Death as an Enemy*.

34. Cf. Karl, "Funktion und Bedeutung einer *weisen Frau*", 136.

35. "Prophet" is a priestly title.

36. Gardiner, *Late-Egyptian Stories*, 89.11–91.10; cf. Fischer-Elfert, *Zaubersprüche*, 92–93.

37. Cf. Edwards, *Oracular Amuletic Decrees*, vol. I, 10, and Fischer-Elfert, *Zaubersprüche*, 111.

38. Cf. Edwards, *Oracular Amuletic Decrees*, vol. I, 12, and Fischer-Elfert, *Zaubersprüche*, 111.

39. Cf. Jelínková-Reymond, *Djed-her*, 123.

40. Cf. Ibid., 124.

41. Cf. Sauneron, *Traité d'ophiologie*, 13, and Leitz, *Schlangennamen*, 109–115.

42. This word is written in hieroglyphs.

43. ē is written with the Greek letter ēta.

44. The gloss above *rotho* shows that this is a mistake for *ortho* (= Greek "correct").

45. Cf. Betz, *Greek Magical Papyri*, 207; explanation of *voces magicae* according to Quack, *Das Ägyptische und die Sprachen Vorderasiens*, 427–507, esp. 468–470.

46. There was probably no necessity to understand these words; cf. Jamblich, *De mysteriis*, vol. VII, 4 ff. for the importance of just sounds.

47. Cf. Betz, *Greek Magical Papyri*, 289.

48. Cf. Ibid., 221.

49. Cf. Ibid., 240.

50. Cf. Johnson, "Introduction to the Demotic Magical Papyri," in Betz, *Greek Magical Papyri*, lv–lvii.

51. Cf. Lichtheim, *Ancient Egyptian Literature*, vol. III, 149.

52. Cf. Kropp, *Zaubertexte*, vol. I, 48, vol. II, 59.

53. For Mary in Coptic magical texts, see Beltz, "Maria in der koptischen Magie", 27–31.

54. van der Vliet, "Spätantikes Heidentum in Ägypten."

55. Cf. Bilabel, *Texte zur Religion*, 176–177.

56. Cf. Fischer-Elfert, *Zaubersprüche*, 128 XI.

Chapter 3

Early Greco-Roman Antiquity

KIMBERLY B. STRATTON

A curse tablet from fourth-century Attica exemplifies many aspects of what has come to be considered magic in Western thought.[1] Inscribed on a thick tablet, this curse emerges from an apparent love triangle or situation of romantic/erotic competition. The petitioner seeks to end the relationship between two lovers, Theodōra and Charias, by binding both Theodōra's ability to attract lovers and Charias's desire for pleasure with her. The second side of the tablet indicates that it was deposited in a grave: "And just as this corpse is without effect (literally incomplete, ἀτελής) may all the words and deeds of Theodōra be without effect (ἀτέλεστα) towards Charias and the other people."[2] There are certain elements in this tablet that resonate with conceptions of magic both ancient and modern. First, this ritual binds the victim in the presence of Hecate (a goddess closely associated with magic and the restless dead in classical Greek thought) and those who died incomplete or unfulfilled (τοὺς ἀτελέστους), indicating either that they died before achieving their natural life span and destiny (being unmarried, for example), were unburied and consequently unable to pass to the underworld and find repose, or were uninitiated and, therefore, lacked the protection of the chthonic deities who granted a better afterlife to initiates.[3] Whichever was the case, they form part of a cohort of ghosts believed to follow Hecate and roam the earth. Like the ghosts of legend and horror films, they were considered to be restive and angry – resentful of living human beings and demanding placation to keep them from causing harm.[4] Additionally, the private goals of this spell, combined with its intention to control and possibly harm another person, signal to most observers (both ancient and modern) an act of magic.

To what extent, however, can we apply the label "magic" to this ritual, and did the practitioners of this and similar rituals consider the activity to be magic? The question is a difficult one, given that the very category of magic has been critiqued in recent decades as a modern imposition on ancient cultures and texts.[5] Furthermore, as scholars of ancient history came to recognize the subjective and pejorative nature of the label "magic" in antiquity, many have argued that no one in the ancient world considered his or her own ritual practices to constitute magic; magic was always a disparaging accusation designed to malign and marginalize another individual or group of people. Although both these observations are decidedly true, it is nonetheless clear that many individuals from different walks of life and social classes engaged in practices that were regarded by their contemporaries as magic, that is, as surreptitious rituals designed to enlist supernatural power to harm or control another person.[6] In some places and times, such practices were illegal. Even where they were not officially proscribed, however, fear of such rituals was widespread; they were enlisted to explain sudden illnesses, professional failures, or similar misfortunes.[7] In this chapter, I will survey the history of magic in Greece and Rome, up to and including the Republic, with the goal of illuminating both the emergence of magic as a discourse of alterity, or othering strategy, in Western thought and the corresponding influence this discourse had on the practice of rituals that came to be considered magic. It is my contention that magic should be conceived not as a specific set of practices but as a form of discourse that shaped stereotypes of magicians and witches as well as the actual practice of certain rituals in antiquity.

Before turning to examine the social history of these types of rituals, I will briefly survey the debate among scholars of antiquity over defining magic and its use as a heuristic category for ancient societies in order to clarify how I understand the operation of magic as a social discourse and in order to delimit the subject matter of this chapter.

Magic in Scholarly Discourse

The past three decades of scholarship on ancient magic bore witness to a radical rethinking of this category, culminating in a debate over whether even to continue using the term magic at all in second-order definitions. The trend represented a corrective to previous generations of scholarship that largely dismissed ancient magic as, in the words of Edward Tylor, "one of the most pernicious delusions that ever vexed mankind" and regarded it as primitive, belonging to the lowest ranks of civilization.[8] Harold Remus in his 1994 presidential address to the Canadian Society of Biblical Studies, which was published subsequently as "'Magic,' Method, Madness," provides a succinct history of this change in attitude. He begins his story at the turn of the twentieth century, when a small number of classical philologists risked censure to investigate and publish the increasing assortment of curses, binding spells, amulets, and magical recipes that had languished in a moldy corner of classical studies since their discoveries around a century earlier. These ancient documents had until that point been considered unworthy of scholarly attention – they were not the elite literary products of a developed society but the creations of uneducated lower classes and "blatant superstition" (*krassen Aberglaubens*) that did not merit the title "literature."[9] Furthermore, these documents threatened to rob classicists of their idealized Greek society: one that was rational and immune to superstition.[10] Preisendanz thus described his efforts among those of a small cohort of like-minded philologists as imprudent to declare publicly.[11] Despite this new attention to these diverse documents, prejudices endured. A. A. Barb, for example, who was heavily influenced by a theological bias, referred to "magical rubbish," which he distinguished from "evangelical truth."[12]

Increasingly, scholars grew uncomfortable with the magic / religion dichotomy and challenged it as theologically biased,[13] colonialist,[14] and inadequate.[15] Alan Segal, for example, in his influential article on defining Hellenistic magic, demonstrates how both categories – magic and religion – collapse when faced with evidence of ancient ritual practices as reflected in the *Greek Magical Papyri* (hereafter *PGM*). Segal points out that "hymns could be written in either magical or religious conditions" and that the people who wrote these texts "saw no distinction between the various sections."[16] The distinction between magic and religion is thus a modern one imposed on ancient practitioners and does not reflect their own state of mind or perceptions of their practices.

Some scholars chose to avoid the debate by using entirely emic terminology,[17] whereas others argued that all ritual practices constituted "religion" for ancient people.[18] Furthermore, many rejected accepting accusations of magic in ancient sources at face value, given that these reflected polemics rather than accurate portrayals of ancient practices.[19] The designation "magic," when wielded by ancients, revealed attempts to define boundaries between us and them, as well as legitimate and illegitimate religious authority, conveying the attitude that my "miracle" is your "magic."[20] The reaction against earlier pejorative attitudes toward magic is clear in the statements of certain scholars from this period who strove to eliminate any dichotomy between magic and religion in ancient studies. John Gager, for example, states that "magic, as a definable and consistent category of human experience, simply does not exist."[21] Christopher Faraone breaks down the perceived distinction between curses and pious prayers, noting that "a *defixio* [curse tablet] employing a prayer formula is exactly that, a prayer to the chthonic deities. Whether the prayer is benevolent or malevolent is immaterial to the pious belief that the gods addressed can and will do what they are asked provided they are approached in a ritually correct manner."[22]

The pendulum began to swing in the opposite direction, however, just as this debate peaked in the early 1990s. A collection of essays on magic published in 2002 by Paul Mirecki and Marvin Meyer includes some that argue for the legitimacy of magic as a category in ancient studies, demonstrating that the religion/magic dichotomy existed in antiquity and was not just a post-Enlightenment, Protestant projection onto ancient practices and beliefs as some had argued. Henk Versnel articulated the view that magic could profitably be used as a second-order definition for comparative scholarship if the material under consideration met a minimum number of predetermined criteria.[23] C. A. Hoffman showed that the same criteria employed by modern scholars to define magic were used also by ancient thinkers,[24] and Fritz Graf demonstrated how several ancient writers had highly developed theories of magic, although these differed from modern conceptions, which have been influenced largely by the work of Edward Tylor and Sir James Frazer.[25] Other scholars sidestep the old debate altogether and persist in using the term "magic" as if it were an unproblematic category.[26]

This is where the present chapter seeks to enter the conversation. Both approaches – accepting and rejecting the term "magic" – have their limitations. On the one hand, as demonstrated by Hoffman, the category "magic" did exist in the ancient world and parallels modern conceptions of this term in many respects, not least because our idea of magic derives from this Greco-Roman origin. Thus, applying the term "magic" to certain ritual practices or people in antiquity is not necessarily anachronistic, as some have argued. On the other hand, ancient terminology for magic often carried highly pejorative connotations in antiquity, so accounts of practicing magic ipso facto should not be regarded at face value but should instead be understood in terms of a discourse of alterity that operated in Greek and Roman society. In other words, researchers should try to understand what ideological work the label "magic" is doing in a particular context. Before discussing the emergence and operation of this discourse, let us look at the rituals themselves.

Curse Tablets and Binding Spells

In this chapter, the discussion of magic will focus on curse tablets and binding spells (Greek *katadesmoi*; Latin *defixiones*).[27] The reason is twofold: first, in order to reconstruct the social history of magic in Greece and Rome, it is important to understand what Greeks and Romans understood to be magic. In many instances, their conceptions coincide with a popular modern understanding. In other cases, they do not. I will not consider the use of amulets in this chapter, for example, because amulets were widely accepted as legitimate aids for healing and protection and were not universally regarded negatively as magic. Most people in antiquity believed in and used amulets. The Babylonian Talmud, for example, sanctions the use of amulets, as long as they have been "proven" to work or come from a producer of proven amulets (b. Shab. 61a–61b, 67a); it also provides recipes for the manufacture of amulets, demonstrating the wide acceptance of this practice as effective and valuable.[28] The famous Greek statesman Pericles is said to have worn an amulet (περίαπτον) when he laid dying of the plague. Plutarch reports that Pericles showed his friend the amulet in order to demonstrate that he was so bad off as to abide this type of folly (ἀβελτερίαν, Per. 38.2). The source of the anecdote, Theophrastus, however, discusses the episode in the context of whether ill fortune and bodily suffering alter the disposition even of those who have excellent character, suggesting that Pericles himself chose to wear the amulet on account of his disease. In either case, despite derision for the practice among certain skeptical elites, wearing amulets was widespread, accepted by many educated authorities and generally not treated under the same semantic constellation as other practices, such as curses, poisoning, and incantations, which were regarded as magic. Thus, although amulets often fall under the category "magic" in a modern rubric, which distinguishes between medicinal practices regarded as effective and labeled as science and those regarded as ineffective or superstitious and labeled as magic, I will not be discussing them here because my object is to understand the practice of rituals that were widely regarded as magic according to ancient definitions.

The second reason this study will focus on the use of *katadesmoi* is that we lack material evidence for other types of practices identified as magic in antiquity. The use of herbs (*pharmakeia*) and singing incantations (*epōidos*), for example, could be considered either legitimate medicine or harmful magic, depending on the context.[29] To the extent that incantations figured in the production and deposition of *katadesmoi* they are included in this discussion.[30] The use of *pharmakeia*, on the other hand, is historically unrecoverable and can only be discussed on the basis of literary portraits and forensic accusations, which are often highly stereotyped, reflecting society's fears and fantasies. Because I have explored literary representations and stereotypes of *pharmakeia* in some depth elsewhere, I will not replicate that discussion here.[31] So, although *pharmakeia* and *epōidos* were common practices identified as magic in antiquity, we simply do not have sufficient material evidence to discuss

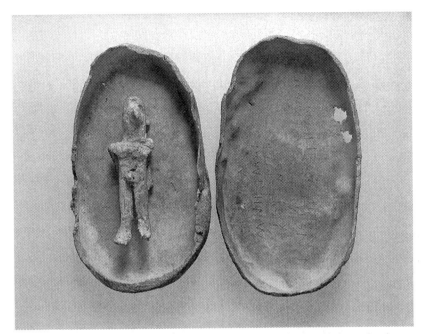

FIGURE 3.1. *Katadesmos* that targets known public figures in what was likely a judicial curse, fifth century BCE, Kerameikos, Athens. Photograph used by permission of the German Archaeological Institute. D-DAI-ATH-Kerameikos 5879. All rights reserved.

them apart from literary representations, leaving us with *katadesmoi* as our only source for the practice of magic independent from imagined or stereotyped performances of it.

Turning then to a discussion of *katadesmoi*, the first questions to ask are what they are and how they were expected to work. *Katadesmoi* are curses inscribed on metal (frequently lead) tablets and often found buried in or near the graves of those who died violently or prematurely. As we saw in the example that opened this chapter, these spells command the ghost of a corpse to bind (literally tie down, *katadeō*) another person or employ ritual analogy to render certain characteristics and talents of the victim cold and useless like the corpse (or sometimes the lead on which the curse is inscribed). Occasionally they are inscribed on a figurine that has been subjected to violent treatment (such as twisting, binding, or piercing), which is the ancient equivalent of a "voodoo" doll (see Figures 3.1 and 3.2). In most cases, these curses appear to target a competitor in some field of action, such as rhetoric, business, or romance (possibly as competing prostitutes or courtesans).[32] One recent study

FIGURE 3.2. *Katadesmos* that targets known public figures in what was likely a judicial curse, fifth century BCE, Kerameikos, Athens. Photograph used by permission of the German Archaeological Institute. D-DAI-ATH-Kerameikos 5882. All rights reserved.

has framed the motivation in terms of risk rather than competition, suggesting that people who commissioned the spells sought to assure success in an uncertain yet vitally important aspect of their lives.[33] If so, risk was nonetheless identified with another person who became the target of the curse's binding action.

These curses debut in the archaeological record around the same time that attitudes toward death appear to have been changing. Whereas formerly the deceased were regarded as impotent wisps of their former selves, devoid of consciousness or power, numerous sources, including *katadesmoi* themselves, indicate that the souls of the dead were increasingly seen as active, powerful, potentially threatening, and needing to be placated or controlled.[34] Sarah Iles Johnston convincingly argues that the correspondence between the appearance of *katadesmoi* and changing beliefs about the dead in Greece is not coincidental. Just as the dead could now pose a threat to living humans and required placation through rituals of propitiation, they also posed an opportunity: they could be compelled into service through curse tablets and incantations.[35] The emergence of *katadesmoi* at this time thus reflects an entrepreneurial exploitation of changing beliefs about the dead, introducing a potent new technology for promoting one's interests and success at the expense of a rival.

These curses, which suddenly appear at the dawn of the Classical era and gain in popularity throughout the Hellenistic and Roman periods, seem to be the result of a dynamic synthesis between existing Greek practices and Near Eastern rituals introduced from Mesopotamia during the preceding centuries. Necromantic oracle sanctuaries (*nekuomanteia*), for example, which were situated at special geographic locations associated with entrances to the underworld, may reflect influences from Assyria and provided a precedent for the invocation of the dead by the living in private rituals, such as *katadesmoi*.[36] The manipulation of figurines to curse someone may also derive from Mesopotamia, where exorcists had long been using various strategies to manipulate ghosts and harm enemies, including binding statues of restless spirits to prevent them from causing harm and burying figurines in the lap of a corpse to consign an enemy to the underworld.[37] In addition to these possible foreign influences, Christopher Faraone explores Greek precedents for *katadesmoi* in the ritual binding of figurines and statues at the civic level to prevent military invasion or plague.[38] Furthermore, Greeks had a tradition of vengeful chthonic spirits, such as the Erinyes, and of restless ghosts who required placation, both of which make appearances in *katadesmoi*.[39] The combination, therefore, of vengeful ghosts, curses, and the manipulation of figurines most likely occurred quite naturally in the context of cultural exchange and creativity that marks the transition to the Classical period, fostering the emergence of a new ritual technology – *katadesmoi*.

Emergence of Magic Discourse

The appearance of *katadesmoi* in the fifth century corresponds chronologically to the emergence of a new conceptual category in Greek roughly equivalent to "magic" in English. Terminology designating foreign, specifically Persian, ritual specialists (*magoi*) combined with terms for herbal medicine or poison (*pharmakeia*), incantation (*epōidē*), manipulation of the restless dead (*goeteia*), and binding spells (*katadesmoi*) to create a semantic constellation that drew on the negative associations of each term to extend and amplify the pejorative meanings of the other terms. Plato, for example, describes the use of incantations and binding spells as a form of *pharmakeia* and laments the deleterious effects such practices had on the psychology of those who fear them or see curses on tombs (Plato, *Leg.* 933a–933b). The Hippocratic author of *On the Sacred Disease* enlists the terms *magos* and *goēs* to denigrate competing healers as charlatans and frauds (*Morb. sacr.* 1). A character in Euripides' *Bacchae* describes Dionysos (disguised as a priest of his own religion) as an effeminate, incantation-chanting magician (*goēs epōidos*) to derogate him and the "foreign" religion he represents.[40] Aeschines and Demosthenes, competing statesmen and orators, both employ the term *goēs* in addition to *magos* to slander each other, demonstrating that these two words had evolved beyond describing particular types of ritual specialists to function as general terms of abuse in political invective.[41] Thus, by the fourth century, an accusation of "magic," using any of the terms just described, marginalized or delegitimized someone by evoking vague associations between deleterious foreign practices, fraud, and charlatanism.[42]

Although it is unwise to accept these accusations simply at face value, *katadesmoi* have been discovered in Athens from the fifth and fourth centuries BCE that target known orators, indicating that the use of magic against a political or rhetorical opponent had some basis in reality at that time. Despite this evidence, Christopher Faraone proposes that most accusations served to excuse an unexpectedly poor performance on the part of a seasoned orator, who was anticipated to succeed, and do not indicate real magical attacks.[43] Magic was thus a rhetorical strategy as well as a reality.

It is also important to note that even the texts that denigrate these practices admit to their popularity. Nevertheless, the dispersal of magic discourse across a broad array of texts over the course of the fifth and fourth centuries suggests that whatever an individual's private attitudes toward these practices may have been, the negative discourse of magic came to define the public transcript, at least among a prominent segment of the population, whose point of view shaped the development of the concept of magic in Western thought.[44] We must assume, for example, that an accusation of being a *goēs* or *magos* in the context of civic debate carried a widely accepted negative charge; otherwise, such accusations would have been meaningless. Similarly, Pentheus's unwise dismissal of Dionysos as a mere *goēs* in Euripides' *Bacchae* works dramatically if we assume it represents a common point of view at that time. If the audience did not identify with Pentheus in his judgment of Dionysos, there would have been less power and poignancy in the tragic denouement of the play. Tragedy works because an audience sees itself – its own desires, fears, and potential mistakes – in the characters on stage.

Magic as a distinct concept and a discourse of alterity thus can be seen to emerge in Greece during the course of the fifth century BCE. Terminology that connoted magic at that time functioned neutrally in pre-classical literature; some practices, such as *epōidos* and *pharmakeia*, had a long history in

Greece, during which, as far as texts reveal, they were regarded neutrally – like taking aspirin.[45] What happens in the fifth century is that these same practices become conflated with others that were regarded negatively, such as *katadesis*, and terms for different practices were combined in such a way that they lost any technical meaning and came to denote aberrant ritual activities more generally. The question to ask, therefore, is why. What circumstances in Greek society could effect such a change in conception and thus create a discourse of alterity out of formerly innocuous medicinal and ritual practices? No laws against magic, for example, appear to have existed in ancient Athens, although killing someone with potions or incantations was prosecutable under laws against murder, and at least two women were known to have been tried on charges of conducting illicit rituals.[46]

The appearance of magic as a discourse of alterity in Greek thought, I propose, can be traced to at least two factors: the first is ideological, and the second relates to the intersection of politics and religion in the ancient *polis*. During the Persian wars, Panhellenism and the espousal of ethnic superiority unified the Greek cities in their joint opposition to Persian imperial expansion.[47] Following the wars, Athens seized on this notion of ethnic and, especially, political superiority to foster allegiance among the Delian League and, later, to justify control over an expanding Athenian empire.[48] Edith Hall delineates the emergence of a "discourse of barbarism" at this time that acted as a foil in the formulation of a new Athenian identity, which was based on democracy and the ideal of equality over hierarchy and tyranny – two characteristics explicitly identified with barbarians in Greek tragedy. This discourse, according to Hall, served the ideological purpose of promoting democracy as a form of government, buttressing Athens's control over its former allies, as well as justifying slavery.[49] The stereotype of the barbarian, which appeared first in tragedy, portrayed barbarians as effeminate, servile, addicted to luxury, cruel, despotic, and lacking emotional self-control (σωφροσύνη).[50] These traits – the antithesis of Athenian values and virtues – were projected onto the foreign Other and thereby reaffirmed for Athenians their rationality, self-control, and superior self-government. Barbarians also conversely constituted an ambivalent source of attraction for Greeks; they represented the exotic Other and purveyors of ancient Oriental wisdom.[51] Magic discourse, I argue, emerged part and parcel of this discourse of barbarism, both reinforcing the perceived Otherness of barbarians and also serving to marginalize certain Greeks by identifying these individuals or groups with threatening outsiders.

The second contributing factor, I propose, is the tension between *polis*-controlled religion and private rites of the household. Sourvinou-Inwood documents the integral role that the *polis* played in Greek religion: religion functioned as the *polis*'s central ideology; it provided structure, meaning, and identity by linking the *polis* and its citizens to their past, their landscape, and, most importantly, to the divine through ritual practices.[52] According to Sourvinou-Inwood, the *polis* regulated and legitimated all religious activity, including rites identified with the household (*oikos*) and family.[53] Although in most cases domestic rites and *polis* religion were complementary, with *polis* religion often mirroring rites of the *oikos* on a grander scale, sometimes tension or conflict between the interests of the *polis* and those of the family arose.[54] Unregulated private rites could be regarded as competing with the *polis* for religious authority and, therefore, raised suspicion.[55] In one extreme example, private celebrations of the Eleusinian mysteries were perceived as sacrilegious mockery and blamed, along with mutilation of the herms, for the disastrous failure of Athens's campaign against Syracuse in 415–413 BCE (Thuc. 6.28). As Deborah Boedeker notes, these private celebrations of the mysteries may have raised questions about the unregulated private harnessing of divine power; political motivations were strongly suspected and led to accusations against Alcibiades for plotting against the democracy.[56] The interlocutor in Plato's *Laws* strongly expresses a similar concern regarding unregulated domestic rites; he loosely links private mysteries and *goētic* incantations (ἐπῳδαῖς γοητεύοντες) with impious disrespect (or even exploitation) of the gods and dangerous political aspirations, such as demagoguery and tyranny (908d, 909b). In this dialogue, the Athenian Stranger states his desire to ban not only the practice of magicians selling curses and cathartic expiation but all household cult, especially the proliferation of women's votive offerings and altars (909d–910c). Interestingly, in this dialogue, Plato conceptually identifies women's private religious devotions with the more sinister activities of "magicians" and political subversion, indicating the intersection of gender, power, and magic that characterizes this discourse in later centuries.[57]

Boedeker perceives in these comments, as well as in certain Attic tragedies, a rising concern in the fifth century about women's control of unregulated domestic rites. She points out that both Aeschylus and Euripides frame the crimes of Clytemnestra and Medea as aberrant sacrifices performed by women in the secret recesses of female domestic space.[58] I propose that magic discourse, which was emerging at this time, provided a way to express this concern over unregulated domestic rites and women's religious practices by associating them with threatening barbarians, political subversion, and illegitimate foreign rituals. Thus, distinct but related social dynamics intersected and reinforced each other in the formulation of magic as a discourse of alterity.

In this context and part of this process, two overlapping stereotypes emerge; both, no doubt, reflect to some extent real characters familiar to fifth-century Greek society, yet their depiction in literature draws on and reinforces the nascent discourse of magic that was emerging at the same time. The first focuses primarily on male ritual experts, whose knowledge of the underworld and ability to manipulate the dead enabled them to offer mystery initiations intended to ensure a better afterlife.[59] According to Plato, for example, begging priests (ἀγύρται) and diviners (μάντεις) performed rituals to expiate the misdeeds of ancestors. Additionally, they sold *katadesmoi*, which could harness and direct the power of the gods to harm an enemy (Plato, *Rep.* 2.364b–2.364c). A similar type of ritual expert is mocked by Hippocrates, who denigrates these competing healers as *magoi*, purifiers (καθάρται), begging priests (ἀγύρται), and quacks (ἀλαζόνες) (*Morb. sacr.* 1). He rejects their claim that epilepsy is sacred and accuses them of fraud and disrespect toward the gods for accusing the gods of causing it. Heraclitus, a sixth-century philosopher from Miletus, denounces *magoi*, along with Bacchants (Βάκχοις), mystery initiates (μύσταις), night-time roamers (νυκτιπόλοις) and Bacchic revelers (λήναις), as impious in a quotation preserved by Clement of Alexandria (*DK* 14). If genuine, this statement indicates that already in the sixth century, *magoi* were associated with mystery initiations, confirming Plato's description more than a century later. Plato, however, never refers to these ritual experts as *magoi*; instead he refers to them as "begging priests" (*agurtai*), which the Hippocratic author of *On the Sacred Disease* uses in combination with *magoi* to describe competing healers who offer to cure with purifications and incantations.

Thus, using the three authors to triangulate, the picture emerges of itinerant male ritual adepts who make a business selling initiations, purifications, and incantations (or curse tablets) to their ancient clientele. All three portraits, however, are strongly condemnatory, so it is possible that the term *"magoi"* and accusations of selling curses have been added to the picture to denigrate these men, who were, at least in the case of the Hippocratic treatise, competitors for clients and legitimacy as healers. What is clear is that various terms for magic and magicians had become interchangeable and that the stereotype of an itinerant priest who could manipulate the dead for protection or to cause harm was active in the fifth and fourth centuries BCE. Sarah Iles

Johnston deftly traces the link between Persian *magoi* and *goētes*, whom she identifies with the ritual experts described earlier in this section. *Goētes* derive their name from *goaō*, a lamentation for the dead traditionally performed by women in the Archaic period and limited thereafter by the laws of Solon. Johnston argues that male ritual experts took over women's funerary dirge and became experts at manipulating the dead, like *magoi* traditionally were in Persia.[60] The evolution occurred sometime between the seventh and sixth centuries, when elements of Mesopotamian culture influenced Greece and the first references to *goētes* as ritual experts in initiation and magic appeared. By the fifth century, the term *goēs* had become synonymous with fraud and foreign chicanery. Thus, Euripides enlists stereotyped conceptions of the *goēs* to dramatic effect in the *Bacchae* when Pentheus accuses the disguised Dionysos of being an effeminate, foreign *goēs*. This denigrating stereotype also appears to be at work in the depictions of *agurtai* and *magoi* discussed in the previous paragraph.

The second stereotype, which focuses on women, similarly acts as a foil for Athenian identity by focusing gendered conceptions of proper social roles through the prism of magic discourse. Women's use of dangerous *pharmakeia* threads itself as a theme through many Attic tragedies and plays a cardinal role in two forensic speeches from the fifth and fourth centuries.[61] The most famous *pharmakis* (usually translated as sorceress, but referring specifically to the use of herbs and potions) is Medea. Medea had already gained a reputation for magic by the beginning of the fifth century, when Pindar referred to her as *pampharmakous*, or skilled in all kinds of herbs (*Pyth.* 4.233). In the seventh century, Hesiod referred to the story of the Argos and Jason's marriage to Medea, but he never alluded to her knowledge of magic or the magical assistance she provided Jason to ensure the success of that heroic voyage (*Theog.* 992–999). We can only assume that her magical role in the epic adventure must have played some part in earlier versions because it is so integral to the story later on. By the time Euripides presented his tragedy, Medea had acquired renown for murder, magic, and deceit. To this list, Euripides likely added infanticide, solidifying Medea's reputation for being not only a sorceress but also a barbarian in the full sense of the word, wholly alien to Greek culture and values.[62] Her horrified husband, Jason, asserts what every audience member must have been thinking: that murdering her children as an act of vengeance is something no Greek woman could have done. Precisely – Medea conceives of her action in masculine heroic terms. She explicitly squelches maternal feelings and feminine emotion to avenge Jason's betrayal. By renouncing maternal devotion in favor of honor and vengeance, she challenges assumptions about proper gender roles, even as her actions confirm to an ancient audience the necessity of the social constructs that keep women in their place. As an infanticidal, barbarian sorceress, Medea corroborates the anxiety over women's domestic religious authority identified by Boedeker.

The plot of Sophocles' *Trachiniae* similarly revolves around a woman's use of magic to resolve a love triangle. Whereas Medea employs magic to take revenge on her rival, the main character in the *Trachiniae*, Deianeira, employs what she believes is a love charm (φρενός σοι τοῦτο κηλητήριον, 575) to control the love of her errant husband, Heracles. As her name, which means man-slayer, forebodes, this potion is not a love charm, but a powerful poison designed to kill the invincible Heracles. Deianeira made the potion from the blood of a centaur as he was dying of a mortal wound inflicted by Heracles himself; the centaur told Deianeira that the potion would prevent Heracles from loving (στέρξει) another woman more than her (577). Significantly, the verb *stergō* indicates the devotion and affection appropriate to spouses, not the fleeting lust of sexual desire. Deianeira's concern, thus, is to protect her status as Heracles' rightful wife and to not have to share her marriage with another woman whom Heracles has just brought home as a captured war bride (546).

In both mythic dramas, women employ *pharmaka* in response to the violation of their social status as wives and mothers. Similarly, in both dramas, the women's use of magic occurs part and parcel of gender role reversals instigated by men. Medea renounces maternal affection and seeks revenge through infanticide after Jason breaks his marital vows to her and leaves her utterly bereft of family or protection. Because she betrayed her natal family to help him, he forces her to assume the male role of protecting her honor and seeking revenge. Deianeira's magic similarly responds to Heracles' failure to exercise good governance and self-restraint by maintaining the proper distinction between concubine and legal wife. His failure to legitimately channel his erotic desire leads to a reversal of gender roles: first, by positioning Deianeira as the *erastēs* (active, desiring partner) pursuing her *erōmenos* (passive object of desire) through magic, and second, by feminizing Heracles with excruciating pain; he declares that he has been transformed into a whimpering woman and discovered to be female (νῦν δ' ἐκ τοιούτου θῆλυς ηὕρημαι τάλας, 1075). Women's use of *pharmakeia* in these two tragedies draws on the emerging discourse of magic to think about proper gender roles, male virtue, and what happens when men lack the self-restraint and wisdom necessary to govern their families, let alone the *polis*. Magic provides a tool for accentuating Otherness in the service of thinking about Self.

Although they are distinct, these two stereotypes gradually came to overlap, with female characters in Hellenistic and Roman literature performing ritual acts that were associated with male *goētes* in the Classical period, such as reanimating corpses (Lucan 6.750–6.830) and engraving curse tablets (Apuleius, *Met.* 3.18). I suggest that this slippage between the two stereotypes was already underway in the Classical period, as is evident from the semantic overlap in many depictions of magic. Herodotus uses a verbal derivative of *pharmakon* (φαρμακεύσαντες) to characterize the rituals of Persian *magoi* (*Hist.* 7.114.1), Circe's *pharmakeia* is described with a term derived from *magos* (μαγγανεύουσαν) in Aristophanes' *Plutus* (310),[63] and Dionysos is described as a flamboyantly effeminate *goēs* in Euripides' *Bacchae*. It is possible that the original association of *goaō* with women's lamentation may have implicitly gendered the perception of *goētes*; at any rate, the gendered inflection was sufficiently present to be exploited by Euripides in the *Bacchae*. Significantly, men's association with magic diminishes over time; in literature of the Roman imperial period, magic becomes primarily a female pursuit.[64]

Hellenistic and Roman Period

It was this discourse of alterity that spread throughout the Hellenistic world and contributed to Roman, Jewish, and eventually Christian ideas of Otherness and illegitimate ritual activity.[65] In the Hellenistic period, an increased interest in things exotic and uncanny can be seen in the detailed attention to magic rituals in literary imaginings.[66] Theocritus's *Idyll* 2, for example, depicts a young female protagonist, Simaetha, and her servant performing a love spell at a crossroads shrine bordered by tombs outside the city. Like the fourth-century Attic "love" spell that opened this discussion, Simaetha seeks to bind her lover and invokes the goddess of ghosts and magic, Hecate, whose arrival is signaled by barking dogs, indicating her presence through her sacred animal. Although Simaetha's love spell does not directly employ a corpse, as does the fourth-century example from Attica, it takes place amid tombs (νεκύων ἀνά τ' ἠρία) and emphasizes Hecate's frightening infernal associations (12–16), which were becoming increasingly stereotyped in literature of this period and later (Horace, *Sat.* 1.8.23–1.8.36; Tibullus 1.2.41–1.2.58; Seneca, *Med.* 797–810). It also portrays Simaetha melting wax (κηρὸν) – probably an effigy of Daphnis – with the intention of causing him to melt with desire for her (28).[67] Effigies in wax, clay, and lead survive in the material record and frequently evidence violent treatment, such as being twisted or pierced with nails – torturing the victim with pangs of love, as Simaetha is described as doing here.[68] Multiple elements of this literary ritual thus conform to what we know about similar practices from material evidence. They endow the dramatic spectacle with verisimilitude.[69] At the same time, however, this idyll attributes magical practices previously associated with men (*magoi*, *goētes*) to a young woman, contributing to the creation of a powerful and enduring stereotype of women's nefarious magic. Furthermore, when Simaetha asks that her spell be as powerful as those of Medea and Circe (15–16), this poem positions her in a genealogy of mythic sorceresses, imagined as a lineage of women manipulating men with magic since time immemorial.

Around the time Theocritus was writing, another Alexandrian poet, Apollonius Rhodius, drew on the discourse of magic to embellish his rendition of the mythic expedition of the Argos. Although magic was already an integral component of the heroes' successful acquisition of the golden fleece, descriptions of Medea's magic in Apollonius's *Argonautica* reflect a similar conflation of the two stereotypes that we saw in Theocritus's *Idyll 2*. For example, Medea is described primarily as wielding the power of herbs and drugs, consistent with the classical stereotype of women's magic; however, she is also said to search for corpses (4.51) and to invoke the heart-eating goddess of death and nimble dogs of Hades (4.1665–4.1666), conforming more with stereotypes of the male *goēs*, who specialized in controlling denizens of the underworld. Furthermore, Medea is able to exert tremendous power through incantation alone, summoning annihilating phantoms (4.1672) to destroy an enemy without the use of herbs or potions, unlike her classical counterpart, who must use a poisonous unguent, when she takes revenge on the princess of Corinth (Euripides, *Med.* 1166–1175).

This presentation of Medea prefigures literary sorceresses of the Roman imperial period who are able to control natural phenomena and reanimate the dead with the power of incantation alone.[70] In these representations, women's magic takes on and exaggerates the macabre aspects of rituals belonging to the *goētes* of earlier times: sorceresses in Roman literature prowl cemeteries and battlefields looking for body parts or commit murder to attain the necessary ingredients for a spell (Horace, *Sat.* 1.8; Horace, *Ep.* 5; Lucan 6.538–6.559). These depictions thus amplify the sinister, subversive, and gendered associations of magic over and above classical Greek representations, laying the groundwork for later stereotypes of women's proclivity to participate in Satanic rites.

It is widely accepted by scholars that the concept of magic was imported to Rome during the Hellenistic period through authors such as Apollonius and Theocritus.[71] The earliest representations of magic that we have in Latin date to the first century CE. They include Virgil's *Eclogue* 8, a creative refashioning of Theocritus's *Idyll* 2, and his portrait of Dido in book four of the *Aeneid*, which is widely believed to have been influenced by Apollonius's portrait of Medea.[72] Prior to these depictions, we have an invective poem by Catullus (90), in which he draws on derogatory stereotypes of *magi* (Latin for *magoi*) to defame an opponent, accusing him of incest, which was a practice attributed to *magoi* by Greek authors.[73] Cicero also mentions *magi*, describing them as Persian priests and diviners, but he disparages them for extravagant tales (*portenta*), which he compares to the ignorant beliefs of the masses (*Nat. d.* 1.43). Both of these references to *magi* employ the term in its technical sense as referring to priests of Persian religion but at the same time identify them with bizarre, outlandish, and even blasphemous beliefs. Thus, although *magi* here are clearly perceived negatively, the term has not yet acquired broader semantic coverage, which would indicate the operation of magic discourse. This occurs with great flourish in the first and second centuries CE with the poets Propertius, Tibullus, and, especially, Horace, as well as the authors Lucan and Apuleius.

Roman law also suggests that there was no distinct concept of magic, nor any laws explicitly against it in the Republican period or earlier. Although statutes against the harmful use of incantations (*carmina*) date back to Rome's earliest law code, the Twelve Tables, these regulations prohibited using *carmina* to steal from or harm someone but did not ban the use of incantation itself.[74] As Hans Kippenberg notes, the law focused on the results of the action, not the means.[75] This is an important distinction because it reveals that magic discourse was not yet operating in Roman law, even though later commentators understood the prohibitions in this manner; their interpretations attest to the recognition of magic as a legal category in their own time but not in the Archaic period.[76]

Another law whose meaning changed over the course of the first centuries BCE and CE also reveals the development of magic as a conceptual category and prosecutable offense. The Lex Cornelia de sicariis and veneficiis, passed by L. Cornelius Sulla in 81 BCE, prohibited murder by various means, including homicide through the administration of potions (*venena*).[77] This law criminalized *venena* for the purpose of killing someone but not the use of potions in general, reflecting the same aim evidenced by the Twelve Tables to prevent inflicting harm without excluding common technologies that bring benefit. Furthermore, the law made no distinction between poison and magic – *venenum* covered both categories. This, no doubt, reflects the inability of ancient forensic science to detect the use of poison: any sudden death generated suspicion and could lead to accusations of *veneficia* against a likely adversary.[78] James Rives argues that an "umbrella category" of magic – what I label "magic discourse" – only emerged in Roman jurisprudence by the second century CE,[79] when *venena* and *carmina* acquire associations with the *magus*, Persian priest, and with *maleficium*, a wicked deed or crime.[80]

Magic Discourse in Practice

Having laid out the emergence and development of magic discourse from fifth-century Athens to the end of the Roman Republic and later, I would like to consider the practice of magic. What did it mean to engage in rituals that a majority of one's neighbors probably considered to be magic and regarded negatively? Is there any evidence that practitioners themselves considered their actions to be within the framework of magic discourse? If so, how did they conceive of their actions, and how might we understand them as social acts?

Stanley Stowers cautions us from over-theorizing religious actions such as sacrifice: "[R]ather than imagining people carrying around highly organized and complete systems of belief that then generate actions, we should imagine that religious inferences and beliefs were evoked as aspects of their practical skills for living life day to day and were dispersed in their practices."[81] This approach might profitably be applied to the making of *katadesmoi*. Stowers argues that a vast majority of religious practices in ancient Greece belonged to the order of what he describes as the "religion of mundane social exchange."[82] This mode of religious activity is not defined by organized and complex belief systems, but rather by intuitive notions about various orders of divine, semi-divine, deceased, and heroic beings who were believed to share the world with humans. This mode of religious activity followed identifiable types of social action analogous to human social interaction. He divides them into: speech acts, such as praying, promising, cursing, or blessing, and actions of social exchange, such as sharing a meal (sacrifice), offering a gift of gratitude (votive), or fulfilling a pledge (offering a plant, animal, or grain).[83] According to this mode of religious activity, *katadesmoi* are just another speech act, petitioning a god or restless ghost to curse someone.[84]

Stowers, however, also addresses the implications of power, which are implicit in all ritual activities:

> One central theoretical and methodological lesson from the embeddedness of religious practices is that the analysis of meaning should not be separated

from the analysis of power and action. Meaning and power are mutually implicated. The researcher should ask two questions: What were the culture's schemes of classification and how did individuals and groups act with or against those schemes so as to produce and distribute social capital?[85]

Precisely! Stowers identifies the crux of the problem as I see it. Scholars have historically considered the distinction between magic and religion to be one of practice; if religion and magic employ the same practices – for example, prayers, hymns, sacrifices, and libations – they can be said to be indistinguishable and the category magic is rejected as a false projection onto ancient culture. Although it is true that the practices themselves are often analogous, the point that Stowers makes, which is crucial to consider when trying to understand ancient magic, is that of classification: researchers need to take fully into account the systems of classification applied by the ancients themselves and the ways that those systems were fundamental to the production of power and the distribution of social capital in the ancient *polis*.[86]

For example, it has been argued that binding spells and curse tablets employed by individuals are equivalent to those employed by *poleis* to protect their inhabitants from restless ghosts or enemy invasion.[87] Although this may be true on a pragmatic level – binding a statue in one case and binding or mutilating a figurine in the other – my assumption is that ancient observers would have classified these acts differently according to context. In virtually every human society, acts of violence sanctioned by the state are regarded differently from those of private individuals. Thus, war, when properly declared according to a society's provision, or the execution of a criminal who has been tried and found guilty according to an accepted legal process are regarded as legitimate acts of killing (except by some pacifists). Private acts of killing, however, are nearly always labeled as murder (or manslaughter) and are prohibited by law.[88] Thus, setting up an electric chair in one's basement to handle conflicts with the neighbors is, to my mind, roughly equivalent to the practice of *katadesmoi*.

Returning again to the Attic curse tablet with which we began, it is not entirely clear to what extent the petitioner in this ritual considered it to be magic. Magic, after all, was still emerging as a concept in the fourth century, and the primary evidence for the operation of the discourse lies in literary depictions and the invective of the educated elite. Yet, the wide dispersal of this discourse across forensic speeches, political invective, philosophical dialogues, and Attic tragedy suggests that a negative conception of magic was widely held, at least in Athens, from where most of our evidence derives. Otherwise, accusations of being a *magos* or *goēs* would not have derogated an opponent in front of a democratic assembly, and depictions of magic in tragedies, such as the *Trachiniae* or *Medea*, would have lost some of their emotional power.

Although it is not clear how the petitioner in this spell regarded his or her actions, a large number of curse tablets from antiquity indicate an awareness that *katadesmoi* were not entirely acceptable and needed to be justified or explained away. Henk Versnel delineated a class of *katadesmoi / defixiones* that he describes as "prayers for justice."[89] These spells conform to many of the criteria that characterize curse tablets – such as consigning their victims to chthonic forces for the purpose of binding or constraining – yet distinguish themselves in significant ways. Unlike ordinary *defixiones*, for example, these curses were sometimes set up in public as monuments or in the temples of the deities they invoked.[90] Rather than hiding their curse from the victim and the larger community, they declared it openly.[91] Perhaps it was thought that knowledge of the curse might encourage the wrongdoer to make amends rather than face divine requital. Whatever the motivation, it is clear that the petitioner of the curse felt there was no need to conceal the action. These rituals also tended to eschew the commanding language typical of curse tablets and used supplicatory speech to win the deity over to their cause.[92]

More importantly for understanding the self-perception of practitioners, these spells often apologized for themselves and sought to excuse their action by explaining it. An example from Attica, dating to the third century BCE, includes the following justification and solicitous language: "Dear Earth, help me. Because I was wronged (ἀδικούμενος) by Euryptolemos and Xenophon I curse (καταδῶ) them" (*DTA* 98).[93] Another example identified by Versnel, from fourth-century BCE Attica, demonstrates an imploring rather than commanding tone – "I beg you" (ἱκετεύω) – and requests that the petitioner – the one who struck the lead (τὴν μολυβδοκόπον) – be spared (*DTA* 100). This added detail strongly suggests that unjustified cursing could result in divine punishment.[94] A rather violent curse from Athens, dating to the first century CE, summons Hecate "to cut the heart of the thieves or the thief" and explicitly states that the petitioner has been compelled to resort to this type of action: "[H]onor me [as suppliant] (σ[έ]βου μὲ), the one inscribing this spell (καταγράφοντα) and destroying [the thieves], because I am not holding back but am forced to do this by the thieves" (*SGD* 21).[95] In this case, the person employing the *defixio* transfers the guilt of using magic to the target of the spell and consequently expresses full awareness that this type of ritual activity is not entirely acceptable. These apologetic curse tablets clearly derive from people who felt helpless and had no other recourse. Most likely they lacked the financial means, social influence, and political capital to defend themselves and seek justice, in which case they may have felt justified to use a form of numinous power proscribed by the political elite. These apologies, however, also suggest that practitioners of other *katadesmoi* probably understood their rituals to be illegitimate to some degree and may even have conceived of their activities in terms of magic discourse.

The literary record presents at least two characters who express a similar reluctance to use magic. In Euripides' *Hippolytus*, Phaedra recoils at the suggestion that she use a *pharmakon* to seduce her chaste stepson (388). Although the connection between love potions – *pharmaka* – and curse tablets – *katadesmoi* – may not have been made yet at that time (it was explicitly made by Plato, *Leg.* 909b in the fourth century), this dramatic portrayal must have appeared realistic to the broad audience that attended the play's performance in the late fifth century. Another literary character to express this sort of shame centuries later is Dido in Virgil's *Aeneid*, which describes her use of *artes magicae* as reluctant (*magicas invitam accingier artis*, 4.493). Although these depictions of an aversion to magic derive from literary products of the elite, they must have drawn on and resonated with cultural attitudes more broadly, even if such outrage was reserved for the public transcript.

In attempting to avoid doing magic, these literary characters and real-life practitioners reveal that a fairly clear idea of what constituted magic existed in antiquity and, consequently, that some people could choose to do it. As Stowers frames it, magic provided a way for them to "[re]distribute social capital" by petitioning gods or the restless dead to punish the guilty or bind the rhetorical ability, romantic charms, or business success of a rival. To this extent, magic was coterminous with religion, seeing as people commonly petitioned the gods for prosperity and security through rituals sanctioned by the *polis*. The difference lies in their unregulated, private, (probably) secret, and detrimental nature.[96] As both Faraone and Boedeker mention, at least some ancient Greeks were uncomfortable with the idea that their neighbors might be concocting spells against them in the privacy of their own homes (Plato, *Laws* 909b).[97] Versnel states this point even more strongly: he accepts Faraone's contention that *katadesmoi* were just another technology for advancing oneself or the interests of one's family and were not indistinguishable from practices commonly labeled religion, yet he argues that those who made and deposited *katadesmoi* "kn[e]w full well that the act [wa]s strongly condemned by all other members of the society, just as they themselves would publicly condemn similar attempts made by others."[98] In other words, Versnel identifies a "double standard of morality" in antiquity regarding the use of curses. Boedeker suggests that private rituals – not only *katadesmoi* but the practice of private mysteries – could be seen as resistance to the *polis*'s uncontested regulation of religion.[99] If so, magic might be regarded as a form of subversive discourse that at least implicitly, if not expressly, challenged the *polis*'s religious hegemony and the power structures it supported.[100] There was certainly a fear of politically motivated and subversive magic in the late Republic and early Roman Empire when Agrippa (33 BCE) and Tiberius (16 or 17 CE) banished magicians from Rome (Dio Cass. 49.43.5, 57.15.8–57.15.9; Tacitus, *Ann.* 2.32).[101]

There is some indication from extant *katadesmoi* and ritual handbooks, dating to the third and fourth centuries CE, that practitioners of *katadesmoi* not only considered their activity to be magic but also actively embraced magic discourse and its alterity. Certain *defixiones*, for example, suggest that their makers were influenced by literary portraits and attempted to conform to expectations in the popular imagination that magic be exotic, esoteric, and bizarre. In other words, we see an escalation in the weirdness and alterity of magic both in literary depictions and extant *defixiones* over the course of the first few centuries CE. Beginning in the first and second centuries, for example, literary portraits of magic highlight the use of grotesque, alien, and obscure ritual ingredients, such as pulsating innards (Apuleius, *Met.* 3.18.1), ossified eyeballs stolen from the corpses of the violently dead, nails from sunken ships, and crucifixion crosses (Lucan 6.538–6.546), and a wolf's beard and the tooth of a mottled serpent (Horace, *Sat.* 1.8.42–1.8.43). Based on extant *defixiones* from the Classical and Hellenistic periods, these depictions appear to be dramatic exaggerations of actual ritual practices. There is substantial evidence, however, that *defixiones* themselves became increasingly complex around this time – perhaps in response to these literary depictions – adding bizarre drawings, obscure symbols, the names of foreign gods, and nonsense language (*voces mysticae*) to the inscribed curse texts to enhance their potency.[102] Certain of these innovations have been explained as naturally occurring developments internal to the specialization of magic and reflecting increased competition among manufacturers of spells. Like any professional guild, venders of *defixiones* must have looked for ways to improve their product and taken advantage of the latest technological improvements.[103]

These changes, however, also suggest a desire to conform to and capitalize on the discourse of magic. Thus, although the prayers for justice indicate a concern that *katadesmoi* are illegitimate and seek to justify themselves, many later spells from the third and fourth centuries CE explicitly cross that line and embrace the alterity of magic discourse in their use of bizarre, uncanny, and grotesque ingredients. These late Roman *defixiones* seem to mimic earlier literary portraits in an escalating use of the exotic and uncanny. For example, one recipe for an erotic *defixio* (*PGM* VII.462–466) requires a copper nail from a shipwrecked vessel, reminding us of the "ruined remains of an unlucky ship" used for magic in Apuleius's *Metamorphoses* a century or more earlier (3.17.4–3.17.5). Another attraction spell (*PGM* IV.1396) employs polluted dirt from a place where heroes or gladiators were slain, recalling the necromantic prowlings of Canidia and her friend in a pauper's cemetery on the Esquiline in Horace's *Satire* 1.8. Another example reminds us of Erichtho's necromancy in Lucan's *Pharsalia* (book 6); this spell directs one to inscribe three Homeric verses on an iron lamella, attach it to an executed criminal, and speak the verses in his ear; he will tell you everything you wish. If you insert the lamella into his wound, you will have great blessings with regard to your superiors and masters (*PGM* IV.2145–IV.2240). Another ritual from the *PGM*, "The Hymn to Selene" (*PGM* IV.2785–IV.2890) employs macabre serpentine imagery that resonates with Seneca's serpentine characterization of Medea in his Stoic rendition of her tragedy (684–688, 701–703, 731–734).

These are just a few examples that suggest that magic technology not only evolved according to internal dynamics and exigencies but responded creatively to social perceptions and literary stereotypes, as well, fostering and contributing to the alterity of magic discourse. David Frankfurter has made a similar argument regarding the appropriation of the *magos* stereotype by Egyptian priests during the Roman imperial period.[104] Bernd-Christian Otto's recent analysis of magic as a self-designation in antiquity also supports this interpretation; he concludes that "ancient ritual practitioners must have picked up the concept 'magic' as a term of self-reference only after it had already circulated as a polemical term in popular discourses."[105] Otto suggests that these self-labeled magicians rehabilitated positive connotations of the term "magic," much as Apuleius does in his *Apologia*, where he argues that magic is "an art acceptable to the undying gods, well versed in honoring and venerating them, pious and, you may be sure, understanding [things] divine" (26.1–26.2). Through analogy with modern movements, such as Neopaganism and Wicca, Otto posits that some ancient "magicians" may have sought to distance themselves from the popular culture of their day, in which case the allure of magic's subversive reputation would have been irresistible.

Conclusion

In this chapter, I have delineated the origin and development of the concept of magic, which operated as a discourse of alterity that was part and parcel of the discourse of barbarism to marginalize certain people and practices, including peripatetic venders of cathartic healing, curse tablets, and unregulated domestic religion and women's control over it. This discourse spread across the Mediterranean during the Hellenistic period and continued to develop what could be described as its "weirdness factor" over the ensuing centuries, influencing both literary stereotypes of women's nefarious magic in Latin literature and the actual practice of magic during the Roman period.[106] By the beginning of the Roman Empire, the concept of magic and its use as a powerful marginalizing stereotype were well developed. Concomitantly, evidence of *defixiones* shows a much more elaborate type of ritual being practiced during the Roman period, one that conforms more closely to the literary imagination, no doubt encouraging further literary embellishment – this appears to be a case of life imitating art imitating life. At the same time, magic becomes criminalized and is particularly linked to sedition and subversion, often being invoked as a charge during politically motivated trials for treason or adultery in the Roman Empire. And that brings us to the threshold of Chapter 4, Roman Antiquity: The Imperial Period.

Notes

1. This chapter substantially reworks a paper I gave at the Early Christian Studies Workshop at the University of Chicago Divinity School in February 2008. I would like to thank the participants of that workshop, especially Christopher Faraone, for their incisive comments and patient criticisms of that earlier paper. Their comments forced me to reconsider many aspects of my argument and have helped me nuance my understanding of the practice of magic as a form of social discourse. I would also like to thank Sarah Iles Johnston for comments and criticisms she made on my book, *Naming the Witch*; I have tried to address her concerns and clarify my earlier argument in the following discussion of gender and magic stereotyping.
2. Audollent, ed., *Defixionum Tabellae*, 96. All translations are my own.
3. Gager, ed., *Curse Tablets*, 90 translates the word as "unmarried," which makes the most sense in this context of erotic separation, given that the next sentence asks that the victim be made ἀτελής. Liddell and Scott, *Greek-English Lexicon*, 9th ed., s.v. ἀτέλ–εια concurs on this specific case. Gager, in n. 26, suggests that this may also be a pun for "one untimely dead." Johnston, *Restless Dead*, 78,

prefers "uninitiated" as a translation. See her n. 127 for discussion and bibliography of the different interpretations of this word.

4. On restless ghosts in Greek thought, see Johnston, *Restless Dead*, for an excellent and full exposition.

5. See the discussion in the next section on Magic in Scholarly Discourse.

6. In my discussion of magic, I am not including many practices that often receive that label in Western parlance: for example, amulets, entertaining tricks, or general superstition. For further explanation, see the discussion in the third section of this chapter on Curse Tablets and Binding Spells.

7. Although perhaps not as often as we might suspect. See Graf, "Victimology," 397–398.

8. Sir Tylor, *Primitive Culture*, vol. 1, 112.

9. Preisendanz, ed., *Papyri Graecae Magicae*, v.

10. Remus, "'Magic,' Method, Madness," 260–261.

11. Preisendanz, *Papyri Graecae Magicae*, v.

12. Barb, "The Survival of Magic Arts," 119, 105.

13. Influenced, for example, by Protestant anti-Catholic polemics. See Smith, *Drudgery Divine*; Styers, *Making Magic*, 9–10.

14. Styers, *Making Magic*, 14–17.

15. Smith, "Trading Places," 16.

16. Segal, "Hellenistic Magic," 352.

17. Gager, *Curse Tablets*, 24; and Janowitz, *Icons of Power*, xiii–xiv.

18. Janowitz, *Magic in the Roman World*, 3.

19. Nock, "Paul and the Magus," 183; Garrett, *Demise of the Devil*, 4–5; Janowitz, *Magic in the Roman World*, 5; and Stratton, *Naming the Witch*, 17.

20. Nock, "Paul and the Magus," 183. Garrett, *Demise of the Devil*, 4–5, 74–75, and Janowitz, *Magic in the Roman World*, 5, among others, echo this view.

21. Gager, *Curse Tablets*, 24.

22. Faraone, "Agonistic Context," 19. This is also largely the view of Smith, "Magic (Greek and Roman)," 269–289.

23. Versnel, "Some Reflections," 186.

24. Hoffman, "Fiat Magia," 184.

25. Graf, "Theories of Magic in Antiquity," 93–104.

26. Dickie, *Magic and Magicians*, 9. Faraone, "Household Religion in Ancient Greece," 223, applies the term "magic" to common Greek domestic practices, such as paying reverence to Hermes and Hekate through their aniconic statutes or worshipping Zeus Ktesios in the image of a storage jar and Dionysos as a phallus.

27. For an excellent discussion of the history, nature, and function of curse tablets, see Ogden, "Binding Spells," 3–90.

28. Abaye, a Babylonian sage, gives directions for making an amulet to cure rabbis (*b. Yoma* 84a) and offers a long list of amulets and other protective

practices that he learned from his mother for treating various afflictions (*b. Shab.* 66b).

29. In Homer's *Odyssey*, for example, Odysseus's uncles staunch blood using an incantation without any hint of derision or derogation (19.457). Similarly, herbal potions are used both to harm and protect (10.210–10.213, 10.290–10.292). For fuller discussion, see Dickie, *Magic and Magicians*, 22–25; Graf, *Magic in the Ancient World*, 28; and Stratton, *Naming the Witch*, 26–27.

30. Gager, *Curse Tablets*, 7; Ogden, "Binding Spells," 9; and Johnston, *Restless Dead*, 111.

31. Stratton, *Naming the Witch*, chs. 2–3.

32. Faraone, "Agonistic Context," is the seminal presentation of this idea. See also Gager, *Curse Tablets*, for a collection of curses organized according to the particular field of competition.

33. Eidinow, *Oracles, Curses, and Risk*, 4.

34. Johnston, *Restless Dead*, 85, 96–97.

35. Ibid., 29.

36. Ibid., 88; Johnston also points out that the νεκεομαντεία began to operate around the same time that the νέκυια of the *Odyssey* (book 11) took its final form and likely influenced it (*Restless Dead*, 84). See Schmidt, "The 'Witch' of En-Dor," 111–130, on the influence of Assyrian necromancy on Israelite religion around the same time. On the topography and archaeology of νεκεομαντεία, see Friese, "Facing the Dead," 29–40.

37. Johnston, *Restless Dead*, 89, cites these examples. For further information on Mesopotamian "magic," see Braun-Holzinger, "Apotropaic Figures at Mesopotamian Temples," 149–172; Abusch, "The Demonic Image of the Witch," 27–58; Scurlock, "Magical Uses," 93–110, on the use of figurines for curing illnesses and for protection against magic; Scurlock, "Translating Transfers in Ancient Mesopotamia," 209–223, on using animals, among other things, as magical surrogates in Mesopotamian ritual; Scurlock, "Soul Emplacements," 4, on using a human skull to cure the gnashing of teeth; Gee, "Oracle by Image," 83–88, on the use of clay images to conjure souls in Middle Kingdom Egypt; and Farber, "How to Marry a Disease," 128, on using a figurine to "marry" a disease to a ghost as part of a cure.

38. Faraone, *Talismans and Trojan Horses*, ch. 4.

39. Johnston, *Restless Dead*, 9–12. See Faraone, "Aeschylus' ὕμνος δέσμιος (*Eum.* 306)," 150–154, on the similarity between the Erinyes' "binding song" and Attic *defixiones*.

40. Although Greek tradition and mythology attributed foreign roots to Dionysos, Linear B tablets indicate that he was most likely worshipped in Greece as early as 1400 BCE, during the Minoan-Mycenaean era. Parker, "Greek Religion," 309. See also Hall, *Inventing the Barbarian*, 151.

41. Aeschines accuses Demosthenes of being a *magos* and *goēs* (*Ctes.* 137); Demosthenes employs *goēs* on a few occasions to signify a liar, deceiver, or someone who "bewitches" others with sophistry (*Cor.* 276; *Fals. leg.* 102, 109; 3 *Aphob.* 32). Additionally, in *De corona*, he ridicules Aeschines' involvement as an assistant in Bacchic mysteries, although there is no way to know if this portrait is accurate or merely designed to marginalize Aeschines with a denigrating stereotype of feminine religious excess (258–260). See the discussion in Stratton, *Naming the Witch*, 48–49.

42. The *Bacchae* expresses this sense already in Pentheus's description of Dionysos as a γόης ἐπωιδός (234).

43. Faraone, "An Accusation of Magic," 156–157, 159–160.

44. On the notion of public transcript, see Scott, *Domination and the Arts of Resistance*, 18. Versnel, "Beyond Cursing," 62, notes that in Mediterranean culture, "a sharp and consistent distinction is maintained between exploits of which one may publicly boast . . . and actions that are *never* confessed publicly or privately" (emphasis in original).

45. See n. 29.

46. See Collins, "Theoris of Lemnos and the Criminalization of Magic," 484–487, which documents this point nicely. An inscription from Teos, dating to around 470 BCE, indicates that magistrates were required to curse publicly those who committed a variety of crimes against the community, including piracy, resisting authority, interfering with the import of corn, and using *pharmaka*. Meiggs and Lewis, *A Selection of Greek Historical Inscriptions*, 65, no. 30, understand φάρμακα to mean "poisoning" here, which supports Collins's thesis regarding the treatment of *pharmakeia* in Athens, although a broader semantic connotation equivalent to "magic" is also possible, given Plato's use of the word to include curse tablets and incantations (*Leg.* 933a).

47. Mitchell, *Panhellenism and the Barbarian*, 29, argues that although the perceived threat from Persia helped unify Greeks, internal conflict among Greek cities and sophistic questioning of the difference between Greek and Other put pressure on this oppositional discourse.

48. Hall, *Inventing the Barbarian*, 1–2.

49. Ibid., 16–17.

50. Ibid., 17. On the feminizing of Persians in particular, see Hall, trans. and ed., *Aeschylus Persians*, 13. Tragedies were performed every year at the annual Dionysia, which served an important ideological function for Athens. See Goldhill, "The Great Dionysia and Civic Ideology," 58–76.

51. Rhodes, "The Impact of the Persian Wars," 37. An inverse version of this discourse involved the idealization of foreigners as holders of ancient and esoteric wisdom. Hall, *Inventing the Barbarian*, 211–223.

52. Sourvinou-Inwood, "What Is *Polis* Religion?" 304.

53. Sourvinou-Inwood, "What is *Polis* Religion?" 322; Sourvinou-Inwood, "Further Aspects of Polis Religion," 270–274. Cicero famously declared that "worship of the gods and the highest interest of the state lay in the same hands" (*De domo suo* 1.1), indicating that the interdependence of politics and religion was equally, if not more, true in Rome.

54. Boedeker, "Family Matters," 236.

55. The *polis* sought to regulate and limit exuberant displays of wealth and mourning at funerals in the interest of subordinating family loyalty and competition, especially among aristocratic families, to *polis*-based identity and solidarity. The establishment of cults on private lands was regarded as promoting private power over the collective interests of the *polis*. Boedeker, "Family Matters," 236–237. The *polis* also administered cults that provided personal initiation and salvation, such as the Eleusinan and Bacchic mysteries. Sourvinou-Inwood, "Further Aspects of *Polis* Religion," 273.

56. Boedeker, "Family Matters," 239.

57. For further discussion of gender and magic discourse, see Stratton, *Naming the Witch*, especially 1–38.

58. Boedeker, "Family Matters," 237–238.

59. Johnston, *Restless Dead*, 102–111.

60. Ibid., 100–111.

61. Euripides *Ion* 616, *Andr.* 32, 159–160, *Med.* 789; Sophocles *Trach.* 575; Antiphon, *In Novercam* 9; Isaeus 6.21.

62. On Medea's foreign origin, see Hall, *Inventing the Barbarian*, 35. On the infanticide, see Johnston, "Corinthian Medea," 65.

63. Collins, *Magic in the Ancient Greek World*, 54.

64. See my discussion in Stratton, *Naming the Witch*, ch. 3.

65. The connections and differences are explicated in Stratton, *Naming the Witch*.

66. Fowler, *The Hellenistic Aesthetic*.

67. For discussion of the implications of gender and power relations, see Faraone, "Clay Hardens and Wax Melts," 294–300.

68. See Faraone, "Molten Wax, Spilt Wine and Mutilated Animals," 62–65, on wax figurines used in execrations and oath ceremonies; Faraone, "Binding and Burying," 165–205; Faraone, *Talismans and Trojan Horses*, 133–135, on the twisting of feet and heads; Gager, *Curse Tablets*, 15–18; Ogden, "Binding Spells," 71–79; Faraone, *Ancient Greek Love Magic*, 152–154, on this passage; and Faraone, "Clay Hardens and Wax Melts," on gender inversion and the melting of wax images in representations of women's love magic.

69. On the problem of treating literary depictions as genuine portraits of events, see Stratton, *Naming the Witch*, 84.

70. Tibullus 1.2.44 (reversing the flow of rivers); Lucan 6.750–6.830 (reanimating the dead); Propertius 4.5.13 (summoning the moon).

71 Tupet, *La magie dans la poésie latine*, 107, 223–224; Graf, *Magic in the Ancient World*, 37–39.

72. Apollonius of Rhodes, *Jason and the Golden Fleece*, xxxi.

73. See discussion in Bigwood, "'Incestuous' Marriage," 311–341.

74. Rome's earliest law code, the Twelve Tables, forbade using incantations (*carmina*) to charm a neighbor's produce into one's own field. Warmington, *Remains of Old Latin*, 479. It also banned using *carmina* to injure someone, although it is not clear if the law intended to ban imprecations or invective. Pliny understood it in terms of cursing (*NH* 28, 18), whereas Cicero understood it as invective (*Resp.* 4.12, quoted by Augustine, *Civ.* 2.9). See the discussion in Rives, "Magic in the XII Tables Revisited," 270–290; Kippenberg, "Magic in Roman Civil Discourse," 145–146; and Graf, *Magic in the Ancient World*, 41–43. In either case, both laws indicate that using incantation itself was not illegal; only using a *carmen* to steal, injure, or slander someone was prohibited.

75. Kippenberg, "Magic in Roman Civil Discourse," 146.

76. James Rives emphasizes that the law at that time clearly did not ban "magic" in the Frazerian sense, because the concept did not yet exist in Rome. Rather, following Richard Gordon and others, Rives argues that magic only appears in the "strong sense" sometime between the first centuries BCE and CE, when it was introduced to Rome by Hellenistic writers. Rives, "Magic in Roman Law," 316.

77. Rives, "Magic in Roman Law," 318.

78. See Graf, *Magic in the Ancient World*, 47; Rives, "Magic in Roman Law," 319–320.

79. Rives, "Magic in Roman Law," 322.

80. Ibid., 321.

81. Stowers, "Religion of Plant and Animal Offerings," 37.

82. Ibid.

83. Ibid., 38.

84. See Faraone, "Agonistic Context," 19.

85. Stowers, "Theorizing the Religion of Ancient Households," 11.

86. One recent study, for example, engages anthropology to understand ancient magic without addressing the biases implicit in definitions, which themselves derive from and reinscribe biases of the ancient authors who first promulgated magic discourse. This approach permits the author to classify reliquaries as magic, betraying a clearly Protestant point of view. Collins, *Magic in the Ancient Greek World*, 7–9, 16.

87. Faraone, "Binding and Burying," 166.

88. Violence, in fact, is closely analogous to magic in the subjectivity of its definition: just as my miracle is your magic, my war is your genocide or terrorism.

89. Versnel, "Beyond Cursing," 61.

90. Gager, *Curse Tablets*, 186.

91. Versnel, "Beyond Cursing," 63, claims that social abhorrence of magic prevented people from inscribing their names on curse tablets or displaying them publicly. He argues that the use of *defixiones*, although widespread, was publicly condemned and denied. Others have proposed alternative reasons for the secrecy surrounding the manufacture and deposition of curse tablets. For example, because the tablet frequently underwent violent manipulation, such as piercing and twisting, one would clearly not desire to have one's name on the same piece of metal and experience the dire effects of the ritual. Another explanation is that curses were only effective when undisturbed; if they were publicly known, the victim could remove the curse by uncovering and removing the tablet, as was the case with Libanius (*Oratio* 1.243–1.250). Both explanations may be valid and not diminish the public outrage over using *defixiones*.

92. Versnel, "Beyond Cursing," 65–66.

93. Wünsch, *Defixionum Tabellae Atticae*, 25.

94. Versnel, "Beyond Cursing," 65.

95. My translation, based on publication of the text in Elderkin, "Two Curse Inscriptions," 390. Versnel, "Beyond Cursing," 66, reconstructs this curse to read: "I make an exception for" (ἐξαιροῦμαι) the one who is inscribing this spell.

96. There is some disagreement about whether practitioners of *katadesmoi* intended them to be secret or not. Gager, *Curse Tablets*, 21, for example, suggests that curses worked psychosomatically on those who knew a "fix" had been put on them. Versnel, "Beyond Cursing," 69, on the other hand, uses the public display of "judicial" curses to distinguish them from regular *katadesmoi*, which were kept secret. See also n. 90.

97. Faraone, "Household Religion in Ancient Greece," 218–219; Boedeker, "Family Matters," 239.

98. Versnel, "Beyond Cursing," 62.

99. Boedeker, "Family Matters," 243.

100. Thomassen, "Is Magic a Subclass of Ritual?" 62, argues in a similar vein.

101. See also the discussion in MacMullen, *Enemies of the Roman Order*, 95–127.

102. See the discussion in Ogden, "Binding Spells," 46–50.

103. Gager, *Curse Tablets*, 10.

104. Frankfurter, *Religion in Roman Egypt*, 224–233.

105. Otto, "Towards Historicizing 'Magic' in Antiquity," 338.

106. Drawing on Malinowski's "coefficient of weirdness." Malinowski, *Coral Gardens and Their Magic*, 220.

PART II

★

THE EARLY LATIN WEST

Chapter 4

Roman Antiquity: The Imperial Period

KYLE A. FRASER

Introduction

In the late Roman imagination, "magic" has decidedly sinister connotations, calling to mind such atrocities as human sacrifice, cannibalism, and gruesome rites of necromancy. The illicit character of magic is not merely a question of its malefic goals (as was typically the case in classical Greece and the Roman Republic), but of its very procedures, which are now imagined to transgress, even *reverse*, the norms of legitimate cult. In short, magic has become the ideological antithesis of religion. The present chapter traces the emergence of this magic-religion dichotomy in the wider context of imperial age culture, with special attention to developments in cosmology, theology, and demonology.

In one direction, then, we are led to examine how the term "magic"[1] was deployed as a polemical category, whether by Roman elites, like Pliny, who were anxious to defend the purity of Roman *religio*, or by philosophers, like Porphyry, who were committed to monotheistic and ascetic ideals. This is magic as seen from the *outside*, as something to be feared, reviled, and even persecuted. In another direction, we shall be concerned with reconstructing the worldview of certain *insiders*, notably those Hellenized Egyptian priests whose secret rites are preserved in the so-called *Greek Magical Papyri* (PGM). Did these priests regard themselves as magicians, and if so, in what sense? Did they embrace the sinister and countercultural connotations of magic? When we examine the Greco-Egyptian spell-books against the background of the imperial stereotypes of the magician, the impression is less one of conformity than one of resistance. The "holy magic" of the papyri operates according to ritual protocols that aim to sanction and empower the magician, distinguishing him from his illegitimate *Other*, the lowly sorcerer. The *PGM* are engaged in a complex process of self-fashioning that is founded on the idealized image of the magician as an initiate, consecrated by the supreme God with the authority to command lesser *daimones* and spirits.

The Greco-Egyptian Formularies and the Professionalization of Magic

One of the characteristic developments of the Roman imperial period was the professionalization of magic as an art, with its own experts and technical manuals. Certainly, the older Greek tradition also had its ritual specialists, chief among them the *goēs*, who could drive away hostile ghosts or rouse them to action in order to satisfy his client's desires.[2] But the extent of the *goēs*'s activities is hard to gauge. No doubt the *goēs* had a hand in fashioning some of the curse tablets that have been discovered in Greece, secreted in tombs and chthonic sanctuaries.[3] However, for the Classical period survivals, it is usually impossible to distinguish between curse tablets created by experts and home-made variants, because the tablets bear only very simple inscriptions; indeed, in many cases only the name of the target appears, with the formula of cursing merely implied.[4] A similar situation holds for amulets: classical sources hint at their use, but we cannot easily identify them in the archaeological record, because typically they were not inscribed. In the older Greek tradition, magical artifacts were consecrated chiefly through verbal incantations, which by their nature leave no trace.[5]

In the imperial period, by contrast, we can trace the proliferation of inscribed amulets, both on gemstones and on thin sheets of gold and silver – the so-called *lamellae*, which were typically rolled up and worn in special capsules.[6] Likewise, the lead curse tablets now display lengthy invocations that specify their purposes.[7] On amulets and curse tablets alike, we find a remarkable uniformity of techniques, especially of new graphic devices, which point to the activity of ritual specialists. It will be useful to outline the chief developments:

1. Magical iconography of gods and *daimones* (see Figures 4.1–4.3);
2. Unintelligible names, the *voces magicae*,[8] often with an Egyptian or Hebrew ring, but usually with no clear etymology[9]; they are sometimes formed in patterns, like wings or triangles (Figure 4.3), or as palindromes (Figures 4.1 and 4.2);
3. Sequences of Greek vowels or, less frequently, consonants, again often structured as graphic patterns (Figure 4.3);
4. Magical "characters" (*charaktēres*) – pseudo-hieroglyphic icons, with a typical "ring-letter" formation (Figure 4.2).

These elements constitute a distinctive magical language, appearing on artifacts unearthed in every corner of the Roman Empire. They are premised on a definite understanding of the techniques by which magical power may be harnessed. A

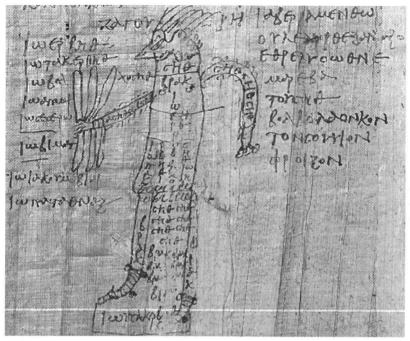

FIGURE 4.1. The formulary instructs the magician to engrave the illustrated figure of Seth-Typhon (or perhaps one of his daimonic servants) on a lead *lamella* along with the secret names of the god: IŌ ERBĒTH, IŌ PAKERBĒTH, IŌ BOLCHOSĒTH (i.e. "Baal who strikes, [that is] Set:" see Gager, *Curse Tablets*, 266), IŌ APOMPS, etc. On the upper right, we note the common, tongue-twisting palindrome, ABERAMENTHŌOULERTHEXAN-AXETHRELUOŌTHNEMAREBA. Detail of *P. Osl.* I, 1 (4th cen. ce), col. 1 (= *PGM* XXXVI. 1–34), courtesy of Gunn Haaland, keeper of the papyrus collection at the University of Oslo Library. Used with permission.

new priority is afforded to ineffable names and symbols, unintelligible in human terms, but meaningful to the gods. Their advantage evidently lies in the fact that they signify their divine referents primitively, bypassing our subjective processes of semantic interpretation.[10] Especially remarkable is the deployment of graphic devices, like the *charaktēres* and word-shapes, which are *literally* "ineffable," that is, incapable of vocal articulation.[11] In general, these techniques reflect a transition from the older Greek idea of magic as an oral practice to the view that magic is embodied in writing and in the ineffable power of visual icons, which concretely embody divine power.[12] Indeed, we can often infer from their formulaic style and complexity that these inscribed artifacts were produced by experts working from spell-books or "formularies" (see Figures 4.1–4.3).[13]

In light of these recurring and widespread technical devices, we are justi-fied in speaking of a kind of tradition. Moreover, the similarities between the

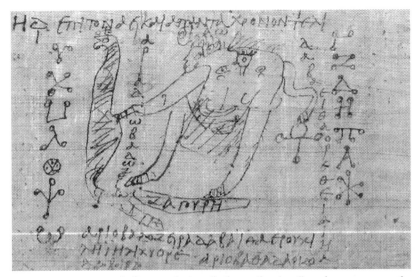

FIGURE 4.2. An apotropaic figure, to be inscribed on a silver *lamella* and worn as an amulet. The figure is flanked by a string of magical names, including (under the feet) the palindrome, EROUCHILĒIĒLICHUORE. Note to the far left and right of the figure, the ineffable *charaktēres*, with their typical ring formation. Detail of *P. Osl.* I, 1, col. 2 (= *PGM* XXXVI. 35–68), courtesy of Gunn Haaland, keeper of the papyrus collection at the University of Oslo Library. Used with permission.

activated survivals (i.e., amulets and curse tablets) and the formularies of the Greco-Egyptian magical papyri (*PGM*) suggest that Egyptian ritual specialists were among the chief contributors to this tradition.[14] Most of the surviving formularies were discovered in Thebes and were certainly produced by priests. Their priestly provenance is evident in their continuity with older Egyptian magical techniques, their adherence to the conventions of the temple *scriptoria*, and above all in their use of Demotic and Hieratic scripts, which were employed exclusively in priestly milieux.[15] Their routes of transmission and influence *beyond* Egypt are unknown. Although the spell-books were intended as secret documents, even one violation of the injunction of secrecy could have led to a wide diffusion. We should not assume that they circulated exclusively within priestly circles. No doubt there were specialists of many types and backgrounds who copied into their own working manuals what they found useful in the Egyptian books. It seems unlikely that the formularies that underpinned the artifacts unearthed in Rome (or regions even farther abroad) would have conformed precisely to the Egyptian models.[16] Indeed, the relation between the Egyptian formularies and the surviving artifacts is not direct – there are almost no exact parallels. Instead, it is a matter of close

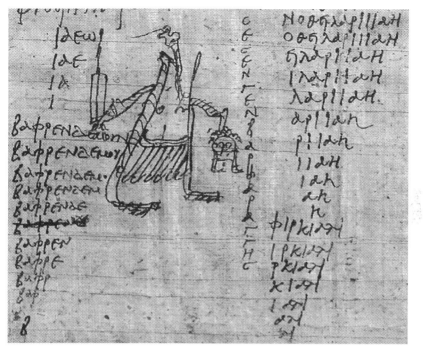

FIGURE 4.3. An erotic binding spell instructs the magician to inscribe the illustrated figure and accompanying names on clean papyrus with myrrh ink. The invoked deity appears to be the fertility god, Min of Coptos (see Betz *GMPT*, 271, n.7). Note the diminishing "wing" formation of the ineffable names (e.g. on the left: baphrendemoun, baphrende-mou, baphrendemo, etc) and of the Greek vowels (upper left: iaeō, iae, ia, i). Detail of *P. Osl.* I, 1, col. 4 (= *PGM* XXXVI. 102–133), courtesy of Gunn Haaland, keeper of the papyrus collection at the University of Oslo Library. Used with permission.

"family resemblances"[17]: the common magical idiom of the *voces magicae* and the *charaktēres*. Above all, the influence of the Egyptian scribal tradition is evident in the working premise, underlying the graphic devices, that magical power is transmitted through writing and embodied in visual icons – a notion alien to the older Greek tradition, but characteristically Egyptian.[18]

It has been suggested, in fact, that the *charaktēres* were modeled on the hieroglyphs, which, in addition to their phonemic significance (as ordinary linguistic signs), also possessed iconographic meaning and power.[19] However, in the *PGM*, this iconic dimension is stressed to an unusual degree, creating the misleading impression that the hieroglyphs were primarily a cipher in which the priests encoded esoteric doctrines. Indeed, it often seems as though these priests are deliberately exaggerating the esotericism of the priesthood and reinventing themselves as wonder-working "magicians." David Frankfurter has introduced the compelling idea of "stereotype appropriation" as a way of explaining this seeming incongruity.

Under Roman occupation, the infrastructure of the Egyptian temples deteriorated because of the cessation of state patronage. At times, the temples were subject not just to neglect but also to active persecution by Roman officials, for whom Egyptian religion was really illicit "magic."[20] It was in this period of decline, roughly between the second and fourth centuries, that most of the formularies were written. Economic pressures seem to have forced the priests to function increasingly as freelance ritual specialists outside of the declining temple institutions. At this point, Frankfurter appeals to stereotype appropriation: in order to attract well-paying foreign clients, these priests had to conform to Hellenistic stereotypes by posturing as esoteric masters.[21] According to his view, this explains the peculiar character of the formularies, which transmit authentic priestly traditions but in a guise that distorts their traditional meaning. Frankfurter's model has merit, but it has been interpreted in narrow socioeconomic terms, as a mere marketing ploy. This way of evaluating the motivations and self-representations of the authors of the *PGM* does not stand up to scrutiny.

The Esotericism of the Greco-Egyptian Formularies: Taking Secrecy Seriously – Stereotype Appropriation – or Resistance?

In principle, Frankfurter's model of stereotype appropriation involves the long-scale absorption and internalization of colonial values, which are blended in complex ways with indigenous traditions.[22] He is fully aware, for instance, that the image of the priest as a wonder-worker was partly based on Egyptian precedents: thaumaturgic priests, like Setne Khamwas, were "folk-hero[es] of the Egyptian scribal world."[23] But often the more subtle possibilities of internalization seem to be downplayed in favor of a rather crude socioeconomic analysis. In his discussions of the magical papyri, Frankfurter suggests that the exotic figure of the magus is really a colonial stereotype that the priests strategically appropriate in order to gain political and economic advantage.[24] Indeed, he suggests that the Greek concept of magic "constitutes no more than a cheap appraisal of Egyptian ritual."[25] The clear implication is that the priests are "selling out" by "buying into" the exotic expectations of their clients. Other scholars, building on Frankfurter's model, have stressed the "marketing" dimensions of the *PGM* even more strongly.[26]

One notices immediately that this way of characterizing the "magician" reaffirms deeply entrenched prejudices. Magic turns out to be a kind of charlatanism that aims to mystify and exploit the gullible client. This is perhaps

not Frankfurter's intention, but it is one consequence of reducing the motivations of the priests to the acquisition of power, prestige, and cash. In support of the marketing model, scholars have highlighted the frequent use of
prestige-building devices in the formularies: assurances of efficacy ("there is
nothing better in the world"); or framing narratives, which attribute the spell
to famous magi or describe the discovery of the spell in a temple.[27] Such devices
have been interpreted as advertisements that are intended to entice foreign
readers who believe in the Hellenistic image of the priest as magician. The
fundamental problem with this view lies in the assumption that the formularies
are directed at an audience beyond the immediate circle of the magician and
his colleagues. In other words, there is a curious failure to distinguish between
a "clientele" and a "readership." It is apparently assumed that the formularies
were intended to be sold along with the magical artifacts – amulets and curse
tablets – produced for the client. This, despite the fact that the formularies insist
over and over that they are secret documents, not to be divulged to outsiders.[28]
In one instance, there is even an explicit injunction that the spells are to be distributed without cost within a closed circle of initiates.[29]

We need to make a distinction between the express intention that the formularies should be kept secret from the uninitiated and the undeniable fact
that they attained a fairly wide diffusion, as evident from their influence on
amulets, gems, and curse tablets throughout the empire. Clearly the injunctions of secrecy were not always observed. It might be argued, I suppose, that
an injunction was itself nothing more than a rhetorical device, another piece
of marketing, intended to seduce the reader by the allure of the mysterious.[30]
But the idea that the formularies were crafted with an external readership in
mind can be shown as unsupportable on other grounds.

Spell "pedigrees" appear not only in the Greek formularies but also in the
Demotic, although here they are less elaborate and show less Hellenistic influence; so, for instance, where the Greek spells may be attributed to a range
of international figures – Greek philosophers, Jewish prophets, or Persian
magi – the Demotic spells appeal only to Egyptian sources. On these grounds,
Jacco Dieleman concludes that the Demotic spells were marketed to a different readership that was less invested in the Hellenistic stereotypes.[31] But
this is a paradoxical conclusion: we know that knowledge of Demotic in this
period was almost exclusively restricted to priestly circles;[32] indeed, this fact is
one of the chief supports for the argument that the authors of the formularies must have been temple scribes. Clearly the prestige-building formulae in
the Demotic papyri were not advertisements at all, because they could not
have been directed at outsiders.[33] Rather, they must be understood as matters of self-definition, ways of imagining and constructing an "authoritative

tradition."[34] As Richard Gordon observes, the need for this kind of assurance may have become more pressing as the priests began to function as freelance ritual specialists outside of the established authority of the temple.[35]

Once we take seriously the claim that the formularies were intended as secret documents, their self-presentation appears in a new light. For instance, it can no longer plausibly be maintained that the mystical devices in the spells – secret names and *charaktēres* – are just "hocus pocus" intended to impress an ignorant clientele.[36] After all, the only magical devices that were ever made visible to the client appeared on the amulets, which were intended to be worn on their person.[37] The formularies were secret manuals, and the curse tablets were secreted by the magician in inaccessible locations, visible only to the gods intended to activate them. Clearly one must conclude that these devices were valued by the magician for their *utility*, as techniques for augmenting ritual power, and had nothing to do with impressing clients.[38] Likewise, the frequent self-description of the priests as initiates cannot be dismissed as window dressing intended to enhance the mystique of the spells.

In my view, the self-definition of the priest-as-magus should be viewed not as an external stereotype, but as an image elaborated within Egyptian priestly circles over the course of centuries, beginning in Ptolemaic times with figures like Manetho. No doubt the Hellenistic reimagining of the priest was at first a self-conscious strategy intended to win position and favor within the Ptolemaic regime. But over time it evolved into an authentic self-understanding. Moreover, this self-understanding does not actually reflect the most prevalent Hellenistic stereotypes of the Egyptian priesthood. We are not dealing here with the passive and wholesale absorption by the colonized of the foreign values of the colonizer. In truth, the reputation of the Egyptian priests was quite bad, even sinister, combining elements of venality, fraud, and religious profanation.[39] It was not a stereotype to be appropriated.

In Heliodorus's *Aithiopika*, the priest Kalasiris complains that Egyptian wisdom has been confused in the popular imagination with sorcery, a vulgar art that "creeps over the earth, waiting upon shades and circling around corpses."[40] In addition to their supposed expertise in erotic magic, Egyptian priests were typically imagined as specialists in necromancy – the summoning of ghosts or (worse) the reanimation of corpses for divinatory purposes.[41] Indeed, necromancy was one of the hallmarks of magic in the Roman imagination, closely linked with other transgressive rites, including human sacrifice and corpse violation.[42] Kalasiris distinguishes this necromantic magic from the true Egyptian wisdom "practiced by priests and the prophetic caste from an early age," which "associates with the gods and shares in their higher nature."[43]

These common stereotypes of the magician were not appropriated by the authors of the *PGM*; rather, they were consciously resisted. When the priests identified themselves as "sacred magicians,"[44] they were resisting the polemical valuations of "magic" and insisting on the more positive, even exalted, understanding of Kalasiris: magic as a transcendental wisdom that aspires to union with the divine. This higher representation of the Egyptian priest as a holy magus was first shaped within the Greek philosophical tradition, and it is especially linked to Pythagorean lore.

Priests and Pythagoreans

Already in classical times, a legend developed that Pythagoras had traveled to Egypt to be initiated into the esoteric wisdom of the temples.[45] This legend was central to the later idealization of Pythagoras as a holy man in the Neo-Pythagorean circles of the imperial age. Greek philosophy was understood as a translation into theoretical categories of an esoteric doctrine that had been concealed by the priests of Egypt in the enigmas of the hieroglyphs. The influence of this tradition in Hellenized priestly circles is evident in Chaeremon's idealized representation of the priest as an ascetic philosopher, wholly dedicated "to the thought and contemplation of God."[46] In his treatise on hieroglyphs, Chaeremon seems to have stressed their importance as ciphers embodying secret knowledge.[47] This was, in part, a concession to the Pythagoreanizing image of the priest as an esoteric master who possessed a wisdom so profound it could not be communicated in ordinary terms. But it may also have been Chaeremon's sincere belief. Over the course of the imperial period, authentic knowledge of the hieroglyphic writing system declined along with the temples.[48] Even within priestly circles, the true meaning of the script was gradually lost. Arguably, the development in the formularies of the ineffable *charaktēres* as secret symbols of the gods was just a further stage in this process, which involved both a forgetting and a mystification of the sacred script of the pharaohs.[49]

We know nothing of the routes through which Pythagorean lore was absorbed by the priests, but its influence on the *PGM* is undeniable. To begin with, there are numerous allusions to figures associated with the "magical current" of Pythagoreanism, developed in Hellenistic times by Bolus of Mendes (ca. 200 BCE). Under the pseudonym of "Democritus," Bolus wrote works on the occult properties of animals, plants, and minerals, effectively creating a new genre of "natural marvels." Central to this tradition was the doctrine of cosmic sympathy: the idea that every natural entity is adapted to the "frequency" of a particular star or planet and is thus connected, in an "occult" manner, to all other entities of that astrological type – just as the rooster, the lotus, and the heliotrope stone are linked as *solar* entities. It appears that Bolus was chiefly responsible for developing the operative implications of this doctrine, which was ultimately of Stoic origin.[50]

In his "pseudo-Democritean" works, Bolus developed the legend that Democritus had acquired his magical lore from the Persian magus Ostanes, who had initiated him in the temples of Egypt.[51] Clearly this image of Democritus as magus and initiate was based on the earlier lore surrounding Pythagoras. In the *PGM*, we encounter spells attributed to Democritus; in one case, he and Pythagoras even appear as a magical duo.[52] This is the Democritus reimagined by Bolus. Other spells are linked to the magus Ostanes himself,[53] and there is one attribution to the notable Pythagorean, Apollonius of Tyana, who belongs loosely in the tradition of Bolus.[54] The Pythagorean ideal of the holy man, with its deeply rooted connection to the wisdom of Egypt, was a natural model for the refashioning of the Egyptian priest as an esoteric master.

The tradition of Bolus is reflected also in the "magical worldview" of the formularies. The doctrine of occult properties is one of the central pillars of the *PGM* spells. In the consecration of statues or amulets, it was important to employ the correct materials, to burn the correct incense, and even to inscribe the symbols with the appropriate ink. Just as the magician had to know the secret names of the deity, so too did the materials have to be "cognate to the gods."[55] For instance, if we wanted to create a portable talisman "charged" with the energies of the sun we would have carved solar symbols (the scarab or ouroboros) and solar names (Helios or Abrasax) on an appropriate stone (jasper or heliotrope) and set it in a golden ring.[56] The knowledge of sympathies, as elaborated especially in the "pseudo-Democritean" tradition of natural magic, was thus one pillar of ritual *praxis*, along with the *gnōsis* of the secret names and invocations.

Pythagoreans and Egyptian priests are frequently linked in other imperial sources. Those who were hostile to Egyptian "magic," whether in virtue of their ideological commitments to the purity of the Roman religion or in virtue of their philosophical distrust of "superstition," poured equal scorn on the Pythagorean holy men *and* their supposed Egyptian masters. Lucian's farcical depiction of the Pythagorean Arignotus and his Egyptian teacher Pancrates – who could ride crocodiles and animate broomsticks – provides a case in point.[57] Interestingly, Pancrates reappears in the formularies as "Pachrates" – now an exalted wonder-worker in the court of the Emperor Hadrian.[58] Over and against the polemical stereotypes, the formularies consistently assert an idealized image. The priest is no vulgar sorcerer; he is, as ever, an initiated servant of the gods. But with the decline of the temples, the sources of hieratic authority had to be internalized. The priest thus becomes a living embodiment of the esoteric wisdom of Egypt.

My aim in the following sections is to explore more closely the boundaries between the polemical representations of "magic" in the literary, legal, and philosophical sources of the imperial age and the reality of magical practice as it appears in the formularies. First, through careful examination of the prevailing stereotypes of the "magician" as portrayed by literary elites, like Pliny and Lucan, and by philosophers, like Plutarch and Porphyry, we shall uncover a set of recurring associations – a typology of religious transgression. Especially prominent are the *topoi* of necromancy and blood sacrifice – rites directed to the gods and *daimones* of the underworld, whose reputation has now acquired a rather sinister cast. Having established the polemical contours of the "sorcerer," we shall then be in a favorable position in the final section of the chapter to evaluate the complex ways in which the magical papyri both acknowledge and react against these stereotypes.

The Polemical Construction of "Magic" in the Imperial Age: Toward a Typology of Religious Transgression

In contrast to earlier periods of antiquity, Roman imperial representations of magic assume a marked degree of coherence, certainly not that of a single concept, but that of a unified syndrome with consistent features. To begin with, magic is definitely something foreign. Pliny, in his *Natural History*, would like to trace it to the Persian magi,[59] although he is uncertain about its routes of diffusion. He is aware that Egyptian priests are also preeminent specialists,[60] and he knows that there is a Jewish branch, as well.[61] Certainly Pythagoras and "Democritus," those supposed disciples of the magi, are blamed for spreading the disease throughout Greek and Roman lands.[62] Although its exact transmissions are unclear, magic is nonetheless a *tradition* with established authorities, handbooks, and procedures. It is an art requiring special initiation and expertise. Indeed, it pretends to be a sacred art, wrapping itself in the seductive veil of mysteries,[63] but its religiosity is really an abomination. Pliny credits the Senate with stamping out the incursions of magic in Rome and its provinces by forbidding human sacrifice: "It is impossible to measure the debt owed to the Romans, who eradicated those monstrous rites, in which to kill a man was an act of high religion, and to eat him was the key to health."[64] Human sacrifice and cannibalism are taken as self-evident markers of magic. Although the claims of magic are, for the most part, fraudulent and illusory, it is nonetheless something dangerous.

The tradition inaugurated by Bolus of Mendes, under the guise of Democritus, strengthened the appearance that magic was a unified worldview with a definite genealogy. Pliny is familiar with the "pseudo-Democritean" writings, in which the Greek philosopher was represented as an initiate of Persian and Egyptian cults. He insists that these works were really written by Democritus, despite the doubts of his contemporaries.[65] He also discusses a work on the magical properties of plants that circulated under the name of Pythagoras, here again taking the attribution at face value.[66] Pliny's texts seemed to confirm the idea of a living magical tradition rooted in the lore of the magi and transmitted to the Greco-Roman world by Greek philosophers. The impression of magic as a tradition was no doubt further strengthened in subsequent centuries by the diffusion of the Greco-Egyptian formularies.

It is important to distinguish from the outset between the polemical view of this magical tradition – that of conservative Roman outsiders – and the self-definition of the practitioners themselves. In the treatment of Pliny, we see the beginnings of a tendency to imagine the secret world of the magicians as constituting an "anti-tradition," subversive of the values of Roman *religio*. The hallmarks of magic are human sacrifice, cannibalism, and related abominations – rites of deliberate transgression.

In imperial discourses on magic, human sacrifice is typically linked to necromancy, an association that is not attested in classical Greek sources. The magician offers human blood to the underworld deities in exchange for foreknowledge. There is a remarkable presumption that this perverse mode of sacrifice is pleasing to the chthonic gods – a point whose theological implications we shall consider in due course. The combined charge of human sacrifice and necromancy appears already in Cicero's invective against the Roman Pythagorean Vatinus. He alleges that Vatinus was accustomed to honoring the chthonic Manes with the entrails (*exta*) of boys and masking his abominable rites (*nefaria sacra*) under the holy veil of Pythagoreanism.[67] The *exta* of animals were used in heptascopy; the charge thus suggests necromancy – a perversion of legitimate divinatory methods. Likewise, Apollonius of Tyana was accused by the Emperor Domitian of divining the future from the entrails of a boy as part of a political conspiracy.[68] Pythagoreans were particularly vulnerable to charges of magic, not only because of their marginal lifestyle but also because they were so closely associated with the secret lore of Persia and Egypt, a connection celebrated in the tradition of Bolus but demonized by Pliny. In his biography, Philostratus assures the reader that the exalted wisdom (*sophia*) that Apollonius and his Greek predecessors inherited from the Egyptians bears no relation to the base art (*technē*) of the magicians.[69] He distinguishes the wonder-working of Apollonius from the "barbaric sacrifices" (*thusias barbarous*) of sorcerers and their "interrogations of ghosts" (*basanous eidōlōn*).[70] We are reminded of Kalasiris's complaint in the *Aithiopika* that the true Egyptian *sophia* had been degraded in popular belief to the magic of the graveyard.

There was a general presumption that witches and sorcerers scoured tombs, funeral pyres, and gallows in search of body parts for use in curses and potions. In his account of the death of the prince Germanicus, Tacitus relates a grisly discovery:

> They found under the floor and in the walls the disinterred remains of corpses, incantations and curses (*devotiones*), and the name "Germanicus" inscribed on lead tablets; there were ashes half-consumed and smeared with corruption, along with other malefic things by which it is believed that souls are consecrated to the infernal deities (*animas numinibus infernis sacrari*).[71]

The terminology is certainly in keeping with the formulae of the Latin curse tablets, which often describe a dedication (*devotio*) or handing over (*donatio*) of the victim to the infernal powers.[72] It is also true that the tablets were frequently deposited in graves, in close contact with human remains. One scholar has suggested that the use of cadaverous materials in the activation of curse tablets would have been a logical extension of the usual method of burying the tablet with the dead – useful in cases where the tablet was secreted above ground.[73] "No doubt," he suggests, "those inserting tablets into graves took the opportunity to avail themselves of supplies for future spells."[74] In fact, there is good reason for doubt. The report of Tacitus should not be taken at face value, despite its factual tone. The image of witches and magicians as grave robbers who skulk around tombs and gallows in the night is typical only of imperial representations. It is part and parcel of a wider typology whose characteristic elements are human sacrifice, cannibalism, and corpse violation. These are markers of transgression embedded in an ideological discourse about the boundaries between licit and illicit *religio*. To read such accounts as empirical descriptions of the actual practice of magic conceals what is most interesting – the tension between the stereotype of the magician and the self-definition of the so-called "magicians" themselves.

If magic is a violation of the normative religion in the Empire, then the most horrifying sorceries will be perpetrated by sociopolitical *outsiders* – by foreign specialists or, worse, by female witches. In contrast to her Greek antecedents, the Roman witch is a figure of utter depravity, wholly dedicated to the forces of death and disorder. She has the power to alter the course of the stars and to draw down the moon – to reverse the normal course of nature. The ultimate transgression is expressed in terms of "necromantic disturbance, the fear of pyres being rifled to obtain unburned parts of corpses, sarcophagi being disturbed, the dead defiled, turned into active dangers."[75] The complex characterization of the Roman witch incorporates the classical figure of the *goēs*, who specialized in negotiations with the world of the dead.[76] In one direction, the legacy of the *goēs* was taken up by the *male* ritual specialists of the imperial age. Egyptian priests and Persian magi were supposed to be experts in necromancy, and the *PGM* certainly confirm that communication with the dead was part of the repertoire of an Egyptian magician.[77] But the Roman witch was a far more sinister successor to the *goēs*: she was not merely a specialist in necromancy, but an embodiment of Hades on earth, living in constant communion with the forces of the netherworld.[78]

In the figure of the necromantic witch, the traditional domain of the *goēs* has undergone a thorough demonization.[79] She not only raises souls, but she also reanimates corpses and desecrates tombs in order to collect ingredients for her noxious spells. Her dedication to the gods of the underworld is so extreme that it sets her in opposition to the gods of heaven. The unfortunate victim of Canidia and Sagana in Horace's *Epodes* pleads for mercy in the name of Jupiter, who is certain to condemn (*improbaturum*) the actions of the witches.[80] Their rites, which are consecrated to Darkness (*Nox*) and the chthonic deities, are illicit in the eyes of the heavenly gods. Lucan, in his *Pharsalia*, provides a lurid depiction of this theme of magical transgression in his account of the necromantic rites performed by Erichtho, at the behest of Sextus Pompey. Not satisfied with the traditional forms of divination, which are "secret but lawful (*tacitum sed fas*)," Pompey sought out the "mysteries of cruel magicians which the gods on high abominate (*supernis detestanda deis*)."[81] Erichtho is wholly given over to the gods of the underworld. She offers heaven no prayer or hymn of supplication. Indeed, her rites are a sinister parody of the proper cultic forms: in place of the prescribed animal sacrifices, she pollutes the altar with the ashes and charred bones of children (*fumantes iuvenum cineres ardentiaque ossa*),[82] or she offers babies torn prematurely from the womb.[83] A remarkable feature of this account is the imagined opposition between the gods of the underworld and the gods of heaven: the rites of the chthonic deities are profanations of proper sacrificial forms.[84] In the background is the transition, characteristic of Hellenistic and imperial times, to a hierarchical understanding of the gods, which introduced new moral and religious polarities.

Philosophers had long been concerned with the infelicities of traditional polytheistic representations of the gods, but in the wake of the cosmological and political transformations of the Hellenistic age, such concerns became widespread. Of crucial importance was the emergence of a hierarchical conception of the divine world, which mirrored the new cosmic hierarchy of the concentric planetary spheres,[85] as well as the imperial "model of the distant emperor, mediated by satraps, governors, or vassal kings."[86] The old gods were reconceptualized as mediating powers of a Supreme Deity. Certainly by the second century CE, this kind of inclusive monotheism or *henotheism* was a typical way of understanding the gods in the Greco-Roman world.[87] The hierarchization of the gods introduced new moral polarities: the gods of heaven, who were associated with light, goodness, and reason, were now ranked above the gods of the underworld, who were associated with darkness, evil, and irrationality. These hierarchical distinctions and valuations are clearly reflected in Lucan's account.

When her initial appeals to the chthonic deities are unsuccessful, Erichtho resorts to compulsive rites, threatening to call on a still greater god: "Do you obey? Or must he be invoked – he, whose invocation always sets the earth quaking ... the one who dwells in a Tartarus unfathomable to you, the one to whom you are the gods above."[88] There is a suggestion here of a supreme ruler of Hades to which all of the infernal gods are subject. The mere threat of invoking his name – which Lucan conceals for dramatic effect – is enough to compel the chthonic deities. Like the supreme God of heaven, this *anti-God* is ineffable, shrouded in mystery. It seems that the diabolical cult of Erichtho, which inverts the sacrifices of the Olympians, also implies what Richard Gordon aptly terms an "inverted theology."[89] This startling suggestion, so foreign to our simplistic views of "pagan polytheism," will reappear more explicitly in our consideration of late Platonic daimonology in the next section.

In Lucan's day (first century CE), it is unclear whether magic as such could be illegal; we know only that malefic uses of magic could be persecuted under a wider rubric of "poisoning," or *veneficium*, on the grounds of the harm done.[90] By the close of the third century, however, there are clear indications that magic had become an art forbidden by law. The essential evidence comes from a commentary (ca. 300 CE) on the *Lex Cornelia* of 81 BCE, in which the earlier charge of *veneficium* has been expanded to a charge against the very practice of magic.[91] At some point during the course of the first three centuries CE, the idea that magic was a violation of divine law found concrete expression in judgments of Roman law. The commentary specifies that the very possession of books of magic could be a capital offense; indeed, it insists quite strongly that even the knowledge (*scientia*) of magic was prohibited.[92] In other words, it is the art itself that is forbidden. Among the chief markers of magic are, as ever, the rites of necromancy and human sacrifice directed to the gods of the dead: "Those who sacrifice a man or obtain omens from his blood, or pollute a shrine or a temple, shall be thrown to the beasts or, if *honestiores*, be punished capitally."[93] No doubt, the primary concerns behind the prohibition were social and political, but they were expressed in religious terms: magic is illegal because it perverts and "pollutes" the rites of *religio*.

Daimonology and the Shifting Boundaries of Legitimate Cult

The new Hellenistic cosmography raised difficult questions relating to divine transcendence.[94] The widening gulf between earth and heaven – between the world of generation and decay below the moon and the expansive ethereal realms above – seemed to preclude any entanglement of the divine in mundane affairs. In the traditional understanding, the gods dwelled just out of sight, at "the distance at which the smoke of sacrifice disappears from view."[95] Now they dwelled in an incorruptible realm beyond the outer reaches of the earth's atmosphere. How was it possible to communicate with such distant gods? Certainly they could not be imagined, in any literal sense, to receive the vapors of sacrifice. Besides, if the gods are changeless, how can they even be affected by our prayers and offerings? The very foundations of cult sacrifice were called into question.

The appeal to hierarchy was a critical strategy in addressing these concerns. The traditional deities of polytheism were reconceptualized as ministers of a transcendent deity, who transmitted His ineffable influence through the cosmic structure of the planetary spheres. The many gods were typically regarded as rulers of the planets, whether they resided in them directly or governed them from a super-celestial domain. Below the moon, the divine hierarchy was extended into the mundane world by the elaboration of a complex daimonology. The *daimones* conveyed the energies of the planetary gods through the earth's atmosphere into the flux of matter, directing and organizing the sub-lunar world in accordance with divine intelligence.

The mediating role of the *daimones* permitted a new rationalization of cult sacrifice that was consistent with the principle of divine transcendence. It was through these daimonic conduits that divine oracles were revealed to humans and human messages were translated to the gods. This way of reconciling cult with correct theology had been suggested much earlier by Plato,[96] but it was developed with a new urgency by the Platonists of the imperial period. For Plutarch, it is inconceivable that gods are directly involved in the administration of rites: "[L]et us entrust these duties to the ministers (*leitourgois*) of the gods ... and let us believe that *daimones* are overseers of the sacred rites (*episkopous thēon hierōn*)."[97] Whereas the gods were impassible, the *daimones* could be moved by prayers and sacrifices. They were believed to have subtle bodies that could distinguish pleasure and pain; thus, they could be imagined to enjoy the sacrificial vapors – even to be nourished by them.

The *daimon* was equally useful in resolving issues of theodicy arising from the old myths, which often describe the gods as licentious and immoral beings. As lesser deities subject to irrational appetites, the *daimones* were convenient scapegoats: unlike their divine superiors, they were fully capable of wickedness and depravity.[98] Thus traditional myth was reconciled with theology but in a way that underscored the moral ambivalence of the *daimones*. If the *daimones* constitute a hierarchy defined by degrees of proximity to the gods, does it not follow that those at the lower end of the spectrum – those most distant from the sources of divine wisdom and goodness – will share increasingly in the chaotic impulses of matter?

In Plutarch's dialogue *On the Obsolescence of Oracles*, we encounter a distinction between propitious *daimones* – the faithful ministers of the gods – and base *daimones* –who are ruled by desire. In the holy mysteries, initiates learn something of the nature of the ministering spirits.[99] As for the evil *daimones*, they have their own cult, which is a profanation of the mysteries, characterized by the consumption of raw flesh, wild lamentation, blasphemy, and human sacrifice.[100] In another treatise, we encounter a similar constellation: frenzied dancing, self-defilement, sorcery and magic (*goēteiai kai mageiai*), and, again, that ultimate marker of religious transgression – human sacrifice.[101] These debased rites are fueled by the superstitious fear of the masses, who presume in their ignorance that divinities, which are wholly good and exempt from desire, are propitiated by acts of depravity and violence. In truth, the spirits that demand this obscene cult are not gods, but bloodthirsty *daimones*.

Plutarch includes sorcery (*goēteia*) within a wider typology of religious transgressions, all of which are rooted in bad theology. False beliefs about the gods breed a misguided fear of the divine, which is expressed in irrational and degrading forms of worship. We have encountered a similar pattern already in our literary sources: magic is defined by an appeal to a series of profanations – necromancy, human sacrifice, cannibalism – which mark it as the ideological Other of true religion. Like Lucan, Plutarch interprets the distinction between licit and illicit cult in *theological* terms, as mirroring an opposition between the gods of light and the gods of death and darkness. But Plutarch's daimonology allows for more precision: the addressees of the cults of human sacrifice and sorcery are actually evil *daimones* who are far removed from the nature of true divinity.

A further parallel with Lucan can be detected in Plutarch's allusions to a supreme agent of evil that is eternally set against the forces of cosmic order. Endorsing what he believes to be the true teaching of Zoroaster and the magi, Plutarch seems to favor something approaching a metaphysical dualism, in which the beneficent creator God is opposed by an arch-*daimon*, the "satanic" adversary called *Areimanios* (i.e., *Ahriman*) in the Persian religion. The gloomy rites of *Areimanios*, which invoke Hades and Darkness, are inversions of the devotional rites offered to the God of Light, *Horomazes*.[102] Again, the forces of the underworld are imagined as constituting a shadow hierarchy that mimics the administration of the true God.[103]

No doubt some of the profane rites imagined by Plutarch had a basis in orgiastic cult practices. But the jump from frenzied dancing to human sacrifice is rather large, and it should remind us that we are dealing with ideological distinctions whose relevance to actual cult practices is far from clear. One is left to wonder, for instance, where Plutarch, as a Pythagorean, stands on the central rite of paganism – animal sacrifice. In one of his early tractates, "On the Eating of Flesh," he characterizes the practice as a form of pollution – unnatural for humans and lawful only in cases of necessity. Although he recognizes that the force of habit will be too powerful for the mass of humanity to resist, he clearly regards abstention from the pollution (*molysmos*) of blood as the mark of the higher spirituality of the philosopher.[104] How far should the condemnation of blood sacrifice extend? Are the *daimones* who feed on the vapors of animal sacrifices legitimate ministers of the gods, or are they the same bloodthirsty fiends who instigated the practice of human sacrifice?

As it turns out, the legitimacy of animal sacrifice would soon become a widespread concern, reaching far beyond marginal Pythagorean circles. For a variety of reasons, the established cult centers declined in the imperial period and reached a crisis point in the economic turmoil of the third century. The evidence is clearest for the Eastern cults in Greece, Syria, and Asia Minor, where "financial restraints and a shift in civic values led to the decline of many priesthoods."[105] The epigraphic evidence reflects a transition from traditional festivals centered on animal sacrifice to less expensive daily offerings involving incense, lamps, and the singing of hymns.[106] Scholars have also noted a resurgence of interest in *oracles*, especially in Asia Minor, where Apollo now, quite remarkably, begins to address pilgrims on matters of theology and cult: "Hapless mortals, what concern have I with bountiful hecatombs of cattle and [gleaming] statues of rich gold ...? The immortal gods indeed have no need of possessions ... Some of you have remembered to sing a hymn in my sanctuaries."[107] Within the emerging monotheistic worldview, the decline of animal sacrifice was legitimated in theological terms: true divinity must transcend material cult. In another famous oracle, the sun-god identified himself as a ministering angel, a mere particle, of the Supreme Deity.[108] By the second century, Plato's transcendental conception of the divine had become a theological commonplace. Certainly animal sacrifice still found ardent supporters, but it was no longer synonymous with pagan religiosity. This surely explains, in part, why the attempts of the Emperor Julian in the fourth century to revive the traditional rites of blood met with such lackluster enthusiasm.[109]

Clearly the boundaries between legitimate and contested forms of ritual were beginning to shift. If we compare the earlier typology of religious transgression in Plutarch (first–second century CE) to the idea of sorcery elaborated by the Neo-Platonist Porphyry (third century CE), we discover that the demonization of blood sacrifice now encompasses not only human sacrifice but animal sacrifice, as well. In his treatise *On Abstinence*, Porphyry paints an idealized picture of the Pythagorean way of life, distinguishing it sharply from the forbidden domain of "sorcery" – a distinction that was not always clear to his contemporaries. The Pythagorean sage observes a wholly inward and spiritualized cult, abstaining from the pollutions of animal flesh, which enflame the passions and corrupt the body.[110] Diametrically opposed to the "divine man" (*theios anēr*) is the sorcerer (*goēs*), who conjures evil *daimones* to indulge his profane and immoderate desires.[111] Porphyry concedes the distinction between ministering *daimones* and evil *daimones*, but in practice he fears it is impossible to tell the two apart. The evil spirits disguise themselves as good *daimones* and perform specious miracles,[112] so that the superstitious masses will continue to nourish them with blood sacrifices.[113] If we cannot tell the good *daimones* from the bad ones, then the distinction between sorcery and legitimate cult becomes impossible to maintain: even if our sacrifices are addressed to good *daimones*, we may be inadvertently worshipping their counterfeits.

The only way to disarm the threat of daimonic subversion is to reject the cult of blood sacrifice, which attracts and empowers the evil *daimones*. We should turn instead to spiritual sacrifices, which properly honor the gods and ennoble the worshipper. Only a purified soul, cleansed of the pollution of blood, is immune to daimonic seduction.[114]

According to the view of Porphyry, pagan sacrifice has become virtually indistinguishable from sorcery. This remarkable conclusion was cleverly exploited by the Christian Fathers because it seemed to offer confirmation, from the mouth of a distinguished philosopher, that the pagan gods were really evil *daimones*.[115] The Christian equation of "paganism" and "sorcery" was persuasive because it exploited instabilities internal to late pagan daimonology. As the sub-lunar world increasingly came to be perceived as the playground of evil *daimones*, the domain of legitimate cult seemed to narrow, whereas the boundaries of sorcery expanded until they threatened to engulf pagan cult entirely.

Scholars often maintain that pagans did not distinguish "magic" from "religion" in theological terms. Instead, they treated magic as a sociopolitical problem, objectionable only in virtue of its antisocial goals.[116] What is supposed to be distinctive about the Christian viewpoint is the total demonization of magic as the ideological inversion of religion. In the eyes of the Christian monotheist, pagan cult is tantamount to "magic" because its addressees are illegitimate: the so-called pagan "gods" are really just demons or fallen angels. This magic-religion dichotomy is held to be alien to paganism because it rests on a distinction between true gods and false gods, which (so the story goes) makes no sense in a polytheistic worldview that is "ever-receptive to new divinities."[117] Already our discussions have cast serious doubt on the supporting premises of this entrenched position.

The claim that the "pagans" viewed magic as a deviant or malefic application of religious rites (and so merely as part of the wider field of religious practices) seems basically correct for the Classical period and for most of the Roman Republic. In neither context do we encounter a firm, "essentializing" distinction between magic and religion. But the situation is strikingly different in the imperial age. We have traced the emergence of a strong conception of magic, embodied in rites of deliberate profanation and reversal: magic is distinct from religion not only in its goals but also in its *form*. Moreover, this distinction is increasingly framed in theological terms: the obscene cult of magic is dedicated to the chthonic deities but condemned by the gods of heaven. Within the hierarchical pantheon of the imperial period, the distinction between high gods and low gods was not merely topological (Heaven above, Hades below) but also moral. The gods of the underworld were still "true gods" (unlike Christian demons), but they were imagined in increasingly horrific terms, and their legitimate worship was becoming hard to distinguish from sorcery. In the Platonic tradition, the elaboration of a complex daimonology allowed for a more precise articulation of these hierarchical valuations: religious rites were officiated by ministering *daimones* or angels of heaven, and magical rites were officiated by infernal, blood-thirsty *daimones*. The modern stereotype of a tolerant and inclusive paganism appears highly dubious in light of these emerging polarities.

Clearly the late pagans were very much inclined to distinguish religion and magic in theological terms. They were, after all, no polytheists – if by this one means the worship of a disparate plurality of gods and the refusal to countenance the idea of a single, all-encompassing deity. Scholars have often overlooked the fact that "pagan polytheism" is a polemical equation. To call pagans "polytheists" in the context of Christian-pagan polemics was to say that their theology was incorrect, that they did not understand the transcendence of the divine, and that they were "idolaters," worshippers of false gods. By treating the stereotype of pagan polytheism as a historical reality and overlooking monotheistic trends in late pagan theology, scholars have lent credence to the polemical representations of the early Christians, who insisted that the pagan "idolaters" did not know or care about the difference between magic and religion. In truth, the late pagans were deeply preoccupied with determining the boundaries between religious cult and "magic." As we have seen, some even wondered whether blood sacrifice was a legitimate mode of worship or a covert form of sorcery.

Now that we have traced the polemical contours of "magic" in the imperial sources, it remains, in the final section, for us to consider the reality of magical practice in the Greco-Egyptian formularies. To what extent do we find evidence in the *PGM* of a tendency to reverse or transgress religious rites? In my view, the formularies consciously resist these transgressive stereotypes not only in their appeals to the ideal of "holy magic" but also in their implicit understanding of *how ritual works*. Lower forms of magic – including such contested rites as necromancy – are sanctioned by their inclusion within a wider initiatory framework in which the authority to command supernatural forces is established through union with the "High God." This implicit henotheism reflects the hierarchization of the Divine World typical of the imperial age, and especially of the Platonic (or Neo-Pythagorean) currents.

The "Holy Magic" of the *PGM* and Its Legitimating Structures

Turning now to the contents and procedures of the Greco-Egyptian formularies, let us consider how they square with the prevailing magical stereotypes of the imperial age. One interesting point of contrast is the practice of necromancy, which literary and legal sources consider central to magic. Necromantic spells are attested in the *PGM*, but they appear rather infrequently; moreover, their ritual procedures do not conform to the literary representations.

In one formulary, we encounter a pair of spells that aim to secure a *daimon* of the dead (*nekydaimon*) as an assistant (*parhedros*), a kind of spirit familiar, who remains permanently linked to the magician and ever-ready to serve his needs.[118] The *nekydaimon* is useful in curses, love spells, and divination: he can be contacted through a necromantic rite of "enquiry" (*anakrisis*), employing a skull wreathed with ivy or flax leaves that have been inscribed with magical formulae.[119] The intended mechanism is unclear, although there is a suggestion that the ghost will appear in the magician's dreams, awaiting his orders.[120] A variant procedure calls for an ass hide, inscribed with elaborate images and formulae, to be placed underneath a corpse.[121] So perhaps there is some basis after all for the popular notion that magicians employed cadaverous materials in necromancy. However, a closer look at the ritual procedures reveals a detail of fundamental importance.

The acquisition of the infernal assistant must be granted by the High God, here identified (as is quite typical) with the sun-god: "Helios, hear me, NN, and grant me power over the spirit of this man, violently slain, from whose body I hold *this* [i.e., his *skull*], so that I may keep him with me … as a helper."[122] In an evocative hymn, the sun-god is then asked to seek out the owner of the skull during his nightly passage through the underworld.[123] Far from constituting an act of transgression, necromancy is here characterized as a fully legitimate extension of the magician's god-given privileges. There is no suggestion of a reversal of proper religious rites: it is not by setting himself against the gods of heaven, but by aligning himself with them, that the magician is able to harness the powers of the underworld.[124]

The magician of the *PGM* understands himself first and foremost as an initiate, specially consecrated and empowered through his intimate connection to the Supreme Deity.[125] This connection was established through the rite of *systasis*, or divine encounter, in which the magician merged with the god and assimilated the god's powers. This rite elevated the initiate to a semi-divine status and could result in a permanent transformation, even "immortalization."[126]

Once the link with the deity was established, the lines of communication were open and various modes of divination could be employed to access transcendental levels of knowledge.[127] The most desirable experience was the "direct vision,"[128] but more common were the indirect techniques employing water bowls or lamps, sometimes with the assistance of a boy medium. Whichever technique was employed, the goal was still to see and hear the god: "You will observe through bowl divination ... beholding the god in the water and hearing a voice from the god which speaks in verses in answer to whatever you want."[129] In many instances, the god appears during sleep: the boundary between waking visions and revelatory dreams was fluid.[130]

This kind of visionary experience was foundational to the ritual system: it provided foreknowledge that was useful in satisfying the needs of clients; but even more importantly, it provided esoteric knowledge, chiefly of the secret icons and names of the deity: "When the god comes in, look down and write the things he says and the Name which he gives you for himself."[131] The magician was above all an initiate of the Divine Name.[132] Unlike the conventional names of the gods, the secret names, or *voces magicae*, were revealed to the initiate in these visionary encounters. Their very *strangeness* is a reflection of their numinous origin; they are attempts at articulating the divine language within the limited range of our vocal apparatus.[133] The holy names were "attuned" to the creative energies of the gods, and they were thus inherently powerful; they had to be wielded with caution and concealed from the uninitiated.[134]

The most prevalent rites in the *PGM*, alongside the erotic spells, are the rites of divination; and within this domain it is not necromancy that is of primary interest, but visionary knowledge of the High God, usually in his solar form as Helios or Apollo – the preeminent god of prophecy.[135] Necromancy had its uses, but it could only be safely and effectively practiced after the magician had realized *systasis* with the divine. The knowledge of the divine names demonstrated the magician's attainment of this initiated status and empowered him to command the infernal spirits.[136] The divine name also functioned as a protective charm that neutralized the threat of *daimonic* attack: "I have your name as a unique phylactery in my heart ... no spirit will stand against me – neither visitation nor any other of the evil beings (*poneroi*) of Hades."[137] The magicians of the *PGM* are clearly mindful of the bad reputation of the infernal *daimones* and spirits, who often disguised themselves as good *daimones* – thus the adjuration that the spirit speak truthfully: "[L]et him tell me however many things I want in my mind, speaking the entire truth, gentle, mild, and pondering no thoughts against me."[138] The dangerous and suspect reputation of necromancy was, to an extent, disarmed by its inclusion within the wider initiatory framework.

But the magicians pushed the boundaries of legitimate ritual still further. They claimed authority not only over infernal spirits but also over the ministering *daimones* or angels of the air,[139] and even, in exceptional circumstances, over the very gods of heaven. In an erotic rite addressed to Aphrodite, compulsive measures are provided in event of delay, and they involve threats and unpleasant fumigations: the sacrifice of a vulture's brains.[140] Even more startling are the compulsive rites occasionally directed against the sun-god, who is typically regarded as the preeminent form of the High God. If he fails to appear, the magician is instructed to sacrifice the brain of a black ram, followed by more extreme measures.[141] But the magician is still operating within the logic of his worldview, because he is convinced that the sun-god, however exalted, is an outer form of the Ineffable Deity. At this point, we reach the limits of compulsion. The magician knows that the Ineffable God cannot be coerced, because it is only through Him that all other beings can be commanded.[142] He responds to his secret names graciously, not by coercion: "I call upon your holy, great and secret names, which you rejoice to hear."[143]

There is only one type of rite, in my view, that is in real danger of breaching the sanctioned boundaries of the ritual system. This is the so-called slander spell. Here the magician aims to fuel the anger of a god by performing blasphemous sacrifices, which he then attributes to his unfortunate target: "'So-and-so' is burning for you, goddess, some horrid incense, the fat of a spotted goat, blood and corruption, the menses of a dead virgin, the heart of one who died before his time ... a woman's embryo ... and – what sacrilege! – she has placed them on your altars."[144] Here we are close to the horrifying images of sorcery in the literary sources: we are reminded of Erichtho's blasphemous offerings of human remains and unborn embryos on the divine altars. Indeed, the magician is consciously engaging in a rite of reversal, which is no doubt partly *inspired* by the literary blasphemies of the day. The procedure is undeniably perverse – this is the key to its effectiveness as slander. The formulary warns that the rite is dangerous, only to be employed in circumstances of dire necessity and with the use of apotropaic charms: the goddess has been known to levitate careless magicians and drop them from a great height.[145] In these slander spells, we see a convergence between magic as it was imagined and feared and magic as it was actually practiced. But these rites are exceptional, as the precautions make plain. Indeed, what is most revealing about these rites is their mindfulness about the boundaries between holy magic and vulgar sorcery – boundaries that could only be trespassed at the magician's peril.

There is no denying the malefic objectives of many of the rites in the formularies. But in the eyes of the practitioners, curses and erotic binding spells were legitimate applications of ritual power, so long as the magician maintained his religious devotion to the One God. This religious justification was not a rhetorical ploy designed to appease the Roman authorities. Although fear of persecution may account in part for the secrecy of the formularies, it cannot fully explain their ideological dimensions. After all, no Roman official would have been persuaded that these were, in fact, holy rites. The depiction of the magician as an initiate was instead a matter of authentic self-understanding, a reaffirmation that, despite the decline of the temples, he was still a consecrated servant of the gods and that his rites, no matter how closely they may at times have resembled "sorcery," were fully in keeping with his priestly status.

Conclusion

In her classic study of the Solomonic tradition, E. M. Butler observed that the essential procedures of the European *grimoires* were anticipated already in the Greco-Egyptian papyri.[146] Indeed, it is surely significant that the earliest exemplar of the Solomonic manuals, the *Testament of Solomon*, began to take shape roughly in the same period as the *PGM*.[147] The *Testament* is not itself, properly speaking, a formulary, but rather a story about the magical powers of Solomon, in which are embedded various technical details of use to the practicing magician: the names of demons, their spheres of influence, their astrological affinities, and most importantly the names of the ruling angels to whom the demons are subject. To the astute magician, the *Testament* reveals a functional system of demonic magic that is premised on the principle that evil spirits can be safely and legitimately deployed by appealing to the higher angelic powers that neutralize their destructive potencies. The power to command infernal spirits is mediated to the "holy magician" through God and His angels. This becomes standard operating procedure in the European *grimoires*: the magician undergoes a protracted period of ritual purity, swearing devotion to God, and then claims authority over the powers of Hell. Monotheistic piety sanctions mundane and even malefic applications of ritual power. The parallel with the magico-religious system of the *PGM* is striking.[148] It is impossible to say whether the tradition of the *PGM* influenced the formation of the *Testament* in this regard. It may be a question of analogy – a common theological response to the perils of demonology. But, at the very least, it is worth noting that the monotheistic approach to neutralizing the dangers of demonic magic was a preoccupation not only of Jewish and Christian magicians but equally of their late pagan contemporaries, who were, after all, monotheists in their own right.

Notes

1. The ideological contours of the term "magic," both positive and negative, will be addressed in due course.
2. See Johnston, "Songs for the Ghosts."
3. Plato tells us that binding spells (*katadesmoi*) were a specialty of the *goēs* (*Republic* 364b–364e). For a handy collection of curse tablets in translation, see Gager, ed., *Curse Tablets*.
4. Faraone, "Agonistic Context," 4–5; Ogden, "Binding Spells," 6–9, 55.
5. Amulets activated by verbal incantation: Kotansky, "Incantations and Prayers for Salvation," 107–110. For the scant evidence of early inscribed amulets, see 110–112.
6. The surviving imperial *lamellae* can be consulted in the edited collection of Kotansky, *Greek Magical Amulets*. For the inscribed gemstones, see Bonner, *Studies in Magical Amulets*.
7. On the increasing complexity of the curse tablets and *lamellae*, see Brashear, "Greek Magical Papyri," 3443–3446. Cf. Gager, *Curse Tablets*, 4–9; Ogden, "Binding Spells," 6–10.
8. In Greek sources, these names are designated variously as: "barbarian" (*barbara*), "senseless" (*asēmata*), "ineffable" (*arrēta*; *aphthenkta*), or "secret" (*krypta*).
9. Brashear ("Greek Magical Papyri," 3576–3603) provides a glossary of *voces magicae* with the various (rather conjectural) etymological derivations that have been proposed by scholars.
10. For this argument, see Iamblichus, *De mysteriis* VII.4 (254, 12–256, 3).
11. The concept of "ineffability" (Gr. *arrētos*; *aphthenktos*) has different nuances: (a) not to be divulged; (b) indefinable, meaningless – equivalent to *asēmatos*; (c) incapable of vocal utterance. The harder it was to vocalize the secret names, the closer they were to the divine tongue: cf. n. 133. On this more stringent sense of "ineffability," see Betz, "Secrecy in the Greek Magical Papyri," 163–165.
12. On the development from oral to scribal magic, see Frankfurter, "Magic of Writing."
13. The term "formulary" highlights the fact that the spell-books contain ritual templates and generic formulae, which were tailored to the special needs of clients.
14. For the standard edition of the magical papyri, see Preisendanz, ed., *Papyri Graecae Magicae*, henceforth cited as *PGM*. For an English translation of the

spells, see Betz, ed., *The Greek Magical Papyri in Translation*, henceforth cited as *GMPT*.

15. See Ritner, "Egyptian Magical Practice," 3345–3353, 3356–3371.

16. Recently discovered curse tablets from the joint sanctuary of Mater Magna and Isis, dating from 80 to 120 CE, are shedding light on the development of indigenous Roman magical practices prior to the widespread influence of the Greco-Egyptian tradition. We should not assume that such regional varieties were entirely supplanted by the Greco-Egyptian models. See Blänsdorf, "Defixiones from the Sanctuary of Isis," esp. 163–165, along with the remarks of Gordon and Marco Simón in their introduction to the same collection, *Magical Practice in the Latin West*, esp. 2–4, 16–17.

17. I follow Richard Gordon's apt use of Wittgenstein's expression in "Shaping the Text," 70–71. On the few close parallels between the formularies and the activated finds, see Brashear, "Greek Magical Papyri," 3416–3419.

18. See Frankfurter, "Magic of Writing," 190–194; Gordon, "Shaping the Text," 96.

19. Frankfurter, "Magic of Writing," 205–211.

20. Ritner, "Egyptian Magical Practice," 3355–3358.

21. On stereotype appropriation, see Frankfurter, *Religion in Roman Egypt*, 224–233; Frankfurter, "Consequences of Hellenism," 171–183.

22. Frankfurter, "Consequences of Hellenism," 162–163.

23. Frankfurter, "Ritual Expertise in Roman Egypt," 119; Frankfurter, *Religion in Roman Egypt*, 226. The historical Prince Khamwas was a son of Ramses II (nineteenth dynasty) and high priest of Ptah at Memphis.

24. Frankfurter, "Consequences of Hellenism," 171, 173–174, 183.

25. Frankfurter, "Ritual Expertise," 120; cf. Frankfurter, *Religion in Roman Egypt*, 237: "[T]raditions that originally function in a total social and economic complex now become merely the hoary accoutrements of a foreign *magos*."

26. Ian Moyer speaks bluntly of the "commoditization" of Egyptian magic in "Thessalos of Tralles and Cultural Exchange," 39–56.

27. Dieleman, *Priests, Tongues, and Rites*, 254–284.

28. On the typical injunction to keep the spells secret, see Betz, "Secrecy in the Greek Magical Papyri," 154–160.

29. *PGM* IV.475–IV.477: "Be gracious to me, O Providence and Psyche, as I write these mysteries handed down [not] for gain" (translation in Betz, *GMPT*).

30. Frankfurter ("Consequences of Hellenism," 174) describes the esotericism of the papyri as a "pretense."

31. Dieleman, *Priests, Tongues, and Rites*, 281–286.

32. Dieleman concedes. Ibid., 286.

33. Indeed, these "spell pedigrees" appear already in the Coffin texts and are traditional priestly conventions, not commercials: see Ritner, "Egyptian Magical Practice," 3367, with notes.

34. See Betz, "Formation of Authoritative Tradition."
35. Gordon, "Shaping the Text," 76.
36. Still a deeply rooted prejudice: see, for example, Brashear, "Greek Magical Papyri," 3397, 3440. The associations of magic with irrationalism are keenly diagnosed by Smith in "Great Scott! Thought and Action One More Time," 85–91.
37. Amongst recent scholars, Richard Gordon ("Shaping the Text," 97) alone seems to have recognized the significance of this crucial point.
38. See, again, Gordon, "Shaping the Text," 97.
39. As Gordon observes in "Shaping the Text," 73–74.
40. Héliodore, *Les Éthiopiques*, vol. I, book 3.16.3.
41. On priests as necromancers, see (pseudo-)Thessalos of Tralles, *De virtutibus herbarum* 22, in *Thessalos von Tralles*, ed. Hans-Veit Friedrich; Apuleius, *Metamorphoses* 2.28–2.29 (the Egyptian priest Zatchlas reanimates a corpse); (pseudo-)Clement, *Recognitions* 1.5.
42. These associations are explored in the next section on "The Polemical Construction of 'Magic.'"
43. Héliodore, *Les Éthiopiques*, vol. I, book 3.16.4.
44. "O blessed initiate of the sacred magic (*mageia hiera*)," PGM I.127; cf. PGM IV.210, 243, 2081, 2450. More commonly the rites are simply described as *mysteries*. See n. 125.
45. His initiation in Egypt first appears in Isocrates (*Busiris* 28).
46. Chaeremon was an Egyptian priest and philosopher of the first century CE. His description of the priesthood is preserved in Porphyry's *On Abstinence*. Translation in Fowden, *Egyptian Hermes*, 54–55.
47. See Dieleman, *Priests, Tongues, and Rites*, 6–7.
48. The last known hieroglyphic inscription dates to 394 CE. See Frankfurter, *Religion in Roman Egypt*, 248–249.
49. As Frankfurter suggests in "Magic of Writing," 207–208.
50. See Festugière, *La révélation d'Hermès Trismégiste*, vol. I, 89–90, with n. 1 (on the doctrine of sympathy), 197–216 (on the role of Bolus in shaping the tradition).
51. On Bolus and the lore of the magi, see Dickie, "Learned Magician." Cf. Beck, "Thus Spake Not Zarathustra," 553–564. Ostanes's initiation of Democritus in Memphis appears in the alchemical "Physical and Mystical Writings" (Beck, "Thus Spake Not Zarathustra," 562).
52. Pythagoras and Democritus: PGM VII.795; Democritus: PGM VII.167; XII.351.
53. Ostanes: PGM IV.2006; XII.121. Zoroaster also appears: PGM XIII.968.
54. Apollonius: PGM XIa. Bolus was an important source for the Pythagorean miracle stories collected by Apollonius in his *Historia Mirabilium*: see Burkert, *Lore and Science in Ancient Pythagoreanism*, 141, with n. 115. Apollonius, in turn, was followed by Porphyry and Iamblichus (Burkert, 100–101). However, as Burkert

notes (100, n. 10), the identification of Apollonius the paradoxographer with the sage of Tyana has been questioned.

55. *PGM* XIII.14–XIII.15. Cf. *PGM* III.500–III.530, on the material symbols of Helios (a different stone, tree, bird, and animal for each hour), and *PGM* VIII.13–VIII.14, VIII.53–VIII.59, on the secret materials of Hermes.

56. See, e.g., *PGM* XII.201–XII.69 and XII.270–XII.350. In the latter spell, the magician is further instructed to consecrate the ring by placing it, for a day, in the entrails of a rooster, i.e., a *solar* animal.

57. *Philopseudes* 33–36.

58. *PGM* IV.2446.

59. *Natural History* 30.3 (henceforth *NH*, cited by book and section of the Latin text).

60. Apollobex the Copt: *NH* 30.9. He also appears in *PGM* XII.121.

61. *NH* 30.11.

62. Ibid. 30. 9–30.10; cf. *NH* 24.156.

63. Ibid. 30.2.

64. Ibid. 30.13 (my translation).

65. Ibid. 30.9–30.10; cf. 24.160. On Pliny's allusions to "Democritus" and the magi, see Dickie, "Learned Magician," 172–192.

66. *NH* 24.156, 24.158–159; cf. 25.13. Pliny rejects the prevailing (and probably correct) opinion that this work – the so-called *De effectu herbarum* – was written by the physician Cleemporus (third century BCE). See also Dickie, "Learned Magician," 190.

67. *In Vatinium* VI.14.

68. Philostratus, *Life of Apollonius* VII.11.

69. Ibid. I.2.

70. Ibid. V.12.

71. Tacitus, *Annals* II.69 (my translation).

72. Gager, *Curse Tablets*, 30, n. 1.

73. Ogden, "Binding Spells," 19–20.

74. Ibid., 19.

75. Gordon, "Imagining Greek and Roman Magic," 206.

76. Ibid., 188.

77. Although, in reality, a rather limited part requiring special precautions. See the final section of this chapter for a full discussion of necromancy in the *PGM*.

78. In the background are complex beliefs concerning women as an embodiment of alterity, an important topic in its own right, which cannot be adequately treated within the parameters of this chapter.

79. Although the classical *goēs* was an ambivalent figure, he was nonetheless a religious functionary and his goals were not always disreputable. See, on this point, Johnston, "Songs for the Ghosts," 95.

80. Horace, *Epode* 5.1–5.10.

81. *Pharsalia* VI.425–VI.434.
82. Ibid. VI.525–VI.526, VI.5533–VI.5535.
83. Ibid. VI.557–VI.558.
84. See the useful discussion in Graf, *Magic in the Ancient World*, 190–194.
85. First elaborated by Eudoxus (fourth century BCE).
86. Smith, "Here, There, and Anywhere," 33.
87. See the collected articles in Athanassiadi and Frede, eds., *Pagan Monotheism in Late Antiquity*.
88. *Phars.* VI.744–VI.749 (my translation).
89. Gordon, "Imagining Greek and Roman Magic," 241–242.
90. The law against *veneficium* was enshrined in the *Lex Cornelia de sicariis et veneficiis* of 81 BCE. It is unclear whether it covered malefic *rites* or merely the deadly use of "magic potions." See Rives, "Magic in Roman Law," 319–320, with n. 20.
91. The text in question is the *Pauli Sententiae* – the "Opinions of Paulus," an influential jurist of the third century CE. But the commentary was not written by Paulus himself; it is "an epitome compiled at the end of the third century CE," (Rives, "Magic in Roman Law," 328).
92. *Pauli Sententiae* 5.23.18.
93. Ibid. 5.23.16 (following the translation of Rives, "Magic in Roman Law," 329).
94. This section builds on the treatment of late Platonic daimonology in Fraser, "Contested Boundaries." The term "daimonology" avoids the implicitly sinister connotations of "demonology," leaving open the moral ambiguities surrounding the pagan *daimones*.
95. Smith, "Here, There, and Anywhere," 28.
96. *Symposium* 202e–203a.
97. *On the Obsolescence of Oracles* 417a–417b.
98. Ibid. 417e–417f; cf. *On Isis and Osiris* 360d–360f.
99. *On the Obsolescence of Oracles* 417c.
100. Ibid. 417c–417d.
101. *On Superstition* 171b–171d.
102. *Isis and Osiris* 369d–369f.
103. Ibid. 370a–370c: the evil minions of Areimanios are created as rivals (*antitechnous*) to the gods of light. Despite the appeal to Persian religious concepts, it would be misguided to insist on the foreign character of this incipient dualism, as though it were unconnected to the inherent problems of demonology we have outlined.
104. *On the Eating of Flesh* 993b.
105. Bradbury, "Julian's Pagan Revival," 351.
106. Ibid. 335, building on the earlier work of Nilsson, "Pagan Divine Service in Late Antiquity."

107. Translation of Bradbury, "Julian's Pagan Revival," 336. On the theosophical oracles, see also Athanassiadi, "Philosophers and Oracles."
108. Athanassiadi, "Philosophers and Oracles," 53.
109. As Bradbury persuasively concludes in "Julian's Pagan Revival," 354–356.
110. *On Abstinence* II.45.4.
111. Ibid. II.45.1–II.45.3.
112. They "[dress] themselves up in the guise (*prosōpa*) of the other gods." Ibid. II.40.3.
113. Ibid. II.42.1–II.42.3.
114. Vegetable offerings to the planetary gods are acceptable (II.32). But the cult of the Supreme Deity should be immaterial (II.34).
115. On Augustine's polemical manipulation of the demonologies of Apuleius and Porphyry, see Fraser, "Contested Boundaries," 140–142.
116. For a full discussion and critique of this standard view, with references to relevant scholarship, see again Fraser, "Contested Boundaries," 132–136.
117. Phillips, "Nullum Crimen sine Lege," 262.
118. *PGM* IV.1928–IV.2005, IV.2006–IV.2125. For a close analysis of this necromantic series, see Faraone, "Necromancy Goes Underground."
119. *PGM* IV.1991–IV.2004; IV.2046–IV.2066. Faraone argues that the unusual use of the term *skyphos* ("cup") for "skull" in these spells reflects a concern to conceal forbidden necromantic rites (Faraone, "Necromancy Goes Underground," 278–281).
120. "[H]e will actually stand beside you through the night in dreams, and he will ask you saying 'Order whatever you wish and I do it.'" *PGM* IV.2052–IV.2054 (translation in Betz, *GMPT*).
121. Ibid. IV.2014–IV.2045.
122. Ibid. IV.1948–IV.1954 (translation in Betz, *GMPT*, slightly modified).
123. Ibid. IV.1955–IV.1989.
124. Graf notes that this "two-level system" is characteristic of the *PGM* (Graf, *Magic in the Ancient World*, 232).
125. On the magician as initiate, see, e.g., *PGM* I.127, IV.172, IV.477, IV.732, 2254, XII.94, XX.6. For the use of the language of the mysteries, with many additional references, see Betz, "Formation of Authoritative Tradition," 164.
126. *PGM* IV.741; cf. *PGM* IV.219–IV.221: "[R]eturn as lord of a god-like nature, perfected through this rite of *systasis*."
127. On the centrality of the rites of divination, see Gordon, "Reporting the Marvellous"; and Graf, "Magic and Divination."
128. The rite of *systasis* and the direct vision (*autopton*) are intimately linked. *Systasis* typically precedes and makes possible visionary experience: "[W]hen you are united with the god, say the formula for a direct vision." *PGM* III.698–III.699; cf. *PGM* IV.162–IV.170, IV.949–IV.950; *PGM* Va.1–Va.3.

129. *PGM* IV.162–IV.166 (translation in Betz, *GMPT*). Whereas Babylonian leca-nomancy was an interpretative technique – a matter of reading patterns in drops of oil – the Egyptian specialists employed it to induce visions. See Gordon, "Shaping the Text," 75; Graf, "Magic and Divination," 288.

130. See Gordon, "Reporting the Marvellous," 83–85.

131. *PGM* XIII.210–XIII.211 (translation in Betz, *GMPT*). For the revelation of the secret name, see also *PGM* II.127–II.128, III.159–III.160, XII.93–XII.94.

132. "I have been initiated into your name." *PGM* XIII.90.

133. "I invoke the immortal names ... which never pass into mortal nature and are not declared in articulate speech by human tongue" *PGM* IV.605–IV.610 (translation in Betz, *GMPT*); cf. XIII.763–XIII.764.

134. *PGM* XIII.872: "If I say it in full, there will be an earthquake." On the injunc-tion to keep the names secret, see Betz, "Secrecy in the Greek Magical Papyri," 160–166.

135. Rites for *systasis* or vision of the High God (inter alia): *PGM* II.73, III.197, III.494–III.611, III.698–III.700, IV.154–IV.285, IV.475–IV.829 (esp. IV.778ff), IV.930–IV.1114, Va.1–Va.3, VI.1–VI.47, VII.570–VII.574, XIII.343–XIII.646, XIII.646–XIII.734, XIII.734–XIII.1077.

136. *PGM* IV.2031–IV.2037: "I adjure you, dead spirit ... by his holy names"; cf. *PGM* IV.219–IV.227 (*systasis* with Helios enables necromancy), IV.435–IV.462, I.262–I.347.

137. *PGM* XIII.795–XIII.799 (translation in Betz, *GMPT*).

138. *PGM* IV.1971–IV.1973 (translation in Faraone, "Necromancy Goes Underground," 259–260).

139. *PGM* V.164–V.170; cf. *PGM* XII.261–XII.263, XIII.740–XIII.746.

140. Ibid. IV.2895.

141. Ibid. II.44–II.50.

142. See Graf, *Magic in the Ancient World*, 226–227.

143. *PGM* IV.1609–IV.1610; cf. *PGM* IV.1786–IV.1788: "I summon you by your great name – you who are unmoved by prayer (*aparaitēton*)."

144. Ibid. IV.2574–IV.2589 (my translation).

145. Ibid. IV.2505–IV.2519.

146. "[T]he preliminary course of preparation, prayers, invocations, constraints, the manifestation of the spirit, the petition and the dismissal ... [that form] has remained essentially the same from that day to this." Butler, *Ritual Magic*, 17.

147. The textual history of the *Testament* is complex. Certainly its main tradi-tions and demonology belong to the early centuries CE. The lore relating to Solomon's use of demonic assistants in constructing the temple was known to the author of the Nag Hammadi *Testimony of Truth* (IX.3, IX.70). That a core version was in circulation in Late Antiquity can be inferred: (a) from a reference to the *Testament* in a Christian work of ca. 400 CE, the *Dialogue of*

Timothy and Aquila; (b) from the survival of papyrus fragments; and (c) from the fact that the work is written in *koinē* Greek. For a translation, with an introductory essay touching on the problems of dating, see *The Old Testament Pseudepigrapha*, trans. Duling, vol.1.

148. See also Fraser, "Contested Boundaries," 149–150, where parallels with the Jewish *Sepher ha-Razim* are also noted.

Chapter 5

The Early Church

MAIJASTINA KAHLOS

For I should not have thought it likely that the same things
could be effected by magicians, even in appearance,
which he who was sent by God performed.[1]

Magic as a Discourse

There is no such thing as magic in and of itself. There are practices, beliefs
and texts that are given – usually by outsiders – the label of being magical. During recent decades, the distinction between religion and magic has
been challenged as untenable. Ancient practices often cross the boundaries between magic and religion that are traditionally followed by modern
scholarship.[2]

Magic functions as a discourse – and most often as a polemic. In order to
avoid essentialistic definitions, I shall treat the concept of magic as a discursive
category that is dependent on the perceiver. I understand magic as a socially
constructed object of knowledge whose content and formulations vary
according to different social contexts and circumstances.[3] For closer definitions of magic, terms such as "unsanctioned religious activity", "ritual power"
or "extra-cultic ritual practices" are preferable.[4] In modern scholarship, magic
has been used to refer to alternative, deviant, private and usually unaccepted
forms of ritual behaviour.[5] When I do make use of the term "magic", it is only
to illustrate how Late Antique writers employed the term in their condemnations of certain practices. I do not take a stand on whether these texts and
practices are magic or religion.

This chapter approaches magic in the early church from two angles. First,
I survey the accusations of magic and the social circumstances surrounding
these accusations. Second, I briefly discuss those Late Antique practices that
both ancient writers and modern scholars have called magical. In the first

part, I examine the ways in which different groups of people performing rituals were depicted as practitioners of magic. I begin my discussion with the accusations of magic against Christian groups and proceed to study the Christian turnover, in which accusations of magic were instead made against Graeco-Roman cults and practices. Moreover, internecine accusations between Christian groups are analysed. What is common to these accusations is that they arise in situations of mutual rivalry. The charge of magic was a frequently used weapon in intergroup and intragroup polemics. In the second part, the discussion of Late Antique practices deemed to be magical focuses on the competition for spiritual authority between ritual experts.

In the survey of the characterizations of early Christianity and Graeco-Roman cults as magical, I interpret these characterizations, or images, as mere reflections of reality. The label of magic tends to tell us more about the fears and anxieties of the accusers than about the people labelled as practitioners of magic. This image is a cognitive mental structure that can be compared to a map in a person's mind, portraying reality but not being real in itself. However, images become real in the sense that they influence human decisions and actions.[6]

In Late Antiquity, magic was used to marginalize those people who were accused of performing magic. I am examining the discourse of magic as part of the general "discourse of ritual censure" in Late Antiquity.[7] The category of magic belonged to the arsenal of polemical strategies against rival and often deviant forms of rituals, texts and behaviour. Magic was by no means the only label; these practices were also branded as idolatrous, superstitious, pagan, barbarian, heretic, Manichaean and so forth. In the manner of magic, all of these categories were versatile and constantly mutating. Therefore, it is imperative not to read Late Antique accusations at face value but rather to interpret them within the context of rhetorical invective and the rivalry for spiritual authority between ritual specialists.

Images and Accusations: Early Christianity Designated as Magic

The narratives in the New Testament canonical gospels and the Acts of the Apostles indicate that the actions of Jesus and his followers were at times labelled as magic by outsiders. Jesus is reported to have cast out demons, healed the sick and even raised people from the dead. In the eyes of outsiders,

Jesus resembled a typical miracle-worker In the gospels and the Acts, the aim of miracle accounts was to manifest Jesus's power and show that this power was of the right kind – divine, not demonic.[8] It was vital for the writers of the gospels and the Acts to anticipate and refute any possible accusations of magic, for instance, by depicting Jesus and his followers as the opponents of magic and demons.[9] In the gospels of Matthew and Luke, the writers efface those elements still present in the gospel of Mark that were commonly regarded as the characteristics of magic and therefore could be used as evidence of magic against Jesus's adherents. Such elements were words of power and ritualistic elements. In the miracle narratives depicted in the gospel of Mark (7.33, 8.23), the use of saliva is an essential part of Jesus's healing miracles, but in the later gospels, it has been glossed over. For the later gospel writers, the saliva became a problem because outside observers would in all probability have regarded it as a magical element.[10]

In the Jewish tradition, Jesus, the rival wonder-worker, was disparaged as a practitioner of magic, and Christianity was disparaged as being permeated with magic.[11] In the eyes of Graeco-Roman outsiders, Christian practices resembled widespread stereotypes of magic. The second-century Platonist Celsus decried Jesus as a magician and compared him to charlatans who performed their tricks for money in marketplaces.[12] Eusebius of Caesarea, Arnobius of Sicca, Lactantius and Athanasius of Alexandria in the fourth century and Augustine of Hippo in the early fifth century report slanders of magic targeted against Jesus.[13] Furthermore, in the eyes of some Graeco-Roman observers, Christian miracle-workers' use of the name of Jesus in their healing practices and exorcisms resembled many practices that were commonly considered magical. Jesus, who had been convicted and crucified as a criminal, could therefore be closely associated with *biaiothanatoi*, people who had died a violent death and whose spirits were invoked in necromancy.[14] The question that was raised decades ago of whether Jesus was a magician is deemed a fruitless inquiry because of its essentialistic nature.[15] One can answer both yes and no – yes in the eyes of outsiders, and especially his rivals, and no in the eyes of his adherents. Needless to say, similar replies could be given in cases of other ancient ritual experts, as well.[16]

In addition to Jesus, the Apostles and other Christian leaders were also labelled as practitioners of magic – even as late as the fourth century by the Emperor Julian. According to Julian, the Apostle Paul outdid every other wizard and charlatan.[17] Charges of ritual murders and cannibalism were connected to these accusations against Christians. These charges are reported by Christian apologists who not only refute them extensively but also issue counttercharges against Graeco-Roman cults and practices.[18]

Origen and Celsus on the Power of Names

Origen was a Christian apologist who addressed allegations of magic against Christians by reframing the terms. Celsus had accused Christians of attaining their powers by using the names of demons in their incantations. In his reply, Origen articulates a distinction between the practices of sorcerers and those of Christians. He states that, whereas magicians use the names of evil spirits, Christians employ the name of Jesus. Origen asserts that Christians obtain their power not by incantations, but by "the name of Jesus" accompanied by the proclamation of the narratives which relate to Jesus. Origen writes that demons have often been cast out of people by the repetition of these names and narratives, adding that the name of Jesus has such power over evil spirits.[19] Here Origen refers to the common ancient practice of using histories (called *historiolae* in modern religious studies) about divine figures, briefly recounted in a ritual context, in healing and exorcism.[20]

In his defence, Origen attempts to articulate a difference. He acknowledged that both Christians and those labelled as magicians aimed to attain power by using the names of supernatural beings, gods and spirits regarded either as evil or good. Sacred names, including the name of Jesus, were abundantly employed in incantations, exorcisms and amulets – Jewish, Christian and non-Christian alike.[21] According to widespread belief, the sacred names were direct manifestations of the supernatural powers and pronouncing the right name in suitable circumstances achieved the epiphany of the supernatural power. Like Celsus, Origen acknowledges the power of names, arguing that "these names therefore, when they are pronounced with the attendant train of circumstances that is appropriate to their nature, are possessed of great power". This applies, for example, to the Egyptian names, which are, Origen claims, efficacious against certain demons, and to other, Persian, names that have a similar effect on other demons. A similar power is found in the names of angels, such as Michael, Gabriel and Raphael, and in Jesus's name, which has expelled myriad evil spirits from human souls and bodies.[22] Because of the power attached to divine names, Christians were forbidden to utter the names of other gods (in the eyes of Christians, demons).[23] Origen declares that a Christian would rather die than pronounce the name Zeus. Zeus was no real god, but he might be a powerful demon posing a real threat to humans.[24]

Magic in the Second- and Third-Century Context of Competition

The label of magic is a marginalizing strategy that reveals the presence of contest over religious authority.[25] Each group declared itself as acting with divine authority, but rivals had to be reviled as charlatans or, even worse, as the accomplices of demons. The mutual accusations thus reflect the rivalry between charismatic miracle-workers and other ritual specialists in the religious marketplace of the Empire.

For instance, the rivalry with other Jewish ritual experts is depicted in the canonical Acts of the Apostles, in which religious rivals are labelled as magicians. In the episode of the seven sons of Sceva (Acts 19:8–19:20), young itinerant Jews try to exorcize demons in the name of Jesus and Paul but fail and are shamefully beaten by the demons. The purpose of the account is to contrast the Apostles, especially Paul, with the flawed Jewish ritual specialists.[26]

There are a number of similar situations in the late second-century and early third-century Apocryphal Acts of the Apostles.[27] Rivalry is apparent in the confrontation between the Apostle Peter and another wonder-worker, Simon the Samaritan, depicted in the apocryphal Acts of Peter. Simon the Samaritan appears already in the canonical Acts of the Apostles (8:5–8:25), where he is depicted as a performer of magic. In the later Christian tradition, he is called Simon Magus.[28] In the Acts of Peter, the Apostle Peter and Simon are engaged in a duel of miracles in which both aim to manifest superiority with signs of power – miracles for the insiders, feats of magic for outsiders. During the course of the second and third centuries, Simon Magus developed into the prototype of a heretic and a magician. In the internecine rivalry between Christian groups, mainstream Christian writers vested the figure of Simon Magus with elements of their own second- and third-century Christian rivals. Thus, magic connected with the image of Simon was an essential tool in reviling rivals in these disputes.[29]

In the Latin epitome of the Acts of Andrew, the Apostle Andrew, who performs miracles in Patras, is regarded as a magician by the local people.[30] Similarly, in the Acts of Thomas, people first take the Apostle Thomas to be a magician because he performs healings and exorcisms. Magic is by no means a harmless label, as can be seen in the Acts of Paul: the Apostle Paul has a profound influence on a young woman called Thecla with his Christian message and is consequently interpreted as having enchanted her. Paul gets into trouble because Thecla's fiancé brands him a sorcerer and incites the populace against him.[31] The Apostle Peter faces similar dangers in the account of the Acts of Peter, as a crowd is about to burn him as a magician in the middle of the dramatic contest with Simon Magus. Ultimately, after Peter's victory, the populace plans to burn Simon instead.[32]

In the contest over religious authority, ritual experts attempted to distinguish themselves as the genuine prophets and downplay any features that could be associated with magic. Hence Christians aimed at distancing themselves from their rivals, whom they labelled as frauds and tricksters.[33] One way of making the distinction was to appeal to unselfish motives, building on the idea that charlatans always aim at personal glory and financial profit, whereas the genuine prophets refuse any reward. In the Apocryphal Acts, Andrew is depicted as declining an offer of reward and Thomas likewise refuses money.[34] The writers attempt to make it clear that their holy men do not perform miracles for their own self-advancement, whereas their rivals, the magicians, do. Tertullian proclaims that Christians cast out demons, thus benefiting all people, without reward or price.[35] However, this seemingly clear dichotomy can be deconstructed, given that there is bargaining involved in all social action: a deity, patron saint or miraculous healer anticipates veneration or respect in exchange for miracles. This is apparent in the Acts of Andrew, in which the Apostle demands that a girl's parents forsake idols in exchange for the healing of their daughter.[36]

Another way of manifesting genuine miracle-working is to underline that Christian holy men perform their miracles without any spectacle of hocus pocus. For instance, in the Apocryphal Acts of the Apostles, it is stressed that the Apostles do not make a show of their miracles but act in modest company – in contrast to impostors such as Simon Magus. There is a clear dialectic relationship between publicity and secrecy. On the one hand, Christians needed to accentuate the modesty and privacy of their activities; on the other hand, they were at risk of being labelled as a surreptitious sect and consequently as practitioners of magic. In Roman society, religion was emphatically public, whereas all secret and private action was regarded with suspicion and could end up being categorized as magic. Graeco-Roman writers such as Celsus accused Christians of acting in secrecy. Pliny the Younger reports that Christians convene in secret and at night.[37] Therefore, we see Christian wonder-workers depicted as acting with great publicity: the scenery of the confrontation between the Apostle Peter and Simon Magus is set in the Forum Romanum, and the Apostle Andrew performs his miracles in a theatre.[38]

Images and Accusations: Christians' Attitudes towards Other Religions

Accusations of magic functioned both as a defence and assault against competitors, and, therefore, polemics and apologetics between religious groups were filled with mutual charges and countercharges. In a rhetorical twist, Christian apologists refuted accusations of magic against Christians and threw the same accusations back at their accusers.

Christian writers held two views on the origin of magic. The first strand followed widespread Graeco-Roman ideas. According to this view, magic had been invented by humans.[39] The second view followed the Jewish tradition, according to which magic had been taught to humans – human women in particular – by the fallen angels.[40] Justin Martyr identifies the traditional Graeco-Roman gods with the fallen angels mentioned in Genesis (6:1–6:4). According to the myth, the fallen angels mingled with human women and taught them magic arts. Demons who were the descendants of the fallen angels and mortal women subjugated humans to themselves, in part by magical writings, in part by fears and chastisement and in part by teaching humans to offer sacrifices, incense and libations. Consequently, sacrifice, incense and libation, the most essential parts of Graeco-Roman religious life, were labelled as magic.[41] This interpretation of Genesis 6:1–6:4 was derived from the Jewish apocryphal Book of Enoch, in which the fallen angels are said to have taught human women "charms and enchantments and the cutting of roots".[42] In the early fourth century, Lactantius refined the theory of demons, making a distinction between demons of heaven, who were the fallen angels, and demons of the earth, who were the descendants of the fallen angels and whom pagans worshipped as their gods in temples. The latter were the demons that the magicians invoked to deceive humans.[43]

The question of whether magic was construed as a human invention or demonic machinery was by no means trivial. In the Christian interpretation of magic as demonic design, magic was not just human charlatanism and trickery, but it was also based on commerce with demons. Consequently, magic was demonized as the work of the Devil.

The Demonization of Graeco-Roman Cults

Christian writers connected magic with demons and, consequently, designated Graeco-Roman cult practices as magic and asserted that they dealt with evil spirits.[44] Tertullian brands Graeco-Roman gods as demons and their priests as magicians. Demons cause diseases and then they remove them, thus cunningly pretending to perform miracles. In this way, he explains, demons make people believe that they are gods.[45] In the early fifth century, Augustine expressed similar views, stating that demons were able to do things that were beyond human capabilities, for example, causing and curing illnesses and predicting the future.[46] As a result, demons misled humans with false miracles and signs so that humans would regard them as gods.[47] The connection between Graeco-Roman religions and magic as demonic deceit is clearly expressed in *The City of God*, in which Augustine discusses Numa Pompilius, the mythical king of the Romans. He represents Numa Pompilius making a pact with demonic forces, thus portraying the legendary founder of the Roman civic religion as a magician.[48]

The demonization of rivals was commonplace in the ancient polemic between religious, philosophical and ethnic groups. In their polemic, Christian writers routinely referred to the presence of demons not only in Graeco-Roman cults and practices but also in all of societal life. Tertullian depicts the surrounding Roman world as filled with demons.[49]

In the Late Antique world-view, demons functioned as the explanation for diseases and other misfortunes of human life. Socially undesirable action and physically strange behaviour (such as disorder and disability) were explained as the result of possession by demons. The early Christian fixation on demons contributed to the darkening of the Late Antique view of the cosmos. However, demons were not a Christian innovation, because supernatural beings that were either good or wicked had also been part of the Graeco-Roman world-view. Christian authors adopted the term "daimon / daemon", which had already been used by Graeco-Roman writers, but they provided the term with a wholly negative connotation. Thus, the Christian input was to repeatedly declare that all demons were evil.[50] Augustine of Hippo declares that in reality demons are spirits "whose only desire is to do harm, who are completely alien from any kind of justice, swollen with arrogance, purple with envy and full of crafty deception".[51]

The Christian contribution was to transform the traditional Graeco-Roman gods into utterly hostile and treacherous demons. In the fourth and fifth centuries, the identification of the traditional Graeco-Roman gods with demons became routine: Christian writers continually referred to the Graeco-Roman gods as demons (*daemonia, daemones*), impure spirits (*spiritus immundi*) and wicked angels (*angeli maligni*).[52] This had a fundamental impact on populating the cosmos with malignant forces. John Chrysostom saw demons abounding in the world between earth and heaven.[53]

Valerie Flint has argued that, in addition to the clearly derogatory use of condemnation, attributing human action to demons could also have a exculpating effect on human weakness and function even as an act of compassion. The Christian hermit Anthony, for instance, excuses from responsibility a young man who has attacked him, explaining the offensive behaviour as the result of demonic possession.[54] A comparable interpretation can be adduced of the story of a Christian girl enchanted by a love charm from a young man. The girl, who earlier committed to chastity as a virgin of God, becomes possessed and is beyond the control of her parents. The holy man Hilarion is asked for help, and he casts out the demon that has troubled the family's life. The possession by demons is used as a means of expelling blame away from the girl herself.[55] Similar accounts of demons and spells causing unacceptable behaviour are found in Graeco-Roman literature.[56] It is true that the concept of the demon could thus serve as a means of escaping responsibility. However, on the other side of the demon coin, the very same Christian leaders who marketed their religion as the redemption of humankind from enslavement to demons stressed the ubiquity of these forces and, ironically enough, enhanced their influence on humans to a greater extent than ever before.[57]

Images and Accusations: Marginalizing Other Christians

In the internecine polemic between Christian groups, Christian writers aimed at undermining the legitimacy and divine authority of rival groups by accusing them of magic. The constructions of heresy and magic were intimately associated with each other. Tertullian connected heretical groups and their leaders closely with magic.[58] As Kimberly Stratton points out, in the first- and second-century polemic between Christian groups, charges of magic were targeted mainly at men. In these accusations, which were often combined with allegations of sexual promiscuity, women appear as the victims of male sorcerers.[59] The second-century heresiologist Irenaeus of Lyon attacks the leader of a rival Christian group, Marcus, accusing him of magical impostures. According to Irenaeus, Marcus used love potions and spells as his magical tools to lead women astray and seduce them.[60]

Furthermore, Irenaeus claims that Marcus used an assistant (*parhedros*) demon through which he uttered prophecies. Irenaeus contrasts the orthodox Christian leaders (that is, Irenaeus and his fellows), who receive their authority from God, with this heretic Marcus, who obtains his power from demons. Justin hurls similar attacks against Simon the Samaritan, who is said to have performed magic "through the art of demons", and against Marcion, who is claimed to act "with the aid of demons".[61] Irenaeus admits that rival Christians do perform miracles, but he questions the nature of their miracles: he claims that they do not act "either through the power of God or in connection with the truth", but only lead people astray. They cannot perform real miracles, healings or exorcisms because they can cast out only those demons that they have themselves sent into people.[62]

In the fourth century, Priscillian, Bishop of Avila, was charged by his ecclesiastical rivals of performing incantations, obscenity, magic and Manichaeism. After years of disputes in church councils, the case was consigned to the imperial court. There, under questioning and probably torture, Priscillian confessed that he had studied obscene doctrines, held nocturnal gatherings with shameful women and prayed while naked. He was sentenced to death for magic (*maleficium*) in 385.[63] In the charges against Priscillian, the elements of nocturnal, thus clandestine, gatherings, sexual promiscuity, sorcery, heretical doctrines and Manichaeism were all intertwined in a concoction of dangerous magic.[64]

Another connection between heresy and magic was woven in 398, when the imperial court led by the chamberlain Eutropius issued a decree against a Christian group called the Eunomians. The Eunomians were compared with sorcerers. This was the first time that a Christian sect deemed as heretical was explicitly associated with magic in legislation. In the imperial decree, mere possession of heretical books were paralleled with the crimes of sorcery. As in other cases, accusations of magic emerged in a situation of rivalry: the Eunomians were considered a political threat to Eutropius's governing clique at the court.[65]

Late Antique Dichotomies and Theories of Magic

Christian ideas of magic and superstition were partly based on earlier Roman views. For the Roman elite and legislators, the Roman civic religion was *"religio"*, whereas foreign, provincial or popular beliefs and practices were bundled under the term *"superstitio"*. Furthermore, beliefs and practices tarred with the brush of magic were assembled into the package of *superstitio*. This concept of *superstitio* was nonetheless a wider concept than magic was. *Superstitio* as such was not illegal, whereas magic was often understood as illegal activity that could be punished by death.[66]

Christian authors, however, worked out a subversion of the Roman concept. In this subversion, the Roman civic religion and other non-Christian cults were deemed *superstitio*, and the Christian cult was regarded as the only proper *religio*. As was discussed earlier in this chapter, the Roman religion and other non-Christian cults were considered magic, because, in the eyes of Christians, they constituted the worship of demons. However, this association between paganism (i.e. polytheistic cults) and magic construed by Christian writers did not immediately break through into Late Roman daily life. Many practices and celebrations constituted an essential part of life in urban and rural communities. In fact, polytheistic cults and magic were not easily coupled. Therefore, two competing interpretations of the term *superstitio* coexisted, for instance, in the fourth-century imperial legislation. However, from the late fourth century onwards, *superstitio* was increasingly understood as referring to polytheistic cults and practices, and to a great extent it was associated with magic.[67]

The package consisting of three protean concepts – paganism, *superstitio* and magic – was gradually established. Ecclesiastical leaders enhanced this package in their argumentation: the most prominent author was Augustine, who in *On the Christian Doctrine* delineated the concept of *superstitio* as comprising "anything established by humans that refers to the making and worshipping of idols, or the worshipping of creation or any part of creation as God, or to consultations and certain agreed codes of communication, settled in collusion with demons".[68] This means that *superstitio* altogether included: the worship of idols, meaning most polytheistic cults; the worship of creation or any part of creation as deity, that is, all philosophical interpretations of the world or its elements as divinities; magical practices; astrology; and divination that involved dealings with demons.

Augustine's model mixed together polytheistic religions (including the Roman civic religion – the former *religio*) with magic under the term "*superstitio*". Because Augustine, in the same manner as other Christian writers, identified the gods of polytheistic cults with evil demons, all of the religious activities dealing with these god-demons were considered magic. Banished into the sphere of magic, polytheistic religions were now transmitted to the area of unsanctioned activity. Augustine also lumped divinatory practices together with magic, and, after Augustine, the association of magic with divination became customary in Late Antique treatises on magic and idolatry. For example, the link between idolatry, magic and various forms of divination appears in the early seventh-century discussion *De magis* by Isidore of Seville.[69]

Augustine explains that the fundamental difference between *religio* and *superstitio* lies in the intentions of the practitioner. He stresses that *religio* is practised in public for unselfish purposes and for the common good, "for the sake of the neighbour and for the love of God". This is contrasted with those who practise *superstitio* out of personal interests and private reasons. Augustine developed a theory of two communication systems in which religion represents the public system of signs shared by a whole community, whereas magic is a private code restricted to a few individuals. Furthermore, religion unites people in the service of God, whereas magic is based on a pact with demons. The forms of performance in rituals as such are not as important as the intention of the participants. If there was an agreed communion with demons, the rituals were condemnable as magic; the agreement with God was acceptable religion. Spells were signs of a contract with demons, whereas sacraments were signs of communion with God.[70]

It is worth noting that the dichotomy between the public and the private, as well as that between the interests of the community and personal aspirations, resemble earlier Roman ideas of the divergence between *religio* and *superstitio*. In that case, *religio* had referred to the official and public religious rituals of the Roman state, whereas *superstitio* had represented the private and unofficial religious sphere.[71] I am therefore inclined to see Augustine's distinction between the public and the private as an important continuation of the Roman ideas of *religio* and *superstitio*.

Magic functioned as the category for unsanctioned practices for other ancient thinkers, too. The early fourth-century Neo-Platonist Iamblichus developed a distinction between religion and magic in which *theurgy* represented good and acceptable religious activity, whereas *goeteia* was objectionable witchcraft.[72] *Theurgy*, which Iamblichus regarded as the supreme form of religion, was classified by Christian writers as magic: Augustine combined *magia* (*mageia*), *goetia* (*goeteia*) and *theurgia* (*theurgeia*) into a single category of magic.[73]

One of the ways in which the boundaries of religion and magic were elaborated in Christian literature was through discussion of the passage regarding Moses and the pharaoh's magicians (Exodus 7:8–8:15).[74] Origen articulates a distinction between the miracles of Moses and the trickery of the pharaoh's magicians based on the difference between divine and demonic power. In *On Different Questions*, Augustine construes a dichotomy between genuine miracles and magical feats by expounding on the confrontation between Moses (and Aaron) and the Egyptian magicians. Here again Augustine explicates the difference between public and private aspirations: God's servants seek the good of their community and God's glory, whereas magicians only look for their own benefit and glory. Moreover, miracles and magic are based on different authorities. Magicians have a private contract with demons, but God's holy men perform miracles as public service.[75]

Magic and Law

In the Roman Empire, religious groups that fell outside of the public civic religion were at risk of being charged with magic. This was a matter of serious concern for Christian groups from the first to the early fourth centuries, especially at the turn of the third century, when there was a clear hardening of popular attitudes towards and imperial repression of practices deemed as magic. The same fears were faced by adherents of polytheistic cults from the fourth century onwards, because the attitudes towards people labelled as magicians were harsher under the Christian emperors.

We do not know of any law that expressly prohibited the practice of magic during the Principate, but there was a Republican law called *lex Cornelia de sicariis et veneficiis* and some decisions of the senate that may have been applied as the basis for legal accusations of magic during the Empire.[76] The exposition of the *lex Cornelia* in Paulus's *Sententiae*, a third-century work of jurisprudence, shows that the law was interpreted to penalize many practices tarred with the designation of magic. Paulus's *Sententiae* mentions that those guilty of the magic art (*magicae artis conscios* – that is, those involved in magic without being themselves magicians) were to be thrown to beasts or crucified, and magicians themselves (*ipsi ... magi*) were to be punished by being burnt alive. This exposition could be applied against many kinds of religious deviance.[77]

There was significant continuity in the attitudes of the Late Roman imperial administration towards private religious activities. The privacy and secrecy of rituals, especially divinatory practices, were considered a threat to imperial rule.[78] Christian emperors proscribed private and secret rituals, such as privately performed sacrifices and divination. Constantine forbade haruspicina and proscribed sacrifices carried out behind closed doors. He nonetheless explicitly allowed haruspices to perform their rituals in public, even though he disparagingly called their practice *superstitio*. Constantine's decree did not classify divination as part of the category of magic, but even so, private and secret gatherings and rituals were always at risk of being associated with magic.[79]

Constantine's son and successor, Constantius II, combined divination and magic in his legislation. In 357, he decreed that nobody was to consult a diviner, an astrologer or a soothsayer. He ordered that augurs and seers were to fall silent, as were Chaldaeans, magicians and "all the rest" who because of the greatness of their crimes were called malefactors by the people. The inquisitiveness (*curiositas*) of divination had to be silenced.[80] The association of magical and divinatory practices is repeated in the early fifth-century legislation of Honorius and Theodosius II.[81]

Late Antique legislators made – probably as a compromise – a distinction between harmful magic and harmless, beneficial magic, often permitting practices and divination that were regarded as harmless and even beneficial to the community. Constantine, for instance, distinguished between practices that were "remedies sought for human bodies" and devices for protecting harvests against rains and hail – these were allowed – and magic that was aimed at killing or seducing someone – this was forbidden. In the case of permitted remedies and protective devices, it was explained, no one's safety or reputation was damaged; on the contrary, they sheltered divine gifts and human labour from harm. It was stressed that the performer acted innocently and the act was beneficent.[82] Similar emphasis on intention and outcome appears in a decree of Valentinian I that allowed the performance of benevolent haruspicina. It was only forbidden to practise it in a damaging way.[83]

Not only were polytheistic cults, divination and astrology packed with magic into a single parcel, but those Christian sects that rivalled Nicene Christianity also became associated with magic in imperial legislation. In the decree issued against the Eunomians in 398, which was discussed earlier in this chapter, the possession of Eunomian heretical books was identified as the crime of *maleficium*; the codices of their crime were to be immediately burned.[84] Another example is the decree by Theodosius II in 435 in which he announces that the Nestorians should be called Simonians because they imitate Simon Magus's crimes in deserting God. In this way, Nestorians were labelled as followers of Simon the Samaritan, who in the Christian tradition had been identified with the arch-heretic Simon Magus, and were thus connected with magic.[85]

Magic as a Political Weapon

The association of magic with paganism and heresy in imperial legislation shows how the imperial government aimed at harnessing magic for various social, political and religious goals. By using magic as a political weapon, they aimed at controlling knowledge of the future. Since the early Principate, Roman emperors had wanted to restrain unsanctioned private soothsaying, which they believed to be connected with conspiracy and treason.[86]

Suspicions sometimes led to politically motivated criminal proceedings. Accusations of magic were often levelled, not only by emperors against persons they regarded as threats but also by senators, courtiers and bishops against their political and ecclesiastical rivals.[87] One of those accused during the reign of Constantius was Athanasius, Bishop of Alexandria, who was charged with illicit divination and "other practices abhorrent to the religion over which he presided".[88] Accusations were linked with the great ecclesiastical disputes as well as imperial politics. The fourth-century historian Ammianus Marcellinus reports of several trials of magic under the reigns of Valentinian I and Valens.[89] At the Second Council of Ephesus in 449, a Syrian bishop, Sophronius of Tella, was charged by his colleagues with astrology, divination, "the vaticinative art of the pagans", and Nestorian "heresy".[90] Another case was the Christian ascetic Priscillian, who, as we saw earlier this chapter, was prosecuted for heresy, Manichaeism and sorcery.

At first glance, one forms the impression of an increased number of magic trials in the fourth century. As Peter Brown has shown, there was hardly any increase in the phenomenon called magic but rather a growing concern of the fourth-century emperors for eliminating political rivals and controlling sources of knowledge in their power struggles. The magic prosecutions were a symptom of the people's and rulers' fears – which were real – rather than any increase in unsanctioned practices – which could have been either real or imagined. The concept of magic was suitably vague and could therefore be adjusted and used in varying circumstances.[91]

The Contest for Ritual Power in the Fourth and Fifth Centuries

After the Constantinian turn, even though (and probably because) Christianity was gradually being established as the prevailing religion in the Empire, the contest for authority between miracle-workers and ritual experts continued. This is visible in the fourth- and fifth-century debates on magic and miracles. In Christian accounts, miracles are the powerful acts of a Christian holy man, bishop or saint, whereas the representatives of the other side (be they polytheists or rival Christians) are involved in magical acts.

Jerome's account of the Christian holy man Hilarion illustrates the roles of magic and miracle in the contest between religions. The episode takes place in Gaza, which Jerome depicts as aggravated by the rivalry between Christians and polytheists, the worshippers of Marnas. A Christian charioteer named Italicus asks Hilarion for help in a circus race, in Jerome's words, "not so much for damaging his opponent as for protecting himself". To Hilarion's objections that one should not waste prayers for such trivialities, Italicus replies that he is acting for the public good. He makes his personal concern a public cause for Christianity: he struggles against "the enemies of God" who would rejoice at the defeat of Christ's church rather than his own defeat. Moreover, Italicus appeals, "a Christian could not employ magic, but rather he could seek for help from the servant of Christ". Persuaded by this argument, Hilarion has his drinking cup filled with water and given to Italicus, who then sprinkles the stable, horses, charioteers, carriage and the barriers of the course with the water. Consequently, Italicus wins the race, which makes the people of Gaza, Christians and pagans alike, cry that the god Marnas has been overcome by Christ. In the eyes of his adversaries, Hilarion resorted to counter-magic, and, in the sequel, they demanded that he should be executed as a Christian sorcerer (maleficus).[92] In Jerome's narrative, competition is taken on many levels: first, on the level of the circus between Italicus and his opponents[93]; second, in the Gazan community between the worshippers of Christ and Marnas; and finally, on the cosmic level between the Christian God and demons.

In Christian narratives, miracles competed in strength and efficacy: the deeds of Christian holy men were depicted as being far greater than those of other miracle-workers. Both Christian miracle-workers and their rivals achieve their acts with the help of supernatural allies. As Fritz Graf remarks, "the difference between the miracles of magicians and the saints, then, is not one of action or cosmology, it is one of magnitude". Augustine articulates the difference as the comparison between the powers of the Christian God and those of lesser divine beings: magicians perform their feats by invoking inferior names.[94] Moses, who was used as a paradigmatic figure in discussions on the boundaries between religion and magic, was also employed to demonstrate the supremacy of God's holy men in comparison with any polytheist ritual expert.

Within a worldview filled with greater and lesser deities, and angels and demons, there was plenty of room for miracles. Augustine understood miracles as events not contrary to nature, but rather contrary to what is known of nature. They appear to be miracles to humans because they are beyond human knowledge. Christian writers could concede that magicians – rival experts – performed miracles, too. Augustine admits that polytheistic experts were able to perform miracles, but he decries these as being based on collaboration with demons and thus distorted.[95] They are phenomena of the wrong sort.

The authenticity of miracles could also be contested. Augustine states that pagan miracles lacked reliable testimony. He mocks pagan miracles as deception and explains that it was no difficulty for demons to create illusions and thus make people believe in them. He gives miracles connected with the cult of Fortuna Muliebris as an example that he rebuts as a mere product of female gossiping. Another case is the ever-burning lamp of Venus, which he describes as simple trickery. This shows that not only demons but also humans with technical skills could achieve illusions that appeared to ignorant people to be miracles. For his part, Augustine had to counter doubts concerning Christian miracles. Contemporary polytheists contested the authenticity of mythical miracles, such as the resurrections of Christ and Lazarus and the restoration of Jonah from the whale.[96]

Self-Assurances and Condemnations

When discussing the debate between Origen and Celsus, I briefly referred to the Christian self-image (or rather, that of the ecclesiastical elite) according to which Christians neither practise magic nor employ any props in their rituals. Origen asserted that Christians exorcized demons without any strange arts of magic or incantations, using only prayers and simple adjurations. In Origen's eyes, Christians did not employ spells but only "the name of Jesus and other words from the sacred Scriptures". Origen stressed that these exorcisms were mainly performed by unlearned Christian folk. Likewise, Tertullian declared that Christians did not rely on astrology, divination or magic.[97]

Christian writers were also inclined to stress that Christian charismatics hardly needed any equipment in their wonder-working. In Late Antique discussions on rituals, a number of Graeco-Roman, Jewish and Christian writers alike accentuated that material equipment belonged to baser practices, whereas rituals with only verbal formulae represented a more advanced level. Thus, the fewer props, the better.[98] In the contest for authority between religious groups, the rituals of one's own group were regarded as superior in this aspect, as well. John Chrysostom states that good Christians only resorted to words in their practices, but he nonetheless acknowledges the sign of the cross as being among the acceptable means.[99] As part of this self-image, rival groups were seen as resorting to all possible apparatuses and mumbo-jumbo. Justin asserted that the Christian use of the name of God was superior to the spells and incense of pagan and Jewish exorcists.[100]

The Late Antique epigraphical and literary evidence, as well as Greek and Coptic papyri, nonetheless indicate that many Christians made ample use of amulets, incantations and rituals that church leaders deemed as magical (Figure 5.1). Bishops, who frequently forbade these practices, insisted on the magicless self-image: genuine Christians did not get involved in magic. Therefore, Origen evades the charges of magic made against Christians by identifying the practitioners of magic as heretical Christians.[101] The Christian self-image has been so convincing that modern scholars have been at odds

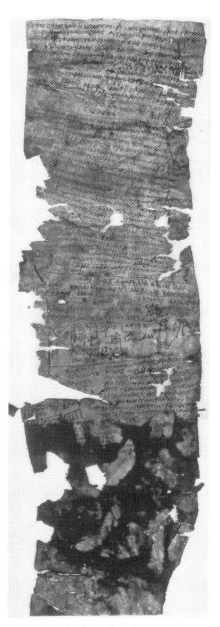

FIGURE 5.1. Spells and recipes written in Coptic on leather, from the London Hay "Cookbook", sixth or seventh century CE, Thebes, Egypt. British Museum 10391. The text is translated in Meyer and Smith, *Ancient Christian Magic*, no. 127. © The Trustees of the British Museum.

with Christian writers such as Julius Africanus, who in his encyclopaedic work *Kestoi* shows ample knowledge of various remedies, incantations and rituals traditionally regarded as magic.[102] Julius Africanus seems to have dwelled in the wide area of ambiguity that did not fit into the clear boundaries set by church leaders.[103]

The vehement self-assertion and condemnation of ecclesiastical writers become more understandable against the background of Christian diversity in the fourth and fifth centuries. The repeated prohibitions of church councils and the complaints of bishops make it clear that many rituals and practices judged as magical continued in the fourth to the seventh centuries and onwards. Again, magic functions as the concept for setting up boundaries when Christian identity, orthodoxy and orthopraxy are negotiated and redefined.

The canons of church councils produced lists of forbidden practices, thus defining proper behaviour through exclusion. In the late fourth century, the Apostolic Constitutions list ritual experts who are excluded from the church, including, among others, magicians, enchanters, astrologers, diviners, wild beast charmers, mendicants, charlatans, makers of amulets, charmers and soothsayers.[104] The Council of Ancyra in 314 forbade people to bring diviners (*divini*) and especially soothsayers (*sortilegi*) into their houses in order to cast out evil (*malum*), detect evil deeds (*maleficia*) or perform pagan purifications (*lustrationes paganorum*).[105]

In the making of boundaries between the accepted religious activities (sacraments) and the unaccepted ones (magic), even members of the ecclesiastical elite were not always capable of delineating borderlines clearly enough. Church leaders and council canons complained about sorcery among the clergy. The late fourth-century Council of Laodicea forbade the clergy to make amulets and to act as magicians, enchanters, mathematicians or astrologers.[106]

Emperors such as Constantius II were troubled about magic that they feared was being practised for seditious purposes at the imperial court. The historian Olympiodorus reports that in 421 a ritual expert marketed his services to the Emperor Honorius at the imperial court, assuring him that he would drive away the barbarians "without resort to weapons". The expert was ultimately put to death.[107] It is nonetheless worth remembering that in the fifth and sixth centuries, the compound accusation of magic and paganism was used as an effective tool in the political struggles in the imperial courts. As Ralph W. Mathisen remarks, the accusations of magic and divination were a ritualistic way of segregating the problematic elements of the community.[108]

The Rise of Magic or Ritual Experts in Rivalry?

This setting and resetting of boundaries by church leaders has stirred modern scholarly discussion on the magicization of Christianity in Late Antiquity and the early Middle Ages. The idea of magicization is connected to the complaints of bishops and church councils about recent Christian converts who brought with them magical or pagan elements to Christianity.

The ecclesiastical elite was inclined to define as pagan, superstitious and even magical those rituals and beliefs that they despised and disliked. Augustine portrayed certain practices as pagan elements that recent converts had carried with them into the church after Constantine's conversion. According to Augustine, these new converts had not abandoned the revelry and drunkenness that belonged to pagan celebration. In this way, he constructs an image of a pure and authentic pre-Constantinian Christianity and represents it as a historical truth.[109] Both Augustine's model of the Christian past and his ideas about the magical use of Christian sacraments have often been adopted in modern scholarship.[110]

I find the idea of magicization problematic. First, it is based on the untenable assumption (already discussed in the introduction of this chapter) that magic and religion are separate and separable phenomena. Second, it implies that before the Late Antique transition, in Christianity there were no such practices and beliefs that ecclesiastical writers, the elite, outsiders and modern scholars together deem as magic. What is inferred here is an essentialistic concept of an authentic primordial Christianity originally untainted by this magic.[111] This presupposition takes at face value the self-assertive claims of a magicless Christianity conveyed by Justin, Tertullian, Origen, Eusebius, Augustine and other writers.

Instead of the rise of magic or magicization, we should speak of the increasing interest in the supernatural in general or in the rise of religion.[112] Moreover, rather than sketch out Late Antique Christianity, especially its local popular forms, as magic (magical survivals) or pagan (pagan survivals),[113] we could analyse various contextualized Christianities – local religious worlds in their different socio-political contexts. Instead of speaking of the simplification of Christian theological concepts and doctrines, we should explore the local creative applications.

David Frankfurter offers an alternative way of perceiving the competitive and complementary relationship between phenomena traditionally distinguished as magic and those distinguished as religion in Late Antiquity. He outlines the struggle in terms of rival ritual experts – between peripheral/

regional experts and local experts. Many of these conflicts are depicted in Late Antique hagiography, Eastern and Western alike, as clashes of regional holy men and bishops with local priests.[114]

The account in "The Life of Theodore of Sykeon", which describes a sixth-century holy man in Galatia, serves as an example in which the rival local expert is branded as a magician and thus distanced from the holy man, whose ritual power is characterized as legitimate. Theodore is involved in competition for authority with another holy man, Theodotus, who lives in the same village and whom the hagiographer calls "a skilled sorcerer, thoroughly versed in wickedness". Theodotus attempts to kill Theodore, driving demons against him at night while he is asleep and later infecting his food and drink. He, however, fails in all of these attempts, acknowledges the greater power of the Christian God and is converted to Christianity. In the sequel, he casts his magical books into the fire.[115]

For the average Late Antique person, the distinction between a holy man and a magician was not too clear. The saint and the sorcerer appear uncomfortably close together. The difference between the legitimate and illegitimate use of supernatural power was also treated in the question-and-answer genre of literature.[116] The boundaries between holy men and magicians were further blurred, because, especially in Egypt, the holy man – the charismatic monk – was often a former pagan priest (in Christian eyes, a sorcerer). Likewise, the writers of ritual texts deemed as magical were probably local priests, deacons and monks.[117]

Signs and Techniques in Rivalry

Techniques such as apotropaic signs, protective objects and rituals, words of power and divinatory practices were not branded as exclusively Graeco-Roman or Jewish or Christian, but rather they were shared by different (often competing) religious groups and sub-groups. Along these lines, I now turn to a number of examples of rituals and objects often condemned or regarded as magical either by the ecclesiastical elite or modern scholarship with the purpose of treating them not as magic, but as belonging to the wide spectrum of methods for coping with the difficulties of human existence and the crises of life.[118]

The cross emerges as a powerful apotropaic sign in Late Antiquity. In amulets it was believed to defend the wearer against the attacks of malign spirits, illnesses and the evil eye. The sign of the cross (often with formulae such as "where there is a cross, no evil can harm" and "by placing your cross, Christ ...

we expel all kind of evil") was incised over entrances in order to protect houses against demons.[119] Theodore of Sykeon is reported to have saved the crops of a Galatian village from damage by hail by uttering a prayer and sticking four crosses of wood into the ground.[120]

Christian writers depicted the cross as the victorious sign opposing the enemies of Christianity. Athanasius (with Anthony of Egypt as his mouth-piece) exulted in the triumph of Christianity over paganism, declaring that the oracles, the charms of the Egyptians and the delusions of magicians ceased and were overturned as soon as the cross of Christ arose. Martin of Braga contrasts the competing signs – the cross and the devilish signs given by birds (*alia diaboli signa per avicellos*).[121] However, a number of ecclesiastical leaders disapproved of the use of the cross in amulets. John Chrysostom reprimands Christians who use amulets with the sign of the cross and the letters of incan-tations. The cross is covered in shame, and the holy mystery is trampled.[122]

In spiritual warfare between religions, the sign of the cross was an effec-tive weapon both in defence and attack. Athanasius insisted that by making the mere sign of the cross, one was able to banish the deceits of demons. He also remarked that where the sign of the cross appeared, magic was weak and witchcraft had no strength.[123]

The sign of the cross was used as an apotropaion to cast out demons from shrines that had been altered into Christian churches. Polytheistic cult places and images were exorcized because demons (the rival, Graeco-Roman gods) that were believed to dwell in shrines and statues had to be expelled.[124] The church historian Rufinus writes that in Alexandria, the images of the Egyptian demon (that is, the god Serapis) were demolished and replaced with the sign of the cross in the walls, entrances and windows of houses.[125]

Likewise, the rite of baptism functioned as an apotropaic ritual that pro-tected against evil forces and brought both bodily and spiritual health and suc-cess. In Late Antiquity, the human body and soul were increasingly perceived as the combat zone in the struggles between supernatural forces of good and evil. In this cosmic conflict, the rite of baptism was thought to exorcize demons from baptismal candidates and mark them as belonging to Christ only. In the Christian baptismal formulae, the catechumen was expected to renounce the Devil, his band and his angels.[126]

In the fourth century, the Eucharist was regarded with great awe; the consecrated bread and wine were thought to possess great supernatural power and were consequently used for various protective and healing purposes, espe-cially for curing eye diseases. It is no wonder that the unsanctioned use of the Eucharist caused trouble for ecclesiastical leaders. The Council of Saragossa in 380 was alarmed by the practice of consuming the Eucharist outside of a church.[127]

The context of rivalry is apparent in the discussion of prayers and incantations by Late Antique Christian writers. In the manner of Irenaeus of Lyon, many later writers stress that Christians utter only pure, sincere prayers, not spells (as their rivals associated with magic do, it is implied). Martin of Braga nonetheless explained to his parishioners that Christian prayers were a form of sacred incantation (*incantatio sancta*) and they replace the incantations (*incantationes*) of magicians and sorcerers.[128]

Christian prayers, incantations or whatever term we decide to employ for ritual utterances have been preserved, for example, from Late Antique Egypt and Hispania. They include curative and protective texts, curses and love spells, covering all kinds of everyday issues, directed not only to the Christian God but also to angels, saints and Biblical figures.[129] In particular, the archangels Michael, Gabriel, Raphael and Uriel, as well as the Biblical figures of Abraham, Jacob, Moses and Solomon are invoked. The invocations of angels were considered with suspicion by church leaders. For instance, Irenaeus of Lyon already condemned the practice. Furthermore, the church councils (for instance, the late fourth-century Council Laodicea) forbade the excessive worship of angels.[130]

Wearing amulets was a wide-spread everyday practice all over the Mediterranean area, in Graeco-Roman, Jewish and Christian circles alike. Amulets with the names of the angels, incantations, Biblical or Homeric verses, small images and letters were designed to provide their wearers with general protection or shield them against specifically named troubles, such as fever, headache or colic.[131]

Bishops complained that Christian sacred objects like the codices of the gospels and the cross were used for various purposes, such as physical healing. For instance, Augustine blames his parishioners who have visited sorcerers for receiving remedies for their illnesses. He advises his listeners to use the gospel rather than an amulet. Even though he is not pleased with the idea of using the codices of the gospels for healing, they are nonetheless preferable to amulets.[132]

The contest over protective objects and rituals is apparent in the depictions by Gregory of Tours: Gregory remarks approvingly that his father was protected from "the violence of bandits, the dangers of floods, the threats of turbulent men and attacks from swords" by a golden medallion with relics that he carried around his neck. Elsewhere he asserts that one has to follow the sign of the cross, the cleansing of baptism and the patronage of the martyrs, not a soothsayer who whispers incantations, casts lots and ties amulets around the neck.[133] In this contest of powers, the presence of the holy man himself could be understood as a talisman that protected communities from harm and evil. For instance, Sulpicius Severus claims that Martin's prayer protected fields near Sens from hail and after his death the hailstorms returned.[134]

Whereas Augustine was distressed about the use of amulets (even though sacred objects were better than the pagan alternatives), Ambrose of Milan was not that strict with phylacteries. He writes with praise of how the Emperor Constantine's mother, Helena, had sent her son a bridle and a diadem prepared from the nails of Christ's cross. With these objects, Helena provided him "the support of divine protection so that he might take his place in battles unharmed and be without fear of danger".[135] Before long, other Christian alternatives were found: the potency of the saints' relics (for instance, a martyrs' blood) in healing illnesses, protecting crops and defeating demons was gradually acknowledged.[136] This made the relics a requisite material for local communities and churches. A seventh-century law of the Visigoths forbids the violation of tombs for the purpose of extracting healing devices (remedium).[137]

Divinatory practices linked with magic were frequently mentioned by Late Antique bishops. Their complaints indicate that despite the prohibitions of secular and church authorities, Christians consulted various diviners and astrologers – or that their bishops at least believed that they were doing so. For instance, John Chrysostom disapproves of Christians who visit professional soothsayers and examine the flights and songs of birds as omens.[138]

Intense rivalry on the authority and influence of oracles and prophecies continued in Late Antique communities. A sharp demarcation was drawn between Christian prophecy and pagan oracles. Augustine contrasts these sanctioned and unsanctioned predictions in his praise of the Emperor Theodosius I. Even in hard times, Theodosius did not lapse into sacrilegious and forbidden inquisitiveness (ad curiositates sacrilegas atque inlicitas), that is, magical divination. Instead, he sent to the Egyptian hermit John to ask about the future and received assurance of victory. In another campaign, the emperor fought his enemy with confidence because he had obtained another prophecy for victory.[139]

The consultation of revered texts was a popular way of seeking solutions for everyday problems or of inquiring about the future. One could do this by opening a book at random and interpreting the first line upon which one's eyes settled as an oracular prophecy. One could also choose at random one of many slips upon which verses from revered books had been copied. The most common texts employed were those by Homer and Biblical writings.

Furthermore, there were collections of oracles, for instance, the so-called *sortes Astrampsychi*, in which there were lists of questions to which answers were allotted. There is ample evidence for the Christian use of lots (*sortes*) from Homeric and Biblical writings alike.[140]

Church leaders and councils both approved and disapproved of the practice of *sortilegium*. Augustine reproaches the use of the Bible for soothsaying for everyday purposes, but, as in the case of using the gospels as healing devices, he thinks it better to read the future by taking at random a text from the gospels than to consult what he calls the demonic (*ad daemonia consulenda*). Furthermore, it is "the worldly affairs and vanity of this life" that he despises, not the practice as such.[141]

Conclusion

I have examined magic in the early church as a discursive social construct whose content is dependent on the perceiver. In Graeco-Roman antiquity, magic functioned as a boundary-making concept in the demarcation between sanctioned and unsanctioned cultic behaviour.

The labels of magic have been analysed as a way of drawing distinctions between insiders and outsiders. First, we have discussed the charges of magic against Christian groups by Graeco-Roman outsiders, then against Graeco-Roman cults by Christian writers and, finally, against Christians by other Christians. What is common to these accusations of magic is the presence of mutual contest over religious authority. In this rivalry, each group considered itself to be practising legitimate forms of piety, whereas the competitors were usually labelled as mere charlatans. The charges of magic inform us about the increasing interest in ritual experts in the religious marketplace of the Empire from the first to the third centuries.

Christian writers held two views of the origin of magic. The first view adapted the Graeco-Roman ideas of the human origin of magic, whereas the second one followed the Jewish tradition, according which magic had been taught to humans by the fallen angels. Consequently, in the Christian interpretation of magic as demonic design, magic was not just human trickery, but it was based on commerce with demons. A single category consisting of three vague concepts – paganism, *superstitio* and magic – was established. The most prominent author to argue for this model was Augustine of Hippo, who in *De doctrina Christiana* bundled together Graeco-Roman religions with magic under the term "*superstitio*". In his theory of magic, Augustine sided with imperial legislation against magic.

The competition for spiritual authority between ritual experts continued after the Constantinian turn as Christianity was gradually being established as the prevailing religion in the Empire. The contest is present in the fourth- and fifth-century debates on magic and miracles. What is striking about these debates is the similar techniques shared by holy men and magicians. Christian writers nonetheless stressed that Christian holy men did not need any equipment in their miracle-working. Despite this magicless Christian self-image, the Late Antique literary, epigraphical and papyrological evidence shows that many Christians made ample use of amulets, incantations and rituals that ecclesiastical leaders deemed to be magical. The repeated complaints of bishops and church councils probably indicate that many rituals and practices judged as magical continued in the fourth to the seventh centuries.

Notes

1. *Pseudo-Clementine Recognitions* 3.57, trans. Smith in *Ante-Nicene Fathers Pseudo-Clementine* 210.
2. To mention but a few scholars, see Segal, "Hellenistic Magic: Some Questions of Definition", 349–375; Gordon and Marco Simón, *Magical Practice*, introduction; Meyer and Mirecki, *Ancient Magic and Ritual Power*, introduction; Remus, "'Magic', Method, Madness", 258–298; Meyer and Smith, *Ancient Christian Magic*, introduction, 1–5; Frankfurter, "Dynamics", 159; Janowitz, *Icons of Power*, xiv–xviii; and Smith, "Trading Places", 16.
3. I follow the theoretical consideration of magic as a discursive formation posed by Stratton, *Naming the Witch*, xi, 2–3, 14–17, 23; also Gordon and Marco Simón, *Magical Practice*, introduction, 5. According to Stratton, *Naming the Witch*, 16, magic as a discourse provides "an understanding of magic that bridges the gulf between those who reject the use of magic as a concept altogether and those who seek a universal heuristic definition".
4. Unsanctioned religious activity: Phillips, "Nullum Crimen sine Lege", 262–263; ritual power: Meyer and Smith, *Ancient Christian Magic*, introduction, 1, and Gordon and Marco Simón, *Magical Practice*, introduction, 4; extra-cultic ritual practices: Frankfurter, "Dynamics", 279.
5. For surveys of the debates on the term "magic" regarding antiquity in particular, see Versnel, "Some Reflections", 177–192; Remus, "'Magic', Method, Madness", 258–272; Stratton, *Naming the Witch*, xi, 4–12; Aune, "Magic in Early Christianity," 1511–1516.
6. For the image as the concept used in the historical research of images (imagology), see Fält, *Looking at the other*, introduction, 7–12; Kahlos, *The Faces of the other*, introduction. For similar observations, although not using the

theoretical concept of the image, see Stratton, *Naming the Witch*, 17; and Ritner, "Parameters", 59.

7. The term is used by Frankfurter, "Beyond Magic", 256.

8. For the miracles in the New Testament and lists of miracles in early Christian writings, see Kelhoffer, *Miracle*, 199–225: e.g. Mark 16:17–16:18 and *Pseudo-Clementine Recognitions* 3.60.

9. E.g. Luke 4:1–4:13 (the testing of Jesus in the wilderness); Luke 11:14–11:23; Mark 3:22; Matthew 12:24 (the Beelzebul dispute); Luke 23:2; Acts 13:11 (Paul's curse of a rival, Bar Jesus); Acts 19:8–19:20 (the seven Jewish exorcists).

10. For discussion on magic in the gospels and the Acts, see Garrett, *Demise of the Devil*; Aune, "Magic", 1523–1539; Hull, *Hellenistic Magic*, 73–141; Smith, *Jesus the Magician*, 21–44, 94–139; Kee, *Miracle*, 156–170.

11. E.g. in the Babylonian Talmud (*Shabbath* 104b), it is implied that Jesus brought his magical skills from Egypt. The narrative of Jesus's visit to Egypt in Matthew 2:12–2:14 was probably turned into an accusation of apprenticeship in the magician's art when he was in Egypt.

12. Celsus in Origen, *Against Celsus* 1.28, 1.38, 1.46, 1.68 (magician), 1.6 (demonic powers), 2.9, 2.14, 2.16, 2.48–2.49, 3.44.

13. E.g. Arnobius, *Against the Pagans* 1.43 reports of accusations that Jesus stole the names of the powerful angels from Egyptian temples.

14. Johnston, *Restless Dead*, 127; Ogden, "Binding Spells", 16. *Biaiothanatoi* in the magical papyri: *Papyri Graecae Magicae* 1.248, 2.48, 4.1390, 4.1950.

15. I am referring here to the discussion started by Morton Smith (*Jesus the Magician*), who regarded Jesus as a magician, thus following the outsiders' label of Jesus as a performer of magic but failing to take into account the views of insiders. For the critique against Smith, see Remus, "'Magic', Method, Madness", 264; Garrett, *Demise of the Devil*, 24–31; and Garrett, "Light on a Dark Subject and Vice Versa", 144–150.

16. In a comparable way, Manichaean texts see the founder-figure Mani as the great healer – whereas outsiders portray him as a magician. BeDuhn, "Magical Bowls", 425–426.

17. Julian, *Against Galileans* 99E. Accusations of magic are reported still in the early fifth century in Augustine, *On the Harmony of the Gospels* 1.9.14, 1.10.15, 1.11.17.

18. E.g. Justin (*First Apology* 14.2) describes his conversion to Christianity as a turning away from magic. Justin (*First Apology* 50.12) aims at portraying the Apostles as teachers, whereas rivals (26) are depicted as charlatans.

19. Origen, *Against Celsus* 1.6.

20. The *historiola* is understood as the performative transmission of power from a mythic realm articulated in narrative to the human present. Such *historiolae* in Christian use included, e.g., gospel stories and saints' legends; see Meyer and Smith, *Ancient Christian Magic*, nos. 8, 13, 43, 47–49, 78, 83, 91, 95. For the

use of *historiolae* in Christian texts of ritual power, see Frankfurter, "Narrating Power", 457–476, esp. 464; van der Vliet, "Satan's Fall", 401.

21. The name of Jesus used in incantations and exorcisms: Mark 9:38; Luke 9:49; Origen, *Against Celsus* 1.6, 1.25, 6.40; *Papyri Graecae Magicae* 4.3007–4.3086; in rabbinic literature: Jerusalem Talmud *Shabbath* 14d.41–14d.44; *Avodah Zara* 2.2.40d, 42–45. For the use of the name of Jesus in exorcisms, also in Graeco-Roman ritual texts, see Aune, "Magic", 1545–1546; Ogden, "Binding Spells", 31.

22. Origen, *Against Celsus* 1.24–1.25, 5.45. See Bosson, "À la croisée", 236–237, on the power of names in Coptic ritualistic texts.

23. E.g. Tertullian, *On Idolatry* 20–21, banned the use of divine names.

24. Origen, *Against Celsus* 4.33–4.34. See Janowitz, *Icons of Power*, 19–43, esp. 36–37, and Sfameni Gasparro, "Gnosi e magia", 32–34, on the power of divine names.

25. Social conflict and contest in the accusations of magic is stressed by, e.g., Garrett, *Demise of the Devil*, 4; Stratton, *Naming the Witch*, 7; Segal, "Hellenistic Magic", 370.

26. For the presence of contest in the Acts of the Apostles, see Garrett, *Demise of the Devil*, 90–95; Stratton, *Naming the Witch*, 7, 124.

27. Acts of John in fragments is dated to about 160, Acts of Paul to shortly after 160, Acts of Peter around the turn of the century (preserved in a late fourth-century Latin version), Acts of Andrew around the turn of the century and Acts of Thomas around 230. See Bremmer, "Magic in the *Apocryphal Acts of the Apostles*", 51–52.

28. For the narrative figure of Simon Magus, see Luttikhuizen, "Simon Magus", 39–51; Czachesz, "Who is Deviant?", 84–96; and Bremmer, "Magic", 62–65, referring to Simon's role as a kind of bogeyman for Christians. Tuzlak, "Magician", 416–426, surveys the early Christian tradition on Simon Magus.

29. Stratton, *Naming the Witch*, 125–129; Knust, *Abandoned to Lust*, 146, 154.

30. Acts of Andrew (Latin) 12, 18. The surviving Acts of Andrew (Latin version) is the sixth-century reworking by Gregory of Tours of a lost Latin translation. Bremmer, "Magic", 53.

31. Acts of Thomas 20. Acts of Paul 15. There is also a nuance of sexual exploitation here as in many other accusations of magic; cf. the image of promiscuity that Irenaeus of Lyons paints of his rivals Marcus and Valentinus.

32. Acts of Peter 28.

33. Cf. Philostratus, who in the third century composed the biography of the first-century polytheist wonder-worker Apollonius of Tyana and, in a manner comparable to the writers of the gospels, aimed at depicting Apollonius's acts of power as genuine miracles and distancing him from any accusations of magic. Luck, "Witches", 130, 134.

34. Acts of Andrew (Latin) 7, 15–16; Acts of Thomas 20. Bremmer, "Magic", 55.

35. Tertullian, *Apology* 37.

36. Acts of Andrew (Latin) 16, see also 7. For the economy of healing miracles, see Neyrey, "Miracles", 22–41.

37. Celsus in Origen, *Against Celsus* 1.7, 8.17. Pliny the Younger, *Letters* 10.96.

38. Acts of Peter 22–23; Acts of Andrew (Latin) 13.

39. E.g. Tertullian, *Treatise on the Soul* 57.

40. E.g. in addition to the view of magic as human invention, Tertullian (*Apology* 22.2–22.3) also promotes the idea of magic as the design of the fallen angels.

41. Justin, *First Apology* 5, 9–10, 14, 25, 54; *Second Apology* 5.

42. Flint, "Demonisation", 293–294; Knust, *Abandoned*, 122–123.

43. Lactantius, *Divine institutes* 2.14–2.16.

44. For the demonization of polytheistic cults and practices, see Kahlos, *Debate and Dialogue*, 172–177; Kühn, *"De divinatione"*, 299–307; Flint, "Demonisation", 279–281.

45. Tertullian, *Apology* 22.

46. E.g. Augustine, *On the Divination of Demons* 3.7, 4.7–4.8, 5.9.

47. The deception of demons: Augustine, *On the Harmony of the Gospels* 1.12.18; *On the Divination of Demons* 6.10; *City of God* 8.22, 18.18.

48. Augustine, *City of God* 7.34–7.35.

49. Tertullian, *On the Shows* 8.7, 10.6, 10.10; *Apology* 29.1.

50. For Greek writers such as Plutarch and Porphyry of Tyre, daimons were supernatural intermediary beings between gods and humans; there were both beneficent daimons and harmful, wicked ones. For the development of the beliefs in daimons/demons, see, e.g., Kahlos, *Debate*, 173–174, with bibliography.

51. Augustine, *City of God* 8.22. Augustine stresses that there are no good demons: 6.4, 9.2, 9.19.

52. E.g. Augustine, *City of God* 2.4, 2.10, 2.25, 2.29, 3.10, 4.1, 4.16, 4.29.

53. John Chrysostom, *Homilies on 1 Thessalonians* 11 in vv. 19–22.

54. Athanasius, *Life of Anthony* 64. Flint, "Demonisation", 290–291, writes that "the weight of a person's own responsibility is, or may be, significantly reduced".

55. Jerome, *Life of Hilarion* 12. Gordon, "Imagining Greek and Roman Magic", 202–203, gives an excellent analysis of the story.

56. Eunapius (*Lives of the Philosophers* 469; ed. Wright, 410–413) writes about the female philosopher Sosipatra, who was attacked by a love spell concocted by an enamoured young man and subsequently suffered from cravings in her breast. A renowned Neo-Platonist, Maximus of Ephesus, cast out the daimon/demon that troubled Sosipatra. As Trombley, *Hellenic Religion*, 63–64, explains, it was easier to confront the otherness of the daimon than it was to sustain the selfness of the inappropriate desires of an upper-class woman.

57. For the redemption of mankind from enslavement to demons, see, for example, the Apostle Paul in Galatians 4:3–4:9 on the elemental powers of the world.

58. Tertullian, *Prescription against Heretics* 33.12, 43.1, 44.5–44.6.

59. Stratton, *Naming the Witch*, 108, 130–140. For charges of sexual promiscuity, see Knust, *Abandoned*, 143–157.

60. Irenaeus, *Against Heresies* 1.13.1, 1.13.5, 7.41.1–7.41.6. For Irenaeus's attack on Marcus, see Förster, *Marcus Magus*, 54–63, 132–138, 360–361.

61. Irenaeus, *Against Heresies* 1.13.3. Justin, *First Apology* 26.

62. Irenaeus, *Against Heresies* 1.4.7, 2.31.2–2.32.4.

63. Sulpicius Severus, *Chronicle* 2.50.8; *Canons of the Council of Saragossa* col. 315–318. For the charges against and trials of Priscillian, see Chadwick, *Priscillian*, esp. 138–148; Burrus, *Making of a Heretic*, 79–98; Van Dam, *Leadership*, 88–106; Girardet, "Trier 385", 577–608; and Breyfogle, "Magic", 435–454.

64. Sexual promiscuity was a stock slander against rival religious groups. In their polemic, mainstream Christian writers linked Manichaeism closely with magic: Burrus, *Making*, 48–49; Humfress, "Roman Law", 130–131.

65. *Codex Theodosianus* 16.5.34 (in 398).

66. For the concept of *superstitio* in Roman discourse, see Gordon, "Religion", 237, 253; Gordon, "*Superstitio*", 72–94; and Kahlos, "*Religio*", 389–408, with further bibliography.

67. For the development and ambiguities of the concept of *superstitio* in the fourth century, see Salzman, "*Superstitio*", 172–188.

68. E.g. Augustine, *On Christian Doctrine* 2.20.30, 2.23.36. In Augustine's model, superstitious divination included augury and *haruspicina* that had traditionally been sanctioned and official activities in Roman society. For Augustine's concept of *superstitio*, see Markus, *Signs and Meanings*, 131–139, 146; Dufault, "Magic and Religion", 77–79; and Graf, "Augustine and Magic", 97–98.

69. Isidore of Seville, *Etymologies* 8.9. Klingshirn, "Isidore", 64–81.

70. Augustine, *On Christian Doctrine* 2.23.36.

71. Gordon, "Imagining Greek and Roman Magic", 210, 215; Kippenberg, "Magic in Roman Civil Discourse", 151–156, 159–160.

72. Iamblichus, *On the Mysteries* 2.11, 3.26, 3.28, 3.31. Dufault, "Magic and Religion", 73–76.

73. Augustine, *City of God* 10.10. The Late Antique Christian labelling of *theurgy* as magic, especially by Augustine, has exerted a strong influence on modern scholars (e.g. Barb, "The Survival of Magic Arts", 100–125, and even Flint, "Demonisation", 286–288) who have traditionally regarded *theurgy* as a form of magical activity (usually high or white magic). For the discussion, see Knipe, "Recycling", 338–339.

74. In Jewish, Christian and Graeco-Roman circles, Moses was renowned as a mighty miracle-worker imbued with Egyptian wisdom. Several spells and writings were attributed to Moses; Gager, *Moses*, 140–161.

75. Origen, *Against Celsus* 2.49–2.51. Augustine, *On Different Questions* 79.1–79.4.

76. *Lex Cornelia de sicariis et veneficis* was issued in 81 BCE by the dictator Lucius Cornelius Sulla in order to restore public order after the civil wars. It was targeted at murderers and poisoners. A performer of magic could be placed in the same category as a poisoner (*veneficus*). Kippenberg, "Magic in Roman Civil Discourse", 147–149.

77. *Sententiae* of Paulus 5.23.14–5.23.18. Rives, "Magic in Roman Law: The Reconstruction of a Crime", 317–335; Rives, "Magic, Religion, and Law", 47–67.

78. Rives, "Magic in Roman Law", 317–321, 331–335; Fögen, *Enteignung*, esp. 254–321.

79. *Codex Theodosianus* 9.16.1 (in 319), see also 9.16.2 (in 319) and 9.18.4 (in 321).

80. *Codex Theodosianus* 9.16.4 (in 357).

81. E.g. *Codex Theodosianus* 9.16.12 (in 409) *de maleficis et mathematicis*. For the connection between magic, divination and astrology, see Graf, "Magic and Divination", 284–295.

82. *Codex Theodosianus* 9.16.3 (in 319 / 321). The rituals of power for protecting fields against hail were a widespread tradition throughout the Mediterranean: e.g. in a Christian phylactery from Late Antique Sicily (late fourth–late sixth century), Jesus Christ, angels, pagan deities and mysterious beings are invoked to protect a vineyard against the demon that raises hail (Manganaro, "Nuovi documenti", 57–67). For Christian phylacteries and spells against hail, see Nieto, "Visigothic Charm", 552–565, with further evidence.

83. *Codex Theodosianus* 9.16.9 (in 371).

84. Ibid. 16.5.34 (in 398). For the destruction of magical books, see Speyer, *Büchervernichtung*, 130–133.

85. *Codex Theodosianus* 16.5.66 (in 435).

86. For attempts at controlling and building the imperial monopoly of knowledge, see Fögen, *Enteignung*, esp. 254–289. For the interconnection between politics, religious policies and magic, see Wischmeyer, "Magische Texte", 95; and Funke, "Majestäts- und Magieprozesse", 145–151.

87. For example, in the middle of power struggles in the imperial court, the Neo-Platonic philosopher Sopater was accused of binding favourable winds by magical means and thus preventing the supply of corn from arriving in Constantinople; he was executed by Constantine (Eunapius, *Lives of the Philosophers* 463, ed. Wright, 384). For the political use of accusations of magic, see Escribano Paño, "Heretical Texts", 123–125; Marasco, "Magia e guerra", 112–117.

88. Ammianus, *Res gestae* 15.7.7–15.7.10.

89. Ibid. 26.4.4, 28.1.8, 28.1.50, 29.1.41, 29.2.3–29.2.4, 30.5.11. Ammianus depicts Valentinian I as an utterly paranoid ruler. Even though the magic trials are historical, one ought not take everything in Ammianus's reports at face value but also analyse them as a drama embroidered in grand style by the

historian. For doubts on Ammianus's reliability, see Wiebe, *Kaiser Valens*, 96–97, 129–130, 173–177. For the trials in the reign of Valentinian I and Valens, see Lenski, *Failure of Empire*, 25–26, 105–106, 211–213; and Funke, "Majestäts- und Magieprozesse", 165–175.

90. The Syrian acts of the Robber Council of Ephesus in 449, in Perry, *Second Synod*, 190–197. See Peterson, "Geheimen Praktiken", 333–345.

91. Brown, "Sorcery", 25–26.

92. Jerome, *Life of Hilarion* 11.

93. Lead curse tablets that were used especially to harm the horses and chari- oteers of rival teams have been excavated in ancient circus areas, e.g., in Carthage and Beirut; see, Jordan, "New *Defixiones*", 117–134; Jordan, "Magica Graeca", 325–335, especially a tablet (no. 4) from Beirut in which "holy angels" (*hagioi angeloi*) are invoked to hold back rival horses and charioteers. The majority of competition curses were targeted against rivals in circus races from the second century onwards.

94. Graf, "Augustine and Magic", 94. Augustine, *On Different Questions* 79.2.

95. Augustine, *City of God* 10.16, 21.8, 22.8.

96. Augustine, *Letters* 102.30–102.32; *City of God* 4.19, 21.6–21.7.

97. Origen, *Against Celsus* 1.6, 7.4. Tertullian, *Apology* 35.12.

98. For discussion on equipment and verbal formulae, see Janowitz, *Icons of Power*, 14–16.

99. John Chrysostom, *Homilies on Colossians* 8.5 in v. 3:15.

100. Justin, *Dialogue with Trypho* 85.3.

101. Origen, *Against Celsus* 1.57.

102. Julius Africanus's interest in protective, healing and execrative rituals and objects led some modern scholars to doubt whether he was Christian at all. For the remedies and rituals in *Kestoi*, see Thee, *Julius Africanus*, 267–299; and Meissner, "Magie", 17–37.

103. For grey areas in Late Antiquity, see Kahlos, *Debate*, 26–42. As Wallraff, "Magie und Religion", 51, remarks, the alleged discrepancy between Africanus's reli- gious conviction and magic disappears when it is placed against the wide spec- trum of different contents and institutions of second-century Christianity.

104. *Apostolic Constitutions* 8.4.32.

105. *Canons of the Council of Ancyra* can. 24 = cap. 71, in Barlow, *Martini Opera*, 140. Klingshirn, "Isidore", 68.

106. *Canons of the Council of Laodicea* can. 36.

107. Constantius II: *Codex Theodosianus* 9.16.6 (in 358); Honorius: Olympiodorus, fragment 36, in Blockley, *Historians* 200–201. See Escribano Paño, "Heretical Texts", 124–125, for further examples.

108. Mathisen, "Crossing", 310–311, 320, referring to Caesarius of Arles.

109. Augustine, *Letters* 29.9. For an illuminating discussion on Augustine's redefi- nitions, see Brown, "Christianization", 662–663.

110. The words of Weltin (*Athens and Jerusalem*, 6) may serve here as an example of the idea of magicization in scholarly discussions: "[H]umble converts to Christianity naturally carried over pagan elements into their new faith" with the attempt "to transfer the potency of old idols to new Christian sacramentals like the sign of cross, shrines, icons, and relics". Even the title of Valerie I. J. Flint's magisterial *The Rise of Magic* (1991) reveals a similar idea of magicization.

111. For a criticism of the idea of magicization, see Markus, *Signs*, 142–143; Kahlos, *Debate*, 112.

112. Cf. Johnston, "Sacrifice", 36, who regards the increasing interest in the magical as part of the wider interest in religion.

113. E.g. Flint, *Rise of Magic*, 4–6, speaks of magical survivals instead of paganism or primitive religion because she wants to avoid the burdens of implicit condemnation that these words carry with them. However, the word "magic" may carry an even heavier burden.

114. Frankfurter, "Beyond Magic", 276–278: Frankfurter, "Dynamics", 161–164.

115. *Life of Theodore of Sykeon* 37–38 (Festugière, *Théodore de Sykéon* I, 34; and Dawes and Baynes, *Three Byzantine Saints*, 113–115). Trombley, "Paganism", 336, 340; and Frankfurter, "Beyond Magic", 276–277, with a number of examples.

116. Stolte, "Magic", 110.

117. For the continuity, see Frankfurter, "Ritual Expertise", 127–130; Frankfurter, "Dynamics", 168, 172; Velásquez Soriano, "Orthodox Belief", 603, 618.

118. Cf. the title of Graf, "How to Cope with a Difficult Life. A View of Ancient Magic".

119. Engemann, "Verbreitung", 42–43, with examples.

120. *Life of Theodore of Sykeon* 144 (Festugière, *Théodore de Sykéon*, vol. I, 45; Dawes and Baynes, *Three Byzantine Saints*, 181). Trombley, "Paganism", 340–341.

121. Athanasius, *Life of Anthony* 79. Martin of Braga, *Reforming the Rustics* 16. Martin refers to the bird signs of the traditional Roman augury. Velásquez Soriano, "Orthodox Belief", 606, 611, 614.

122. John Chrysostom, *Homilies on Colossians* 8 in v. 15.

123. Athanasius, *On the Incarnation of the Word* 47; *Life of Anthony* 78.

124. The statues of gods were associated with great supernatural powers. For Late Antique Christian views of idols, see Karivieri, "Magic", 403–405; Kahlos, *Debate*, 169–172; Saradi-Mendelovici, "Christian Attitudes", 56–57.

125. Rufinus, *Church History* 2.29, col. 537. Engemann, "Verbreitung", 44–45, with other examples.

126. E.g. Tertullian, *On the Shows* 4.1; Hippolytus, *Apostolic Tradition* 20. For the use of baptism as a rite of exorcism, see Thraede, "Exorzismus", 7; Magoulias, "Lives", 228. For the differences and similarities between the exorcism rituals in Graeco-Roman, Jewish and Christian circles, see Kotansky, "Exorcistic Amulets", 246–276. The rite of the Eucharist was regarded with suspicion

by Graeco-Roman outsiders, and Justin (*First Apology* 61–62, 65–67) had to defend it against charges of magic.

127. This concern was connected to the disputes over Priscillian: *Canons of the Council of Saragossa* col. 315. For the ritual power of the Eucharist, see Dölger, "Segnen", 231–244; Breyfogle, "Magic", 440–441.

128. Irenaeus, *Against Heresies* 2.32.5. Martin of Braga, *Reforming the Rustics* 16. For the difficulties of making distinctions between prayers and spells, see Janowitz, *Icons of Power*, 95–96; Velásquez Soriano, "Orthodox Belief", 616.

129. Egypt: Meyer and Smith, *Ancient Christian Magic*, e.g. nos. 88–112 (curses); nos. 72–82 (erotic spells); Hispania: Velásquez Soriano, "Orthodox Belief", 620–625. For curses in the New Testament writings (e.g. Galatians 1:8–1:9; 1 Corinthians 5:3–5:5; 1 Timothy 1:20), see Remus, "'Magic', Method, Madness", 267, and Aune, "Magic", 1552–1554.

130. Irenaeus, *Against Heresies* 2.32.5; *Canons of the Council of Laodicea* can. 35.

131. For the Christian use of amulets, see Ogden, "Binding Spells", 51; Janowitz, *Magic*, 56–57; Sfameni, "Magic", 450–453, 461–467. E.g. Kotansky, "Christian Lamella", 45, for an early second-century Christian gold *lamella* for headache; Lambert, "Celtic Loricae", 642, for a Late Antique Christian amulet on papyrus, requesting the name of Jesus to protect the wearer from all illnesses, fevers, headaches, the evil eye and evil spirits (*Supplementum Magicum* 31).

132. Augustine, *Tractates on the Gospel of John* 7.7, 7.12. Augustine refers to little copies of gospels that were used as amulets. For the ritual power of the gospels and other sacred books, see Escribano Paño, "Heretical Texts", 129.

133. His father's medallion: Gregory of Tours, *Glory of the Martyrs* 83, trans. Van Dam, *Gregory of Tours: Glory of the Martyrs*, 108; the rival medallion: Gregory of Tours, *Miracles of Saint Julian* 45. Van Dam, *Saints and their Miracles*, 192; Brown, *Rise of Western Christendom*, 105–106.

134. Sulpicius Severus, *Dialogues* 2(3).7.

135. Ambrose, *Oration on the Death of Theodosius I* 41, 47–51, transl. Liebeschuetz, *Ambrose*, 197–198.

136. Relics of saints: Brown, *Rise*, 198; Magoulias, "Lives", 252–256.

137. *Leges Visigothorum* 11.2.2. The law has usually been read as being connected with magic, especially necromancy (McKenna, "Paganism", 125, and Flint, *Rise of Magic*, 216 n. 54), but, as Klingshirn ("Isidore", 80) points out, it is probably an attempt to restrict the vigorous hunt for saints' relics.

138. Visiting professional soothsayers: John Chrysostom, *Homilies on Second Timothy* 8 in v. 3.14; birds: *Homilies on First Timothy* 10 in v. 3.7.

139. Augustine, *City of God* 5.26. Augustine refers to Theodosius's campaigns against the usurper Maximus in 388 and against the usurper Eugenius in 394. Chadwick, "Oracles", 125–126.

140. For the techniques of *sortilegium* in Graeco-Roman, Jewish and Christian circles, see van der Horst, "*Sortes*", 144–166; Youtie, "Questions", 252–257.

Christian oracular texts, e.g., Papini, "Fragments", 395–401; Meyer and Smith, *Ancient Christian Magic*, nos. 29–35.

141. Augustine, *Letters* 55.20.37 (in 400). Augustine himself resorted to consulting the Bible by randomly opening the book in the famous conversion scene (*"Tolle, lege"*) in Augustine, *Confessions* 8.12.29. Klingshirn, "Defining", 126.

Chapter 6
The Early Medieval West

YITZHAK HEN

Some time around the turn of the eighth century, in an Insular learning centre on the European continent, a diligent scribe copied a short list of magical practices and superstitions into a codex that comprises mostly canonical material and Carolingian capitularies.[1] This short text, commonly known to modern scholars as the *Indiculus superstitionum et paganiarum* ("a short list of superstitions and pagan practices"), is an appropriate starting point for this chapter because it not only stands at the core of any discussion of magic in the early medieval West,[2] but it also exemplifies in a straightforward manner the numerous stumbling blocks one has to tackle when studying early medieval magical practices in their cultural, religious and social context. Let us, then, cite this short text in full:

A SHORT LIST OF SUPERSTITIONS AND PAGAN PRACTICES
1. Of sacrilege at the graves of the dead.
2. Of sacrilege over the departed, that is, *dadsias*.
3. Of the *spurcaliae* in February.
4. Of the little houses, that is, sanctuaries.
5. Of sacrilegious acts in connection with churches.
6. Of the sacred rites of the woods which they call *nimidas*.
7. Of those things which they do upon stones.
8. Of the sacred rites of Mercury and Jupiter.
9. Of the sacrifice which is offered to any of the saints.
10. Of amulets and knots.
11. Of the fountains of sacrifices.
12. Of incantations.
13. Of auguries according to birds, or according to the dung or sneezing of horses or cattle.
14. Of diviners or sorcerers.
15. Of fire made by friction from wood, that is, *nodfyr*.

16. Of the brains of animals.

17. Of the observance of the pagans on the hearth or in the inception of any business.

18. Of undetermined places which they celebrate as holy.

19. Of the bed-straw which good people call Holy Mary's.

20. Of the days which they make for Jupiter and Mercury.

21. Of the eclipses of the moon, [during] which they call *vince luna!* ("Triumph, moon!")

22. Of storms, and horns, and snail shells.

23. Of furrows around villas.

24. Of the pagan course which they call *yrias*, with torn garments and footwear.

25. Of this, that they feign for themselves that dead persons of whatever sort are saints.

26. Of an idol made of dough.

27. Of idols made of rags.

28. Of an idol which they carry through the fields.

29. Of wooden feet or hands in a pagan rite.

30. Of this, that they believe that [some] women command the moon, and that they may be able to take away the hearts of men, according to the pagans.[3]

Any discussion of this intriguing text must begin with a clear pronouncement of our sheer ignorance of the circumstances that led to its composition and transmission. We do not know who wrote it, when, where and for what purpose it was composed or subsequently copied, and any attempt to answer these questions with any amount of certainty is nothing but intellectual guesswork, based on bits and pieces of indirect information conveyed by the available sources. The manuscript evidence, as well as the *Indiculus's* linguistic peculiarities, led scholars in the past to associate it with the circle of Boniface (d. 754).[4] In the Vatican manuscript that preserves it, the *Indiculus* follows the decrees of two reform councils held in 742/743 and 743/744 under the auspices of Boniface and in collaboration with the Frankish *major domus* Carloman.[5] Moreover, a passage from Gregory the Great's *libellus responsionum* (to which I shall return later in this chapter) and an Old-Saxon baptismal formula, which also precede the *Indiculus* in the very same manuscript, add a certain missionary flair to the text, which fits extremely well with Boniface's aims and objectives.[6] These assertions, although highly plausible, cannot be ascertained beyond any reasonable doubt, and they clearly expose our most acute problem in the study of early medieval magic – the nature of our sources.

Scarcity, Brevity and Ambiguity

Combing through the sources from the early medieval West (roughly the fifth through the tenth centuries), it is quite amazing how very few of them refer to magic in any detail.[7] Various sorts of magical practices and professions, such as the use of amulets, the manipulation of fortune-tellers and soothsayers or the application of magical potions, are indeed mentioned in a plethora of texts from the period – ranging from sermons and theological tracts to law codes and penitentials and to chronicles and letter collections. But these references to magic are very brief and extremely ambiguous, just like the succinct and abstruse entries of the *Indiculus*. Moreover, the terminology used by our sources is exceptionally vague and prone to misinterpretation. Bernadette Filotas, for example, had found almost fifty different technical terms to denote magicians and sorcerers, such as *ariolus*, *cocriocus*, *maleficus* and *obligator*, but, as she herself admits, it is not at all clear what these terms actually mean and whether their meaning changed across time and space.[8]

This ambiguity is extremely disconcerting whenever one attempts to delineate the various aspects of magic and its uses in the early medieval West. What Caesarius of Arles (d. 542) means by "paying attention to and observing sneezes (*sternutationes*)" is as clear as the meaning behind the *Indiculus*'s "bed-straw which good people call Holy Mary's".[9] One can guess, but it seems we shall never know for sure until some new evidence is unearthed. It is very rare to find detailed descriptions of magical and semi-magical practices and beliefs, like the account of the *tempestarii* given by Agobard of Lyon (d. 840) or the idiosyncratic incantations recorded by Burchard of Worms (d. 1025) in his *Corrector sive medicus* (i.e. book XIX of his *Decretum*),[10] and even these detailed descriptions, as we shall see in the next section, are not always comprehensible and straightforward.

Yet, it is not only the scarcity, brevity and ambiguity of references to magic that pose difficulties of interpretation; it is also the fact that the lion's share of magical practices mentioned in our sources are repetitive. As a matter of fact, most of the beliefs mentioned in the *Indiculus* were also denounced by a long list of authors in Late Antiquity and the early Middle Ages. Let us take, for instance, the practice of observing sneezes that was just mentioned, which Caesarius of Arles had characterised as "not only sacrilegious, but also ridiculous".[11] The very same condemnation was repeated with minor changes and variations by Martin of Braga (d. 580),[12] Pseudo-Eligius of Noyon,[13] as well as the eighth-century *Homilia de sacrilegiis*,[14] to give just a few examples. Similarly, the *Indiculus's* "auguries according to birds" was denounced time and again.[15] In his sermon against those who consult fortune-tellers and soothsayers, Caesarius of Arles admonishes his flock not to "observe auguries, pay attention to certain singing birds when on the road, or dare to announce diabolical divinations according to their singing".[16] Likewise, Martin of Braga condemns "men who entice demons by bird's song",[17] and following the example of Martin's treatise,[18] later authors, as well as numerous penitentials, rehearse this condemnation in one way or another.[19] Do these repetitions imply that throughout the early medieval West (from Galicia and Arles in the south to Noyon and the Rhineland in the north), auguries according to singing birds or according to sneezing were performed by professional seers and soothsayers?

Whenever this question and its implications are discussed, two schools of interpretation are immediately mentioned. Whereas some scholars argue that the repetitions and copying of certain texts are clear signs of submission to literary conventions (topoi) and thus abolish any documentary value of the texts in question,[20] others claim that such repetitions prove the continued existence of certain practices or beliefs and therefore present an accurate reflection of reality.[21] Although one has to acknowledge that both schools have some strong points in support of their arguments, neither position is completely convincing. A combination of the two is needed in order to understand the texts with which we are dealing.

No doubt the repetition of various unauthorised magical practices, such as the *auguria* according to singing birds and their classification as "pagan" or "diabolical", are, in a sense, the result of some well-rooted literary conventions. Even though the *Indiculus's* "course which they call *yrias*",[22] which is otherwise unattested, clearly refers to a local practice well known to the author and the audience but unknown to us (and all past attempts to understand it stretched the human imagination *ad absurdum*),[23] most of the recurring condemnations of magical practices are not like that. They seem to repeat mechanically and rather inconsiderately previous convictions and denunciations. Nevertheless, it would be wrong to assume that these repetitions bear no relation to reality. Although they should not be understood as reflections of the mundane reality in which such practices were actually performed, it is well justified to accept these repetitive condemnations as evidence for what the people who composed these documents thought ought to be prohibited.[24] Hence, they should be regarded as expressions of norms, not documentary facts. Such an interpretation gives a whole new meaning to the repetition in our sources, and it forces us to re-evaluate them against a broader Christian background.

Christianity, Paganism and the Survival of Magic

Understanding the repetitive feature of our sources as reflecting something other than actual reality brings to light another major flaw in our documentary evidence, that is, its heavy ecclesiastical bias. Most, if not all, of the texts that document magic in the early medieval West were composed by clerics and missionaries, whose Christian prism on daily life and social practices is undeniable. This ecclesiastical myopia is extremely worrying when one attempts to evaluate the accuracy of these reports. Did the bishops, monks or itinerary priests who incorporated short references to magical lore in their works actually document real beliefs and magical rituals that were practised by the local communities in their region? This is, of course, an open question, yet it seems that the vast majority of magical practices mentioned in our ecclesiastically biased sources are not only repetitive ad nauseam but also somewhat irrelevant to the context in which they were supposedly performed.

Once again, the *Indiculus* provides some excellent examples. Twice in this short text are the cults of Jupiter and Mercury mentioned – first, the author refers to "the sacred rites of Mercury and Jupiter",[25] and then "the days which they make for Jupiter and Mercury" are mentioned.[26] Are we to assume that Jupiter and Mercury were still venerated in mid-eighth-century eastern Francia? Such an assertion, of course, is untenable, and scholars in the past were quick to argue that by Mercury and Jupiter, the author of the *Indiculus* surely meant Wodan and Thor,[27] thus assuming that the author possessed enough knowledge (or lack thereof) of Roman religion and Germanic mythology to draw the similarity between these gods. But this is not what the *Indiculus* says. The *Indiculus* simply denounces the cults of Jupiter and Mercury in a straightforward manner, in what appears to echo tens, if not hundreds, of past condemnations.[28] A well-established topos that goes back to Tacitus's *Germania* and Augustine's *De civitate Dei* (*On the City of God*),[29] rather than an oblique reference to actual rites, seems to have been the case. After all, the author of the *Indiculus* was versed enough in the region's cultural and religious language to be able to use specific terms, such as *dadsias, nimidas, nodfyr*, and *yrias*,[30] to denote indigenous local practices. Moreover, we can trust a companion of Boniface to recognise the cult of Wodan or Thor and to refer to it with the correct terms.

The Christian partiality of our sources is also disclosed by the fact that the various magical practices listed and condemned were regularly coupled with denunciations of paganism and superstitious beliefs. The title of the *Indiculus*, "A Short List of Superstitions and Pagan Practices", although modern, relies on a deep-rooted Late Antique and early medieval trend to associate magic with paganism and superstitions. For example, in one of his sermons, Caesarius of Arles writes that "no one should consult enchanters for his/her own sake, for whoever does that evil loses the sacrament of baptism at once, and immediately becomes sacrilegious and pagan".[31] Similarly, Martin of Braga, after mentioning numerous superstitions and magical practices, admonishes that "these observances are all pagan practices, devised by the inventiveness of demons"[32]; and Pirmin of Reichenau (d. 753), to give just one more example, classifies as pagan and diabolical a long list of superstitious beliefs and magical rites, which reads very much like the list of the *Indiculus*.[33] By doing this, early medieval authors plunged into the murky waters of traditional Christian teaching on superstitions and pagan rituals, and it seems they had a good reason to do so.

From the fourth century onwards, various practices that the Christian authorities could not abolish, transform or control were defined by Christian authors as "pagan". Hence, a certain image of what was considered pagan emerged in the writings of Christians, such as Ambrose of Milan (d. 397), Jerome (d. 420) and Augustine (d. 430), and this image was later used and recycled by preachers, theologians, missionaries and legislators.[34] Needless to say, magical practices, such as various forms of divination, amulets or the use of incantations, were part and parcel of that concept of paganism, and they helped Christianity set up clear-cut boundaries by defining what is permitted from a Christian point of view and what is not.[35] Often, the past practices that survived the conversion of the West had no religious meaning anymore. And yet, they were a crucial part of Christianity's view of paganism and, consequently, of itself. To paraphrase Robert Markus, the condemnation of pre-Christian patterns of behaviour helped define the identity of the Christian community, united with its bishop under a shared loyalty and value system.[36] Hence, we should be extremely cautious when attributing the label "pagan" to social or magical customs practised by people converted to Christianity. Not everything that survives from the pagan past or described in our sources as superstitious retained its pagan religious meaning, and in fact many of the magical practices condemned in the early Middle Ages as pagan did not necessarily bear the heavy charge of religious significance one might attribute to them in a different context.

Taking these condemnations at face value, several modern historians argued for the persistence of pagan religious practices among the newly converted Christians and thus failed to take into account the sheer vitality of non-religious social institutions and traditions and their power to resist change.[37] True, auguries and other forms of divination had some pagan religious meanings in the Roman past.[38] But when mentioned by eighth-century authors, these supposedly magical practices were part of a social tradition that was completely detached from its original pagan connotations. Even Caesarius of Arles at the beginning of the sixth century was well aware of the fact that many of the practices he condemned as pagan were often detached from their original pagan meaning,[39] and for us, who live in an age in which every major newspaper publishes a daily horoscope, this should come as no surprise. Not everything that survives from the pagan past or that is described in our sources as pagan retained its pagan religious meaning.

But the classification of magical practices as pagan survivals is even more intriguing. It raises a whole series of problems concerning the artificiality, in a sense, of written models and traditions. Given the repetitive, prescriptive and biased nature of our sources, one should ask what relationship the resurfacing of particular practices bears to changing realities. The pairing of magic with paganism is extremely indicative in that respect. Surprisingly, but not unexpectedly, the volume of references to magic and magical observances in our sources went hand in hand with the increasing preoccupation with paganism and superstitions in the early medieval West, which in itself was stimulated by a variety of social, religious and political developments.

Let us first consider the matter of conversion. Although most scholars agree nowadays that by the end of the sixth century, a vast majority of the inhabitants of Western Europe were, in fact, baptised Christians, there is little consensus regarding the degree to which Christianity had been adopted by them. On the one hand, some historians argued that conversion to Christianity includes very little apart from two obvious things – baptism and the renunciation of all pagan gods and worship rituals. According to these criteria, Western Europe of the early Middle Ages was indeed a Christian society. On the other hand, it has been argued that true conversion entails a change in every aspect of an individual's life, thought and belief. Arthur Darby Nock, for example, wrote in his 1933 vanguard study of conversion that "by conversion we mean the reorientation of the soul of an individual, his deliberate turning from indifference or from an earlier form of piety to another, a turning which implies a consciousness that a great change is involved, that the old was wrong and the new is right".[40] Subsequently, Ramsey MacMullen suggested that "so disturbing and difficult must be conversion, or so incomplete".[41] According to Nock, MacMullen and many of their followers, early medieval Europe was, perhaps, Christian by name but still pagan by practice and spirit.

However, to understand conversion as "the reorientation of the soul of an individual" and "the adhesion of the will to a theology" is to impose modern perceptions on the past. It further assumes deep knowledge and understanding of Christianity's theology and doctrine on the side of the people. Yet, very few Christians have ever attained deep and thorough theological understanding, like Saint Augustine (d. 430) did, and to judge the conversion of a society according to an Augustinian yardstick is, to my mind, misleading. The Christianity of the "ordinary" men and women, which manifested itself mainly in ritual acts and participation in ceremonies, was not the Christianity of theologians, and it is unreasonable to expect a total reorientation of the soul and a complete adhesion to a theology.

Whichever school of interpretation one chooses to follow, it is obvious that the conversion of the post-Roman West was a teleological process. From the fourth century onwards, Christianity expanded its horizons and established itself among the inhabitants of Western Europe.[42] The work of missionaries, bishops and monks, as well as the ecclesiastical reforms at the behest of both churchmen and secular rulers, clearly made a huge difference, and as time progressed, Christianity's hold of the early medieval West was strengthened and deepened. And yet, the more prevalent and widespread Christianity became, the more obsessed it became with pagan survivals and magical practices.

Throughout the fifth and the sixth centuries, the references to paganism and magical practices were very few and trite. A few were mentioned in the admonitory dossier of Caesarius of Arles and Martin of Braga, and a few more can be found in the works of Gregory of Tours, in several hagiographical treatises and in the canons of the Merovingian church councils that were convened in the sixth and early seventh centuries.[43] But, as we noted earlier in this chapter, in all of these cases, the references are repetitive, derivative and dull. Things, however, were about to change.

The late seventh and early eighth centuries marked an important turning point in the references made to magic and paganism in Western Europe. From that period onwards, the number of references to magical practices and superstitious observances was rising at an exponential rate, and their tone became more zealous and abrasive. There is a sharp contrast between, on the one hand, the general terms in which practices are condemned in the sixth century and, on the other hand, the numerous, wide-ranging prohibitions in later sources.[44] This gradual change continued well into the eleventh century, and Burchard of Worms's *Corrector sive medicus* epitomises the culmination of this phenomenon, while at the same time inaugurating a new phase in the history of medieval magic.[45]

It has been suggested in the past that the preoccupation with paganism and magic in the late seventh and early eighth centuries was influenced by Insular missionaries who operated on the continent.[46] It may well be that missionary activity in remote regions, such as Frisia and Saxony, where pagan religions were still alive and active, helped kindle interest in pagan practices closer to home. It would be difficult to disprove this theory, but on balance, the view that the rising number of references to magic and paganism had more to do with ecclesiastical strategies and political manoeuvres seems more likely to be right.

The abundant and explicit evidence concerning Boniface and his activities – the *vitae* of Boniface himself and of his Anglo-Saxon followers, as well as his copious correspondence – might give the false impression that Boniface was sent by the Pope to convert the heathens in a virgin pagan territory.[47] Reality, however, was quite different. From other contemporary sources and thanks to modern research, it is now clear that the regions to which Boniface was sent and in which he operated were far from being pagan; nor was he the only missionary working there. In fact, Boniface hardly converted any pagans to Christianity. A close examination of the sources reveals that Boniface was mainly preoccupied with the enhancement of ecclesiastical rules and regulations and with the reorganisation of the Frankish church.[48] Like Caesarius of Arles two hundred years before him, Boniface wanted to bring the Frankish church into line with ecclesiastical norms from which he thought it had deviated. Thus, promoting Roman norms in doctrine, canon law and liturgy in an already Christianised territory, rather than Christianising pagan tribes, was the heart of Boniface's labour on the continent.

It was the ecclesiastical vocation and reformatory zeal of missionaries and ecclesiastics like Boniface that fostered the growing use of denounced pagan and magical practices as Christian boundary markers. This strategy was further encouraged by the fact that Carolingian propagandists were quick to realise the compelling qualities of such a topos and consequently manipulated it against their Merovingian predecessors. It is a well-known fact that anti-Merovingian propaganda, whose purpose was to undermine and discredit the Merovingian dynasty and to pave the way for legitimising the Carolingian usurpation of 751, was created by the Carolingians, their supporters and court scholars.[49] By repeating old condemnations of magical and pagan practices, Carolingian authors highlighted the Christian and reformatory fervour of their own kings and, at the same time, undermined the Merovingians by suggesting their supposed carelessness in religious matters and by describing their religious culture as a mainly pagan one, in which magical practices were rife.[50]

Hence, the condemnation of pagan practices and magical lore became in the early medieval West a rhetorical trope devised by churchmen and rulers alike, and this accounts for the increasing volume of references to such abhorred practices in the sources from the early eighth century onwards. This tendency also accords extremely well with yet another trend that characterised the literary culture of the period and which was inspired by the Carolingian preoccupation with authority, orthodoxy and correctness.[51] This preoccupation is attested by the successive attempts made at the behest of the Carolingian kings to create a new, corrected and, most of all, orthodox repertoire of ecclesiastical texts, which eventually would become the standard Christian handbooks throughout the Frankish realm. In some cases, as with Paul the Deacon's homiliary,[52] authoritative texts were commissioned and prepared at home, but more often such texts were acquired from well-known centres of authority abroad, mainly from Rome.[53]

The preoccupation with authority, orthodoxy, and correctness, which was one of the most prevailing characteristics of what is commonly known as the "Carolingian Renaissance", sent Carolingian authors to excavate old sources for definitions of orthodoxy, and what they found was a large corpus of texts that made ample use of magic and paganism in an attempt to portray a mirror image of Christian orthodoxy and correctness. But, as they did in so many things, the Carolingians were much more systematic and extravagant in collecting and organising these topoi and hence produced larger, fuller and more elaborate canonical compilations that recycled old prohibitions. Reading, for example, Regino of Prüm's (d. 915) *De synodalibus causis et disciplinis ecclesiasticis (On Synodical Cases and Ecclesiastic Discipline)*,[54] one cannot escape the feeling of walking a well-trodden path but in a flashy Carolingian disguise.

What had started as a genuine concern with orthodoxy and correctness shortly became an obsession. More and more magical practices found their ways into the texts. Some of these were new, but the vast majority were pretentious variants on old themes. Regino's compilation is already larger and more comprehensive than any other penitential or canonical composition written before the ninth century, and Burchard's *Corrector sive medicus* makes even Regino's compilation look like a flimsy and sloppy list of forbidden magical observances and superstitious beliefs. This tendency is also apparent in the liturgical corpus of the time, in which the sacramentaries of the so-called Gelasianised-Gregorian type became large books packed with prayers and benedictions taken from older sacramentaries and assembled by churchmen and liturgists because of what Emmanuel Bourque has described as "a compiling mania".[55] The more churchmen became preoccupied with orthodoxy and correctness, the more references to magic and superstitions were incorporated into our sources. This is a simple injective equation.

The Rise of Magic and the Fall of Scholarship

The rising number of references to magic in our sources from the fifth to the tenth centuries and the increasing variety of practices mentioned by churchmen and legislators were often taken to reflect the "rise" of magic and the prevalent use of magical practices in the early medieval West. Needless to say, this assessment was deeply couched in the dim view of early medieval culture and society that characterised modern scholarship, at least from the time of Petrarch (d. 1374).[56] However, as we just saw in the previous section, the multiplying references to various magical practices in the sources from the fifth to the tenth centuries reflect all sorts of things, but they should not be taken to imply that magic was on the rise in Western Europe during the early Middle Ages.

Adopting the paradigm of rise and fall, suggested by the title of Keith Thomas's seminal study of magic in early modern Europe,[57] Valerie Flint has argued for the rise of magic in early medieval Europe not as a mere revitalised pagan survival but as Christianised pagan practices that were adopted by the church and its representatives.[58] In her book *The Rise of Magic in Early Medieval Europe*, which is still the most comprehensive treatment of references to magic in the early Middle Ages, Flint maintains that the church, after rejecting all forms of magic, realised how important it was for the people and therefore "rescued" it by incorporating some magical practices into Christianity's own world of beliefs, perceptions and attitudes.[59]

Ignoring the peculiar nature of our sources, as well as the unique contexts in which they were written, Flint adopted a baffling synoptic approach, making little allowance for chronological or geographical differences. Hence, for her, the problems that Roman magic raised for late antique bishops, such as Ambrose of Milan and Augustine of Hippo, were basically the same kind of problems that Germanic paganism raised for missionaries and churchmen in Carolingian Francia or late Anglo-Saxon England. The ways in which each culture coped with these practices, according to Flint, was different. Whereas the former merely condemned magical practices and classified them as pagan and diabolical, the latter rescued these practices, Christianised them and adopted them. In both cases, magic was tolerated and allowed to be transported across centuries in what seems like a continuous saturnalia of magical lore.

Taking her cue from Pope Gregory the Great's *Libellus responsionum* (*Booklet of Answers*), Flint argues that the rescuing of competing magical practices and the calling of them to the aid of the church was part of an official papal policy. In his famous letter to Abbot Mellitus of Canterbury (d. 624), Gregory offered some guidance on various matters pertaining to the conversion of pagans:

> I have decided after long deliberation about the English people, namely that the idol temples of that race should by no means be destroyed, but only the idols in them. Take holy water and sprinkle it in these shrines, build altars and place relics in them. For if the shrines are well built, it is essential that they should be changed from the worship of devils to the service of the true God. When this people see that their shrines are not destroyed they will be able to banish error from their hearts and be more ready to come to the places they are familiar with, but now recognizing and worshiping the true God. And because they are in the habit of slaughtering much cattle as sacrifices to devils, some solemnity ought to be given them in exchange for this. So on the day of the dedication or the festivals of the holy martyrs, whose relics are deposited there, let them make themselves huts from the branches of trees around the churches which have been converted out of shrines, and let them celebrate the solemnity with religious feasts.[60]

Gregory's instructions to Mellitus, which constitute a dramatic change in papal missionary strategy,[61] were aimed at bolstering the missionary activity in England. After scolding the English king for not doing enough to promote Christianity, Gregory realised that the slow progress in the Christianisation of the English was not due to insufficient zeal and motivation on the king's part. The whole concept of conversion as a ruthless confrontational process suddenly seemed to him unsuitable for the conversion of pagans, and he entertained the thought that maybe a lenient flexible approach would do the job more effectively. Hence, according to Gregory's new approach, Christianisation should entail as little disruption as possible to everyday life.

Gregory's *Libellous responsionum*, according to Flint, is the launcher and the inspiration behind the Christianisation of magic and pagan practices in the early Middle Ages. But Gregory, one should stress, did not suggest the adoption of pagan practices and their incorporation into the Christian rhythm of everyday life. On the contrary; he simply advised that Christian feasts should be introduced as proper replacements of pagan ones. Flint also believes that unrelenting pressure of competing non-Christian magical practices and active sorcerers forced the Christian authorities, which, strangely enough, she equates with the "Benedictine Order [sic!]",[62] to react either by condemning these practices, which proved to be inefficient, or by embracing these practices and giving them a Christian guise. An excellent case in point is the practice of divination by casting lots (*sortes*), which was unequivocally condemned as pagan and superstitious by various Christian authors and policymakers.[63] In various sources from the early medieval West, the condemned *sortes* appear in what seems to be a Christianised form of a pagan practice. For example, in the first council of Orléans, which was convened on 10 July 511 at the initiative of King Clovis (d. 511),[64] the Merovingian bishops resolved (among other things) that:

> If any cleric, monk or laymen shall think he should observe divination or auguries or casting the lots (*sortes*), which they say are "of the saints" (*sanctorum*) to whomever they should believe they should make them known, they are to be expelled from the Church's communion with those who believe in them.[65]

This resolution was subsequently repeated by several regional and "national" church councils, such as the diocesan council of Auxerre (561–605),[66] which declared that:

> It is forbidden to turn to soothsayers or to augurs, or to those who pretend to know the future, or to look at what they call "the lots of the saints" (*sortes sanctorum*), or those they make of wood or bread. But whatever a man wishes to do, let him do it in the Name of God.[67]

Moreover, it was further recycled by many penitentials, such as the one appended to the Bobbio Missal and dated to around 700[68]:

> If anyone consult what is called without reason "lots of the saints" (*sortes sanctorum*) or any other lots (*sortes*), she/he shall do penance for three years, one [of which] on bread and water.[69]

These canons are simple and straightforward. They rule against any form of divination or fortune-telling, and they clearly associate the use of the *sortes* with unorthodox superstitious behaviour, a reminiscent survival of the pagan past. The fact that a peculiar practice called *sortes sanctorum* (whatever that means) was listed in the very same canons along with other forms of condemned divinations is, according to Flint, a clear indication of the persistent use of *sortes*, albeit in a Christianised form, among the newly converted Christians. This notion gets impressive support from numerous contemporary sources.

In his *Ten Books of History*, Gregory of Tours (d. 594) relates how Merovech, King Chilperic's son, consulted the *sortes* to check whether he would inherit his father's kingdom, as was predicted by a certain female soothsayer:

> Merovech had no faith in Guntram's soothsayer. He placed three books on the Saint's [i.e. Saint Martin's] tomb, the Psalter, the Book of Kings, and

the Gospels: then he spent the whole night in prayer, beseeching the holy confessor to show him what was going to happen and to indicate clearly whether or not he would be allowed to inherit the kingship. He spent three days and nights in fasting, vigil and supplication: then he went up to the tomb and opened the first volume, which was the Book of Kings. This was the first verse on the page which he opened: "Because thou hast forsaken the Lord thy God and hast taken hold upon other gods and hast not walked uprightly before him, the Lord thy God will deliver thee into the hands of thy enemies" [I Kings 9.9]. He found the following verse in the Psalms: "Surely thou didst set them slippery places, thou castedst them down into destruction. How are they brought into desolation, as in a moment! They are utterly consumed because of their iniquities" [Psalms 73.18–73.19]. This was what he found in the Gospels: "Ye know that after two days in the feast of the Passover, and the son of man is betrayed to be crucified" [Matt. 26.2]. Merovech was dismayed by these answers and for a long time he wept at the tomb of the Holy bishop.[70]

This is by no means the only example for the use of the *sortes* in an utterly Christian disguise. In the middle of the struggle between King Lothar I (d. 561) and his rebellious son Chramn (d. 560), to give just one more example, the *sortes* were consulted again, this time in an attempt to reach a political decision:

[The] priests placed three books on the altar, the Prophets, the epistles and the Gospels. They prayed to the Lord that in His divine power He would reveal to them what would happen to Chramn, whether he would ever prosper and whether or not he would come to the throne. At the same time they agreed among themselves that each should read at Mass whatever he found when he first opened the book. The Book of the Prophets was opened first. There they found: "I will take away the hedge thereof, and it shall be eaten up. When I looked that it should bring forth grapes, it brought forth wild grapes" [Isaiah 4.4–4.5]. Then the Book of the Apostle was opened and they found this: "For yourselves know perfectly that the day of the Lord so cometh as a thief in the night. For when they shall say, peace and safety; then sudden destruction cometh upon them, as travail upon a woman with child; and they shall not escape" [I Thess. 5.2–5.3]. Finally the Lord spoke through the Gospel: "And every one that heareth these sayings of mine, and doeth them not, shall be likened unto a foolish man, which built his house upon the sand. And the rain descended, and the floods came, and the winds blew, and beat upon that house, and it fell, and great was the fall of it" [Matt. 7.26–7.27]. Chramn was welcomed in his churches by the Bishop whom I have named and he was allowed to take communion.[71]

If the former incident could be dismissed as a deviant aberration, brought about by Merovech's own distress and insecurity, the latter is much more compelling. It was the priests of Dijon Cathedral who consulted the *sortes*, ignoring the unambiguous conciliar decrees mentioned earlier in this section, and Gregory found nothing wrong in it.[72] Could it be that Gregory, the famous Bishop of Tours, understood the use of the *sortes* as a harmless and non-threatening superstitious practice that had nothing to do with religious beliefs or pagan cults?

If taken at face value, the two incidents reported by Gregory and just cited prove unequivocally that the church silently adopted magical practices, Christianised them and gave its consent to their use. But things were much more complicated than that. First, chronologically, the Christianisation of the *sortes*, if indeed that is what we are describing, must have taken place at a fairly early stage. Our sources, including Caesarius of Arles, Gregory of Tours and the Merovingian church councils, clearly imply that by the end of the fifth or the very early sixth century, the *sortes* were already Christianised and practised by the Christian inhabitants of Gaul. This predates significantly the chronology suggested by Flint for the "rise of magic" in the early Middle Ages.

Moreover, by understanding the *sortes sanctorum* or the *sortes biblicae* as a deliberately Christianised form of a pagan rite, one shuns the crucial role and tenacious strength of non-religious social behaviours and their perseverance, even if religious authorities had instructed against them. Magic was always there, as a social practice, from the beginning of civilisation through the Greek and the Roman world and into the Middle Ages. It did not always bear the heavy charges of religious deviation, and it did not have to be Christianised or rescued in order to be practised by pagans, Jews, Christians and Muslims alike. An illuminating case in point is provided by Augustine of Hippo himself. The turning point in his conversion was brought about by a *sortes*-like practice he had performed after hearing the kids in his backyard playing and singing *"Tolle lege! Tolle lege!"* ("Pick up and read! Pick up and read!").[73] Reflecting on this event more than ten years later, when he was already the Bishop of Hippo and a respectable Christian theologian, Augustine found nothing wrong or diabolical in his actions. He clearly saw the message he had received when opening the New Testament as a divine omen, sent to him by God and not by a deceiving demon. Condemned magical practices are one thing, and the persistent use of supposedly magical practices as part of society's cultural and social heritage is another thing. The difference between them is like the difference between a fictitious reality, created by means of Christian rhetoric, and the reality of everyday life. One should not confuse the two, and any attempt to portray the everyday practices of a Christian society as the rise of magic in a Christianised form is idiosyncratic and anachronistic. Furthermore, it completely ignores the nature of our sources, the contexts in which they were written and the dispositions of the societies in question.

The Thin Line between Magic and Religion

The case of the *sortes sanctorum* clearly highlights the inadequacy of modern terminology to describe and classify early medieval cultural-religious phenomena, and it emphasises how very fine, and often blurred, the line that separates magic from religion, *superstitio* from *religio licita*, is. The exchange between the anthropologist Hildred Geerze and the historian Keith Thomas, which appeared in the *Journal of Interdisciplinary History*,[74] is extremely enlightening in this respect.

In her review of *Religion and the Decline of Magic*, Geerze criticised Thomas on account of the clear distinction he makes between religion and magic as two separable cultural complexes which can be in competition and whose fortunes may sometimes rise and fall separately.[75] Religion according to Thomas, writes Geertz, "is a term that covers the kind of beliefs and practices that are comprehensive, organized and concerned with providing general symbols of life", whereas magic is a label he uses to denote "those beliefs and practices which are specific, incoherent, and primarily oriented toward providing practical solutions to immediate problems and not referable to any coherent scheme of ideas".[76]

Thomas responded to Geertz's critique by reiterating his argument that the various definitions of magic and religion with which scholars in the past attempted to assess systems of beliefs and practices are, in fact, products of the early modern period. It was the sixteenth-century Protestant Reformers who first declared that "magic is coercive and religion intercessory, and that magic was not a false religion, but a different sort of activity altogether".[77] Hence, these early modern categories are culture bound and cannot be applied to many premodern cultures without qualms or reservations. The risk of anachronism and incomprehensibility is simply too high.

As far as the early Middle Ages are concerned, the early modern categories of magic and religion are ill-suited to illuminate the complex reality of the Christianised West, not the least because the line between magic and religion is extremely frail and blurred, and therefore it is impossible to draw. Certain essential characteristics of early medieval Christianity, such the cults of saints and relics, or even the sacraments themselves, would be viewed by Protestant reformers as magical, because they present a picture of incoherent, specific means of coercing supernatural power to achieve particular ends. A brief look at the so-called Old Gelasian Sacramentary (*Sacramentarium Gelasianum*) will clarify that point. In the third book of the *Gelasianum*, which is dedicated to private and votive masses, one finds masses for those who embark on a journey,[78] for the death of animals,[79] for infertility,[80] for all kinds of weather,[81] for health,[82] for trees and for many other occasions.[83] If looked at from a cynical point of view, this list of masses reads very much like a Christian replica of the *Indiculus*. What is the difference between the Old Gelasian prayer *pro sterillitate mulierum* and the condemned acts of barren women who, according to Caesarius of Arles, desperate to conceive, turn to "herbs, diabolic signs, and sacrilegious objects"?[84] Whereas the former is an appeal to God to interfere and change the course of nature, the latter is an attempt to interfere with the course of nature by entreating unspecified supernatural powers. Obviously these two "solutions" are on the same continuum, and they both entice extraordinary intervention in everyday life. The elusive criteria that differentiate them, and subsequently classify the one as a legitimate Christian act and the other as a condemned magical practice, is not so much in the nature of the act itself but in the eyes of the beholder.

Medicine, Protection and the Extraordinary

When stripped of the typological references to magic, the sources from early medieval Europe tell us very little about actual encounters with magicians or about the performance of magical procedures, and in all of these cases, the magic mentioned is situated on a hazy continuum between condemnation and approval. Two examples will suffice to illustrate this point.

In his book *De virtutibus sancti Martini* (*On the Virtues of Saint Martin*), Gregory of Tours relates an incident that happened near Tours during his own episcopacy:

> The wife of Serenatus, one of my servants, was retuning from working in the field. Her husband had gone on ahead. Suddenly she fell into the hands of her companions and slipped to the ground; because her tongue was tied and she was unable to pronounce any words with her mouth, she became mute. Then the soothsayers (*hariolii*) came and said that she had experienced an attack by a midday demon. They prescribed amulets of herbs (*ligamina herbarum*) and verbal incantations (*incantationum*); but as usual they could provide no medicine for the woman on the verge of death. While her family mixed shouts with their weeping, her son ran breathlessly to my niece Eustenia. He announced that his mother had reached the final point of her life. Eustenia went and visited the ill woman, and after removing the amulets that the silly [soothsayers] had attached, she poured oil from [Martin's] blessed tomb on

her mouth and rubbed it with wax. Soon the ill woman's speech was restored, and after the evil deception [of the demon] was removed, she recovered.[85]

Nothing exemplifies the overlap of magic and religion better than this passage. The fuzziness of the boundaries that separate the doctor (*medicus*) from the magician (*magus, maleficus, hariolus*, etc.) and from the saint (*sanctus*) is seen here at its best.[86] Gregory used all of his dramatic literary skills and the common arsenal of Christian topoi to deliver a purely Christian message – a message that had already been articulated by Caesarius of Arles when admonishing his flock:

> What is deplorable is that there are some who seek soothsayers in every kind of infirmity. They consult seers and diviners, summon enchanters, and hang diabolical phylacteries and magic letters on themselves. Often enough they receive charms even from priests and religious, who, however, are not really religious or clerics but the Devil's helpers. See, brethren, how I plead with you not to consent to accept these wicked objects, even if they are offered by clerics. There is no remedy of Christ in them, but the poison of the Devil, which will not cure your body but will kill your poor soul with the sword of infidelity. Even if you are told that the phylacteries contain holy facts and divine lessons, let no one believe it or expect health to come to him from them.[87]

Christians, according to Caesarius and Gregory, should turn to God and his saints when in distress. But what is interesting in the passage just cited from Caesarius is the great variety of other solutions that were at hand, ranging from practicing magicians to local doctors (whom our Christian authors may have mistaken for magicians) to clerics who offered all sorts of medications. These were all condemned as diabolical and inappropriate, even if they had some Christian and holy elements in them. One keeps wondering how Caesarius would have classified Gregory of Tours's own amulet, which falls into the very same category of condemned practices. Gregory tells us that:

> At the time when Theudebert ordered the sons of Clermont to be sent off as hostages [in 533], my father had been recently married. Because he wished himself to be protected by relics of saints, he asked a cleric to grant him something from these relics, so that with their protection he might be kept safe as he set out on this long journey. He put the sacred ashes in a gold medallion and carried it with him. Although he did not even know the names of the blessed men, he was accustomed to recount that he had been rescued from many dangers.[88]

Is this phylactery, which contained some holy material and which was given by a cleric, not exactly like the one condemned by Caesarius in the passage just cited? Needless to say, Gregory was not impressed by Caesarius's severe judgement on amulets and phylacteries. On the contrary, he felt very privileged and honoured to own the very same amulet later on, and to put it to good use:

> Many years later I received these relics from my mother. While I was travelling from Burgundy to Clermont, a huge storm appeared in my path. The storm frequently flashed with lightning in the sky and rumbled with loud crashes of thunder. Then I took the holy relics from my pocket and raised my hands before the cloud. The cloud immediately divided into two parts and passed by on the right and the left; it threatened neither me, nor anyone else.[89]

A *tempestarius* ("conjuror of storms") par excellence! So, where is the line between magic and Christian practice to be drawn?

Gregory's behaviour in the incident just adduced leads us to the second, and final, example I wish to discuss here. In a treatise entitled *Liber in contra insulsam vulgi opinionem de grandine et tonitruis* (*A Book against the Irrational Belief of the People about Hail and Thunder*), Agobard of Lyon goes out of his way to refute the popular belief that certain *tempestarii* have the power to cause thunder- and hailstorms.[90] Who these *tempestarii* are is not at all clear. Agobard, one should stress, does not associate them with paganism or portray them, like many earlier authors did, as remnants of an old and pagan magical lore. They could have been local men and women dabbling with magic – the local village sorcerers – as suggested by Monica Blöcker,[91] but, as suggested by Rob Meens, Agobard's *tempestarii* were more probably local clerics who pretended to control the weather and who exacted a kind of payment in return for their services – an aberrant clerical behaviour in the eyes of the rigorous Bishop of Lyon.[92]

Agobard's treatise against the *tempestarii* is, perhaps, the most conspicuous evidence of our inability to differentiate between magic and religion in the early Middle Ages. Any attempt to do so and to set up clear-cut boundaries or to describe various supposedly magical practices in terms of "survival", "rise" or "Christianisation" would result in a drastic oversimplification, not to say a travesty, of a much more complicated and nuanced situation. In ninth-century Lyon, as we have just seen in this section, the categories of magic and religion were so inextricably mixed and confused that the perplexed bishop of the city had to gather his actions, arm himself with all the venomous arsenal of Christian admonition and attack a practice that was otherwise sanctioned by various prayers, which were added by Benedict of Aniane (d. 821) at about the same time to the standard sacramentary of the Frankish church.[93]

Epilogue

"Magic has to be extraordinary. If it is not, there is no reason to suppose that it will work".[94] But so does religion. Hence, when considering the nature of magic and magical practices in the early medieval West, one has to keep in mind that magic was closely intertwined with the Christianised world-view of the post-Roman Barbarian world. No doubt people in the early medieval West possessed amulets and phylacteries (with or without holy dust),[95] turned to "witch doctors" in times of illness and distress and attempted to intervene in the course of nature by swallowing potions or reciting incantations. These acts were interpreted by various Christian authors as magical and, more often than not, as pagan and diabolical. However, at the very same time, similar solutions were offered by the church and its clerics, who sometime resorted to questionable behaviours. Reality, it appears, was much more complicated, nuanced and multilayered than the dichotomy suggested by our biased sources.

Given the nature of our sources and the nature of the human society with which we are dealing, one should be extremely cautious of the interpretation of magic, its survival and its practice in the early medieval West. Large margins of misinterpretation and misrepresentation must be allowed. Should the horoscope in the daily newspaper be interpreted as a magical act of divination? Is serving chicken soup to someone with a flu an act of Jewish magic? Or should the baking of gingerbread men (the *Indiculus*'s "an idol made of dough") before Halloween or Christmas be considered as magical, as well?[96] Agobard and many of his fellow bishops in the early Middle Ages would have answered these questions with a passionate "Yes!" But we, as sensible historians, may and should question their judgement.

Notes

1. Vatican, Biblioteca Apostolica Vatinana, Pal. lat. 577, fols. 7r–7v. On this codex, see Mordek, *Biblioteca capitularium regum Francorum manuscripta*, 774–779.
2. See, for example, Flint, *The Rise of Magic*; Bernadette Filotas, *Pagan Survivals*.
3. *Indiculus superstitionum et paganiarum*, ed. Boretius, 222–223, no. 108. I cite (with minor changes and variations) the English translation by McNeill and Gamer, *Medieval Handbooks of Penance*, 419–421. Note that the title is modern, and it does not appear in the original manuscript.
4. On Boniface and his circle, see Schieffer, *Winfrid-Bonifatius*; Wood, *The Missionary Life*, 57–78; von Padberg, *Bonifatius: Missionar und Reformer*. See also the various papers collected in Reuter, ed., *The Greatest Englishman*; Felten, Jarnut, Mostert and von Padberg, eds., *Bonifatius: Leben und Nachwirken*.

5. Dierkens, "Superstitions", 9–26; Homann, Eckhard and Schmidt-Wiegand, "Indiculus superstitionum et paganiarum", 369–384.

6. See Glatthaar, *Bonifatius und das Sakrileg*, 435–455.

7. This was also noted by Murray, "Missionaries and Magic in Dark-Age Europe", 186–205, esp. 189.

8. Filotas, *Pagan Survivals*, 218–269.

9. Caesarius of Arles, *Sermones* 54.1, ed. Morin, 236; *Indiculus* 19.

10. See Agobard of Lyons, *De grandine et tonitruis*, ed. van Acker, 3–15; Burchard of Worms, *Decretum* XIX, ed. Schmitz, vol. II, 403–467. On the *Corrector sive medicus*, see Körntgen, "Canon Law and the Practice of Penance", 103–117; on Burchard's *Decretum* in general, see Austin, *Shaping Church Law*.

11. Caesarius of Arles, *Sermones* 54.1, ed. Morin, 236.

12. Martin of Braga, *De correctione rusticorum* 12, ed. Barlow, 183–203, esp. 191.

13. This sermon was partly edited in *Vita Eligii episcopi Noviomagensis* 16, ed. Krusch, 705–708; the full sermon is printed in PL 87, cols. 524D–550C. On this sermon, see McCune, "Rethinking the Pseudo-Eligius Sermon Collection", 445–476.

14. *Homilia de sacrilegiis* 9, ed. Caspari, 7.

15. *Indiculus* 13.

16. Caesarius of Arles, *Sermones* 54.1, ed. Morin, 236.

17. Martin of Braga, *De correctione rusticorum* 12, ed. Barlow, 191.

18. On the influence of Martin's treatise, see Hen, "Martin of Braga's *De correctione rusticorum*", 35–49.

19. See Filotas, *Pagan Survivals*, 241–242.

20. See Harmening, *Superstitio*, esp. 49–73.

21. Schmitt, "Les superstitions", 425–453; Schmitt, "'Religion populaire' et culture folklorique", 941–953. See also Künzel, "Paganism, syncrétisme, et culture religieuse populaire", 1055–1069.

22. *Indiculus* 24.

23. See Filotas, *Pagan Survivals*, 185.

24. Hen, *Culture and Religion*, 154–206, esp. 167–172; Hen, "Paganism and Superstitions", 229–240; Meens, "Magic and the Early Medieval World View", 285–295.

25. *Indiculus* 6.

26. Ibid. 20.

27. McNeil and Gamer, *Medieval Handbooks of Penance*, 420; Harmening, *Superstitio*, 159–161; Dierkens, "Superstitions", 19, 21.

28. Filotas, *Pagan Survivals*, 70–73, 136–137.

29. Tacitus, *De origine et situ Germanorum (Germania)* 9, ed. Winterbottom and Ogilvie, 42.; Augustine, *De civitate Dei* VII.14, ed. Dombart and Kalb, 197–198.

30. *Indiculus* 2, 6, 15 and 24, respectively.

31. Caesarius of Arles, *Sermones* 54.1, ed. Morin, 236.

32. Martin of Braga, *De correctione rusticorum* 11, ed. Barlaw, 190.

33. Pirmin of Reichenaus, *Scarapsus* 22, ed. Hauswald, 74–82.

34. See Hen, *Culture and Religion*, 154–206; Filotas, *Pagan Survivals*, 12–28; Palmer, "Defining Paganism in the Carolingian Worlds", 402–425.

35. See Hen, *Culture and Religion*, 167–172; Hen, "Paganism and Superstitions"; Zeddies, *Religio et sacrilegium*.

36. Markus, *The End of Ancient Christianity*, 207.

37. Ibid. 9.

38. Beard, North and Price, *Religions of Rome*, 21–24.

39. Caesarius of Arles, *Sermones* 54.6, ed. Morin, 239–240.

40. Nock, *Conversion*, 7, 14.

41. MacMullen, *Christianizing the Roman Empire*, 74.

42. Brown, *The Rise of Western Christendom*.

43. On all of these, see Hen, *Culture and Religion*, 154–206. See also Filotas, *Pagan Survivals*, especially 365–383.

44. Hen, *Culture and Religion*, 189–205.

45. See Rampton, "Burchard of Worms and Female Magical Ritual", 7–34.

46. Markus, "From Caesarius to Boniface", 154–172, esp. 171–172.

47. Schieffer, *Winfrid-Bonifatius*, 139–157; Löwe, "Pirmin, Willibrord und Bonifatius", 327–372; McKitterick, *Anglo-Saxon Missionaries in Germany*.

48. Wood, *The Missionary Life*, 57–78; Clay, *In the Shadow of Death*.

49. See, for example, Nelson, "Kingship and Empire in the Carolingian World", 52–87; Hannig, *Consensus fidelium*, 227–237.

50. Hen, *Culture and Religion*, 197–206; Hen, "The Annals of Metz and the Merovingian Past", 175–190.

51. This preoccupation was already noted by McKitterick, *The Carolingians and the Written Word*, esp. 200–210.

52. See Hen, "Paul the Deacon and the Frankish Liturgy", 205–221.

53. Bullough, "Roman Books and Carolingian *Renovatio*", 1–38.

54. Regino of Prüm, *Libri duo de synodalibus causis et disciplinis ecclesiasticis*, ed. Wasserschleben.

55. Vogel, *Medieval Liturgy*, 102–105; Bourque, *Étude sur les sacramentaires romains*, 292–299.

56. See Hen, *Roman Barbarians*, 3–21.

57. Thomas, *Religion and the Decline of Magic*.

58. Flint, *The Rise of Magic*.

59. Ibid. esp. 59–84.

60. Bede, *Historia ecclesiastica gentis Anglorum*, I.30 ed. and trans. Colgrave and Mynors, 106. I cite the English translation by McClure and Collins, 57.

61. Markus, "Gregory the Great and a Papal Missionary Strategy", 29–38; Markus, *Gregory the Great and His World*, 177–187.

62. Flint, *The Rise of Magic*, 376.

63. For a short introduction on the *sortes sanctorum*, see Flint, *The Rise of Magic*, 273–286.

64. On the first Church Council of Orléans, see Pontal, *Histoire des conciles*, 47–58.

65. *Concilium Aurelianenses I (511) 30*, in *Les canons*, ed. Gaudemet and Basdevant, vol. I, 88. I cite the English translation from Hillgarth, *Christianity and Paganism*, 103.

66. On the council of Auxerre, see Pontal, *Histoire des conciles*, 192–193.

67. *Synodus diocesana Autissiodorensis (561–605) 4*, in *Les canons*, ed. Gaudemet and Basdevant, vol. II, 488 (trans. Hillgarth, *Christianity and Paganism*, 103).

68. On this penitential, see Meens, "Reforming the Clergy", 154–167.

69. *Poenitentiale Bobbioense 26*, in *The Bobbio Missal: A Gallican Mass-Book*, ed. Lowe, 175.

70. Gregory of Tours, *Libri historiarum* V.14, ed. Krusch and Levison, 212. I cite the English translation by Thorpe, *Gregory of Tours*, 271–272.

71. Gregory of Tours, *Libri historiarum* IV.16, ed. Krusch and Levison, 149–150 (trans. Thorpe, *Gregory of Tours*, 212–213).

72. For a fine discussion of these passages, see Zeddies, *Religio et sacrilegium*, 260–270.

73. Augustine, *Confessiones* VIII.29, ed. Verheijen, 131.

74. Geertz, "An Anthropology of Religion", 71–89; Thomas, "An Anthropology of Religion", 91–109.

75. Geertz, "An Anthropology of Religion", 72.

76. Ibid.

77. Thomas, "An Anthropology of Religion", 96.

78. *Liber sacramentorum Romanae aecclesiae ordinis anni circuli (Sacramentarium Gelasianum)* III.xxiii.1308–III.xxiv.1320, ed. Mohlberg, Eizenhöfer and Siffrin, 191–193.

79. *Sacramentarium Gelasianum* III.xlii.1393–III.xlii.1397, ed. Mohlberg et al., 202.

80. *Sacramentarium Gelasianum* III.xliii.1398–III.xliii.1401 and liv.1461–liv.1470, ed. Mohlberg et al., 203 and 212–213, respectively.

81. *Sacramentarium Gelasianum* III.xliv.1402–III.xliv.1406, xlv.1407–xlv.1412, xlvii.1418–lvii.1421, ed. Mohlberg et al., 203, 204 and 205, respectively.

82. *Sacramentarium Gelasianum* III.lxx.1539–III.lxxi.1543, ed. Mohlberg et al., 222.

83. *Sacramentarium Gelasianum* III.xc.1606, ed. Mohlberg et al., 233.

84. For the *pro sterillitate mulierum*, see *Sacramentarium Gelasianum* III.liv.1461–III.liv.1470, ed. Mohlberg et al., 212–213. Caesarius of Arles, *Sermones* 51.4, ed. Morin, 229.

85. Gregory of Tours, *De virtutibus sancti Martini* IV.36, ed. Krusch, 208–209. I cite the English translation by Van Dam, *Saints and Their Miracles in Late Antique Gaul*, 299–300.

86. See Flint, "The Early Medieval 'Medicus'", 127–145.

87. Caesarius of Arles, *Sermones* 50.1, ed. Morin, 225; I cite the English translation by Mueller, *Caesarius of Arles: Sermons*, vol. I, 254.

88. Gregory of Tours, *Liber in Gloria martyrum* 83, ed. Krusch, 94. I cite the English translation by Van Dam, *Gregory of Tours: Glory of the Martyrs*, 107–108.

89. Gregory of Tours, *Liber in Gloria martyrum* 83, ed. Krusch, 95 (trans. Van Dam, *Gregory of Tours: Glory of the Martyrs*, 109).

90. See Agobard of Lyons, *De grandine et tonitruis*; on this treatise, see Jolivet, "Agobard de Lyon et les faiseurs de pluie", 15–25; Meens, "Thunder over Lyon", 157–166.

91. Blöcker, "Wetterzauber", 117–131.

92. Meens, "Thunder over Lyon", esp. 160–166.

93. Benedict of Aniane, *Supplementum* XCIII.1366–XCIII.1369, in *Le sacramentaire grégorien*, ed. Deshusses, 449.

94. Meens, "Magic and the Early Medieval World View", 291.

95. This is corroborated by numerous archaeological findings. See, for example, Dierkens, "The Evidence of Archaeology", 39–64; Meaney, *Anglo-Saxon Amulets and Cursing Stones*.

96. *Indiculus* 26.

PART III

★

PARALLEL TRADITIONS

Chapter 7

Magic in Medieval Byzantium

ALICIA WALKER

In Byzantium, magic was consistently categorized as a body of non-Christian knowledge and practices, which in turn was often associated with pre-Christian, pagan traditions. As a consequence, modern scholarship often recounts the history of magic in Byzantium in conjunction with the history of Christianization and the gradual abandonment of pagan culture. Scholarship on Byzantine magic is therefore significantly more abundant regarding the early Byzantine period (ca. 320–726), the era when the Empire's transition from a predominantly pagan society to a predominantly Christian one transpired. In recent decades, attention has begun to turn toward the study of magic in the middle Byzantine era (ca. 843–1204), that is to say, the epoch after Iconoclasm (ca. 726–843).[1] Still, the topic of magic cannot be said to have established itself in the mainstream of Byzantine historiography, a point illustrated by the fact that none of the three large-scale handbooks for Byzantine studies published between 2008 and 2010 includes an essay devoted specifically to the topic of magic or the occult.[2]

Other essays in this volume discuss magic in the Late Antique world, a period when the Roman-Byzantine Empire still encompassed both the East and West. The current chapter focuses instead on attitudes toward and practices of magic in the middle Byzantine era, by which time the Eastern Roman Empire had emerged as a geographic and cultural entity separate from Western medieval Europe. The chapter first evaluates the definition of magic in the civil and canon law of the middle Byzantine period, as well as that of related terminology in other textual genres, such as historical chronicles. Issues of gender in middle Byzantine conceptions of magic are addressed, including the particular roles that women were understood to play as practitioners and victims of occult and demonic activities. Attention then turns to a deeper exploration of learned magic in medieval Byzantium, especially its content and forms of transmission. Finally, the late and post-Byzantine magical traditions that have roots in the middle Byzantine era are briefly mentioned, and the particular continuities with medieval Byzantine magic that they maintained are noted. Throughout this chapter, written sources are considered in tandem with the visual and material evidence of Byzantine magic: artifacts not only complement but also augment the available record, shedding light on aspects of Byzantine magic that are unattested in written documentation.[3]

Defining "Magic" in Medieval Byzantium: Texts, Images, Objects

As in the West, church authorities played a significant part not only in the social approval and rejection of magic but also in the very definition of what magic was. The specific natures of different magical endeavors varied greatly from one another, and judgment regarding whether a particular activity was acceptable to Christian Orthodoxy could change over time. A consistent defining element for occult practices across the middle Byzantine period was the belief that such endeavors involved the marshaling of supernatural powers outside of ecclesiastical authority and rituals. Extra-institutional and extra-liturgical activities and devices might employ Christian imagery and language, but they did so in a manner not sanctioned by the church. Occult traditions can also be distinguished in relation to class, with individuals of lower social echelons typically being associated with what might be labeled as superstitious activities transmitted through popular practice and oral tradition, whereas educated people engaged in the exploration of more esoteric, book-based occult knowledge. Such distinctions were by no means absolute, however, as indicated by certain practices (for example, the use of amulets) and beliefs (in, for example, the supernatural power of antique statues) that are evident across the social spectrum of medieval Byzantium.

References to occult practices and practitioners are found in a wide range of written sources, including law codes, historical accounts, homilies, and saints' lives. Middle Byzantine legislation provides definitions of unsanctioned activities, and these sources offer useful guidelines for understanding the position of the Byzantine State and the Orthodox Church regarding what constituted magic.[4] Although middle Byzantine civil law generally reiterates the regulations articulated in early Byzantine imperial codes, a noteworthy shift occurred with the promulgation of Novel 65 under Emperor Leo VI (r. 886–912), which terminated the long-standing toleration of benign magic (such as spells and amulets intended to aid a harvest or cure an illness).[5] In the post-Iconoclastic era, only the power of Christ and his saints could be marshaled against threats or beseeched for assistance, and their aid was secured by means of objects, language, and rituals authorized by the church. Magic was judged to be inherently evil, regardless of the practitioner's intentions, and those who participated in it were, technically speaking, apostates.

Although individual types of magic are not precisely defined in the middle Byzantine civil codes, canon law of the era is more specific. An important source for middle Byzantine ecclesiastical definitions of magic is the commentary begun in the 1170s by the scholar Theodore Balsamon (d. ca. 1195), which discussed the rulings on magic found in Canon 61 of the famous late seventh-century ecclesiastical synod, the so-called Council in Trullo (691/692). Balsamon cites a variety of occult practices and the individuals who participated in them, thereby clarifying the kinds of activities that were denounced by the church. He definitively condemns astrology and astronomy, judging the two to be one and the same. This position is of interest because Balsamon's prominent forerunner, the canonist John Zonaras (d. ca. 1159), had distinguished between the two types of knowledge, condoning astronomy as a legitimate academic field of inquiry.[6] Balsamon was writing, however, in the wake of a campaign spearheaded by the Emperor Manuel I Komnenos (r. 1143–1180) to defend the orthodoxy of astrology, and Balsamon's definitive rejection of both domains of knowledge can be read as an uncompromising response to the emperor's efforts.[7]

Other practitioners of magic censured by Balsamon included: diviners (μάντεις), both those who observed the natural world in order to prognosticate (e.g., palm readers and augurs) and those who used tools to reveal hidden information (e.g., lecanomancers, who performed divination by means of interpreting the surface of liquid contained within a vessel); the so-called *hekantontarchos* (ἑκαντόνταρχος), an ambiguous category of magicians who deceived and manipulated ordinary people by means of their cunning; amulet peddlers; snake charmers; *engastrimythoi* (ἐγγαστρίμυθοι, literally "belly-talkers"), a type of false prophet who claimed to deliver oracles while feigning demonic possession; and so-called *ghitevtai* (γητευταί), people, especially priests and monks, who distorted Orthodox religion by invoking the names of Christian holy people in their incantations and purveying sacred objects and images to be used as amulets or in divinatory rituals.[8] This last group no doubt raised particular concern for the church because the *ghitevtai* employed Christian terms, emblems, and objects in their machinations, thereby blurring the line between Orthodox and unorthodox practices and potentially confusing the ignorant, who might easily mistake these rituals and devices as legitimate.[9]

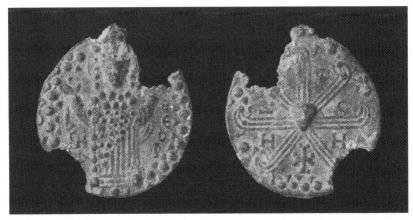

FIGURE 7.1. Amulet depicting Saint Theophano (obv) and the Wandering Womb (rev), middle Byzantine, 900–1200, lead, diam. 3.2 cm. Harvard Art Museums / Arthur M. Sackler Museum, bequest of Thomas Whittemore, 1951.31.4.1869. Photo: Katya Kallsen. © President and Fellows of Harvard College.

Material evidence for the combination of Christian and magical imagery is found in a sizable corpus of middle Byzantine amulets.[10] The group includes objects in a variety of media, such as enamel, bronze, and semi-precious stone. Most of these charms were intended to provide medical assistance. They frequently depict the so-called wandering womb (a motif that visualizes the inflicted body part that the amulet was intended to cure) or the Chnoubis (a pre-Christian apotropaic emblem in the shape of a lion-headed serpent), both of which are often presented in tandem with portraits of the Virgin Mary, a saint (Figure 7.1), or a narrative scene from the New Testament. These talismanic objects share many features with early Byzantine magical devices and therefore point to either the revival or survival in the middle Byzantine era of Late Antique magical techniques, especially those of a medical nature.[11] Based on the high quality and relatively valuable substances of these amulets, Jeffrey Spier suggests that they were used by the middle Byzantine elite. An apparent tenth-century surge in their production may reflect a renewed scholarly interest in occult treatises around that time.[12]

As regards the penalties for unorthodox activities, middle Byzantine historical accounts report the prosecution of prominent individuals found guilty of malicious magic, particularly spells or other machinations against emperors or their close associates. Civil authorities exercised jurisdiction over individuals who committed serious crimes by occult means; they could (and did) issue punishments as severe as blinding, banishment, or even execution. For instance, the monk Theodore Santabarenos (d. ca. 919) was reported to have used magic to gain the favor of the Emperor Basil I (r. 867–886) and to turn him against his son and heir, Leo, who had denounced Theodore as a sorcerer. Theodore's schemes were eventually exposed, and after being found guilty at trial, he was flogged, exiled, and later blinded.[13] In the 1160s, the Emperor Manuel I commanded that the courtiers Skleros Seth and Michael Sikidites be blinded with hot irons as punishment for their use of malicious magic: in the former case, to seduce a young virgin and, in the latter case, to conjure deceptive, destructive visions that attacked and tormented his victims.[14] In these high-profile examples, however, it must be noted that the condemned individuals were involved not only in magic but also in court intrigue, including treason, and the severity of their sentences reflected the seriousness of these political crimes.

Ecclesiastical authorities dealt with the lesser transgressions of common people. Balsamon instructs that the rulings against those found guilty of magic should be determined in relation to the degree of their intentionality and malice. Those who performed or sought magical intervention could be punished with six years of excommunication, and clerics might be defrocked, but ecclesiastical judgments tended to be more clement in instances of mild violations. Indeed, the naïve, the simpleminded, and the repentant could reasonably hope for more relaxed sentences. This conciliatory attitude was not apparent in the earliest Byzantine civil codes of the fourth century, which roundly condemned practitioners of any form of occult activity and equated their actions with the capital offenses of murder and treason.[15] This strident attitude initially shaped earlier canon law as well, but church authorities rapidly made finer distinctions among magical acts, and already in the later fourth century, they had begun to differentiate between categories of magical practice that fell, for example, alongside the serious but more redeemable transgressions of apostasy and heresy.[16] Balsamon affirmed this position by recommending forbearance toward individuals whose social background or level of education rendered them ill-equipped to identify practitioners of the occult or to reject their aid.[17] This dispensation was justified on the grounds that some sorcerers and amulet purveyors were themselves monks and priests, and the objects they proffered often employed Christian motifs and names. Balsamon reasoned that common people might be confused about the legitimacy of the services and products being purveyed.[18]

The concern to distinguish Orthodox religious practices from pagan and/or magical acts also affected the reintroduction of images into Christian devotion following Iconoclasm. Iconophile theologians set strict guidelines for the depiction of holy people and the veneration of them through icons, an effort geared toward guaranteeing that the faithful did not inadvertently stray into idolatry when paying homage to Christ or the saints via their images. Post-Iconoclastic icons portrayed holy people according to established criteria that were designed to affiliate the depicted figure with a particular, unmistakable individual; labels identifying the saints by name furthered this effort and became an essential feature of Orthodox representation.[19] This change reflected a new understanding about how icons worked: the post-Iconoclastic theology specified that images rendered in icons did not operate as independent, powerful objects; nor could the image's potency be magnified through repetition.[20] Rather, the post-Iconoclastic icon was qualified as impotent material, which served as a mere conduit for prayers to the holy person who was the prototype of the image and the source of its spiritual power.[21] Aimed at preventing idolatry, these new criteria identified by exclusion a variety of other kinds of images and objects – such as amulets, repeating emblems that were thought to increase in power by means of their multiplication, and non-canonical portraits of holy people – that had been less controlled and less frequently condemned before Iconoclasm but that now were definitively relegated to a position outside of officially sanctioned Christian practices.

In Byzantine texts more broadly, the words commonly used in reference to the occult include μαγεία (magic), μάγος (magician), φαρμακεία (spells and/or potions), γοητεία (sorcery), and γόης (sorcerer).[22] Terms such as these were often deployed in Iconophile rhetoric as a means to discredit religious and political enemies, especially Iconoclast authorities. For example, Iconophile sources affiliate the Iconoclast patriarch John the Grammarian (d. ca. 867) with sorcery and divination, a claim that may reflect his actual interest in branches of learning that the Orthodox Church considered heretical.[23] The condemnation of John is also apparent in the visual culture of post-Iconoclastic Byzantine. A marginal illustration in the ninth-century Khludov Psalter creates a typological parallel between John and Simon Magus, the Samarian sorcerer who offended God by trying to buy from the apostles Peter and John the ability to channel the Holy Spirit (Acts 8:9–8:24) (Moscow, Hist. Mus., MS. 129. D, fol. 51v) (Figure 7.2). The manuscript illumination shows John the Grammarian trampled by his historical opponent, the Iconophile Patriarch Nikephoros I (d. 828), while Simon Magus writhes under the foot of St. Peter. Much as Peter revealed Simon to be an enemy of God and a sinner, Nikephoros is credited with exposing the false teachings and spiritual corruption of John the Grammarian and his Iconoclast cohort.

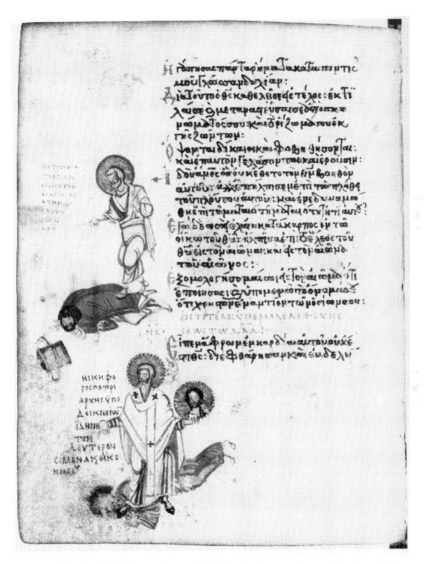

FIGURE 7.2. Patriarch Nikephoros I trampling John the Grammarian and the Apostle Peter trampling Simon Magus, Khludov Psalter, middle Byzantine, mid-ninth century, pigment on vellum, 19.5 × 15 cm. Hist. Mus., Moscow, MS. D.129, fol. 51v. © State Historical Museum, Moscow.

FIGURE 7.3. John the Grammarian performing lecanomancy, *History* of John Skylitzes, Norman-Byzantine, twelfth century, Sicily, pigment on vellum, 35.5 × 27 cm. Biblioteca Nacional de España, Madrid, vitr. 26–2, fol. 58r. © Biblioteca Nacional de España, Madrid.

The late eleventh-century chronicle of the Byzantine historian John Skylitzes is one of several middle Byzantine accounts that refer to John the Grammarian as a sorcerer and accuse him of honing abilities in various occult techniques, including lecanomancy, heptoscopy (reading the omens in animal livers), *stoicheiosis* (manipulating statues to influence fortune and bring about desired results), and necromancy (conjuring the dead).[24] An illustrated twelfth-century manuscript of Skylitzes's chronicle, thought to have been produced in Norman Sicily, depicts John the Grammarian exercising his unorthodox skills. In one scene, he is labeled as a lecanomancer and shown leaning over a large bowl as he divines the name of the successor to the Iconoclast Emperor Theophilos (r. 829–842). With one hand, John stirs the waters in the vessel and with the other, he points to a star in the heavens. Theophilos sits enthroned to the right and observes intently the lecanomantic ritual (Madrid, Biblioteca Nacional de España, vitr. 26–2, fol. 58r) (Figure 7.3).[25]

Numerous references to lecanomancy in middle Byzantine texts suggest that it was a prevalent divinatory practice. The tools used in medieval magic are rarely preserved, but a middle Byzantine glass bowl, now outfitted as a chalice and held in the treasury of the Church of San Marco in Venice, may have served in lecanomantic rituals.[26] It shows around the exterior wall seven medallions framing classicizing figures, several of whom are related to divination, including an augur, the Greco-Roman god Mercury, and Odysseus

FIGURE 7.4. San Marco bowl, middle Byzantine, eleventh or twelfth century, enameled and gilded glass, h. 17 cm, diam. 17 cm (with handles, 33 cm). Treasury of San Marco, Venice. Per gentile concessione della Procuratoria di San Marco, Venezia, Italia.

FIGURE 7.5. Detail of pseudo-inscription, San Marco bowl. Per gentile concessione della Procuratoria di San Marco, Venezia, Italia.

(Figure 7.4). Around the base and rim of the vessel (Figure 7.5) are inscribed pseudo-Arabic bands (combinations of letter-like forms that resemble Arabic but that do not form consistently legible letters or words). In the middle Byzantine period, magic in general and divination in particular were understood to have grown from both Greco-Roman and ancient Near Eastern roots. Medieval Islamic cultures were often referred to by the names of their purported ancestors (such as the Chaldeans or the Egyptians), a convention that may have led to associating magical expertise with contemporary Muslims and that was certainly affirmed by the expertise in astrology and other divinatory arts that medieval Islamic groups had developed during the tenth and subsequent centuries.[27] The combination of classicizing iconography and Islamicizing script on the San Marco bowl may therefore reflect an understanding of both ancient and foreign cultures as potent sources of divinatory knowledge.[28] Together the imagery and "inscriptions" on the object would have empowered it for use in supernatural rituals.

Various additional forms of magic are mentioned in other middle Byzantine historical accounts. These references are often to types of divination, a trend that may be due to the importance that prognostication played in Byzantine politics, which was a topic of greatest interest to most chroniclers.[29] The early thirteenth-century account by Niketas Choniates, for example, records several cases of individuals performing supernatural acts at the request of emperors who sought to gain information about the future, including a (false) seer, Basilakes, whose followers interpreted his enigmatic utterances as prophecies, and a sorcerer, Skleros Seth, who had been trained since childhood as a lecanomancer.[30] These and other illicit activities mentioned by Byzantine historians closely parallel the occult practices condemned by Balsamon, a correlation that suggests the vitality and pervasiveness of these unorthodox pursuits at all levels of medieval Byzantine society. Indeed, a tenth-century text that provides instructions on how to prepare for an imperial expedition specifies that manuals for the interpretation of dreams (βιβλίον τὸν Ὀνειροκρίτην) and "chances and occurrences" (βιβλίον Συναντηματικόν, presumably a book for interpreting omens) be included in the baggage taken on campaign, a recommendation that is made without any indication that the use of such books would be controversial.[31] Other types of prognostication attested in the middle Byzantine period include chremetismomancy (the interpretation of horses' neighs) and palomancy (divination based on the inadvertent twitching of an individual's body).[32]

Accusations of magical transgressions were not only leveled at prominent Iconoclasts but were also used as a form of political calumny more generally. For example, the courtier Alexios Axouch, who had served faithfully under the Emperor Manuel I Komnenos, was falsely accused of sorcery by enemies in the twelfth century (ca. 1167).[33] These allegations may have gained traction because Axouch was of Seljuq origin. His "Persian" background could have encouraged prejudices that associated occult learning and practices with foreigners, especially Muslims. In some cases, such as that of Axouch, the denunciation of a high-ranking courtier as a sorcerer can be dismissed as a form of political invective that was unrelated to "real" magic. Yet in other instances, these indictments remain consistent with a broader definition of magic as any act that exercises power or promotes beliefs that reside outside of Christian Orthodoxy. Such actions and ideas could include heresies like Iconoclasm, which were believed by some Byzantine commentators to operate in an "unofficial" domain and to have been inspired by Satan or his demons.[34]

Another important textual source for middle Byzantine conceptions of magic is saints' lives, in which the supernatural machinations and moral weakness of sorcerers and their clients are sharply contrasted with the virtue and spiritual strength of Christian holy people and their followers.[35] These stories often recount how a naïve person engages a magician to help solve a persistent problem, not realizing that this relationship will ensnare him or her in evil forces. After suffering the assaults of demons, the individual seeks the aid of a holy person to escape these supernatural tormentors. Following further anguish, the petitioner and the saint successfully repulse the demons, and the Christian repents for having failed in his or her vigilance against the deceptions of Satan. The moral of these stories typically affirms that prayers directed to Christian holy people are the only means of gaining legitimate supernatural assistance. In some accounts, magicians are so impressed by the superior power of Christ that they convert to Christianity.

An intriguing middle Byzantine visual depiction of occult practice and the besting of demonic forces through Christian faith is found in a ninth-century (ca. 879–883) manuscript recording the homilies of the late fourth-century Bishop (and later Saint) Gregory of Nazianzus. One illustration depicts a scene from the life of the early Christian saint Cyprian, who had been a sorcerer prior to his conversion. In the upper register, Cyprian is portrayed in the clothing of an ancient philosopher (Paris, Bibliothèque nationale, ms. Gr. 510, fol. 332v) (Figure 7.6). This iconography no doubt reflects the belief, established in early Byzantine sources, that pagan philosophers were practitioners of the occult.[36] He is surrounded by magical devices, including a globe (used for astrological projections), a pagan cult statue (which was believed to be inhabited by demons), and a large bowl (in which stand two miniature figures that likely represent the effigies used in love spells).[37] According to his vita, Cyprian attempted to seduce the Christian virgin, Justina, through demonic influence. His advances were thwarted, however, by Justina's prayers to Christ, an event conveyed in visual terms by the black-figured demon (mostly effaced) who flies back to Cyprian after being repulsed.[38] Inspired by the efficacy of Christ's

FIGURE 7.6. Scenes from the life of Saint Cyprian, *Homilies* of Gregory of Nazianzus, middle Byzantine, ca. 879–883, pigment on vellum. Bibliothèque nationale, Paris, ms. Gr. 510, fol. 332v. © Bibliothèque nationale de France.

intervention, Cyprian converted to Christianity. His baptism is depicted in the lower register; beside him, a pile of tablets representing his occult knowledge has been cast to the flames. Cyprian was a victim of the infamous late third-century persecutions of Christians during the reign of the Roman Emperor Diocletian (r. 284–305). The images represent, therefore, a middle Byzantine conception of a Late Roman pagan sorcerer and the tools of his trade, as well as the power of Christ and his devotees to triumph over the dark arts of the occult.

Women and Magic in Byzantium

Although "witches" in the Western sense (i.e., women who form pacts with Satan and perform rites of demonic worship) never comprised a significant category in the history of Byzantine magic, there were gendered notions of how demons and humans interacted.[39] A common topos in saints' lives is the woman possessed by, unwittingly in league with, or desired as the object of demonic forces. Women are also commonly characterized by hypersexual desires, either being consumed by such temptations themselves (often as the result of a spell cast against them) or ensnaring others with the unnatural intensity of their own physical allure.[40] In cataloging John the Grammarian's travesties, for instance, Skylitzes recounts that John lured nuns to an underground workshop, where he consorted with them indecently and manipulated them to collaborate in his sorcery.[41] We might understand these stories as exposing a societal anxiety surrounding the control of female bodies, as well as the affirmation of a belief in the spiritual vulnerability of women, who were thought to be too naïve to recognize and too weak to resist the magician's or demon's deceptions.

Women also appear as the practitioners of magic, often in the form of the drunken old woman who peddles false prophecies or who manufactures illicit amulets.[42] In this respect, the middle Byzantine era saw the continuation of a Late Antique topos that tagged marginal women as the agents of unorthodox supernatural actions.[43] In a few instances, specific women of high social status were associated with the occult, but usually they thwarted Byzantine expectations for female behavior in other ways as well, and their magical activities can be understood as a subset of a broader range of traits that made them unconventional characters.

Perhaps the most prominent of such women to bear the taint of the occult was the Empress Zoe (d. 1050). In describing her reign, the historian Michael Psellos

FIGURE 7.7. Amulet depicting the Holy Rider attacking the demon Gyllou (obv) and magical signs (rev), Byzantine, tenth or eleventh century (?), from Asia Minor, silver, diam. 5 cm. Ashmolean Museum, University of Oxford, AN1980.53. © Ashmolean Museum, University of Oxford.

(ca. 1018–1081) insinuated her involvement with two activities of questionable nature: she mixed unguents and perfumes in her chambers, which may be an allusion to the production of magical potions; and she prayed to an unusual icon of Christ that changed colors in response to the questions that she posed, a practice that can be interpreted as a form of prognostication and that represents a use of icons that was unconventional, if not unorthodox.[44] These allusions must be read, however, in relation to Psellos's broader attitude toward Zoe, which was not favorable. The suggestion of her involvement in occult practices may be, therefore, part of his larger effort to demonstrate her unfitness to rule.

A final domain of supernatural manipulation commonly ascribed to women in the Byzantine literature was medical magic, particularly that having to do with conception, birth, and gynecological disorders.[45] Many middle Byzantine amulets appear to have been designed to assist women, as indicated by their depiction of the wandering womb and/or the Holy Rider (an apotropaic figure who was believed to repel the infamous miscarriage-inducing, child-stealing demon Gyllou) (Figure 7.7).[46] Seeking unconventional means to combat medical conditions was a path not limited to women of lower social standing. At the urging of her husband, Romanos III (r. 1028–1034), the aforementioned Empress Zoe, who was significantly past childbearing age at the time of their marriage, hung charms and chains from her body that were intended to assist her in conception, an effort that Michael Psellos dismissed as futile nonsense.[47] We can speculate that midwives may have been particularly knowledgeable about medico-magical amulets, an expertise that would have been of obvious value, if not necessity, in their line of work.[48]

Magic and Erudition: The "Occult Sciences" of Medieval Byzantium

In addition to popular magical practices and the objects associated with them, the middle Byzantine period also witnessed substantial interest among members of the Byzantine elite in the study of what modern scholars have termed the "occult sciences." Maria Mavroudi and Paul Magdalino differentiate the occult sciences from magic more broadly based on former's literate, sophisticated character, which required significant preparatory education on the part of those who attempted to master it.[49] Generally speaking, these erudite pursuits were decidedly outside of Orthodox Christian practice, but they could be defended as potentially acceptable domains of intellectual exploration. Learned people who perused occult texts were careful to emphasize that their interests remained purely theoretical and that they did not practice the methods in which these books instructed.[50] They justified their study of unorthodox wisdom as a way to combat un-Christian teachings or promoted this learning as a necessary part of their broader effort to understand and preserve ancient knowledge in all its forms.

The types of learning that can be classified within the occult sciences include astronomy and astrology, as well as dream interpretation, alchemy, the reading of omens, and the understanding of the sympathetic properties of natural materials, like stones. As articulated in the work of the middle Byzantine scholar of "pagan" learning Michael Psellos, who was mentioned in the previous section, all of these fields of study were understood to be related to ancient philosophy and specifically to theories of cosmic sympathy, which accounted for natural phenomena that were otherwise inexplicable.[51] From the perspective of learned men like Psellos, such knowledge was fundamentally separate from the popular magic peddled by crazy old women and shifty charlatans on street corners and the unorthodox machinations employed by members of the imperial court.[52] The occult sciences represented an erudite and exclusive body of wisdom that carried the authority of an ancient textual tradition inherited from the Greco-Roman and Near Eastern worlds.

This esoteric learning was also deeply imbricated with bodies of scientific knowledge that were of interest to other medieval cultures. In particular, the tenth century witnessed a massive effort on the part of the medieval Islamic Abbāsid Dynasty (750–1250) to obtain and translate into Arabic numerous manuscripts that preserved ancient scientific and philosophical knowledge. Medieval Byzantine scholars were very aware of the Islamic engagement with and accomplishments in a broad range of scientific fields. In some instances,

Byzantine intellectuals were in direct contact with foreign students and scholars from the Islamic world, particularly those with connections to the sophisticated courtly and intellectual communities of the Ummayads in Spain (711–1031), the Fatimids in Egypt and Syria (909–1171), and the ʿAbbāsids in the Near East.[53] Arabic manuscripts on occult sciences were also translated into Greek, a phenomenon that is particularly well documented in the field of dream interpretation.[54]

Western European connections with Byzantine magic are less evident in the surviving record, although they certainly existed. The Lombardian diplomat Liudprand of Cremona (d. ca. 972), who visited Constantinople at least twice in the tenth century as an emissary from the court of Otto I (r. 936–973), speaks of political prophecies circulating at the court that compelled Emperor Nikephoros II Phokas (r. 963–969) to go on campaign against the Arabs. Liudprand reports that the Byzantines interpreted a prophecy that "[t]he lion and the cub together shall exterminate the wild donkey" to mean that Nikephoros (as the lion) and Otto (as the cub) would together defeat the Arabs (as the wild donkey). Liudprand disagrees with this reading, however, proposing instead that Otto was the triumphant lion, his heir was the cub, and the Byzantines were the donkey.[55] The passage demonstrates that interpreting omens was a practice in which both the Byzantines and Lombards engaged.

The translation of Arabic scientific and occult texts into Latin, particularly during the eleventh and twelfth centuries, is well known.[56] Byzantium participated in this phenomenon indirectly, because many of the Arabic manuscripts transmitted to the Latin West had been translated from Byzantine Greek sources in the immediately preceding centuries. But Byzantium also contributed directly to the growth in Western European knowledge of the occult at this time through the translation into Latin of medieval Greek manuscripts. These included texts on the magical properties of animals, plants, and stones; manuals for dream interpretation; and treatises on astrology.[57] At least some of these manuscripts are known to have been translated in Constantinople and then exported to the West.[58] It has been suggested that the Western European interest in astronomy during the mid-twelfth century may have been an impetus for the defense of astrology endorsed by Manuel I, who both emulated Latin fashions and competed with Latin powers; he may have viewed the Western use of astral prognostication as a skill that demanded cultivation and legitimation in Byzantium as well.[59] The topic of Byzantine-Latin connections in the domain of magic is only now beginning to receive sustained attention and is a topic that requires further research.

The pursuit of occult knowledge as part of an education in ancient learning is attested for a number of middle Byzantine intellectuals. Michael Psellos (discussed in the previous section) and the learned twelfth-century imperial princess Anna Komnena (d. 1153/1154) wrote about having surveyed such literature.[60] However, the cautious and circuitous manner in which they and other middle Byzantine scholars refer to these undertakings points to the risk that engagement with unsanctioned intellectual domains could carry. Indeed, a student of Michael Psellos, John Italos (ca. 1025–1082), was put on trial in 1082 for offenses that included paganism, a charge that refers to his efforts at interweaving the study of ancient philosophy and Christian theology.[61] It must be noted, however, that the percentage of the population capable of reading texts on philosophy and the occult sciences in the middle Byzantine era was extraordinarily small, and within the very limited group equipped to pursue the mastery of such erudite knowledge, it is possible that even fewer educated people would have risked this potentially unorthodox undertaking.[62]

Michael Psellos is a particularly noteworthy figure in the study of the occult sciences because of the extensive preservation of his writings and the unusually detailed justifications he offers for his interest in ostensibly unorthodox learning.[63] Also of note is Psellos's terminology for the occult knowledge he explored, which includes vocabulary different from that usually applied to magic in Byzantium. As Paul Magdalino observes, Psellos employed words that emphasize the inaccessible, mysterious, and even dangerous nature of the specialized knowledge he has plumbed, including ἀπόκρυφος ("apocryphal," but in the sense of the Latin equivalent, *occultus*), ἀπόρρητος ("forbidden" or "secret"), and ἄρρητος ("unspoken," "unutterable," or "inexplicable").[64] He is known to have studied alchemy, astronomy, the magical attributes of stones, and the talismanic properties of statues. Furthermore, he wrote treatises on some of these topics. It must be emphasized, however, that Psellos does not represent the norm for middle Byzantine attitudes toward magic. He was a man of exceptional erudition with privileged access to some of the richest libraries in the medieval world and clearly possessed an intellectual drive that pushed him in directions few others followed. Even after factoring in the extent to which he introduced his students to unconventional fields of knowledge, it remains unclear whether he set in motion a broad-based revival of occult learning. Nor is it yet possible to determine if his articulation of the relationship between ancient philosophy and the occult sciences was widely understood or shared.[65]

Among the fields of occult science that Psellos and others explored, the most significant arena for the continuation of ancient theories and practices was astrology.⁶⁶ Although Byzantine sources sometimes differentiated astronomy as an objective science from astrology as the application of celestial observations for oracular interpretations, such distinction was not consistently applied. In particular, astronomy (ἀστρονομία) could include astrology (ἀστρολογία), and astronomy / astrology could encompass orthodox activities (such as determining the liturgical calendar or navigation), as well as unsanctioned practices (like prognostication). Furthermore, there was no strict terminological distinction for those who studied the stars, with *astronomos* (ἀστρονόμος), *astrologos* (ἀστρολόγος), and *mathematikos* (μαθηματικός) being used interchangeably.⁶⁷ Predictably, church officials condemned astral prognostication uncompromisingly, but the practice was actively pursued in imperial circles. Horoscopes were cast for some emperors, including Constantine VII Porphyrogenitus (r. 945–949).⁶⁸ As noted in the previous section, Manuel I commissioned a defense of astrology justifying the consultation of the stars on the basis of their being part of the natural world created by God. Gathering knowledge that could be gained through them was therefore argued to be within the domain of Orthodox learning and practice.⁶⁹

The interpretation of dreams was another field that received extensive attention, as demonstrated by the significant corpus of manuscripts that preserve *oneirocritica* (ὀνειροκριτικά, or manuals for dream interpretation). The *oneirocritica* saw a surge in popularity during the middle Byzantine period and were consulted by people throughout Byzantine society.⁷⁰ The so-called provincial magnate Eustathius Boilas inventoried an *oneirocriticon* in his will of 1059, a record that indicates not only the ownership of such books but also the acceptability of their use.⁷¹ Some of these texts were the products of a shared Byzantine-Islamic tradition, with cross-cultural transmission and traces of the translation process evident in their content.⁷² Like astrology, dream interpretation was defended on the basis of divine sanction; it was claimed that God sent dreams as a means of guiding the recipient, although the Orthodox Church was not always in agreement with this claim and only recognized some prophetic dreams as legitimate.⁷³ The deep interest that prognostication of various kinds garnered at the Byzantine court and among the aristocracy is not surprising. The emperor and his circle often faced extremely demanding responsibilities and uncertain circumstances. They no doubt sought all means possible to maintain perspective on and control over the future, even if that effort took them to the shadowy depths of lecanomantic vessels and the dark voids encircling the stars.⁷⁴

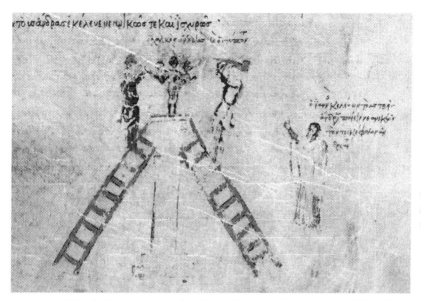

FIGURE 7.8. John the Grammarian performing *stoicheiosis* with a statue in the Hippodrome, *History* of John Skylitzes, Norman-Byzantine, twelfth century, Sicily, pigment on vellum, 35.5 x 27 cm. Biblioteca Nacional de España, Madrid, vitr. 26–2, fol. 65r. © Biblioteca Nacional de España, Madrid.

The Byzantines believed that pagan statuary, especially cult statues, could be inhabited by demons, and the ability to manipulate the supernatural power of these sculptures (their *stoicheion*, στοιχεῖον) was recognized as an occult skill with direct connections to pagan learning. Constantinople possessed a large number of ancient Greek and Roman statues that had been transported to the city shortly after its founding in the fourth century.[75] An eighth-century description of Constantinople and its monuments, the *Parastaseis syntomoi chronikai*, is replete with references to the magical properties of these sculptures.[76] *Stoicheiosis* is also one of the black arts that the ninth-century Iconoclast patriarch John the Grammarian is claimed to have practiced. The illustrated version of the chronicle of John Skylitzes depicts John orchestrating the disfigurement of a statue in order to predict and influence the demise of the emperor's foreign enemies (Madrid, Biblioteca Nacional de España, vitr. 26–2, fol. 65r) (Figure 7.8).[77] Like many domains of magic, belief in the supernatural powers of statuary and monumental apotropaioi was not unique to the Byzantine world. In particular, medieval Islamic sources demonstrate a strong connection with Byzantine traditions in this field and offer intriguing opportunities for future cross-cultural study.[78]

Although the lines between magic and religion were in some respects clearer in the more distinctly Christian culture of the middle Byzantine era than they had been in the transitional period of early Byzantine history, there was still ambiguity regarding the nature of supernatural powers. For instance, a common feature of numerous middle Byzantine churches is the use of animals (including those that show a distinct stylistic similarity to motifs in Islamic art) and/or pseudo-Arabic motifs in the decoration of the exteriors and interiors of these sacred spaces, especially at liminal junctures, including doors, windows, and the iconostasis (the barrier between the nave and the sanctuary of a church).[79] The use of natural and foreign motifs, which represent seemingly profane iconography, may at first appear incongruous in these holy buildings. Yet these emblems and the supernatural power they were thought to convey can be productively understood as essentially neutral in character; their potentially "magical" versus "sacred" status was generated not intrinsically but instead through the contexts of their use.[80] These powerful signs could be legitimized through their placement in holy buildings, where their supernatural power helped ward off evil and protect sanctified spaces.[81] This final example emphasizes once again an essential aspect of magic in Byzantium: the meaning of the term was never fully fixed, varying over time and among different divisions of society, or even among individuals in a single place and time.

The Legacy of Medieval Byzantine Magic

In conclusion, a word should be said about the afterlife of medieval Byzantine magic. Conventional periodization ends the middle Byzantine era in 1204 with the Crusaders' sacking of Constantinople, which remained in Western hands until it was reclaimed by the Byzantines in 1261. Late Byzantine (ca. 1261–1453) and early modern Greek magic show clear continuities and intriguing discontinuities with earlier traditions.[82] A possible survival of middle Byzantine occult practices is found in a fifteenth-century Italo-Byzantine Greek manuscript attributed to a doctor, John of Aron. In one scene is illustrated a lecanomantic ritual (Bologna, Biblioteca Universitaria, ms. 3632, fol. 350v) (Figure 7.9), which shows the diviner seated on a chair and enclosed in a circle.[83] The image recalls the visual representations and textual descriptions of lecanomancy that appear with surprising frequency in middle Byzantine sources. On a more popular level, the continued use of

FIGURE 7.9. Detail of a scene showing a lecanomantic ritual, Dioscorides, *Materia medica*, Italo-Byzantine, 1440, Italy, pigment on vellum. BUB, Bologna, ms. 3632, fol. 350v. Su concessione della Biblioteca Universitaria di Bologna.

amulets emblazoned with the evil eye and other apotropaic devices in the modern Greek world implies the long endurance of such popular beliefs and practices, although the exact nature of the diachronic relationships between medieval and modern Greek magic awaits further investigation.[84] Beyond this internal legacy, Byzantine magic also made important contributions to the Western European medieval and early modern occult sciences; Ottoman and Persian traditions of popular and learned magic, especially astrology and dream interpretation; and medieval and modern Slavic – particularly Russian – magical practices, including the use of amulets, spells, and dream interpretation.[85]

Notes

1. See esp. select essays in Maguire, ed., *Byzantine Magic*; Magdalino and Mavroudi, eds., *The Occult Sciences in Byzantium*; Petropoulos, ed., *Greek Magic: Ancient, Medieval and Modern*; the abstracts for a recent conference session moderated by Spieser, "Magie, croyance, superstition," vol. 2, 197–202; the sources in n. 3.

2. Jeffreys, Haldon, and Cormack, eds., *The Oxford Handbook of Byzantine Studies*; James, ed., *A Companion to Byzantium*; Stephenson, ed., *The Byzantine World*. Several entries of relevance to magic are found in Kazhdan, ed., *The Oxford Dictionary of Byzantium*, cf. "amulet," "astrology," "Chnoubis," "divination," "*engastrimythos*," "evil eye," "Hermes Trismegistos," "Holy Rider," "horoscope," "incantation," "magic," "magician," "Oneirokritika," "oracles," "popular religion," "ring signs."

3. Magic has been an increasingly common theme in publications on Byzantine material and visual culture since the late 1980s. See, for example, Maguire, Maguire, and Duncan-Flowers, *Art and Holy Powers in the Early Christian House*; Spier, "Medieval Byzantine Magical Amulets," 25–62; Russell, "The Archaeological Context of Magic," 35–50; Maguire, "Magic and Money in the Early Middle Ages," 1037–1054; Maguire, "'Feathers Signify Power,'" 383–398; Heintz, "Health: Magic, Medicine, and Prayer," 275–281; Peers, "Magic, the *Mandylion*, and the *Letter of Abgar*," 163–174; Walker, "Meaningful Mingling," 32–53; Ryder, "Popular Religion."

4. For an overview of Byzantine secular and canon laws relating to magic, see Troianos, "Zauberei und Giftmischerei in mittelbyzantinischer Zeit," 37–51.

5. Fögen, "Legislation und Kodifkation des Kaisers Leon VI," 27.

6. Magdalino, "Occult Science and Imperial Power," 158.

7. Magdalino, "The Byzantine Reception of Classical Astrology," 35–57, esp. 44–45, 50.

8. Fögen, "Balsamon on Magic," 100–102. See also Magdalino, "Occult Science and Imperial Power," 158–160.

9. Regarding the use of magical charms recounted in middle Byzantine saints' lives, see Abrahamse, "Magic and Sorcery in the Hagiography of the Middle Byzantine Period," 12–13.

10. Spier, "Medieval Byzantine Magical Amulets," 25–62.

11. For examples of early Byzantine medico-magical and other apotropaic devices, see Vikan, "Art, Medicine, and Magic in Early Byzantium," 65–86; Russell, "Byzantine *Instrumenta Domestica* from Anemurium," 133–163.

12. Spier, "Medieval Byzantine Magical Amulets," 50–51. Regarding the spike in Byzantine interest in pagan learning, including categories of magical and occult knowledge, during the tenth century, see Lemerle, *Le premier humanisme byzantin*; Gutas, *Greek Thought, Arabic Culture*, esp. 175–186.

13. Theophanes Continuatus, *Chronographia*, ed. Bekker, 348–351; Karlin-Hayter, *Vita Euthymii*, 4–5 (ll. 28–32), 8–9 (ll. 6–14).

14. Nicetas Choniates, *O City of Byzantium*, trans. Magoulias, 84–85.

15. Fögen, "Balsamon on Magic," 108–110.

16. Ibid., 109–110.

17. Ibid., 108.

18. See, for example, the stories recounted in middle Byzantine saints' lives of the false holy men Bigrinos and Gourias, who deceived the faithful into participating in demonic rituals, with predictably unfortunate results. Abrahamse, "Magic and Sorcery in the Hagiography of the Middle Byzantine Period," 10–12.

19. Maguire, "Other Icons," 9–20.

20. As discussed in Maguire, "Garments Pleasing to God," 215–224.

21. Maguire, "Magic and the Christian Image," esp. 66–71.

22. Kazhdan, *The Oxford Dictionary of Byzantium*, cf. "magic" and "magician."

23. Regarding John the Grammarian's possible engagement with unorthodox learning and his negative reputation in Iconophile literature, see Magdalino, *L'orthodoxie des astrologues*, 58–69; Magdalino, "Occult Science and Imperial Power," 122–124, 128, 135–137.

24. John Skylitzes, *A Synopsis of Byzantine History*, trans. Wortley, 86–87 (ch. 5, 3–4 [85–86]).

25. John Skylitzes, *A Synopsis of Byzantine History*, 74 (ch. 4, 21 [72]); Grabar and Manoussacas, *L'illustration du manuscrit de Skylitzès*, 47, no. 140, fig. 61; Tsamakda, *The Illustrated Chronicle of Ioannes Skylitzes*, 101, fig. 139.

26. Walker, "Meaningful Mingling," 32–53.

27. Magdalino, "The Byzantine Reception of Classical Astrology," 36–48, esp. 39–40.

28. Regarding the recognition of magic as a dynamically cross-cultural, diachronic phenomenon, see Mavroudi, "Occult Science and Society in Byzantium," 39–95.

29. Magdalino, "Occult Science and Imperial Power," 120–122.

30. Nicetas Choniates, *O City of Byzantium*, for Basilakes: 246–247; for Skleros Seth: 84–85, 187.

31. Constantine VII, *Three Treatises on Imperial Military Expeditions*, trans. Haldon, 106–107 ([C] l. 199), with commentary at 211.

32. Costanza, "La palmomanzia e tecniche affini in età bizantina," 95–111; Costanza, "Nitriti come segni profetici," 1–24.

33. Choniates, *O City of Byzantium*, 82–84. Greenfield, "Sorcery and Politics at the Byzantine Court," 73–93; Magdalino, "Occult Science and Imperial Power," 127–128, 148–149.

34. Trojanos, "Magic and the Devil," 48.

35. Abrahamse, "Magic and Sorcery in the Hagiography of the Middle Byzantine Period," 3–17; Maguire, "From the Evil Eye to the Eye of Justice," 217–239; Calofonos, "The Magician Vigrinos and His Victim," 64–71.

36. Magdalino, "Introduction," in *The Occult Sciences in Byzantium*, ed. Magdalino and Mavroudi, 14.

37. Brubaker, *Vision and Meaning in Ninth-Century Byzantium*, 141–144, fig. 33; Maguire, "Magic and Sorcery in Ninth-Century Manuscript Illumination," 199.

38. Regarding the iconography of demons in middle and late Byzantine art, see Greenfield, "Fallen into Outer Darkness," 61–80.

39. The exception that proves the rule is found in the tenth-century vita of Basil the Younger, which recounts the saint's own encounter with a female seductress who had inherited supernatural powers from her mother and was able to harm those who resisted her advances. Abrahamse, "Magic and Sorcery in the Hagiography of the Middle Byzantine Period," 15–16.

40. Abrahamse, "Magic and Sorcery in the Hagiography of the Middle Byzantine Period," 15–16; Kazhdan, "Byzantine Hagiography and Sex," 140–142.

41. John Skylitzes, *John Skylitzes. A Synopsis of Byzantine History*, 86–87 (ch. 5, 3 [85–86]).

42. Fögen, "Balsamon on Magic," 105–109.

43. Dickie, *Magic and Magicians in the Greco-Roman World*, 281–284, 300–303.

44. Psellos, Michel. *Chronographie, ou, Histoire d'un siècle de Byzance (976–1077)*. Edited and translated by Émile Renauld. 2 vols. Paris: Société d'édition "Les Belles lettres," 1926–1928. Also see Mavroudi, "Female Practitioners of Magic," 200.

45. Mavroudi, "Female Practitioners of Magic," 200; Heintz, "Health: Magic, Medicine, and Prayer," 275–281.

46. Patera, "Gylou, démon et sorcière du monde byzantin," 311–327.

47. Michel Psellos, *Chronographie*, 1.34–1.35 (book 3, para. 5).

48. Mavroudi, "Female Practitioners of Magic," 200. For possible connections between popular medicine practiced in the medieval and modern Greek worlds, see Clark, *A Cretan Healer's Handbook in the Byzantine Tradition*.

49. For the most recent studies on these branches of magical knowledge in Byzantium, see the essays gathered in Magdalino and Mavroudi, eds., *The Occult Sciences in Byzantium*, which also cite the important earlier bibliography on these topics.

50. On this point, see Duffy, "Reactions of Two Byzantine Intellectuals," 83–90; Magdalino, "Introduction," 16, 19–20, 27–29.

51. Magdalino and Mavroudi, *The Occult Sciences in Byzantium*, 11–13, 18, esp. 20–21, 27–28; Ierodiakonou, "The Greek Concept of Sympatheia," 97–118.

52. For a summary of accusations and insinuations of occult practices made by Psellos against members of the imperial court, see Kaldellis, *The Argument of Psellos' Chronographia*, 109–115.

53. Gutas, *Greek Thought, Arabic Culture*; Mavroudi, *A Byzantine Book on Dream Interpretation*; Magdalino, "Introduction," 32–35.

54. See esp. Mavroudi, *A Byzantine Book on Dream Interpretation*.

55. Liudprand of Cremona, *The Complete Works*, trans. Squatriti, 262–265.

56. For instance, see Pingree, "The Diffusion of Arabic Magical Texts," 57–102.

57. Burnett, "Late Antique and Medieval Latin Translations of Greek Texts," 325–359, esp. 329–331, 334–341.

58. Ibid. 329–330.

59. Magdalino, "The Byzantine Reception of Classical Astrology," 44; Magdalino, "The Porphyrogenita and the Astrologers," 30–31.

60. Magdalino, "Introduction," 16–17, 27; Magdalino, "The Porphyrogenita and the Astrologers."

61. Clucas, *The Trial of John Italos*.

62. Regarding the low percentage of the Byzantine population educated at this high level, see Browning, "Literacy in the Byzantine World," 39–54, esp. 40.

63. On Psellos and his interests in the occult, see Magdalino, "Introduction," 15–21, 28–35, which summarizes the earlier bibliography.

64. Ibid., 15–19.

65. Duffy, "Hellenic Philosophy in Byzantium," 139–156.

66. See esp. Magdalino, *L'orthodoxie des astrologues*; and the relevant essays in Magdalino and Mavroudi, eds., *The Occult Sciences in Byzantium*.

67. Regarding these terms and their use in Byzantine sources, see Magdalino, "The Byzantine Reception of Classical Astrology," esp. 34–37.

68. Pingree, "The Horoscope of Constantine VII Porphyrogenitus," 219–231. Regarding horoscopes cast on the occasion of imperial coronations in the eleventh and twelfth centuries, see Pingree, "Gregory Chioniades and Palaeologan Astronomy," 138–139, esp. 138 n. 29.

69. Magdalino, *The Empire of Manuel I Komnenos*, 377–379; Magdalino, *L'orthodoxie des astrologues*, 109–132.

70. Oberhelman, *Dreambooks in Byzantium*, 55–58.

71. Vryonis, "The Will of a Provincial Magnate, Eustathius Boilas (1059)," 269.

72. Mavroudi, *A Byzantine Book on Dream Interpretation*.

73. Oberhelman, *Dreambooks in Byzantium*, 23–24, 47–55.

74. Magdalino, "Occult Science and Imperial Power," 119–162.

75. Mango, "Antique Statuary and the Byzantine Beholder," 55–75; James, "'Pray Not to Fall into Temptation and Be on Your Guard,'" 12–20.

76. Cameron and Herrin, eds., *Constantinople in the Eighth Century*; Simeonova, "Magic and the Warding-Off of Barbarians in Constantinople," 207–210, with earlier bibliography.

77. John Skylitzes, *A Synopsis of Byzantine History*, 86–87 (ch. 5, 3 [85–86]); Tsamakda, *The Illustrated Chronicle of Ioannes Skylitzes*, 109, fig. 160.

78. For work in this direction, see Flood, "Image against Nature," 143–166.

79. For discussion of these decorations, see Walker, "Islamicizing Motifs in Byzantine Churches."

80. Maguire and Maguire, "Animals and Magic in Byzantine Art," 58–96.

81. On this point, see Maguire, "The Cage of Crosses," 169–172.

82. See Cupane, "La magia a Bisanzio nel secolo XIV," 237–262; Clark, *A Cretan Healer's Handbook in the Byzantine Tradition*; Greenfield, *Traditions of Belief in Late Byzantine Demonology*; Stewart, *Demons and the Devil*; Greenfield, "A Contribution to the Study of Palaeologan Magic," 117–154; Magdalino,

"Introduction," 21–26; Tselikas, "Spells and Exorcisms in Three Post-Byzantine Manuscripts," 72–81.

83. Maguire, "'Feathers Signify Power,'" 384–385.

84. For example, see Herzfeld, "Meaning and Morality," 560–574; Veikou, "Ritual Word and Symbolic Movement," 95–105; Chryssanthopoulou, "The Evil Eye among the Greeks of Australia" 106–118.

85. Regarding the late and post-Byzantine contributions to Western European and Islamic traditions of magic, see Saliba, "Revisiting the Astronomical Contacts," 362–373; Mavroudi, "Exchanges with Arabic Writers," 62–75; Farhad, ed., *Falnama: The Book of Omens*. On Slavic magic and its roots in the Byzantine occult traditions, see Ševčenko, "Remarks on the Diffusion of Byzantine Scientific and Pseudo-Scientific Literature," 321–345; Spier, "Medieval Byzantine Magical Amulets," 44–51; Ryan, "Magic and Divination," 35–58; Ryan, *The Bathhouse at Midnight*.

Chapter 8

Magic, Marvel, and Miracle in Early Islamic Thought

TRAVIS ZADEH

Introduction: The Western Study of Islamic Magic

The modern study of magic in Islam is intimately connected to the history of Orientalism as it developed during the course of the nineteenth century. During this period, anthropologists and scholars of religion identified magic with the primitive and irrational, set in opposition to true religion, reason, and empiricism.[1] For instance, in his account of the customs of Egyptians, the famed Arabic philologist, traveler, and English translator of *The Arabian Nights*, Edward Lane (d. 1876), observed that Arabs on the whole are a very superstitious people and that the most prominent of the superstitions among them is their belief in jinn. He gives examples of the practice of conjuring jinn, the use of jars and other vessels to bottle them, and the general Solomonic background to the art of subjugating jinn, all of which, he notes, help explain the marvelous tapestry of *The Arabian Nights*, replete as it is with magical transformations and the black arts of sorcery.[2]

In addition to the belief in supernatural spirits, as well as the omnipresent power of saints, one of the more remarkable superstitions for Lane was the use of written charms and amulets, the composition of which is "founded upon magic." These charms, he explains, commonly consist of particular Qur'ānic passages and the names of God, along with angels, jinn, prophets, and saints, all mixed with combinations of numerals and secret diagrams (Figure 8.1). Lane continues that "the most esteemed of all 'ḥegábs' (or charms) is a 'muṣḥaf' (or copy of the Ḳur-án),'" which in its miniature form is worn by both men and women in an embroidered leather case and is used as a prophylactic against "disease, enchantment, the evil eye and a variety of other evils."[3]

It is not at all surprising that, in the course of his travels, Lane encountered such beliefs and practices. Indeed, the deployment of the Qur'ān for protective and curative purposes can be traced back to the earliest history of Islamic devotion. It is also true that the belief in jinn and their occult power is rooted

FIGURE 8.1. Print block amulet, ca. 11th century, 23 x 8.4 cm. The top of the amulet features a Solomonic seal. © The Metropolitan Museum of Art, 1978.546.32.

in the Qur'ān and the fabric of early Islamic cosmography. Similarly, the practice of shrine veneration and the acceptance and promotion of saintly miracles is intimately connected to the structures of religious authority and piety in Islamic history. To be sure, one can point to factions among the religious elite that, in various historical and geographical contexts, have debated the probity of beliefs and practices that Lane would have deemed superstitious. Yet, in the general framework of religious orthopraxy, Qur'ānic charms, a belief in jinn, and the visiting of tombs of prophets and saints have historically occupied a rather normative place in Islamic soteriology. The categorization of such religious practices and beliefs as manifestations of superstitious magic forms part of the broader epistemological foundations of Orientalism, which viewed the Orient in general and Islam in particular as decadent, effeminate, and irrational.

The anthropological encounter with native Muslims could also be largely substituted with a close reading of texts, particularly *The Arabian Nights*, considered in the development of Orientalism as a key for understanding the Muslim mind. The Orientalist Duncan Black Macdonald (d. 1943) notes in his Haskell lectures on comparative religion, which were delivered at the University of Chicago in 1906, that there still reigns across the Muslim world "an unquestioning faith in the magician." He continues by stating that the shell separating "the Oriental from the Unseen is still very thin," easily broken by the charms and amulets of magicians, for "the world of the *Arabian Nights* is still his world."[4] Throughout his scholarship, Macdonald drew extensively from *The Arabian Nights*, with its magical twists and turns, which he viewed as reflecting "the common soul of Islam." In his advice to missionaries, he notes that this collection of tales of powerful jinn and seductive enchantresses can actually "take the place of contact with the Muslim world," for unlike direct interactions with Muslims, it neither "misleads nor misinforms."[5]

There is, however, much about the Western study of Islam and magic that has both misled and misinformed. Part of this arises from the raw exoticism shaping the literary, artistic, and scholarly discourses of Orientalism, an exoticism that represents Muslims as blindly following religious law and ritual while maintaining practices rooted in pagan traditions of magic and superstition.[6] It is a common strategy in polemical interactions between differing religious communities to present what an opposing group views to be sacred as truly unlawful, irrational, or magical. What Orientalists or missionaries identified as magical rites would not necessarily constitute magic within the framework of Islamic devotion. Such is the case, for example, with the assertion in the first edition of the *Encyclopaedia of Islam* (1913–1934) that Muslims do not study the Qur'ān in order to understand it; rather, it is learned by heart for "the reward promised in the next world," and to "benefit by the virtue or *baraka* [blessing] of the divine word." This, the author concludes, is in keeping with "the mentality of Muḥammadan peoples with [their] strong belief in magic."[7] Recourse to the salvific power of the Qur'ān in its oral and written forms is thus reduced to a primitive belief in magic. Here, as elsewhere, the concept of magic is applied largely without consideration to autochthonous discourses on what constitutes the magical or the occult. Rather, the category is treated as though it has universal applicability with a common ontology of superstition, fakery, and ignorance that transcends the particularities of any given context.

Needless to say, for Islamic intellectual and cultural history, the line between magic and religion does not follow the same course that defined the Enlightenment, with its critique of magic as primitive superstition. To be sure, there are important examples of Muslim theologians who saw magic as nothing more than mere trickery; however, they did so largely within a religious framework that was designed to protect the singularity of miracles as the probative basis for determining the authenticity of prophets.

Similarly, although sorcery was generally considered a capital offense in juridical discourse, historically Muslim societies did not participate in anything akin to the persecution of witches and other "deviants" that shapes significant chapters in medieval and early modern European history. In the development of Islamic legal, philosophical, and theological discourses, the boundaries of magic prove to be incredibly porous. In certain contexts, magic is defined as the opposite of religion, akin to disbelief in and disobedience toward God. Yet, there are also traditions that were quite dominant in the formation of Islamic thought that view magic as not substantively distinct from miracle; rather, they advance magic as constituting an integral part of the natural fabric of the cosmos, as a mysterious force to be harnessed and controlled. This process of defining magic, marvel, and miracle fits into a larger pattern of demarcating internal divisions while maintaining external boundaries.

Early Background: Neither Poet nor Soothsayer

The categorization of magic as the opposite of religion can be found in the earliest stages of Islamic history. In an account preserved in several early Arabic sources, al-Walīd b. al-Mughīra (d. 1/622), an aristocratic opponent of the Muslim community in Mecca, heard the Prophet recite the Qur'ān. Recognizing that Muḥammad neither was possessed by a jinn (*majnūn*), nor was he a poet (*shāʿir*), al-Walīd argued: "I have seen soothsayers (*kuhhān*) and he does not murmur (*zamzama*) like one, nor does he use rhymed prose (*sajʿ*) like one." Ultimately, al-Walīd settled on *sāḥir*, a term that signifies a sorcerer or magician to describe him.[8] In the exegetical tradition, al-Walīd's assessment is generally read as the occasion for the following Qurʾānic passage: "Then he turned away, full of pride. And he said, 'This is just magic imitated [from others], just the speech of a human being.'"[9] This critique fits into a rhetorical configuration in the Qurʾān, in which the opponents of Muḥammad and of the early Muslim community repeatedly refer to the revelation as clear or obvious magic (e.g., Q. 27:13, *hādhā siḥrun mubīn*).[10] In the ethical framework of the Qurʾān, such refrains of disbelief are matched with descriptions of the revelation as a clear scripture (*kitāb mubīn*) and the prophetic message as a clear warning (*nadhīr mubīn*).[11] Thus, in the binary logic of the revelation, what appears to unbelievers as *siḥr*, that is, magic, sorcery, or enchantment, is truly salvific guidance from God.

The charge of deceptive magic is leveled at the revelation, at the resurrection, at divine signs (*āyāt*), and at divine truth (*ḥaqq*).[12] Just as Muḥammad's prophecy is ridiculed, the Qurʾān relates that earlier disbelievers had rejected the miracles of Moses and Jesus as mere magic.[13] Similarly, accusations of sorcery are directly attributed to Muḥammad:

> A. L. R. These are the signs of the wise book. Is it a wonder to people that We have revealed to a man among them so that he should warn people – and give those who believe good tidings that they are on a sure footing before their lord? [But] those who disbelieve say, "He is clearly a sorcerer."[14]

This process of discursive maneuvering reflects how the categories of the licit and illicit are bound within a broader formulation of religious authority and authenticity, where magic is opposed to miracle and defined as inauthentic and specious in contrast to the legitimacy of divine truth. As these passages highlight, the Qurʾān makes every effort to reject for itself the label of magic or trickery in a rhetorical structure designed to establish its divine origin. It is not entirely surprising that Muḥammad's opponents in Mecca would have disparaged the revelation as magic or trickery, considering the strong oracular currents running throughout the body of the text. This oracular dimension is generally designed to foretell the end of time and the final judgment, drawing on various rhetorical strategies, including, most notably, oaths, enigmas, and mysterious letters that open many suras (e.g., the letters A. L. R. just cited).[15]

The Qurʾān speaks of magic as illicit and harmful and generally associates it with evil or trickery. The final two suras of the Qurʾān (113–114), known as the suras of refuge (i.e., *al-muʿawwidhatān*), both begin with "Say: I seek refuge in the Lord (*qul aʿūdhu bi-rabb*)" and serve as prayers of protection against various evils, including, most notably, witchcraft. This is made explicit with the reference to the evil of women who blow on knots (*al-naffāthāt fī l-ʿuqad*, Q. 113:4). In the Qurʾān, the word *naffāthāt*, or blowing women, is a *hapax legomenon*.[16] However, its meaning (i.e., witches) is apparent from the various ancient traditions of guarding against magical knots, as reflected, for instance, in incantations preserved in the Akkadian *Maqlû* (*Burning*) tablets of ancient Mesopotamia.[17] The Akkadian *kiṣrū* (knots) is a cognate of *qṭar* and *qeṭrā* in Aramaic and Syriac and all three carry the sense of magical knots.[18] Thus, for instance, in the Bible, Daniel has the power to untie knots (*šĕrâ qiṭrîn*), meaning he can guard against witchcraft.[19]

The final apotropaic verses in the Qurʾān also describe a search for protection against the one who whispers (*waswās*), which in the exegetical tradition is generally interpreted as the whispering temptation of the Devil, by way of demonic insinuation.[20] This may also be an allusion to the whispering or murmuring associated with magical incantations. In the Hebrew Bible, Isaiah warns against consulting magicians who chirp and whisper (*hamĕsapsĕpîm wĕ-hammahgîm*); they are contrasted with the Law (*tôrāh*), in which there is no magic (*ʾên-lô šāḥar*).[21] The term used is also a cognate with the Arabic *siḥr* (magic or sorcery) and with the Akkadian *saḫāru*, meaning to encircle with sorcery or magic.[22] The etymology of *siḥr* points to ancient Mesopotamian magical practices, a link that resonates with the Qurʾānic account of the residents of Babel obtaining knowledge of magic from the fallen angels Hārūt and Mārūt (Q. 2:102).[23]

Word Play

The word "magic" itself warrants further consideration. The Greek loanwords *magos* (a Persian priest) and *mageia* (a cognate with the English word "magic") were fused relatively early with Greek notions of black magic (e.g., *goēteia*).[24] In Aramaic, the association of the *magus* with sorcery (*ḥiršē*) finds expression in the Babylonian Talmud (e.g., Šab. 75a).[25] The history of the word reminds us that, as a discursive category, magic is often identified with the religious practices of others. However, although *majūs* in Arabic is generally associated with heretical dualism and fire worship, the word itself does not carry with it a sense of magic or sorcery; rather, it is used as a general term for Magians.[26] This signification is already attested in the Qurʾān, which refers to Magians (*majūs*) alongside Jews, Nazarenes, Sabeans, and polytheists as separate groups that will be judged individually by God at the end of time (Q. 22:17).

A profound cosmographic reordering took place through the early absorption of Persian converts in the burgeoning Islamic urban centers. In addition to the historical record,[27] we can readily trace the impact of this encounter in the lexicographical residue with the importation of Persian loanwords into Arabic. A relevant example for our discussion of magic can be found in Arabic with *nīranj*, from the Middle Persian *nērang* [nylng]. This term originally signifies ritual directions or formulae, as expressed, for instance, in the Middle Persian commentary of the *Nērangestān*, which treats the valid means of performing rituals. The word is used to describe Avestan rites (*Abestāgīg nērang*, Dēnkard 7.7.2) and ritual directions for the *drōn* ceremony (*nērang ī drōn*), for the sacrifice (*nērang ī kardan*), and for consecrating water and bull's urine (*nērang ī āb ud pādyāb*).[28] The *Bundahišn* (*Primal Creation*) relates how the *gāhānīg nērang*, or sacred hymnic power of the *Gathas*, will smash the Foul Spirit (*Ganāg-mēnōy*) and the demon Āz.[29] Similarly, *nērang* signifies the recitation of the Avesta, with the aim of healing or warding off demons, in the sense of a ritual speech act designed to obtain beneficial results. However, in Arabic and in Early New Persian, *nīranj* often conveys a negative connotation, meaning charm, spell, or incantation, generally with a sense of illicit magic and trickery.

A similar process is at work with the Middle Persian *afsōn* ['pswn], which signifies an incantation or formulaic recitation often used to ward off evil or illness with the recitation of sacred Avestan words. For example, the Pahlavi *Rivāyat* accompanying the *Dādestān ī Dēnīg* records a recitation for curing fever (*afsōn ī tab*) that includes Avestan formulae written in the Avestan script.[30] Similarly, the Pahlavi commentary (*zand*) on the *Wīdēwdād* of the Avesta describes *afsōn* as healing with the beneficent *manθra* or sacred word (*mānsarspand bēšāzēnēd*).[31] In the *Shāh-nāma* (*Book of Kings*) of Abū l-Qāsim Firdawsī (d. 411/1020), *afsun* continues to signify the enunciation of a sacred formula for warding off demons. However, in New Persian, the term also comes to evoke illicit magical practices.[32]

Other categories from pre-Islamic Persian cosmography are reinscribed in Islamic salvation history in what we might call an *interpretatio islamica*. Thus, for instance, the Arabic *shayāṭīn* (or demons) and jinn are often translated in Early New Persian as *dīv* and *parī*, cognates of the Middle Persian *dēw* and *parīg*. In Zoroastrian eschatology, *dēw*, written in Book Pahlavi with the arameogram ŠDYA, function as baleful adversaries in the battle between Ohrmazd and Ahriman, who represent the forces of good and evil, respectively. Similarly, the term *parīg* has the general sense of evil witches or sorceresses; they feature as malevolent forces in the broader cosmological struggle for good. In addition to "demon," the New Persian *dīv* can also be used to translate the word jinn, a pattern of equivalence found, for instance, in early Persian translations and commentaries of the Qur'ān. In New Persian, however, the term *parī* soon sheds the negative connotations of witchcraft. Although they are also identified with jinn,[33] which in Islamic eschatology can be, like humans, either good-natured or wicked, the *parī* also have the general sense of angelic benevolent creatures from the realm of the spirits, akin to the English cognate fairy; thus, we have such common Persian appellations as Parīzād (fairy born) and Parīpaykar (fairy countenance).[34] In contrast, the Middle Persian *jādūg* (sorcerer) and *jādūgīh* (sorcery) generally maintain the same negative connotations in the New Persian cognate *jādū* for magic, witchcraft, and sorcery. As with the early Islamic association of *siḥr* with practices demarcated as ancient, foreign, or liminal, the Middle Persian *jādūgīh* also serves as a relational concept that is set in opposition to true religion (*dēn*). In the eschatological currents of the *Ayādgār ī Jāmāspīg* (*Memorial of Jāmāsp*), a late Zoroastrian world history, we read that although there are many followers of Ohrmazd, much of the world, which includes the Indians, Chinese, and Arabs (*tāzīgān*), as well as Turkestan and Barbary (*barbarestān*), sides with the evil Ahriman and openly practices witchcraft (*jādūgīh āškārag kunēnd*).[35] This process of marking religious others as in league with demonic sorcery is tied to a nearly ubiquitous practice among religious communities of identifying external boundaries while regulating internal divisions. The absorption and subsequent inscription of Persian vocabulary in Islamic cosmography is itself a testament to this process.

Magical Reasoning

Pre-Islamic Persian history, culture, and religious traditions profoundly shaped the development of Islamic civilization. This is expressed notably in the sheer number of Persian converts from the ranks of the religious elite and state administration. Throughout Islamic history, conversion has been a multidirectional process of transculturation: non-Muslims did not simply enter a fixed religious system; they were also active agents in its construction. What conversion meant beyond the circles of the urban elite remains largely unknown, although there is much to suggest that indigenous religious practices and beliefs developed side by side in the course of Islamization.

A telling example is found in the comments by the chief Ḥanafī jurist of Baghdad, Abū Bakr al-Jaṣṣāṣ (d. 370/981), in his legal exegesis, the *Aḥkām al-Qur'ān*, on the origins of magic. Commenting on Q. 2:102, a verse that associates magic with ancient Babel, Jaṣṣāṣ relates the account of Bīwarāsb, the demon king of Babel:

> The ignorant masses and the women among us claim that Afarīdūn imprisoned Bīwarāsb in one of the highest mountains of Danbāwand and that he lives there chained and that magicians come to him there and they have learned magic (siḥr) from him and that one day he will escape and will conquer the world and that he is the Deceiver (al-dajjāl, i.e., the false messiah), whom the Prophet described and warned us about. I reckon that they also took this account from Magians.[36]

This is a reference to the famous story in Zoroastrian mythology of the ancient Persian king Frēdōn (Afarīdūn), who conquered the demon Bēwarāsp (Bīwarāsb); according to Jaṣṣāṣ, the Arabs also call him Ḍaḥḥāk, corresponding to the Middle Persian Dahāg, a cognate with the Avestan aždahā for "dragon" or "serpent." Elements of this story stretch back to the Avesta, in which Frēdōn slays Aži Dahāka.[37] Celebrated in Firdawsī's Shāh-nāma, details of this account have long featured in early Muslim sources. For instance, the foundational lexicography, the Kitāb al-ʿAyn, composed by Khalīl b. Aḥmad (d. ca. 170/786) and redacted by his companion al-Layth b. al-Muẓaffar (d. 187/803), relates that Bīwarāsb, known as Ḍaḥḥāk, was a sorcerer (sāḥir) imprisoned in Mount Damavand, and he was known as the "possessor of two serpents (dhū l-ḥayyatayn)," a reference to the serpents that grew out of his shoulders and that fed on human brains (Figure 8.2).[38]

Several of the accounts related by Jaṣṣāṣ have direct parallels in Zoroastrian scriptural material. As for the association of Dahāg with sorcery, we read in the Dēnkard (Acts of Religion), a ninth-century encyclopedia composed in Book Pahlavi, that Dahāg had spread sorcery throughout Babel (jādūgīh andar Bābēl kard), leading humankind into idol worship (uzdēs-paristišnīh).[39] Likewise, the Bundahišn identifies Dahāg as Bēwarāsp and relates that Frēdōn, unable to kill the demon, bound him to Mount Damavand.[40] Eschatological currents are also found in Zoroastrian material. Thus, for instance, we read a millenarian prediction in the Bundahišn that, at the end of the world, Dahāg will break free from his chains and cause immense destruction on earth through his demonic desire (dēw-kāmagīh).[41]

With Jaṣṣāṣ's account, we see the identification of Ḍaḥḥāk with the Dajjāl, the Deceiver who, in the early hadith corpus, plays a role akin to the antiChrist in the eschatological unfolding of the end of time.[42] This equation of Ḍaḥḥāk with the Dajjāl can also be found in other early Muslim sources,[43] and it reflects a broader pattern of grafting pre-Islamic Persian history onto the

FIGURE 8.2. The demon king Ḍaḥḥāk bound in chains on Mount Damavand with two brain-eating serpents that have grown out of his shoulders, Abū l-Qāsim Firdawsī (d. 411/1020), from a dispersed Ilkhānid manuscript, ca. 1335, known as the Demotte, or the Great Mongol *Shāh-nāma*. The Trustees of the Chester Beatty Library, Dublin Per 104.3, reconstructed folio 11b.

arc of Islamic salvation. Likewise, the connection with magic is echoed in other material of the period, such as in the *Tārīkh-i Sīstān* and the Sāmānid *Tafsīr-i Ṭabarī*, both of which recount that Ḍaḥḥāk seized control of the world through sorcery.[44]

Jaṣṣāṣ relates that these beliefs are held by "the ignorant masses and women among us," concluding that the material itself is taken from Zoroastrian sources. His account thus situates this particular cosmography of magic in the sphere of "popular," or non-elite, beliefs and practices associated with religious outsiders and evidently transposed by Persian converts into an Islamic soteriology. Yet, there is reason to suspect, given the appearance of similar material in other Islamic sources,[45] that what Jaṣṣāṣ imputes to the ignorant masses does not reflect popular currents as such; rather, this anecdote fits into Jaṣṣāṣ's larger theological rejection of the reality of magic. Working in the structure of Muʿtazilī theology, Jaṣṣāṣ develops a robust argument against the ontological power of magic, which he presents as nothing more than sleight-of-hand deceit, enacted through tricks and illusions. In his treatment of the topic, Jaṣṣāṣ positions belief in magic on a par with ignorance. Thus, for instance, he argues that the masses foolishly believe that "a person can be transformed into an ass or a dog and that if they wish they can return to their original form and that people can mount ostrich eggs, brooms, or jars and fly in the air, passing from Iraq to India or to whatever regions they wish and then return all in one night."[46]

The rejection of the possibility of flying on brooms across the evening sky fits into Jaṣṣāṣ's larger attempt to theologically circumscribe and define the boundaries of the paranormal. Jaṣṣāṣ ridicules the masses, women, and the ignorant as foolishly believing in the power of magic. Rather, it is deception, trickery, and ignorance that form the basis of all magical activity. Jaṣṣāṣ's account presents optical illusions as things that appear as the opposite of what they really are, that are only produced when their true natures are hidden. He also discusses the deceptive acts of swindlers or tricksters (mushaʿwidhūn), who through legerdemain (i.e., shaʿwadha) practice various forms of trickery, such as changing thread into variegated colors, swallowing swords, and bringing dead birds back to life.[47] Included in his treatment of the topic is an anecdote concerning an automaton statute that guarded a royal sepulcher in the Levant, which, through secret mechanical levers connected to a staircase, decapitated all who tried to enter the king's burial chamber. In this regard, Jaṣṣāṣ's examples of magic as deception echo classical definitions of astonishment and wonder in the face of the unknown. For example, Jaṣṣāṣ's contemporary in Baghdad, the Muʿtazilī theologian Abū l-Ḥasan al-Rummānī (d. 384/994), describes astonishment (taʿajjub) as obscurity or confusion. Rummānī explains that it is normal for people to be astonished by that for which they do not know the cause (sabab), adding that the more the cause of something is obscured, the greater the sense of wonder becomes.[48] This definition of wonder can be found throughout Arabic writings on nature,[49] and it parallels the Arabic absorption of Greek learning that is reflected, in this particular instance, in the Platonic association of wonder with the development of philosophy.[50] Aristotle stresses this point in the opening to the Metaphysica, where he argues that it is through the act of being astonished that humankind begins to philosophize.[51]

Remaining astonished without uncovering the cause of the bewilderment is itself a form of ignorance. This is the foundation of Jaṣṣāṣ's argument that if magicians indeed had the power that they claimed to possess, in terms of the benefit and harm they could produce and their capacity to fly and their knowledge of the unseen, then they would surely be capable of killing kings, unearthing vast treasures, and defeating entire countries. He concludes that this is simply not the case; rather, "the majority of [magicians] are greedy and deceptive, and try to steal dirhams by tricking people; they are poor and impoverished and we know they are not capable of anything."[52]

Normative Definitions

The difficulty with Jaṣṣāṣ's Muʿtazilī position on magic is that the broader sote-riology of the Qurʾān and the prophetic Sunna affirm an array of supernatural phenomena that extend far beyond prophetic miracles. From the power of the unseen or occult (*ghayb*) to the workings of angels, demons, and jinn to the mysterious and malignant influence of the evil eye, reality is, in a fundamental sense, pregnant with the marvelous. Thus, for instance, despite his firm rejec-tion of magic, Jaṣṣāṣ acknowledges the power of the evil eye and sanctions the prophylactic recitation of Qurʾānic verses and the names of God to ward off evil through the use of incantations (*ruqyā*, pl. *ruqā*).[53]

This entire discussion fits into a larger set of debates about the nature of miracles and their relationship to prophecy. Many Muslim theologians came to define the prophetic miracle, or *muʿjiza* (literally an act that incapacitates another from repeating or imitating), as a rupture with customary phenom-ena that only a prophet was capable of producing. This particular defini-tion served as a probative basis for authenticating the claim to prophethood. Because the Prophet Muḥammad was recognized as the final prophet, or the seal of all the prophets, the door to further miraculous workings was closed, as it were, in any prophetic sense. However, in traditional Sunni theological circles, the wonderworking of holy men and women, known broadly as the *awliyāʾ*, the friends or saints of God, was generally grouped under the label of *karāmāt,* favor or gifts bestowed by God (compare with the Greek *charismata*). The various branches of Shiʿi theology distinguished the marvelous power of the Imams from the miraculous deeds achieved by the prophets often in very similar terms. However, as with magic, several Muʿtazilī theologians rejected the possibility of miraculous workings produced by anyone other than a prophet, regardless of what terminology was used to describe the phenom-enon in question. This line of argument was designed to limit miracles to a distant prophetic age and thus to safeguard the miracle as a basis for establish-ing prophethood. Needless to say, the theological stance that neither magic nor saintly miracles had any ontological reality was a source of considerable debate, particularly as it competed with a vision of a cosmos that was filled with both wonder and enchantment.

The supernatural fabric governing Islamic theodicy gave the religious elite ample space to systematize a range of phenomena regulated within the sphere of the occult sciences ('ulūm al-ghayb). This systematization forms part of a larger process of rationalizing magic and its power through epistemological structures and categories developed in natural science. In turn, much of the treatment of magic was profoundly shaped by the absorption and naturalization in Arabic letters of philosophical learning from Late Antiquity, specifically Neo-Platonism and Hermeticism.[54] In terms of the categorization of magic, particularly well known are the models advanced by such later authorities as Fakhr al-Dīn al-Rāzī (d. 606 / 1209), Ibn Khaldūn (d. 808 / 1406), and Ḥājjī Khalīfa (d. 1067 / 1657), all of whom to some degree approach the various disciplines of magic through the rubrics of natural science and philosophy.[55]

The Ashʿarī theologian Fakhr al-Dīn al-Rāzī treats a broad range of occult sciences in various writings. In his voluminous Qurʾān commentary, Mafātīḥ al-ghayb (Keys to the Unseen), Rāzī addresses the question of magic, focusing much of his attention on refuting the theologian al-Qāḍī ʿAbd al-Jabbār (d. 415 / 1025) and the Muʿtazilī argument that magic is nothing other than trickery. He does this by affirming the scientific existence of occult forces through arguments rooted largely in Neo-Platonic natural philosophy on the relationship between the heavenly spheres, the human body, and the soul.[56] Under the broader rubric of enchantment or magic (siḥr), Rāzī lists a range of activities and phenomena that have real and measurable effects on the physical world. These include trickery and deceit, as well as the transformation of substances by harnessing occult forces in nature and commanding spirits through incantations and through the power of the rational soul (al-nafs al-nāṭiqa).[57]

Rāzī elaborates further on an array of occult activities that fall under the broad category of siḥr in his theological summa, al-Maṭālib al-ʿāliya min al-ʿilm al-ilāhī (Sublime Pursuits in the Divine Science).[58] These practices include: (1) judicial astrology (i.e., aḥkām al-nujūm); (2) purification of the rational soul, which is generated from celestial spirits (al-arwāḥ al-falakiyya), through spiritual exercises to obtain occult powers; (3) the use of the magical properties of mineral, plant, and animal medicaments[59]; (4) the deployment of incantations and charms to draw the aid of the lower spirits (al-arwāḥ al-safaliyya), which Rāzī identifies with jinn and demons[60]; (5) obtaining the aid of celestial spirits to produce phenomena that break with custom; (6) sleight of hand and deception, particularly through optical tricks; (7) automata and the marvels of hidden mechanisms; (8) the use of omens (faʾl) and divination (zajr), which itself consists of eight categories – physiognomy (firāsa), geomancy ('ilm al-raml), palmoscopy ('ilm ikhtilāj al-aʿḍāʾ, i.e., divination through the twitching of limbs); omoplatoscopy or scapulomancy (al-naẓar fī l aktāf, i.e., divination by examining the shoulder bones of animals), lithomancy (ḍarb al-aḥjār, which, according to Rāzī, is generally practiced by women), reading palms and foot-prints, augury through the flight and call of birds, and determining omens (tafāʾul) through the occurrence of various events;[61] (9) manipulating the fool-ish and those of little intellect by producing food and gaining their trust; and (10) employing various kinds of lies, tricks, and deceptions to instill fear in others and to gain control over them.

With regard to the ultimate power of magic, Rāzī explains that within the structure of Sunnī theology, as represented here by the ahl al-Sunna, a magician is indeed able to fly through the air and transform a person into an ass or an ass into a person through the recitation of specific incantations and charms. The power animating such magical feats – as well as that behind astrological forces and talismans – rests solely with God.[62] Likewise, Rāzī holds the same to be true for astrological forces and the talismans used to harness them.[63] This view of absolute divine power is entirely congruent with broader currents in Ashʿarī theodicy that relate to the absolutely transcendent nature and omnipotence of God in the face of all creation, including the existence of evil.[64] Yet both in jurid-ical and theological terms, the lawfulness of magic in general and astrology in particular was a topic of considerable debate. The occult is a field of study that Rāzī, nonetheless, appears to have both promoted and explored in great depth. This is reflected in the work generally ascribed to him on astrological and talismanic arts, al-Sirr al-maktūm fī mukhāṭabat al-nujūm (The Occult Secret on Discoursing with the Stars),[65] which includes various prophylactic recipes to protect against sorcery and other afflictions, as well as directions on how to harness celestial and earthly powers, such as the planets and the jinn.[66]

As for the lawfulness of magic, Rāzī, in his commentary on the Qurʾān, argues that there is nothing inherently wrong with studying the various branches of the occult, for it is through such pursuits that one is able to distin-guish magic from miracle; furthermore, it is from such study that knowledge of the licit and illicit use of magic is obtained.[67] A similar epistemological rationale guides his examination of celestial and talismanic magic in al-Sirr al-maktūm.[68] Additionally, in the course of al-Maṭālib al-ʿāliya, Rāzī argues that rational structures govern a variety of talismanic and divinatory practices.[69] Justifying his examination of the topic, Rāzī further argues that those who practice this art should have a full knowledge of how these affairs work, so that the magical procedures enacted will not be riddled with errors.[70]

This argument fits into Rāzī's larger rationalization of occult learning as a licit branch of the natural sciences. For Rāzī, magic, along with the miracles of saints and prophets, forms part of the fabric of the cosmos. Such a view holds that the ability to harness magical or miraculous powers hinges on the internal senses of the *nafs* – the soul or psyche (Greek *psukhē*). These paranormal workings relate to a broader hierarchical system of natural forces and faculties. Central to Rāzī's exposition is the role of the estimative faculty (*al-quwwa al-wahmiyya*, Latin *vis aestimativa*), which can be manipulated by the rational soul of the intellect to produce ruptures with customary phenomena.[71]

Rāzī's rationalization builds on the psychological system of the imagination developed by the famed Persian philosopher Ibn Sīnā (d. 428/1037), known in the Latin West as Avicenna. For Ibn Sīnā, the estimative faculty is the highest of the internal senses of the soul and can be used to influence other bodies without any physical intermediary, solely through its own power, which in its most perfected form is linked to prophecy.[72] Ultimately, the faculties of the intellect form the natural basis for the thaumaturgic capacity of the soul to act directly on other bodies or other souls through a form of paranormal causation.[73] For both Ibn Sīnā and Rāzī, prophetic miracles are the realization of this natural capacity within the form of an individual who, through inherent disposition, has obtained a level of intellectual and spiritual perfection in both a theoretical and a practical expression.[74]

Such a framework makes distinguishing miracle from magic a rather difficult endeavor. Rāzī raises a series of doubts about the validity of miracles as a rational basis for a demonstrable proof of prophethood. He further questions how one can ascertain with utter certainty that it was God, and not demons or jinn, who was responsible for the miraculous acts of the prophets.[75] To address this problem, Rāzī advances the a priori argument that the spread of Islam was inherently good and beneficial to humankind and in its own right can confirm the legitimacy of Muḥammad as a divinely guided prophet.[76] In such a structure, the focus on prophecy solely in moral terms, rather than on miraculous phenomena, strips magic of any inherent evil quality.[77] This hinges on a line of inquiry advanced by Ibn Sīnā that the only phenomenological difference between magic and miracle is the natural disposition of the soul toward either good or evil.[78] This vision of the ontological status of the prophetic miracle was also taken up by the Ashʿarī theologian Abū Ḥāmid al-Ghazālī (d. 505/1111).[79] As a force in nature, the occult can thus be used to achieve both beneficial and harmful results. Thus, for Rāzī the study of magic is entirely legitimate, as the question is not the field itself, but the ends to which it is used. Needless to say, this kind of argumentation was not universally accepted, even among fellow Ashʿarī theologians.[80]

On Subjugating Occult Forces

Although we can trace a strong current of condemnation toward various forms of magic in normative branches of Islamic law and theology, there is a sizable corpus of writing that seeks to legitimize the study and practice of occult sciences. Furthermore, other than the general limitations governing access to writing and literacy in premodern societies, historically the dissemination of this material was not restricted to any particular region or context of production; additionally, this body of writing was supported by courts as well as by religious authorities. For instance, although much separates the two works in terms of scope, Rāzī's *al-Sirr al-maktūm* has long been associated with the *Ghāyat al-ḥakīm* (*The Goal of the Sage*),[81] a grimoire of astral magic and talismanic arts that appears to have been written by the Andalusian religious scholar Maslama b. Qāsim al-Qurṭubī (d. 353/964).[82] The *Ghāya* circulated in its Arabic original well beyond al-Andalus and North Africa and exists in numerous manuscripts, a testament to its continued popularity.[83] During the reign of Alfonso X (r. 1252–1284), it was translated into Spanish under the title *Picatrix*. The work was then subsequently translated into Latin and as such represents the movement of Arabic writings on astral magic to the West.[84]

With its strong emphasis on planetary influences, the *Ghāya* offers a testament to the spread of Hellenistic philosophy, Hermeticism, alchemy, and Mesopotamian astrology, along with Indic astronomic traditions.[85] The cosmological system of astral influences detailed in the *Ghāya* builds heavily on the Arabic reception of Neo-Platonic thought, particularly the power of the soul and the interconnections governing the relationship between the celestial and earthly spheres.[86] In this framework, the *Ghāya* divides magic (*siḥr*) into theoretical (*ʿilmī*) and practical (*ʿamalī*) domains connecting the heavens and the earth,[87] and it defines magic as a phenomenon whose cause (*sabab*) is hidden from the majority of intellects and is difficult to discover.[88] This nominal definition speaks both to an emphasis on the esoteric and secret nature of the occult and to earlier philosophical approaches to wonder and astonishment.

As for its broader thaumaturgy of the soul and the categorization of magic as a legitimate branch of natural science, the *Ghāya* appears to have drawn directly from the encyclopedic, epistolary writings of the Ikhwān al-Ṣafāʾ, the Brothers of Purity, writings that were composed during the middle of the fourth/tenth century.[89] Although the identity of the authors and the composition of the letters has been a matter of some scholarly dispute, the general consensus is that the Ikhwān were a coterie of Ismāʿīlī intellectuals based in Basra and Baghdad.[90] The Ikhwān locate the study of the occult as a branch of natural science that includes alchemy (*kīmīyā'*), judicial astrology (*aḥkām al-nujūm*), magic and talismans (*al-siḥr wa-l-ṭillasmāt*), medicine (*ṭibb*), and the ascetic discipline (*tajrīd*) of the soul.[91] Central to this exposition is their theory of the universal soul (*al-nafs al-kulliyya*), which emanates throughout existence. This vision of creation also posits the capacity of the rational soul to influence other bodies. Thus, for instance, charms (*ruqā*), spells (*nushar*), and incantations (*'azā'im*) draw their power from subtle spiritual influences (*āthār laṭīfa ruḥāniyya*) that emanate from the rational soul and influence the bestial soul (*al-nafs al-bahīmiyya*).[92] As for the question of legitimacy, the Ikhwān argue that it is ultimately the moral or ethical value that determines the lawfulness of magic. In this regard, they categorize prophetic miracles as examples of licit magic (*al-siḥr al-ḥilāl*), for such prodigious signs call humankind to God, whereas any spell or enchantment that instills doubt or leads people away from God is illicit (*ḥarām*), invalid (*bāṭil*), and has no basis.[93]

This theoretical work on magic and the occult intersects with a diverse range of socio-religious practices, which include among other facets the figure of the *mu'azzim*, the conjurer or enchanter, who can summon and control occult forces. The practice of subjugating such occult forces is given prophetic sanction through the figure of King Solomon and his power over demons and jinn (Figure 8.3). The most famous conjurer of the Umayyad period was Ibn Hilāl of Kūfa. Known as the *makhdūm*, the one who is served by the jinn, Ibn Hilāl features in early belletristic and historical writing as a contemporary of and sometime rival to the Umayyad commander of Iraq, Ḥajjāj b. Yūsuf (d. 95/714). Ibn Hilāl could conjure jinn and had the power of teleportation, a skill that allowed him to travel vast distances in an instance. Much of the early polemical material on the controversial mystic, thaumaturge, and itinerant preacher al-Ḥusayn b. Manṣūr al-Ḥallāj (d. 309/922) also focuses on his ability to summon demons and jinn. This motif is also expressed in the famed religious scholar Abū Ya'qūb Sirāj al-Dīn al-Sakkākī (d. 626/1229), who is known to have performed marvels through occult forces when he was a minister for the Mongol Emperor Chatagai Khan (d. 642/1244?). These three conjurers all shared run-ins with the authorities, which for Ḥallāj and Sakkākī ultimately led to their demise.

Despite the patently liminal status of magical practices, there exists a vast corpus on the occult arts, which also gives further insight into the spheres in which magic was enacted. There is much to suggest that the religious elite not only circulated such literature but also used it to harness occult powers. In this regard, the example of Abū l-Faḍl Muḥammad al-Ṭabasī (d. 482/1089), who lived much of his life in Nishapur, is particularly illustrative. Ṭabasī features in

FIGURE 8.3. Solomon enthroned above the orders of humankind and the jinn, from the poem the *Sulaymān-nāma* (*The Book of Solomon*), ca. 1500. The Trustees of the Chester Beatty Library, Dublin, T 406, f. 1b. The poem was composed by Firdawsī-i Rūmī for the Ottoman sultan Bayezid II (r. 1481–1512), as was this particular manuscript. The painting represents both Solomon's power over the jinn, as well as his ability, also affirmed in the Qur'ān, to understand the speech of birds.

Rāzī's *Sirr al-maktūm* as one of many authorities cited on the occult.[94] However, Ṭabasī was also known to be a trusted religious authority trained in Shāfiʿī law and Ashʿarī theology, a pious ascetic, and a Sufi, who composed numerous works and delivered lectures in madrasas of the region.[95]

Nonetheless, Ṭabasī is most famous for *al-Shāmil fī l-baḥr al-kāmil* (*The Comprehensive Compendium to the Entire Sea*), a treatise on subjugating demons and jinn through incantations, spells, and talismans.[96] One of the primary focuses of the work is explaining how to subjugate various spirits, demons, and jinn. According to Ṭabasī, there are two methods of doing so. The first is illicit and prohibited magic founded on disbelief; the other is completely licit, as it is based on profound piety, probity, purity, and ascetic seclusion, turning from the temptations of creation and devoting oneself to God.[97] This particular classification not only legitimates the various occult practices detailed in Ṭabasī's book of spells, but it also situates them in a broader setting of mystical devotion and asceticism. The *Shāmil* offers a testament to the interconnections that tie thaumaturgy and mystical devotion together. On this point, Ṭabasī argues that masters of this art have attained the rank of saints, and he offers several examples, including most prominently the mystic Ḥallāj. Ṭabasī also includes here Ibn Hilāl, who had befriended the Devil and obtained from him the power of incantation. We are told that Ibn Hilāl gained such a mastery over the occult arts that he was able to transport a man from Baghdad to Samarqand and back again in a single night.[98]

The *Shāmil* offers instructions for the preparation of various incantations that usually prescribe a combination of written and recited formulae. The incantations (ʿazīma, pl. ʿazāʾim) are designed to impose obligation on spirits, forcing them into submission in order to obtain supernatural powers through their aid.[99] Central to this process is the preparation of charms referred to as *khawātīm* (sg. *khātim*, literally seal or ring).[100] These are written on various mediums, such as paper, parchment, or leather hides, or they are engraved on tablets, metal disks, or signet rings. Instructions for drawing magical symbols and figural forms feature throughout the *Shāmil*. Also frequently used is the magic circle (*mandal*), which is drawn when casting various spells.

The incantations generally invoke otherworldly powers, holy figures, or sacred objects. In addition to the jinn, this often includes addressing the divine names of God, an array of angels, and the entire host of Islamic prophets from Adam to Muḥammad. However, dark forces are also called on and are featured in a colorful demonology that focuses on Iblīs (the Devil) and his countless progeny, represented most prominently with his daughter ʿAyna, who had married a jinni and was known by enchanters as the Lady Queen

FIGURE 8.4. A diagram of a magic seal (*khātim*) for casting an incantation to inflict harm on others, Abū l-Faḍl Muḥammad al-Ṭabasī (d. 482/1089), *al-Shāmil fī l-baḥr al-kāmil*. Princeton University, Islamic MSS, New Series, no. 160, fol. 37b. The anthropomorphic diagram, representing the object of the incantation, is surrounded by apocalyptic Qurʾānic verses referencing particular body parts of the damned (Q. 2:7, 12:23, 12:24, 12:30, 36:8–36:9, 36:65).

(*al-sayyida al-malika*). Like other books of spells, the incantations prescribed in the collection are used to obtain a variety of ends (Figure 8.4). Spells to ward off illness, demon possession, the evil eye, and sorcerers are prominent, as are love potions and charms for seduction.

Needless to say, the juridical and theological probity of many of these practices would be questionable in normative frameworks of Islamic theology and orthopraxy. Invoking the names of demonic forces would appear to be at odds with strict monotheism; similarly, the demonology detailed in the work speaks to a profoundly dualistic vision of the cosmos. Yet the fact that this material was produced by and circulated among the religious elite in the region also gives room for pause.

FIGURE 8.5. Bronze cast talismanic pendant, ca. 10th century, Nishapur, Iran, diam. 2.4 cm, thick. 0.5 cm © The Metropolitan Museum of Art, 40.170.245. The zodiac signs of Leo and Scorpio feature beneath three Solomonic seals and are surrounded by pseudo-writing that resembles the expression "There is no deity but God" in Arabic script.

Many of Ṭabasī's spells call for amulets and charms to be buried in certain locations or to be hung from particular areas of the home. The practice of trapping demons and jinn within vessels to be buried is a procedure used in many of the incantations. The application of spices, drugs, and various medicaments also features prominently. The archeological evidence both in the region during this period and broadly throughout the diverse landscapes of Islamic religious devotion points to the widespread use of amulets, charms, magical vessels, and clothing marked with various talismanic and astrological symbols, as well as Qur'ānic verses and supplications (Figure 8.5). Many of the talismanic practices described in the *Shāmil* find parallels today in diverse contexts; this is attested in an array of anthropological scholarship on the modern period, as well as by primary sources in Arabic and a host of vernacular dialects. The ubiquity of manuals on talismans, spells, and amulets and their circulation in premodern Islamic manuscript culture further adumbrates the religious networks across which this material traveled and was used.[101]

Exorcism, Charisma, and Religious Authority

Another field of the occult that directly intersects with the religious elite can be found in the diverse practices of exorcism. The religious literature on exorcism makes a concerted effort to distinguish licit religious practices from sorcery. In traditionalist circles, the arguments for the lawfulness of exorcism by the Ḥanbalī reformist Ibn Taymiyya (d. 728/1328) are rather illuminating. Along with an array of other intercessory practices, such as astrology, the veneration of saints, and shrine visitation, the Damascene scholar takes a particularly tough stance on the abuses of enchanters: he states that they make oaths to jinn and demons; their incantations are based on disbelief and polytheism; they write material from the Qurʾān in blood and other impurities in an attempt to please demons; they steal money from the ignorant; and furthermore, many of them are not truly capable of defending against jinn and end up actually harming those who seek their help.[102] Although his critique is clearly polemical, much of it appears to be based on actual practices developed by professional enchanters.

In contrast to what he terms polytheistic and illicit forms of commanding spirits, Ibn Taymiyya roots the lawful practice of exorcism in the actions of the prophets, from Solomon to Muḥammad, who defended humankind against demons. He offers numerous examples in the Sunna of the Prophet and the early Companions, concluding that, if done properly, exorcism is both lawful and righteous. The licit method of casting out demons and jinn is based solely on the power of God, as articulated by the divine names, the Qurʾān, and prophetically sanctioned formulae.[103] According to Ibn Taymiyya, the throne verse (Q. 2:255) is particularly efficacious and has been shown by countless authorities to have the proven ability of defending the soul against demons and to aid the possessed.[104]

In addition to reciting sacred formulae, Ibn Taymiyya advises striking the possessed repeatedly. Drawing on the personal experience of countless exorcisms that he personally performed, Ibn Taymiyya recommends hitting the afflicted hundreds of times with a cane and explains that it is the evil spirit that cries out in agony, not the body of the possessed, and that no harm will come to the person afflicted.[105] The Ḥanbalī scholar Ibn Qayyim al-Jawziyya (d. 751/1350), a chief disciple of Ibn Taymiyya, relates that he saw his master perform numerous such exorcisms. On some occasions, Ibn Taymiyya could cast out the spirit merely by commanding it to leave. Often, however, the spirit would be much more recalcitrant and his master would take to striking the body of the possessed with a rod. During one such intervention, Ibn Taymiyya related, "I struck the possessed with a rod on the veins of his neck until my very hands grew tired from so much striking. Those present thought that the possessed would surely die from this abuse." Ibn Taymiyya succeeded in casting the demon out of the man's body by reciting from the Qur'ān, invoking the name of God and the Prophet, and arguing directly with the evil spirit. As for the severe physical punishment, Ibn Taymiyya concludes that the man gained consciousness once the spirit had left and did not feel anything from all of the beating.[106]

Underlying the antagonistic engagement with demons and jinn is the rejection of any form of appeal for assistance or intercession to powers other than God. On this point, Ibn Taymiyya ridicules many of the wonders ascribed to Sufi saints (awliyā'), which he says the ignorant believe to be divine miracles (karāmāt); rather, he explains, these are demonic deceptions worked not by the divinely guided, but by the misled followers of demons.[107] This fits into Ibn Taymiyya's larger critique of the veneration of saints and the visitation of shrines, a critique that is directed, in great measure, at the intercessory structures of Ash'arī theology. Additionally, Ibn Taymiyya takes aim at the theory that prophetic miracles are not ontologically distinct from magic, a theory developed, as we saw earlier in the chapter, by the likes of the philosopher Ibn Sīnā and the Ash'arī theologians Ghazālī and Rāzī.[108] Likewise, in his broad rejection of astrology and other occult practices,[109] Ibn Taymiyya attacks Rāzī's al-Sirr al-maktūm as a work of magic based on worshiping stars and seeking the intercession of spirits to obtain illicit powers. Furthermore, he argues that the cataclysmic Mongol invasions and mass devastation that followed were brought on as a divine punishment for the apostasy, hypocrisy, and heresy that had run rampant among Muslims living in Eastern lands. Ibn Taymiyya singles out as an example of this excess Rāzī's al-Sirr al-maktūm, which he claims calls for worshiping stars and teaches people how to work magic. In this vein, Ibn Taymiyya argues that the Mongol sacking of Baghdad in 656/1258 and the consequent collapse of the 'Abbāsid caliphate was a divine retribution for the promotion and cultivation of the magical arts.[110]

In contrast to various occult practices deemed illicit, Ibn Taymiyya embraces the use of the Qur'ān, in both its written and oral forms, as a means of warding off illness and protecting against evil. Among the practices Ibn Taymiyya promotes is the ingestion of Qur'ānic verses for their curative power.[111] Similar uses of the Qur'ān are also detailed in occult writings, as in Ṭabasī's Shāmil, a fact that highlights the difficulty of distinguishing unlawful magic from sanctioned religious practice in normative terms. In a similar vein, Ibn Taymiyya rejects the use of unknown symbols or words commonly found on charms, incantations, and talismans as illicit, even if they are accompanied by Qur'ānic verses. He reasons that because the meaning is unknown, such material could very well consist of demonic or polytheistic statements that contravene the tenets of Islamic monotheism.[112] This position is in marked contrast to Ṭabasī, who includes in his book of spells countless incantations recited and written in an unintelligible language. In this context of unintelligible ciphers, it is of note that Fakhr al-Dīn al-Rāzī developed a theoretical basis for the use of unknown phrases and symbols as a means of enhancing the effectiveness of talismans.[113]

The nearly ubiquitous use of amulets and charms written with Qur'ānic material further demonstrates the difficulty of delineating the boundaries of magic in Islamic soteriology. Such deployments of the Qur'ān should not be considered magical in the sense of being unlawful or irreligious, for the source of their power lies precisely in their divine nature. The phrase "Qur'ānic the-urgy" may well help describe the copious literature on the special properties of the Qur'ān promoted by the likes of Aḥmad b. 'Alī al-Būnī (d. 622/1225) and 'Abd Allāh al-Yāfi'ī (d. 768/1367). This body of writing advances the occult power of the Qur'ān and the names of God, deployed through talismans, charms, magic squares, numerology, and mystical letters (ḥurūf) (Figure 8.6). Also found in such works are various recipes for ingesting the Qur'ān.[114]

From an early period, religious authorities in traditionalist circles, generally referred to as the people of tradition (ahl al-ḥadīth), actively promoted Qur'ānic theurgy within the normative bounds of piety and devotion. The descriptions contained in the hadith corpus on how to prepare Qur'ānic amulets, charms, and recipes for ingesting the Qur'ān indicate as much. Particularly illuminat-ing in this regard are reports in the collections on juridical questions (masā'il) posed to Aḥmad b. Ḥanbal (d. 241/855) and redacted by his son 'Abd Allāh (d. 290/903) and his disciples; these reports give further insight into how various material and corporeal engagements with scripture crossed into a domestic domain. 'Abd Allāh recounts that his father wrote out amulets containing Qur'ānic material to be worn on the body. Likewise, the student of Aḥmad b. Ḥanbal, Abū Dāwūd al-Sijistānī (d. 275/889), recounts that he saw a young son of his master wearing a leather amulet around his neck. Often parents attached such amulets to their children as preventative measures to guard against the evil eye. This is made explicit when Sijistānī follows with a question he put to Ibn Ḥanbal concerning the lawfulness of a charm (ruqya) to guard against the evil eye. Ibn Ḥanbal responds that he sees no problem with such a practice. Sijistānī also inquires about the practice of Qur'ānic ingestion or erasure, to

(a)

(b)

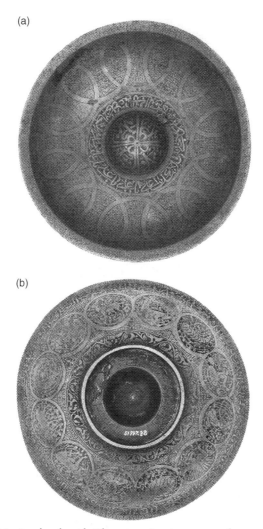

FIGURE 8.6. Divination bowl, mid-16th century, Iranian, engraved copper, 5.7 × 19.8 cm. The Arthur M. Sackler Gallery, Washington, DC, s1997.38. The inside of the bowl (a) contains ciphers in the form of magic numbers and Arabic prayers. The central calligraphic band consists of an Arabic invocation to Imam ʿAlī, referred to here as the manifestation of marvels (mazhar al-ʿajāʾib). The bowl's outer body (b) is decorated with the twelve signs of the zodiac, as well as magic squares and numbers and invocations to the Prophet Muḥammad and various Shīʿī Imams.

which Ibn Ḥanbal replies that there is also no issue with ingesting the Qurʾān dissolved in water or using that water to perform ritual ablution and that he has never heard of there being a problem with it.[115] This is a practice also affirmed by ʿAbd Allāh in his discussion of his father's use of amulets.

The charismatic presence in the written and oral forms of the Qurʾān fits into a larger topography of sacred materiality, which included a range of physical objects and locations invested with intercessory powers. The conceptual link between Qurʾānic theurgy and a sacred landscape populated with powerful relics is readily apparent in ʿAbd Allāh's treatment of the subject. Continuing with his discussion of amulets and erasure, ʿAbd Allāh relates that his father, Ibn Ḥanbal, was in possession of a hair from the Prophet and that his father would put it to his mouth and kiss it. His father would also place it on his head and eyes, submerge it in water, and then drink that water. ʿAbd Allāh also relates that Abū Yaʿqūb, the grandson of the ʿAbbāsid caliph Abū Jaʿfar al-Manṣūr (d. 158/775), sent the famed bowl of the Prophet to his father and that his father washed it in a cistern and then drank from it, adding, "On more than one occasion, I saw [my father] drink the water from the Zamzam well [of Mecca] in order to be cured by it and he would wash his hands and face with it."[116] Taken as a whole, this account links the various intercessory engagements with the Qurʾān to a wider universe of sacred matter that is to be directly touched and ingested.

The Shāfiʿī jurist and historian Shams al-Dīn Abū ʿAbd Allāh al-Dhahabī (d. 748/1348) records a parallel version of this report, also related on the authority of ʿAbd Allāh. However, he adds that ʿAbd Allāh asked his father about the legality of touching the pomegranate-shaped handle of the Prophet's *minbar*, as well as the tomb of the Prophet, to which Ibn Ḥanbal replied that he saw no harm in such practices.[117] A similar statement can be found in ʿAbd Allāh's transmission of his father's *Kitāb al-ʿIlal wa-maʿrifat al-rijāl* (*The Book of Hadith Errors and Knowledge of Hadith Transmitters*). Here Ibn Ḥanbal grants permission to those who seek divine blessing, or *baraka*, from the tomb or the *minbar* of the Prophet by touching or kissing it in order to draw themselves closer to God.[118]

As for Dhahabī, he prefaces this report with the rhetorical question, "[W]here is the obstinate disowner (*al-mutanaṭṭiʿ al-munkir*) of Aḥmad b. Ḥanbal now?" This is not only an allusion to the prophetic hadith "those who are obstinate perish" (*halaka l-mutanaṭṭiʿūn*),[119] but it is also a cryptic jab at Dhahabī's former teacher, the Ḥanbalī jurist Ibn Taymiyya, who wrote extensively against those who visited shrines for the intercessory benefits associated with them. Ibn Taymiyya claimed that the early religious authorities agreed that it was illicit to touch or kiss the tomb of the Prophet, and he concluded that the reason for this was "to protect monotheism (tawḥīd), for making tombs into mosques is one of the foundations of attributing partners to God (min uṣūl al-shirk bi-llāh)."[120] In explicit contradistinction with Ibn Taymiyya, Dhahabī comes out in support of shrine veneration and sees particular merit in making a pilgrimage to the tomb of the Prophet and the intercessory blessings gained from sacred matter associated with him.[121] By quoting Ibn Ḥanbal in support of these intercessory practices, Dhahabī characterizes Ibn Taymiyya's position on shrine visitation as a radical break with earlier Ḥanbalī juridical praxis. This was also a line of attack that Dhahabī's student, the Ash'arī theologian and Shāfi'ī judge of Damascus, Taqī l-Dīn Abū l-Ḥasan 'Alī l-Subkī (d. 756/1355), took against Ibn Taymiyya in an entire treatise, entitled Shifā' al-siqām fī ziyārat khayr al-anām (The Cure for the Ill in Visiting the Best of Humankind), which was dedicated to defending the practice.[122]

Ibn Taymiyya's censure of shrine visitation was repugnant to many and famously served as the basis for his final imprisonment, which led to his death. In his writings on the topic, Ibn Taymiyya set out a highly sophisticated treatment of shrine pilgrimage (ziyāra) that is much more complex than an outright ban on visiting tombs.[123] At a theological level, however, his main concern with seeking intercession from the tombs of saints and prophets was that it invests created matter (makhlūq) with divine power and thereby runs afoul of strict monotheism.[124] It is the specific implication of material mediation that was problematic for Ibn Taymiyya. To be sure, there is an internal consistency between his aversion to drawing on relics and tombs for their intercessory power and his support of ingesting verses of the Qur'ān for similar ends; for Ibn Taymiyya, the Qur'ān is uncreated divine speech and thus is theologically distinct from the necessarily temporal manifestations of relics and shrines.[125] Ibn Taymiyya's chief pupil, Ibn Qayyim, advanced a similar resistance to shrine veneration. Likewise, he promoted the Qur'ān's charismatic power in his al-Ṭibb al-nabawwī, an influential treatment of prophetic medicine in which he advances the legitimacy of amulets written with Qur'ānic verses and draws on the authority of Ibn Taymiyya and Aḥmad b. Ḥanbal, whom he claims both employed such amulets. He further argues that the act of writing verses of the Qur'ān in ink, immersing the paper in water, and then drinking the water was also a tradition accepted by the early community (salaf).[126]

One is hard-pressed to find urban centers across the lands of Islam in the premodern period without active cultures of shrine visitation. Likewise, various manifestations of Qur'ānic theurgy, from charms and amulets to inscriptions on bowls and garments are equally ubiquitous, intersecting with ancient attitudes

toward divine language and sacred writing. Both spheres of religious performance build on the power of *baraka* (divine blessing or charisma) obtained
through sacred matter. Just as tomb visitation evoked censure in certain traditionalist circles, so too did the talismanic use of the Qur'ān in charms and
amulets.[127] The same holds true for magic in its sundry manifestations, which
reveals a good deal about how the boundaries of the licit and the illicit have historically been defined and negotiated. In the modern period, faced with diverse
discourses of demystification, the spheres of the magical and the enchanted
have undergone significant reconfigurations in the expressions of Islamic piety,
devotion, and learning. For Muslim societies, the process of modernization,
with its roots in European colonialism and post-Enlightenment thought, as
well as in Islamic reformism, has challenged and reconfigured an array of historically traditional practices, often viewing them as being based on ignorance
and superstition. This can be seen, for instance, rather prominently in critiques
or correctives leveled by a range of Muslim authorities toward such activities
as exorcism, shrine devotion, and the preparation of amulets. As we have seen
in this chapter, many of these debates are rooted in classical Islamic thought;
however, they take on profoundly distinct expressions in the context of modern
Islamic reform. Yet through it all, in the competing poles of normativity, magic,
marvel, and miracle ultimately function as normative categories designed not
only to understand the world but also to shape it.

Notes

1. See Styers, *Making Magic*, 14–17; Francis, "Magic and Divination," 625–628.
2. Lane, *Account*, 222–223.
3. Ibid., 247.
4. Macdonald, *Religious Attitude*, 126.
5. Macdonald, "Concluding Study," 216; cited in Bodine, "Magic Carpet to Islam," 4.
6. Examples are legion. See, for instance, Mauchamp, *La sorcellerie au Maróc*, 86–98; Westermarck, *Pagan Survivals*; Donaldson, *Wild Rue*, 64, 130.
7. Brunot, "Maktab," in *Encyclopaedia of Islam*, 1st ed.; see Travis Zadeh, *Vernacular Qur'an*, 8–9.
8. Ibn Hishām, *Sīra* 1:288–1:289.
9. Q. 74:23–74:25, "*thumma adbara wa'stakbara, fa-qāla in hādha illā siḥrun yu'tharu, in hādhā illā qawlu l-bashari.*" On the exegetical tradition, see, for instance, Zarkashī (d. 794/1392), *Burhān* 1:110–1:111. Cf. Wāḥidī (d. 486/1076), *Asbāb* 468; 'Abd al-Razzāq (d. 211/826–827), *Tafsīr* 2:328–2:329; Ṭabarī (d. 310/923), *Jāmiʿ* 23:429, on the authority of 'Ikrima (d. 105/723–724), and more broadly, 23:429–23:432.

10. On the occurrence of words with the root *s-ḥ-r* in the Qurʾān, see Badawi and Abdel Haleem, *Qurʾanic Usage*, 425–426.

11. On *kitāb mubīn*, see Q. 5:15, 6:59, 10:61, 11:6, 12:1, 26:2, 27:2, 27:75, 28:2, 34:3, 43:2, 44:2; on *nadhīr mubīn*, see Q. 11:25, 15:89, 22:49, 26:115, 29:50, 38:70, 46:9, 51:50–51:51, 67:26, 71:2. As for the self-reflexivity in the Qurʾān vis-à-vis the conception of *kitāb*, see Madigan, *Qurʾân's Self-Image*, 53–77.

12. Q. 6:7, 11:7, 37:15, 54:2, 34:43, 46:7, 43:30, respectively.

13. On Moses, see Q. 10:76, 27:13; on Jesus, see Q. 5:110, 61:6.

14. Q. 10:1–10:2, "*alif, lām, rāʾ, tilka āyātu l-kitābi l-ḥakīm. a-kāna lil-nāsi ʿajaban an awḥaynā ilā rajulin minhum an andhiri l-nāsa wa-bashshiri l-ladhīna āmanū anna lahum qadama ṣidqin ʿinda rabbihim, qāla l-kāfirūna inna hādhā l-sāḥirun mubīn.*"

15. See Stewart, "Mysterious Letters."

16. See Badawi and Abdel Haleem, *Qurʾanic Usage*, 952–953.

17. See Abusch, *Mesopotamian Witchcraft*, 288.

18. CAD 8(k):437, 1a; see Smith, *Thesaurus*, 2:3591, col. 1.

19. See Dan. 5:6, 5:11–5:12, 5:16. Wolters, "Untying the King's Knots," 117–122; Paul, "The Mesopotamian Background of Daniel 1–6," 61–62.

20. Q. 114:4, cf. Q. 20:120; Badawi and Abdel Haleem, *Qurʾanic Usage*, 1027.

21. Isa. 8:19–8:20. See Schmidt, *Israel's Beneficent Dead*, 148–149; Jeffers, *Magic and Divination*, 170.

22. CAD 15(s):46, 3d.

23. See Vajda, "Hārūt wa Mārūt," in *Encyclopaedia of Islam*, 2nd ed.

24. See Benveniste, *Les mages*, 11–12; de Jong, *Zoroastrianism*, 221–222, 387–403.

25. See Secunda, "Studying with a Magus," 151–152.

26. The Arabic lexicographers generally view the word as Persian in origin but do not associate it with magic as such; see Ibn Fāris, *Muʿjam* 5:297; Ibn al-Manẓūr, *Lisān* 6:214–6:215.

27. On the impact of this process in early Arabic historiographical discourse, see Savant, *The New Muslims of Post-Conquest Iran*.

28. See, for instance, *Nērangestān, Fragard* 1, ch. 2, para. 15, ch. 10, paras. 14, 28, etc.; Boyce, "'Pādyāb' and 'Nērang,'" 284–285.

29. *Bundahišn* 387, para. 34.30.

30. *Pahl. Riv.* 1:228–1:229, ch. 63, paras. 1, 5, cf. 1:198–1:199, ch. 56, paras. 6, 11.

31. *Pahl. Ven.* 170, ch. 7, para. 44; cf. *Pahl. Riv.* 2:250.

32. See Omidsalar, "Magic ii. In Literature and Folklore in the Islamic Period," in *Encyclopaedia Iranica*.

33. E.g., Ṭabarī (attrib.), *Tarjuma-i Tafsīr-i Ṭabarī* 7:1946; see also, Zadeh, *Vernacular Qurʾan*, 528.

34. See Asmussen, "De-Demonization," 116–117.

35. *Ayādgār ī Jāmāspīg* 50–51, ch. 8, paras. 1, 4; cf. Shapira, *Studies in Zoroastrian Exegesis*, 180–181.

36. Jaṣṣāṣ, *Aḥkām* 1:53. Cf. Bīrūnī (d. ca. 442/1050), *Jamāhir* 185–186.

37. See Skjærvø, "Aždahā," in *Encyclopaedia Iranica*.
38. Khalīl, *Kitāb al-ʿAyn* 8:104; cf. Firdawsī, *Shāh-nāma* 1:83–1:84, ll. 464–481.
39. *Dēnkard* para. 7.4.72, translated in Molé, *La légende de Zoroastre*, 57.
40. *Bundahišn* 342, ch. 29, para. 13.
41. Ibid., 372, ch. 33, para. 40.
42. See Cook, *Muslim Apocalyptic*, 92ff.
43. E.g., *Tārīkh-i Sīstān* 60.
44. Ibid., 50; Ṭabarī (attrib.), *Tarjuma-i Tafsīr-i Ṭabarī* 5:1151.
45. See Ṭabarī, *Tārīkh* 1:201–1:211.
46. Jaṣṣāṣ, *Aḥkām* 1:54.
47. Ibid., 1:55; on *shaʿwadha*, see Bosworth, *Mediaeval Islamic Underworld*, vol. 2, 333.
48. As quoted by Suyūṭī (d. 911 / 1505), *Itqān* 2:99.
49. See Travis Zadeh, "The Wiles of Creation," 32–43.
50. Plato, *Theaetetus* 155d2–155d4.
51. Aristotle, *Metaphysica* 982b12–982b13.
52. Jaṣṣāṣ, *Aḥkām* 1:59.
53. Ibid., 5:379.
54. On this historical process, see Sabra, "The Appropriation and Subsequent Naturalization"; and more broadly, Gutas, *Greek Thought*. For the Hermetic tradition, see van Bladel, *Arabic Hermes*.
55. See Rāzī, *Mafātīḥ* 3:221–3:234; Ibn Khaldūn, *Tārīkh* 1:655–1:664; Ḥājjī Khalīfa, *Kashf* 1:12, 1:15; Fahd, "Siḥr," in *Encyclopaedia of Islam*, 2nd ed.; Fahd, "Le monde du sorcier en Islam"; Asatrian, "Ibn Khaldūn on Magic and the Occult."
56. Rāzī, *Mafātīḥ* 3:224–3:225.
57. Ibid., 3:223–3:230; treated in Macdonald, "Siḥr," in *Encyclopaedia of Islam*, 1st ed.
58. Rāzī, *Maṭālib* 8:143–8:146. This is an expanded version of the eight categories found in Rāzī's *Mafātīḥ*; it leaves out the eighth category, that is, sowing discord through slander (*namīma*), and expands the seventh, that is, tricking the foolish, into two separate fields. Missing from the *Mafātīḥ* is the discussion of divination, the eighth category in the *Maṭālib*.
59. By way of example, Rāzī cites a work by Ibn Waḥshiyya, presumably his book of poisons, *Kitāb al-Sumūm*, ed. Levey.
60. Rāzī notes that he examines the topic of lower spirits, the jinn, and demons earlier in his summa; see *Maṭālib* 7:315–7:331.
61. Rāzī examines the topic of physiognomy, along with other related divinatory practices in greater depth in a separate study; see Rāzī, *Kitāb al-Firāsa* 100–108; see Ḥājjī Khalīfa's classifications of *firāsa* in *Kashf* 1:15; also see Fahd, *La divination arabe*, 39–40, 188–195 (divination by casting stones), 196–204 (geomancy), 369ff (physiognomy), 393–395 (palmistry), 397–402 (palmoscopy), 440–446 (augury by flight of birds), 438–439 (*zajr*).
62. Rāzī, *Mafātīḥ* 3:230–3:231.

63. Ibid., 13:62, 14:128.
64. Ashʿarī, *Lumaʿ* 47, 71, paras. 107, 170. For Rāzī on theodicy, see Shihadeh, *Teleological Ethics*, 146, 160–169. More broadly, see von Grunebaum, "Observations on the Muslim Concept of Evil"; Ormsby, *Theodicy in Islamic Thought*, 16–31.
65. Although the text clearly references Rāzī as its author, the medieval reception of *al-Sirr al-maktūm* raised questions concerning its provenance. Relatively early on, there circulated theories that Rāzī did not author the collection, or if he did, he did not believe what was contained in the collection and repented and repudiated the work; see Tāj al-Dīn al-Subkī (d. 771/1370), *Ṭabaqāt* 8:87; Ibn Kathīr, *Tafsīr* 1:367; Ḥājjī Khalīfa, *Kashf* 2:990–2:991; cf. Ibn Khallikān (d. 681/1282), *Wafayāt* 4:249; for a further overview of the classical reception of the work, see al-ʿAlwānī, *Imām* 211–214. See also Maʿṣūmī, "Imām Fakhr al-Dīn al-Rāzī and his Critics," 362–363. On the work and its ascription to Rāzī, I follow Ullmann, who upholds its authenticity, *Die Natur- und Geheimwissenschaften*, 388–390. Furthermore, the metaphysical and cosmological positions, particularly on the psyche, are internally consistent with Rāzī's Neo-Platonism and his reception of Avicennan philosophy, pointing either to the authenticity of the ascription or to a writer who was profoundly engaged with Rāzī's thought and terminology. See also Shihadeh, *Teleological Ethics*, 8; Vesel, "Occult Sciences." On the Persian translation, see Vesel, "The Persian Translation of Fakhr al-Dīn Rāzī's *al-Sirr al-maktūm*."
66. The text itself remains only in manuscript and lithograph. The nineteenth-century lithograph published in Cairo is incomplete: al-Rāzī, *al-Sirr al-maktūm*, cited hereafter. For the contents of the work, see Ahlwardt, *Verzeichnis*, vol. 5, 282–284 (ms. Berlin 5886/Pet. 207).
67. Rāzī, *Mafātīḥ* 3:231–3:232. Ibn Kathīr heavily criticizes Rāzī for this very argument: *Tafsīr* 1:366–1:367.
68. Rāzī, *Sirr* 1–5 (ms. 5886, fols. 1b–3a).
69. Rāzī, *Maṭālib* 8:179–8:185, cf. 8:187–8:196.
70. Ibid., 8:184–8:185, cf. 8:179.
71. See Rāzī, *Maṭālib* 8:137, 8:144; Rāzī, *Mafātīḥ* 3:225; Rāzī, *Sirr* 11–12. The treatment here of Rāzī's theology of the soul draws from Zadeh, "Commanding Demons and Jinn," 152–154.
72. Ibn Sīnā, *Kitāb al-Nafs* 200–201, para. 4.4; see also Marmura, "Avicenna's Psychological Proof."
73. See Hall, "Intellect, Soul and Body," 68–69.
74. Rāzī, *Maṭālib* 8:121–8:123. See also Abrahamov, "Religion Versus Philosophy," 420–424; Marmura, "Avicenna's Psychological Proof."
75. Rāzī, *Maṭālib* 8:46, 8:50.
76. Ibid., 8:122.
77. Ibid., 8:137; Rāzī, *Mabāḥith* 2:424.

78. Ibn Sīnā, *Ishārāt* 4.156–4.157; see Rāzī's commentary, *Sharḥ al-ishārāt* 2:661

79. See Griffel, "al-Gazālī's Concept of Prophecy," 110–113.

80. See, for instance, Ghazālī, *Tahāfut* 290–291; Ghazālī, *Iḥyā'* 1:16, 1:29, 1:39.

81. Ibn Khaldūn, *Tārīkh* 1:660; Qalqashandī (d. 821 / 1418), *Ṣubḥ* 1:474. On the broader astrological parallels between the two, see Vesel, "Le *Sirr al-maktūm*."

82. See Fierro, "Bāṭinism in al-Andalus," 92–102.

83. Ps-Majrīṭī, *Picatrix* ix–x; Sezgin, *GAS* 4:297.

84. See Pingree, "Between the *Ghāya* and *Picatrix*," 27–28.

85. Pingree, "Some of the Sources," 2–3.

86. Ps-Majrīṭī, *Ghāya* 3–6, trans. 4–7.

87. Ibid., 8–9, trans. 9. Cf. Ikhwān al-Ṣafā', *Rasā'il* 4:313.

88. Ps-Majrīṭī, *Ghāya* 7, trans. 8.

89. See Fierro, "Bāṭinism in al-Andalus," 106–108; Ps-Majrīṭī, *Picatrix* lix–lxi; Pingree, "Some of the Sources," 3; Ikhwān al-Ṣafā', *On Magic*, 15–16.

90. El-Bizri, "Prologue," 3–13.

91. Ikhwān al-Ṣafā', *Rasā'il* 4:286–4:287, trans. 95–96, cf. 13–14.

92. Ibid., 4:309, trans. 153.

93. Ibid., 4:313–4:315, cf. 330–331.

94. Ullmann, *Die Natur- und Geheimwissenschaften*, 390. The following examination of Ṭabasī and the *Shāmil* is treated in further depth in Zadeh, "Commanding Demons and Jinn," 144–151.

95. See Fārisī, *Muntakhab* 61; Samʿānī, *Ansāb* 8:209. See also Yāqūt, *Buldān* 4:20; Dhahabī, *Siyar* 18:588. On the intellectual history of the religious elite of Nishapur during this period, see Bulliet, *Patricians*, as well as Zadeh, *The Vernacular Qur'an*, 331–359.

96. The complete title as given in the work itself is *al-Shāmil fī l-baḥr al-kāmil fī l-dawr al-ʿāmil fī uṣūl al-taʿẓīm wa-qawāʿid al-tanjīm* (*The Comprehensive Compendium to the Entire Sea for the Governing Element in the Foundations of Enchantment and the Rules for Casting Spells*). On Ṭabasī's use of the word *tanjīm* to signify casting spells and the technical meaning of astrological determinations or prognostication, see Zadeh "Commanding Demons and Jinn," 147–148.

97. Ṭabasī, *Shāmil* fols. 2a–2b.

98. Ibid., fols. 4b–5a.

99. On the etymology of *ʿazīma*, see Ibn al-Manẓūr, *Lisān* 12:400.

100. See Allan, "Khātam, khātim," *Encyclopaedia of Islam*, 2nd ed.; Porter, "Islamic Seals"; Stevenson, "Some Specimens," 112–114.

101. For examples of amulets and talismanic seals from the region during this period, see Allan, *Nishapur*, 60–61, 68–70.

102. Ibn Taymiyya, *Majmūʿ* 19:35, 19:45–19:46; Shiblī, *Ākām* 102–103.

103. Ibn Taymiyya, *Majmūʿ* 19:42, 19:56–19:59; Ibn Taymiyya, *Ṣafadiyya* 1:169.

104. Ibn Taymiyya, *Majmūʿ* 19:55.

105. Ibid., 19:60; Shiblī, *Ākām* 112–113.

106. Ibn Qayyim, *Ṭibb* 52–53.

107. Ibn Taymiyya, *Majmūʿ* 19:55.

108. Ibn Taymiyya, *Ṣafadiyya* 1:136–1:138, 1:142–1:143, 1:171.

109. See Michot, "Ibn Taymiyya on Astrology."

110. Ibn Taymiyya, *Majmūʿ* 13:180–13:181; Ibn Taymiyya, *Bayān talbīs* 3:53–3:55; Ibn Taymiyya, *Ṣafadiyya* 1:66–1:70, 172. See also Ibn Qayyim, *Badāʾiʿ* 1:758.

111. Ibn Taymiyya, *Majmūʿ* 27:340–27:342; Shiblī, *Ākām* 104; Ibn Qayyim, *Ṭibb* 277–278.

112. Ibn Taymiyya, *Majmūʿ* 19:61.

113. Rāzī, *Mafātīḥ* 1:161; Rāzī, *Maṭālib* 8:183–8:184.

114. See, for instance, Būnī, *Shams* 218; Yāfiʿī, *Durr* 11; on Būnī, see Francis, *Islamic Symbols*.

115. Sijistānī, *Masāʾil* 349.

116. ʿAbd Allāh b. Aḥmad, *Masāʾil* 447; Iṣfahānī, *Ḥilyat* 9:183–9:184.

117. Dhahabī, *Siyar* 4:484–4:485.

118. Ibn Ḥanbal, *ʿIlal* 2:492.

119. See, for instance, Muslim, *Ṣaḥīḥ* 2:1128–2:1129.

120. Ibn Taymiyya, *Majmūʿ* 27:223; cf. Ibn Taymiyya, *Jawāb* 11–13, 27.

121. Dhahabī, *Siyar* 4:485, editor's note, n. 1.

122. Abū l-Ḥasan al-Subkī, *Shifāʾ* 202–232, esp. 205–209; Taylor, *In the Vicinity*, 195–218.

123. Taylor, *In the Vicinity*, 168–194.

124. Ibn Taymiyya, *Jawāb* 21–12; Ibn Taymiyya, *Majmūʿ* 27:340–27:342.

125. See Zadeh, "Fire Cannot Harm It," 61–63.

126. Ibn Qayyim, *Ṭibb* 277–278.

127. Zadeh, "Touching and Ingesting," 465–466.

Chapter 9

Jewish Magic in the Middle Ages

GIDEON BOHAK

For students of medieval Christian magic, the most striking feature of medieval Jewish magic is that within the Jewish community it was never considered heretical or diabolical.* Some medieval rabbis frowned upon it, others practiced it with zeal, and most members of the Jewish elite utilized some magical practices but ignored or rejected others. But no one ever tried to persecute its practitioners, burn its handbooks, or punish its users, and only a handful of rabbis saw it as inherently "un-Jewish." In some places, Jewish practitioners of magic could run into trouble with the non-Jewish authorities, but of their fellow Jews they had little to fear, save for the condescending rebuke or mocking sneers of a few die-hard Maimonideans. And when debates about the legitimacy of certain magical activities did erupt, the issues involved had little to do with the legitimacy of magic per se and more to do with the legitimacy of practices that verged on idolatry, and thus could be classified as forbidden. Moreover, in many cases, the practice of Jewish magic was complementary to the practice of mainstream Judaism, as codified in Judaism's elaborate law-codes.[1]

The implications of this peculiar feature for the historian of Jewish magic cannot be exaggerated. First and foremost, it means that the evidence for the study of medieval Jewish magic is extremely detailed and comes in many different types of sources. Looking at the "insider" evidence (i.e., the texts and objects produced by the magicians themselves), we may note many hundreds of manuscripts of Jewish magic, usually copied by individual practitioners for their own use and often providing their copyists' names without any attempt at self-censorship or disguise. In some cases, we even find these copyists inserting their own names into the magical recipes themselves (instead of the generic formula of "so-and-so son of so-and-so"), especially in recipes for protection and those for charm and grace in the eyes of others.[2] We may also note magical recipes written on the margins of non-magical manuscripts – including, in fact, the margins of the most important talmudic manuscript from the Middle Ages.[3] And when we turn to the "outsider" evidence (i.e., that produced by persons who did not practice magic themselves, at least not in a professional manner), we note many hundreds of references to, and detailed discussions of, magical texts and activities. Some of these are polemical in nature, but many others are matter-of-fact discussions of amulets, exorcisms, apotropaic and medical magic, astral-talismanic magic, and numerous forms of divination, all adduced within biblical commentaries, philosophical tracts, religious responsa, popular stories, mystical writings, secular poetry, and even personal letters.[4] Assembling all of the evidence from these two types of sources and reconstructing a detailed and nuanced picture of medieval Jewish magic remain scholarly desiderata, in spite of some important contributions by earlier scholars.[5] In what follows, we shall make no attempt to offer such a reconstruction, but instead attempt to sketch the basic contours of this overall picture of medieval Jewish magic.[6]

The following discussion shall be divided in three sections. First, we shall look at the medieval Jewish discourse of magic by focusing on four specific examples of rabbinic discussions of magic and magic-related practices. Then, we shall look at some of the texts and technologies that may be grouped under the heading of "medieval Jewish magic," with special emphasis on their origins, transmission, and adaptation in different times and places. We shall then turn, in the third section of this chapter, to a brief examination of the rise of Kabbalah and its contribution to medieval Jewish magic.

The Discourse of Magic in Medieval Jewish Culture

Magic and divination are repeatedly forbidden by the Hebrew Bible, and their practitioners are condemned to death (Ex. 22:17; Lev. 19:26, 20:6; Dt. 18:9–18:15). But the Bible never really explains which practices are forbidden and instead provides a list of prohibited practitioners, including the *mekhasheph*, the *qosem*, the *ba'al 'ov*, and many others, without offering any specific details about what it is that they do and why it is that they are forbidden. Moreover, the Bible sometimes depicts legitimate Jewish leaders performing feats of magic and divination, be it Moses and Aaron beating the Egyptian magicians at their own game (Ex. 7–11), Joshua crossing the Jordan River (Josh. 3–4) and conquering Jericho (Josh. 6), Elijah and Elisha producing food ex nihilo (1 Ki. 17:10–17:16; 2 Ki. 4:1–4:7), reviving the dead (1 Ki. 17:17–17:24; 2 Ki. 4:18–4:37; 2 Ki. 13:20–13:21) and harming offensive children (2 Ki. 2:23–2:25), or Joshua, Saul, and David consulting the oracular *Urim and Thummim* (e.g., Num. 27:21; 1 Sam. 23:9–23:12; 1 Sam. 28:6). Thus, Jewish readers of the Hebrew Bible were confronted with a very inconsistent set of attitudes toward magic and its practitioners and had no overarching criteria with which to decide where to draw the line between what is acceptable in the realms of magic and divination and what lies beyond the pale.[7]

Among these readers, the rabbis of Late Antique Palestine and Babylonia, who between the first and fifth centuries CE developed the kind of Judaism that has survived until our own time, are remarkable for their even greater flexibility on this issue. They, too, noted that the *mekhasheph* should be put to death (*Mishna*, Sanhedrin 7.4), but they also noted that this applied only to one who performs an actual deed, whereas a mere sleight of hand is exempt from punishment (*Mishna*, Sanhedrin 7.11). Moreover, they permitted numerous magical practices that were deemed to have apotropaic and medical value (including, for example, the production and use of amulets), provided their hearers and readers with numerous magical spells and recipes for apotropaic and healing purposes, told stories of famous rabbis who practiced magic in order to fight magicians, and insisted that studying magic was not only legitimate but also desirable. Perhaps most surprising, they explicitly developed a category of licit magic when they noted that whereas some types of *keshaphim* are forbidden and deserving of the death penalty, others are forbidden but entail no punishment, and yet others are a priori permitted. As an example of the latter category, they told a story of two rabbis who created a calf ex nihilo and then ate it, clearly admitting that this was magic, and that rabbis too practice such magic, but insisting that this was a legitimate type of magic (Babylonian Talmud, Sanhedrin 67b, cf. also 65b). Thus, although they opposed some specific magical practices (especially healing in the name of Jesus) and occasionally frowned upon others (such as the magical use of Torah scrolls and biblical verses), the rabbis' overall discourse of magic took for granted that magic is effective and that in most cases it could be practiced, unless the praxis itself entailed a gross violation of their religious sensibilities. And as rabbinic literature became the starting point and yardstick for later Jewish culture, its lenient discourse of magic became the norm in later Judaism.[8]

There were, however, two major exceptions. The first was the challenge posed by the Karaites, a medieval Jewish group that broke away from the Rabbanites and their *halakha* (religious law) and sought to bring their own behavior in line with the biblical legislation. One major aspect of their anti-Rabbanite polemic was their claim that both rabbinic literature and the Rabbanite leadership of their own days were shot through with magic.[9] To the modern historian, their polemics are an excellent source for the study of medieval Jewish magic, especially their references to specific magical texts and practices popular among the rabbis of their own days, references that often are corroborated by the other evidence at our disposal.

The Karaite polemics made little difference to the practitioners of Jewish magic, because these attacks came from the outside and were a part of an all-out assault against all aspects of rabbinic culture. But a second challenge, which was influenced partly by the Karaite polemics and partly by Greek philosophy (as transmitted to the Jews through Arabic channels), was far more significant. This was the rationalists' war on magic, especially on linguistic and ritual magic and on the belief in the magical power of words, names, signs, and symbolic actions, often conducted within specific time frames. The most outspoken opponent of Jewish magic on this score was Moses Maimonides, whose attempt to utterly reform Judaism and rid it of all its magical beliefs and practices proved extremely controversial (as we shall see later in this section). And although Maimonides' injunctions proved successful in some cases, his anti-magic crusade as a whole may only be seen as a glorious failure: some Jewish leaders and thinkers accepted his views, but many others, including some of the leading rabbis of the Middle Ages, flatly rejected them as contradicting both the Hebrew Bible and classical rabbinic literature. Thus, magic and divination were not only widely practiced by Jews in the Middle Ages, but they were also often seen as utterly acceptable within the Jewish religious legislation. The only practices that aroused sustained and heated resistance were those that smacked of idolatry, or of Christianity, and even in such cases, exceptions could always be made.

To get a sense of some of the dynamics of these debates, let us look at four specific examples, each of which will illuminate different aspects of the medieval Jewish discourse of magic.

(a) Around the year 1000 CE, the rabbis of Kairouan, in North Africa, asked the Babylonian Gaon (head of the *yeshivah*, the rabbinic academy) Hai (939–1038) about the effectiveness and permissibility of the use of powerful names to achieve various mundane aims and about the scope of forbidden magical practices. Dissatisfied by his response, which apparently dismissed the stories of marvelous deeds performed by manipulating secret names and limited the scope of forbidden magic to the offering of incense to demons, they reformulated their question in greater detail. He responded once again, and this second exchange was copied down by later scribes and is currently preserved in several different manuscripts.[10] A full analysis of this fascinating document, which runs to some twenty pages, is out of the question here, but several points that emerge from this exchange are relevant to our discussion. First, both the rabbis of Kairouan and the Babylonian Gaon display their familiarity with numerous magical techniques, most of which are well documented in the "insider" sources.[11] The Babylonian rabbi even mentions three well-known books of magic – *Sepher ha-Yashar* (*The Book of the Upright*), *Harba de-Moshe* (*The Sword of Moses*), and *Raza Rabba* (*The Great Secret*) – as well as numerous booklets and smaller textual units.[12] As both the Kairouan rabbis' question and Hai's response make clear, most of these magical texts consisted of long sequences of magical recipes of the type "If you want to achieve X, do Y," which was the most common basic structure of Late Antique and medieval Jewish magical literature.[13] Second, although Hai Gaon generally denies the claims that "masters of the name" can work great deeds by following the instructions found in these texts, he also admits that rabbis too (not perhaps in his own *yeshivah* of Pumbedita, but those in the one in Sura, which was not far from there) also dabbled in such practices. He also admits that God's sacred name, when uttered or written down, can work great wonders, as was narrated in several celebrated talmudic stories.[14] Third, his attempt to re-explain what exactly is included under the rubric of forbidden magic is neither very clear nor too consistent, but its bottom line seems to be that some types of spells recited for demons, and often accompanied by the offering of incense, are forbidden under Jewish law.[15] Finally, he emphatically insists that the deeds performed by magicians are utterly different from the miracles performed by the biblical prophets, because the former do things that are humanly possible, whereas the latter performed miracles that no other human being could have accomplished, such as turning the water of the Nile into blood.[16]

Although this brief summary does not do full justice to Hai's detailed response, it does highlight the fact that here we see a medieval Jewish rabbi who is extremely knowledgeable about magical texts and practices, even though he insists that he never studied magic.[17] Moreover, even though he expresses his derision at those who take the magicians' claims seriously (and quotes Prov. 14:15, "a fool will believe anything!"),[18] he also admits that rabbis too use this supposedly useless technology and finds it virtually impossible to draw a clear line between licit and illicit magic. If this was the view of the most prominent rabbi of the early eleventh century, it is no wonder that there are hundreds of fragments of magical recipe books (including both *Sepher ha-Yashar* and *The Sword of Moses*), as well as numerous amulets, curses, dream requests, and erotic spells, in the Cairo Genizah, the used-paper storeroom of a medieval synagogue, most of whose manuscripts date from the tenth to the thirteenth centuries.[19]

(b) From Kairouan and Babylonia of the early eleventh century we move to Southern Italy and the year 1054. There, the writer Ahimaaz son of Paltiel produced a family chronicle, in rhymed prose, recounting his ancestors' history from the mid-ninth century onward.[20] His account is full of stories of miracles, magic, and the uses of the power inherent in God's name, of which we may focus on one specific example. The *Chronicle* relates how Ahimaaz's ninth-century forefathers, R. Shephatiah, R. Hananel, and R. Eleazar, all dwelling in Oria (in the "heel" of the Italian peninsula), displayed a great interest in Jewish esoteric knowledge, including a close study of the *Sepher ha-Yashar* described in the previous paragraphs.[21] Ahimaaz then dwells at some length on the figure of Rabbi Aharon, or Abu Aharon, of Baghdad, a miracle-working maverick who was exiled by his father after he harnessed to his mill a lion that had killed the donkey that had been harnessed there first. He then set sail to Italy, where he performed many more such feats, and, the poet notes, when he came to Oria he settled there,

> and his wisdom poured forth, and his teaching was implanted,
> and he demonstrated his powers, and the judgment of legal cases,
> as in the times of the *Urim* and the days of the Sanhedrin.
> And the law of the *sotah* he there set up and enacted,
> and instead of "dust of ... the earth of the Tabernacle" (Num. 5:17),
> the dust from below the Torah-ark was taken.[22]

In other, more prosaic, words, this Abu Aharon is said to have revived the old *sotah* ritual for detecting whether a woman had committed adultery (Num. 5:11–5:31), a ritual that, according to rabbinic literature, went out of use already in the Second Temple period (*Mishna*, Sotah 9.9). And as the original ritual had to be carried out in the Desert Tabernacle or in the Jerusalem Temple, Abu Aharon used the synagogue as a substitute and replaced the requisite dust from the floor of the Tabernacle or the Temple with dust from the floor of the synagogue – from right under the ark of the Torah. The rest of his ritual reenactment of this ancient ordeal must have followed the biblical model, including the mixing of the dust into pure water, the writing of a special text, and the "erasing" of its ink in the water, as well as the presentation of this concoction to the woman suspected of adultery, who would be forced to drink it. If she was innocent, nothing would happen, but if she was guilty, her thigh would fall and her belly would swell (in line with Num. 5:21–5:22, 5:27–5:28), thus proving her guilt.

Ahimaaz's account thus provides us with an interesting example of the revival of an old Jewish ritual after a hiatus of eight hundred years or more, but its most interesting feature is the fact that this "outsider" account is corroborated by "insider" evidence. Two Genizah fragments with magical recipes provide instructions for precisely the kind of praxis supposedly carried out by Abu Aharon (including the taking of the dust from under the Torah ark of the synagogue), thus confirming the revival of the *sotah* ordeal in the early Middle Ages and its circulation among Oriental Jews.[23] Ahimaaz's chronicle may be full of fantasy, but he did not make up this ritual in his own imagination, for it apparently was quite widely known, regardless of whether it was still being practiced in Italy in the mid-eleventh century.

A second point that is worth noting here is that the Abu Aharon whose exploits are celebrated in the *Scroll of Ahimaaz* is mentioned in later Ashkenazi sources as a major conduit of esoteric knowledge from the Orient to Italy, from where it then traveled across the Alps and reached the Jews of northern France and Germany (the so-called *Hasidei Ashkenaz*, or Ashkenazi pietists). And although the scholarly attempts to "rediscover" the exact nature of the secrets transmitted by this shady figure have not yet been successful, his historicity seems to be beyond any reasonable doubt.[24] As we see throughout the *Scroll of Ahimaaz*, as well as in Hai Gaon's responsum, firsthand knowledge of the mechanics of magic and divination was quite common among medieval rabbis. In this case, we also see that stories of some rabbis' successful exploits could be recited with great pride by their descendants and followers even several centuries later. Moreover, here too we see how the efficacy of such rituals was taken for granted by most medieval Jews and how their legitimacy could hardly be questioned in light of the biblical (or, in other cases, talmudic) precedents.[25] And once again, we see how the "outsider" evidence, this time in a family chronicle written by a poet with an interest in magic, matches well with what we find in the "insider" evidence, namely the handbooks copied and utilized by the medieval practitioners of Jewish magic.

(c) From southern Italy we move to Spain, North Africa, and especially Cairo, where the great Jewish philosopher, physician, and leader Moses Maimonides (the Rambam, d. 1204) finally settled and wrote his great works, especially the *Mishne Torah* (his encyclopedic summation of Jewish law) and the *Guide of the Perplexed*. In all of his works, including these two, Maimonides' war on magic is repeatedly manifested, and – as he assures his readers – it is a war based on his intimate familiarity with the magical texts themselves. Looking at his reading list (*Guide* 3.29–3.30), we find none of the works mentioned by Hai Gaon or the Karaites, but rather a whole range of works of astral-talismanic magic, some of which were falsely attributed to Hermes or Aristotle, and all of which Maimonides attributed to the so-called Sabeans.[26] This difference between the two rabbis' magical libraries accurately reflects the transformation of the

Jewish magical tradition in the eleventh and twelfth centuries, with the massive entry, through Arabic channels of transmission, of new magical technologies, an issue to which we shall return in the next section of this chapter. But it is especially a result of Maimonides' own interests, which lay squarely in the realm of learned magic, as opposed to the popular magical practices discussed in Hai's responsum, and of his wider philosophical agenda throughout the *Guide*. From his perspective, these Sabean books and the practices prescribed in them offered an illustration of the kind of "paganism" against which the Hebrew Bible was fighting, both with its prohibitions of magic and divination in Dt. 18:9–18:15 and with its recurrent prohibitions of idolatry (*Guide* 3.37).

We shall return to the issue of astral-talismanic magic and to its extensive use by medieval Jews later in this chapter, but for the time being, we must note that Maimonides' objections to what he found in the Sabean books he had read, and to other forms of magic and divination, run on two parallel tracks. On the one hand, he insists that magical practices – especially those that involve the use of supposedly potent words and names and are accompanied by ritual actions conducted at specific times – are sheer nonsense and a complete waste of their followers' time (and, just like Hai Gaon, he too quotes Prov. 14:15 in this context). On the other hand, he insists that most of these magical practices are included under the rubric of illicit magic and are thus forbidden to all God-fearing Jews in any case.[27]

Maimonides' two-pronged attack on magic has often been studied, not least because it was deemed extremely suitable for the needs of modern Jewish rationalists, especially those of the *Haskalah* of the eighteenth century, the *Wissenschaft des Judenthums* of the nineteenth century, and the Jewish Studies of the twentieth century.[28] What has less often been noted is how futile this huge effort eventually proved to be, because both contemporary and later Jewish practitioners of magic either argued vehemently against Maimonides' views (and we shall see one such example later in the chapter) or politely ignored them, and the Jewish magical tradition proudly sailed onward.[29] There were, however, some cases in which his rebukes proved more successful. For example, his vehement objection to the addition of "magic words," angel names, and magic signs to the *mezuzah* (the scroll with specified biblical verses that Jews affix to their doorposts) in an effort to enhance its apotropaic value did not bring about the complete demise of this practice, which is well attested in the Cairo Genizah. But it did set off a fierce debate, in which many different rabbis expressed their divergent opinions, and at some point this practice indeed petered out.[30] But other practices that Maimonides disliked, including the adjuration of demons with spells and incense offerings, continued to be practiced extensively among the Jews of later generations, and in many cases, they are still being practiced today.

(d) From Maimonides' Cairo we move to Barcelona and to the world of Rabbi Shlomo ben Abraham ibn Adret (the Rashba, 1235–1310) who lived roughly one century after Maimonides. Of his many references to magic, we may focus on a single responsum, dating from the early fourteenth century.[31] As in the case of Hai's responsum, here too we are reading a second exchange of letters, which followed a first round of questions and answers.[32] In that first round, the Rashba had been asked whether making a metal image (i.e., a talisman) of a lion for medicinal purposes is permitted, and he responded that it is. As a precedent, he adduced the mishnaic permission to wear a coin on a gouty limb and the talmudic admission that it is the image on the coin that does some of the healing.[33] He also noted that although making the image of a lion might seem especially problematic, given that this is one of the four faces of the "animals" that carry God's chariot (as in Ezek. 1:10) and rabbinic literature explicitly forbids making images of God's servants, a major talmudic authority limited that prohibition to the making of all four faces side by side (Babylonian Talmud, Rosh ha-Shana 24b), and therefore making a self-standing image of a lion is permitted. Finally, as a third and concluding argument, the Rashba claimed that his revered teacher, the great Rabbi Moses ben Nahman (the Ramban), both permitted the use of such images and even used them himself.

Rashba's first response apparently failed to satisfy the rabbis of Montpellier, who kept on flooding him with angry refutations of his arguments and providing more details of the praxis involved in the making of such images, including the offering of incense and fumigations, which clearly fall under the rabbinic definitions of idolatry and therefore had to be strictly forbidden.[34] In his long response, the Rashba does not really answer these questions directly, but he does embark on a long diatribe in which he seeks (a) to show that Maimonides' objections to various magical practices are far from consistent, given that he too insisted that if something *really* heals it cannot be forbidden, and especially (b) to provide an almost endless series of talmudic examples that prove that the rabbis of old had permitted numerous magical practices, especially those practiced for apotropaic and healing purposes. Analyzing all of his examples would take us too far afield, but his bottom line is important – namely, that making metal talismans in line with the instructions of astral magic is fine, as long as one does not offer incense to the image itself, nor worship the angel in charge of the day or hour on which the image is to be made, because both these actions would be considered idolatrous.[35] When one of the main opponents of astral magic insisted that the Rashba's responsum was far from satisfactory, the revered rabbi responded by complaining about the Aristotelian Jews, whose views (including the derisive citation of Prov. 15:14 against whomever believes in the reality of the biblical and talmudic stories!) both he and his opponent found offensive, and by curtly dismissing all objections to the permissibility of astral magic.[36]

The image that emerges from all of this is quite clear – magic was widely practiced by the rabbinic elite in thirteenth- and fourteenth-century Spain, and medical magic was the easiest to justify. Even astral magic, including the making of talismanic images, was deemed acceptable to many rabbis, and only the offering of incense, or other practices that could be seen as worshipping an object or a power other than God, were considered beyond the pale. And although Maimonides' views were greatly respected, they so blatantly contradicted everything that was found in the Hebrew Bible or in classical rabbinic literature that they could easily be refuted.[37] To put things in more modern terms, we may conclude that for many rabbis in the Middle Ages, magic was very "Jewish," and the objection to its efficacy or legitimacy was very "un-Jewish." The end of this debate, we may add, was the famous ban promulgated by the Rashba against the study of philosophy by anyone who had not yet reached the age of twenty-five, a ban that was fiercely opposed by philosophy's many Jewish supporters.[38]

The Cultural Makeup of Medieval Jewish Magic

Looking at the history of the Jewish magical tradition (and of Jewish culture as a whole), one may visualize it as a stream, into which more and more fountains and tributaries keep on flowing, but whose water is constantly evaporating because of the heat of the sun. When looking at medieval Jewish magic, one may see four streams flowing into it – (a) that of Late Antique Jewish magic, which was transmitted into the Middle Ages in written manuscripts that were continuously copied, redacted, and adapted for more than one thousand years; (b) that of medieval Muslim magic, which made a lasting impression on medieval Jewish magic; (c) that of Christian magic, whose impact on medieval Jewish magic was much less significant; and (d) that of medieval Kabbalah, the Jewish mystical-esoteric tradition. In what follows, we shall first examine the survival of Late Antique Jewish magic into the Middle Ages, and then turn to the Muslim and Christian influences on medieval Jewish magic. We shall then turn, in the third and final section of this chapter, to a brief examination of the relations between the Jewish magical tradition and Kabbalistic ideas and practices.[39]

(a) The Transmission of the Jewish Magical Tradition
from Late Antiquity to the Middle Ages

Looking at the history of the Jewish magical tradition, one may note some modest and poorly documented beginnings already in the Second Temple period and an impressive growth in Late Antiquity, roughly from the third and fourth centuries CE to the rise of Islam. This sudden growth may also be the result of the "scribalization" of the Jewish magical tradition – that is, the shift to magical practices that often were transmitted in written form and whose execution often entailed the production of written objects – a shift that helped secure the survival of numerous written objects of Jewish magic from Late Antiquity, and thus enabled their detailed study.[40] This "scribalization" of ancient Jewish magic, especially in Palestine and in the Greek-speaking Jewish diaspora, also ensured the smooth transmission of much Late Antique Jewish magical lore into the Middle Ages, especially in the form of recipe books and manuals of Jewish magic, most of which were written in Aramaic and in Hebrew.[41] In Sasanian Babylonia, on the other hand, Jewish magical spells seem to have been transmitted mostly in oral form, even when they were written down on hundreds of clay bowls, a praxis that makes them partly accessible to the modern historian.[42] The result of this process of oral transmission is that whereas medieval Jewish magic displays many signs of continuity from the older, "Western" branch of Late Antique Jewish magic, continuities from the "Eastern" branch, that of the Jews of Sasanian Babylonia, are not as prevalent.[43]

The smooth flow of Late Antique Palestinian Jewish magic into the Middle Ages has several important implications. First and foremost, the older Jewish magical texts were characterized by their deep exposure to the Greco-Egyptian magical tradition and by their selective borrowings and adaptations from that tradition. To put things rather crudely, one may note that the "pagan" gods were mostly left out of the Jewish magical tradition, but less offensive elements, such as the magic signs and magic names strewn throughout the Greco-Egyptian magical tradition, were warmly adopted by the Jewish magicians. This is why in Late Antique Jewish magical texts, and in medieval ones as well, one often finds the *charaktêres*, those mysterious-looking ring-letters, or the name Abrasax, or word-triangles made up of gradually diminishing words, "magic words," and powerful names.[44] This also is one more reason why medieval Jewish magic differs from medieval Christian magic: whereas the *charaktêres*, for example, were frowned upon by Augustine and therefore were deemed problematic in medieval Christian culture (where the tainted term often was replaced by less offensive terms, such as *figurae*), in the Jewish

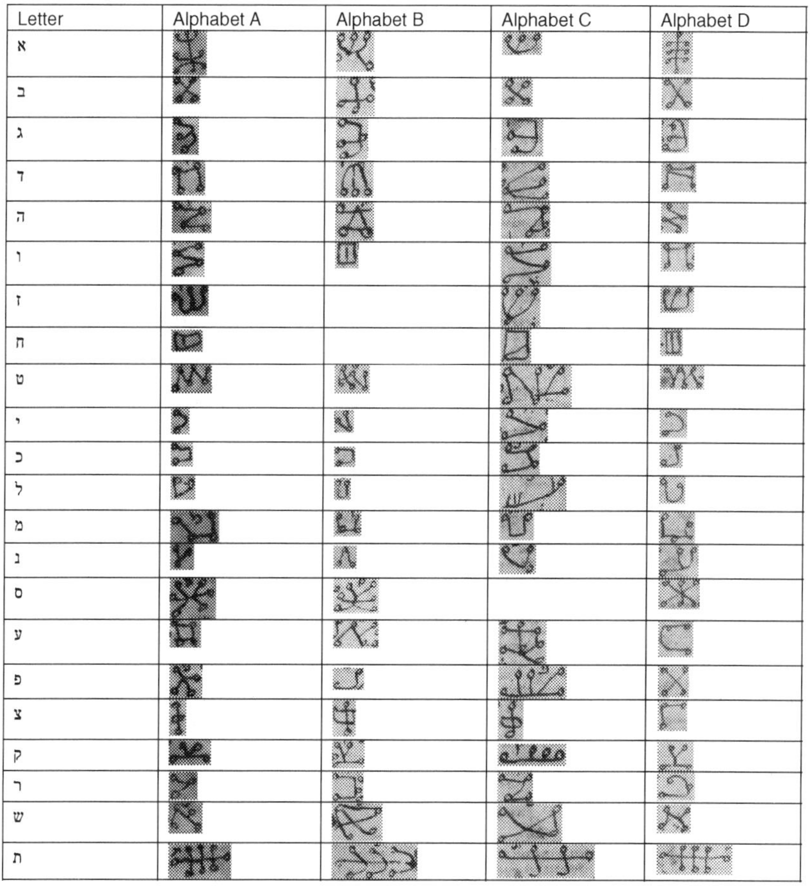

Letter	Alphabet A	Alphabet B	Alphabet C	Alphabet D
א				
ב				
ג				
ד				
ה				
ו				
ז				
ח				
ט				
י				
כ				
ל				
מ				
נ				
ס				
ע				
פ				
צ				
ק				
ר				
ש				
ת				

FIGURE 9.1. Angelic Alphabets. Alphabet A is taken from T-S K 12.60; B is from NYPL Heb. 190 (olim Sassoon 56), 181; C is from NYPL Heb. 190, 182; D is from Geneva 145 (olim Sassoon 290), 186. There are many more alphabets in these and other manuscripts.

magical tradition, they were fully naturalized already in Late Antiquity and therefore aroused no objections.[45] In Jewish magical texts, they appear either as powerful signs devoid of any "pagan" or diabolical connotations or as secret "seals" used by the angels in heaven. In the Middle Ages there were many attempts by Jewish magicians and mystics to "decipher" the meaning of these mysterious signs and to decode the "angelic alphabets" that supposedly lay behind them (see Figure 9.1).[46] Such speculations facilitated the reentry of some of these magic signs into the Christian magical tradition and their adoption by the likes of Cornelius Agrippa von Nettesheim.

The smooth flow of Late Antique Jewish magic into the Middle Ages assured the continuous transmission and use of many magical texts, including the Late Antique Palestinian *Sepher ha-Razim* (*The Book of the Mysteries*), the *Sepher ha-Yashar* and *The Sword of Moses* mentioned earlier in the chapter, and a plethora of similar, but mostly shorter, magical texts.[47] It also assured the transmission, adaptation, translation, and use of individual magical recipes, including one magical recipe whose transmission history may even be traced in a continuous manner from the fifth or sixth century all the way to the twentieth century.[48] It also assured the transmission of the basic techniques of the Jewish magical tradition, namely, the recitation and/or inscription of spells, often accompanied by the manipulation of readily available mineral, vegetal, animal, or human substances, in order to achieve various apotropaic, medical, divinatory, aggressive, erotic, or other aims.[49] But as we shall see in the next two subsections, medieval Jewish magic was not merely the reheated remains of older Jewish magic; it was deeply enriched by the entry of new, and unprecedented, magical technologies borrowed from the Jews' new neighbors in the Middle Ages.

(b) The Impact of Muslim Magic on Medieval Jewish Magic

Looking at Oriental Jewish manuscripts that transmit magical texts and recipes, such as those found in the Cairo Genizah and those in many other collections, we find copious documentation of Oriental Jewish magic from the tenth to the twentieth centuries. One of the most striking features of this branch of medieval Jewish magic is its enthusiastic adoption of Islamic magical technologies borrowed from the Jews' Arabic-speaking neighbors. This is a small part of a much wider phenomenon, namely, the deep cultural impact of Arabic-Muslim culture on medieval Judaism. This process was greatly facilitated by the use of a shared language, Arabic (which the Jews often wrote in Hebrew letters, a form known as Judaeo-Arabic), and by the fact that the Jews never denied Islam's deep commitment to monotheism and therefore were less fearful of borrowing some Muslim practices and of participating in the cultural exchange of the Muslim intellectual elite. This process is apparent in all spheres of Jewish cultural activity in the lands of Islam, from philosophy and medicine to *belles-lettres* and poetry, and it has often been described in the past.[50] Focusing solely on magic, we may note that in this field, too, we can speak of Judaeo-Arabic culture as a true "hyphen culture" – so much so that when we read some Judaeo-Arabic magical texts from the Cairo Genizah, we might be tempted to classify them as "Muslim" and "Jewish" at the same time, given that the process of "Judaizing" them consisted mostly of transliterating them from one alphabet to another, often with very little censorship and very few modifications.[51] The best sign of this cultural openness is the appearance in the Jewish world of completely new types of magical texts and technologies, which would have been quite unthinkable to the Jewish magicians of a few centuries earlier.[52] Of these, the two novel magical technologies that had the greatest impact on the later course of the Jewish magical tradition were the rituals for summoning demons, on the one hand, and the practice of talismanic, or astral, magic, on the other hand. Let us briefly examine each of these.

Turning first to demonology, we may note that the Jewish infatuation with demons goes back a long way, at least to the third century BCE and probably much earlier, and it is extremely well attested in the centuries preceding the rise of Islam.[53] But whereas the Jews of the Second Temple period and of Late Antiquity were mostly occupied with trying to keep demons at bay, exorcizing them out of the persons whom they had entered, or (less frequently) sending them back upon the magicians who had set them on their evil mission, in later periods we also find Jews actively trying to attract demons.[54] This new magical technology often consisted of long and elaborate rituals for gathering demons to a single place (the Hebrew term for such a gathering is *qevitzah*), interrogating them, and subduing them so as to be able to use them for various tasks. In many cases, the ritual necessitated the drawing of a large circle or a square, inside of which the magician would stand, the offering of incense (a practice that, as we noted earlier in the chapter, was forbidden even by Hai Gaon, not to mention Maimonides), and the recitation of long spells. In some cases, the detailed instructions were accompanied by images of the demons themselves (see Figure 9.2), and especially those of the "seals" of the different demons, which had to be produced (usually in bronze or other metals) and shown to them as a part of the ritual (see Figure 9.3). The instructions for such rituals often were transmitted in Judaeo-Arabic, but Hebrew translations and adaptations were quick to follow, and these were spread far and wide, including to the Jews of Christian Europe.[55] There, the new technology even gave rise to the medieval image of the demon-summoning Jew (an image that unfortunately corroborated the Christian anti-Jewish stereotype of the Jews' pact with the Devil) and to Hebrew as a preferred language for such practices.[56]

A second type of magical activity that became very popular among Jews in the Middle Ages, and that was entirely unattested in earlier periods, is the use of talismanic, or astral, magic. This was a technology that was based on the astrological assumption that the planets and the stars have a great impact on

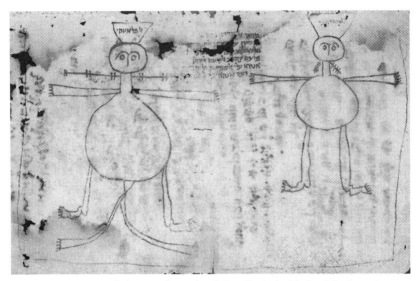

FIGURE 9.2. Images of demons from the Cairo Genizah. Taylor-Schechter Ar. 51.95. Reprinted by courtesy of the Syndics of Cambridge University Library.

	Sunday
	Monday
	Tuesday
	Wednesday
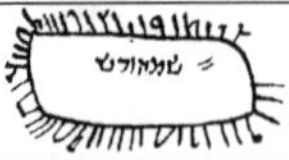	Thursday
	Friday
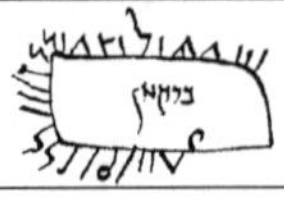	Saturday

FIGURE 9.3. The seals of the seven kings of the demons ruling over the days of the week. Based on ms. NYPL Heb. 190, 156.

everything that happens on earth and the conviction that these powers could be harnessed through ritual techniques. The praxis consisted of choosing an astrologically suitable moment, preparing an appropriate talisman, placing it in an appropriate position, and performing elaborate rituals, including the offering of incense and the recitation of special prayers and adjurations, all of which were intended to "charge" the talisman with the astral powers. Once "charged," the talisman could be used to achieve the usual aims of the magical practices – for love, for hate, to fend off evil forces, to heal the sick, to destroy a city wall, and so on. This technology – which in the Middle Ages was avidly used by Muslim, Christian, and Jewish magicians and physicians alike – was transmitted in special handbooks, with detailed instructions on how to produce each of the talismans and how to use them. Such handbooks circulated in the Jewish world both in Judaeo-Arabic versions transliterated from Arabic sources and in Hebrew translations made from Arabic or Latin originals.[57] Their great popularity in medieval Jewish culture and the impact of astral magic on Jewish physicians, philosophers, and Bible commentators have often been noted by earlier scholars and need not detain us here.[58]

Side by side with these two new magical technologies, many more elements of medieval Jewish magic can be shown to have been borrowed from the Arabs, including the use of (numeric) magic squares, the citation of Qur'ānic verses and Muslim blessing formulae, the use of Arabic magic signs, and so on. Even the so-called "Star of David" was borrowed from the Muslim magical tradition by the Jewish one, and it thus began its long and tortuous road from a magical design to a Jewish national symbol.[59] The same holds true in the realm of divination, where the Jewish contact with Arabic culture entailed the adoption of new divinatory techniques, such as geomancy or treasure hunting, and the great expansion of others, such as dream interpretation.[60] Thus, one may safely conclude that the contact with Arabic magic and divination greatly enriched the Jewish magical tradition, with new textual sources and new magical techniques joining and supplementing the old ones and spreading not only to the Arabic-speaking Jews of the lands of Islam but also to the Hebrew-speaking Jews of Christian Europe.

(c) The Impact of Christian Magic on Medieval Jewish Magic

Having briefly examined the Muslim-Arabic contributions to the Jewish magical tradition, we now turn to the Christian ones. In the medieval Christian world, there never was a cultural middle ground between Christians and Jews, both because very few Jews knew Latin – the vehicle of learned discourse in medieval Europe – and because Jews saw Christians and their culture as a threat and therefore were wary of the overt absorption of Christian texts and traditions.[61] Moreover, the relative absence of social circles in which Jews and Christians could exchange manuscripts and practices, and the dangerous status of magic within Christian society, all made Christian magic less accessible to Jews. We therefore find many specific Christian magical practices that entered the Jewish magical tradition, and even some Latin magical texts in Hebrew translation or transliteration, but we do not find the systemic and pervasive entry of foreign magical technologies into the Jewish world that we find in the lands of Islam.

Looking at Jewish magical texts and practices from medieval Europe, we may easily note items that were borrowed from the Christian magical tradition, including the ubiquitous appearance of the famous palindromic square, SATOR AREPO TENET OPERA ROTAS, or the recurrence of the magic word "Abracadabra," which is first attested in Latin literature in the third century CE and becomes extremely popular in the Middle Ages, first in Christian magical texts and then in Jewish ones, as well.[62] We even find more specifically Christian names, such as Lucifer and Beelzebub or the three Magi who had once adored the baby Jesus, namely, Gaspar, Melchior and Belthazar, and specifically Christian terms, such as *nigromancia* (in many different spellings).[63] We also find elements borrowed from European folk beliefs, such as the evil demoness Striga or magical signs resembling those of the *Ars notoria*, whose shapes differ both from those of the earlier *charaktêres* and from those of the Arabic ones.[64] Sometimes we even find whole recipes that clearly came from Christian sources and were translated by the Jewish magicians from Latin or Greek, usually with some modifications.[65] And, in what is perhaps the most interesting phenomenon, we find several examples of Christian Latin spells and prayers that were transcribed by the Jewish practitioners in Hebrew letters and may thus be viewed as "Judaeo-Latin" magical spells (see Figure 9.4).[66]

Such examples of the Jewish borrowing of Christian magical spells, signs, and practices are of great importance, and they deserve a closer study. However, one should not forget that such examples are few and far between, and they are the exception rather than the rule. The one area in which this kind of cross-cultural borrowing was more common was the realm of medicine and "experimental science" (in its medieval version), where technical knowledge flowed more smoothly from the Christian to the Jewish world. In this area, we also find some of the clearest examples of the Jewish borrowing and translation of Latin Christian texts.[67] One such example is the so-called *Experimenta duodecim Johannes Paulini*, which begins with the instruction to

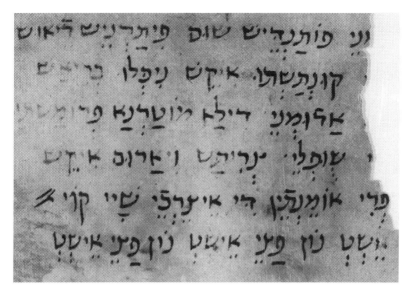

FIGURE 9.4. A thirteenth-century "Judaeo-Latin" prayer from the Cairo Genizah. Taylor-Schechter K 1.115. Reprinted by courtesy of the Syndics of Cambridge University Library.

burn the skin of a snake when the moon is waxing in the first degree of Aries and then lists twelve uses of the resulting powder, from healing head wounds to winning scientific disputations.[68] This well-known Latin text is said to have been translated from an Arabic text called *Salus vitae*, and although the Arabic original has not yet been identified, its name, "The Health of Life," makes perfect sense, given that in Arabic the word for "life" and the word for "snake" are almost identical. This text was translated into Hebrew on several different occasions, and although one of the translations may have been directly from the Arabic original, the others probably were based on the Latin version.[69]

To summarize what we have seen, we may note that although a systematic survey of all the Jewish magical manuscripts of medieval Europe – not just the Hebrew ones, but also those written in Yiddish and in Ladino – has yet to be carried out, it seems clear that the systemic and pervasive influences on the Jewish magical tradition that we find in the Arabic-speaking Muslim world are not paralleled in the Latin- or Greek-speaking Christian world. There, too, Jewish magicians borrowed words of power, magic signs, and even whole spells from their non-Jewish neighbors, but they rarely borrowed new magical technologies, and even when they borrowed Christian prayers, they often censured all of those elements that they found religiously offensive.[70]

Jewish Magic and Kabbalah in the Middle Ages

In the previous section, we focused mainly on the enrichment of medieval Jewish magic by external influences, and this might give the impression that the Jewish magical tradition is nothing but the mixture of older Jewish magic with newer, foreign magical technologies. This, however, is not the case; the Jewish magical tradition was greatly enriched by internal Jewish developments as well, and especially by the rise of the so-called Kabbalah, the Jewish mystical-esoteric tradition.

The full relations between Jewish magic and the early Kabbalah are an enormous topic that still awaits a full scholarly treatment.[71] On the one hand, there is much evidence for some Kabbalists' great interest in magical techniques – including, for example, dream requests or techniques of automatic writing – and their use of such techniques in their search for the attainment of celestial secrets.[72] On the other hand, there is much evidence for the contribution of the Kabbalah, especially the so-called "Kabbalah of the names" (as opposed to the "Kabbalah of the (Divine) Sephirot," which is today often referred to as the theosophic branch of Kabbalah), to the growth of the Jewish magical tradition in the Middle Ages.[73] From the point of view of the Jewish magical tradition, this contribution consisted of an ever-growing stream of powerful names and their uses, often at the expense of more elaborate magical rituals.[74]

The obsession with powerful names is evident already in Late Antique Jewish magic, where it was shaped by two complementary processes. On the one hand, the biblical infatuation with powerful verbal utterances (as in Gen. 1), with secret names (e.g., Judg. 13:18), and especially with the powerful name of God, which no one may utter (e.g., Lev. 24:11, 24:16), gave rise to some traditions of esoteric names and their great powers.[75] On the other hand, the Greco-Egyptian magical tradition provided an endless variety of "magic words" and displayed its own infatuation with the power of such words, an infatuation that is common in many other magical traditions.[76] The Jewish interest in such issues is also manifest in the Hekhalot literature, which is one of the earliest stages of the Jewish mystical tradition, where meaningless "words" and powerful names are a major theme. It is even visible in rabbinic literature, especially in the discussion of God's esoteric names of four, twelve, and forty-two letters, and the strict rules of secrecy under which they were transmitted (Babylonian Talmud, Kiddushin 71a). Furthermore, Hai Gaon, in the responsum that we analyzed in the first section of this chapter, refers to this issue and notes that the exact pronunciation of God's name of forty-two letters was transmitted in his days *be-kabbalah*, that is, by word of mouth from one tradent to another, and this is the earliest known use of the word *kabbalah* in this specific sense.[77] Moreover, as we noted in our analysis earlier in the chapter, much of his responsum deals with the issue of the efficacy of such names and the permissibility of their use, and such issues continued to trouble the Jewish elite, especially the philosophers and the Kabbalists, throughout the Middle Ages. The Jewish magicians, on the other hand, were less bothered by the theory and more troubled by the praxis, and thus they found in the Kabbalists' contributions much that was suitable for their own needs.[78] In what follows, we shall not try to disentangle all of these different threads but merely note two examples of the influence of Kabbalistic name speculations on the Jewish magical tradition.[79]

(a) One of the earliest and most common practices of the "Kabbalah of the names" was the addition of powerful names to existing Jewish prayers in an effort to enhance their effectiveness. This practice is well attested in Hai Gaon's responsum, because it was a part of the question sent by the sages of Kairouan to the Babylonian rabbi. If, they ask, one is innocent, is old, is humble, and fulfills all of the other criteria for the transmission of God's names as specified in the Babylonian Talmud and he wishes to use the name – how should he do it? Should he insert it into the usual supplicatory prayers, mention his specific need, and then recite the secret name wherever the prayer uses the Tetragrammaton (which is written YHWH but would normally be pronounced "Adonai")? Or should he use it in the Eighteen Benedictions prayer, which is the standard Jewish daily prayer and use its benedictions to ask for something that is related to the benediction's contents (e.g., asking in "Blessed are thou, who heals the sick" for health for someone who is sick), but inserting the secret name at the end of the blessing where the Tetragrammaton would usually be found? Such were their questions.[80] Hai's response is complex. At first, he insists that for reasons of sanctity, God's name may only be recited in the Holy Land – that is, neither in Kairouan nor in Babylonia. Moreover, because no one really knows its exact pronunciation, one may make a mistake in pronouncing it, and this would be a great sin. This would have been an elegant way out of the whole crux, given that it renders the whole question moot, but Hai immediately adds that even in places where one may recite the name, one should not simply insert it into a blessing, but instead first recite the name, then recite praises and glorifications along the lines of the Throne hymns (known to us from Hekhalot literature), and then ask God whatever he wishes.[81] Thus, in a single sentence, Hai has made it clear that, in his opinion, and within strict limitations on who may conduct the ritual and on where and how it may be conducted, one may use God's esoteric name(s) to beg for one's specific needs.

The practice of adding special names to the standard prayers is, of course, a close parallel to the addition of angel names and powerful signs to the *mezuzah*, a practice to which we already devoted some attention. As noted in the first section of this chapter, the Cairo Genizah furnishes us with several examples of such *mezuzot*, but it also provides interesting evidence of the addition of magical names to the regular prayers, presumably of the type known to the rabbis of Kairouan and to Hai Gaon.[82] Thus, in one Genizah fragment, we find the Eighteen Benedictions prayer turned into a set of magical spells.[83] For each Benediction, an aim is specified ("If you wish to raise the dead from the grave . . . if you wish to talk to the sun," etc.), as well as a list of "magic words," but no ritual instructions whatsoever. It is, of course, possible that the meaningless "words" in fact are ritual instructions, which have been encrypted by way of some yet undeciphered code. It seems more likely, however, that here we have an example of the addition of powerful "words" to the daily prayer, which turn each of its constituent Benedictions into a powerful spell recited in order to achieve a specific aim.

Examples such as these could be multiplied, especially because the "magicalization" of the standard Jewish prayers is a recurrent phenomenon in the history of the Kabbalah and of the Jewish magical tradition.[84] But rather than adducing more such texts, we should pause for a moment to consider their wider implications. First, we may note that the practice of adding God's esoteric names to the regular prayers was not seen by the rabbis of Kairouan or by Hai Gaon as directly related to magic. In fact, we may assume that for many of their developers and users, the names were seen as a *substitute* for the magical rituals found in the magicians' handbooks. Thus, if you wish to speak to the sun (which travels around the whole world and therefore is extremely knowledgeable), you need perform neither the elaborate ritual for this purpose that is set out in *Sepher ha-Razim*, nor the simpler magical ritual suggested by *The Sword of Moses*, but merely recite one of the Benedictions of the standard daily prayer along with its secret name and the sun will reveal its secrets to you.[85] Thus, it is quite possible that this and many other practices associated with the use of powerful names were developed by "masters of the name," who were rather suspicious, or who thought that their clients or followers might be rather suspicious, of the fanciful rituals found in the Jewish magical texts. We shall return to this possibility later in the chapter, when we see yet another example of this process.

A second implication of the magical uses of the prayers is just as intriguing. Assuming that not all copyists and readers of the Genizah fragments in which these prayers are found were pious and humble elders, who were worthy of using the secret names, we may note here one recurrent feature of the Kabbalah of the names, namely, the "trickle down" effect apparent in its transmission and application. In theory, God's secret names were inserted into the prayers only by those worthy of doing so, and as long as such names were transmitted *be-kabbalah*, by word of mouth, such elitist monopolization could still be secured.[86] But once the texts were written down, they started circulating far and wide, and they were available for all to use. This is a recurrent phenomenon in the history of the Kabbalah and its relations with the Jewish magical tradition, namely, the development by the "masters of the name" of new names and their uses, which were in some cases aimed as alternatives to the magicians' elaborate rituals, but once these names and uses were written down, they ended up joining all of the other magical practices found in the magicians' handbooks.

(b) As a second example of the impact of the "Kabbalah of the names" on the development of Jewish magic, we may compare two different texts – *The Sword of Moses*, which was mentioned earlier in the chapter, and the text known as *Shimmush(e) Torah (The Use(s) of the Torah)*. The former, and older, text consists of an introductory section, a "sword" (basically a long list of "magic words"), and a list of around 140 recipes that describe how to use different sections of this "sword." The recipes are quite short and usually involve the uttering or the writing down of a specific sequence of powerful "words" (as found in the "sword" itself) as well as additional ritual activities, such as reciting these "words" over oil and rubbing a demoniac with that oil, reciting them over dust and throwing that dust at the enemy, and even preparing a "voodoo doll" and shooting it with palm-thorn arrows.[87] All of these practices are extremely common in Late Antique and medieval Jewish magic, and in this respect, *The Sword of Moses* offers a typical example of the logocentric nature of much of Jewish magic, with its firm belief that words have the power to create, to destroy, and to change whatever needs changing, coupled with its assumption that rituals too are efficacious and that the manipulation of various objects and substances also has its own great powers. This combination of "words" and "deeds," transmitted in the form of practical recipes ("to achieve X, do Y and say/write Z") is highly typical of Jewish magic in Late Antiquity and the Middle Ages, and it is common to most of the texts and practices that have been mentioned thus far, with some texts laying more stress on the ritual actions and others focusing more on the words to be spoken or written down.

Seen from this perspective, the *Shimmush(e) Torah (The Use(s) of the Torah)* seems like a very unusual text.[88] It is preceded by a long and detailed introduction, which also circulated separately under the title of *Maayan ha-Hokhma*

(*The Fountain of Wisdom*).[89] *Maayan ha Hokhma* relates the story of Moses' encounters with various angels as he ascended to heaven to receive the Torah and the secrets that they passed on to him. In the version that served as the introduction to *Shimmush(e) Torah*, this knowledge includes the secret name associated with every *parasha* (lectionary portion) of the Torah, as well as its magical uses.[90] This esoteric lore is then detailed at some length in the *Shimmush(e) Torah* itself, which is arranged according to the Torah portions, from the beginning of Genesis to the end of Deuteronomy. For each portion, and sometimes even for individual verses, it lists the secret name associated with it, often adding an explanation of how this name is derived from that specific portion or verse through elaborate letter permutations. For many of the Torah portions, it also describes for which (magical) uses the portion and its secret name can be employed – for charm and grace, to avoid evil dreams, for a newlywed couple, against robbers, to have a beautiful voice, and so on. The date and provenance of this text are far from clear – Gershom Scholem thought that it belonged in Late Antiquity or the early Middle Ages and was of Oriental Jewish origins, and this assumption has been shared by most subsequent scholars.[91] However, this assumption has recently been challenged in favor of a twelfth- or thirteenth-century European provenance.[92] But be that as it may, what we have here is a book of magic that is entirely different from the likes of *The Sword of Moses* or most other Jewish and non-Jewish magical texts of Late Antiquity and the Middle Ages. Here, the structure of the book is determined by the order of the biblical portions, and the main focus is on the names to be derived from them; the magical uses are presented as a sort of a by-product to the text's main interest. Moreover, although the aims of the magical uses are quite similar to those found in *The Sword of Moses* and other Jewish magical texts, the praxis certainly is not. In fact, the use of the names and the verses surveyed by *Shimmush Torah* requires very little ritual – in almost all cases, it is the mere *uttering* of the name or the verse that is supposed to be effective for a given purpose. Much less frequent is the injunction to *write* the names or the verses, and more complex rituals of the kind that is so common in other Jewish magical texts are almost entirely absent.[93] In short, the producers and users of such a text may rightly be called "masters of the name," because it is their knowledge of the secret names associated with each Torah portion that gives them their special powers. Of course, once the book was written down, it could be used by other Jewish magicians, as well, and the names found therein could travel to other magical recipe books and join the main stream of the Jewish magical tradition.[94] But in its "pure" form, this text represents a separate, and much more Kabbalistic, tributary that flowed into the wider stream of the Jewish magical tradition, joining the Late Antique, the Muslim, and the Christian tributaries that we surveyed in the preceding sections. In passing, we may note that in the Renaissance, this text was translated into Latin and joined the rich world of the so-called "Christian Kabbalah," which lies outside the scope of the present chapter.[95]

Summary

As noted throughout the chapter, medieval Jewish magic was widely and openly studied and practiced by many learned Jews.[96] To be sure, some philosophically minded Jews objected to almost all magical practices, and many rabbis objected to specific magical practices, especially those that smacked of idolatry. But although such objections helped filter some magical practices out of the Jewish magical tradition and prevented the entry of others (especially in Christian Europe), they neither eradicated the Jewish magical tradition nor drove it underground. Widely practiced, transmitted in thousands of manuscripts, and constantly absorbing and developing new techniques and practices, the Jewish magical tradition grew in Late Antiquity and thrived in the Middle Ages. But in spite of many important contributions to the study of medieval Jewish magic, its full story has yet to be told; the survey in this chapter is but a preliminary sketch of some of its salient features and a modest attempt to encourage further research in this richly documented but poorly studied field.

Notes

*   I am grateful to Ortal-Paz Saar, Katelyn Mesler and Yuval Harari for their helpful comments on an earlier draft of this chapter and to Yasmin Bohak for her help in preparing the figures.
1. See also Trachtenberg, *Jewish Magic and Superstition*, 12–19.
2. For some of the earliest examples of this phenomenon, see Saar, "Success, Protection and Grace," 101–135.
3. See Veltri, "'Watermarks' in the MS Munich, Hebr. 95," 255–268; Shoham-Steiner, "'This Should Not Be Shown to a Gentile,'" 53–59.
4. This evidence has never been collected in a systematic manner, but useful starting points may be found in Zimmels, *Magicians, Theologians and Doctors*; Kanarfogel, *"Peering through the Lattices."* And cf. Chajes, "Rabbis and Their (In)Famous Magic," 58–79, 349–358, which makes extensive use of such evidence for the reconstruction of Jewish magic in the sixteenth to eighteenth centuries.

5. See especially Trachtenberg, *Jewish Magic and Superstition*

6. For a broader outline of the desiderata in the study of Jewish magic, see Bohak, "Prolegomena to the Study of the Jewish Magical Tradition," 107–150.

7. For a detailed substantiation of this claim, see Bohak, *Ancient Jewish Magic*, 11–35.

8. For detailed discussions of the rabbinic discourse on magic, see Harari, "The Sages and the Occult," 521–564; and Bohak, *Ancient Jewish Magic*, 357–386.

9. For these polemics, see Mann, *Texts and Studies in Jewish History and Literature*, vol. 2, 55–57, 75–83; Harari, "Leadership, Authority, and the 'Other,'" 79–101.

10. For this responsum, see Emanuel, *Newly Discovered Geonic Responsa*, 124–146 (Heb.). For the manuscript evidence, see ibid., 121–123. The first set of letters has not been preserved, but its contents may roughly be reconstructed from the Kairouan rabbis' second question (ibid., 124–127) and from Hai Gaon's second response (ibid., 127–146). For earlier analyses of this responsum and of related responsa attributed to Hai Gaon, see Joël, *Der Aberglaube und die Stellung des Judenthums*, vol. 2, 30–56; Hildesheimer, "Mystik und Agada im Urteile," 259–286; Dan, *History of Jewish Mysticism and Esotericism*, vol. 4, 143–195 (Heb.); Harari, "Leadership, Authority, and the 'Other,'" 87–90. However, a fuller analysis of this important text and an adequate English translation remain scholarly desiderata.

11. Note, for example, the detailed descriptions (Emanuel, *Newly Discovered Geonic Responsa*, 126, 137–138) of the practice of "dream request" (for summoning a revelatory dream) and the evidence for that practice assembled by Bellusci, "Dream Requests from the Cairo Genizah."

12. Emanuel, *Newly Discovered Geonic Responsa*, 131–132. For *Sepher ha-Yashar*, see Wandrey, "Das Buch des Gewandes," 183–314; for *The Sword of Moses*, see Gaster, *The Sword of Moses*, vol. 1, 288–337, vol. 3, 69–103; Harari, *Harba de-Moshe (The Sword of Moses)* (Heb.); Harari, "The Sword of Moses (*Harba de-Moshe*)," 58–98. The *Raza Rabba*, a Babylonian Jewish work of magic, has yet to be identified in our "insider" sources.

13. Emanuel, *Newly Discovered Geonic Responsa*, 125, 131.

14. For "masters of the name," see Emanuel, *Newly Discovered Geonic Responsa*, 124; for the claims about Sura, see ibid., 130: "And in the *yeshivah* at Sura these things were widespread, since they are close to the city of Babylon and to the house of Nebuchadnezzar, but we are far away from there." For this assertion, see also Assaf, *The Gaonic Period and Its Literature*, 261–264 (Heb.). For the power of God's name, see Emanuel, *Newly Discovered Geonic Responsa*, 133–134.

15. Emanuel, *Newly Discovered Geonic Responsa*, esp. 140–141.

16. Ibid., 145.

17. See ibid., 138, where Hai comments on a magical praxis mentioned in the Talmud, noting that "magic (*keshaphim*) is only permitted to be taught to

members of the Sanhedrin (the supreme court) who pass judgments on matters of life and death, but we did not study *keshaphim*, and this thing is a matter of *keshaphim*," whence his ignorance of the exact nature of this specific
praxis.

18. Ibid., 131.

19. For the magical texts from the Cairo Genizah, see Schäfer, "Jewish Magic
Literature in Late Antiquity," 75–91; and Bohak, "Towards a Catalogue of the
Magical, Astrological, Divinatory and Alchemical Fragments," 53–79, with an
extensive bibliography.

20. For the *Scroll of Ahimaaz*, see Klar, ed., *Megillat Ahimaaz* (Heb.); for a new critical
edition, with an English translation and a full commentary, see Bonfil, *History
and Folklore*. For its stories of magic and miracles, see Benin, "The Chronicle
of Ahimaaz," 237–250 (Heb.); Harari, "The *Scroll of Ahimaaz*," 185–202 (Heb.);
Dan, *History of Jewish Mysticism and Esotericism*, vol. 4, 222–242 (Heb.).

21. See Bonfil, *History and Folklore*, 234–237.

22. For the Hebrew text, see Bonfil, *History and Folklore*, 255; the English translation is my own.

23. For the Genizah fragments, see Schäfer and Shaked, *Magische Texte*, vol. 1,
no. 1 (=JTSL ENA 3635.17), and no. 2 (=T-S K 1.56), and Veltri, "'Inyan Sota,"
23–48. For their connection with the story in the *Scroll of Ahimaaz*, see Harari,
"The *Scroll of Ahimaaz*," (Heb.). Note that the *Scroll* itself relates that Abu
Aharon boarded a boat to Egypt on his way back to his native Babylonia
(Bonfil, *History and Folklore*, 279).

24. See Weinstock, "Discovered Legacy of Mystic Writings," 153–159 (Heb.);
Scholem, "Has A Legacy Been Discovered," 252–265 (Heb.).

25. This issue was further compounded by the fact that many medieval magical texts were pseudepigraphically attributed to biblical or rabbinic figures
(for example, to King Solomon), and as these attributions often were taken
by medieval rabbis at face value (cf. Maimonides, *Commentary on the Mishna*,
Pessahim 4.10), claiming that such books were "un-Jewish" became even more
difficult.

26. For Maimonides' Sabeans, see esp. Hjärpe, *Analyse critique des traditions arabes*;
and Stroumsa, "Sabéens de Harrân et Sabéens de Maïmonide," 335–352. In the
same volume, see also Paul B. Fenton, "Maïmonide et l'*Agriculture nabatéenne*," 303–333.

27. See esp. *Guide* 1.61–1.62, 3.37; *Mishne Torah*, Avodat Kokhavim 11.4–11.18. For
detailed analyses of Maimonides' anti-magic crusade, see Lewis, "Maimonides
on Superstition," 475–488; Schwartz, *Studies on Astral Magic*, esp. 27–54;
Halbertal, *Maimonides*, 189–194 (Heb.); Ravitzky, "'The Ravings of Amulet
Writers,'" 93–130. See also Schwartz, "Magic, Philosophy and Kabbalah,"
99–132 (Heb.), which notes that even some medieval followers of Maimonides
found in his writings a bit of leeway for the practice of magic.

28. See Harris, "The Image of Maimonides," 117–139; for the overevaluation of Maimonides in the academic study of "Jewish philosophy," see Sirat, "Should We Stop Teaching Maimonides?" 136–144. The number of scholarly monographs devoted to Maimonides that were published since Sirat's paper was written proves that her call has yet to be heeded.

29. For a refreshing exception to this scholarly silence, see Kellner, *Maimonides' Confrontation with Mysticism*, esp. 17–18, 286–296.

30. See Maimonides, *Mishne Torah*, Hilkhot Mezuzah 5.4, and Aptowitzer, "Les noms de Dieu et des anges dans la mezouza"; Trachtenberg, *Jewish Magic and Superstition*, 145–152; Bohak, "Mezuzoth with Magical Additions from the Cairo Genizah," 387–403 (Heb.).

31. This responsum (no. 413 in his collected responsa) forms part of a dossier, *Minhat Qena'ot (An Offering of Zeal)*, compiled by Abba Mari of Lunel, a major player in the whole affair. In what follows, I have used the edition by Dimitrovsky, *Teshuvot ha-Rashba*, 281–308 (Heb.). For Adret's view of magic, see also Klein-Braslavy, "The Concept of Magic," 105–129; Davidson, "Perceptions of Medicine and Magic," 104–141 (Heb.). For the whole controversy, see Schwartz, *Studies on Astral Magic*, 123–165.

32. The first response is mentioned both by the Rashba himself (Schwartz, *Studies on Astral Magic*, 281–283) and by Abba Mari (ibid., 273–274), whose objection to Rashba's permissiveness generated the more detailed response. That Abba Mari was not the only French rabbi to object to the Spanish rabbi's leniency is made clear by the Rashba himself (ibid., 283).

33. *Mishna*, Shabbat 6.6, and Babylonian Talmud, Shabbat 65a. For the wider context of these practices, see Bohak, *Ancient Jewish Magic*, 383.

34. For the "Book of Figures" in which these instructions were found, see Shatzmiller, "In Search of the 'Book of Figures,'" 383–407; Shatzmiller, "The Forms of the Twelve Constellations," 397–408 (Heb.); Leicht, *Astrologumena Judaica*, 310–316. See also Leicht, "Le chapitre II,12," 295–330.

35. For these two limitations, see Leicht, "Le chapitre II,12," 283, 303.

36. For Abba Mari's objections, see ibid., esp. 319–325. For the Rashba's response, see ibid., esp. 342, 347–348.

37. And cf. Trachtenberg, *Jewish Magic and Superstition*, 20: "In short, the Talmudic classification plagued the efforts of medieval codifiers to bring the law into relation with contemporary procedures. Yet, from a practical standpoint, they succeeded in effectively excluding from the proscribed 'magic' all the forms current among Jews."

38. For a lucid survey of these events, see Stern, "Philosophy in Southern France," 281–303.

39. A full-fledged history of the Jewish magical tradition has never been attempted, but see the preliminary sketches by Vajda, "La magie en Israël," 127–153; Idel, "On Judaism, Jewish Mysticism and Magic," 195–214; the illustrated catalogue

in Vukosavović, ed., *Angels and Demons*; and especially the recent survey by Yuval Harari, "Jewish Magic: An Annotated Overview," 13–85 (Heb.).

40. For detailed surveys of this evidence, see Alexander, "Incantations and Books of Magic," 342–379; Swartz, "Jewish Magic in Late Antiquity," 699–720; Bohak, *Ancient Jewish Magic*, 143–226; Harari, *Early Jewish Magic*, 159–228 (Heb.).

41. For a fuller discussion of this point, see Bohak, "The Jewish Magical Tradition," 324–339; for a more specific example, see Bohak, "From Qumran to Cairo," 31–52. Many other examples may be found in Leicht, "Some Observations on the Diffusion of Jewish Magical Texts," 213–231; and in Saar, "Jewish Love Magic" (Heb.).

42. For a useful introduction to the Sasanian Jewish incantation bowls, with much further bibliography, see Levene, *Curse or Blessing, What's in the Magical Bowl?*.

43. There are, however, some important exceptions, such as the *Pishra de-Rabbi Hanina ben Dosa* (ed. Michelini Tocci, "Note e documenti di letterature religiosa," 101–108); the *Havdala de-Rabbi Akiba* (ed. Scholem, "Havdala de-Rabbi Aqiva," 243–281 (Heb.); and the *get* formula analyzed by Levene and Bohak, "Divorcing Lilith," 197–217.

44. For a fuller discussion, see Bohak, *Ancient Jewish Magic*, 247–278.

45. For the medieval Christian discourse of the *charaktêres*, see Véronèse and Grévin, "Les 'caractères' magiques au Moyen Âge," 305–379; for Augustine's condemnations of the *charaktêres*, see ibid., 309–317.

46. And see, for example, Weinstock, "The Alphabet of Metatron and Its Interpretation," 51–76 (Heb.); Idel, "The Anonymous *Commentary on the Alphabet of Metatron*," 255–264 (Heb.); Bohak, "The *Charaktêres* in Ancient and Medieval Jewish Magic," 25–44.

47. For *Sepher ha-Razim*, probably the most influential book of ancient Jewish magic, see Margalioth, *Sepher ha-Razim* (Heb.); Morgan, *Sepher ha-Razim*; Rebiger and Schäfer, *Sefer ha-Razim I und II*.

48. For this specific example, see Bohak, *Ancient Jewish Magic*, 156–158.

49. For the aims and techniques of ancient Jewish magic, see Harari, "Early Jewish Magic," 136–226 (Heb.).

50. See, for example, Drory, *The Emergence of Jewish-Arabic Literary Contacts* (Heb.); Wasserstrom, *Between Muslim and Jew*.

51. For a case in point, see Friedländer, "A Muhammedan Book on Augury," 84–103; many other examples remain unpublished.

52. See Shaked, "Between Judaism and Islam," 4–19 (Heb.); Shaked, "Medieval Jewish Magic in Relation to Islam," 97–109; Zoran, "Magic, Theurgy and the Knowledge of Letters," 19–62 (Heb.). The following passages are partly based on my forthcoming chapter on medieval Oriental Jewish magic in Rustow and Chazan, eds., *The Cambridge History of Judaism*, vol. 5, *Jews and Judaism in the Islamic World*.

53. And see Eshel, "Demonology in Palestine" (Heb.).

54. Such practices are already attested in the Greek magical papyri (e.g., PGM I.1–I.195); see also Ciraolo, "Supernatural Assistants in the Greek Magical Papyri," 279–295. Although such techniques may have been known to Jews in Late Antiquity, they seem to have entered the Jewish magical tradition only in their Arabic versions, which are far more elaborate than the earlier Greek ones were.

55. For some pertinent examples, see Scholem, "Bilar the King of Devils," 112–127 (Heb.); and Scholem, "Some Sources of Jewish-Arabic Demonology," 1–13; Golb, "Aspects of the Historical Background of Jewish Life," 12–18; Patai, "The Love Factor in a Hebrew-Arabic Conjuration," 239–253; Schäfer and Shaked, *Magische Texte*, vol. 1, no. 5 (=JTSL ENA 2643.6–2643.7), 6a/5, vol. 1, no. 6 (=T-S K 1.1), vol. 3, no. 62 (=T-S K 1.3), 1a/1–1b/8, vol. 3, no. 66 (=T-S AS 142.15 + T-S NS 246.14), 1b.

56. For pertinent examples, see the *qevitzah*-type ritual performed by two Jews described in a mystery play of 1541 in Schwab, "Mots hébreux dans les Mystères du Moyen Âge," 148; and Trachtenberg, *The Devil and the Jews*, 61, which also refers to Benvenuto Cellini's celebrated account of a demon-summoning ritual performed by a Sicilian priest in the Colosseum in 1533 or 1534: "Now the necromancer began to utter those awful invocations, calling by name on multitudes of demons who are captains of their legions, and these he summoned by the virtue and potency of God, the Uncreated, Living, and Eternal, in phrases of the Hebrew, and also of the Greek and Latin tongues." (Symonds, trans., *The Autobiography of Benvenuto Cellini*, 118).

57. For astral magic in the Middle Ages, see Weill-Parot, *Les "images astrologiques" au Moyen Âge*; for the Judaeo-Arabic texts, see Burnett and Bohak, "A Judaeo-Arabic Version of Thābit ibn Qurra's *De imaginibus*," 179–200; for the Hebrew texts, see the detailed survey by Leicht, *Astrologumena Judaica*, 295–359.

58. See esp. Schwartz, *Astral Magic in Medieval Jewish Thought* (Heb.); Schwartz, *Amulets, Properties and Rationalism* (Heb.); and Schwartz, *Studies on Astral Magic*.

59. And see Scholem, "The Star of David: History of a Symbol," in *Haaretz Almanac 1948–1949*, 148–163 (Heb.); for an English version, see Scholem, "The Star of David: History of a Symbol," in Scholem, *The Messianic Idea in Judaism*, 257–281; Idel, "R. Nehemia ben Shlomo the Prophet," vol. 1, 1–76 (Heb.). A fuller survey of all the Genizah evidence on the six-pointed star will add much to their discussion.

60. For geomancy, see Villuendas Sabaté, "La geomancia judía." For treasure hunting, see Golb, "The Esoteric Practices of the Jews of Fatimid Egypt," 533–535. For dream interpretation, see Lamoreaux, *The Early Muslim Tradition*

of Dream Interpretation, 166, who rightly notes that this topic demands much further research.

61. This issue has been discussed by numerous scholars; see also Freudenthal, "Arabic and Latin Cultures as Resources," 74–105, with further bibliography.

62. For Sator Arepo, see Trachtenberg, *Jewish Magic and Superstition,* 201–202, and Barkai, *A History of Jewish Gynaecological Texts,* 183; for Abracadabra, see Bohak, *Ancient Jewish Magic,* 266.

63. For the three Magi, see Mesler, "The Three Magi,"161–218; for *nigromancia,* see Leicht, "Nahmanides on Necromancy," 251–264.

64. For the demons, see Trachtenberg, *Jewish Magic and Superstition,* 37–43. For magic signs, see Bohak, "The *Charaktêres,*" and for the *Ars notoria,* see Leicht, *Astrologumena Judaica,* 369–370.

65. For two specific examples, see Leicht, "The Legend of St. Eustachius (Eustathius)," 325–330; Saar, "A Genizah Magical Fragment and Its European Parallels."

66. See Güdemann, *Geschichte des Erziehungswesens,* vol. 1, 218, vol. 2, 333–337; Trachtenberg, *Jewish Magic and Superstition,* 102–103; Loewe, "A Mediaeval Latin-German Magical Text," 345–368; and Bohak, "Catching a Thief," 344–362; in the future, I hope to edit more such texts.

67. See, for example, García-Ballester, Ferre, and Feliu, "Jewish Appreciation of Fourteenth-Century Scholastic Medicine," 85–117; Barkai, *A History of Jewish Gynaecological Texts;* Mesler, "The Three Magi"; Caballero-Navas, *The Book of Women's Love;* Bos and Zwink, *Berakhyah Ben Natronai ha-Nakdan, Sefer Ko'ah ha-Avanim (On the Virtue of the Stones);* Ferre, "The Incorporation of Foreign Medical Literature into the Medieval Jewish Corpus," 171–183; Mesler, "The Medieval Lapidary of Techel/Azareus."

68. The Latin text was edited by Schibby Johnsson, "Les 'Experimenta duodecim Johannes Paulini,'" 257–267, who also mentions two of the Hebrew manuscripts in which it appears. For its place in the history of Western "experimental" literature, see Thorndike, *A History of Magic and Experimental Science,* vol. 2, 794–796.

69. See Zonta, "Medieval Hebrew Translations of Philosophical and Scientific Texts," 17–73, 58, no. 424. For a fuller survey of the manuscript evidence, see Bohak, "Rabbanite Magical Texts in Karaite Manuscripts," 26–27.

70. For such self-censorship, see Bohak, "Catching a Thief," 358.

71. For the time being, see Baron, *A Social and Religious History of the Jews,* vol. 8, 3–54, 273–295; Scholem, *Kabbalah,* 182–189; Idel, "Between the Magic of the Holy Names and the Kabbalah," 79–96 (Heb.); Garb, "Mysticism and Magic," 97–109 (Heb.).

72. See Idel, *Nocturnal Kabbalists* (Heb.), and Goldreich, *Automatic Writing in Zoharic Literature and Modernism* (Heb.), respectively.

73. For the Kabbalists' own distinction between these two types of Kabbalah, see Idel, "Defining Kabbalah," 97–122.

74. For the importance of the distinction in medieval Jewish magic between "name magic" and "ritual magic," see also Harari, "Jewish Magic: An Annotated Overview," 44–49, with further references to Moshe Idel's emphasis of this distinction. And cf. Trachtenberg, *Jewish Magic and Superstition*, 86–89.

75. See, for example, Harari, "Moses, the Sword, and *The Sword of Moses*," 293–329, with further bibliography.

76. For examples from Greco-Roman and Greco-Egyptian magic, see Versnel, "The Poetics of the Magical Charm," 105–158; for a wider anthropological perspective, see Tambiah, "The Magical Power of Words," 175–208.

77. See Hai's responsum (in Emanuel, *Newly Discovered Geonic Responsa*), 135, where he also explains how this oral transmission was carried out. The importance of the word *kabbalah* in this context was highlighted by Idel, "Defining Kabbalah," 100–101.

78. Let me add, in passing, that the question of whether the traditions studied later in this chapter should be labeled "Kabbalistic" (contrary to Scholem's famous decision to identify the beginnings of Kabbalah proper with *Sepher ha-Bahir*) or "proto-Kabbalistic" (as was done, for example, by Kellner, *Maimonides' Confrontation with Mysticism*, 18–25), seems to me more semantic than substantial, and it need not detain us here.

79. Another important example is provided by Moshe Idel's attempts to identify within a vast body of anonymous short Kabbalistic treatises and magical texts the "fingerprints" of Nehemiah ben Shlomo, the thirteenth-century mystic-prophet-magician of Erfurt. For the most pertinent of these studies, see Idel, "Between Ashkenaz and Castille in the Thirteenth Century," 475–554 (Heb.), with further bibliography.

80. See Hai's responsum (in Emanuel, *Newly Discovered Geonic Responsa*), 126.

81. Ibid., 137.

82. For what follows, see also Schäfer, "Jewish Liturgy and Magic," vol. 1, 541–556.

83. Schäfer and Shaked, *Magische Texte*, vol. 2, no. 26 (=T.-S. K 1.35 + T.-S. K 1.48), 1a/11–2a/26.

84. See also the pertinent examples in Schäfer and Shaked, *Magische Texte*, vol. 2, nos. 22–30, with references to the appearance of some of these texts not only in the Cairo Genizah but also in European Jewish manuscripts.

85. For *Sepher ha-Razim*'s famous adjuration of the sun, see Morgan, *Sepher ha-Razim*, 69–72; for *The Sword of Moses*, see Harari, "The Sword of Moses," 86–87; see also *Sepher Raziel* (Amsterdam: Moses b. Abraham Mendes Coutinho, 1701), fol. 6b.

86. Hai's own responsum is a case in point – when discussing God's esoteric names (in Emanuel, *Newly Discovered Geonic Responsa*, 134–135), he provides some data

about their actual contents, but he never divulges the entire name, even when it is clear that he himself knows it!

87. See Harari, "The Sword of Moses," 83, 86, 89, respectively.

88. My citations from this text are based on the popular edition, *Sepher Shimmush Torah* (Jerusalem: n.p., 2001) (Heb.). A critical edition and a detailed study of the manuscript evidence for this work, which clearly was very popular throughout the Middle Ages, remain scholarly desiderata.

89. Ed. Jellinek, *Bet ha-Midrasch*, vol. 1, 58–61.

90. See *Shimmush Torah*, 5 = *Maayan ha-Hokhma*, 61: "And all the angels of service became his [Moses'] friends, and each one of them transmitted to him a word of healing and the secret of the names that are derived from each Torah-portion in all their uses."

91. For Scholem's view, see, for example, *Kabbalah*, 20, 170: "The magical uses of the Torah are discussed in the book *Shimmushei Torah*, which dates at the very latest from the geonic period."

92. See Rebiger, "Bildung magischer Namen im *Sefer Shimmush Tehillim*," 7–24; and especially Rebiger, *Sefer Shimmush Tehillim*, 29, 39–40.

93. Out of sixty-nine magical uses listed in the printed text, only fourteen require writing (found on pp. 17, 20, 26, 28, 29, 30, 31, 33, 34 [two cases], 36 [two cases], 37, and 38). In this respect, even the book *Shimmush Tehillim* (*The Use of the Psalms*), recently edited by Bill Rebiger, displays a far greater emphasis on ritual actions than the *Shimmush(e) Torah*.

94. And I note, for example, that in the fifteenth-century manuscript of Jewish magic, New York Public Library Heb. 190, of which I am now preparing a critical edition, one may find several examples of recipes known from the *Shimmush(e) Torah* – e.g., 103, ll. 6–8, and 240, l. 1.

95. For the Latin version, made by Flavius Mithridates, see Buzzetta, "Aspetti della magia naturalis e della scientia cabalae," 680–681.

96. This holds true for later periods, as well; see, for example, Idel, "Jewish Magic from the Renaissance Period to Early Hasidism," 82–117; Etkes, "The Role of Magic and *Ba'alei Shem* in Ashkenazic Society," 69–104 (Heb.); and Chajes, "Rabbis and Their (In)Famous Magic."

PART IV

★

OLD EUROPE

Chapter 10

Common Magic

CATHERINE RIDER

As in many other places and periods, many magical practices between the eleventh and the eighteenth centuries were rooted in everyday life. They responded to widespread and fundamental concerns, such as curing illness, seeking prosperity or love and explaining and averting misfortune. In an influential book on medieval magic first published in 1989, Richard Kieckhefer called these practices the "common tradition" of magic because, he argued, they were widely used and not limited to any specific group of people.[1] Since then, the "common tradition" has received less attention from scholars than the better-documented, learned forms of magic, but historians of premodern Europe have nevertheless identified a huge variety of common magical practices.[2] Within this broad category, there is much diversity. Some forms of "common magic" were probably a well-known part of everyday life, but others were less mundane. Some might require a trip to a specialist (often known in English as a cunning man or woman) whose services did not necessarily come cheap. Others tapped into powerful emotions in a way that would not have felt routine to the people involved. For example, accusations that someone had used magic to cause illness or death were often rooted in neighbourhood quarrels and interpersonal tensions which could be deeply distressing to both "victim" and alleged perpetrator and which could sometimes lead to witch trials and executions. Love magic could have equally dramatic consequences, including inappropriate relationships and marital breakdowns. Nevertheless, even these disruptive kinds of magic can be seen as "common" in the sense that they are likely to have been widely known, even if they were not commonly used. They are also common in the sense that they (or a specialist who offered them) are likely to have been accessible to a wide range of people.

The wide accessibility of common magic distinguishes it from the other forms of magic which are discussed in Part IV of this book. Unlike learned magic, common magic did not require a high level of education, and it was therefore not confined to a small, mostly male group of educated practitioners. Unlike diabolic magic, common magic usually did not invoke demons openly, although its opponents often argued that it relied on demonic forces. And in contrast to the forms of "magic" associated with priests, common magic did not necessarily make use of religious rituals or language, although sometimes it did. Common magic was never entirely distinct from these more specialized practices, and the relationship between them changed over time as ideas and practices spread. In the sixteenth and seventeenth centuries, for example, the translation into English of Latin magical texts which described (among other things) how to communicate with angels led to a "democratization" of learned angel magic as some literate cunning folk began to conjure angels to help them find stolen goods or identify thieves.[3] Despite these overlaps, however, common magic remains distinct from learned, diabolic and priestly magic. It is set apart by its wide range of practitioners: priests and laity, educated and uneducated, men and women, specialists and occasional users.

When writing the history of common magic, scholars face several problems. One is the diversity of practices that can be defined as "common". We can view the commonness of common magic in several different ways: widely practised, widely known, or widely accessible through specialists who had particular skills. A second problem relates to what should be considered "magic". In the cases of healing and some methods of predicting the future, in particular, there was considerable room for debate about what constituted magic, rather than a legitimate way of manipulating the natural world or a religious exercise. In these areas, some kinds of common magic overlapped substantially with religious rituals, invoking Christ and the saints and employing phrases from the Bible or the liturgy. Other kinds overlapped with medieval and early modern science and medicine, for example, when herbs or stones were worn about the neck in order to benefit the wearer. When they thought about these practices, scientific and medical writers were often willing to recognize a category of practices that they called *empirica* or *experimenta*.[4] These were not "experiments" in the modern sense. Instead, they were phenomena which could not be explained by contemporary scientific theories and were known from experience. One example given by Marbode of Rennes, an eleventh-century bishop who wrote a treatise on the powers of precious stones, was the "fact" that if a magnet was placed on a woman's head while she slept, she would fall out of bed if she was guilty of adultery, but if she was innocent, she would turn to embrace her husband.[5] When they speculated about how *empirica* worked, scientific writers argued that they relied on "occult" or "hidden" forces in the natural world. As such, they did not rely on demons, and they were considered a branch of science rather than magic.[6]

Modern scholars have taken many approaches to defining magic and analysing its relationship to religion and science, but when discussing common magic, it is useful to start with the definition of magic that was formulated by medieval intellectuals. These writers defined magic as a means of influencing the world which did not work through physical forces (even unexplained "occult" ones) or through the power of God and so must rely on the powers of demons instead.[7] More importantly for our purposes, from the twelfth century onwards, theologians had a standard list of practices which fitted this general definition. This was set out in the *Decretum* of Gratian, a hugely influential textbook of canon law compiled in the mid-twelfth century. Gratian's *Decretum* described a series of hypothetical legal cases and then put together passages from earlier theological writings and church councils which related to each one. Case 26 focused on a priest who had been a magical practitioner: the term Gratian used was *sortilegus*. This had originally been a term for someone who foretold the future by casting lots but under this heading Gratian gave information about a much wider range of magical practices. These included various ways of predicting the future, for example, casting lots, astrology and interpreting omens; the use of spoken charms and amulets for healing; unspecified "magical" practices performed on January 1st, presumably to guarantee good fortune in the coming year; and attempts to harm others by ritual means. Gratian also discussed a few unorthodox beliefs in addition to these practices, such as the belief that certain women could leave their bodies and fly around at night with the goddess Diana – a myth which in the fifteenth century became part of the stereotype of the flying, devil-worshipping witch.[8]

Gratian's chapter was important for shaping later definitions of common magic because many later churchmen used it as the basis for their own writings. There was still room for debate about what counted as magic – theologians debated whether all forms of astrology should be seen as magical and where the exact boundaries lay between an illicit magical charm and a prayer, for example. Many uneducated people may also have questioned whether everything in Gratian's chapter was really magic. But Gratian's list is a useful place to start because it tells us the kinds of practices contemporaries considered when they thought about common magic, and they show us how decisions were made about whether something was, or was not, magic.

Sources for Common Magic

Before looking at what common magic was and who did it, we need to address two important questions: How do we know about it, and how much can we know about it? In contrast to the authors of learned magical texts, most people who performed common magic did not write down what they were doing or what they hoped to achieve. Instead, our records of these practices come from the educated. It is likely that to some extent educated people shared many of the beliefs of their uneducated contemporaries: they talked to family and friends, and they observed what people did in the world around them. Nevertheless, they may also have misunderstood or misrepresented widespread beliefs. This is a problem faced by any scholar who wishes to write about popular culture in premodern society, and since the 1970s, it has attracted much attention from historians. There has been much debate about the extent to which it is possible to reconstruct popular culture from sources produced by the elites and also about how useful it is to imagine a "popular culture" or "popular religion" that was distinct from elite culture or religion at all.[9] As we will see, studies of common magic have played an important part in these debates.

Much of our information about common magic comes from the writings of clergy, especially for the Middle Ages. Magic appears in the statutes of church councils, penitentials (guides to giving penance which list various sins), sermons, *exempla* (short stories for use in preaching) and devotional treatises which discussed religious topics for the benefit of the clergy and devout, literate laypeople. These sources were written to encourage correct belief and behaviour, and not surprisingly they are hostile to magic, but they give valuable details about what they claim are popular magical practices. For example, *Fasciculus Morum*, a manual for preachers written in early fourteenth-century England, describes "witches" called *tilsters* who offered magical healing. The book's anonymous author complained that "when somebody's stomach is heavy and sick because he has eaten and drunk too much, they say 'his mother has fallen', and then it is necessary to call in some wretched old woman who knows this craft to rub his stomach and sides".[10] Works like this were written throughout the period, but they are most numerous and detailed in periods when ecclesiastical concerns about "superstition" were particularly intense. This happened in the fifteenth century as part of a wider movement concerned with pastoral care and church reform and again after the Reformation, when Protestants labelled many Catholic practices as magic and Catholics in turn became more critical of some traditional rituals.[11] In the early modern period, some educated laypeople as well as clergy also wrote to criticize popular magic. A famous example is the late sixteenth-century English gentleman Reginald Scot, who denounced contemporary witchcraft beliefs in his *Discoverie of Witchcraft*. In the process, he described these beliefs in great detail – so much so that later readers often used his book as a guide for doing the very kinds of magic Scot himself condemned.[12]

These sources were written to persuade: to show why magic was wrong and to tell people not to do it. Other sources were produced as part of more active attempts at repression by both the church and the secular authorities. Some of the most detailed descriptions of common magic come from court records, which record occasions when people were prosecuted for doing magic. In the Middle Ages, prosecution was not especially common, but scattered examples do survive. An inquisition into heresy in early fourteenth-century Montaillou, in the Pyrenees, uncovered a few individuals who had consulted soothsayers, and the secular courts of Florence prosecuted a handful of cases of magic between 1375 and 1430, resulting in three executions.[13] From the fifteenth century onwards, judicial records survive in greater numbers. Many of these are from witch trials, which began in the fifteenth century in parts of modern Switzerland, Alpine France and northern Italy and spread slowly across Europe, peaking in many places in the late sixteenth and early seventeenth centuries.[14] At the same time, in Catholic parts of Europe and America, the inquisition also prosecuted magic.[15] These trial records give details about the kinds of magic which people did, or were believed to do. They also describe widespread beliefs and practices, including methods for healing, identifying witches and turning spells back on the people who cast them.

The information about common magic in all of these sources needs to be read sensitively. It was recorded by hostile observers, and it was also highly selective. What the authors of these texts chose to focus on was not necessarily the same as what the people who used common magic found important. Thus, a text written to denounce magic will focus on the practices its author found most troubling, not necessarily on those which were most common, whereas trial records will tell us about the forms of magic that were most likely to be prosecuted but perhaps ignore others.

A further problem is that the authors of these texts often approached common magic with their own preconceptions about what it was. Their descriptions of it were shaped by a long tradition of writing against magic. Thus, the anonymous author of *Fasciculus Morum* quoted extensively from Gratian's twelfth-century canon law textbook in addition to adding the details about *tilsters*, and many other writers also copied much material from earlier sources. Because of this, it can be difficult to know how well *Fasciculus Morum's* description of common magic reflects the situation in early fourteenth-century England and how much was pieced together from Gratian and did not bear much relation to contemporary practice. Trial records present similar problems because the questions that were asked in witch trials and before the inquisition were often determined by what judges or inquisitors expected to find – which may in turn have been shaped by written sources like Gratian. Leading questions, imprisonment and, in some cases, torture could cause defendants to confess to things which may not have been common practices or beliefs and which only reflected the concerns of the educated elite. Over the past few decades, many historians have sought to separate elite beliefs from popular beliefs in witch trial records, but there is still disagreement about the extent to which this is possible and about which elements should be seen as "elite" and which as "popular".[16]

Occasionally, we can see how the records produced by educated observers altered popular beliefs about magic as judges and inquisitors struggled to interpret their witnesses' testimonies. Some of the best known examples are the *benandanti* cases discovered by Carlo Ginzburg.[17] The *benandanti* were healers from the Friuli, in what is now north-east Italy. Their powers were linked to a complex mythology, according to which they believed that (among other things) they went into a trance and travelled out of their bodies on certain nights of the year to fight witches. Ginzburg shows how during the late sixteenth and early seventeenth centuries, the *benandanti* came to the attention of the Venetian inquisition. The inquisitors were initially baffled by what they heard, but eventually they concluded that the *benandanti* must be witches themselves and they succeeded in convincing some *benandanti* of this. Here, very detailed records show how over time, one group of educated inquisitors radically reshaped the beliefs they encountered, and the same thing may have happened less obviously in other times and places. However, despite these problems, Ginzburg and many other historians have shown that sources which were written as part of a process of repression can still tell us much about common magic. Witnesses and defendants described the practices and beliefs they claimed existed in the world around them, and educated writers also gave details even as they complained about popular beliefs.

There are also sources for common magic written from a less hostile perspective: they recorded magical practices because they were useful or interesting. Despite condemnation by the church, texts which described how to do various forms of divination were written down from the twelfth century onwards.[18] Healing practices which could be seen as magical were also written down in a range of places, from academic medical texts to the blank pages of prayer books.[19] As we will see later in the chapter, many of these practices may not have been viewed as magic by the people who copied them, but some do correspond to practices denounced by contemporary theologians. Other sources described what they claimed were widespread magical beliefs without explicitly condemning them. The expansion of literacy in the sixteenth and seventeenth centuries led to the publication of pamphlets aimed at a popular audience which described extraordinary phenomena, including cases of witchcraft.[20] More recently, in the nineteenth and early twentieth centuries, folklorists recorded popular beliefs, including "superstitions" and magical practices, in order to preserve them before they died out. It is difficult to tell how old this folklore is, but some of the practices and beliefs they describe are attested in earlier texts, and therefore it can be useful to compare them with the early modern and medieval sources.[21]

These sources pose their own challenges. They were written by people with some education, so it is difficult to know exactly how well they reflect the beliefs of the illiterate. It is also difficult to know how well they reflect widespread beliefs and practices: many seventeenth-century observers criticized pamphlets as unreliable,[22] and some were written to support particular religious or political agendas and so are not necessarily representative of what most people believed. For example, David Harley has shown that pamphlets which described cases of witchcraft and demonic possession in seventeenth-century England were written to back up different positions in wider religious controversies.[23] Nevertheless, the fact that charms and methods of divination were copied at all suggests that they were seen as useful and that they were used by some people. Pamphlets, too, despite their bias and exaggeration, suggest there was a widespread interest in magical phenomena, and folklore evidence, when used carefully, can also shed light on some earlier forms of magic. These sources therefore provide a valuable supplement to sources produced by the critics of common magic.

Another way of getting at common magic is through material culture.[24] Much has not survived. Small items were easy to lose, whereas objects made from organic materials would often have decomposed. It is also difficult to know which archaeological finds should be seen as "magical", because often we do not know how they were perceived and used at the time. Was it magic or unofficial religion to bury a pilgrim badge brought back from a saint's shrine under a house or in a garden or to place it on the entrance to a stable or cowshed to protect the inhabitants?[25] However, some surviving items can be classified as magical with more certainty, especially when they correspond to descriptions of magical objects found in written sources.[26] The material culture of magic is still little studied compared with the written sources, but it has the potential to expand our knowledge in important ways, given that so much common magic was probably never written down.

Taken together these sources tell us much about common magic despite the difficulties they pose in interpretation. They tell us about particular beliefs, practices and practitioners. More broadly, they also show that common magic was persistent. Despite the efforts of some clergy and educated laypeople, many people used common magic, and some practices and ideas seem to have continued throughout the period and beyond. The sources also show that attitudes towards common magic varied considerably, depending on what exactly was done, why and by whom. It is to these issues that the chapter now turns.

The Uses of Common Magic

Common magic had very many uses and could be employed in almost any sphere of life. It could be used actively to bring about a result, for example, to heal, predict the future or cause harm, and it could also be used defensively to ward off evil influences and protect people, animals and crops against the things that threatened them.[27] The boundaries between these active and defensive uses of common magic were sometimes blurry: one of the charms discussed later in this section was designed both to cure an illness and to protect against the witchcraft that was believed to be causing it. However, the two often seem to have been viewed differently. Most of the time, the secular authorities and even the clergy focused their condemnations on active uses of magic and seem to have been more willing to tolerate unofficial practices which were designed to ward off witchcraft and other evils.[28] Following the sources, this section will focus primarily on the more active forms of magic which are best documented, but it is important to remember that they were part of a much wider body of practices, some of which attracted more condemnation than others.

One of the best-documented uses of common magic was for healing. Healing magic also poses some of the most serious problems of definition, because it overlapped both with prayers asking for healing and with non-magical medicine. When they thought about magical healing, the clergy generally focused on two kinds of remedies in particular. These were charms (words which were spoken over the sick person or written down and given to that person to wear) and amulets (objects which were worn on the body to benefit the wearer in some way). As early as the fourth century AD, St Augustine had argued that both charms and amulets were magic because they could not have a physical effect on the body, and so if they worked, they must rely on demons.[29] His words were quoted in the influential *Decretum* of Gratian, and they influenced many later writers.[30] However, medieval and early modern attitudes towards both charms and amulets were more complex than Augustine's was.

Charms were recorded throughout the period, and some travelled long distances, migrating from one language to another along trade and communication routes. Long-distance trade routes probably explain how versions of the same verse charm to stop bleeding can be found all around the North Sea in English, Scots, Low German, Dutch, Danish, Swedish and Norwegian.[31] Charms also varied over time, however. Some tenth- and eleventh-century charms invoked pagan gods such as Woden, often placing these pagan gods alongside Christian prayers and language in ways that make it difficult to separate "magic" from "religion" or "Christianity" from "paganism".[32] In later centuries, the pagan gods dropped away and charms relied increasingly on Christian language and imagery. Many took the form of short prayers which mentioned Christ or the saints and asked God to cure the sick person. For example, the fifteenth-century English physician Thomas Fayreford recorded the following charm to restrain excessive menstrual bleeding in women: "Saint Veronica suffered a flux of blood + she touched the hem of Christ's garment + she was cured. + May this woman, N[ame], be healed of a flux of blood through our Lord Jesus Christ".[33] The crosses in the text are directions to the practitioner to make the sign of the cross at those points.

If charms were written down, more elaborate combinations of words and diagrams were possible.[34] One example survives in the records of a court case heard in Norwich, England, in 1654 and is discussed by Frederick Valletta.[35] It was written on a small piece of paper which was given by a cunning man named Christopher Hall to the wife of John Smithbourne (Figure 10.1). Smithbourne's wife had fallen ill and was believed to be bewitched; the charm was designed to cure her and protect her against witchcraft. It included four circular diagrams and several magical symbols, but the bulk of it was devoted to words interspersed with crosses: names of God, such as "Iesus. Christus. Messias. Sother. Emmanuel. Sabbaoth [sic]"; the names of the three magi from the New Testament (whose names were often used in charms, especially to cure epilepsy); the names of the four evangelists; phrases from the Latin liturgy, such as "Kyrie Eleison"; and, finally, a prayer in English asking Jesus to "defend the bearer of this wrighting by thy power vertue and might from all enemyes visible and invisible at this present and for evermore amen".[36]

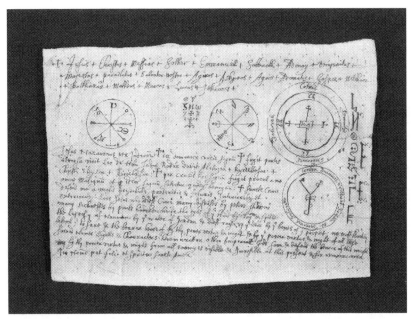

FIGURE 10.1. Charm from Norfolk quarter sessions papers, 1654. Norfolk Record Office, C/S 3/Box 41a. © Norfolk Record Office.

Because most charms used religious language and appealed to God and the saints, many people probably regarded them as prayers rather than as magic. Eamon Duffy and Don C. Skemer have argued persuasively that some of them were accepted by clergy and laity, educated and uneducated alike.[37] Nevertheless, even if many verbal cures were accepted, certain educated observers still found some of them problematic. Thomas Aquinas (d. 1274) and other medieval theologians conceded that people could write down prayers and quotations from scripture and wear them as an expression of religious devotion, but they forbade any charm which included strange, unknown words or characters, because these might be the names of demons. They also deemed it magic if people recited prayers, wrote them down or tied them on the body in specific ways which would not affect the power of a genuine prayer: for example, when people believed that a charm was more powerful if it was written down at a certain time.[38] For this reason, people who used well-known prayers or words in unorthodox ways might occasionally fall foul of the church. In 1527, William Brown was brought before the court of the bishop of London, accused of curing horses by collecting certain herbs and saying the Lord's Prayer five times, the Ave Maria five times and the Apostles'

Creed three times. In principle, there was nothing wrong with saying any of these prayers, but the court records describe Brown's actions as "magic art" and "incantation", presumably because of the requirement to say the prayers a certain number of times.[39] However, court cases like this are not very common, and many people probably used prayers and holy words in ways that strict theologians would have found questionable.

According to St Augustine, wearing amulets on the body for healing was also magic, but in practice many medieval and early modern people do not seem to have viewed these practices negatively. Theologians did not denounce them as regularly as they did charms, and medical and scientific texts throughout the period included some of them.[40] Thus, the thirteenth-century Portuguese cleric and physician Petrus Hispanus (d. 1276), who went on to become Pope John XXI, noted that "a red *celidonis* stone [a stone which was believed to be found in the womb of a swallow], worn bound in a linen cloth and placed under the left armpit" could cure epilepsy, and wearing the root of bryony protected against both epilepsy and magically caused impotence.[41] Petrus's collection of remedies was a mainstream medical work and was presumably not regarded as magical: it circulated widely, was translated into many vernacular languages and was printed in the sixteenth century.

Recommendations like Petrus's were also put into practice. The religious inscriptions on some surviving pieces of medieval and early modern jewellery suggest that their stones were worn for the benefits they could bring to the wearer, as well as for their beauty. A ring from fourteenth-century Italy now in the British Museum (Figure 10.2) includes a toadstone (a kind of fossil) and is inscribed with two quotations from the Bible: "Iexus [sic] auten [sic] transiens per mediun [sic] illorum ibat" ("But Jesus passed through their midst", Luke 4:30) and "Et verbum caro factum est" ("And the word was made flesh", John 1:14). Both of these quotations can be found inscribed on other objects, and the opening of St John's Gospel, in particular, was widely believed to offer protection against demons.[42] A strict theologian could have viewed this ring as magical, but in practice there is little evidence that most churchmen included objects like this in their condemnations of magic.

Charms and amulets were used for a variety of conditions but not, it seems, for everything. They could be used to protect against illnesses caused by magic, as Christopher Hall's charm shows. Charms were also used for some conditions which were deemed to have physical causes, including fevers, bleeding, difficulties in childbirth, epilepsy and toothache. It is not clear why these conditions attracted charms, but it may have been because parallels could be found for them in the Bible or in religious tradition, such as the

FIGURE 10.2. Toadstone ring with inscription. © Trustees of the British Museum.

parallel between excessive menstrual bleeding and St Veronica with her flux of blood, in the charm quoted earlier in this section.[43] However, even for these conditions, charms were not used to the exclusion of other cures. Many people were eclectic in their choice of cures, combining different kinds of remedy from different sources, especially if they were rich enough to be able to consult more than one medical practitioner.[44]

Charms and amulets were widely used and recommended by educated people as well as uneducated ones, but attitudes towards them varied. Some educated medical practitioners and laypeople dismissed them as "fables" or "women's chatter", but many others were willing to accept them as tried and tested remedies.[45] Attitudes were also affected by wider religious, cultural and social changes. During the sixteenth and seventeenth centuries, physicians increasingly rejected them because they were trying to define their own professional status against that of other practitioners, and labelling certain unexplained cures as superstitious or magical was one way to do so.[46] Ecclesiastical attitudes hardened at the same time, because during the Reformation and Counter-Reformation, both Protestant and Catholic authorities attempted to repress healing practices that they deemed magical.[47] However, the campaigns against magical or "superstitious" remedies were slow processes, and it seems that many people, even some among the well educated, continued to use them into the seventeenth century and beyond.[48]

Another common use of magic was divination, either to predict the future or to uncover information about the present. For some people, this meant interpreting omens in the world around them. Robert Mannyng, who wrote a manual of religious instruction in English verse in early fourteenth-century England complained that:

> Many believe in the [mag]pie,
> When she cometh low or high,
> Chattering, and hath no rest,
> Then say they we shall have guest.[49]

There also existed many other ways of foretelling the future, from reading palms to gazing into a shiny surface. As with healing, these practices were probably widespread and not confined to the poor or uneducated. Thus, the twelfth-century writer and bishop John of Salisbury told of how when he was a boy, his tutor made him look into a polished fingernail and other shiny surfaces (children were believed to be especially good at this because they were virgins), but John saw nothing there, much to his relief.[50] Members of the educated elite might also pay less learned specialists to do divination for them. In 1564, in Augsburg, Germany, the healer Anna Megerler claimed that one of the foremost merchants of the period, Anton Fugger, had employed her to do crystal-gazing on his behalf, and used the information he gained in his business dealings.[51]

One of the major uses of divination was to identify thieves and find lost or stolen property, and this seems to have been a potentially lucrative trade for magical practitioners. Techniques varied, but one common one was the "sieve and shears". The practitioner balanced a sieve on the point of a pair of shears and read out the suspects' names one by one; when they spoke the name of the guilty person, the sieve would rotate.[52] Accusations made by magical methods could be taken seriously and sometimes led to arrests, but the opponents of thief divination stressed that magic could also lead to false accusations.[53] As with healing, it was difficult to decide whether all of these ways of predicting the future or uncovering information about the present were truly magic.

It was widely accepted that some things could legitimately be predicted by observing the natural world: weather forecasting was the obvious example, and some forms of astrology also fell into this category, because it was widely believed that the stars did influence certain events on earth. However, medieval and early modern theologians were more dubious about methods of predicting the future that did not rely on the observation of natural causes and effects. If people claimed to be able to predict the future in impossible ways, either they were lying or they were performing magic.

Preachers told a range of stories that made both of these points. The Dominican friar and preacher Etienne de Bourbon (d. 1262), based at Lyons in France, collected several. One of his stories told of a female diviner who was able to tell visitors who they were and why they had come by means of a clever trick: her servants would stop the visitors as they approached and ask them what their business was. Then, while one servant delayed the visitors, the other relayed the information to their mistress, who was then able to amaze the visitors by her uncanny knowledge. However, Etienne was not so willing to dismiss every form of divination as a fraud. "When I was studying at Paris", he said, a fellow student had his books stolen and employed a magician to find them. The magician invoked demons who pointed the finger at the wrong person.[54] Nevertheless, despite the efforts of preachers like Etienne, healing magic and divination seem to have been perceived as effective and to have been very common. Ecclesiastical literature on superstition complained repeatedly about this and argued forcefully that the use of magic even for good purposes was wrong.[55] Their repeated complaints suggest that not everyone agreed.

Magic was also used in another area of human life that provoked anxiety and strong emotions: in the realm of love and sex. It could arouse love or sexual desire; break up a relationship by causing hate or impotence; cause infertility or miscarriages, or conversely help a couple conceive a child.[56] Popular attitudes towards all of this were often more ambivalent than they were towards divination and healing. Love magic was especially condemned when it caused disruption to existing relationships. For example, in 1345, a woman testified at the canonization process of the Italian friar Gerard Cagnoli that her son had been "bewitched and taken away by a woman who was unfaithful to her husband". He had lived with this woman for two years before the saint intervened and caused him to come home.[57] Magic also attracted condemnation if it caused impotence, as when the early thirteenth-century cleric Thomas of Chobham claimed to have heard of a woman in Paris who made her former lover impotent with his new wife.[58] We hear much less about love magic that did not cause scandals or marital problems like these. It is even possible that when magic led to appropriate marriages, it could be seen as socially useful,[59] but it is hard to be certain because cases in which everyone was happy rarely came before the courts and so we know little about them.

Accusations of love magic like the ones just described were not necessarily based on any hard evidence that magic had taken place. Rather, they arose to explain an inappropriate relationship or a mysterious case of impotence, attacking the person held responsible while absolving the "victim" of blame. Nevertheless, it is clear that some people did try to use magic to gain control over the emotions and behaviour of others. The inquisitions of early modern Catholic Europe were especially interested in this, and their records give detailed information about magic used for a variety of sexual and emotional purposes.[60] Some kinds of love magic were highly aggressive, both in their purpose and in the symbolism they employed. The Venetian inquisition records describe a form of love magic known as *dare Martello*, "giving the hammer", which aimed to torment the victim until he or she came to the person who performed the magic. A method for doing this was taught by Elisabetta Giantis to a widow named Anna and her daughter. Elisabetta told them to conjure the Devil to afflict the person they wanted "and not let him walk, nor do any business, nor come near, nor read, nor write, nor go with man or woman, until he comes to me to do my desire".[61]

At this point, love magic blurs into *maleficium*, the use of magic to harm others. Most of the time, however, the problems allegedly caused by harmful magic had nothing to do with love. It was believed that magic could cause sickness or even death in people or animals, as well as other agricultural problems, such as the drying up of cows' milk. Studies of witch trials from the fifteenth century onwards have shown that it was this aspect of magic which most worried ordinary people, and many trials started with an accusation that the "witch" had caused harm to another person.[62]

Records of witch trials like these tell us much about the fear of harmful magic in the early modern period. (They are not very numerous before the fifteenth century, so medieval attitudes towards harmful magic are more difficult to assess.) They tell us what some people thought witches did and how they tried to resolve the situation if they thought they had been bewitched. They show that accusations of harmful witchcraft often arose among people who lived in close proximity to one another and grew out of interpersonal tensions which sometimes went back many years. In this context, the studies of English witchcraft accusations conducted in the 1970s by Keith Thomas and Alan Macfarlane (inspired by anthropological studies of witchcraft in twentieth-century Africa) were important in drawing attention to the importance of socio-economic tensions within early modern communities and the relationship between accuser and accused.[63] Since then, historians have investigated these relationships in more detail for various parts of Europe and have argued that the situation was more complex than Thomas and Macfarlane suggested, but they continue to stress the importance of neighbourhood relationships and tensions in creating suspicions and accusations of witchcraft.[64] Other recent studies have explored in more detail how widespread beliefs about harmful magic led to trials. Often witchcraft was suspected if a person fell ill or suffered misfortune after a quarrel with someone – particularly if the person with whom they quarrelled already had a reputation as a witch or if they had made threats such as "you'll regret this". In this situation, the first step was often to seek a cure from the suspected witch. Legal action was usually the last resort: it was expensive and witchcraft was difficult to prove conclusively, so accusers who could not prove their allegations risked being sued for slander.[65]

As these studies have shown, trial records tell us much about who was accused of witchcraft and how accusations arose, but they say much less about the reality of harmful magic. Given that harmful magic was believed to work, it seems likely that some people would have tried to use it, but it is difficult to get at this from the surviving evidence, because in most cases accusations were based on a quarrel followed by misfortune and not on any hard evidence of magical practices.

Not surprisingly, common magic also included techniques to counter harmful witchcraft and to identify witches. Medieval and early modern medical writers recorded some ways of warding off magic, especially when they discussed impotence, a condition that was sometimes thought to be caused by magic.[66] Often these remedies were derived from earlier written sources, but Petrus Hispanus recorded one that he claimed came from popular culture: St John's wort kept away all demons if it was kept in the house, he said, and for this reason it was popularly known as "demons' bane".[67] Some techniques for warding off witchcraft were widely known: for example, there are many references in England to a method of identifying a witch by boiling the victim's urine. It was believed that this would cause the witch pain, forcing her to reveal herself.[68] There were also more elaborate ways of protecting oneself or one's house from evil influences. One solution from early modern England was to bury in the house a witch bottle: a jar or bottle containing a selection of objects that were designed to reflect evil spells back onto the witch who cast them. One witch bottle, dated between 1650 and 1700 and now in the Museum

FIGURE 10.3. Post-medieval bellarmine jar. © Museum of London.

of London, contains several iron nails and a piece of felt in the shape of a heart, pierced with five pins. (Figure 10.3).[69] As well as these self-help methods, cunning folk could also be called in to identify witches and cure witchcraft, and their word could lead to legal action, although the authorities did not always view such accusations sympathetically, any more than they trusted accusations of theft that were made by magical means.[70]

319

Common magic was also used for a range of other purposes. Medieval preachers warned their listeners against stealing consecrated hosts for "magical" purposes, such as sprinkling them on their fields to improve the crops.[71] Early modern soldiers as far apart as Venice and England carried written charms to protect them from injury in battle.[72] Magic could also be used for financial gain: to find buried treasure or, more modestly, to win at gambling.[73]

When faced with this mass of practices, it is tempting for a modern reader to ask why particular forms of magic appealed so widely to people and why they were believed to work. Keith Thomas and Alan Macfarlane suggested several reasons why common magic was believed to be useful and effective on the basis of their reading of anthropological evidence. For example, divination to identify a thief might work by confirming the victim's existing suspicions, and it might even intimidate the guilty party into returning the stolen goods. In cases of illness, taking counteractions against witchcraft might provide psychological comfort to the victim and give him or her a way of taking control of the illness.[74] More recently, Edward Bever has turned to another discipline, cognitive science, to explore how magic could be thought to work, and he has argued that thanks to psychological phenomena like the placebo effect, many witchcraft beliefs may have had more basis in reality than historians have often thought.[75] His theories have proved controversial, but the debate about the extent to which common magic affected the people who used it or believed that it had been used on them looks set to continue.[76]

It is clear, however, that many uses of common magic were pragmatic responses to common needs and problems: to foresee and influence the future; to gain health, love or prosperity; and to explain and counter misfortune and, in some cases, to cause it in others. For this reason, it can be found in many places throughout the medieval and early modern periods. However, there was much scope for variation in the details of the practices and the ways in which they were regarded.

Practitioners: Real and Imagined

Who used these long-established techniques? As we have seen, for historians one of the defining features of common magic is that it was accessible to many different kinds of people. Many forms of common magic were probably very common indeed, being orally transmitted and widely used. Sometimes ecclesiastical condemnations implied this. A fourteenth-century German friar named Rudolf described a series of what he claimed were local magical practices, focusing particularly on forms of love and fertility magic performed by women. He implied that women and girls commonly used them, saying that if priests asked in confession, they would learn about very many of them.[77] Occasionally, people who were not specialists in magic also wrote down common practices for their own use. Richard Kieckhefer has described a fifteenth-century book of household management probably compiled at Wolfsthurn Castle in the Italian Alps which, alongside all kinds of information relevant to running a large estate, includes healing charms and methods for warding off harmful magic. As we have seen, these things were not necessarily regarded as magic, but the later owners of the manuscript certainly viewed some of them with suspicion, adding notes that described one remedy as "superstitious" and commenting of another that "this would be good – if it were true".[78]

There were also people who specialized in magic. They were called cunning folk or wise men or women in English, and they went by a multitude of names elsewhere: *devins* in Lorraine, *saludadores* in Spain and Portugal and *magare* in southern Italy.[79] They identified thieves and witches, predicted the future and diagnosed and cured illnesses, including illnesses that were believed to have been caused by magic. These specialists could be male or female, clergy or laity.[80] They interacted with their clients in a variety of ways. Some offered their services for free, even claiming that to accept money would damage their powers (although they sometimes accepted gifts), whereas others charged, sometimes considerable sums of money. A few worked as cunning folk full time, but most combined it with other trades, partly because it was common in premodern Europe to make extra money from part-time occupations and partly because full-time cunning folk were more visible and so more likely to attract negative attention from the authorities.[81] But whoever they were, these diverse practitioners had specialist skills or knowledge which most people did not have.

Their knowledge could come from various different sources. In some parts of Europe, cunning folk claimed to be in contact with beings and worlds beyond our own. Angels, saints and fairies were all believed to initiate healers and seers into their gifts in places as widely scattered as Scotland, Hungary, Switzerland and Portugal, and they were also believed to help cunning folk heal, predict the future and identify witches.[82] Claiming to be in touch with the fairies or angels could strengthen a cunning person's reputation for having special powers, but it was not essential, and many cunning folk seem to have managed without it, relying instead on specialist knowledge or a family tradition of magical practice.

Other magical specialists distinguished themselves from their clients and demonstrated their special knowledge through literacy and their access to books. Some cunning folk owned magical texts, and these works served as inspirations for magical practice and probably also as a way of impressing clients.[83] Writing also played an important role in some forms of magic. Many healing charms required the practitioner to write something down, as well as say it aloud. Sometimes they required a considerable amount of writing, as in the seventeenth-century charm in Figure 10.1, although it did not necessarily require a great deal of education to produce these charms if the formula was copied from an exemplar. Love magic, too, might rely on writing: the educated courtesans of sixteenth-century Venice used written prayers to bind love and seem to have copied these prayers amongst themselves.[84] Beyond this, education to a higher level and knowledge of Latin opened the way to more sophisticated forms of magic, particularly in the Middle Ages, before magical works were translated into vernacular languages.[85]

The importance of reading and writing meant these practices were not truly common, but even uneducated people could get some access to them. It was possible to pay someone else to use magical books or write charms for you: one thirteenth-century friar complained about people (probably clergy) who wrote healing charms to give or sell to others.[86] Moreover, literacy rates steadily increased during the medieval and early modern periods, although with much variation between areas and social groups, so written forms of magic were increasingly accessible to a wider audience as time progressed. As the audience for written information about magic increased, so too did the supply of information available, and magical texts began to be translated into vernacular languages and printed during the early modern period.[87] Thus, by 1800, a far wider range of people are likely to have had at least a basic ability to access written forms of magic than in 1100, making common magic an increasingly literate activity.

When it came to written magic, clergy were more likely than laypeople to have the education necessary to read magical books, especially in the Middle Ages. They also had other advantages as magical practitioners: their role as mediators between God and man, involvement in sacred rituals and access to consecrated substances gave them an additional source of power. Many of the practices clergy used were adaptations of official rituals, and many clergy probably saw them as legitimate, if unofficial, religious activities, even though strict theologians condemned some of them as magic.[88] Beyond this, some clergy can be found acting as cunning folk and performing the same activities as other magical specialists, but by the eighteenth century these "cunning clergy" were becoming rare, as Protestant and Catholic churches alike began to keep a closer eye on clerical behaviour and distinctions between educated and uneducated medical practitioners sharpened.[89]

In addition to genuine magical practitioners, some groups of people were also believed to be especially likely to do magic, whether or not they actually did so. Here historians have emphasized the importance of various factors. One is gender. Practitioners of common magic could be men or women, but certain practices were associated especially with women. It is well known that in the early modern period more women than men were put on trial for harmful witchcraft (although there are some exceptions, such as in Iceland and Estonia), and the reasons for this are much debated.[90] Behind the trials, the association between women and magic was deeply rooted in the ecclesiastical culture of the Middle Ages. The eleventh-century bishop Burchard of Worms gave a detailed description of magical practices which he claimed women performed, as did the fourteenth-century friar Rudolf.[91] From the fifteenth century onwards, however, some churchmen increasingly associated women with harmful magic in particular. This was done most forcefully by the *Malleus Maleficarum*, a treatise on witchcraft written by the Dominican friars Heinrich Kramer and Jacob Sprenger in 1486. In a chapter which has become notorious among modern historians, Kramer and Sprenger gave several reasons why women were especially likely to be witches: they lacked moderation and so were prone to extreme goodness or excessive evil; they were more gullible than men and so more easily deceived by demons; they lacked reason and were prone to strong emotions, and they were vain and lustful.[92] The *Malleus* influenced some later writers and was reprinted in twenty-nine editions, but its position on gender was extreme, and other writers were more willing to acknowledge that either men or women could be witches, even if women predominated.[93]

The association between women and harmful magic was not simply a product of clerical misogyny, however. As numerous studies have shown, many accusations of witchcraft arose "from below" when people accused their neighbours, and people were more likely to accuse women than men.[94] Women as well as men accused other women of witchcraft, and in some cases, witchcraft accusations among women could be a way of expressing fears that were closely connected with female roles. This is clear in the cases from seventeenth-century Augsburg, Germany, studied by Lyndal Roper, in which women who had recently given birth accused their lying-in maids of bewitching them or their newborn children.[95] Even before the witch trials, women seem to have been especially linked to harmful magic. A study of the fifteenth-century church courts of Canterbury has found that although both men and women were accused of most forms of beneficent magic, accusations of harmful magic were made overwhelmingly against women.[96] It is almost impossible to know from these sources whether women really did use harmful magic more often than men did, but widespread belief certainly seems to have associated them with it – both in the church and among the laity.

Women were also more likely than men to be accused of love magic. Some historians have suggested this was because women were genuinely more likely to perform love magic than men were, because they had few other ways of influencing the men in their lives. The case of Matteuccia di Francesco, who was burned for witchcraft in Todi in 1428, might be an example of this. Matteuccia was accused of (among other things) using love magic to help several women who were being ill-treated by their husbands or sexual partners. The magic was designed to make their menfolk treat them better.[97] Similarly, in eighteenth-century Mexico, Magdalena de la Mata told the inquisition she had sought magical help after her husband beat her badly. Not every woman who sought love magic was in this position, but these cases suggest one reason why women might use love magic more often than men did.[98] On the other hand, it is also likely that women were more likely to be accused of love magic than men were. In this case, accusations might reflect men's fears that women might try to control them, or they might have arisen as a way of blaming men's unacceptable sexual behaviour on a female temptress – as in the case of the man whom Gerard Cagnoli miraculously "cured" of his liaison with an adulterous woman, described in the previous section.[99]

Other groups were also especially likely to be accused of magic or to be suspected of using it. One of these was the clergy, perhaps because of their access to sacred substances and to books. The belief that priests could affect the weather seems to have been relatively widespread,[100] but accusations against priests sometimes also reflected local circumstances. In a study of La Rochelle, a coastal town in south-west France, Kevin Robbins has suggested that priests were suspected of impotence magic (which was normally associated with women) because of anxieties specific to the area. He argues that many La Rochelle men were away for long periods fishing, leaving the priests alone with the women, and in these circumstances, priests became the focus of men's fears about leaving wives and households behind and vulnerable.[101] In other areas, accusations of magic fed on other local anxieties. Thus, studies of love magic in the Catholic parts of America in the early modern period discuss the way in which accusations were motivated by concerns about race as well as gender in the specific ethnic circumstances of the New World.[102]

Other factors cut across broad groupings, such as gender, race and clerical status. Throughout Europe, certain kinds of women and men were more likely to be accused of magic than others. Occupation might be one factor. As we have seen, among men priests might be particularly vulnerable to accusations of some kinds of magic. Because of their status as magical practitioners, cunning folk might also be more likely than other people to end up accused of harmful witchcraft. In the case of women, research into the detailed inquisition records of sixteenth-century Venice has shown that prostitutes were especially likely to be accused of using love magic on their male clients to keep their love. This was a good way of attacking a woman who seemed to have too much power over high-status men, but the accusations were not always unfounded, given that methods of love magic really did seem to circulate among prostitutes.[103] Other groups of women were also vulnerable to accusation, including unmarried women and widows who were not subject to a husband's guidance; foreigners, such as Greek and Slav women; and women who had a poor reputation.[104]

Reputation was also crucial in trials elsewhere. Because witchcraft accusations were often based on neighbourhood tensions, a person who did not get along with their neighbours was more likely to be suspected of witchcraft. Moreover, once a person gained a reputation as a witch, it could snowball, because further suspicions were likely to become attached to them. A reputation for immorality also did not help. Conversely, a good reputation could make accusations of magic seem less plausible. In 1467 in what is now Switzerland, Françoise Bonvrin was accused of witchcraft, but her lawyer offered a defence that rested, in part, on the fact that she was a pious woman whose family had never been suspected of witchcraft – and she was acquitted.[105] A family history of witchcraft (or a lack of one) also played a role in trials elsewhere.[106]

Inquisition records and witch trials have thus helped historians identify patterns connected with gender, occupation and reputation which can help explain why some people were especially likely to be suspected of using magic and why they might actually be tempted to use it. However, in many cases, the exact reasons why some people were accused when others (presumably) were not remain complex and must have depended on many individual factors.

Studies of magical practitioners and suspected witches are often based on court cases, and the fact that some magical specialists ended up in court prompts questions about how they were regarded by the people around them. Strict theologians throughout the period argued that the apparently benign magic of the cunning folk was just as demonic as the more visibly dangerous activities of the witch were. Popular attitudes towards cunning folk could also be ambivalent, and people believed that those who knew how to heal might also know how to harm.[107] Sometimes accusations arose against a cunning person who was unsuccessful in healing somebody, especially if the sick person got worse instead of better. In this case, they might be suspected of causing or worsening the illness. In a few other cases, cunning folk who made accusations of witchcraft became caught up in the resulting trials themselves. This happened to Chonrad Stoeckhlin, a Swiss herdsman in the late sixteenth century who claimed to be able to identify witches. Stoeckhlin said that his ability to identify witches came from the mysterious "phantoms of the night", and his neighbours seem to have accepted this: when he named a woman as a witch, they arrested her and she later died in prison. But then the bishop of Augsburg's officials took over the case, and they regarded Stoeckhlin's "night people" with more suspicion. For them, it looked suspiciously like trafficking with demons, and Stoeckhlin ended up being executed for witchcraft himself.[108]

However, the accusations made against individuals never developed into large-scale hostility towards all cunning folk. Only a minority of witch trials were directed against cunning folk, and probably only a minority of cunning folk ended up in court on charges of witchcraft.[109] Meanwhile, successive generations of educated writers complained about how the common people could not be persuaded to see the activities of cunning folk as bad.[110] In most parts of Europe, witch trials began when people denounced their neighbours for witchcraft, and it seems that people were not often willing to denounce cunning folk whom they believed offered a useful service. If their relationship with a client broke down, cunning folk ran a greater than average risk of being accused of witchcraft, but many others probably went about their business unaccused.

Conclusion

The history of common magic is very broad, and it intersects with many other aspects of medieval and early modern culture, including the histories of illness and healing, crime (both with the prosecution of magical practitioners and with the use of magic to detect thieves and other malefactors) and sexuality and gender. Moreover, many of the surviving sources were influenced by much wider social and cultural processes, notably the attempts by educated elites, especially within the church, to influence popular religion and culture. Regional studies have shown that common magic has much to tell us about popular culture and which aspects of it attracted elite disapproval, as well as how they went about persuading others of their views.[111]

Many other questions also require further exploration, including some basic ones. How truly "common" was common magic, and what factors might have influenced who practised it? To what extent was it known and practised by any interested party, and to what extent was it the province of specialists? To what extent was it viewed as legitimate, or as "magic" at all, and which factors determined how it was regarded? To what extent was it perceived as effective, and how significant were the concerns expressed by some writers that cunning folk were frauds? The relationships between common magic and the other forms of magic discussed in this volume are also important. The influence of magical texts on early modern English cunning folk has received some attention, but more could be done to determine how much common magic borrowed from learned magic, and vice versa. What was borrowed, and how was it understood? Did practices change their meaning when they moved from learned into common magic, or from common magic into learned?

There are also important questions about continuity and change. Studies of common magic often point to striking continuities, showing how similar ideas and practices can be found over long periods and in widely scattered geographical areas.[112] It can be very useful to approach common magic in this way. The evidence is often fragmentary, and parallels from different periods or regions help illuminate the meaning or context of obscure references in the surviving sources. These studies do not argue that nothing changed between 1100 and 1800, but it would be useful to explore the extent of this continuity further. How universal were the goals and techniques of common magic? How did it adapt to different societies, and how was it adapted by different social groups within those societies (for example, by women, men, clergy or prostitutes)? Some of the studies discussed in this chapter suggest ways in which beliefs about magic might reflect local anxieties, but everywhere there must have been a variety of interactions between local and universal beliefs.

Change over time brings us back to the relationship between common magic and wider cultural changes. Europe between 1100 and 1800 witnessed rising literacy, campaigns against "superstition", attempts to reform popular culture and the rise and fall of witch trials. How much did these change common magic, or attitudes towards it? For example, do the early modern witch trials reflect a genuine increase in the fear of harmful magic (and if so, what might lie behind that?), or do they simply suggest that by the late sixteenth century it was easier to take suspects to court? Attitudes towards the supernatural itself also changed. In particular, historians have debated whether the early modern period witnessed a process of "disenchantment" in which religious leaders began to place less emphasis on the idea that divine forces intervened regularly in everyday life and on the power of ritual to channel supernatural forces, although the extent and significance of this disenchantment have been much debated.[113] All of these major changes, as well as others, are likely to have had an effect on common magic: on what was done, what was feared, what was seen as magic and how magic was regarded. Conversely, a deeper understanding of common magic has much to contribute to our view of these wider historical processes.

Notes

1. Kieckhefer, *Magic in the Middle Ages*, 56.
2. For surveys, see Clark, "Popular Magic", 99–121 and Wilson, *The Magical Universe: Everyday Ritual*.
3. Davies, "Angels in Elite and Popular Magic, 1650–1790", 298.
4. Olsan, "Charms and Prayers in Medieval Medical Theory and Practice", 347–351.
5. Boudet, *Entre science et nigromance*, 123–124.
6. Kieckhefer, *Magic in the Middle Ages*, 12–13.
7. Ibid., 9–17.
8. Gratian, *Decretum*, ed. Friedberg, causa 26, cols. 1020–1046.
9. Overviews of this debate include Biller, "Popular Religion", 221–246; Scribner, "Is a History of Popular Culture Possible?" 175–191; Arnold, *Belief and Unbelief*, ch. 1.
10. Wenzel, ed. and trans., *Fasciculus Morum*, 577.
11. See Bailey, "Concern over Superstition", 115–133 and Cameron, *Enchanted Europe*.
12. Davies, *Cunning Folk*, 125–127.
13. Le Roy Ladurie, *Montaillou*, 289–290; Brucker, "Sorcery in Early Renaissance Florence", 8–9.
14. The historiography on this is vast. See the works by Behringer, Briggs, Macfarlane, Lyndal Roper and Thomas cited in subsequent notes. For an overview, see Barry and Davies, eds., *Palgrave Advances in Witchcraft Historiography*.
15. Again there is a large historiography but see the works by Behar, Gentilcore, Ginzburg, Martin and Ruggiero cited in subsequent notes.
16. For a recent overview see Nenonen, "Culture Wars", 108–124.
17. Ginzburg, *The Night Battles*.
18. Boudet, *Entre science et nigromance*, ch. 2.
19. Olsan, "Charms and Prayers"; Duffy, *Marking the Hours*, 91–96.
20. Sharpe, *Instruments of Darkness*, 60.
21. Wilson, *Magical Universe*, xxix.
22. Valletta, *Magic, Witchcraft and Superstition*, 6.

23. Harley, "Mental Illness", 114–144.

24. Merrifield, *The Archaeology of Ritual and Magic*; Gilchrist, "Magic for the Dead?" 119–159.

25. Spencer, *Pilgrim Souvenirs*, 18.

26. Cheape, "Charms against Witchcraft", 233–235; Merrifield, *Archaeology of Ritual and Magic*, 169–172.

27. Wilson, *Magical Universe*, xviii.

28. Bailey, "The Disenchantment of Magic", 394, 397–398.

29. Augustine, *De doctrina christiana*, trans. Green, 91–93.

30. Gratian, *Decretum*, cols. 1021–1022.

31. Roper, *English Verbal*, 161–162.

32. See Murdoch, "But Did They Work?" 358–369; Jolly, *Popular Religion in Late Saxon England*.

33. Olsan, "Charms and Prayers", 361–362.

34. On written charms, see Skemer, *Binding Words*; Davies, *Cunning Folk*, ch. 6.

35. Valletta, *Magic, Witchcraft and Superstition*, 111–112.

36. Charm, Norfolk Record Office, C/S 3/box 41a.

37. Eamon Duffy, *The Stripping of the Altars*, 278–287; Skemer, *Binding Words*, 5.

38. Skemer, *Binding Words*, 63–64.

39. Hale, *A Series of Precedents and Proceedings in Criminal Causes Extending from the Year 1475 to 1640*, 102.

40. Rider, "Medical Magic and the Church in Thirteenth-Century England", 100.

41. Petrus Hispanus, *Thesaurus Pauperum*, 109, 113, 239.

42. Kieckhefer, *Magic in the Middle Ages*, 102–103; Skemer, *Binding Words*, 87–88.

43. Olsan, "The Corpus of Charms", 228–229.

44. Park, "Medicine and Magic", 130–131; Rankin, "Duchess, Heal Thyself," 110.

45. Olsan, "Charms and Prayers", 349; Park, "Medicine and Magic", 130.

46. Briggs, *Witches and Neighbors*, 184.

47. Thomas, *Religion*, 256–257; Gentilcore, *From Bishop to Witch*, 139.

48. Briggs, *Witches and Neighbors*, 103; Gentilcore, "Was There a 'Popular Medicine' in Early Modern Europe?" 161.

49. Robert Mannyng of Brunne, *Handlyng Synne*, 12.

50. John of Salisbury, *Policraticus*, book 2, ch. 28, 147. See also Boudet, *Entre science et nigromance*, 101–106.

51. Roper, "Stealing Manhood", 5.

52. Thomas, *Religion*, 213.

53. Sharpe, *Instruments of Darkness*, 67–68.

54. Lecoy de la Marche, ed., *Anecdotes historiques*, 315–318.

55. Bailey, "Disenchantment of Magic", 390.

56. See Kieckhefer, "Erotic Magic", 30–55.

57. Goodich, "Sexuality", 504–505.

58. Thomas of Chobham, *Summa confessorum*, 184; Rider, *Magic and Impotence*, 97–98.
59. A suggestion made by Ruggiero, *Binding Passions*, 134.
60. See Ruggiero, *Binding Passions*, and Behar, "Sexual Witchcraft", 178–201. For a different view, see von Germeten, "Sexuality, Witchcraft and Honor", 374–383.
61. Martin, *Witchcraft*, 103.
62. Kieckhefer, *European Witch Trials*, 48; Thomas, *Religion*, 444; Briggs, *Witches and Neighbors*, 23.
63. Thomas, *Religion*, ch. 17; Macfarlane, *Witchcraft*, chs. 18–19.
64. See Briggs, *Witches and Neighbors*, 119–123.
65. Ibid., 97–98; Behringer, *Witchcraft Persecutions*, 85–89. Johannes Dillinger argues that in some areas legal action was a more common response: Dillinger, *"Evil People"*, 61.
66. Clark, "Demons and Disease", 38–58; Rider, *Magic and Impotence*, ch. 9.
67. Rider, *Magic and Impotence*, 167.
68. Thomas, *Religion*, 543–544.
69. On this and similar items, see Merrifield, *Archaeology of Ritual and Magic*, 163–175.
70. Thomas, *Religion*, 185–187; Dillinger, *"Evil People"*, 58.
71. Thomas, *Religion*, 34–35.
72. Martin, *Witchcraft*, 98; Valletta, *Magic, Witchcraft and Superstition*, 97–98.
73. Thomas, *Religion*, 234–237; Martin, *Witchcraft*, 110.
74. Thomas, *Religion*, 216–219; Macfarlane, *Witchcraft*, 223.
75. Bever, *The Realities of Witchcraft*.
76. For different views, see Bailey, Clark, Jenkins, Voltmer, de Blécourt, Sørenson, and Bever, "Forum: Contending Realities", 81–121.
77. Franz, "Des Frater Rudolfus Buch", 418–431.
78. Kieckhefer, *Magic in the Middle Ages*, 3–5.
79. Briggs, *The Witches of Lorraine*, 180–217; Campagne, "Charismatic Healers", 44; Gentilcore, *Bishop to Witch*, 129.
80. On cunning folk, see Macfarlane, *Witchcraft*, 115–134; de Blécourt, "Witch Doctors", 285–303; and Davies, *Cunning Folk*.
81. Briggs, *Witches and Neighbors*, 148.
82. Pócs, *Between the Living and the Dead*, 149–150; Behringer, *Shaman of Oberstdorf*, 22; Campagne, "Charismatic Healers", 46; Purkiss, *Troublesome Things*, 126–127.
83. Davies, *Cunning Folk*, ch. 5; Gentilcore, *Bishop to Witch*, 229.
84. Ruggiero, *Binding Passions*, 3–5.
85. Davies, *Cunning Folk*, 120.
86. Rider, "Medical Magic", 96–97.
87. Thomas, *Religion*, 227.

88. Gentilcore, *Bishop to Witch*, ch. 4.

89. Davies, *Cunning Folk*, 80–82.

90. For an overview, see Briggs, *Witches and Neighbors*, ch. 7.

91. Burchard of Worms, *Decretum*, book 19, ch. 5, in *PL* 140, cols. 971–976; Shinners, *Medieval Popular Religion 1000–1500*, 450–456; Franz, "Frater Rudolfus Buch", 425.

92. Kramer and Sprenger, *The Hammer of Witches*, 160–170.

93. See Schulte, *Man as Witch*, 92–159.

94. Sharpe, *Instruments of Darkness*, 174.

95. Roper, "Witchcraft and Fantasy", 199–225.

96. Karen Jones and Michael Zell, "'The Divels Speciall Instruments': Women and Witchcraft before the 'Great Witch Hunt'", *Social History* 30 (2005), p. 55.

97. Kieckhefer, "Erotic Magic", 30.

98. Behar, "Sexual Witchcraft", 184. For a different view, see von Germeten, "Sexuality, Witchcraft and Honor", 378–379.

99. Kieckhefer, "Erotic Magic", 30.

100. Wilson, *Magical Universe*, 397.

101. Robbins, "Magical Emasculation", 67.

102. von Germeten, "Sexuality, Witchcraft and Honor", 379.

103. Ruggiero, *Binding Passions*, 44–45, 92–94.

104. Martin, *Witchcraft*, 227–235.

105. Strobino, *Françoise sauvée des flammes?*, 87–89.

106. Briggs, *Witches and Neighbors*, 215.

107. Gentilcore, *Bishop to Witch*, 143; Briggs, *Witches and Neighbors*, 146.

108. Behringer, *Shaman of Oberstdorf*, 91–93.

109. Briggs, *Witches of Lorraine*, 196; Dillinger, *"Evil People"*, 60.

110. Briggs, *Witches and Neighbors*, 159–160.

111. See, for example, Thomas, *Religion*; and Gentilcore, *Bishop to Witch*.

112. Kieckhefer, *Magic in the Middle Ages*, 57; Wilson, *Magical Universe*, xxvii; Clark, "Popular Magic", 103.

113. Walsham, "The Reformation", 497–528; Bailey, "Disenchantment of Magic", 383–388.

Chapter 11

Learned Magic

DAVID J. COLLINS, S.J.

The Renaissance humanist and monastic reformer Johannes Trithemius (1462–1516) rarely hesitated to express skepticism about claims of magic as practiced in his own day or in the past. In his *Annals of Hirsau*, he introduced readers to a thirteenth-century *praestigiator admirabilis* from Frisia named Theodo. Theodo was reputed to have restored a servant to life whom he had decapitated an hour earlier. He could also walk in the air, devour armed men whole, swallow cartloads of hay in one gulp, and drag great weights of wood and stone single-handedly. Trithemius denounced him not for deriving power from demons, as might be claimed of someone suspected of necromancy, but for deluding simple people.[1] Elsewhere, in correspondence with an astrologer at the court of the Elector Palatine in Heidelberg, Trithemius reflected on an encounter with a man who identified himself as "Master George Sabellicus, a new Faustus, a font of necromantics, an astrologer, a magician, and a prolific diviner through the reading of palms, soil, fire, and water." Trithemius derided this "prince of necromantics" as a deadbeat in an invective that counts among the earliest written references to that most renowned of Renaissance magicians, Dr. Faustus.[2]

But Trithemius was not merely, or even most famously, magic's detractor. Quite to the contrary, he enjoyed notoriety in his own day, and has since, as a sorcerer, accomplished in his own right, and as the teacher of such other celebrated Renaissance magicians (or *mages*) as Heinrich Cornelius Agrippa von Nettesheim (1486–1535) and Paracelsus (1493–1541). Martin Luther even denounced Trithemius as a master of black magic in his table talk of 1539.[3] This aspect of his fame was inspired by a letter he wrote in 1499 to a sympathetic poet and theologian in Ghent, in which he mentioned his work in progress on steganography, a form of coded communication by angelic transmission. A third party with heightened sensitivity to the demonic intercepted the letter and publicized its contents with an insinuation of Trithemius's depraved curiosity.[4] As distressing as this development may have been for the abbot, his reaction – remaining engaged, if more surreptitiously, in the study of magic and committed to discerning a distinction between illicit, demonic magic and licit forms of magic that were closely associated with approved natural philosophy – represents a common characteristic of practitioners of magic in the Renaissance.

The struggle to carve out an intellectually and morally legitimate field of magic, which included for Trithemius such topics as steganography and was distinct from the demonic magic of Sabellicus and the chicanery of Theodo, was indeed much larger than one person's private battle. It was a constitutive component to a widespread interest in the fifteenth- and sixteenth-century Western world in "learned magic." Although a practitioner of such magic was commonly referred to in Latin as a *magus*, what he – and mages were even more exclusively male than *maleficiae* (witches) were female – practiced was not categorized in its day as "learned."[5] It is a modern sense of similarities among various kinds of magic that has led to their association as "learned magic," a classification that encompasses significant portions of what more particularly can be identified as natural magic, image magic, divination, alchemy, and ritual magic.[6] The similarities include, for example, a shared presupposition that hidden but natural forces were embedded in the created world and could be tapped and manipulated; an expert – a *magus* or adept – who practiced them; the ways in which the expert became proficient in them; the areas of expertise – linguistic, mathematical, and technical – necessary to acquire that proficiency; the expense of the paraphernalia required for their practice; an expressed relationship – sometimes real, sometimes imagined or contrived – through sources, texts, and concepts to Mediterranean antiquity; the milieus – monastic, academic, and courtly – where they were practiced; the role of the book as a repository for the relevant knowledge and as an apparatus in their practice; the identification of the practices as *scientia*, that is, as corresponding to contemporaneous notions of rationality, by critics and defenders; and the generally inconsistent and non-violent ways in which academic, civil, and ecclesiastical authorities discouraged the practices, when and where they were discouraged at all.

This sketch of learned magic, especially in those forms with resemblances to modern academic disciplines, points to another difficulty in studying it, namely, that modern identification of the medieval and early modern phenomena gravitates toward what appears unmodern. As learned as such forms of magic might appear in comparison to common magic and much superstition, at the core of what is identified as learned magic is that which most readily strikes present-day scientific sensibilities as rationally deficient and malformed. These analytic tendencies can be so deeply ingrained as to go unnoticed even in the most sophisticated interpreter of historical documents and can put a historical analysis in danger of anachronism by treating as a whole what is, in fact, the detritus. The oddness of learned magic consequently resolves in misleadingly sharp contrast. The nineteenth- and early twentieth-century study of alchemy offers an especially illuminating example of this problem, insofar as the scholarship tended either to highlight that which seemed most like alchemy and thus laid the groundwork for modern chemistry or to derogate cursorily alchemy's outmoded physics and the mystical and supernatural imaginings of its practitioners. Although the task of modern historians includes organizing the relevant material they find to make their analyses more accessible, their challenge in the case of magic is to account for, or at least to portray with precision, the absence of a conscious structure among the practitioners. We will return to this problem when we consider the eighteenth-century developments that close the chapter.[7] More immediately, the aim of this chapter is to elucidate the forms and practice of magic that can be called "learned," with attention to shared characteristics and developments from the twelfth to the eighteenth centuries.

The High Medieval Rise of Learned Magic

Well before the twelfth-century rise of learned magic, there were kinds of magic that required formal learning, at the very least insofar as they were transmitted through written materials and so required the literacy of their practitioners. Consideration of them offers helpful background to the high medieval watershed. The origins of medieval magic are to be found in the intersecting magical imaginations of Greco-Roman and barbarian societies in the first millennium CE as Mediterranean and northern European societies appropriated Christianity. This grand process of European enculturation yielded a salmagundi of magical beliefs and practices, whose aims included healing, divining, protecting, cursing, and harming. Richard Kieckhefer has influentially christened the results "the common tradition," because they can be found across wide swaths of medieval society.[8] The principal mode of transmitting the common tradition was oral, even though written traces can be found throughout the early medieval period. The expansion of the manuscript and then the printing culture that defined learned culture in the later Middle Ages led to the even wider dissemination of the common tradition.[9] This medieval transmission allowed practitioners to be much more than a specially trained subset of medieval society and to include just as easily the monk, whose access to the literature of magic was relatively easy, as the lavender, whose was not.[10]

The two factors most constitutive of the rise of learned magic beginning in the twelfth century were, first, the expansion of educational institutions with the burgeoning of urban schools and the emergence of universities and, second, a rapidly intensifying interest in ancient, most especially Aristotelian, learning. These, along with successful new efforts at discovering and reproducing ancient texts, at learning the languages necessary for translating the ancient texts and their subsequent commentaries from Greek, Hebrew, and Arabic into Latin, and at creating the infrastructure to make books available, effected the watershed in Western society that is often designated the renaissance of the twelfth century. The schools served as the nexus for the mutually vitalizing occurrence of these events. The slightly expanded period shaped by these characteristics – the eleventh through the thirteenth centuries – is often also called the High Middle Ages.[11]

Kinds of Learned Magic

The particular kinds of magic that benefited from the invigorated interest in Mediterranean Antiquity and that required the linguistic and mathematical skills that higher learning fostered can be organized conveniently, if arguably, into six groups, largely on the basis of how they were collected in volumes of magic at the time: natural magic, image magic, astral magic, divination, alchemy, and ritual magic.[12] These forms of magic were informed not only by the rediscovered texts of ancient Greece and Rome but also by the commentaries and treatises produced by Muslim and Jewish scholars in more recent centuries thanks to the learned West's willingness to engage these too for the first time. This engagement with learned magic tended to occur in several key locations: the traditional centers of learning, such as the monasteries, which had preserved many ancient books in their libraries through the early Middle Ages and which were the most important centers of learning in the West until the High Middle Ages; the new centers of learning, the universities; and courts, royal and ecclesiastical, largely on account of their financial resources, most famously including the Castilian court of Alphonse X the Wise (r. 1252–1284) and the imperial court of Frederick II (1194–1250).

Natural Magic

Natural magic operated on the assumption that created objects – minerals, plants, animals, and even parts of the human body – are interconnected in ways that are hidden, or "occult," but nonetheless discoverable and susceptible to human manipulation. According to the university philosopher and Bishop of Paris William of Auvergne (1180–1249), who had conceptualized natural magic more seminally than any other high medieval thinker, the interconnections are rational in the sense that they are structured in patterns and follow rules. The philosopher can learn these patterns and rules and through experimentation take advantage of the object's powers, or "virtues," to produce "marvels" that are neither demonic nor merely human. William's understanding of the hidden powers and the ways they might be utilized made possible a theoretical defense of natural magic as congruous with Christian faith and morals: the virtues of created objects are part of God's creation, and so the knowledge required for its practice was in the first instance not so removed from natural philosophy proper. At the same time, natural magic distressed many medieval thinkers as wicked, even if it was neither demonic nor unnatural, because of its operations and goals.[13]

One widespread text of natural magic, the *Liber aggregationis*, or *Experimenta*, was at least in part authored by the eminent Dominican philosopher Albertus Magnus (1196–1288). The work systematically details both the apparent and occult powers of herbs, minerals and gems, and animals. The book explains how, through occult powers, particular items can be used to accomplish such feats as silencing a dog, making the practitioner invisible, and burning flesh without fire. Parts of the book describe using occult powers to gain wisdom, to stir up and quiet storms, and to extract knowledge from a reluctant source. The lodestone was an object of particular interest in this and other volumes of natural magic. Used for navigation in compasses by the twelfth century, its attractive properties were finally associated with electricity, rather than the occult virtues, only as recently as the nineteenth century. In the *Liber aggregationis*, its use is recommended for determining the chastity of one's spouse. Throughout the work, the author appealed to Aristotle as the ultimate authority for his knowledge, a common contrivance in works of this sort and very much in keeping with the spirit of the age, which was so enamored with the Greek thinker that the foremost Scholastic, Thomas Aquinas, called him simply "the Philosopher." The concern implicit in these examples for the proper discernment of the real, if hidden, properties of created objects is what has led to much scholarly investigation of the links between high medieval natural magic and the development of the early natural sciences.[14]

A more controversial volume of natural magic is the *Liber vaccae* (*Book of Cows*), whose origins were in the ninth-century Arab world and Latin fragments of which began appearing in the West in the twelfth century. The work instructs in the making of humanoid creatures and the use of their blood and entrails to win unusual powers for the practitioner. To take one procedure as an example: impregnating a ewe with his own semen and carefully tending to the resulting pregnancy, the magician can create a being that will reveal future and faraway events, as well as offer such powers as the ability to walk on water and change the phase of the moon. As bizarre as the magic of the *Liber vaccae* might appear to the modern reader and despite the lack of expressed theoretical underpinnings, various typical principles of natural magic are evident throughout it: for example, the principle of sympathy suggests that magic's causes are related to its goals; thus, for example, the yellow sap of a tree might help cure jaundice.[15]

Image Magic

Image magic comprises a second form of learned magic. Like natural magic, image magic was conceived as a way to manipulate the occult powers of natural objects in relation to each other and to human beings. The distinctive aspect of image magic was its reliance on special characters, ciphers, and figures to activate or transform the occult, natural powers of given objects. Common materials used in image magic included wax figures modeled into purposeful shapes and gems engraved with special signs. The effects its practitioners sought ranged from the protection of the wearer in battle to the destruction of a business rival's resources. The level of expertise required for the practice of image magic varied greatly. Certain forms were so widespread that they can be ascribed to Europe's common culture.[16] At the same time, technical manuals and other guides to image magic of a more sophisticated sort were a significant part of the medieval library.[17] Most books of image magic in the Latin West had their origin in the Arab world and arrived via the Iberian peninsula.

An especially well-known volume of image magic, *Picatrix* (Figure 11.1), arrived in the court of the mid-thirteenth-century king of Castile and Leon, Alphonse X.[18] Moreover, both before and after the Reformation and on all resulting sides of the Christian confessional fissure, many practices drew on easily accessible objects and symbols of religious significance, blurring the sharp lines theological experts wanted to draw between religion and magic.[19] Conversely, in the minds of the theologically elite, the application of special markings and possible ceremonial enhancements placed image magic closer to demonic magic, and its open practice could thus attract greater legal hostility.[20]

The debate over image magic's lawfulness and validity, akin to the evaluation of natural magic, was linked to the larger Scholastic debate over the extent and limits of natural philosophy. The framing question was whether an image worked because of occult natural powers or because of demonic intervention. In the former case, use of the image would be lawful; in the latter, it would be unlawful. The urge to make image magic lawful then situated it alongside or even in the field of natural philosophy. The alignment shaped

FIGURE 11.1. Albrecht Dürer, Melancholia, 1514. Above the image of the angel in the upper right-hand corner of the engraving is a magic square. Magic squares were introduced to the Latin West in the *Picatrix*. The origins of the *Picatrix*, a handbook of talismanic magic, are in the Arab-Muslim world, perhaps in the tenth century. It arrived in the Latin West by way of thirteenth-century Castille. The magic square contains sequences of numbers adding up to 34. The bottom line includes the engravings year of production, 1514, framed by 1 and 4, the values assigned to the letters A and D. © The Trustees of the British Museum, Art Resource, New York.

the debate and can be seen in the usual placement of works of image magic among the *naturalia*. This tendency toward keeping image magic in the intellectual orbit of natural philosophy was shaped by certain authoritative works, most famously the *Speculum astronomiae*, which scribes and printers used to guide their selection of particular magical texts for reproduction on the basis of philosophical validity and moral lawfulness. Their use had a constraining effect, and the number and titles of texts of image magic reproduced through the late Middle Ages decreased.[21]

Astral Magic

Medieval and early modern image magic frequently depended on astronomical knowledge: the ciphers etched into precious gems were commonly astronomical symbols, and the preparation and use of talismans is often linked to carefully designated celestial phenomena. Astral magic had as its goal the harnessing of powers alleged to emanate from the planets and stars. *Picatrix*, which was mentioned in the previous section, is an important repository of astral magic and evidence of its close association with image magic,[22] as is the *De imaginibus*, attributed to Muslim scholar Thabit ibn Qurra (826–901),[23] which offered careful instructions on the making of talismans.[24]

Astral magic was related to astronomy and astrology, that is, the study of celestial bodies, their movements, and their influences on the human world. The question of how they are related (and distinguished) can be a vexing one, as suggested by the equivocal and overlapping use of words like *astronomus*, *mathematicus*, and *astrologus* in medieval documents. The beginnings of a general, if elastic, tendency toward distinguishing between astronomy, astrology, and astral magic was derived in large part from Ptolemy's definitions of kinds of astronomy, and it reached its most influential form in the *Speculum astronomiae*. The second-century Greco-Egyptian's four-volume work on astrology, the *Tetrabiblos*, was translated into Latin in 1138 and circulated under the title *Quadrapartitum*; the more mathematical *Almagest* was translated some decades later.[25] Both works had tremendous influence on the Mediterranean world – Christian, Jewish, and Muslim alike – and were revisited by astronomical thinkers both wittingly and not wittingly throughout the Middle Ages. In the *Tetrabiblos*, Ptolemy distinguished between the study of the cosmos that determines the placement and motions of celestial bodies relative to one another and to the earth, and the study of the influence that those bodies' natural properties have on earthly objects and on human beings: competence in these two sciences empowers one to prognosticate. Ptolemy proceeded to investigate and explain the latter of the two "preliminary sciences" and to teach its usefulness in issues of personal and civic importance. He also explained the various influences that given celestial bodies have on the terrestrial world and on human society, tribes, and individuals. The constellations, for example, have considerable influence on climate and weather: Virgo "excites moisture and thunder"; Sagittarius excites wind; and Leo excites heat. Celestial bodies can also influence physical characteristics: Jupiter, associated with heat and moisture, when in the east, makes a person's complexion fair, hair growth moderate, and stature dignified. In the West, however, it encourages long, straight hair and middling stature. Various celestial bodies have influence relative to a given person's status in society: thus the motions of the Sun and Saturn have particular influence on a father, whereas the Moon and Venus have influence on a mother. Ptolemy ascribed many ethnic stereotypes to the position of celestial bodies relative to the geographical coordinates of given regions in the Mediterranean world of his day.

The Latin Christian literature, beginning influentially with Saint Augustine's fifth-century *City of God*, distinguished between astronomy's capacity to predict the future, a power that was usually at least tolerated, and the capacity to change it, which was rejected as either false or immoral. Isidore of Seville (560–636) distinguished further between *astrologia naturalis* and *astrologia superstitiosa* in his seventh-century *Etymologies*: the former encompassed acceptable forms of celestial analysis in medicine and meteorology; the latter reinforced earlier condemnations of astrology that threatened human free will and moral responsibility through its use of horoscopes and other astral charts to determine human actions. By the later Middle Ages, the term "judicial astrology" came into use, and its most popular forms included "interrogations" – uncovering hidden knowledge with reference to the position of constellations at the time a question is posed – and "elections" – ascertaining with reference to the stars the most fortuitous time to undertake an activity.[26] In short, early medieval Christian writers laid the groundwork for a distinction that occupied Western astronomers for centuries to come: on the one hand, the reality of celestial influences on human society and an understanding of the heavens as a repository for information about the present and the future were recognized, and related discussions examined questions of degree and extent, rather than outright validity. On the other hand, the morality of using celestial powers to change the future or to access hidden knowledge was, although open to debate on finer points, more generally rejected.

At this point, astrology abuts astral magic. Astral magic involves the use of talismans with astrological signs to tap into occult celestial powers. Condemnations were justified with reference to the real harm that astral magic was thought to accomplish and for the ways in which it restricted human moral freedom.[27] The distinction between the signs used in astral magic and the effects celestial bodies could have on human world was fundamental to the negative judgment of astral magic in the eyes of orthodox religion and natural philosophy.[28]

The study of astrology in the most encompassing sense was reinvigorated by the general high medieval enthusiasm for Mediterranean learning. Adelard of Bath (1080–1152) translated the significant Arabic work of astral magic *De numero Indorum* by the ninth-century Persian astronomer al-Khwarismi. The thirteenth-century philosopher Albertus Magnus (1193–1280), who played such a key role in the early appropriation of Aristotelian thought and Muslim and Jewish commentaries on that thought into the West, wrote extensively on the influences of celestial bodies and the manipulation of their power through signs. His student, Thomas Aquinas, who wrote much less on the topic, prohibited it.[29]

In the later Middle Ages, the distinctions between astronomy and astrology would continue to shift. A crucial mark of astronomy's legitimacy after the thirteenth century was its nearness to the academic curriculum. Astronomy numbered among the seven liberal arts as the study of form in motion and had a place in the teaching program in the faculty of the arts at the medieval university. Even though it was taken as axiomatic that celestial bodies exercise influence on Earth, the range of influence on human personality and fortune was not taught in the schools officially, but it did on occasion find its way into astronomy lectures and was examined as a moral issue by theologians. A general tendency can also be identified in the later Middle Ages toward integrating the ancient mathematical sciences – astronomy, geography, and geometrical optics – with Aristotelian natural philosophy; and along these lines, scholars of mathematics, medicine, and natural philosophy were incorporating "the science of the stars" – the study of heavenly bodies, the measuring of their movement, and the study of their effects on earthly bodies – into their curriculums by the fifteenth century. The idea that celestial bodies and their motions influenced human personality and fate was only gradually rejected from formal academic circles at the end of the early modern period. An effective process of marginalizing astrology from the academy has been representatively dated by D. Rutkin to its exclusion from a textbook by the Jesuit mathematician Christopher Clavius (1537–1612) in 1570.[30] In short, astrology was a field of knowledge that straddled numerous fences of intellectual legitimacy. Few boundaries separating what might be recognized today as astrology and astronomy, or astrology and astral magic, remained fast throughout the several centuries examined in this chapter.

Divination

A fourth category of learned magic, divination, aims at foretelling the future and discerning hidden truths by reading signs in configurations of natural objects. As with the other forms of learned magic, medieval Westerners appropriated basic ideas about divination from ancient Near East and Greco-Roman traditions. Isidore of Seville cited the Roman scholar Varro (116–27 BC) as associating divination in the first instance with the four elements of earth, air, fire, and water.[31] Mantic arts, as the various forms of divination are also known, are thus identified by the objects used in the interpretation: geomancy relies on patterns discerned in tossed handfuls of sand or rocks;[32] aeromancy relies on atmospheric conditions, such as wind, clouds, thunder and lightning, comets, and meteors; pyromancy relies on shapes, colors, and patterns in flames or in burned objects; and hydromancy relies on signs in water, such as the ripples caused by pebbles thrown into it. Other means of prognosticating discussed in the medieval and early modern periods included catoptromancy, divination using a mirror[33]; crystallomancy, which requires a crystal ball[34]; gyromancy, which claims to interpret the collapse of a person who is spun into dizziness, relative to a circle drawn on the ground; scapulimancy divines from tossed shoulder blades (of sheep)[35]; and so forth. Physiognomy – the prediction of people's fate from certain physical characteristics – was among the most seriously analyzed forms of divination in the later Middle Ages and early modern period. Western thinkers drew ideas from both Greco-Roman and Arab traditions and developed those ideas energetically.[36] Albertus Magnus was a vigorous advocate for physiognomy.[37] Michael Savonarola incorporated extensive anatomical reflections in his mid-fifteenth-century *Speculum physionomiae*. Indeed, by the fifteenth century, aspects of physiognomy can be found in university lectures; and it has inspired, especially in the form of chiromancy, or palm reading, learned interest to the present day (see Figure 11.2).[38]

Physiognomy, of all the mantic arts, challenges divination's easy categorization as magic. Although Isidore made no effort to distinguish divination from magic, medieval theologians and church councils generally did. By the High Middle Ages, divination was customarily treated in treatises on its own. Authoritative, if largely derivative, authors on divination in this period, such as Hugh of Saint Victor (1096–1141) in his *Didascalicon* and Thomas Aquinas (1225–1274) in the *Summa theologiae*,[39] treated divination as a distinct category of magic. A consensus that mantics were necessarily demonic, and so condemnable, which began in the high medieval period, reached full expression in the *Book of All Forbidden Arts* by the Bavarian court physician, poet, and

FIGURE 11.2. This famous image of "Astronomical Man" is taken from the early fifteenth-century prayer book, the *Tres Riches Heures du duc de Berry*. Here the connection is drawn between the constellations of the zodiac and parts of the human body, giving evidence of the Renaissance association of medicine and astrology. London, Victoria and Albert Museum, Photo: Eileen Tweedy, Art Resource, New York.

translator Johannes Hartlieb (1400–1468).[40] Regardless, mantics were discouraged, insofar as they were considered at the least presumptuous explorations into a knowledge that belonged to God alone.[41]

Alchemy

Alchemy – the science of transforming natural substances into other substances – constitutes a fifth form of learned magic. Like astronomy, alchemy could include practices and base itself on presuppositions that can be placed along a long spectrum measuring degree of rationality. Much current scholarship prefers not to regard alchemy as magic at all, defining it separately as an occult art. At the very least, it merits consideration in this volume as a marker of how inapt modern distinctions between magic, science, and religion can be when applied to premodern periods. What alchemy might encompass could vary by practitioner and context. Medieval guides to alchemy could include processes as simple as reducing a substance to ashes (cineration) or as complicated as transmuting baser substances into nobler ones – most notoriously, lead to gold – by a process called projection. Medieval alchemists sought after the so-called "philosopher's stone," a red powder considered to be essential to the successful transmutation of substances, as well as the "elixir of life," which embodied alchemists' most ardent medical aspirations. Also like astronomy, medieval alchemy was based on principles of Aristotelian physics, but the texts and ideas attracting most attention in the Latin West from the twelfth century onward came from the Muslim world.

Like the other forms of learned magic, alchemy's practice in the medieval and early modern periods drew from various ancient traditions in ancient Near Eastern and Mediterranean cultures and was invigorated by the new appropriation of Muslim-Arabic literature beginning in the twelfth century.[42] Among the most influential and quickly translated texts shaping the invigorated interest in alchemy in the Latin West were Jabir's *Kitab al-Sab'een* (*Book of the Seventy*) and *Kitab al-Kimya* (*Book of the Composition of Alchemy*),[43] Rhazes's *al-Asrar* (*Book of Secrets*) and *Sirr al-Asrar* (*The Secret of Secrets*), and another work under the same name, *Book of the Secret of Secrets*, which was ascribed to Aristotle but was in fact also of Muslim-Arabic origin. The Persian alchemist Jabir (or Geber, as he was commonly known in the West: Abu Musa Jabir ibn Hayyan, 721–815), in addition to the works he authored, is associated with the Arabic version of the *Emerald Tablet*, a text that is ascribed to the legendary Hermes Trismegistus and that became an important part of the West's alchemical canon. Precise designation of his enormous corpus on alchemy, astrology, and medicine is controverted to this day on account of a fourteenth-century Western alchemist who used Geber as his pen name, some of whose misascribed alchemical texts proved as influential among medieval and early modern alchemists as the writings of Jabir himself.[44] The two works ascribed to Rhazes (Muhammad ibn Zakariya al-Razi, 865–925), a Persian alchemist, offered the West theoretical underpinnings and practical guides for alchemical research. Aristotle's place in high medieval Western thought about alchemy was later shaped by Ibn Sina, known in the West as Avicenna (980–1037). Indeed, Avicenna's alchemical writings – the *De anima in arte alchemiae* most notably – were in part so influential on account of their misascription to Aristotle: his *De congelatione et conglutinatione lapidum*, which expressed skepticism about the possibility of achieving real transmutation through alchemy, was incorrectly thought to be by Aristotle.[45] Alchemy appropriated a mystical dimension in the fifteenth century with the rise of Neo-Platonism in Western thought on magic, a development that will be discussed in the next section.

The two early Scholastic thinkers most responsible for ensuring that alchemy, or at least certain kinds of it, were taken seriously on a scholarly level were Albertus Magnus and Roger Bacon (1219–1294). Albert's position developed in his *Book of Minerals* and his commentary on Aristotle's *Meteorology*. He affirmed the theoretical underpinnings of alchemy but at the same time expressed skepticism at alchemy's ability to achieve its goals and admitted he had never seen most of what he understood as possible ever being carried out with success. Albert's position was favorable enough – and his authority on matters of physical nature was sterling enough – that subsequent generations of alchemical theorists ascribed their most important writings to him, and he gained a posthumous reputation for having been an avid practitioner. The most widely circulating pseudo-Albertine alchemical text up to the sixteenth century was the *Semita recta*, dubbed by Pearl Kibre to be "an excellent introduction to the alchemical art of the late thirteenth and fourteenth centuries."[46] Unlikely legend made Roger Bacon Albert's most promising student in the alchemical arts. He came to an even more sympathetic position on the effects of alchemy and developed a set of its medical implications, most dramatically those associated with the elixir of life.[47]

Alchemy might be thought the quintessential learned magic to the extent that its practitioners imagined it, like astrology, to be a fully legitimate and rational field of knowledge. But what distinguished alchemy from astrology in this regard was a very practical issue: alchemy included hands-on experimentation, which was excluded from the accepted disciplines in the medieval university. Experimentation smacked not of rational reflection – the business of a university – but of craftsmanship. Consequently, alchemy was excluded from the university's curriculum with a vigor not applied to astrology.[48] At the same time, medieval alchemy included a desire not simply to change nature but to perfect it, and that goal – of making the impure pure – could be understood by practitioners as a religious duty. Nonetheless, the complexities of the rituals and formulae, the necessity of instruction manuals, and the obscurantist use of ancient and pseudo-ancient languages and ciphers kept the practice of alchemy in limited hands not far from centers of learning.

With the rise of Platonism in the fifteenth century, alchemy became correspondingly detached from the Aristotelian physics that had undergirded the possibility of its success by medieval reckoning, mystically more complex in its procedures, and the extracurricular activity of persons associated with universities. Alongside these developments, both alchemy and astrology developed further associations with medicine (see Figure 11.3). The scholarship on medieval and early modern medicine is enormous and growing, and anything beyond the most cursory mention is not possible here. In the early modern period, doctors commonly referred to astronomical phenomena in treating patients, and the standard pocket calendar – or now, the calendar app – can be regarded as the descendant of the schedules of celestial events that doctors carried with them. There were healing practices that made no appeal to occult forces, and those that did. Like the study of the heavens, knowledge regarding human health and sickness could be found within and beyond the university curriculum. Like image magic, there was healing magic that qualified as "learned magic" by the definition outlined at the outset of the chapter and healing magic that qualified as "common magic."[49]

Emblematic of the Renaissance shift in alchemy is the figure of Paracelsus.[50] Paracelsus's key medical insights were reactions to the contempt with which he held the ancient medical fundamentals taken from Hippocrates and Galen on humors and temperaments. He developed instead a notion of toxins and pharmacologists called iatrochemistry.[51] The art and practice of alchemy, by Renaissance reckoning, furthered an evolution that was facilitated by the structure of creation itself. Philosopher's stones could transform human beings into divinities. Paracelsus added salt to the key ingredients of sulfur and mercury, and with his encouragement in opaque writings that gained followers, alchemists and physicians began to experiment in the direction of chemical medicine. By expanding alchemy to encompass consideration of the structure, composition, and properties of matter, Paracelsus and his disciples contributed to the transition from alchemy to chemistry. Other prominent Renaissance alchemists included Andreas Libavius, Michael Sendigovius, and Robert Fludd.[52]

FIGURE 11.3. This engraving by the Dutch artist and publisher Philip Galle (1537–1612) follows the painting "The Alchemist" by Pieter Bruegel the Elder (1558). The prominence of the equipment, ingredients, and books is noteworthy, as is the placement of the alchemical laboratory in monastic precincts. The enigmatic caption, added by Galle, reads, "The ignorant ought to acquire things and afterward work hard. The power of a precious, cheap, but ultimately rare stone is a thing singularly certain, cheap, and everywhere to be found. Mingled with the four natures and stuffed in a cloud, it is no unique mineral, but where found as such it is universally nearby." Berlin, Kupferstichkabinett, Staatliche Museen, Photo: Jörg P. Anders, Art Resource, New York.

Alchemy's transformation continued into the eighteenth century: dimensions of what had been the activity of medieval and early modern alchemists become appropriated into the new discipline of chemistry, which began to take a respectable place at the university. What remained would later be dismissed and was sometimes ridiculed. Paul-Jaques Malouin (1701–1777), a medical doctor and contributor to Diderot's famous *Encyclopédie* distinguished between alchemy and chemistry as that which is unexplained and appears marvelous as opposed to that which is explained and rational: alchemy, to the extent that it had real and measurable effects, moved according to this definition into chemistry.[53] Throughout the period under consideration in this chapter, there was also a mystical dimension to alchemy that intensified with the Platonism of the Renaissance and was likewise invigorated in certain Catholic and Protestant circles in conjunction with the Reformation. Alchemy, in short, straddled ambiguous and fuzzy boundaries with both science and religion, and it opens up the relationship between magic and esotericism.[54]

Ritual Magic

Ritual magic concerns itself with the conjuration of spirits – both good and evil – for particular tasks through complex ceremonies. Its complexity led to an extensive and thriving literature in the medieval and early modern periods, and the rituals often mimicked approved ecclesiastical rituals. The family resemblance to church rituals and the bookishness of ritual magic suggest significant clerical involvement, which is all the more striking given the decidedly negative view taken by church authorities toward what became known by the later Middle Ages as necromancy.[55] The meaning of necromancy had also shifted. In antiquity, it referred in a morally ambiguous way to the conjuring of the spirits of the dead. By the later Middle Ages, necromancy was understood to entail commerce with demons.[56] Here it will be noted that the transition of necromancy from amoral conjuration of the dead to deeply immoral cooperation with the demonic began with a development in monotheistic thinking – first Neo-Platonic, then Christian – that ultimately led the Christian church to associate the *daemones* of ancient thought, which were morally neutral or ambivalent beings, with the inherently wicked demons of Jewish and Christian scriptures.[57] In a later but analogous development, the principal referent of necromancy shifted from conjurations of the dead in the ancient and early medieval periods for divinatory purposes to commerce with demons by the late Middle Ages.[58]

Various other forms of magic addressed thus far in this chapter also required ceremonies for their effectiveness. The distinctiveness of ritual magic as a category distinct from image magic and the rites associated with it has to do with the powers being tapped: the learned magic described up to this point took as its goal the identification and manipulation of the occult powers in created objects, whether those powers were embedded in celestial bodies or inherent to certain words and ciphers. Ritual magic was aimed at gaining the assistance of spirits. By medieval and early modern Christian reckoning, demons were, on the one hand, created beings and thus part of the natural world; but on the other hand, on account of their spiritual nature and angelic origins, they were immensely more familiar with the occult properties of the rest of the created world. Furthermore, by virtue of the Satanic *non serviam*, demons were to be shunned at all costs.[59]

A few words about angelic magic are warranted here (with Michael Bailey addressing specifically demonic magic at length in Chapter 12). Two significant texts of angelic magic that circulated in the medieval and early modern periods were the *Ars notoria* and the *Sworn Book of Honorius*. The rituals in these works are not different from those attending to demons, insofar as they demand complicated rites of preparation, including fasting and meditation. The obvious difference is that the instructions themselves consist of prayers to God and the angels. From the thirteenth to the seventeenth centuries, the *Ars notoria* was a widely disseminated example of theurgic magic, with its principle end being an increase in the practitioner's knowledge and insight. The *Ars notoria* earned condemnation on account of its use of long lists of words in ancient languages and notes (thus the "notoria" of the title) appended to intricate diagrams dedicated to the field of knowledge or virtue. The text claims the authorship of the Israelite king Solomon and has strong Neo-Platonic resonances, but unlike many texts of learned magic in circulation in the later Middle Ages, no evidence has been found to directly connect the *Ars notoria* with the Neo-Platonists of Late Antiquity.[60] The *Sworn Book of Honorius* is a systematic guide to the performing of two spells, the first, lengthier, and more complicated of which aims at bringing the conjurer to the Beatific Vision; the other aims at conjuring elemental spirits. The *Sworn Book*, especially the first spell, exemplifies the high level of intricacy angelic ritual magic could attain with its extensive preparatory requirements that addressed not only the materials to use and the rites to perform but also the state in which the adept must approach the ritual. Indeed, ritual magic in general required of its practitioners a certain moral and mystical state of being in order for it to work. And to attain that state the practitioner was instructed to fast, to engage in penances, to remain continent, and so on. In this respect, ritual magic distinguishes itself from image magic: its effectiveness was intimately associated with the condition of the practitioner; consequently, as Frank Klaassen has incisively put it, the texts of ritual magic were "less a repository of truth than a vehicle for its discovery."[61]

Ritual magic enjoyed sustained interest throughout the six centuries under consideration in this chapter. It has recently been pointed out that, contrary to a certain conventional wisdom, ritual magic continued attracting sustained interest through and beyond the Renaissance, because, unlike the more "natural" forms of learned magic, it developed quite independently of the natural philosophical debate over material and physical "virtues." And so ritual magic remained largely unaffected by the challenge in the early modern period to the physics that undergirded a material world held together by occult powers.[62]

Moments of Transformation from the Eleventh to the Eighteenth Centuries

Appreciation of learned magic as an overarching category is complicated not only by the often unclear ways in which the types described in this chapter related to one another but also by the different rates at which and ways in which they changed over the six centuries under consideration. All drew from some ancient sources and were invigorated by the intellectual revolution of the twelfth and thirteenth centuries. At the same time, divination in particular had roots in the early medieval "common tradition" and flourished through oral transmission as much as written transmission. Later medieval concerns about demonic influences on society, for example, made certain kinds of ritual magic more suspect than astral magic, and Neo-Platonic ideas in the Renaissance transformed alchemy more than it did ritual magic. Nonetheless, all of the forms outlined here transmuted in part into specifically learned forms of magic in conjunction with what we have defined as the renaissance of the twelfth century. This is particularly obvious in the cases of ritual magic, alchemy, and astrology, all three of which produced enormous amounts of literature, increasing the book dependency of each as a discipline and demanding of their experts significant literacy and numeracy. In addition, these forms of learned magic rested on significant bodies of mainstream learning that had ancient roots and had been newly reinserted into the foundations of the new university learning, namely, Aristotelian physics, Ptolemaic astronomy, and Galenic medicine. Ptolemy proved to be of most direct significance, because he had written extensively not just on mathematical astronomy in the *Almagest* but also on astrology in the *Tetrabiblios*.

If the renaissance of the twelfth century can be thought of as a first watershed moment for learned magic, a second can be identified in the intellectual and cultural developments associated with the Renaissance, properly named, of the fourteenth to sixteenth centuries. The transformation was powered by factors analogous to those in the twelfth century, especially a renewed interest in ancient thought. This time, rather than Aristotelianism, it was the third-century development of Platonism that attracted most Western attention. Neo-Platonism, as the new movement has since been dubbed, infused traditional Platonism with an ontological mysticism based on cycles of emanation and return that bound together a primeval source of Being, the One, with Intelligence and Soul. As a religious philosophy, Neo-Platonism encouraged humans to seek an ascent out of the material world to the hypostases of

One, Intelligence, and Soul. As these ideas spread, they had profound influence on ancient Mediterranean culture and religion, both pagan and monotheist alike.[63] The newest orthodox articulations of Christianity, most prominently those of the fifth-century theologian Augustine of Hippo, appropriated many Neo-Platonic ideas, most famously through the writings of Plotinus and Porphyry. These Neo-Platonic thinkers and others such as Iamblichus, Proclus, and Synesius provided ritual, magical models for the attainment of hidden knowledge that proved highly attractive to the mages of the Renaissance.[64]

Neo-Platonism inspired Renaissance thinking about magic in many ways, none of which was more influential, or vexing to later generations, than Hermeticism. Hermeticism is an unsystematic body of knowledge that is rooted in Greco-Egyptian culture and associated with the legendary figure of Hermes Trismegistus. Hermes has obscure links to the Egyptian deity Thoth, a messenger between the divine and mortal realms and the inventor of hieroglyphs. Writings associated with the "Thrice Great Hermes" circulated throughout the medieval West but were never studied with the same level of exuberance that is exhibited in the Florentine philosopher Marsilio Ficino's translation of the Greek tracts known as the *Corpus hermeticum* from 1463. Misattributed in Ficino's *On the Power and Wisdom of God* to an Egyptian contemporary of the Hebrew Prophet Moses, the collection had been redacted throughout the first millennium, especially in the first through third centuries AD, and it shows the influence of late ancient Neo-Platonism and Gnosticism. Despite a lack of philosophical coherence across Hermetical texts, they share presuppositions regarding a mystical interconnectedness within the universe, a fundamental analogy between microcosm and macrocosm, and the effective powers of sympathy and antipathy linking and repelling created entities, such as human beings and the stars, through the cosmos.[65]

Figuring out the appropriate relationships between Hermes and the *Corpus hermeticum*, between the *hermetica* and Renaissance Hermeticism, and between Hermeticism and Renaissance magic still presents intricate challenges, and debates over basic questions are far from being settled.[66] For the schools of thought that impute conceptual coherence to Hermeticism and assert its distinctive influence on how magic was understood and practiced, Hermeticism shaped magic in the Renaissance in two distinct ways: the first derived from Ficino's translations of the *Corpus* and an eighteenth tract in Latin, the *Asclepius*. Ficino's colleague, as it were, was Pico della Mirandola, who proposed nine hundred theses on magic and other topics for debate in Rome in 1486, at which time he defended Neo-Platonic "natural magic" as the means to gain full insight into the nature of Creation, and thus as a real science and not magic in the traditional, condemned sense.[67] Along similar lines, Mirandola was also a strong advocate of the Kabbalah.[68] The other Hermetic tradition appealed principally to the *Emerald Tablet* and had little to do with the Corpus. Paracelsus is the chief representative of this latter tradition, and through him, alchemy became associated with the healing arts.[69]

Although the challenges taken up in magical inquiry during the Renaissance – the desire to find, understand, and manipulate hidden powers in nature – were not novel to this period, the emblematic figure undertaking these investigations, the so-called *magus*, was. He is well represented by such fascinating personalities as Ficino; Heinrich Cornelius Agrippa von Nettesheim, a German Neo-Platonist who distinguished between the manifest and occult properties of objects and argued in his *On Occult Philosophy* for the legitimacy of a natural magic derived from natural philosophy, an idea that he was influential in spreading but that he had derived largely from Ficino; and Paracelsus, a Neo-Platonic mystic who wrote extensively on medicine, alchemy, and astrology.

The critique of Renaissance thinkers, even when it is characterized by an initial sympathy toward the learned magical traditions around them, can be seen as laying the groundwork for more substantial skepticism. Pietro Pomponazzi (1462–1525) argued in his *On Incantations* against the intervention of angels and demons in the world on the Aristotelian grounds that incorporeal beings could not suspend through magic or miraculous operations the ordinary workings of the material world. Instead, he argued for a notion of celestial causality that allowed for heavenly influences on earthly events, one that human efforts could naturally influence.[70]

John Dee (1527–1608) made eclectic efforts to synthesize various forms of learned magic, especially astrology, and Hermetic philosophy in an attempt to learn the language of angels, the universal language of creation, and so to effect a pre-apocalyptic unity of human kind. Since the last century, his thinking has been considered characteristic of ways in which magic influenced the development of modern scientific thought.[71] In the fourth book of his *On the Sense of Things and on Magic*, Tommaso Campanella (1568–1639) considered natural magic. His historical approach to magic in general starts with a critique of contemporary magical practice, which he denounces as intellectually derelict and morally corrupt. Drawing from Giambattista della Porta, Campanella argued that magic is an ancient, Persian wisdom that gives insight into the real workings of the natural world, both earthly and celestial. From this, Campanella divided magic into three types: divine, natural, and deceitful. This tripartite division of magic dominated the schematic evaluation of magic offered in the learned encyclopedias of the eighteenth century, most prominently Diderot's *Encyclopédie*.[72]

Despite something of a chronological correspondence, the sixteenth-century Reformation had a different, and overall lesser, impact on learned forms of magic than the Renaissance. When differences and developments can be traced, they are related not to new theological ideas but rather to new ecclesiastical concerns about defining and distinguishing what belongs to orthodox religion, be it from a Catholic or a Protestant perspective. To be sure, Catholic rituals came under severe criticism for smacking of magical chicanery, and every side of the new confessional fissure was convinced of the inefficacy of the rites of the others (see also Chapter 13, "Magic and Priestcraft"). Yet, as has been often noted, the learned evangelical theologian Philipp Melanchthon accepted the legitimacy of much astrology, and early modern popes commissioned the drafting of horoscopes. Furthermore, the Consistory in Geneva was as eager as the Roman Inquisition to uncover and purge the church of superstition.[73]

As has been suggested earlier this chapter, the eighteenth century marks for learned magic a watershed moment on the same order as the watershed moment identified in the twelfth century, only this one marks its substantial decline rather than its burgeoning. It included a skepticism about the possibility of magic's efficacy and the rejection and replacement of the physical presuppositions that explained magical happenings. In point of fact, as far as learned magic goes, although the eighteenth century did not provide a complete break with the past and although learned magic hardly disappeared from the scene, larger intellectual movements in the seventeenth and eighteenth centuries did lead to a change in the perspective on, skepticism toward, and significant rejection of the forms of learned magic described in this chapter. Three points bear highlighting.

First, to the extent that much learned magic rested on natural philosophical presuppositions, its credibility was seriously undermined by the gradual obsolescing of Aristotelian physics and the increasing discounting of occult forces as explanations for natural causes. Astronomers, whose observations had been newly enhanced by the telescope, dealt debilitating blows to the old physics: the moons of Jupiter showed that celestial objects could revolve around points other than a single cosmic center point; the pockmarked surface of the moon gave evidence that celestial bodies were not perfect spheres; and Kepler's laws of planetary motion explained that planets moved with changing velocities and on elliptical orbits. None of this made sense in an Aristotelian cosmos.[74] The first attempt at a coherent replacement to

Aristotelian physics, mechanical philosophy, did not itself prove to be all that durable; it was key, nevertheless, in interrupting the force that had been propelling the Renaissance worldviews that accommodated natural magic. Mechanical philosophy, whose foremost exponent was René Descartes (1596–1650), took all phenomena to be explicable in terms of particles of passive matter that could be put in motion only by direct contact with another particle. By reducing the explanation of natural phenomena to mechanical causes, mechanical philosophy eliminated occult qualities – the stuff of most learned magic – from natural philosophy.[75]

A second factor contributing to the decline of learned magic, as defined in this chapter, in the seventeenth and eighteenth centuries was the appropriation of certain aspects of it into acceptable academic disciplines. Both medieval astrology and alchemy were, albeit in different ways and at different rates, much affected by this kind of transformation. The chemistry that eventually took the place of alchemy as an acceptable discipline in the early modern university was both defined over and against medieval alchemy.[76] Astrology, although in much diminished terms still practiced today, likewise bequeathed aspects of its aims, its raison d'être, and its content to proper astronomical research, even as the validity of its outright impact on human fate and personality, at least in the university, was rejected.[77]

Third, these developments were accompanied by a broader change that has famously, or notoriously, been described as the process of "disenchantment." The *Encyclopédie* entries on the forms of magic discussed in this chapter – such as Maulouin's on alchemy – all argue a similar idea: between antiquity and Diderot's own epoch, learned magic subsumed under its authority some genuinely rational and scientific activity without pursuing real causes and natural explanations. Once the rational is extracted, what remains is religious superstition and nonsensical thinking. Full consideration of "disenchantment" is, of course, beyond the scope of this chapter (although every chapter in this volume struggles with it). Two aspects of the historical process as developed by Max Weber and his disciples at the beginning of the last century and his disciples warrant highlighting: disenchantment effectively *absolutizes* the rejection of occult causation and the acceptance of discernible, comprehensible natural causation for natural phenomena and *standardizes* it across Western society, so that the skepticism toward supernatural causation and the confidence in natural causation is shared by the unskilled laborer taking the bus to work (Weber's image) and the educated elite at his desk. Later chapters in this volume call into question how absolute and standardized the disenchanted Western imagination has become.[78]

Nonetheless, when one compares learned magic in its ascendency from the twelfth to the fifteenth centuries to its status in the eighteenth century, the contrast is stark. The identifying components outlined at the beginning of this chapter and well exemplified in the person and works of Trithemius had lost their propelling force: in the very centers of learning that had cultivated the study of learned magic – the monastery, the university, and the princely court – the *magus* was now ridiculed as a charlatan, the notion of occult forces had been rejected, and the natural theories and practices had been sifted through and divided into that which had their place in learned societies and the academy and that which was dismissed as charlatanry.

Notes

1. Johannes Trithemius, *Annales Hirsaugienses* 1:608.
2. Letter 48, to Johann Virdung of Hasfurt, 20 August 1507, in Johannes Trithemius, *Opera Historica*, vol. 1, 559–560. Leo Ruickbie offers a fuller telling of the encounter and addresses the identification of Trithemius with Faustus himself in later literature: Ruickbie, *Faustus*, 39–66.
3. Martin Luther, *WA TR* 4:319 (no. 4450).
4. Brann, *Trithemius and Magical Theology*, 7; Arnold, *Trithemius*, 180–200.
5. E.g., *acquisita, docta, erudita, litteralis, litterata*, etc.
6. Astrology and necromancy are closely related to image magic and ritual magic, respectively. Astrology will be considered in a later section, as will necromancy, which is treated more thoroughly in Chapter 12. Benedek Láng has recently offered a useful set of distinctions in defining learned magic and justifying his exclusion of astronomy from consideration in his research into book culture and magic in Central Europe. Norbert Henrichs's work represents another, older, and more conceptual approach to taxonomizing kinds of magic, especially in distinguishing the licit from the illicit. Láng, *Unlocked Books*, 17–43; Henrichs, "Scientia magica," 607–624.
7. On this point I follow closely Henry, "The Fragmentation," 1–48.
8. Kieckhefer, *Magic in the Middle Ages*, 56–94.
9. Page, *Magic in Medieval Manuscripts*; Rouse and Rouse, *Manuscripts and Their Makers*, 17–97.
10. See Davies, *Grimoires*, 6–32.
11. The literature on the intellectual developments of the High Middle Ages is enormous. The notion of a twelfth-century renaissance comes from Haskins's 1927 work: Haskins, *The Renaissance of the Twelfth Century*. See also Colish, *Medieval Foundations of the Western Intellectual Tradition*, 175–182. Luscombe puts the developments in a broader context: Luscombe, "Thought and Learning," 461–498, 835–842. The specific development of the university is outlined in Verger's chapter in an edited volume that is worth referring to

as a whole: Verger, "Patterns." A sketch of the implications of the general academic and intellectual developments can be found in Bailey, *Magic and Superstition in Europe*, 77–79, 91–96; Kieckhefer, *Magic in the Middle Ages*, 116–144. On the complexity of Aristotle's contribution to the rise of learned magic and his reception by later authors, see Burnett, "Arabic, Greek, and Latin Works on Astrological Magic," 84–96. On the central importance of the translator's skill, see Burnett, "Translating Activity," 1036–1058. The last two items have conveniently been reprinted: Burnett, *Magic and Divination in the Middle Ages*. For an overview of the medieval Muslim and Jewish thought that Westerners were engaging, see Colish, *Medieval Foundations of the Western Intellectual Tradition*, 129–159.

12. The organization is adapted from Láng, *Unlocked Books*, 17–43.

13. Ibid., 36, 51–78; Thorndike, *A History of Magic*, vol. 4, 1342–1344; de Mayo, *The Demonology of William of Auvergne*, 11–90, 150–153.

14. Albertus Magnus, *Le liber de virtutibus herbarum, lapidum et animalium*. See also Sturlese, *Storia della filosofia tedesca nel Medioevo*, 124–125; Draelants, "Expérience et autorités," 89–122; Draelants and Paulmier-Foucart, "Échanges dans la societas des naturalistes," 219–238; Draelants and Sannino, "Albertinisme et hermétisme," 223–255; Láng, *Unlocked Books*, 55–58.

15. van der Lugt, "'Abominable Mixtures,'" 232–243; Page, *Magic in Medieval Manuscripts*, 49–72.

16. Kieckhefer, "The Specific Rationality of Medieval Magic," 833.

17. Klaassen, "English Manuscripts of Magic," 3–31.

18. For an analysis of the interest in magic at the courts of Frederick II and Alfonso X, see Boudet, *Entre science et nigromance*, 157–203.

19. Here we have in mind the seminal work of Bob Scribner: e.g., Scribner, "Incombustible Luther"; Scribner, "Magie und Aberglaube"; Scribner, "The Reformation, Popular Magic, and the 'Disenchantment of the World'"; Scribner, "Reformation and Desacralization."

20. Kieckhefer, *Forbidden Rites*, 1–21.

21. A critical edition and translation of the *Speculum* can be found in Zambelli, *The Speculum astronomiae and Its Enigma*, 203–273. See Klaassen, *Transformations*, 44–47; Boudet, *Entre science et nigromance*, 205–278; Hackett, "Albert the Great," 437–449; Page, *Magic in Medieval Manuscripts*, 73–92.

22. al-Majriti, *Picatrix: Un traité de magie médiéval*; al-Majriti, *Picatrix: The Latin Version of the Gāyat al-Hakīm*. See also Boudet, Caiozzo, and Weill-Parot, eds., *Images et magie*; Weill-Parot, *Les "images astrologiques" au Moyen Age*, 645–674, esp. 477–488, 643–675; Weill-Parot, "Astrology," 201–230.

23. Thābit ibn Qurrah, *The Astronomical Works of Thabit b. Qurra*. See also Carmody, *Arabic Astronomical and Astrological Sciences*, 116–128; Weill-Parot, *Les "images astrologiques" au Moyen Age*, 63–77.

24. Burnett, "Talismans," 1–15.

25. Ptolemy, *Tetrabiblos*. In 1138, Plato of Tivoli translated the Arabic version of the *Tetrabiblos* into Latin. Charles Burnett identifies nine manuscripts and five Renaissance printings of Plato's translation.

26. *Studies in History and Philosophy* dedicated its second issue in 2010 to the challenge of developing a history of astrology through the period from 1100 to 1800. Most pertinent here are: Carey, "Judicial Astrology," 90–98; Boudet, "A 'College of Astrology and Medicine'?" 99–108.

27. Weill-Parot, *Les "images astrologiques" au Moyen Age*, 223.

28. Boudet, *Entre science et nigromance*, 33–87.

29. Weill-Parot, "Astrology," 223–302. For the question of the transmission of ideas about magic more generally from late antiquity to the Renaissance, see Dasen, *Les savoirs magiques*.

30. Lindberg, *The Beginnings of Western Science*, 270–277; Rutkin, "Astrology, Natural Philosophy and the History of Science," 62; Rutkin, "Various Uses," 167–182; Rutkin, "Astrology," 541.

31. Isidore of Seville, *Etymologies* VIII.ix.13.

32. Charmasson, *Recherches sur une technique divinatoire*.

33. Delatte, *La catoptromancie grecque et ses dérivés*; Melchior-Bonnet, *The Mirror: A History*, 105, 105 n. 106, 192.

34. The Welsh mage John Dee was a prominent sixteenth-century practitioner of crystallomancy: Parry, "John Dee," 649–651; Harkness, *John Dee's Conversations*, 96–99.

35. Burnett, "Scapulimancy," vol. XII, 1–14.

36. Foerster, *Scriptores physiognomonici graeci et latini*.

37. Albertus Magnus, *Questions Concerning Aristotle's "On Animals."*

38. Resnick, *Marks of Distinction*, 13–34; Boudet, *Entre science et nigromance*, 89–117.

39. Hugh of St. Victor, *The "Didascalicon" of Hugh of St. Victor*, 154–155 (appendix B); Thomas Aquinas, *Summa theologiae* Iia–IIae 95.

40. Hartlieb, *Das Buch der verbotenen Künste*. See also Bailey, "The Disenchantment of Magic," 391; Láng, *Unlocked Books*, 123–126; Kieckhefer, *Forbidden Rites*, 33; Fürbeth, *Hartlieb*; Fürbeth, "Das Johannes Hartlieb zugeschriebene 'Buch,'" 449–479; Schnell, "Neues," 444–448.

41. Láng, *Unlocked Books*, 38, 123–143.

42. Newman, *Promethean Ambitions*, 11–33.

43. Ibn Hayyan, *Names, Natures, and Things*.

44. Geber, *The "Summa perfectionis" of Pseudo-Geber*, ed. Newman. The helpful introduction and commentary by William R. Newman that addresses the historical and textual problems involved in untangling the eighth-century Persian from the thirteenth-century Italian runs pp. 1–248.

45. Moureau, "Elixir atque fermentum," 277–325.

46. Albertus Magnus, *The Book of Minerals*; Albertus Magnus (Pseudo-), *Libellus de alchimia*. See Kibre, "Alchemical Writings Ascribed to Albertus Magnus,"

499–518; Kibre, "An Alchemical Tract Attributed to Albertus Magnus," 303–316; Kibre, "The *Alkimia minor* Ascribed to Albertus Magnus," 267–300; Kibre, "Albertus Magnus on Alchemy," 187–202.

47. DeVun, *Prophecy*, 81–89; Newman, "An Overview," 313–336.

48. Crisciani, "La *quaestio de alchimia* fra duecento e trecento," 119–168; Newman, "Technology and Alchemical Debate," 423–445.

49. A recent survey of the history of medicine addresses only in passing the tapping of occult powers for healing purposes: Hardman, *The History of Medicine*. Helpful consideration of the high medieval complexities can be found in: Rider, "Medical Magic and the Church in Thirteenth-Century England." In the later medieval and Renaissance periods: Siraisi, *History, Medicine, and the Traditions of Renaissance Learning*; Siraisi, *Medieval and Early Renaissance Medicine*. In the early modern period: French, *Medicine before Science*; Lindemann, *Medicine and Society in Early Modern Europe*; Jerry Stannard, Kay, and Stannard, eds., *Herbs and Herbalism in the Middle Ages and Renaissance*; Gijswijt-Hofstra, Marland, and de Waardt, eds., *Illness and Healing Alternatives in Western Europe*; Willem de Blécourt and Cornelie Usborne, eds., *Cultural Approaches to the History of Medicine*. See also Jacquart, "Médecine et alchimie"; Paravicini Bagliani and Santi, eds., *The Regulation of Evil*; Rigo, "From Constantinople"; DeVun, *Prophecy*, 52–79; Pereira, "Heavens on Earth," 131–144; Newman, "Technology and Alchemical Debate," 423–445. On the astrological calendar and medicine, see Carey, "What is the Folded Almanac?" 481–509.

50. E.g., Gilly and van Heertum, eds., *Magic, Alchemy and Science*; Compagni, "'Dispersa Intentio'"; Eamon, "Alchemy in Popular Culture"; Jacquart, "Médecine et alchimie"; Moran, *Distilling Knowledge*.

51. The seminal work on Paracelsus and medicine is Pagel, *Paracelsus*. More recent works include Schaffer, "The Astrological Roots of Mesmerism"; Heinz, "Die Natur als Magierin"; Webster, *Paracelsus*; Copenhaver, "Magic"; Williams and Gunnoe, eds., *Paracelsian Moments*; Webster, "Paracelsus, Paracelsianism, and the Secularization of the Worldview"; Hammond, "Paracelsus and the Boundaries of Medicine"; Webster, "Paracelsus Confronts the Saints"; Meier, *Paracelsus*.

52. Debus, ed. *Alchemy and Early Modern Chemistry*; Dobbs, *The Foundations of Newton's Alchemy*; Webster, "Paracelsus Confronts the Saints."

53. Diderot and d'Alembert, eds., *Encyclopédie*, vol. 1, 248–249.

54. Newman and Principe, *Alchemy Tried in the Fire*, 1–91, 315–320. For insight into the contemporary *status quaestionis* among historians of science, see also Newman, "What Have We Learned," 313–321, and Principe, "Alchemy Restored," 305–312.

55. Kieckhefer, *Forbidden Rites*, 1–21.

56. Boudet has pointed out that there is a tendency toward using the term "nigromancy" for ceremonies that were not condemned or that an author did not

want condemned, and "necromancy" was used more consistently as the term of opprobrium.

57. See Chapter 4.

58. Láng identifies three overlapping understandings of necromancy in the later Middle Ages: a reproving term for illicit magic, a demonic subtype of ritual magic, and the science of the hidden: Láng, *Unlocked Books*, 41–42.

59. For the relation of demonology to early modern science and theology, see Clark, *Thinking with Demons*.

60. "Ars Notoria." See also Boudet, *Entre science et nigromance*, 150–154; Klaassen, *Transformations*, 33–34; Láng, *Unlocked Books*, 89–94; Page, *Magic in Medieval Manuscripts*, 44–45.

61. White and White, *Index to the Spirits Given in 'Honourius'*; Driscoll, ed., *The Sworn Book of Honourius the Magician*; Hedegård, ed., *Liber iuratus Honorii*. See also Mathiesen, "A Thirteenth-Century Ritual to Attain the Beatific Vision," 143–162; Klaassen, *Transformations*, 4, 102–111; Fanger, *Invoking Angels*, esp. 1–35; Page, *Magic in Medieval Manuscripts*, 112–130.

62. Klaassen, *Transformations*.

63. See Chapter 4.

64. See Hadot, "Neoplatonism," 240–242. See also Armstrong, ed., *The Cambridge History of Later Greek and Early Medieval Philosophy*; Beierwaltes, *Denken des Einen*; Copenhaver, "Hermes Trismegistus," 79–110.

65. Burnett and Ryan, eds., *Magic and the Classical Tradition*; Ebeling, *Secret History*; Faivre, *The Eternal Hermes*; Hanegraaff, "Beyond the Yates Paradigm"; Paolo Lucentini, Parri, and Compagni, eds., *Hermetism*.

66. By way of contrast, compare the two following items for their opposed understandings: Compagni, "Hermetism"; Copenhaver, ed., *Hermetica*.

67. Pico della Mirandola, *Oration*; Pico della Mirandola, *Syncretism*. See also Rabin, "Unholy Astrology," 151–162.

68. Idel, "Hermetism," 389–408; Wirszubski, *Pico della Mirandola's Encounter with Jewish Mysticism*. As an issue in Europe beyond the Italian peninsula: Gilly, "Hermes oder Luther."

69. Moreschini, *Storia dell'ermetismo cristiano*; Gilly and van Heertum, *Magic, Alchemy and Science*. Kühlmann and Telle, eds., *Corpus Paracelsisticum*.

70. Pomponazzi, *De incantationibus*.

71. Clulee, "At the Crossroads of Magic and Science," 57–71; Stark, *Rhetoric, Science, and Magic in Seventeenth-Century England*.

72. Headley, *Tommaso Campanella and the Transformation of the World*; Campanella, *Del senso delle cose e della magia a cura di Germana Ernst*; Walker, *Spiritual and Demonic Magic from Ficino to Campanella*.

73. See Chapters 12 and 13. See also Bailey, *Magic and Superstition in Europe*, 193–200; Herzig, "The Demons and the Friars," 1025–1058; Westman, *The Copernican*

Question; Watt, "Calvin's Geneva," 215–244; Rutkin, "Various Uses," 167–182; Barbierato, "Magical Literature," 159–175.

74. Grant, *Planets, Stars, and Orbs*, 189–323, 488–568; Randles, *The Unmaking of the Medieval Christian Cosmos*, 1–105, 183–218.

75. Grant, *A History of Natural Philosophy*, 274–293; Eamon, "Magic and the Occult," 614–616.

76. Principe, *Chymists and Chymistry*; Newman and Principe, *Alchemy Tried in the Fire*; Principe, "Alchemy Restored," 305–312.

77. Hunter, "The Royal Society and the Decline of Magic," 103–119; Kassell, "Stars, Spirits, Signs," 67–69; Hayton, "Instruments and Demonstrations in the Astrological Curriculum," 125–134; Rutkin, "Astrology," 541–562; Donahue, "Astronomy," 562–595.

78. Green, "Two Meanings of Disenchantment: Sociological Condition vs. Philosophical Act," 51–84; Hanegraaff, "How Magic Survived," 357–380; Jenkins, "Disenchantment, Enchantment and Re-Enchantment," 11–32; Sherry, "Disenchantment," 369–386; Walsham, "The Reformation and 'The Disenchantment of the World' Reassessed," 497–528; Weber, "Scholarship as Profession," 129–156; Davies, *Grimoires*, 93–138.

Chapter 12

Diabolic Magic

MICHAEL D. BAILEY

"All superstitious arts of this sort, therefore, whether foolish or harmful, constituted through a certain pestiferous association of human beings and demons, as if by a pact of faithless and deceitful friendship, must be utterly repudiated and shunned by a Christian." So proclaimed Saint Augustine in the second book of his *De doctrina Christiana*, written around 396.[1] And so it remained for the next millennium and beyond. The great Bishop of Hippo was not the first Christian authority to associate superstitious and magical practices with demons, but he was surely the most influential, at least for the Latin West throughout the medieval and early modern periods. His discussions of demonic power and his statements about the inevitable entanglement of any human who sought to invoke or control that power with diabolical evil "as if by a pact" provided a solid foundation for most subsequent learned discourse on diabolic magic.[2] Two centuries later, the encyclopedic Isidore of Seville recapitulated Augustine almost exactly when he declared that "in all these things [magical practices] is the art of demons, arising from a certain pestiferous association of human beings and evil angels."[3] Amidst a bewildering variety of actual practices, what defined magic at a theoretical level for most Christian authorities, and what epitomized its evil, was a perceived unholy alliance between human sorcerers and the forces of hell.[4]

Yet in terms of the overall history of magic in the premodern West, many centuries were to elapse before authorities, be they intellectual, ecclesiastical, or judicial, became truly energized by the demonic menace that they were convinced lay at the heart of almost all magical practice. Often presented as an example of the relatively moderate concern of earlier centuries (when compared to the bonfires to come) and an important foundation for later skepticism are the statements in the canon *Episcopi* about the essentially illusory nature of demonic power and of human engagement with demons.[5] The first known copy of the canon appears in the early tenth-century law collection of Regino of Prüm, but medieval authorities believed that it dated from the fourth-century Council of Ancyra. It appears to consist of two separate documents fused into one. First, it exhorts bishops and their officials to eradicate the "pernicious and diabolical art of sorcery and harmful magic" from regions under their jurisdiction and to expel any practitioners of this art, male and female alike. It then recounts at much greater length the case of "certain wicked women" who believe themselves to travel at night in the train of the goddess Diana, whom they imagine that they serve. The figure of Diana is, of course, understood to be a demon, but there is no reality to these diabolical escapades, for the women are merely "seduced by illusions and phantasms."[6] A similar attitude can be found in the legislation against magical practices collected in Burchard of Worms's *Decretum*, composed around 1010, especially books 10 and 19 of this work, the latter of which is known separately as *Corrector sive medicus*. Here, in particular, statutes often condemn not so much magical actions themselves as the belief that they might have real effects, whether those effects were to harm, heal, or protect.[7]

This (somewhat) restrained view of demonic capabilities, and hence the nature of the threat represented by demonic magic, which was evident into the early 1000s, changed dramatically during the eleventh through eighteenth centuries, the era of "Old Europe." Old doubts and hesitancies never vanished entirely, but other, considerably more dramatic concerns arose and gained wide credence across much of Western Christendom. The most spectacular manifestation of those concerns, of course, was the concept of diabolical, conspiratorial witchcraft and the tens of thousands of witch trials that occurred between the fifteenth and eighteenth centuries. Hundreds of thousands of people were accused or threatened with accusation, and across the continent, probably fewer than 50,000 were executed not just for performing what was then generally conceived as terribly real, effective harmful magic (*maleficium*) but also for being sworn agents of the Devil and operatives in a covert diabolical campaign against Christian society.[8] Witchcraft and witch trials were multifaceted phenomena reflecting social, legal, political, and economic tensions, as well as both "elite" and "popular" understandings of the demonic. This chapter, however, approaches them as the major evidence for and consequence of a particular Western European view of diabolical magic, and in order to understand that aspect of the complex conglomeration that was witchcraft, we need to look back several centuries before the earliest witch hunts.

The story of Europe's mounting diabolical obsession is frequently presented as one of steadily increasing credulity and fear, and validly so. Yet through all of these centuries, there also existed enduring currents of skepticism, typically not in the basic existence of demons, but certainly in the various possibilities of demonic power. The survey offered here will therefore trace the "rise" of diabolical concerns and of witchcraft, but it will also stress ongoing tensions between concern(s) and skepticism(s). The ultimate skepticisms of the seventeenth and eighteenth centuries that ended witch hunting and contributed to the at least partial undoing of the notion of an "enchanted" world rife with materially active demonic (and divine) power will then be understood, when we encounter them, not entirely as innovative or unprecedented eruptions of the radically "modern" but rather as another phase in a long tradition of vacillating concerns and convictions about the magical and the diabolic.

New Knowledge and New Magic in the Eleventh, Twelfth, and Thirteenth Centuries

The significance of the "renaissance of the twelfth century," which really began in the eleventh century and extended into the thirteenth, on conceptions of magic in Western Europe, especially elite conceptions, is well known.[9] "New" learning flowed into the West, mainly in the form of ancient texts, some of which were rediscovered in the recesses of monastic libraries, but most of which were transmitted via the far more intellectually advanced Muslim world and complemented by the learned commentaries of generations of Muslim scholars. A number of these texts addressed magical knowledge, much of it astral or alchemical, and a significant portion also included discussion of spiritual magic, that is, rites intended to invoke and harness the power of spirit beings that Western clerical authorities inevitably identified as demons. Perhaps the best known such text, although it entered the West only late in the thirteenth century, was *Picatrix*, which dealt extensively with rites focused on astral spirits, thus blurring the lines that medieval authorities hoped to draw between varieties of magical practice.[10] Dangerous and morally disreputable as it was understood to be, magic of this sort nevertheless carried a powerful intellectual pedigree. Magicians who entangled themselves in demonic operations could no longer be dismissed as foolish *illiterati*, and the power of demons, in their hands, could not be reduced to simple trickery and illusion.

New fears of diabolical magic began to become manifest in tales set, not surprisingly, in zones of intense Christian contact with Muslim culture, namely southern Italy and Iberia. Among the more famous accounts was that concerning Gerbert of Aurillac (ca. 940–1003), later Pope Sylvester II. As a scholar, he had traveled to Spain to study and subsequently rose through the German imperial and ecclesiastical hierarchy to attain the papal throne. Within a century after his death, rumor held that Gerbert had studied diabolical sorcery in Toledo (which developed an enduring reputation as the site of a legendary school of satanic magic) and that he used his alliance with demons and the power it conferred to achieve his startling rise within the church. Other eleventh-century popes supposedly studied magic in a secret diabolical school in Rome itself.[11] As magical knowledge moved north, so did tales of shadowy demonic rites set amid the learned culture and often at the very real schools that developed in these years. In the mid-eleventh century, the rhetorician and imperial bureaucrat Anselm of Besate included vivid accounts of demonic invocation in his *Rhetorimachia*. Born at Besate, just outside Milan, he studied at the schools of northern Italy before entering the service of the German emperors, ultimately dying in the service of the Bishop of Hildesheim in the 1060s. In his major work, he constructed a rhetorical critique of his cousin Rotiland (who may or may not have actually existed) as an educated magician who was entangled with diabolical forces. In one account, for example, he related how Rotiland took a young boy outside the walls of a city – perhaps the city of Parma, where Anselm had himself studied. He buried the lad up to his waist, suffumigated him with acrid fumes, and uttered incantations involving strange, diabolical words, all as part of a spell to compel a woman to fall in love with him. Emphasizing the learned component of such magic, Anselm noted that Rotiland possessed a book of demonic magic, and, drawing an explicit connection to Muslim learning, he also accused him of sometimes performing magic in the company of a Saracen physician.[12]

A century later, in the mid-1100s, the English scholar John of Salisbury wrote in his *Policraticus* about how, when he was just a schoolboy, his teacher had involved him and another student in a ritual for conjuring demons to appear in a polished basin, or even in the boys' own fingernails made shiny with oil. Supposedly, young boys could more easily see such demonic apparitions because of their unpolluted, impressionable nature, although John saw nothing and the other boy perceived only uncertain, cloudy figures.[13] Stories such as these indicate not just a new level and locus of concern about diabolical magic, but they also point to a new type of magician taking his (and the gender here is decidedly male) place in Europe – the educated cleric who worked in, or at least in a shadowy world linked to, the great schools and later universities of the High Middle Ages, as well as the increasingly bureaucratic courts where many university-trained clerics obtained employment (Figure 12.1 illustrates

FIGURE 12.1. An illustration of magicians from an eleventh-century copy of Rabanus Maurus's *De universo*. Credit: A. M. Rosati / Art Resource, NY.

learned magicians in a courtly context). These men comprised what Richard Kieckhefer has called a "clerical underworld" of necromancy.[14]

Thus far, my account of new magical concerns has been basically anecdotal – schoolmen telling tales out of school, so to speak, but not yet addressing diabolical magic as part of their main intellectual activity. For that type of engagement with magic, we might think to look at high medieval canon law, the codification of which was certainly part of the great systematizing effort that emerged out of twelfth-century Scholasticism. The central figure here is Gratian, a scholar at the law school of Bologna in the mid-twelfth century and author of the *Decretum*, which became the fundamental basis for all subsequent canon law. Yet law, which is conservative by nature, is actually not the place to get a good view of new concerns about magic in this period.[15] The principal case that forms the basis of Causa 26, the main section of the *Decretum* that addresses magic, deals with a clerical magician, but this is not novel. Many early medieval accounts discussed village priests, who were no better educated or less superstitious than their parishioners were, succumbing to magical demonic fraud, but certainly not practicing the learned and elaborate conjurations of later schoolman-necromancers. In terms of making some statement about the nature of demonic power, the *Decretum*, like earlier legal collections, mainly reiterated the canon *Episcopi*.[16]

In the thirteenth century, however, how magic might operate by diabolical agency and how it bound or obligated a human magician to a demonic spirit became important subjects not of legal commentary but of Scholastic reflection, both philosophical and theological. The great theologian Thomas Aquinas, for example, discussed the nature and operation of demonic power at length in his famous *Summa theologiae*, as well as in other works, such as *Summa contra gentiles* and *De malo*.[17] Like most Scholastics, Aquinas set the power of demons entirely within the divinely ordered parameters of the created world. Their abilities were preternatural, in that they could manipulate aspects of that world in marvelous ways, but they were not truly supernatural, that is, exceeding the limits of natural law, like God could through a miracle. Perhaps the most famous illustration of amazing, but nonetheless naturally bounded, demonic operation came with Aquinas's parsing of how demons might impregnate human women. As spiritual entities, demons had no natural sexual capacity, and in any event, divinely ordered nature did not allow sexual generation between creatures of different species. By manipulating natural processes, however, demons could mimic sexual potency. First assuming the artificial physical form of a female succubus, a demon would have sex with a man, collecting his semen. Then, using its capacity for near-instantaneous motion, the demon would appear to a woman as a male incubus and impregnate her with the stolen semen.[18] In principle, such a notion of demonic operation harkened back to basic Augustinian thinking that a demon's main abilities lay in moving and transporting matter at great speed and in manipulating human perceptions. Aquinas and other thirteenth-century Scholastics, however, provided a more fully developed framework for thinking systematically about demonic power that became the basis for almost all subsequent demonology in the medieval and early modern eras, at least for those authorities who adhered to a basically Aristotelian tradition. They also created a fundamental intellectual problem that would haunt all later thought about diabolic magic. Namely, if demons operated only by manipulating natural processes, albeit sometimes in fantastic ways, how could authorities reliably discern demonic magic from natural occurrences, especially from possibly rare and wondrous ones?

In recognition of the possible marvelous, mysterious, and occult virtues in nature that human beings might learn to manipulate, a category of "natural magic" emerged in thirteenth-century Christian thought, which would further complicate notions of demonic magic for the remainder of the era of Old Europe. The key figure here was not Aquinas but his contemporary William of Auvergne, who was also a scholar at the University of Paris and ultimately became Bishop of Paris from 1228 until his death in 1249. Aquinas discussed aspects of what could have been conceived as natural magic, mainly astral magic purporting to manipulate natural forces emanating from the stars and planets, but he concluded that such rites were actually directed toward demonic spirits.[19] By contrast, in the early work in which he first introduced the term *magia naturalis*, William argued that many authorities were too ready to attribute to demons what could, in fact, be entirely natural operations.[20] In a later, more detailed treatment, however, he stressed that most kinds of magical practices did involve demons, and he also noted that these wicked spirits, possessing great knowledge of the physical world, might instruct humans in forms of natural magic or even manipulate occult natural forces themselves once they had been invoked by a diabolic rite.[21] Indeed, in a sense, all demonic magic was "natural," given that Scholastics maintained that demons always operated within the strictures of natural law.[22] What mattered, as it had for Augustine centuries earlier, was whether, by some magical rite, human beings could be thought to have entangled themselves with demonic forces in any way. Concern about such magic clearly grew in Paris during the thirteenth century, and in 1277, Bishop Etienne Tempier, in the course of condemning more than two hundred philosophical propositions drawn from Aristotle and his Arabic commentators, also condemned books of divination, sorcery, and demonic invocation.[23] Early in the next century, such concerns reached a crescendo not in Paris but at the papal court in Avignon.

Diabolical Concerns in the Fourteenth Century

An argument can be made that Christian demonology, including the elaborate analysis of the nature of demonic being and power, as well as hardening condemnations that human interaction with demons via invocation and conjuration necessarily entailed supplication, worship, and ultimately conspiratorial alliance, began only in the early fourteenth century and was in large measure inaugurated by Pope John XXII (1316–1334).[24] He was deeply concerned throughout his papacy with the sort of magic addressed in the previous section – learned, clerical, and demonic. Fearing magical attacks on his own person, as well as against Christian society, John ordered the prosecution, on charges of demonic invocation, of numerous clergy, including some bishops, and in 1320, he ordered the inquisitors of Carcassonne and Toulouse to direct their attention to cases of demonic invocation in magical rites.[25] Also commonly attributed to him is one of the most fundamental condemnations of diabolic magic in the Western tradition, the decretal *Super illius specula* (*Upon His Watchtower*), which was reportedly issued in 1326.[26] It excommunicated any Christian who invoked demons for magical purposes. Curiously, however, it was not registered in standard canon law collections of the time and seems to have remained essentially unknown for fifty years, until the inquisitor Nicolau Eymerich cited it as an essential legal basis for the prosecution of sorcerers in his influential handbook *Directorium inquisitorum*, which was written in 1376.[27] This has caused some scholars to question its authenticity and attribution to John. Yet, as Alain Boureau has rightly pointed out, establishing appropriate grounds to condemn demonic magicians was certainly a major and heated issue of John's papacy. In 1320, the pope assembled a commission of ten theologians and canon lawyers to consider the vexing question of whether demonic invocation automatically constituted heresy. The answer was by no means straightforward, because heresy was, by most definitions, a matter of belief and not behavior, so the question became whether certain actions, in this case magical rites deemed to be demonic, so thoroughly demonstrated illicit belief that the act itself became heretical. Although a range of opinions were advanced, the majority of the commission ultimately agreed with the pope's preferred position that demonic invocation equated to heresy, primarily because, it was determined, such invocation necessarily involved some type of devotion shown toward demons and constituted a pact involving the magician in an alliance with the Devil against God.[28]

Inquisitorial literature can help us gauge how rapidly these concerns spread outward from the papal court. As noted in the previous paragraph, Nicolau Eymerich eventually made *Super illius specula* a centerpiece of his condemnation of demonic magic in *Directorium inquisitorum*. More immediately, however, we can look to Bernard Gui, the inquisitor of Toulouse in the early 1320s, to whom John's letter directing action against demonic sorcery had been addressed. Despite the papal imperative, Gui appears not to have prosecuted any cases of sorcery personally, but other inquisitors in this region certainly did so, and Gui himself included some influential discussion of demonic magic in his 1324 manual *Practica inquisitionis*.[29] When addressing diabolism directly, he dealt mainly with the sort of magicians who troubled John, namely, learned necromancers who were often clerics, performing elaborate rites and utilizing intricate ritual objects that could be construed as demonstrating devotion to and allegiance with demons (see Figure 12.2). Yet he also included relatively simple practices of common sorcery: spells performed with herbs or basic household items in order to heal or protect from injury, divine the identity of thieves, or arouse affection or animosity between spouses.[30] Here we see a pattern that would persist throughout the rest of the fourteenth century and into the era of the first witch hunts in the early fifteenth century: authorities constructed notions of diabolic magic based mainly on elite practices but extended the diabolism they believed to be evident in such practices either tacitly or explicitly to simpler rites of common sorcery, as well.

The world of elite necromancy that authorities directly targeted in the fourteenth century was quite real, and it involved a learned tradition transmitted through texts that became well known to magistrates. Nicolau Eymerich, for example, listed several manuals of demonic magic seized from necromancers whom he had tried.[31] Whereas alchemists or practitioners of astral magic could argue that their rites drew exclusively on natural forces (a defense that authorities regularly rejected), necromancers generally admitted that their rites relied on demons. Their most common defense was that they commanded and controlled these creatures rather than being in any way subservient or bound to them. After all, Christ had promised that any faithful Christian could wield power over demons, exorcizing them in his name, and most necromancers were clergymen employing what were often quasi-liturgical rites.[32] Authorities rejected this defense, as well, often stressing the elements of necromantic magic that seemed to smack of blatant demon worship: lighting candles, burning incense, saying prayers, and even animal sacrifices and blood offerings.[33] More basically, they responded with the line of argument first

FIGURE 12.2. Medieval necromancers often employed ritual objects similar to this elaborate talisman associated with John Dee in the sixteenth century. Credit: © The Trustees of the British Museum.

advanced by John XXII and his commission: that simply to invoke a demon entailed a heretical act of worship and consecrated a pact that bound, and to some extent subjugated, the human magician to diabolical masters.[34]

Some traditions of elite learned magic claimed to invoke not demons but beneficent spirits.[35] The so-called *ars notoria*, for example, purported to bestow on its practitioners knowledge and wisdom through invocations of God, the Virgin Mary, and angels.[36] Here too, authorities dismissed such assertions, contending that practitioners of these arts, if they were not simply lying to protect themselves, were deceived about the nature of the spirits they conjured. Satan could, after all, present himself as an angel of light. Although normally, before the law, ignorance of one's crime reduced one's culpability, succumbing to demonic deception was itself a violation, both for educated clerics (who, it could be argued, should have known better) and for the common laity.

By the end of the fourteenth century, many notions regarding diabolical magic that would be manifested in the idea of witchcraft had been established. Authorities (and although I have focused on ecclesiastical authorities thus far, one could include secular officials, as well) were increasingly concerned about the materially harmful power of demons. They were convinced that most forms of magic were demonic, whether they explicitly appeared to be so or not. And they had developed a battery of arguments stating that any type of demonic invocation necessarily entailed not just engagement with but also subservience to the minions of the Devil. Nevertheless, in the late fourteenth century, such notions remained focused mainly on only one end of the social scale, with authorities worrying about educated clerical necromancers rather than simple village witches. Also still absent was the notion of demonic sorcerers operating as members of diabolical cults of the sort that inquisitorial and other officials had long imagined to characterize other forms of heresy. These final elements emerged in the fifteenth century, as the full stereotype of diabolical, conspiratorial witchcraft coalesced in Western Europe.

The Emergence of Diabolical Witchcraft

Witchcraft is many things. Most broadly, it can mean almost any kind of harmful magic (*maleficium*). It can mean magic performed mainly by women. It nearly always means magic performed in relatively simple ways (a few words, a gesture, or even a threatening glance) by people of relatively low social status. It can be imagined as magic performed as part of a vast diabolical conspiracy, with witches gathering in sometimes great numbers at terrible nocturnal assemblies where demons or the Devil himself preside, obeisance and offerings are made to them, and horrific rites of sexual depravity, murder, and cannibalism are enacted. In all of these ways except the first, witchcraft is quite different from the learned elite (and male) tradition of diabolic magic we have been tracing thus far. Although most authorities were convinced that clerical necromancers bound themselves to demons when performing magical rites, they did not imagine those necromancers as members of great cults of sorcerers, like they sometimes did with witches. In some respects, the phenomenon of witchcraft, as it was conceived in the fifteenth century, represents a return to the more typical early medieval pattern of authorities focusing their magical concerns mainly on simple, uneducated people. What carried over from the world of elite magic were ideas of demons as more actively threatening and powerful agents of physical harm than they had typically appeared to be in earlier centuries and the notion that witches were not just dupes of demonic illusion but that they deliberately surrendered themselves to Satan.

This new image of diabolic magic proved highly successful and endured for several centuries. Yet we should not imagine it being so powerful as to sweep aside all elements of skepticism. We would do well to remember that toward the end of the fifteenth century, the inquisitor Heinrich Kramer witnessed the utter collapse of a series of trials he had been conducting in Innsbruck in the face of substantial opposition and skepticism, certainly of him as a reliable and responsible prosecutor, if not of the possible existence of witches themselves. Still stinging from this defeat, he began his infamous *Malleus maleficarum* with the pronouncement that failing to believe in the existence of witches, and by extension in the intensely diabolical image of witchcraft that the *Malleus* would present, was itself a grave heresy.[37] Although the extent of such skepticism was certainly limited, especially from a modern point of view, because the acceptance and successful diffusion of the witch stereotype is an often told story, I want here at least somewhat to stress the very real, although always mitigated, degrees of skepticism that accompanied the notion of diabolical witchcraft.

As Richard Kieckhefer reminds us, we should not think of a single, coherent conception of witchcraft, at least in terms of its origin in the fifteenth century, and I would extend his caution to the entire period of the witch trials.[38] One of the remarkable facts about the emergence of Western European notions of diabolical witchcraft is just how localized their origins really were. Many of the earliest trials and the initial theoretical literature that proposed the notion of a devil-worshiping cult of maleficent sorcerers appeared in the space of only a few years in the early 1400s, and they occurred in lands that all ringed the Western Alps: present-day western Switzerland, northern Italy, and French Dauphine.[39] These were, importantly, borderland regions where different cultures (legal, linguistic, and otherwise) came into contact. A strong inquisitorial presence, particularly the Dominican inquisition based in Lausanne, overlapped with growing secular jurisdictions as city governments and territorial lords in this region sought to consolidate their power. The blurring of language is best exemplified by the various uses of the francophone term *vaudois*. The word could be applied to Waldensian heresy, to heretical or just disreputable behavior of a more general sort, or ultimately to witches. How exactly the meanings shifted is uncertain, now and probably then, as are the effects such shifts may have had on the process of accusations and trials.[40]

Having just cautioned against advancing any single stereotype of witchcraft, let me sketch at least some basic characteristics of that construct before noting some of the discrepancies and skepticisms that always pertained to it. One important, although not always essential, component of witchcraft, that was central to its diabolic character was the notion that witches operated not individually but as members of satanically orchestrated sects. This concept of cultish organization and activity underlay almost all of the other horrors of witches' "synagogues," an initial term for the imagined gatherings that later became known as "sabbaths." The conviction that witches met in groups and thus could identify one another was a major component of the mentality that supported expansive hunts as opposed to more contained individual trials. Helpfully, we can see this concept emerging in a single source. The Dominican theologian Johannes Nider's *Formicarius* (*Ant-Hill*) of 1437–1438 described groups of witches gathering at assemblies, swearing service to presiding demons, and engaging in horrible rites at their command. Yet Nider also presented several accounts of an individual witch named Staedelin who operated alone or with a single accomplice. He performed demonic *maleficium*, summoning demons and making crude offerings to them so they would carry out nefarious tasks on his behalf, but none of the other elaborate mythology of the sabbath is evident in Nider's descriptions of him. As I have argued elsewhere, he seems to represent an older view of individual diabolic sorcery at the very moment it began to give way to a new, more elaborate vision of witchcraft in the minds of authorities.[41]

As the idea of diabolical cults of witches developed, it was perhaps only natural that extreme notions derived from earlier polemics against heretical groups should be extended to witchcraft: that witches worshiped the Devil or demons at sabbaths, that they proclaimed their homage to these creatures through words and gestures, often including the ritual of the obscene kiss, that they feasted and engaged in perverse sexual orgies with demons and with each other, and that they desecrated the cross and sacraments. Pope Gregory IX had articulated such an image as early as 1233 in his decretal *Vox in Rama* when he addressed the supposed depravity of heretics, but not yet witches.[42]

The relationship of witchcraft to heresy, as opposed to or in conjunction with the history of magic and diabolism, has long been debated. In the late nineteenth and early twentieth centuries, such founding fathers of witchcraft studies as Henry Charles Lea and Joseph Hansen came to witchcraft by way of their histories of medieval inquisitions.[43] In the 1970s, when the study of witchcraft underwent a major resurgence, Jeffrey Russell argued forcefully that witchcraft emerged from medieval heresy, whereas Norman Cohn and

FIGURE 12.3. Fifteenth-century marginalia of flying witches from Martin le Franc's *Champion des dames*. Credit: Snark / Art Resource, NY.

Richard Kieckhefer tied it more to traditions of demonic magic.[44] More recently, Kathrin Utz Tremp has revisited this question, providing a detailed study of diabolic elements of heresy and how they eventually informed ideas of witchcraft in the fifteenth century.[45]

The exact image of a witches' sabbath was always contested. Among the earliest demonological sources from the 1430s, the brief, anonymous *Errores gazariorum* (*Errors of the Gazarii*; *gazarius*, like *vaudois*, being a generic term for heretic that blended with the notion of "witch" at this time) contains the most vivid description of a sabbath (here "synagogue").[46] In addition to elements mentioned already – diabolical homage, orgies, and desecration – this text recounts how witches murdered children, cannibalized their corpses, and also boiled them down to make poisons and other magical unguents, including some to smear on brooms and staves, which were then used to travel to future gatherings (see Figure 12.3). The notion that witches killed children sprang from several roots, among them various beliefs in creatures of folklore and legend, such as the *strix* or *lamia* (both later terms for witches), which were originally vampiric monsters that haunted the night.[47] Another major root of ideas of the sabbath, some scholars have argued, was a continent-wide web of belief in various forms of shamanism and mystical healing that revolved around spirit journeys. The most notable scholar here is Carlo Ginzburg, who contends that such notions comprise the principal root of the idea of the sabbath, although others have advanced similar arguments in a more moderate vein.[48]

Possible shamanistic notions of nocturnal spirit journeys intrude most obviously into stereotypes of witchcraft in the form of witches' suspected night-flight to sabbaths. But such flight was also the most broadly contested idea associated with diabolic witchcraft. Skepticism here was founded on the ancient decree of the canon *Episcopi* (five hundred years old by the early fifteenth century and believed by ecclesiastical authorities to be more than a thousand years old), which declared in no uncertain terms that nocturnal journeys in the service of a demon were pure illusion. This did not obviate the crime – swearing oneself to Satan's service was just as severe a transgression whether it was done in the flesh or only in the mind. Still, if flight, and hence the sabbath itself, was purely illusory, this raised serious questions about the sexual congress, murder of children, and other activities that supposedly took place.[49] Some authors were content to leave nocturnal travels to the realm of erroneous imagination. Johannes Nider, for example, presented a supposedly contemporary account that echoed the canon *Episcopi*. A Dominican friar, he related, once observed an old woman who claimed that she flew with Diana. To do so, she slathered herself with ointments and entered a trance while perched in a large pasta bowl balanced on a stool. Although she thrashed about under the force of her delusion, physically she never traveled any farther than the serious tumble she took from her perch to the floor in the course of her gyrations.[50] Another approach was to argue that *Episcopi* pertained to a much earlier era and had no bearing on the "new sect" of witches that was believed to manifest in the fifteenth and subsequent centuries. The strongest early voice here was that of the Dominican inquisitor Nicolas Jacquier in his *Flagellum haereticorum fascinariorum*, which was written in 1458.[51] Almost thirty years later, Heinrich Kramer had his cake and ate it, too, reporting the supposed testimony of a witch who confessed that sometimes she journeyed to the sabbath in the flesh, but when this was inconvenient for her she could also travel there in spirit, in the form of a blue vapor that emitted from her mouth while she slept.[52]

The reality of flight, and of the sabbath, remained an open question throughout the sixteenth, seventeenth, and eighteenth centuries. In addition to being a matter of considerable skepticism itself, it provided an obvious point of departure for any skeptic who sought to challenge the possibility of effective demonic power in the physical world more generally (we will encounter examples of that sort of skepticism later in the chapter). The debate around flight also provides an excellent illustration of the mixed nature of the concept of diabolical witchcraft. Although in part it revolved around purely intellectual issues – the accepted potentials of demonic power, for example, or the degree of authority ceded to a centuries-old legal document – the issue was never one of purely abstract Scholastic debate. Depending on their own inclinations, church inquisitors and lay magistrates either reluctantly accommodated or actively sought out the testimony of people who, whether because of some shamanistically tinged experience or because of the threat of torture or because of some other reason entirely, admitted to encountering demons, flying with them, or having sex with them in real physical terms. The power balance in these interactions was, of course, massively unequal, but we would be wrong to think that certain ideas that became constituent of witchcraft never flowed up from popular or common belief to the level of the legal and intellectual authorities or that authorities simply overlaid their own demonological conceptions and concerns onto a body of more popular or common belief that had to do only with healing, harming, and magical protection. Although the heavy framework of diabolism that came to envelope witchcraft was undoubtedly primarily a construct of educated elites reading their own and earlier demonological works, all the way back to the foundational pronouncements of Augustine, nevertheless, in this as in every other aspect of its complicated and variable structure, witchcraft emerged not solely by means of authoritative pronouncement but also through discourse and debate that drew on ideas from a multitude of sources.

Diabolic Magic in an Age of Witch Hunts

If the concept of witchcraft is multifaceted and mutable, with even its overtly diabolic elements emerging from a number of traditions – earlier notions of diabolic magic, certainly, but also ideas about demonically inspired heresy and a broad but diffuse gamut of folkloric beliefs in spirit travel, spirit beings, and so forth – what are we to make of the witch hunts themselves as expressions of concern over the diabolic? Scholars have long identified intense, specifically Christian, diabolism as the principal element that distinguishes the historical Western European notion of witchcraft from conceptions of malevolent magicians who might be called witches elsewhere in the world, and as was noted earlier in the chapter, these diabolic fears and conceptions of satanic cults stoked the flames that allowed more contained and limited trials to expand into full-fledged hunts.[53] But major hunts, which were capable of claiming hundreds or even thousands of victims, were always sporadic and localized, even at the absolute height of Europe's trials in the late sixteenth and early seventeenth centuries. They also tended to be clustered in lands of the German Empire, especially in the politically fragmented western regions of the empire, the zone of diverse territories (not all of them Germanophone) stretching from the Western Alps up the "Lotharingian corridor" to the Low Countries.[54] Everywhere major hunts occurred, they did so because multiple factors converged – political, legal, economic, and social, as well as some basic underlying fear of diabolical agents being loose in Christian society – to create the particular circumstances that allowed accusations and trials to spiral out of control.

Below the level of major hunts, among the individual trials or small clusters that comprised much of Europe's "witch hunt," again multiple factors always had to converge, and overt diabolism often appears to have played a relatively minor role. The most essential root of individual suspicions, and ultimately accusations, leading to a trial was the conviction that *maleficium* had been performed – animals had sickened, crops had withered, or children had been injured or taken ill. All of these things could, of course, happen quite naturally, so there had to be something (almost anything, if suspicion already ran high enough) that marked the harm or misfortune as particularly sudden or strange. Those suspected of causing such harm were typically neighbors, even family members, and so accusations, when they finally came, were generally heavily loaded with all of the various intense animosities and tensions that split small, tightly knit societies: conflicts about property, inheritance, charity, good motherhood, sexuality, and proper gender roles, to name only a few.[55] In all of this, diabolic concerns figure lightly, if at all. If there was any one element that might be said to have been overriding (or underlying), it would likely be fertility and all of the multifarious anxieties that revolved around maintaining precarious human, animal, and agricultural reproduction in this era.[56] This very basic fear of witchcraft as an assault on fertility and hence on the continued survival of society itself did, however, loop back into notions of witches as diabolical agents, and tracts and treatises on the subject are replete with images of demons instructing witches to kill children, impede conception, and steal crops or blast them with thunderstorms or hail.

The relationship of witchcraft to gender, which is a central concern in much modern scholarship, also illustrates the complex place of diabolism within processes of suspicion and accusation. Witches were predominantly women;

that is, women were generally suspected, accused, tried, and convicted of this crime at substantially higher rates than men were, and depictions of witches typically show women, often in a highly sexualized way (see Figure 12.4). Nowhere was witchcraft an exclusively female crime, and in some regions, such as Normandy or remote Iceland, the majority of witches were men.[57] Yet across Europe, roughly three out of every four victims of witch trials were women. As with every other major aspect of witchcraft, multiple factors interwove to produce this preponderance. Women were generally more legally vulnerable than men were, especially widows or the unmarried. Women who were not under the control of some immediate male family member raised concerns about supposedly unrestrained female sexuality. Unmarried daughters could be an economic burden on their families, particularly as they aged, and women who had married but were then widowed could obstruct (ideally patrilineal) inheritance patters. Ingrained cultural beliefs about both women and magic also played a significant role, insofar as a great deal of witchcraft (harmful magic that often affected fertility) was associated with areas of predominantly female activity: childbirth, the care of sick children, food preparation (with attendant possibilities for poisoning), and so forth.[58]

Demonologists and other elite authorities had definite ideas about why witches tended to be women, and those ideas derived from their view of witchcraft as an intensely diabolic practice. Weaker than men physically, mentally, and spiritually, women were more vulnerable to outright demonic assaults, such as possession, and also more susceptible to the alluring wiles of demonic temptation. Among witchcraft theorists, the Dominican Johannes Nider first articulated such an argument in the early fifteenth century, and toward century's end, Heinrich Kramer expanded upon it significantly in *Malleus maleficarum*.[59] As Stuart Clark has rightly cautioned, however, among demonological authors, Kramer was singularly gender-obsessed, and most theoretical literature treats witchcraft's strongly gendered character only slightly, if at all.[60] This is not to say that gender and sex – especially sex with demons – did not enter into the thinking of the male authors of these treatises,[61] but it was not typically at the forefront of their stated concerns, as it so clearly was in the *Malleus*. In fact, there is some reason to believe that early witchcraft theorists may have hesitated slightly before accepting the predominance of women suspected and accused of witchcraft in the course of the trials. The image of the wicked female sorceress was of course deeply rooted in medieval traditions, and it rested on venerable classical antecedents. Yet prior to the fifteenth century, when authorities had thought seriously about diabolic magic, they had thought primarily of male necromancers. In the dialogue of his *Formicarius*,

FIGURE 12.4. Hans Baldung Grien, *Witches' Sabbath*, 1510. Credit: © The Trustees of the British Museum.

Johannes Nider had the character of a befuddled student express surprise that women, too, were capable of such powerful and terrible magic, and this may have been more than a rhetorical device allowing Nider to launch into his explanation for why witches were predominantly women.[62] Throughout the period of the trials, the predominance of women as witches (where they did predominate) seems to have been more a matter of popular consensus than an imposition of elite demonology.

In a broad sense, demonology and conceptions of diabolic magic underwent relatively little change during the period of the witch trials, and such change as there was related only tangentially to witchcraft. Theories of witchcraft, like notions of diabolic necromancy before them, were based firmly in Scholastic, Aristotelian thought. Yet even as stereotypes of diabolic witchcraft were coalescing in the fifteenth century, rival intellectual systems grounded in Neo-Platonism were on the rise in Italy, offering new perspectives on old questions about the nature and power of demons and other spirit entities. "Renaissance magic" is a vague category, but in general it may refer to learned systems of magic grounded in new modes of thought that emerged initially out of Italy. Such magic was frequently aimed at attaining knowledge or some sort of spiritual or intellectual elevation on the part of the practitioner, although it could certainly also be intended to achieve more practical ends, whether those were to heal, protect, or divine the future.[63] Pope Urban VIII had the *magus* Tommaso Campanella transferred from an inquisitorial prison in Naples to Rome in 1626, for example, so that he could serve the pontiff as an astrologer and magician, performing rites to protect the pope from inimical magical or astral forces.[64]

Recent scholarship has pointed to the limitations of any notion of absolutely distinct "Renaissance magic."[65] Recognizing that some medieval mages also attempted to summon angels or benevolent spirits to achieve personal edification or elevation or claimed that their rites drew exclusively on natural forces, we should undoubtedly see the elite spiritual and natural magic of the fifteenth and sixteenth centuries as building on certain thirteenth- and fourteenth-century developments, just as conceptions of witchcraft did. Yet in the era of the trials, this elite magic and witchcraft largely diverged. The greatest connection between them was the concern many learned mages felt that they might be linked to or condemned as witches. True, sometimes humanist intellectuals opposed witch trials, but they usually did so by focusing on procedures or evidence, not by voicing any broad objections to the basic demonology on which the idea of diabolic witchcraft rested. Famously in 1519, the German humanist and occultist Cornelius Agrippa, who was then civic orator in Metz, defended a woman accused of witchcraft by the local Dominican inquisitor, arguing that she was old and senile, not a sworn agent of Satan. But in his major work *De occulta philosophia*, although he rather daringly blurred the lines between purely natural and demonic magic, he also strove to separate elite magic from the diabolic practices associated with witches.[66] Nevertheless, he was plagued by suspicions of him being a diabolical sorcerer all his life, and after his death, he became a likely model for the developing Faust legend (there was also an actual Faust who lived at roughly the same time).[67]

The other classic historiographic watershed of this period, the Reformation, produced no substantial change in demonology or conceptions of diabolic witchcraft whatsoever. Protestant authorities conceptualized and condemned witchcraft in almost exactly the same terms as Catholics did, although Catholicism allowed for certain means of defense against witchcraft via the power of church rituals and sacramental items, which Protestantism denied. Condemnation of witchcraft was closely tied to Reformist concerns among all Christian confessions in this period, primarily through efforts to promote greater piety while stamping out superstition among the laity.[68] The inter- and intra-confessional strife of the Reformation era certainly also contributed to a range of other factors that promoted witch hunting, such as social tension, political uncertainty, and even economic privations. But religion per se was not a primary factor determining whether a given prince, magistrate, or court pursued witches intensely or with lenience. Most of the so-called German superhunts, for example, occurred in the territories of Catholic prince-bishops or in mini-states controlled by individual monastic houses.[69] Yet at the other end of the spectrum, such aggressively Counter-Reformation institutions as the Roman and Spanish inquisitions prosecuted very few witches.[70] Such variance stemmed from differences in the juridical and bureaucratic structures of these courts, not from any fundamental disagreement about the nature of the diabolic threat that witches represented. Similar comparisons could be developed for Protestant jurisdictions. In general (although of course not always), larger, more bureaucratic, and more professional courts tended to inhibit prosecutions for witchcraft by an insistence on strict rules of evidence and procedure.[71]

All of this calls into question how central diabolic aspects of witchcraft really were to actual dynamics of witch hunting or to the functioning of witchcraft beliefs within society in general. On the one hand, the perceived relationship between witches and the Devil, which was broadly believed across Europe, was, along with the basic practice of *maleficium*, one of the two fundamental components of what "witchcraft" usually meant in the period of the trials.[72]

On the other hand, the ways in which diabolism interacted with and influenced all of the other factors that shaped beliefs, concerns, and ultimately trials varied dramatically from region to region and across more than two centuries. In some times and places, diabolic fears loomed large, whereas in others, they were muted or virtually nonexistent. England, for example, has typically been seen as more resistant to the "cumulative concept" of witchcraft, including the more intense diabolism of "continental" demonology.[73] Yet, there in fact never was any continental norm, and numerous regions throughout Europe proved resistant to severe diabolic concerns, at least as reflected in the dynamics of their trials.

Several decades ago, Richard Kieckhefer argued that, at least in early trials, diabolism was primarily an elite concern that magistrates imposed on accusations having to do mainly with *maleficium,* and this observation has been frequently confirmed.[74] People who believed themselves afflicted by witchcraft generally focused on the harm done to them and how it might be alleviated – which could well involve having recourse to a cunning person, magical healer, even to the witch herself – rather than making a formal accusation in some court. Once a case entered the courts, however, magistrates familiar with learned demonology began to inquire about cults, sabbaths, and other diabolic elements. This picture must be nuanced in two ways, however. First, as has already been touched on in this chapter, although diabolism may not have been the primary practical concern that drove people to bring formal charges of witchcraft against their neighbors, that does not mean that common images of witchcraft were not infused with diabolic elements, either learned from authorities through such mechanisms as sermons, popular broadsheet literature, or even the process of the trials themselves or stemming from widely held folkloric beliefs. Second, not all magistrates were equally obsessed with the diabolic. In reality, every official had his own level of concern or, alternately phrased, his own degree of skepticism about the clear and present danger of the diabolic. In general terms, we can say that the higher up in any court system a case went (and, hence, assumedly the more trained and expert the judges), the less the likelihood that a trial would be affected by rampant diabolic fears. This was not because more educated magistrates were skeptical about basic demonology, but because they tended to question the means by which the diabolic aspects of witchcraft could be proven legally. The "evidence" for sabbaths was inevitably the testimony of other witches or of the accused herself, often extracted under torture or threat of torture. Rather, mid-level courts, which were staffed by educated jurists but still able to be affected by potentially explosive local concerns, may have been the most likely to fixate on diabolic elements in witchcraft trials. Once again, we confront the inherently mixed nature of witchcraft, particularly regarding its diabolical components.

Skepticism about Diabolic Magic

"Skepticism" and "decline" are often linked terms in witchcraft historiography. As I have tried to illustrate throughout this chapter, however, various degrees of skepticism about certain components of witchcraft actually manifested in every period and form a continuous component of the history of this topic. Moreover, as suggested earlier in the chapter (and as is well known to experts), nothing like complete skepticism about the entire construct of diabolic witchcraft was necessary to restrict or reduce the number of trials. One often-drawn contrast is that made between full skepticism and a more limited "judicial" sort, which focused on doubts about the validity of evidence and procedure in the trials.[75] In broad terms, judicial skepticism took root first, being fairly firmly established (although, as with every aspect of the history of witchcraft, by no means universally accepted and applied to different degrees in different jurisdictions) in the early seventeenth century. Fundamental skepticism about the power of demons and the basic possibility of demonic *maleficium* became widely accepted only in the eighteenth century.[76] Yet in more precise terms, the two skepticisms cannot be neatly isolated from one another. Although they achieved greater levels of acceptance at different times, they actually developed alongside one another. Moreover, it is fair to assume that most authorities who tended to oppose judicial skepticism, arguing that witchcraft was a *crimen exceptum* (an exceptional crime to which normal judicial restraints, rules of evidence, restrictions on torture, and so forth could not be allowed to apply), did so because of the exceptional fear generated by the notion of witches as both powerful malefactors and sworn agents of Satan. Conversely, authorities who upheld various forms of judicial skepticism were self-evidently less inclined to cast aside established rules of procedure even in the face of a (perceived) monstrous threat, although whether that also means they were to any degree more skeptical about the scope or reality of that threat is another matter.

As we have seen, some degree of doubt about the nature and extent of demonic power, and hence about the severity of diabolic threat, was actually the earlier form of skepticism, as it was encoded in the canon *Episcopi* and in many early medieval legal condemnations of magic. As Scholastic theories of magic and demonology developed in the twelfth and thirteenth centuries, they also spawned certain forms of skepticism about the potentialities of demonic power. William of Auvergne, especially, developed the notion of natural magic and at least initially warned that most other authorities were too eager to attribute to demons what were likely entirely natural operations, although he subsequently mitigated his own "skepticism" on this point somewhat. That demons were largely powerless and that most magic was either natural or simply unreal was never a widely appreciated position in the fourteenth and fifteenth centuries, yet there were some powerful voices that articulated just that sort of skepticism. Possibly the greatest was the French schoolman Nicole Oresme, who, writing in the decades after 1350, advanced the position that demons essentially did not interfere in the physical world in any way.[77] In the fifteenth century, as stereotypes of diabolic witchcraft coalesced, many authorities were skeptical at least of certain elements of those stereotypes, above all the physical reality of flight and the sabbath. Judicial skepticism also began to manifest with the earliest witch trials. The bishop of Brixen who opposed the trials at Innsbruck in 1485, for example, did not question the possibility of demonic menace, but he did doubt the capacity of Heinrich Kramer to identify and prosecute witches responsibly, ultimately calling the inquisitor senile and banishing him from his diocese (admittedly a rather ad hominem form of skepticism).[78]

Beginning in the fifteenth century and continuing into the sixteenth, a number of humanist thinkers became opponents of witch trials. Some challenged certain aspects of Scholastic demonology upon which notions of diabolic magic rested, but they also frequently objected to the extreme and (in their view) excessive nature of witchcraft prosecutions. In 1515, for example, the Milanese jurist Andrea Alciati labeled the hunts developing in northern Italy a "new holocaust."[79] Other major intellectual figures, such as Erasmus and, as we have seen, Cornelius Agrippa, challenged various aspects of witch trials, casting doubt on procedures and questioning the degree to which the often poor old women targeted as witches were actually entangled with demonic forces as opposed to being merely deluded and confused. Agrippa's student Johann Weyer, the court physician to the duke of Cleves, is often considered the first truly major skeptical authority, having published the treatise *De praestigiis daemonum* (*On the Deceptive Illusions of Demons*) in 1563. His attack on witchcraft, and the forms of skepticism underlying it, took various forms. Theologically, he did not deny the power of demons in the physical world, but he did question why they would choose to act through human agents rather than exercise their power directly. He also subverted the notion of the pact whereby powerful demonic agents supposedly submitted to apparent human control. To explain why so many accused witches themselves believed they were in league with Satan, he turned to medical explanations – they were sick, senile, or deluded.[80]

In 1584, the Englishman Reginald Scot published his *Discoverie of Witchcraft*, frequently hailed as the first radically skeptical work in the Western European demonological tradition, in which he denied the reality of any spiritual operations in the physical world and, hence, any real possibility for diabolic magic.[81] As we have seen in this chapter, Scot was not the first thinker to assert that degree of skepticism about spiritual operations in the world. Nicole Oresme had done so more than two centuries earlier, although there is no evidence that Scot had read Oresme.[82] The Englishman was the first, however, to make such skepticism the foundation of a sustained attack on witchcraft and witch trials, and in this he was still too precocious – his book was banned and his ideas would not gain widespread acceptance for more than a century. More successful was the German Jesuit Friedrich Spee, who published (anonymously) his *Cautio criminalis* in 1631. This work was a landmark of judicial skepticism, lambasting the severity and procedural iniquities of witch trials, particularly the unrestricted use of torture. Some modern scholars have suggested that Spee's own skepticism ran deeper, to a rejection of the reality of witchcraft rather than just a criticism of trial procedures. His tactic of more limited critique was successful, however. Although the book sparked some controversy, it found a sympathetic audience almost immediately.[83] By the end of the seventeenth century, European intellectuals were ready for a full rejection of diabolic witchcraft. This came in the form of the Dutchman Balthasar Bekker's *De betoverde weereld*, published in four volumes in the early 1690s (see Figure 12.5). His rejection of any real demonic operations in the world was based at least in part on the new philosophy of Cartesian rationalism, which imposed a sharp separation between the worlds of matter and mind or spirit.[84] The book was banned in some places, and Bekker was tried for blasphemy and stripped of his ministerial position, because his arguments applied equally to divine as well as diabolic power operating in the world. But the time for such skepticism had clearly come, and his ideas would carry the day in the coming century.

Thus told, the spread of opposition to witch hunting and skepticism about the reality of witchcraft appears to be a relatively straightforward story. Any simple, teleological narrative of intellectual progress culminating in "modern rationality" will be deceptive, however. Given that belief in diabolic witchcraft and magic did decline precipitously in the eighteenth century, at least among intellectual and political elites, there is a tendency to view the great skeptics

DE
BETOVERDE
WEERELD,
Zynde een
GRONDIG ONDERSOEK
Van 't gemeen gevoelen aangaande de GEESTEN, derselver
Aart en Vermogen, Bewind en Bedryf: als ook 't gene de
Menschen door derselver kraght en gemeenschap doen

In vier Boeken ondernomen

Van

BALTHASAR BEKKER S. T. D.
Predikant tot Amsterdam.

t'AMSTERDAM,
By DANIEL VAN DEN DALEN
Boekverkoper op 't Rockin / bezijden de Beurs. 1691.

FIGURE 12.5. Title page of Bekker's *Betoverde Weereld*.

of earlier periods, clear back to Oresme in the fourteenth century, as bold
harbingers of modern thought and daring rebels ahead of their times. In fact,
however, although their positions could be radical and extreme, they all operated within the skeptical possibilities of their own eras. Such possibilities had
always existed, not as some entirely external challenges to ideas of diabolic
magic, but as parts of those very systems of thought. A major illustration of

this point is the relation of the scientific revolution to belief in diabolic magic and witchcraft. The old whiggish paradigm would tell us that as "modern scientific thinking" developed in the seventeenth century, it clashed with and ultimately conquered those premodern, superstitious systems of thought that gave rise to diabolic magic and witchcraft. In fact, early science and witchcraft theory developed side by side, and they were just as capable of supporting as of conflicting with one another.[85] In 1681, only a decade before Bekker's *De betoverde weereld*, Joseph Glanvill's *Saducismus triumphatus* advanced a powerful defense of spiritual forces and diabolic witchcraft grounded in the most current scientific thought.[86]

The significance of the great works of skepticism, with their neatly ordered publication dates, in terms of charting waning concern over diabolic magic and witchcraft is hard to say. Many major jurisdictions were already curtailing witch trials in the early seventeenth century. The Parlement of Paris, for example, executed its last witch in 1623, and the famously tolerant Dutch Republic did so in 1609.[87] But neither do the dates of "last executions" or "last trials" in any given region always correlate securely to a moment of major decline in concern. The Spanish Inquisition, for example, had always kept fairly good control over trials, and in 1623, its central council had ordered all tribunals to adhere to strict guidelines that made capital convictions extremely rare. Nevertheless, the last execution in Spain came in 1781, and the final trial was held in 1820, among the latest in all of Europe.[88] In general, though, across much of the continent, trials were already being restricted to a significant degree and authorities were becoming intent on stamping down, rather than fanning, diabolical concerns by the time that what is often meant by "skepticism toward witchcraft" took major hold.

What that decline indicates, I suggest, is the importance of less spectacular but more practically effective varieties of skepticism about diabolic magic. Doubts always existed about the possible extent of demonic powers, and about how likely it might be that this or that person had actually become entangled with diabolic forces in the manner described by the most extreme visions of sabbaths and necromantic ceremonies. Rarely rising to the level of complete disbelief in diabolic magic or witchcraft per se, they were nevertheless surely a major factor in restraining concern over witchcraft and the ruthless hunting of witches. We have the examples of truly out-of-control hunts to remind us just how deadly the matrix of beliefs centered around diabolic magic could be. Yet we will understand those beliefs more fully if we focus not just on the obvious credulities but also on the constant skepticisms that accompany the entire history of diabolic magic.

In most regions of Europe, witch trials ended mainly in the seventeenth century, and in the course of the eighteenth, most elite authorities came to deride any notion of direct demonic action in the physical world, and hence of any "real" diabolic magic. Yet not all belief in magic and certainly not in the real existence and power of the Devil vanished as Europe entered its modern era. The curtain does not come down entirely on diabolic magic, therefore, as we pass the boundary year of 1800. Instead, we enter another era of its long history.

Notes

1. *De doctrina Christiana* 2.23(36), ed. Martin, 58: "Omnes igitur artes huiusmodi uel nugatoriae uel noxiae superstitionis ex quadam pestifera societate hominum et daemonum quasi pacta infidelis et dolosae amicitiae constituta penitus sunt repudianda et fugienda christiano." Unless otherwise noted, all translations are my own.

2. Aside from *De doctrina Christiana*, see Augustine, *De divinatione daemonum*, and *De civitate dei* (esp. books 8–10).

3. Isidore, *Etymologiarum sive originum libri XX* 8.9.31, ed. Lindsay, 2 vols., n.p.: "In quibus omnibus ars daemonum est ex quadam pestifera societate hominum et angelorum malorum exorta."

4. Kieckhefer, "The Specific Rationality of Medieval Magic," 813–836. For a valuable discussion of how central diabolism should be to investigations of European magic and witchcraft, see Midelfort, "Witch Craze?" and Kivelson, "Lethal Convictions," 11–33 and 34–61, respectively.

5. See Tschacher, "Der Flug durch die Luft," 225–276; Ostorero, *Le diable au sabbat*, 574–617.

6. Hansen, ed., *Quellen und Untersuchungen*, 38–39.

7. Burchard of Worms, *Decretorum libri viginti*, ed. Migne, esp. cols. 831–854, 951–976.

8. Levack, *The Witch-Hunt in Early Modern Europe*, 20–24, estimates 45,000 total executions. Monter, "Witch Trials in Continental Europe," 13, estimates 40,000 executions. Behringer, *Witches and Witch-Hunts*, 149, estimates 50,000 executions.

9. Kieckhefer, *Magic in the Middle Ages*, 117–119; Peters, *The Magician, the Witch*, 63.

10. Pingree, ed., *Picatrix*.

11. Peters, *The Magician, the Witch*, 28; Kieckhefer, *Magic in the Middle Ages*, 143–144.

12. Analysis and edited portions of text in Manitius, "Magie und Rhetorik bei Anselm von Besate," 52–72; see also Peters, *The Magician, the Witch*, 21–28.

13. John of Salisbury, *Policraticus* 2.28, ed. Keats-Rohan, 167–168.

14. Kieckhefer, *Magic in the Middle Ages*, 153.

15. For a survey into later periods, see Hersperger, *Kirche, Magie, und "Aberglaube."*

16. Gratian, *Decretum*, causa 26, q. 5 c. 12; *Corpus Iuris Canonici*, ed. Friedberg, vol. 1, 1030–1031.

17. See Linsenmann, *Die Magie bei Thomas von Aquin*.

18. Aquinas, *Summa theologiae* 1.51.3.

19. Aquinas, *Summa contra gentiles* 3.104–3.106.

20. William of Auvergne, *De legibus* 24, in *Opera omnia*, 67. On this as the first usage of *magia naturalis*, see Boudet, *Entre science et nigromance*, 128.

21. William of Auvergne, *De universo* 2.3.22, in *Opera omnia*, 998–1000. On William as a demonologist, see de Mayo, *The Demonology of William of Auvergne*.

22. The term *magia naturalis*, however, always meant non-demonic magic in Scholastic usage.

23. Piché, ed., *La condamnation parisienne de 1277*. See Peters, *The Magician, the Witch*, 90–91; Boudet, *Entre science et nigromance*, 251–258.

24. Boureau, *Satan the Heretic*, esp. 8–42.

25. On John's positions regarding magic in general, see Cohn, *Europe's Inner Demons*, 130–133; Peters, *The Magician, the Witch*, 129–133. For a sympathetic reading of John's concerns, see Decker, *Witchcraft and the Papacy*, 23–31. His letter to the inquisitors of Carcassonne and Toulouse is in Hansen, *Quellen und Untersuchungen*, 4–5.

26. Hansen, *Quellen und Untersuchungen*, 5–6. The title phrase likely refers to Isaiah 21:8–21:9, in which a sentry observes approaching horsemen proclaiming the fall of Babylon and the destruction of that city's demonic idols.

27. Eymerich, *Directorium inquisitorum* 2.43.9, ed. Peña, 341–342. See comment in Peters, *The Magician, the Witch*, 132–133; Boureau, *Satan the Heretic*, 12–14.

28. In addition to Boureau, *Satan the Heretic*, 43–67, see Boureau, *Le pape et les sorciers*. For another interpretation, see Iribarren, "From Black Magic to Heresy," 32–60.

29. Bailey, "From Sorcery to Witchcraft," 967–971.

30. Gui, *Practica inquisitionis heretice pravitatis* 5.6.2, ed. Douais, 292–293.

31. Eymerich, *Directorium inquisitorum* 2.43.1, ed. Peña, 338.

32. On necromantic practice, see Kieckhefer, *Forbidden Rites*.

33. Eymerich, *Directorium inquisitorum* 2.43.3, ed. Peña, 338.

34. Eymerich, *Directorium inquisitorum* 2.43.14, ed. Peña, 344.

35. On various types of medieval spirit magic, see Fanger, "Introduction," in *Conjuring Spirits*, esp. vii–ix, as well as several other essays in that volume; see also Veenstra, "Venerating and Conjuring Angels," 119–134.

36. Véronèse, *L'ars notoria au Moyen Âge*.

37. Kramer, *Malleus maleficarum* 1.1, ed. and trans. Mackay, vol. 1, 217. On the failed hunt, see Kieckhefer, "Magic at Innsbruck," 11–29.

38. Kieckhefer, "Mythologies of Witchcraft in the Fifteenth Century," 79–108.

39. These trials and literature have been studied extensively by historians working in Lausanne. For an overview, see Utz Tremp, "Witches' Brooms and Magic Ointments," 173–187.

40. Utz Tremp, *Von der Häresie zur Hexerei*, 441–447; Behringer, "How Waldensians Became Witches," 155–192.

41. Bailey, "From Sorcery to Witchcraft," 981–983; Bailey, *Battling Demons*, esp. 43–45.

42. Kors and Peters, eds., *Witchcraft in Europe 400–1700*, 114–116.

43. Lea, *A History of the Inquisition of the Middle Ages*; Hansen, *Zauberwahn, Inquisition, und Hexenprozesse*.

44. Russell, *Witchcraft in the Middle Ages*; Cohn, *Europe's Inner Demons*; Kieckhefer, *European Witch Trials*.

45. Utz Tremp, *Von der Häresie zur Hexerei*.

46. Edited in Ostorero, Paravicini Bagliani, and Utz Tremp, eds., *L'imaginaire du sabbat*, 267–353. One version of the text, which is misdated, is also in Hansen, *Quellen und Untersuchungen*, 118–122.

47. Kieckhefer, "Avenging the Blood of Children," 91–110.

48. Ginzburg, *Ecstasies: Deciphering the Witches' Sabbath*. For other positions and an overview of current debates, see the special forum on "Shamanism and Witchcraft" in *Magic, Ritual, and Witchcraft*, 207–241.

49. See Ostorero, *Le diable au sabbat*, 571–720.

50. Nider, *Formicarius* 2.4, in *L'imaginaire du sabbat*, ed. Ostorero, 134–136.

51. See esp. ch. 7 of Jacquier, *Flagellum*, 36–51: "De differentia inter sectam et haeresim fascinariorum modernorum et illusionem mulierum de quibus loquitus c. Episcopi".

52. Kramer, *Malleus* 2.1.3, ed. and trans. Mackay, 410.

53. On witchcraft and witch hunting in a global context, see Behringer, *Witches and Witch-Hunts*, esp. 3–4, 8–9.

54. Behringer, *Witches and Witch-Hunts*, 105, maps major "hot-spots" of witch hunting. For an overview of the German *Sonderweg*, see Monter, "Witch Trials in Continental Europe," 16–29.

55. A good introduction to witchcraft at this level is Briggs, *Witches and Neighbors*.

56. Roper, *Witch Craze*.

57. On the phenomenon of male witches, which is now beginning to receive serious scholarly attention, see Schulte, *Hexenmeister*; Apps and Gow, *Male Witches in Early Modern Europe*; Rowlands, ed., *Witchcraft and Masculinities in Early Modern Europe*.

58. See Roper, *Witch Craze*; Willis, *Malevolent Nurture*; Karlsen, *The Devil in the Shape of a Woman*.

59. On Nider, see Bailey, "The Feminization of Magic," 120–134. Kramer's misogyny has been the focus of much study, but there is no definitive account. See variously Broedel, *The Malleus Maleficarum and the Construction of Witchcraft*, 167–184; Herzig, "Witches, Saints, and Heretics," 24–55; Herzig, "Flies, Heretics, and the Gendering of Witchcraft," 51–80.

60. Clark, "The 'Gendering' of Witchcraft in French Demonology," 426–437; Clark, *Thinking with Demons*, 106–133.

61. See Stephens, *Demon Lovers*.

62. Nider, *Formicarius* 5.8, ed. Colvener, 388 (this section is not excerpted in *L'imaginaire du sabbat*). For a more extensive argument along these lines, see Bailey, "The Feminization of Magic." On conceptions of women in fifteenth-century demonology, see Chène and Ostorero, "Démonologie et misogynie," 171–196.

63. A good introduction to "Renaissance" magic remains Walker, *Spiritual and Demonic Magic*.

64. Walker, *Spiritual and Demonic Magic*, 205–207.

65. Klaassen, "Medieval Ritual Magic in the Renaissance," 166–199; Kieckhefer, "Did Magic Have a Renaissance?" 199–212.

66. Lehrich, *The Language of Demons and Angels*.

67. Baron, *Doctor Faustus from History to Legend*.

68. The interface of witchcraft and other religious concerns is explored with great sophistication in Clark, *Thinking with Demons*, 437–545.

69. On German superhunts, see Monter, "Witch Trials in Continental Europe," 22–29.

70. Monter, "Witch Trials in Continental Europe," 44–49. See also Monter, *Frontiers of Heresy*, 255–275; Duni, *Under the Devil's Spell*, esp. 32–37; Decker, *Witchcraft and the Papacy*, esp. chs. 8–10.

71. See Levack, *The Witch-Hunt in Early Modern Europe*, 212–217, on Germany and France; likewise Monter, "Witch Trials in Continental Europe," 31–34, 40–44. See also Moeller, *Dass Willkür über Recht ginge*, esp. 353–468, on the effects of different judicial environments in a Protestant region.

72. Levack, *The Witch-Hunt in Early Modern Europe*, 7.

73. Ibid., 218; Ankarloo, "Witch Trials in Northern Europe 1450–1700," 79.

74. Kieckhefer, *European Witch Trials*.

75. Levack, *The Witch-Hunt in Early Modern Europe*, 254.

76. I emphasized this model of progressive skepticisms in my *Magic and Superstition in Europe*, 173–174, 212.

77. Oresme, *De causis mirabilium*, in Hansen, *Nicole Oresme and the Marvels of Nature*, 136–138.

78. Kieckhefer, "Magic at Innsbruck."

79. Hansen, *Quellen und Untersuchungen*, 310.

80. *De praestigiis daemonum* has been translated into English, with an extensive introduction, as Weyer, *Witches, Devils, and Doctors in the Renaissance*, ed. Mora and Kohl, trans. Shea. An abridgement, with a new introduction, appeared as Weyer, *On Witchcraft*, ed. Kohl and Midelfort.

81. Anglo, "Reginald Scot's *Discoverie*," 106–139, esp. 126–129; Estes, "Reginald Scot and His *Discoverie*," 444–456, esp. 446.

82. Anglo, "Reginald Scot's *Discoverie*," 130, notes similarities to Oresme.

83. Spee, *Cautio Criminalis, or a Book on Witch Trials*, trans. Hellyer. Hellyer deals succinctly with the possible extent of Spee's skepticism in his "Translator's Introduction," xxiii.

84. Fix, *Balthasar Bekker, Spirit Belief, and Confessionalism*.

85. Clark, *Thinking with Demons*, 294–311.

86. Bostridge, *Witchcraft and Its Transformations*, 73–77.

87. Levack, *The Witch-Hunt in Early Modern Europe*, 280. The fullest general study of decline is also by Levack, "The Decline and End of Witchcraft Prosecutions," 1–93.

88. Europe's last legal execution for witchcraft took place in the Swiss canton of Glarus in 1782; a trial of debatable legality resulted in executions in the Polish city of Posnan in 1793. See Levack, "The Decline and End of Witchcraft Prosecutions," 88–89.

Chapter 13

Magic and Priestcraft: Reformers and Reformation

HELEN PARISH

In the months that followed the lifting of printing restrictions early in the reign of Edward VI, Luke Shepherd published *The Vpcheringe of the Messe*, in which a narrator, in the form of a conservative cleric, lamented the apparent fall of the Mass and the elevation of scripture above the teachings and traditions of the Catholic Church. "Mistress Missa" emerged in what was rapidly becoming her standard guise as the daughter of the pope, the companion of Eve, forced to leave England in the face of evangelical criticism. In her defence, Shepherd's narrator suggested that the Mass brought many benefits:

> [S]he bringeth weather clere
> And ceasonable yere
> And if it neade agayne
> They say she bringeth rayne
> She seaceth thunder lowed
> And scattereth euery cloude
> They say the plague and pestile[n]ce
> The feuer and the epilence
> The popish masse expelleth he[n]ce
> And grasse she maketh growe
> And fayre wynde to blowe.[1]

And so the list continues. Shepherd's poetic talents may have been limited, but he was certainly not alone in the approach that he took in his criticisms of Catholic sacramental theology and practice. Particularly in 1548, this kind of vocabulary, and the more general method, was commonplace in vernacular writing against the Mass and its place in the life of the church and the devotions of the faithful. The act of the first Edwardian parliament, "Against revilers of the Sacrament and for Communion in both kinds", failed to bring an end to the debate, and the fires of controversy were stoked from press and pulpit.[2] The Mass, it was suggested, was the illegitimate daughter of several popes, nurtured by centuries of doctrinal innovation, and supporting the lifestyle of a degenerate and godless priesthood. The banishment of Mistress Missa was established as a necessary priority of religious reform in England. Guilty by virtue of her parentage and her association with popes and priesthood, the figure of the Mass was put on trial in print in William Turner's *A New Dialogue Wherein is Conteyned the Examination of the Masse*, whereas *A New Dialogue called the Endightment Agaynste Mother Masse* dragged the Mass from church to face accusations of blasphemy and murder.[3] In *A Breife Recantation of Maystres Missa*, the eponymous villain complained that she had been deceived by her chaplains and their false claims that Catholic theology was rooted in scripture.[4] Rather, it appeared that her birth was the fruit of a union between her father the pope and "dame Avaritia", with the intention of bolstering the power of the papacy, increasing the wealth of the church, and supporting the reputation of "Ihon lacklatyne that could do nothynge but mumble vp matens".[5] Other pamphleteers engaged with specific questions: Edmund Guest argued with vigour against private Masses, William Salisbury denounced the assertion that the Mass served as a propitiatory sacrifice, and Luke Shepherd's *Antipus* presented a satire on the theology of transubstantiation. The dramatic moment of the consecration and elevation of the elements was commonly portrayed as theatricality and show, a "popish play" designed to entertain and deceive the faithful. Performance and pageantry, it was argued, both concealed and communicated false doctrine. Thomas Becon denounced priests as "gay, gaudy, gallant, gorgeous game-players", whereas John Jewel complained that the sacrament had become, in the hands of popes and priests, a "stage play".[6] However, the highly fictionalised tone of some of the tracts need not imply a disengagement from the reality of religious reform in the late 1540s; even the most comic or bawdy polemic could have a clear resonance with what might loosely be termed the "official" agenda and with the key players in debates about the direction of reform in the Edwardian church. Thus, Stephen Gardiner as the object of some of Shepherd's sharp-tongued criticism in *A Pore Helpe, Doctor Double Ale* was at least in part a caricature of a conservative London cleric, and Salisbury's attempt to undermine the theology of the Mass as sacrifice would not have been an unwelcome companion to the removal of altars from churches. In a similar vein, the reference in the Council of 1549 to "their conjured bredde and water" sits readily alongside the language of sorcery, witchcraft and magic that permeated writing against the Mass in evangelical polemic.[7]

This representation of the Mass as a form of ecclesiastically sanctioned magic was a familiar trope in Protestant writing in the mid-sixteenth century and beyond. Luke Shepherd's mockery of the apparent benefits and capacities of the Mass reflected a broader body of writing in which the powers attributed to the consecrated host – both sanctioned and unsanctioned by the church – provided ample fodder for those seeking to undermine traditional theology. Indeed, Shepherd's mocking assertion that the Mass acted as a protective against the hazards of daily life, pestilence, fever, and inclement weather was all the more potent because it shared a rhetorical lexicon with pre-Reformation writing and preaching on the sacrament. Items laid on the altar during Mass were believed by some to acquire healing and protective properties, and hosts removed from churches were claimed to have the ability to extinguish fire.[8] The early fifteenth-century English *Alphabet of Tales*, derived from the fourteenth-century *Alphabetum narrationum*, included several miracle narratives associated with the consecrated host, ranging from the discovery of counterfeit coins to the apparently spontaneous veneration of the sacrament by animals.[9] Some forty-six miracle collections which included accounts of miracles associated with the Mass were circulating in the three centuries before the Reformation, and such miracle narratives were possessed of a pedagogic and pastoral value.[10] Accounts of such wonders were not confined to miracle collections; *Gregory's Chronicle*, for example, described how a London locksmith who had conspired with thieves to remove pixes from churches was rendered incapable of seeing the host at Mass. Driven to confess his sin, his sight was restored in a tale that reinforced both the centrality of seeing the host and the importance of sacramental confession.[11] Indeed, simply seeing the host brought its own benefits, benefits which were not only embedded in popular devotion but also described and detailed by and for the clergy. Both Mirk's *Instructions for Parish Priests* and Lydgate's *Merita Missa* encouraged the belief that witnessing the consecration, or seeing the host, was a central and valuable part of religious life.[12] The section of the *Festial* that dealt with the feast of Corpus Christi included the assurance that "Christ left thus this sacrament to be used evermore in Holy church ... first for man's great helping ... both in lyfe and death". Seven gifts were given to those who attended Mass, including the assurance that the faithful would not want for food, the forgiveness of idle speech and oaths, the preservation of sight on that day and preservation from sudden death.[13] John Audeley's *De meritis misse, quomodo debemus audire missam*, written in the 1420s, informed the pious observer that to see the consecrated host was to be assured of the company of angels and to be protected from blindness, sudden death and hunger and thirst for the day.[14] Such literature, albeit intended to inculcate orthodox private devotion and devotion to the sacrament, also provided evangelical polemicists with a broad range of exempla with which to illustrate their denunciations of the apparently magical properties and uses of the host. Thus, under pressure from her accusers, the character of Mistress Missa confessed that she had begotten many children with the pope, including "missa pro defunctis, missa pro pluvial, masse de nomine Jesu, and the masse of Scala Coeli, which was of greater power and virtue than all the others".[15] Hugh Hilarie's *Resurreccion of the masse* claimed for the host, in a mocking tone, the ability to heal every disease of man, "messeled swine and mangye horses", to help women find husbands (and husbands be rid of women with whom they were dissatisfied) and to release the souls of the damned from hell.[16] In a similar vein, John Ramsey listed the powers associated with the host, which served "for rayne, for drowthe for pestilence and shepe, for pygges, for pylgrimes, for shippes that be saylynge, for corne for the cough and for those that cannot slepe".[17] The humour that resided in such outlandish claims was a powerful polemical weapon, but so too was the fact that there was a grain of truth here in the coincidence of popular belief, orthodox pastoral and Protestant propaganda.

However, it was not simply the uses to which the host might be put that attracted criticism from evangelical theologians and polemicists but also the mechanism by which such uses were efficacious and the means by which that efficacy was imbued. The association between the Mass and magic was not made simply on the basis that the consecrated bread was believed to be possessed of such an impressive array of miraculous powers. Rather, the link between magic and the Mass reached to the heart of the liturgy, and of late medieval devotion, in the assertion that transubstantiation was itself no miracle, but rather a magical or quasi-magical manipulation by the priest. The image of the priest not as celebrant but as conjuror cast the central rite of the church as a diabolic act; at worst, the Mass became a display of false wonderworking; at best, it was an act of deception, theatre and fraud. The language and gestures of the liturgy, the vestments worn by the celebrant and the heightened sense of mystery construed and constructed as the priest stood with his back to the people contributed to the sense of drama that attended the moment of consecration and the "seeing" of the bread and wine at the elevation that had become established as the pivotal moment in lay devotion. This sense of the significance of the moment, and the witnessing of that moment, fed into evangelical criticisms of Catholic theology and practice; the assault on the superstition and magic of traditional Eucharistic theology was all the more resonant and compelling because it struck at the heart of church, and of parish religion. The author of *Here begynneth a booke called the fal of the Romish church* painted a picture of the priest "standinge at the aultar in players garments telling a straunge tale to the dead walles in a forren language", using words and actions that led the people into idolatry.[18] John Bale described how he had rebutted the demands of his flock in Ossory that he should say Mass, "for of all occupacions me thinke / it is most folish. For there standeth the preste disgysed / lyke one that wolde shewe some co[n]ueyau[n]ce or iuglyng playe. He turneth his back to ye people / and telleth a tale to the walle in a fore[n] language".[19] The mockery of transubstantiation in evangelical polemic, accounts of fraudulent attempts to re-create, physically and visibly, the transformation of the substance and the assertion that the words of con-secration were little more than magical mumblings were made all the more potent by the depth of their roots in the theology of the Catholic Church and the practice of parish religion.

It is hardly surprising that a critique of the theology of transubstantiation was central to the mockery of the Mass in evangelical polemical writing. "At the centre of the whole religious system of the later middle ages", writes Miri Rubin, "lay a ritual which turned bread into flesh – a fragile, small, wheaten disc into God".[20] But much of this ritual was hidden from the laity, occurring physically behind a screen, linguistically in words that were not audible, and morally in that it was not proper to make public this most central rite of the church.[21] Such was the power and mystery behind these barely audible words that Caxton's *Golden Legend* included, as a warning and devotional aid, the story of a group of shepherds who were burned alive after saying the words of consecration over bread.[22] The words spoken by the priest, and the visible moment of the elevation, acquired a pivotal significance as the moment of miracle, as the focal point for devotion and as a tool of pedagogy and pro-paganda.[23] The elevation itself became associated with miracles; those who raised their eyes in a state of sin found that they could not see the bread, those without sight had it restored and those who doubted the truth of the doctrine of the church perceived not bread, but Christ, in the hands of the priest.[24] The significance of the moment had been recognised by critics of the church before the Reformation, and Lollards were reported to have exclaimed and declaimed loudly at the elevation to make clear their distaste for the Catholic theology of the Eucharist.[25] At the heart of criticisms of traditional devotional practice lay the disparity between the experience of the ears and the eyes. The words "hoc est corpus meum" asserted the physical presence of Christ in the bread and wine, but those occasions on which, to the eyes, bread became flesh and wine became blood were the staple of miracle collections precisely because they were so rare. Traditional theology had emphasised the disparity between the visible accident and invisible substance, but this very contrast was to provide much of the ammunition for evangelical criticisms.

In attempting to break apart the image of the host as the body of Christ, evangelical writers presented the Mass as a cult of bread and wine, and hence as idolatry and superstition.[26] Shepherd's dialogue between *Iohn Bon and Mast Person* exposed a bewildered priest to the naïve questioning of John Bon (Figure 13.1). The consecrated host, he suggested, was too small to contain the body of Christ. The priest claimed that bread was indeed the body of Christ, yet to John and his senses, the species still tasted and looked like bread and wine even after the consecration.[27] Shepherd's satire was a popular piece, and even in this moment of apparently open debate, it aroused the concern of the Lord Mayor. It opened with a woodcut, reused from Richard Pynson's *Rule of Seynt Benet* (1516), depicting a Corpus Christi procession, which in Shepherd's text was underlaid – and undermined – by a stanza mocking the "wafer cake" and the priestly "poore foole" who made a god that he could not carry. The encounter between the priest and John Bon itself took place on the eve of the feast of Corpus Christi, and it included a comic debate over the feasibility of containing the man "copsi curtsy" within the processional monstrance. As the parson explained the theology that underpinned the celebration and bemoaned its imminent suppression, John Bon retorted that the sacrament was a "devilish masse", and the celebrant a trickster was "juggling [and] craftye".

Robert Crowley argued that the corruptibility of the consecrated elements was proof enough that they did not contain the body of Christ, for what else filled the belly of the mouse, burned in the flames or became putrid with mould?[28] The words of consecration, if they had any physical effect at all, positioned the priest not as the servant of Christ, but in the role of magician, conjuring with bread and wine to deceive the faithful. John Bale sneered that the Catholic clergy "are very connynge worke men that ... can do so moche in so lyttle tyme and with so fewe wordes", suggesting that it was more likely that the "breathynge of yours vpon the breade is but a newe founde toye of your owne sorcerye".[29] Catholic priests were not priests at all, but "dau[n]cing apaes, whose natural property is to counterfeit al things that they se done afore them", including the suffering of Aaron and the sacrifice of Christ.[30] It was surely not possible, one anonymous author contended, that the priest "ca[n] with feue words make both god and man".[31] Priests were instead "conning artificers" who could make neither beast nor fowl, yet claimed to be able to make God; these "cakes of John Podyngmakers making ... is not holy nor of no virtue, tyll these chattering charmers haue charmed it".[32] Robert Crowley, in response to Miles Hogarde's defence of Catholic theology, argued that the utterances of the priest at Mass showed that "cunning is

FIGURE 13.1. Title page from John Bon and Mast Person. Reprinted with permission of the Trustees of the British Library.

a greate thinge, and helpeth as much in this matter as quick conueighaunce doth in legerdemayne".[33] In *A declaration of the masse*, Marcourt complained that the Mass had "seduced and begyled" the world "under shadow and colour of holynesse" in which the "sely pore sacrificiers" were "enchaunters and ydle people".[34] The Mass, Peter Moone lamented, was simply one among the "feattes of legerdemayne, by these iugglers inuented" to delude and deceive the faithful. The bread and the faithful were both bewitched by the words and the rituals of the priest.[35] The Last Supper, Thomas Cranmer suggested, had been instituted as a sacrament that was meant to bind the faithful together and create a brotherly love, but the Devil had "iuggled herein" to make it a focus for discord, with the papists being "wonderfull iuglers and coniurers that with certain words can make God and the dyuell to dwel together in one man".[36] Bale invited the reader to examine "the popes prodygyouse Masse" and the miracles worked in its name. Its "disgisynges, instrumentes, blessynges, turnynges and legerdemaynes", he protested, "serueth all wytches in theyr wytchery, all sorcerers, charmers, inchaunters, dreamers, sothsayers, necromansers, coniures, crosse dyggers, deuyll raysers, myracle doers, doggeleches, and bawdes. For wythout a Masse, they can not well worke theyr feates ... Where are the names of God, of his Angels, & of his sayntes, more ryfe than among witches, charmers, inchau[n]ters, & sorcerers?"[37]

Chief among these "charmers, inchau[n]ters, & sorcerers" were the Catholic clergy, and the vocabulary of "juggling", "legerdemain" and "charming" punctuated evangelical denunciations of the Mass in particular, and of the Catholic priesthood and liturgies more generally. Whereas the Mass provided perhaps the most obvious, and fruitful, location for discussion of the magical manipulations of the Catholic Church and clergy, the representation of the priest as magician and conjuror extended into a broader discussion of sacraments and sacramentals. In the use of blessings, oils, wax, lights, ashes and palms, Bale claimed, the Catholic clergy "coniured / crossed / sensed / spatled / and breathed / with turne and halfe turne / and with seyst me and seyst me not / and a thousande feates more of cleane legerde mayne / to vpholde that mart of theyr maintenaunce".[38] Hugh Hilarie mocked the priest who, like "Brandon the iuglare", used his arms "like charmers and coniurers" in gestures and blessings.[39] In Thomas Becon's denunciation of the Mass, the Catholic clergy occupied themselves with "consecrating, blowing, blasting and breathing" to "charm the bread" so that "it trudgeth straightways away beyond the moon".[40] Thomas Crowley likened the ritual gestures of the priest at Mass to the movements of a magician, "full of turnes & halfe turnes, beckeinges and duckeinges, crosseynges, tosseynges and tumblings" and contrasted the elaborate liturgy of the Mass with the simple celebration of the Lord's Supper. Christ had taken bread, broken it and distributed it, but, Crowley protested, the priests "take bread & blowe vpo[n] it breathinge out certaine wordes in the maner of enchau[n]ters & sorcerers, to turne the substaunce therof".[41] If transubstantiation was magic, so the blessing of water was "coniuring", and the Catholic clergy were "false fayning Iuglers", "crafty iuglers" and workers of legerdemain.[42]

The suggestion that the priest used magic at the consecration to manipulate the bread and wine and to deceive the faithful had the potential to turn the central sacrament of the church into a diabolic wonder, placing the priest not in the position of *alter Christus*, but of the servant of Satan. Evangelical polemic echoed with the assertion that the Antichrist sought to deceive the faithful with "spiritual sorceryes" and that the miracles that were claimed for the saints of the Catholic Church were false wonders.[43] But these false wonders were not necessarily actual or tangible events, and the language of conjuring, juggling and legerdemain implied as much a sleight of hand and a deception of the eyes as a physical transformation. This linguistic ambiguity was not unique to the polemical literature of the 1540s; the boundary between magic, demonic magic and superstition in the later Middle Ages could be equally permeable, as Richard Kieckhefer has demonstrated. Definitions of magic often involved little specific reflection on the differences, or similarities, between what was referred to as "magic" and what was discussed under the umbrella of "superstition". The improper use of the relics of the saints, or indeed of the consecrated host, was rarely considered to be magic, and to succumb to the temptations of the Devil to engage in such practices need not, explicitly or implicitly, involve the conjuring of demons.

In a similar vein, where the miraculous properties of the object were rooted in the saintly or divine, their abuse was not necessarily understood as natural magic.[44] In a discussion that was to shape much later writing on the magical arts, Isidore of Seville's *Etymologies* located under the heading of "magic and magicians" a range of occult and other practices, ranging from malefici and sorcery to necromancy, hydromancy, geomancy, aeromancy, pyromancy, divination and the sortilege of those who "profess the science of divination under the pretended guise of religion".[45] Isidore's headings found their way into the writings of Maurus, Burchard of Worms and Ivo of Chartres, as well as, in the twelfth century, Gratian's *Decretum*, the works of Hugh of St Victor and those of John of Salisbury. Isidore located his discussion of magic in a section of the *Etymologies* that debated religion and religious sects, and his summary reflected the position of the eighth-century church as it was articulated in councils and canons.[46] However, Isidore and his successors debated the legality of magic but not its efficacy; magic was a form of moral and religious perversion, but it was not, perhaps, something that needed to be explained. By the twelfth century, John of Salisbury thought it appropriate to locate a discussion of magic in the section of the *Policraticus* that dealt with courtly entertainment, so that magic became as much jest and trickery as demonic practice. Magic and sorcery were discussed alongside mimicry, wrestling and *praestigium*, or juggling, a trickery and deception of the eyes.[47] Trickery of the eyes in other contexts was a popular spectacle. The notebook of a fifteenth-century monk of Syon Abbey, for example, explained how to give the impression of manipulating an egg by attaching a hair which could be tugged with the fingers.[48] Terms such as prestidigitation and legerdemain, which poured from the pages of Protestant polemic against the priesthood, embodied a similar imprecision. What occurred with the uttering of the words "hoc est corpus meum", if it was not miracle, was condemned either as magic or as sleight of hand. To enchant might be to use magic to bring about a real effect, but it might equally be to entertain, enthral and deceive the audience by theatrical display and gesture.

Thus, the criticism of the words of the priest at Mass as "legerdemaynes" and "dreamynges" could open the door to a discussion of the deception of the eyes of the faithful at the hands of a quick-fingered priest.[49] Narratives of physical forgeries of the Eucharistic miracle were a commonplace of polemical mockery of the sacrament and the celebrant. The attempt of the Surrey priest Nicholas Germes to provide his congregation with incontrovertible proof of the veracity of Catholic theology was to become a staple of evangelical writing against the Mass in the 1540s. Germes, identified by Bale as a "popysh priest", pricked his fingers with a pin at the moment of the consecration to give the illusion of Christ's blood on the altar.[50] Germes's sleight of hand was also to feature in the discussion of the feigned miracles of the medieval church in the *Confutation of Unwritten Verities*. Here, it was accompanied by an account of the wondrous proofs claimed by a Marian monk of Christ Church Canterbury who had attempted to demonstrate the physical presence of Christ in the consecrated elements by feeding the host to a horse, which piously refused to consume it, by using a host fed to a horse to expose the Devil and by describing the horror of a woman who had taken a host home from Mass in her mouth, only to find the Christ child in the pot where she had concealed it.[51]

The chronology was current, but the exempla was traditional and familiar. Mirk's *Festial* had described the miracle attributed to Archbishop Odo of Canterbury, in which the doubting clergy were convinced of the real presence

FIGURE 13.2. *Mass of Saint Gregory*, early sixteenth century, Dutch style, engraving. Pope Gregory I, seen from behind and flanked by two monks, worships before an altar with Christ as the Man of Sorrows standing in the tomb. Reprinted with the permission of the Trustees of the British Museum.

of Christ in the consecrated elements when blood was seen to run over the fingers of the archbishop and into the chalice.[52] A similar story underpinned the popular iconography of the *Mass of St Gregory*; Edward the Confessor witnessed the appearance of the infant Christ in the hands of Archbishop Wulfstan; and the broken host bleeding was a central theme in narratives of host desecration, particularly when it came at the hands of Jews (Figure 13.2). The Mass of St Gregory was a popular image in late medieval art, although the earliest narrative dates from the eighth century. In thirteenth-century editions of the *Golden Legend*, the narrative had been conflated with other similar stories to include the physical appearance of the entire body of Christ on the altar, and this formulation of the legend was the most commonly depicted in late medieval paintings and engravings.[53] In a similar vein to the horse which refused to devour the host, the *Alphabet of Tales* included a miracle narrative in which a swarm of bees venerated the consecrated bread placed in its hive, constructing a chapel around it.[54] Such familiar topoi in sermons and miracle collections could readily acquire new meaning when viewed through the lens of evangelical criticism. Odo's miracle was mocked by Bale and Foxe, who cast the legend as evidence of devious practice on the part of the archbishop and his supporters. In Bale's account, Odo feigned the miracle in an attempt to silence those clerics who argued that the bread and wine were simply figures of Christ's body and blood. The narrative was recast as a clash between these proto-Protestants and the archetypal manipulative monks who, finding scriptural support for their belief wanting, "were driuen to false miracles or playne experymentes of sorcerye. For Odo, by a cast of legerdemayne, shewed vnto the people a broken host bledynge".[55] Odo's false miracle was not a neutral event but rather, in Bale's hands, a clear demonstration of the possibilities for fraud and deception at this most central moment of traditional piety.

In such cases, seeing was very definitely not believing. Whereas the transformation of bread into body and wine into blood had been invisible and insensible, it became in evangelical rhetoric, irrelevant, impossible and incomprehensible. Where flesh and blood *were* visible, such transformation was made apparent only by fraud, trickery and deception on the part of the priest. In denouncing transubstantiation and the role and function of the priest as magic and fraud, evangelical writers struck at the heart of Catholic devotion by exploiting the lexicon, the imagery and the spectacle that it afforded. Richard Morison had advised that for "the common people, things sooner enter by the eyes than by the ears: remembering more better that they see than that they hear".[56] Yet what the faithful *saw* at the consecration and elevation remained unchanged. Indeed, in response to evangelical criticism, the English Catholic Richard Smith wrote that to see "rawe fleshe and bloud" would lead the faithful to hold the sacrament in contempt.[57] The miracle of the visible transformation of the bread and wine was the exception, not the rule. If the theology of transubstantiation was to be undermined and expunged from the minds and memories of the believer, it was not enough to change what was seen. Rather, that which was seen required a new explanation that was anchored in the familiar but gnawed away at it from within. The link between the invisible body and the visible bread needed to be broken, a fracture that was accomplished by casting the words of the priest as prestige, his gestures as disguise and juggling and the language of liturgy as theatre, as an illusory and delusory spectacle.

It was not only the Mass which was to be represented in light of these competing and proximate interpretations. The language of conjuring, charming and enchanting in writing against the theology of transubstantiation was also a staple of evangelical polemic against traditional religion, particularly the roles of saints, images and relics in Catholic devotion. The specific assertion that the priest at the moment of consecration was engaged in magical manipulation, deception or conjuring was expanded and turned against the veneration of the saints, the saintly miraculous and the sense that the sacred inhered in particular times, places and persons. "Wyth thy preuye legerdimain, with the iulginge castes, with the craftes and inchauntments of thy subtyle charmers", Bale responded to his critics, "were all the nacions of the worlde deceyued with lies in hypocrisye, were the great gouernors most miserable blinded and with errours in supersticion the common people seduced".[58] The magic and sorcery of the Catholic clergy, Bale contended, extended beyond the sacraments and into a panoply of beliefs and practices that served to support the authority of the church and blind the faithful to the gospel. In place of true religion, popes and priests had introduced "straunge worshippynges", "charminge", "iuglinge", and "wretched wytchery".[59] Princes and people had been "drowned with dreames" and led into captivity by their ignorance and by the preaching of doctrines that had their roots in the traditions of men rather than the truth of scripture.[60] Derision was heaped on the "feates of legerdemayne, by these iugglers inuented that God's word shulde not florysshe, the light of our salvation".[61] Priestly magic, manipulation and necromancy, it was argued, was evident in the chronicles, in the lives and legends of the saints and in the miracles they were claimed to have performed.

By far the most straightforward assertion among evangelical writers was that the age of miracles had passed. Miracles might have had a place and function in the primitive church, it was argued, but they had long since ceased to be a necessary feature of Christianity. This was, for example, the line of argument pursued by Martin Luther in his *Commentary on Matthew*, by William Tyndale in his *Answer to Sir Thomas More's Dialogue* and by Richard Sheldon in his *Survey of the Miracles of the Church of Rome*.[62] Miracles had been, for a time, a guarantor of the legitimacy of innovation, appropriate to the nascent Christian church, but not to the established institutional church or, it was argued, to the reformed churches. The presentation of the Reformation as restoration rather than innovation, as a return to the practices of the primitive church purged of the accretions of medieval Catholicism, carried with it an assumption that no further testimony to the truth of the Gospel was necessary. In his prefatory address to Francis I in the *Institutes of the Christian Religion*, John Calvin made precisely this point. Opponents of the Reformation, he complained, "in demanding miracles of us act dishonestly, for we are not forging some new gospel but are retaining that very gospel whose truth all the miracles of Jesus Christ and his disciples ever wrought to confirm".[63]

Whereas the miracles presented in the pages of medieval hagiography had established the individual saint as part of a chain of holy men and women that stretched back into scripture, these same miracles in the hands of critics of the church were the fulfilment of a rather different biblical promise. The "false hue" of Catholic miracles, John Calvin suggested, could readily dazzle the eyes of the believer, were it not for the warnings contained in the Gospel (Matt. 24.24) and the Pauline Epistles (2 Thess. 2.9) against the false wonders that would be used to support the doctrines of the Devil. William Tyndale, John Bale and John Foxe applied these same texts to the miracles of the Catholic saints: the ability to work false wonders was within the capacity of those who "love not the truth", and these "strange delusions" and "lyenge signes and wonders" raised the possibility that the faithful might be "deuylishly deceyued". The Mass appeared on the title page of Foxe's *Actes and Monumentes* as one of the defining characteristics of the false church (Figure 13.3). Catholic priests are depicted venerating the consecrated host beneath an image of their fellows falling into the jaws of Hell, whereas in the opposite column, the trumpets of the evangelical martyrs echo the trumpets of the angels above.[64]

Such vocabulary was far from new in the first decades of the sixteenth century. For John Wycliffe, the miracles claimed by and for the Catholic Church in the post–Apostolic Era were evidence less of the intrusion of the divine into the mortal world through the mediation of saints and clerics than of the posturing of a priesthood which was virtually impotent in the face of its critics and in its capacity to preach, evangelise and comprehend the word of God. Miracles were neither necessary nor granted by God in an era where faith was long established: "[Q]uantum ad miracula, patet quod cessant hodie in nostris episcopis, cum satis est post fidem in evangelio divulgatum ipsam impressam sanctis exhortacionibus confirmare".[65] Such was true not only of the miracles of the saints, Wycliffe argued, but also of that central miracle of Catholicism, the miracle of the Eucharist. Miracles, and the veneration of the miraculous, whether in relics or in the elements, were the work of the Devil, as was the apparently commonly held belief that the priest in each consecration made infinite miracles, as Christ had done.[66] There were two overlapping arguments here: the first was that the age of miracles had passed and that the veneration of the saints and their wonders was at best superfluous, and the second, more specific assertion was that the daily, repeated miracle in which the faithful encountered blood and flesh in wine and bread was deception, or conjuring, on the part of the priest. The danger was that from this central rite, the faithful tended to extrapolate a more general capacity of the Catholic Church and its clergy to make present the miraculous and divine, and thus

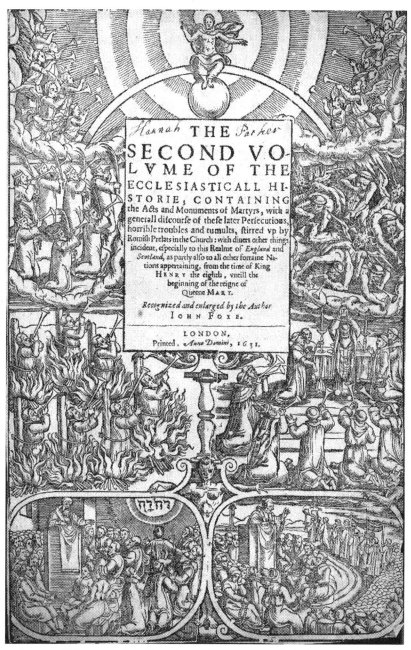

FIGURE 13.3. Title page for John Foxe, *Acts and Monuments (Book of Martyrs)*, second volume edition, 1631. Christ and angels in heaven above, with a scene from hell at the upper right; along the left are burning martyrs and a Protestant congregation; along the right, the Mass and a Catholic sermon. Woodcut. Reprinted with the permission of the Trustees of the British Museum.

in the hands of Wycliffe and his successors, the critique of transubstantiation implied and facilitated a more general re-evaluation of the miracles attributed to saints and priests. In a similar vein, Robert Barnes warned against the dangers of perceiving the miraculous in all that was wondrous; after all, miracles had been claimed for false images and prophets in the past, whether for the brazen serpent, the goddess Diana, or the "Turks" who had worked wonders in defence of their beliefs.[67] The miracles associated with the saints of the medieval church, Bale claimed, were false wonders, feigned and devilish deceptions. Guised as "virginall votaries", these "angels of darkenesse" practised "gostlye conueyaunces" and "strange delusions" that were more fitting for hell than for heaven, despite their reputation for sanctity.[68] The Antichrist, as scripture taught, preached contrary to Christ and, cloaked in hypocrisy, "doth many false myracles" which were evident in the "ydolatrie and necrolatrie" of the clergy. Christ alone had the ability and the authority to work miracles, but by the sufferance of God, the Devil had been permitted to use marvels and wonders to deceive the eyes of the multitude, including princes and governors. The "preuye legerdemain [and] ... iuglinge castes ... craftes and ... inchauntments of ye subtyle charmers" had allowed the faithful to be deceived by lies and hypocrisy, but as the light of the Gospel was permitted to shine on the church of the past and present, Bale anticipated, "theyr sorceryes and inchauntme[n]tes shall come to derysyon".[69] In Bale's apocalyptic historical scheme, the Catholic clergy became the conjurers of Egypt and the "lecherouse locusts" released from the bottomless pit, bringing with them sorcery, superstition, charms and "straunge worshippings".[70]

Bale's relentless assault on the mission, morality and miracles of Catholic saints and clergy hammered home the message that the magic of the priesthood was to be both exposed and eradicated. The persuasiveness of his polemic owed much to the all-encompassing nature of the assault, which ranged from the mockery of individual miracles to a detailed criticism of the sacraments to an appeal for reform which was imbued with an eschatological ambition. The image of the priest as conjuror and magician was a potent one, as we saw earlier in the chapter, given its location at the intersection between the experience of the reader, the theology of the church and the rhetoric of the reformers. There was also, perhaps significantly, an already established popular or polemical tradition in which Catholic miracles, relics, priests and sacraments were presented as fraud, magic and objects of derision. Modelled on Faus Semblant, Chaucer's Pardoner presents the bones of pigs as the relics of the saints and appears as "a professional hypocrite who pretends to a holiness that he possesses not at all".[71] Feigned wonders, feigned relics and feigned holiness coincide in the caricature. In the Canon's Yeoman's Tale, the (ex-) Yeoman recalls with a hint of nostalgia his life of old and his practice of "that slidynge science" of alchemy. The capacity to deceive, however, remains, as the Yeoman tempts the "sely preest" to experience and experiment with magic in both complex forms and in mere sleight-of-hand. The range of magical deception is broad, and the appetite of the priest is swiftly whetted. However, the willingness to perceive magic and to believe that magic had been performed was founded on a reciprocal relationship between the practitioner and the observer. Acceptance that an event had a supernatural cause was contingent on the audience's willing participation in the act and the ritual or drama that surrounded it, but perhaps also on the presence of doubt or objection: the audience should first be willing to be deceived, then question and then concede to the trick.[72] The success of the canon's illusion depends on both its theatricality and the willingness of the priest to accept and participate in it. The same, perhaps, might be said of the miracles, or alleged magic, of the clergy; the delineation between miracle and feigned wonder, and the positioning of the priest or saint in the spectrum, was accomplished in intellectual, moral, polemical and also practical terms.

The apparent malleability of magic and miracle was, in part, a reflection of the fact that both were perceived and understood in their subjective visible manifestations, not in terms of their objective causes.[73] Medieval writing on miracles, including that of Aquinas, Gerald of Wales and John of Salisbury, was emphatic in its insistence that the miraculous was distinct from marvel and magic, but the multiplicity of miracles claimed for the church and its holy men and women, coupled with the predispositions of their audience, ensured that in practice the boundary between miracle, magic and nature remained permeable. Despite this apparent osmotic relationship, the erection of a barrier between magic and miracle was an essential part of the defence of the distinctiveness of the Christian church. The nascent church was not, after all, alone in laying claim to an apparent ability to manipulate the natural world. The promotion of Christian miracles as just that, miraculous, required a determined reconsideration of the wonders associated with paganism and demonic magic as neither miracles, nor even innocuous illusions. For Augustine, the godly miracles of the saints were the antithesis of the demonic theurgy practised outside the church, and Christian miracle was established in stark opposition to the magical wonders of its opponents.[74] Condemnations of magic and necromancy punctuated the literature and laws of the medieval church, and the repeated rejection of magic as worthless wonder and illusion perhaps reflected the very real fear that the sorcery of a demonic sect posed a fundamental threat to the integrity of the faith.[75] By the twelfth century, the practice of magic, which was forcefully condemned by the church, had become associated with heresy and thus with the conscious rejection or parody of orthodox doctrine and liturgy that the term "heresy" implied. Rudolf Herzog's assertion that "magic is always other people's faith" offers a simple, if not simplistic, summary of the attitude of Christian apologists towards the wonders claimed for their opponents,[76] but the meaning of godly miracle was often imparted in a dialogue between saint and sorcerer in which the similarities between miracle and magic seemed more significant than the differences did.[77]

As Stuart Clark has argued, miracle and magic "provided competing but proximate imageries of power; only something entirely contingent – legitimacy – separated them".[78] The acceptance of the legitimacy of certain actions reflected underlying assumptions about the conflicting nature of miracle and magic, and thus a common distinction was drawn between the elements of hope and expectation inherent in religious observation. Prayer, miracles and requests for the intercession of the saint, for example, were in essence acts of supplication, appeals for supernatural assistance that held the promise, but not the guarantee, of success. Magic, by contrast, relied on elements of compulsion, with the intended result being obtained by the recitation of specific words or the enactment of defined gestures.[79] The separation of magic from religion was accomplished, or at least attempted, not only in the issue of compulsion but also in the wider context provided by evidence of intent and purpose. Magic, it is suggested, encompassed those actions that were directed towards the fulfilment of short-term goals, including the defeat of an enemy or the preservation of crops. Religious ritual, in contrast, was concerned with goals that were both more abstract and less immediate, primarily the salvation of the soul. Magic remained a "specific art for specific ends", whereas religion was based on the participation of the community, whose unity stemmed from the function that it fulfilled.[80] However, such a distinction is made difficult both by the problems inherent in understanding the precise motivation behind a ritual or act and by the belief that the manipulation of the supernatural in the present moment provided an assurance that future salvation had been secured. The miracles associated with the Rood of Boxley that continued into the early modern period were a case in point; an encounter with the miraculous at Boxley was possible only for those pilgrims with a suitably pure heart and pious aspect.[81]

Religious aspirations within magic and perceptions of magical elements in religion point to evidence of practical accommodation alongside the theoretical opposition. The magical and the folkloric were interwoven with threads of orthodox piety in the fabric of medieval religious life, as traditional non-Christian practices were adapted to the Christian world-view, sustaining a contested amorphous middle ground between religion and magic.[82] Such difficulties were no less acute in the era of the Reformation, but there the contrast between miracle and sorcery was to become a powerful weapon in the hands of propagandists and polemicists seeking to define the boundary between not only religion and magic in the past but also true and false belief in the present.

If the recognition of magic as such was the result of its reception and acceptance by its audience, was it this same element of plausibility, or willingness to believe, that made the accusations of magic and sorcery levelled against the clergy in polemic and propaganda such a convincing part of anti-Catholic rhetoric? Certainly, there are examples to be found of clerical dabbling in magic, necromancy and superstition, although the definitions of the magic involved, and indeed of "cleric", are notoriously imprecise. In what is still the most substantial study of late medieval clerical necromancy, Richard Kieckhefer reminds his reader that the clerics of the clerical underworld who explored a shared interest in demonic magic and necromancy were not necessarily the parish clergy encountered by the faithful on a daily or weekly basis. Similarly, the actions and ideas that fell under the umbrella of "necromancy" might equally be understood as magic not in the demonic sense, but rather in the performative sense.[83] The representation of saints as sorcerers in evangelical polemic served a particular purpose in the redefinition of the boundary between miracle and magic and in the identification of the Catholic Church as the congregation of Satan, but it also reflected a reality in which an interest in magic might well be part of the intellectual environment or inheritance of the educated religious. John of Vallambrosa, for example, collected and explored forbidden writings, developing a fascination with the occult that was to result in his confinement in solitude, an existence which was to leave him determined to pursue a life of repentance and austerity. Cases of clerical magic were reported in the alpine Val Camonica in the mid-fifteenth century, with reports and complaints against clerics for divination and "nefarious arts". In Brescia, "multa maleficia" were committed by the clergy, suggesting an overlap between the culture of priesthood and the practice of magic that was more than simply a rhetorical device of opposition.[84] Concern about such practices at an institutional level is evident in the writings of Nicolas Eymeric, whose 1376 Directorium inquisitorum contained references to clerical magic, necromancy and superstition. Yet at a more basic level, the debate about religious observance, superstition and magic was conducted around questions of the legitimate or illegitimate use of holy water, talismans, amulets or semi-Christian charms. Here, as Keith Thomas noted, the line between magic and religion was "impossibly fine", with the result that the actions of the priest (or the perception of these actions) could be variously located.[85]

The very possibility that a priest might extend the scope of his knowledge beyond the Christian supernatural, however, facilitated a rift between general and specific accusations of such practices, simultaneously making plausible some of the more outlandish actions attributed to key individuals and using such legends as the starting point for a more broadbrush representation of Catholic theology and practice as quasi-magical. The broad rhetoric of sorcery, witchcraft, magic and juggling that was used against the Catholic Church and clergy had a more specific application in the denunciation of particular individuals, particularly popes and saints, as magicians and workers of false wonders. This reconstruction of medieval history and hagiography in the service of the Reformation underpinned much of John Bale's work, particularly the *Actes of the English Votaries*, in which the heroes of the past emerged as the villains of the present and the miracles of the saints appeared as demonic delusions. Augustine arrived in Canterbury, Bale claimed, as a member not of the order of Christ but of the "supersticiouse sect of Benet", armed with Aristotle's artillery and "crafty sciences" rather than the word of God in scripture. The "incantacyons" of the missionaries deluded the Saxon kings and convinced them to embrace the Roman faith and the monastic life. In the centuries that followed, it was alleged, the legends of such "sanctified sorcerers" were allowed to distort the history of the church in England, bolstering the authority of the monastics and promoting idolatry, superstition and magical manipulation in place of true religion.[86] In some cases, the association between saintly miracles and clerical magic was more direct and explicit. St Oswald, Bale claimed, had been schooled in necromancy during his time at Floriac, and the Roman priest Palumbanus was guilty of sorcery, necromancy and "knaueries spiritual".[87] The miracles of St Dunstan were likewise presented as magic and "legerdemain", whereas the accident that befell the pro-clerical marriage party at Calne was attributed to necromancy and sorcery.[88] The manipulation of the natural world could no longer be seen as an indication of divine approbation or doctrinal truth.

The equation of Catholic miracle with clerical and saintly magic extended beyond the reinterpretation of the *vitae* of the saints and into the criticism of papal authority, the papal office and its occupants in evangelical histories of the medieval church. Thus, it was alleged, ecclesiastical magicians were to be found upon the chair of St Peter, with Silvester II and Gregory VII emerging as the favoured targets. The pontificate of Silvester, spanning the crucial year 1000, was presented in evangelical writing as a critical moment in the history of the church, and the relationship between Catholicism, magic and the expansion of the influence of the Antichrist in Christian history. The use of biblical prophecy as a means of interpreting the past lent weight to the notion that the end of the first millennium was a portentous moment, but the activities of Silvester, both in the realm of church reform and in pseudoscientific exploration, left him open to more specific criticism. The availability of the medieval chronicle literature in which the sixteenth-century "legend" of the pope might be rooted made the evangelical narrative all the more compelling. It was Silvester, so the story ran, who had been responsible for the loosing of Satan from the pit, in accordance with the prophecies of John.[89] In an attempt to secure his position in the church and eventually lay claim to the papal throne, Silvester had entered into a pact with the Devil that had both secured his safe flight from Spain and established the priorities of his pontificate (Figure 13.4). Such was the influence of diabolic magic in the church of the eleventh century, one commentator alleged, that "the com[m]on people do knowe evidently that the moset conyngest doctours and maistres of magical artes and other sciences . . . were always either sacrificeing priestes or elles monkishe or frierishe cloisterours".[90] The emerging narrative of Silvester's pontificate drew heavily from the work of Platina, whose *Vitæ Pontificum Platinæ historici liber de vita Christi ac omnium pontificum qui hactenus ducenti fuere et XX* (1479) had established the basic details of Silvester's biography. The first full edition of Bartolomeo Platina's *Lives of the Popes* was presented to Pope Sixtus V in 1475 and printed in 1479, and the text emerged as the definitive Renaissance study of the medieval papacy, running to more than eighty editions and being adapted and augmented until the eighteenth century. Platina's work was blunt in its criticisms of those popes who failed to live up to the obligations of the office or whose character fell below the high standards that Platina expected of the successors of St Peter. For this reason, the *Vitae* proved popular with evangelical polemicists, who used Platina's histories as a source for evidence of papal corruption. Platina described how Silvester had "got the popedom (as they say) by ill arts", lending support to the Protestant claim that Gerbert's elevation to the papacy could be ascribed to his skill in necromancy. Platina outlined Gerbert's education in Fleury and his subsequent journey to Spain to study human sciences and, allegedly, to follow the Devil. Gerbert had eventually secured his promotion to Ravenna, after which "at last the devil helping him with an extraordinary lift he got the popedom,

FIGURE 13.4. *Pope Silvester II and the Devil*. Illustration from Martin of Poland, *Chronicon pontificum et imperatorum*, ca. 1460. Heidelberg, University Library, Heidelberg, Cod. Pal. germ. 137, fol. 216v). Image in the public domain.

upon this condition that after his death he should be wholly the devil's". The necromancy legend, however, had its origins in earlier chronicle writing, particularly William of Malmesbury's *Gesta regum Anglorum*, which Bale had used in his commentary, and in the summary of Silvester and his pontificate that appeared in Benno's account of the predecessors of Gregory VII and their interests in the occult. Although William of Malmesbury saw fit to record the stories that were reported of Silvester in writing, it would seem that he was sceptical that they had their foundation in truth. Having completed his account of the flight of Gerbert from Spain, William admitted "probably some may regard all this as a fiction because the vulgar are used to undermine the fame of scholars saying that the man who excels in his admirable science holds converse with the devil". In his support, William cites Boethius's *Consolation of Philosophy*, perhaps giving vent to his own frustrations that scholarship was poorly respected and the learned were treated with suspicion. Whatever the polemical intention, the narrative is complicated by the fact that William himself seems to have identified Silvester with Pope John XVI, the anti-pope to the imperially sanctioned Gregory V ("tunc vero papa Romanus Johannes qui est Gerbertus"), and by the replication of this error at the hands of sixteenth-century readers of the *Gesta*.[91] The suggestion of papal necromancy in the *Gesta* and in Benno's commentary, however, assured Silvester a prominent place in evangelical anti-papal writing and in discourse on the relationship between magic and miracle in the lives of the popes.

Although the pontificate of Silvester II provided a clear demonstration of the polemical potential inherent in the rewriting of papal biographies in light of shifting doctrinal priorities, Silvester was not the only pope whose interactions with the demonic and the illicit supernatural acquired a prominent position in Protestant histories. Hildebrand, later Pope Gregory VII, it was alleged, had used his knowledge of magic to impose celibacy on an unwilling clergy and to work false miracles, including the transformation of communion bread into a finger.[92] Like Silvester's, the pontificate of Gregory VII was to occupy a critical space in evangelical histories and polemics, in which accusations of clerical magic and necromancy were to loom large. The reforms enacted in Gregory's name, and particularly the determined imposition of clerical celibacy, featured prominently in the Protestant narrative, but the denunciation of the pope as the agent of the Antichrist, a necromancer and a conjuror was made possible by the availability of contemporary tales, accusations and legends in which accusations of deceit, magical manipulation and diabolic interventions were at the fore. Reformation critics accused Gregory of "monstrouse wytchcraftes" and the ability to deceive the eyes of the observer with false wonders and feigned miracles.[93] Again, Benno's letters were to provide much of the ammunition against the pope, supplemented by accusations made by Gregory's critics and opponents at the Council of Worms (1076) and at the Synod of Brixen (1080), where the pope was denounced as an "open devotee of dreams and divinations, and a necromancer working with an oracular spirit".[94]

By 1611, John Napier had identified some twenty-two popes who were "abhominable Necromancers" in a list that was no doubt informed by the earlier accusations levelled against the popes by Bale, Barnes, Swinnerton and Foxe.[95] Swinnerton claimed that Benedict IX used magic and sacrifices to demons to draw women to him, whereas Bale claimed that Benedict IX's artifice had first secured the accession of his father and uncle to the papal throne, and then "by his magicke [Benedict] brought to passe that he succeeded them". Benedict's advisers, Bale alleged, including Lawrence and John Gratian were both "notorious coniurers", educated in the magical arts by Pope Silvester, but the pontiff's Reformation reputation was perhaps influenced all the more by criticisms levelled against him by influential opponents, including Peter Damian, whose *Liber Gomorrhianus* denounced Benedict as "a demon from hell in the guise of a priest".[96] Boniface VIII's conflict with secular authority in the form of Philip of France was unlikely to endear him to English evangelicals who were keen to secure the subordination of the church to the king, but again, accusations that the pope was a magician and necromancer loomed large in a narrative that was informed by the claims of earlier critics. In a posthumous trial, the French king accused the pope of a myriad of offences, including conjuring and maintaining demons, practicing ritual magic and consulting sorcerers.[97] This was not the first such accusation that Philip had levelled against a senior figure in the church; the practice of magic and witchcraft had also featured prominently in the proceedings against Guichard of Troyes. The bishop was arrested in 1308 and accused of using black magic to bring about the death of Philip's wife, Queen Jeanne, in 1305 and of plotting against other French princes and nobility. The bishop, it was alleged, was the fruit of a union between his mother and an incubus, had himself conjured up the Devil in the form of a monk and had committed various other crimes against the church and the laws of the realm.[98] Evangelical writers also hurled accusations of magic and necromancy against more recent occupants of the throne of St Peter, on occasion reflecting the activities of the popes along the malleable boundary between licit and illicit engagement with the supernatural. Bale described Paul III (1534–1549) as "very conning in astrologie, southsaying, and coniuring ... an astrologian, a Magician, [and] a wyzard" who had in his service a number of individuals who were "raysers of euyl spirites in the bodies of dead men" and who were employed to cast his nativities and destiny by the stars.[99] Bale's accusations had their roots in contemporary comments on the academic, and perhaps practical, interest that the pope took in the occult sciences. Paul III was not alone in this; several Renaissance popes acted as patrons to alchemists, astrologers and astronomers, including Leo X, who was described as "superstizioso credente anch' egli nei pronostici".[100] There were certainly astrologers in Rome during the pontificate of Paul III who dedicated their prognostications to the pope, or to members of the curia, and Luca Gauricio was summoned to the papal court by Paul III and appointed as Bishop of Giffani. Vincentius Abstemius credited the pope with the restoration of astrology to a position of respectability, and the pontiff certainly continued to receive astrological predictions throughout his occupation of the throne of St Peter.

Accusations of witchcraft and magic were used against the papal office and against individual popes in order to undermine the reputation of the individual and the respectability of the institution or in the service of political or personal rivalries and ambitions. In some cases, particularly in the accusations levelled against Silvester II and Gregory VII, there is a clear confessional motive to the reinvigoration of the legends of papal necromancy in the sixteenth century; these were long-standing representations of papal magic, into which new life was breathed by the imperatives of evangelical history writing and propaganda. But the origins of these accusations lay in the condemnations of contemporaries and in divisions opening up within the medieval church or between church and empire or pope and prince. Pressed into the service of sixteenth-century debate, stories of papal necromancy acquired a new agenda, but witchcraft had long been a weapon in the armoury of those hostile to the papacy or to particular popes. Perhaps the best-studied example is that of Benedict XIII, who was charged with a series of "magical" offences that have been summed up as a "tissue of nonsense" but that raise some significant questions about the relationship between clerical interest in the occult and the reality of accusations of magic.[101] What is most interesting is not the accuracy of the charges but the fact that at specific times and locations in the life of the church, evidence that was at other times dismissed as folklore could be presented by and to senior churchmen in a court of law. Benedict XIII and Gregory XII were tried before the Council of Pisa in 1409, in the hope that the papal schism could be brought to an end by their deposition. Two sets of charges were brought against them, including the allegation that both, but particularly Benedict, were, among other offences, guilty of witchcraft.[102] Against Benedict, the accusations included "multos nigromanticos, divinatores, magicos et libros migromancie et alios perquiri mandavit et perquisivit ac habuit", as well as further attempts to blacken the reputation of the pope both by direct charge, by association with apparently known practitioners of the occult arts, including Francesco Eximenis, and by rather tenuous means. Benedict was alleged to have read, possessed or attempted to procure various books on necromancy, demonology and astrology, although, as Harvey notes, there is little damning in this testimony, which simply demonstrates that the pope, like most of his contemporaries, was possessed of an interest in astrology and prophecy (but nothing more serious).[103] The momentum behind the charges was provided not by the strength of the evidence, but by the readiness of those who spoke against the pope to believe in the reality of witchcraft and, indeed, papal witchcraft. Like Chaucer's Canon's Yeoman, the pope's detractors gained their authority from the credulity of their audience. However, in Benedict's case, the audience was, it seems, located in the court rather than the tavern, and the specific charges of witchcraft made against the pope did not feature in his formal condemnation by the Council. The suggestion that the pope was guilty of witchcraft was a potentially useful addition to the more general charges against him, had these proved sufficient to justify deposition, and these allegations afforded the possibility of a reference back to the charges against Gregory and Silvester, as well as Boniface VIII, who was cited at Pisa as a precedent for the case against Benedict.

The iconoclastic hammers of the evangelicals broke apart, physically and intellectually, the images of saints and of sanctity, the miracles enshrined in medieval hagiography, the authority of the papacy and the sacramental powers of the "conjuring" priest. Yet the separation of miracle from magic, at least in theoretical terms, still owed much to the legacy of the Catholic past. In their assault on traditional assumptions about the miraculous, evangelical writers, like their Catholic counterparts, debated miracles on the basis of the following: scriptural precedent and example; the assertion of Christian truth in the face of heresy and the false wonders of the Antichrist; the confirmation of the doctrines of the church; and the holiness of life manifested by the individual by whose agency the miracle was obtained. However, the application of these conceptual principles to the history and theology of the Catholic Church produced a markedly different outcome, in which priests became sorcerers, miracles became evidence of doctrinal error, and the lives and legends of the saints testified to the false foundations of their cults. The traditional lexicon of debate, refracted through the prism of evangelical understanding, produced a dramatically different delineation between magic and miracle.

As this boundary shifted, the magic rather than miracle of the Mass, as represented in evangelical polemical writing, positioned the central rite of the Catholic Church as (potentially diabolic) fraud and the celebrant as a conjuror, deceiver or false preacher. It is hardly surprising that controversy over the theology of the Eucharist assumed centre stage at critical moments in the definition of reformed doctrine. But evangelical writing against the Mass informed, and was informed by, broader debates about the role of see-ing and believing, the role of the "audience" in making the link between idea and event, and the function and intentions of the priesthood. It was in the Mass that the eyes of the body and the eyes of faith collided, and it was in the evangelical attack on transubstantiation that a new vision and perception of sacrament and celebrant was constructed.[104] Whereas Catholic theology had asserted the central significance of that which could not be seen, evangelical writers argued for the supremacy of that which was recognised by "our eyes, our nose, our mouth, our taste" in the physical elements, and they turned to the vocabulary of magic, juggling and deceit to condemn traditional belief. Transubstantiation, the invisible transformation of the substance of the ele-ments into flesh and blood, was a false wonder, but so too was the appar-ent manipulation of the eyes of the faithful, who were deceived by the false promises of the church and the sleight of hand of the priest.[105] By the 1580s, the link between Catholicism and deception, and between priest and conjuror, had become firmly established in Reginald Scot's *Discoverie of Witchcraft*. The words and actions of the Catholic clergy were intermingled with Scot's mock-ery of supposed witchcraft and magic, with the result that "oracling priests and monks" became not the faithful servants of God, but rather the work-ers of "cousening tricks", "strange illusions" and "counterfet visions".[106] Such rhetoric was applied with a broad brush to the Catholic clergy, from parish priest to pope, and with rather more precision to individuals in whose reputa-tion the role of celebrant and conjuror coalesced in past and present. It found expression in the popular, scurrilous anti-Mass tracts of the late 1540s, in the defence of the Edwardian settlements of religion and in John Jewel's academic defence of the reformed church in England. The proximate activities of priest and sorcerer, whether they were real or constructed, were a shared concern for the medieval church and for its Reformation critics. Writing on the origins of medieval hagiography and the cult of the saints, Delehaye argued for the presence of a "material but wholly external link between the new religion and the old", a link that was forged by observances and symbols.[107] In the England of the 1540s, the link between the old and new lay rather in the refraction of these observances and symbols through the prism of competing but contigu-ous interpretations; John Bale's priestly charmers, enchanters, conjurers and dogleeches (and, indeed, Richard Pynson's *Corpus Christi*, Figure 13.1) had a central role to play in the drama of religious reformation.

Notes

1. Shepherd, *The Vpcheringe of the Messe*, sigs. A4r–A4v.
2. Brigden, *London and the Reformation*, 434–436.
3. King, *English Reformation Literature*, 249–250; Punt, *A New Dialogue called the Endightment Agaynste Mother Masse*, sig. A5r.
4. I. M., *A Breife Recantation of Maystres Missa*, sig. A1v.
5. Ibid., sig. A3v.
6. Turner, *A New Dialogue Wherin is Conteyned the Examination of the Masse*, sig. A3r; Marshall, *The Catholic Priesthood*, 34–35; Becon, *Displaying of the Popish Masse*, 259–260; Jewel, *Apologie of the Church of England*, 35–36.
7. Dugmore, *The Mass and the English Reformers*, 142.
8. Scribner, *Popular Culture and Popular Movements*, 10; Huizinga, *The Waning of the Middle Ages*.
9. de Besançon, *Alphabet of Tales*, nos. 577, 695.
10. Rubin, *Corpus Christi*, 111.
11. Gairdner, ed., *The Historical Collections of a Citizen of London*, 224–225.
12. Mirk, *Instructions for Parish Priests*, ed. Peacock, 149; Lydgate, *Merita Missa*, 148–154.
13. Mirk, *Instructions*, 155–156.
14. *The Poems of John Audeley*, 67, quoted in Rubin, *Corpus Christi*, 108.
15. Anon., *Breife Recantation of Mistress Missa* (1548?), sig. A3r.
16. Hilarie, *The resurreccion of the masse*, sig. A3r.
17. Ramsey, *A Plaister for a Galled Horse*, n.p.
18. Anon., *Here begynneth a booke*, sig. B5v.
19. Bale, *The vocacyon of Ioha[n] Bale to the bishiprick of Ossorie in Irela[n]de his persecucio[n]s in ye same, & finall delyueraunce.*
20. Rubin, *Corpus Christi*, 1.
21. Bossy, "The Mass as a Social Institution", 33.
22. de Voraigne, *The Golden Legend*, trans. Caxton, "The Storie of the Masse", 438r.
23. Brooke, "Religious Sentiment and Church Design", 162–182; Grant, "The Elevation of the Host", 228–250.
24. Duffy, *The Stripping of the Altars*, 101; Furnivall, ed., *Robert of Brunne's Handlynge Synne*; Erbe, ed., *Mirk's Festial*; Dugmore *The Mass and the English Reformers*, 75–77; Messenger, *The Reformation, the Mass and the Priesthood*, 96–105; Rubin, *Corpus Christi*, 115–118.
25. Duffy, *The Stripping of the Altars*, 103.
26. Veron, *The godly saiyngs of the old auncient faithful fathers vpon the Sacrament of the bodye and bloude of Chryste*, sigs. A5r–A5v; F8r–F8v.
27. Shepherd, *Doctour Dubble Ale*, sig. A4r.
28. Crowley, *The confutation of the mishapen aunswer*, sigs. E1r–E1v.

29. Bale, *A mysterye of inyquyte*, sigs. G7r, H2r.
30. Bale, *The apology of Iohan Bale agaynste a ranke papyst anuswering both hym and hys doctours*, sig. A8r.
31. Punt, *A New Dialogue called the Endightment Agaynste Mother Messe*, sig A5r.
32. Anon., *Here begynneth a booke*, sigs. A4v, C4r.
33. Crowley, *The confutation of the mishapen aunswer*, sig. C1r.
34. Marcourt, *A declaration of the masse*, sigs. A6r–A6v, B7r.
35. Moone, *A short treatyse of certayne thinges abused*, sig. A2v.
36. Cranmer, *A defence of the true and catholike doctrine*.
37. Bale, *The lattre examinacyon of Anne Askewe*, sigs. C8v–D1r.
38. Bale, *A mysterye of inyquyte*, 5.
39. Hilarie, *The resurreccion of the masse*.
40. Becon, *Displaying of the Popish Mass*, 261, 262, 266.
41. Crowley, *The confutation of the mishapen aunswer*, sigs. D3r, F7v.
42. Moone, *A short treatyse of certayne thinges abused*, sig. A3r; Anon., *Here begynneth a booke*, sigs. A3v, A4r.
43. Bale, *The Image of Both Churches*, part II, 7v; Parish, *Monks, Miracles and Magic*; Marshall, *The Catholic Priesthood*; Walsham, *Providence in Early Modern England*.
44. Kieckhefer, *Magic in the Middle Ages*, 80.
45. Thorndike, *A History of Magic and Experimental Science*, part 2, 628–630.
46. Veenstra, *Magic and Divination at the Courts*, 154.
47. John of Salisbury, *Policraticus*, trans. Nederman, I.8, I.9.
48. Kieckhefer, *Magic in the Middle Ages*, 91.
49. Bale, *A mysterye of inyquyte*, sigs. F1r, F3r, G7r, H2r; cf. Anon., *Here begynneth a booke*, sigs. A4v, B5v, C4v.
50. Bale, *The First Two Partes of the Actes*, part I, sig. G6v; MacLure, *Register of Sermons preached at Paul's Cross*, 26 (8 February 1545).
51. E. P., *A Confutation of Unwritten Verities*, sigs. O3v–O4v.
52. Erbe, ed., *Mirk's Festial*, 170–171. The miracle attributed to Odo is unusual, in that such physical appearances of flesh and blood at the Eucharist were less frequently reported before the twelfth century. However, the same incident is recorded among the miracles of Odo in William of Malmesbury's *Gesta Pontificum*, which provided Foxe with his information: William of Malmesbury, *Gesta Romanorum Pontificum*, ed. Preest, 18.
53. For a fuller discussion of these themes, see Rubin, *Corpus Christi*, 308–310; Kamerick, *Popular Piety and Art in the Late Middle Ages*.
54. Parish, *Monks, Miracles and Magic*; Rubin, *Corpus Christi*, 135–136; de Besançon, *Alphabet of Tales*, no. 695; Stacey, "From Ritual Crucifixion to Host Desecration", 11–28; Teter, *Sinners on Trial*.
55. Bale, *Actes of the English Votaries*, part I, sigs. G6r–G6v; Foxe, *The first volume of the Ecclesiasticall History*, fol. 199 [henceforth *Actes and Monuments*].

56. MacCulloch, *The Reign of Henry VIII*, 187.

57. Smith, *The assertion and defence of the sacramente*, 24r.

58. Ibid., part III, sig. Dd3r.

59. Bale, *The Image of Both Churches*, part I, sigs. E4r, Q1r–Q1v; Bale, *A mysterye of inyquyte*, sig. E3v.

60. Moone, *A short treatyse of certayne thinges abused*, sig. A2r.

61. Ibid., sig. A2v.

62. Quoted in Walker, "The Cessation of Miracles", 12; Tyndale, *An Answer to Sir Thomas More's Dialogue*, 130–131; Sheldon, *Survey of the Miracles of the Church of Rome*, sig. C1r; Turner, *The Huntyng of the Romishe Vvolfe*, sigs. A8r–A8v.

63. Calvin, *Institutes of the Christian Religion*, ed. McNeill, 16.

64. Tyndale, *An Answer to Sir Thomas More's Dialogue*, 129; Bale, *Actes of the English Votaries*, sigs. A5r–A5v; Foxe, *Actes and Monuments* (referring to the miracles of Becket).

65. Wycliffe, *Tractatus de Potestate Pape*, ed. Loserth, 106–107.

66. "Quilibet sacerdos consecrando eucharistiam facit infinita miracula et tanta quanta fecit dominus Jhus Christus"; Wycliffe, *Dialogus Sive Speculum Ecclesie Militantis*, ed. Pollard, 32.

67. Barnes, *A Supplicacion vnto the most gracious prynce H. the viij*, sig. S3r.

68. Bale, *Actes of the English Votaries*, sig. A5r.

69. Bale, *A mysterye of inyquyte*, sigs. H6r, K3r; Bale, *The Image of Both Churches*, part II, sig. G4v, part III, sig. Dd3r.

70. Bale, *The Image of Both Churches*, part I, sigs. B2r, B3r, E4r; Bale, *A mysterye of inyquyte*, sig. C8v.

71. Donaldson, *Speaking of Chaucer*, 1091.

72. Steinmeyer, *Hiding the Elephant*, 17.

73. Aquinas, *Summa theologiae*, trans. Fathers of the English Dominican Province, vol. I, 520; Aquinas, *Summa contra gentiles*, trans. Fathers of the English Dominican Province, vol. III, part ii, 65ff.

74. Augustine, *City of God*, 10:9; Clark, *Thinking with Demons*, 167. For a further discussion of these themes, see Kieckhefer, *Magic in the Middle Ages*, 35–36, 38–40; Murray, "Missionaries and Magic in Dark Age Europe", 37; Jolly, Raudvere and Peters, eds., *Witchcraft and Magic in Europe*, vol. 3, 1–2; Kieckhefer, "The Holy and the Unholy", 815; Remus, *Pagan Christian Conflict in the Second Century*.

75. Gregory the Great, "Life of St Benedict", 75–77. For biblical prohibitions of magic, see Leviticus 20:6, 20:27; Deuteronomy 13; 1 Sam. 15:23; 1 Cor. 10:20; 2 Thess. 2; 1 Tim. 4:1; Augustine, *City of God*, book 9; for a discussion of these themes in the medieval penitentials, see MacNeill and Gamer, *Medieval Handbooks of Penance*. Indeed, the triumph of the figure of the Christian

missionary often testified to the truth of his preaching. Bede's *Life of St Cuthbert* emphasised not only role of the miracles worked by Cuthbert in promoting his preaching in Northumbria but also their superiority to pagan magic; see Harmening, *Superstitio*; Gurevich, *Medieval Popular Culture*. Magic, and particularly clerical magic, was condemned at the synods of Elvira (306), Carthage (398) and Orleans (511); C. H. Talbot, *The Anglo-Saxon Missionaries in Germany*; Bede, *Vita Sancti Cuthberti*, ed. Colgrave, 184.

76. Herzog, *Die Wunderheilungen von Epidauros*, 140.

77. Parish, *Monks, Miracles and Magic*, 15.

78. Jolly, Raudvere and Peters, eds., *Witchcraft and Magic*, 2; Clark, *Thinking with Demons*, 552.

79. Kee, *Miracle in the Early Christian World*, pursues this distinction to the full. It is worth noting in this context the difference between the orthodox view of the Mass, in which the efficacy of the sacrament was independent of the character of the priest (*ex opere operato*), and those rites of the church which required an honest priest and devout laity (*ex opere operantis*). Peter Brown argued that in fact both saint and sorcerer were able to command, "but the saint has an effective 'vested' power, whereas the sorcerer works with a technique that is unreliable, and above all, cumbersome". Brown, "Sorcery, Demons and the Rise of Christianity", 14–45; Malinowski, *Magic, Science and Religion*, esp. 38, 87.

80. Malinowski, *Magic, Science and Religion*, esp. 38, 87.

81. Marshall, "Forgery and Miracles in the Reign of Henry VIII", 39–73. For a criticism of claims that the sinful were unable to witness miracles, see Corrie, ed., *Sermons and Remains of Hugh Latimer*, 364.

82. Thomas, *Religion and the Decline of Magic*, ch. 2. See also the discussion between Thomas and Geertz over the nature of religion and magic: Geertz, "An Anthropology of Religion and Magic", 71–89; and Thomas's reply, "An Anthropology of Religion and Magic II", 91–109. Other significant contributions to the debate include Gentilcore, *From Bishop to Witch*; Gentilcore, *Healers and Healing in Early Modern Italy*; Cameron, "For Reasoned Faith and Embattled Creed", 165–187; Klaniczay, *The Uses of Supernatural Power*; Hill and Swan, eds., *The Community, the Family and the Saint*; Dinzelbacher, "Heilige oder Hexen", 41–60.

83. Kieckhefer, *Magic in the Middle Ages*, 152.

84. Bowd, *Venice's Most Loyal City*, 179.

85. Thomas, *Religion and the Decline of Magic*, ch. 2.

86. Bale, *Actes of the English Votaries*, part 1, sigs. C7v, D8r.

87. Ibid., part II, sig. C7r.

88. Bale, *Actes of the English Votaries*, part I, 17vff; Flacius, Judex and Wigand, *Ecclesiastica historia*, cent. X, cols. 453–455; Foxe, *Actes and monuments*, vol. 1, fol. 207; Parish, "Impudent and Abhominable Fictions", 45–65.

89. Swinnerton, *A Mustre of Scismatyke bysshopes of Rome*, sig. B5v; Bietenholz, *Historia and Fabula*, ch. 2; Oldoni, "Gerberto a la sua storia", 629–704.

90. Gualther, *Antichrist, that is to say A true reporte that Antichriste is come*, sig. L6r.

91. See William Stubbs, introduction to the *Gesta* of William of Malmesbury, in Stubbs, ed., *De gestis regum Anglorum*, ix–cxiv. Rollo notes that Malmesbury was an accomplished papal historian who supervised the compilation of the *Liber Pontificalis* and had research widely in the writing of the *Gesta*. Yet, if he was aware of the error, he made no attempt to correct it, leading Rollo to conclude that Malmesbury had composed his biography of Silvester for a proficient but small audience, for whom the error would be clear, thereby justifying the mocking of the illiterate majority who could not distinguish fact from fiction. Rollo, *Glamorous Sorcery*, 12–13.

92. Bale, *A mysterye of inyquyte*, 16; Bale, *Acta Romanorvm Pontificum*, sigs. K8v, I1v; Bale, *Actes of the English Votaries*, part 2, sigs. B1r, D6v; Foxe, *Actes and monuments*, vol. I, fols. 217–218, 228; Flacius, Judex and Wigand, *Ecclesiastica historia*, cent. X, cols. 547–548; Swinnerton, *A Mustre of Scismatyke bysshopes of Rome*, sig. A6v.

93. Swinnerton, *A Mustre of Scismatyke bysshopes of Rome*, sigs. A1–A7v; Barnes, *A Supplicacion vnto the most gracious prynce H. the viij*, sig. M5v; Foxe, *Actes and monuments*, part I, fol. 225.

94. Mommsen and Morrison, eds., *Imperial Lives and Letters*, doc. 15a.

95. Napier, *A Plaine discovery of the whole revelation of St John*, fols. 56–58.

96. Bale, *The Pageant of Popes*, trans. Studely, fols. 75–76. Peter Damian's denunciation was informed by his detestation of Benedict's apparent homosexuality, echoed in Pope Victor III's *Dialogues*, in which Benedict was denounced as having a "life as a pope so vile, so foul, so execrable, that I shudder to think of it".

97. A long list of allegations made against the pope was presented by Guillaume de Plaisians on 14 April 1303; see Boase, *Boniface VIII*, 333–334; Dupuy, *Histoire du différend*, 342ff.

98. Ibid., fol. 125ff. A full discussion of the accusations against the bishop can be found in Rigault, *Le procès de Guichard*.

99. Bale, *The Pageant of Popes*, fol. 231.

100. Thorndike, *A History of Magic and Experimental Science*, part 9, 252.

101. Harvey, "Papal Witchcraft", 109–116.

102. Valois, *La France et le Grand Schisme d'Occident*, vol. IV, 94–97; Vincke, "Acta Concilii Pisani", 213–294.

103. Harvey, "Papal Witchcraft", 114.

104. On the theme of the senses, particularly sight, and the Reformation, see Clark, *Vision in Early Modern European Culture*, 182ff; Milner, *The Senses and the English Reformation*; Iliffe, "Lying Wonders and Juggling Tricks", 185–209.

105. Bradford, *Two Notable Sermons*, sig. G1r. It is worth noting here, as Clark suggests, that Catholic writers continued to argue that the "juggling" for which the Catholic clergy were condemned would surely relate to a change in substance and not accident. See, for example, Dorman, *A Proufe of Certeyne Articles in Religion Denied by M. Iuell*.

106. Scot, *The Discoverie of Witchcraft* 176–177.

107. Delehaye, *The Legends of the Saints*, 149.

PART V

★

COLONIAL ENCOUNTERS

Chapter 14

Spain and Mexico

LOUISE M. BURKHART

Spain's colonial enterprise in the Americas brought Europeans into contact with hundreds of peoples previously unknown to what was now the "Old World." These diverse societies included nomadic foragers, village horticul- turalists, and the urban civilizations of Mesoamerica and the Andes. When in 1494 Pope Alexander VI granted Isabella and Ferdinand sovereignty over the newly discovered lands, he also demanded that they Christianize the inhab- itants. Although rapacity frequently overrode religion among the colonists' priorities, Spanish colonialism – more than that of any later European power – always concerned itself with the state of its new subjects' souls. Even as much of Europe rejected Roman Catholicism, Spain proudly replenished Rome's territories with great tracts of American soil.

This chapter focuses on Spain's encounter with Mexico, the jewel added in 1521 to the crown of the newly elected Emperor Charles V, Ferdinand and Isabella's young Habsburg grandson. In August of that year, the Mexicas' twin cities of Tenochtitlan and Tlatelolco, center of the Aztec Empire and one of the world's largest urban settlements, fell to a combined force of long-time enemies, rebelling subjects, and Spanish adventurers led by Hernando Cortés. The Mexica defeat allowed Spain to establish its first large mainland colony, which endured until 1821. The Viceroyalty of New Spain encompassed Aztec and neighboring territories, and it expanded into what is now Central America and the southwestern United States.

It was in the central Mexican highlands that indigenous civilization was most thoroughly documented, by indigenous as well as European authors. Hence, most information in this chapter relates to this region, where the clash between native and Christian religious and magical ideas and practices can be most closely examined. Here the largest language group was the Nahuas, as it is called by historians and anthropologists today; at the time, speakers of Nahuatl divided themselves into local ethnic-political groups, among which the Mexica, the leading power in the Aztec Empire, were one of many.

The idolatry, witchcraft, and magic that Spaniards associated with indigenous Mesoamericans served the same ideological function that tropes of savagery or racial inferiority did for later colonial projects: keeping the colonized perpetually in a condition of otherness and subjection. The sections that follow examine several specific battlegrounds of the fractious encounter that used to be considered a "spiritual conquest."[1] First is the missionaries' association of indigenous deities and their temple rituals with worship of the Devil – the entity that early modern Europeans constructed as the master of witchcraft and sorcery. Eliminating sacrificial rituals and the worship of "idols" was the evangelizers' foremost concern. The idea that Indians were in thrall to the Devil – and if freed might easily fall back into his service – colored churchmen's views of all native religious practices.

Magic and witchcraft were lesser concerns for the evangelizers than idolatrous sacrifice was; however, because Europeans associated them with the Devil, they too violated the First Commandment. Indigenous religious practice can be roughly divided into two spheres. One comprises public, collective temple ritual. In charge of these rites were professionals whom Spanish observers viewed as a priesthood despite the "idolatrous" nature of their services; friars were content to be called by the same term: *teopixque*, or "god-keepers." The other consists of individualized and more instrumental rites, which were associated with issues of personal fate and fortune. These somewhat correspond to what such early theorists as Sir James Frazer, Marcel Mauss, and Bronislaw Malinowski set apart as the domain of "magic" – although the rites were not purely mechanical, given that practitioners had to appease and appeal to capricious superhuman entities.[2] Spanish observers characterized these practices variously, and somewhat interchangeably, as witchcraft (*brujería, hechicería*), sorcery (*sortilegio*), and superstition (*superstición, abusión*), although they also saw signs of idolatry (*idolatría*) where indigenous sacred forces were invoked. These rites were the province of full- or part-time specialists who operated out of their homes and thus could not be disenfranchised like the temple priests were. Their diversity of techniques struck Marcel Mauss as "a complete specialization of magical rites and practices."[3]

This duality of religious domains is encoded in the Mesoamerican calendrical system. One calendar organized collective worship and supplication of the gods through temple rituals. Another calendar governed the art of divination. The second section of this chapter introduces Mexican "magic" by discussing this divinatory calendar.

One factor complicating the introduction of Christianity was the absence of moral dualism in Mesoamerican thought. The third section of this chapter examines the extent to which a domain of malefice or black magic existed in indigenous conceptions of magical practitioners and considers how European observers imposed their notions of witchcraft and the demonic pact on these darker figures.

The fourth section discusses divination and healing. Europeans were impressed by native medicine but repelled by the magical techniques it employed in diagnosis and treatment. Seeing magic as diabolical, and Indians as extremely susceptible to demonic influence, some churchmen grouped all native doctors and midwives with the workers of malefice.

The fifth section complements the discussion of unsanctioned native religion with a brief look at indigenized Christianity, especially the cult of the saints. The multiplicity of the Roman Catholic divine, concretized in images, made it easy for indigenous Christians to continue to see sacred forces infusing the material world, manifesting their presence in wondrous ways and making their assistance available to devotees. Because the same basic conceptions underlay divination and magical healing, churchmen's attempts to separate matters of faith from matters of magic were ill fated.

The final section, drawing from the expanding literature on the Mexican Inquisition, places Indian magic in the multiethnic context of colonial society, extending into the seventeenth and eighteenth centuries.

"A Likeness of Hell"

> To them it was a great nuisance to listen to the word of God, and they did not want to do anything but give themselves to vices and sins, sacrifices and festivals, eating and drinking and getting drunk at them, and feeding the idols with their own blood, which they drew from their own ears, tongues, and arms, and other parts of their bodies ... This land was a likeness of hell, to see the inhabitants of it crying out at night, some calling to the devil, others drunk, others singing and dancing.[4]

The evangelization of Mexico formally began when a party of twelve Spanish Franciscans arrived in 1524. In this quotation, fray Toribio de Benavente (ca. 1490–1569), one of the famed twelve, who adopted the Nahuatl name Motolinia ("he is poor"), recalls his first impression of indigenous religion. Such an infernal scene contrasts to good effect with the Franciscans' notable early successes, which Motolinia, writing in 1540 or 1541, documents with enthusiasm. The more hellish pre-Columbian religion was, the more glorious were the friars' victories, and the more impressive were their converts' signs of piety. Nahuas themselves sometimes accentuated the more violent aspects of their old rites, painting scenes of blood-soaked temples, monstrous idols, and cannibal feasts or inflating the numbers of their sacrificial victims.

However, pre-Columbian religion really was bloody, especially the major festivals in the Aztec capital. Most human sacrifices were of enemy warriors, who were captured in battle rather than killed outright. Some were male or female slaves; the rain gods favored children. Heart extraction was the most common technique of sacrifice; other methods included scaffold sacrifice and gladiatorial sacrifice. The dead bodies were further modified through beheading, dismemberment, and sometimes flaying. Heads were displayed on racks; priests donned flayed skins. Some human flesh was consumed: for example, a warrior whose captive was sacrificed would serve a meal prepared with flesh from his captive's thigh, retaining the femur for his wife to use in rituals that would protect him in future battles. And, as Motolinia observed, native people also frequently cut their own flesh and offered their blood to the gods.[5]

Examining these practices, it is helpful to realize that, for indigenous Mexicans, a human being was not a stable, bounded entity, one soul inhabiting one body, in whom reason strove to keep emotion in check. Rather, a person was a composite formed of flesh, bone, blood, and soul-like components. This composite was subject to, and easily invaded by the cosmic forces that inhabit and flow through all of creation, manifesting themselves as heat, light, rain, wind, fire, maize, and so on. Identity could be ritually deconstructed and reconstructed, turning a person into a vessel for a cosmic force. Gods were similarly composite, constructed as temporary images or impersonators and then dismantled, their identities unfixed and overlapping, unfolding into male-female pairs or into groups of four, five, or four hundred. These gods had sacrificed themselves to make human life possible, and they were owed reciprocal services, given that people continued to depend on them for life and sustenance.[6]

The blood and the bodies were, thus, the wreckage left behind when gods passed into and out of human beings. They indicated neither exceptional cruelty nor the exceptional love that fray Bartolomé de Las Casas tried to find there. The Dominican crusader for Indian rights, obliged to defend Aztec religion in his famous 1550–1551 debate with theologian Juan Ginés de Sepúlveda, argued that Aztec human sacrifice evidenced the most profound, albeit misdirected, religious devotion, because human life is the most precious thing that can be offered to any god. He also made the case that Spanish greed took more human lives in one year than sacrificial rituals had taken in the full century before the conquest.[7] The much more typical European reaction, however, was revulsion.

Although the earliest observers, including Cortés, attributed the shortcomings of Mexican civilization more to ignorance and weakness than to the Devil, Europeans soon became convinced that the newly conquered lands were the domain of Satan.[8] Although some deities could be interpreted as apotheosized men (Quetzalcoatl, Huitzilopochtli), for the most part, Spanish commentators considered indigenous deities to be actual devils, even though they adopted native terms for "deity," *teotl* in Nahuatl, to refer to God. The crafty Tezcatlipoca, a shape-shifting trickster god, was equated to Lucifer.[9] Not until the Enlightenment, when the exiled Jesuit Francisco Javier Clavigero wrote his *Ancient History of Mexico* (1780–1781), would even the most learned and sympathetic non-Indian chroniclers cease to interpret pre-Columbian religion as being free from demonic interference (Figure 14.1).[10]

Certain aspects of indigenous religion challenged European understandings not because of their otherness but because of their familiarity: myths of paradises lost, great floods, and magical conceptions; rites that resembled baptism, confession, and communion; priestly celibacy; priests called *papahuaque*, which is similar to the Spanish word for pope (*papa*); and chaste young women, akin to nuns, who served in the temples. Observers disagreed as to whether the pagan Indians found their way to some truths by the light of their natural reason or whether the Devil invented these things in mockery of the true faith. Some, notably the Dominican chronicler Diego Durán, who was struck by certain legends about Quetzalcoatl, posited that a Christian evangelist, possibly Saint Thomas, might once have preached in Mexico.[11]

Within a few decades of the Aztec defeat, Christianity had made significant inroads. A stable ecclesiastical structure was established in central Mexico, and missionaries began to extend their work into the provinces. The temples, whose cults had been suppressed by civil authority, were dismantled; their ruins supplied building materials for churches, which were often constructed in the same or adjacent locations. Human sacrifice was virtually eliminated. Many people were baptized, learned the basic catechism, and attended church services. Civil life was reorganized around the church calendar. A shortage of priests left many functions in the hands of indigenous religious officials, and native Christianity took on its own distinctive and variable forms.[12]

Putting an end to idolatry was the gravest concern for the missionaries, including first the Franciscans, who were soon joined by the Dominicans, the Augustinians, and, in 1572, the Jesuits. They treated as violations of the First Commandment any practices associated with idols – images of stone, wood, or clay that some people continued, clandestinely, to keep. Also idolatrous was anything that hinted too strongly at the old gods and rituals, especially

Quema y Quandio de los templas idolatricos de la prouinᵈ de Jaxcala por los frayles y Españoles y conrentinᵒ de los naturales

FIGURE 14.1. Franciscan Friars burn temples in the city of Tlaxcala, driving out gods whom the indigenous artist depicts as devils. Drawing in Diego Muñoz Camargo's *Descripçion de la çiudad y prouincia de Tlaxcala*, late sixteenth century, f. 240v. University of Glasgow Library, Special Collections. Image reproduced with permission of the Bridgeman Art Library International.

blood sacrifice. For the baptized, sins against the First Commandment were considered manifestations of heresy and even apostasy, and as such they were punishable by ecclesiastical courts.

Indigenous people had no conception of their religious practices as a defined or bounded domain of "religion" or "faith" that could simply be exchanged for another. Corresponding European categories translated only clumsily into indigenous languages. In the case of Nahuatl, missionaries and their indigenous linguistic assistants developed the term *tlateotoquiliztli*, "following things as gods," to refer to idolatry. They contrasted this with *tlaneltoquiliztli*, "believing things" or "following things as true," to refer to the Christian faith.

The desire to root out idolatry motivated churchmen to document indigenous religion in detail. Franciscans proved to be the most prolific ethnographers; Dominicans, Jesuits, and a few secular clergy also produced important records. The Franciscan friar Bernardino de Sahagún (1499?–1590) compiled the most significant single source, a text unique in European colonialism.[13] Sahagún's three decades of collaboration with Nahua scholars and consultants resulted in the so-called *Florentine Codex*, a twelve-book account of indigenous civilization. The material was collected in the Nahuatl language and illustrated by native artists. Sahagún added Castilian prologues, asides, and a rough translation (perhaps partly written by bilingual Nahuas) to the final version, which was prepared in the mid-1570s. The codex depicts a complex, functioning society in which elders are respected, children are cherished, gods are served, and everyone knows his or her station: it is as much a defense of Nahua cultural legitimacy as it is a guide for anti-idolatry crusaders.

The shortage of clergy precluded any thorough and consistent surveillance of native practice. Anti-idolatry campaigns could be oppressive, but they were intermittent and localized, never attaining the scale of the seventeenth-century suppressions of idolatry carried out in the Andes.[14] If caught, a practitioner could receive a whipping, other public humiliations, and jail time and could see his or her ritual items confiscated and destroyed.

Indians were rarely put to death for idolatry alone. The most notorious exception occurred far from central Mexico, among the Mayans of the Yucatan Peninsula. In 1562, Franciscan provincial superior Diego de Landa led an illegal inquisitorial investigation of idolatry among Mayan converts, during which more than 4,500 people were tortured. One hundred fifty-eight died from this torture. Many others were maimed; some committed suicide.[15] In the famous case of don Carlos Chichimecatecuhtli, a Nahua ruler put on trial in 1539 by Mexico's first bishop, the Franciscan Juan de Zumárraga, the defendant was acquitted of idolatry charges. His conviction and execution rested instead on the more serious charge of heretical dogmatizing: actively preaching against Christianity.[16]

The Day Count

God gets especially angry if you seek out a deceiver, a healer, or a day-counter, so that he or she will tell you whether or not you will recover from an illness, or if something will happen to you that is painful and afflicting, scary and frightening. Nor are you to ask that he or she tell you whether it is on a good day that you were born, or that you plan to marry, or plan to build a house, or whatever you plan to do.[17]

In 1553, the Franciscan Andrés de Olmos (1480?–1568), who had participated in a witchcraft investigation in Basque country shortly before sailing to Mexico in 1528, translated into Nahuatl parts of Martín de Castañega's 1529 treatise on sorcery and superstition. Olmos believed the "simple Indian natives" were as deep in the Devil's service as European witches were and thus could benefit from this Spanish inquisitor's wisdom.[18] In this quotation, Olmos supplements Castañega's material with a warning against indigenous divinatory practice.

A defining characteristic of the Mesoamerican cultural area is a 260-day divinatory calendar that had been in use for more than 2,000 years before Columbus sailed. The count combines twenty day names, mostly animals, plants, and other natural phenomena, with numerical coefficients from one to thirteen, to make 260 distinct signs (One Flower, Six Water, Twelve Eagle, and the like). Each day sign with the coefficient of one started a distinct thirteen-day period, breaking the count into twenty units, each with different deities as patrons.

Temple rituals and divinatory arts had separate calendars. The day count interlaced with a 365-day solar calendar, or year count, which parsed the same day signs into eighteen twenty-day segments that the priests used to schedule the major, public ceremonies. The five leftover days, unpatronized by deities, were a "useless" period when "people just lay around in their houses."[19] Once every fifty-two years, the solar and divinatory calendars began on the same day, forming a cycle that was called in Nahuatl a *xiuhmolpilli*, or "year bundle."

Of the various explanations for the 260-day span, the most persuasive derives it from a natural human cycle: the typical time between a pregnant woman's first missed menstruation and the birth of her baby. This gestational connection, supported by ethnographic evidence from Guatemala,[20] is not attested in colonial sources. However, women's use of the cycle to predict their delivery dates may have simply gone undocumented by Spanish observers, as most information was recorded from and by men. Because a major function of the calendar was, as Olmos complains, to make predictions on the basis of a person's date of birth, a link to conception and gestation is logical (Figure 14.2).

In Nahuatl, the divinatory calendar was called the *tonalpohualli*, or "day count." Specialists called *tonalpouhque*, "those who count (or read) the days," kept books in which the day signs and prognosticative images were painted. As Olmos indicates, people consulted the calendar not only when their children

FIGURE 14.2. A mother consults a diviner about her child, born on the day Ten Rabbit. Illustration from the *Florentine Codex*, book four, f. 34v. Reprinted with permission from fray Bernardino de Sahagún, *Historia general de las cosas de Nueva España, Códice florentino.* Facsimile of the *Codex Florentinus* of the Biblioteca Medicea Laurenziana, published by the Archivo General de la Nación, 1979.

were born but also when planning marriages and for other important undertakings. Day signs were entangled with cosmic and human identities: *tonalli*,
the word for day or day sign, derived from the verb *tona*, which refers to the
heat of the sun, a basic life-giving force. A soul housed in the crown of the
head was also a person's *tonalli*. This entity provided body heat and influenced
a person's well-being and destiny. It could be harmed or dislodged, especially
from a child, and therefore require a specialist's treatment.[21]

A person's *tonalli* – soul and day sign – determined his or her fate, for good
or ill, although a poor prognosis could be countered by holding a birth ceremony on some better day. For example, parents of a baby born on the dreaded
One Grass, who would likely see their grandchildren perish as easily as grass,
could partly neutralize the ill effects by bathing and naming their child on
Two Reed, a propitious day associated with the god Tezcatlipoca. Diligent
behavior – such as fasting, serving the gods, and abstaining from alcohol –
could also counteract a poor *tonalli*.

Each number, symbol, and thirteen-day unit had different fortunes associated with it. There were also interlacing series of nine Lords of the Night
and thirteen avian patrons associated, respectively, with the nine layers of
the underworld and the thirteen layers of the heavens. Specific deities were
associated with certain day signs. Thus, a day counter had various criteria
to consider when divining the fortune of any particular day and could tailor
his or her readings to suit the client's needs and circumstances. The detailed
accounts in Sahagún's book on this divinatory art show that day signs could
have different implications depending on whether a person was a noble or a
commoner or a man or a woman.[22]

To the most optimistic Franciscan observers, the fact that the Indians had
developed a 365-day calendar demonstrated their rationality and ingenuity.[23]
The divinatory calendar received no such defense, even though its resemblance to Old World zodiacal astrology might seem to provide some grounds
for recognition and respect. Although astrology was the object of suspicion
and condemnation within Latin Christendom to the extent that it seemed to
hamper the exercise of free will, the notion that constellations and planets
influenced human life and fortune was so well rooted in the Bible and in
ancient philosophy that it was accepted throughout European Christian society. However, to Catholic priests, the day count did not seem to be tied to any
natural effects of stars and planets. As the Franciscan Sahagún argued:

> [T]his manner of divination can in no way be valid, because it is not based on
> the influence of the stars or on any natural thing, nor does its cycle conform

with the cycle of the year, because it contains no more than 260 days, which, when finished, return to the beginning. This counting trick is either a necromantic art or a pact and invention of the devil, which should, with all diligence, be eradicated.[24]

Some Nahuas translated zodiacal materials into their own language.[25] The day count itself was forced underground; in some areas it survived for a long time through oral tradition or written texts.[26] Manuscripts harvested by an anti-idolatry campaign in the Villa Alta region of Oaxaca in 1704–1705 show that at least forty Northern Zapotec communities still kept 260-day calendars.[27] The day count endured to the present only in Guatemala, where it now flourishes amid the post–civil war resurgence of Mayan religion.

The Question of Evil

The *nahualli* is a sage, a counselor, trustworthy, serious, honored, respected, dignified, not reviled, not subject to insults.

The *nahualli* is properly called a witch, who frightens people at night and sucks [blood from] children.[28]

Roman Catholic priests saw all practitioners of magic arts as wicked, but the figure they most avidly associated with witchery was the shaman who could change into an animal. The most powerful shape-shifters changed into predators, such as jaguars or pumas, whereas less powerful ones changed into smaller creatures. Called *nahualli* (pl. *nanahualtin*) in Nahuatl, this figure is found throughout Mesoamerica and extends deep into prehistory. In a variant of the tradition, individuals do not change form; instead, they have an animal alter-ego whose fate they share, such that harm to one is harm to the other.[29]

The quotation at the beginning of this section captures the disjuncture between indigenous and European evaluations: the first statement is a Nahua consultant's description of the *nahualli*; the second is the same passage rendered into Spanish by fray Bernardino de Sahagún. So similar was this shape-shifting to Europeans' concepts of the witch's familiar and the metamorphic illusions the Devil created in his followers that they did not hesitate to call it witchcraft and to assume that these shamans had pacts with the Devil. Feared but respected by Indians, and feared and reviled by Spaniards, *nanahualtin* prowled colonial imaginations, although they apparently narrowed their area of expertise to focus on the rain gods and rain control.[30]

Mexico's first major sorcery trial, held in 1536 under Bishop Zumárraga, was of a reputed *nahualli*, although Martín Ocelotl's ability to change into a jaguar

FIGURE 14.3. The *tlacatecolotl*, shown with a monstrous head like a European-style devil, approaches a sleeping victim. Illustration from the *Florentine Codex*, book ten, f. 21r. Reprinted with permission from fray Bernardino de Sahagún, *Historia general de las cosas de Nueva España, Códice florentino*. Facsimile of the *Codex Florentinus* of the Biblioteca Medicea Laurenziana, published by the Archivo General de la Nación, 1979.

(Nahuatl *ocelotl*; this was probably also his day sign), puma, and dog was but one of his alleged offenses. A self-proclaimed prophet and conjurer of rain, he also preached against Christianity. Spanish colonists were convinced that he consorted with the Devil. Martín was sent off to be jailed by the Spanish Inquisition in Seville, but his ship was lost at sea.[31]

Indigenous Mesoamericans had no general concept corresponding to malefice or necromancy or, indeed, to "evil" as such. However, the *nahualli* and other magicians could use their power to cause harm, and some categories of practitioner seem to have been unambiguously malevolent. One of these is the *tlacatecolotl*, or "human owl," a type of *nahualli*. Sahagún again imposed his European model and declared that, like the *nahualli*, the *tlacatecolotl* was "the man who has a pact with the demon." However, about this figure his Nahua consultants, too, have nothing good to say. Owls were omens of death and emissaries of underworld gods; the *tlacatecolotl* took owl form when casting sickness and death on people. When the friars selected a Nahuatl term to use for "devil" (*diablo, demonio*), they chose *tlacatecolotl*. The term became ubiquitous in Nahuatl to refer to the devils of Christian teachings and thus also to the pre-Columbian deities. Graphic pictorial and verbal imagery established the frightful nature of these creatures and their infernal abode (Figure 14.3).[32]

Also to be feared was the *tlahuipochin*, whom Olmos describes as a necromancer who walks about at night spitting fire and terrorizing people so that they lose their wits, sicken, or die.[33] Nor did the *temacpalitotique*, "they who make people dance with the palm of the hand," have any redeeming qualities. These sorcerers stole a forearm from the body of a woman who had died in her first childbirth – such women were deified, and their fingers protected warriors on the battlefield – and with it cast an enchanted sleep on their victims, whom they proceeded to plunder and rape.[34]

Other dangers posed by ill-intentioned magicians can be seen in the Nahuatl words for magical harm: as well as the generic "do things to people" or "enchant people," they could "flower" people (work a love charm), "owl" people, burn wooden figures of people, kill with potions, blow on people, oppress people's hearts, eat people's hearts, eat people's legs, make people's hearts spin (drive them crazy), cast away people's roads (make them lose their way), or turn people's faces. All of these were subsumed, in dictionaries and other sources, into the Spanish notion of *hechicería* (spell casting, witchcraft).[35]

Malevolent practitioners had a place in Aztec history, although their powers were perhaps evaluated more negatively when Christianized authors converted pictorial chronicles into alphabetic writing. Chimalpahin, a Nahua church steward and historian, gives this description, in Nahuatl, of Malinalxochitl, a sister of the Mexica patron deity Huitzilopochtli, to explain why her brother abandoned her as he led the Mexicas' ancestors on their long migration to the site of their future city:

> [T]hey abandoned her as she slept because she was not human, she undertook great perversity, she was a heart-eater, a foot-twister, a deceiver, one who casts away people's roads, one who puts people to sleep, one who makes people eat snakes, one who makes people eat scorpions. She called all the centipedes and spiders, and became a *tlahuipochin*. She was exceedingly perverse.

Malinalxochitl raised a *nahualli* son, Copil, who grew up to challenge his uncle. Huitzilopochtli killed the "exceedingly perverse" Copil and removed his heart, and then he sent a man to throw the heart into the marshes of Lake Tetzcoco. From his heart grew the cactus that marked the spot where Tenochtitlan would be founded.[36] Chimalpahin describes the magical powers of Malinalxochitl and Copil in very indigenous terms, but he may have felt compelled to emphasis that they were "perverse," just as later in the story he attributes a mystical voice to the Devil (*diablo*).[37]

Magical harm could be caused unintentionally by people in a morally polluted condition, such as adulterers or other promiscuous persons, thieves, or drunkards. Such individuals exuded emanations that were dangerous, especially to the very young, but that could also affect their spouses or their possessions or disempower a ritual. Called "killing with filth," this phenomenon's similarity to the "evil eye" may have facilitated that Old World complex's widespread adoption into Mexican folk culture.[38]

Spaniards widely assumed that indigenous practitioners had pacts, explicit or implicit, with the Devil. Olmos translated Castañega's discussion of the pact into Nahuatl, glossing *pacto* with a word meaning "vow" or "promise."[39] Jacinto de la Serna, a seventeenth-century archbishop of Mexico, asserted that the word *tizitl*, although often equated with *médico*, or "physician," also meant "diviner, sage, and sorcerer," and that such a one "has a pact with the Devil."[40] Hernando Ruiz de Alarcón, a secular priest who completed a treatise about Nahua practitioners in 1629, also assumed these individuals had made pacts with the Devil. However, a *nahualli*'s pact differed from that of a European witch. Ruiz de Alarcón, distorting the day-count consultation made upon a child's birth, surmised that a child's parents forge a pact with the Devil by dedicating the child to an animal that would become its *nahualli*, and the Devil then creates the illusion that this animal carries out the child's commands. Undoubtedly, the child, "after arriving at the use of reason, reiterates the pact or ratifies it tacitly or expressly, because without this condition it is unbelievable that the Devil would have such power, especially against a baptized person." Ruiz de Alarcón also recounts several cases, reported by Spanish witnesses, of Indians taking animal form or suffering death or injury simultaneously with their animal alter-egos.[41]

Even if indigenous people accepted the identification of their deities and magical practices with the Devil, in the absence of moral dualism they would not necessarily reject them for that reason. Mesoamerican cosmology balanced creation against destruction, chaos against order. All superhuman entities required respect and service, and the Devil could have his uses, just as God and the saints did.[42] Indians came to associate the Devil with states of disorder – drunkenness, violence, sexual tensions, and jealousy – and the destructive emotions associated with these conditions.[43]

Divination and Healing

And the same people [who worship the Devil] at other times go out into the countryside by day, or late at night, and take certain beverages of herbs and roots, like the one they call peyote, or herb of Santa María, or whatever other name, with which they become enraptured, and dull their senses and illusions. And the fantastic visions they have there they afterwards judge and publicize as revelations or definite news of what is going to happen.[44]

Of all the indigenous divinatory techniques, the one that most troubled Spanish priests was the use of hallucinogens to induce a trance. In this altered state of consciousness, the practitioner would seek knowledge helpful to the client or even recover a lost soul. Prescribed to patients, the drugs would help them provide additional diagnostic clues.

The statement at the beginning of this section comes from the Edict of the Faith of 1617, a list of religious offenses the Mexican Inquisition circulated to encourage people to report themselves or others. In addition to peyote (*Lophophora williamsii*) – both the cactus bud and the flower, the latter variously called herb or flower of Santa Rosa, Santa María, or Rosa María – trancers ingested morning glory seeds (*Rivea corymbosa*), mushrooms, tobacco, and other plants, which were easily available in colonial native markets. Spanish priests assumed such practices entailed a pact with the Devil, who appeared in the visions.[45]

Diviners, male and female alike, had a large repertoire of techniques in addition to drug-induced trance for determining the causes of illness or misfortune, finding lost objects or missing persons, forecasting the future, or otherwise assisting their clients. They gazed into vessels of water, cast maize grains or crystals and analyzed the resulting pattern, knotted and unknotted cords, measured the client's arm with their palm, or felt the client's pulse.[46] According to legend, the first diviners learned their techniques from Cipactonal and Oxomoco, a man and woman who were a manifestation of the benign male-female creator deity. Images of this elderly couple were painted in divinatory almanacs (Figure 14.4).

Mesoamerican healers supplemented their magic with an immense herbal pharmacopeia. For some plants, experimental data indicate physiological effects consistent with their use; for example, the plant called "heart flower" (*Talauma mexicana*), employed for heart problems and as a diuretic, has vasoconstrictive and other cardiological effects and relaxes bladder tissue.[47] Spaniards were impressed by the skill of native doctors and hoped to benefit from New World remedies. Two diaphoretics, holywood (*Guaiacum sanctum*) and sarsaparilla (*Smilax* sp.), were shipped in large quantities to Europe to treat syphilis, which humoral theory associated with an excess of phlegm.[48]

The oldest Mexican medical treatise is a manuscript created in 1552 at the college for indigenous youth that the Franciscans founded in Tlatelolco in 1536. A Nahua healer named Martín de la Cruz collaborated with Juan Badiano, a Latin-trained scholar from the college, and an anonymous artist to compile an illustrated herbal with Latin explanations of curing techniques. Commissioned by a son of the former viceroy, the herbal was sent to Charles V

FIGURE 14.4. Oxomoco and Cipactonal, the ancient patrons of the divinatory arts, pictured in the *Codex Borbonicus*, an early colonial day-count book. Oxomoco demonstrates divination with cast maize kernels. Cipactonal holds an incense burner, incense bag, and bloodletter. Both have tobacco gourds on their backs. Image courtesy of Akademische Druck-u. Verlagsanstalt, Graz, Austria.

to encourage his support for indigenous education.[49] Sahagún's consultants created a numbered catalog of 150 medicaments, mostly plants but also things like jaguar meat and fossilized bones.[50] The largest study was commissioned by Philip II, Charles's son and successor as King of Spain, who sent one of his country's premier physicians, Francisco Hernández, to study the medicinal plants of Mexico and Peru. Hernández spent five years touring Mexico and never reached Peru. The illustrated manuscript he sent to Philip in 1576 identified 3,076 New World plants and included many ethnographic details.[51]

Midwifery was one medical specialty that attracted Spanish scrutiny. Skilled in the use of massage, native midwives could manipulate a fetus into proper position for delivery. Two substances they administered to speed birth, a plant called "woman medicine" (*Montanoa tomentosa*) and a potion prepared from possum tail, have been shown to induce uterine contractions.[52] Midwives saved some women's lives by passing an obsidian blade through the cervix to cut up and remove a dead fetus when delivery proved impossible.[53] Some reproductive knowledge seemed evil to the friars. Like European witch hunters, Olmos associated abortion with witchcraft: he includes practitioners who provide abortifacients ("they cast things out for people"), as well as those who treat sterility ("they place children for people"), in his list of witches and necromancers.[54]

Precautions that midwives urged on their patients included, in addition to eating well and not lifting anything heavy, not sleeping during the day, lest the baby have abnormally large eyelids, not chewing gum, lest the baby be born with perforated lips, and not having intercourse with their husbands late in their pregnancy, lest the semen glue the fetus to the womb.[55] People also warned pregnant women against viewing a lunar eclipse, lest the baby be born with a cleft lip, and walking around at night, lest the child cry excessively.[56] These sorts of beliefs struck Spaniards as superstitions (*abusiones*), a category Sahagún defines as the attribution of bad effects to something that does not actually cause them. He distinguishes these from auguries or omens (*agüeros*), which attribute something to animals that is not part of their nature (such as the owl's call that augurs death) and which represent illicit attempts "to know of the things which our Lord God has not willed that we should know." Both omens and superstitions were, in his view, all too common among the Indians.[57]

Archbishop Serna lamented that midwives administering possum potion did not simply employ it for the effect God gave it, but added conjurations and invocations of their gods.[58] In practice, it was impossible to suppress only those elements of native healing that offended Spanish priests – divination, sympathetic magic, and invocation of the fire or other sacred forces – because the healers themselves did not conceptually separate supernatural from natural effects. Therefore, preachers felt compelled to categorically impugn indigenous curers. In an effort to arm other priests with necessary knowledge, Ruiz de Alarcón penned detailed, step-by-step descriptions of healing procedures, including the Nahuatl incantations employed by the men and women he interrogated.

These chants layer the healer's simplest acts with sensory images and references to the day count and to myth. For the patient, these would provoke visualizations and organize disturbing symptoms into reassuring cosmic patterns. Water for bathing an afflicted body part becomes "she of the jade skirt," the goddess of water.[59] The curer's five fingers are "those of the five day-signs," signs in the day count with the coefficient five, which was associated with deities of pulque, the native alcoholic drink. Diagnosing the patient, called "child of the gods," the fingers climb his or her arm, or the "jade ladder."[60] To fix bone fractures, healers used splints and poultices of a plant called "fracture medicine." They also associated the broken bone with the bones of extinct people that the god Quetzalcoatl stole from the underworld in order to create the human beings of the current era, dropping and breaking them as he fled.[61]

Other techniques included massage, sweat baths, sweeping the patient's body with *estafiate* and other purifying plants,[62] the use of the breath or saliva, and "taking things from people": the classic shamanic technique of extracting small objects or animals from the patient's body, whether by sucking, rubbing with the hands, or cupping with gourds.

Healers also interpreted their own and their patients' dreams. Like omens, dream interpretation was an attempt to gain knowledge of hidden things, and confessors grouped dreams with omens when they questioned native penitents about offenses to the First Commandment. The Dominican Martín de León asks, "Have you believed in dreams, or have you considered as an omen the horned owl, barn owl, or some other creature, saying 'maybe something bad will happen to me, maybe I will die'?"[63] Bartolomé de Alva, a priest of mixed Spanish and Nahua ancestry, adds hallucinogens to a similar list: "Do you believe in dreams, peyote, ololiuhqui, fire, horned owls, barn owls, snakes or some other thing your grandfathers the ancients used to worship?"[64] Today, dream interpretation remains integral to the recruitment and training of Mesoamerican shamans.[65]

From Magic to Miracles

[A]nd when he was about to die, the angel Saint Gabriel and the angel Saint Michael appeared to him, and he saw them come down from heaven, and they brought from there a lancet, which they gave to him, and they told him, "My son, Juan de la Cruz, on behalf of our Lord God we come to teach you how you are to let blood, to serve God" ... and he saw the Most Holy Virgin ... with the baby Jesus naked in her arms, and above her she brought a golden arch, and from the said arch came hanging the following herbs: coane-nepilli, tlatlanquaie, xoxotlatzin, quapopoltzin.[66]

Thus did a native curer explain to Archbishop Serna in 1646 how he learned the European technique of bleeding with a lancet and which herbs to prescribe (all four medicines appear in Sahagún's catalog). Some colonial native healers ascribed their powers to a saint, associated their hallucinogens and other plants with saints, attributed illnesses to angry saints, and incorporated prayers from the catechism into their cures.[67] Some such actions were subterfuge; many were sincere attempts to benefit from the new sources of power. Churchmen like Serna and Ruiz de Alarcón found the admixture of Christian elements into pagan practice particularly offensive.

Because indigenous people did not share the Spaniards' moral dualism or their distinction between natural and supernatural realms, it is not surprising that their appropriations of Christianity took on a distinctive cast or that they saw no contradiction in practicing Christian and pre-Columbian traditions side by side. Whereas Spaniards tried to eradicate customs they deemed idolatrous or superstitious, indigenous Christians infused their Christianity with many of the same attitudes and aspirations encoded in those older ways. A brief look at native Christianity may, thus, complement the preceding account of unsanctioned religious culture.

Preachers went to great pains to emphasize that there was only one god, but at the same time, they avidly propagated devotion to the Virgin Mary and other saints. Each indigenous community received a patron saint, whose name was prefaced to the town's existing name. The saint took on the functions of a patron deity and sometimes bore a resemblance to earlier local divinities. For example, Chiautempan, a site of devotion to the goddess Toci, "Our Grandmother," became Santa Ana Chiauhtempan and began to revere Saint Anne, Jesus's grandmother – to the chagrin of Sahagún, who saw too much continuity between the two grandmothers.[68] Patron saints entered local legend, as in the town of Santiago Sula, where a late seventeenth-century account explained how two wise elders entrusted with the task of choosing a saint had had identical dreams in which Saint James (Santiago) declared that he would be Sula's patron.[69] Mesoamerican peoples imbued their local landscapes with sacred forces, which governed the availability of water and the growth of crops; inevitably, they imposed seasonal meanings onto the saints' calendar and associated their patron saints with sacred mountains, caves, or water sources.[70]

Crosses and images of Christ, Mary, and the saints became foci of devotion in churches, chapels, and homes. Native artists painted and sculpted Christian images, copying imported woodcuts. Wealthy donors, or members of religious brotherhoods who pooled their funds, commissioned elaborate altarpieces and other regalia for the churches. Households strove to acquire at least one, and often several, images.[71] For a while, the Spanish term *imagen* sometimes appears in Nahuatl documents in reference to statues and pictures of saints, but it virtually vanishes after the mid-seventeenth century, as if people abandoned any pretense of distinguishing between the representation and the personage represented, and they "reverted to their habit ... of looking at the spiritual being and the tangible form as fully integrated."[72] Such attitudes struck Spanish churchmen as evidence of the Indians' idolatrous tendencies and the weakness of their Christian faith; throughout the colonial period, their Christian devotions were denigrated as showy performances that lacked spiritual depth.[73] A succinct statement of the Spanish perspective appears in inquisition testimony provided in 1768 by the Dominican friar Francisco Larrea. Although he defended actors in Passion plays who borrowed costume elements from statues in their churches, Larrea criticized their Christianity: "[I]n them it is not disrespect of the holy images; rather, in these peoples one experiences such an excessive veneration that ministers must reprimand them, for because of their simplicity one may suspect that they place the ultimate end of the adoration on the statue or painting, with no relation to the original."[74]

Contrary to what Spaniards imagined, indigenous people had never worshipped mere objects of wood and stone. Images and deity impersonators were inhabited and animated by the figures they represented. The care that people took of their Christian images – building and decorating their churches, providing them with clothing and ornaments, offering them candles along with the traditional copal incense, lavishing them with flowers that marked the presence of the sacred, taking them on processions, celebrating their festivals with music and dances, sweeping in front of them, asking to be buried near them, tending them on household altars, bequeathing them to their heirs, and writing about them as if they were people – represented a style of devotion that Spaniards were ill disposed to understand or accept.[75] Observers were likewise troubled by the reverence shown to actors playing Jesus in those controversial Passion plays, for people would kiss them, offer them incense, and collect their blood – real or imitation – to use in healing.[76] The occasional religious movement that elevated an indigenous man or woman to the status of Jesus or Mary was ruthlessly suppressed.[77]

Miracle-working images dotted Spain's landscape,[78] and native people readily embraced this aspect of Christianity, for why should images not appear and disappear, move about, heal the sick, raise the dead, stop floods and epidemics, prove impervious to damage, and otherwise exhibit agency? Nahuas labelled such events tlamahuizolli, "things to be marveled at," a term used to translate the Spanish milagro and Latin miraculum. The term does not imply divine intervention or any suspension of "natural" law. It suggests an attitude of awe similar to that inspired by the omens of old, but applied now to something that brings good fortune or sets a positive example. The same term was used for preachers' exempla and sometimes for dramatic adaptations of Christian narratives.

In his chronicle of notable Mexico City events, the Nahua historian Chimalpahin recounts several tlamahuizolli, such as the following, dated December 11, 1600:

San Diego revived a small child; it was a great miracle that he performed. When [the child] died, its mother brought it to the church and laid it before San Diego. With much weeping she prayed to God's precious one, San Diego. And he accepted her petition. Then the child revived, and after it revived the bells began to peal everywhere because of it. All the friars saw it, as well as the Spaniards.[79]

Here, as in many of his other references to saints, Chimalpahin makes no distinction between personage and image. In two of his other miracles, women who try to stop Indians from setting up crosses on street corners take sick and die, punished by God for opposing such a pious act.[80]

Among wonder-working images, crucifixes, such as Our Lord of Chalma, which was found one morning in a cave where a pre-Columbian deity had been worshipped, vied for popularity with miracle-working Virgins, of whom Mexico City alone boasted at least forty-four by 1650; their country cousins included Our Lady of the Remedies, which was lost by Spaniards during the conquest and found under an agave plant by an Otomi Indian.[81] The most famous Marian devotion, Our Lady of Guadalupe, began in the 1550s when Spaniards attributed miracles to an Immaculate Conception painted on cloth by a native artist; in the 1640s, the devotion gained its origin story, in which the Virgin appeared in 1531 to a Nahua named Juan Diego and left her image imprinted on his cloak.[82]

Shrines became pilgrimage centers, their visitors supporting local commerce. A desire to profit from the pilgrim trade prompted Spaniards in the town of Tepaltzingo to wrest control of a miracle-working Christ from an Indian religious brotherhood in 1724, starting a dispute that lasted well into the next century.[83] When in the eighteenth century Spain's new Bourbon rulers introduced "reforms" that undermined the communal property base of indigenous towns, many miracle-working images became pilgrims themselves and were taken on alms-gathering tours to raise funds for their own maintenance, as well as that of their shrines.[84]

Most indigenous Christians had – like European peasants – only a rudimentary knowledge of formal doctrine. Many knew at least the Our Father, Hail Mary, Creed, and other bits of the catechism, adapted into their own language; others knew less. This may be one reason they enthusiastically embraced the rosary and the *corona*, or crown, of Mary – repetitive prayer cycles through which they could parlay minimal knowledge into maximum spiritual merit, keeping themselves in the Virgin's good graces (Figure 14.5). The imagery of a rose chaplet, or a crown, appealed to their penchant for accoutering the sacred images. In miracle narratives translated into Nahuatl, the Virgin helps

¶ Ynicoronatzin sctā maria:
Ynicquac ticmopobuiliz, achtopa cruz
tica timomachiyotiz niman tiquitoz yn
Credo ycuepca yn neltoconi/niman to
tocompehualtiztiquitoz.

¶ Marimopaql
titia ynticenqzca
tlapanabuica tla
matcatzintli ynti
sancta Maria. j.
Pater nr̄/matla
tlactetl. Aue ma
rias.
¶ Marimopaql
titia yn ticenquiz
ca tlapanabuica
ichpochtzintli in

FIGURE 14.5. The *corona* of Saint Mary, a prayer cycle employing repetition of the Our Father and the Hail Mary, published in a Nahuatl-language catechism, fray Pedro de Gante's *Doctrina christiana en lengua mexicana*, 1553, f. 128v. Image courtesy of the Nettie Lee Benson Latin American Collection, University of Texas Libraries, The University of Texas at Austin.

devotees who do no more than pray the rosary or just the Hail Mary. The Virgin filled some of the space vacated by the female deities but also added a benevolent, indulgent role appreciated by devotees bearing the burden of colonial rule.[85]

The colonial power structure precluded Spaniards from granting indigenous Christianity equal status to their own, however sincerely or fervently Indians expressed their devotion. Yet what Spaniards evaluated as weakness or inferiority did correspond to real differences. Spanish Catholicism had indeed gone native, in a way that other early modern Christian confessions – those that had rejected the cult of the saints, the veneration of images, and associated popular traditions – simply could not have done. The evangelizers aimed to replace the Devil with God and idolatry and witchcraft with the true faith; what they actually achieved was to add Jesus and the saints to the sacred personages whom Mesoamericans served and called on for aid.

Policing the Magical Marketplace

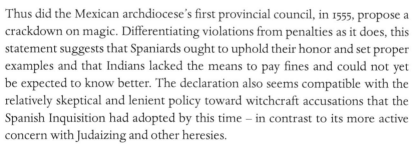

> Because many people, men as well as women, forgetting the fear of God and of the faith, and the trust they should have in Divine Providence, make use of divinations and spells, sorceries, and enchantments, and go or send others to consult with those who make such witchcraft, who are servants of the Demon ... we command that from now on all people who make use of the said spells, sorceries, incantations, or divinations, or other witchcraft, or consult with the said sorcerers or diviners, or go to them, or in any way participate in their offenses, in addition to all other penalties applicable by law in such a case, incur a sentence of excommunication *ipso facto*, and a penalty of fifty pesos for the first time, and double for the second time, and that they be publicly shamed, and exiled, as and for the time that the judges who know about [the case] think fit; which penalty applies to Spaniards, and not Indians ... And if the sorcerers are Indians, they must do public penance in the church on a feast day, along with whatever else the judge thinks fit, provided the penalty is not monetary.[86]

Thus did the Mexican archdiocese's first provincial council, in 1555, propose a crackdown on magic. Differentiating violations from penalties as it does, this statement suggests that Spaniards ought to uphold their honor and set proper examples and that Indians lacked the means to pay fines and could not yet be expected to know better. The declaration also seems compatible with the relatively skeptical and lenient policy toward witchcraft accusations that the Spanish Inquisition had adopted by this time – in contrast to its more active concern with Judaizing and other heresies.

In 1526, a committee of ten inquisitors, convened in Granada, had concluded that the homicides to which accused witches often confessed might be illusory, and four of the ten were convinced that the witches' sabbath was itself an illusion. In response to a 1549 Barcelona case in which an inquisitor, without authorization from the tribunal's Supreme Council, had seven women burned for witchcraft, the council sent an investigator who drafted "one of the most damning denunciations of witchcraft persecution ever recorded." Thereafter, with the single exception of a witch hunt that spilled across the French border in 1609 – which led to another investigation and scathing condemnation of the judges' procedures – the Spanish Inquisition did not allow accused witches to be tortured or killed, and it assumed that testimony describing acts of witchcraft was delusionary. Although neither the inquisition nor the royal courts had the jurisdiction to prevent local courts from occasionally executing witches and the inquisition did continue to investigate cases of "superstition," which increased in number in the seventeenth century, local prosecutions of witchcraft declined in the seventeenth century, and in inquisitorial proceedings, even the most egregious magical crimes received no punishment more severe than obligatory abjuration and flogging.[87]

In New Spain, local bishops held inquisitorial authority as an extension of the Spanish tribunal until 1571, when Mexico's own Holy Office of the Inquisition was established. Philip II authorized tribunals for New Spain and Peru in response to a wave of petitions alleging abuses of clerical power, as in the Landa affair, and increasing problems policing both the book trade and the religious affiliations of foreign merchants and seamen.[88] The king instructed the colonial inquisitors "not to take proceedings against the Indians of your district, because ... it is our will that you only act against Old Christians and others within these Spanish realms against whom it is customary to take proceedings."[89]

The exemption of Indians from the inquisition's jurisdiction acknowledged that they were novices in the faith. Also, as the land's original inhabitants, they were juridically separated from Spaniards into a "republic of Indians," which paid tribute to the Crown and was formally under its protection. In any case, inquisitorial methods were poorly suited to policing the pervasive, small-scale irregularities in Indian religion.[90] Jurisdiction over Indian religious affairs remained in the hands of local clergy and ecclesiastical judges, with policing performed through confessional interrogation and the occasional larger-scale campaign against idolatry.

In early modern Europe, witchcraft and magic were associated especially with women, who accounted for approximately 80 percent of those executed as witches.[91] Authors of witch-hunting handbooks explained that women turned to supernatural means to compensate for their weakness, ignorance, and lack of power – and to satisfy unmet sexual needs.[92] In Mexico, indigenous people were, in a sense, categorically feminized by colonial discourses that cast them as similarly weak, irrational, and carnal. Such views upheld the privileged position of Spanish males, but it also opened up an alternative or inverse domain of unsanctioned, supernatural, demonic, and magical power in which Indians, not Spaniards, held authority.[93]

The approximately 200,000 Africans brought to Mexico as slaves, together with their descendants, enjoyed no such exemption. Some enslaved Africans were already Christians; all others were obliged to undergo baptism at African slaving ports, on ship, or upon arrival in the colony. Unless their masters were particularly conscientious – like the Jesuits, who kept slaves on their haciendas – they received little formal catechesis. Afro-Mexicans, even those of partially Indian parentage, lacked the legal status that Indians had as "natural" citizens of the colony; like the mestizo descendants of Spaniards and Indians, they belonged to the "republic of Spaniards." Nor were they perceived as weak or feminine; on the contrary, they were placed in roles of enforcement, mediating between Spaniards and Indians as overseers and forced to perform the hard labor to which Indians seemed ill suited.[94]

Over time, Afro-Mexicans became increasingly of mixed African and native and/or Spanish ancestry and increasingly free: the slave trade declined after the mid-seventeenth century, some people bought themselves out of slavery, and the children of enslaved fathers and free mothers of any ethnicity were born free. They also vastly outnumbered the Spaniards.[95] Subjection to the inquisition obliged Afro-Mexicans to be spiritually responsible for themselves, but it also gave Spaniards a tool of surveillance over people they kept in servile economic positions and from whom they feared violent rebellion.

Mexican Inquisition records, which extend to the end of the colonial era, depict indigenous, Afro-Mexican, mestizo, and Spanish people interacting in an increasingly multiethnic magical landscape. Although testimony was necessarily molded to inquisitors' procedures and expectations, the Mexican Inquisition did not torture or execute defendants charged with magic, and so the transcripts mirror social reality more closely than in European cases where defendants suffered torture or feared death. And even though Indians were not prosecuted, other people testified to being clients or victims of Indian witchcraft, and the implicated Indians were sometimes hauled in for questioning. Some inquisitors apparently believed that any case involving the Devil must involve an Indian, as well.[96]

However much Spanish churchmen might want to suppress Indian practitioners, separate Indians from non-Indians, and hold other Spaniards to their own moral standards, one problem made this impossible: the colony's shortage of licensed medical specialists, be they physicians, surgeons, or even blood-letting barbers. Even where men credentialed by the colony's medical tribunal did practice, most people – certainly most non-Spaniards – could not afford their fees.[97] Also, even though Juan de la Cruz proudly wielded the lancet the archangels gave him, indigenous medicine had much to recommend it over humoral pathology.

That Indian healers were also magicians did not deter sick lay people. Indeed, many non-Indian clients sought to improve their health, economic opportunities, or social lives by magical means, and they sought out those best equipped to provide such assistance, not caring in times of crisis if the Indians' power came from the Devil. And they paid these practitioners for their services.[98]

In this underground economy, Indians – men and women alike – were the primary sources of knowledge and magical wares. Indians from rural or frontier regions, especially the nomadic Chichimecs of northern Mexico (where the peyote came from), had greater magical credibility than those from more central, settled locales.[99] Magic spread from Indians to others; Ruiz de Alarcón wrote that "those who have many dealings with the Indians, especially if they are low persons, are easily infected by their customs and superstitions."[100] Those "low" persons were typically Afro-Mexican servants, who were often sent as intermediaries to consult Indian practitioners on behalf of their mistresses: a respectable Spanish lady did not frequent Indian markets or travel to Indian villages.

Afro-Mexicans also set themselves up as practitioners, using hallucinogens and even claiming to be shape-shifting *nanahualtin*, a risky enterprise if they became too successful at their craft, for even their own clients might turn on them. Those most likely to get arrested for magical activity were Afro-Mexican women, such as Gerónima de Barahona, a meat seller notorious in seventeenth-century Santiago, Guatemala, for the witchery she claimed to have learned from two Indians – and for daring to direct her magic at elite men, including the inquisitor who interrogated her. However, Afro-Mexican men, mestizos, and Spaniards – especially women – also passed in considerable numbers through the inquisition's halls. Spanish women received the lightest penalties. An Afro-Mexican woman was much more likely to have her goods confiscated, go to jail, or be banished from her home – these were Gerónima's punishments – even if she claimed to have acted at the behest of her Spanish mistress or other higher-class clients.[101]

Love charms were the magical marketplace's hottest commodity. Even cases involving an alleged demonic pact usually centered on domestic relations.[102] Like women described in the *Malleus maleficarum*,[103] a woman typically sought to "tame" (*amansar*) or "tie" (*ligar*) her husband or lover so that he would be more attentive to her and unable to perform sexually with other women; men thus rendered impotent sometimes denounced their jealous paramours to the inquisition. Amulets made with dead hummingbirds could attract a lover, but much love magic employed the indigenous chocolate beverage. Grainy and opaque, it concealed the menstrual blood, pubic and underarm hairs, and other substances that could ensorcel a man.[104] One Cecilia de Arriola so unmanned her unfaithful husband that he found himself in the kitchen preparing her morning chocolate, while she slept late.[105] Afro-Mexican slaves and servants used similar remedies to "tame" cruel masters, hoping to end beatings or gain freer run of the household. When men sought love magic, it was to enhance their powers of seduction.[106]

Colonial magic was a melting pot; it can be difficult to separate European, African, and indigenous ingredients, especially given that all three regions had many similar practices in the first place. Such Spanish elements as divining with eggs passed easily into wider practice.[107] Enslaved Africans, who were less able to import their culture, added their own interpretations to the many local customs – such as divination, amulets, and supernatural illness – that were familiar to them. Some specifically African traditions, such as spirit mediumship and the associated practice of ventriloquism, came under the inquisition's scrutiny.[108] African spiritual beliefs, along with indigenous beliefs in soul loss, may have influenced Mexican mystics: their visionary experiences, sometimes enhanced by peyote, centered on the condition of other people's souls, much more so than the visions of their European counterparts did. The otherworldly spirits who possessed them were known to demand chocolate or tobacco.[109]

The most prevalent European ingredient was the Devil, an alternate authority figure who might provide an instant solution to intractable problems. In 1614, eighteen-year-old Diego de Cervantes, an Afro-Mexican serving a sentence in a workhouse, promised himself to the Devil after a supervisor scalded his feet to punish him for laziness. Diego offered to write out a pact in his own blood, but he got spooked after something hairy touched him and told him where to go to fulfill his pledge.[110] Sometimes the Devil appeared in Indian form, as he did to a mestizo named Pedro de Castillo in 1677. An Indian woman directed Pedro to a cave, where the Aztec Emperor Moteuczoma, seated in a golden chair, ordered him to relinquish his rosary and relics, as well as his soul.[111] In 1598, a Spanish woman described a veritable witches' sabbath, at which people danced and "sinned" and cavorted with horned demons. One demon, complete with claws and a huge penis, told her he was her father and master. Her escort to these events was an Indian woman.[112]

Accounts this close to the classic sabbath are quite rare, but inquisitors heard many tales of interactions with the Devil. Like their Spanish counterparts, and increasingly as time went on, they tended toward skepticism and leniency, not even bothering to pursue many of the accusations and self-denunciations. Those involved in magical crimes were overwhelmingly the sorts of people whom these elite judges saw as "low" or "vile": blacks, Indians, anyone of mixed ancestry, Spaniards from the lowest social rung, and loose women of any category.[113] In a sense, all buyers and sellers in the magical marketplace became honorary Indians, people of limited capacity from whom little was expected. By 1771, when clerics at the fourth provincial council fretted once again about Spaniards who patronized Indian practitioners,[114] Mexico's ethnic landscape was profoundly different from what it was in 1555. But it was the spiritual health only of the Spanish elite that troubled these clergymen.

The first Franciscans in New Spain dreamed of establishing a millennial kingdom, the Age of the Holy Spirit foreseen by Joachim of Fiore.[115] As that dream faded, they began to see the Devil in every corner. The idolatry and superstitions attributed to Indians justified their subjugation; eventually, Africans and all ethnically mixed persons joined them in a vast underclass of "vile" people, who were as susceptible to religious lapses as the old women targeted by Europe's witch hunters. Pre-Columbian, European, and African magic merged into a dynamic and diverse panoply of practices eagerly exploited by people seeking authority or assistance.

Mexico remains a place where magic is an everyday thing, from the charms and powders sold in any of its market to the Virgins and Christs who appear on subway tiles or scorched tortillas. Shamans and other traditional specialists still practice their arts. The magical marketplace has a global reach: a Nahua healer travels annually to Manhattan to ritually cleanse her wealthy clients; and tourists seek shaman-guided spiritual experiences at Mesoamerican ruins.[116] And anyone in the world can consult the 260-day calendar on the internet.[117]

Notes

1. As in Robert Ricard's classic, missionary-centered analysis, first published in French in 1933, *The Spiritual Conquest of Mexico*.
2. Frazer, *The Golden Bough: A Study in Magic and Religion*, ch. 4; Mauss, *A General Theory of Magic*; Malinowski, "Magic, Science and Religion."
3. Quoted in Quezada, *Enfermedad y maleficio*, 61.
4. Motolinia, or Toribio de Benavente, *Historia de los indios de la Nueva España*, 19.

5. The best descriptions of these rituals are Sahagún, *Florentine Codex*, vol. 2 (the wives' treatment of the femurs is p. 60), and Durán, *Book of the Gods and Rites*.

6. López Austin, *Cuerpo humano*; Clendinnen, *Aztecs: An Interpretation*.

7. Keen, *The Aztec Image in Western Thought*, 97.

8. On this shift, see Cervantes, *Devil in the New World*, 13–15.

9. Burkhart, *Slippery Earth*, 40–42.

10. Cervantes, *Devil in the New World*, 149–154.

11. Durán, *Book of the Gods and Rites*, 59.

12. See, for example, Farriss, *Maya Society under Colonial Rule*; Lockhart, *Nahuas after the Conquest*; Tavárez, *Invisible War*.

13. Sahagún, *Florentine Codex*.

14. Tavárez, *Invisible War*.

15. Clendinnen, *Ambivalent Conquests*, 76. Only bishops had inquisitorial authority; Landa did not become bishop until 1573.

16. Greenleaf, *Zumárraga and the Mexican Inquisition*, 68–74.

17. Olmos, *Tratado de hechicerías*, 18–20.

18. Ibid., 3; de Castañega, *Tratado de las supersticiones y hechicerías*.

19. Sahagún, *Florentine Codex*, vol. 2, 171

20. Tedlock, *Time and the Highland Maya*, 93.

21. On the *tonalli*, see López Austin, *Cuerpo humano*, vol. 1, 223–251; Furst, *The Natural History of the Soul in Ancient Mexico*; on the *tonalpohualli*, see Sahagún, *Florentine Codex*, vol. 4.

22. Sahagún, *Florentine Codex*, vol. 4.

23. Baudot, *Utopia and History in Mexico*, 484–485.

24. Sahagún, *Florentine Codex*, introductory vol., 61.

25. Tavárez, *Invisible War*, 133–139.

26. Tedlock, *Time and the Highland Maya*, 92.

27. Tavárez, *Invisible War*, 146.

28. Sahagún, *Florentine Codex*, vol. 10, 31; Sahagún, *Historia general de las cosas de Nueva España*, vol. 10, 20v.

29. López Austin, *Cuerpo humano*, vol. 1, 416–432; Aguirre Beltrán, *Medicina y magia*, ch. 5; Foster, "Nagualism in Mexico and Guatemala," 85–103.

30. Aguirre Beltrán, *Medicina y magia*, 102–104.

31. Greenleaf, *Zumárraga and the Mexican Inquisition*, 53–54, Lopes Don, "Franciscans, Indian Sorcerers, and the Inquisition," 34–47.

32. Burkhart, *Slippery Earth*, 40–42, 53–56; López Austin, "Cuarenta clases de magos," 88–90.

33. Olmos, *Advertencias*, 112r–112v.

34. Sahagún, *Florentine Codex*, vol. 4, 102–106; López Austin, "Los temacpalitotique," 97–118.

35. Molina, *Vocabulario en lengua castellana y mexicano y castellano*, 70r.

36. Chimalpahin Quauhtlehuanitzin, *Codex Chimalpahin*, 76–79, 86–89.

37. Ibid., 102–103.

38. Burkhart, *Slippery Earth*, 95–97; López Austin, *Cuerpo humano*, vol. I, 287–299; Ortiz de Montellano, *Aztec Medicine*, 223–225.

39. Olmos, *Tratado de hechicerías*, 40–43.

40. Serna, "Manual de los ministros," 101.

41. Ruiz de Alarcón, *Aztec Sorcerers*, 64–66.

42. Cervantes, *Devil in the New World*, 41–43; Burkhart, *Slippery Earth*, 34–39.

43. Sousa, "The Devil and Deviance," 163, 171.

44. Quezada, *Enfermedad y maleficio*, 46.

45. Ibid., 46–48, 51.

46. On the range of techniques, see López Austin, "Cuarenta clases"; Quezada, *Enfermedad y maleficio*, 61–106.

47. Ortiz de Montellano, *Aztec Medicine*, 261.

48. Ibid., 25, 121, 257–258, 261.

49. Ibid., 20–22; Cruz, *The Badianus Manuscript*.

50. Sahagún, *Florentine Codex*, vol. 10, 141–191.

51. Ortiz de Montellano, *Aztec Medicine*, 25–29. Although a poorly edited portion of Hernández's work was published in 1648, the original text was lost when the royal library at El Escorial burned in 1671.

52. Ibid., 185–186, 191.

53. Sahagún, *Florentine Codex*, vol. 6, 157, 160.

54. Summers, *Malleus maleficarum*, 66; Olmos, *Advertencias*, 112r–112v.

55. Sahagún, *Florentine Codex*, vol. 6, 156.

56. Ibid., vol. 5, 189.

57. Ibid., introductory vol., 63–64.

58. Serna, "Manual de los ministros," 250.

59. Ruiz de Alarcón, *Aztec Sorcerers*, 234.

60. Ibid., 203.

61. Ibid., 267–269.

62. *Artemisia mexicana*, Nahuatl *iztauhyatl*, which is still ubiquitous in Mexican folk practice: Quezada, *Enfermedad y maleficio*, 57–59.

63. León, *Camino del cielo en lengua mexicana*, 111v.

64. Sell and Schwaller, eds. and trans., *Don Bartolomé de Alva*, 91; *ololiuhqui* refers to morning glory seeds.

65. Tedlock, *Time and the Highland Maya*; Knab, *The Dialogue of Earth and Sky*.

66. Serna, "Manual de los ministros," 103–104.

67. Quezada, *Enfermedad y maleficio*, 47–48, 54, 57–58; Ruiz de Alarcón, *Aztec Sorcerers*, 205.

68. Sahagún, *Florentine Codex*, introductory vol., 90–91.

69. Lockhart, *Nahuas after the Conquest*, 236.

70. Wake, *Framing the Sacred*.

71. Lockhart, *Nahuas after the Conquest*, 237–240.

72. Ibid., 238.

73. Burkhart, "Pious Performances," 361–381.

74. "Las representaciones teatrales de la pasión," 353.

75. Burkhart, "Pious Performances"; Clendinnen, "Ways to the Sacred," 105–141; Wood, "Adopted Saints," 259–293.

76. Archivo General de la Nación, Bienes Nacionales, vol. 990, exp. 10; transcribed by Jonathan Truitt.

77. Bricker, *The Indian Christ, the Indian King*; Gosner, *Soldiers of the Virgin*.

78. On Spanish practices associated with saints, images, and miracles, see William A. Christian's works: *Local Religion in Sixteenth-Century Spain* and *Apparitions in Late Medieval and Renaissance Spain*.

79. Chimalpahin Quauhtlehuanitzin, *Annals of His Time*, 68–69. The sex of the child is not mentioned.

80. Ibid., 68–69, 250–257, 304–305; all of the events occurred between 1600 and 1615.

81. Hughes, *Biography of a Mexican Crucifix*; Weckmann, *La herencia medieval de México*, vol. 1, 342, 345–348.

82. Burkhart, "The Cult of the Virgin of Guadalupe in Mexico," 198–227.

83. Reyes Valerio, *Tepalcingo*, 10–11.

84. Osowski, *Indigenous Miracles*, chs. 3, 4.

85. Burkhart, *Before Guadalupe*, 119–127, 133–134, 143–146.

86. Lorenzana, *Concilios provinciales*, 45–46.

87. Kamen, *The Spanish Inquisition*, 271–276, esp. 273.

88. Greenleaf, *Zumárraga and the Mexican Inquisition*, 17–19.

89. Moreno de los Arcos, "New Spain's Inquisition for Indians," 36 n. 28.

90. Klor de Alva, "Colonizing Souls," 14.

91. Behringer, *Witches and Witch-Hunts*, 158.

92. Summers, *Malleus maleficarum*, 41–48; the misogyny expressed in the *Malleus maleficarum* may represent an extreme case, but it is echoed, at less length, in a section of Martín de Castañega's Spanish treatise (*Tratado*, 63–65) that Olmos translated into Nahuatl (*Tratado de hechicerías*, 46–49).

93. Lewis, *Hall of Mirrors*, 5–7.

94. Bristol, *Christians, Blasphemers, and Witches*.

95. Ibid., 4.

96. Lewis, *Hall of Mirrors*, 147.

97. Quezada, *Enfermedad y maleficio*, 11, 16–21, 29; Bristol, *Christians, Blasphemers, and Witches*, 164.

98. Lewis, *Hall of Mirrors*, 122

99. Ibid., 108–109.

100. Ruiz de Alarcón, *Aztec Sorcerers*, 93.

101. Lewis, *Hall of Mirrors*, 152–154; Quezada, *Enfermedad y maleficio*, 30–31; Gerónima's adventures are documented by Few, *Women Who Live Evil Lives*.

102. Behar, "Sex and Sin," 34.

103. Summers, *Malleus maleficarum*, 54–55.

104. Behar, "Sex and Sin," 37–43; Few, *Women Who Live Evil Lives*, 52–55; Behar, "Sexual Witchcraft, Colonialism, and Women's Powers," 178–206.

105. Few, *Women Who Live Evil Lives*, 32–33.

106. Bristol, *Christians, Blasphemers, and Witches*, 167–170; Lewis, *Hall of Mirrors*, 143, 157–159.

107. Quezada, *Enfermedad y maleficio*, 69.

108. Bristol, *Christians, Blasphemers, and Witches*, 153–156, 158; Lewis, *Hall of Mirrors*, 151, 153; Villa-Flores, "Talking through the Chest," 299–321.

109. Jaffary, *False Mystics*, 102–103.

110. Bristol, *Christians, Blasphemers, and Witches*, 142–143; Cervantes, *Devil in the New World*, 84.

111. Cervantes, *Devil in the New World*, 38–39.

112. Lewis, *Hall of Mirrors*, 127–129.

113. Behar, "Sex and Sin," 35.

114. Jaffary, *False Mystics*, 102.

115. Phelan, *The Millennial Kingdom of the Franciscans*.

116. Guy Trebay, "The Age of Purification," *New York Times*, May 22, 2011; one such tour company is Sacred Earth Journeys in British Columbia (http://www.sacredearthjourneys.ca).

117. For example, "Aztec Calendar" (http://www.azteccalendar.com) and "Tzolkin – Maya Calendar Explorer" (http://www.xcone.com.au/maya/).

Chapter 15

Folk Magic in British North America

RICHARD GODBEER

When several girls and young women living in Salem Village, Massachusetts, began to have strange fits in January 1692, their worried families and neighbors wanted to know what was causing the afflictions and how to end them. Mary Sibley, a member of the local church and the aunt of one of the afflicted girls, Mary Walcott, suspected that her niece was bewitched and turned to defensive magic in an attempt to identify the culprit. Sibley asked two Indian slaves who lived and worked in the local minister's home, Tituba and John, to bake a cake consisting of meal and the afflicted girl's urine, which they then fed to a dog. If the experiment worked, the witch responsible would be revealed. Sure enough, once the cake had been baked, the girls could see "particular persons hurting of them."[1]

Over the coming months, as a growing number of local inhabitants were accused of witchcraft, both accusers and accused gave testimony that included descriptions of colonists using defensive magic, divination, and image magic. That testimony confirmed what earlier witch trials had already shown – that folk magic, although condemned by the Puritan faith as an instrument of the Devil, was deeply embedded in New England's culture and that many settlers saw nothing wrong with such practices. One of the accused, Dorcas Hoar of Beverly, Massachusetts, had "a book of palmistry" in which "there were rules to know what should come to pass." She also claimed that she could predict a neighbor's future by the "veins about her eyes." When Hoar's minister, John Hale, confronted her in 1670, explaining that "it was an evil book and evil art," she "seemed ... to renounce or reject all such practices." Yet the minister came to believe that Hoar had merely been humoring him. Several years later, Hale heard that she was still in possession of a fortune-telling book and perhaps still offering her services to neighbors.[2]

John Hale was by no means alone in seeking to dissuade his parishioners from the use of magic. When Samuel Parris, the minister in Salem Village, discovered that Mary Sibley had asked his own slave to bake a urine cake in hope of identifying whomever was responsible for her niece's affliction, he summoned her to his home and "discoursed" her in his study, reducing her to "tears and sorrowful confession" for what he saw as her "grand error." Two days later, he denounced Sibley from the pulpit of the village meetinghouse.[3] Yet combating the use of magic techniques was an uphill struggle. Despite strident clerical condemnation, magical beliefs and techniques were common currency throughout New England. Scattered evidence from other British colonies suggests that the use of divining, healing, and defensive magic was by no means limited to the northern colonies. And those opposed to magic had to worry not only about folk traditions that had survived efforts by English reformers to expunge "superstitious" practices and made their way across the Atlantic.[4] They also had to face the grim possibility that occult techniques used by Indians and Africans might infiltrate colonial settlements in North America. According to ministers, the Devil had enjoyed dominion over the Americas until the English arrived and was furious that his control of the region was now under threat. Many colonists saw Indians and Africans as devil worshippers, and so they anticipated facing in the New World an array of demonic threats, in guises that were both familiar and new. In 1692, one of the afflicted girls claimed that French Catholics in Canada and Indian chiefs from throughout the region had attended witch meetings "to concert the methods of ruining New England."[5]

The folk magical traditions that colonists brought with them from England assumed that men and women could manipulate supernatural forces for their own ends. Many settlers believed that through the use of simple techniques passed down from one generation to the next, they could harness occult forces so as to achieve greater knowledge and control over their lives: they could predict the future, heal physical ailments, inflict harm, and defend themselves against occult attack. Most magical techniques were quite straightforward, and so colonists often experimented on their own. But in times of need, they also turned to neighbors who were known to have occult skill. These local experts – often called cunning folk – performed an important social service, as they told fortunes, claimed to heal the sick, and offered protection against witchcraft.[6]

Magical divination enabled people to locate lost or stolen goods and to predict future events. The latter seems to have been of particular concern in New England, perhaps in reaction to the uncertainties and anxieties that Puritan theology engendered regarding each person's ultimate fate. Cunning folk used a variety of fortune-telling techniques that they sometimes learned from manuals that circulated on both sides of the Atlantic. As we saw earlier in the chapter, Dorcas Hoar had "a book of palmistry" that she used to tell fortunes. Samuel Wardwell of Andover, Massachusetts, told people's fortunes by "look[ing] in their hand and then ... cast[ing] his eyes down upon the ground always before he told anything." Robert Roman of Chester County, Pennsylvania, had a reputation for "practicing geomancy" and "divining by a stick."[7] Some divining techniques required no particular expertise and thus could be used independently of cunning folk. One such technique involved balancing a sieve on a pair of shears or scissors and asking a question; if the sieve turned or fell to the floor, the answer was positive. At the Salem witch trials, Rebecca Johnson of Andover "acknowledged the turning of the sieve in her house by her daughter" in an attempt to find out "if her brother Moses Haggat was alive or dead." Sarah Hawkes, daughter-in-law to cunning man Samuel Wardwell, had also "turned the sieve and scissors." One of the girls who became afflicted in early 1692 had apparently been trying to find out who her future husband would be by suspending the white of an egg in a glass of water and using it as a form of crystal ball.[8]

People also used magic to protect themselves from harm and to heal the sick. When Edward Cole of Northumberland County, Virginia, suspected that a neighbor was bewitching his wife, he hung a horseshoe over their door to ward off evil. When the woman whom he suspected was still able to enter their house, he concluded that his suspicions must have been unfounded.[9] Cotton Mather, a minister in Boston, knew a woman "who upon uttering some words over very painful hurts and sores did ... presently cure them." Indeed, Mather had heard that in some New England towns, it was "a usual thing for people to cure hurts with spells." Traditional folk medicine often combined the application of plants and minerals with the use of charms or incantations. The verbal formulae used in these "spells" often originated as Catholic prayers; their use for this particular purpose was a survival from the medieval belief that sanctioned church rituals could protect against harm and heal the sick. According to Cotton's father and fellow minister, Increase Mather, a healer in Boston had prescribed as "an effective remedy against the toothache" a "sealed paper" containing the words, "In nomine Patris, Filii, et Spiritus Sancti, Preserve thy servant, such a one."[10]

But magic could be used to harm as well as to heal. Those suspected of deploying magical skill for malevolent ends were distrusted by their neighbors and labeled as witches. From this perspective, witchcraft was the misuse of occult skill, the dangerous underside of an otherwise valued local resource. The most notorious magical technique for inflicting harm was image magic, which operated on the principle that damaging an object taken to represent an enemy would also injure the person represented. At the Salem witch trials, a remarkable number of testimonies mentioned the use of "poppets" to injure enemies. Susannah Sheldon claimed that Job Tookey had "run a great pin into a poppet's heart which killed" Gamaliel Hawkins. Mary Bridges, Jr., testified that "[t]he way of her afflicting was by sticking pins into things and clothes and think[ing] of hurting them." And workers who were demolishing a wall in Bridget Bishop's cellar found there several cloth "poppets" with pins stuck into them. Whether or not these accused witches had in fact used image magic in the hope of harming their enemies, residents of Salem Village and the surrounding communities were evidently familiar with this magical technique and its underlying assumptions.[11]

Fortunately for those who feared occult attack, there were straightforward defensive or counter-magical techniques that could defend them against witchcraft, identify the person responsible, and inflict retribution. When someone used occult means to harm their enemies, a two-way channel of communication was believed to open between the malefactor and victim. By damaging a bewitched object or something associated with the bewitched person, the witchcraft would be undone and the harm would be translated back onto whomever had caused it. This might involve burning something associated with the bewitched creature or person, such as the tail of an animal or the hair of a human being. If the experiment worked, the person responsible for the witchcraft would be drawn to the fire or would suffer injuries supposedly caused by the counter-magic. When Margaret Garrett of Hartford, Connecticut, suspected that one of her cheeses had been bewitched, she flung it into the fire. Elizabeth Seager, who was at the time in Garrett's barn, came into the house and "cried out she was full of pain, and sat wringing of her body and crying out, 'What do I ail? What do I ail?'" Goodwife Garrett concluded that Seager must be the culprit.[12] In Surry County, Virginia, Joan Wright told a neighbor that she had successfully countered a bewitchment by heating a horseshoe until it was "red hot" and then throwing it into the urine of the victim: "[S]o long as the horseshoe was hot," she averred, "the witch was sick at the heart. And when the iron was cold, she was well again."[13]

The belief that magic could be used for both good and evil purposes placed cunning folk in an ambiguous and vulnerable position. Neighbors who possessed occult powers performed an important service in predicting futures and healing the sick, but they were also potentially deadly enemies. When New Englanders feared that they were bewitched, they often blamed men and women in their local communities who already had a reputation for occult skill and with whom they had quarreled: they might conclude that skills previously used for their own benefit were now being turned against them. Anyone known for their magical expertise had reason to worry if they argued with a neighbor who then suffered a mysterious illness or mishap. Indeed, much of the surviving information about the use of folk magic comes from depositions presented at witch trials: witnesses would often testify that the defendant had assisted them or their neighbors by divining or healing on their behalf, which proved the defendant to have occult skill; that expertise was now apparently serving less benign ends. Healers were especially vulnerable to accusations of witchcraft if they applied their skills to a patient whose condition then worsened.

Suspicions that magical skill had been used for malicious ends were much more likely to be directed against female practitioners. Cunning women, in other words, were much more likely to be accused of witchcraft than their male counterparts were. The power wielded by cunning folk was potentially threatening in the hands of either a man or a woman, but it was especially threatening if the cunning person was female, because the aura of power surrounding cunning folk contradicted gender norms that placed women in subordinate positions. On both sides of the Atlantic, witchcraft was perceived as a largely female phenomenon, and so it is hardly surprising that female cunning folk were disproportionately targeted. Yet neither magical beliefs nor magical practices were gender-specific: men as well as women resorted to and functioned as cunning folk.[14]

As English colonists turned to magic in hopes of divining the future, curing ailments, and protecting themselves or their loved ones from harm, their options were not limited to English techniques and English cunning folk. When English migrants crossed the Atlantic to settle in North America, they entered a world in which Indian, African, and European cultural traditions coexisted and sometimes comingled.[15] Indian and African cultures varied among themselves just as much as those within Europe did, but they did share fundamental beliefs relating to magic and witchcraft that had some similarities to those held by European colonists. Indians and Africans generally assumed that the natural and supernatural worlds could intersect in both positive and negative ways. Those who had the ability to access occult forces or act as intermediaries between the human and spirit realms could use that skill for benevolent or malevolent ends. Such powers often proved helpful to individuals and the community at large, but they and those who wielded them were also potentially dangerous.

It is difficult to tell from the surviving documentation whether cunning folk or other colonists incorporated Indian and African occult techniques into their magical repertoire. Tituba, whom the minister of Salem Village had purchased when he was living in Barbados, was known for her occult skill. Apparently "her mistress in her own country ... had taught her some means to be used for the discovery of a witch." Whether the urine cake recipe used by Tituba in early 1692 came from Mary Sibley or had been passed on to Tituba by her mistress in Barbados is unclear, but it seems to have been English in origin.[16] That Sibley and Tituba settled on an English method for identifying those responsible for bewitching Sibley's niece points to the danger of assuming that the involvement of an Indian would necessarily have resulted in the use of a Native American technique, but the experiment did clearly constitute a convergence of peoples and cultures in defense of a terrified young woman. We do know that settlers appropriated Indian and African medical knowledge. English accounts of contact with Indians often recognized their skill in the use of indigenous plants to heal a range of illnesses.[17] And when an enslaved African healer in South Carolina known as Doctor Caesar developed a cure for snakebites, he was granted his freedom by the colonial assembly in return for sharing his remedy. But the description of Caesar's cure in the colonial records makes no mention of any charms that Caesar may have used when administering the cure to African patients. Africans and Indians, like many English settlers, believed that the treatment of illness should incorporate both natural and supernatural therapies. Yet some white colonists may have been unwilling to adopt occult charms proffered by people whom they believed to be pagans and devil worshippers. Or Caesar may have withheld such information. Or if he did pass it on, those responsible for the official record may not have wanted to acknowledge either that settlers used magical charms or that they were adopting African occult practices.[18]

The frequent assertion by ministers and others that Indians and Africans worshipped the Devil would have discouraged at least some colonists from using occult techniques that originated within those cultures. But in many instances, they may not even have realized that a particular activity had a supernatural component. White southerners often failed to appreciate the religious or occult significance of slave behavior. Dancing, for example, functioned for whites as a form of relaxation and exercise, as an opportunity to display physical grace and prowess, and as a component of courtship. Few whites seem to have understood that a form of circular dance movement referred to by historians as the Ring Shout played a crucial role in African spirituality; when slaves joined together in dance, the occasion most likely had a strong religious component. Just as African healing techniques often included a charm of some kind, so too did Africans use amulets or charms in conjunction with poison against their enemies. Slaves in the eighteenth-century South frequently used poison to murder their masters or overseers, but white court prosecutors and newspaper reports treated these attacks as straightforward murder (and as petit treason when a slave poisoned his master), stripping the attacks of any occult component. Yet not all whites were that oblivious: when Thomas Jefferson's son-in-law, Thomas Mann Randolph, described a black man who was suspected of poisoning a slave family living on Jefferson's estate at Monticello as a "conjuror," he recognized that the alleged murderer might have deployed supernatural weapons in combination with poison.[19]

The surviving records do contain occasional hints of supernatural exchange across racial lines, but they are little more than suggestive. A story circulated in mid-seventeenth-century Fairfield, Connecticut, about an Indian who had apparently visited the home of Mary Staples and offered her "two things brighter than the light of the day ... Indian gods, as the Indian called them." When Staples was later tried for witchcraft, locals resurrected the story as incriminating evidence. Staples admitted having been offered these objects, but she claimed that she had refused to accept them.[20] Farther south, a white South Carolinian wrote down a charm for warding off witchcraft that consisted of Christian phrases and crosses on a paper that was then to be put "in a small rag tied round the neck." This bears a close resemblance to Nkisi charms for protecting against evil spirits, although English men and women also carried protective charms in bags hung around their necks, so it is impossible to tell whether this prescription reflected African influence or shared beliefs.[21]

Evidence of magical belief and examples of magical experimentation survive from each region of British America, but most of the extant documentation comes from seventeenth-century New England. The War of Independence and later the Civil War inflicted disproportionate damage on the southern colonies, destroying lives, property, and also historical records that might otherwise have given us much more detailed information about early Southern culture. But even had these wars not taken place, there would most likely survive more information about early New England than colonies farther south, in part because more of those who settled in the northern colonies could read and write. Puritans believed that becoming literate was a crucial part of becoming a person of faith, because it was through reading the Bible that individual men and women could gain access to divine truth.[22] Learning how to write was less crucial than learning how to read, yet a significant minority of New Englanders could do both. Literate colonists left behind a remarkable written testimony of their struggles against temptation and the forces of evil – individually and in concert, informally and through institutional channels. One of the dangers that Puritan leaders saw as threatening their spiritual enterprise was the persistence, even within New England's godly settlements, of folk magic, which they categorized as witchcraft. The transcripts from witchcraft cases constitute a major source of information about magical beliefs and practices. Court records included depositions from colonists who were not themselves literate but who gave oral testimony about the services provided by cunning folk and the use of defensive magic against suspect witches that was then entered into the official record. Although witchcraft prosecutions occurred throughout the British colonies in North America, the powerful influence of religious culture in New England produced a disproportionate number of cases and thus a disproportionate amount of information about magical beliefs and techniques.[23]

The basic assumption underlying folk magic – that people could harness occult powers for their own ends – contrasted sharply with the teachings of Puritan theology, which placed supernatural power firmly in God's hands. Clergymen were horrified by the popularity of magical techniques. They insisted that scripture gave no sanction for such experiments and that human beings could not wield supernatural forces on their own. The Puritan clergy did not doubt that magic worked, but according to them, it did so because the Devil provided assistance to the person conducting the experiment. Divination served "a vain curiosity to pry into things God ha[d] forbidden and concealed from discovery by lawful means," declared John Hale, the minister at Beverly. People could gain access to "forbidden" knowledge, he warned, only "through the assistance of a familiar spirit." Ministers were particularly shocked by the use of religious words and phrases in protective and healing spells. According to Samuel Willard, a minister in Boston, this was "an horrible abusing of the name of God to such purposes as serve egregiously to the establishing of the Devil's kingdom in the hearts of men." Defensive magic, clergymen insisted, was no less dependent on demonic intervention than were the bewitchments that it sought to undo. Deodat Lawson, who had served as minister in Salem Village prior to Samuel Parris, condemned such techniques as "using the Devil's shield against the Devil's sword." Individuals might think that they were successfully harnessing occult powers, but in fact the Devil was doing it for them and so luring them into his service.[24]

Ministers had similar concerns about the use of astrology to predict human affairs. Interest in astrological prognostication was widespread in New England and, indeed, throughout British America.[25] Puritan theologians accepted that celestial bodies had a direct influence over natural events and had no quarrel with the use of astronomical information to predict the weather, farming conditions, and even physical health; however, they would not countenance "judicial" astrology – the application of astronomical information to human affairs. In common with magical divination, they argued, judicial astrology intruded into "things secret" that could not be revealed by "lawful means." Its claim to foreknowledge must, therefore, be false, unless the Devil was intervening to provide the information. Charles Morton, who preached in Cambridge, Massachusetts, declared that when astrologers predicted accurately, Satan "had a greater stroke therein than the art." The Devil thereby encouraged people "to think slightly of God's providence."[26] This was not the only connection between magic and astrology: the latter's assumption of a direct causal linkage between celestial and terrestrial phenomena bore a close resemblance to a belief in image magic. Puritans also worried that the signs of the zodiac were potential objects of idolatry; their dominion over different parts of the body was disturbingly reminiscent of Catholic saints' responsibility for the cure of various diseases.[27]

In addition to sanctioning "natural" astrology, Puritan ministers were also interested in the broad providential significance of extraordinary celestial phenomena, such as comets and eclipses, which they believed God sent either as "signal[s] of great and notable changes" or as "heralds of wrath."[28] They were just as convinced as other English men and women that the universe was filled with awe-inspiring portents, prodigies, and wonders that carried supernatural significance. Puritans drew on a "wonder lore" that derived from folklore, classical meteorology, apocalyptic prophecy, and natural philosophy. But ministers condemned specific interpretations of any such phenomena as "too much boldness" and insisted that heavenly movements were "only signal and not causal" of human events – a crucial distinction for them. To think otherwise was blasphemy against God's omnipotence and an invitation to Satan, who was always ready and eager to exploit human presumption.[29]

Yet many colonists were much less fastidious than their ministers were and used astrology as well as divination to foretell human events. They saw no harm in benevolent magic or astrological predictions and branded as witches only those who sought to harness occult forces for malevolent purposes. Such distinctions were, from a clerical perspective, either dangerously naïve or disingenuous. Folk magic and judicial astrology were, insisted ministers, dependent on a diabolical agency, regardless of whether the intention was benign or malevolent. Particularly worrisome was the apparent failure of some covenanted believers to recognize the dangers inherent in magical experimentation, including believers like Mary Sibley, the church member in Salem Village who responded to her niece's affliction by turning to counter-magic.

Parris denounced Sibley for "going to the Devil for help against the Devil." According to her minister, Mary Sibley had, in effect, "raised" the Devil and so was "instrumental" in the "calamities" now befalling the community. That a member of his own congregation would act in this way was "a great grief" to Parris, yet he did not believe that Sibley had self-consciously forsaken her commitment to obey God's commandments. "I do truly hope and believe," Parris declared, "that this our sister doth truly fear the Lord, and am well satisfied from her that what she did, she did it ignorantly, from what she had heard of this nature from other ignorant, or worse, persons."[30]

According to other clergymen serving in New England, Sibley was by no means anomalous. There were, declared Cotton Mather, "manifold sorceries practiced by those that ma[d]e a profession of Christianity." Nor was Parris unique in concluding that church members who turned to folk magic did so "ignorantly." When ministers acknowledged the unpalatable truth that magical practices had persisted even within New England's covenanted communities, they generally took the view that most of those who turned to magic did so because they failed to understand how dangerous it was. Increase Mather believed that some people "practice[d] such things in their simplicity, not knowing that therein they gratifie[d] the Devil." Cotton Mather also acknowledged that those who used "magical ceremonies" were not "well aware of what they have been adoing." John Hale believed that such people used magical techniques simply because they believed that they worked, without considering how they worked. "Such have an implicit faith," he wrote, "that the means used shall produce the effect desired, but consider not how; and so are beguiled by the serpent that lies in the grass unseen."[31]

New England ministers thus acknowledged that they had been less than entirely successful in communicating their perspective on the workings of the supernatural world and that even seemingly devout colonists sometimes behaved in ways that were inconsistent with their profession of Puritan faith. Recent historians of religious culture in the North American colonies have drawn our attention to what Patricia Bonomi describes as a lay "fluidity of allegiance." Annette Laing has pointed out that "many colonists were not as heavily invested in denominational identities and distinctions as were their ministers." Sometimes settlers crossed denominational lines because there was no church or minister of their own preferred faith available in a particular neighborhood. But lay pluralism was not merely a product of circumstances. It also reflected what Laing terms "a latitudinarian spirituality." Many colonists adhered to or disregarded specific doctrines and procedures as it suited them, switching back and forth between different perspectives and options with scant regard for intellectual consistency or institutional loyalty.[32] That "latitudinarian" sensibility, which was so alien to the intellectual instincts and professional interests of clergymen, incorporated ideas and practices from well beyond the bounds of Protestant Christianity. As David Hall has noted, early New Englanders combined Puritan faith with a wonder lore that drew on a dazzling array of traditions and beliefs. Scholars such as Jon Butler have stressed the "spiritual eclecticism" of men and women who turned not only to Christianity but also to folk magic and astrology as they sought to negotiate the uncertainties and vicissitudes of their lives.[33]

One might perhaps expect that Puritan New England would have been the one cultural venue in British North America where official principles and popular behavior would have coincided quite closely, but this was by no means always the case. Many New England colonists clung to traditional beliefs and assumptions, even when these beliefs and assumptions contradicted ideals to which they were supposedly committed. Some colonists were doubtless rigorous and exclusive in their commitment to Puritan faith, but others were more inclusive and drew on folk magic, astrology, and religious faith in combinations that were intellectually inconsistent and yet worked well for them. It may well be that some colonists did not understand why magic was offensive from a Puritan perspective. We cannot assume that most ordinary folk shared the intellectual self-consciousness that prompted ministers to probe the assumptions underlying magical techniques. Nor can we assume that logical consistency was more important to the average colonist than the needs of the moment and the widespread assumption that such techniques did work. Others may have understood that magic was heterodox but quietly ignored clerical injunctions when it suited them. This appears to have been true of Dorcas Hoar, who was still in possession of a palmistry book several years after promising her minister that she would "reject all such practices."[34]

Some individuals seem to have believed that magical power came from God. John Hale met one man who used as medicinal charms words and phrases that he believed to be taken from scripture; he told Hale that God had given him "the gift of healing." This fellow was clearly not unique. Winifred Holman of Cambridge, Massachusetts, offered to cure a neighbor's illness "with the blessing of God." Increase Mather was concerned that lay men and women might think they were drawing on divine power when using magical techniques: he cautioned that people who turned to counter-magic should not declare that "[t]he Lord was my healer," because it was in fact the Devil who had come to their aid. And Deodat Lawson also found it necessary to remind listeners that divinatory powers came "from the Devil, not from God."[35]

Magic may have appealed to some New Englanders in part because it enabled them to alleviate anxieties created by Puritanism itself. Those anxieties arose from the uncertainty created by predestinarian theology. Even those who believed that they had felt within themselves the transformative power of divine love and mercy were supposed to remain doubtful of their salvation. Ministers warned their congregations that intimations of grace were elusive, unreliable, and dangerous. Recognizing one's own spiritual worthlessness was, they taught, a crucial part of becoming worthy of God's forgiveness. A growing emphasis on the importance of preparation in Puritan sermons gave believers some sense of agency in their own redemption: according to preparationist theology, believers should nurture within themselves a desire for grace that would make them fit receptacles for that gift, should it be proffered. Yet preparatory exercises offered no guarantees: just as nobody could be certain that they were elect, so nobody could tell if they were fully prepared. Indeed, the whole purpose of preparation was to cultivate a sense of one's own spiritual inadequacy, so that the more successfully people prepared, the more they would doubt their worthiness of God's mercy.[36]

Some believers accepted doubt and anxiety as normative and desirable, but others sought at least occasional relief from spiritual anxiety. Magic offered one potential outlet, and among those who turned to divination, there were devout people who yearned for some sense of certainty about the future. Knowing how long one's children would live or who one's future husband would be paled into insignificance when compared to the question of whether one would be saved, but such knowledge did offer some degree of certitude, however limited or short term it was. Some New Englanders went further and attempted to penetrate the mystery of election itself through divination. Cotton Mather was horrified to discover that some colonists took their Bibles, let them fall open, and then determined "the state of their souls" from the first word upon which their eyes fell. Such practices were clearly inconsistent with the religious principles taught by New England's clergy, but the men and women using them may either not have fully grasped that inconsistency or ignored it because of the comfort that divination offered.[37]

Folk magic also met needs that had previously been answered by a repertoire of ecclesiastical magic within the Catholic Church but that Protestants in England had abolished. The medieval church had taught that holy water, coins, candles, and relics could offer protection against harm and heal the sick. Theologians stressed that the efficacy of such rituals depended on the spiritual sincerity of those who used them, yet ordinary folk seem to have endowed religious objects and rituals with an automatic power, often treating ecclesiastical magic and folk techniques as virtually interchangeable, much to the dismay of church officials.[38] Protestant reformers rejected the notion that performing specific rituals could bring about a desired effect: they insisted that the only way to achieve safety or release from suffering was to appeal to God's mercy. Thus, it is hardly surprising that ecclesiastical magic had no place in the Church of England or in the religious culture that the Puritans established in New England. But suppressing folk magic turned out to be much more challenging on both sides of the Atlantic, in large part because the knowledge and control that it offered was so appealing, even among those who identified with a reformed sensibility.

Ambiguities within Puritan theology may also have encouraged New Englanders to use magic. When colonists suspected that a particular affliction had been caused by witchcraft and turned to counter-magic in a bid to undo the harm and identify the person responsible, their ministers were horrified. Clergymen insisted that all suffering should be understood as a providential judgment: looking inward, repenting for one's spiritual failings, and begging God to forgive one's sins was the only acceptable route to recovery. Yet those same ministers delivered through their sermons very mixed messages when it came to responsibility for suffering and sin. On the one hand, any misfortune should be understood as a punishment for sin, which was itself the product of human corruption. The Devil was assuredly eager to tempt men and women into sin, but those who entertained wicked thoughts or committed sinful acts were culpable in giving way to the Devil's advances. Satan was thus empowered by humanity's own moral depravity. "If there were no Devil to tempt," declared Nicholas Noyes, the minister in Salem Town, "yet the inbred corruption of men's hearts, that are deceitful above all things and desperately wicked, is enough to undo all." Yet, on the other hand, ministers often depicted Satan as a formidable force in his own right and a serious threat to the human soul, luring men and women away from their obedience to God's commandments. At times, the Devil figured in sermons as an almost invincible force: Samuel Parris warned that "if the Devil do but hold up his finger, give the least hint of his mind, his servants and slaves will obey."[39]

Some New Englanders were temperamentally more inclined to blame themselves for their afflictions and sinful impulses, whereas others tended to blame Satan. Samuel Willard condemned the latter for trying "to extenuate [their] own fault by seeking to throw it upon Satan." This was, he lamented, "a thing too frequent among such as profess themselves to be the children of God."[40] Yet the implicit tension in clerical teaching on the subject of liability between diabolical power and human responsibility gave layfolk considerable leeway in deciding whom to blame for their sins and misfortunes. The ministers' portrayal of the world as a dangerous place troubled by an active devil may well have encouraged even devout believers to focus on external sources of evil and to protect themselves against such threats by resorting to counter-magic. These were not mutually exclusive responses: New Englanders often looked both inward and outward for the sources of their troubles, blaming both their own moral failings and external forces, such as Satan or a human enemy. Indeed, it seems quite plausible that in the opening months of 1692, Mary Sibley was praying to God, as well as using counter-magic to identify whomever was bewitching her niece.[41]

When people became convinced that a neighbor had used witchcraft against them, they could respond in a number of ways. They could focus on their own spiritual failings as the ultimate reason for God's having unleashed the Devil and his minions, in which case they would commit to a regimen of repentance and reformation in the hope that God would withdraw his chastising rod. Or they could seek revenge through the use of counter-magic, perhaps burning the hair or urine of the bewitched person in the hopes of identifying and injuring the witch responsible. Or they could lodge a formal complaint and initiate a criminal prosecution. The first response placed at least some blame for what was happening on the victims themselves. The second responded to supernatural affliction by blaming someone else and seeking retribution through occult means. A legal response offered victims the possibility of official and public retribution: the penalty for witchcraft throughout the New England colonies was death.

Yet convincing oneself and one's neighbors of an individual's guilt was not the same as convincing a court. Puritan theology depicted witches as heretics who had renounced Christianity and sworn allegiance to the Devil. New England laws defined witchcraft in theological terms, demanding proof of diabolical allegiance. Yet ordinary men and women were more inclined to think about witchcraft as a practical problem: having concluded that a particular misfortune was caused by occult attack, they wanted to know who the witch was, and they wanted her punished. When claiming that a local cunning man or woman had used his or her skill to harm or destroy, they focused on showing that the individual had magical expertise that had allegedly been misused for malevolent ends. In other words, the logic of their evidence was driven by magical, not theological, assumptions. The evidence presented at most witch trials reflected that orientation and rarely made any mention of the Devil. That deponents did not adapt their testimony to fit legal criteria indicates that ordinary colonists were quite stubbornly focused on practical threats to their safety when thinking about witchcraft, and that at least some people were much less thoroughly schooled in official ideology than persistent stereo-types of early New Englanders would suggest. That disjunction between legal requirements and the nature of most popular testimony resulted in frequent acquittals. Of the sixty-one known prosecutions for witchcraft in seventeenth-century New England, excluding the Salem witch hunt, sixteen resulted in conviction, a rate of slightly more than one-quarter. Four of these individuals confessed, which made the court's job much easier. If they are omitted, the conviction rate falls to just less than one-fifth.[42]

The depositions given against New England's accused witches generally fell into one of four categories. Most frequently, villagers and townsfolk described quarrels with the accused individual that had been followed by a misfortune or illness for which they could find no natural explanation; the witnesses claimed that the alleged witch had afflicted them as a direct consequence of these arguments. Second, deponents claimed that the accused had a reputation for skill as a fortune-teller or healer; this established that the accused had occult powers that could also have been used for malign purposes. Third, witnesses described having used counter-magic, perhaps cutting off part of a bewitched animal's tail and throwing it in a fire or boiling the urine of a bewitched child; if a neighbor suffered an analogous injury soon afterward or was drawn inexpli-cably to the house in which the experiment had taken place, that information was offered up to the court as incriminating testimony. And finally, neighbors described the accused's suspicious behavior or preternatural characteristics, such as extraordinary strength.

These depositions demonstrated beyond any doubt the fear that alleged witches aroused among their neighbors, but they were mostly unconvincing from a legal perspective. Magistrates and the learned ministers whom they consulted during many of these trials dismissed testimony relating "strange accidents" following quarrels as "slender and uncertain grounds" for convic-tion. Clergymen denounced counter-magic as "going to the Devil for help against the Devil" and warned that Satan was a malicious liar, which hardly encouraged magistrates to rely on testimony describing counter-magical experiments. They were occasionally willing to conclude that divination or other magical practices that ministers condemned as diabolical proved collu-sion between the accused witch and the Devil, but even here magistrates were mostly reluctant to convict unless there was explicit mention of the Devil.[43]

New England magistrates were ready and willing to convict and execute accused witches if the evidence against them prove convincing. But they insisted that the evidence before them should satisfy rigorous standards of proof: this meant either a voluntary confession or at least two independent witnesses to any incident demonstrating the individual's guilt. It was difficult enough to secure two witnesses for other offenses that carried the death penalty, but the challenge was compounded when dealing with an invisible crime involving alleged collusion with supernatural agents. Only in a minority of cases were New England magistrates convinced that the evidence did satisfy the established criteria for conviction. At other trials, their fastidious adherence to evidentiary standards resulted in acquittal. In some instances, they overturned jury verdicts, rejecting the instincts of local jurymen who were convinced of the accused person's guilt.

The neighbors and enemies of accused witches who had given what they considered to be damning testimony were often infuriated by the reluctance of magistrates to convict on the basis of their depositions. Sometimes they would confer with each other, gather new evidence against the acquitted individual, and then renew legal charges. Three individuals were each prosecuted on three separate occasions; another five appeared in court twice on charges of witchcraft. All of these cases resulted in acquittal.[44] Repeat prosecutions expressed an unshaken belief in an individual's guilt and also dissatisfaction with the courts' handling of witchcraft cases. That dissatisfaction sometimes resulted in extralegal retaliation: Mary Webster of Hadley, Massachusetts, was tried and acquitted in 1683; however, a year later, when another of her neighbors fell ill and accused her of bewitching him, several young men paid Webster a visit and brutally assaulted her.[45]

As the difficulty of securing a legal conviction for witchcraft became increasingly apparent, New Englanders became less and less inclined to initiate legal prosecutions against suspected witches: there were nineteen witch trials during the 1660s, but only six during the 1670s and eight during the 1680s. That dramatic decline did not occur because of a lessening fear of witches, as would become clear in 1692, when official encouragement of witchcraft accusations in and around Salem Village unleashed a deluge of allegations. It is perhaps not a coincidence that ministers became much more vociferous in their denunciations of counter-magic during the 1680s. As it became clear that the court system was not an effective tool against witches, New Englanders may have turned increasingly to counter-magic instead.

At first it seemed that the evidentiary problems that had plagued previous witch trials would not thwart the proceedings at Salem. More than fifty of the accused in 1692 confessed, describing in graphic detail their initiation into the Devil's service and often naming other individuals who had allegedly joined the Satanic confederacy. These confessions lent a horrifying credibility to the accusations pouring in from communities throughout Essex County. The evidence given by witnesses against the accused contained, moreover, countless references to the Devil and his involvement with the alleged witches; these also facilitated conviction. By the end of the summer, however, a growing number of critics were casting doubt on the court's proceedings. Many of the confessing witches had recanted, claiming that their confessions had been forced from them by overly zealous officials through the use of physical torture and psychological pressure. Some of them had been promised that those who confessed, renounced their allegiance to Satan, and then cooperated with the authorities would be spared from execution. In a ghastly irony, only those who refused to perjure themselves by admitting to crimes that they had not committed went to their deaths. Other than confessions, most of the testimony describing the Devil's involvement in the alleged witch conspiracy came from the afflicted girls whose torments had sparked the witch hunt. They claimed to be repeating information provided by the specters of witches that appeared to them. A growing chorus of ministers and magistrates warned that Satan might represent innocent persons in spectral form so as to incriminate them falsely. Because the Devil was a liar, critics warned, evidence that originated with him could not be trusted.

Once spectral testimony and the confessions came under attack, the court found itself in an extremely difficult position. There were many depositions against the accused from witnesses other than the afflicted girls, but hardly any of that testimony included references to diabolical involvement such as the law demanded, and so, in early October, Governor Phips halted the trials. From the perspective of people who wanted the courts to take decisive actions against witches living among them – including cunning folk who had apparently used their skills to harm or even murder their neighbors – the acquittal and release of many suspects in the weeks and months following the suspension of the trials must have been frustrating and also frightening. Popular disillusionment combined with official embarrassment following the debacle at Salem to bring about an end to witch trials in New England.

By the early eighteenth century, a degree of skepticism about certain kinds of allegedly supernatural phenomena began to take hold among those who embraced Enlightenment ideas. But belief in magic and astrology would prove to be resilient among other Americans.[46] In 1728, the pastor at Medford, Massachusetts, condemned young people for "sieve-turning" and "palmistry." In 1755, the pastor at Westborough, Massachusetts, had to preach "against the foolish and wicked practice of going to cunning men to inquire for lost things." And in 1773, a minister in Newport, Rhode Island, noted in his diary the death of a local cunning man "who was wont to tell where lost things might be found and what day, hour, and minute was fortunate for vessels to sail."[47] People continued to blame their misfortunes on witchcraft: counter-magic remained a popular weapon against occult attack, and the popular fear of witchcraft occasionally erupted into physical violence. In the summer of 1787, as delegates met in Philadelphia to draft the federal constitution, a woman sustained fatal injuries inflicted by a mob in a street nearby because they believed that she had used witchcraft to kill a child in her neighborhood. Fifteen years later, a young man was convicted in New York for assaulting an elderly woman because he believed that she had bewitched him and that he could undo the bewitchment by cutting her three times across the forehead. Meanwhile, treasure seekers across the newly independent states were using divining rods and peep stones that they scrutinized in the darkness of their hats to locate pirate hoards in the hopes of instant enrichment. Belief in the occult as a credible and valuable tool might no longer have been intellectually respectable, but the nineteenth century would show just how powerful a force it remained within American culture.[48]

Notes

1. Hale, *A Modest Enquiry*, 23, 25; Lawson, *A Brief and True Narrative*, 9.
2. Rosenthal, ed., *Records of the Salem Witch Hunt*, 593–595.
3. Boyer and Nissenbaum, eds., *Salem-Village Witchcraft*, 278–279.
4. Mather, *Discourse on Witchcraft*, 19.
5. Mather, "A Brand Pluck't Out of the Burning," 281–282.
6. This essay does not discuss the use of "learned" or "natural" magic in British North America; on this, see Woodward, *Prospero's America*; Butler, *Awash in a Sea of Faith*; and Leventhal, *In the Shadow of the Enlightenment*.
7. Rosenthal, ed., *Records of the Salem Withc-Hunt*, 593, 645; *Records of the Courts of Chester County, Pennsylvania, 1681–1697* (Philadelphia, 1910), 363.
8. Rosenthal, ed., *Records of the Salem Witch Hunt*, 573, 597; Hale, *A Modest Enquiry*, 132–133.
9. Edward LeBreton and Thomas Bandmill, Depositions, April 11, 1671, Northumberland County Record Book.
10. Mather, "Paper on Witchcraft," 265–266; Mather, *Wonders of the Invisible World*, 96; Mather, *Essay for the Recording of Illustrious Providences*, 261.
11. Rosenthal, ed., *Records of the Salem Witch Hunt*, 371, 393, 552.
12. Margaret Garrett, Testimony, June 17, 1665, Willys Papers W–4.
13. McIlwaine, ed., *Minutes of the Council and General Court of Colonial Virginia, 1622–1632, 1670–1676*, 112.

14. Around four-fifths of the New Englanders tried for witchcraft were women. Roughly half of the men charged with this crime were married or otherwise close to accused women; they were, in other words, guilty by association. See Demos, *Entertaining Satan*, 60–62; and Karlsen, *The Devil in the Shape of a Woman*, 47–48. Puritan ministers did not teach that women were by nature more evil than men, but they did see them as weaker and thus more susceptible to sinful impulses. Clergymen reminded New England congregations that it was Eve who first gave way to Satan and then seduced Adam. All women inherited that potential for collusion with the Devil from their first mother, yet some were much more likely than others to be accused of witchcraft. Throughout the seventeenth century, women in New England became especially vulnerable to such allegations if they were seen as challenging their prescribed place in a gendered hierarchy that Puritans held to be ordained by God. Any behavior or circumstance that seemed disorderly could easily become identified as diabolical and associated with witchcraft: the Devil had, after all, led a rebellion against God's rule in heaven. See Karlsen, *The Devil in the Shape of a Woman*; and Reis, *Damned Women*.

15. For a helpful overview of this complex subject, see Games, *Witchcraft in Early North America*.

16. For references to urine cakes in England, see Kittredge, *Witchcraft in Old and New England*, 435 n. 237.

17. See, for examples, Lawson, *A New Voyage to Virginia*, 17–18; and Maurice Mathews, Letter, May 18, 1680, South Caroliniana Library.

18. See Galvin, "Decoctions for Carolinians," esp. 82–84, 88–89.

19. For the poisoning of white southerners by slaves, see Games, *Witchcraft in Early North America*, 52–55, 153–158; for the poisonings at Monticello, see ibid., 158–159. For more on the use of divination, charms, and invocations by African slaves, see Morgan, *Slave Counterpoint*, 621, 624.

20. Hoadly, ed., *Records of the Colony or Jurisdiction of New Haven*, vol. 2, 80, 86. For tantalizing references to African fortune-tellers in early eighteenth-century Boston, see Butler, *Awash in a Sea of Faith*, 94.

21. Ellison and Mulligan Receipt Book, Hutson Family Papers, 34/570. I am grateful to Mary Calvin for bringing this evidence to my attention. For the interplay between English and African cultures, see Sobel, *The World They Made Together*.

22. See Hall, *Worlds of Wonder, Days of Judgment*, ch. 1.

23. There were far fewer prosecutions for witchcraft in the middle and southern colonies than there were in New England. There was one execution in Maryland, and three women were hanged onboard ships heading for the Chesapeake; five witch suspects were convicted and executed in Bermuda (to which, not coincidentally, several Puritan ministers had emigrated).

24. Hale, *A Modest Enquiry*, 165; Willard, *The Danger of Taking God's Name in Vain*, 10; Lawson, *Christ's Fidelity*, 62.

25. For the use of astrology in British North America, see Godbeer, *The Devil's Dominion*, ch. 4; and Butler, *Awash in a Sea of Faith*, ch. 3.

26. Morton, "Compendium Physicae," 29.

27. See Thomas, *Religion and the Decline of Magic*, 435–440.

28. Danforth, *An Astronomical Description of the Late Comet or Blazing Star*, 16–17.

29. Mather, *Heaven's Alarm to the World*, 16–17; Mather, *Kometographia*, 133. For wonder lore in New England, see Hall, *Worlds of Wonder, Days of Judgment*, ch. 2.

30. Boyer and Nissenbaum, eds., *Salem-Village Witchcraft*, 278–279.

31. Mather, *Discourse on Witchcraft*, 25; Mather, *Essay for the Recording of Illustrious Providences*, 260; Mather, "Paper on Witchcraft," 258; Hale, *A Modest Enquiry*, 131.

32. Bonomi, *Under the Cope of Heaven*, 57; Laing, "A Very Immoral and Offensive Man," 8; Laing, "All Things to All Men," 11.

33. Hall, *Worlds of Wonder, Days of Judgment*, ch. 2; Butler, *Awash in a Sea of Faith*, 1. Several historians have considered the place that folk magic occupied in the culture of seventeenth-century New England. Richard Weisman emphasizes the "rift between magic and religion," posits a fundamental antipathy between what he sees as two "competing cosmologies," and depicts "the proponents of magic" as engaged in a direct confrontation with the clergy. David Hall rejects altogether the notion of two distinct traditions, arguing that ministers and lay colonists combined religious theology with pagan and folk beliefs in a syncretic worldview that was remarkably inclusive and tolerant. He writes that there was no "war ... between magic and religion, in part because the clergy also were attracted to occult ideas ... [and] relied on older lore as much any layman." Instead, there was "an accommodation" between the two that enabled occasional interpretive disagreements within an overall framework of consensus. Jon Butler and I see little "accommodation" on the part of clergymen when it came to folk magical techniques that purportedly enabled people to wield supernatural forces; and yet, we argue, many colonists did not see folk magic as antagonistic to religious faith and continued to use magical techniques, much to the dismay of pastors, who demanded in vain exclusive loyalty from their flocks. See Weisman, *Witchcraft, Magic, and Religion in Seventeenth-Century Massachusetts*, 53, 54, 66; Hall, *Worlds of Wonder, Days of Judgment*, 5–7, ch. 2; Butler, *Awash in a Sea of Faith*, ch. 3; and Godbeer, *The Devil's Dominion*, 55–84.

34. Rosenthal, ed., *Records of the Salem Witch Hunt*, 593–594.

35. Hale, *A Modest Enquiry*, 131–132; Middlesex Court Files, fol. 25, no. 4; Mather, *Essay for the Recording of Illustrious Providences*, 266; Lawson, *Christ's Fidelity*, 65.

36. See Pettit, *The Heart Prepared*; McGiffert, ed., *God's Plot*, 198; Hambrick-Stowe, *The Practice of Piety*; and Delbanco, *The Puritan Ordeal*.

37. Mather, *Discourse on Witchcraft*, 27.

38. See Flint, *The Rise of Magic in Early Medieval Europe*; Kieckhefer, *Magic in the Middle Ages*; Klaniczay, *The Uses of Supernatural Power*; and Thomas, *Religion and the Decline of Magic*, esp. ch. 2.

39. Noyes, *New England's Duty and Interest*, 55–56; Cooper, Jr., and Minkema, eds., *The Sermon Notebook of Samuel Parris*, 202.

40. Willard, *The Christian's Exercise by Satan's Temptations*, 149.

41. For a more extended version of this argument, see Godbeer, *The Devil's Dominion*, ch. 3. The likelihood of individuals deciding to blame their troubles on outside forces instead of their own moral failings would have depended on their own psychological inclinations and also those of their minister, their mood at the time of the misfortune, and the broader influences being exerted on them by their cultural environment. Recent scholarship on the underlying causes of the Salem witch hunt has argued that a chain of recent crises in the region encouraged the colonists to blame their misfortunes on external threats: see ibid., 179–203; Norton, *In the Devil's Snare*; and Boyer and Nissenbaum, *Salem Possessed*.

42. Godbeer, *The Devil's Dominion*, 158.

43. Hall, ed., *Witch-Hunting in Seventeenth-Century New England*, 348; Boyer and Nissenbaum, eds., *Salem-Village Witchcraft*, 278.

44. Godbeer, *The Devil's Dominion*, 173.

45. Drake, *Annals of Witchcraft in New England*, 179.

46. Jon Butler refers to this as "the folklorization of magic" in *Awash in a Sea of Faith*, 83.

47. Turrell, "Detection of Witchcraft," 19–20; Wallett, ed., *The Diary of Ebenezer Parkman*, 288; Dexter, ed., *The Literary Diary of Ezra Stiles*, vol. 1, 385.

48. *Independent Journal* (New York), July 18, 1787; *Pennsylvania Gazette*, 18 & 25 July, 1787; *Massachusetts Centinel*, August 1, 1787; *Boston Weekly Magazine*, December 18, 1802; Taylor, "The Early Republic's Supernatural Economy," 6–34. For more detailed discussion of the persistent belief in witchcraft, magic, and the occult throughout the eighteenth and into the nineteenth centuries, see Butler, *Awash in a Sea of Faith*, 83–97, ch. 8; Leventhal, *In the Shadow of the Enlightenment*; Demos, *Entertaining Satan*, 393–394; and Godbeer, *The Devil's Dominion*, 225–233.

Chapter 16

Colonial Magic: The Dutch East Indies

MARGARET J. WIENER

Histories and anthropologies of magic and witchcraft rarely meet in the spacetime of a single scholarly reflection.[1] By this, I mean more than the self-evident fact that historians attend to past events and that anthropologists usually (although not always) research their contemporaries. By and large, historians have restricted themselves to the geographic imaginary of Europe and the nation-states that currently comprise it. Until relatively recently,[2] their major temporal concern was the era of organized witch trials; they tended to treat magic as an aberrant feature of Europe's past and to focus on its decline. Although now many emphasize that magic and witchcraft did not vanish with the Enlightenment, most treat it as a survival mostly found among less-educated or rural European populations.[3]

For anthropologists, magic and witchcraft mainly constitute elements of everyday life in regions beyond Europe's borders, with Africa as the heart of magical darkness. As the discipline coalesced around the figure of the "primitive" in the late nineteenth century, armchair ethnologists unproblematically recognized magic in reports streaming back to European metropoles from outposts of empire, penned by travelers, merchants, missionaries, colonial officials, and other "men on the spot." Declaring magic fundamental to the primitive, and thus a phenomenon with worldwide distribution, they assumed contemporary accounts recounted forms of life unchanged from a past once shared by all of humanity, and overcome by only a few. As anthropologists turned from speculative human history to careful ethnographic description, with some even arguing that magic might itself become altered in response to changing circumstances,[4] treatment became resolutely local, a feature of specific non-European ethnic groups, regions, and nations.

As this suggests, whatever their differences historians and anthropologists clearly have much in common. Like most academics, they presume their readers are (or should be) disenchanted, in contrast to those about whom they write; both treat witchcraft and magic as products of false belief. More to the point for this chapter, both also presume clear boundaries – both temporally, as neatly demarcated decades or centuries, and spatially, corresponding to the borders of nations or to specific regions.

Such boundaries are inherently artificial. This is evident in regard to temporal categories based as they are on multiples of the magical unit of 10, as in the "nineteenth century." But national and cultural boundaries are equally arbitrary. Ideas and practices have always traveled across both time and space.[5] People continually rework concepts and activities that they understand to belong to some past, making them potent actors in present projects. And, of course, ideas and practices cross borders by being carried in books, in objects, and in stories over roads and across oceans. This is highly relevant for rethinking reports of magic and witchcraft in colonized regions.[6]

Thus, we have studies of Europe, on the one hand, and non-Europe, on the other hand, with the two remaining clearly apart, as if those who think of themselves as Europeans and others as non-European (which is never just a matter of geography, but also a question of culture and history) had nothing to do with one another. Yet during the period that magic supposedly declined in the West, Europeans were busy trading, spreading the gospel, conquering, and otherwise colonizing the rest of the world. They brought with them on these expeditions world-producing frames and practices that found themselves both reinforced and stretched in novel applications.

How might we think about the history of witchcraft and magic without falling into these familiar temporal and geographic habits? How can we track claims about witches and magic as they travel across time and space, looking at what they gather and at the friction they generate?[7] In short, can we think about these topics both historically and globally?

I use the concept of colonial magic to attend to such connections. Colonial magic refers to the hybrid formations resulting from efforts to extend familiar concepts to novel situations involving clashes about what counts as real. Both those situations and the concepts themselves are embedded in relations of power – not only those power relations of colonialism itself but also those that maintain hegemonic meanings and valuations: thus, for Europeans the idea that magic and witchcraft implicitly belong to a benighted past. At the same time, colonial magic refers to the sleight of hand that distracts readers of European reports and publications from the work that is being done to produce *equivalences* between now and then and here and there, which simultaneously generates differences and hierarchies. Finally, colonial magic is multi-sited. It is never just about people from European countries at odds with persons from a particular non-European site. Not only did (and do)

Europeans bring ideas that sediment centuries of formation that included earlier moments of conquest, movement, and struggle in many places, but also on the other end different and equally complex formations that did not – prior to the imposition of European rule – coalesce into concepts such as witchcraft or magic.

Colonial magic is not, then, about the practices or values of colonized subjects. Nor is it about the projection of European categories onto the blank slate of a *terra incognita*, or new terrain. Instead, it speaks to efforts to make sense that alter what they touch – both for colonized and for colonizer populations. What makes colonialism useful for rethinking the history of magic is that it inherently yields unanticipated fusions. Colonial relations form sites of translation, in the sense of movement as well as of commensuration. Inevitably, European colonizers sought to turn the unfamiliar into the familiar. But in the process, the familiar mutated in unpredictable ways.

That magic took shape at critical (in both senses) sites of engagement in colonial transactions should come as no surprise. Historically, parsing activities and ideas as magic constituted a front line of advancing Christian theologies, legal systems, and commercial relations as the church spread outward from Rome. It constituted one of several tools through which the church could splice existing and alternative collectivities into its fold, offering a way to envelop non-Christian entities and practices (such as deities, spaces, and rites) that posed intellectual, moral, and political challenges. Beginning in the era in which Europeans began to intervene in the Americas, Africa, and Asia, magic traveled back and forth on merchant ships and in documents, between European metropoles and expanding networks of entrepôts, inquisitions, offices, courtrooms, missionary fields, doctors' consulting rooms, museums, and learned societies. Voyages of discovery, mercantile transactions, and empires translated magic to the rest of the world – and translated the rest of the world through magic.

The Netherlands and its colonies provide intriguing, if comparatively unfamiliar, vantage points from which to introduce colonial magic. Historians long represented the Netherlands as a place that achieved cosmopolitan tolerance early and served as a refuge for dissenters from elsewhere. This Netherlands exemplifies Weber's disenchantment theory. Indeed, historians writing of the "decline of magic" and of growing skepticism among the learned about the very possibility of witchcraft often grant the Dutch Calvinist theologian and minister Balthasar Bekker the distinction of having authored the first book to raise such doubts.[8] Recent scholarship notes that such images of the Dutch date only to the late eighteenth century, with the publication of a book by

Scheltema in 1794.[9] As in other parts of Europe, the dominant view in the Netherlands, and among historians, was that witch beliefs lingered only in remote rural areas, a position recently disputed by de Blécourt.[10] Dutchmen residing in the Dutch East Indies in the nineteenth and twentieth centuries often described themselves as *nuchter*, or disenchanted and level-headed. Indeed, such level-headedness formed a crucial element of colonizer subjectivity, as Dutch residents compared themselves to Indonesians, Eurasians, and creolized "Indies people."[11]

In the Netherlands, contemporary secular magic is imbued with a subtly geo-historical tinge. It is inflected by the Dutch colonial experience, especially by the Netherlands' long involvement with the archipelago known since its independence as the nation-state of Indonesia. Even Dutch people with little direct (e.g., family) engagement with colonial Indonesia have some familiarity with *keris* (Indonesian daggers), *guna-guna* (often understood as Indonesian "black magic"), and "hidden force" (the title of a famous colonial novel) from ambient culture, especially television, novels, movies, and museums.

As I show later in the chapter, Dutch merchants played a pivotal early role in colonial magic by putting into general circulation crucial concepts and attitudes that emerged through mercantile transactions on the west coast of Africa in the seventeenth century. The central figure was the fetish, although what was said about this hybrid object also helped to position Africa as the heart of magical darkness in European imaginations. In Africa itself, the twentieth century saw a shift from fetishism to witchcraft as a central concern of colonial states, which was not the case in the Indies. In this chapter, I address where and how practices termed "witchcraft" *did* emerge as a matter of concern in the Indies, even if it remained a relatively minor worry (especially when compared to the fetish).

Ideally, to speak of colonial magic in relation to the Indies would require attending to what Dutch actors (from different regions and different social classes) brought with them, rethinking their accounts of what Indonesians were doing, considering how Dutch efforts to render Indonesian activities as magic and/or witchcraft changed those activities, and noting which reworked concepts returned to the Netherlands – and also traveled beyond it. It also would entail tracking closely the entangled relations among many times and places. Colonial magic forces us not only to notice relations between colonizer cultural formations and those of the peoples they colonized or even the complex new entities and practices that took shape as they struggled to deal with one another. It pushes us beyond even semi-national assemblages – to, for instance, British colonizers and their African colonies. It would also require more attention to the historical formation of that complex conglomeration of differing peoples who became unified as residents of the Dutch East Indies and who for centuries and even millennia before any European ships docked had engaged in trade – of ideas as well as goods and genes – with people residing in the areas now called India, the Middle East, and China.

This chapter has two goals. One is ambitious: to argue that the history of magic and witchcraft must necessarily be multi-sited. Our contemporary concepts are the sedimented products of global history, a history involving movement, partial connection, and obstruction.[12] The second is more modest: to explore the necromantic work involved in bringing the figure of the witch to the Dutch East Indies.

It is important to state from the start that witchcraft never emerged as a major concern in the Indies.[13] After tracking where and when it did arise as a translation of occurrences in the Indies and a source of difficulty for colonial authorities, I offer a hypothesis about why it remained a minor issue. I contend that it is worth attending as much to colonial magic's failures to coalesce productively as to its successes. As part of that demonstration, I periodically remind readers of other colonial territories where, by contrast, witchcraft and the figure of the witch congealed all too firmly. And I indicate throughout how such terms elided significant differences between European and Indonesian realities, even as they (partially) connected them.

Focusing on witchcraft, a topic well known to historians of Europe, not only highlights relations between places usually discussed in isolation from one another but also reveals how historical memory became articulated with projects of colonial domination. At the same time, given historians' long interest in witch trials, it is of no little interest that the law served as the institutional domain through which the witch was translated around the globe (albeit in different ways).

The Entwined Story of Witches and Fetishes: A Brief Demonstration of Colonial Magic

To make the best case for my argument about colonial magic, I begin with a short detour to the west coast of Africa and the formation of the fetish, the intercultural and multi-sited object par excellence.[14] The witch and the fetish belong together in forgotten, but nonetheless inherited, pasts that span multiple continents. The fetish is intimately entwined with the story of the witch in at least three ways. First, European witchcraft concepts initially gave birth to the fetish. Intending simply to name unfamiliar objects and practices for what they seemed to resemble, the Portuguese traders who called these *feitiço* (witchcraft) unleashed something unanticipated. Second, the fetish's narrative circulation contributed to slaying the idea of the witch as a European figure of fear. Third, tropes and attitudes honed in describing fetish practices entered the toolkits of European intellectuals as broad critiques of non-European gullibility and irrationality, positions that were crucial to later colonizing projects.

As Pietz has demonstrated in his masterful essays on the topic, the idea of the fetish arose from interactions between European and African traders on Africa's west coast in the fifteenth century.[15] Fetish derived from *feitiço*,[16] the Portuguese word for witchcraft. Portuguese traders used the term to refer to African activities centering on certain objects that reminded them of witchcraft practices.[17] The term quickly morphed into the pidgin *fetisso* among those trading with Europeans.

Two Dutch Protestant merchants, Pieter de Marees and Willem Bosman, proved to be key actors in moving the fetish into the conceptual armature of European intellectuals. De Marees's account of his visit to the Gold Coast to trade in 1602 offered the first description of these objects and practices and transported the term *fetisso* into northern European languages, including not only Dutch but also German and English. His account of fetishes is rife with terms such as "sorcerer"; the fetish's separation from witchcraft was not yet complete.

If European witchcraft gave birth to the fetish, the fetish in turn helped to unmake the European witch. De Marees's text helped undermine discourses about spirits, bodies, and their relationship, a topic crucial to theories that witches made pacts with Satan, who used them to do evil. Most significantly, Balthasar Bekker, the minister in the Dutch Reformed Church mentioned in the previous section, drew on de Marees's and other voyage literature in his lengthy consideration of whether purely spiritual beings could indeed intervene in worldly affairs.[18] Many later writers heralded Bekker's controversial 1691–1693 multivolume tome as the first – and certainly the most coherent – conceptual blow struck against prevailing ideas about witchcraft.[19]

Willem Bosman, chief merchant for the Dutch West India Company in Guinea, drew on Bekker's work in a 1703 book that not only displaced de Marees as the authority on the fetish (Bosman, unlike de Marees, lived in Guinea for many years) but also shaped the "problem of the fetish" by refracting it through the lenses of ignorance and irrationality. As Pietz observes:

> Only because it was safe and acceptable to rule out absolutely the devil as a
> causal agent could a Bosman explicitly characterize African superstition as

being based on ignorance of the fact (the knowledge of which was rationality itself) that natural events happened according to impersonal laws and chance conjunctures, not according to the intentional purposes of unseen spiritual agents.[20]

Bosman presented the fetish as a fundamental misunderstanding of the proper properties and value of things, and he depicted Africans as both unscrupulous and credulous – by contrast with Europeans such as himself.

The experiences of Protestant merchants that produced the problem of the fetish eventuated in Enlightenment philosophies that discredited a host of agents, practices, and experiences as both unreasonable and (importantly) archaic and subjected those agents, practices, and experiences to ridicule, reform, and efforts at eradication. The fetish itself became embroiled in speculative debates about the origins of religion with Charles de Brosses's fabrication of fetishism in 1760, as European intellectuals sought to pin down exactly which misunderstandings of the world indexed "primitive" mentalities. As trade gave way to conquest and control in the nineteenth century, such positions became entwined with an understanding of the bourgeois European as the pinnacle of human achievement, whose rule would benefit benighted others.[21] Through such projects, the fetish became reacquainted with the witch, and both formed evidence of non-European backwardness.

Colonial Witches in the Age of the Witch Trials

Europeans conjured witches during two different periods of colonizing activity: first, during the initial era of European expansion that began in the fifteenth century, when the settler colonialism taking form in the New World contrasted with the largely mercantile adventures that got Europeans involved with Africans and Asians; second, in the heyday of European imperialism, roughly from the mid-nineteenth century up to World War II, after which Asian and African imperial formations began to break into independent nation-states. The witch herself formed a different entity in each of these two periods and aroused quite different anxieties.

Voyages of discovery, trade, and conquest began during the moral panic that historians refer to as the witch hunt. Both narratives and the new forms of wealth brought back from distant places in turn contributed to the witch's disappearance from mainstream European public life – a disappearance that shaped the later period of colonial rule. In this section, I briefly comment on the manifestation of witches outside of Europe in the earlier moments of colonial encounter, drawing on the limited material available to me from the Dutch East Indies.

If the witch initially hitched a ride to Africa on Portuguese caravels before morphing into the novel formation of the fetish, his or her journeys elsewhere had different, if equally unpredictable, outcomes. In the aftermath of conquest, conversion, and settlement in the Spanish Empire in the Americas, witches materialized in inquisitions in Mexico and Peru, but they most commonly took the form of African slaves and mulattoes – or even creoles – rather than the people that are now called Indians. Inquisitors treaded cautiously when it came to recently Christianized native populations, even as Indians began to acquire a reputation as healers and sorcerers.[22] In the Dutch East Indies, where, compared to Latin America, colonialism certainly took much less intrusive (and much more geographically restricted) forms at this time, natives whose acts led Europeans to associate them with witches could provoke the occasional surprisingly strong response, and it was even more surprising given the relative inattention to prosecuting witches among Dutch authorities in Europe.

When traders from the newly chartered Dutch East India Company (VOC) began to infiltrate trade routes to Asia at the start of the seventeenth century, little incentive existed to invest concern about witches in the scattered ports where the company established its trading posts and forts. Europeans remained few and far between outside of company headquarters in the town of Batavia on Java's northwest coast, and the company's focus was monetary profit rather than conquest, glory, or spreading Christianity. Because the Company discouraged settlers, the Dutch community not only remained tiny but also became strongly creolized as merchants cohabited with or married Indonesian and Eurasian women.[23] Having rebelled against Spanish domination (and for many, the Catholic Church), Dutch merchants had no interest in patrolling anyone's faith – and many consulted local experts (misleadingly referred to as Muslim "priests") to heal, uncover the causes of misfortune, and carry out prophylactic rites.[24] Because wealth came from access to and commodification of agricultural products (at first mainly spices but soon also indigo, coffee, tea, and sugar), the objects a later colonial regime would find to be troublesome fetishes remained curiosities rather than, as on Africa's west coast, impediments to trade to which terms such as witchcraft might stick. Moreover, not only had the judicial prosecution of witches in the Netherlands already ended before Dutch merchants arrived in the Indies, but accounts of foreign lands by the company's merchants (as described in the previous section for Guinea) further transformed dominant attitudes.[25]

Still, witches did form a real part of the world from which company employees came. And in 1638 in Batavia, authorities prosecuted and burned an Indonesian "witch" (*tovenaar*) who originally came from the island of Banda.[26] With two assistants (his brother and a woman), the witch offered a variety of services for clients. Trouble started when rumors began to circulate that the trio had caused a European family a series of illnesses and other misfortunes and had killed two European men. They were subsequently tried and convicted of witchcraft. In rendering judgment, the bench of magistrates ruled:

> [T]hey had led many weak people astray by their ungodly and chilling practices and brought them from the Lord God to the devil, which matters are of very pernicious consequence, that being conducive to the destruction and ruin of this community as fighting directly against the glory of God must not be [treated] patiently in a Christian domain but punished in the strictest way as an example. (This and all translations from Dutch are mine.)

Thus they sentenced the witch "to be briskly burned with fire and consumed to ash … along with his magically enticing books and papers."[27] The witch's confederates were flogged, branded, and exiled.

As both Dutch and Iberian colonial formations show, European and non-European lives tended to be enmeshed in this period.[28] Consulting local experts to deal with adversity or to advance good fortune did not entail much of a stretch, despite the novelty of their practices. At the same time, because witches constituted a fixture of European experience, it was not surprising to discover them in distant places and occasionally to find them as troubling there as they could be at home – and requiring similar treatment.

Resurrecting the Witch in Nineteenth-Century Colonial Rule

The colonialism that took shape during the course of the nineteenth century differed considerably from earlier forms. In the New World, for example, "liberation" by wars for national independence meant that colonialism no longer involved rule by distant monarchs but rather by agents of new republics (whose attitudes toward indigenous populations were no less colonial). In Asia and Africa, European nation-states, rather than corporations, took up the business of extracting wealth, an activity accompanied by extended government functions that included administering justice and that entailed the study – and eventually was justified by the reform – of indigenous populations. The Dutch East Indies came into existence when the assets and debts of the Dutch East India Company, bankrupt at the turn of the nineteenth century, reverted to the Netherlands, which paid little attention to its new possessions halfway across the world until the 1830s. For much of the nineteenth century, the Netherlands retained the company's focus on the extraction of wealth, often through the forced production of agricultural commodities. More regions across the archipelago came under Dutch control, however, through treaties and military conflicts.

By the time this second phase of colonial expansion began, witchcraft no longer counted as part of reality in dominant European nature-cultures. A European who invoked witchcraft to explain misfortune risked derision as a superstitious fool. Witchcraft purportedly belonged to the past.[29] And that judgment accompanied all decisions to render non-European actors and acts in such terms. Indeed, the use of words such as "witchcraft" to describe facts of contemporary non-European life constituted necromancy, a summoning of ghosts.

Courts of law served as the primary venue in which colonial officials drew on their understanding of witchcraft to make sense of Indonesian claims and acts. The law, of course, is the institution through which historians originally tracked the rise and fall of witchcraft as an object of intense concern in Europe's own past – and, as we will see later in this chapter, it was not only in the Indies that such conjuring occurred. In regional tribunals, administrators called witchcraft back from the gray halls of Europe's dead past to speak of Indonesian motivations. In doing so, they resurrected a specter that some warned could threaten the very possibility of establishing justice.

Rendering Indonesian practices as witchcraft occurred in legal proceedings from at least the mid-nineteenth century onward. On the whole, different laws applied to Europeans, natives, and "foreign Orientals" (persons of Indian, Chinese, or Middle Eastern extraction residing in colonized portions of the archipelago). Matters involving native violations were adjudicated in district tribunals, with the ranking district officer presiding over a bench of magistrates consisting of local native authorities and Indonesians serving as prosecutors and investigators (Figure 16.1). Cases heard in such tribunals usually remained resolutely local, but on occasion, verdicts were appealed, some even coming before the Supreme Court in Batavia. Beginning in the middle of the century, new law journals published occasional summaries of regional cases that struck them as interesting, especially (but not only) those that reached the Supreme Court. In the following section, I draw on summaries from the best known of these journals, *Law in the Netherlands Indies (Regt van Nederlandsch-Indië;*

FIGURE 16.1. Court in session, 1899, Koetoardjo, Central Java. Courtesy of KITLV/Royal Netherlands Institute of Southeast Asia and Caribbean Studies.

hereafter *RNI*) to consider the emergence of witchcraft as an object of sporadic concern in the Indies and some of the issues that it raised.

"Witchcraft Beliefs" in Dutch Colonial Tribunals

Most references to witchcraft in *RNI* (although not all) occurred in cases where defendants indicted for homicide confessed to killing someone but claimed they acted in self-defense. From 1848 to 1897, *RNI* summarizes eleven such cases, mainly on the island of Java, with two from Timor and one each from North Bali and South Sulawesi. Defendants invariably testified that the "victim" already had killed family members and/or neighbors by making them fatally ill; generally, they expressed fear for their own lives, too.

Although by no means capturing all incidents or statements that might have reminded officials of witchcraft, these eleven arraignments illuminate the friction generated when local forms of justice collided with European ontological hegemonies and a particular understanding of Europe's history. The label of witchcraft connected myriad Indonesian acts and terms with a particular understanding of European history. For administrators, witchcraft evoked a shameful interlude of irrationality in Europe's past, during which innocents had been sacrificed. These judgments repeatedly infiltrate their efforts to administer justice to colonized subjects.

The Dutch officials presiding over each of these tribunals zeroed in on one pragmatic issue: Did testimony about what sounded like witchcraft constitute a mitigating circumstance and justify a reduced sentence? Murder, particularly when premeditated, as was usually true in these cases, was a capital crime. In every case, however, rather than death by hanging, courts sentenced such defendants to forced labor, mostly in chains outside of their home district. Some sentences were reduced further on appeal to the colonial Supreme Court in Batavia, resulting in fewer years, no chains, and/or no exile.

For both the Dutch officials who heard these cases and the lawyers digesting them for *RNI*, native testimony could only be explained in the same Enlightened terms through which they retrospectively judged historical witch trials. Thus, the official presiding in an 1848 case attributed the defendant's act to "fanatic enthusiastic superstition";[30] the phrase "native superstition" occurs often in headings to these articles. References also are made to failures of reason.[31] In determining a sentence, however, care is taken to clarify that what is at stake is not the mistaken beliefs of an individual; the community to which he or she belongs shares those views about either the possibility that a person could cause others to sicken and/or die or about the particular person killed (usually both). In the 1848 case, on appeal, the Supreme Court added to the theme of superstition that of "nationality," suggesting that superstition characterized all Javanese.[32] Another case refers to "folk beliefs".[33] Most cases specify more precisely with whom such "beliefs" are shared, however. In pronouncing judgment in a case from Sumenep (Java) in 1895, the court noted that not only did the defendant believe the victim "possessed the power to kill or make people ill by magical means (*toovermiddelen*)," but other witnesses, including the village head, also agreed, persuading the magistrate that the defendant "really was convinced" that the victim had harmed his family.[34] Several cases, in fact, refer to the fact that indigenous leaders held such positions. Thus, the Resident adjudicating an 1854 case observed that even among the chiefs (who presumably should have known better), "firm belief exists in sorcerers and witches who by their evil practices can spread illnesses and death as they please, the persons suspected of sorcery being so feared and hated that they do not consider it as a criminal offence to take their lives."[35] Long before the formation of an anthropology advocating cultural relativism or its Dutch equivalent in customary law studies, colonial administrators had to recognize in practice that judgments of wrongdoing differed, even if the law treated those killed as unfortunate innocents.

Read against this legal grain, however, the testimony presented at these tribunals shows the ontological violence that the phrase "witchcraft beliefs" obscures. Such terms did not merely commensurate; they performed colonial power by making one reality – that of European colonizers – prevail over others. Testimony, on the other hand, offers glimpses into how colonized populations constructed reality. This means attending to the evidence that defendants persistently offered to justify their acts.

For instance, in 1855 Java, Mudin and a confederate hacked to death a woman named Bok Gendruk. When arrested, both immediately confessed but explained that she had been a witch (*tooverheks*) who had caused the death of one defendant's mother and the other's father-in-law and had made both of them ill. On several occasions, Mudin had dreamed that Bok Gendruk seized him by the throat and groped his body; when he woke, he would be sick. The last time it had happened, his illness lasted a year. Moreover, he insisted that many suffering from that illness told him before they died that they had had the same dream.[36]

Dreams also are relevant in another case from Java, as is the decedent's odd behavior. When Pa Tipah sidled up to Pa Pasri on his verandah one morning and refused to speak, Pa Pasri became very anxious; whenever he did this, people fell fatally ill. In the past, he had dreamed that Pa Tipah gave him meat, and when he woke he was sick. This had happened to his mother, too. So he asked the silent Pa Tipah if he had not already made enough people sick. Pa Tipah retorted that he had only caused four deaths and named his victims. Pa Pasri's efforts to have him admit to three more (including Pa Pasri's father) led to an altercation that resulted in Pa Tipah's death.[37]

The deceased person's non-coerced confession crops up again in an 1891 case from North Bali involving Men Mukiari's death at the hands of I Urip and Ketut Sasak. I Urip testified that not long ago he had awakened in the middle of the night to find a large animal beside him that turned into Men Mukiari and then into a monkey, which squeezed his throat for more than half an hour before releasing him and vanishing. After that, he fell ill. Ketut Sasak declared that Men Mukiari was widely known as a witch (*tooverkol*). After she had visited his mother a few months earlier, the latter fell unconscious. The following morning, Men Mukiari came by again and his mother fell into a coma. Before dying that evening, she briefly regained consciousness long enough to gasp that Men Mukiari had been sitting on her and strangling her all day. Soon after, Men Mukiari gave his son some beans. After eating them, he cried out in pain and died. When they confronted her, "Men Mukiari answered that she really did bewitch his co-defendant I Urip and his, defendant's, mother and child," whereupon they beat her to death.[38]

A different kind of evidence of the decedent's status figured in an 1888 case from Segeri. La Patta and a neighbor killed Sanro Boa after La Patta found Sanro Boa eating dirt under his house, which is part of the way that *suangi* inflict harm on a household. Calling *"suangi, suangi,"* they followed Sanro Boa, who suddenly turned into a pig and tried to eat them. When they attacked the pig with lances, it ran away but then turned back, and they killed it. The following morning, Sanro Boa's body was found on precisely that spot. The court noted that their story "may not be judged entirely according to Western concepts": not only is it "a generally popular belief that suangi really exist and can bring misfortune by their acts," but others also testified that Sanro Boa "passed as a suangi."[39]

The perceiving of humans as animals also makes an appearance in a trial in Java. A few days after telling his boss that a coworker was bewitching him, Sidin killed three other coworkers and wounded a fourth in a nighttime rampage. At his trial, he claimed that he thought animals were attacking him – presumably because of the witchcraft. Investigators had examined all of the workers' rooms to look for "magical agents" (*toovermiddelen*, specified as *gambar*, Indonesian for "picture"[40]) that might explain his misperception but found nothing. The tribunal decided he had been in his right mind and sentenced him to death.

Although it may seem obvious that the content of such testimony had no place in the reality of Dutch officials, less evident is its failure to mesh seamlessly with the specificities of historical European witchcraft that those officials implicitly invoked. Only occasionally do they appear to meet, as in a case from 1856 Priangan in which the village head Kertadiwangsa ordered six villagers to kill Bapa Adim and Ambu Jaib, a married couple widely regarded as "possessed by the devil and the cause of ... many deaths."[41] Several other references to possession by the Devil also occur in this transcript, although it affects not people but their goods and houses.[42] Here, Europe's past echoes more strongly, although the defendant again takes pains to establish the couple's guilt: when a serious illness claimed numerous lives some years earlier, many called the husband or wife by name with their dying breaths, crying "let me go, don't torment me."[43]

Courts of law, of course, formed only one of many sites in the Dutch East Indies where Dutch and Indonesian ontologies – their experience of what entities populate the world and what capacities those entities possess – came into conflict As we saw in the previous examples, and as was typical of such moments of confrontation, officials addressed the conflict by moving it to an epistemological register, speaking not of witches but of a *belief* in witches, in contrast to the superior *knowledge* of Europeans. Dutch officials had to interpret defendants' testimony as proof of belief, because that was the only slot the phenomena described could occupy in hegemonic formations. Thus, instead of concerning themselves with the potential guilt of decedents, courts could focus instead on defendants' ideas and values.

Officials across the archipelago apparently came to similar conclusions independently of one another: namely, that Indonesian claims mitigated what the Dutch legal code classified as murder. The Supreme Court accepted the need for mitigation. Even though none of the cases the Court considered refers to precedents – only to statutes, which is not surprising, given that precedents play little role in Dutch legal practice, based as it is on the Napoleonic Code – so that only their appearance in the journal itself connects them, those serving on the Court time and again took what we now call culture into partial account. In no case, however, did they dismiss the charge of murder and let the perpetrators go free or treat them, as they might have been treated in their own communities presuming that their assessment of the deceased was indeed widely shared, as heroes. Such developments formed part of a burgeoning concern with cultural relativism in colonial law, which would, around the turn of the twentieth century, coalesce into a scholarly field devoted to customary law (*adatrecht*) in the Netherlands.

"Witch Murders" as a Colonial Problem in the Early Twentieth Century

Cases reported in *RNI* acknowledge that defendants acted according to the values of their communities and occasionally on behalf of those communities (as Kertadiwangsa did). Yet the difficulty of adjudicating such matters involved more than the legal outcomes suggest. Not only could the killing of witches elude discovery, posing a serious problem for colonial law and order, but even when exposed, such matters presented conundrums for conscientious officials attempting to mete out justice. This was particularly true after 1900, when the colonial state conquered and otherwise incorporated areas of the archipelago that were hitherto independent in the name of bringing the benefits of civilization. To see how troubling such situations could be, I turn to an article that appeared in a journal for colonial civil servants by G. W. Mazee, who at that time held the post of Civil Authority in the Poso district of Central Sulawesi, about a rash of "murders of witches" (*heksenmoord*) he accidentally uncovered among the Toraja in 1911.

Taking for granted a distinction between human and natural causality, Mazee explains the mistake that in his view underlies witchcraft accusations: "heathens," seeking moral explanations for natural occurrences, blame epidemics on persons whose behavior marks them as odd. Before the colonial state established its authority in the area in 1906, the Toraja settled such cases through ordeals, which offered virtually no chance for the witch to prove his or her innocence. Following the trial, villagers beat the proven witch to death, urging young boys to take part to build their courage. The Dutch outlawed such "witch trials" and in 1907 imposed a fine on anyone taking part in them. But in 1909, a contagious lung disease spread to the region. Prohibited from taking action publicly, village heads ordered the witches to be killed surreptitiously.

Mazee found this out purely by chance, although the man he caught then disclosed the existence of numerous other such instances. The tribunals established to try these cases consisted of three "chiefs," with Mazee presiding. Mazee noted that this meant that the chiefs had to try persons that they "in their heart granted [were] right"; the chiefs also "believed in witches" and likely would have given the same orders as those they judged. Expanding upon this sentiment, he observed: "In their eyes anyway a witch is no less dangerous than, e.g., a mad dog; to protect such people thus appears to them extremely absurd, or better said extremely stupid and besides very unjust."[44] Moreover, public opinion supported village leaders who put witches to death in defiance of colonial law. Thus, it was unsurprising that the chiefs only found the defendants guilty of failure to abide by the government's orders. Because they could hardly be expected to impose the punishment that Dutch authorities deemed proper for homicide, Mazee handled sentencing on his own.

Mazee followed the "usual solution": imposing the harshest sentence (ten–fifteen years of forced labor in chains on another island) on the chiefs who ordered the deaths, as they had abused their authority in addition to having been accessories to murder.[45] The actual killers (in one case, nine twenty-year-olds) received milder punishments.

But the "usual solution" struck Mazee as woefully ineffective, given that it failed to resolve the multiple clashes between the colonial state and its subjects that such cases revealed. First, Europeans governments should not only protect the welfare of all, but they also should have a monopoly on capital punishment; hence, local authorities could not order anyone's death. Moreover, a compromise already existed in this region: the Dutch were willing to send those accused of witchcraft to live under government protection; killing them was not necessary. Second, punishment neither acted as a deterrent nor affected people's understandings of the causes of misfortune or the best way to remedy it. Colonial law had only engendered more devious ways to dispense of a purported witch, for example, by felling a tree on him or her or by pushing him or her off a precipice. Third, Toraja sent far from home fared poorly. And the usual punishment (forced labor in a chain gang in a distant place) exposed people whose major failings were not sharing European values and not distinguishing between good and evil (which Mazee treats as self-evident moral distinctions) but relying instead on tradition to the corrupting influence of hardened criminals, which could likely lead to problems of reintegration on their return home.

Mazee also amplifies the bankruptcy of efforts to address witchcraft beliefs by removing those accused of witchcraft from their communities. Such a response totally failed to fulfill local desires for justice. Perhaps sending witches farther away would help, but given that Indonesians appeared to find separation from familiar places stressful, this would pose problems for the state, which judged such persons innocent of any crime. He then notes (in parentheses) that "[i]t is curious that the accused acknowledged themselves to be witches," but he says nothing further about this.

By his use of the term "witch" and his assertion that those accused of witchcraft were innocent, Mazee had already dragged a figure from the Dutch past through time and across space to a region sharing no common culture or history with the Netherlands. But he then makes the equivalence between the Dutch past and the Toraja present explicit by rhetorically asking what might be the appropriate verdict to impose on people who, prior to their incorporation into the colonial state, were "no higher in development than our Batavians when the Romans found them" and who now find themselves "in collision with a civilization that is more than eighteen centuries older" that itself only relatively recently, and "perhaps still not entirely," vanquished belief in witches.[46]

Mazee ends by asking readers with more experience for a solution. His own conclusion is that the state lacked the right kind of power to address the problem: what is needed are not better sentences but more "civilization," in order to rid Toraja of their superstitions and "fear of evil spirits." Thus, he urges support of the missions. For Mazee, no administrative or judicial remedy existed; only drastic cultural change could resolve the clash between colonizers and colonized.

Taken together with the reports in *RNI*, several conclusions may be drawn from Mazee's distressed article. Clearly, defendants on trial did not consider their acts to be criminal, seeing as they readily confessed when caught. As I noted in the previous section, they offered evidence to justify their deeds: stories of visits or gifts from those they killed; troubling dreams; conversations with family members about their dreams, followed by illness and/or death; dying words by those harmed; and seeing the person shift into animal form. Tribunals often invited testimony by others in the community to confirm that not just the defendants regarded the deceased as being responsible for harming others. Most intriguingly, when confronted, the witch had often confessed. Although we mainly have only the testimony of their killers for that, Mazee also mentions it in puzzled passing.[47]

As I show later in the chapter, Dutch scholars readily took up the matter of community norms as an interesting concern. And Mazee's article shows how administrators grappled with such matters and their implications for colonial justice. As Guha has noted, colonial states exercised dominance without hegemony.[48] The state could and did prosecute acts leading to death as murder, but it could not ignore the motives that led to such acts and had to recognize that those it ruled at the very least saw the world quite differently. Acting violently against those perpetrating violence could not prevent similar acts in the future or change local values. For that, as Mazee concludes, institutions beyond the judiciary were necessary, in order to effect a radical reconstruction of reality. Although for Mazee, Protestant missionaries hopefully could lead the way to that disenchanted Promised Land, in general to achieve such an end, colonialism had to invade not just territories but worlds, carving out a domain of "nature" to account for illness and rendering deluded or deceived by culture those who claimed otherwise, whether about themselves or others.

In this the Dutch failed, judging by the present. Although they did manage to stop what they called witch trials and the execution or exile of persons they categorized as witches, persons exercising malign power still retain their potency throughout Indonesia.[49] Moreover, the notion of "native belief" may have assured Dutch authorities that they had identified where Indonesians mistook the imaginary for the real, but their trials embroiled them more than they acknowledge in Indonesian realities. Of course, the regional courts that tried these cases always consisted, as in Mazee's district, of Indonesian members, along with Indonesian prosecutors and police investigators. Although the presiding Dutch official heard in the testimony by defendants and community members "witchcraft beliefs" that mitigated guilt, native authorities likely heard something different: proof that the decedent had merited death. And it is hard to imagine that a Dutch official would have ordered, for instance, a search for images that might prove that Sidin really was being bewitched.

These law cases formed occasions when the Dutch past was transported to an Indonesian present through the mediation of words such as witch. At times, the Dutch attempt to translate vernacular terms. Thus, cases from Timor and Segeri refer to *suangi*, although translations differ: sorcerer (*tovenaar*) in Timor and an evil spirit in Segeri. The difference might lie in distinct Indonesian cultures, although the events in Segeri presented in the previous section make "evil spirit" unlikely. But in the many cases from Java and the one from Bali, no vernacular appears. Instead, reports speak of witches, using old Dutch terms such as *tovenaar* or terms imported during the period of the witch trials (*heks, tooverheks, tooverkol*, all of which were gendered female).[50] Occasionally, Dutch officials make sense of what witnesses say by speaking about "the devil." Thus, one district officer (who speaks of precolonial "witch trials," or *hexenprocessen*, the term used historically in the Netherlands) writes: "[I]t is generally known that the Balinese believe that people can put themselves in connection with devils and witches," a claim that sounds suspiciously like *maleficium* but not much like Bali.[51] The Priangan case involving Kertadiwangsa repeatedly refers to possession by "the devil," an idea that is conceivably plausible in a Muslim community, although a vernacular would clarify how closely the author hews to Sundanese, rather than Dutch, ideas. There is no evidence, however, that colonial authorities put much thought into these words. A situation reminded an official of discredited European concepts, and because he viewed Indonesians as inherently backwards, translation proceeded without further ado.

Comparative Interlude: Witchcraft in Twentieth-Century British Colonial Africa

Around the same time that Mazee penned his article about witch killing in the Celebes, Africa was becoming the territory most associated with the necromantic language of witchcraft. For centuries, the fetish had defined Africa for European intellectuals as a land "enveloped in the dark mantle of Night," as Hegel put it in *The Philosophy of History*.[52] But not long after the European powers began to divide the continent among themselves, the witch displaced the fetish as the dominant figure in images of Africa and Africans.[53]

In the early years of the twentieth century, British district officers all over the recently acquired regions of Africa began to draw up a series of "anti-witchcraft ordinances" that were to be repeatedly revised during the subsequent decades. Taking as their model Britain's own 1735 anti-witchcraft act, they were not directed at witches but rather at activities involving what the British considered supernatural.[54] Thus, although some ordinances prohibited acts aimed at harming others by witchcraft activities, they tended as well to target those who claimed to be able to detect witchcraft or to counteract its effects. Such ordinances led to myriad complications and unanticipated outcomes for both Africans and colonial administrators. Among other things, they embroiled colonial officials in contradictory positions and initially convinced many Africans that the British were on the side of the witches.[55]

Administrative alarm over witches and the African "witch-doctors" who promised to uncover or eradicate them also gave birth to a vast anthropological literature, as anthropologists, sometimes working for colonial states, sought to explain the phenomenon for European readers. Indeed, the fact that anthropologists adopted the state's translation of African practices as witchcraft in their increasingly nuanced descriptions and analyses gave their work surprising traction beyond their own discipline and beyond colonial administration. Thus, Evans-Pritchard's famous study of the Azande led not only to several rounds of attention to African witchcraft (the first, in the 1950s, was sociological in emphasis, stressing the conflicts that resulted in accusations; the second, in the 1970s, was epistemological, attending to the rationality of African claims) but also to considerable interest by historians in the social relations of accusations in European witch trials and in the forms of thought that made witchcraft plausible. Another consequence of such British interventions is that both the practices colonial regimes sought to eradicate and the term "witchcraft" itself became increasingly relevant to Africans, even as countless studies showed that the word failed to capture important indigenous distinctions. Thus, witches continue to be an intense focus of concern for Africans (and Africanists) long after independence.

Although the anti-witchcraft ordinances did the most to solidify witchcraft as a matter of concern for both governments and scholars when it came to Africa, the colonial judiciary found itself confronted with the same kinds of cases already discussed in relation to the Indies. The killing of witches in British Africa appears to have attracted the attention of the courts between the two world wars.[56] Unlike the Dutch in the Indies, the Supreme Court that heard cases in British Africa was reluctant to commute death sentences by accepting "witchcraft beliefs" as a mitigating circumstance unless specific legal conditions obtained. The Court did, however, come up with criteria for such situations.

By contrast with British Africa, in the Indies, the Supreme Court never established specific guidelines for adjudicating "witch murders"; nor did witchcraft ever become the target of ordinances or particular policy interventions.

Officials treated phenomena that reminded them of witchcraft on an ad hoc basis as they surfaced in the course of everyday governance, and for the most part only when it led to outcomes they considered murder. Consequently, witchcraft never achieved stability as an object of knowledge. Yet there was at least one effort to change that, and there was one rejected opportunity. These are my topics in the next two sections.

Drawing Together Archipelago Witchcraft as a Matter of Colonial Concern

British Africa suggests that for witchcraft to emerge as a focus for colonial activity, and in turn as an incitement for scholarly investigation, the dispersed occasions on which specific colonial officers made sense of particular events in regions that did not necessarily share any common history had to be brought together. In British Africa, this happened in two ways: through the passing of ordinances that criminalized certain types of activities and gathered them under the label of witchcraft; and through the establishment of generalizable procedures for criminal prosecution and sentencing in cases involving the deliberate killing of figures whom officials translated as witches. Thus, the notion of the witch had to travel from isolated incidents through colonial hierarchies into texts and then make its way back through the chain of scattered officials into the territories under their authority. At the same time, such texts cemented the witch as a problem for empirical investigation, and the texts that such efforts generated could then circulate as knowledge through and beyond disciplinary networks, being distributed through books, articles, translations, conferences, and classrooms.

As already indicated earlier in the chapter, in the Dutch East Indies, no similar codification of the witch occurred in legal codes or court proceedings. But in the 1930s, an effort was made to produce such an outcome. In this case, the site for both drawing things together and for recommending alterations in colonial policies took place in the Netherlands itself at the University of Leiden, which had long been established as the center for producing scholarly knowledge about the Indies and for training men for the colonial civil service. The medium was a doctoral dissertation in jurisprudence at the university on the topic of customary law (*adatrecht*) offences in the "magical worldview" of Indonesians. Its author, Nicolaas Lesquillier, proudly noted under his name on the title page that he was born in Aceh in the Indies.

Adat law was a uniquely Dutch field of scholarship and policy recommendations that focused entirely on the Indies. Established around the turn of the twentieth century at Leiden by Cornelis van Vollenhoven (who borrowed the term from Snouck Hurgronje, a famous expert on Islam who had served the colonial regime as advisor on native affairs), the discipline's name was as hybrid as its products. *Adat* is an Arabic loan word that in Indonesian refers to customs or traditions. Adat law sought to uncover the underlying unwritten laws constituting indigenous practices. A brilliant scholar, van Vollenhoven was indefatigable in eliciting materials from "men on the spot" and in making legislators take them into account. An advocate of not only understanding but also accommodating Indonesian values, he inspired detailed studies of virtually every corner of the archipelago.[57]

Lesquillier was the first customary law scholar to organize this project around the novel notion of a magical worldview. For Lesquillier, what counted as offenses against adat made sense through the expedient of imagining a radically different worldview, in which a dynamic force operated in all things – humans, gods, ancestors, plants, animals, and inanimate objects, both natural and manufactured. All of these entities existed in a delicate balance: acts that upset equilibrium constituted offenses; sanctions sought to restore it.

For our purposes, the most relevant portions of Lesquillier's book are those that draw together materials from all over the archipelago to address offenses involving homicide by "poisoning, by 'black magic,' and by witchcraft or werewolves." Although he uses some of the same language, Lesquillier turns periodic administrative interventions that mentioned witchcraft on their head. Temporarily leaving aside poisoning, he notes that Dutch law has nothing to say about the others, which Indonesians rank as serious offenses. The problem that adat raises is not that Indonesians killed innocents accused of imaginary acts but that the Dutch failed to recognize and remediate serious crimes.

Lesquillier draws on the writing of scholar-administrators who worked this terrain where ethnology met jurisprudence, bringing the extensive archive of studies of regional adat into conjunction with actual criminal prosecutions. In the process, he reviews the cases reported in *RNI* (and covers more than just the trials for homicide). Examining the sentences, he critiques the colonial state's failure to establish a unified policy not only on the matter of mitigation but also on appropriate sentencing rather than letting each district officer decide for himself. He further condemns the judgments as much too harsh. Lesquillier mentions approvingly the mild sentence imposed on Pa Latta – a year of hard labor without chains – as a vast improvement over earlier verdicts, but he suggests that a suspended sentence would be better still.[58]

Unlike officials who produced witchcraft through problems of governance, the adat law studies he cites did concern themselves with vernaculars. This is why Lesquillier speaks of "witches or werewolves," although "werewolf" is an inadequate rendering of Indonesian therianthropy. For Europeans of that time, witches and werewolves constituted two different categories of unreal beings.[59] But in many parts of Indonesia, some humans learned to take animal form (recall Sanro Boa the *suangi* or I Urip's nocturnal encounter with Men Mukiari), occasionally assuming the innocuous shape of a domesticated animal to gain entrée to a victim's home and sometimes becoming a wild animal, such as a monkey or a more deadly tiger. (There are no mentions of wolves, though.) In the hands of the scholar-administrators that Lesquillier cites, we discover "werewolves" among the Toraja and learn that the Balinese witch is actually a shape-shifting *leyak*, "corresponding with the *swangi*-belief in the Moluccas."[60]

Like other adat law scholars, Lesquillier asserts that colonial law and policy should accommodate community values. He makes two recommendations. First, the regime should "meet the superstitious primitive halfway" in regard to witches or werewolves. Anticipating objections that this would penalize the innocent, he insists that popular opinion does not choose targets arbitrarily. Those accused tend to be eccentrics who seriously transgress social norms; moreover, such persons know where their strange conduct will lead. (Sanro Boa serves as an example for him of someone who performed an act associated with *suangi*.) When a rash of odd deaths raises concern about such people and brings public life to a halt, the fact that the government does nothing generates frustration. He cites a famous missionary-scholar who claimed the Toraja found the government's protection of witches as irresponsible as Europeans would find the shielding of a rabid dog: "Is it then surprising," Lesquillier asks, "that, no longer being able to offer resistance to this untenable situation, they kill the person in question by taking the law into their own hands?"[61] Unfortunately, they then discover that the regime not only refuses to bring witches to justice but also severely punishes those who do so extralegally.

What, then, is Lesquillier's solution? Indonesians should be able to lodge a formal complaint against witches, and the government should act on such complaints, either by removing the witch from the community (if need be, he suggests, for psychological treatment) or by overseeing purification oaths or rites. Dismissing local concerns only encourages what Dutch law defines as criminal acts – and what adat law requires. (Lesquillier apparently did not know that such a solution had been tried and had failed; Mazee is not in his bibliography.)

FIGURE 16.2. Dukun from Kandangan, near Lumajang (East Java). Courtesy of KITLV/ Royal Netherlands Institute of Southeast Asia and Caribbean Studies.

Lesquillier notes that since the turn of the century, few cases of witch killing had appeared in the law journals, but he does not take this to mark the success of existing policies. To the contrary. Severe sentences only compound suspicion that the government sides with witches. Instead of changing people's minds about the reality of witchcraft, such sentences encourage an insidious creativity: "The case does not reach our ears, or the murderers appear untraceable."[62]

Lesquillier's second recommendation involves a distinction he draws between witches/werewolves and "black magicians."[63] The difference seems to lie in the fact that witchcraft is an attribution by others that may or may not have anything to do with the deliberate actions of the one accused (apart from general weirdness). "Black magic," though, is an intentional act that typically involves material mediations and may even leave material traces as evidence. The introduction of black magic touches on two other topics of periodic colonial concern in the Indies: Indonesian "cunning men," commonly known by their Javanese name, *dukun* (see Figure 16.2), and activities that

European residents of the Indies called *guna-guna* after Javanese practices that were intended to generate desire.[64] Lesquillier notes here that what we call "magic" Indonesians call "knowledge"; the purview of indigenous experts encompasses curing the sick, warding off danger, and provoking love or sympathy (1934: 134), as well as doing harm. Because Europeans regard magic as based on fantasy or a failure of reason, they have failed to recognize when the activities of indigenous experts veer into the domain of criminality, especially when Europeans allow doctors and scientists to serve as arbiters of the factual basis of the activities involved. European doctors, Lesquillier notes (and here he is a true Indies boy), regularly fail to explain sudden deaths, illnesses, or psychological disturbances (even insanity) in the Indies. Medicine, of course, continually evolves: substances that doctors now consider toxic were once deemed safe. Moreover, little is understood about the power of suggestion or other matters that the new field of parapsychology may explain. In short, rather than treating the efficacy of the means employed as the basis for deciding whether the use of black magic has been criminal, the perpetrator's intention should serve as guide. If someone is popularly understood to be capable of making people ill or killing them, then he or she is dangerous to the welfare of the community and should be treated as a criminal. In the "East," he declares, "occult sciences" are widespread. By ignoring when they aim at felonious ends, the government encourages criminality.

To make his point, Lesquillier reviews several cases of black magic in *RNI* and other sources. In one, a man obtained from an expert a series of materials that he used (unsuccessfully) to try to seduce a married woman; in another, a servant added substances to his mistress's soup to put her in a good mood. Lesquillier agrees that the expert in the former case deserved his guilty verdict (although he disputes the legal justification, which was "fraud"), but in the second case, the court acquitted the servant because the substances he administered could not produce the desired effect; nor were they toxic and therefore dangerous. He ends with a case of poisoning known to him personally, in which a *dukun* gave a client a bamboo cylinder containing locusts to release in front of an enemy's home. The cylinder also contained a powdered poison that stuck to the locusts' feet. When released, they flew up to the lights and then fell onto the food the family was eating. The victims refused to file a complaint, instead enlisting a more powerful *dukun*. Knowing that they cannot be tried for any crime empowers such unscrupulous persons.

Lesquillier's solution to the problem that black magic posed involves a legal document that had been, on the whole, highly controversial among customary law experts. In 1918, the colonial regime decided for the first time to establish a single penal code for all residents of the Indies. It was almost entirely based on the Dutch Penal Code. But there were several deviations from the European original that were largely focused on what became known as "occult offenses." One took aim at persons engaging in activities deemed inherently fraudulent: telling fortunes, interpreting dreams, or forecasting the future in any form.[65] Another made it a crime to offer instruction in occult knowledge that might encourage someone to think he or she could commit a crime without fear of being caught. The remaining articles addressed the manufacture, circulation, and use of amulets (which by this time were treated in scholarly works as fetishes) and sanctioned some of their uses.[66]

Although thinking that only one of these articles (the one about instruction in occult knowledge) made sense, Lesquillier proposed adding a regulation to criminalize black magic. He even suggested its form: "Anyone who by magical means intentionally tries to cause another harm, whether misfortune, illness, psychological disturbance, death . . . is punished," noting that the details could be worked out later.[67] Elsewhere, he indicates that "misfortune" could include seduction or exerting undue influence on authorities.[68]

Unlike the British in Africa (although very much in line with the ways in which the anti-witchcraft laws came to be administered by officials, and for similar reasons), his ordinance and other suggestions take "the native point of view" seriously by treating witchcraft and black magic as criminal offenses. At the same time, it is worth noting that the positions he takes, particularly in his discussion of black magic, reiterated claims more often expressed by non-academic (and Indies-identified) writers: namely, that European science might not be capable of recognizing the occurrence of a crime and was too arrogant in abrogating to itself the ability to judge, for instance, whether or not certain substances were poisons.[69] Moreover, his distinction between witchcraft and black magic might have puzzled some Indonesians. Consider, for example, that in Eastern Indonesia *sanro* (as in Sanro Boa the *suangi*) commonly refers to indigenous experts whose activities overlap with those of Javanese *dukun*.

Finally, it is worth emphasizing that the material Lesquillier reviews comes from across the archipelago, from places with markedly different languages and distinct forms of life. Bringing them together in the pages of his book makes them equivalent, commensurating them not only with European terms such as black magic, witch, and werewolf but also with each other. Such yoking together is what makes terms such as magic and witchcraft appear so self-evident to us today. Yet connections between practices and entities are more fragile than they appear.

Witchcraft's Emergence as a Matter of Dutch Concern Comes to a Halt

In 1936, toward the end of Dutch rule in Indonesia (although no one knew it yet), Catholic missionaries, colonial officials, and academics gathered for the fourteenth consecutive year in Leuven for a week-long discussion of a topic that was meant to be relevant to all. That year, the organizers chose the theme of witchcraft (*hekserij*) in mission lands. In planning the conference, some committee members wondered if it would engage everyone's interest, but when the well-known British journal *Africa* devoted a special issue to witchcraft in October 1935, and soon after other articles and theses appeared on the topic, they felt sure it would prove productive. The only question was whether non-Africanists would find it equally relevant.[70]

Bringing together in a single time and place parties that had different investments and represented myriad colonized terrains, such conferences enabled ideas and practices both to travel and to achieve solidity. They are therefore important sites for the construction of witchcraft as a purportedly easily recognizable phenomenon transcending time and space. The Leuven conference offered an opening for Indies experts to suture hitherto local involvements and translations to a concept that was on the verge of taking off.

To facilitate that project, the conveners carefully carved out a definition for witchcraft (*hekserij*), distinguishing it from a host of other practices that colonial agents, missionaries, and ethnologists tended to merge together. Magic (*magie*), they announced, encompasses witchcraft; greater specificity about the latter will advance knowledge.[71] They proposed defining witchcraft as "a real or imaginary act with real or imaginary consequences" (in contrast to superstition, which only deals with the imaginary, witchcraft is efficacious), "dictated or done by a living human being" (not, they stress, by forces of nature, ghosts, ancestors, or spirits), "to the detriment of one's fellow man" (not covering, therefore, the diviner, fortune-teller, or witch-doctor or medicine man whose role is to discover and respond to acts of witchcraft), using means not amenable to objective, scientific research (hence, inherently outside the domain of nature).

What might Lesquillier have done with this? Oddly, although his book is listed in the bibliography of the published proceedings, Lesquillier was not invited to address the group on the Dutch East Indies. Perhaps he was invited but not able to attend or perhaps he was too junior – or simply not Catholic. Instead, the conveners asked Professor C. C. Berg of Leiden University, an expert on Old Javanese literature and historiography, to speak. His talk certainly contributed to the making of magic as a phenomenon with global reach, as he knit magic into the skein of a world that had been connected for millennia. Yet he sidestepped witchcraft, the conference focus. His disciplinary specialty undoubtedly had something to do with this: Old Javanese texts shed little light on the messy business of living together, which is how witchcraft took shape in colonial societies. He himself does not cite Lesquillier. Possibly, although both were experts on Indies cultures, and although they overlapped at Leiden, the paths of the authority on the literate traditions of an ancient civilization and the doctoral student of the unwritten customs shaping everyday life across the archipelago never crossed.

To explain why he chose to address "refined" forms of magic (*toverij*) on Java instead of witchcraft in the Dutch East Indies, however defined, Berg introduced the Indies as shaped by "four powers ...: heathenism, Hinduism, Islam, and Western influence." Anthropologically, it forms the meeting point of two culture areas – the "thousand and one forms of primitive culture found in the Pacific" and civilized Asia.[72] On the sea route between the Middle and Far East, the archipelago had absorbed wave after wave of cultural influences from China, Arabia, and especially India. Interference by European merchants (first Portuguese, then Dutch) broke these ancient trade relations with the subcontinent, but the blended products of those connections remained. Even conversion to Islam had not eradicated Java's Hinduized culture, particularly among aristocrats.

Given the ample talks scheduled that week on primitive societies, Berg felt he could safely ignore the "heathen" stratum, seeing as magic "comes to expression in similar cultural circumstances in nearly similar ways everywhere."[73] He also sidestepped Islam, defining it as a religion focused on doctrinal duties. And because Western influences were by definition "through and through rationalist and thus directed against magic," they too could be ignored. "Hinduized" cultures, however, merited attention. Not only had Indian religions never rejected magic, but "India ... is the classical land of magic." Quite apart from its famous fakirs and yogis, since the time of the Rgveda, Indian religion had devolved into a form of "systemized magic" that aimed to master (rather than worship) cosmic forces.[74] Thus, Berg claims, in Hinduized Java, "magic plays as great a role as it plays in central Africa or on the Salomon [sic] islands," albeit in spheres of activity usually associated with civilization, such as in kingship and in literature.

Central to this is the concept of *mana*, a Polynesian term that the French ethnologist Marcel Mauss introduced to the analysis of magic in 1902, which Berg glosses as "magical force." In a triadic translation, Berg asserts that Javanese call it *sekti*, "'power,' 'force', that became with them [as opposed to Sanskrit *shakti*], however, purely and only *magical* power."[75] Although Berg draws *sekti* out of texts, he offers several anecdotes to suggest its ongoing relevance to Javanese life.

Berg does not, however, connect magical power to witchcraft, as it was elaborated by the conveners or otherwise. Had he tracked it further into everyday life rather than focusing on texts and high culture, magical power might have led Berg to witchcraft. Some persons deemed magically powerful (*sekti*) – including the indigenous experts that Lesquillier highlighted – performed acts that fit the conveners' definition of witchcraft. But *sekti* is morally neutral, a power that could be used to help as well as harm (the difference often being a matter of perspective); witchcraft, for Europeans of that time, was not.

Rather than seeing Berg as having studied an arcane topic only of concern to a small Indonesian ruling class and fellow philologists, one could argue that he substituted an intriguing Indian Ocean concept for a European one that had been overdetermined by history. Colonial magic offers easy passage for European concepts, which dominate scholarly and administrative discourses. Berg interposed friction. Mauss pulled *mana* into the anthropological world, and to some extent it has traveled beyond that world. Berg potentially gave *sekti* (which was already well traveled, given that it had moved to Java from India) a push outside of Asia, as a conceivable improvement on witchcraft. Could *sekti* have found traction among Africanists or Africans? Might a term without the witch's religious, political, and historical baggage help to construct a less Eurocentric world?

In the published proceedings, conveners observed that those working in Asia reported much less concern with witchcraft than Africanists did, happily for them.[76] Berg's paper no doubt contributed to this conclusion. Despite his startling statements about India and magic (still not witchcraft), witchcraft's continental associations in the 1930s appeared decidedly African. Berg did nothing to advance witchcraft as a matter of Indies concern, even if colonial officials, not to mention a colleague in another discipline, regularly reached back into the past for that term to facilitate their projects.[77]

Concluding Remarks

This chapter has engaged constructions of the witch in engagements between Europeans and non-Europeans, focusing on the Dutch and the archipelago now known as Indonesia. A brief discussion of the formation and elaboration of the concept of the fetish showed the global connectedness of colonial magic, including its ultimate capacity to undermine the very distinctions between rational Europe and irrational non-Europe that it originally made. Once a way to translate African practices that reminded Portuguese visitors of minor forms of witchcraft, by the twentieth century, "fetish" and "witch" had thoroughly diverged. Moreover, the inherently intercultural fetish has proved to be a continually surprising machine for new theoretical insights. This is in contrast to the witch, which to a surprising degree remains thoroughly enmeshed with its European past. Moving around the globe with different waves of colonialism, its mode of ontological production always entailed implicit equations between a European original (increasingly, a disgraced *then*) and a non-European echo (an inferior *now*).

Although my focus has been the Indies,[78] I have touched on other geographic locations where crucial elements of colonial magic were elaborated. Most important of these was Africa, the site of origin of the most famous forms of colonial magic and a field for the elaboration of both the fetish and the witch.

In the Indies, fetishes provoked both mockery and alarm. The ubiquity of amulets, which were so often of sizes and materials that made them easy to overlook and easy to conceal and which enabled their possessors to act in ways that were otherwise unlikely, made them especially threatening, which is why two of the "occult offenses" in the 1918 Penal Code referred to them. Yet apart from the fear that amulets might provoke rebellion by promises of invulnerability, the offenses they made possible – such as theft and lying under oath – were by no means as serious in European law as murder was. And it was in relation to cases that the Dutch judged to be homicide that the Dutch conjured the witch in Indonesia. Certainly, we have seen ample evidence that Dutch bureaucrats – and residents – encountered practices they described as witchcraft (*hekserij* or *toverij*), and they even refer to "witch trials" (*hexenprocessen*) as traditional practices. Yet witchcraft never stabilized as an object of concern for Dutch scholar-administrators or, for that matter, even for missionaries in Indonesia.

Although this is speculative, I suspect that witchcraft might have eventually emerged as an object of greater administrative and/or scholarly interest. In 1942, the Japanese invaded the Indies and imprisoned Dutch officials. Following the war, Dutch efforts to reestablish authority encountered fierce and ultimately successful resistance by Indonesian nationalists. Certainly, even before the war, anti-colonial nationalism alarmed the colonial state considerably more than other activities did; "witchcraft beliefs," unless they led to murder, and only then if the deaths had been identified as unnatural, were at least part of the "traditional" practices of indigenous populations, unlike struggles for political autonomy. Still, it is worth considering that the growing interest in witchcraft in Africa and in the academy mainly took shape in the 1950s, when the Indies no longer existed. If it had, it is hard to imagine that witchcraft would not have sparked a response among at least Dutch anthropologists. As it is, witchcraft remains closely associated with Africa in the anthropological imagination. By contrast, the main "magical" topic that finds its way into the work of foreign scholars writing about Indonesia, although often more as a metaphor than a phenomenon, is the fetish.

Notes

1. Clearly, I am not referring here to the way that historians of European witchcraft found inspiration in anthropological studies of African magic, which directed them to productive studies of the social tensions underlying accusations of witchcraft and a broader concern with mentalities.

2. See in particular Gijswijt-Hofstra and Frijhoff, *Witchcraft in the Netherlands*; Ankarloo and Clark, *Witchcraft and Magic in Europe*, vol. 5, *The Eighteenth and Nineteenth Centuries*; Ankarloo and Clark, *Witchcraft and Magic in Europe*, vol. 6, *The Twentieth Century*; and de Blécourt and Davies, *Witchcraft Continued*.

3. But see de Blécourt, who not only offers evidence of twentieth-century urban examples ("Boiling Chickens and Burning Cats") but also highlights in general the problem of inadequate sources when it comes to documenting cases of bewitchment and unwitching in contemporary Europe (in that article, as well as in "The Witch, Her Victim").

4. See Gluckman, "The Magic of Despair."

5. Understanding magic as distant in time and space becomes implausible as soon as one considers the enormous range of practices and objects sorted under the category. Rather than disappearing, these have proliferated and become omnipresent, even in the very heart of "first world" metropolitan centers. The remarkable success of the Harry Potter franchise – the books, translated into some seventy languages; the films; the Florida theme parks; the costumes and fake wands available for online purchase – is only one symptom of this. The genre of fantasy, which is rife with (vaguely medieval) figures called wizards and sorcerers that further extend these terms, flourishes, as do other entertainment venues centered on magical tricks and illusions (see During, *Modern Enchantments*). Religions such as Wicca and Neo-Paganism seek to undermine the historically drawn boundaries between religion and magic. In short, interest in magic is hardly limited to the long ago and far

away; rather, it flourishes in cosmopolitan popular culture. Scholarly analysis has not kept pace with such worldly developments. And it is remarkable how little dialogue has existed between the magic that concerns most historians and the "secular" magic of contemporary culture, which During argues involves a complex attitude toward reality and experience that is shaped by staged illusion and the "as-if" experience of fiction.

6. I leave aside here the important question of what exactly the category of magic has meant historically, through the slow accretion of an ever-increasing array of activities and things.

7. I take the concept of friction here from Tsing, *Friction: An Ethnography of Global Connection*.

8. See Stronks, "The Significance of Balthasar Bekker's *The Enchanted World*," 149–156, as well as Ankarloo and Clark, *Witchcraft and Magic in Europe*, vol. 5, *The Eighteenth and Nineteenth Centuries*.

9. Stronks, "The Significance of Balthasar Bekker's *The Enchanted World*," 149.

10. For the view that witchcraft lingered in the countryside, see, e.g., Gijswijt-Hofstra and Frijhoff, *Witchcraft in the Netherlands*. For Willem de Blécourt's challenge, see "Boiling Chickens and Burning Cats."

11. See Wiener, "Dangerous Liaisons."

12. I borrow the term "partial connection," although not the complications of her use of the concept, from Strathern, *Partial Connections*.

13. Or elsewhere in Southeast Asia. See Watson and Ellen, *Understanding Witchcraft and Sorcery in Southeast Asia*.

14. Given the exemplary nature of the fetish, it would seem the logical focus of a chapter on colonial magic. If I spend less time on the fetish than it deserves, it is because I have followed certain paths that its story takes elsewhere (see Wiener, "Hidden Forces," "The Magical Life of Things," and my forthcoming book, "Magic in Translation") and because the witch has been such a crucial figure in both history and anthropology.

15. See Pietz, "The Problem of the Fetish, I," "The Problem of the Fetish, II," and "The Problem of the Fetish, IIIa."

16. This word is related to the Dutch *hekserij*.

17. Most likely, they thought these resembled *veneficium*, or vain observances, rather than *maleficium*, with its more serious pacts with demons. See Pietz, "The problem of the Fetish, II."

18. For instance, Balthasar Bekker discusses fetishes as gods, as well as forms of witchcraft and magic in *The World Bewitch'd*, vol. I, 72–73.

19. See, for instance, Levack, "The Decline and End of Witchcraft Prosecutions," 1–93; Porter, "Witchcraft and Magic in Enlightenment, Romantic, and Liberal Thought," 191–282; and Stronks, "The Significance of Balthasar Bekker's *The Enchanted World*," 149–156.

20. Pietz, "The Problem of the Fetish, II," 117 n. 27

21. Later uses of the concept brought the fetish to bear on the lives of modern Europeans themselves, especially via Freud's theory of sexual fetishes and Marx's theory that commodity fetishism was crucial to understanding capitalism. Thus, fetishism rebounded back on European lives, although it has always retained the primitivist tinge that allows it to serve as a tool of critique.

22. For an account of New World inquisitions, Silverblatt, *Modern Inquisitions*.

23. Taylor, *The Social World of Batavia*.

24. According to the historian Leonard Blussé, "black magic was a common occurrence in Batavia" among Dutch residents (*Strange Company*, 242). In a particularly rancorous divorce, for instance, the husband suspected his wife of trying to harm him when he discovered a jar sealed with a black substance, and he called in five "Moorish priests" to investigate. Finding a paper with Arabic script attached to the jug's bottom and a "small dog or image of devilish appearance" inside confirmed a malign intent. By "Moorish," Europeans of this era meant Muslim, the (technical) religion of most Indonesians. Islam does not, however, have priests. Whether these experts were *hajis* (men who had visited Mecca, which was relatively uncommon at that time given existing modes of transport) or what the Dutch later referred to as *dukun* (a Javanese term for people versed in the arts of healing and harming) is unclear.

25. According to Gijswijt-Hofstra, the judicial prosecution of witches ended (except for one province under Spanish rule) by 1600, much earlier than elsewhere in northwest Europe, and in any event executed no more than 150 people total. The extrajudicial killing of witches, however, continued for some time. See Gijswijt-Hofstra, "Six Centuries of Witchcraft in the Netherlands," esp. 25–34. The Dutch East India Company was chartered in 1602, and established headquarters for its operations in the Indies in 1619 on Java's northwest coast.

26. Although native residents of Batavia (now Jakarta) would be Sundanese, Indonesians from many areas of the archipelago populated the city, including, for instance, slaves traded from the island of Bali. Banda, the source of nutmeg, was one of the famous spice islands and so under Dutch control at this time.

27. I know of this incident only because it was resurrected in a law journal in 1866. The author found it surprising that witches had been burned in the Indies as well as in Europe. See de Roo, "Een toovenaar in Batavia verbrand," 13–14.

28. Such enmeshment continued throughout the colonial era, although it took different forms – and elicited different reactions – over time. See Wiener, "Dangerous Liaisons."

29. So, at least, authorities maintained. On the ground, matters proved more complicated, as de Blécourt shows in "Boiling Chickens and Burning Cats."

30. This phrase occurs in *Law in the Netherlands Indies* (*Regt van Nederlandsch-Indië*; hereafter *RNI*) 1, no. 2 (1850).

31. See, for example, *RNI* 57 (1892).

32. *RNI* 1, no. 2 (1850): 105–107.

33. *RNI* 5, no. 10 (1854).

34. *RNI* 64 (1895).

35. *RNI* 5, no. 10 (1854): 785.

36. *RNI* 6, no. 12 (1856): 66–69.

37. *RNI* 6, no. 12 (1856): 70–73.

38. *RNI* 57 (1892): 403–410.

39. *RNI* 67 (1897): 385.

40. *RNI* 3, no. 6 (1851): 71–75.

41. Der Kinderen, "Bijgeloof in de Preanger Regentschappen," 299.

42. After consulting the Javanese district head, Kertadiwangsa asked the couple to leave; when they refused, he recruited villagers to kill them and to burn their bodies and houses. On their own initiative, the villagers also divvied up the couple's possessions, except for one participant who feared "that the devil, who in his view lived in those things, would pass into him." Kertadiwangsa himself received seven water buffaloes but got rid of them to avoid "being possessed by the devil." He claimed he ordered the houses burned so no one else would live in them and "be bewitched."

43. Der Kinderen, "Bijgeloof in the Preanger Regentschappen," 300.

44. Mazee,"Over Heksen-Moord en de Berechting Daarvan," 398.

45. Was Mazee speaking here of the way similar matters had been adjudicated in other colonized regions of the archipelago? Or was he only referring to a general principle of holding instigators (and / or native authorities) more responsible than those who actually carried out a crime?

46. Mazee, "Over Heksen-Moord en de Berechting Daarvan," 398.

47. Anthropologists have on occasion offered explanations for confessions to acts that they too regard as impossible a priori, perhaps most famously Lévi-Strauss, in "The Sorcerer and His Magic."

48. Guha, *Dominance without Hegemony*.

49. This is not to say that executions ended completely, especially given what Mazee says about deaths that were made to appear accidental. And for three months in 1998–1999, people in East Java killed more than one hundred "witches," according to Siegel, *Naming the Witch*.

50. For a discussion of these terms, see also Gijswijt-Hofstra, "Six Centuries of Witchcraft in the Netherlands," 2–3, 14.

51. *RNI* (1892): 409–410.

52. He adds that "even Herodotus called the Negroes sorcerers," a somewhat different association. Hegel, *The Philosophy of History*, 111.

53. This shift is remarked upon by Peter Pels in "The Magic of Africa," although he does not explain it. One possibility is that the concern of colonial states (as opposed to trading companies) with maintaining order made responses to harm attributed to the malevolence of neighbors or kin immediately problematic and put the issue of commensurating values that generated discourse on the fetish on the back burner. It is also worth asking, however, about the relevance of transatlantic colonial magic. What role did British experiences with African slaves on New World plantations, where novel practices such as *obeah* became associated simultaneously with sorcery and rebellion, play?

54. Mesaki, "Witchcraft and the Law in Tanzania," 133.

55. Fields, "Political Contingencies of Witchcraft."

56. Luongo, *Witchcraft and Colonial Rule in Kenya*.

57. For adat law, see Sonius, "Introduction" in *Van Vollenhoven on Indonesian Adat Law*, and Burns, *The Leiden Legacy*. Since the publication of Hobsbawm and Ranger's famous edited volume *The Invention of Tradition*, it has also become evident that "tradition" is hardly an unproblematic notion. Indeed, Ranger himself has tracked the way in which the gathering of information about "custom" in colonial Africa froze what had been dynamic relations and processes into forms of life that conferred unprecedented authority on older men in particular. Similar arguments have been made about other colonial situations, as well. In short, descriptions of adat law were interventions, with unpredictable consequences, rather than mere representations of a preexisting reality.

58. Lesquillier, *Het Adatdelichtenrecht*, 218–219.

59. At the time of the witch trials, some witches were werewolves, but would Lesquillier or his readers have been aware of that?

60. Lesquillier, *Het Adatdelichtenrecht*, 130–131.

61. Ibid., 131.

62. Ibid., 227.

63. The distinction may seem reminiscent of one that Evans-Pritchard draws between the witch, who unintentionally harms others because of inherited capacity, and the sorcerer, who must use substances to carry out such work. Lesquillier suggests that in the Indies a distinction might rest on how the harm is effected. In Bali, for instance, the "werewolf/witch" (*leyak*) definitely learns his or her skills (as addressed by de Kat Angelino in "De leak op Bali"), although people are born with differential capacities for exercising them; however, I am fairly confident that these skills do involve the manufacture of substances that must come into contact with the target. The real distinction that Lesquillier draws is between people whom others suspect of being "witches" but who may or may not be acting as such and people who do in fact possess and exercise the requisite abilities.

64. Lesquillier's treatment of these topics speaks to his experiences growing up in Indonesia and suggests – as does his proud notation of his place of birth on the title page of his book – that his was an old (creolized) Indies family. For extensive discussions of *guna-guna* within colonial popular culture and scholarship, see Wiener, "Dangerous Liaisons," and "Magic, (Colonial) Science, and Science Studies."

65. This is reminiscent of Great Britain's 1735 ordinance and some statements in various African anti-witchcraft ordinances, but whether or not it was inspired by these, I have not been able to ascertain.

66. Hekmeijer, *Wetboek van Strafrecht voor Nederlandsche Indië*, 180.

67. Lesquillier, *Het Adatdelictenrecht*, 138.

68. Ibid., 228

69. See Wiener, "Dangerous Liaisons."

70. Van Reeth et al, *Hekserij in de missielanden*, 7. Contributors to the *Africa* issue included colonial administrators and anthropologists, among them E. E. Evans-Pritchard, who provided a glimpse into his not-yet-published research among the Azande.

71. More fully, magic includes *toverij*, as well.

72. Berg, "Verfijnde Vormen van Tooverij," 67.

73. Ibid., 69.

74. Others at the conference echoed the distinction he makes between religion, which refers implicitly to Christian concepts of the proper relation of human to god, and magic, which draws on ethnologists such as Frazer.

75. Berg, "Verfijnde Vormen van Tooverij," 74. *Sekti* is one of two concepts that Berg elaborates; the other (involving the treatment of things classified together as identical for certain purposes) is not relevant here. Although Berg's analysis draws on an accumulated ethnological legacy (especially British and French), the language of magic (*magie, magisch*) was relatively new to Dutch scholars (see Wiener, "Magic, (Colonial) Science, and Science Studies").

76. Van Reeth et al, *Hekserij in de missielanden*, 11

77. It is surprising that no missionaries working in the Indies received an invitation to Leuven. They might well have offered a different perspective on whether "witchcraft" constituted a problem for them. See, e.g., Hoekendijk, *De Toovenaar der Soendalanden*. Although it was published in 1941, and thus after the conference, and although the author was Protestant rather than Catholic, he narrates the tale of a Sundanese "witch" (*tovenaar*) or witch-doctor who engages in some of the activities that Lesquillier labeled as black magic.

78. In particular, the island of Java, where the Dutch maintained the longest presence and had the most intimate relations with subject populations.

Chapter 17

Magic in Common and Legal Perspectives

OWEN DAVIES

The laws against the crime of witchcraft, or *maleficium*, instituted across Europe during the early modern era also prohibited the practice of magic more generally. For some theologians, Protestant and Catholic alike, those who practised magic to combat witchcraft and misfortune were worse criminals than those who were accused as witches. Magic was blasphemous, even a heresy; there was no such thing as good magic. The lure of magic to resolve mundane difficulties tempted people from the path of God. Only the divinity could perform the miracles that cunning folk and sorcerers claimed for themselves. To resort to magic and magical practitioners was, therefore, an implicit renunciation of Christianity. Witches killed people yet did not damn their souls, but the practitioners of "good" magic damned those who procured their services.

As we shall see in this chapter, the redefinition of these notions regarding the legal and religious status of magic during the seventeenth and eighteenth centuries was messy and inconsistent, and it continued to perplex and embarrass in the next century. Magic was not a unified and inextricably linked set of beliefs that unravelled simultaneously when one aspect, such as witchcraft, waned or was undermined by new social, intellectual or religious developments. Astrology has maintained its currency in the West, as has spirit communication. In the eighteenth and nineteenth centuries, furthermore, science and religion generated new or rehashed notions of the occult or hidden world that could be encompassed within the magical realm, such as Spiritualism and mesmerism.

The German sociologist Max Weber posited that the disenchantment, or "demagification", of the world followed as a consequence of the advent and spread of Protestantism, which engendered a scientific rationalism and a capitalist ethic that fundamentally undermined the "recourse to magical means". The Enlightenment finished the job. This model of the development of Western thought has received considerable revision in recent years.[1]

Neither the Reformation nor the Enlightenment heralded an irreversible and pervasive shift towards a rational Western world. The rational and irrational – both mutable and slippery definitions – continued to coexist through the eighteenth century and beyond in elite, middling and popular cultures: modernity and magic have proven not to be mutually exclusive in the West, nor anywhere else around the globe, for that matter, as this chapter will demonstrate.[2]

In Weberian terms, then, the eighteenth to the twentieth centuries continued to be "enchanted", expressed in the same forms as those found in the worlds of ancient, medieval and early modern magic, such as astrology and divination, sometimes as reformulations of old concepts, namely, the nineteenth-century enthusiasm for mesmerism, Spiritualism and modern ritual magic. Furthermore, the criminal records and newspapers and the work of folklorists and early anthropologists reveal popular cultures of magic and witchcraft as rich as those uncovered in the early modern archives.[3] So the place of magic in the modern West was complex and variable culturally, chronologically and intellectually, making its legal position all the more problematic. Let us begin, naturally enough, with the end of the witch trials.

Ending the Crime of Witchcraft, Punishing "Superstition"

There was no one defining moment when Europe's legislatures came to the conclusion that the prosecution of witchcraft and magic was indefensible.[4] Science certainly influenced growing intellectual caution about the reality of witchcraft during the seventeenth century, but the key to the end of the witch trials was the developing sophistication of jurisprudence and the increasing centralisation of judicial authority as absolutist states extended their control over their citizens. The growing reluctance to use torture, for instance, stemmed the spiralling, self-confirming reality of confessed witchcraft. Scepticism about the validity of spectral evidence kicked away another of the pillars that held up witchcraft prosecutions. Expert medical testimony as to the role of mental illness in accusations began to have an influence. The last of the trials of the late eighteenth century usually occurred in areas where the central judicial authority failed to impose its will over local courts that were presided over by magistrates, sheriffs and the like. These were men who were often closer to the world of the common people and their concerns than the university-educated lawyers and judges of the central judiciary were. The trials ended when parliaments decided to use the legislature to impose "new realities" on the peripheries once and for all.

The various statutes, codes and edicts that snuffed out the trials did not explicitly refute the existence of witches – this is by no means a story about the triumph of scepticism. Many in educated society continued to cling to a belief in diabolic magic, supported by references in the Bible and the weight of history. So the 1766 edict of the Austrian Empress Maria Theresa, which brought an end to witch hunting in Habsburg lands, decreed merely that all judicial decisions to torture or execute witches had to be submitted to the King or Empress for royal sanction. Although it did not deny the existence of witches, it did state concerns about the pernicious consequences of belief in them. Further ordinances two years later ordered local magistrates to refrain from instituting legal proceedings against magical practices "unless they have very clear proofs in the matter". Witchcraft only ceased to be a crime in Habsburg territories in the late 1780s.[5] In Poland in 1776, the *Sjem*, or lower house of the Polish parliament, abolished the death penalty "in cases of malefice and witchcraft", effectively ending the witch trials in the country. Although, again, the law did not explicitly deny existence of the crime, a Royal Chancellor ended the *Sjem* session with a classic Enlightenment speech stating, "at last these trials for witchcraft, with their horrible consequences disgraceful to the human race, will have no place in our nation".[6] In some states, witchcraft was not decriminalised until more than a century after the last of the trials, because of a mixture of oversight and embarrassment. The 1587 witchcraft law in Ireland was only repealed by the British parliament in April 1821, whereas in Denmark, a law authorising the burning of witches was not repealed until 1866.[7]

France and England present two interesting case studies in terms of how the laws regarding magic were framed and changed during the Enlightenment period and beyond, and they highlight the need to be sensitive to the semantics. In July 1682, Louis XIV issued a royal edict that did not explicitly refer to witchcraft but effectively prevented its prosecution. The new law was directed at the "so called" magic of "diviners, magicians and enchanters". In other words, it reconfigured magic as a pretence and its practitioners as being guilty of fraud or sacrilege. Banishment and corporal punishment such as flogging were considered appropriate sentences, although the use of poisons in magic carried the death sentence. During the late seventeenth and early eighteenth centuries, the Parisian authorities launched a campaign against these *"faux sorciers"*, or "false sorcerers", who were thought, with some justification, to be plaguing high and low society with their treasure-hunting, love-inducing, satanic pact-making, protection-giving, and influence-attracting magical services.[8] Elsewhere in the French provinces, the suppression of magical practice was less systematic, although summary punishments were periodically meted out in lower courts, such as in a case heard before the *sénéchaussée* court of Bazas, Gironde, in 1770. A watchmaker named Philippe Elie, and a herbalist named Laurent Lavigne were charged with "irreligion, impiety, and abuse of the credulity of the people under the pretext of putting into use supposed secrets for curing illnesses". They had been arrested for healing people with magic, and several magic manuscripts and a metal talisman were confiscated (Figure 17.1). They were fined ten *livres* each and banished from the district for three years.[9]

The term *faux sorciers*, used in French legal records of the early part of the century, disappeared in the latter half as the crime of magic was subsumed intellectually and legally into the general category of *escroquerie* ("fraud"). Then a decree of 1791 left magic as a *"crime imaginaire"*, prosecutable as *escroquerie*.[10] In 1811, during the Empire, article 405 of the penal code against fraud laid down heavier punishment for those who persuaded others of "the existence of false undertakings, of a power or of an imaginary influence". The punishment was now between five and ten years in prison and heavy fines. This did little to dent the magic trade, though, with a string of prosecutions over the next few years, such as that of a curer of witchcraft named Roger of Vicq, in central France, who was condemned to five years' imprisonment in 1827. The presiding judge told him, "you outrage him, our righteous God, with all your juggleries".[11]

A similar shift in language and interpretation is evident in the British laws against magic. Witchcraft was decriminalised and demoted to the status of a false belief by the Witchcraft Act of 1736, which punished those who

> pretend to exercise or use any kind of Witchcraft, Sorcery, Inchantment, or Conjuration, or undertake to tell Fortunes, or pretend, from his or her Skill or Knowledge in any occult or crafty Science, to discover where or in what manner any Goods or Chattels, supposed to have been stolen or lost, may be found.

The punishment was one year's imprisonment, quarterly stints in the pillory for one hour and the payment of sureties for good behaviour (Figure 17.2).[12] The strict application of the law in Scotland was problematic, though, as there were no appropriate institutions to imprison convicts for the length of a year and no pillories in which to punish them.

The statute was an explicit attack on the numerous cunning folk and fortune-tellers who plied their trade by unbewitching, healing, detecting stolen property, provoking love and performing a myriad other magical services. These were the very same magical practitioners who had been targeted, along

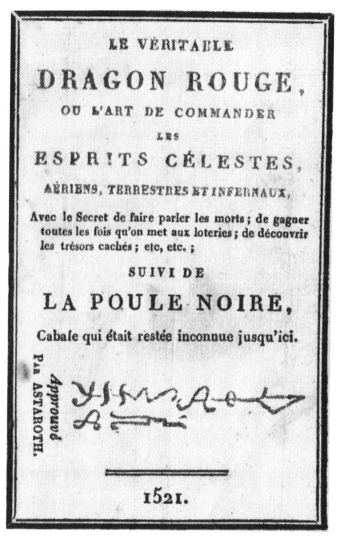

LE VÉRITABLE

DRAGON ROUGE,

OU L'ART DE COMMANDER

LES

ESPRITS CÉLESTES,

AÉRIENS, TERRESTRES ET INFERNAUX,

Avec le Secret de faire parler les morts ; de gagner
toutes les fois qu'on met aux loteries ; de découvrir
les trésors cachés ; etc, etc. ;

SUIVI DE

LA POULE NOIRE,

Cabale qui était restée inconnue jusqu'ici.

Approuvé Par ASTAROTH.

1521.

FIGURE 17.1. *The Dragon Rouge.* One of the most notorious nineteenth-century French grimoires. It sold tens of thousands of copies and was named in numerous prosecutions for
magical practice.

with witches, in the English and Welsh Conjuration Act of 1604 as Satan's
acolytes: their crimes then were diabolic, but now they were deemed fraudulent. A few cunning folk, fortune-tellers and spiritualists were tried under
the 1736 law during the next two centuries, but there was evidently some

VISITORS AT GYPSY CAR

FIGURE 17.2. A romanticised depiction of gypsy fortune-telling. Numerous such fortune-tellers were prosecuted under laws against vagrancy and fraud in the eighteenth and nineteenth centuries.

embarrassment on behalf of magistrates about invoking a law that referred explicitly to witchcraft even as a fraud. In 1894, for instance, a Cornish cunning man named William Rapson Oates, known popularly as the "Ludgvan wizard", was charged at the assizes under the 1736 act, having promised a client that he could remove the spell that was upon her with the aid of the stars and planets. The presiding judge observed, though, that the charge "was framed on an almost obsolete statute" and recommended that the case be treated as one of false pretences. "It was rather a pity the case was sent to the assizes", he said. "Such roguery should be dealt with summarily". Oates was sent to gaol for seven months with hard labour. He was no stranger to such institutions. He had already served more than twelve years in prison during his life for fraudulent pretences and other crimes.[13] Most magical practitioners in nineteenth-century Britain were prosecuted instead under the laws against vagrancy, particularly after the promulgation of the 1824 Vagrancy

Act, section four of which allowed for the prosecution of "persons pretending or professing to tell fortunes, or using any subtle craft, means, or device, by palmistry or otherwise, to deceive and impose".[14]

The implementation of laws against the pretence of magic was even more complicated in North America, where English Common Law was adopted and adapted differently by each state. Well into the eighteenth century, witchcraft and magic remained a criminal offence in an early modern sense. It was only in the 1770s that Thomas Jefferson proposed Virginia enact a version of the 1736 statute, recommending that: "All attempts to delude the people, or to abuse their understanding by exercise of the pretended arts of witchcraft, conjuration, enchantment or sorcery or by pretended prophecies, shall be punished by ducking and whipping". In Pennsylvania, the 1604 act was not repealed until September 1794.[15]

Various states also adopted variations of the British vagrancy laws that lumped the services of cunning folk and fortune-tellers in with "immoral" street activities. So in the 1840s, the revised statutes of Maine included a section that referred to nightwalkers, brawlers, railers, pilferers, common pipers, fiddlers and those "feigning themselves to have knowledge in physiognomy, palmistry, or, for the like purpose, pretending that they can tell destinies or fortunes, or discover where lost or stolen goods may be found".

Returning to witchcraft as a *real* crime and not a *pretence*, and in much of Europe, what were for all intents and purposes witch trials also continued under the remit of other capital offences. So the French edict of 1682 also made sacrilege a capital offence and, although it was usually invoked for such crimes as theft of church property, it was sometimes prosecuted in cases of ritual magic where clerical paraphernalia or sacred objects such as the crucifix and communion host were used or when the accused were believed to have sought relations with the Devil. Numerous rogue Catholic clergymen were rounded up in France during the eighteenth century for abusing the sacraments, their sacerdotal clothes and the offices of the church in the service of magic – men such as L'abbé Marchand, priest of Saint-Hilaire-du-Mont, who was arrested in 1760 for magically invoking spirits.

A series of magician trials in Lyon and Dijon during the early 1740s ended with the burning alive in 1743 of a defrocked priest named Guillaudot. Evidence against him stated that he, along with two accomplices, went to a chateau near Bois-d'Oingt, Beaujolais, and celebrated four masses during the night. The altar was encircled with hazel tree wood, and the words JEIAH, JEHOVA, EMMANUEL and TETRAGRAMMATON were written at the four compass points; four lit wax candles containing asafoetida resin were placed in the angles. At the moment of the consecration, Guillaudot placed a piece of virgin parchment from the skin of a goat, on which was depicted the pentacle of Solomon, under the corporal cloth, pronouncing a spirit invocation that ended:

> Come therefore in the name of Adonay, Zebaoth, Adonay, Amioram, come, hurry on the wings of the winds, it is the king of kings Adonay, Saday who commands you, el Aty, Titciep, Azia, Hin, Jen, Minosel, Achadan, Vay, Vaa, Ey, Haa, Eye, Ael, El, El, Ahy, Hau, go, go, go.

Guillaudot then consecrated a host that he broke into three pieces, giving one each to his two accomplices and keeping the third for himself to protect them all from the violence of any demons that might appear.[16]

The sacrilege laws were forcefully employed in French Canada, too. In 1742, a soldier employed a candle, knife, some powders and a crucifix to detect the location of a Montreal cobbler's stolen savings. He was sentenced to stand at the parish church door in only his shirt with a placard hung around his neck stating "Profaner of Holy Things". He was then flogged at every crossroads in the parish before being sent to the galleys for three years.[17]

In early modern Lutheran Sweden, the crimes of harmful magic and poisoning had been described under the same name, *förgörning*, but by the end of the seventeenth century, they were separated and placed in different sections of the legal code, with magic being defined as supernatural and poisoning as natural. People who attempted pacts with the Devil, mostly men – particularly soldiers – were prosecuted under laws against blasphemy. The crime of intentional blasphemy carried the death penalty in Sweden until 1864, but analysis of the fifteen cases of pacts with the Devil heard by the King's Council between 1741 and 1789 shows that the crime was increasingly couched in pathological rather than religious terms, the product of ignorance and illness rather than spiritual iniquity. Then in 1789, the act of making a pact with the Devil, or using the host in magic rituals, was redefined in legal terms as *vidskepelse* – mere superstition.[18]

Witch trials continued in German states well into the mid-eighteenth century, and at the same time, a series of poisoning trials in France and Germany turned out to be witch trials in all but name. The last accused witch to be officially executed in Europe was actually found guilty of poisoning: her name was Anna Göldi, a domestic servant in the service of Dr Johann Tschudi, in Glarus canton, Switzerland.[19] In 1782, Tschudi's eight-year-old daughter accused Göldi of putting pins in her milk. Göldi was dismissed and left the area. Then the daughter began to vomit pins and nails. Suspected of vengeful witchcraft, Göldi was arrested, and the town councillors, led by Tschudi, threatened her with torture if she did not cure his daughter – a local healer had concluded that only the person who had afflicted the girl could reverse the torment. Facing a Catch-22 situation, Göldi agreed to treat the girl, thereby implicitly confirming she had been responsible for the girl's affliction in the first place. The malicious young girl then accused Göldi of having given her a magic biscuit that caused her pin spewing, which she claimed was baked by one of Göldi's friends, a metalworker named Rudfolf Steinmüller. Göldi was then tortured and confessed to her conspiracy with Steinmüller. The latter hanged himself while awaiting trial, and on 13 June, Göldi was beheaded for poisoning. The case was widely reported in Switzerland and neighbouring German states, apparently inspiring a rash of copycat pin spitting. The German journalist Wilhelm Ludwig Weckhrlin was declared an outlaw by the canton of Glarus for publishing a sarcastic critique of the trial, but Swiss criticism in general seems to have been muted, perhaps because of the remarkable threat stated in the death sentence:

> Whosoever dares to condemn, disparage or attempt to avenge the poor sinner's death, now or in the future, or vilify, hate or denigrate anyone for it, he or she will, according to the edict and decree of our Penal Code, follow in the poor sinner's footsteps, be treated in a like manner, and be subject to the same sentence.[20]

The illegality of treasure hunting by magical means had long been enshrined in legal codes across Europe.[21] In England, for instance, the 1604 Witchcraft and Conjuration Act covered those who took "upon him or them by Witchcrafte Inchantment Charme or Sorcerie to tell or declare in what place any treasure of golde or silver should or had in the earth or other secret places". By the eighteenth century, the activity was deemed a pernicious consequence of popular "superstition" and sometimes blasphemous in terms of the magic used. In 1758, a priest was sent to the galleys for life by the Paris Parlement for using treasure-hunting magic, whereas lesser punishment were meted out in 1773 to a group of treasure seekers at Günzburg in south-western Germany. Their punishment consisted of kneeling twice a day for an hour in the marketplace on three successive days, brandishing their magical paraphernalia.[22] In the state of Württemberg, there were no laws against treasure hunting on the statute books, leading the law faculty of the University of Tübingen in 1748 to criticise the government for the omission. The activity encouraged avarice, they opined, and the use of God's name in magical rituals was blasphemous and deserved the death penalty.[23]

Even without the use of magic, seeking treasure usually had to be sanctioned by the appropriate authorities because of land rights and royal prerogatives over such bounty. In the duchy of Württemberg, permits had to be acquired, and eighteenth-century applications reveal the continued idea that treasures were guarded by ghosts and other spirits, which required Catholic exorcism or magic to deal with them. Magical treasure hunting was an equally popular activity in eighteenth- and nineteenth-century Spain and Italy. Between 1700 and 1820, more than two hundred cases were heard by inquisition tribunals across Spain.[24]

North America is known for the gold rushes of the nineteenth century, but there were many European settlers who did not search for natural mineral gold but rather continued the quest for *hidden* gold and employed the magic traditionally thought to reveal and capture it. Legends abounded of pirate booty and Spanish silver mines. Joseph Smith, the founder of the Mormon faith, was an active seeker in New York State during the 1820s, and he was known for using his seer-stone to locate treasures.[25] When, in the early 1860s, the Pennsylvania General Assembly beefed up its laws against fortune-telling, it included in its list of prohibitions to tell for "lucre or gain ... where treasure, property, money or valuables are hid, or to tell the places where to dig or to search for gold, metals, hidden treasure".[26] Later in the century, in 1899, newspapers reported that numerous attempts, including the resort to magic, had been employed to find the bushel of gold and silver coins reputedly hidden in the deserted settlement of Bertrand, Michigan, by the French trader who founded it, Joseph Bertrand.[27]

A Moral and Spiritual Offence

So far the emphasis has been on the secular legal status of magic, but in the modern era, ecclesiastical courts and tribunals still played a part in the policing of magic, despite their diminishing role in society. The practices of magical practitioners transgressed the moral codes laid down by the church by luring people into committing sin by resorting to magic and not God or his ordained representatives in times of need. The inquisitions are the most obvious examples of continued ecclesiastical judicial power. The Portuguese Inquisition investigated more than five hundred magical practitioners and healers between 1715 and 1770, although its interest subsided subsequently and cases were few and far between until its demise in 1821. It should be noted that none of the five hundred or so defendants were handed over to be executed for their blasphemous activities. The last century of the Spanish Inquisition, which was abolished in 1834, reveals a similar picture. Some 1,384 cases of magic were considered by tribunals across Spain, the Balearics and Canaries between 1700 and 1820. Accusations of magic swirled around a female mystic and diviner named Dolores López, for instance, who was the last person to be burned at the stake for heresy in Spain, at Seville in 1781. López claimed that since the age of four, she had regular conversations with the Virgin Mary. Most late cases were more run-of-the-mill. In Majorca in 1816, Antonia Mañana was investigated for providing a client with a charm to punish her adulterous husband which consisted of a black and red silk ribbon and the man's pubic hair. The practice of impotence magic by another female healer, Tomasa Bueno, led to her being hauled before a tribunal on several occasions and resulted in her incarceration in an inquisitorial prison in 1801.[28]

In those countries with inquisitions, there were also other local ecclesiastical courts dealing with popular magic, as David Gentilcore has shown for eighteenth-century southern Italy, whereas in the Catholic lands of northern Europe it was the local church courts and secular courts that shared the task. In 1772, for instance, a man from the Polish village of Krzyżanowice who lodged a complaint of witchcraft against another found himself having to undergo penance, deliver a public apology at the church door to the accused and pay a fine of beeswax candles to the church.[29] We shall discuss such slander cases in more detail shortly.

Although in Protestant Europe, the clergy frequently denounced "superstition" from the pulpit and in print as a relic of Catholicism, or as the product of sinful ignorance, evidence for the continued role of church courts in policing popular magic is patchy, in part because of a lack of detailed research in the archives. The paucity of material also reflects the reality that the official churches' responsibilities for punishing moral offences were diminishing at the parish level. In England, for example, most Anglican visitation articles, which were sent to parishes in advance of the sitting of a church court, ceased to call for the presentment of magical practitioners by the mid-seventeenth century. In the Dutch province of Zeeland, the last case heard by the Dutch Reformed Church was in 1729, whereas magic cases continued to be heard in Scottish and Manx ecclesiastical courts during the first half of the eighteenth century.[30] In Lutheran Sweden, an ecclesiastical visitation questionnaire that circulated in 1795 asked: "Do you think enlightenment, fear of God and good manners are increasing or decreasing?" and "What are the secrets of the folk? Which superstitions and bad customs are common?" In much of Europe, there is little evidence of the courts continuing this interest into the next century, though.[31]

The councils and elders of close-knit Protestant religious groups maintained more of a policing role regarding magical belief and practice amongst their brethren for longer. In German Pietist communities, there are instances of church councils arbitrating in cases of witchcraft accusations into the nineteenth century, whereas a Methodist Society in southern England struck off fifty members from its class register in 1816 for holding to the belief in witchcraft.[32] In the many small and isolated communities in nineteenth-century America made up of recently emigrated Europeans, the myriad churches assumed perhaps even greater responsibility for policing the magical beliefs and practices of their flocks in the absence of other structures. In November 1877, the Joint Columbus Conference of Lutheran ministers debated the problem of witchcraft and magic amongst their mainly German members and came to an agreement that the practice of such "superstition" overstepped "the boundaries prescribed in God's Word to execute that which lies beyond the ordinary effect of nature, and is contrary to the employment of rightful means".[33] A few years later, the Swedish Lutheran Church in Belgrade, Nicollet County, Minnesota, stepped in to adjudicate over a witchcraft dispute among its Swedish immigrant flock, and a rare ecclesiastical court case was instituted by the Methodist Episcopal Church in Columbiana County, Ohio, in 1893 to try a woman who repeatedly made accusations of witchcraft against another member of the church.[34]

The early modern ecclesiastical courts used to play a prominent role in prosecuting defamation and slander – moral offences that sometimes derived from accusations of witchcraft. During the era of the trials, those accused of witchcraft could also take advantage of secular laws. In the German territory of Mensfelden, for instance, the authorities in 1618 allowed that anyone who called a married woman a witch could be fined a hefty six florins. After all, with witchcraft being a capital offence, such slander was deadly serious.[35] But across Europe, few of those accused resorted to slander prosecutions. It cost money to bring a suit, and besides, the danger for those who did prosecute was the amplification of the accusations.

Ignoring the slander was, perhaps, the best option. That changed, of course, once witchcraft was relegated to an imaginary crime. Yet, still, the resort to court for slander had its dangers, particularly in the nineteenth century, when newspapers were likely to report the case and so broadcast the slander far beyond one's community.

By the nineteenth century, slander was primarily a civil offence handled by secular courts, but in much of Europe, cases were few and far between by this time. When, in 1712, the legislature of the Dutch province of Drenthe removed the laws against "real" harmful witchcraft, they left in place a law that punished those who scolded someone for being a "Thief, Murderer, Witch". Numerous slander cases were heard up until the late 1780s, and then they stopped.[36] Across the North Sea, in England, the ecclesiastical courts continued to deal with sexual defamation up until 1855, but witch slander cases had long been consigned to the secular realm, and even there they were rare. In 1813, Thomas Starkie wrote in his *Treatise of the Law of Slander* (1813) that the case law regarding witch slander was so inconsistent "as to appear incapable of affording any illustration of the subject of this treatise".[37] Still, the occasional instances occurred into the twentieth century. In 1927, Isabella Hazleton of Dungannon, Northern Ireland, faced repeated accusations from neighbours that she bewitched their cows. Straws from her thatch were taken to burn under the cows' noses as a counter-spell. As a result of the accusations, no one for miles around would speak to her, so she sued her persecutors for slander, receiving damages of £5 from one neighbour, even though the case against the other defendants was dismissed.[38]

In imperial Germany, insult laws that were bolstered in the 1870s led to an avalanche of slander cases brought by people from all social levels. Malicious slander intended to sully a person's reputation was punishable with imprisonment, and it was even a criminal offence to defame the memory of a dead person.[39] This was different from British Common Law, where slander was treated as a civil and not a criminal offence and usually required evidence of material injury to the plaintiff. The burgeoning German population in late nineteenth- and early twentieth-century America brought this recent litigious custom with them, and numerous slander trials involving witchcraft were heard in courts across the United States. Slander prosecutions were also brought as a consequence of other forms of magical belief. In 1913, a Berlin court heard the case of Adelheid Gebhardt of the village of Bohnsdorf, now a suburb of the city, who accused a barber's wife of theft. Gebhardt, who was in her seventies, suspected some money of hers had been stolen, so she employed the Bible and Key method of divination, variations of which were practised across Europe. She put an old key in her Bible, holding the key by the ring end with one hand and the Bible in her other hand. She then repeated a verse from the Bible, followed by the names of possible suspects. The Bible sprang out of her hand when it came to the barber's wife. On this evidence, Gebhardt made a formal complaint against the woman, but the case fell through due to a lack of evidence, and Gebhardt was sued for slander and fined a small sum.[40]

Dealing with Witches

As has been shown for England and the United States, ignorance of the decriminalisation of witchcraft was widespread into the nineteenth century. People continued to believe that accused witches could and should be punished under the law. Suspicions of witchcraft were reported to the police and magistrates, and there was shock, bemusement and anger when accusers were told there were no laws against witchcraft (other than as a fraud) and that they should not be so foolish as to believe in such things. So it is not surprising that people sometimes took the law into their own hands – just as they had done in the era of the witch trials. Hundreds of cases of individual and mob violence against suspected witches have been recorded during and beyond the nineteenth century.

The most spectacular manifestation of popular justice was the trial by water, or swimming test (Figure 17.3), which survived into the mid-nineteenth century in northern parts of Europe. Witch swimmings watched by hundreds took place at Hela, near Danzig, in 1836, and the last known swimming in England occurred in Essex in 1863, when a deaf and dumb cunning man died from ill health after being badly beaten and forced under the water. The details of the case suggest that by this time, the intention of the water test was more of a punishment than a trial.[41] Although swimmings were sometimes violent and vicious affairs, on some occasions, it was the accused witches who requested they be swum in order to prove their innocence before their communities. This was the case in 1823 when Hendrika Hofhuis of Deldenerbroek, in the Netherlands, was accused of bewitching a neighbour in childbed. Hofhuis duly sank, thereby proving her innocence, before several hundred villagers.[42]

Some suspected witches were badly beaten and abused by accusers pursuing counter-magic rituals. In England, for instance, there are numerous cases of scratching, whereby blood was drawn from the accused witch with a knife or other sharp instrument. A study of court cases from such actions in nineteenth-century Somerset reveals that most witch scratchers were between twenty and forty years old – a generation younger than most of the victims of the attacks. In 1852, Grace Webb, a thirty-year-old handloom weaver, accused her sixty-six-year-old aunt, Charity Furzer, of tormenting her at night. She saw visions of Furzer and felt a heavy load on her stomach. Grace attacked Furzer and drew blood. Prosecuted for assault, she told the magistrate, "I have felt better ever since I gave the scratch; it was a lucky scratch for me".[43] In some other European cultures, the blood of the witch was forcibly collected and

499

ILLUSTRATION, No. LXXVIII.

A TALISMAN FOR LOVE.

" But this most sweet and lighted calm,
    Its blue and midnight hour,
    Wakened the *hidden* springs of his heart,
    With a *deep* and *secret* power."—IOLE.

THIS talisman is said to be wonderfully efficacious in procuring success in amours and love adventures; it must be made in the day and hour of *Venus,* when she is favourable to the planet *Mars.* It should be made of pure *silver,* or purified copper. If *Venus* be in the sign of *Taurus* or *Libra,* it is still better.

2 K 2

FIGURE 17.3. A talisman for provoking love from the British magical manual, *The Astrologer of the Nineteenth Century* (London, 1825), by the occultist Robert Cross Smith (1795–1832).

535

applied to the body of his or her victim. After a cabinet-maker's daughter of Schonbeck, West Prussia, had been bedridden by witchcraft for three years, he was advised in 1883 to make her drink the blood of the suspected witch. Neighbours duly trapped the women, her finger was pricked and the blood was given to the girl. The father and his accomplices were subsequently prosecuted and sentenced to three days in prison. In Poland, in 1907, the authorities in the village of Wieliszew, some sixteen miles north of Warsaw, dealt with a similar case. Marya Zhroh, daughter of farmer Jan Zhroh, fell ill and claimed that a neighbour named Josephine Zlolkow bewitched her when she was milking the cows. Marya told villagers that she would feel better if she drank some of the witch's blood. A crowd of sympathisers then visited Josephine and beat her till blood was running from her nose and ears, which they then collected to administer to Marya. On ingesting some of the blood, she declared she felt much better. The badly injured Josephine sent for the priest, who informed the police, leading to the arrest of two of the main offenders.[44]

Supposed witches were also tortured into removing the spells they were accused of casting. This sometimes took the form of whipping or simply beating the witch to a pulp. In France during the early nineteenth century, a series of court cases resulted from the practice of burning or grilling witches, that is, forcing them into hearths and bonfires – the flames were to make them talk. The same practice also led to the death of a woman in Belgian Flanders in 1815.[45] The infamous Irish Clonmel burning of 1895, although described at the time as a "witch burning" was actually concerned with the fear of changelings. Twenty-six-year-old Bridget Cleary was beaten and then burned by her husband, who believed his wife had been abducted by the fairies and replaced with one of their kind, a changeling. Bridget died from her treatment, and her husband subsequently served fifteen years' imprisonment for manslaughter.[46]

The ultimate method for dealing with witches was to kill them, and the Old Testament provided the sanction for doing so. Did it not say in Exodus chapter 22, verse 18, as printed in the King James Bible, that "thou shalt not suffer a witch to live"? This popular appeal to Biblical authority was echoed in witchcraft conversations across Europe. To give just a couple of examples of the numerous witch killings that occurred in nineteenth- and early twentieth-century Europe, in 1892, a widowed fortune-teller named Heil of Salmünster, Hesse, Germany, was accused of witchcraft and then found murdered on her doorstep. Three crosses in blood were smeared above the door. Two women were arrested.[47] In 1904, it was reported that Antonia Lojacono and her husband of Terrasini Favarotta, Sicily, were brutally murdered in their bed by Bartolo Frontieri and his wife, who believed Antonia had bewitched one of their children to death. One night they entered the Lojaconos' bedroom and stabbed Antonia's husband before proceeding to pour petrol over her and setting her alight. The Frontieris fled Sicily, but the police investigation was further held up because many locals supported the murder of a witch and refused to co-operate.[48]

Witch killers were sometimes diagnosed as suffering from insanity, meaning that they were sent to asylums rather than facing execution or penal servitude. Some clearly were suffering from conditions that we understand today, such as schizophrenia and paranoid delusions, but others exhibited no clear signs of pathology from retrospective diagnoses. Yet the emerging science of psychiatry during the nineteenth century adopted the "enlightened" view that, in such a progressive age, people who expressed strong fears of witches and convictions that they were bewitched, must suffer some degree of mental disease beyond mere credulity. Divorced from the environment, society and culture in which witches were an everyday reality, some psychiatrists could not contemplate that the fear of witchcraft, the experience of heavy misfortune and the intensity of the experience of *thinking* oneself bewitched could lead otherwise healthy individuals to the resolution that their well-being, their very existence, could only be secured through the death of their tormentors. The Leipzig physician and philosopher Ernst Platner (1744–1818) dealt with one young man who shot dead a friend under the conviction that he was plotting to kill him by witchcraft. Before and after the crime, he knew quite well that he would be executed for his act – in other words, he knew right from wrong, which was a key test of sanity – but he said "it is a thousand times better to die on the scaffold, than to perish miserably by the artifices of magic".[49] Platner diagnosed him as suffering from a category of insanity known as monomania.

Personal retribution against witches was often the end point of a period of consultation with family and friends. Lurking in the background, we also often find cunning folk. As we have seen, their activities were criminalised by laws against fraud and vagrancy, but the legislation did little to dent their ubiquity during the nineteenth century.[50] Dealing with witches was one of the mainstays of their business, providing charms and amulets to ward off bewitchment, rituals for detecting the identity of witches, magical and herbal remedies for the bewitched or instructions on how clients could deal with the culprits. It was sometimes cunning folk who advised clients to scratch witches, for example. Their rituals were numerous and diverse, although there are common themes, such as the piercing of animal hearts. In 1829, a fifty-nine-year-old cunning man named Dupleune was prosecuted for *escroquerie* before the assize of St Pol, in northern France, for, amongst other acts, receiving thirty francs for instructing a client that his daughter could be cured of witchery by taking the heart of a lamb that had not yet eaten and pricking it with an awl that had yet to be used. This would cause the evil spirit great torment.[51] The power of such magic could work across oceans, too. In 1904, Pietro Masganini of Livorno, Italy, was suspected by some of murdering a love rival, Guiseppe Pozzello, who had recently left Italy for New York. Friends of Pozzello spotted Masganini dropping some objects in a shallow well after consulting a cunning woman. They fished out three packages and took them to the police office. In the first bundle was a leather pouch containing a sheep's heart pierced by fifty pins or skewers, along with scraps of brightly coloured cloth and a stamped envelope bearing the name of the woman at the centre of the love triangle, Paula Legardis. The second bundle contained a fragment of a tombstone inscribed "Here lies the body of Joseph [Guiseppe]" wound with red cotton thread. The third package contained a glass jar covered with parchment, inside of which was a dried, shrivelled toad wrapped in a tress of woman's hair, which was also pierced with fifty steel pins. Masganini was questioned by the police, but no charges were laid. Nine days later it was reported that Pozzello had died in New York.[52]

Cunning folk were not the only professional unwitchers, of course. The Catholic clergy had the weapon of exorcism at their disposal, although the context and language in which they employed it was usually that of possession rather than bewitchment; in other words, the origins of the cases they dealt with often stemmed from popular suspicions of witchcraft that, through clerical intervention, were redefined as diabolic possession. The confessional propaganda battles that began with the Reformation continued to be played out at the end of the nineteenth century in regions such as the Netherlands and southern Germany where Catholic and Protestant clergy rubbed alongside each other and vied for influence. Catholic authorities used exorcism as an example of the practical protective potency of the faith and its sacraments, whereas some Protestant polemicists denounced its use as no better than the "superstitious" frauds of cunning folk. The confluence of confessional rivalry, Catholic demonology, popular belief and secular law are apparent in the build up to and aftermath of an exorcism conducted in 1891 by one Father Aurelian (Figure 17.4).

On Shrove Tuesday 1891, the ten-year-old son of Michael Zilk, a miller of Wemding, Bavaria, began to exhibit the signs of possession. He would fall into fits of rage at the sight of churches and shrines and was unable to say his prayers. The physicians could no nothing. Michael Zilk was a Catholic, but his wife was a Protestant, and the boy had been educated in the Protestant faith.

A WITCH! A WITCH!   p. 215

FIGURE 17.4. Depiction of a witch swimming from *The Cunning Woman's Grandson* (London, 1889) by Charlotte M. Yonge.

So at first the local pastor was consulted, but his benedictions had no effect. This was clearly a matter for the Catholics. So the Zilks made a request to the nearby Capuchin cloister. Father Aurelian was sent to investigate. He believed it to be a genuine case of diabolic possession and was granted authorisation by the Bishop of Augsburg and Eichstätt to conduct an exorcism. This was duly done in July. During Aurelian's struggle with the evil spirit, the following dialogue ensued:

> You must depart from the child; there is no help for you.
> I can't.
> Why can't you?
> Because she is always banning.
> Who is banning? Some woman?
> Yes.
> What is her name?
> Hertz.

On hearing this, the boy's parents exclaimed that this was one of their neighbours – a Protestant of course! Further conversation with the spirit revealed that Hetz had cast her spell when the boy had eaten some dried pears she had offered him on Shrove Tuesday. Aurelian published an authorised version of the exorcism, *Die Teufelsaustreibung in Wemding* (1892), and an account also appeared in the *Kölnische Zeitung* newspaper.

This was not the end of the story, though, for Hertz took advantage of German slander laws and sued Aurelian in an Eichstätt court. She gave testimony that she had not bewitched the boy and that the dried pears had actually been given to the boy by her maidservant. Her own children had eaten the pears without any ill effects. Since the reports had been published, she had been called a witch by others in the community and her children had been taunted at school as "witch-children". The public prosecutor ruled that Aurelian had uttered a slander and imposed a fine of fifty marks with costs or five days' imprisonment. Following this successful outcome, Hertz intended to take proceedings against the *Kölnische Zeitung*, as well.[53] The hugely embarrassed church authorities set about recalling and destroying any copies of the pamphlet they could find, so within a short time it was nearly impossible to obtain.[54]

Although such cases provided fine ammunition for the anti-Catholic polemicists, it is important to stress that various evangelical Protestant denominations were willing to perform similar services. Instead of the authorised ritual exorcisms of the Catholic Church, they would perform lengthy and repeated praying over the possessed. One group of English Primitive Methodists accrued the name "Magic Methodists" in the early nineteenth century because of their preoccupation with trances, visions and the healing of the possessed at a time when Wesleyan Methodism was being drained of the vibrant providentialism inspired by its founder.[55] In Germany in 1842, the Pietist Pastor Johann Christoph Blumhardt (1805–1880) of Möttlingen, Württemberg, became famed for his ability to expel demons after he apparently cured a female parishioner named Gottliebin Dittus by using two years of prayers and counselling, aided by other pastors. The demon immediately swapped to Gottliebin's sister, and when it was finally expelled from her, it was reported that the demon cried "*Jesus ist Sieger!* (Jesus is Victor!)". A "Christian awakening" ensued, with numerous people coming forward claiming to be possessed. The demand led Blumhardt to set up a clinic in the spa town of Bad Boll. Before his exorcism of Gottliebin, Blumhardt had little understanding of the rich world of popular belief regarding witchcraft, magic and spirits, but after years of treating the possessed, he wrote "that everything that had hitherto been reckoned under the most ridiculous popular superstition, stepped over from the world of fairy tales into reality".[56] Blumhardt's son took over his father's work after his death. The advent of Spiritualism would further polarise the Protestant world with regard to the nature of spirit communication and its place in Protestant theology and practice.

Continuation

By the end of the nineteenth century, the pervasiveness of the popular belief in witchcraft and magic was still evident to those who were neither ignorant of popular cultures nor blinded by confidence in the supposed advancement of humanity in the Industrial Age. It could not be eradicated by redefining it is a fraud, and religious authority was too compromised to do the job – an accusation levelled at the Catholic Church in particular. The American historian and linguist Professor Edward Payson Evans, son of a Presbyterian clergyman and author of the seminal *Criminal Prosecution and Capital Punishment of Animals*, wrote in 1892 that popular superstition was rife in the "vast low-lying plains of humanity" and that although modern science was eroding it at the edges, much education was required. He warned, however, that wherever the schoolmaster "wears the cassock or the cowl, or is placed under strict clerical supervision, as the recent Prussian Education Bill proposed to do, the progress of intelligence ... will be exceedingly slow".[57] Much confidence continued to be placed on the expansion of popular secular education, but noticeable progress on that front was opaque.

Learning to read and write was no spell against the belief in magic. Perhaps another profession – the medical one – could deal the death blow through its campaign against the myriad irregular healers who upheld a popular belief in the power of magic and spiritual succour.[58]

The French medical profession was in the vanguard of the campaign, and indeed, the power of the profession depended in part on suppressing the diversity of the medical market. The Napoleonic state provided the perfect political and structural conditions for imposing medical control, and in 1803, the Law of Ventôse imposed a national system of medical licensing. Successive further restrictions on medical practice over the next century reinforced the professionalization of dentistry and veterinary practice. In Britain, the 1858 Medical Act created a medical register that made it easy to identify unlicensed medical practitioners, thereby enabling the police to better pursue quacks and cunning folk. Similar developments occurred across much of Europe at the time. Yet, judging from the number of prosecutions of magical healers under these laws, such medical legislation patently failed, an observation that is supported by the reportage of folklorists and ethnographers during the late nineteenth century.

The continued resorting to traditional folk medicine, with its mixture of natural and magical remedies and charms, has been well documented across much of twentieth-century Europe.[59] In the mid-1950s, the Communist authorities in Yugoslavia launched a campaign to extinguish folk magic beliefs using travelling exhibitions and publicity campaigns. Around ninety folk healers of various sorts were prosecuted by Serbian courts in the mid-1950s.[60] In 1954, the German Society for Protection against Superstition was formed, uniting Protestant and Catholic campaigners. The north German schoolteacher Johann Kruse carried out a widely reported public campaign against cunning folk and grimoires (Figure 17.5), which he saw as perpetuating the pernicious belief in witchcraft. At the other end of the country, the Lutheran minister Kurt Koch attracted international attention for his struggle against the "flood of magical conjuration which washes the Alps".[61] Suspected witches were still being shot dead in France and the United States into the mid-twentieth century. The world of magic and witchcraft that we like to define as medieval or early modern continued to exist three hundred years later not as a relic or a peculiar survival but as an expression of perennial fears, anxieties and suspicions.

P. SUTTER

Curé de Wickerschwihr
près Colmar (Haut-Rhin)

Le Diable

SES PAROLES, SON ACTION

DANS LES POSSÉDÉS D'ILLFURT (Alsace)

d'après des documents historiques

QUATRIÈME ÉDITION FRANÇAISE,
Revue par l'abbé WARIN, du Diocèse d'Arras

AUGMENTÉE DU RÉCIT DE LA

POSSESSION D'UNE JEUNE CAFRE

des Missions Catholiques du Natal (Afrique du Sud)

LIBRAIRIE BRUNET

32, Rue Gambetta, ARRAS *(France)*

FIGURE 17.5. Pamphlet account of the possession and exorcism of two boys from Illfurt, Alsace, during the 1860s.

Notes

1. Hunter, "The Decline of Magic", 399–423; Hunter, "The Royal Society and the Decline of Magic", 103–119; Walsham, "The Reformation and 'The Disenchantment of the World'", 497–528; Cameron, *Enchanted Europe*; Marshall, "Disenchantment and Re-Enchantment in Europe", 599–606; Bever, "Witchcraft Prosecutions and the Decline of Magic", 263–293; Bell, "Breaking Modernity's Spell – Magic and Modern History", 115–123.

2. See, for example, Hanegraaff, "How Magic Survived the Disenchantment of the World", 357–380; Bell, *The Magical Imagination*; Davies, *Magic: A Very Short Introduction*; Freytag and Sawicki, eds., *Wunderwelten*; Doering-Manteuffel, *Okkultismus*. For a more global approach, see Meyer and Pels, eds., *Magic and Modernity*.

3. See the important overviews: Gijswijt-Hofstra, "Witchcraft after the Witch-Trials", 95–191; de Blécourt, "The Witch, Her Victim, The Unwitcher and the Researcher", 141–220; Davies and de Blécourt, eds., *Beyond the Witch Trials*; de Blécourt and Davies, eds., *Witchcraft Continued*.

4. For a detailed overview, see Levack, "The Decline and End of Witchcraft Prosecutions", 1–95.

5. Kern, "An End to Witchcraft Trials in Austria", 159–185; Klaniczay, "The Decline of Witches and the Rise of Vampires", 168–188; Klaniczay, *The Uses of Supernatural Power*.

6. Ostling, *Between the Devil and the Host*, 59–60.

7. Davies, *Witchcraft, Magic and Culture*, 48–49; Henningsen, "Witch Persecution after the Era of the Witch Trials", 106–107.

8. See Krampl, *Les secrets des faux sorciers*.

9. Ruff, *Crime, Justice and Public Order*, 167.

10. Krampl, *Les secrets des faux sorciers*, 16.

11. Mozzani, *Magie et superstitions*, 230–232. See also Devlin, *The Superstitious Mind*.

12. Davies, "Decriminalising the Witch", 207–232.

13. *Royal Cornwall Gazette*, 31 July 1869; 14 March 1874; 1 February 1894. More generally, see Davies, *Witchcraft, Magic and Culture*, 61–75.

14. Davies, *Witchcraft, Magic and Culture*, 54–55, 61–75; Perkins, *The Reform of Time*.

15. See Davies, *America Bewitched*; Leventhal, *In the Shadow of the Enlightenment*; Freeman and Banning, "Rogues, Vagabonds, and Lunatics", 31–43.

16. Beaune, *Les sorciers de Lyon*, 42–43.

17. McManners, *Church and Society*, 235–236.

18. Oja, "The Superstitious Other", 72; Olli, "Blasphemy in Early Modern Sweden", 457–470; Olli, "The Devil's Pact", 100–117. See also Sörlin, *Wicked Arts*.

19. Levack, "The Decline and End of Witchcraft Prosecutions", 80–81; Behringer, *Witchcraft Persecutions in Bavaria*, esp. 345. See also Roper, *Witch Craze*, ch. 10; Fiume, "The Old Vinegar Lady", 65–87.

20. For a discussion of the case, see Kord, *Murderesses in German Writing*, 24–33; Hauser, *Der Justizmord an Anna Göldi*.

21. For recent studies of magical treasure hunting in the period, see Davies, *Grimoires*, esp. ch. 3; Dillinger, *Magical Treasure Hunting*; Tschaikner, *Schatzgräberei in Voralberg und Liechtenstein*.

22. McManners, *Church and Society*, 236; Dillinger, *Magical Treasure Hunting*, 123.

23. Dillinger and Feld, "Treasure-Hunting", 168.

24. Molero, *Magie et sorcellerie en Espagne*, 159.

25. See Davies, *Grimoires*, 145–148; Walker, "The Persistent Idea of American Treasure Hunting", 429–459; Quinn, *Early Mormonism and the Magic World View*.

26. Laws of the General Assembly of the State of Pennsylvania, Passed at the Session of 1861 (Harrisburg, 1861), 270–271.

27. *Daily Herald* (Mississippi), 11 January 1899.

28. Walker, *Doctors, Folk Medicine and the Inquisition*; Molero, "Heterodoxia y here-jía"; Molero, *Magie et sorcellerie en Espagne*, 195–196, 213–214.

29. Gentilcore, *From Bishop to Witch*; Ostling, *Between the Devil and the Host*, 59.

30. Davies, *Cunning-Folk*, 17–18; Gijswijt-Hofstra, "Witchcraft before Zeeland Magistrates and Church Courts", 117; Maxwell-Stuart, "Witchcraft and Magic in Eighteenth-Century Scotland", 88–91; Sharpe, "Witchcraft in the Early Modern Isle of Man", 11–28.

31. Cited in Van Gent, *Magic, Body, and the Self*, 44, n. 88.

32. Gestrich, "Pietismus und Aberglaube", 269–286; Gijswijt-Hofstra, "Witchcraft after the Witch-Trials", 166–167; Davies, *Witchcraft, Magic and Culture*, 15.

33. *Cincinnati Daily Gazette*, 8 November 1877.

34. See Davies, *America Bewitched*.

35. Dillinger, *"Evil People"*, 79.

36. de Blécourt, "'Evil People'", 145. See also de Blécourt, and Pereboom, "Insult and Admonition", 119–132.

37. Starkie, *A Treatise of the Law of Slander*, 87.

38. *San Diego Union*, 8 October 1927.

39. See Goldberg, *Honor, Politics and the Law in Imperial Germany*, esp. 33–74.

40. *Colorado Springs Gazette*, 2 March 1913.

41. Freytag, "Witchcraft, Witch Doctors and the Fight against 'Superstition'", 29–46; Davies, *Witchcraft, Magic and Culture*, 99.

42. Gijswijt-Hofstra, "Witchcraft after the Witch-Trials", 112.

43. Davies, *A People Bewitched*, 125, 131–132.

44. *Berlin Vossische Zeitung*, reported in *Galveston Weekly News*, 5 July 1883; *Times-Picayune*, 15 September 1907. For further Polish cases, see Schiffmann, "The Witch and the Crime", 147–165.

45. See, for example, Traimond, *Le pouvoir de la maladie*; Devlin, *The Superstitious Mind*.

46. Bourke, *The Burning of Bridget Cleary*; Hoff and Yeates, *The Cooper's Wife is Missing*.

47. *Morning Olympian*, 27 February 1892.

48. *Plain Dealer*, 11 September 1904.

49. Quoted in Henke, "Observations on Some of the Forms of Monomania", 221.

50. See, for example, Davies, *Cunning-Folk*; Davies, *A People Bewitched*; the essays in de Blécourt and Davies, eds., *Witchcraft Continued*; de Blécourt, "Witch Doctors, Soothsayers and Priests", 285–303; de Blécourt, "On the Continuation of Witchcraft", 335–352; Allen, "Wizards or Charlatans", 68–84; Tallis, "The Conjuror, the Fairy, the Devil and the Preacher"; Waters, "Belief in Witchcraft in Oxfordshire and Warwickshire", 98–116. For Europe, see, for example, Tangherlini, "'How Do You Know She's a Witch?'", 279–303. For North America, see Benes, "Fortunetellers, Wise Men, and Magical Healers", 127–149; Davies, *America Bewitched*, ch. 5.

51. *Gazette des Tribunaux*, reported in *The Standard*, 23 September 1829.

52. *Chicago Daily Tribune*, 11 September 1904. A Giuseppe Pozzillo arrived in New York on 12 October 1903 having sailed on the Victoria.

53. *Evening Post*, 28 January 1893.

54. Frazer, "A Recent Chapter in the Modernist Controversy", 258. For other major cases of possession in the period, see Burton, *Holy Tears, Holy Blood*, ch. 7; Harris, "Possession on the Borders", 451–478; Davies, "Witchcraft Accusations in France", 107–133.

55. Davies, "Methodism, the Clergy, and the Popular Belief", 252–265; Brittain, "Hugh Bourne and the Magic Methodists", 132–140.

56. Midelfort, *Exorcism and Enlightenment*, 147; Meyer, *Translating the Devil*, 46–49; Zahl, *Pneumatology and Theology of the Cross*, 13–17.

57. Evans, "Modern Instances of Demoniacal Possession", 168.

58. See Ramsey, *Professional and Popular Medicine in France*; Ramsey, "Magical Healing, Witchcraft and Elite Discourse", 14–38; Marin-Courtoud, "Les procès de sorcellerie pendant la IIIe République", vol. 2, 161–173; Perdiguero, "Magical Healing in Spain", 133–151; Davies, "Cunning-Folk in the Medical Market-Place", 55–73.

59. See Davies, "European Folk Medicine", 25–44.

60. *Omaha World-Herald*, 7 March 1955.

61. See Davies, *Grimoires*, 247–261.

Chapter 18

Elite Magic in the Nineteenth Century

DAVID ALLEN HARVEY

In January 1893, two men from the bohemian literary subculture of Paris, accompanied by their seconds, marched paces in opposite directions and faced off with dueling pistols. The occurrence of such a duel was far from uncommon, for as Robert Nye has shown, dueling played a central role in the social performance of elite male honor in fin-de-siècle France.[1] The motive of this particular duel, however, was anything but ordinary. One of the duelists, the journalist Jules Bois, a friend of the author Joris-Karl Huysmans and an intrepid chronicler of the magical, mysterious, and heretical, had accused the other, the bohemian poet, Neo-Rosicrucian, and practicing magician Stanislas de Guaita, of using his occult powers to commit murder from a distance of several hundred miles. Joseph Boullan, the man whom Guaita was accused of slaying, was an apostate priest, the leader of a marginal Lyon sect called the Oeuvre de la Miséricorde, and the inspiration for the character of Dr. Johannes in Huysmans's novel *Là-bas* (1891), and he died suddenly on the night of January 3 after complaining of a choking sensation. In an article published in *Gil Blas* the following week, Bois declared that Boullan had been "struck by invisible rage and by criminal hands armed with occult thunderbolts, with unknown and awesome power." Bois multiplied his accusations in the following days, claiming that Guaita was a master in the use of poisons, commanded a familiar spirit that inhabited a cupboard in his apartment, and regularly performed alchemical experiments, invoked spirits, and cast magic spells. Guaita ridiculed the charges that Bois brought against him, calling them "more damaging for the malicious or naïve authors of this canard than for myself," and he declared that "if it sufficed to raise one's finger toward the sky to strike down one's enemy at a distance, we would see many sudden deaths." Nevertheless, Guaita felt it necessary to defend his honor as a gentleman, and he issued a formal challenge to the offending journalist. Bois was spared from the brunt of whatever occult powers Guaita might have possessed, however, as the two men exchanged shots without injury to either party, and the dispute was quickly laid to rest thereafter.[2]

The story of Guaita and Bois, Huysmans and Boullan, and their occult confrères clashes sharply with what most of us think we know about nineteenth-century European culture. The early Third Republic is well known as the period in which the political power of Catholicism was decisively broken in France and the doctrines of science, progress, and militant secularism were carried to the most remote corners of the French hexagon by an army of schoolteachers, the so-called "black hussars of the Republic." Moreover, theorists of modernization, from Max Weber to the present, have emphasized the secularization of Western intellectual life during this period, with its naïve faith in progress and in the power of science and human reason to overcome all obstacles and resolve all mysteries and the positivist ambition to achieve in all fields of knowledge the level of certitude reached by the physical sciences. Randall Styers, noting that Weber's term for "disenchantment" – *Entzauberung* – literally means "removing the magic," argues that "magic has assumed the role of modernity's foil, and debates over magic have provided an important site for the articulation of modernity's norms."[3] Magic and modernity, it has often been assumed, are fundamentally antithetical to one another; however, Styers argues that they have in fact been interdependent, with the former serving as a sort of catch-all residual category against which the latter has defined itself.

The importance of magic in nineteenth-century European popular culture and folklore has never been in dispute, as belief in miracles, prophecies, and magical talismans remained strong, particularly in rural areas. Thomas Kselman and Raymond Jonas have emphasized the significance of miracles, apparitions of the Virgin, and other magical occurrences in the post-Revolutionary revival of French Catholicism, whereas David Blackbourn's work highlights the significance of Marian piety and miracle cults in German Catholicism during the same period.[4] Nor were such phenomena limited to Catholic continental Europe, despite a persistent Protestant tendency to equate magic and superstition with Catholic obscurantism.[5] The English-speaking world was also shaken by waves of religious fervor and millenarianism in the early Industrial Era, as many Englishmen and Americans who were deeply concerned by the transformations of their age sought certainty in apocalyptic prophecies and new divine revelations. Nineteenth-century Europe and America teemed with communes, phalansteries, and other such experiments in social and spiritual regeneration. Nevertheless, outside the field of the cultural history of religion, many scholars and general readers alike implicitly accepted the modernization=secularization thesis, and historians such as Keith Thomas and Eugen Weber have argued that peasant belief in magic was an archaic survival, dispelled by the advances of orthodox religion and modern education.[6]

A belief in magic was not limited to the superstitious masses, however, and particularly in the fin de siècle, it attracted the attention of the artistic and intellectual elite, who saw in it a wellspring of new creative energies, a medium for the exploration of the invisible world beyond the reach of the senses, and a higher wisdom capable of reconciling the increasingly opposed forces of science and religion. Styers has observed that "modern occultism is thus as modern as it is occult, and it demonstrates the deep level at which the 'secular' and the 'sacred,' the 'rational' and the 'irrational' refuse separation."[7] James Webb, one of the first credible historians of modern esotericism, wrote in 1974 that "to ignore the occult revival of the nineteenth century is to ignore a large slice of modern intellectual development."[8] This chapter will attempt to restore that slice to its proper place in the history of the rise of modern Western culture.

The Western Esoteric Tradition from the Renaissance to the Enlightenment

Nineteenth-century Europe inherited a rich, complex esoteric tradition from the early modern era. Antoine Faivre argues that Western esotericism emerged in the late fifteenth century, "when scientists and humanists undertook to appropriate various traditions of the past – Neo-Pythagoreanism, Neo-Platonism, Alexandrian Hermetism, Jewish Kabbalah – with the concern to show that some of them, indeed all of them, mutually enrich each other and represent more or less the branches of a common trunk, that is, of a *philosophia perennis*, an 'eternal philosophy.'"[9] Faivre has further elaborated a systematic definition of the Western esoteric tradition, in which he has identified the following six key tenets: a belief in correspondences between the macrocosm (the universe) and microcosm (man); a vitalistic understanding of nature as a living force rather than inanimate matter; the importance of imagination and meditation as paths to knowledge; the experience of transmutation (both the physical transformation of lead into gold and the spiritual or symbolic transformation of the alchemist or magician's soul); the search for concordances between apparently different "exoteric" religious traditions; and a belief in the continuous transmission of a primordial tradition through initiation into secret societies.[10] This tradition, which was a mixture of Neo-Platonism, Renaissance Hermeticism, borrowings from Kabbalah, astrology, alchemy, and so on, had been subsumed somewhat by the advance of Newtonian science and the mechanistic philosophy of Descartes and his successors, but it never entirely disappeared. Indeed, from the seventeenth through the nineteenth centuries, many practitioners and popularizers of the new knowledge recoiled from the religious and metaphysical implications of their own work, and men of science (Newton not least among them) dabbled in the occult.

Ironically, the Enlightenment's own respect for antiquity contributed to the survival of a belief in the "Egyptian mysteries" associated with the legendary figure of Hermes Trismegistus, as well as that of the Pythagorean and Neo-Platonist elements that formed part of the classical heritage. Antoine Court de Gebelin's *Monde primitif* (1781), which sought to recover information regarding the language, culture, and beliefs of a primordial, prehistoric root civilization for mankind, launched the false but widely influential belief that the Tarot deck (a playing card game that emerged in Renaissance Italy and Provence with no magical pretentions) concealed in allegorical form the sacred wisdom of the ancient Egyptians, whereas his contemporary Jean-Baptiste Alliette, a onetime wigmaker who earned notoriety as a fortune-teller, popularized the use of the Tarot in divination. Their dual legacy would have profound impact on both elite and popular magic in the nineteenth century and beyond. Another contemporary, the Italian mystic and mountebank Giuseppe Balsamo Cagliostro, also claimed to be an initiate of the ancient Egyptian mysteries, and he developed an elaborate branch of esoteric "Egyptian" freemasonry in the years immediately prior to the Revolution.[11]

The institution of Freemasonry, which emerged in its modern form in seventeenth-century Britain, provided a convenient vehicle for the transmission of a variety of esoteric beliefs. In its origins, Freemasonry was a craft guild among stonemasons, similar to many other corporate bodies in early modern Europe. However, seventeenth-century lodges in England and Scotland, for reasons that are still unclear, began to admit non-practicing, honorary members who were attracted to Masonry because of the secrets the order was believed to maintain. These "speculative Masons" increasingly came to dominate the organization, as Freemasonry became a site of sociability for men from the upper and middle classes and lost the craft character of its artisanal roots. English Freemasonry, organized around the Grand Lodge of London from 1717 onward, retained this mundane, clubby social atmosphere, along with the three original degrees (Apprentice, Fellow Craft, and Master Mason) derived from artisanal practice.[12]

The Scottish Rite, however, that was transmitted to continental Europe by Jacobite exiles, soon developed a system of higher grades and a more elaborate mythology, which traced the history of the order back to the construction of the Temple of Solomon in ancient Israel. Esoteric Freemasonry flourished in continental Europe in the eighteenth century, especially in the smaller states of western and central Germany. Many of these new orders fused the form of Masonic lodges and associations with the legends of the Rosicrucian manifestoes (seventeenth-century texts that told of the spread of spiritual enlightenment from East to West by Christian Rosenkreutz, the legendary founder of a supposed secret brotherhood of initiates), which had left their greatest influence on German Central Europe, and with the mystical belief systems of seventeenth-century mystics, such as Jakob Boehme.[13] Enthusiastic Masons often joined multiple orders, seeking new initiations and new secrets. An international assembly of esoteric Freemasonry, the Wilhelmsbad conference of 1782, sought, without success, to adopt a uniform system of higher degrees and to establish a semblance of unity amid the bewildering diversity of rival orders. Although the conference failed in that regard, it would later take on a central role in post-Revolutionary conspiracy theories, which saw Freemasonry as an immense plot against the established order.

The Enlightenment made its own contributions to the esoteric tradition. Robert Darnton has observed that the rapid advances of scientific knowledge left many people dazzled and disoriented, ready to believe the most marvelous tales, because so many marvels had already been proven true. If men could defy gravity through balloon flights or seize lightning from the heavens in the form of electricity, who could say with certainty whether the much-heralded new science of animal magnetism was true or false? For a brief time, the Austrian doctor Franz Anton Mesmer captivated French society with his promises to cure disease through the regulation of the "magnetic fluid" that kept the mind and body alike in proper balance. Although a scientific commission empowered by Louis XVI and including luminaries such as Benjamin Franklin, Antoine Lavoisier, and Jean-Sylvain Bailly demonstrated that Mesmer's claims lacked scientific merit, animal magnetism established itself in late eighteenth-century French belief. The Marquis de Puységur experimented with magnetic cures and reported positive results among his patients, and esoteric circles, notably in Lyon, made use of magnetism to induce a trancelike state, by which the hypnotized subject, or *somnambule*, was believed to come into contact with the extrasensory world.[14]

If the Enlightenment itself exercised influence over the subsequent development of elite magic in the nineteenth century, however, the Illuminist reaction against Enlightenment rationalism and materialism played an even greater role. Although only a minority of Enlightenment thinkers – such as La Mettrie, Helvétius, and the baron d'Holbach – were avowed materialists who rejected all notions of a supreme being or supernatural forces, the rather austere Deist concept of God as a "great watchmaker" or "grand architect of the universe" who created the world and then withdrew from it left many contemporaries cold.[15] Against the "mechanistic philosophy" suggested by Descartes and popularized by his eighteenth-century heirs, Illuminists and Romantics imagined a living universe suffused with vital forces and energies, in which all things were connected and acted reciprocally on one another, a vision that, as we have observed earlier in this section, had been central to Renaissance Neo-Platonist and Hermetic thought. The concept of a living, interconnected universe was most fully elaborated in Germany, where the Romantic philosopher Friedrich Schelling developed a theory of *Naturphilosophie* that, Corinna Treitel observes, envisioned "nature as a living organism endowed with a 'world soul.'"[16] This unitary and vitalist conception of the universe would serve, directly or indirectly, as the theoretical foundation for the subsequent revival and reinvention of ritual magic in the nineteenth century, as magicians and visionaries sought to interpret, balance, and command the hidden forces of nature.

Although Mesmer and Schelling refused to believe in a disenchanted universe, in which nothing existed except matter and motion, their conception of the forces of nature was largely naturalist and impersonal in character, and it had little of the traditional Christian belief in the regular intervention of divine Providence in human affairs. Other late eighteenth-century Illuminists, however, imagined a more explicitly Judeo-Christian cosmos, in which angels and demons populated the invisible world and battled for the allegiance of human souls. This belief system led to the revival of a form of ritual magic known as theurgy, sometimes also called white magic, in which the operant, through the combination of abstinence, elaborate ritual, and personal piety, sought contact with divine messengers. A mysterious figure, Martinès de Pasqually, who is often described as a Portuguese Jewish convert to Christianity, introduced a new system of theurgic ritual into France in the 1760s, under a quasi-Masonic order called the Temple des Elus Coëns, or the "temple of chosen priests." Preoccupied with the question of original sin and humanity's consequent fall from divine grace, Martinès de Pasqually sought to enter into communication with spirits in the astral plane, who could intervene with the deity on humanity's behalf, and to ward off the malignant influence of demons who sought to preserve man's fallen state. Martinist adepts prepared for theurgic rituals with a full day of fasting, and at midnight they placed themselves in circles inscribed with hieroglyphic symbols while wearing black clothing and red and white robes, and they beseeched the spirits to make their presence known through flashes of light, sounds or voices, or even direct apparitions. Such signs, which Martinès de Pasqually called *passes*, would signify that the initiate had received divine favor and would, after his death, recover the virtues and spiritual powers lost by Adam after the Fall.[17]

Martinès de Pasqually's most prominent convert, Louis-Claude de Saint-Martin, developed "Martinism" into a system of belief as well as of magical practice, emphasizing traditional Christian faith and piety, but also advancing a belief in multiple incarnations and the ultimate redemption of all of humanity through a series of trials. Following Martinès de Pasqually's death in 1774, Saint-Martin took control of the movement, yet without the founder's charismatic presence, the remaining Temples des Elus Coëns closed their doors within the following decade, and Saint-Martin withdrew from active organizational life into contemplation. The Alsatian publisher Rudolf Salzmann introduced him to the works of the Baroque German mystic Jakob Boehme (1575–1624), whose influence led Saint-Martin to turn increasingly in a less ritualistic direction. Saint-Martin combined a largely Christian theological and ethical system with the theory of metempsychosis (which he probably adopted from Greek Pythagoreanism rather than from Buddhism or other Eastern religions, given that the latter remained little known to Europeans at the time), according to which souls would pass through a series of incarnations and trials, through which, by a gradual process of self-purification, they would ultimately achieve reintegration with their divine origins. Saint-Martin's fusion of Christianity and esoteric philosophy into a religion of progress anticipates in most of its details the development of spiritualist doctrines by Allan Kardec in the following century, a topic to which we will return later in the chapter.

The French Revolution marked an important caesura between the esoteric Freemasonry and Illuminism of the late Enlightenment and the rise of new currents of magic and esotericism in the nineteenth century. Not only were many adepts scattered by the dramatic events of war and revolution and divided into opposing camps, but the nationalist antagonisms engendered by the Revolutionary and Napoleonic wars also shattered the international republic of letters that had allowed (to take the example of Martinism) French magicians and mystics to synthesize elements of Jewish Kabbalism introduced from Iberia with German Baroque mysticism within an organizational framework (Freemasonry) that had been imported from the British Isles. Although such transnational borrowings would continue, the occult revivals of the nineteenth century would be more nationally distinct from one another, as we will soon see. The scope of such borrowings, however, would widen in the second half of the nineteenth century, incorporating not just Europe but also America and (through the idiosyncratic and frequently distorting prism of Madame Blavatsky (1831–1891) and her followers) Asia, as well.

Elite and Popular Magic: Spiritualism and Theosophy

The Western esoteric tradition was, in the nineteenth century, enriched by two imports from beyond Europe: Spiritualism in the 1850s and the Theosophical Society in the 1880s. Both were imports from the Anglophone world, with Spiritualism originating in Hydesville, New York, in 1848, and the Theosophical Society having been founded in 1875 in New York City and later transferred to British India by the charismatic Russian expatriate Helena Petrovna Blavatsky. Although these imports had their sources outside of what we, following Faivre, have identified as the Western esoteric tradition, they were taken up quickly because they resonated with elements already present in that tradition.

Modern Spiritualism emerged out of the "burned-over district" of upstate New York, the same fertile ground that also gave rise to Mormonism, Seventh-Day Adventism, and the free-love communalism of Oneida. In 1848, two adolescent girls, Kate and Margaret Fox, heard noises in their home, which they took as a sign of the presence of an invisible spirit. They engaged the spirit in a sort of conversation, which revealed that he was the ghost of a peddler who had been murdered and buried in the house years earlier. From this humble beginning, the Fox sisters became celebrities in antebellum America, and the craze for communication with the spirits of the dead swept across the United States and across the Atlantic, reaching France in 1853. French observers were most struck by the physical manifestations of spirit communication, and these phenomena, specifically the *tables tournantes*, or "turning tables," gave their name to the movement as a whole. Within little time, French citizens of both genders and all classes began to participate in spiritualist séances, where they joined hands to create a "magnetic chain" to attract the spirits of the deceased. As the code of binary communication through percussive responses to yes or no questions proved limiting, more sophisticated tools were developed to allow the spirits to speak more freely. These included the *planchette*, a forerunner of the Ouija board, with which a medium moved a sliding hand tool across a table of the alphabet to spell out messages from the beyond, and the practice of "automatic writing," in which the medium essentially took dictation from the spirits, who guided his or her hand.

Why did American Spiritualism catch on so quickly in Second Empire France? As an essentially experiential phenomenon based on communication with the spirits of the dead, Spiritualism bore striking affinities to the practice of magnetic somnambulism, a tradition native to France and deriving from the doctrines of Mesmer and the researches of the Marquis de Puységur. Even before news of the exploits of the Fox sisters crossed the Atlantic, magnetic somnambulism was a well-established practice, in which a magnetizer, or hypnotist (almost always male), induced a trancelike state in a medium (usually, but not always, female) and asked her a series of questions dealing with health and healing, the prediction of future events, or religious and metaphysical concerns. The connection between the *somnambule* and *magnétiseur* was a uniquely intimate one, and such professional closeness frequently led to marriage, as was the case of Louis-Alphonse Cahagnet and Adèle Maginot and that of J.-J. Ricard and Virginie Plan. There were some significant differences between French magnetic somnambulism and American Spiritualism: French *somnambules* entered the trance state under the direction of a *magnétiseur* and remained under his influence, and they revealed information about the future, the astral plane, or their own physical condition or that of their petitioners through the extrasensory perception that they were believed to achieve through hypnosis, rather than as a result of direct communication with the spirits of the dead.[18] The practices were sufficiently similar, however, for the latter to be received and assimilated into the former, changing the content of both in the process.

A French former schoolteacher, Allan Kardec (born Hippolyte Léon Denizard Rivail) transformed Spiritualism by integrating it with existing "magnetic somnambulist" practice and by developing a cosmology that owed much to Hermetic philosophy. Kardec's first major book, *Le livre des esprits* (1857), which was supposedly a compilation of around a thousand questions and answers assembled over the course of several years of spirit communication, offered a comprehensive metaphysical, religious, and ethical system and functioned in the following years as a sort of spiritualist bible. According to Kardec, human souls passed through a series of incarnations, on this world and on others like it, in order to face and overcome a series of "trials," through which they gradually perfected themselves and advanced toward a higher state. Although it was separated from the tragic theological overtones of the Fall from Paradise and integrated into a more secularized teleology of progress, Kardec's system bore substantial resemblance to that elaborated by

Louis-Claude de Saint-Martin at the end of the previous century. Kardec's doctrines of Spiritualism also offered consolation to bereaved parents, spouses, and children for the loss of their loved ones, and many French citizens, from the humble denizens of working-class spiritualist circles to the poet and novelist Victor Hugo, who invoked the spirit of his deceased daughter Léopoldine from his home in exile on the island of Jersey, were attracted to it for this reason. Other factors also contributed to the appeal of Spiritualism. Nicole Edelman and Lynn Sharp have both noted the empowerment that the movement gave to women, with Sharp noting that because "feminine qualities were considered desirable for contacting the spirits," Spiritualism offered them a forum for public speech lacking in other sectors of society.[19] John Warne Monroe also notes the political context, arguing that many former romantic socialists and chastened liberals, demoralized by the failure of the Revolution of 1848 and the imposition of a virtual dictatorship under Louis-Napoleon Bonaparte, found in Spiritualism and other esoteric movements the promise of a better world to come.

As reshaped by Kardec, Spiritualism became a major cultural movement in the middle decades of the nineteenth century in France, and it sparked a journal, the *Revue spirite*, a national organization, and local chapters scattered throughout France. The repressive and autocratic Bonapartist regime tolerated it, perceiving it as a harmless diversion unthreatening to the political order, although Catholic conservatives and secular republicans alike denounced it as a dangerous folly. Nicole Edelman notes that the politics of Spiritualism were in fact quite ambiguous, writing: "If spiritualism is a doctrine of docility and submission, because the fate of each person is deserved by a previous life, it is also a doctrine of emancipation and equality between men and women, between blacks and whites, between rich and poor. Each place being interchangeable, it encourages each person to intervene here below against inequality and poverty."[20]

In 1875 in New York, a generation after the initial appearance of American Spiritualism in Europe, the charismatic Russian émigrée Helena Petrovna Blavatsky and Henry Steele Olcott, an attorney and former Union officer in the Civil War, founded the Theosophical Society as a "universal brotherhood of humanity, without distinction of race, creed, sex, caste, or color," which was dedicated to "the study of comparative religion, philosophy, and science." Blavatsky's spiritual teachings, compiled in the vast, rambling syntheses *Isis Unveiled* and *The Secret Doctrine*, were a blend of Hinduism, Buddhism, and other Eastern religions, transformed and explained for Western consumption. Blavatsky herself was one of the first in a succession of amateurs of the occult who, disillusioned with modern science and traditional Christianity alike, argued that contemporary Westerners must look to the East to find true spiritual enlightenment.[21] Blavatsky's teachings struck a chord with European audiences already predisposed to look upon the Orient as a repository of ancient esoteric wisdom, and Western sages from Pythagoras to Christian Rosenkreutz had traveled there to seek initiation to its gnosis. The German author Annie Francé-Harrar later wrote that the 1890s had witnessed "a spiritual wind blowing from East to West."[22] A generation later, in the interwar period, the French mystic René Guénon would argue that as the decadent, materialist West had lost contact with the roots of its own esoteric tradition, it was only in the Orient that true spiritual enlightenment could be found.[23] To the extent that religion and spirituality in the contemporary West have been transformed by a "wind from the East," it is Blavatsky who was primarily responsible for summoning and directing it.

As the historian of esotericism Joscelyn Godwin has noted, the sudden emergence of Spiritualism and Theosophy, in 1848 and 1875 respectively, marked substantial milestones in the history of magic and the occult in the modern West.[24] Certainly no other movements, organizations, or currents of thought can rival these two in terms of their breadth of popular interest and participation or their broader cultural influence. As we have seen, Spiritualism attracted many followers because it appeared to resolve the increasingly broad divide between science and religion by offering empirical proof of life after death and because its doctrines, as elaborated by Allan Kardec, corresponded neatly with the nineteenth century's faith in progress and in the perfection of humanity. A generation later, with the "culture wars" between reason and faith growing ever more bitter, Theosophy held out the promise of ancient wisdom from the mysterious Orient that could transcend the sterile binary opposition at which Western culture had arrived and create a new (or rather a new/old) higher synthesis.

At the same time, however, neither movement was without its critics. Scientific rationalists and Voltairean skeptics found the credulous Spiritualists and their *tables tournantes* easy to mock, whereas devout churchmen worried that such phenomena were the work of the Devil. Similarly, the Theosophical Society's rejection of Christianity in favor of its own idiosyncratic hodgepodge of Eastern religions, as well as the imperious personality of its founder, Helena Petrovna Blavatsky, made it suspect to many contemporaries. Such doubts and negative reactions surfaced, however, not only among those milieus that were predisposed to hostility toward esoteric organizations but also among many persons who were initially attracted to them. The occult revival of the

1880s and 1890s, although probably impossible without the prior influence of Spiritualism and Theosophy, was to a large degree a reaction against both of these movements.

The Fin-de-Siècle Occult Revival

The reaction, and the revival, led in two distinct and opposed directions. On the one hand, many scientists were intrigued by the "phenomena" produced by the Spiritualist movement, ranging from the *tables tournantes* themselves to the practice of automatic writing to the alleged clairvoyant or telekinetic powers of famous spirit mediums, such as Eusapia Palladino, and the use of new technologies, particularly photography, to attempt to record empirical evidence of the spirit world. Although many of these scientists and scholars found the Spiritualist movement foolish and misguided, they believed that the mediums had unwittingly stumbled on proof of the existence of the invisible world beyond the reach of the senses. The German philosopher Arthur Schopenhauer called animal magnetism "the most significant and pregnant of all the discoveries that have ever been made ... [I]t is really practical metaphysics."[25] Corinna Treitel argues that the neologism and apparent oxymoron "practical metaphysics" reveals why anti-materialist philosophers and scholars found Spiritualist phenomena so compelling, as these "might open a doorway to the transcendent ... [which] scientific materialists were attempting to dismiss as useless metaphysical speculation."[26]

Many of the scientists interested in spirit phenomena came together in the Society for Psychical Research, which was created by a group of Cambridge scientists and philosophers led by William Crookes, Henry Sidgwick, and others, or in its French or German equivalents led by like-minded men such as Charles Richet, Pierre Janet, Eduard von Hartmann, and Albert von Schrenck-Notzing. Although they were sometimes dismissed as overly credulous by their more skeptical scientific peers, these "psychical researchers" remained committed to scientific explanations and standards of evidence, and they gradually became convinced that the "phenomena" produced in Spiritualist séances were not physical manifestations of the spirit world but rather evidence of heretofore unsuspected faculties of the human mind. The special commission created by Louis XVI a century earlier to evaluate the claims of Franz Anton Mesmer had reached similar conclusions, but contemporaries failed to develop the implications of the commission's observation that the effects of "animal magnetism" were mental rather than physical. In the late Victorian era, however, as scholars such as Treitel, M. Brady Brower, and

Sofie Lachapelle have demonstrated, the "psychical researchers" played a critical, catalyzing role in the emergence of modern psychology.[27]

If the "psychical researchers" were particularly interested in empirically observable "phenomena," the bohemian circles of artists, dandies, and mystics whose spiritual quests gave rise to a plethora of new, mostly ephemeral, secret societies and mystical orders in the fin de siècle explicitly rejected these manifestations as crude theatrics, unworthy of the true initiate. Consequently, the esotericism of the Neo-Rosicrucians, Martinists, and members of the Golden Dawn was more secretive and subjective, based on a retreat from the physical world into the unexplored regions of the self and of individual consciousness. Informed by Neo-Platonist and Neo-Hermetic notions such as the correspondences between the macrocosm and the microcosm, the existence of other, hidden planes of being, whether in other dimensions or on distant planets, and a vitalistic vision of the cosmos as suffused throughout by hidden forces, such as the "astral light" or "elemental" beings like gnomes, sylphs, sprites, and salamanders, they believed that a retreat into absolute interiority would enable the magician to understand the hidden forces of nature, to gain access to higher knowledge unattainable by empirical, scientific means, and perhaps even to act upon the cosmos, although in largely imperceptible ways. For this reason, their magical operations were not public, physical phenomena such as levitating tables but rather private, deeply personal, and evidently quite intense experiences, such as astral projection, crystal-gazing, and the evocation of spiritual beings from other planes of existence.

The bohemian mystics of the occult revival therefore embraced the subjectivity of individual consciousness and sought out altered states of being in order to explore and expand it. Alex Owen has argued that although those members of the Golden Dawn, such as Annie Horniman and Frederick Leigh Gardner, who engaged in spiritual voyages to other planets along the "astral light" must have known that in a literal, physical sense, they never left the London house that served as their base of occult operations, they nonetheless believed strongly in the subjective reality of their experiences and in the transcendent value of the esoteric gnosis that they gained thereby.[28] Similarly, Aleister Crowley firmly believed that his magical experiences in the Algerian desert – a series of elaborate rituals and incantations followed by an act of sodomy performed on him by his neophyte, Victor Neuburg, in the guise of a satyr – had brought him into contact with alternate realities and endowed him with tremendous magical powers.[29]

In contrast to the largely rough and ready atmosphere of the Spiritualist séance, which, although generally conducted in a private home, was usually open to neophytes and curiosity-seekers and usually publicized its results (if there were any) widely, the new esoteric orders of the fin de siècle stressed secrecy, initiation, and elaborate ritual preparations as necessary prerequisites for magical operations. Much like medieval hermits and Christian mystics, many of these occultists believed that long periods of fasting, physical privation, and meditation were necessary to cultivate the mental and spiritual powers necessary for magical work. In some extreme cases, these preparations could take on strongly sadistic or masochistic overtones: Crowley subjected Neuburg to a harsh regime of fasting, isolation, and periodic scourgings in order to prepare him for initiation. Some mystics added to these preparations the use of hallucinogenic drugs, such as hashish, opium, and cocaine, which Stanislas de Guaita praised as restoring man's primeval creative faculties, but which were finally the cause of his untimely death at the age of thirty-seven.

The revival of an interest in ritual magic, shared by both the French Martinists and the British members of the Golden Dawn, was largely inspired by the writings and private teachings of a mid-century French apostate priest, Alphonse-Louis Constant, who achieved fame as an esoteric teacher and magician under the name Eliphas Levi (a Hebraization of his given names). Levi's Martinist biographer Paul Chacornac called him "the renovator of the occult tradition in France," whereas Decker, Depaulis, and Dummett, authors of a scholarly history of the Tarot deck, have written that Levi's work "formed the narrow channel through which the whole Western tradition of magic flowed to the modern era."[30] James Webb credits Levi with "almost single-handedly turning the Secret Traditions into a romantic mixture suitable for popular consumption."[31] Although the fin-de-siècle mystics who read Levi and adopted his ideas would likely have discovered the esoteric tradition through other means had he not existed, his influence on the fin-de-siècle occult revival was undeniable.

Constant, the son of a Parisian shoemaker, was born in 1810 and trained from an early age for the priesthood, but a series of romantic entanglements and an inclination toward utopian socialism led him to abandon his religious vocation by the mid-1840s. After the twin disappointments of the failure of the Revolution of 1848 and that of his marriage to the feminist writer Claude Vignon (Noémi Cadiot), Constant was introduced to esotericism by the Polish mystic Hoenë Wronski, adopted the name and the persona of the *magus* Eliphas Levi, and went into a brief exile in London. During this visit, Levi met with English occultists, thereby starting a cross-Channel communication that would last for the remainder of his life, and claimed to have conjured the spirit of the ancient Neo-Platonist Apollonius of Tyana.[32] In his later years,

Levi attracted a number of British disciples, notably Kenneth Mackenzie and Mrs. Hutchinson, the wife of the English consul in Paris, and these personal connections, along with his writings on the theory and practice of magic, helped ensure his influence on both sides of the English Channel.

Levi's magical theories, elaborated in the dense and rambling tomes *Dogme et rituel de la haute magie* and *La clef des grands mystères*, offered a synthesis of existing esoteric philosophy, along with a variety of new additions. His system was predicated on principles that Faivre has identified as central to the Western esoteric tradition, such as the notion of correspondences between the macrocosm and the microcosm, the possibility of transmutation, and the continuous secret transmission of the *prisca theologia*. However, Levi also added new elements that, although not part of Renaissance Hermetic philosophy or German Romantic *Naturphilosophie*, were to be broadly influential in the fin-de-siècle occult revival. One of these was his association of the Tarot deck with the Kabbalah, because of the coincidence between the twenty-two trump cards and the twenty-two letters of the Hebrew alphabet. Although the Tarot, originally a simple playing card game, had been used in divination since at least the late eighteenth century, it was Levi who attributed symbolic meanings to each card and made the Tarot central to magical practice. Another of Levi's central contributions was the concept of the *lumière astrale* or "astral light," a modification of Mesmer's "great magnetic agent" or of the "ether" of early modern scientists, who assumed that objects that exerted force on one another had to be physically in contact. According to Levi, the "astral light" suffused the universe with vital forces, connecting the macrocosm to the microcosm and enabling the one to influence the other.[33] Although Levi's body of work was unsystematic and somewhat muddled, he bequeathed to the following generation an elaborate and flexible system of divination based on the Tarot, which contributed to both elite philosophizing and popular fortune-telling in the following decades, and a theory of magic offering pseudoscientific explanations of how magical rites, talismans, and incantations could impact the physical world and connect multiple planes of existence.

When, in the 1880s, both the British and the French Neo-Rosicrucians broke with Blavatsky's Theosophical Society because of the latter's rejection of Christianity and emphasis on Eastern religions and sought instead to recover a distinctly Western and Judeo-Christian esoteric tradition, Levi's body of work offered them exactly what they were seeking. John Warne Monroe has written that Guaita and Encausse were originally attracted to the Theosophical Society, but that "they found the Theosophical emphasis on non-Western religious traditions disconcerting," and he notes that when

Blavatsky and Olcott attempted to impose greater doctrinal unity on the Paris chapters of the society, "this local variant, which stressed the importance of Christ and the central role of France in humanity's spiritual development, proved too deep-rooted to eliminate."[34] The French "Catholic Rosicrucian" Joséphin Péladan declared in 1890, "I could not take occultism in its entirety with me to mass, and I refuse to rub shoulders with spiritualism, masonry, or Buddhism."[35] Also symbolic of this Western, Christian orientation in the fin-de-siècle occult revival is Edouard Schuré's treatise *The Great Initiates*, which presents ancient Hinduism, the Egyptian mysteries, Greek Platonism and Pythagoreanism, and the teachings of Moses as diverse manifestations of an underlying esoteric wisdom that finds its most complete expression in the life and teachings of Jesus Christ.[36] This view was, of course, not Schuré's innovation; on the contrary, as D. P. Walker has shown, it formed a common thread with Renaissance Hermetism and Neo-Platonism from Marsilio Ficino in the fifteenth century to Athanasius Kircher in the seventeenth.[37]

It is surely significant that the occult revivals of the 1880s in both Britain and France, independently of one another and apparently without any direct coordination between them, each appealed to the seventeenth-century Central European legend of Christian Rosenkreutz and the Rosicrucian brotherhood, who styled themselves as latter-day Rosicrucians and claimed a direct line of intellectual descent through initiation from their early modern predecessors. Frances Yates has argued that the Rosicrucian manifestoes, which appeared in the context of the wars of religion and bitter confessional conflict between Catholics and Protestants, offered a message of harmony and fraternity founded on esoteric wisdom and the quest for self-perfection, expressed metaphorically in alchemical terms. The fin-de-siècle Neo-Rosicrucians, like their predecessors, found the intellectual culture of their age similarly fractured, although in their case between the opposing poles of scientific materialism and religious dogmatism, and hoped that ancient esoteric wisdom could restore wholeness to Western culture and usher in a new golden age of society.

There were other parallels between the seventeenth-century Rosicrucians and their fin-de-siècle heirs. In both cases, the community of initiates was a textual creation before it became a social one, as the founders, or "restorers" of the "traditions," encountered and then propagated their ideas first in writing, before attempting to (re-)create actual secret societies based on rites of initiation. Yates demonstrates that the two founding manifestoes of Rosicrucianism, the *Confessio* and the *Fama fraternitas*, predated any actual Rosicrucian organizations, and that many of the readers inspired by them sought first to make contact with the supposedly already extant secret brotherhoods before subsequently settling for founding new societies of their own upon Rosicrucian principles.[38] As will be seen later in the chapter, the founders of the Hermetic Order of the Golden Dawn claimed to be restoring a long-forgotten Rosicrucian sect whose rituals they had rediscovered, a claim that enabled their new organization to challenge the then-thriving Theosophical Society of Madame Blavatsky with an appeal to an ancient and venerable tradition of which they were the sole custodians. Similarly, Stanislas de Guaita founded his *Ordre cabbalistique de la Rose-Croix* on principles he encountered not through personal initiation, but rather through his reading of the seventeenth-century Rosicrucian manifestoes and other Hermetic and esoteric texts, although his collaborator, Gérard Encausse (better known as Papus), claimed to have received direct initiation in the occult mysteries from a chain of initiates stretching back to the eighteenth-century founders of Martinism.

The trope of the "unknown superiors" who are believed to be at the pinnacle of esoteric secret societies was another element introduced by the seventeenth-century Rosicrucians, popularized by eighteenth-century esoteric Freemasonry, and widely adopted by the various sects and movements of the fin-de-siècle occult revival. H. P. Blavatsky claimed to be in regular communication with her Indian "Mahatma" Koot Hoomi, whereas Joseph-Alexandre Saint-Yves d'Alveydre claimed a telepathic link to the Grand Lama of Tibet.[39] Samuel Liddell MacGregor Mathers, the increasingly erratic and authoritarian leader of the Golden Dawn, cited his personal obedience to the unknown superiors of the Order as a defense against fellow initiates who questioned his authority, and he warned that the psychological impact of being in the presence of such great magicians was such that "I cannot conceive a much less advanced Initiate being able to support such a strain even for five minutes, without Death ensuing."[40] Although the claim of the existence of such powerful secret superiors lent cachet and authority to small, marginal esoteric sects, the reality was frequently more prosaic; Victor-Emile Michelet, a follower of Guaita and Encausse, later confessed that "in reality, the six unknown members [of the leadership committee of Guaita's Rose-Croix] never existed."[41]

The most famous magical society produced by the fin-de-siècle occult revival was the Hermetic Order of the Golden Dawn.[42] Although it existed for little more than a decade, the Golden Dawn attracted some of the most colorful, prominent, and notorious personalities of late Victorian Britain, gave rise to several notable scandals, and ultimately collapsed into public acrimony. The Order was the brainchild of two members of an already existing esoteric society called the Societas Rosicruciana in Anglia, the physician

William Wynn Westcott and the charismatic bohemian intellectual Samuel Liddell MacGregor Mathers. Westcott claimed to have discovered in August 1887 an ancient Rosicrucian manuscript written in cipher containing descriptions of five quasi-Masonic rituals for a previously unknown secret society that was similar to esoteric Freemasonry but admitting both women and men. After translating the manuscript and recreating the rituals described therein, Westcott learned that an authentic ancient Rosicrucian society called *Die Goldene Dämmerung* still existed in Germany and requested and received from one of its leaders, a certain Fräulein Anna Sprengel, permission to establish an English chapter of the order, translating its name as the "golden dawn." Along with a third esoteric Freemason, the Reverend A. F. A. Woodford, who died soon thereafter, Westcott and Mathers founded a new initiatory society, whose members studied the Hermetic corpus, the Kabbalah, astrology, alchemy, and Tarot divination, among other esoteric subjects, and passed, through a series of examinations from being neophytes to advanced degrees that were numbered from zero to ten. These degrees were grouped into a relatively inclusive "first order," a more secretive "second order," into which the most promising adepts were initiated, and a "third order" (that did not actually exist) of super-magicians, hidden from the eyes of the profane but allegedly offering secret guidance to the visible masters of the order.

Despite its small size (with never more than a few hundred initiates) and secrecy, the Golden Dawn quickly became one of the most prominent esoteric societies in Britain. Its most famous convert was the Irish poet and playwright William Butler Yeats, who was among the leaders of the society throughout the 1890s, attracting other members of the artistic community, such as the actress Florence Farr and the patron of the arts Annie Horniman, to join as well. Other notable members included Arthur Edward Waite, who was the author of a number of works on magic and esotericism and the designer, along with the art nouveau artist Pamela Colman Smith, of a new Tarot deck (their vivid illustrations and rich symbolism have made it perhaps the most widely used fortune-telling tool in the contemporary English-speaking world), and Aleister Crowley, about whom more will be said shortly.

The history of the Golden Dawn was conflictive from the outset, as might perhaps be expected of a very small organization with a large proportion of dynamic, strong-willed personalities who were more suited to leading or debating than to passive obedience. These problems worsened in 1892 when Mathers moved from London to Paris, the home of his wife, Mina, sister of the philosopher Henri Bergson, yet insisted on maintaining autocratic control over the Golden Dawn. For four years, the Matherses lived in Paris in genteel poverty, supported by their benefactor Annie Horniman. In 1896, however, Horniman withdrew her financial support, and Mathers retaliated by expelling her from the Order, despite the objections of Yeats and others. Westcott, under pressure from his superiors in the Coroner's Office, resigned from the Order in 1897, removing the last moderating influence between Mathers in Paris and the remaining leadership in London. Seeking to discredit his erstwhile rival, Mathers wrote to Florence Farr in 1900 that Westcott had never been in contact with the secret chiefs of the Rosicrucian Order and had forged the letters from "Fräulein Sprengel" authorizing the creation of the British chapter of the Golden Dawn. This revelation backfired badly, however, seeing as Mathers had shared complicity in Westcott's deception, and the historic legitimacy of the entire Order was thereby called into question. The feud between Mathers and the remainder of the leadership worsened thereafter, and it peaked in an April 1900 confrontation in which Crowley, on Mathers's orders, seized possession of the Order's meeting hall, wearing kilts and a ritual mask. Crowley was soon expelled from the building by the police, but the Golden Dawn never recovered from the schism that followed. Soon after, in 1901, a scandal erupted when two supposed masters of the Order raped a young woman in what they claimed was a ritual of initiation. Although no actual leaders of the Golden Dawn appear to have been implicated in the crime, the resultant scandal led most of its prominent members to withdraw from active participation, and the society withered thereafter. Although several successor groups lingered on until at least the First World War, the Golden Dawn's moment of splendor had passed.

The association of magic with immorality and aberrant sexuality in the public imagination, to which the scandal of 1901 contributed greatly, was advanced still further by the notorious acts of Aleister Crowley. Although some latter-day admirers of the Golden Dawn insist that Crowley was never truly a member of the Order (he was, in fact, initiated by Mathers despite the objections of its other leaders), he is without question the most (in)famous of the early twentieth-century magicians. After leaving the Golden Dawn, Crowley was initiated into the German Ordo Templi Orientis in 1912 and subsequently founded his own Abbey of Thelema, which apparently more than lived up to its Rabelaisian name. Adopting the new titles "Baphomet" (the goat-headed, hermaphroditic demon supposedly worshipped by the medieval Templars and pictured on the fifteenth trump of the Tarot deck, commonly called "the Devil") and "the Beast 666," Crowley embraced blasphemy and Satanism, inaugurating a new form of "Magick" involving blood, excrement, and sadomasochistic sexual rituals. Dubbed "the wickedest man in the world" by the British press, Crowley attracted a few disciples and admirers, both in his own lifetime and thereafter (including the British rock star Ozzy Osbourne and his band Black Sabbath, who immortalized him in song), but he also did more than any other figure to discredit magic, esotericism, and the occult in the eyes of most of the general public.[43] With Crowley, the fin-de-siècle occult revival entered a blind alley, from which it would only emerge much later, and was transformed into a very different sort of "new Age" spirituality.

Magic and Modernity: The Lure of the Occult

Why were so many of the brightest and most original minds of the fin de siècle attracted to magic and the occult? In his 1974 lecture "The Occult and the Modern World," Mircea Eliade attributes the enduring popularity of astrology, divination, and other "occult" practices to their "parareligious function," which responds to moral and metaphysical questions that modern science has by and large not deigned to answer. Eliade argues that contemporary initiates, repulsed by the notion of a disenchanted world and an existence without transcendent meaning, embrace the notion that "the universe moves according to a preestablished plan ... The ultimate goal is secret or beyond human understanding; but at least it gives meaning to a cosmos regarded by most scientists as the result of blind hazard, and it gives sense to the human existence declared by Sartre to be *de trop*."[44]

The declarations of fin-de-siècle dabblers and enthusiasts of the occult confirm Eliade's argument. The novelist Joris-Karl Huysmans was drawn to occultism and magic out of disillusionment with late nineteenth-century positivism and scientific materialism, a stage in a personal spiritual quest that ultimately led him from materialism back to a particularly rigorous, anti-modern Catholicism. Huysmans, whose novel *Là-bas* was perhaps the most enduring literary monument to fin-de-siècle occultism, told his friend Gustave Guiches in 1887 of his thirst for "genuine occultism – not above but beneath or beside or beyond reality! ... [T]here's a mystery there which ... haunts me."[45] In his letter of introduction to the apostate priest and cult leader Joseph Boullan (represented in the novel as the good magician Dr. Johannes), Huysmans wrote that "I want to show Zola, Charcot, the spiritualists, and the rest that nothing has been explained ... to show that all the materialist theories ... are false."[46] Although Huysmans was, at most, a "fellow traveler" of the fin-de-siècle occult revival, similar sentiments were expressed by those of his contemporaries who were most deeply engaged in esoteric pursuits. Oswald Wirth, a Swiss hypnotist who became Guaita's closest disciple in the fin-de-siècle Martinist Order, later wrote that he was drawn to esotericism out of a sense of existential longing and deep alienation from the sharply polarized intellectual world of the fin de siècle. "Why struggle to live with the perspective of ending in nothingness?" he wrote. "A materialist consequent with his doctrines has the choice between suicide and the unbridled pursuit of his appetites.... If our ephemeral existence has no consequences, why should we bother?"[47]

If, as I have argued elsewhere,[48] the spirit of the post-Enlightenment wave of Illuminism and esoteric Freemasonry was Faustian, seeking to unlock the hidden mysteries of the universe through obscure and forbidden knowledge, the spirit of fin-de-siècle occultism was Nietzschean, seeing in ritual magic and esoteric study a means to the self-cultivation of an artistic and intellectual elite. Victor-Emile Michelet's memoir of the French occult revival of the fin de siècle stresses the affinities between the magician's quest for occult gnosis and the artist's pursuit of the ideal; he wrote: "The initiate who attempts the Great Work, by whatever means, is an artist, a creator, a poet."[49] These concerns are made most explicit by the French "Catholic Rosicrucian" Joséphin Péladan, who wrote in his treatise on practical magic, *Comment on devient mage*, that the true meaning of life was "to make a masterpiece of the block of soul which God has given him [or her] to labor over." Addressing himself to aspiring magicians, Péladan declared:

> Until now Hermetic pedagogy has told you of omnipotence, of making gold, of talismans and charms. These are all impostures; you will never be more than the spiritual king of a body and a soul, but if you succeed, if your mind makes of your body a slave, and of your soul a virtuous minister, then you will act upon others to the same degree to which you act upon yourself.[50]

Péladan went on to define magic as "the art of the sublimation of man" and declared that great geniuses, such as Leonardo da Vinci or Richard Wagner, were divine messengers beyond terrestrial morality, for "the earth does not produce these beings who create like God."[51] Péladan, whose personal cult combined traditional Catholicism with an apotheosis of the great men of the past, defined greatness in largely aesthetic terms, declaring that the *magus* must have "a horror for the mediocre, and a perception of the sublime."[52]

Péladan's onetime collaborator and subsequent rival, Stanislas de Guaita, held a similar view of magic as a means to self-realization. In a particularly megalomaniacal moment, Guaita proclaimed that the study of the occult sciences permitted the master magician "the exercise of a relative omnipotence, delegated from the power of God ... It is the taking possession, by right of conquest, of the mysteries of Heaven." Guaita contrasted this "active reintegration" of humans into their original "Adamic faculties" favorably to the "passive reintegration" of saints and religious ascetics, calling the former "more advantageous, richer in prerogatives."[53] A contemporary critic, Fernand Divoire, recognized the elitist and antidemocratic overtones in the magical quest of Guaita and Péladan, particularly in the latter's contention that the magician and other men of genius were above ordinary moral laws. Calling Eliphas Levi "Nietzschean avant le mot," Divoire concluded: "No, one should not become a *magus*. One should not sacrifice one's life to the pursuit of an illusory scepter. One should not have the goal of leaving humanity in order to dominate it."[54] Divoire found fin-de-siècle occultism Nietzschean in its entirety, calling it "truly a new religion, the old religion of the man-god, adapted to contemporary tastes."[55]

It would be incorrect, however, to suggest that the fin-de-siècle occult revival was a purely individualistic quest for personal self-cultivation or self-aggrandizement. Many of those who were drawn to esoteric movements, as we have seen in the previous sections of this chapter, were deeply alienated from what they perceived as a decadent, deeply fractured modern civilization caught between the extremes of outmoded religious dogmatism and the sort of simplistic materialism that Flaubert satirized in the character of the pharmacist Homais. They hoped, as Treitel has written of the colonial propagandist-turned-Theosophist Wilhelm Hübbe-Schleiden, "to reform society by first changing individuals from the inside."[56] The two leading figures of the French fin-de-siècle occult revival, Stanislas de Guaita and Gérard Encausse, expressed in their writings the hope that the recovery of ancient esoteric wisdom could restore wholeness and harmony to a deeply fractured modern world. Encausse, trained as a medical doctor but drawn by his own temperament and interests toward esoteric and magical pursuits, wrote that "materialism has given all that can be expected of it" and argued that "if we deign for a moment no longer to believe in indefinite progress ... we will discover that the colossal civilizations of the past also possessed a Science, Universities, and Schools."[57] Similarly, Guaita wrote in the introduction to his 1891 treatise *Le temple de Satan* that "the intellectual world is in complete disorder," signaled by "the triumph of the worse epidemic, that of agnosticism." Guaita praised the civilizations of remote antiquity for being "based on the unity of Synthesis and not on the fragments of Analysis," in which "religion consecrated the teachings of Gnosis, while Gnosis verified the dogmas of religion." "The men of that blessed age were giants," Guaita concluded, "we are but pygmies ... At the sight of our rotten society, Rama or

Zoroaster would scoff, if they did not rather feel the urge to weep for us and our presumptuous decadence."[58]

Not all of the occult enthusiasts of the fin de siècle shared Guaita's cultural pessimism; on the contrary, many of them, particularly Spiritualists and Theosophists, believed that society was on the threshold of dramatic progress and spiritual regeneration. Most of them, progressives and pessimists alike, believed that the secret and arcane wisdom proffered by esoteric movements and societies held the key to restoring wholeness and authenticity to a deeply fractured and alienating modern society. In fact, it was, I would argue, the paradox between the perception of present decadence and the hope for imminent regeneration that gave fin-de-siècle occultism its unique character. If fin-de-siècle occultists despaired of a purely materialist modern civilization and looked longingly backward to an idealized past, many of them also, as early as the 1880s, heralded the dawning of the Age of Aquarius.

Suggestions for Future Research

Recent scholarship on the fin-de-siècle occult revival has begun to restore its centrality to the cultural and intellectual genesis of high modernity. Alex Owen and Corinna Treitel have highlighted the connections between esotericism and artistic modernism in Britain and Germany, respectively, and John Warne Monroe, Sofie Lachapelle, and M. Brady Brower have argued for its importance in the emergence of modern psychology and its conception of a "multivalent self" ridden with unconscious drives and conflicting forces. Treitel also argues for close affinities between the occult sciences and the *Lebensreform* movement of the early twentieth century in Germany, encompassing such practices as vegetarianism, nudism, homeopathic medicine, and the valorization of homosexuality as a natural and legitimate expression of desire.[59]

Certain connections, such as the importance of the Golden Dawn in the career of the Irish poet W. B. Yeats, or the role of "psychical researchers" such as William Crookes in the emergence of modern psychology, are now generally established. However, there is much more that could be done to examine the "ripple effect" of fin-de-siècle occultism on the broader society beyond the small circle of active adepts. Many fin-de-siècle artists, writers, and intellectuals dabbled in the occult during the 1880s and 1890s, including the playwright George Bernard Shaw, the novelist Paul Adam, and the composer Erik Satie, whereas many others, such as the poets Stéphane Mallarmé, Arthur Rimbaud, and Rainer Maria Rilke and the painters Gustave Moreau, Odilon Redon, and Wassily Kandinsky, although not direct participants in the occult revival, incorporated esoteric themes into their works. One can also extend the circle to include close family members: the sister of philosopher Henri Bergson and the wife of novelist Oscar Wilde were active in the Golden Dawn. Although neither of these men seems to have been particularly convinced by occultism, it would be instructive to explore how, if at all, their own work was affected by their close encounters with the movement.

The First World War has often been taken as marking the end of the fin-de-siècle occult revival, and for good reason. Much as the French Revolution brought to a close the age of late-Enlightenment Illuminism and esoteric Freemasonry, the Great War claimed the lives of many occult adepts and enthusiasts, scattered and scarred many of the others, left Europe more bitterly divided along national lines than ever before, and brought with it so much suffering and death that such pursuits as crystal-gazing, astral travel, and ritual magic can only have seemed like frivolous indulgences suitable for the levity of the Belle Époque but unworthy of the gravity of the post-war moment. The timelines of intellectual and cultural history do not divide themselves as neatly into discrete periods as does that of political history, however, and some, at least, of the surviving members of esoteric orders like the Martinists, the Golden Dawn, or the Theosophical Society sought to rekindle the flames of these fading movements in the 1920s and beyond. We know relatively little, however, of the aftereffects of fin-de-siècle occultism in the interwar period. Many of the most noteworthy cultural manifestations of the period – Surrealism, Freudian and especially Jungian psychoanalysis, and the plethora of movements, from Futurism to Négritude, that celebrated the vital, the primitive, and the irrational over the allegedly cold, sterile rationalism of the Enlightenment and Positivist traditions – bear at least a sort of "elective affinity" with the occult revival of the fin-de-siècle years. It would be interesting and instructive to see whether, and to what degree, the legacies of nineteenth-century elite magic played a role in their formulation, dissemination, and reception. If this is true for the interwar modernist avant-garde, it is all the more true for those new religious movements – from Wicca to various forms of New Age spirituality – that emerged in Europe and the United States after the Second World War.

With the exception of Spiritualism and Theosophy, both of which were transnational from the outset, there has been surprisingly little study of how the different occult revivals of the fin de siècle were related to one another, even though the leader of the Golden Dawn, S. L. MacGregor Mathers, long resided in Paris and was married to a Frenchwoman (Mina Bergson, sister of the philosopher Henri), the Paris-based occultists Guaita and Wirth were equally at home in French and German circles, and both Gérard Encausse and the French faith healer "Maitre Philippe" traveled to the Russian imperial court at St. Petersburg. Such influences across national boundaries could be tracked in several ways: through the history of personal interactions between occultists and their fellow travelers; through the history of the book, by documenting the translation and circulation of esoteric texts from one country to another; or through a "history of ideas" approach, examining in detail the development of esoteric beliefs and practices and tracing the lines of their transmission.

Another potentially fruitful line of inquiry, which I have explored although certainly not exhausted in my own monograph, is the politics of fin-de-siècle occultism. Although Nicholas Goodrick-Clarke has made a persuasive case for the importance of fin-de-siècle Ariosophy to the witches' brew of pan-Germanism, racism, and metahistorical speculation that ultimately gave rise to National Socialism and documented links between various contemporary esoteric movements and the radical right, it would clearly be inaccurate to label occultism tout court as racist, reactionary, or proto-fascist.[60] Numerous scholars have demonstrated the affinities between mid-century Spiritualism and the republican left in Second Empire and Third Republic France, and H. P. Blavatsky (and even more so her disciple Annie Besant) combined an admiration for Indian spirituality with criticism of British imperial rule of the subcontinent. Similarly, Joseph-Alexandre Saint-Yves d'Alveydre situated an imaginary utopia of initiates in a hidden corner of British India (rather similar to the supposedly unconquered village of Astérix the Gaul celebrated in a French comic strip) and sketched a model for a benevolent, paternalist world government that he called the "synarchy." There were certainly suggestive connections between Martinism and the French integralist right – Guaita was a lifelong friend of the anti-Dreyfusard intellectual Maurice Barrès and another prominent anti-Dreyfusard, Gaston Méry, took an active interest in occult phenomena, even launching a new journal, *L'echo du Merveilleux*, to publicize them. It remains to be explored, however, how substantial these connections were and what light, if any, they can shed on either the development of fin-de-siècle occultism or the rise of the radical right during the same period.

The national and cultural politics of the Golden Dawn are particularly ripe for further exploration. The cofounder and dominant figure of the Order, S. L. MacGregor Mathers, invented a false Scottish aristocratic pedigree (calling himself the Comte de Glenstrae), affected staunch Jacobite political sympathies and militaristic poses, developed a fascination with Celtic mysticism and mythology (angrily rebutting W. B. Yeats's reminder that the epic poetry of Ossian had been proven a forgery), and drew attention to himself in Paris by dressing in kilts. Yeats himself blended Celtic mysticism with Neo-Rosicrucian doctrine, and his Irish patriotism and yearning for a new age of cultural rebirth remained closely intertwined, although he became wary of Mathers's Jacobite leanings and autocratic tendencies. By contrast, Maud Gonne, an object of Yeats's affection who briefly flirted with membership in the Golden Dawn, rejected the order because of its links to Freemasonry and therefore, in her view, with British imperialism. As the Golden Dawn flourished at a moment in which the Irish Home Rule issue convulsed British politics, the British Empire was nearing its zenith, and the Indian National Congress was coming into being, such a reexamination would, I believe, be well worth the effort.

Finally, although this is hardly an unexplored topic, there is undoubtedly more that could be said with regard to the relationship between magic and issues of gender and sexuality. As noted earlier in the chapter, spirit medium-ship was often perceived in the nineteenth century as a particularly feminine gift, because of the nervous sensibility that was also believed to make women uniquely susceptible to "hysteria," and certain mediums seem to have made use of their faculties to advance their own views and interests in a way that would otherwise have been closed to them because of their gender. The asso-ciation of mediumship with femininity was so strong that male spirit medi-ums, such as Daniel Dunglas Home, were often mocked as effeminate and their sexual orientation called into question.[61] By contrast, the French Neo-Rosicrucians, particularly Guaita, defined their magical quest as a particularly masculine one, which they contrasted to frivolous and feminine Spiritualism.

Both of these positions are founded on the normative and essentialist notions of femininity and masculinity that were unthinkingly shared by most nineteenth-century Europeans. There has been less study of the ways in which magic destabilized traditional gender norms. Randall Styers has observed that the figure of the magician "violates the basic norms of modern, rationalized, masculine, and heterosexual subjectivity ... the magician is, in a word, queer," a double entendre that suggests both the magician's marginal social status and his or her defiance of traditional gender norms.[62] Aleister Crowley is, of course, the most prominent example of a magician who openly flouted conventional gender norms, embracing bisexuality as a higher state of being that synthe-sized both masculine and feminine identities. Alex Owen, observing that the scandal involving Oscar Wilde had brought the issue of "unnatural vice" to the center of public discourse in late Victorian Britain, has noted that the enemies of fin-de-siècle British occultism used charges of pederasty against some of its leaders, including, notably, Crowley himself and the prominent Theosophist Charles Leadbeater, to discredit the enterprise as a whole.[63] Naomi Andrews has analyzed the ways in which French romantic socialism embraced the figure of the androgyne as representing future social regeneration through the transcendence of the male/female duality, and Owen has also noted that both the Theosophists and members of the Golden Dawn celebrated the "divine hermaphrodite" as an ideal toward which both men and women should aspire, for it represents the original perfection of humanity prior to the separation of Adam and Eve and their Fall from Paradise.[64] The fin de siècle was also the period in which early sex researchers and reformers such as Magnus Hirschfeld and Havelock Ellis began to defend homosexuality as a "third sex" and a valid and natural lifestyle, rather than as a perversion of "normal" sexuality. It would be interesting to explore whether and to what degree the occult revival provided a forum for fin-de-siècle gays and lesbians to define and defend their gender identities in a more positive light than that allowed by mainstream society.

Whatever directions future research on the topic of elite magic and the occult in the nineteenth century may take, it is unlikely that twenty-first-century scholars will ever again be able to dismiss it as an aberration in the grand narrative of progress, secularization, and the "disenchantment of the world," as Max Weber famously did at the start of the twentieth century. On the contrary, as Treitel has argued, magic and occultism have been central to the elaboration of "alternative modernities," which were and continue to be constitutive of contemporary society and culture.[65] The Western world's fascination with magic, unexplained "paranormal" phenomena, and allegedly ancient and esoteric wisdom is neither a vestigial relic of a bygone, superstitious age nor a sign of contemporary malaise and cultural decadence. Rather, it is a central, if often unacknowledged, part of the Western tradition itself, the exploration of which continues to provide a rich and nuanced understanding of Europe's past and present alike.

Notes

1. Nye, *Masculinity and Male Codes of Honor*.
2. On the feud between Guaita and Bois regarding Boullan's death, see Laver, *The First Decadent*; Joany Bricaud, *L'abbé Boullan (Docteur Johannes de Là-Bas)*; and Harvey, *Beyond Enlightenment*.
3. Styers, *Making Magic*, 13.
4. Kselman, *Miracles and Prophecies in Nineteenth Century France*; Jonas, *France and the Cult of the Sacred Heart*; Blackbourn, *Marpingen*.
5. On this point, see Styers, *Making Magic*, 36–38.
6. For this interpretation, see Weber, *Peasants into Frenchmen*; Thomas, *Religion and the Decline of Magic*.

7. Styers, *Making Magic*, 19.
8. Webb, *Occult Underground*, 1.
9. Faivre, *Theosophy, Imagination, Tradition*, xiv.
10. Ibid., xxi–xxiv.
11. For Court de Gebelin and Etteilla's "Egyptian" theory of the Tarot, see Harvey, *Beyond Enlightenment*, as well as Decker, Depaulis, and Dummett, *Wicked Pack of Cards*. For *Egyptomanie* more generally, see Iversen, *The Myth of Egypt*; and Curran, *The Egyptian Renaissance*.
12. For the origins of Freemasonry, see Stevenson, *The Origins of Freemasonry*; and Jacob, *Living the Enlightenment*.
13. For the Rosicrucian manifestoes, see Yates, *Rosicrucian Enlightenment*. For early modern German esotericism, see Faivre, *Theosophy, Imagination, Tradition*.
14. For Franz Mesmer and his reception in late Old Regime France, see Darnton, *Mesmerism and the End of the Enlightenment*. For the subsequent development of "animal magnetism" and "magnetic somnambulism" in France after Mesmer, see Edelman, *Voyantes, guérisseuses et visionnaires*.
15. For the religious and metaphysical debates of the Enlightenment in France and elsewhere, see Israel, *Radical Enlightenment*; and Jacob, *Living the Enlightenment*.
16. Treitel, *Science for the Soul*, 34–35.
17. On Martinès de Pasqually and Louis-Claude de Saint-Martin, see Harvey, *Beyond Enlightenment*; von Rijnberk, *Un thaumaturge au XVIIIe siècle*; and Le Forestier, *La Franc-Maçonnerie Templière*.
18. For "magnetic somnambulism" in France prior to the arrival of American Spiritualism, see Edelman, *Voyantes, guérisseuses et visionnaires*, esp. 15–73.
19. Sharp, "Rational Religion, Irrational Science," 208, 224. See also Sharp, *Secular Spirituality*.
20. Edelman, *Voyantes, guérisseuses et visionnaires*, 122.
21. For the history and doctrines of the Theosophical Society, see Blavatsky, *An Abridgement of the Secret Doctrine*; and Dixon, *Divine Feminine*.
22. Cited in Treitel, *Science for the Soul*, 66.
23. Faivre, *Access to Western Esotericism*, 100–102.
24. Godwin, *The Theosophical Enlightenment*, 187.
25. Cited in Treitel, *Science for the Soul*, 36.
26. Treitel, *Science for the Soul*, 36.
27. Treitel, *Science for the Soul*; Brower, *Unruly Spirits*; Lachapelle, *Investigating the Supernatural*.
28. Owen, *Place of Enchantment*, 1–3.
29. Ibid., 195–202.
30. Decker, Depaulis, and Dummett, *Wicked Pack of Cards*, 169.
31. Webb, *Occult Underground*, 257.

32. Information taken from McIntosh, *Eliphas Levi and the French Occult Revival*, 74–77, 89–91, 100–103.
33. McIntosh, *Eliphas Levi and the French Occult Revival*, 148–150.
34. Monroe, "Evidence of Things Not Seen," 304. See also Monroe, *Laboratories of Faith*.
35. Cited in McIntosh, *Eliphas Levi and the French Occult Revival*, 171.
36. Schuré, *The Great Initiates*.
37. Walker, *The Ancient Theology*.
38. Yates, *Rosicrucian Enlightenment*.
39. Cited in Webb, *Occult Underground*, 271–272.
40. S. L. MacGregor Mathers, October 29, 1896 manifesto, cited in Howe, *Magicians of the Golden Dawn*, 130.
41. Michelet, *Les compagnons de la hiérophanie*, 23.
42. The following account of the rise and decline of the Hermetic Order of the Golden Dawn is taken from Owen, *Place of Enchantment*; Harper, *Yeats's Golden Dawn*; and Howe, *Magicians of the Golden Dawn*.
43. This discussion of Aleister Crowley's career is taken primarily from Owen, *Place of Enchantment*.
44. Eliade, *Occultism, Witchcraft, and Cultural Fashions*, 61.
45. Cited in McIntosh, *Eliphas Levi and the French Occult Revival*, 178.
46. Ibid., 185.
47. Wirth, *Stanislas de Guaita, l'occultisme vécu*, 70.
48. Harvey, *Beyond Enlightenment*, 9.
49. Michelet, *Les compagnons de la hiérophanie*, 12.
50. Péladan, *Comment on devient mage*, 23, 27.
51. Ibid., 135, 200.
52. Ibid., 215.
53. de Guaita, *La clef de la magie noire*, 205–207.
54. Divoire, *Faut-il devenir mage?*, 51, 59.
55. Ibid., 67.
56. Treitel, *Science for the Soul*, 90.
57. Papus (Gérard Encausse), *Le Tarot des Bohémiens*, 15.
58. de Guaita, *Le temple de Satan*, 13–15.
59. On this point, see Treitel, *Science for the Soul*, 68–76, 154–161.
60. Goodrick-Clarke, *The Occult Roots of Nazism*. By contrast, Corinna Treitel argues that Ariosophy formed only a small and unrepresentative part of fin-de-siècle German occultism.
61. Monroe, "Evidence of Things Not Seen," 127–128.
62. Styers, *Making Magic*, 191.
63. Owen, *Place of Enchantment*, 104–111.
64. Andrews, *Socialism's Muse*; Owen, *Place of Enchantment*, 108–111.
65. Treitel, *Science for the Soul*, 51.

Chapter 19

Magic in the Postcolonial Americas

RAQUEL ROMBERG

A Brief Introduction

The first time I saw the altar of a *bruja* (witch-healer) in Puerto Rico, I was astounded by the bizarre mishmash of Catholic saints and African- and Amerindian-looking deities side by side with a Buddha and a chromolitho-graph of a blonde Jesus surrounded by all sorts of tall, colored candles. Hanging from a large bronze cross, I also noticed a small packet, obsessively wrapped with a cord – a magic work, I later learned, that had been left there to be empowered by the cross (Figure 19.1). What was the meaning of this carefully displayed, yet, to my view, incongruent configuration of icons and religious symbols that had crossed geographical, temporal, and, most impor-tantly, cultural boundaries?

These apparently incongruous mixtures – what for many would be exam-ples of syncretism or creolization – tell just one side of the story, as will become clearer later in the chapter. They could be seen as sediments comprising the strata of past and present ritual practices, the products of recurrent, non-official, irreverent religious appropriations of hegemonic religious symbols, rather than just mixtures. Elsewhere I have characterized these power-laden processes as "ritual piracy" as an alternative, and more historically precise, way of discussing "creolization" processes and creole (vernacular) religions (Romberg 2005b, 2011c). The other story that creole religions tells has to do with the rewriting of these harsh creolization histories in ways that reflect the experiences and agency of their practitioners in the present. The shape and form of altars today may reveal to the ethnographically curious, then, not only the particular ritual practices of their owners, but they may also, in a broader sense, manifest the layered histories of volatile religious, cultural, economic, and political encounters in the Americas and their ongoing reinter-pretation.[1] In this latter sense, as will be outlined in this chapter, they provide a window to both those embodied, counterhegemonic histories that otherwise

FIGURE 19.1. Magic work hanging from the cross.

would have likely escaped the explorations of cultural historians and anthropologists (cf. Stoller 1995; Romberg 2011a) and those more consciously intentional self-displays of politically minded practitioners.[2]

Several contemporary creole vernacular religions such as Cuban Santería (Lucumí), Abakuá, and Palo Monte; Brazilian Candomblé, Macumba, and Umbanda; Haitian Vodou; and Puerto Rican *brujería* have persisted centuries of colonial and postcolonial persecution. This persistence suggests that, in fact, magic – understood as the illicit summoning of supernatural entities to aid in human affairs, in opposition to such summoning by the hegemonic official religion – has never completely disappeared in the Americas, even though it went underground and camouflaged its faces at times and redefined its terms and meaning at others.[3] Despite, or perhaps because of, countless attempts to extirpate these vernacular religions, whether in the name of religion during colonial times or in the name of progress in the post-independence era, magic has persisted to live under various, more tolerable, guises until today in the protected worlds of global tourism, music performances, and art museums.

Even if an engagement with disenchantment and re-enchantment theories of modernity is outside the scope of this chapter, addressing theories

and discourses of modernity is inevitable when discussing nineteenth- and
twentieth-century magic. Just as the Enlightenment's opposition between
magic and reason has served to define the meaning of each since the seventeenth century, the opposition itself has subsequently taken a life of its
own and developed new oppositions over time, such as dogma vs. rationality
and magic vs. science.[4] Short of engaging in an extended anthropological
discussion of magic as a social category, it is important to note that after the
Enlightenment, magic did acquire a separate ontological existence in opposition to religion and also in opposition to science in various evolutionist and
social-racist explanations of human difference and inequality.[5] It became one
of the essential, reified, empirical attributes by means of which "primitives"
were to be scientifically distinguished from "civilized" men. Therefore, when
I refer to magic here, I mean it as a category that has been historically constituted in opposition to religion, not as a descriptive analytical term (see Asad
1983, 1988, 1993; Styers 2004).

In the colonial and postcolonial Americas, the term "magic" has been used
in all sorts of official documents and travelers' diaries in order to index the
"heathen," "exotic," or "outlandish" customs and nature of marginalized
African and indigenous populations. However, attributing magic practices
solely to these marginalized groups (first by the inquisition and then by scholars) has been grossly misleading, to say the least: some of the magical practices attributed to Africans were hardly different from some of the rituals of
medieval Catholicism. But the latter were labeled as pertaining to religion.[6]
During an interview with Puerto Rican anthropologist Ricardo Alegría (1995),
he reflected on the pervasive attitude in the Puerto Rico of the 1990s of blindly
assigning anything that looked like magic (masks being involved, for example)
to African influences, which prevented an open discussion of similar masquerades being performed within the Catholic Church but not considered "magical practices."[7] Indeed, at various periods, creole religious practices have been
labeled by non-practitioners as "witchcraft," "magic," "sects," and "cults," and
only recently, following the political-legal involvement of practitioners, have
they been officially recognized in most places as religions.

The anthropological untangling of these histories will be the task of this
chapter.[8] This journey will entail tracing the different threads that have led
to the various attitudes toward magic in nineteenth- and twentieth-century
Latin America and the Spanish and French Caribbean, societies that have been
affected consecutively by colonialism, slavery, emancipation, and postcolonial nation- and state-building processes. This exploration will unravel various social locations of magic, ruled by distinct moral geographies, which

have positioned peasants, elite urbanites (including cultural, political, and commercial elites), and low and middle working class people on different scales of civility, modernity, and morality. Given the designated scope of this chapter, its aim is to provide an overview of the topic and to suggest a few road maps for further research, rather than to examine each location in depth. The analytical framework that guides this essay is based on a practice approach that highlights interrelations between culture, power, and history.[9]

Such a framework, in this case, places a high value on instances of agency in order to unravel how vernacular creole religions contested, punctuated, and tamed various hegemonic religious and cultural practices that had meant to vilify and control them. For example, it helps unravel the ambiguity of the Spaniards' "success" in imposing their own culture on the Amerindians, even as the Amerindians subverted Spanish religious laws and representations "not by rejecting or altering them, but by *using them* with respect to ends and references foreign to the system they had no choice but to accept" (de Certeau 1984: xiii, emphasis added). Furthermore, a practice approach also underscores the agency of practitioners who may capitalize on the academic interest in Afro-Latin religions and of politically minded practitioners who actively rewrite the histories of their religions by highlighting their pre-slavery African sources and by dismissing their Euro-Catholic vestiges.

Often, creole religious practices have retained hegemonic symbols long after they ceased to be relevant in the mainstream (cf. Williams 1980). As such, they illustrate what Anna Tsing terms the "margins," or those "zones of unpredictability at the edges of discursive stability, where contradictory discourses overlap, and where discrepant kinds of meaning-making converge" (1994: 3). For this reason, assessing the emergence of creole religions in the Americas will entail tracing the various sociohistorical contexts that informed the complex, uneven encounters of different African, European, and indigenous religious and healing traditions.[10] What kinds of laws and edicts were established in order to control creole magic during various periods in the Americas since emancipation, and why? How did the organization of social relations and particular ecologies determine the relative access to resources necessary for the performance of divination, healing, and magic?[11] In the name of which ideologies and social programs were "witches" and "sorcerers" persecuted at certain times and celebrated at others? How should we account for their recent re-Africanization and politicization?

A few general explanatory remarks about the organizational differences between the creole religions that will be discussed here are needed. Some, such as Candomblé and Santería, are organized and transmitted by means of initiation within a hierarchy of practitioners around house-temples; and some, such as Abakuá and Palo, were historically organized as secret societies (Cabrera 1958, 1979). Others, such as Puerto Rican *brujería*, Haitian and Dominican Vodou, various forms of Latin American *chamanismo*, and Mexican *curanderismo*, are based on the spiritual charisma of the individual healer – with no theology or hierarchy to authorize them – and thus are highly sensitive to change and internal variation. All of them entail heterogeneous sets of medical, magic, and religious practices that vary according to particular house-temples or practitioners.[12] For the purposes of this essay, however, the local differences of how a host of practitioners – including *brujos*, *curanderos*, *mães de santos*, *santeros*, *houngans*, *mambos*, and *chamanes* – are named and what their different modes of healing, divining, and making magic works are will be glossed for the most part, except in cases where these differences are invoked by practitioners within the field of religious practices.[13] Following a practice approach, then, I will bracket the ontological questions of belief (from the practitioners' perspective) and instead discuss creole magic as a form of communication between humans and spirits (see Palmer et al. 2010) that has been shaped by particular historical conditions and discourses. Expanding on this framework, recent studies in the anthropology of the body have proposed "embodiment" as a way to move away from discourse to the body, that is, to focus on communication that takes place from bodies to bodies and not only from discourse to discourse (see Csordas 1990, 1993; Stoller 1997; Romberg 2009) (see Figure 19.2).

Social scientists and students of religion have used many terms to define processes of religious contact in the Americas: for example, the interpenetration of civilizations, syncretism, symbiosis, and creolization, just to name a few (see Herskovits 1937, 1938; Bastide 1978; Brandon 1993; Desmangles 1992). I will use some of these terms in ways that might not necessarily correspond to the way they have been used elsewhere.[14] What guides me here is the assumption that rather than merely addressing the fusion or mixture of various religious and magic traditions as if they had equal social value, the postcolonial history of magic needs to account for the history of racial, gender, and class inequality that informed the nature of these mixtures in the first place (see Romberg 2005b, 2011c).

Among them, the most used one, syncretism, has been referenced in religious studies to speak of religious mixtures; in colonial situations, it has meant the unintelligent juxtaposition of indigenous beliefs with Catholicism (the colonizers' religion).[15] Syncretism assumed the "imitation" of Catholic rituals without a real faith in or understanding of the theological implications of the

FIGURE 19.2. The gestures of possession and healing.

religion and the mixture of those implications with indigenous elements.[16] Although syncretism has been extensively debated in academic circles, it has also entered actual religious practices, or their politics, when practitioners characterize the practices of others as syncretic in order to disavow and disdain them (as will be developed later in the chapter).[17] Michael Taussig writes that the colonial meeting of three continents was guided not by "an organic synthesis or 'syncretism' of the three great streams of New World History – African, Christian, Indian – but as a chamber of mirrors reflecting each stream's perception of the other" (1987: 218). Thereby, the attention to representations of creole religions among various publics – such as devotees, politicians, church officials, artists, and scholars – is crucial for assessing the agency of practitioners in each historical crossroad.

This essay is about the frictions that were created at the intersection of the imposition of medieval Catholicism, the incomplete evangelization of indigenous and African enslaved populations, and the persistence of indigenous and African religious and medical practices, as well as the latest frictions among practitioners about the direction that their religions should take. Frictions informed the birth of creole religions in the Americas, as well as their more recent developments.[18] For example, despite the efforts of the inquisition to promote religious uniformity, the religious heterodoxy that was forged through the centuries at the interstices of colonial social life was irrepressible, as will become evident later in the chapter. As anthropologist Ruth Behar notes for the Mexican case, the popular practices of magic and witchcraft "had acquired a life of their own, becoming part and parcel of the belief system of the new lower classes that were coming into being in Mexico at the end of the colonial period. By the time the inquisitors lost interest in the dialogue with the lay folk, their participation no longer mattered; a popular magical and religious culture had already taken form, which was beyond erasure or redemption" (1987: 51). To these heterodox waves, recent developments have added renewed quests for orthodoxy, which also reflect frictions, but of other kinds.

One of the main threads that connect the various sections in this essay is that the waves and accidents of history in economic, religious, and political terms have shaped, in many ways, the form and meaning of creole vernacular religions. Some of the most vivid ways are manifested in the relentless recreation of pantheons of spirits and deities and their worship (see Dayan 1995, 1997), which in turn reflect their devotees' dreams and fears, as well as their desires and conflicts. For instance, in addition to the deities (*orishas* and *lwas*) that the enslaved imported to the Americas from Africa and the saints the *peninsulares* brought from Europe, indigenous and creole religions opted to canonize a number of local political leaders and military heroes who were believed to have been endowed with unique spiritual powers. In Haiti, revolution heroes Jean Jack Dessalines and Touissant Louverture figure prominently in the pantheon of Vodou spirits, especially as conduits for "fighting" poverty and inequality.[19] In the rest of Latin America, similar processes have taken place: brave indigenous caciques (called *caboclos* in Brazil), ex-slaves, wise black men and women, independence military heroes, and, more recently, medical doctors, prominent scientists, and artists have become protective spirits, summoned by devotees who want to channel their particular powers and expertise.[20]

The unique spiritual charisma and vision of ritual experts have relentlessly reshaped established pantheons and rituals and thereby added regional variations over time. These ritual changes may have been adopted or rejected by new generations of healers, who, through the years, potentially determined the rise and fall of deities and their worship. Like in the ranking of popular music in radio shows, the fame and decline of healers and their protective spirits have depended on the relevance of their spiritual expertise to the lives of followers, their status in the field of spiritual healing, and the number and prestige of their worshipers.[21] One can safely suggest, then, that "innovation" and "invention," no less than continuity, have created almost as many orthodoxies as heterodoxies in postcolonial religious "traditions" and that multifaceted earthly devotions, as well as divination, magic, and healing practices, have continued to summon those divine interventions that are most relevant to the lives and experiences of their devotees.[22]

Maroon Catholicism and Creole Magic

Alternative Worship Spaces

We *brujos* and *espiritistas* pray and plead to God either in the church or here [at home, in our altar rooms]. You don't need to be kneeling in the church, with a black heart. You'd be better off here [in my altar-room] with a white heart and *espiritismo*. You are your church. The church is within us. (Haydée Trinidad, a Puerto Rican *bruja*, 1996)

The first layer of postcolonial creole magic emerges as the result of more than three centuries of Spanish and Portuguese colonial rule in the Americas. During this period, not only did Catholicism become the official religion, but ecclesiastical officials in numerous instances also took on the responsibilities of civil government. However, as a result of chronic colonial underfunding in most of the colonies (the majority of which did not provide massive colonial profits), several interstitial zones emerged in which maroon societies developed their own ways of life in economic, political, and religious terms. The emergence of sociocultural spaces at the margins of colonial government is especially striking: groups of runaway slaves, shipwreck survivors, and landless peasants operated in parasitic relation to the colonial order, insofar as they were dependent on yet autonomous from it. In matters of religion, this meant the creation of home chapels and altars where devotees were able to develop their own particular forms of Catholic worship that incorporated their own miracles and offerings without ecclesiastic supervision.[23] Expressions of frustration from church officials at their impotence in preventing such irreverent acts of appropriation are ubiquitous, appearing in numerous ecclesiastical documents and edicts.[24] Against this background, a predominantly individualistic, anti-institutional religiosity developed at the margins of the institutional church, and it included the creation of home chapels and magic rituals that "pirated" the gestures, symbols, and functions of the Catholic Church. For example, popular healers have prayed Our Fathers and Hail Marys since colonial times, and they have continued to illicitly use both water from the baptismal fountain and the cross in order to empower their healing and magic works and to conduct all sorts of priestly functions long after these alternative creole forms of religiosity were tacitly approved by the Church out of necessity.

A closer look at various interstitial spaces and groups, as well as points of friction between marginalized and hegemonic groups, reveals that magic in the postcolonial Americas emerges as a result of the recognition of colonial religious power and its irreverent transfiguration by the marginalized. Elsewhere I characterize such dual responses of creolization processes as "ritual piracy" (Romberg 2005b, 2011c). Often practical, rather than theological, decisions created the conditions – unintentionally, of course – for the creation of alternative modes of religiosity.

Ermitas (country chapels), which were erected under the sponsorship of the Catholic Church,[25] soon created the conditions for the takeover of Catholic priestly roles by female devotees (*rezadoras* and *mantenedoras*).[26] In the long run, processes such as these worked against the overt goals of the church to control the population's modes of worship. Historian Robert Wright, when discussing the history of the Catholic priesthood in northern New Mexico, suggests the notion of a "priestless Catholicism" in order to explain the emergence of popular forms of Catholicism in the colonies (quoted in Padilla 2003: 74). Demographic isolation, the colonial scarcity of funds, and a basic anti-official attitude that had created "interstitial" zones of resistance (Mintz 1974) since the very beginning of colonization inspired and fostered individualist, anticlerical, and popular forms of Catholic worship, such as *curanderismo, brujería,* and *chamanismo.*[27] These forms of popular Catholicism originated in the countryside as forms of anticlerical worship that took over the usual functioning of priests. Initially, this was a mechanism sponsored by the church out of necessity, and it was meant to resolve the church's endemic lack of priests and funding, but inadvertently it produced its own seeds of resistance.[28]

The Magic of the Church

Since the early decades of colonization, villages and towns commonly traced their origins to miraculous events and apparitions that had occurred there. The intervening saint became the patron saint of that place. When sacred objects that had once been lost in colonial voyages were inexplicably rediscovered on a certain site, a new chapel or convent would commonly be erected there. A sacred geography was thus established, which was a precondition for the development of future pilgrimages, devotional liturgies, and yearly festivals. The decisive element, however, was that the ecclesiastical officials, not the faithful, were to be the arbiters and interpreters of such miraculous events. In contrast, as colonies gradually gained their independence during the nineteenth century, the authorizing power shifted from prelates to popular devotees. If during colonial times the spatial hagiography served to symbolize the godly driven state power, in postcolonial times, it reflected the devotional impetus of the population and their quest for miracles.[29] In either case, what was not foreseen at the moment of legitimation at these sites was that subsequent determinations of the legitimacy of miracles there would be popularly ascertained without reference to ecclesiastical authority. In the postcolonial context, reports of miracles did indeed continue, and out of some of them there emerged genuinely popular (even international) pilgrimage sites, despite the lack of formal ecclesiastical approbation.[30]

Another important institutional colonial practice that left its mark in postcolonial times was the *cofradía*, or church-sponsored lay fraternity, which unintentionally helped forge and maintain various forms of popular Catholicism, *curanderismo*, *brujería*, and shamanism throughout the Americas.[31] In charge of organizing religious festivities and rituals, these fraternities became a matter of concern because of their elaborate wakes and funeral rituals. The regulations that were issued with the purpose of controlling the "commemorations of the dead" and the elaborate festivities that would follow (see Murga & Huerga 1989: 433–434) are indications of the pervasive beliefs in the magical power of the dead, their power to affect the lives of the living, and the possibility to communicate and summon them.[32] The preoccupation with maintaining close relationships with the recent dead and more distant ancestors by African and Amerindian groups has been crucial in shaping creole healing and magic rituals (later also enhanced by Spiritism, as will be shown in a later section).[33]

For example, the influence of African-based funerary rituals in Puerto Rico (even though the number of slaves was extremely small compared to Cuba) can be gleaned from the threat that the communal aspects of *baquines* – the Afro-Latin-based funerary rite for infants – posed for the authorities. Because it was believed that young children died as *angelitos* ("little angels"), their death provided the occasion for merriment and feasting of a sort that could also result in social disorder and revolt.[34]

By the beginning of the nineteenth century, during the height of the sugar boom in Cuba, black *cabildos* (church-sponsored fraternities) were flourishing among first- and second-generation enslaved Africans (López Valdés 1985; Brandon 1993; Howard 1998). These *cabildos* were part of the church's "sponsored syncretism," which encouraged members of the various *cabildos*, organized according to African "nations" (ethnic-linguistic groups), to adapt their drumming and dancing to the celebration of the Catholic saints. *Cabildos* also offered urban slaves and free people of color venues for upward mobility, political power, and leadership (given that real political power was outside of their reach). They provided safe places for African initiation rituals under the guise of orthodox Christian worship. Under the noses of white priests, Abakuá, Congo (Bantu), Yoruba, Carabalí, and Mandinga elements, just to name a few, were introduced and concealed in the *congadas* (masquerades during Carnival) as the veneration of saints.[35] Thus, the *cabildos* of Cuba and Brazil – rather than the plantations – are considered by scholars to be the main spaces in which traditional orthodox Catholicism, on the one side, and African deity (*orisha*) and ancestor worship, on the other side, met in the New World and where Santería and Candomblé emerged (see Brandon 1993 for Cuba; Bastide 1978 for Brazil) and African religions survived.

Images and Magic Objects: Regulation and Devotion

Throughout the period under investigation, ecclesiastical authorities attempted to bring popular appreciation of spiritual power into harmony with official understandings of sacral materiality. The images of saints (both sculpted and pictorial) located in churches, and the miraculous stories that legitimized their worship lent themselves to the vernacular creativity of slaves and peasants alike. In response, ecclesiastical authorities attempted to protect public images in chapels and churches and to prevent the adoption of new heterodox imagery in private homes. Controlling the iconography was a vital gatekeeping aspiration. Church edicts suggest genuine concern among ecclesiastical officials over the unchecked profusion of "Catholic devotions" – called *milagros*, or miracles – among the people and the "corruption" of its symbols outside of the church walls with non-Catholic adornments.[36]

Today, as in medieval times, worshiping the saints by praying and making occasional offerings to them (especially when making pleas) is considered decisive in assuring their protection. Since early colonization, certain objects have been viewed as manifestations and emblems of contracts made between a devotee and a saint. Just as *promesas* (ex votos) – silver medallions – were left at church altars in colonial times as offerings and as emblems of pleas to the saints (Figure 19.3), manufactured objects, from photos, pacifiers, and locks to pieces of clothing, serve the same purposes today.[37] In fact, mass-produced teddy bears, plastic hearts, and flowers may have changed the shape of these devotional acts but not their essence: the belief in summoning the unseen world via objects that have been imbued with spirit – that is, with the unwavering faith of the devotee.[38]

The same logic operates in the making of *resguardos* and protective amulets. Any object can turn into an amulet if it belongs to the chain of resemblances associated with the saint's symbols and if the right spiritual powers are transferred to it. Priests were the ones empowered to perform that transfer in colonial times, but *brujos* and *curanderos* have since taken on that role, as well. Today, when making amulets, *brujos* "consecrate" them by "baptizing" them with holy water – either taken from the nearby church or produced in their altar-rooms with rainwater – reminding us that much of what popular healers do today had been done at earlier times by priests in the colony.

The Invention of the Devil and the End of the Inquisition

By the beginning of the nineteenth century, the Inquisition (Tribunal del Santo Oficio de la Inquisición) in the New World turned its attention more to the political settling of scores than to theological heresy, and hence their proceedings became less public and dramatic. Even before the suppression of the inquisition in 1834, cases of "magic and superstition" had been gradually decreasing in number since mid-eighteenth century, and such cases that did occur were often dismissed in theological terms as being more the function of ignorance than heresy on the part of the uneducated *mestizos* and childish Indians.[39] According to anthropologist Ruth Behar (1987), by the end of the eighteenth century and certainly by the beginning of the nineteenth, "the inquisitors treated witchcraft and superstition cases not merely with paternal lenience but with contempt," because the lower classes were only capable, in the eyes of the inquisition, of having "low ideas" and "base superstitions," and

FIGURE 19.3. *Promesas* pinned on the painting of a saint at the Cathedral of Mexico City.

therefore intervention was pointless (Behar 1987: 48).[40] Henceforth, all but the most serious cases of "magic and superstition" were handled by local priests and bishops, while the inquisition busied itself mostly with political dissidents, anti-royalist and independence leaders, and freemasons.[41]

Most cases of violations of the slave and Indian population in Cartagena, Colombia, were perceived as mild and labeled as "magic and superstition." When slaves were involved, cases were managed by the secular powers, and those that involved Indians fell under the jurisdiction of the Protectorate of Natives.[42] According to historian Juan Blázquez Miguel (1994), however, many white incarcerators and other penal administrators who believed in the magical powers of detained mulatto and black witches refused to incarcerate them for fear of their potential retaliation. Notably, also at the high ranks of the religious establishment, the boundaries between the accusers and accused were blurred, as in cases in which bishops were punished for consulting *curanderos* instead of medical doctors and in cases in which inquisitors lost their memory by drinking potions that their mulatto lovers gave them.[43] Indeed, the inquisition's lenience toward baptized blacks and mulattoes who kept their "African idolatrous beliefs" was evident.

Those accused of making pacts with the Devil received different treatment indeed. The Devil, it bears noting, had to be invented in the Americas before the inquisition could prosecute. The indigenous populations and enslaved Africans had no concept of the Devil before their contact with Europeans (Blázquez Miguel 1994: 73). Once the idea of the Devil was imported, then the notion of a pact with it followed suit. In New World Christianity as in Old, responsibility for all evils, natural and moral alike, were imputed to the Devil (see Moreno de los Arcos 1991). In reaction, exorcism – of lands, animals, plants, and people – became an important part of New World Christian religious ritual that indigenous and mestizo groups began progressively to incorporate into their own social and religious imagination: including stories about the Devil, descriptions of its shape, and accounts of its words. The Devil itself became the intercultural product in the Americas of diverse agents – priests, inquisitors, white colonists, and those accused of being possessed by the Devil.[44]

From a practice approach, this ritualistic obsession with the finding, identifying, and exorcising of the Devil created the reality of the Devil.[45] The Devil became, according to Michael Taussig, a central character in colonial nightmares of terror and capitalist exploitation (1980, 1987). Writing about Colombian peasants and Bolivian miners, he notes that pacts with the Devil were believed to be easily identified because of their mixed blessings: first, they would guarantee incredible yields of production, but soon after they would bring the total destruction of all achieved profits. One of the often-cited cases of colonial magic that combines the fascination and fear of capitalist accumulation involves the baptizing of money (analyzed by Taussig 1980: 126–139).

The idea is that by illicitly baptizing money instead of a child, the "godfather" of the bill could call it back endlessly after it was used, reversing the actual fate of money exchanged for goods, on the one hand, and materializing the idea of the interest of capital, on the other hand.

In places where there were large indigenous populations, such as Mexico, Peru, Colombia, Ecuador, and Venezuela, the development of postcolonial creole magic owes much of its healing practices to the indigenous use of medicinal and hallucinogenic plants in healing and curing rituals. The status of such popular healers has been always ambiguous – reactions toward them range from extreme reverence to fear. Indeed, cases of sorcery accusations including the use of native hallucinogenic plants that were reported in Peru, Colombia, Venezuela, and Panama (cf. Blázquez Miguel 1994) are extremely similar to those reported in other parts of the Americas where there was a large indigenous population, such as in Mexico (cf. Quezada 1991).

The role of indigenous people in forging the forms and meaning of postcolonial creole shamanism and magic is undeniable (see Bacigalupo 2007). In a profound reading of this history, Taussig (1987) suggests that the magic potency that has been ascribed to Indian shamans until today stems in no small measure from the ambiguity that had been manifested by white colonists toward Indians since colonial times. Revered and consulted for their magic and healing powers, Indians were also tortured and killed for the very wildness that had inspired awe for their spiritual powers. This ambiguity, Taussig argues, lays at the basis of the culture of terror from which generations of shamans have since drawn their magic potency.

In sum, the composite practices of creole healing and magic paradoxically owe much to the imposition of Catholicism in the New World and to the various institutions that had aimed at managing, controlling, and persecuting the religiosity of the various groups under colonial rule. In the suggestive words of Ruth Behar:

> If the Inquisition records are an indication, in the interchange of magical cures and remedies that took place in colonial Mexico, the social groups that juridically formed different castes interacted closely, sharing and spreading a complex repository of supernatural knowledge about marital and sexual relationships that the inquisitors simply called "superstition" and "witchcraft." Indian women gave hummingbirds to Spanish healers for use in sexual attraction, mulatta women told mestiza women how to tame their husbands, a *loba* sorceress introduced a *coyota* to the Devil. This, shall we say "popular," system of belief ran parallel to the system of belief of the Church, and it spread as quickly as Christianity did in the New World, so that after a while it became

impossible to distinguish what in it was "Indian" or "Spanish" or "African." (1987: 48)

Curanderos, Brujos, *and* Chamanes

Popular healers who combine various Catholic and Amerindian, and in some cases also African, ritual elements in their spiritual curing have been called generically *curanderos, brujos,* and *chamanes* throughout the Spanish Americas.[46] Because the church allowed only priests to perform and supervise healing procedures leading to spiritual cures (which were carefully defined in a series of laws), everyone else by virtue of proceeding outside of the confines of the church was labeled as a *curandero, chaman,* or *brujo. Curanderos* today use all sorts of ancient healing techniques mingled with elements of Christianity, adding selected elements of modern medicine in order to heal and comfort the sick.[47] The differences among the various popular healers stem from the particular ecology in which they work and the Amerindian or African traditions from which they draw. Many cases of famous *curanderos* were reported in Latin America and the Caribbean in the nineteenth century, and some of them became objects of devotion by other *curanderos* after their deaths. But, as will be shown later in the chapter, also the controversies surrounding these popular healers are telling (see Sowell 2001).[48] In some cases, their homes or graves became sites of pilgrimage. Such was the case with Don Pedrito Jaramillo, which was reported in the film *Spirit Doctors* by Monica Delgado and Michael Van Wagenen (1997). During the nineteenth century, Jaramillo, who was raised in a poor labor neighborhood in Mexico, first came to prominence as a healer in the low Rio Grande Valley. Jaramillo used a variety of spiritual and herbal remedies to heal thousands until his death in 1907.[49] As a result, he rose to the status of folk saint, and his grave in Falfurrias, Texas, became a site where pilgrims came to supplicate for healing miracles and cures. Another *curandero* who rose to the level of national folk saint was El Niño Fidencio, who was born in 1898 as José Fidencio Síntora Constantino. Born into an impoverished Mexican family, he became Mexico's most renowned healer in the 1920s, establishing a healing mission in the Mexican border state of Nuevo León. El Niño Fidencio employed a variety of techniques to heal his patients, such as using only a piece of broken glass to remove tumors and perform other similar "surgeries"; he also prescribed the use of herbs and desert plants and used a variety of spiritual healing techniques. In 1928, El Niño Fidencio was reported to have cured the president of Mexico of a serious illness, and doing so dramatically increased his following throughout the country.

After his death at the age of forty in 1938, his temple attracted hundreds of thousands of believers from throughout the continent.[50] Some folk healers have been recognized as saints (e.g., the Mexican Mayo Indian "San" Damián) or as "venerated" people in their communities (e.g., the Venezuelan medical doctor José Gregorio Hernández).[51]

The legacy of the Catholic Church is felt in the daily rituals and healing and magic works performed by *brujos*, who still occasionally shroud what they do with a veil of mystery and secrecy (because fear and prejudice have not completely disappeared). For instance, Puerto Rican *brujos* draw their spiritual legitimacy directly from Jesus, or Papá Dios, who might appear to them in dreams or revelations to announce to them their special gifts (see Romberg 2003b, 2009). *Brujos* not only emulate the life and teachings of Jesus to assure his continued protection, but they also summon his power in performing healing and magic rituals, similar to those performed by *curanderos* and *chamanes*, by ritually pirating the gestures and symbols of Catholic ritual. For example, the actions and objects described in the second section of this chapter – praying Our Fathers and Hail Marys, and using the cross and water from the baptismal fountain – serve to empower their magic works and assure their success (Romberg 2005b, 2011c).

The integration of Catholic and African forms of worship found in Afro-Latin religions, such as Haitian Vodou and Brazilian Candomblé, offer comparable examples of the de-territorialization of the sacred or the relocation of hegemonic religion to the margins. For instance, in Candomblé *terreiros* (temples), there is a separate altar for the Catholic saints and a separate time for Catholic prayer. Likewise, the role of the *prêt savann* ("bush priest," or specialist versed in Catholic prayers) is crucial in Vodou for initiating the ceremonies at the *hounfò* (temple). Recognizing the exclusive power invested in the colonial state to constitute the idea of civility, the relocation of Catholic worship to *terreiros* and *hounfòs* may have been more than a complacent gesture to Catholic rule (or a form of "defensive syncretism"); rather, it may be indicative of the irreverent, symbolic translocation of Catholic legitimacy to the *terreiro* and the *hounfò*, along with the migration of Catholic prayers that have empowered since colonial times the ritual spaces of vernacular creole religions.[52]

The iconographic, functional, ecological, and temporal referents of Catholicism are still powerful references in the making of magic works and in all sorts of cleansing, divination, and exorcism rituals within some vernacular creole religions. These ways of using past hegemonic symbols of Catholicism contrasts with other Afro-Latin religions today, particularly with certain house-temples of Santería and Candomblé, which have engaged in the "extirpation" of any Catholic references from their practices, following their politically motivated re-Africanization projects, as will be shown in later sections.

Science and Spirits

Spiritism

The legacy of European nineteenth-century esoteric movements and Freemasonry have been as crucial as indigenous and Catholic religious practices for creole vernacular healing and magic practices in the Americas. The main difference perhaps is that the esoteric movements were imported by the creole elites, many of whom were educated in Europe. Of all these movements, Scientific Spiritism – as encoded by the French scientist and man of letters Allan Kardec (1804–1869) in the 1850s and 1860s – spread fastest through Latin America.[53] Providing a form of progressive "secular spirituality" (Sharp 2006), it adapted the major tenets of esotericism and Freemasonry to the prevailing evolutionist, positivist, and scientific theories of that time. Scientific Spiritism converted the prevailing discourses of physics about the behavior of physical elements and phenomena such as waves, gravity, light, and fluids into a cosmopolitan utopia that spoke of spiritual evolution and progress.[54] By adding Theosophy – mainly the Buddhist and Brahmanic theories concerning pantheistic evolution and the reincarnation of spirits, spirit mediumship, and the communication of humans with "enlightened" spirits – Scientific Spiritism offered a timeless and spaceless discourse on human values and progress. In short, scientific discourses of evolution were translated into a spiritual discourse of immeasurable evolution.

At a time when most societies in the Americas were undergoing processes of independence and nation-building, Scientific Spiritism was a spiritual philosophy that offered the possibility of being both modern and moral.[55] Its appeal for the creole professional and intellectual elites (who had hopes of becoming also the ruling classes) stemmed from its philosophically antireligious, moral, and scientific explanations of the spiritual world, which the elites embraced as the basis for guiding society toward progress and social justice.[56] The content and rhetoric of pamphlets and booklets published by centers of Scientific Spiritism since its founding in the second half of the nineteenth century reflect the influence of social positivism and the hopes that "village enlightenment" philosophies would reach the quasi-literate "folk" (Hazen 2000).[57] After translating complex metaphysical and scientific progressive ideas into more simple forms, Spiritists published and distributed educational pamphlets among the folk as a way to democratize and popularize the universal "enlightenment of the spirit." Together with charitable activities, which included the founding and funding of asylums and hospices, Spiritist centers aimed at leading the new nations in progressive directions. Through the years, via intensive educational outreach programs, several diffusion publications, and the founding of hospitals and orphanages, Spiritists in the Americas transformed nineteenth-century French Spiritism into a local, moral idiom of progress and patriotism that called for combined social-moral changes and the creation of a post-independence "enlightened" modern society.[58]

A brief summary of the major Spiritist ideas can explain its appeal to anticlerical Catholics. Born Catholic and later becoming a student of medicine and literature and a disciple of the humanist educator Johann Heinrich Pestalozzi (1746–1827), Kardec proposed a form of secular spirituality based on the following principles: there is a superior infinite intelligence (God) that finite men cannot completely comprehend; spiritual life is eternal and the soul is immortal; all enlightened spirits (preeminently Christ) are projections of God and should be emulated; the evocation of and communication with spirits are possible in certain circumstances (and everyone can develop these faculties); humans must live many material lives in order to evolve and reach perfection; the divine Law of Cause and Effect makes us pay for our wrongdoings in subsequent reincarnations; through good deeds and charity toward our fellow humans, we can compensate for the social debts (wrongdoings to fellow humans) we acquired in previous existences; there is no hell or Satan, for these were religious myths that contradict the essential goodness of God; and, finally, there are other inhabited worlds in the universe (Yañez Vda. de Otero 1963; Mesa Redonda Espírita 1969; Machuca 1982; Rodríguez Escudero 1991).

It was, therefore, not by chance that the popular classes were also fascinated with Spiritism. The generalized belief in the existence of spirits and the ability to communicate with them existed among Amerindian populations centuries before Kardec's Spiritism reached the Americas. These beliefs were combined with popular Catholicism in all sorts of healing and magic practices by rural and urban *curanderos, chamanes* and *brujos*. Indeed, in the *Gospel According to Spiritism*, Kardec adapted Christianity, especially miracles involving God, Jesus, Mary, and the Saints to his philosophy of spiritual enlightenment and mediumship.[59] This resonated with anticlerical Catholics throughout the Americas, and it offered them the possibility of being both Spiritists and Christians.[60] By the end of the nineteenth century, Spiritist centers were founded all over the Americas, mostly by doctors, lawyers, and radical intellectuals. The historian

FIGURE 19.4. Spiritists gathered for a night séance of the Mesa Blanca.

Lidio Cruz Monclova notes about Puerto Rico that the "evocation of spirits was in great vogue at fashionable parties ... as early as 1856" (1958: 643). *Veladas* (nighttime spiritual gatherings) were held communally at Spiritist centers, and during them, the messages of *espíritus de luz* (enlightened spirits) were heard.[61] The most common layout of these séances – taking place around a table covered by a white cloth, on top of which were placed a bowl of water, a white candle, the Bible, and Kardec's books – defined this type of Spiritism as *Espiritismo de Mesa Blanca* (Spiritism of the White Table; Figure 19.4).

By the beginning of the twentieth century, these elite forms of spirituality were adopted and transformed by people of different socioeconomic statuses who added to the austere, scientific communication with spirits popular Catholic, indigenous, and African forms of communication with and worship of the dead.[62] In time, these centers attracted a wide variety of participants, including white, black, and mulatto middle- and low-class people.[63] Gradually, *curanderos*, *chamanes* and *brujos* formed new private centers in their homes, where private consultations and weekly gatherings were held on a regular basis. They contributed an array of ritual objects and offerings that included: icons of saints and deities, candles, incense, and flowers; spiritual healing practices, such as *santiguos* (curing blessings) and *despojos* (spiritual cleansing); special prayers and spells; and magic works of mixed indigenous, medieval Catholic, and African roots.[64] In contrast to early Spiritists who aimed at a secular, "modern" form of worship devoid of any signs of popular Catholicism, these new forms of Spiritism included a strong religious idiom and functions taken from folk Catholicism; for example, altars (like those in the church), baptism, Catholic saints, prayers, and the rosary were added to the more austere Spiritism of the White Table.[65]

However, Spiritist appropriations of Catholicism have not been uncontested (see Fernández Olmos & Paravisini-Gebert 2003: 178). The church, since the nineteenth century, has waged a strong public war campaign against Spiritists of all kinds (often together with attacks on Freemasons) through the publication of books, newspaper articles, sermons that denounced them as heretics, and the more practical means of refusing to perform Catholic marriage, baptismal, or funerary ceremonies for alleged Spiritists, as well as Freemasons (see Benito y Cantero 1886; Cruz Monclova 1957: 856–864).

Rationalism and Science: Magic on Trial Again

Following emancipation and independence, state-building processes inspired a number of laws and regulations that were detrimental to large numbers of poor, unemployed groups of mixed ancestry, mostly of African and indigenous origin.[66] Among these "problematic" groups, popular healers – who concomitantly fascinated folklorists and artists for their pastoral authenticity – began to be framed within new progressive discourses of the state as dangerous, atavistic remnants of "primitive" eras. In the early decades of the twentieth century, attacks on popular religions were launched not on religious grounds but rather as a result of discourses of progress, science, and rationality.[67] As part of the rationalization of newly created creole states (e.g., Cuba, Brazil, and Puerto Rico) and coinciding with the institutionalization of national schools of medicine, concerted attacks against popular religions, such as popular Spiritism, Santería, Candomblé, *brujería*, and *curanderismo*, were launched by state agencies (legal, medical, and educational alike).[68] Framing these religions as superstitions and the evils of modernization, these programs criminalized popular healers as charlatans.[69]

In Puerto Rico, the war against popular healers was launched as part of new federal and state programs that were designed during the 1940s and 1950s to help "modernize" the island. This was an attack framed not in religious terms but in the language of the newly adopted philosophy of social progress (Romberg 2003a). The medical establishment – which took over the role of bringing progress to Puerto Rico – made a conflation between popular Spiritism (not Scientific Spiritism) and witchcraft.[70] Recruiting the Puerto

La superstición:
producto de
la ignorancia
y el miedo

FIGURE 19.5A. "Superstition: The Product of Ignorance and Fear," from the booklet *Science against Superstition.*

Rican Department of Health and Education, a booklet entitled "La ciencia contra la superstición" ("Science against Superstition") was published in 1951 and distributed in the countryside (Figures 19.5a–19.5b). The goal was to "extirpate primitive healing practices" and promote newly formed public health centers (Departamento de Instrucción 1951). Through the story of a family that used to consult popular healers and was the object of a tragic event – the death of their son – a general message against superstition was constructed. It encompassed all the healing- and spirit-related practices outside of the medical profession. The medical establishment appeared as the "rational" savior of this family when the oldest daughter decided to become a medical doctor and the savior of Puerto Rico as a whole against the dangerous effects of popular and Spiritist healing practices.[71] These campaigns were meant to eliminate the *embaucadores* (charlatans) who pretended to have healing powers; they were not meant to persecute those popular healers who "did not charge for their services," that is, those that performed *"la obra espiritual"* (spiritual work) for *"caridad"* (charity).[72]

La ciencia:
producto de
la investigacion
y la verdad

FIGURE 19.5B. "Science: The Product of Investigation and Truth," from the booklet *Science against Superstition*.

It is crucial to mention that the conversation between Spiritism and medicine in places such as Brazil since the first half of the twentieth century has been intense and filled with unrealized hopes of empirically proving the scientific basis of mediumship, especially with regard to "psychic surgery." As medicine was being institutionalized in postcolonial creole states, most elite Spiritists believed in and promoted alternative therapies that were conveniently framed as "scientific," in contrast to those labeled as "magic." In Brazil, David Hess tells us (1991: 129 n. 4, 223), a famous healer known as Zé Arigó, or "the surgeon with the rusty knife," was accused (by the Catholic Church and medical doctors) and convicted (by the state) of *curanderismo* (according to the law by the same name) on repeated occasions; he was pardoned but then convicted again in 1956 and 1964.[73] His biographers claim that he had a "multinational" phalanx of spirit doctors, and among them, by far the most important was "Dr. Fritz" – a German physician who had died during World War I and who had decided to finish his work on earth through Arigó.[74]

Today, the legacy of Spiritism is very much embedded in the collective memory of many in the Americas, and it has been integrated into the rituals and proceedings of almost all, or perhaps all, creole religions.[75] In Puerto Rico, it is so pervasive that elements of Spiritism can be identified even among those who do not define themselves as *espiritistas*. As a professor at the University of Puerto Rico said to me, "if you scratch the surface a little, all of us in Puerto Rico are Spiritists." He explained that most people routinely decipher their own or their kin's dreams to uncover messages sent by spirits about matters such as family issues or the winning lottery numbers. Candles and incense are lit each week as a commemoration or an offering – but usually people do not like to mention this publicly, because saying that someone "lights candles" means that the person is involved in witchcraft. Spiritism appears also in linguistic expressions, adding new meanings to common words: for example, *limpiar* (to clean) has an attached spiritual meaning of cleansing the house or the body of bad influences. Body language also shows the influence of Spiritism, as when a person, by touching his or her arms, refers to the appearance of goose bumps as the actual presence of spirits, or *los fluidos* (spiritual fluids).

But the legacy of state persecution remains engraved in the minds of the oldest *brujos* and *espiritistas*. For instance, some are careful not to mention anything that would place them outside of the acceptable or "progressive" forms Spiritism. Therefore, expressions like *"hacer la obra espiritual* (to perform spiritual deeds)," *"levantar causas* (to lift causes or bewitchments)," or even the word "Spiritism" are used as generic, acceptable euphemisms that help hide from the public eye less acceptable practices, such as the performance of *trabajos* (a broad category that encompasses all sorts of magic and healing works).

Africa in the Americas: From Racism to Celebration

During my fieldwork in Puerto Rico in 1995, when I asked the director of a Spiritist center about syncretism, he handed me a book and said the answers were there. That book, *Africanismo y espiritismo* (1994 [1958]), first published in Portuguese by the Brazilian Spiritist journalist Deolindo Amorim in 1947, was a blunt attack on Brazilian versions of Spiritism (Umbanda) for their inclusion of African and popular Catholic practices. Stating that Umbanda is a second level of syncretism of already syncretic Afro-Catholic beliefs in Brazil (Ibid.: 32–33), Amorim emphasizes that it has nothing to do with Kardecean Spiritism. Umbanda practices, he continues, should be the focus of "folkloric" or "ethnological" studies because they deal with superstitions, mediumship, and animism, but they should be kept out of the study of Spiritism, which should be studied strictly according to its doctrine (Ibid.: 59). A new term – *"espiritismo folklórico* (folkloric Spiritism)" – came to designate, according to the Puerto Rican historian of Spiritism Rodríguez Escudero, the practices "of people who did not study this philosophy from the books of its exegetes but who have learned somehow by going to centers and by listening to certain orators who had developed healing abilities and were the object of popular admiration" (1991: 328–330).[76]

Indeed, by rejecting "folkloric Spiritism" and aiming to monopolize the social ownership of Spiritism, centers began making changes in their proceedings by the mid-twentieth century, such as confining the famous collective *veladas* of the past to private sessions with selected mediums.[77] This was done, paraphrasing the director of one center, to prevent *espiriteros* (a derogatory word used to designate false Spiritists) or "ignorant people from learning the techniques of mediumship, which could be then used for communicating with backward spirits." Scientific Spiritists argue that the spirits worshiped by popular Spiritism – those that "drink rum and smoke tobacco" (these are their offerings) – have to be "raised" and "enlightened" (*"hay que levantarlos"* or *"darles luz"*), because they operate at "lower levels of vibration."[78]

The next ethnographic vignettes illustrate how these implicitly classist and racist idioms often live on even when the historical circumstances, ideologies, and power relations that shaped them in the first place have ceased to be relevant (cf. Williams 1980). They also exemplify the interrelation between vernacular religious practices, history, and power that was mentioned in the introduction to this chapter. One man I met at a botanica during my fieldwork in 1995 told me that he stopped going to a Spiritist center because the director scolded him for letting such "primitive" spirits possess him (he had made contortions that were too expressive while in trance) and suggested that he must "educate" them. Similarly, at a metaphysics class I attended, a woman in trance was seriously hurt after the coordinator instructed the participants to leave and avoid touching her – a request that clearly contradicted the normative practice of protecting the "material" body from injuries during trance that I had seen at all sorts of spiritual gatherings. Instead, she explained, "spiritual energies are like children, you have to educate them. You know when they arrive and you have to stand up, control them, receive the energy, process it and then give out (verbalize) the message." To educate means, in these contexts, to avoid letting the spirits dominate your body movements in ways that are reminiscent of African forms of possession. Instead, one should "teach" them to communicate through those forms that have been accepted and institutionalized by Scientific Spiritism: for example, automatic writing, telekinesis, telepathy, clairvoyance, psychometry, and so forth.

I have chosen these ethnographic vignettes as a segue to my discussion on Africa in the Americas partly because they help me situate the fluctuations between the de-Africanization and re-Africanization processes that are discussed in the following sections.[79] These processes also unravel centuries of implicit racist assumptions about African religions, especially their ecstatic and magical aspects. Even when these assumptions were neither consciously held nor sustained by lived experiences, they have still misinformed innumerable interactions between practitioners and outsiders. As Stuart Hall (1992: 16) notes, racism is a "structure of knowledge and representations" that separates us from them. Indeed, for centuries, Africa has been "invented," becoming an "idea" in various European intellectual projects, according to renowned African philosopher V. Y. Mudimbe (1988, 1994). These European projects have positioned Africa in opposition to Europe – in line with Edward Said's Orientalism – in order to serve their own civilizatory agendas. Rather than being a representation, the idea of Africa has thus been constituted as a misrepresentation. Until roughly the 1980s, anything that had to do with African religions carried very negative connotations, except for practitioners and insiders (and occasionally intellectuals engaged in artistic projects, as will be discussed later in the chapter), as tokens of primitive, anti-modern, superstitious, magic practices.[80] Even though this racist structure, which is a legacy of slavery, still persists today mostly at unofficial levels, such racist assumptions have ceased both to guide public culture and to appear as publicly acceptable since roughly the 1980s, for reasons I will only be able to sketch briefly in the following sections.

Anti-Superstition Wars and De-Africanization

As part of the rationalization quests of the newly independent states mentioned earlier in the chapter, racist programs of "social hygiene," which were administered by the various state agencies, began criminalizing the work of popular healers as quackery and fraud.[81] Physicians, lawyers, criminal anthropologists, sociologists, and state administrators took on the task of "solving" these social problems, which they saw as threatening social progress. Examples of this process abound and cover places like Brazil (Bastide 1978; Hess 1991; Harding 2000; Borges 2001; Matory 2005) and Cuba (Brandon 1993; Palmié 2002; Román 2007). In some cases, social scientists, along with journalists and other intellectuals joined in the overall attack on popular healers during the early decades after emancipation (see, for example, Ortiz 1906 and Castellanos 1916).[82] What is remarkable is that in most cases medico-legal jargon was used to depict popular healers as "parasites" of society. Similarly to the health campaigns designed to "extirpate" epidemic diseases in the newly independent nations in the Americas, popular healers were the objects of "cleansing" campaigns of "social hygiene" aimed at "annihilating ... parasites" (Ortiz 1906: 368).[83] In Brazil, Cuba, and Haiti, "anti-superstition wars" were launched directly against practitioners of Afro-Latin religions. Even though in each case the timing was slightly different because of the particularities of each country's history, these wars are evidence of the initial fear of these religions – then labeled as cults – being seeds of social disorder and criminal behavior that could threaten the "civilizing" process embarked by these new states. Rachel Harding discusses the repression that Candomblé suffered throughout the nineteenth and well into the twentieth centuries; she points to the symbolic associations made by the dominant society between Afro-Brazilian religions and notions of "noxiousness and marginality," as well as to the public reporting of practitioners as "uncivilized, ignorant, or criminal in their nature" (2000: 61–62). Their gatherings were denounced, prohibited, and punished through all sorts of local edicts and police orders for being threats not just to the "slavocratic social and economic apparatus but also to elite ideas about 'Brazilian civilization'" (Ibid.: 139). When the new republican government decreed the Penal Code of 1890 (only two years after abolition), the persecution of Candomblé in Brazil by the state apparatus (and by physicians aiming at institutionalizing modern medicine) "criminalized spirit possession, love magic, and herbal folk healing as forms of the illegal practice of medicine" (Borges 2001: 181, 184). Another wave of persecution, this time promoted by journalists, public health officers, and police inspectors, followed between 1920 and 1930 under the guise of rationalizing and modernizing the state apparatus, which enabled racist attitudes to be legally protected and enforced (Ibid.: 190).

In Cuba, similar forms of state persecution and criminalization of Afro-Cuban religions took place in the early decades after its independence in 1902. As part of the de-Africanization of Cuba, Cabildos were persecuted, religious paraphernalia was confiscated, and drums were destroyed (Brandon 1993: 82–85). In this context, Fernando Ortiz, who studied in Italy under the infamous biological criminologist Cesare Lombroso, published *La hampa Afrocubana* in 1906. Unlike in his later works, Ortiz writes here as a criminal-lawyer, using the rhetoric of forensic medicine and psychiatry. Criminalizing Afro-Cuban religious practices and its practitioners, he proposes a concerted medical and legal program of "social hygiene [sanitation]" programs (Ortiz 1906: 368).[84] Ortiz portrays the houses of Afro-Cuban practitioners as "sores" and "centers of infection" that need to be "wiped out" (Ibid.: 20, 223, 230) through "energetic repressive and preventive measures" that are in line with "the guidelines of contemporary scientific progress" (Ibid.: 373). This is how Ortiz portrayed Afro-Cuban religions before his ideological conversion from critic to folklorist and founding member of the Afrocubanismo movement, which was instrumental in recognizing the cultural value of Afro-Cuban heritage in forging Cuban nationalism in the 1930s–1940s. Under Castro's revolution, the practices of Santería were prohibited again, this time for political-ideological reasons that coincided, on some points, with the reasons given by the builders of the scientific/modern/rational state half a century earlier.

The timing and trajectory of Vodou in Haiti is quite different from the Brazilian and the Cuban cases, mainly because Haiti became the first Black republic in the Americas in 1804. All sorts of non-academic records tell us that African dances were performed as early as the seventeenth century in Haiti. But the form that today we know as Vodou developed in the period between 1730 and 1790, when large numbers of enslaved Africans were imported. As a result of the economic, cultural, and religious embargoes that followed the end of slavery and independence, Haiti was very much left on its own, with Vodou developing steadily for sixty years outside of any interference of the Catholic Church until 1860 – when the concordat between Haiti and the Vatican was signed, priests returned to Haiti, and all confiscated possessions of the church were returned. Thus, the persecution of Vodou by the church came relatively late in the history of Haiti via successive anti-superstition campaigns in 1896, 1913, and 1941 (Desmangles 1992: 53–55). These campaigns resulted in the burning and destruction of hundreds of *hounfòs* (temples) and ritual paraphernalia. During the American occupation of Haiti (1915–1935), Haitians saw again the persecution of Vodou, which had gained a reputation for being a conduit for plots against invaders as a result of the Vodou ritual that allegedly initiated the Haitian revolution in 1790. During the dictatorship of François Duvalier ("Papa Doc," 1957–1971), Haiti suffered from what Laguerre calls the "Duvalierization of Vodou," which entailed the recruitment of Vodou priests and networks to the secret police in order to sustain his dictatorship and marginalize the great majority of Vodou practitioners among the peasantry (Laguerre 1989; Johnson 2006).

One can argue that in most cases the intentional de-Africanization of vernacular religions by practitioners only followed, not preceded, the sponsored de-Africanization processes by the state apparatuses in their national cultures. For instance, practitioners of Umbanda – which had coalesced as a national religion around the 1920s in southeast Brazil – were keen to de-Africanize and whitewash Umbanda's origins by dissociating it from any Afro-Brazilian influences (Jensen 2010). As if internalizing and responding to the criticism of Amorim described in the previous section, Umbanda practitioners sought to identify with white elite conceptions of Spiritism – a trend that would only be reversed after the 1970s, when Africanness became a guarantee of authenticity and ritual efficacy.

Rewriting Africa: Estheticization, Folklorization, and Re-Africanization

"Afro-American magic," which for centuries had marked the margins of colonial rule, has been repeatedly rewritten in various postcolonial cultural projects in order to serve a variety of multivalent agendas promoted by scholars, governmental and commercial agents, and practitioners.[85] But, as Kevin Yelvington warns, even when the re-Africanization of religious practices is framed in a positive light as a way of resisting racist connotations of Africanness, images of Africa are always constructed within "cultural spaces inhabited by power" (2006b: 36). Roughly between the 1930s and the 1950s, creole intellectuals appropriated some aspects of Afro-Latin religions, especially their indigenous and African elements, to construct a cultural creole ideology of their nations. I am referring to various artistic (political) movements such as Afrocubanismo (Cuba), the pan-Francophone Négritude movement, the Latin American *indigenismo* movement (Cuba, Haiti, and Brazil), Luso-tropicalism (Brazil), and Operation Serenity (Puerto Rico).[86] Except for the Négritude movement, which black intellectuals framed as a separate entity that connected blacks in the French colonies, the key element in these intellectual reworkings was the celebration of the creole aspects (in cultural terms) of their newly formed nations. The anti-African attitudes of the state apparatuses stood in stark contrast to the estheticizing gaze of creole intellectuals, who, inspired by avant-garde, modernist attitudes, celebrated syncretism and the African influences in their national cultures.[87] Instead of framing African religions within criminal and biological deterministic theories, some of the intellectual and professional elites drew on the ideology of Romantic primitivism (which was also guided by biological determinism) to frame (and tame) African culture in a more positive, that is, European, light as a way out of what they perceived as the maladies and alienation of modernization. For example, the modern artistic movement Afrocubanismo (influenced by the European Surrealist and Dadaist fascination with primitivism) promoted works that celebrated Afro-Cuban music, dance, and religion in the process of safely "nationalizing blackness" between 1920 and 1940 (Moore 1997). This process of estheticization, one must remember, was inflected by the elite's experiences of Afro-Cuban culture and their local aspirations to fit their work within the European modernist "discovery" of Africa following either the primitivist, Surrealist, or socialist movements that were in vogue at that time. For practitioners, this meant the recognition and celebration of their religious practices at a national level (even if racism still prevented people of African descent from attaining socioeconomic mobility).

In Brazil, a similar effervescence also yielded more tangible effects for practitioners. Because the intellectual elite (who were often also part of the political elite) were sponsors of various Candomblé *terreiros*, they were instrumental in securing the recognition of Candomblé in 1970 as an official religion (see Bastide 1978; Hess 1991; Matory 2005). But it is important to note that the elite supported the Yoruba elements of Candomblé, not the creole origins of Macumba, which were associated with *caboclos* (Amerindian deities) and *preto-velhos* (old slaves' spirits), and with Bantu forms of ancestor worship and the performance of "black magic." As will be discussed later in this section, this division of labor – between Yoruba and Bantu influences –acquired an ontological existence and cultural currency that would keep defining the future value of religious practices and practitioners until very recently.

Concomitantly, the interest that social scientists took in African-based cultural expressions shifted in the 1940s from a psychological to a cultural/religious perspective, mainly following the work of American anthropologist Melville J. Herskovits. He was instrumental in placing the study of African cultures in the Americas, particularly its religious aspects, at the center of academic research by focusing on what he termed "Africanisms" – cultural traits transported from Africa to the New World. With major institutional support, Herskovits and his wife and collaborator, Frances S. Herskovits, were able to expand research on Afro-American religions and cultures to several locations in the Americas. Herskovits assumed the existence of an African diaspora even before he found the necessary evidence. Rather than dwell on the extensive, scholarly critique of this assumption (Apter 1991; Yelvington 2001), I want to note that the cultural celebration of Africanity, although inspired by a laudable anti-racist approach, did not translate into more equitable conditions for those whose religions and cultural forms were being celebrated; racial discrimination was still rampant in the Americas.[88]

With the support of several influential creole elites in the Americas and prominent groups in Africa, Afro-Latin religious practices and their practitioners gained prestige and recognition as a result of the increased local and international scholarly attention. This in turn helped create new orthodoxies that were in line with the agendas of these interest groups. Even though this support was basically paternalistic in most cases, its consequences for practitioners was unexpectedly long lasting. In Brazil, the sponsorship of social and political leaders, as well as scholars, was important for providing the basis for the subsequent revaluation of Candomblé as a "pure" African religion in the national imagination (Matory 2005). In recent years, the marketing of Africanness within tourist circuits and its incorporation into national (or regional) heritage programs have added other layers of meaning and guiding agendas. One can see the current commodification of "Africa" as an upshot of the earlier self-conscious reorganization of Candomblé houses in response to state persecution (Giesler 2000).

Similar processes occurred also in Castro's Cuba with the folklorization of Santería, which provided a safe synthesis of Lucumí (a local reference to Yoruba), Palo, and Abakuá traditions by intellectuals and practitioners (Matibag 1996; Hagedorn 2001). The change of discourse – from a criminal to a cultural one – resulted, as in the case of Candomblé, in the estheticization of Afro-Cuban religions, especially by intellectuals and artists, as illustrated in the literary works by Alejo Carpentier and Nicolas Gillén in the 1940s (Murphy 1988: 34–35; Brandon 1993, Matibag 1996; Shefferman 2006) and in various Afro-Cuban musical genres, such as *son, rumba,* and *guanguancó* (Moore 1994, 1997). After Castro's revolution, Santería practices were forbidden, but they paradoxically became part of Cuba's national heritage. Even though the early Cuban revolutionary government was against all religions, it recaptured Santería as a symbol of anti-colonial, anti-Catholic, and anti-capitalist resistance (in ways that were not necessarily congruent with the practitioners' political attitudes) by drawing a parallel between it and the heroism of the maroon societies (*palenques*, where African-based religions were kept alive) in their opposition to colonialism. From the world of criminality and persecution, Santería and the other creole religions in the Americas had entered the protected worlds of folklore and heritage.

In Puerto Rico, a new form of national identity began to be forged from the 1980s onward around nativistic and conservationist versions of national identity. In this context, Afro–Puerto Rican elements of national identity were highlighted, giving *brujería, curanderismo,* and Spiritism, as well as African-based cultural expressions, the protective label of "our heritage." The unintended effects were important for practitioners: freed from the demands of secrecy and marginality, their practices began to be imagined as contributions to the nation's heritage, not as threats to its modernity.[89] The public revaluing of Africanity and popular medicine in Puerto Rican culture acquired yet another meaning in light of Puerto Rico's unresolved political status as a commonwealth of the United States. Aware of the politics of national culture, especially the ideologies of "multiculturalism" and "cultural nationalism," *brujos* and *santeros* were able to capitalize on the conservationist cultural policies of the 1990s.[90]

Explorations of vernacular religions in a temporal perspective reveal that idioms of ritual purity often reflect extra-religious ideologies of culture and transnational contact, in addition to the most obvious intra-religious considerations of solidarity, secrecy, and effectiveness. In the following paragraphs, I draw primarily on some aspects of the ethnohistory of Candomblé in order to illustrate the complex ways in which notions of ritual purity may be shaped by a host of religiously unrelated social agents operating in a variety of local and transnational social arenas.

Although the state engaged in persecuting Afro-Brazilian religions in the 1930s, an alternative move in the northern cities of Recife and Salvador was driven by avant-garde psychiatrists and anthropologists aimed at protecting respectable and traditional "pure African religions," such as Candomblé, in opposition to the "dangerous eclecticisms" of Umbanda (Borges 2001: 190). Around 1935–1937, "they negotiated with governors and police chiefs to form boards of cult leaders and doctors that would certify traditional centers as authentic folkloric religions," exempting them from persecution as "sects" (Ibid.: 190). In this context, priests and scholars gathered in the 1937 Afro-Brazilian congress, which culminated with the organization of the Union of Afro-Brazilian Sects (Bastide 1978: 22).[91] Such forms of organization were instrumental for protecting Candomblé houses from persecution, but at the same time, they established authoritative criteria for authenticity and, by default, also for exclusion. Matory (2005: 219–222) shows that through subsequent meetings between scholars and priests particular ideological alliances emerged, which in turn acquired "the credibility to structure new communities and hierarchies in the present" (Ibid.: 221). Via claims of African "purity" and tradition and the disavowal of "black magic," Nagô-based houses (of authentic Yoruba origins) were now to be protected from persecution.[92]

Matory traces the claims of purity and purification in twentieth-century Candomblé in Bahia by means of an exploration of the selective reproduction and amplification of certain elements of its worship. One such amplification was the veneration of Oxalá (considered by many to be the counterpart of Jesus Christ) during the yearly Washing of the Church of Our Lord of Bonfim, which had been famous since the 1890s. "Oxalá's meteoric rise within the Candomblé and his symbolic association with purity appear uniquely indebted to the efforts of Professor Martiniano and Mãe Aninha [a Candomblé priestess], which are in turn rooted in the Lagosian Cultural Renaissance [an African cultural nationalism movement]" (Ibid.: 140); his veneration thus illustrates the joint economic, political, and religious local and transnational agendas informing the rise and fall of certain *orishas* and rituals.

Coinciding with the aftereffects of the Civil Rights movement and the emergence of multicultural ideologies on a local and global scale, Africanness – in fact, Yorubanness – acquires an unprecedented cultural-political patina in the postcolonial Americas that exceeds, in effect, the previous early twentieth-century modernist fascination with Africa and African things (see Yelvington 2006b). Of course, the re-Africanization of creole religions also entailed the extirpation of any Catholic elements from their practices. This was the case with the de-Cubanization of Santería in the United States and the founding of the Orisa-Voodoo temple in the United States, following the black nationalist movement of the 1960s, which divided Cuban practitioners living in the United States (some of which were white Cubans) from African-American practitioners (Brandon 1993; Palmié 1995; Capone 2005).[93]

According to Matory, another wave of orthodoxy or internal purification of Afro-Brazilian religions was the result of the rekindling of trade relations between Brazil, Nigeria, and Dahomey, Benin, after World War II. In the 1980s, Nigerian travelers, traders, diviners, and publishers flooded into Brazil with a well-precedented combination of religious zeal and profit in mind. Hence, like in the 1930s, the 1980s witnessed a trade-empowered drive and a literature-backed push to "Africanize" the Afro-Brazilian religions and "purify" them of their allegedly non-African elements. Carrying this out were Yoruba-centric professors from West Africa and Brazilian Candomblé priestesses.

What is fascinating about Matory's account is the complex mixture of transnational trade with non-commercial and non-religious influences, all of which eventually shaped religious practices. Some of the influences on Candomblé that Matory explores included, to name just a few: the power of itinerant and local intellectuals, the internal mobility created within religious hierarchies, the competition among religious houses, and the indirect effects of local economic and political interests. The initiation of Afro-Atlantic practitioners in Africa became a rightful means of certifying the purity of the religious expertise of Candomblé spiritual leaders, but it contested the existing normative religious hierarchy, which had been based on genealogical priestly seniority on a local level.[94] Several Brazilian practitioners in positions of power, however, such as the directors of cultural centers and associations devoted to the promotion of African-based practices in the Black Atlantic, questioned the monopolization of purity by African intellectuals (Matory 2005: 414 n. 8–9). As the stakes seemed to run very high, competition and dissent among practitioners increased in direct relation to the position that Afro-Brazilian temples had taken vis-à-vis the revitalization and commodification of Africa.

The diversity of the various Candomblé houses reflects the religious genealogies (which were mostly the result of imagined religious ancestry) that formed them. These genealogies have been carefully traced and diacritically displayed by house-temples in order to assert their connection to a particular African ethnic group or nation within a "national market of consumers of religious goods and services" (Motta 1994: 67). Especially after the publication of books and articles by both Brazilian and international researchers that have implicitly "canonized" Nagô as the norm of a good, authentic Afro-Brazilian religion, these genealogies have formed the basis for claims of authenticity and purity in matters of ritual, doctrine, and even metaphysics (Motta 1994; Matory 2005). Ethnic affiliation, as a guarantee of orthodoxy, had become a marketing strategy in a world of intense competition for alternative healing traditions. Africanness, once devalued for its connection to "primitiveness," had become a seal of authenticity and purity since the 1970s, and its standards were placed in opposition to all sorts of "syncretic" vernacular religions.

The practices of *brujería* and Umbanda have defied these regimes of value for the most part until quite recently, when some Umbanda houses began to re-Africanize their proceedings (Prandi 1991, referenced in Matory 2005: 228). These were understandable processes, if one takes into account the disparaging ways in which some of the "purist" Candomblé centers had referred to Umbanda centers as simply "watered-down versions of Candomblé" because they drew on both European Spiritism and African sources (Matory 2005: 165). Yet, even as Candomblé *terreiros* are re-Africanized, their followers do not necessarily follow that trend. The followers often are not even of Afro-Brazilian decent or do not identify with Black Nationalist movements. It is only paradoxical that as followers of Candomblé have become ethnically heterogeneous – Candomblé becoming a universalistic religion that appeals without any discrimination of color or ethnic origin to all Brazilians (Motta 1994: 73) – *terreiros* have re-ethnicized its rituals and image.

Like Candomblé houses that aimed at recovering the Africanness of their practices, some Santería houses sought not just to "purge" any vestiges of their Catholic colonial past but also to recover their "authentic" West African Yoruba components. This particular type of "re-Africanization" is characterized by Cuban scholar Lázara Menéndez Vázquez (1995) as "Yorubanization," because it is the Yoruba influence, not just any African influence, that is assigned high cultural currency in constructing an Afro-creole heritage in the African diaspora (see Brandon 1993; D. Brown 2003b; Matory 2005, Capone 2010 [1999]).

A spiritual/moral division of labor resembling Weber's (1960) distinction between the ideal-types of priests and magicians has been thus construed, and in it, the Yoruba spirits are benevolent and guided by a holistic cosmological system of moral reciprocity (characterized as healing) with humans, in contrast to Congolese-Bantu ancestor spirits that intervene in human affairs by means of magic works (characterized as sorcery) that are aimed at serving the particularistic interests and agendas of the living.[95] Not surprisingly, this division corresponds to the non-academic, generic distinction between "white" and "black" magic. It has also been adopted in construing the opposition within Vodou between the Rada family of lwas (associated with West African "cool" traditions) and Petwo lwas (primarily of Kreyòl and Native Indian origins, characterized as violent, and associated with the worlds of warfare and slavery). This distinction acquires a similar significance within Afro-Cuban religions, where Lucumí, or Santería (corresponding to "cool" African traditions of harmony and healing) has been opposed to Palo Monte, or Palo Mayombe (associated with the dead and sorcery) (see Palmié 2002, 2004, 2006; Wedel 2004; Routon 2010).[96] Needless to say, for practitioners, these lay and academic oppositions, unless they are used for political purposes, lack any relevance in their daily worship and special rituals (cf. Sharot 2001), some of which usually combine so-called white and black magic techniques without distinguishing between them.

An important point that Lorand Matory makes with respect to the revitalization of the idea of Africa in the Americas is that even before the modernist recognition of the esthetic value of African culture in the first decades of the twentieth century by intellectuals and artists, transnational relations between Brazilian Candomblé practitioners and African intellectuals had yielded important cultural and religious exchanges. As Afro-Brazilians and Afro-Cubans traveled to West Africa and West Africans traveled to Brazil and the rest of the African diaspora during the nineteenth and twentieth centuries, the idea of Africa and the African diaspora became jointly construed by means of these transnational dialogues (Matory 2005; Yelvington 2006a; Otero 2010). This point will be further elaborated in the next section, along with developments that have drawn on other sources than the African roots of creole religions.

Multicultural Magic and Healing in Nationalist and Environmentalist Colors

The literary appropriation of the folk in nineteenth-century nation-building processes is widely known. What is less known is the recovery of "folk medicine and popular doctors" within new environmentalist definitions of cultural nationalism, which is especially relevant for Puerto Rico, following the late 1980s and 1990s multicultural turn. If during the modernist rationalization of the state, "popular doctors" were criminalized as "charlatans," within the new politics of multiculturalism, they are celebrated as the descendants of their nation's ancient herbalists and early environmentalists. Popular medicine became recast as an inspirational token of the nation's ancient connection to its land, nature, and people (see Laguerre 1987; Fernández Olmos & Paravisini-Gebert 2011) – as evidenced by the special archive dedicated by the Puerto Rican school of medicine to folk healing, in particular, and the publication of articles on vernacular religions in ethnobotany journals, in general.

By the 1980s, the vilification of *brujería* in Puerto Rico not only stopped but was actually reversed. As a result of the discourse of multiculturalism and the civil rights movement, Puerto Ricans began to publicly recognize their Afro and Taíno heritage. In line with New Age and environmental discourses, *brujería* practices and *brujos* began to enjoy the protection and cultural recognition afforded to them as tokens of Puerto Rican popular wisdom and popular medicine. Ethnobotany, as a national exploration, became relevant and connected to the patriotic and folkloric rewriting of *brujos* and *curanderos* as popular doctors (see Núñez Meléndez 1982). Likewise, trade books that teach how to use the invaluable "national" flora in home remedies (see Hajosy 1991) became coveted resources among Yuppie consumers living both in and outside of Puerto Rico. As "popular doctors," *brujos* could now be left alone and even enjoy the relative prestige ascribed to them for being the embodiment of quintessential Puerto Ricanness. The irony is that at that very point in time, most *brujos* were least motivated by nationalist or patriotic attitudes. Having to assert their spiritual power and charisma without the support of an organization or formal institutional recognition (as Candomblé and Santería practitioners did), *brujos* tended to respond to the transnational market of spiritual goods in more pragmatic ways. That is, regardless of the national, ethnic, or racial origin of spirits and deities, *brujos* incorporated them in accordance with their assumed spiritual efficacy and power. On the other hand, one can argue that because of their ethnic differences, an increased pool of cosmic energies could be accessed. For instance, the various "courts" of deities associated with the Venezuelan cult of María Lionza, which includes Negro Felipe and Guaicaipuro, illustrate the advantages of combining heterogenous sets of spiritual powers, because they offer a gamut of expert help that could be ritually summoned: the court of Amerindian caciques; of black slaves; of *malandros* (urban, petty criminals); of medical doctors and scientists, led by Dr. José Gregorio Hernández; of political leaders, led by Simón Bolivar; and of Vikings, depicted as ancient Germans but considered African (see Pollak-Eltz 2003).[97]

Almost at the same time, the intensification of ritual contact between transnational healers in the Americas has forged as many heterodoxies – plural, "pidgin religions" – as new orthodoxies – self-conscious attempts at "purifying" those religions (as shown earlier in the chapter). How can we make sense of the increased eclecticism of vernacular religions, on the one hand, and their radical re-ethnicization, on the other hand? Ethnographic evidence of the blurring of boundaries between Candomblé, Santería, Vodou, *brujería*, *chamanismo*, *curanderismo*, and *espiritismo* among healers of various orientations during joint spiritual events held in major Caribbean and US mainland cities contrasts with the redrawing of boundaries by some practitioners who regard cultural ownership, not ritual pragmatics, as a critical aspect of their religious practices. In such cases, ritual eclecticism might coexist with the idiom of ritual purity, and the circulation of a ritual lingua franca might coexist with attempts at regimenting its flow. Having discussed processes of orthodoxy and purification earlier, I now address those of eclecticism and heterodoxy.

Botanicas: Sites of Unorthodoxy

Adding to the whims of the spirits – which, *brujos* claim, determine their healing and magic rituals – commercial forces and entrepreneurs that are engaged in the production and marketing of religious commodities on a global scale expand the array of deities that may be summoned and then included in the pantheon of individual healers. For instance, in most botanicas, one might find various options for increasing one's luck (Figure 19.6), such as: an *Ekeko*, the Peruvian midget spirit of wealth; *Kwan Yin*, a Buddhist goddess of fortune; or *Ganesh*, the elephant-headed Hindu deity of opulence. Besides icons of Catholic saints, one can find the *Indio* (a Native American warrior), the *Madama* (a powerful black woman), and *Don Gregorio* (the white Colombian medical doctor mentioned earlier), as well as Japanese and Hindu

FIGURE 19.6 A well-supplied botanica signifying good luck.

deities, each with its own particular character. Local and imported icons from various places of the world – including South, Central, and North America, South Asia, and the Caribbean – representing a gamut of ethnic, racial, class, and gender social-types make up an ever-changing pantheon of cosmopolitan spirits that is placed together with New Age healing stones and quartz, as well as trade books on meditation and extraterrestrial encounters. In contrast to the purist tendencies mentioned earlier, botanicas attest to the cosmopolitan character and relentless change of charismatic vernacular religions. The variety, not the specificity, of the national and ethnic origins of the icons increases their combined ritual efficacy, which draws on their specific translocal powers in order to form a comprehensive nondiscriminatory pantheon of spiritual commodities (see Romberg 2003b). Botanicas are, therefore, ideal places to trace the merging of practices such as Catholicism, popular Spiritism, Santerismo, Santería, Vodou (the Haitian and Dominican Republic versions), New Age self-help techniques, and other emergent healing and magic systems – the selection of ritual commodities depending on the religious practices of the clientele in a particular area (Long 2001; Romberg 2003b; Murphy 2010). It is important to note that global marketing strategies are also shaping the form and meaning of rituals and, by extension, are creating new belief patterns that are becoming in some ways increasingly similar in different parts of the world. For instance, books that contain local recipes for spiritual works using herbs, candles, and other materials, like the *Manual esotérico* (1988) by the Venezuelan Celia Blanco and *El monte* (1975) by the Cuban Lydia Cabrera, are best sellers in Puerto Rico and other parts of the Americas. These, along with products imported from China, India, Mexico, Japan, and Peru are reshaping healing and magic rituals by transcending local practices and erasing their apparent differences. Such eclectic trends toward spiritual entrepreneurship point to a potentiality for a commodity-based transnational (or international) syncretism that is in most cases devoid of actual contact between practitioners.

Transnational Encounters

In contrast, the initial (forced) transnational contact forged by colonialism and the transatlantic slave trade played a great part in shaping the heterodox, eclectic nature of Afro-Latin religions. But subsequent transnational movements between diasporic and African merchants and intellectuals in the nineteenth and twentieth centuries also propelled new forms of religious orthodoxy and purity. In this light, the more recent processes of eclecticism and orthodoxy are not as new as some globalization and transnationalism social theorists seem to suggest. What seems to be new are the ideologies, motivations, and life experiences of these "new" transnational publics and circuits. For example, the contact between an increasing number of Haitian and other Caribbean immigrants in American cities such as New York, Miami, and Los Angeles has produced new venues for ritual heterodoxy and eclecticism, as well as for orthodoxy and purity (see Laguerre 1987; Romberg 2005a).

Yet, most scholarship about the religions of the Black Atlantic have been framed in recent years by and large via celebratory metaphors, such as *ajiaco*, *sancocho*, and *callaloo*, thus highlighting the creative contestation, appropriation, revision, and mutual transformation of creole religions (Fernández Olmos & Paravisini-Gebert 2003). Along these lines, some have focused on the role of African religious cosmologies, regardless of their origins, in constituting a pan-African diaspora in the public sphere. In looking comparatively at Candomblé, Vodou, and Santería, for instance, Murphy highlighted the importance of "ceremonial spirituality" in constituting what he called "spiritual diasporas" (1994: 6). Much less scholarship has been produced about the primordialist, often racist, outcomes of transnational flows and contact (Capone 2005; Matory 2005; Stewart 2005). It has recently become more evident that alongside processes that could be characterized as religious pidginization or creolization, there are concurrent social and religious forces invested in standardization and essentialism. In this sense, I can only agree with Matory's reevaluation (2005: 73–76) of the theoretical hype of transnationalism in social theory. It seems that transnationalism is a term that is good not just for thinking about hybridity and the creative mutual transformations that break the isomorphism between a people, a land, and a culture (Ferguson & Gupta 1992), but it also helps us discuss new forms, arenas, and agendas of ritual orthodoxy and purity.

Secondary Religious Diasporas: Orthodoxies and Heterodoxies

This essay would be incomplete had it not discussed, even briefly, important ritual changes that occurred as a consequence of the transnational migration of practitioners and their spirits from their home countries to other countries in the Americas – characterized as secondary religious diasporas (Frigerio 2004). One of the organizing principles of the literature on this topic focuses on the question of how changes in the material and social conditions of practitioners have promoted changes at the ritual and cosmological levels (see K. Brown 1991, 1999; Cornelius 1992; D. Brown 1999; Romberg 2005a, 2012a). This literature highlights the flexibility and adaptability of these religions to various social contexts and the malleability shown by practitioners who fit their worship to new social, cultural, and environmental situations (see especially the documentary film *Legacy of the Spirits* by Kramer [1985]).

Also, under the auspices of international cultural and political organizations aimed overtly at connecting various creole religions under one umbrella,[98] secondary religious diasporas have undergone crucial ideological changes. In addition to promoting the official recognition of their religions and to protecting practitioners from unjust persecution, these international organizations have also interfered de facto in establishing new criteria of religious authenticity.[99] These, in turn, have created new tensions and debates, especially among those who reject the idea that the goals of these organizations should be the setting of standards, because, in their view, these religions were never meant to be institutionalized. The debates, of course, continue, and they include issues of inclusion and exclusion, such as the plights of women, homosexuals, and individuals whose religious practices have not yet been validated.

In a review of Stefania Capone's *Les Yoruba du Nouveau Monde* (2005), Terry Rey (2007) notes the top-down direction of these organizations and Capone's focus on mostly key figures in the priestly ranks of *orisha* religion, leaving out of her discussion the voices of the laity. Rey rightly argues that, for the most part, devotees (those who have entered these religions not as the result of a conscious political move) are usually less concerned with political-cultural maneuvers, such as those that inspired the re-Africanization of their religions, and more concerned with solving their daily problems with the spiritual aid and direction of their religions.[100]

But surely the tensions between top-down interpretations and bottom-up ritual practices are often resolved in a continuum, where the agency of practitioners and exegetes might interweave (see Capone 2010 [1999]). The exploration of plural, transnational religious markets in secondary diasporas has yielded works, inspired by recent debates within medical anthropology and religious revitalization movements, such as those discussed earlier in the chapter, that welcome the variety of traditional systems of spiritual, or faith-based, healing available in the Americas and their potential compatibility with biomedicine, as well as health care and hospice systems (Maduro 1983; Trotter 1997; Barnes & Starr Sered 2004; Craig 2007).

Representations of Multicultural Magic: Between Pluralism and Exoticism

One of the important channels through which the wider public has learned about the local and global aspects of creole religions – engulfed until very recently in veils of secrecy and damaging stereotypes – has been the arts. Musicians, dancers, and visual artists as well as art historians who have taken an interest in the sensuous, material aspects of these religions have contributed in the past three decades to enlighten the wider public about their complex, profound spiritual and intellectual aspects.[101] They also have contributed to the popularity of these religions, their acceptance in the public sphere, and the ease with which practitioners can openly assert their religious affiliations (see Alvarez 1997).[102] Conveying for the most part the embodied spirituality of these religions via the display of altars, sacred objects, and garments, exhibitions of their material cultures – accompanied by contextual explanations – have materialized for the public the connection between ritual manifestations and spiritual meanings. The screening of dancing and drumming events that accompanied these exhibitions helped further materialize, for instance, how preverbal experiences inscribed during heightened events (such as initiation rituals and religious festivities) have the power to elicit emotions in an unconscious manner simply by means of a reactivation of certain bodily gestures and somatic predispositions (see Csordas 1990, 1993; Romberg 2012b).[103] Indeed, whereas the somatic predispositions, religious gestures, and bodily movements of practitioners during worship are anchored in particular cosmologies, eschatological myths, and ancestral beings, they are nonetheless experienced as second nature. These ideas, encapsulated in Pierre Bourdieu's "practical belief" (1990 [1980]: 66–69), have also been conveyed in vivid form in the filmic works by dancer and artist Maya Deren (1985) on Vodou possession, the personal field notes of dancer Katherine Dunham (1969) about her initiation into Vodou, and the curatorial efforts of Donald Consentino (1995) and Robert-Farris Thompson (1993; Exhibition Program Guide 1994) in their large-scale, comprehensive exhibitions of the material culture of these religions (accompanied by catalogues with thorough photographic and textual documentation). I stress the importance of these efforts as corrective representations of creole religions in the Americas, after much damage had been done by exoticising Hollywoodian misrepresentations of their rituals – of the very sacred manifestations of spirituality mentioned earlier in the chapter – and their practitioners in horror films (see Hurbon 1995; Paravisini-Gebert 1996).[104] Although I am also aware of the problems of representation and of the estheticization and exhibition of these religions in museums and festivals outside of the practitioners' contexts, these problems shy in contrast to those in, say, fictionalized horror-film representations.

The Modernity of Creole Magic

In this last section, I want to reflect on the influences of non-religious economic and bureaucratic values on religious practices, especially those of consumer and welfare capitalism, in order to discuss the modernity of creole religions from an ethnographic perspective. An exploration of the ways of "using" modern forms of consumption and redistribution by *brujos*, and the moral economy of Puerto Rican *brujería* in a modern colony will serve as a test case that also speaks in various degrees and forms to other vernacular religions in the Americas (see Sansi Roca 2007; Romberg 2012a). The purpose is to situate the discussion of magic in the postcolonial Americas within larger social processes, stressing the coevalness of the modernity of non-practitioners and practitioners of creole religions from an empirical perspective.[105] When individuals bring documents produced by welfare state agents to consultations with *brujos*, they are seeking to achieve the material benefits that might be garnered from the appropriate spiritual and material interventions

FIGURE 19.7. Magic work with Social Security documents.

(Figure 19.7). Indeed, as a consequence of the centrality of consumer and welfare capitalist values in the lives of Puerto Ricans, the most savvy and powerful *brujos* also intervene as brokers between their clients and welfare agencies and businesses – performing similar roles to those of some global religions and mega-churches. Having thus acquired additional cultural capital pertaining to new systems of production and redistribution under consumer and welfare capitalism, *brujos* are often at the center of commercial and bureaucratic networks. In this capacity, they are able, for example, to recommend their unemployed clients to companies headed by their influential clients and to inform their needy ones of new welfare regulations that may become available. As a result, as will become evident in the following analysis, the healing and magic styles of powerful *brujos* – those blessed by both the spirits and influential clients – encompass not only the spiritual but also the material welfare of their clients. Because they now intercede more directly in the material conditions of their clients and are no longer persecuted as heretics or vilified as charlatans, *brujos* have begun to function implicitly as "spiritual entrepreneurs": as brokers between state, business, and professional networks (Romberg 2003b). As such, they are able to accumulate additional "spiritual capital" and enter into competition with other healers for fame and recognition by the public – not unlike media preachers (see Romberg 2011b).

Within this new moral economy, material acquisitiveness and a desire for success have been elevated to a higher moral and spiritual order of aspiration: *brujos* and their followers see material and spiritual progress, as well as the attainment of high social status, as not only morally legitimate quests but also visible signs of being "blessed" by the spirits. In response to dominant capitalist and welfare desires and opportunities (not alternative or outlandish values, as outsiders might assume), the moral economy of *brujería* strategically articulates, in unorthodox ways, capitalist and welfare values with the ethical values of Spiritism in order to promote their clients' prosperity or blessings (see Romberg 2012a). Current reworkings such as these should make us rethink not only disenchantment but also re-enchantment theories.

Weber's term for the modern disenchantment of the world was *Entzauberung*, or "removing the magic" (Styers 2004: 13), which conveys that the basis of his modernity theory assumed a separation between the worlds of faith and those of reason. This theory of modernity has been recently revisited not just by critical theorists of modernity and secularization but also, more specifically, by scholars who address the recent flourishing of global religions and religious healing in so-called first world countries.[106] Overall, this revision suggests that we should revisit the secularization thesis implied in modernization theories.[107] If, in fact, the world has never ceased to be enchanted – meaning the assignation of spirit to things in, but not limited to, commodity fetishism à la Marx (1983 [1867]) – the idea of "re-enchantment" ceases to have real import in the theorizing of religious revivals in late modernity.[108] On this note, I can end with a play on Latour's *We Have Never Been Modern* (1993) and suggest, "we have never been disenchanted," or rather, faith and reason or religion and economy have never been separated. The current alleged re-enchantment of the world is just a phantom that covers up its unfulfilled disenchantment.

Notes

1. My discussion of societies that had been Catholic colonies in the Luso-Hispanic-French Americas includes the Spanish and French Caribbean; these areas will be referred to as the Americas and the New World interchangeably, for brevity's sake. Also, in reviewing common trends, I refrain from specifying particular places, unless it is crucial that I note them to advance my argument. It is not my intention, however, to "invent" a region of postcolonial magic in opposition to regions where there is no magic or to gloss over meaningful differences between, say, Andean and Mexican shamanism or between various Afro-creole spiritual and healing systems.

2. Some aspects of my anthropological research provide ethnographic insights into the historical processes I am discussing here. They are based on eighteen months of ethnographic fieldwork (in 1995–1996) working intensively as an apprentice of a Puerto Rican self-defined *bruja* and interacting with many other

brujos, espiritistas, and *santeros.* Participation in various types of rituals allowed me to experience the world of healing and magic from the inside. It yielded a vast corpus of audio and visual documentation of divination, healing, and magic rituals, some of which are published in Romberg (2003b, 2009). Photos in this essay are my own, except when noted. All translations of Spanish sources are mine.

3. I purposely conflate the discussion of secret societies, such as Abakuá and Palo, with the other creole religions in order to convey the blurring and current redrawing of boundaries between secret societies (which have recently ceased to be so "secret"), their historical participation in religious festivals, and their established religious practices, all of which further complicate the politics of naming.

4. Encyclopedists established these categories and the distinction between "superstition," "magic," and "enlightened" religions as a result of empirical "facts" gathered by travelers and antiquarians about exotic Others and ignorant folk, as well as a result of their personal rejection of dogmatic religions and embrace of deism (Gay 1977 [1966]: 145–149; Flaherty 1992). Enlightenment philosophes placed institutional dogmatic religions and magic in opposition to the rule of reason and the practice of criticism, with little regard for scientific discoveries that were made by scientists who were also alchemists and astrologers. See Beltran (2000) for an excellent discussion of the blurring between science, healing, and magic.

5. See Stanley Tambiah (1990) for a learned exploration of the anthropological side of these dichotomies and Pels (2003) for a critical discussion of magic and modernity through the eyes and practices of nineteenth-century anthropologists.

6. The literary genre of "magical realism" seems to have aimed at capturing (and naturalizing), since the 1960s, an assumedly essential Latin American obsession with magic in everyday life (see Hegerfeldt 2005). Christopher Warnes (2005: 1) notes the oxymoronic nature of "magical realism," suggesting that it adds a "numinous quality to the everyday, and it thus promises somehow to reconcile the modern, rational, 'disenchanted' subject of the West with forgotten but recoverable spiritual realities."

7. At that time, in the 1990s, a series of conferences about the African roots of Puerto Rican culture – its music, dance, festivities, and religiosity – were held, after centuries of these roots having been completely silenced (see Zenón 1974). If throughout the colonial period this served to assert the hegemony of Catholic rule, in the postcolonial era, it reflects the cultural politics of the African diaspora and the re-Africanization of creole cultures.

8. Vernacular religions in the Americas have been studied from various other frameworks, including medicine, psychology, and art; some of them will be mentioned later in the chapter, especially when their interpretations have influenced practitioners.

9. A brief caveat: although these processes are discussed here within a postcolonial context, Puerto Rico, as a commonwealth of the United States is characterized by political scientist Ramón Grosfoguel (1997, 2003) as a "modern colony" like other cases of "postcolonial colonies," such as the French overseas regions in the Caribbean.

10. For a quick, well-documented overview of the formation and main rituals of several of these and other creole religions, see Fernández Olmos & Paravisini-Gebert (1996, 2001, 2003).

11. I am thinking here about the different opportunities that plantation and urban slaves had to conduct initiation rituals and worship. The urban context (according to both Bastide and Herskovits) offered more opportunities for free associations and cultural creativity. Free people of color could survive better in urban centers (often composing one-third of the total population). According to Herbert Klein (1967), the system of *coartación* that allowed slaves to buy their freedom helped many urban slaves free themselves either by means of moonlighting or through the sponsorship of members of trade and church fraternities of people of color.

12. This is the reason for the difficulties, or perhaps impossibility, of defining the practices of creole religions in fixed ways.

13. Perhaps the major difference is that *chamanes* summon animal spirits as guides, and they may take hallucinogens in order to enter into trance.

14. For example, due to an unintentional partnership, academic uses of syncretism can also become part of local meaning-making processes. But beyond the recognition that by appropriating or excising syncretism either global or distinct identities could be constructed, we are confronted with an equally important issue: the attributed cultural value of syncretism. Stewart rightly asserts that when syncretism occurs, "a parallel discourse which might be termed meta-syncretic" engulfs the "commentary, and registered perceptions of actors as to whether amalgamation has occurred and whether this is good or bad" (1995: 36). The compelling questions are: What is the status of these competing forms of knowledge, and to what use should they be put?

15. Creole religions in the Americas have been discussed using concepts such as "syncretism" (Herskovits 1937; Droogers 1989); "acculturation" (Herskovits 1938); "symbiosis" (Bastide 1978; Murphy 1988; Desmangles 1992); "juxtaposition" (Desmangles 1992); "parallelism" (Thompson 1983; López Valdés 1995; Abimbola 1996); "interpenetration" (Bastide 1978); "inter-system" (Drummond 1980); and "transculturation" (Ortiz 1995 [1940]). Desmangles shows that processes of ecological symbiosis, for example, shaped the concerted calendrical observances and the particular locations for the celebration of saints and lwas. Because each was celebrated in its typical form and space – saints celebrated by a mass in the church and lwas by sacrifices and possession in the countryside – Desmangles claims that rather than syncretism or fusion,

a more precise term to describe these processes would be "juxtaposition" (1992: 138).

16. Take note of the assumption about the purity of the great religions and the impurity of New World, "syncretic" religions.

17. About the social politics of "syncretism," see Stewart (1995) and the volume edited by Stewart & Shaw (1994). For excellent discussions and case studies of creolization from a multidisciplinary perspective, see Stewart (2005) and Cara & Baron (2011).

18. Haitian writer and supporter of the Négritude movement Jean Price-Mars (1876–1969) noted in his *So Spoke the Uncle* (1928) that behind syncretism lay forced Christianity, camouflage, and caricature conversions (quoted in Dayan 1995: 255).

19. At the end of the twentieth century, Hollywoodian military heroes such as Rambo were also included as contemporary manifestations of those more ancient ones.

20. For instance, the trinity of Venezuelan spirits, also termed the three powers (*potencias*) in reference to the magic of the races, is comprised of Maria Lionza (a native woman who was raped by a Spaniard), Negro Primero (a black general in the army of liberator Simón Bolivar), and Guaicaipuro (the most powerful of the Amerindian caciques) (Pollack-Eltz 2003). In some versions, Negro Felipe, a slave who was killed by Europeans, is part of the trinity instead of Negro Primero.

21. Elsewhere I characterize the dynamics of the spiritual charisma and power of healers as "spiritual capital" (Romberg 2003b, 2011b).

22. These innovations might have started even before the arrival of enslaved Africans to the New World. It is most likely that the various forms of deity and ancestor worship of the enslaved Congolese, Senegalese, Dahomeyans, and Yorubas, among others, who had been brought to the Americas by force, were combined even before they had contact with Catholicism. Therefore, it seems that the merging, or syncretism, of the religious practices of various African peoples into one worship community preceded the second wave of syncretism with Catholicism.

23. Indeed, the personal worship of spirits persisted in conjunction with the practices of medieval Mediterranean popular Catholicism (Vidal 1994: 13).

24. Some analysts, such as Jaime R. Vidal (1994), argue that this was because of Puerto Rico's geography, its demographic distribution, and its underfunded established church. These factors, in addition to the circulation of runaway slaves from the Caribbean, contributed to the formation of a "maroon society" – "*sociedad cimarrona*" in A. Quintero-Rivera's words (1995) – that was both geographically and culturally located on the margins of colonial centers, thereby allowing for a wide range of vernacular creativity and individuality.

25. In Puerto Rico, Archbishop López de Haro proclaimed in 1647 that churchgoers who lived more than six *leguas* (approximately eighteen miles) from the nearest church were exempted from weekly mass, except during Los Días Santos (Holy Week, concluding on Easter Sunday) (Díaz Soler 1974: 171).

26. *Rezadoras* would conduct the liturgy and pray the novenas during wakes for nine days in order to help the spirit of the dead depart in peace. Imagine the importance of these women among people who believed in reincarnation and communication with the dead. *Mantenedoras* were women who were in charge of guarding ritual objects after they had been used and returning them when necessary (see Vidal 1994: 21, 213 n. 36).

27. Similar processes occurred in Brazil and Cuba, where maroon societies, or *quilombos*, were established on remote mountainous areas away from the control of the colonial powers (see Bastide 1978 for Brazil; Brandon 1993 for Cuba).

28. Some aspects of the history of Puerto Rican popular devotions in the eighteenth century are well documented in López Cantos (1992). For a current representation of popular religions, see the catalogue of the exhibition organized and introduced by Alegría-Pons (1988) and Curbelo de Díaz (1986).

29. Symbolizing the sacred nature of Catholic rule over the colonies, a calendar-based schedule of devotion to the patron saints was created in each colony. In addition to a special mass for patron saints, these public celebrations included games, singing, and dancing. Apparently, these forms of religious merriment facilitated the inclusion of activities other than church-approved devotions (or, as they are often described in ecclesiastical records, "less than purely Catholic forms of veneration") in the lives of the people.

30. By way of example, Puerto Rican cases are described in Agosto Cintrón (1996) and Duany (1998).

31. For example, Anna María Padilla (2003: 76–77) writes about the tradition of *rezadoras* within the *penitentes* confraternity in northern New Mexico who had the purpose of protecting the community by means of their personal sacrifice during the Holy Week observance, when bodily penances were ritually practiced in a live reenactment of the Calvary drama. Also, a cursory search of the word *rezadora* on the internet reveals that in Honduras, the tradition of *rezadoras* is still alive and crucial – although in danger of dwindling – among rural populations, as in many other parts of the Hispanic Americas, today.

32. For example, fearing that the assumed magical power emanating from the ritual management of the dead during these commemorations would be used in un-Christian ways, the church prohibited the confreres from conducting the ritual of keeping vigil over the open casket throughout the night. Oddly, in spite of the religious precept to conduct vigils for the dead throughout the night and against the typical custom of leaving churches open both day and night, it was ordered that all churches be closed to devotees at night.

33. The tradition of praying the novenas and the belief in *muertos* (the dead) in *brujería*, the special rituals for the *lwa* Gede (owner of the cemetery) in Vodou, and the *egunguns* in Candomblé, Umbanda, Santería, and Palo are just a few examples. See Cabrera (1979), Murphy (1988, 1994), Desmangles (1992), Dayan (1995, 1997), and Palmié (2002, 2004, 2006).

34. The "Bando de Policía y Buen Gobierno" of 1862 (article 113) prohibited the dances performed during the *baquiné*. Addressing also the funerary practices of slaves, this civil ordinance also prohibited kin from "[the ritual] carrying of [deceased] blacks from house to house" and "singing for [the deceased] in the style of the nation to which they belong" (Díaz Soler 1974: 172).

35. According to Bastide (1978: 120), slaves re-created the King and Queen tradition of their land in their brotherhoods and *congada* festivals; those elected to be the King and Queen were addressed by the other members of the fraternity as "your Majesty," or "your Excellency." David Brown (2003b) draws on these kingship traditions imported from Africa as the basis of his analysis of the form and meaning of "coronation" rituals in Cuban Santería.

36. With the aim of restricting the creation and propagation of unauthorized images, Constitution CIX reserved to the church alone the right to certify miracles and to incorporate into its liturgy new holy relics (*reliquias*) (Murga & Huerga 1989: 437).

37. In a visit to Mexico's City Metropolitan Cathedral of the Ascension (Catedral Metropolitana de la Asunsión) in 2008, I noticed (and photographed) large paintings representing the saints, framed by wide pieces of red velvet on which a plethora of silver ex votos (representing different parts of the body) were pinned.

38. In the Metropolitan Cathedral, I also saw, to my great surprise, offerings very similar to those made by *curanderos*, *brujos*, and *santeros* placed at the altars of specific saints. One of those dedicated to San Ramón Nonato (whose day of celebration is August 31) had a lengthy explanation of his miracles. He is the guardian saint of pregnant women (because he was born alive from a dead mother), and he is the patron saint against gossip and for keeping secrets (because his mouth was locked as a punishment for proselytizing among non-Christians). The offerings placed in his altar at the cathedral were profusely placed together and included plenty of pacifiers and baby booties, as well as locks hanging from long strings of colored ribbons with long inscriptions on them. The official sign placed next to the altar included prayers for protecting pregnant women and for fighting gossip; at the end, there were clearly written instructions for placing locked locks near the saint after having thrown the keys into a special box by the side of the saint's icon.

39. Here, I use "Indians" to mean Native Americans or Amerindians, fully acknowledging the origin of this misnomer since the time of conquest.

40. Notably, the racial status of those accused of magic and superstition made no difference to the inquisitors. Behar (1987: 49) suggests that socioeconomic position was of greater importance than racial or caste categories in determining a person's status by the nineteenth century. She insightfully remarks: "Although 'the people' had not yet developed a class consciousness, the inquisitors had begun to develop one for them."

41. Indeed, the "Inquisition became increasingly secular, developing political interests in combating sedition and the spread of French revolutionary ideology in the New World. For instance, the inquisition excommunicated Hidalgo, the priest who led the Independence movement. By 1810, however, such efforts had become merely theatrical means of bolstering Spanish rule" (Farris 1968: 202–203, referenced in Behar 1987: 51). Bishops and parish priests were in charge of administering the sacraments and of reporting any irregularities in the fulfillment of these sacraments or trespasses made to the liturgy – which was carefully defined in various ecclesiastical edicts. Elsewhere I track the vernacular anti-institutional religious practices of colonial Puerto Rico back through the various ecclesiastical and governmental regulations that were meant to address the many infractions made by *brujos* and other popular healers, and I also shed light on those who were assumed to have made them (Romberg 2003b). This is how we can learn about what the illegitimate behaviors of those labeled as *nigromantes* (conjurers), *agoreros* (diviners), and *hechiceros* (sorcerers) were.

42. Blázquez Miguel notes that although the number of "superstition" cases brought to the Spanish Tribunals were statistically minimal, this was not so in the Americas, where 584 superstition cases figured in third place, after bigamy and crypto-Judaism (1994: 96).

43. These examples show how thin the line dividing Catholicism and "superstition" was. Legitimate versus illegitimate forms of spiritual endeavors were defined according to an institutionalized cosmological taxonomy that specified both who was entitled to contact the supernatural realm and which purposes were deemed acceptable for mediation (see Romberg 2003b).

44. Creole images of the Devil were also adopted in folkloric dances and masquerades. See, for example, the masks of *vegigantes* (devils) worn in Catholic festivities in Puerto Rico (Alegría 1956) and *La diablada* (dances of devils) performed by the indigenous people in Chile, Peru, and Bolivia. These dances were recently the object of international controversy; Bolivia claimed at an international court of justice to be the sole owner of *La diablada*, after it was recognized by the UNESCO World Heritage Centre as a Bolivian folkloric dance.

45. See the excellent study by Michel de Certeau (1990 [1970]), *The Possession at Loudon*, on the modes in which the reality of possession was created in

seventeenth-century Loudon, France, by a host of agents at the interstices of diabolical seizure and divine illumination.

46. Although Spanish *curanderos* claimed to heal "through the grace of God" (Quezada 1991: 52), mestizos, mulattos, Indians, and blacks also included their traditional healing systems and use of medicinal and magical plants in addition to the invocation of both their spirits – pre-Hispanic or African – and the Catholic saints.

47. Since roughly the 1970s, American medical anthropologists have taken an interest in *curanderos* and their role as folk healers or popular doctors among Latinos living in the United States. For more on ethnomedicine, see Maduro (1983), Scheper-Hughes & Stewart (1983), Trotter (1997 [1981]), and Reiff et al. (2003). Renaldo Maduro (1983), for example, notes the advantages of integrating biomedicine and *curanderismo* into the treatment of Latino communities in the United States.

48. Sowell (2001) investigates the controversies surrounding the nineteenth-century Andean healer Miguel Perdomo Neira.

49. At a time when medical doctors were scarce in southern Texas, he played an important role in the border society.

50. Nancy Scheper-Hughes & David Stewart (1983) report on the practices of *curanderismo* in New Mexico in the 1980s, arguing that they have been dwindling for the most part, except when they are used as an alternative in cases of pediatric disorders, chronic illnesses and pain, and maladies that are defined as spiritual, according to traditional beliefs.

51. See June Macklin & Ross Crumrine (1973: 89) for the trajectories of three folk healers toward sainthood in Mexico: they include "'Santa' Teresa of Sonora who achieved her fame in the 1880s; El Nino 'Santo' Fidencio of Nuevo Leon, who reached the height of his renown in the 1920s; and 'San' Damian, the pseudonym of a Mayo Indian of Sonora who received recognition as recently as 1958."

52. The *prèt savann* (a ritual specialist versed in Catholic prayers), for instance, was in charge of opening Vodou ceremonies.

53. The books by Allan Kardec (born Hippolyte Léon Denizard Rivail in 1804) that codified Scientific Spiritism include: the *Book of Spirits* (1857), the *Book of Mediums* (1861), and the *Gospel According to Spiritism* (1864). In Cuba and Puerto Rico, these books had to be initially introduced illegally because the Spanish colonial government had banned them. In Brazil, Kardec's Spiritism came to be named Kardecismo.

54. According to the transcendental topology of Spiritism, "enlightened" is used for a spirit whose light has achieved the greatest wavelength, whose ethereal fluids have reached the highest "frequency," and who thereby has "risen" to the higher spheres of the cosmos, coming in close proximity with other

enlightened spirits – such as, preeminently but not only, Jesus – who are projections of God and should be emulated.

55. Rodríguez Escudero, a Puerto Rican Spiritist-historian, refers to Spiritism as "a force that is called out to play an important role in the modern world and in our homeland" (1991: 4). Indeed, as part of their functions, Spiritist centers saw their involvement with society by and large as morally and socially necessary for the foundation and further funding of humanitarian organizations, such as orphanages, hospitals for the poor, and asylums (Yañez Vda. de Otero 1963: 29).

56. The scientific-empirical aspect of Scientific Spiritism needs clarification. Similarly to other esoteric and occult movements in Europe and the Anglo-Americas, Kardec's Spiritism operated within a general scientific interest in the observation and measurement of metaphysical phenomena – a practice that would later be established as the study of parapsychology.

57. See, for example, the transcription of aphorisms delivered by spirits that are gathered and published in the booklet *Club Amor y Ciencia* (1913).

58. Today there is a global Spiritist organization and new Spiritist centers in countries that were not traditionally Spiritist, such as the United States, the United Kingdom, and Japan. According to a blog by a Brazilian psychologist and Spiritist, Brazil has the largest Spiritist following, with about 2.2 million people who declare to be Spiritists (about 1.3 percent of the Brazilian population, according to the IBGE (Brazilian Institute of Geography Statistics, an official organization), and it plays a major activist role in society (http://spiritism-discussed.blogspot.com/2007/11/who-is-spiritist-in-brazil.html). See also the website of the Federação Espírita Brasileira (Brazilian Spiritist Federation, http://www.febnet.org.br/).

59. It is significant that Spiritists use the Christian theological virtues of "faith, hope and charity" as welcome and farewell greetings. These are the three theological virtues recognized also by Masons.

60. By the beginning of the twentieth century, the only book that had sold more copies than the Bible in Puerto Rico was Kardec's *The Gospel According to Spiritism* (Díaz-Quinones 1996).

61. Yañez Vda. de Otero writes that in Puerto Rico, between 1879 and 1889, the Spanish government became suspicious about these night gatherings and decreed that organizers must request municipal permissions in advance. Notwithstanding these provisions – and fearing their potentially subversive nature – the police also assigned armed guards at the gates of the centers during these spiritual events (1963: 19).

62. Mario Núñez Molina aptly coined the expression "indigenous Spiritism" in order to refer to local popular reworkings of Spiritism (mentioned in Fernandez Olmos & Paravisini-Gebert 2003: 186).

63. In some areas in Cuba, a new form of Spiritism was called *Espiritismo de Cordón* (Spiritism of the Circle) because members would stand in a circle and move in circles, dancing counterclockwise while stepping forcefully and lifting their arms in order to promote possession, with the purpose of healing its members (Fernández Olmos & Paravisini-Gebert 2003: 179–185). Similarly, in Puerto Rico there are Spiritist Healing Circles, or *Círculos de Sanación*. The more African-based forms of Spiritism are called *Espiritismo Cruzao* (in Cuba).

64. Since the 1950s, Spiritism has also incorporated more visible ritual and musical elements from related African spirit possession religions, such as Cuban Santería and Haitian Vodou, giving rise to what today is called "Santerismo," which is very similar to Brazilian Umbanda.

65. Spiritists, who followed the tradition of folk Catholicism that was practiced also by peasants in the mountain areas for centuries, thereby never ceased to see themselves as Catholics, not even after the more recent introduction of African deities into their pantheon.

66. These processes occurred almost at the same time, depending on the specific years in which independence was granted. It is worth noting that Cuba and Puerto Rico were the last slave-owning Spanish colonies; the abolition of slavery took effect in 1873 in Puerto Rico and in 1886 in Cuba. Although they were still held as Spanish colonies at the time of the Spanish American War of 1898, Cuba achieved its independence in 1902, and Puerto Rico became first a territory of the United States in 1898 and then a commonwealth in 1952.

67. According to Sowell (2003), the introduction of scientific medicine into Latin America during the eighteenth and nineteenth centuries shaped the form and meaning of colonial medical pluralism. This has had a lasting effect on state formation processes and the scientific modernization impetus of the twentieth century, as well as on the development of contemporary medical pluralism. Writing specifically about Colombia, Sowell's (2003) analysis is also pertinent to other places in the Caribbean and Latin America.

68. In Puerto Rico, this process took place in the 1940s. See Romberg (1998, 2003a). Sowell notes that many scholars have examined state formation in Latin America through the study of medical history and the institutionalization of medical systems.

69. The association of medical doctors in Colombia determined that the well-being of their profession "was closely linked to the perceived dangers of charlatanism." They defined a charlatan as "an empiric who presents himself as a titled medical doctor ... and one who 'sought the mysterious' instead of the 'true knowledge' of science" (quoted in Sowell 2003: 913).

70. Medical doctors were found among the members of Scientific Spiritism. They disparaged any popular forms of it as "superstitious" in comparison to the "authentic" Spiritism that they followed (see Romberg 1998).

71. Paradoxically, in recent years, there has been a tendency to reappropriate "popular medicine" within the Puerto Rican medical establishment apparently as a response to the worldwide interest in herbal and unobtrusive healing practices. The first three issues of *Buhiti*, a journal published by the Puerto Rican School of Medicine at the University of Puerto Rico in July 1970, October 1970, and January 1971, show the medical relevance of these renewed interests.

72. Compare this statement with the principles of Scientific Spiritism mentioned in the previous section, particularly the one that refers to the important role of charity for "true" Spiritists.

73. The Brazilian law against *curandeirismo* (which has parallels in Argentina and Peru) "provides a catchall category for the prosecution of popular healers who might not be punishable under the other articles of the penal code, such as stellionate (unspecified types of fraud), the illegal practice of medicine, and charlatanism" (Hess 1991: 143). It establishes that making diagnoses and habitually prescribing, administering, or applying any substance, using gestures, words, or any other means could be punishable with detention from six months to two years.

74. His fame began after he allegedly operated on the senator Lúcio Bittencourt in 1950 and cured him of lung cancer (Hess 1991: 129). Since then, "Dr. Fritz" has been responsible for many spiritual surgeries in Brazil. See S. M. Greenfield (1987) for spiritual surgeries and other healings performed without antiseptics and anesthesia by two Brazilian Spiritist healers. Sowell mentions the impact of another medical doctor who became an international Spiritist entity. He writes:

> The healing cult of the Venezuelan doctor José Gregorio Hernández is particularly strong in Colombia. San Gregorio often appears to people in a dark suit, carrying a medical bag, and heals them, using either doses of medicine or surgery. Holy water with curative powers seeps from his tomb. *Promesas* with his image are sold outside churches and in *curanderos'* shops. As the church has come to claim José Gregorio's powers, his image is displayed on murals, in many homes, and in automobiles. In some areas the healing cult has Spiritist ramifications, such as in Brother Walter's Puerto Tejada "Centro Hospitalario de José Gregorio," where Brother Walter calls upon the doctor's spirit to guide him in his surgical procedures. Indian healers in Putumayo also use José Gregorio's curative powers. San Gregorio has been "venerated" by the Vatican, the status preceding sainthood, in large part because of the many healing miracles attributed to him. Hundreds of thousands of Colombians seeking relief from illnesses turn to San Gregorio as naturally as they take an aspirin, or visit a scientific healer. (2003: 924–925)

See also Pollak-Eltz (1994, 2003) and Taussig (1987).

75. Some scholars have looked at Spiritism in psychological terms and interpret its centrality among Latin Americans and Latinos in the United States

as a folk mental health system. See Bram (1957), Garrison (1977), Finkler (1985), Harwood (1987), Koss (1992), Núñez Molina (1990), and Santo (2010).

76. It is worthwhile to note how by referencing "folklore," these Spiritists differentiate the "tainted" from the "authentic" forms of Spiritism and implicitly exclude popular classes from the original, learned version of Spiritism.

77. After a brief amount of fieldwork at some Spiritist centers in Rio de Janeiro in 2009, I got the impression that this has become standard practice in all centers of Spiritism around the world.

78. Also, it is worth mentioning that the spirits channeled by Scientific Spiritism mediums, whose words are then transcribed and published in Spiritist publications, were usually famous national heroes, Western and Eastern ancient philosophers, physicians, lawyers, and scientific, artistic and musical geniuses, and other such figures of local and international stature recognized by elite cultural canons (see Hess 1991: 31).

79. There is extensive scholarship on these religious processes in the Americas and in their "second religious diasporas" (Frigerio 2004), which I am only able to briefly sketch here. See, for instance, Palmié (1995), Jensen (2001), Frigerio (2004), and Matory (2005).

80. Yelvington characterizes the positive invention of Africa and things African by people of African descent in Latin American and Caribbean as inventions "from below" (2006b: 36). See Palmié (2008) for how notions of Africanity are inscribed in all sorts of social projects in the Afro-Atlantic context.

81. It should be noted that Afro-Cuban religions always attracted whites, some of which were accepted as members in black secret societies, such as Abakuá. The state was extremely harsh and critical of these occurrences and believed they were signs that the lower white classes had fallen for these "retrograde" practices, thus becoming a threat to the culture and civilization of the Cuban nation (Howard 1998: 155–156).

82. Notably, in Haiti, the new black republic, which legend tells became a reality as a result of a Vodou ceremony that initiated the revolts leading to the Haitian revolution, was the one that persecuted Vodouisants in several anti-superstition campaigns in 1896 and 1913 (see Laguerre 1989; Desmangles 1992; Dayan 1995).

83. These are quotes I translated from *Los negros brujos* (Ortiz 1906). It is important to note that the same Fernando Ortiz who has been lauded for his pioneering contributions to the study of Afro-Cuban culture is also the author of these impugnable expressions against the practitioners of Afro-Cuban vernacular religions. For a more detailed discussion of Ortiz's extreme shift in attitude, see Moore (1994) and Romberg (2003a).

84. Interestingly, the Brazilian forensic psychiatrist and ethnologist Raimundo Nina Rodriguez, who wrote about Afro-Brazilian religions in this same vein in the 1900s, shares this same intellectual background.

85. J. Lorand Matory (2005) contributed significantly to this point, stressing how Afro-Brazilian practitioners of Candomblé have shaped the place that Africa played in Candomblé, and vice versa.

86. In Puerto Rico, Operation Serenity was a state-sponsored cultural and educational program launched in the late 1940s, at a time when the national identity and spiritual integrity of Puerto Ricans were perceived by its leaders as being threatened by its politico-economic affiliation with the United States under the commonwealth. The cultural and educational programs that were designed at that time idealized the past and romanticized the indigenous and peasant populations, not their African constituents and roots – this would happen only after the 1970s (see Dávila 1997; Guerra 1998; Romberg 2003a, 2007).

87. In Puerto Rico, this process took place later, around the 1980s.

88. For Cuba, see De la Fuente (1998) and Bronfman (2004).

89. African-based religious and musical elements have been rescued from oblivion since the 1980s in government- and university-sponsored festivals, conferences, and events intended to "recover" the African roots of Puerto Rican culture and history. For example, the Centro de Estudios de la Realidad Puertorriqueña (CEREP) began issuing special publications – such as the two books *El machete de Ogún* (1989) and *La tercera raíz* (1992) – on the forgotten African components of Puerto Rican culture and history. Several biannual international symposiums on Afro-Caribbean religions were held at the University of Puerto Rico in the 1990s, and these symposiums also reconnected Puerto Rico with a concerted Pan-Afro-Antillean identity.

90. See Charles Taylor (1994) for a revealing discussion of the complex sociocultural relations involved in "multiculturalism" and the "politics of recognition" within modern democracies, where particular groups' claims for national, civil, gender, and / or ethnic identities replace the previously held universalistic notion of the "general will."

91. The consecutive Afro-Brazilian congresses of 1934, 1937, and 1939 gathered together ethnographers, psychiatrists, anthropologists, folklorists, historians, linguists, and sociologists, who then would become leading figures in interpreting the meaning of these religions from their specific disciplinary perspectives.

92. During World War II, Herskovits engaged in research in Brazil, contributing a culturalist approach to the interpretation of Afro-Brazilian religions, in contrast to local psychopathological interpretations of ecstatic religions – and of possession and trance in particular (see Bastide 1978).

93. The re-Africanization of creole religions acquires another meaning once practitioners migrate from their home countries to other places, carrying with them their traditions (Frigerio (2004) termed this a "second religious diaspora").

94. This trend has also been instrumental in constituting authenticity claims among Cuban and African-American *babalawos* who chose to be initiated in Africa (D. Brown 2003b). During my fieldwork, I heard Cuban and Puerto Rican *babalawos* resist this new criteria for religious authority and hierarchy, claiming that initiation in Africa is in itself no guarantee of true knowledge, because many initiates have been taken in by savvy West Africans who "fed them" inaccurate information about the religion in exchange for large sums of money. A similar argument appears in Alejandro Frigerio (2004) about Nigerian religious entrepreneurs who visit Candomblé houses in Argentina and have almost no qualms "in stamping their seal of African purity in any temple or practitioner that pays enough respect – in whatever kind of species is needed."

95. Evidencing the pervasive yet misleading power of these dichotomies, Bastide claims that Bantu-based, more so than Yoruba-based, Candomblés merge Catholic and African elements, because they are more inclined toward magic (1978: 280).

96. Notably, Todd R. Ochoa (2010a, 2010b) refers to Palo as a set of "Cuban-Kongo societies of affliction," not a religion, in which worship of the dead and the care of *nagangas* or *prendas* (entities lodged in cauldrons) figure prominently in healing and harming rituals.

97. Michael Taussig (1997) draws on the cult of María Lionza in an original ethnography about an imaginary Latin American country in order to explore the "magic of the state" – the eerie partnership between the sacred powers released in state rituals of violence and religious healing pilgrimages. For an eye-opening investigation of the magic of mimesis in colonial encounters mediated by modern reproduction and amplification technologies, see Taussig (1993).

98. Several international congresses with the words "African religions," "Yoruba religions," and *"orisha"* in their titles have gathered together practitioners of creole and African religions in various places in the Americas and elsewhere. A brief internet search can identify hundreds of such organizations and current events.

99. One such conscious reorganization of creole religions and the excising of any vestiges of Catholicism according to the new politically motivated criteria mentioned earlier in the chapter is the Oyotunji African Village and Orisa-Vodou Spiritual Lineage in South Carolina, which was founded in 1970 by the African-American nationalist Walter Eugene King, who became the

babalawo Oba Efuntola Oseijeman Adelabu Adefunmi I (see Brandon 1993; Capone 2005).

100. As mentioned earlier in the chapter, practitioners who need to compete today in a market of religious services, however, might draw on their real or construed closeness to "original" Yoruba religious practices and genealogies in order, for instance, to raise their currency.

101. Following the influential work of Robert-Farris Thompson (1983), an extensive academic corpus that ties creole religions in the Americas to African religions and cosmologies through material culture and the arts has been created. See also, for instance, Flores-Peña & Evanchuk (1994), K. Brown (1995a, 1995b), and D. Brown (2003a, 2003b).

102. In 1993, after much controversy in Hialeah, Florida, the Supreme Court in Miami recognized the religious rights of Santería practitioners to perform animal sacrifices.

103. The contributions of Jean Rouch (1960, 1971) and Paul Stoller (1989, 1995, 1997), among others, to the exploration of embodiment and the sensuous aspects of possession religions in the African context are noteworthy, and they inform my own explorations (Romberg 2009, 2011a, 2012).

104. The Hollywoodian "voodoo-horror film" *The Serpent and the Rainbow*, directed by Wes Craven (1988) – after the sensationalist and controversial book by Wade Davis, *Serpent and the Rainbow: A Harvard Scientist's Astonishing Journey into the Secret Societies of Haitian Voodoo, Zombis and Magic* – comes to my mind. It adds to the misrepresentations of Vodou that were initiated by *White Zombie* by Victor Halperin (1932), and *I Walked with a Zombie* by Jacques Tourneur (1943) (see Boutros 2011). For a sociological analysis of the overall fascination with, and consumption of, these and other Caribbean representations, see Sheller (2003).

105. The modernity of dominant and subaltern groups in the Caribbean has been extensively discussed in relation to metropolitan capitalist forms of entrepreneurship, exploitation, production, accumulation, and consumption, as well as Enlightenment civilizatory projects involving the scientific management, accounting, and dominance of people and nature. More specifically, the modernity of subaltern groups (which was historically denied to them) has been recently recognized in postcolonial studies by circumscribing their participation in capitalist and civilizatory forms of domination and exploitation as either victims or resilient, inventive bricoleurs (see Romberg 2012a).

106. See the edited volumes by Barnes & Starr Sered (2004), Helen Berger (2005), and Csordas (2009) on the variety of current modes of religious healing in a global/transnational context in America and the Caribbean. In more general terms, discussions on the production and validity of the connection between

secularism and modernity have been conducted in Habermas (2008), Styers (2004), Wexler (2007), Landy & Saler (2009).

107. This scholarship is extensive and growing. See, for example, Beyer (1990, 1994), Latour (1993), Casanova (1994, 2001), P. L. Berger (2001, 2006), Asad (2003), Scott & Hirschkind (2006), M. Taylor (2007), and Gillespie (2009).

108. See Meyer & Pels (2003), Masquelier (2004), and Meyer (2010) for anthropological discussions about the modernity of magic and the magic in/of modernity. Cf. a political science discussion of the secularization thesis, for example, in C. Taylor (2007).

Chapter 20

New Age and Neopagan Magic

SABINA MAGLIOCCO

The term "magic" in the context of New Age and Neopagan movements differs from magic as it was previously conceptualized in Western culture. Instead of implying surreptitious or irregular ways of controlling the natural world, it refers to a set of techniques for altering consciousness and bringing about personal transformation. Although the movements themselves also strive to transform the culture surrounding them in significant ways, such change is thought to begin at the individual level with personal enlightenment and self-realization. Magic thus becomes a technology for human growth and potential, for transforming human consciousness and creating a new perception of the world as sacred and enchanted.[1] What sets New Age and Neopagan magic apart from mysticism is the element of agency: adherents actively seek to alter their consciousness by following specific techniques. Enlightenment is thus the logical consequence of a volitional process, rather than the grace of God or the result of prayer or supplication.

Scholars have traditionally distinguished sharply between religion and magic. Magic has been categorized either as a primitive practice reflecting the erroneous conception that humans could control phenomena through ritual or as surreptitious ritual practices whose ends were individualistic rather than aimed at the well-being of the larger society. These distinctions have been critiqued by anthropologists, who have demonstrated that the dividing line between magic and religion is necessarily arbitrary, given that both practices involve maintaining relations with an invisible spirit world by means of ritual. In this chapter, I take an anthropological perspective on the question of the nature of religion and the relationship between religion and magic – a question I will explore more fully later in the chapter. I consider attempts to distinguish religion from magic to be grounded in a concept of religion as an analytic category that privileges Christian monotheism as the norm and views religions that deviate from it as deficient.[2] Magic is used as a foil against which to define legitimate religious practice, perpetuating a pattern going back to classical times.[3] My definition of religion is based on that of the anthropologist Clifford Geertz, who views it as a cultural system that provides:

> (1) a system of symbols which acts to (2) establish powerful, pervasive and long-lasting moods and motivations in men by (3) formulating conceptions of a general order of existence and (4) clothing these conceptions with such an aura of factuality that (5) the moods and motivations seem uniquely realistic.[4]

This is important when dealing with Neopaganism and the New Age movement because both involve practices that may be categorized as magic either by the practitioners themselves (in the case of Neopagans) or by outside observers (in the case of the New Age movement) but that are essentially religious according to a Geertzian definition. Although they are part of a Western cultural and spiritual trajectory, these movements challenge established notions of magic and religion as separate, irreconcilable categories. They demonstrate how the application of anthropological analytical tools can be useful within a Western context, and they decenter prevailing notions that are based on Christianity as a normative religion.

Both "New Age" and "Neopagan" are umbrella terms for spiritual movements comprising a wide diversity of practices and beliefs. The two communities are contiguous and share certain common features – a worldview that privileges experience over belief, the location of spiritual authority within the self, and a focus on self-realization and human potential – inspired by the spiritual and esoteric movements of the nineteenth and early twentieth centuries and sustained by the countercultural stance of various social movements of the 1960s.[5] They generally reject the idea of a supernatural world separate from the natural one, and they perceive what mainstream religions might label as supernaturalism – for example, divination or communication with the dead – as part of the skills that humans are accorded within the natural world. Both lack a single authoritative sacred text or a recognized prophet and instead eclectically combine spiritual material from a variety of cultural and historical sources. New Agers and Neopagans are also non-exclusive: participation in these movements does not preclude belonging to other religious or spiritual communities or belonging to multiple denominations within the movements themselves. Given these commonalities, scholars have tended to group them together.[6] However, these groups' self-perceptions are not congruent with scholarly classifications. Both New Agers and Neopagans are quite individualistic and resist being stereotyped or grouped into categories. Most modern Pagans object to being identified with the New Age movement, which they perceive as shallow, simplistic, and commercialistic. Likewise, most New Agers reject being classified with Neopagans, whom they deride for their colorful ritual costumes or dark, Goth-inspired looks.[7] There may also be significant class differences between the two groups, with New Agers tending to have a higher level of income than Neopagans.[8] Wouter Hanegraaff sees modern Pagans as constituting a specific and separate subculture within the New Age movement.[9] Although this classification has its drawbacks, the two movements share enough of a common history and worldview that they can be treated together in terms of their conceptualization of magic.

One of the primary differences between Neopagans and New Agers is that the former actively embrace magic. They define it as a set of spiritual techniques to change consciousness at will, and they use it to re-enchant the universe, expand human potential, achieve self-realization and planetary healing, and ultimately bring humans into contact with the sacred. Neopagans locate spiritual authenticity in ancient, pre-Christian religions. They see Christianity and monotheistic religions more generally as the source of many contemporary problems, including the alienation of humans from the natural environment, the exploitation of natural resources and native peoples, and a moralism that stigmatizes and curtails natural expressions of sexuality. Modern Pagans seek to reclaim ancient religious traditions as a way of reconnecting with the sacred in the natural world and creating a greater sense of community among peoples and other living beings. They view the practice of ritual magic as central to this enterprise.

In contrast, New Age practitioners are less likely to embrace the concept of magic than Neopagans are, and they foreground instead the "science" of their worldview. Certain scientific theories, particularly those that seek to explain the universe through a single unitary model (e.g., Stephen Hawking's *A Brief History of Time* and Fritjof Capra's *The Tao of Physics*), are interpreted as legitimating a New Age spiritual worldview that seeks unity behind all phenomena and may be used to argue against the scientific establishment, which is perceived as alienating, reductionist, and responsible for many modern ills.[10] However, saying that magic has little significance for New Agers ignores both the religious dimensions of New Age science and important changes in the way that scholars understand magic.

Most scholars of the New Age movement acknowledge that although, unlike Neopaganism, it does not constitute a group of religions, it nevertheless has a strong spiritual dimension. New Agers seek a deep personal transformation at the spiritual or psychological level. This transformation frequently has a mystical component: the individual departs from an earlier stage of life dominated by negative aspects (e.g., illness, purposelessness, hopelessness, rigidity, adherence to orthodox modes of thought, or participation in an exploitative relationship) as a result of a transformative experience that imparts enlightenment and endows life with meaning, hope, and purpose. A variety of technologies may be used to bring about this transformation; these are often described or understood in terms that use the language of science as a legitimizing discourse. Regardless of the technology employed, the nature of personal transformation and enlightenment is spiritual, and it often involves adopting an ongoing practice or set of rituals intended to uphold the results of the original transformation and create similar experiences in others. In this sense, the transformative experience and practices employed to maintain the experience of enlightenment it engendered can be seen as having something in common with magic.

To attempt to delineate the role of magic in the New Age movement and modern Paganism entails entering one of the central scholarly conversations in contemporary anthropology on the nature of magic and its relationship to two other important categories in anthropological thought: religion and science. The common Western concept of magic encompasses both a cosmology in which supernatural forces play a significant role and a set of technologies that are applied by the magician to attempt to control those forces and bend them to his or her will. Western attitudes toward magic have generally been negative, especially in the comparison of magic with religion and science. Juxtaposed against religion, magic has been portrayed as instrumental, mechanical, manipulative, anti-social, and coercive, aimed at achieving specific short-term goals for the individual. Religious ritual, by contrast, allegedly entreats supernatural powers for their general benevolence, and it is designed to unify society for the good of all.[11] Anthropologist Stanley J. Tambiah, in his critique of the anthropological study of magic, argued that this dichotomy between magic and religion had its roots in the Protestant Reformation, which, in seeking a more direct relationship between the individual and God, denounced certain Catholic doctrines, such as transubstantiation and traditions associated with saints' feasts and seasonal liturgical rites, as vestiges of pagan magic.[12] This perspective continued to be reflected in the views of early anthropologists such as Edward B. Tylor and Sir James G. Frazer, for whom magic represented a primitive and ultimately false method for understanding how the world worked and attempting to control it. In their unilinear conception of cultural evolution, magic was destined to be replaced first by organized religion and eventually by modern science. When contrasted against science, magic again fared badly, coming off as irrational and based on mistaken notions of how the world operates. Magical practitioners were assumed to lack rationality, either because they did not have the scientific knowledge necessary to understand how the world worked, as in the case of indigenous cultures, or because they were in a powerless position within a culture, as in the case of disadvantaged minorities living within a modernized Western state. For the latter, magic was understood as a compensatory mechanism that would eventually disappear as they became educated and fully integrated into the dominant culture. Some early studies of Neopaganism and New Age movements construed the construct of magic as a way of thinking that is opposed to rationality, although they struggled with the fact that adherents did not fit the expected categories of believers, in that they were typically middle class and belonged to the majority culture. The anthropologist T. M. Luhrmann's *Persuasions of the Witches' Craft* (1979), an ethnography of Neopagan witches and ritual magicians in London, questioned how educated, middle-class people could believe in and claim to practice magic. Luhrmann showed how modern magicians used metaphorical language and imaginative narrative to overcome their doubts, and she hypothesized that members came to interpret their experiences as magical through gradual exposure to other members' narratives, a process she called "interpretive drift."[13]

Another line of thinking in anthropology that began in the mid-twentieth century critiqued the separation of magic, religion, and science as inherently flawed because of the ethnocentric nature of early anthropological inquiry and the consequent imposition of Western categories and values on the cosmologies of non-Western peoples. The British sociocultural anthropologist E. E. Evans-Pritchard first called attention to the dangers of superimposing Western terms such as "witchcraft" and "magic" onto non-Western systems, where native categories might not correspond closely to Western ones. He also demonstrated that indigenous people such as the Azande of western Sudan were perfectly capable of performing rational deductive thinking while simultaneously maintaining a firm belief in the power of witches and oracles.[14] A broader critique was presented by the American anthropologists Murray Wax and Rosalie Wax, who noted that the separation of magic from religion was a uniquely Western construct, one that the majority of indigenous religions did not share. They called for the abandonment of magic as an analytical category on the basis of its inadequacy and ethnocentrism.[15]

A second critique attacked the notion of magic as a pre-rational or irrational way of understanding the world. The French anthropologist Lucien Lévy-Bruhl hypothesized in his posthumously published notebooks that rational-logical and mystical, or "participatory," ways of thought coexisted in all human societies. Although the latter could perhaps be more easily observed in premodern societies, he cautioned that it was present in every human mind and that without it "would perhaps disappear ... poetry, art, metaphysics and scientific invention – almost everything, in short, that makes for the beauty and grandeur of human life."[16] This view was taken up by the anthropologist Stanley J. Tambiah, who warned that "[a] narrow yardstick of 'rationality' misses the theatrical and illocutionary aspects of ritual performance."[17] He characterized the participatory way of thought as involving all of the senses and emotions and as being expressed through art forms such as poetry, narrative, and ritual. British social anthropologist Susan Greenwood, an ethnographer of New Age and Neopagan movements, has further characterized participatory consciousness as creating emotional connections to the world, using holistic language, expressing itself through metaphor, seeing the world as "inspirited" or animated by spiritual forces, and making use of alternative states of consciousness.[18]

In the twenty-first century, therefore, anthropologists are beginning to interpret magic as a form of participatory consciousness accessible to humans living in any form of society in all historical periods. In contrast with a logical-causal mode of thought, with which it always coexists, participatory consciousness sensorially involves the individual in an animated universe filled with spiritual forces and perceived as a unified, coherent, and meaningful whole. It finds expression through creative means, be they poetry, narrative, ritual or other forms of art, and it communicates through metaphor. It connects individuals to the world around them through strong emotional bonds, emphasizing feeling over detachment. It often operates through alternate states of consciousness – states that differ from ordinary waking consciousness and that range from dreams and light trances, such as those brought on by listening to a story or becoming involved in a performance, to dramatic dissociative states in which the individual may feel disconnected from the self and fully merged with another being or consciousness. According to this understanding, "magic" may include techniques used to achieve a participatory state of consciousness, as well as the insights and personal transformations that are derived as a result of experiences of participatory consciousness. Given this revised definition, it will become clear that magic is central to both Neopagan and New Age practices and worldviews.

The American religious historian J. Gordon Melton, one of the first scholars to seriously study the New Age movement, sees the idea of transformation as the key to defining and understanding the movement.[19] Transformation, in this context, refers both to a personal transformation of the individual and to the transformation of culture and humanity more broadly. Both New Agers and Neopagans share a yearning for a better future – one characterized by world peace, social justice, and ecological renewal. In both, global transformation generally begins at the individual level with a transformative spiritual experience – one that forces the individual into a more participatory mode of consciousness. The insights gleaned from this participatory consciousness are then used to transform material aspects of life – for example, the adoption of new dietary practices – that promise to eventually effect broader changes in culture.

In addition to the importance of experiences of participatory consciousness in New Age and Neopagan practice, both groups also cultivate relationships with a variety of spiritual beings, such as gods and goddesses, nature spirits, spirits of the dead, angels, and aliens. Both reject mainstream monotheism, although some may perceive the existence of a single divine principle in the universe, of which spirits are aspects or "emanations."[20] Spirits may be perceived either as existing in their own right or as "archetypes" representing those parts of the human experience whose existence has a sociocultural reality. Communication with spirits can take place through meditation, "channeling," and exchange with spirit guides during ritual or trance. Spirit beings become an intimate part of practitioners' lives: they help with material goals, such as getting jobs or finding apartments, as well as spiritual growth and planetary healing. Spirits may enter into the lives of New Agers and Neopagans unbidden: the New Age author J. Z. Knight first perceived Ramtha, her spirit guide, at her bedside; Peter and Eileen Caddy and Dorothy MacLean, the founders of Findhorn, a New Age farming community in Scotland, were contacted by plant devas who instructed them in gardening techniques; and Laurel Olson Mendes, a Neopagan priestess and seið practitioner,[21] first experienced communication from a goddess while singing the soprano recitatives from Handel's "Messiah" in her church choir (see Figure 20.1). New Age and Neopagan belief systems and practices normalize such encounters, creating contexts in which practitioners learn to control and understand them. It could be argued that given the stigmatization of spiritual encounters in Western secular culture and mainstream religions, Neopagan and New Age subcultures create spaces where those who have undergone them can find acceptance and understanding and also learn techniques to harness their experiences for personal development and self-actualization.

FIGURE 20.1. Community Center at Findhorn, an intentional New Age community in Scotland. Image under Creative Commons License.

Magical Roots

Although both the New Age movement and Neopaganism emerged during the twentieth century, they share historical roots in Western esotericism going back to classical times. Esotericism includes a number of interrelated philosophies and religious traditions dating to antiquity, including Neo-Pythagoreanism, Stoicism, Hermeticism, Gnosticism, Neo-Platonism, and Christianity. The French scholar Antoine Faivre identifies six characteristics common to esoteric philosophies. These include: the idea of correspondences between all parts of the visible and invisible worlds, such that the macrocosm is reflected in and can be understood by studying the microcosm, and vice versa; the view of nature as inspirited by a divine force; the possibility of mediating between worlds through rituals that manipulate the correspondences between them, as well as seeing the imagination as an instrument for self-knowledge and gnosis; the belief that transformation is possible through an inner process or mystical path that reveals the mysteries of the cosmos and brings the initiate closer to God; the tendency to seek commonalities between and among traditions in order to gain further illumination; and the transmission of knowledge from master to disciple as part of an initiatory path, with the notion of a historical genealogy of knowledge transmission as an authenticating discourse.[22] These elements can be found in the philosophies of Neo-Platonism and Hermeticism; the premodern sciences of astrology, alchemy, and *mageia* (high magic or theurgy); and the theosophical current of from the Kabbalah, a set of Jewish mystical texts, all of which contributed to the development of magic in New Age and Neopagan thought.[23]

These disparate sources were brought together for the first time in Renaissance Florence through the work of Marsilio Ficino (1433–1499) and Giovanni Pico della Mirandola (1463–1494). Under the patronage of Cosimo de' Medici, Ficino was responsible for compiling and translating into Latin various Greek manuscripts known as the *Corpus Hermeticum*, or *Hermetica*, which consisted of mystical and philosophical writings drawing from Platonism, Stoicism, Neo-Platonism, and Egyptian Gnosticism dating from the second half of the second century CE to the end of the third century CE. The central figure in these texts was Hermes Trismegistus, a syncretic fusion of the Greek god Hermes with the Egyptian god Thoth. According to the Hermetic material, the central principle in the universe was that of sacred unity: everything in the universe derived ultimately from a single divine source. The universe consisted of multiple spheres, or "emanations": nature, stars, spirits and "guardians," and *nous*, or angelic spirits closest to the source of creation. The goal of Hermetic magic was to achieve oneness with the Godhead by entering into the realms of divine thought. Pico della Mirandola further developed Ficino's work by combining it with his knowledge of the Kabbalah, astrology, Christian mysticism, and theurgy, or *mageia*. Pico believed that humans could raise themselves to the level of gods through the practice of *mageia*: magic was a route to enlightenment and understanding, because it could raise earthly matter to the level of the Godhead.[24]

The theme of spiritual transformation was also important to early modern alchemists, the successors of the Renaissance magi. Alchemists' work was based on the Hermetic concepts of the fundamental unity of the universe and the correspondences between the physical and spiritual realms, or "microcosm and macrocosm." Thus, chemical alchemy was concerned with the process of transmuting base metals into gold, but this process also had a metaphorical dimension: it represented the transmutation of the human soul from its base nature to its highest possible state: a union with God. These concepts in turn were influential to the development of the symbolic elements of Freemasonry in the seventeenth century and to the emergence of the Society of the Rose Cross, or Rosicrucian Fraternity, in the eighteenth; through them, a set of magical symbols and concepts entered Western esoteric culture that continue to be used today in Neopaganism and some branches of New Age practice.

The first part of the nineteenth century saw a revival of interest in magical practice as a method of spiritual transformation in France, where the occultist Eliphas Levi rediscovered and reinterpreted the Kabbalah, linking it with ancient Egyptian religion and with the Tarot. By the final decades of the century, Levi's works had inspired the members of the Hermetic Order of the Golden Dawn. Practicing in England in the final decade of the nineteenth century and the early decades of the twentieth, the founders of this organization "gather[ed] together the threads of the Western esoteric tradition and initiat[ed] a transformative process that continued into the twenty-first century."[25] The Order of the Golden Dawn was one of the most influential esoteric organizations in modern history; all modern magical systems derive from it to some degree.[26] The goal of Golden Dawn initiates was to ascend the Kabbalistic Tree of Life in order to emerge ritually into the Light, a term that was synonymous with union with the divine. This was accomplished through a ritual process in which the initiate identified with a sphere of consciousness symbolized by each of the nine stations on the Tree of Life. The Order of the Golden Dawn was among the first modern magical organizations to use and document alternate states of consciousness – including trance, out of body, and mystical experiences – for the purpose of personal spiritual transformation.[27] It also developed a precise technology using visualization and "willed imagination" to allow adepts to achieve an altered state. Symbols and correspondences were of central importance to the Golden Dawn magicians, who believed that stimulation of all five senses was necessary in order for the adept to communicate successfully with the unconscious mind and with the deities. Associations with particular deities and qualities were based on a system of magical correspondences derived from Renaissance and classical magic, whereby each god or goddess was linked with specific colors, plants, minerals, precious stones, and perfumes. Samuel Liddell MacGregor Mathers and Wynn Westcott, two founders of the Hermetic Order of the Golden Dawn, compiled a table of these associations entitled *The Book of Correspondences* in the 1890s; the list was later published by the ceremonial magician Aleister Crowley under his own name.[28] These same associations continue to be used in Neopagan magic today.

Renaissance Hermeticism and its successors can be interpreted as syncretizing the emerging discovery of nature as a documentable entity with a desire to maintain the sacred dimension of the cosmos.[29] In the period between the Renaissance and the nineteenth-century magical revival, Western magic underwent an increasing process of secularization on account of the development of science, the Enlightenment, and the disenchantment of the world. The result was not an esotericism opposed to the Enlightenment or scientific thought but one that sought to come to terms with them.[30] The doctrines of Swedenborgianism and Spiritualism incorporated a Darwinian evolutionary framework into a discourse of the transmutation of the soul, whereas Mesmerism, a movement established by the seventeenth-century German physician Franz Anton Mesmer (1735–1815), sought to integrate emerging scientific knowledge about magnetism and electricity into a spiritual framework that promised personal healing. The development of chiropractic and naturopathic medicine in the nineteenth century also synthesized science with spirituality and contributed to the formation of New Age concepts of alternative healing. As will be delineated in the next section, a concern with synthesizing spirituality and science continues to be a key interest of the New Age movement today. Ironically, Hanegraaff argues, these philosophies and practices were based on an acceptance of the disenchanted world; they represented "an attempt to adapt esotericism to a disenchanted world: a world which no longer harbors a dimension of irreducible mystery ... based upon an experience of the sacred as present in the daily world."[31] In contrast, the emergence of Romanticism at the end of the eighteenth century represented a rejection of this compromise and a genuine attempt to re-enchant the world by reintroducing the element of mystery. The nineteenth-century rediscovery of magic was part of this drive toward re-enchantment: it was an attempt to re-create a participatory worldview.[32] Neopaganism embodies this impulse to a much greater degree than the New Age movement does. Thus, although the New Age movement and Neopaganism share roots in Western esotericism, the former is heir to philosophies and practices whose goal was to reconcile the scientific with the mystical, whereas the latter is the successor to Romantic movements whose goal was the re-enchantment and re-sacralization of the world.

Two additional cultural strains contributed to the development of Neopagan and New Age magic. The first was the psychologization of spirituality. Sigmund Freud's (1856–1939) concepts of the unconscious and the link between the unconscious, dreams, and myth had a revolutionary impact on early twentieth-century thought. Individual consciousness was now understood as riddled with motivations, impulses, and anxieties that were not apprehensible to rational thought, because they were lodged deep in the unconscious. They emerged only through dreams, poetry, and mythology, making both the individual and culture more complex and multivalent than previous understandings had allowed. The work of the soul became not the attainment of salvation in the next life but the achievement of harmony and mental health in the present life through the healing of traumas and neuroses whose roots were buried in early experience, perhaps not even accessible to memory. The American poet Ralph Waldo Emerson (1803–1882) and the psychologist William James (1842–1910) each reflected these ideas in their works, albeit in different ways.[33] As a result, popular understandings of the cosmos, the universe, and the infinite acquired a psychological flavor: these notions, which were previously linked to religion, became understandable as psychological constructs, as aspects of the individual psyche. "Spiritual" and "psychological" became increasingly interchangeable terms. At the same time, new technologies – such as hypnosis, psychoanalysis, and dream analysis – emerged to integrate the hidden aspects of the soul with the conscious, rational ones, thus achieving healing. The work of Freud's disciple Carl Jung (1875–1961) was enormously influential, in that it aimed at harmonizing science and rationalism (Jung was a trained physician) with esotericism. Jung was able to translate esoteric principles in psychological terms, "providing a 'scientific' alternative to occultism."[34] He sacralized psychology to an even greater degree than his predecessors had; as a result, people could talk about gods and mean a part of their own psyches, or they could refer to their own psyches as part of the divine. The equivalence between God, mind, and psyche is fundamental to the New Age worldview; it is what makes the New Age and Neopagan emphasis on self-realization religious in nature.

Finally, the introduction of Asian philosophies and practices greatly contributed to the development of New Age thought. Central to this were the works of Helena P. Blavatsky (1831–1891) and Alice Bailey (1880–1949). In 1875, Blavatsky founded the Theosophical Society, a group dedicated to spirit communication and mediumship. Blavatsky's incorporation of Eastern philosophies and esoteric traditions, such as the idea of reincarnation, distinguished Theosophists from the earlier Spiritualists and led to a rift between these two groups. "While Theosophists rejected Spiritualism as philosophically unsophisticated and uncosmopolitan, Spiritualists rejected Theosophy as unscientific occultism."[35] Bailey, an evangelical turned Theosophist, popularized the term "New Age" in reference to the coming transformation. Claiming to receive messages from an "Ascended Master," a Tibetan monk known as "D. K.," Bailey promoted Theosophical concepts, reconciled them with Christian doctrine, and introduced her own interpretations of esoteric astrology, including the prophecy of a coming Aquarian Age.[36]

These various currents of esoteric thought blossomed in 1960s counterculture, a movement that rejected orthodoxy of any kind and privileged points of
view that were marginalized by the mainstream. In that crucible, the modern
New Age movement emerged.

Magic in the New Age Movement

"New Age" is an umbrella term comprising a wide variety of practices and
beliefs that share a desire to transform society by transforming the self and
an eschatological belief that the world is on the cusp of a great change that
will lead to the dawning of a new age in human consciousness, sometimes
referred to as the "Age of Aquarius." The movement is characterized by eclecticism, and it includes such disparate practices as channeling, psychic readings, astrology, past-life regression, astral projection, (neo-)shamanic journeys, naturopathic medicine, crystal healing, color- and aromatherapy, yoga,
mantras, positive affirmations, an interest in lost civilizations, and earth goddesses. Participation in these practices is non-exclusive; because practice is
individual, rather than group-based, people can combine practices and beliefs
in their own unique ways. Individuals typically become devotees of a small
number of technologies and may devalue others.[37] Although most scholars
have emphasized the highly individualistic and personal dimensions of the
New Age movement, others have understood it as a sociopolitical movement
focused on countercultural values and sustainability.[38]

Because it is difficult to define the boundaries of the New Age movement by
listing some of its component technologies and practices, another approach is
to examine the common underlying beliefs of many New Age practitioners.
These include:

- Theism. God is understood as the ultimate unifying principle in the universe rather than as a personal, anthropomorphized deity. Some New Agers
  are panentheists, seeing God as the ultimate animating force present in the
  universe, whereas others are pantheists, believing that God is the physical
  manifestation of the universe;
- A belief in a variety of spiritual beings, such as gods, angels, devas, faeries,
  ghosts, spirit guides, and aliens;
- A belief in a universal power, or "energy," as the basic life force. Often
  equated with the concept of energy in quantum physics, this universal
  energy is thought to permeate all living beings as well as inanimate features,
  such as rocks, trees, rivers, mountains, oceans, and the earth itself. Different

FIGURE 20.2. Cathedral Rock in Sedona, Arizona, a New Age attraction. Image by Kenneth Thomas, under Creative Commons License.

from heat, light, or electricity, it is more akin to the Asian concept of *chi*. Energy derives ultimately from the unifying principle, and it can be passed between individuals and manipulated and channeled using meditation and various other therapies for the purpose of healing. Certain locations, especially those deemed sacred by ancient civilizations, are thought to emanate spiritual energy (see Figure 20.2);

- A belief in reincarnation and karma as frames through which the long-term transformation of the individual are viewed. A single lifetime is not considered long enough to reach enlightenment; the individual must reincarnate multiple times to learn lessons and reach full potential. In addition to providing the reassurance of life after death, this belief can also be used to explain and justify social inequalities and negative events in life, to speculate on past lives, and to suggest the possibility of soul mates transcending numerous lifetimes;

- A belief that all religions and spiritual traditions share a common, universal core and that, in the coming New Age, there will be a single universal religion that will draw on all of the world's major faiths. This religion will emphasize self-knowledge, personal growth, healing, transformation, and harmony with the earth and all its creatures;

- A belief that earlier prophets, such as Christ, Buddha, and Krishna, were bearers of the divine principle of unity and its message of universal love and acceptance. These prophets are sometimes called "Ascended Masters" or "The Great White Brotherhood";

- A lack of the concepts of evil and sin. All is God, therefore all is good. Evil is understood as ignorance, a lack of compassion, or a lack of enlightenment. Sex is a natural, positive force; all sexual orientations and gender manifestations, from cisgender to transgender, are accepted as part of the natural order and variety of the universe;
- A belief that meditation and techniques of personal transformation, as taught by various teachers, are techniques for attaining unity with the Godhead;
- Eschatology. The world is on the cusp of a great transformation, the coming of a New Age, sometimes called the Age of Aquarius, which will bring positive change. Some believe a new prophet akin to Christ or Buddha will appear to usher in the New Age;
- Teleology. Life has a purpose, even if it is unclear to humans; everything happens for a reason;
- A belief in the power of thought. "Thought Creates," therefore it is important to focus one's thinking on positive outcomes in order to engender them. Negative outcomes are the result of negative thoughts, and reality can be shifted by thought alone. A critical mass of highly evolved thinkers concentrating on a particular thought can bring about change in the world. Humans have a responsibility to think and act positively and creatively in order to heal themselves and the world;
- Microcosm/macrocosm ("as above, so below"). Phenomena are linked through correspondences; therefore, for example, astrology can shed light on human behavior, one's personality, and events on earth.[39]

The concept of magic is not central to the New Age movement like it is in Neopaganism. New Agers on the whole do not think of themselves as practicing magic; they are more oriented toward science as ontology. Nevertheless, there are a number of ways in which magic can be understood as playing a role in the movement's beliefs and practices. By using the definition of magic as a type of participatory consciousness, it is evident that many New Age tenets partake in, or encourage adherents to partake in, a frame of mind that is more participatory than it is strictly logical or rational. The threads going back to Hermetic teachings, which are consistent throughout the history of Western esotericism, are evident in many New Age beliefs. At the most fundamental level, naturopathic medicine, crystal healing, color- and aromatherapy, and astrology assume a unitary cosmos in which the microcosm can stand for and influence the macrocosm, and vice versa. Faith in the power of thought to affect reality is also indicative of a degree of magical thinking. The notion of the universe as animated by energy and permeated by a divine force that is manifested through other types of spirits is characteristic of a participatory worldview. Practices designed to expand and transform the self, such as meditation, astral projection, channeling, past-life regression, shamanic journeying, and communication with spirit guides all involve the altering of consciousness to some degree and thus by definition involve magic as participatory consciousness.

What is as at least as striking as the numerous ways New Age beliefs and practices correlate to Western understandings of the magical is the resistance on the part of New Agers to the categorization. Rather than embracing the language of magic, New Agers more typically attempt to ground their practices in the language of science as a way of authenticating and legitimizing their beliefs. Scientists and skeptics, on their part, view this as New Agers misusing scientific discourse by making reference to spiritual elements that are regarded as survivals from older religious cosmologies. As David Hess notes, "[n]otions of the ascientific, pseudoscientific, or less scientific range from (as the skeptics would see it) the whole gamut of paranormal, spiritual and occult beliefs to (as the New Agers and their predecessors would see it) a dogmatically materialistic scientific orthodoxy."[40] Paradoxically, although they regard science as rigid and dogmatic and construct themselves as persecuted liberators of truth, New Agers lionize a number of scientists whose works are recognized as profoundly advancing their fields and also seem to have metaphysical implications. Among them are theoretical physicist David Bohm and the neurologist Karl Pribram, who independently developed what is referred to as the "holographic paradigm" – the belief that the entire description of something (the universe, in Bohm's case, and the mind, in Pribram's) is fully contained in its smallest fragment; the physicist and Nobel laureate Wolfgang Pauli, whose work with Carl Jung led to the development of the theory of synchronicity, the idea that temporally coincident events can be linked together by an inherently meaningful relationship independent of ordinary cause and effect; Ilya Prigogine, another Nobel laureate whose theory of a self-organizing universe appears to suggest the principle of unity; and Rupert Sheldrake, who developed the concept of "morphogenetic fields," a kind of holistic aether through which entities in the world organize and communicate.[41] To these could be added Stephen Hawking's *A Brief History of Time*, Fritjoff Capra's *The Tao of Physics*, and Gary Zukav's *The Dancing Wu Li Masters*. For all of their mixed feelings toward science, New

Agers align themselves firmly with a tradition of reconciling the scientific and the mystical in a disenchanted world.

Magic in Neopaganism

Neopaganism approaches the concept quite differently. Neopaganism – also called modern Paganism to distinguish it from its classical antecedents – is an etic term for a variety of religions that revive, reclaim, and experiment with pre-Christian polytheistic worship. Thus, whereas New Agers speak of a scientific orientation toward the future, Neopagans turn to the past for inspiration. Because of the great diversity of denominations and worldviews contained within this movement, it is perhaps more correct to discuss modern Paganisms in the plural. Although they are rooted in the Western tradition of esotericism, they emerged as full-blown religions only in the twentieth century.[42] Modern Paganisms expanded during the 1970s as a result of counterculture, environmentalism, feminism, and the search for more meaningful forms of spirituality divorced from the norms of established religions. Often calling themselves nature-based religions, they share with New Agers a view of the natural world as sacred and divinity as immanent in it. In those terms, modern Pagans name and embrace magic as a natural force.

As was the case for New Age practices, modern Pagan religions are difficult to systematize. Although many of their practices derive from literary sources, they share no sacred texts. Certain individuals within them may rise to prominence, but the movement lacks prophets or gurus. The basic unit of organization is the small group, called a circle, coven, or grove, but recent surveys indicate that the highest growth rate in Neopaganism is among solitary practitioners.[43] These individuals may meet with other adherents at regular "moots" or for seasonal celebrations, but they are essentially independent agents. Further complicating the picture is the fact that modern Pagan religions are non-exclusive; individuals may affiliate with a number of denominations, both within the movement and outside of it. For example, it is not unusual for Pagans of Jewish origin to identify both as Jews and as Pagans or for members to belong to several Pagan denominations simultaneously. Neopaganism currently represents one of the fastest-growing new religious movements in the world, with more than one million adherents in Europe and North America alone. There are branches of modern Paganisms on every continent in the world.

Modern Paganisms can be divided into two main groups, depending on their association with Revival Witchcraft, also known as Wicca. Wicca first came to public attention through the work of the British civil servant Gerald B. Gardner (1884–1964). In a book entitled *Witchcraft Today* (1954), he claimed to have been initiated into the last living coven of witches in England. Drawing from the theories of the Egyptologist Margaret Murray (1863–1963) and the amateur folklorist Charles G. Leland (1824–1903), he interpreted witchcraft as the survival of a pre-Christian religion that venerated a goddess associated with the moon and earth and a horned god of the hunt and vegetation. This religion, which he hypothesized had once existed all over Europe, had been misunderstood as diabolism by medieval persecutors and was forced into hiding. Its adherents had met during full moons, as well as during the cross-quarter days of the calendar (the midpoint days between each solstice and equinox, or February 1, May 1, August 1, and November 1) to worship the deities and work magic.[44] There is much disagreement among scholars as to whether such a group actually existed in England during the 1930s and 1940s; if one did, it probably did not date back much further than the last decade of the nineteenth century.[45] "The Brotherhood of the Wica,"[46] as Gardner said the adherents called themselves, incorporated elements from Freemasonry (Gardner was a Co-Mason), Golden Dawn ceremonial magic, folk customs and traditions, literature, and anthropological and historical interpretations of magic and witchcraft. By the late 1950s, Gardner had established at least two working covens in southern England and appeared in newspaper, radio, and television interviews to promote the religion. Inevitably, other individuals emerged claiming to practice equally old and more authentic forms of pagan witchcraft. By the late 1960s, the various forms of modern Pagan Witchcraft, including those descended from Gardner's covens, had begun to gain adherents not only in Britain but also in North America, Australia, and parts of continental Europe.

Neopagan Witchcraft was strongly influenced by two social movements: environmentalism and second-wave feminism. Gardner had portrayed Wicca as a fertility religion, and its year-cycle rites are grounded in metaphors that are linked to natural processes of birth, growth, maturation, reproduction, death, and regeneration. Under the influence of environmentalism, its focus on fertility and belief in the immanence of the sacred in the natural world attracted adherents who felt a strong commitment to ecology and the preservation of nature and who saw the spirituality of an earlier time as a vehicle to re-enchant the world and right the wrongs that had been committed against the planet. Witchcraft also appealed to feminists who rejected the patriarchal nature of Abrahamic religions and sought active liturgical roles, as well as a connection with the divine feminine embodied in the witches' goddess.

Feminist interpretations of Craft arose from the broader movement of women's spirituality that sought to reinterpret facets of mainstream religion in a feminist vein and provide more opportunities for women to access liturgical roles and spiritual authority, be it in mainstream or alternative religions. They often focused on the goddess exclusively and practiced in women-only groups where women could fully experience their spirituality without the interference of male authority. Although some forms of Goddess Spirituality embraced the word "witch," reclaiming it as an index of women's power, others avoided it, preferring instead to align with the myth of prehistoric matriarchal religions. It was also in the United States that ethnic varietals of modern Witchcraft began to emerge, allegedly deriving from parallel survivals of goddess-centered pagan religions in other parts of Europe and appealing to those who sought a spiritual dimension in their ethnic heritage.

The other, non-witchen Paganisms developed parallel to, but separately from, Revival Witchcraft, either derived from Gardner or elsewhere. Non-witchen Paganisms likewise can be subdivided into their own traditions, and foremost among them is Reconstructionism. Reconstructionist Paganisms attempt to re-create the religious practices of pre-Christian people with as much accuracy as possible even as they adapt those practices to modern times. Reconstructionists base their practice on surviving texts from the cultures and historical periods they emulate, as well as on archeological and historical scholarship. Heathenism, for example, includes modern Pagan religions inspired by the practices of ancient Norse and Germanic peoples. Druidry comprises a number of orders based on the practices of the ancient Celtic priesthood. Celtic Reconstructionism distinguishes itself from Druidry by focusing on the daily, domestic spiritual practices of ordinary Celtic peoples. Hellenic Reconstructionism revives aspects of ancient Greek paganism. And Kemetic Reconstructionism is inspired by the religion of ancient Egypt. In some parts of Europe, Reconstructionism has taken on a strongly nationalist flavor, at times appealing to elements of the New Right.[47] Finally, some non-witchen traditions were inspired by literature: the Church of All Worlds was founded in 1962 by Tim Zell and Richard Lance Christie in an attempt to re-create the religion portrayed in Robert A. Heinlein's science fiction novel *Stranger in a Strange Land* (1961), and it also incorporates material from the Western esoteric tradition, as well as an environmental ethos in its rites and practices.[48]

Neo-shamanism is a separate group of traditions whose spiritual techniques are based on the practices of indigenous shamans, religious specialists who journey in spirit to communicate with the supernatural realm for the benefit of the community they serve. Neo-shamans typically work with animal spirits who serve as guides to the otherworld, which they visit while in alternate states of consciousness. They use a number of techniques, such as drumming and dancing, to achieve these states, during which they communicate with otherworldly spirits. Whereas traditional shamans use spirit communication to serve their communities, neo-shamans' journeys primarily lead them to self-realization and personal healing, although many also work to heal others and the planet. Neo-shamanism owes much of its popularity to the anthropologists Carlos Casteneda (1925–1998) and Michael Harner (b. 1929). Both men wrote about their experiences studying traditional shamanism, the former with Yaqui healer Don Juan Matus,[49] the latter among the Jívaro Indians of the Ecuadorian rainforest,[50] before founding their own organizations to teach and disseminate shamanic techniques in a Western context. Harner's *The Way of the Shaman: A Guide to Power and Healing* (1980) has become a guidebook for many New Agers and Neopagans interested in alternate states of consciousness and spirit journeys. Neo-shamanism is more of a technology than a religion; its techniques are used and adapted in many variants of modern Paganism, as well as by New Agers.

Magic is more central to modern Pagan traditions to a much greater extent than it is to New Age groups. Neopagan mythic history, with its references to witchcraft and ancient pagan cults, foregrounds magic as a technology. As might be expected in such an individualistic movement, magic has different meanings in different Pagan denominations, and it is more important to some than to others. Some Neopagans define magic as "the ability to change consciousness at will," drawing on the definition of the early twentieth-century English ceremonial magician Aleister Crowley. This definition does not require any transformation outside of the individual's own perception, and it is in harmony with the anthropological definition of magic as participatory consciousness. Other Neopagans prefer a definition that allows for the possibility that magic can also transform material reality. For them, magic is the ability to harness natural forces in harmony with one's will in order to bring about a transformation. As heterodox as they are, modern Paganisms nevertheless share a view of magic as a natural force and an organizational principle for the cosmos.

Mainstream perceptions of magic have tended to emphasize its supernatural qualities – that is, if it exists at all, magic is presumed to operate through supernatural agents existing outside of the fundamental laws of nature. Among modern Paganisms, however, magic is perceived to be a force inherent in nature. Modern Pagans share with New Agers the concept of energy as a force that permeates the entire natural world. It is inherent in every living thing, as well as in the four Aristotelian elements: air, fire, water, and earth. It can be raised, manipulated, and directed toward specific ends. The art and skill of "working" energy is what Neopagans call "magic." Energy can be harnessed by an adept to change consciousness as well as to transform reality, effecting changes in both the self and the material world. Magic to change consciousness usually has the goal of connecting with a spiritual entity: a deity, ancestor, spirit of a place, or the spirit of another living being, such as an animal or plant. Its broader aim is to bring the practitioner into closer touch with the sacred, in some cases even to merge with a deity or other spiritual being, thereby becoming god-like for a brief time. Some practitioners refer to this type of magic as theurgy, a term borrowed from the Neo-Platonists and meaning a union with a deity or other spiritual entity. This form of magic is common to a wide variety of Neopagan denominations, from Wicca, in which the goddess and god are "drawn down" into the bodies of the priestess and priest at the climax of the ritual, to neo-shamanic practices in which practitioners seek to merge with a spirit guide that often takes the form of an animal.

- Magic can also be practiced to transform physical reality in conformity with the magician's will. This form of magic is often called thaumaturgy. Even in thaumaturgy, however, Neopagans believe that magic follows certain universal laws. They can be synthesized into the following principles: Magic follows natural laws. Thus, magic intended to enhance the natural properties of a thing (e.g., to make seeds grow) is more likely to succeed than magic that violates natural laws (e.g., turning people into toads);
- The more simple the means that are available to achieve something, the less successful magic will be. Thus, it is easier to order pizza from the pizza place than to make a pizza magically appear;
- Invisible entities. Neopagans see the world as filled with spiritual entities, such as goddesses, gods, ancestor spirits, spirits of place, and faeries; they believe it is possible to communicate with them using magic – that is, by altering consciousness in ritual;
- Unity or sympathy. All phenomena are linked, directly or indirectly; the universe operates as an interconnected whole. This principle can be further broken down as follows:

  - Contagion. Items once in contact continue to influence one another, even after they are separated. Essence can be transferred through touch; for example, in healing magic, energy can be transmitted by the laying on of hands;

- Homeopathy (like causes or cures like). Things that look alike are alike and can substitute for each other in ritual magic. Thus, one way to make something happen is to enact that change using a symbol in ritual;
- Commonality controls. If two or more things have elements in common, they are linked through their commonality. For example, in the United States, money is green; thus, a spell to bring financial prosperity might use green candles, a green altar cloth, and green objects to enhance wealth through that common characteristic;
- Microcosm/macrocosm ("as above, so below"). Larger patterns can reflect or influence smaller ones, and vice versa;
- Synchronicity. Coincidences are meaningful;
- Knowledge is power. To know the name of someone or something is to know its essence and to be able to control it;
- Animism or personification. Any phenomenon can be considered alive and sentient. Thus, for example, in ritual, Neopagans might address a personal fear, asking that it depart.[51]

Margot Adler, a groundbreaking researcher of the movement, describes an incident that illustrates how Neopagans use magic as a natural force both to change consciousness and to bring about changes in the material world. While working on a communal farm, she and other volunteers were given the task of collecting dying fish from a muddy riverbed and loading them onto a truck so they could be converted into fertilizer. The day was hot, the creek bed was awash with mud, and the slippery fish slid every which way, making the task well-nigh impossible. After several hours of struggle with no progress, the group leader suggested that the volunteers imagine themselves as hungry bears whose very survival depended on catching the fish. The volunteers began to imagine their hands as great paws; they brought them together to catch the fish and threw them into the truck. Within an hour, the truck bed was full of fish.[52] In this example, only the participants' consciousness changed: the day was equally hot, the creek was equally muddy, the fish did not leap willingly into the truck bed, and the volunteers did not actually change into bears. Yet by using their imaginations, the participants were able to change their approach to a material problem and solve it. That, many Neopagans would say, is magic.

There are two important aspects highlighted by this example. The first is that magic involves a change in consciousness – an altered or alternative state of consciousness, some would say – and not simply a change of attitude. By tapping into "Bear Consciousness," participants were able to act as if they were bears and successfully complete the task. The second is that, in anthropological terms, the volunteers were able to temporarily shift from a rational/logical form of consciousness into one that was participatory in nature. This form of consciousness is more creative, making use of the imagination and what many might call "make-believe." Yet it was exactly through this shift that they were able to complete the difficult task at hand. When modern Pagans seek to change their consciousness, it is this magical or participatory consciousness that they seek and that they say allows them to transform reality in accordance with their will.

When practicing thaumaturgy, Neopagans often distinguish "working for essence" from "working for form." Working for form involves doing magic with a very specific goal in mind: x job at y company, for example, or a car of a specific make, model, year, and color. In contrast, working for essence involves analyzing one's will to discover the essence of one's desire: a feeling of financial security and stability by being gainfully employed in work that is personally rewarding, for example, or reliable transportation to and from work. Pagans say that magic for form is less likely to succeed than magic for essence is, because the latter leaves more room in the universe for reality to shift in accordance with will. Thus, a specific job at a particular company might not be available, or it could turn out to be a nightmare, but working for a feeling of financial security and stability through rewarding employment may open up opportunities that the practitioner had not previously considered and would find equally satisfying. Magic for a particular car might not yield results, but if the magician is open to a variety of cars, or to car-pooling with a neighbor, the desired effect could be gained by different means. This idea is sometimes expressed with the proverb: "Magic won't get you what you want, but it will get you what you need."

Neopagan magic is governed by two overriding ethical principles. The first is captured in the dictum: "An it harm none, do as thou wilt." Possibly an adaptation of Aleister Crowley's "Do as thou wilt shall be the whole of the law," this principle indicates that magicians are free to practice according to their will, as long as others are not harmed in the process. This may extend not only to other persons but also to animals, plants, the environment, and the greater good of the planet. Interference with the will of others is considered a form of harm; therefore, a spell to make an individual fall in love is unethical. The ethical way of working in such a case would involve asking for love to come into one's life. The second ethical principle of magic, sometimes called the Threefold Law, holds that whatever the magician puts out is bound to return three times over. Thus, benevolent magic will bring positive results, whereas aggressive, irresponsible, or negative magic will have adverse effects on the practitioner. Magic may, however, be used in self-defense, and some practitioners hold that it is ethical to use magic against another person if it stops them from doing harm – as in binding a rapist so he or she can no longer hurt anyone.

Most Neopagans believe that magic must be accompanied by actions in the material world in order to get results; they are much less likely than New Agers to believe in the power of thought alone. Magical actions require work; wishing alone is not enough to cause change to occur. Thaumaturgical work requires some kind of symbolic enactment of the desired result, often using magical correspondences based on a deity's color, numbers, plants, minerals, and planetary associations drawn from ceremonial magic. Usually, several of these are combined in an amulet or talisman that symbolizes the result the magician hopes to obtain from the spell. The symbol is then "charged" by raising, focusing, and directing energy into it. Energy can be raised by using the imagination, stimulating emotions, or moving the body – preferably all three – through a process involving dancing in a circle and chanting while imagining the desired goal. As the energy builds to a peak, the magician focuses on the talisman or object containing the spell, aims, and "fires" the energy at this goal.[53] Any excess energy is "grounded" (directed into the earth).

The magic of theurgy, or union with a spirit, typically involves a trance induced through guided visualization or guided meditation, a process of storytelling in which participants are asked to imagine themselves in a scenario. The story may include a poetic invocation of the deity, or it may simply invite participants to imagine their interactions with the spirit world. In Wiccan traditions, the goddess and god are "drawn down" on the priestess and priest, respectively; they briefly possess the bodies of their hosts and interact with other coveners in that form. Non-Wiccan traditions may or may not involve deity possession. In the modern Heathen practice of seið, a diviner enters into trance to communicate with ancestors in the spirit world to answer questions from the audience. Neo-shamanic spirit journeys generally also involve an alteration of consciousness; the shaman experiences a feeling of flying outside of the body and journeying to the spirit world, where communion with animal spirits takes place.

Although magic may be performed by Pagans alone, group rituals, which take place at set times in the lunar or calendrical cycle (during full moons, solstices, equinoxes, and cross-quarter days), are more typical settings where magic occurs. Neopagan rituals may be thought of as performance art pieces that transform ordinary parks, backyards, and living rooms into enchanted spaces where participants can have extraordinary experiences. Modern Pagans

use elaborate costumes, decorations, and music to create a feeling of separation from the ordinary, everyday world during their rituals. They create
sacred space by "casting the circle," marking an imaginary ring to contain the
participants and the powers they invoke; but whereas the circle served their
medieval and Renaissance predecessors by containing and controlling the spiritual powers invoked, modern Pagans use it to demarcate a sacred space and
time within which their imaginations can have full rein. The quarters, represented by the directions of east, south, west, and north, and their corresponding Aristotelian elements of air, fire, water, and earth, are called and saluted.
Deities and other spirits may be invoked, and the purpose of the ritual is
stated: "We are gathered here at Midsummer to journey to the realm of Faery
so we may bring back the power to re-enchant and heal the earth," for example. Now begins the core of the ritual: the actions the planners have devised
to encourage participants to personally experience the magical, the sacred.
Suburban gardens are transformed by twinkling fairy lights, spooky jack-o'-
lanterns, arbors draped in fabric, or other seasonal accoutrements; participants may take the parts of goddesses and gods, enacting the drama between
Demeter and Persephone, the Oak King and the Holly King, or other mythical
characters. Participants interact with the characters, chant, sing, dance around
a bonfire (safely contained by a fire pit), and raise energy, lifting their arms up
to the stars to direct it and send it toward their goal. After the energy peaks,
there is often a shared meal – "cakes and wine," although juice is frequently
substituted in respect of those who avoid alcohol for various reasons – or a
potluck. For a brief time, adherents have altered their consciousness, transforming themselves into deities and the ordinary world into a participatory,
enchanted realm. That is the essence of Neopagan magic.

Ultimately, although Neopagan magic strives to re-enchant the world, it,
too, is grounded in participants' experiences of disenchanted modernity. It calls
for a degree of suspension of disbelief, of engrossment in a framed experience,[54] in order to be successful. Both New Age and Neopagan magic are thus
quintessential products of modernity: less rejections of rationality than creative responses to a disenchanted world in which personal spiritual experiences
are both necessary to the human spirit and deeply distrusted by the dominant
paradigm.

Trends in Current Research

The literature on magic and esotericism in Western cultures has grown
exponentially in the first decade and a half of the twenty-first century. One

category emerging from this expansion is the field of Pagan Studies, which has given rise to several journals (e.g. *The Pomegranate* and *Journal for the Academic Study of Magic* [2003–2007; now defunct]) as well as a series of books under the imprint of Altamira Press dedicated to the academic study of Neopagan magic and culture. In 2009, the venerable publisher Brill issued the *Handbook of Contemporary Pagan Studies*, a compendium of scholarly essays on a broad range of subjects and approaches to the field that includes a section specifically devoted to magic.[55]

In contrast, the term "New Age" has lost popularity as both participants in the movement and the scholars who study them have rejected the term. Stephen Sutcliffe argues in *Children of the New Age: A History of Spiritual Practice* (2002) that after the 1970s, the label "New Age" came to have too broad a variety of meanings to be useful, and he advocates for its elimination from academic discourse.[56] In keeping with that theme, Matthew Wood's *Possession, Power and the New Age: Ambiguities of Authority in Neoliberal Societies* (2007) disputes the idea of New Agers as bricoleurs for whom the self is the ultimate spiritual authority, focusing instead on how groups construct "nonformative" authority by incorporating various authorities within the self.[57] Whereas early studies of New Age and Neopagan groups were largely sociological in nature and focused on the origins, nature, and ethos of the movements, recent studies have focused more closely on the cultures of subgroups within these movements and engaged with how they intersect with themes of power, gender, and politics in Western neoliberal democracies. They frequently apply postmodern and feminist theory to analyze how New Age and Neopagan practices reproduce and contest established systems of power. In so doing, they challenge some of the generalizations of earlier studies. Among these are Stephen Sutcliffe and Ingvlid Gilhus's *New Age Spirituality: Rethinking Religion* (2014) and Paul Heelas's *Spiritualities of Life: New Age Romanticism and Consumptive Capitalism* (2008).[58] Although published in the late 1990s, Michael F. Brown's *The Channeling Zone: American Spirituality in an Anxious Age* (1997) is also in this category.[59] Anna Fedele and Kim Knibbe's *Gender and Power in Contemporary Spirituality: Ethnographic Approaches* (2013) applies gender and feminist theory to analyze ritual and magical practices in a variety of new religious movements on a global scale, examining the influence of movements of people and religions into new cultural contexts. New Age and Neopagan spiritualities have been criticized for their appropriation of material from non-Western sources; Fedele and Knibbe's volume also illustrates the complexities of these global flows of spiritual ideas. As a counter-impulse to intercultural borrowing, the localization and nationalization of some forms of Neopaganism, along with some of their racialist implications, are addressed by Michael Strmiska in *Modern Paganism in World Cultures* (2006), Mattias Gardell in *Gods of the Blood: The Pagan Revival and White Separatism* (2003), and Mariya Lesiv in *The Return of Ancestral Gods: Modern Ukrainian Paganism as an Alternative Vision for a Nation* (2013). Lee Gilmore's *Theatre in a Crowded Fire: Ritual and Spirituality at Burning Man* (2010) explores the spirituality and confluence of New Age ideas in the phenomenon of Burning Man, a week-long festival in the Nevada Desert that has become a form of pilgrimage for many attendees who otherwise eschew religion. A spate of yet-unpublished research investigates the relationships between New Age and Neopagan worldviews, perceptions of nature, and sustainable practices. In conclusion, a great deal of research remains to be done in order to understand the variety of movements subsumed under the rubric of "New Age" and "Neopaganism," their individual worldviews, and their relationships with larger structures of power.

Notes

1. Drury, *Stealing Fire from Heaven*, 7.
2. See Asad, "Anthropological Conceptions of Religion," 237–259; Styers, *Making Magic*, 4.
3. Hutton, "The New Old Paganism," 107.
4. Geertz, "Religion as a Cultural System," 87–125.
5. Pike, *New Age and Neopagan Religion*, 22.
6. See Hanegraaff, *New Age Religion*; Melton, Clark, and Kelly, eds., *The New Age Encyclopedia*; Pike, *New Age and Neopagan Religion*; and York, *The Emerging Network*.
7. Pike, *New Age and Neopagan Religion*, 22.
8. Magliocco, *Witching Culture*, 85.
9. Hanegraaff, *New Age Religion*, 79.
10. Ibid., 62.
11. Durkheim, *The Elementary Forms of the Religious Life*, 55.
12. Tambiah, *Magic, Science, Religion*, 19.
13. Luhrmann, *Persuasions of the Witches' Craft*, 308–323.
14. Evans-Pritchard, *Witchcraft, Oracles and Magic among the Azande*.
15. Wax and Wax, "The Notion of Magic," 495–503.
16. Lucien Lévy-Bruhl, in Tambiah, *Magic, Science, Religion*, 91–92.
17. Tambiah, *Magic, Science, Religion*, 24.
18. Greenwood, *The Nature of Magic*, 42.
19. Melton, Clark, and Kelly, eds., *The New Age Encyclopedia*, xiii.
20. Pike, *New Age and Neopagan Religion*, 27.
21. Seið is a modern Pagan practice that reclaims an ancient Norse rite of prophesy and divination. See Blain, *Nine Worlds of Seid-Magic*.

22. Antoine Faivre, in Hanegraaff, *New Age Religion*, 398–400.

23. Hanegraaff, *New Age Religion*, 388.

24. Drury, *Stealing Fire from Heaven*, 12–13; see also Burnett and Ryan, *Magic and the Classical Tradition*; Faivre, *The Eternal Hermes*, 181–185; Hanegraaff, "Beyond the Yates Paradigm," 5–37; and Lucentini, Parri, and Compagni, eds., *Hermetism from Late Antiquity to Humanism*.

25. Drury, *Stealing Fire from Heaven*, 7.

26. Ibid.

27. Ibid., 120.

28. Ibid., 59.

29. Hanegraaff, *New Age Religion*, 396–397.

30. Ibid., 401–421.

31. Ibid., 429.

32. Ibid., 423.

33. See Bender, *The New Metaphysicals*.

34. Ibid., 513.

35. Hess, *Science and the New Age*, 20.

36. Lewis and Melton, *Perspectives on the New Age*, xi.

37. Melton, Clark, and Kelly, eds., *New Age Encyclopedia*, xiv.

38. See Satin, *New Age Politics*; Roszak, *Person/Planet*; McLaughlin, *Spiritual Politics*.

39. Adapted from Melton, Clark, and Kelly, eds., *New Age Encyclopedia*, xvi–xvii.

40. Hess, *Science and the New Age*, 17.

41. Hanegraaff, *New Age Religion*, 63.

42. See Hutton, *Triumph of the Moon*; and Hutton, *The Druids*.

43. Berger, "Fifteen Years of Continuity and Change."

44. During the late 1950s, the solstices and equinoxes were added to the ritual calendar through the influence of Ross Nichols, one of the founders of modern Druidry, on Gerald Gardner. See Hutton, "Modern Pagan Festivals," 251–273.

45. For a discussion of this, see Hutton, *Triumph of the Moon*, 205–240; and Heselton, *Witchfather: A Life of Gerald Gardner*.

46. The spelling was later changed to "Wicca," the form used today, based on the Old English word *wicce*, meaning "witch."

47. See Strmiska, *Modern Paganism in World Cultures*; and Hale, "John Michell, Radical Traditionalism," 77–97.

48. See York, "Invented Culture/Invented Religion," 135–136, 141; and Cusack, *Invented Religions*, 53–82.

49. Casteneda, *The Teachings of Don Juan*. Critiques by other anthropologists have alleged that Casteneda's book is fictional; this is the accepted position in contemporary anthropology.

50. Harner, *The Jivaro*.

51. Magliocco, *Witching Culture*, 102–104.

52. Adler, *Drawing down the Moon*, 6–8.
53. Bonewits, *Real Magic*, 159–160.
54. Goffman, *Frame Analysis*.
55. Lewis and Pizza, eds., *Handbook of Contemporary Paganism*.
56. Sutcliffe, *Children of the New Age*, 39–40.
57. Wood, *Possession, Power and the New Age*, 4–5.
58. Sutcliffe and Gilhus, *New Age Spirituality*; and Heelas, *Spiritualities of Life*.
59. Brown, *The Channeling Zone*.

Bibliography

Introduction (by David J. Collins, S.J.)

Abusch, Tzvi, and Daniel Schwemer, eds. *Corpus of Mesopotamian Anti-Witchcraft Rituals.* Vol. 1. Ancient Magic and Divination 8.1. Leiden and Boston: Brill, 2011.

Abusch, Tzvi. *Mesopotamian Witchcraft: Toward a History and Understanding of Babylonian Witchcraft Beliefs and Literature.* Ancient Magic and Divination 5. Leiden and Boston: Brill Styx, 2002.

Abusch, Tzvi, and Karel van der Toorn, eds. *Mesopotamian Magic: Textual, Historical, Interpretative Perspectives.* Groningen: Styx Press, 1999.

Ankarloo, Bengt, and Stuart Clark, eds. *Witchcraft and Magic in Europe.* 6 vols. Philadelphia: University of Pennsylvania Press, 1999–2002.

Bailey, Michael D. *Battling Demons: Witchcraft, Heresy, and Reform in the Late Middle Ages.* University Park: Penn State University Press, 2003.

Fearful Spirits, Reasoned Follies: The Boundaries of Superstition in Late Medieval Europe. Ithaca: Cornell University Press, 2013.

de Blécourt, Willem, and Owen Davies, eds. *Witchcraft Continued: Popular Magic in Modern Europe.* Manchester: Manchester University Press, 2004.

Boureau, Alain. *Satan the Heretic: The Birth of Demonology in the Medieval West.* Translated by Teresa Lavender Fagan. Chicago: University of Chicago Press, 2006.

Bremmer, Jan N., and Jan R. Veenstra, eds. *The Metamorphosis of Magic from Late Antiquity to the Early Modern Period.* Vol. 1, *Groningen Studies in Cultural Change.* Leuven: Peeters, 2002.

Cameron, Euan. *Enchanted Europe: Superstition, Reason, and Religion, 1250–1750.* Oxford: Oxford University Press, 2010.

Clark, Stuart. *Thinking with Demons: The Idea of Witchcraft in Early Modern Europe.* Oxford: Clarendon Press, 1997.

Davies, Owen. *Grimoires: A History of Magic Books.* Oxford: Oxford University Press, 2009.

Magic: A Very Short Introduction. Oxford: Oxford University Press, 2012.

Davies, Owen, and Willem de Blécourt, eds. *Beyond the Witch Trials: Witchcraft and Magic in Enlightenment Europe.* Manchester: Manchester University Press, 2004.

Flint, Valerie I. J. *The Rise of Magic in Early Medieval Europe.* Princeton: Princeton University Press, 1991.

Games, Alison. *Witchcraft in Early North America.* American Controversies Series. Lanham, MD: Rowman & Littlefield Publishers, 2010.

Gilly, Carlos, and Cis van Heertum, eds. *Magic, Alchemy and Science, 15th–18th Centuries: The Influence of Hermes Trismegistus.* 2 vols. Florence: Centro Di, 2002.

Golden, Richard M., ed. *Encyclopedia of Witchcraft: The Western Tradition.* Santa Barbara: ABC-CLIO, 2006.

Harvey, David Allen. *Beyond Enlightenment: Occultism and Politics in Modern France.* DeKalb: Northern Illinois University Press, 2005.

Jolly, Karen Louise. *Popular Religion in Late Saxon England: Elf Charms in Context.* Chapel Hill: University of North Carolina Press, 1996.

Kieckhefer, Richard. *Forbidden Rites: A Necromancer's Manual of the Fifteenth Century.* University Park: Penn State University Press, 1998.

Klaassen, Frank F. *Transformations of Magic: Illicit Learned Magic in the Later Middle Ages and Renaissance.* Magic in History. University Park: Penn State University Press, 2013.

Kramer, Heinrich. *Malleus maleficarum.* Edited and translated by Christopher S. Mackay. 2 vols. Cambridge: Cambridge University Press, 2006.

Láng, Benedek. *Unlocked Books: Manuscripts of Learned Magic in the Medieval Libraries of Central Europe.* Magic in History. University Park: Penn State University Press, 2008.

Levack, Brian P., ed. *Articles on Witchcraft, Magic, and Demonology.* 12 vols. New York: Garland, 1992.

——— ed. *New Perspectives on Witchcraft, Magic, and Demonology.* 6 vols. New York: Routledge, 2001.

Magliocco, Sabina. *Witching Culture: Folklore and Neopaganism in America.* Philadelphia: University of Pennsylvania Press, 2004.

Meyer, Birgit, and Peter Pels, eds. *Magic and Modernity: Interfaces of Revelation and Concealment.* Stanford: Stanford University Press, 2003.

Mirecki, Paul Allan, and Marvin Meyer, eds. *Magic and Ritual in the Ancient World.* Religions in the Graeco-Roman World 141, edited by R. van den Broek, H. J. W. Drijvers, and H. S. Versnell. Leiden, Boston, and Cologne: Brill, 2002.

Owen, Alex. *The Place of Enchantment: British Occultism and the Culture of the Modern.* Chicago: University of Chicago Press, 2004.

Paravicini Bagliani, Agostino. *Le "Speculum astronomiae," une énigme?: Enquête sur les manuscrits.* Micrologus' Library. Florence: SISMEL Edizioni del Galluzzo, 2001.

Park, Katharine, and Lorraine Daston, eds. *The Cambridge History of Science.* Vol. 3, *Early Modern Science.* Cambridge: Cambridge University Press, 2006.

Pócs, Éva, and Gábor Klaniczay, eds. *Demons, Spirits, Witches.* 3 vols. Budapest and New York: Central European University Press, 2005–2008.

Rutkin, Darrel H. "Astrology." In *The Cambridge History of Science: Early Modern Science,* edited by Katharine Park and Lorraine Daston, 541–562. Cambridge: Cambridge University Press, 2006.

Stephens, Walter. *Demon Lovers: Witchcraft, Sex, and the Crisis of Belief.* Chicago: University of Chicago Press, 2002.

Styers, Randall. *Making Magic: Religion, Magic, and Science in the Modern World.* New York and Oxford: Oxford University Press, 2004.

Veenstra, Jan R. *Magic and Divination at the Courts of Burgundy and France: Text and Context of Laurens Pignon's "Contre les devineurs" (1411).* Brill's Studies in Intellectual History, edited by Arie Johan Vanderjagt. Leiden: Brill, 1998.

Weill-Parot, Nicolas. *Les "images astrologiques" au Moyen Âge et à la Renaissance: Spéculations intellectuelles et pratiques magiques, XIIe–XVe siècle.* Sciences, techniques et civilisations du Moyen Âge à l'aube des Lumières 6. Paris: Honoré Champion, 2002.

Williams, Gerhild Scholz, and Charles D. Gunnoe, eds. *Paracelsian Moments: Science, Medicine, and Astrology in Early Modern Europe.* Kirksville, MO: Truman State University Press, 2002.

Zambelli, Paola. *The "Speculum astronomiae" and Its Enigma: Astrology, Theology, and Science in Albertus Magnus and His Contemporaries.* Boston Studies in the Philosophy of Science, edited by Robert S. Cohen. Dordrecht: Kluwer Academic Publishers, 1992.

White Magic, Black Magic in the European Renaissance. Studies in Medieval and Reformation Traditions, edited by Andrew Colin Gow. Leiden: Brill, 2007.

Zika, Charles. *Exorcising Our Demons: Magic, Witchcraft, and Visual Culture in Early Modern Europe.* Studies in Medieval and Reformation Thought. Leiden: Brill, 2003.

Reuchlin und die okkulte Tradition der Renaissance. Pforzheimer Reuchlinschriften. Sigmaringen: Jan Thorbecke Verlag, 1998.

1 The Ancient Near East (by Daniel Schwemer)

Primary Sources

AMT — Thompson, Reginald Campbell. *Assyrian Medical Texts from the Originals in the British Museum.* London and Oxford: Oxford University Press, 1923.

BAM — Köcher, Franz. *Die babylonisch-assyrische Medizin in Texten und Untersuchungen.* Vols. I–VI. Berlin and New York: Walter de Gruyter, 1963–1980.

FHL — Durand, Jean-Marie, and Emmanuel Laroche. "Fragments hittites du Louvre." In *Mémorial Atatürk: Etudes d'archéologie et de philologie anatoliennes*, 73–107. Éditions recherche sur les civilisations: Synthèse 10. Paris: Institut Français d'études anatoliennes and Éditions recherche sur les civilisations, 1982.

KAL 2 — Schwemer, Daniel. *Rituale und Beschwörungen gegen Schadenzauber.* Keilschrifttexte aus Assur literarischen Inhalts 2; Wissenschaftliche Veröffentlichungen der Deutschen Orient-Gesellschaft 117. Wiesbaden: Harrassowitz, 2007.

KAR — Ebeling, Erich. *Keilschrifttexte aus Assur religiösen Inhalts.* 2 vols. Wissenschaftliche Veröffentlichungen der Deutschen Orient-Gesellschaft 28, 34. Leipzig: Hinrichs, 1915–1919, 1920–1923.

KBo — *Keilschrifttexte aus Boghazköi.* Leipzig: Hinrichs, 1916–23. Berlin: Mann, 1954-.

KUB — *Keilschrifturkunden aus Boghazköi.* Berlin: Deutsche Akademie der Wissenschaften zu Berlin, Institut für Orientforschung, 1921-.

LKA — Ebeling, Erich, and Franz Köcher. *Literarische Keilschrifttexte aus Assur.* Berlin: Akademie-Verlag, 1953.

STT — Gurney, Oliver R. (vol. I with Jacob J. Finkelstein, vol. II with Peter Hulin). *The Sultantepe Tablets.* Vols. I–II. London: The British Institute of Archaeology at Ankara, 1957, 1964.

Further Abbreviations:

A — Museum siglum, İstanbul Arkeoloji Müzeleri, Istanbul.

BM — Museum siglum, British Museum, London.

K — Museum siglum, British Museum, London.

Sm   Museum siglum, British Museum, London.

VA   Museum siglum, Vorderasiatisches Museum, Berlin.

WA   Museum siglum, British Museum, London.

CAD   *The Assyrian Dictionary of the Oriental Institute of the University of Chicago.* 21 vols., edited by Martha T. Roth. Chicago: OIUC, 1956–2011.

PSD   *The Sumerian Dictionary of the University of Pennsylvania Museum.* Philadelphia: University of Pennsylvania's Museum of Archaeology and Anthropology, 1974–.

Secondary Sources

Abusch, Tzvi. *Mesopotamian Witchcraft. Toward a History and Understanding of Babylonian Witchcraft Beliefs and Literature.* Ancient Magic and Divination 5. Leiden and Boston: Brill / Styx, 2002.

Abusch, Tzvi, and Daniel Schwemer. "Das Abwehrzauber-Ritual Maqlû ('Verbrennung')." In *Texte aus der Umwelt des Alten Testaments. Neue Folge*, vol. 4, edited by Bernd Janowski and Gernot Wilhelm, 128–186. Gütersloh: Gütersloher Verlagshaus, 2008.

"The Chicago Maqlû Fragment (A 7876)." *Iraq* 71 (2009): 53–87.

eds. *Corpus of Mesopotamian Anti-Witchcraft Rituals.* Vol. 1. Ancient Magic and Divination 8.1. Leiden and Boston: Brill, 2011. [*CMAwR* 1]

Ambos, Claus. *Mesopotamische Baurituale aus dem 1. Jahrtausend v. Chr.* Dresden: ISLET, 2004.

Beaulieu, Paul-Alain. "Late Babylonian Intellectual Life." In *The Babylonian World*, edited by Gwendolyn Leick, 473–484. New York and London: Routledge, 2007.

Beckman, Gary M. *Hittite Birth Rituals.* 2nd ed. Studien zu den Boğazköy-Texten 29. Wiesbaden: Harrassowitz, 1983.

Biggs, Robert D. "Liebeszauber." In *Reallexikon der Assyriologie und Vorderasiatischen Archäologie*, vol. 7, 17–18. Berlin: Walter de Gruyter, 1987–1990.

Biggs, Robert D. "Medicine, Surgery, and Public Health in Ancient Mesopotamia." In *Civilizations of the Ancient Near East*, edited by Jack M. Sasson, 1911–1924. New York: Charles Scribner's Sons, 1995.

van Bimsbergen, Wim, and Frans A. M. Wiggermann. "Magic in History. A Theoretical Perspective, and Its Application to Ancient Mesopotamia." In *Mesopotamian Magic. Textual Historical, and Interpretative Perspectives*, edited by Tzvi Abusch and Karel van der Toorn, 3–34. Ancient Magic and Divination 1. Groningen: Styx Publications, 1999.

Borger, Rykle. "Die Weihe eines Enlil-Priesters." *Bibliotheca Orientalis* 30 (1973): 162–176.

Braarvig, Jens. "Magic. Reconsidering the Grand Dichotomy." In *The World of Ancient Magic. Papers from the First International Samson Eitrem Seminar at the Norwegian Institute at Athens, 4–8 May 1997*, edited by David R. Jordan, Hugo Montgomery, and Einar Thomassen, 21–54. Papers from the Norwegian Institute at Athens 4. Bergen: The Norwegian Institute at Athens, 1999.

Butler, Sally A. L. *Mesopotamian Conceptions of Dreams and Dream Rituals.* Alter Orient und Altes Testament 258. Münster: Ugarit-Verlag, 1998.

Caplice, Richard I. *The Akkadian Namburi Texts: An Introduction.* Sources from the Ancient Near East 1. Malibu: Undena Publications, 1974.

Cunningham, Graham. *"Deliver Me from Evil." Mesopotamian Incantations 2500–1500 BC.* Studia Pohl series maior 17. Rome: Editrice Pontificio Istituto Biblico, 1997.

Religion and Magic. Approaches and Theories. New York: New York University Press, 1999.

Delling, Gerhard. *"Mageía, mágos, mageúein."* In *Theologisches Wörterbuch zum Neuen Testament*, vol. 4, edited by Gerhard Kittel, 360–363. Stuttgart: Kohlhammer, 1942.

van Dijk, Johannes J. A., and Markham J. Geller, with the collaboration of Joachim Oelsner. *Ur III Incantations from the Frau Professor Hilprecht-Collection, Jena.* Texte und Materialien der Frau Professor Hilprecht Collection of Babylonian Antiquities im Eigentum der Friedrich Schiller-Universität Jena 6. Wiesbaden: Harrassowitz, 2003.

Farber, Walter. *"Rituale und Beschwörungen in akkadischer Sprache."* In *Texte aus der Umwelt des Alten Testaments*, vol. 2, edited by Otto Kaiser, 212–281. Gütersloh: Gütersloher Verlagshaus, 1987.

"Tamarisken, Fibeln, Skolopender. Zur philologischen Deutung der 'Reiseszene' auf neuassyrischen Lamaštu-Amuletten." In *Language, Literature, and History. Philological and Historical Studies Presented to Erica Reiner*, edited by Francesca Rochberg-Halton, 85–105. American Oriental Series 67. New Haven: American Oriental Society, 1987.

Finkel, Irving L. *"Adad-apla-iddina, Esagil-kīn-apli, and the Series sa.gig."* In *A Scientific Humanist: Studies in Memory of Abraham Sachs*, edited by Erle Leichty, Maria deJong Ellis and Pamela Gerardi, 143–159. Occasional Publications of the Samuel Noah Kramer Fund 9. Philadelphia: University Museum, 1988.

Finkel, Irving L. *"A Study in Scarlet: Incantations against Samana."* In *Festschrift für Rykle Borger zu seinem 65. Geburtstag am 24. Mai 1994*, edited by Stefan M. Maul, 71–106. Cuneiform Monographs 10. Groningen: Styx Publications, 1998.

"On Some Dog, Snake and Scorpion Incantations." In *Mesopotamian Magic. Textual Historical, and Interpretative Perspectives*, edited by Tzvi Abusch and Karel van der Toorn, 213–250. Ancient Magic and Divination 1. Groningen: Styx Publications, 1999.

Foster, Benjamin R. *"Humor and Cuneiform Literature." Journal of the Ancient Near Eastern Society* 6 (1974): 69–85.

Before the Muses. An Anthology of Akkadian Literature, 3rd ed. Bethesda, MD: CDL Press, 2005.

Frame, Grant, and Andrew R. George. "The Royal Libraries of Nineveh: New Evidence for King Ashurbanipal's Tablet Collecting." *Iraq* 67 (2005): 265–284.

Frazer, James. *The Golden Bough: A Study in Magic and Religion.* Abr. ed. London: Macmillan, 1922. Reprint, London: Penguin Books, 1996.

Geller, Markham J. "New Duplicates to SBTU II." *Archiv für Orientforschung* 35 (1988): 1–23.

"The Aramaic Incantation in Cuneiform Script (AO 6489 = TCL 6, 58)." *Jaarbericht van het Voor"aziatisch-Egyptisch Genootschap "Ex Oriente Lux"* 35–36 (1997–2000): 127–146.

"Incipits and Rubrics." In *Wisdom, Gods and Literature: Studies in Assyriology in Honour of W. G. Lambert*, edited by Andrew R. George and Irving L. Finkel, 225–258. Winona Lake: Eisenbrauns, 2000.

"Akkadian Evil Eye Incantations from Assur." *Zeitschrift für Assyriologie und Vorderasiatische Archäologie* 94 (2004): 52–58.

Evil Demons. Canonical Utukkū lemnūtu Incantations. State Archives of Assyria Cuneiform Texts 5. Helsinki: The Neo-Assyrian Text Corpus Project, 2007.

George, Andrew R. "Model Dogs." In *Art and Empire. Treasures from Assyria in the British Museum*, edited by John E. Curtis and Julian E. Reade, 116–117. London: British Museum Press, 1995.

Babylonian Literary Texts in the Schøyen Collection. Cornell University Studies in Assyriology and Sumerology 10. Bethesda, MD: CDL Press, 2009.

Grensemann, Hermann. *Die hippokratische Schrift "Über die heilige Krankheit"*. Ars Medica II.1. Berlin: Walter de Gruyter, 1968.

Haas, Volkert, with contributions by Daliah Bawanypeck. *Materia Magica et Medica Hethitica. Ein Beitrag zur Heilkunde im Alten Orient*. Berlin and New York: Walter de Gruyter, 2003.

Hauptmann, Harald. "Die Felsspalte D." In *Das hethitische Felsheiligtum Yazılıkaya*, edited by Kurt Bittel, 62–75. Berlin: Gebr. Mann, 1975.

Heeßel, Nils P. *Pazuzu. Archäologische und philologische Studien zu einem altorientalischen Dämon*. Ancient Magic and Divination 4. Leiden and Boston: Brill and Styx Publications, 2002.

"Neues von Esagil-kīn-apli. Die ältere Version der physiognomischen Omenserie *alamdimmû*." In *Assur-Forschungen. Arbeiten aus der Forschungsstelle "Edition literarischer Keilschrifttexte aus Assur" der Heidelberger Akademie der Wissenschaften*, edited by Stefan M. Maul and Nils P. Heeßel, 139–188. Wiesbaden: Harrassowitz, 2010.

Hutter, Manfred. "Aspects of Luwian Religion." In *The Luwians*, edited by H. Craig Melchert, 211–280. Handbuch der Orientalistik I.68. Leiden and Boston: Brill, 2003.

Jaques, Margaret. "'Mon dieu, qu'ai-je donc fait?' Les prières pénitentielles (dingir-šà-dab-ba) et l'expression de la piété privée en Mésopotamie." Habilitation thesis, Universität Zurich, 2011.

Jean, Cynthia. *La magie néo-assyrienne en contexte: Recherches sur le métier d'exorciste et le concept d'āšipūtu*. State Archives of Assyria Studies 17. Helsinki: The Neo-Assyrian Text Corpus Project, 2006.

Koch, Heidemarie. "Texte aus Iran." In *Texte aus der Umwelt des Alten Testaments. Neue Folge*, vol. 4, edited by Bernd Janowski and Gernot Wilhelm, 387–392. Gütersloh: Gütersloher Verlagshaus, 2008.

Krebernik, Manfred. *Die Beschwörungen aus Fara und Ebla. Untersuchungen zur ältesten keilschriftlichen Beschwörungsliteratur*. Texte und Studien zur Orientalistik 2. Hildesheim: Georg Olms, 1984.

Kümmel, Hans Martin. *Ersatzrituale für den hethitischen König*. Studien zu den Boğazköy-Texten 3. Wiesbaden: Harrassowitz, 1967.

Lambert, Wilfred G. *Babylonian Wisdom Literature*. Oxford: Oxford University Press, 1960.

"A Catalogue of Texts and Authors." *Journal of Cuneiform Studies* 16 (1962): 59–77.

"DINGIR.ŠÀ.DIB.BA Incantations." *Journal of Near Eastern Studies* 33 (1974): 267–322.

Linssen, Marc J. H. *The Cults of Uruk and Babylon. The Temple Ritual Texts as Evidence for Hellenistic Cult Practises*. Cuneiform Monographs 25. Leiden and Boston: Brill, 2004.

Maul, Stefan M. "Der Kneipenbesuch als Heilverfahren." In *La circulation des biens, des personnes et des idées dans le Proche-Orient ancien. Actes de la XXXVIIIe Rencontre Assyriologique Internationale (Paris, 8–10 juillet 1991)*, edited by Dominique Charpin and Francis Joannès, 389–396. Paris: Éditions recherche sur les civilisations, 1992.

Zukunftsbewältigung. Eine Untersuchung altorientalischen Denkens anhand der babylonisch-assyrischen Löserituale (Namburbi). Baghdader Forschungen 18. Mainz: von Zabern, 1994.

"Die Tontafelbibliothek aus dem sogenannten 'Haus des Beschwörungspriesters.'" In *Assur-Forschungen. Arbeiten aus der Forschungsstelle "Edition literarischer Keilschrifttexte aus Assur" der Heidelberger Akademie der Wissenschaften*, edited by Stefan M. Maul and Nils P. Heeßel, 189–228. Wiesbaden: Harrassowitz, 2010.

Mayer, Werner R. "Das Ritual *KAR* 26 mit dem Gebet 'Marduk 24.'" *Orientalia Nova Series* 68 (1999): 145–163.

Meier, Gerhard. *Die assyrische Beschwörungssammlung Maqlû*. Archiv für Orientforschung supp. 2. Berlin: Gerhard Meier, 1937.

Metcalf, Christopher. "New Parallels in Hittite and Sumerian Praise of the Sun." *Welt des Orients* 41 (2011): 168–176.

Miller, Jared L. *Studies in the Origins, Development and Interpretation of the Kizzuwatna Rituals*. Studien zu den Boğazköy-Texten 46. Wiesbaden: Harrassowitz, 2004.

Myhrman, David W. "Die Labartu-Texte. Babylonische Beschwörungsformeln nebst Zauberverfahren gegen die Dämonin Labartu." *Zeitschrift für Assyriologie und Vorderasiatische Archäologie* 16 (1902): 141–200.

Niehr, Herbert. "Texte aus Ugarit." In *Texte aus der Umwelt des Alten Testaments. Neue Folge*, vol. 4, edited by Bernd Janowski and Gernot Wilhelm, 243–257. Gütersloh: Gütersloher Verlagshaus, 2008.

Oettinger, Norbert. *Die militärischen Eide der Hethiter*. Studien zu den Boğazköy-Texten 22. Wiesbaden: Harrassowitz, 1976.

Oppenheim, A. Leo. *The Interpretation of Dreams in the Ancient Near East. With a Translation of an Assyrian Dream-Book*. Transactions of the American Philosophical Society 46.3. Philadelphia: The American Philosophical Society, 1956.

Ancient Mesopotamia. Portrait of a Dead Civilization, edited by Erica Reiner. Chicago and London: University of Chicago Press, 1977.

Otten, Heinrich. *Puduḫepa. Eine Königin in ihren Textzeugnissen*. Mainz: Akademie der Wissenschaften und der Literatur, 1975.

Pardee, Dennis. "Les documents d'Arslan Tash: Authentiques ou faux?" *Syria* 75 (1998): 15–54.

Ritual and Cult at Ugarit. Writings from the Ancient World 10. Atlanta: Society of Biblical Literature, 2002.

Parpola, Simo. *Letters from Assyrian Scholars to the Kings Esarhaddon and Assurbanipal*. Vols. I–II. Alter Orient und Altes Testament 5.1–2. Kevelaer and Neukirchen-Vluyn: Butzon & Bercker and Neukirchener Verlag, 1970, 1983.

"Assyrian Library Records." *Journal of Near Eastern Studies* 42 (1983): 1–29.

Pedersén, Olof. *Archives and Libraries in the City of Assur*. Parts I–II. Acta Universitatis Upsaliensis Studia Semitica Upsaliensia 6, 8. Uppsala: Almqvist & Wiksell, 1985, 1986.

Prechel, Doris, and Thomas Richter. "Abrakadabra oder Althurritisch. Betrachtungen zu einigen altbabylonischen Beschwörungstexten." In *Kulturgeschichten. Altorientalistische Studien für Volkert Haas zum 65. Geburtstag*, edited by Jörg Klinger, Doris Prechel, and Thomas Richter, 333–371. Saarbrücken: SDV, 2001.

Reiner, Erica. *Šurpu. A Collection of Sumerian and Akkadian Incantations*. Archiv für Orientforschung supp. 11. Vienna: Institut für Orientalistik, 1958.

Astral Magic in Babylonia. Transactions of the American Philosophical Society 85.4. Philadelphia: The American Philosophical Society, 1995.

Ritter, Edith K. "Magical-Expert (= *āšipu*) and Physician (= *asû*): Notes on Two Complementary Professions in Babylonian Medicine." In *Studies in Honor of Benno*

Landsberger, edited by Hans Gustav Güterbock and Thorkild Jacobsen, 299–321. Assyriological Studies 16. Chicago: University of Chicago Press, 1965.

Salje, Beate. "Siegelverwendung im privaten Bereich. 'Schmuck' – Amulett – Grabbeigabe." In *Mit sieben Siegeln versehen. Das Siegel in Wirtschaft und Kunst des Alten Orients*, edited by Evelyn Klengel-Brandt, 125–137. Mainz: von Zabern, 1997.

Schwemer, Daniel. "Ein akkadischer Liebeszauber aus Ḫattuša." *Zeitschrift für Assyriologie und Vorderasiatische Archäologie* 94 (2004): 59–79.

Abwehrzauber und Behexung. Studien zum Schadenzauberglauben im alten Mesopotamien (Unter Benutzung von Tzvi Abuschs Kritischem Katalog und Sammlungen im Rahmen des Kooperationsprojektes Corpus of Mesopotamian Anti-Witchcraft Rituals). Wiesbaden: Harrassowitz, 2007.

"Witchcraft and War: The Ritual Fragment Ki 1904-10-9, 18 (BM 98989)." *Iraq* 69 (2007): 29–42.

"Washing, Defiling and Burning: Two Bilingual Anti-Witchcraft Incantations." *Orientalia Nova Series* 78 (2009): 44–68.

"Empowering the Patient: The Opening Section of the Ritual *Maqlû*." In *Pax Hethitica. Studies on the Hittites and Their Neighbours in Honor of Itamar Singer*, edited by Yoram Cohen, Amir Gilan, and Jared L. Miller, 311–339. Studien zu den Boğazköy-Texten 51. Wiesbaden: Harrassowitz, 2010.

"Entrusting the Witches to Ḫumuṭ-tabal: The ušburruda Ritual BM 47806+." *Iraq* 72 (2010): 63–78.

"Magic Rituals: Conceptualization and Performance." In *Oxford Handbook of Cuneiform Culture*, edited by Karen Radner and Eleanor Robson, 418–442. Oxford: Oxford University Press, 2011.

"Evil Witches, Apotropaic Plants and the New Moon: Two Anti-Witchcraft Incantations from Babylon (BM 35672 and BM 36584)." *Welt des Orients* 41 (2011): 177–190.

"Gauging the Influence of Babylonian Magic: The Reception of Mesopotamian Traditions in Hittite Ritual Practice." In *Diversity and Standardization. Perspectives on Ancient Near Eastern Cultural History*, edited by Eva Cancik-Kirschbaum, Jörg Klinger, and Gerfrid G. W. Müller, 145–172. Berlin: Akademie Verlag, 2014.

Scurlock, JoAnn. "Was There a 'Love-Hungry' Ēntu-Priestess Named Eṭirtum?" *Archiv für Orientforschung* 36–37 (1989–1990): 107–112.

"Physician, Exorcist, Conjurer, Magician: A Tale of Two Healing Professionals." In *Mesopotamian Magic. Textual Historical, and Interpretative Perspectives*, edited by Tzvi Abusch and Karel van der Toorn, 69–79. Ancient Magic and Divination 1. Groningen: Styx Publications, 1999.

"Sorcery in the Stars. STT 300, BRM 4.19–20 and the Mandaic Book of the Zodiac." *Archiv für Orientforschung* 51 (2005–2006): 125–146.

Magico-Medical Means of Treating Ghost-Induced Illnesses in Ancient Mesopotamia. Ancient Magic and Divination 3. Leiden and Boston: Brill, 2006.

Shehata, Dahlia. *Musiker und ihr vokales Repertoire. Untersuchungen zu Inhalt und Organisation von Musikerberufen und Liedgattungen in altbabylonischer Zeit*. Göttinger Beiträge zum Alten Orient 3. Göttingen: Universitätsverlag Göttingen, 2009.

Spronk, Klaas. "The Incantations." In *Handbook of Ugaritic Studies*, edited by Wilfred G. E. Watson and Nicholas Wyatt, 270–286. Handbuch der Orientalistik I.39. Leiden and Boston: Brill, 1999.

Stol, Marten. "Diagnosis and Therapy in Babylonian Medicine." *Jaarbericht van het Vooraziatisch-Egyptisch Genootschap "Ex Oriente Lux"* 32 (1993): 42–65.

Epilepsy in Babylonia. Cuneiform Monographs 2. Groningen: Styx Publications, 1993.

Birth in Babylonia and the Bible. Its Mediterranean Setting. Cuneiform Monographs 14. Groningen: Styx Publications, 2000.

Versnel, Henk. "Some Reflections on the Relationship Magic–Religion." *Numen* 38, no. 2 (1991): 177–197.

Waerzeggers, Caroline, and Michael Jursa. "On the Initiation of Babylonian Priests." *Zeitschrift für altorientalische und biblische Rechtsgeschichte* 14 (2008): 1–38.

Walker, Christopher B. F., and Michael Dick. *The Induction of the Cultic Image in Ancient Mesopotamia. The Mesopotamian Mīs Pî Ritual.* State Archives of Assyria Literary Texts 1. Helsinki: The Neo-Assyrian Text Corpus Project, 2001.

Wasserman, Nathan. "From the Notebook of a Professional Exorcist." In *Von Göttern und Menschen. Beiträge zu Literatur und Geschichte des Alten Orients. Festschrift für Brigitte Groneberg,* edited by Dahlia Shehata, Frauke Weiershäuser, and Kamran V. Zand, 329–349. Cuneiform Monographs 41. Leiden and Boston: Brill, 2010.

Westenholz, Aage. "The Graeco-Babyloniaca Once Again." *Zeitschrift für Assyriologie und Vorderasiatische Archäologie* 97 (2007): 262–313.

Wiggermann, Frans A. M. *Mesopotamian Protective Spirits. The Ritual Texts.* Cuneiform Monographs 1. Groningen: Styx Publications, 1992.

"Lamaštu, Daughter of Anu. A Profile." In *Birth in Babylonia and the Bible. Its Mediterranean Setting,* by Marten Stol, 217–249. Cuneiform Monographs 14. Groningen: Styx Publications, 2000.

"The Four Winds and the Origins of Pazuzu." In *Das geistige Erfassen der Welt im Alten Orient. Sprache, Religion, Kultur und Gesellschaft,* edited by Claus Wilcke, 125–165. Wiesbaden: Harrassowitz, 2007.

Wilcke, Claus. "Liebesbeschwörungen aus Isin." *Zeitschrift für Assyriologie und Vorderasiatische Archäologie* 75 (1985): 188–209.

Ziegler, Nele. *Le harem de Zimrî-Lîm.* Florilegium Marianum 4; Mémoires de N.A.B.U. 5. Paris: Societé pour l'Étude du Proche-Orient Ancien, 1999.

2 Ancient Egypt (by Friedhelm Hoffmann)

Primary Sources

Abubakr, Abdel Moneim, and Jürgen Osing. "Ächtungstexte aus dem Alten Reich." *Mitteilungen des Deutschen Archäologischen Instituts Abteilung Kairo* 29 (1973): 97–133.

Betz, Hans Dieter, ed. *The Greek Magical Papyri in Translation, Including the Demotic Spells.* 2nd ed. Chicago and London: University of Chicago Press, 1992.

Bilabel, Friedrich, and Adolf Grohmann. *Griechische, koptische und arabische Texte zur Religion und religiösen Literatur in Ägyptens Spätzeit.* Heidelberg: Verlag der Universitäts-Bibliothek, 1934.

Borghouts, J[oris] F[rans]. *The Magical Texts of Papyrus Leiden I 348.* Leiden: Brill, 1971.

Ancient Egyptian Magical Texts. Leiden: Brill, 1978.

Bresciani, Edda. *Letteratura e poesia dell'antico Egitto. Cultura e società attraverso i testi.* New ed. Turin: Einaudi, 1999.

Daressy, G[eorges]. *Textes et dessins magiques.* Cairo: Institut Français d'Archéologie Orientale, 1903.

Edwards, I[orwerth] E[iddon] S[tephen]. *Oracular Amuletic Decrees.* 2 vols. London: British Museum, 1960.

Erman, Adolf. *Reden, Rufe und Lieder auf Gräberbildern des Alten Reiches.* Berlin: Akademie der Wissenschaften, 1919.

Fischer-Elfert, Hans-W[erner], with contributions by Tonio Sebastian Richter. *Altägyptische Zaubersprüche.* Stuttgart: Reclam, 2005.

Fischer-Elfert, Hans-Werner, and Friedhelm Hoffmann. *Die magischen Texte und Vignetten des Papyrus Nr. 1826 in der Griechischen Nationalbibliothek zu Athen.* (forthcoming).

Gardiner, Alan H[enderson]. *Chester Beatty Gift.* 2 vols. London: British Museum, 1935.

    The Ramesseum Papyri. Oxford: Griffith Institute, 1955.

    Late-Egyptian Stories. Brussels: Fondation Égyptologique Reine Élisabeth, 1981.

Griffith, F[rancis] Ll[ewllyn], and Herbert Thompson. *The Demotic Magical Papyrus of London and Leiden.* 3 vols. London: Grevel, 1904–1909.

Helck, Wolfgang. *Urkunden der 18. Dynastie. Übersetzung zu den Heften 17–22.* Berlin: Akademie-Verlag, 1961.

Jelínková-Reymond, E[va Anne Elisabeth]. *Les inscriptions de la statue guérisseuse de Djed-her-le-Sauveur.* Cairo: Institut Français d'Archéologie Orientale, 1956.

Johnson, Janet H[elen]. "Louvre E 3229: A Demotic Magical Text." *Enchoria* 7 (1977): 55–102.

Kitchen, K[enneth] A[nderson]. *Ramesside Inscriptions. Historical and Biographical.* 8 vols. Oxford: Blackwell, 1975–1990.

Koenig, Yvan. "Les textes d'envoûtement de Mirgissa." *Revue d'égyptologie* 41 (1990): 101–125.

Kropp, Angelicus M. *Ausgewählte koptische Zaubertexte.* 3 vols. Brussels: Fondation Égyptologique Reine Élisabeth, 1930–1931.

Lange, H[ans] O[stenfeldt]. *Der magische Papyrus Harris.* Copenhagen: Høst, 1927.

Leitz, Christian. *Tagewählerei. Das Buch ḥ3t nḥḥ pḥ.wy ḏt und verwandte Texte.* 2 vols. Wiesbaden: Harrassowitz, 1994.

    "Die Schlangensprüche in den Pyramidentexten." *Orientalia* 65 (1996): 381–427.

    Magical and Medical Papyri of the New Kingdom. London: British Museum Press, 1999.

Lexa, François. *La magie dans l'Égypte antique de l'Ancien Empire jusqu'à l'époque copte.* 3 vols. Paris: Geuthner, 1925.

Lichtheim, Miriam. *Ancient Egyptian Literature. A Book of Readings.* 3 vols. Berkeley, Los Angeles, and London: University of California Press, 1975–1980.

Massart, Adhémar. *The Leiden Magical Papyrus I 343 + I 345.* Leiden: Brill, 1954.

Meyer, Marvin, and Richard Smith, eds. *Ancient Christian Magic. Coptic Texts of Ritual Power.* San Francisco: Harper, 1994.

Müller-Winkler, Claudia. *Die ägyptischen Objekt-Amulette. Mit Publikation der Sammlung des Biblischen Instituts der Universität Freiburg, Schweiz, ehemals Sammlung Fouad S. Matouk.* Freiburg Schweiz: Universitätsverlag; Göttingen: Vandenhoeck & Ruprecht, 1987.

Osing, Jürgen. "Ächtungstexte aus dem Alten Reich (II)." *Mitteilungen des Deutschen Archäologischen Instituts Abteilung Kairo* 32 (1976): 133–185.

Parkinson, R[ichard] B[ruce]. *The Tale of Sinuhe and Other Ancient Egyptian Poems 1940–1640 BC.* Oxford: Oxford University Press, 1998.

Pernigotti, Sergio. *Testi della magia copta*. Imola: Mandragora, 2000.

Posener, Georges. *Cinq figurines d'envoûtement*. Cairo: Institut Français d'Archéologie Orientale, 1987.

Quack, Joachim Friedrich. *Studien zur Lehre für Merikare*. Wiesbaden: Harrassowitz, 1992.

Roccati, Alessandro. *Papiro ieratico n. 54003. Estratti magici e rituali del Primo Medio Regno*. Turin: Pozzo, 1970.

    Magica Taurinensia. Il grande papiro magico di Torino e i suoi duplicati. Rome: GBPress, 2011.

Sauneron, Serge. *Le papyrus magique illustré de Brooklyn. Brooklyn Museum 47.218.156*. Brooklyn: Brooklyn Museum, 1970.

    Un traité égyptien d'ophiologie. Papyrus du Brooklyn Museum nos. 47.218.48 et 85. Cairo: Institut Français d'Archéologie Orientale, 1989.

Sethe, Kurt. *Die Ächtung feindlicher Fürsten, Völker und Dinge auf altägyptischen Tongefäßscherben des Mittleren Reiches*. Berlin: Verlag der Akademie der Wissenschaften, 1926.

    Urkunden des Alten Reichs. Leipzig: Hinrichs, 1933.

Vernus, Pascal. "Omina calendériques et comptabilité d'offrandes sur une tablette hiératique de la XVIIIe dynastie." *Revue d'Égyptologie* 33 (1981): 89–124.

Yamazaki, Naoko. *Zaubersprüche für Mutter und Kind. Papyrus Berlin 3027*. Berlin: Dürring, 2003.

Zauzich, Karl-Theodor. "Aus zwei demotischen Traumbüchern." *Archiv für Papyrusforschung und verwandte Gebiete* 27 (1980): 91–98.

Secondary Sources

Altenmüller, Hartwig. "Magische Literatur." In *Lexikon der Ägyptologie*, vol. 3, edited by Wolfgang Helck and Wolfhart Westendorf, 1151–1162. Wiesbaden: Harrassowitz, 1980.

Andrews, Carol. *Amulets of Ancient Egypt*. London: British Museum Press, 1994.

Assmann, Jan. "Magic and Theology in Ancient Egypt." In *Envisioning Magic. A Princeton Seminar and Symposium*, edited by Peter Schäfer and Hans G. Kippenberg, 1–18. Studies in the History of Religions 75. Leiden, New York, and Cologne: Brill, 1997.

Beltz, Walter. "Maria in der koptischen Magie." In *Zeit und Geschichte in der koptischen Frömmigkeit bis zum 8. Jahrhundert. Beiträge zur VIII. Internationalen Halleschen Koptologentagung vom 15.–18. Mai 1998, gefördert durch das Land Sachsen-Anhalt und die Deutsche Forschungsgemeinschaft*, edited by Walter Beltz and Jürgen Tubach, 27–31. Halle (Saale): Universität Halle-Wittenberg, 1998.

Bonner, Campbell. *Studies in Magical Amulets, Chiefly Graeco-Egyptian*. Ann Arbor: University of Michigan Press, 1950.

Borghouts, J[oris] F[rans]. "Magical Texts." In *Textes et languages de l'Égypte pharaonique. Cent cinquante années de recherches. 1822 – 1972. Hommages à Jean-François Champollion*, part 3, 7–19. Cairo: Institut Français d'Archéologie Orientale, [1974].

    "Magie." In *Lexikon der Ägyptologie*, vol. 3, edited by Wolfgang Helck and Wolfhart Westendorf, 1137–1151. Wiesbaden: Harrassowitz, 1980.

    "ꜣḫ.w (akhu) and ḥkꜣ.w (hekau). Two Basic Notions of Ancient Egyptian Magic, and the Concept of the Divine Creative Word." In *La magia in Egitto ai tempi dei faraoni. Atti convegno internazionale di studi, Milano 29–31 ottobre 1985*, edited by Alessandro

Roccati and Alberto Siliotti, 29–46. Milan: Rassegna Internazionale di Cinematografia Archeologica, Arte e Natura Libri, 1987.

Brashear, William M. "The Greek Magical Papyri: An Introduction and Survey; Annotated Bibliography (1928–1994)." In *Aufstieg und Niedergang der römischen Welt. Geschichte und Kultur Roms im Spiegel der neueren Forschung*, part II, *Principat*, vol. 18, *Religion*, fasc. 5, *Heidentum: Die religiösen Verhältnisse in den Provinzen (Forts.)*, edited by Wolfgang Haase, 3380–3684. Berlin and New York: de Gruyter, 1995.

von Deines, Hildegard, and Wolfhart Westendorf. *Wörterbuch der medizinischen Texte*. 2 vols. Berlin: Akademie-Verlag, 1961–1962.

Dieleman, Jacco. *Priests, Tongues, and Rites. The London-Leiden Magical Manuscripts and Translation in Egyptian Ritual (100–300 CE)*. Leiden and Boston: Brill, 2005.

——— "Scribal Practices in the Production of Magic Handbooks in Egypt." In *Continuity and Innovation in the Magical Tradition*, edited by Gideon Bohak, Yuval Harari, and Shaul Shaked, 85–117. Leiden: Brill, 2011.

Eschweiler, Peter. *Bildzauber im alten Ägypten. Die Verwendung von Bildern und Gegenständen in magischen Handlungen nach den Texten des Mittleren und Neuen Reiches*, Freiburg Schweiz: Universitätsverlag; Göttingen: Vandenhoeck & Ruprecht, 1994.

Étienne, Marc, ed. *Heka. Magie et envoûtement dans l'Égypte ancienne. Les dossiers du musée du Louvre*. Paris: Réunion des musées nationaux, 2000.

Gnirs, Andrea M[aria]. "Nilpferdstoßzähne und Schlangenstäbe. Zu den magischen Geräten des so genannten Ramesseumsfundes." in *Texte – Theben – Tonfragmente. Festschrift für Günter Burkard*, edited by Dieter Kessler, Regine Schulz, Martina Ullmann, Alexandra Verbovsek, and Stefan Wimmer, 128–156. Wiesbaden: Harrassowitz, 2009.

Goedicke, Hans. "Was Magic Used in the Harem Conspiracy against Ramses III? (*Papyrus Rollin* and *Papyrus Lee*)." *Journal of Egyptian Archaeology* 49 (1963): 71–92.

Hawass, Zahi. "The Tombs of the Pyramid Builders – The Tomb of the Artisan Petety and His Curse." In *Egypt, Israel, and the Ancient Mediterranean World. Studies in Honor of Donald B. Redford*, 21–39. Leiden and Boston: Brill, 2004.

Hopfner, Theodor. *Griechisch-ägyptischer Offenbarungszauber mit einer eingehenden Darstellung des griechisch-synkretistischen Daemonenglaubens und der Voraussetzungen und Mittel des Zaubers überhaupt und der magischen Divination im besonderen*. Leipzig: Haessel, 1921, 1924. Reprint, Amsterdam: Hackert, 1974.

Kákosy, László. *Zauberei im alten Ägypten*. Leipzig: Koehler & Amelang, 1989.

Karl, Doris. "Funktion und Bedeutung einer *weisen Frau* im alten Ägypten." *Studien zur Altägyptischen Kultur* 28 (2000): 131–160.

Klasens, Adolf. "Amulet." In *Lexikon der Ägyptologie*, vol. 1, edited by Wolfgang Helck and Eberhard Otto, 232–236. Wiesbaden: Harrassowitz, 1975.

Koenig, Yvan. *Magie et magiciens dans l'Égypte ancienne*. Paris: Pygmalion, 1994.

——— ed. *La magie en Égypte. À la recherche d'une définition. Actes du colloque organisé par le Musée du Louvre, les 29 et 30 septembre 2000*. Paris: Documentation Française, 2002.

Kousoulis, P[anagiotis] E. M., ed. *Ancient Egyptian Demonology. Studies on the Boundaries between the Demonic and the Divine in Egyptian Magic*. Leuven: Peeters, 2011.

Kyffin, Joanna. "'A True Secret of the House of Life': Prosody, Intertext and Performance in Magical Texts." In *Narratives of Egypt and the Ancient Near East. Literary and Linguistic Approaches*, edited by Frederik Hagen, John Johnston, Wendy Monkhouse, Kathryn

Piquette, John Tait, and Martin Worthington, 225–255. Leuven, Paris, and Walpole, MA: Brill, 2011.

Lacau, Pierre. "Les 'statues guérisseuses' dans l'ancienne Égypte." *Monuments Piot* 25 (1921–1922): 189–209.

Leitz, Christian. *Die Schlangennamen in den ägyptischen und griechischen Giftbüchern.* Mainz: Akademie der Wissenschaften; Stuttgart: Steiner, 1997.

von Lieven, Alexandra. "Divination in Ägypten." *Altorientalische Forschungen* 26 (1999): 77–126.

Meyer, Marvin, and Paul Mirecki, ed. *Ancient Magic and Ritual Power.* Leiden and New York: Brill, 1995.

Momigliano, Arnaldo, ed. *The Conflict between Paganism and Christianity in the Fourth Century.* Oxford: Clarendon Press, 1963.

Otto, Bernd-Christian. *Magie: Rezeptions- und diskursgeschichtliche Analysen von der Antike bis zur Neuzeit.* Berlin: De Gruyter, 2011.

Pernigotti, Sergio. "La magia del quotidiano nell'Egitto copto: Introduzione." *Ricerche di egittologie e di antichità copte* 1 (1999): 77–94.

Petrie, William Matthew Flinders. *Amulets. Illustrated by the Egyptian Collection in University College London.* London: Constable, 1914. Reprint, Warminster: Aris & Phillips, [1972].

Pinch, Geraldine. *Magic in Ancient Egypt.* London: British Museum Press, 1994.

Quack, Joachim Friedrich. "Kontinuität und Wandel in der spätägyptischen Magie." *Studi epigrafici e linguistici sul Vicino Oriente antico* 15 (1998): 77–94.

———. "Magie und Totenbuch – Eine Fallstudie (pEbers 2,1–6)." *Chronique d'Égypte* 74 (1999): 5–17.

———. "Explizite Aufzeichnungsmeidung im Alten Ägypten." *Lingua Aegyptia* 10 (2002): 339–342.

———. "Griechische und andere Dämonen in spätdemotischen magischen Texten." In *Das Ägyptische und die Sprachen Vorderasiens, Nordafrikas und der Ägäis. Akten des Basler Kolloquiums zum ägyptisch-nichtsemitischen Sprachkontakt. Basel 9.–11. Juli 2003*, edited by Thomas Schneider, 427–507. Münster: Ugarit-Verlag, 2004).

———. "Postulated and Real Efficacy in Late Antique Divination Rituals." *Journal of Ritual Studies* 24, no. 1 (2010): 45–60.

Reisner, George Andrew. *Amulets.* 2 vols. Cairo: Institut Français d'Archéologie Orientale, 1907, 1958.

Richter, Siegfried G. "Jedes Mittel ist recht – Facetten koptischer Magie." *Kemet* 16, no. 2 (2007): 41–45.

Ritner, Robert K[riech]. "Egyptian Magical Practice under the Roman Empire: The Demotic Spells and Their Religious Context." In *Aufstieg und Niedergang der römischen Welt. Geschichte und Kultur Roms im Spiegel der neueren Forschung*, part II, *Principat*, vol. 18, *Religion*, fasc. 5, *Heidentum: Die religiösen Verhältnisse in den Provinzen (Forts.)*, edited by Wolfgang Haase, 3333–3379. Berlin and New York: de Gruyter, 1995).

———. *The Mechanics of Ancient Egyptian Magical Practice.* Chicago: Oriental Institute of the University of Chicago, 2008.

Roccati Alessandro, and Alberto Siliotti, ed. *La magia in Egitto ai tempi dei faraoni. Atti convegno internazionale di studi, Milano 29–31 ottobre 1985.* Milan: Rassegna Internazionale di Cinematografia Archeologica, Arte e Natura Libri, 1987.

Schneider, Thomas. "Die Waffe als Analogie. Altägyptische Magie als System." In *Das Analogiedenken. Vorstöße in ein neues Gebiet der Rationalitätstheorie*, edited by Karen Gloy and Manuel Bachmann, 37–85. Freiburg im Breisgau and Munich: Alber, 2000.

Tait, W[illiam] J[ohn]. "Theban Magic." In *Hundred-Gated Thebes. Acts of a Colloquium on Thebes and the Theban Area in the Graeco-Roman Period*, edited by S[ven] P[eter] Vleeming, 169–182. Leiden, New York, and Cologne: Brill, 1995.

van der Vliet, Jacques. "Spätantikes Heidentum in Ägypten im Spiegel der koptischen Literatur." In *Begegnung von Heidentum und Christentum im spätantiken Ägypten*, 99–130. Riggisberg: Abegg-Stiftung, 1993.

Westendorf, Wolfhart. *Handbuch der altägyptischen Medizin*. 2 vols. Leiden, Boston, and Cologne: Brill, 1999.

Zandee, J[an]. *Death as an Enemy According to Ancient Egyptian Conceptions*. Leiden: Brill, 1960.

3 Early Greco-Roman Antiquity (by Kimberly B. Stratton)

Primary Sources

Aeschylus. *The Persians*. Edited and translated by Edith Hall. Warminster, England: Aris and Phillips, 1996.

Apollonius of Rhodes. *Jason and the Golden Fleece: The Argonautica*. Translated with introduction and explanatory notes by Richard Hunter. Oxford: The Clarendon Press of Oxford University Press, 1993.

Audollent, A., ed. *Defixionum Tabellae*. Frankfurt: Minerva, 1967.

Elderkin, G. W. "Two Curse Inscriptions." *Hesperia* 6, no. 3 (1937): 382–395.

Gager, John G., ed. *Curse Tablets and Binding Spells from the Ancient World*. Oxford: Oxford University Press, 1992.

Meiggs, R., and D. M. Lewis, eds. and trans. *A Selection of Greek Historical Inscriptions*. Oxford: Oxford University Press, 1969.

Preisendanz, Karl, ed. *Papyri Graecae Magicae: Die griechischen Zauberpapyri*. Stuttgart: Verlag B. G. Teubner, 1973.

Warmington, E. H. *Remains of Old Latin*. Vol 3. Loeb Classical Library. Cambridge, MA: Harvard University Press, 1935.

Wünsch, R. *Defixionum Tabellae Atticae*. Inscriptiones Graecae 3.3. Berlin: Königlich-Preußische Akademie der Wissenschaften, 1897.

Secondary Sources

Abusch, Tzvi. "The Demonic Image of the Witch in Standard Babylonian Literature: The Reworking of Popular Conceptions by Learned Exorcists." In *Religion, Science, and Magic in Concert and Conflict*, edited by Jacob Neusner, Ernest Frerichs, and Paul Virgil McCracken Flesher, 27–58. New York and Oxford: Oxford University Press, 1989.

Barb, A. A. "The Survival of Magic Arts." In *The Conflict between Paganism and Christianity in the Fourth Century*, edited by Arnaldo Momigliano, 100–125. Oxford: Clarendon Press, 1963.

Bigwood, Joan M. "'Incestuous' Marriage in Achaemenid Iran: Myths and Realities." *Klio* 91, no. 2 (2009): 311–341.

Boedeker, Deborah. "Family Matters: Domestic Religion in Classical Greece." In *Household and Family Religion in Antiquity*, edited by John Bodel and Saul M. Olyan, 229–247. Ancient World: Comparative Histories. Malden, MA and Oxford: Blackwell, 2008.

Braun-Holzinger, Eva A. "Apotropaic Figures at Mesopotamian Temples in the Third and Second Millennia." In *Mesopotamian Magic: Textual, Historical, and Interpretive Perspectives*, vol. 1, edited by Tzvi Abusch and Karel van der Toorn, 149–172. Ancient Magic and Divination. Groningen: Styx, 1999.

Collins, Derek. "Theoris of Lemnos and the Criminalization of Magic in Fourth-Century Athens." *Classical Quarterly* 51, no. 2 (2001): 477–493.

Magic in the Ancient Greek World. Blackwell Ancient Religions. Malden, MA: Blackwell, 2008.

Dickie, Matthew W. *Magic and Magicians in the Greco-Roman World*. London and New York: Routledge, 2001.

Eidinow, Esther. *Oracles, Curses, and Risk among the Ancient Greeks*. Oxford and New York: Oxford University Press, 2007.

Faraone, Christopher. "Aeschylus' ὕμνος δέσμιος (Eum. 306) and Attic Judicial Curse Tablets." *The Journal of Hellenic Studies* 105 (1985): 150–154.

"An Accusation of Magic in Classical Athens (AR. Wasps 946–48)." *Transactions of the American Philological Association (1974–)* 119 (1989): 149–160.

"Clay Hardens and Wax Melts: Magical Role-Reversal in Vergil's Eighth Eclogue." *Classical Philology* 84 (1989): 294–300.

"The Agonistic Context of Early Greek Binding Spells." In *Magika Hiera: Ancient Greek Magic and Religion*, edited by Christopher A. Faraone and Dirk Obbink, 3–32. New York and Oxford: Oxford University Press, 1991.

"Binding and Burying the Forces of Evil: The Defensive Use of 'Voodoo Dolls' in Ancient Greece." *Classical Antiquity* 10, no. 2 (1991): 165–205.

Talismans and Trojan Horses: Guardian Statues in Ancient Greek Myth and Ritual. New York: Oxford University Press, 1992.

"Molten Wax, Spilt Wine and Mutilated Animals: Sympathetic Magic in Near Eastern and Early Greek Oath Ceremonies." *The Journal of Hellenic Studies* 113 (1993): 60–80.

Ancient Greek Love Magic. Cambridge, MA: Harvard University Press, 1999.

"Household Religion in Ancient Greece." In *Household and Family Religion in Antiquity*, edited by John Bodel and Saul M. Olyan, 210–228. Ancient World: Comparative Histories. Malden, MA and Oxford: Blackwell, 2008.

Farber, W. "How to Marry a Disease: Epidemics, Contagion, and a Magic Ritual Against the 'Hand of the Ghost.'" In *Magic and Rationality in Ancient Near Eastern and Graeco-Roman Medicine*, edited by H. F. J. Horstmanshoff and M. Stol, 117–132. Leiden: Brill, 2004.

Fowler, Barbara Hughes. *The Hellenistic Aesthetic*. Madison: University of Wisconsin Press, 1989.

Frankfurter, David. *Religion in Roman Egypt: Assimilation and Resistance*. Princeton: Princeton University Press, 1998.

Friese, Wiebke. "Facing the Dead: Landscape and Ritual of Ancient Greek Death Oracles." *Time and Mind: The Journal of Archaeology, Consciousness and Culture* 3, no. 1 (2010): 29–40.

Garrett, Susan. *The Demise of the Devil: Magic and the Demonic in Luke's Writings*. Minneapolis: Fortress Press, 1989.

Gee, John. "Oracle by Image: Coffin Text 103 in Context." In *Magic and Divination in the Ancient World*, edited by Leda Ciraolo and Jonathan Seidel, 83–88. Leiden: Brill, 2002.

Goldhill, S. "The Great Dionysia and Civic Ideology." *Journal of Hellenic Studies* CVII (1987): 58–76.

Graf, Fritz. *Magic in the Ancient World*. Translated by Franklin Philip. Cambridge, MA: Harvard University Press, 1997.

——. "Theories of Magic in Antiquity." In *Magic and Ritual in the Ancient World*, edited by Paul Mirecki and Marvin Meyer, 93–104. Religions in the Graeco-Roman World 141. Leiden, Boston, and Cologne: Brill, 2002.

——. "Victimology or: How to Deal with Untimely Death." In *Daughters of Hecate: Women and Magic in the Ancient World*, edited by Kimberly B. Stratton, with Dayna S. Kalleres, 386–417. New York: Oxford University Press, 2014.

Hall, Edith. *Inventing the Barbarian: Greek Self-Definition through Tragedy*. Oxford: Clarendon Press, 1989.

Hoffman, C. A. "Fiat Magia." In *Magic and Ritual in the Ancient World*, edited by Paul Mirecki and Marvin Meyer, 179–194. Religions in the Graeco-Roman World 141. Leiden, Boston, and Cologne: Brill, 2002.

Janowitz, Naomi. *Magic in the Roman World*. London and New York: Routledge, 2001.

——. *Icons of Power: Ritual Practices in Late Antiquity*. University Park: Penn State University Press, 2002.

Johnston, Sarah Iles. "Corinthian Medea and the Cult of Hera Akraia." In *Medea: Essays on Medea in Myth, Literature, Philosophy, and Art*, edited by James J. Clauss and Sarah Iles Johnston, 44–70. Princeton: Princeton University Press, 1997.

——. *Restless Dead: Encounters between the Living and the Dead in Ancient Greece*. Berkeley, Los Angeles, and London: University of California Press, 1999.

Kippenberg, Hans G. "Magic in Roman Civil Discourse: Why Rituals Could Be Illegal." In *Envisioning Magic: A Princeton Seminar and Symposium*, edited by Peter Schäfer and Hans G. Kippenberg, 137–163. Studies in the History of Religions 75. Leiden, New York, and Cologne: Brill, 1997.

Liddell, Henry George, and Robert Scott. *Greek-English Lexicon*. 9th ed. Oxford: Clarendon Press, 1996.

MacMullen, Ramsay. *Enemies of the Roman Order: Treason, Unrest, and Alienation in the Empire*. London: Routledge, 1966.

Malinowski, Bronislaw. *Coral Gardens and Their Magic: A Study of the Methods of Tilling the Soil and of Agricultural Rites in the Trobriand Islands*. New York and Cincinnati: American Book Company, 1935.

Mitchell, Lynnette G. *Panhellenism and the Barbarian in Archaic and Classical Greece*. Swansea: The Classical Press of Wales, 2007.

Nock, Arthur Darby. "Paul and the Magus." In *The Beginnings of Christianity*, part I, edited by F. J. Foakes-Jackson and Kirsopp Lake, 164–188. London: Macmillan and Co., 1933.

Ogden, Daniel. "Binding Spells: Curse Tablets and Voodoo Dolls in the Greek and Roman Worlds." In *Witchcraft and Magic in Europe*, vol. 2, *Ancient Greece and Rome*, edited by Bengt Ankarloo and Stuart Clark, 1–90. Philadelphia: University of Pennsylvania Press, 1999.

Otto, Bernd-Christian. "Towards Historicizing 'Magic' in Antiquity." *Numen* 60 (2013): 308–347.

Parker, Robert. "Greek Religion." In *The Oxford History of Greece and the Hellenistic World*, edited by John Boardman, Jasper Griffin, and Oswyn Murray, 306–329. Oxford and New York: Oxford University Press, 1986.

Remus, Harold. "'Magic,' Method, Madness." *Method and Theory in the Study of Religion* 11 (1999): 258–298.

Rhodes, P. J. "The Impact of the Persian Wars on Classical Greece." In *Cultural Responses to the Persian Wars*, edited by Emma Bridges, Edith Hall, and P. J. Rhodes, 31–46. Oxford: Oxford University Press, 2007.

Rives, James B. "Magic in the XII Tables Revisited." *Classical Quarterly* 52, no. 1 (2002): 270–290.

——— "Magic in Roman Law: The Reconstruction of a Crime." *Classical Antiquity* 22, no. 2 (2003): 313–339.

Schmidt, Brian B. "The 'Witch' of En-Dor, 1 Samuel 28, and Ancient Near Eastern Necromancy." In *Ancient Magic and Ritual Power*, edited by Marvin Meyer and Paul Mirecki, 111–130. Leiden and New York: Brill, 1995.

Scott, James C. *Domination and the Arts of Resistance: Hidden Transcripts*. New Haven: Yale University Press, 1990.

Scurlock, JoAnn. "Magical Uses of Ancient Mesopotamian Festivals of the Dead." In *Ancient Magic and Ritual Power*, edited by Marvin Meyer and Paul Mirecki, 93–110. Leiden and New York: Brill, 1995.

——— "Soul Emplacements in Ancient Mesopotamian Funerary Rituals." In *Magic and Divination in the Ancient World*, edited by Leda Ciraolo and Jonathan Seidel, 1–6. Leiden: Brill, 2002.

——— "Translating Transfers in Ancient Mesopotamia." In *Magic and Ritual in the Ancient World*, edited by Paul Mirecki and Marvin Meyer, 209–223. Religions in the Graeco-Roman World 141. Leiden, Boston, and Cologne: Brill, 2002.

Segal, Alan F. "Hellenistic Magic: Some Questions of Definition." In *Studies in Gnosticism and Hellenistic Religions Presented to Gilles Quispel on the Occasion of His 65th Birthday*, edited by R. van den Broek and M. J. Vermaseren, 349–375. Leiden: Brill, 1981.

Smith, Jonathan Z. *Drudgery Divine: On the Comparison of Early Christianities and the Religions of Late Antiquity*. Chicago: University of Chicago Press, 1990.

——— "Trading Places." In *Ancient Magic and Ritual Power*, edited by Marvin Meyer and Paul Mirecki, 13–27. Leiden and New York: Brill, 1995.

Smith, Kirby Flower. "Magic (Greek and Roman)." In *Encyclopaedia of Religion and Ethics*, vol. 8, edited by J. Hastings, 269–289. Edinburgh: T & T Clark, 1916.

Sourvinou-Inwood, Christiane. "Further Aspects of Polis Religion." *Annali Istituto Orientale de Napoli: Archaeologia e Storia Antica* 10 (1988): 259–274.

——— "What is Polis Religion?" In *The Greek City: From Homer to Alexander*, edited by Oswyn Murray and Simon Price, 295–322. Oxford: Clarendon Press; New York: Oxford University Press, 1990.

Stowers, Stanley. "Theorizing the Religion of Ancient Households and Families." In *Household and Family Religion in Antiquity*, edited by John Bodel and Saul M. Olyan, 5–19. Ancient World: Comparative Histories. Malden, MA and Oxford: Blackwell, 2008.

"The Religion of Plant and Animal Offerings versus the Religion of Meanings, Essences, and Textual Mysteries." In *Ancient Mediterranean Sacrifice*, edited by Jennifer Wright Knust and Zsuzsanna Várhelyi, 35–56. New York: Oxford University Press, 2011.

Stratton, Kimberly. *Naming the Witch: Magic, Ideology, and Stereotype in the Ancient World*. New York: Columbia University Press, 2007.

Styers, Randall. *Making Magic: Religion, Magic, and Science in the Modern World*. New York and Oxford: Oxford University Press, 2004.

Thomassen, Einar. "Is Magic a Subclass of Ritual?" In *The World of Ancient Magic. Papers from the First International Samson Eitrem Seminar at the Norwegian Institute at Athens, 4–8 May 1997*, edited by David R. Jordan, Hugo Montgomery, and Einar Thomassen, 55–66. Papers from the Norwegian Institute at Athens 4. Bergen: The Norwegian Institute at Athens, 1999.

Tupet, Anne-Marie. *La magie dans la poésie latine*. Paris: Les Belles Lettres, 1976.

Tylor, Sir Edward Burnett, with an introduction by Paul Radin. *Primitive Culture*. Vol. 1, *The Origins of Culture*. The Library of Religion and Culture. New York: Harper and Brothers, Harper Torchbooks, 1958.

Versnel, H. S. "Beyond Cursing: The Appeal to Justice in Judicial Prayer." In *Magika Hiera: Ancient Greek Magic and Religion*, edited by Christopher A. Faraone and Dirk Obbink, 65–69. Oxford: Oxford University Press, 1991.

"Some Reflections on the Relationship Magic-Religion." *Numen* 38, no. 2 (1991): 177–197.

4 Roman Antiquity: The Imperial Period (by Kyle A. Fraser)

Primary Sources

Betz, Hans Dieter, ed. *The Greek Magical Papyri in Translation, Including the Demotic Spells*. Chicago: University of Chicago Press, 1989. [GMPT]

Cicero. *In Vatinium*. In *Cicero XII: Pros Sestio; In Vatinium*. Translated by R. Gardner. Loeb Classical Library. 1958. Reprint, Cambridge, MA: Harvard University Press, 1984.

Clement. *The Recognitions of Clement*. Translated by Thomas Smith. In *Ante-Nicene Fathers*, vol. 8, edited by Alexander Roberts and James Donaldson. New York: Christian Literature Publishing Company, 1886.

Duling, D. C. trans., *The Testament of Solomon*. In *The Old Testament Pseudepigrapha*, vol. 1, edited by James H. Charlesworth, 935–987. London: Darton, Longman & Todd, 1983.

Friedrich, Hans-Veit, ed. *Thessalos von Tralles: Griechisch und Lateinisch*. Meisenheim am Glan: Verlag Anton Hain, 1968.

Gager, John G., ed. *Curse Tablets and Binding Spells from the Ancient World*. Oxford: Oxford University Press, 1992.

Héliodore. *Les Éthiopiques*. Edited by R. M. Rattenbury and Rev. T. W. Lumb. Translated by J. Maillon. 2nd ed. 3 vols. Paris: Les Belles Lettres, 1960.

Horace. *Epodes*. In *Horace: Odes and Epodes*. Edited and translated by Niall Rudd. Loeb Classical Library. Cambridge, MA: Harvard University Press, 2004.

Jamblique. *Les mystères d'Égypte (De mysteriis)*. Edited and translated by Édouard des Places. Paris: Les Belles Lettres, 1996.

Kotansky, Roy, ed. *Greek Magical Amulets: The Inscribed Gold, Silver, Copper and Bronze Lamellae I: Published Texts of Known Provenance*. Opladen: Westdeutscher Verlag, 1994.

Lucan. *The Civil War (Pharsalia)*. Translated by J. D. Duff. Loeb Classical Library. 1928. Reprint, Cambridge, MA: Harvard University Press, 1988.

Lucian. *Philopseudes*. In *Lucian*, vol. 3, translated by A. M. Harmon. Loeb Classical Library. Cambridge, MA: Harvard University Press, 1960.

Philostratus. *The Life of Apollonius*. Edited and translated by Christopher P. Jones. 2 vols. Loeb Classical Library. Cambridge, MA: Harvard University Press, 2005.

Pliny. *Natural History*. Vols. 7–8. Translated by W. H. S. Jones. Loeb Classical Library. Cambridge, MA: Harvard University Press, 1963.

Plutarch. *On Isis and Osiris*. In *Plutarch's Moralia*, vol. 5, translated by F. C. Babbitt. Loeb Classical Library. Cambridge, MA: Harvard University Press, 1969.

On the Eating of Flesh. In *Plutarch's Moralia*, vol. 12, translated by William C. Helmbold. Loeb Classical Library. Cambridge, MA: Harvard University Press, 1957.

On the Obsolescence of Oracles. In *Plutarch's Moralia*, vol. 5, translated by F. C. Babbitt. Loeb Classical Library. Cambridge, MA: Harvard University Press, 1969.

Porphyre. *De l'abstinence*. Edited and translated by Jean Bouffartigue and Michel Patillon. 3 vols. Paris: Les Belles Lettres, 1979.

Preisendanz, Karl, ed. *Papyri Graecae Magicae: Die griechischen Zauberpapyri*. 2 vols. 1928–1931. 2nd ed., 1973–1974. Reprint, Leipzig: K. G. Saur, 2001. [PGM]

Tacitus. *Annals*. In *P. Cornelii Taciti libri qui supersunt*, vol. 1, edited by Erich Koestermann. Leipzig: Teubner, 1960.

Secondary Sources

Ankarloo, Bengt, and Stuart Clark, eds. *Witchcraft and Magic in Europe*, vol. 2, *Ancient Greece and Rome*. Philadelphia: University of Pennsylvania Press, 1999.

Athanassiadi, Polymnia. "Philosophers and Oracles: Shifts of Authority in Late Paganism." *Byzantion* 62 (1992): 45–62.

Athanassiadi, Polymnia, and Michael Frede, eds. *Pagan Monotheism in Late Antiquity*. Oxford: Oxford University Press, 1999.

Beck, Roger. "Thus Spake Not Zarathustra: Zoroastrian Pseudepigrapha of the Greco-Roman World." In *A History of Zoroastrianism*, vol. 3, edited by Mary Boyce and Frantz Grenet, 553–564. Leiden: Brill, 1991.

Betz, Hans Dieter. "The Formation of Authoritative Tradition in the Greek Magical Papyri." In *Self-Definition in the Greco-Roman World*, edited by Ben F. Meyer and E. P. Sandars, 161–170. Philadelphia: Fortress Press, 1982.

"Secrecy in the Greek Magical Papyri." In *Secrecy and Concealment: Studies in the History of Mediterranean and Near Eastern Religions*, edited by Hans G. Kippenberg and Guy G. Stroumsa, 153–175. Leiden: Brill, 1995.

Blänsdorf, Jürgen. "Defixiones from the Sanctuary of Isis." In *Magical Practice in the Latin West, Papers from the International Conference Held at the University of Zaragoza, 30 Sept.–1 Oct. 2005*, edited by Richard L. Gordon and Francisco Marco Simón, 141–190. Leiden: Brill, 2010.

Bonner, Campbell. *Studies in Magical Amulets, Chiefly Graeco-Egyptian*. Ann Arbor: University of Michigan Press, 1950.

Bradbury, Scott. "Julian's Pagan Revival and the Decline of Blood Sacrifice." *Phoenix* 49, no. 4 (Winter 1995): 331–356.

Brashear, William M. "The Greek Magical Papyri: An Introduction and Survey; Annotated Bibliography (1928–1994)." In *Aufstieg und Niedergang der römischen Welt. Geschichte und*

Kultur Roms im Spiegel der neueren Forschung, part II, *Principat*, vol. 18, *Religion*, fasc. 5, *Heidentum: Die religiösen Verhältnisse in den Provinzen (Forts.)*, edited by Wolfgang Haase, 3380–3684. Berlin and New York: de Gruyter, 1995.

Burkert, Walter. *Lore and Science in Ancient Pythagoreanism*. Translated by Edwin L. Minar, Jr. Cambridge, MA: Harvard University Press, 1972.

Butler, Elizabeth M. *Ritual Magic*. Cambridge: Cambridge University Press, 1949.

Dickie, Matthew. "The Learned Magician and the Collection and Transmission of Magical Lore." In *The World of Ancient Magic. Papers from the First International Samson Eitrem Seminar at the Norwegian Institute at Athens, 4–8 May 1997*, edited by David R. Jordan, Hugo Montgomery, and Einar Thomassen, 163–193. Papers from the Norwegian Institute at Athens 4. Bergen: The Norwegian Institute at Athens, 1999.

Dieleman, Jacco. *Priests, Tongues, and Rites. The London-Leiden Magical Manuscripts and Translation in Egyptian Ritual (100–300 CE)*. Leiden and Boston: Brill, 2005.

Faraone, Christopher A. "The Agonistic Context of Early Greek Binding Spells." In *Magika Hiera*, edited by Christopher A. Faraone and Dirk Obbink, 3–32. New York and Oxford: Oxford University Press, 1991.

"Necromancy Goes Underground: The Disguise of Skull-and-Corpse-Divination in the Paris Magical Papyri." In *Mantikē: Studies in Ancient Divination*, edited by Sarah I. Johnston and Peter T. Struck, 255–282. Leiden: Brill, 2005.

Faraone, Christopher A., and Dirk Obbink, eds. *Magika Hiera: Ancient Greek Magic and Religion*. New York and Oxford: Oxford University Press, 1991.

Festugière, André-Jean. *La révélation d'Hermès Trismégiste*. Vol. 1: *L'astrologie et les sciences occultes*. 1950. Reprint, Paris: Les Belles Lettres, 2006.

Fowden, Garth. *The Egyptian Hermes: A Historical Approach to the Late Pagan Mind*. 1986. Reprint, Princeton: Princeton University Press, 1993.

Frankfurter, David. "The Magic of Writing and the Writing of Magic: The Power of the Word in Egyptian and Greek Traditions." *Helios: Journal of the Classical Association of the Southwest* 21 (1994): 189–221.

"Ritual Expertise in Roman Egypt and the Problem of the Category 'Magician.'" In *Envisioning Magic: A Princeton Seminar and Symposium*, edited by Peter Schäfer and Hans G. Kippenberg, 115–135. Studies in the History of Religions 75. Leiden, New York, and Cologne: Brill, 1997.

Religion in Roman Egypt: Assimilation and Resistance. Princeton: Princeton University Press, 1998.

"The Consequences of Hellenism in Late Antique Egypt." *Archiv für Religionsgeschichte* 2 (2000): 162–194.

Fraser, Kyle. "The Contested Boundaries of 'Magic' and 'Religion' in Late Pagan Monotheism." *Magic, Ritual and Witchcraft* 4, no. 2 (Winter 2009): 131–151.

Gordon, Richard. "Reporting the Marvellous: Private Divination in the Greek Magical Papyri." In *Envisioning Magic: A Princeton Seminar and Symposium*, edited by Peter Schäfer and Hans G. Kippenberg, 65–92. Studies in the History of Religions 75. Leiden, New York, and Cologne: Brill, 1997.

"Imagining Greek and Roman Magic." In *Witchcraft and Magic in Europe*, vol. 2, *Ancient Greece and Rome*, edited by Bengt Ankarloo and Stuart Clark, 159–275. Philadelphia: University of Pennsylvania Press, 1999.

"Shaping the Text; Innovation and Authority in Graeco-Egyptian Malign Magic." In *Kykeon: Studies in Honour of H. S. Versnel*, edited by H. F. J. Horstmanshoff, H. W. Singor, F. T. van Straten and J. H. M. Strubbe, 69–111. Leiden: Brill, 2002.

Gordon, Richard L., and Francisco Marco Simón, eds. *Magical Practice in the Latin West. Papers from the International Conference Held at the University of Zaragoza, 30 Sept.–1 Oct. 2005*. Leiden: Brill, 2010.

Graf, Fritz. *Magic in the Ancient World*. Translated by Franklin Philip. Cambridge, MA: Harvard University Press, 1997.

"Magic and Divination." In *The World of Ancient Magic. Papers from the First International Samson Eitrem Seminar at the Norwegian Institute at Athens, 4–8 May 1997*, edited by David R. Jordan, Hugo Montgomery, and Einar Thomassen, 283–297. Papers from the Norwegian Institute at Athens 4. Bergen: The Norwegian Institute at Athens, 1999.

Johnston, Sarah Iles. "Songs for the Ghosts." In *The World of Ancient Magic. Papers from the First International Samson Eitrem Seminar at the Norwegian Institute at Athens, 4–8 May 1997*, edited by David R. Jordan, Hugo Montgomery, and Einar Thomassen, 83–102. Papers from the Norwegian Institute at Athens 4. Bergen: The Norwegian Institute at Athens, 1999.

Jordan, David R., Hugo Montgomery, and Einar Thomassen, eds. *The World of Ancient Magic. Papers from the First International Samson Eitrem Seminar at the Norwegian Institute at Athens, 4–8 May 1997*. Papers from the Norwegian Institute at Athens 4. Bergen: The Norwegian Institute at Athens, 1999.

Kotansky, Roy. "Incantations and Prayers for Salvation on Inscribed Greek Amulets." In *Magika Hiera: Ancient Greek Magic and Religion*, edited by Christopher A. Faraone and Dirk Obbink, 107–137. New York and Oxford: Oxford University Press, 1991.

Moyer, Ian. "Thessalos of Tralles and Cultural Exchange." In *Prayer, Magic and the Stars in the Ancient and Late Antique World*, edited by Scott Noegel, Joel Walker, and Brannon Wheeler, 39–56. Pittsburgh: Penn State University Press, 2003.

Nilsson, Martin P. "Pagan Divine Service in Late Antiquity." *Harvard Theological Review* 38, no. 1 (1945): 63–69.

Noegel, Scott, Joel Walker, and Brannon Wheeler, eds. *Prayer, Magic and the Stars in the Ancient and Late Antique World*. Pittsburgh: Penn State University Press, 2003.

Ogden, Daniel. "Binding Spells: Curse Tablets and Voodoo Dolls in the Greek and Roman Worlds." In *Witchcraft and Magic in Europe*, vol. 2, *Ancient Greece and Rome*, edited by Bengt Ankarloo and Stuart Clark, 1–90. Philadelphia: University of Pennsylvania Press, 1999.

Phillips, C. R., III. "Nullum Crimen sine Lege: Socioreligious Sanctions on Magic." In *Magika Hiera: Ancient Greek Magic and Religion*, edited by Christopher A. Faraone and Dirk Obbink, 260–276. New York and Oxford: Oxford University Press, 1991.

Ritner, Robert K. "Egyptian Magical Practice under the Roman Empire: The Demotic Spells and Their Religious Context." In *Aufstieg und Niedergang der römischen Welt. Geschichte und Kultur Roms im Spiegel der neueren Forschung*, part II, *Principat*, vol. 18, *Religion*, fasc. 5, *Heidentum: Die religiösen Verhältnisse in den Provinzen (Forts.)*, edited by Wolfgang Haase, 3333–3379. Berlin and New York: de Gruyter, 1995.

Rives, James B. "Magic in Roman Law: The Reconstruction of a Crime." *Classical Antiquity* 22, no. 2 (2003): 313–339.

Schäfer, Peter, and Hans G. Kippenberg, eds. *Envisioning Magic: A Princeton Seminar and Symposium*. Studies in the History of Religions 75. Leiden, New York, and Cologne: Brill, 1997.

Smith, Jonathan Z. "Great Scott! Thought and Action One More Time." In *Magic and Ritual in the Ancient World*, edited by Paul Mirecki and Marvin Meyer, 73–91. Religions in the Graeco-Roman World 141. Leiden, Boston, and Cologne: Brill, 2002.

"Here, There, and Anywhere." In *Prayer, Magic and the Stars in the Ancient and Late Antique World*, edited by Scott Noegel, Joel Walker, and Brannon Wheeler, 21–36. Pittsburgh: Penn State University Press, 2003.

5 The Early Church (by Maijastina Kahlos)

Primary Sources

The Acts of Paul. Edited by W. Scheemelcher. Translated by R. McL. Wilson. In *New Testament Apocrypha*, vol. 2, edited by Wilhelm Scheemelcher, 322–390. Philadelphia: The Westminster Press, 1992.

The Acts of Peter. Edited by W. Schneemelcher. Translated by G. C. Stead. In *New Testament Apocrypha*, vol. 2, edited by Wilhelm Scheemelcher, translation edited by R. McL. Wilson, 259–322. Philadelphia: The Westminster Press, 1992.

The Acts of Thomas. Edited By G. Bornkamm. Translated by R. McL. Wilson. In *New Testament Apocrypha*, vol. 2, edited by Wilhelm Scheemelcher, 425–531. Philadelphia: The Westminster Press, 1992.

Ambrose. *Oration on the Death of Theodosius I*. In *Ambrose of Milan. Political Letters and Speeches*, translated by J. H. W. G. Liebeschuetz, with the assistance of Carole Hill, 395. Liverpool: Liverpool University Press, 2005.

Ammianus Marcellinus. *Res Gestae*. Translated by John C. Rolfe. 3 vols. Cambridge, MA: Harvard University Press, 1935–1940.

Apostolic Constitutions. In *The Ante-Nicene Fathers*, vol. 7, edited by Alexander Roberts, James Donaldson, and A. Cleveland Coxe, 385–508. Grand Rapids: Eerdmans, 1957.

Arnobius. *Arnobe: Contre les gentils* [Against the Pagans] Book I. Edited by Henri Le Bonniec. Paris: Les Belles Lettres, 1982.

Athanasius. *On the Incarnation of the Word*. In *Contra gentes and De incarnation*, edited and translated by Robert W. Thomson, 104–289. Oxford: Clarendon Press, 1971.

Vie d'Antoine [Life of Anthony]. Edited by G. J. M. Bartelink. Sources chrétiennes 400. Paris: Cerf, 1994.

Augustine. *De civitate Dei* [City of God]. Edited by Bernard Dombart and Alphonse Kalb. 2 vols. Stuttgart: Teubner, 1981.

Confessions. Vol. 1. Edited by James J. O'Donnell. Oxford: Clarendon Press, 1992.

De doctrina Christiana [On Christian Doctrine]. Edited and translated by R. P. H. Green. Oxford: Clarendon Press, 1995.

Letters. In *Sancti Aurelii Augustini: Hipponensis episcopi epistulae*, 2 vols, edited by A. Goldbacher. Corpus Scriptorum Ecclesiasticorum Latinorum 34.1–2. Vienna: Österreichische Akademie der Wissenschaften, 1895, 1898.

On Different Questions. In *Sancti Aurelii Augustini: De diversis quaestionibus octoginta tribus*, edited by Almut Mutzenbecher. Corpus Christianorum Series Latina 44A. Turnhout: Brepols, 1975.

On the Divination of Demons. In *Sancti Aurelii Augustini opera*, edited by Joseph Zycha, 597–618. Corpus Scriptorum Ecclesiasticorum Latinorum 41. Vienna: Österreichische Akademie der Wissenschaften, 1900.

On the Harmony of the Gospels. In *S. Aurelii Augustini opera omnia editio latina*. www.augustinus.it/latino/consenso_evangelisti/index.htm

Tractates on the Gospel of John. In *S. Aurelii Augustini opera omnia editio latina*. www.augustinus.it/latino/commento_vsg/index2.htm

Babylonian Talmud (Shabbath). In *Der Babylonische Talmud*, vol. 1, *Berakhoth. Mishna Zeraim. Shabbath*, translated by Lazarus Goldschmidt. 3rd ed. Königstein: Jüdischer Verlag, 1980.

Betz, Hans Dieter, ed. *The Greek Magical Papyri in Translation, Including the Demotic Spells*. 2nd ed. Chicago and London: University of Chicago Press, 1992.

Canones Concilii Ancyrani, Capitula ex orientalium patrum synodis a Martino episcopo ordinata atque collecta. In *Martini episcopi Bracarensis opera omnia*, edited by Claude W. Barlow. New Haven: Yale University Press, 1950.

Canons of the Council of Laodicea. In *Nicene and Post-Nicene Fathers*, vol. 13, second series, edited by Philip Schaff and Henry Wace. Grand Rapids: Eerdmanns, 1957.

Canons of the Council of Saragossa. In *Patrologia Latina*, vol. 84. Alexandria: Chadwyck-Healey, 1995. pld.chadwyck.co.uk/

Codex Theodosianus. In *Theodosiani libri XVI cum constitutionibus Sirmondianis*, vol. I.1, edited by Theodor Mommsen and Paul Krüger. Berlin: Weidmann, 1905.

Eunapius. *Lives of the Philosophers*. In *The Lives of Sophists*, by Philostratus and Eunapius, translated by W. C. Wright. Cambridge, MA: Harvard University Press, 1921.

Gager, John G. *Curse Tablets and Binding Spells from the Ancient World*. Oxford: Oxford University Press, 1992.

Gregory of Tours. *Liber de miraculis beati Andreae apostoli* [The Acts of Andrew]. In *Monumenta germaniae historica. Scriptorum rerum Merovingicarum*, vol. I.1, *Gregorii turonensis miracula et opera minora*, edited by Max Bonnet. Hannover: Hahnsche Buchhandlung, 1885.

Miracles of Saint Julian, Libri octo miraculorum. In *Monumenta germaniae historica. Scriptorum rerum Merovingicarum*, vol. I.1, *Gregorii Turonensis Miracula et opera minora*, edited by Bruno Krusch. Hannover: Hahnsche Buchhandlung, 1885.

Miracles of Saint Julian. In *Saints and Their Miracles in Late Antique Gaul*, by Raymond van Dam. Princeton: Princeton University Press, 1993.

Glory of the Martyrs, Libri octo miraculorum. In *Monumenta germaniae historica. Scriptorum rerum Merovingicarum*, vol. I.1, *Gregorii Turonensis Miracula et opera minora*, edited by Bruno Krusch. Hannover: Hahnsche Buchhandlung, 1885.

Glory of the Martyrs. Edited and translated by Raymond van Dam. Translated Texts for Historians 3. Liverpool: Liverpool University Press, 1988.

Hippolytus. *La tradition apostolique d'après les anciennes versions* [Apostolic Tradition]. Edited by Bernard Botte. Sources chrétiennes 11 bis. Paris: Cerf, 1968.

Iamblichus. *Les mystères d'Egypte* [On the Mysteries of Egypt]. Edited by Édouard des Places. Paris: Les Belles Lettres, 1996.

Irenaeus. *Contre les heresies* [Against Heresies]. Edited by Adelin Rousseau and Louis Doutreleau. 2 vols. Sources chrétiennes 263, 294. Paris: Cerf, 1979–1982.

Isidore of Seville. *Etymologiarum sive originum libri XX*. Vol. 1. Edited by W. M. Lindsay. Oxford: Clarendon Press, 1911.

Jerome. *Life of Hilarion*. In *Trois vies de moines (Paul, Malchus, Hilarion)*, edited by Edouard M. Morales and Pierre Leclerc. Sources chrétiennes 508. Paris: Cerf, 2007.

John Chrysostom. *Homilies on Colossians*. In *Nicene and Post-Nicene Fathers*, vol. 13, first series, edited by Philip Schaff. Grand Rapids: Eerdmanns, 1956.

   Homilies on 1 Thessalonians. In *Nicene and Post-Nicene Fathers*, vol. 13, first series, edited by Philip Schaff. Grand Rapids: Eerdmanns, 1956.

   Homilies on First Timothy. In *Nicene and Post-Nicene Fathers*, vol. 13, first series, edited by Philip Schaff. Grand Rapids: Eerdmanns, 1956.

   Homilies on Second Timothy. In *Nicene and Post-Nicene Fathers*, vol. 13, first series, edited by Philip Schaff. Grand Rapids: Eerdmanns, 1956.

Julian. *Against Galileans*. In *The Works of the Emperor Julian*, vol. 3, translated by W. C. Wright. Cambridge, MA: Harvard University Press, 1923.

Justin. *Dialogue with Trypho*. In *Iustini Martyris dialogus cum Tryphone*, edited by Miroslav Marcovich. Berlin: de Gruyter, 1997.

   First Apology. In *Iustini Martyris apologiae pro Christianis*, edited by Miroslav Marcovich. Berlin: de Gruyter, 1994.

   Second Apology. In *Iustini Martyris apologiae pro Christianis*, edited by Miroslav Marcovich. Berlin: de Gruyter, 1994.

Lactantius. *Institutions divines* [Divine Institutes]. Vol. II. Edited by Pierre Monat. Sources chrétiennes 337. Paris: Cerf, 1987.

Leges Visigothorum. In *Monumenta Germaniae Historica. Leges nationum Germanicarum*, vol. I.1, *Leges Visigothorum*, edited by Karl Zeumer. Hannover: Hahnsche Buchhandlung, 1902.

Life of Theodore of Sykeon. In *Three Byzantine Saints: Contemporary Biographies*, translated by Elizabeth Dawes and Norman H. Baynes. London: Mowbrays, 1977.

Martin of Braga. *Reforming the Rustics*. In *Martini episcopi Bracarensis opera omnia*, edited by Claude W. Barlow. New Haven: Yale University Press, 1950.

Meyer, Marvin, and Richard Smith, eds. *Ancient Christian Magic. Coptic Texts of Ritual Power*. Princeton: Princeton University Press, 1999.

Mosaicarum et romanarum legum collatio. In *Fontes Iuris Romanae antejustiniani*, vol. II, edited by S. Riccobono, J. Baviera, and J. Furlani. Florence: Barbèra, 1968.

Olympiodorus. "Fragments." In *The Fragmentary Classicising Historians of the Later Roman Empire: Eunapius, Olympiodorus, Priscus and Malchus*, vol. 2, edited by R. C. Blockley. Liverpool: Cairns, 1983.

Origen. *Contre Celse* [Against Celsus]. Edited by Marcel Borret. 4 vols. Sources chrétiennes 132, 136, 147, 150. Paris: Cerf, 1967–1969.

Paulus. *Sententiae*. In *Fontes Iuris Romanae antejustiniani*, vol. II, edited by S. Riccobono, J. Baviera, and J. Furlani. Florence: Barbèra, 1968.

Pliny the Younger. *Letters*. Vol. II. Edited by W. M. L. Hutchinson. Cambridge, MA: Harvard University Press, 1915.

Pseudo-Clementine Recognitions. Translated by Thomas Smith. In *The Ante-Nicene Fathers*, vol. 8, edited by Alexander Roberts and James Donaldson. Grand Rapids: Eerdmans, 1957.

Rufinus. *Church History*. In *Patrologia Latina*, vol. 21. Alexandria: Chadwyck-Healey, 1995. pld.chadwyck.co.uk

Sulpicius Severus. *Chronicle*, edited by Karl Halm. Corpus Scriptorum Ecclesiasticorum Latinorum 1. Vienna: Österreichische Akademie der Wissenschaften, 1866.

Dialogues. In *Sulpicii Severi libri qui supersunt,* edited by Karl Halm. Corpus Scriptorum Ecclesiasticorum Latinorum 1. Vienna: Österreichische Akademie der Wissenschaften, 1866.

Supplementum Magicum. Vol. 1. Edited and translated by Ralph W. Daniel and Franco Maltomini. Papyrologica Coloniensia 16.1. Opladen: Westdeutscher Verlag, 1990.

The Syrian Acts of the "Robber" Council of Ephesus. In *The Second Synod of Ephesus Together with Certain Extracts Relating to It,* edited by S. G. F. Perry. Dartford: Orient Press, 1881.

Talmud Yerushalmi. Vol. II.1, *Shabbat.* Translated by Frowald Gil Hüttenmeister. Tübingen: Mohr Siebeck, 2004.

Talmud Yerushalmi. Vol. IV.7, *Avoda Zara.* Translated by Gerd A. Wevers. Tübingen: Mohr Siebeck, 1980.

Tertullian. *Apologétique* [Apology]. Edited by Jean-Pierre Waltzing and Albert Severyns. Paris: Les Belles Lettres, 1971.

    De idololatria [On Idolatry]. Edited and translated by J. H. Waszink and J. C. M. van Winden. Supplements to Vigiliae Christianae 1. Leiden: Brill, 1987.

    On the Shows. In *Tertulliani opera,* edited by A. Reitterscheid and G. Wissowa. Corpus Scriptorum Ecclesiasticorum Latinorum 20. Vienna: Österreichische Akademie der Wissenschaften, 1890.

    Traité de la prescription contre les hérétiques [The Prescription against Heretics]. Edited by R. F. Refoulé and P. de Labriolle. Sources chrétiennes 46. Paris: Cerf, 1957.

    Treatise on the Soul. In *Tertulliani opera,* edited by A. Reitterscheid and G. Wissowa. Corpus Scriptorum Ecclesiasticorum Latinorum 20. Vienna: Österreichische Akademie der Wissenschaften, 1890.

Vie de Théodore de Sykéon [Life of Theodore of Sykeon]. Vol. 1. Edited by André-Jean Festugière. Subsidia hagiographica 48. Brussels: Société des Bollandistes, 1970.

Secondary Sources

Aune, David E. "Magic in Early Christianity." In *Aufstieg und Niedergang der römischen Welt: Geschichte und Kultur Roms im Spiegel der neueren Forschung,* part II, *Principat,* vol. 23, fasc. 2, edited by Wolfgang Haase, 1507–1557. Berlin: de Gruyter, 1980.

Barb, A. A. "The Survival of Magic Arts." In *The Conflict between Paganism and Christianity in the Fourth Century,* edited by Arnaldo Momigliano, 100–125. Oxford: Clarendon Press, 1963.

BeDuhn, Jason David. "Magical Bowls and Manichaeans." In *Ancient Magic and Ritual Power,* edited by Marvin Meyer and Paul Mirecki, 419–434. Leiden and New York: Brill, 1995.

Bosson, Nathalie. "À la croisée des chemins: Réflection sur le pouvoir du nom dans la magie copte traditionelle." In *La magie,* vol. 1, *Du monde babylonien au monde hellénistique,* edited by Alain Moreau and Jean-Claude Turpin, 233–243. Montpellier: Université Paul Valéry Montpellier III, 2000.

Bremmer, Jan N. "Magic in the *Apocryphal Acts of the Apostles.*" In *The Metamorphosis of Magic from Late Antiquity to the early Modern Period,* edited by Jan N. Bremmer and Jan R. Veenstra, 51–70. Leuven: Peeters, 2002.

Breyfogle, Todd. "Magic, Women, and Heresy in the Late Empire: The Case of the Priscillianists." In *Ancient Magic and Ritual Power,* edited by Marvin Meyer and Paul Mirecki, 435–454. Leiden and New York: Brill, 1995.

Brown, Peter. "Sorcery, Demons and the Rise of Christianity: From Late Antiquity in the Middle Ages." In *Witchcraft: Confessions and Accusations*, edited by Mary Douglas, 17–45. London: Tavistock, 1970. Reprint in Peter Brown, *Religion and Society in the Age of Saint Augustine*, 119–146. London: Faber and Faber, 1972.

The Rise of Western Christendom: Triumph and Diversity, AD 200–1000. Oxford: Blackwell, 1996.

"Christianization and Religious Conflict." In *The Cambridge Ancient History*, vol. XIII, *The Late Empire, A.D. 337–425*, edited by Averil Cameron and Peter Garnsey, 632–664. Cambridge: Cambridge University Press, 1998.

Burrus, Virginia. *The Making of a Heretic. Gender, Authority, and the Priscillianist Controversy.* Berkeley: University of California Press, 1995.

Chadwick, Henry. *Priscillian of Avila. The Occult and the Charismatic in the Early Church.* Oxford: Clarendon Press, 1976.

"Oracles of the End in the Conflict of Paganism and Christianity in the Fourth Century." In *Mémorial A. J. Festugière: Antiquité païenne et chrétienne*, edited by E. Lucchesi and H. Saffrey, 125–129. Geneva: Cramer, 1984.

Czachesz, I. "Who is Deviant? Entering the Story-World of the *Acts of Peter*." In *The Apocryphal Acts of Peter. Magic, Miracles and Gnosticism*, edited by Jan N. Bremmer, 84–96. Leuven: Peeters, 1998.

van Dam, Raymond. *Leadership and Community in Late Antique Gaul.* Berkeley: University of California Press, 1985.

Dölger, F. J. "Das Segnen der Sinn mit der Eucharistie." In *Antike und Christentum*, vol. III, 231–244. Münster: Aschendorff, 1932.

Dufault, Olivier. "Magic and Religion in Augustine and Iamblichus." In *Religious Identity in Late Antiquity*, edited by Robert M. Frakes and Elizabeth DePalma Digeser, 59–83. Toronto: Edgar Kent, Inc., Publishers, 2006.

Engemann, J. "Zur Verbreitung der magischen Übelabwehr in der nichtchristlichen und christlichen Spätantike." *Jahrbuch für Antike und Christentum* 18 (1975): 22–48.

Escribano Paño, Maria Victoria. "Heretical Texts and *Maleficium* in the *Codex Theodosianus* (*CTh* 16.5.34)." In *Magical Practice in the Latin West. Papers from the International Conference Held at the University of Zaragoza, 30 Sept.–1 Oct. 2005*, edited by Richard L. Gordon and Francisco Marco Simón, 105–138. Leiden: Brill, 2010.

Fält, Olavi K. "Introduction." In *Looking at the Other: Historical Study of Images in Theory and Practise*, edited by Kari Alenius, Olavi K. Fält, and Seija Jalagin, 7–12. Oulu: Oulu University Press, 2002.

Flint, Valerie I. J. *The Rise of Magic in Early Medieval Europe.* Princeton: Princeton University Press, 1991.

"The Demonisation of Magic and Sorcery in Late Antiquity: Christian Redefinitions of Pagan Religions." In *Witchcraft and Magic in Europe*, vol. 2, *Ancient Greece and Rome*, edited by Bengt Ankarloo and Stuart Clark, 279–348. London: The Athlone Press, 1999.

Fögen, Marie Theres. *Die Enteignung der Wahrsager. Studien zum kaiserlichen Wissensmonopol in der Spätantike.* Frankfurt am Main: Suhrkamp, 1993.

Förster, Niclas. *Marcus Magus.* Tübingen: Mohr Siebeck, 1999.

Frankfurter, David. "Narrating Power: The Theory and Practice of the Magical Historiola in Ritual Spells." In *Ancient Magic and Ritual Power*, edited by Marvin Meyer and Paul Mirecki, 457–476. Leiden and New York: Brill, 1995.

"Ritual Expertise in Roman Egypt and the Problem of the Category 'Magician.'" In *Envisioning Magic: A Princeton Seminar and Symposium*, edited by Peter Schäfer and Hans G. Kippenberg, 115–135. Studies in the History of Religions 75. Leiden, New York, and Cologne: Brill, 1997.

"Dynamics of Ritual Expertise in Antiquity and Beyond: Towards a New Taxonomy of 'Magicians.'" In *Magic and Ritual in the Ancient World*, edited by Paul Mirecki and Marvin Meyer, 159–178. Religions in the Graeco-Roman World 141. Leiden, Boston, and Cologne: Brill, 2002.

"Beyond Magic and Superstition." In *A People's History of Christianity*, vol. 2, *Late Ancient Christianity*, edited by Virginia Burrus, 255–284. Minneapolis: Fortress Press, 2005.

Funke, Hermann. "Majestäts- und Magieprozesse bei Ammianus Marcellinus." *Jahrbuch für Antike und Christentum* 10 (1967): 145–175.

Gager, John G. *Moses in Greco-Roman Paganism*. Nashville: Abingdon Press, 1972.

Garrett, Susan. *The Demise of the Devil: Magic and the Demonic in Luke's Writings*. Minneapolis: Fortress Press, 1989.

"Light on a Dark Subject and Vice Versa: Magic and Magicians in the New Testament." In *Religion, Science, and Magic: In Concert and in Conflict*, edited by J. Neusner, E. S. Frerichs, and P. V. M. Flesher, 142–165. New York: Oxford University Press, 1989.

Girardet, Klaus M. "Trier 385. Der Prozess gegen die Priszillianer." *Chiron* 4 (1974): 577–608. Reprint in Klaus M. Girardet, *Kaisertum, Religionspolitik und das Recht von Staat und Kirche in der Spätantike*, 419–454. Bonn: Habelt, 2009.

Gordon, Richard. "Religion in the Roman Empire: The Civic Compromise and Its Limits." In *Pagan Priests*, edited by Mary Beard and John North, 233–255. London: Duckworth, 1990.

"Imagining Greek and Roman Magic." In *Witchcraft and Magic in Europe*, vol. 2, *Ancient Greece and Rome*, edited by Bengt Ankarloo and Stuart Clark, 159–275. London: The Athlone Press, 1999.

"*Superstitio*, Superstition and Religious Repression in the Late Roman Republic and Principate (100 BCE–300 CE)." In *The Religion of Fools? Superstition Past and Present*, edited by S. A. Smith and Alan Knight, 72–94. Oxford: Oxford Journals, 2008.

Gordon, Richard, and Francisco Marco Simón. "Introduction." In *Magical Practice in the Latin West. Papers from the International Conference Held at the University of Zaragoza, 30 Sept.–1 Oct. 2005*, edited by Richard L. Gordon and Francisco Marco Simón, 1–49. Leiden: Brill, 2010.

Graf, Fritz. "How to Cope with a Difficult Life. A View of Ancient Magic." In *Envisioning Magic: A Princeton Seminar and Symposium*, edited by Peter Schäfer and Hans G. Kippenberg, 93–114. Studies in the History of Religions 75. Leiden, New York, and Cologne: Brill, 1997.

"Magic and Divination." In *The World of Ancient Magic. Papers from the First International Samson Eitrem Seminar at the Norwegian Institute at Athens, 4–8 May 1997*, edited by David R. Jordan, Hugo Montgomery, and Einar Thomassen, 283–298. Papers from the Norwegian Institute at Athens 4. Bergen: The Norwegian Institute at Athens, 1999.

"Augustine and Magic." In *The Metamorphosis of Magic from Late Antiquity to the Early Modern Period*, edited by Jan N. Bremmer and Jan R. Veenstra, 87–103. Leuven: Peeters, 2002.

van der Horst, Pieter W. *"Sortes*: Sacred Books as Instant Oracles in Late Antiquity." In *The Use of Sacred Books in the Ancient World*, edited by L. V. Rutgers, P. W. van der Horst, H. W. Havelaar, and L. Teugels, 143–173. Leuven: Peeters, 1998.

Hull, John M. *Hellenistic Magic and the Synoptic Tradition*. London: SCM Press, 1974.

Humfress, Caroline. "Roman Law, Forensic Argument and the Formation of Christian Orthodoxy (III–VI Centuries)." In *Orthodoxie, christianisme, histoire*, edited by Susanna Elm, Éric Rebillard, and Antonella Romano, 125–147. Rome: École française de Rome, 2000.

Janowitz, Naomi. *Magic in the Roman World*. London and New York: Routledge, 2001.

––––. *Icons of Power: Ritual Practices in Late Antiquity*. University Park: Penn State University Press, 2002.

Johnston, Sarah Iles. *Restless Dead: Encounters between the Living and the Dead in Ancient Greece*. Berkeley, Los Angeles, and London: University of California Press, 1999.

––––. "Le sacrifice dans les papyrus magiques grecs." In *La magie*, vol. 2, *La magie dans l'antiquité grecque tardive. Les mythes*, edited by Alain Moreau and Jean-Claude Turpin, 19–36. Montpellier: Université Paul Valéry Montpellier III, 2000.

Jordan, David R. "New *Defixiones* from Carthage." In *The Circus and a Byzantine Cemetery at Carthage*, vol. 1, edited by J. H. Humphrey, 117–134. Ann Arbor: University of Michigan Press, 1988.

––––. "Magica Graeca Parvula." *Zeitschrift für Papyrologie und Epigraphik* 100 (1994): 325–335.

Kahlos, M. *Debate and Dialogue. Christian and Pagan Cultures, c. 360–430*. Aldershot: Ashgate, 2007.

––––. *"Religio* and *superstitio*: Retortions and Phases of a Binary Opposition in Late Antiquity." *Athenaeum* 95, no. 1 (2007): 389–408.

––––. "Introduction." In *The Faces of the Other. Religious Rivalry and Ethnic Encounters in the Later Roman World*, edited by M. Kahlos. Brepols: Turnhout, 2011.

Karivieri, Arja. "Magic and Syncretic Religious Culture in the East." In *Religious Diversity in Late Antiquity*, edited by David M. Gwynn and Susanne Bangert, 401–434. Late Antique Archaeology 6. Leiden: Brill, 2010.

Kee, Howard Clark. *Miracle in the Early Christian World. A Study in Sociohistorical Method*. New Haven: Yale University Press, 1983.

Kelhoffer, J. A. *Miracle and Mission*. Tübingen: Mohr Siebeck, 2000.

Kippenberg, Hans G. "Magic in Roman Civil Discourse: Why Rituals Could Be Illegal." In *Envisioning Magic: A Princeton Seminar and Symposium*, edited by Peter Schäfer and Hans G. Kippenberg, 137–163. Studies in the History of Religions 75. Leiden, New York, and Cologne: Brill, 1997.

Klingshirn, William E. "Defining the *Sortes Sanctorum*: Gibbon, Du Cange, and Early Christian Lot Divination." *Journal of Early Christian Studies* 10, no. 1 (2002): 77–130.

––––. "Isidore of Seville's Taxonomy of Magicians and Diviners." *Traditio* 58 (2003): 59–90.

Knipe, Sergio. "Recycling the Refuse-Heap of Magic: Scholarly Approaches to Theurgy since 1963." *Cristianesimo nella storia* 31 (2009): 337–345.

Knust, Jennifer Wright. *Abandoned to Lust: Sexual Slander and Ancient Christianity*. New York: Columbia University Press, 2005.

Kotansky, Roy. "Greek Exorcistic Amulets." In *Ancient Magic and Ritual Power*, edited by Marvin Meyer and Paul Mirecki, 243–477. Leiden and New York: Brill, 1995.

"An Early Christian Gold *Lamella* for Headache." In *Magic and Ritual in the Ancient World*, edited by Paul Mirecki and Marvin Meyer, 37–46. Religions in the Graeco-Roman World 141. Leiden, Boston, and Cologne: Brill, 2002.

Kühn, K. "Augustins Schrift *De divinatione daemonum*." *Augustiniana* 47 (1997): 291–337.

Lambert, Pierre-Yves. "Celtic Loricae and Ancient Magical Charms." In *Magical Practice in the Latin West. Papers from the International Conference Held at the University of Zaragoza, 30 Sept.–1 Oct. 2005*, edited by Richard L. Gordon and Francisco Marco Simón, 629–648. Leiden: Brill, 2010.

Lenski, Noel. *Failure of Empire. Valens and the Roman State in the Fourth Century A.D.* Berkeley: University of California Press, 2002.

Luck, Georg. "Witches and Sorcerers in Classical Literature." In *Witchcraft and Magic in Europe*, vol. 2, *Ancient Greece and Rome*, edited by Bengt Ankarloo and Stuart Clark, 93–158. London: The Athlone Press, 1999.

Luttikhuizen, Gerard. "Simon Magus as a Narrative Figure." In *The Apocryphal Acts of Peter. Magic, Miracles and Gnosticism*, edited by Jan N. Bremmer, 39–51. Leuven: Peeters, 1998.

Magoulias, H. J. "The Lives of Byzantine Saints as Sources of Data for the History of Magic in the Sixth and Seventh Centuries A.D.: Sorcery, Relics and Icons." *Byzantion* 37 (1967): 228–269.

Manganaro, Giacomo. "Nuovi documenti magici della Sicilia orientale." *Rendiconti della Classe di Scienze morali, storiche e filologiche dell'Accademia dei Lincei* 18 (1963): 57–74.

Marasco, Gabriele. "La magia e la guerra." *Millennium* 1 (2004): 83–132.

Markus, R. A. *Signs and Meanings. World and Text in Ancient Christianity.* Liverpool: Liverpool University Press, 1996.

Mathisen, R. W. "Crossing the Supernatural Frontier in Western Late Antiquity." In *Shifting Frontiers in Late Antiquity*, edited by R. W. Mathisen and H. S. Sivan, 309–320. Aldershot: Ashgate, 1996.

McKenna, Stephen. *Paganism and Pagan Survivals in Spain up to the Fall of the Visigothic Kingdom.* Washington, DC: Catholic University of America Press, 1938.

Meissner, Burkhard. "Magie, Pseudo-Technik und Paratechnik: Technik und Wissenschaft in den Kestoi des Julius Africanus." In *Die Kestoi des Julius Africanus und ihre Überlieferung*, edited by Martin Wallraff and Laura Mecella, 17–37. Berlin: de Gruyter, 2009.

Meyer, Marvin, and Paul Mirecki. "Introduction." In *Ancient Magic and Ritual Power*, edited by Marvin Meyer and Paul Mirecki, 1–10. Leiden and New York: Brill, 1995.

Meyer, Marvin, and Richard Smith. "Introduction." In *Ancient Christian Magic. Coptic Texts of Ritual Power*, edited by Marvin Meyer and Richard Smith, 1–9. Princeton: Princeton University Press, 1999.

Neyrey, Jerome H. "Miracles, in other Words: Social Science Perspectives on Healings." In *Miracles in Jewish and Christian Antiquity: Imagining Truth*, edited by John C. Cavadini, 19–55. Notre Dame: University of Notre Dame Press, 1999.

Nieto, Francisco Javier Fernández. "A Visigothic Charm from Asturias and the Classical Tradition of Phylacteries against Hail." In *Magical Practice in the Latin West. Papers from the International Conference Held at the University of Zaragoza, 30 Sept.–1 Oct. 2005*, edited by Richard L. Gordon and Francisco Marco Simón, 551–599. Leiden: Brill, 2010.

Ogden, Daniel. "Binding Spells: Curse Tablets and Voodoo Dolls in the Greek and Roman Worlds." In *Witchcraft and Magic in Europe*, vol. 2, *Ancient Greece and Rome*, edited by Bengt Ankarloo and Stuart Clark, 1–90. London: The Athlone Press, 1999.

Papini, Lucia. "Fragments of the *Sortes Sanctorum* from the Shrine of St. Colluthus." In *Pilgrimage and Holy Space in Late Antique Egypt*, edited by David Frankfurter, 393–401. Leiden: Brill, 1998.

Peterson, Erik. "Die geheimen Praktiken eines syrischen Bischofs." In *Frühkirche, Judentum und Gnosis. Studien und Untersuchungen*, 333–345. Rome: Herder, 1959.

Phillips, C. R., III. "*Nullum Crimen sine Lege*: Socioreligious Sanctions on Magic." In *Magika Hiera: Ancient Greek Magic and Religion*, edited by Christopher by Faraone and Dirk Obbink, 260–281. New York and Oxford: Oxford University Press, 1991.

Remus, Harold. "'Magic,' Method, Madness." *Method and Theory in the Study of Religion* 11 (1999): 258–298.

Ricks, Stephen D. "The Magician as Outsider in the Hebrew Bible and the New Testament." In *Ancient Magic and Ritual Power*, edited by Marvin Meyer and Paul Mirecki, 131–143. Leiden and New York: Brill, 1995.

Ritner, Robert K. "The Religious, Social, and Legal Parameters of Traditional Egyptian Magic." In *Ancient Magic and Ritual Power*, edited by Marvin Meyer and Paul Mirecki, 43–60. Leiden and New York: Brill, 1995.

Rives, James B. "Magic in Roman Law: The Reconstruction of a Crime." *Classical Antiquity* 22, no. 2 (2003): 313–339.

"Magic, Religion, and Law: The Case of the *Lex Cornelia de sicariis et veneficiis*." In *Religion and Law in Classical and Christian Rome*, edited by Clifford Ando and Jörg Rüpke, 47–67. Stuttgart: Steiner, 2006.

Salzman, M. R. "*Superstitio* in the Codex Theodosianus and the Persecution of Pagans." *Vigiliae Christianae* 41 (1987): 172–188.

Saradi-Mendelovici, Helen. "Christian Attitudes towards Pagan Monuments in Late Antiquity and Their Legacy in Later Byzantine Centuries." *Dumbarton Oaks Papers* 44 (1990): 47–61.

Segal, Alan F. "Hellenistic Magic: Some Questions of Definition." In *Studies in Gnosticism and Hellenistic Religions Presented to Gilles Quispel on the Occasion of His 65th Birthday*, edited by R. van den Broek and M. J. Vermaseren, 349–375. Leiden: Brill, 1981.

Sfameni, Carla. "Magic in Late Antiquity: The Evidence of Magical Gems." In *Religious Diversity in Late Antiquity*, edited by David M. Gwynn and Susanne Bangert, 435–473. Late Antique Archaeology 6. Leiden: Brill, 2010.

Sfameni Gasparro, Giulia. "Tra gnosi e magia: Spazio e ruolo della prassi magica nell'universo religioso dello gnosticismo." In *Il tardoantico alle soglie del duemila. Diritto, religione, società*, edited by Giuliana Lanata, 1–35. Pisa: Edizioni ETS, 2000.

Smith, Jonathan Z. "Trading Places." In *Ancient Magic and Ritual Power*, edited by Marvin Meyer and Paul Mirecki, 13–27. Leiden and New York: Brill, 1995.

Smith, Morton. *Jesus the Magician*. San Francisco: Harper and Row, 1978.

Speyer, Wolfgang. *Büchervernichtung und Zensur des Geistes bei Heiden, Juden und Christen*. Stuttgart: Hiersemann, 1981.

Stolte, Bernard H. "Magic and Byzantine Law in the Seventh Century." In *The Metamorphosis of Magic from Late Antiquity to the Early Modern Period*, edited by Jan N. Bremmer and Jan R. Veenstra, 105–115. Leuven: Peeters, 2002.

Stratton, Kimberly. *Naming the Witch: Magic, Ideology, and Stereotype in the Ancient World.* New York: Columbia University Press, 2007.

Thee, Francis C. R. *Julius Africanus and the Early Christian View of Magic.* Tübingen: Mohr Siebeck, 1984.

Thraede, Klaus. "Exorzismus." In *Reallexikon für Antike und Christentum*, vol. 7, edited by Theodor Klauser, 44–117. Stuttgart: Hiersemann, 1969.

Trombley, Frank R. "Paganism in the Greek World at the End of Antiquity: The Case of Rural Anatolia and Greece." *Harvard Theological Review* 78 (1985): 327–352.

Hellenic Religion and Christianization c. 370–529. Vol. I. Leiden: Brill, 1993.

Tuzlak, Ayse. "The Magician and the Heretic: The Case of Simon Magus." In *Magic and Ritual in the Ancient World*, edited by Paul Mirecki and Marvin Meyer, 416–426. Religions in the Graeco-Roman World 141. Leiden, Boston, and Cologne: Brill, 2002.

Velásquez Soriano, Isabel. "Between Orthodox Belief and 'Superstition' in Visigothic Hispania." In *Magical Practice in the Latin West. Papers from the International Conference Held at the University of Zaragoza, 30 Sept.–1 Oct. 2005*, edited by Richard L. Gordon and Francisco Marco Simón, 601–627. Leiden: Brill, 2010.

Versnel, H. S. "Some Reflections on the Relationship Magic-Religion." *Numen* 38, no. 2 (1991): 177–197.

van der Vliet, Jacques. "Satan's Fall in Coptic Magic." In *Ancient Magic and Ritual Power*, edited by Marvin Meyer and Paul Mirecki, 401–418. Leiden and New York: Brill, 1995.

Wallraff, Martin. "Magie und Religion in den Kestoi des Julius Africanus." In *Die Kestoi des Julius Africanus und ihre Überlieferung*, edited by Martin Wallraff and Laura Mecella, 39–52. Berlin: de Gruyter, 2009.

Weltin, E. G. *Athens and Jerusalem. An Interpretative Essay on Christianity and Classical Culture.* Atlanta: Scholars Press, 1987.

Wiebe, Franz Josef. *Kaiser Valens und die heidnische Opposition.* Habelt: Bonn, 1995.

Wischmeyer, W. "Magische Texte. Vorüberlegungen und Materialen zum Verständnis christlicher spätantiker Texte." In *Heiden und Christen im 5. Jahrhundert*, edited by J. van Oort and D. Wyrwa, 88–122. Leuven: Peeters, 1998.

Youtie, Herbert C. "Questions to a Christian Oracle." *Zeitschrift für Papyrologie und Epigraphik* 18 (1975): 253–257.

6 The Early Medieval West (by Yitzhak Hen)

Manuscripts

Vatican, Biblioteca Apostolica VAticana, Pal. lat. 577, fols. 7r-v *(Indiculus superstitionum et paganiarum).*

Primary Sources

Agobard of Lyons. *De grandine et tonitruis.* Edited by L. van Acker. Corpus Christianorum Continuatio Mediaevalis 52. Turnhout: Brepols, 1981.

Augustine. *De civitate Dei.* Edited by Bernard Dombart and Alphonse Kalb. 2 vols. Corpus Christianorum Series Latina 47–48. Turnhout: Brepols, 1955.

Confessiones. Edited by Lucas Verheijen. Corpus Christianorum Series Latina 27. Turnhout: Brepols, 1981.

Bede. *Historia ecclesiastica gentis Anglorum.* Edited and translated by Bertram Colgrave and Roger A. B. Mynors as *Bede's Ecclesiastical History of the English People.* Oxford: Oxford University Press, 1969. Translated by Judith McClure and Roger Collins. Oxford: Oxford University Press, 1994.

The Bobbio Missal: A Gallican Mass-Book. Edited by E. A. Lowe. Henry Bradshaw Society 58. London: Henry Bradshaw Society, 1920.

Burchard of Worms. *Decretum.* In *Die Bussbücher und das kanonische Bussverfahren nach handschriftlichen Quellen,* edited by Herman J. Schmitz, vol. II. Düsseldorf: Akademische Druck-u. Verlagsanstalt, 1898.

Caesarius of Arles. *Sermones.* Edited by Germain Morin. 2 vols. Corpus Christianorum Series Latina 103–104. Turnhout, 1953. Translated by Mary M. Mueller as *Caesarius of Arles: Sermons.* 3 vols. Washington, DC: Catholic University of America Press, 1956–1973.

Les canons des conciles mérovingiens (VIe–VIIe siècles). Edited by Jean Gaudemet and Brigitte Basdevant. 2 vols. Sources chrétiennes 353–354. Paris: Cerf, 1989.

Eligius of Noyon. *Sermones.* PL 87, cols. 524D–50C.

Gregory of Tours. *Liber in gloria martyrum.* In *Monumenta germaniae historica. Scriptorum rerum Merovingicarum,* vol. I.2, edited by Bruno Krusch, 484–562. Hannover: Hahnsche Buchhandlung, 1885. Translated by Raymond van Dam as *Gregory of Tours: Glory of the Martyrs.* Translated Texts for Historians 3. Liverpool: Liverpool University Press, 1988.

Libri historiarum X. In *Monumenta germaniae historica. Scriptorum rerum Merovingicarum,* vol. I.1, edited by Bruno Krusch and Wilhelm Levison. Hannover: Hahnsche Buchhandlung, 1951. Translated by Lewis Thorpe as *Gregory of Tours: History of the Franks.* New York: Penguin Books, 1974.

De virtutibus sancti Martini. In *Monumenta germaniae historica. Scriptorum rerum Merovingicarum,* vol. I.2, edited by Bruno Krusch, 134–210. Hannover: Hahnsche Buchhandlung, 1885. Translated by Raymond van Dam as *Saints and Their Miracles in Late Antique Gaul.* Princeton: Princeton University Press, 1993.

Hillgarth, J. N. *Christianity and Paganism, 350–750: The Conversion of Western Europe.* Rev. ed. Philadelphia: University of Pennsylvania Press, 1986.

Homilia de sacrilegiis. Edited by Carl P. Caspari as *Eine Augustin fälschlich beilegte Homilia de sacrilegiis.* Christiania: Dybwad, 1886.

Indiculus superstitionum et paganiarum. In *Monumenta germaniae historica. Capitularia regum Francorum,* edited by Alfred Boretius, vol. I, no. 108, 22–223. Hannover: Hahn, 1883.

Liber sacramentorum Romanae aecclesiae ordinis anni circuli (Sacramentarium Gelasianum). Edited by Leo C. Mohlberg, Leo Eizenhöfer, and Peter Siffrin. Rerum Ecclesiarum Documenta series maior 4. Rome: Herder, 1960.

Martin of Braga. *De correctione rusticorum.* In *Martini episcopi Bracarensis opera omnia,* edited by Claude W. Barlow, 183–203. New Haven: Yale University Press, 1950.

McNeill, John T., and Helena Gamer. *Medieval Handbooks of Penance: A Translation of the Principal "Libri Poenitentiales" and Selections from Related Documents.* New York: Columbia University Press, 1938.

Pirmin of Reichenaus. *Scarapsus.* Edited by Eckhard Hauswald. *Monumenta germaniae historica.* Quellen zur Geistesgeschichte des Mittelalters 25. Hannover: Hahn, 2010.

Regino of Prüm. *Libri duo de synodalibus causis et disciplinis ecclesiasticis.* Edited by F. G. A. Wasserschleben. Leipzig: Engelmann, 1840.

Le sacramentaire grégorien. Ses principales formes d'après les plus anciens manuscrits. Edited by Jean Deshusses. Spicilegium Friburgense 16. Freibourg: Editions universitaires, 1979.

Tacitus. *De origine et situ Germanorum (Germania).* Edited by Michael Winterbottom and R. M. Ogilvie. Oxford: Oxford University Press, 1975.

Vita eligii episcopi Noviomagensis. In *Monumenta germaniae historica. Scriptorum rerum Merovingicarum,* vol. 4, edited by Bruno Krusch, 663–741. Hannover: Hahn, 1902.

Secondary Sources

Austin, Greta. *Shaping Church Law around the Year 1000: The Decretum of Burchard of Worms.* Aldershot: Ashgate, 2009.

Beard, Mary, John North, and Simon Price. *Religions of Rome.* Vol. I, *A History* Cambridge: Cambridge University Press, 1998.

Blöcker, Monica. "Wetterzauber: Zu einem Glaubenskomplex des frühen Mittelalters." *Francia* 9 (1981); 117–131.

Bourque, Emmanuel. *Étude sur les sacramentaires romains.* Vol. II.2. Rome: Pontificio Istituto di Archeologia Cristiana 1958.

Brown, Peter R. L. *The Rise of Western Christendom: Triumph and Diversity, AD 200–1000.* 2nd ed. Oxford: Wiley-Blackwell, 2003.

Bullough, Donald A. "Roman Books and Carolingian *renovatio.*" In *Renaissance and Renewal in Church History,* edited by Derek Baker, 23–50. Studies in Church History 14. Oxford: Wiley-Blackwell, 1977. Reprint in Donald A. Bullough, *Carolingian Culture: Sources and Heritage,* 1–38. Manchester: Manchester University Press, 1991.

Clay, John-Henry. *In the Shadow of Death: Saint Boniface and the Conversion of Hesia, 721–754.* Cultural Encounters in Late Antiquity and the Middle Ages 11. Turnhout: Brepols, 2011.

Dierkens, Alain. "Superstitions, christianisme et paganism à la fin de l'époque mérovingienne." In *Magie, sorcellerie, parapsychology,* edited by Hervé Hasquin, 9–26. Brussels: Éd de l'Université de Bruxelles, 1984.

"The Evidence of Archaeology." In *The Pagan Middle Ages,* edited by Ludo J. R. Milis, 39–64. Woodbridge: Boydell Press, 1998.

Felten, Franz J., Jörg Jarnut, Marco Mostert, and Lutz E. von Padberg, eds. *Bonifatius: Leben und Nachwirken. Die Gestaltung des christlichen Europa im Frühmittelalter.* Mainz: Gesellschaft für Mittelrheinische Kirchengeschichte, 2007.

Filotas, Bernadette. *Pagan Survivals, Superstitions and Popular Cultures in Early Medieval Pastoral Literature.* Toronto: University of Toronto Press, 2005.

Flint, Valerie I. J. "The Early Medieval 'Medicus,' the Saint – and the Enchanter." *Social History of Medicine* 2 (1989): 127–145.

The Rise of Magic in Early Medieval Europe. Princeton: Princeton University Press, 1990.

Geertz, Hildred. "An Anthropology of Religion and Magic, I." *Journal of Interdisciplinary History* 6 (1975): 71–89.

Glatthaar, Michael. *Bonifatius und das Sakrileg: Zur politischen Dimension eines Rechtsbegriffs.* Freiburger Beiträge zur mittelalterlichen Geschichte 17. Frankfurt am Main: Peter Lang, 2004.

Hannig, Jürgen. *Consensus fidelium: Frühfeudale Interpretationen des Verhältnisses von Königtum und Adel am Beispiel des Frankenreiches.* Monographien zur Geschichte des Mittelalters 27. Stuttgart: Hiersemann, 1982.

Harmening, Dieter. *Superstitio. Überlieferungs- und theoriegeschichtliche Untersuchungen zur kritisch-theologischen Aberglaubensliteratur des Mittelalters*. Berlin: E. Schmidt, 1979.

Hen, Yitzhak. *Culture and Religion in Merovingian Gaul, A.D. 481–751*. Leiden: Brill, 1995.

——— . "Paul the Deacon and the Frankish Liturgy." In *Paolo Diacono: Uno scrittore fra tradizione longobarda e rinnovamento carolingio*, edited by Paulo Chiesa, 205–221. Udine: Forum, 2000.

——— . "The Annals of Metz and the Merovingian Past." In *The Uses of the Past in the Early Middle Ages*, edited by Yitzhak Hen and Matthew Innes, 175–190. Cambridge: Cambridge University Press, 2001.

——— . "Martin of Braga's *De correctione rusticorum* and Its Uses in Frankish Gaul. In *Medieval Transformations: Texts, Power, and Gifts in Context*, edited by Esther Cohen and Mayke de Jong, 35–49. Leiden: Brill, 2001.

——— . "Paganism and Superstitions in the Time of Gregory of Tours – *Une question mal posée!*" In *The World of Gregory of Tours*, edited by Kathleen Mitchell and Ian Wood, 229–240. Leiden: Brill, 2002.

——— . *Roman Barbarians: The Royal Court and Culture in the Early Medieval West*. Basingstoke and New York: Palgrave-Macmillan, 2007.

Homann, Holger, Meineke Eckhard, and Ruth Schmidt-Wiegand. "Indiculus superstitionum et paganiarum. In *Reallexikon der germanische Altertumskunde*, vol. 15, 369–384. Berlin: de Gruyter, 2000.

Jolivet, Jean. "Agobard de Lyon et les faiseurs de pluie." In *La method critique au Moyen Âge*, edited by Mireille Chazan and Gilbert Dahan, 15–25. Turnhout: Brepols, 2006.

Körntgen, Ludger. "Canon Law and the Practice of Penance: Burchard of Worms' Penitential." *Early Medieval Europe* 14 (2006): 103–117.

Künzel, Rudi. "Paganism, syncrétisme, et culture religieuse populaire au haut Moyen Âges. Réflexions et méthodes." *Annales ESC* 47 (1992): 1055–1069.

Löwe, Heinz. "Pirmin, Willibrord und Bonifatius: Ihre Bedeutung für die Missionsgeschichte ihrer Zeit." In *La conversione al cristianesimo nell'Europa dell'alto medioevo*, 327–372. Settimane di studi del Centro italiano di studi sull'alto medioevo 14. Spoleto: Centro italiano di studi sull'alto Medioevo, 1967. Reprint in Heinz Löwe, *Religiosität und Bildung im frühen Mittelalter*, 133–137. Weimar: Böhlau, 1994.

MacMullen, Ramsey. *Christianizing the Roman Empire, A.D. 100–400*. New Haven and London: Yale University Press, 1984.

Markus, Robert A. "Gregory the Great and a Papal Missionary Strategy." In *The Mission of the Church and the Propagation of the Faith*, edited by G. J. Cuming, 29–38. Studies in Church History 6. Cambridge: Cambridge University Press, 1970. Reprint in Robert A. Markus, *From Augustine to Gregory the Great*, chapter XI. Aldershot: Ashgrove, 1983.

——— . *The End of Ancient Christianity*. Cambridge: Cambridge University Press, 1990.

——— . "From Caesarius to Boniface: Christianity and Paganism in Gaul." In *Le septième siècle: Changements et continuities / The Seventh Century: Changes and Continuity*, edited by Jacques Fontaine and J. N. Hillgarth, 154–172. London: The Warburg Institute, 1992.

——— . *Gregory the Great and His World*. Cambridge: Cambridge University Press, 1997.

McCune, James. "Rethinking the Pseudo-Eligius Sermon Collection." *Early Medieval Europe* 16 (2008): 445–476.

McKitterick, Rosamond. *The Carolingians and the Written Word*. Cambridge: Cambridge University Press, 1989.

Anglo-Saxon Missionaries in Germany: Personal Connections and Local Influences. Vaughan Papers 36. Leicester, 1991. Reprint in Rosamond McKitterick, *The Frankish Kings and Culture in the Early Middle Ages,* chapter I. Aldershot: Ashgrove, 1995.

Meaney, Audrey L. *Anglo-Saxon Amulets and Cursing Stones.* BAR British Series 96. Oxford: British Archeological Reports, 1981.

Meens, Rob. "Magic and the Early Medieval World View. In *The Community, the Family and the Saint: Patterns of Power in Early Medieval Europe. Selected Proceedings of the International Medieval Congress, University of Leeds, 407 July 1994, 10–13 July 1995,* edited by Joyce Hill and Mary Swan, 285–295. Turnhout: Brepols, 1988.

   "Reforming the Clergy: A Context for the Use of the Bobbio Penitential." In *The Bobbio Missal: Liturgy and Religious Culture in Merovingian Gaul,* edited by Yitzhak Hen and Rob Meens, 154–167. Cambridge: Cambridge University Press, 2004.

   "Thunder over Lyon: Agobard, the *tempestarii* and Christianity." In *Paganism in the Middle Ages and the Renaissance,* edited by C. Steel, J. Marenbon, and W. Verbeke, 157–166. Mediaevalia Lovaniensia Studia 42. Leuven: Leuven University Press, 2013.

Mordek, Hubert. *Biblioteca capitularium regum Francorum manuscripta: Überlieferung und Traditionszusammenhang der fränkische Herschererlasse. Monumenta germaniae historica.* Hilfsmittel 15. Hannover: Hahn, 1994.

Murray, Alexander C. "Missionaries and Magic in Dark-Age Europe." *Past and Present* 136 (1992): 186–205.

Nelson, Janet L. "Kingship and Empire." In *The Cambridge History of Medieval Political Thought, c. 350–c. 1450,* edited by J. H. Burns, 211–251. Cambridge: Cambridge University Press, 1988, Reprint as "Kingship and Empire in the Carolingian World," in *Carolingian Culture: Emulation and Innovation,* edited by Rosamond McKitterick, 52–87. Cambridge: Cambridge University Press, 1994.

Nock, Arthur Darby. *Conversion. The Old and the New in Religion from Alexander the Great to Augustine of Hippo.* Oxford: Oxford University Press, 1933.

von Padberg, Lutz E. *Bonifatius: Missionar und Reformer.* Munich: C. H. Beck, 2003.

Palmer, James. "Defining Paganism in the Carolingian Worlds." *Early Medieval Europe* 15 (2007): 402–425.

Pontal, Odette. *Histoire des conciles mérovingiens.* Paris: Cerf, 1989.

Rampton, Martha. "Burchard of Worms and Female Magical Ritual." In *Medieval and Early Modern Ritual: Formalized Behaviours in Europe, China and Japan,* edited by Jöelle Rollo-Koster, 7–34. Leiden: Brill, 2002.

Reuter, Timothy, ed. *The Greatest Englishman: Essays on St Boniface and the Church at Credition.* Exeter: Paternoster Press, 1980.

Schieffer, Theodore. *Winfrid-Bonifatius und die christliche Grundlegung Europas.* Freiburg: Wissenschaftliche Buchgesellschaft, 1954.

Schmitt, Jean-Claude. "'Religion populaire' et culture folklorique." *Annales ESC* 31 (1976): 941–953.

   "Les superstitions." In *Histoire de la France religieuse,* edited by Jacques Le Goff, vol. 1, 425–453. Paris: Seuil, 1988.

Thomas, Keith. *Religion and the Decline of Magic.* New York: Charles Scribner's Sons, 1971.

   "An Anthropology of Religion and Magic, II." *Journal of Interdisciplinary History* 6 (1975): 91–109.

Vogel, Cyrille. *Medieval Liturgy: An Introduction to the Sources*. Translated and revised By William Storey and Niels Rasmussen. Washington, DC: Catholic University of America Press, 1986.

Wood, Ian N. *The Missionary Life: Saints and the Evangelisation of Europe, 400–1050*. London and New York: Routledge, 2001.

Zeddies, Nicole. *Religio und Sacrilegium: Studien zur Inkriminierung von Magie, Häresie und Heidentum (4.–7. Jahrhundert)*. Frankfurt am Main: Peter Lang, 1999.

7   Magic in Medieval Byzantium (ca. 843–1204) (by Alicia Walker)

Primary Sources

Cameron, Averil, and Judith Herrin, eds. and trans. *Constantinople in the Eighth Century: The* Parastaseis syntomoi chronikai. Columbia Studies in the Classical Tradition 10. Leiden: Brill, 1984.

Choniates, Nicetas. *O City of Byzantium: Annals of Niketas Choniates*. Translated by Harry J. Magoulias. Detroit: Wayne State University Press, 1984.

Constantine VII, Emperor of the East. *Constantine Porphyrogenitus: Three Treatises on Imperial Military Expeditions*. Translated by John F. Haldon. Corpus fontium historiae Byzantinae 28. Vienna: Verlag der Österreichischen Akademie der Wissenschaften, 1990.

Karlin-Hayter, Patricia, trans. and ed. *Vita Euthymii*. Brussels: Éditions de Byzantion, 1970.

Liudprand of Cremona. *The Complete Works of Liudprand of Cremona*. Translated by Paolo Squatriti. Washington, DC: Catholic University of America Press, 2007.

Psellos, Michel. *Chronographie, ou, Histoire d'un siè cle de Byzance (976–1077)*. Edited and translated by Émile Renauld. 2 vols. Paris: Société d'édition "Les Belles lettres," 1926–1928.

Skylitzes, John. *John Skylitzes. A Synopsis of Byzantine History, 811–1057*. Translated by John Wortley. Cambridge: Cambridge University Press, 2010.

Theophanes Continuatus. *Chronographia*. Edited by I. Bekker. Corpus Scriptorum Historiae Byzantinae 33, edited by Barthold Georg Niebuhr. Bonn: Impensis Ed. Weberi, 1838.

Secondary Sources

Abrahamse, Dorothy de F. "Magic and Sorcery in the Hagiography of the Middle Byzantine Period." *Byzantinische Forschungen* 8 (1982): 3–17.

Browning, Robert. "Literacy in the Byzantine World." *Byzantine and Modern Greek Studies* 4 (1978): 39–54.

Brubaker, Leslie. *Vision and Meaning in Ninth-Century Byzantium. Image as Exegesis in the Homilies of Gregory Nazianzus*. Cambridge: Cambridge University Press, 1999.

Burnett, Charles. "Late Antique and Medieval Latin Translations of Greek Texts on Astrology and Magic." In *The Occult Sciences in Byzantium*, edited by Paul Magdalino and Maria Mavroudi, 325–359. Geneva: La pomme d'or, 2006.

Calofonos, George Th. "The Magician Vigrinos and His Victim. A Case of Magic from the *Life of St. Andrew the Fool*." In *Greek Magic: Ancient, Medieval and Modern*, edited by J. C. B. Petropoulos, 64–71. London: Routledge, 2008.

Chryssanthopoulou, Vassiliki. "The Evil Eye among the Greeks of Australia: Identity, Continuity and Modernization." In *Greek Magic: Ancient, Medieval and Modern*, edited by J. C. B. Petropoulos, 106–118. London: Routledge, 2008.

Clark, Patricia Ann. *A Cretan Healer's Handbook in the Byzantine Tradition: Text, Translation and Commentary*. Farnham, Surrey: Ashgate, 2011.

Clucas, Lowell. *The Trial of John Italos and the Crisis of Intellectual Values in Byzantium in the Eleventh Century*. Miscellanea Byzantina Monacensia 26. Munich: Institut für Byzantinistik, Neugriechische Philologie und Byzantinische Kunstgeschichte der Universität, 1981.

Costanza, Salvatore. "La palmomanzia e tecniche affini in età bizantina." *Schede medievali: Rassegna dell'Officina di studi medievali* 44 (2006): 95–111.

"Nitriti come segni profetici: Cavalli fatidici a Bisanzio (XI–XIV sec.)." *Byzantinische Zeitschrift* 102, no. 1 (2010): 1–24.

Cupane, Carolina. "La magia a Bisanzio nel secolo XIV: Azione e reazione. Dal registro del patriarcato costantinopolitano (1315–1402)." *Jahrbuch der österreichischen Byzantinistik* 29 (1980): 237–262.

Dickie, Matthew W. *Magic and Magicians in the Greco-Roman World*. London and New York: Routledge, 2001.

Duffy, John. "Reactions of Two Byzantine Intellectuals to the Theory and Practice of Magic: Michael Psellos and Michael Italikos." In *Byzantine Magic*, edited by Henry Maguire, 83–90. Washington, DC: Dumbarton Oaks, 1995.

"Hellenic Philosophy in Byzantium and the Lonely Mission of Michael Psellos." In *Byzantine Philosophy and Its Ancient Sources*, edited by K. Ierodiakonou, 139–156. Oxford: Clarendon Press, 2002.

Farhad, M., ed. *Falnama: The Book of Omens*. Washington, DC: Arthur M. Sackler Gallery, Smithsonian Institution Press, 2009.

Flood, Finbarr Barry. "Image against Nature: Spolia as Apotropaia in Byzantium and the dār al-Islām." *The Medieval History Journal* 9 (2006): 143–166.

Fögen, Marie Theres. "Legislation und Kodifikation des Kaisers Leon VI." *Subseciva Groningana: Studies in Roman and Byzantine Law* 3 (1989): 23–35.

"Balsamon on Magic: From Roman Secular Law to Byzantine Canon Law." In *Byzantine Magic*, edited by Henry Maguire, 99–115. Washington, DC: Dumbarton Oaks, 1995.

Grabar, André, and M. Manoussacas. *L'illustration du manuscript de Skylitzès de la Bibliothèque Nationale de Madrid*. Bibliothèque de l'Institut hellénique d'études byzantines et post-byzantines de Venise 10. Venice: Institut hellénique d'études byzantines et post-byzantines de Venise, 1979.

Greenfield, Richard. *Traditions of Belief in Late Byzantine Demonology*. Amsterdam: Adolf M. Hakkert, 1988.

"Fallen into Outer Darkness: Later Byzantine Depictions and Conceptions of the Devil and the Demons." *Etnofoor* 5, nos. 1/2 (1992): 61–80.

"Sorcery and Politics at the Byzantine Court in the Twelfth Century: Interpretations of History." In *The Making of Byzantine History. Studies Dedicated to Donald M. Nicol*, edited by R. Beaton and C. Roueché, 73–93. Aldershot: Variorum, 1993.

"A Contribution to the Study of Palaeologan Magic." In *Byzantine Magic*, edited by Henry Maguire, 117–154. Washington, DC: Dumbarton Oaks, 1995.

Gutas, Dimitri. *Greek Thought, Arabic Culture: The Graeco-Arabic Translation Movement in Baghdad and Early 'Abbāsid Society (2nd–4th/8th–10th Centuries)*. London: Routledge, 1998.

Heintz, Molly Fulghum. "Health: Magic, Medicine, and Prayer." In *Byzantine Women and Their World*, edited by Ioli Kalavrezou, 275–281. Cambridge, MA: Harvard University Art Museums, 2001.

Herzfeld, Michael. "Meaning and Morality: A Semiotic Approach to Evil Eye Accusations in a Greek Village." *American Ethnologist* 8, no. 3 (1981): 560–574.

Ierodiakonou, Katerina. "The Greek Concept of Sympatheia and Its Byzantine Appropriation in Michael Psellos." In *The Occult Sciences in Byzantium*, edited by Paul Magdalino and Maria Mavroudi, 97–118. Geneva: La pomme d'or, 2006.

James, Liz. "'Pray Not to Fall into Temptation and Be on Your Guard': Pagan Statues in Christian Constantinople." *Gesta* 35, no. 1 (1996): 12–20.

——, ed. *A Companion to Byzantium*. Malden, MA: Wiley-Blackwell, 2010.

Jeffreys, Elizabeth, John Haldon, and Robin Cormack, eds. *The Oxford Handbook of Byzantine Studies*. Oxford: Oxford University Press, 2008.

Kaldellis, Anthony. *The Argument of Psellos'* Chronographia. Leiden: Brill, 1999.

Kazhdan, Alexander. "Byzantine Hagiography and Sex in the Fifth to Twelfth Centuries." *Dumbarton Oaks Papers* 44 (1990): 131–143.

Kazhdan, Alexander, ed. *The Oxford Dictionary of Byzantium*. 3 vols. Oxford: Oxford University Press, 1996.

Lemerle, Paul. *Le premier humanism byzantin. Notes et remarques sur enseignement et culture à Byzance des origines au Xe siècle*. Paris: Presses universitaires de France, 1971. Translated by Helen Lindsay and Ann Moffatt as *Byzantine Humanism: The First Phase*. Canberra: Australian Association for Byzantine Studies, 1986.

Magdalino, Paul. *The Empire of Manuel I Komnenos, 1143–1180*. Cambridge: Cambridge University Press, 1993.

——. "The Byzantine Reception of Classical Astrology." In *Literacy, Education and Manuscript Transmission in Byzantium and Beyond*, edited by Catherine Holmes and Judith Waring, 35–57. Leiden: Brill, 2002.

——. "The Porphyrogenita and the Astrologers. A Commentary on *Alexiad* VI.7.1–7." In *Porphyrogenita. Essays on the History and Literature of Byzantium and the Latin East in Honor of Julian Chrysostomides*, edited by Charalambos Dendrinos, Eirene Harvalia-Crook, Jonathan Harris, and Judith Herrin, 15–31. Aldershot: Ashgate, 2003.

——. "Occult Science and Imperial Power in Byzantine History and Historiography (9th–12th centuries)." In *The Occult Sciences in Byzantium*, edited by Paul Magdalino and Maria Mavroudi, 119–62. Geneva: La pomme d'or, 2006.

——. *L'orthodoxie des astrologues. La science entre le dogme et la divination à Byzance (VIIe–XIVe siècle)*. Paris: Lethielleux, 2006.

Magdalino, Paul, and Maria Mavroudi, eds. *The Occult Sciences in Byzantium*. Geneva: La pomme d'or, 2006.

Maguire, Eunice Dauterman, and Henry Maguire. *Other Icons. Art and Power in Byzantine Secular Culture*. Princeton: Princeton University Press, 2007.

Maguire, Eunice Dauterman, Henry Maguire, and Maggie Duncan-Flowers. *Art and Holy Powers in the Early Christian House*. Urbana: University of Illinois Press, 1989.

Maguire, Henry. "Garments Pleasing to God: The Significance of Domestic Textile Designs in the Early Byzantine Period." *Dumbarton Oaks Papers* 44 (1990): 215–224.

——. "The Cage of Crosses: Ancient and Medieval Sculptures on the 'Little Metropolis' in Athens." In *Thymiama stē mnēmē tēs Laskarinas Boura*, 169–172. Athens: Benaki Museum, 1994.

"From the Evil Eye to the Eye of Justice: The Saints, Art, and Justice in Byzantium." In *Law and Society in Byzantium, Ninth–Twelfth Centuries*, edited by Angeliki Laiou and Dieter Simon, 217–239. Washington, DC: Dumbarton Oaks, 1994.

ed. *Byzantine Magic*. Washington, DC: Dumbarton Oaks, 1995.

"Magic and the Christian Image." In *Byzantine Magic*, edited by Henry Maguire, 51–75. Washington, DC: Dumbarton Oaks, 1995.

"Magic and Money in the Early Middle Ages." *Speculum* 72, no. 4 (1997): 1037–1054.

"'Feathers Signify Power.' The Iconography of Byzantine Ceramics from Serres." In *Diethnes Synedrio Hoi Serres kai hē periochē tous apo tēn archaia stē metavyzantinē koinōnia, Serres 29 Septemvriou–3 Oktōvriou 1993: Praktika*, vol. 2, 383–398. Thessaloniki: Dēmos Serrōn, 1998.

"Other Icons: The Classical Nude in Byzantine Bone and Ivory Carvings." *The Journal of the Walters Art Museum* 62 (2004): 9–20.

"Magic and Sorcery in Ninth-Century Manuscript Illumination." In *Proceedings of the 22nd International Congress of Byzantine Studies, Sofia, 22–27 August 2011*, vol. 3, 199. Sofia: Bulgarian Historical Heritage Foundation, 2011.

Mango, Cyril. "Antique Statuary and the Byzantine Beholder." *Dumbarton Oaks Papers* 17 (1963): 55–75.

Mavroudi, Maria. *A Byzantine Book on Dream Interpretation: The Oneirocriticon of Achmet and Its Arabic Sources*. Leiden: Brill, 2002.

"Exchanges with Arabic Writers during the Late Byzantine Period." In *Byzantium: Faith and Power (1261–1557). Perspectives on Late Byzantine Art and Culture*, edited by Sarah T. Brooks, 62–75. New York: Metropolitan Museum of Art, 2006.

"Occult Science and Society in Byzantium: Considerations for Future Research." In *The Occult Sciences in Byzantium*, edited by Paul Magdalino and Maria Mavroudi, 39–95. Geneva: La pomme d'or, 2006.

"Female Practitioners of Magic in the Middle Byzantine Period." In *Proceedings of the 22nd International Congress of Byzantine Studies, Sofia, 22–27 August 2011*, vol. 2, 200. Sofia: Bulgarian Historical Heritage Foundation, 2011.

Oberhelman, Steven M. *Dreambooks in Byzantium. Six Oneirocritica in Translation, with Commentary and Introduction*. Aldershot: Ashgate, 2008.

Patera, Maria. "Gylou, démon et sorcière du monde byzantin au monde néogrec." *Revue des Études Byzantines* 64–65 (2007): 311–327.

Peers, Glenn. "Magic, the *Mandylion*, and the *Letter of Abgar*. On a Greco-Arabic Amulet Roll in Chicago and New York." In *Intorno al Sacro Volto. Genova, Bisanzio e il Mediterraneo (secoli XI–XIV)*, edited by Anna Rosa Calderoni Masetti, Colette Dufour Bozzo, and Gerhard Wolfe, 163–174. Collana del Kunsthistorisches Institut in Florenz 11. Venice: Marsilio, 2007.

Petropoulos, J. C. B., ed. *Greek Magic: Ancient, Medieval and Modern*. London: Routledge, 2008.

Pingree, David. "Gregory Chioniades and Palaeologan Astronomy." *Dumbarton Oaks Papers* 18 (1964): 133–160.

"The Horoscope of Constantine VII Porphyrogenitus." *Dumbarton Oaks Papers* 27 (1973): 219–231.

"The Diffusion of Arabic Magical Texts in Western Europe." In *La diffusione delle scienze islamiche nel medioevo europeo*, edited by B. Scarcia Amoretti, 57–102. Rome: Accademia Nazionale dei Lincei, 1987.

Russell, James. "Byzantine *Instrumenta Domestica* from Anemurium: The Significance of Context." In *City, Town, and Countryside in the Early Byzantine Era*, edited by R. L. Hohlfelder, 133–163. Boulder: East European Monographs, 1982.

———. "The Archaeological Context of Magic in the Early Byzantine Period." In *Byzantine Magic*, edited by Henry Maguire, 35–50. Washington, DC: Dumbarton Oaks, 1995.

Ryan, W. F. "Magic and Divination. Old Russian Sources." In *The Occult in Russian and Soviet Culture*, edited by Bernice Glatzer Rosenthal, 35–58. Ithaca: Cornell University Press, 1997.

———. *The Bathhouse at Midnight: An Historical Survey of Magic and Divination in Russia*. University Park: Penn State University Press, 1999.

Ryder, Edmund C. "Popular Religion: Magical Uses of Imagery in Byzantine Art." *Heilbrunn Timeline of Art History*. New York: Metropolitan Museum of Art, 2000–, http://www.metmuseum.org/toah/hd/popu/hd_popu.htm

Saliba, George. "Revisiting the Astronomical Contacts between the World of Islam and Renaissance Europe: The Byzantine Connection." In *The Occult Sciences in Byzantium*, edited by Paul Magdalino and Maria Mavroudi, 362–373. Geneva: La pomme d'or, 2006.

Ševčenko, Ihor. "Remarks on the Diffusion of Byzantine Scientific and Pseudo-Scientific Literature among the Orthodox Slavs." *The Slavonic and East European Review* 59, no. 3 (1981): 321–345.

Simeonova, Liliana. "Magic and the Warding-off of Barbarians in Constantinople, 9th–12th Centuries." In *Material Culture and Well-Being in Byzantium (400–1453)*, edited by Michael Grünbart, Ewald Kislinger, Anna Muthesius, and Dionysios Ch. Stathakopoulos, 207–210. Vienna: Verlag der Österreichischen Akademie der Wissenschaften, 2007.

Spier, Jeffrey. "Medieval Byzantine Magical Amulets and Their Tradition." *Journal of the Warburg and Courtauld Institutes* 56 (1993): 25–62.

Spieser, Jean-Michel. "Magie, croyance, superstition: Des gemmes aux eulogies et au-delà." In *Proceedings of the 22nd International Congress of Byzantine Studies, Sofia, 22–27 August 2011*, vol. 2, 197–202. Sofia: Bulgarian Historical Heritage Foundation, 2011.

Stephenson, Paul, ed. *The Byzantine World*. New York: Routledge, 2010.

Stewart, C. *Demons and the Devil: Moral Imagination in Modern Greek Culture*. Princeton: Princeton University Press, 1991.

Troianos, S. "Zauberei und Giftmischerei in mittelbyzantinischer Zeit." In *Fest und Alltag in Byzanz*, edited by Günter Prinzing and Dieter Simon, 37–51. Munich: C. H. Beck, 1990.

Trojanos, Spyros N. "Magic and the Devil. From the Old to the New Rome." In *Greek Magic: Ancient, Medieval and Modern*, edited by J. C. B. Petropoulos, 44–52. London: Routledge, 2008.

Tsamakda, Vasiliki. *The Illustrated Chronicle of Ioannes Skylitzes in Madrid*. Leiden: Alexandros Press, 2002.

Tselikas, Agamemnon. "Spells and Exorcisms in Three Post-Byzantine Manuscripts." In *Greek Magic: Ancient, Medieval and Modern*, edited by J. C. B. Petropoulos, 72–81. London: Routledge, 2008.

Veikou, Christina. "Ritual Word and Symbolic Movement in Spells against the Evil Eye." In *Greek Magic: Ancient, Medieval and Modern*, edited by J. C. B. Petropoulos, 95–105. London: Routledge, 2008.

Vikan, Gary. "Art, Medicine, and Magic in Early Byzantium." *Dumbarton Oaks Papers* 38 (1984): 65–86.

Vryonis, S. "The Will of a Provincial Magnate, Eustathius Boilas (1059)." *Dumbarton Oaks Papers* 11 (1957): 263–277.

Walker, Alicia. "Meaningful Mingling: Classicizing Imagery and Islamicizing Script in a Byzantine Bowl." *The Art Bulletin* 90, no. 1 (2008): 32–53.

"Islamicizing Motifs in Middle Byzantine Church Decoration." In *The Cambridge World History of Religious Architecture*, edited by Ann Marie Yasin and Richard Etlin (forthcoming).

8 Magic, Marvel, and Miracle in Early Islamic Thought (by Travis Zadeh)

Primary Sources

ʿAbd Allāh b. Aḥmad. *Masāʾil Imām Aḥmad b. Ḥanbal*. Edited by Zuhayr al-Shāwīsh. Beirut: al-Maktab al-Islāmī, 1981.

ʿAbd al-Jabbār. *al-Mughnī fī abwāb al-tawḥīd wa-l-ʿadl*. Edited by Ṭāhā Ḥusayn and Ibrāhīm Madkūr, 20 vols. Cairo: Wizārat al-Thaqāfa wa-l-Irshād al-Qawmī, 1958–1965.

ʿAbd al-Razzāq b. Hammām al-Ḥimyarī. *Tafsīr al-Qurʾān*. Edited by Muṣṭafā Muslim Muḥammad. 3 vols. Riyadh: Maktabat al-Rushd, 1989.

Aristotle. *Metaphysica*. Edited by W. Jaeger. Oxford: Clarendon Press, 1957.

al-Ashʿarī, Abū l-Ḥasan. *Kitāb al-Lumaʿ / The Theology of al-Ashʿarī*. Edited and translated by Richard McCarthy. Beirut: Imprimerie Catholique, 1953.

Ayādgār ī Jāmāspīg / Libro apocalittico persiano: Ayātkār i Zāmāspik. Edited and translated by Giuseppe Messina. Rome: Pontifico istituto biblico, 1939.

Bundahišn / Zoroastrische Kosmogonie und Kosmologie. Edited by Fazlollah Pakzad. Tehran: Markaz Dāʾirat al-Maʿārif, 2005.

al-Būnī, Aḥmad b. ʿAlī. *Shams al-maʿārif al-kubrā*. Beirut: al-Maktaba al-Thaqāfiyya, n.d.

al-Dhahabī, Abū ʿAbd Allāh. *Siyar aʿlām al-nubalāʾ*. Edited by Shuʿayb al-Arnāʾūṭ, Ḥusayn Asad, ʿImād Ṭayyār, ʿIzz al-Dīn Ḍalī, and Yāsir Ḥasan. 24 vols. Beirut: Muʾassasat al-Risāla, 1982.

al-Fārisī, ʿAbd al-Ghāfir. *al-Muntakhab min Kitāb al-Siyāq lil-Tārīkh Nīshābūr*. Redacted and abridged by Ibrāhīm b. Muḥammad al-Ṣarīfīnī. Edited by Muḥammad Kāẓim al-Maḥmūdī. Qom: Jamāʿat al-Mudarrisīn fī l-Ḥawza al-ʿIlmiyya, 1983.

Firdawsī, Abū l-Qāsim. *Shāh-nāma*. Edited by Jalāl Khāliqī Muṭlaq and Maḥmūd Umīdsālār. 8 vols. New York: Bibliotheca Persica, 1988–2008.

al-Ghazālī, Abū Ḥāmid. *Tahāfut al-falāsifa*. Edited by Maurice Bouyges. Beirut: Imprimerie Catholique, 1927.

Iḥyāʾ ʿulūm al-dīn. 4 vols. Beirut: Dār al-Maʿrifa, 1982.

Ḥājjī Khalīfa (Muṣṭafā b. ʿAbd Allāh). *Kashf al-ẓunūn ʿan asāmī l-kutub wa-l-funūn*. Edited by Muḥammad Sharaf al-Dīn Yāltaqāyā and Rifʿat Bīlka al-Kilīsī. 2 vols. Istanbul: Wikālat al-Maʿārif al-Jalīla, 1941.

The Hērbedestān and the Nērangestān. Edited and translated by Firoze Kotwal and Philip Kreyenbroek. 4 vols. (vol. 1. *Hērbedestān*; vol. 2. *Nērangestān, Fragard* 1; vol. 3. *Nērangestān, Fragard* 2; vol. 4. *Nērangestān, Fragard* 3). Paris: Association pour l'avancement des études iraniennes, 1992–2009. [*Nērangestān*]

Ibn Fāris, Abū l-Ḥusayn. *Muʿjam al-maqāyīs fī l-lugha*. Edited by Shihāb al-Dīn Abū ʿAmr. 6 vols. Beirut: Dār al-Fikr, 1994.

Ibn Ḥanbal, Aḥmad. *Kitāb al-ʿIlal wa-maʿrifat al-rijāl*. Edited by Waṣī Allāh b. Muḥammad ʿAbbās. 4 vols. Riyadh: Dār al-Khānī, 2001.

Ibn Hishām. *al-Sīra al-nabawiyya*. Edited by Muṣṭafā al-Saqqā, Ibrāhīm al-Ibyārī, and ʿAbd al-Ḥafiẓ Shalabī. 4 vols. Cairo: Maṭbaʿat al-Bābī l-Ḥalabī, 1955.

Ibn Kathīr. *Tafsīr al-Qurʾān al-ʿAẓīm*. Edited by Sāmī b. Muḥammad al-Salāma. 8 vols. 2nd ed. Riyadh: Dār al-Ṭība, 1999.

Ibn Khaldūn. *Tārīkh / Dīwān al-mubtadaʾ wa-l-khabar fī tārīkh al-ʿArab wa-l-Barbar*. Edited by Khalīl Shiḥāda. 8 vols. Beirut: Dār al-Fikr, 1981–1983.

Ibn Khallikān. *Wafayāt al-aʿyān wa-anbāʾ al-zamān*. Edited by Iḥsān ʿAbbās. 8 vols. Beirut: Dār Ṣādir, 1977.

Ibn al-Manẓūr. *Lisān al-ʿArab*. 15 vols. Beirut: Dār al-Ṣādir, 1955–1956.

Ibn Qayyim al-Jawziyya. *al-Ṭibb al-nabawī*. Edited by ʿAbd al-Ghānī ʿAbd al-Khāliq. Beirut: Dār al-Fatḥ, 1957.

Badāʾiʿ al-fawāʾid. Edited by ʿAlīm b. Muḥammad al-ʿUmrān. 5 vols. Mecca: Dār ʿĀlam al-Fawāʾid, 2004–2005.

Ibn Sīnā. *al-Ishārāt wa l-tanbīhāt maʿa sharḥ Nāṣir al-Dīn Ṭūsī*. Edited by Sulaymān Dunyā. 3 vols. Cairo: Dār al-Maʿārif, 1957–1960.

al-Shifāʾ: Kitāb al-Nafs. Edited by Fazlur Rahman. Oxford: Oxford University Press, 1959.

Ibn Taymiyya. *al-Jawāb al-bāhir fī zuwwār al-maqābir*. Edited by Sulaymān b. ʿAbd al-Raḥmān al-Ṣanīʿ and ʿAbd al-Raḥmān b. Yaḥyā al-Yamānī. Cairo: al-Maṭbaʿa al-Salafiyya, 1956–1957.

Kitāb al-Ṣafadiyya. Edited by Muḥammad Rashād Sālim. 2 vols. Riyadh: Dār al-Faḍīla, 2000.

Majmūʿ al-fatāwā. Edited by ʿAbd al-Raḥmān b. Muḥammad b. Qāsim and Muḥammad b. ʿAbd al-Raḥmān. 37 vols. Riyadh: Maṭābiʿ al-Riyāḍ, 2004.

Bayān talbīs al-Jahmiyya fī taʾsīs bidaʿihim al-kalāmiyya. Edited by Yaḥyā b. Muḥammad al-Hunaydī. 10 vols. Medina: Majmaʿ al-Malik Fahd li-Ṭibāʿat al-Muṣḥaf al-Sharīf, 2005–2006.

Ibn Waḥshiyya. *Kitāb al-Sumūm / Medieval Arabic Toxicology: The Book on Poisons of Ibn Waḥshīya and Its Relation to Early Indian and Greek Texts*. Edited by Martin Levey. Philadelphia: The American Philosophical Society, 1966.

Ikhwān al-Ṣafāʾ. *Rasāʾil Ikhwān al-Ṣafāʾ*. Edited by Buṭrus al-Bustānī. 4 vols. Beirut: Dār Ṣādir, 1957.

Epistles of the Brethren of Purity. On Magic I. An Arabic Critical Edition and English Translation of Epistle 52a. Edited and translated by Godefroid de Callataÿ and Bruno Halflants. Oxford: Oxford University Press, 2011.

al-Iṣfahānī, Abū Nuʿaym. *Ḥilyat al-awliyāʾ wa-ṭabaqāt al-aṣfiyāʾ*. 10 vols. Cairo: Maktabat al-Khānjī, 1932–1938.

Jābir b. Ḥayyān. *Kitāb Usṭuqus al-Uss*. Edited and translated in Peter Zirnis, "Kitāb Usṭuqus al-Uss of Jābir ibn Ḥayyān." PhD diss., New York University, 1979.

al-Jaṣṣāṣ, Abū Bakr. *Aḥkām al-Qurʾān*. Edited by Muḥammad al-Ṣādiq Qamḥāwī. 5 vols. Beirut: Dār al-Iḥyāʾ al-Arabī, 1992.

al-Khalīl b. Aḥmad al-Farāhidī. *Kitāb al-ʿAyn*. Edited by Mahdī al-Makhzūmī and Ibrāhīm al-Sāmarrāʾī. 8 vols. Baghdad: Dār al-Rashīd, 1980–1985.

al-Majrīṭī, Maslama b. Aḥmad. *Ghāyat al-ḥakīm wa-aḥaqq al-natījatayn bi-taqdīm*. Edited by Hellmut Ritter. Berlin: B. G. Teubner, 1933.

Picatrix: Das Ziel des Weisen. Translated by Hellmut Ritter and Martin Plessner. London: Warburg Institute, University of London, 1962.

Muslim b. al-Ḥajjāj al-Qushayrī. *Ṣaḥīḥ*. 2 vols. In *Mawsūʿat al-ḥadīth al-sharīf*. Vaduz: Jamʿiyyat al-Maknaz al-Islāmī, 2000–2001.

The Pahlavi Rivāyat Accompanying the Dādestān ī Dēnīg. Edited and translated by Alan Williams. 2 vols. Copenhagen: Munksgaard, 1990. [*Pahl. Riv.*]

Pahlavi Vendidâd (Zand-î Jvît-Dêv-Dât). Edited and translated by Behramgore T. Anklesaria. Bombay: K. R. Cama Oriental Institute, 1949. [*Pahl. Ven.*]

Plato. *Theaetetus*. In *Platonis Opera*, edited by J. Burnet, vol. 1. Oxford: Clarendon Press, 1900.

al-Qalqashandī, Abū l-ʿAbbās. *Ṣubḥ al-aʿshā fī ṣināʿat al-inshāʾ*. 14 vols. Cairo: Dār al-Kutub al-Khidiwiyya, 1913–1922.

al-Rāzī, Fakhr al-Dīn. *Muḥaṣṣal afkār al-mutaqaddimīn wa-l-mutaʾakhkhirīn min al-ʿulamāʾ wa-l-mutakallimīn*. Edited by Ṭāha ʿAbd al-Raʾūf Saʿd. Cairo: Maktabat al-Kullīyāt al-Azhariyya, 1978.

   Mafātīḥ al-ghayb. 32 vols. Beirut: Dār al-Fikr, 1981.

   Kitāb al-Firāsa. In Yūsuf Murād, *al-Firāsa ʿind al-ʿArab / La physiognomonie arabe*, translated from the French by Murād Wahba, 95–154. Cairo: al-Hayʾa al-Miṣriyya al-ʿĀmma li-l-Kitāb, 1982.

   al-Maṭālib al-ʿāliya min al-ʿilm al-ilāhī. Edited by Aḥmād Ḥijāzī al-Saqqā. 9 vols. Beirut: Dār al-Kitāb al-ʿArabī, 1987.

   Sharḥ al-ishārāt wa-l-tanbīhāt. Edited by ʿAlī Riḍā Najaf-zāda. 2 vols. Tehran: Anjuman-i Āthār wa Mafākhir-i Farhangī, 2005.

   al-Sirr al-maktūm. Cairo: al-Ḥajariyya, n.d.

al-Samʿānī, ʿAbd al-Karīm. *al-Ansāb*. Edited by Yaḥyā al-Muʿallimī al-Yamānī, et al. 13 vols. Hyderabad: Dāʾirat al-Maʿārif al-ʿUthmāniyya, 1962–1982.

Shiblī, Badr al-Dīn. *Kitāb al-Ākām al-marjān fī aḥkām al-jānn*. Cairo: Maṭbaʿat al-Saʿāda, 1908–1909.

al-Sijistānī, Abū Dāwūd. *Masāʾil Imām Aḥmad*. Edited by Abū Muʿādh Ṭāriq b. ʿAwaḍ. Cairo: Maktabat Ibn Taymiyya, 1999.

al-Subkī, Abū l-Ḥasan ʿAlī. *Shifāʾ al-siqām fī ziyārat khayr al-anām*. Edited by Ḥusayn Muḥammad ʿAlī Ibn Shukrī. Beirut: Dār al-Kutub al-ʿIlmiyya, 2008.

al-Subkī, Tāj al-Dīn. *Ṭabaqāt al-Shāfiʿiyya al-kubrā*. Edited by Muḥammad al-Ṭanāḥī and ʿAbd al-Fattāḥ Muḥammad al-Ḥilw. 9 vols. Cairo: ʿĪsā l-Bābī l-Ḥalabī, 1967.

al-Suyūṭī, Jalāl al-Dīn. *al-Itqān fī ʿulūm al-Qurʾān*. 2 vols. Mumbai: Abnāʾ Mawlawī Muḥammad b. Ghulām al-Sūratī, 1978.

al-Ṭabarī, Abū Jaʿfar. *Tārīkh al-rusūl wa-l-mulūk / Annales*. Edited by M. J. de Goeje. 15 vols. in 3 vols. Leiden: Brill, 1879–1901.

   (attrib.). *Tarjuma-i Tafsīr-i Ṭabarī*. Edited by Ḥabīb Yaghmāʾī. 7 vols. Tehran: Intishārāt-i Tūs, 1961–1988.

   Jāmiʿ al-bayān fī tafsīr al-Qurʾān. Edited by ʿAbd Allāh Allāh b. ʿAbd al-Muḥsin al-Turkī. 26 vols. Cairo: Dār Hajar, 2001.

al-Ṭabasī, Abū l-Faḍl. *al-Shāmil fī l-baḥr al-kāmil fī l-dawr al-ʿāmil fī uṣūl al-taʿzīm wa-qawāʿid al-tanjīm*. Islamic MSS, n.s., no. 160, Princeton University.

Tārīkh-i Sīstān. Edited by Muḥammad Taqī Bihār. Tehran: Intishārāt-i Maʿīn, 2002–2003.

al-Wāḥidī, Abū l-Ḥasan. *Asbāb nuzūl al-Qurʾān*. Edited by Kamāl Basyūnī Zaghlūl. Beirut: Dār al-Kutub al-ʿIlmiyya, 1991.

al-Yāfiʿī, ʿAbd Allāh b. Asʿad. *al-Durr al-naẓīm fī khawāṣṣ al-Qurʾān al-ʿaẓīm*. Edited by Muḥsin ʿAqīl. Beirut: Dār al-Rasūl al-Akram, 1999.

Yāqūt b. ʿAbd Allāh. *Muʿjam al-buldān*. 5 vols. Beirut: Dār Ṣādir, 1955–1957.

al-Zarkashī, Badr al-Dīn Muḥammad b. Bahādur. *al-Burhān fī ʿulūm al-Qurʾān*. Edited by Muḥammad Abū l-Faḍl Ibrāhīm. 4 vols. Cairo: Dār Iḥyaʾ al-Kutub ʿArabiyya, 1957.

Secondary Sources

Abusch, Tzvi. *Mesopotamian Witchcraft: Toward a History and Understanding of Babylonian Witchcraft Beliefs and Literature*. Ancient Magic and Divination 5. Leiden and Boston: Brill/Styx, 2002.

Ahlwardt, Wilhelm. *Verzeichnis der arabischen Handschriften*. 10 vols. Berlin: A. W. Schade, 1887–1899.

Allan, James. *Nishapur: Metalwork of the Early Islamic Period*. New York: The Metropolitan Museum of Art, 1982.

Asatrian, Mushegh. "Ibn Khaldūn on Magic and the Occult." *Iran and the Caucasus* 7, nos. 1–2 (2003): 73–123.

Asmussen, Jes. "A Zoroastrian 'De-Demonization' in Judeo-Persian." *Irano-Judaica* 1 (1982): 112–121.

The Assyrian Dictionary of the Oriental Institute of the University of Chicago. 21 vols. Chicago: Oriental Institute, 1956–2010. [CAD]

Badawi, Elsaid, and Muhammad Abdel Haleem. *Arabic-English Dictionary of Qurʾanic Usage*. Leiden: Brill, 2008.

Benveniste, Émile. *Les mages dans l'ancien Iran*. Paris: G.-P. Maisonneuve, 1938.

van Bladel, Kevin. *The Arabic Hermes: From Pagan Sage to Prophet of Science*. Oxford: Oxford University Press, 2009.

Bodine, J. Jermain. "Magic Carpet to Islam: Duncan Black Macdonald and the Arabian Nights." *Muslim World* 67, no. 1 (1977): 1–11.

Bosworth, C. E. *The Mediaeval Islamic Underworld: The Banū Sāsān in Arabic Society and Literature*. 2 vols. Leiden: Brill, 1976.

Boyce, Mary. "'Pādyāb' and 'Nērang': Two Pahlavi Terms Further Considered." *Bulletin of the School of Oriental and African Studies* 54, no. 2 (1991): 281–291.

Bulliet, Richard. *The Patricians of Nishapur: A Study in Medieval Islamic Social History*. Cambridge, MA: Harvard Middle Eastern Studies, 1972.

Cook, David. *Studies in Muslim Apocalyptic*. Princeton: Darwin Press, 2002.

Donaldson, Bess Allen. *The Wild Rue: A Study of Muhammadan Magic and Folklore in Iran*. London: Luzac and Co., 1938.

El-Bizri, Nader. "Prologue." In *The Ikhwān al-Ṣafāʾ and Their Rasāʾil: An Introduction*, edited by Nader El-Bizri, 1–32. Oxford: Oxford University Press: 2008.

Encyclopaedia of Islam. Edited by M. Th. Houtsma. 1st ed. Leiden: Brill, 1913–1934.

Encyclopaedia of Islam. Edited by E. van Donzel. 2nd ed. Leiden: Brill, 1954–2005.

Encyclopaedia Iranica. Edited by Ehsan Yarshater. London: Routledge, 1982–.

Fahd, Toufic. *La divination arabe*. Leiden: Brill, 1966.

"Le monde du sorcier en Islam." *Sources Orientales* 7 (1966): 157–204.

Fierro, Maribel. "Bāṭinism in al-Andalus. Maslama b. Qāsim al-Qurṭubī (d. 353/964), Author of the *Rutbat al-Ḥakīm* and the *Ghāyat al-Ḥakīm (Picatrix)*." *Studia Islamica* 84 (1996): 87–112.

Francis, Edgar. "Islamic Symbols and Sufi Rituals for Protection and Healing: Religion and Magic in the Writings of Ahmad ibn Ali al-Buni (d. 622/1225)." PhD diss., University of California, Los Angeles, 2005.

"Magic and Divination in the Medieval Middle East." *History Compass* 9, no. 8 (2011): 622–633.

Griffel, Frank. "al-Ġazālī's Concept of Prophecy: The Introduction of Avicennan Psychology into Ašʿarite Theology." *Arabic Sciences and Philosophy* 14 (2004): 101–144.

Al-Ghazālī's Philosophical Theology. Oxford: Oxford University Press, 2009.

von Grunebaum, Gustave. "Observations on the Muslim Concept of Evil." *Studia Islamica* 31 (1970): 117–134.

Gutas, Dimitri. *Greek Thought, Arabic Culture: The Graeco-Arabic Translation Movement in Baghdad and Early ʿAbbāsid Society (2nd–4th/8th–10th centuries)*. London: Routledge, 1998.

Hall, Robert. "Intellect, Soul and Body in Ibn Sīnā: Systematic Synthesis and Development of the Aristotelian, Neoplatonic and Galenic Theories." In *Interpreting Avicenna. Science and Philosophy in Medieval Islam. Proceedings of the Second Conference of the Avicenna Study Group*, edited by Jon McGinnis, 62–86. Leiden: Brill, 2004.

Jeffers, Ann. *Magic and Divination in Ancient Palestine and Syria*. Leiden: Brill, 1996.

Jong, Albert de. *Zoroastrianism in Greek and Latin Literature*. Leiden: Brill, 1997.

Lane, Edward. *An Account of the Manners and Customs of the Modern Egyptians*. Edited by Edward Stanley Poole. London: John Murray, 1860.

Macdonald, Duncan. *The Religious Attitude and Life in Islam*. Chicago: University of Chicago, 1909.

"Concluding Study." In *The Vital Forces of Christianity and Islam: Six Studies by Missionaries to Moslems*, 215–239. London: Oxford University Press, 1915.

Madigan, Daniel. *The Qurʾân's Self-Image: Writing and Authority in Islam's Scripture*. Princeton: Princeton University Press, 2001.

Marmura, Michael. "Avicenna's Psychological Proof of Prophecy." *Journal of Near Eastern Studies* 22, no. 1 (1963): 49–56.

Maʿṣūmī, M. Ṣaghīr Ḥasan. "Imām Fakhr al-Dīn al-Rāzī and His Critics." *Islamic Studies* 6, no. 4 (1967): 355–374.

Mauchamp, Émile. *La sorcellerie au Maróc*. Paris: Dorbon-ainé, 1911.

Michot, Yahya. "Ibn Taymiyya on Astrology: Annotated Translation of Three Fatwas." *Journal of Islamic Studies* 11, no. 2 (2000) 147–208.

Molé, Marijan. *La légende de Zoroastre selon les textes pehlevis*. Paris: C. Klincksieck, 1967.

Ormsby, Eric. *Theodicy in Islamic Thought: The Dispute over al-Ghazālī's Best of All Possible Worlds*. Princeton: Princeton University Press, 1984.

Paul, Shalom. "The Mesopotamian Background of Daniel 1–6." In *The Book of Daniel: Composition and Reception*, edited by John Joseph Collins and Peter Flint, vol. 1, 55–68. Leiden: Brill, 2001.

Pingree, David. "Between the *Ghāya* and *Picatrix*. I: The Spanish Version." *Journal of the Warburg and Courtauld Institutes* 44 (1981): 27–56.

Sabra, A. I. "The Appropriation and Subsequent Naturalization of Greek Science in Medieval Islam: A Preliminary Statement." *History of Science* 25 (1987): 223–243.

Savant, Sarah. *The New Muslims of Post-Conquest Iran: Tradition, Memory, and Conversion.* Cambridge: Cambridge University Press, 2013.

Schmidt, Brian. *Israel's Beneficent Dead: Ancestor Cult and Necromancy in Ancient Israelite Religion and Tradition.* Tübingen: J. C. B. Mohr, 1994.

Secunda, Shai. "Studying with a Magus / Like Giving a Tongue to a Wolf." *Bulletin of the Asia Institute* 19 (2009): 151–157.

Sezgin, Fuat. *Geschichte des arabischen Schrifttums.* 15 vols. Leiden: Brill, 1967–2010. [*GAS*]

Shapira, Dan. "Studies in Zoroastrian Exegesis: Zand." PhD diss., Hebrew University of Jerusalem, 1998.

Shihadeh, Ayman. *The Teleological Ethics of Fakhr al-Dīn al-Rāzī.* Leiden: Brill, 2006.

Smith, Payne. *Thesaurus Syriacus.* 2 vols. Oxford: Clarendon Press, 1879–1901.

Stewart, Devin. "The Mysterious Letters and Other Formal Features of the Qur'ān in Light of Greek and Babylonian Oracular Texts." *New Perspectives on the Qur'ān: The Qur'ān in Its Historical Context 2*, edited by Gabriel Said Reynolds, 323–348. London: Routledge, 2011.

Styers, Randall. *Making Magic: Religion, Magic, and Science in the Modern World.* New York and Oxford: Oxford University Press, 2004.

Taylor, Christopher. *In the Vicinity of the Righteous: Ziyāra and the Veneration of Muslim Saints in Late Medieval Egypt.* Leiden: Brill, 1999.

Ullmann, Manfred. *Die Natur- und Geheimwissenschaften im Islam.* Leiden: Brill, 1972.

Vesel, Živa. "The Persian Translation of Fakhr al-Dīn Rāzī's *al-Sirr al-maktūm* ('The Occult Secret') for Itutmish." *Confluence of Cultures: French Contributions to Indo-Persian Studies*, edited by Françoise Delvoye Nalini, 14–22. New Delhi: Manohar, 1994.

——— "Occult Sciences: Compilers and Authority." *Texts of Power, the Power of the Text: Readings in Textual Authority Across History and Cultures*, edited by Cezary Galewicz, 113–27. Kraków: Homini, 2006.

——— "Le *Sirr al-maktūm* de Fakhr al-Dīn Rāzī face à la *Ghāyat al-ḥakīm*." In *Images et magie: Picatrix entre Orient et Occident*, edited by Jean-Patrice Boudet, Anna Caiozzo, and Nicolas Weill-Parot, 77–93. Paris: Honoré Champion, 2011.

Westermarck, Edward. *Pagan Survivals in Mohammedan Civilization.* London: Macmillan and Co., 1933.

Wolters, Al. "Untying the King's Knots: Physiology and Wordplay in Daniel 5." *Journal of Biblical Literature* 110, no. 1 (1991): 117–122.

Zadeh, Travis. "Fire Cannot Harm It: Mediation, Temptation and the Charismatic Power of the Qur'ān." *Journal of Qur'ānic Studies* 10, no. 2 (2008): 50–72.

——— "Touching and Ingesting: Early Debates over the Material Qur'ān." *Journal of the American Oriental Society* 129, no. 3 (2009): 443–466.

——— "The Wiles of Creation: Philosophy, Fiction, and the *'Ajā'ib* Tradition." *Middle Eastern Literatures* 13, no. 1 (2010): 21–48.

——— *The Vernacular Qur'an: Translation and the Rise of Persian Exegesis.* Oxford: Oxford University Press, 2012.

"Commanding Demons and Jinn: The Sorcerer in Early Islamic Thought." In *No Tapping around Philology: A Festschrift in Honor of Wheeler McIntosh Thackston Jr.'s 70th Birthday*, edited by Alireza Korangy and Daniel Sheffield, 131–160. Wiesbaden: Harrassowitz Verlag, 2014.

9 Jewish Magic in the Middle Ages (by Gideon Bohak)

Alexander, P. S. "Incantations and Books of Magic." In E. Schürer, *The History of the Jewish People in the Age of Jesus Christ*, revised and edited by G. Vermes, F. Millar, and M. Goodman, vol. 3, part 1, 342–379. Edinburgh: T & T Clark, 1986.

Aptowitzer, V. "Les Noms de Dieu et des Anges dans la Mezouza." *Revue des Études Juives* 60 (1910): 39–52; 65 (1913): 54–60.

Assaf, Simcha. *The Gaonic Period and Its Literature* [Hebrew]. Edited by Mordechai Margalioth. Jerusalem: Mossad ha-Rav Kook, 1955.

Barkai, Ron. *A History of Jewish Gynaecological Texts in the Middle Ages*. Brill's Series in Jewish Studies XX. Leiden: Brill, 1998.

Baron, Salo W. *A Social and Religious History of the Jews*. 2nd ed. 18 vols. New York: Columbia University Press, 1952–1983.

Bellusci, Alessia. "Dream Requests from the Cairo Genizah." MA thesis, Tel Aviv University, 2011.

Benin, Stephen D. "The Chronicle of Ahimaaz and Its Place in Byzantine Literature." [Hebrew.] *Jerusalem Studies in Jewish Thought* 4 (1985): 237–250.

Bohak, Gideon. "Catching a Thief: The Jewish Trials of a Christian Ordeal." *Jewish Studies Quarterly* 13 (2006): 344–362.

——— *Ancient Jewish Magic: A History*. Cambridge: Cambridge University Press, 2008.

——— "The Jewish Magical Tradition from Late Antique Palestine to the Cairo Genizah." In *From Hellenism to Islam: Cultural and Linguistic Change in the Roman Near East*, edited by Hannah M. Cotton, Robert G. Hoyland, Jonathan J. Price, and David J. Wasserstein, 324–339. Cambridge: Cambridge University Press, 2009.

——— "Prolegomena to the Study of the Jewish Magical Tradition." *Currents in Biblical Literature* 8 (2009): 107–150.

——— "Mezuzoth with Magical Additions from the Cairo Genizah." [Hebrew.] In "Festschrift for Mordechai Akiva Friedman," special issue, *Dinei Israel: Studies in Halakha and in Jewish Law* 26–27 (2009–2010): 387–403.

——— "Towards a Catalogue of the Magical, Astrological, Divinatory and Alchemical Fragments from the Cambridge Genizah Collections." In *"From a Sacred Source": Genizah Studies in Honour of Professor Stefan C. Reif*, edited by Ben Outhwaite and Siam Bhayro, 53–79. Études sur le Judaïsme Médiéval 42; Cambridge Genizah Studies Series 1. Leiden: Brill, 2010.

——— "The *Charaktêres* in Ancient and Medieval Jewish Magic." *Acta Classica Universitatis Scientiarum Debreceniensis* 47 (2011): 25–44.

——— "From Qumran to Cairo: The Lives and Times of a Jewish Exorcistic Formula (with an Appendix by Shaul Shaked)." In *Ritual Healing: Magic, Ritual and Medical Therapy from Antiquity until the Early Modern Period*, edited by Ildikó Csepregi and Charles Burnett, 31–52. Micrologus' Library 48. Florence: SISMEL Edizioni del Galluzzo, 2012.

"Magic." In *The Cambridge History of Judaism*, vol. 5, *Jews and Judaism in the Islamic World, Seventh through Fifteenth Centuries*, edited by Marina Rustow and Robert Chazan. Cambridge: Cambridge University Press (forthcoming).

"Rabbanite Magical Texts in Karaite Manuscripts." *Karaite Archives* 1 (2013): 17–34.

Bonfil, Robert. *History and Folklore in a Medieval Jewish Chronicle: The Family Chronicle of Ahima'az ben Paltiel*. Studies in Jewish History and Culture 22. Leiden: Brill, 2009.

Bos, Gerrit, and Julia Zwink. *Berakhyah Ben Natronai ha-Nakdan, Sefer Ko'ah ha-Avanim (On the Virtue of the Stones): Hebrew Text and English Translation, with a Lexicological Analysis of the Romance Terminology and Source Study*. Études sur le Judaïsme Médiéval 40. Leiden: Brill, 2010.

Burnett, Charles, and Gideon Bohak. "A Judaeo-Arabic Version of Thābit ibn Qurra's *De imaginibus* and Psuedo-Ptolemy's *Opus imaginum*." In *Islamic Philosophy, Science, Culture, and Religion: Studies in Honor of Dimitri Gutas*, edited by Felicitas Opwis and David Reisman, 179–200. Leiden: Brill, 2012.

Buzzetta, Flavia. "Aspetti della magia naturalis e della scientia cabalae nel pensiero di Giovanni Pico della Mirandola (1486–1487)." PhD diss., Università degli Studi di Palermo – École Pratique des Hautes Etudes, Palermo, 2011.

Caballero-Navas, Carmen. *The Book of Women's Love and Jewish Medieval Medical Literature on Women (Sefer Ahavat Nashim)*. London: Kegan Paul, 2004.

Chajes, J. H. "Rabbis and Their (In)Famous Magic: Classical Foundations, Medieval and Early Modern Reverberations." In *Jewish Studies at the Crossroads of Anthropology and History: Authority, Diaspora, Tradition*, edited by Ra'anan S. Boustan, Oren Kosansky, and Marina Rustow, 58–79, 349–358. Philadelphia: University of Pennsylvania Press, 2011.

Ciraolo, Leda Jean. "Supernatural Assistants in the Greek Magical Papyri." In *Ancient Magic and Ritual Power*, edited by Marvin Meyer and Paul Mirecki, 279–295. Leiden and New York: Brill, 1995.

Dan, Joseph. *History of Jewish Mysticism and Esotericism* [Hebrew]. Vol. 4. Jerusalem: Shazar, 2009.

Davidson, Hannah R. "Perceptions of Medicine and Magic within the Jewish Community of Catalonia in the 13th and 14th Centuries." [Hebrew.] PhD diss., Hebrew University of Jerusalem, 2004.

Dimitrovsky, Hayyim Zalman. *Teshuvot ha-Rashba*. 2 vols. Jerusalem: Mosad ha-Rav Kook – Makhon le-hotsa'at rishonim ve-aharonim, 1990.

Drory, Rina. *The Emergence of Jewish-Arabic Literary Contacts at the Beginning of the Tenth Century* [Hebrew]. Tel Aviv: Porter Institute, Tel Aviv University, 1988.

Emanuel, Simcha. *Newly Discovered Geonic Responsa* [Hebrew]. Jerusalem and Cleveland: Ofeq Institute, Friedberg Library, 1995.

Eshel, Esther. "Demonology in Palestine during the Second Temple Period." [Hebrew.] PhD diss., Hebrew University of Jerusalem, 1999.

Etkes, I. "The Role of Magic and Ba'alei Shem in Ashkenazic Society in the Late Seventeenth and Early Eighteenth Centuries." [Hebrew.] *Zion* 60 (1995): 69–104.

Fenton, Paul B. "Maïmonide et l'*Agriculture nabatéenne*." In *Maïmonide, philosophe et savant (1138–1204)*, edited by Tony Lévy and Roshdi Rashed, 303–333. Leuven: Peeters, 2004.

Ferre, Lola. "The Incorporation of Foreign Medical Literature into the Medieval Jewish Corpus." In *Late Medieval Jewish Identities: Iberia and Beyond*, edited by Carmen

Caballero-Navas and Esperanza Alfonso, 171–183. The New Middle Ages, New York: Palgrave Macmillan, 2010.

Freudenthal, Gad. "Arabic and Latin Cultures as Resources for the Hebrew Translation Movement: Comparative Considerations, Both Quantitative and Qualitative." in *Science in Medieval Jewish Culture*, edited by Gad Freudenthal, 74–105. Cambridge: Cambridge University Press, 2011.

Friedländer, I. "A Muhammedan Book on Augury in Hebrew Characters." *Jewish Quarterly Review* 19 (1907): 84–103.

Garb, Jonathan. "Mysticism and Magic: Objections, Doubts, Accommodation." [Hebrew.] *Mahanaim* 14 (2002): 97–109.

García-Ballester, Luis, Lola Ferre, and Eduard Feliu. "Jewish Appreciation of Fourteenth-Century Scholastic Medicine." In *Renaissance Medical Learning: Evolution of a Tradition*, edited by Michael R. McVaugh and Nancy G. Siraisi, 85–117. Osiris 2nd series 6. Chicago: University of Chicago Press, 1990.

Gaster, Moses. *The Sword of Moses*. London: Nutt, 1896.

⸺ *Studies and Texts in Folklore, Magic, Medieval Romance, Hebrew Apocrypha and Samaritan Archaeology*. 3 vols. London: Maggs Brothers, 1928. Reprint, New York: Ktav, 1971.

Golb, Norman. "The Esoteric Practices of the Jews of Fatimid Egypt." *American Philosophical Society Yearbook* (1965): 533–535.

⸺ "Aspects of the Historical Background of Jewish Life in Medieval Egypt." In *Jewish Medieval and Renaissance Studies*, edited by A. Altmann, 1–18. Cambridge, MA: Harvard University Press, 1967.

Goldreich, Amos. *Automatic Writing in Zoharic Literature and Modernism* [Hebrew]. Los Angeles: Cherub Press, 2010.

Güdemann, Moritz. *Geschichte des Erziehungswesens und der Cultur der abendländischen Juden während des Mittelalters*. 3 vols. Vienna: Alfred Hölder, 1880–1888. Reprint, Amsterdam: Philo Press, 1966.

Halbertal, Moshe. *Maimonides* [Hebrew]. Jerusalem: Shazar, 2009.

Harari, Yuval. *Harba de-Moshe (The Sword of Moses): A New Edition and a Study* [Hebrew.]. Jerusalem: Academon, 1997.

⸺ "Early Jewish Magic: Methodological and Phenomenological Studies." [Hebrew.] PhD diss., Hebrew University of Jerusalem, 1998.

⸺ "Moses, the Sword, and *The Sword of Moses*: Between Rabbinical and Magical Traditions." *Jewish Studies Quarterly* 12 (2005): 293–329.

⸺ "The Sages and the Occult." In *The Literature of the Sages*, part II, *Midrash and Targum, Liturgy, Poetry, Mysticism, Contracts, Inscriptions, Ancient Science, and the Languages of Rabbinic Literature* edited by Shmuel Safrai, Zeev Safrai, Joshua Schwartz and Peter J. Tomson, 521–564. Assen: Van Gorcum, 2006.

⸺ "The *Scroll of Ahimaaz* and the Jewish Magical Culture: A Note on the *Sotah* Ordeal." [Hebrew.] *Tarbiz* 75 (2006): 185–202.

⸺ "Leadership, Authority, and the 'Other' in the Debate over Magic from the Karaites to Maimonides." *The Journal for the Study of Sephardic and Mizrahi Jewry* 1 (2007): 79–101.

⸺ *Early Jewish Magic: Research, Method, Sources* [Hebrew]. Jerusalem: Mossad Bialik and Yad Ben-Zvi, 2010.

⸺ "Jewish Magic: An Annotated Overview." [Hebrew.] *El Prezente: Studies in Sephardic Culture* 5 (2011): 13–85.

"The Sword of Moses (*Harba de-Moshe*): A New Translation and Introduction." *Magic, Ritual and Witchcraft* 7 (2012): 58–98.

Harris, Jay. "The Image of Maimonides in Nineteenth-Century Jewish Historiography." *Proceedings of the American Academy for Jewish Research* 54 (1987): 117–139.

Hildesheimer, Esriel Erich. "Mystik und Agada im Urteile der Gaonen R. Scherira und R. Hai." In *Festschrift für Jacob Rosenheim*, 259–286. Frankfurt am Main: Kauffmann Verlag, 1931.

Hjärpe, J. "Analyse critique des traditions arabes sur les Sabéens harraniens." Ph.D. dissertation. Uppsala Universitet, 1972.

Idel, Moshe. "Jewish Magic from the Renaissance Period to Early Hasidism." In *Religion, Science, and Magic in Concert and in Conflict*, edited by Jacob Neusner, Ernest S. Frerichs, and Paul V. M. Flesher, 82–117. New York and Oxford: Oxford University Press, 1989.

"Defining Kabbalah: The Kabbalah of the Divine Names." In *Mystics of the Book*, edited by R. A. Herrera, 97–122. New York: Peter Lang, 1993.

"On Judaism, Jewish Mysticism and Magic." In *Envisioning Magic: A Princeton Seminar and Symposium*, edited by Peter Schäfer and Hans G. Kippenberg, 195–214. Studies in the History of Religions 75. Leiden, New York, and Cologne: Brill, 1997.

"Between the Magic of the Holy Names and the Kabbalah of the Names of R. Abraham Abulafia." [Hebrew.] *Mahanaim* 14 (2002): 79–96.

Nocturnal Kabbalists [Hebrew]. Jerusalem: Karmel, 2006.

"The Anonymous *Commentary on the Alphabet of Metatron*: A Treatise by Rabbi Nehemiah ben Shlomo." [Hebrew.] *Tarbiz* 76 (2007): 255–264.

"Between Ashkenaz and Castille in the Thirteenth Century – Adjurations, Lists and Gates of Derashot in the Circle of R. Nehemiah ben Shlomo ha-Navi and Their Impact." [Hebrew.] *Tarbiz* 77 (2008): 475–554.

"R. Nehemiah ben Shlomo the Prophet on the Star of David and the Name Taftafia: From Jewish Magic to Practical and Theoretical Kabbalah." [Hebrew.] In *Ta Shma: Studies in Judaica in Memory of Israel M. Ta-Shma*, edited by Avraham (Rami) Reiner, vol. 1, 1–76. Alon Shevut: Tevunot Press, 2011.

Jellinek, Adolph. *Bet ha-Midrasch*. 2nd ed. Jerusalem: Bamberger and Vahrman, 1938.

Joël, David. *Der Aberglaube und die Stellung des Judenthums zu demselben*. Jahresbericht des jüdisch-theologischen Seminars "Fraenckel'scher Stiftung". Breslau: Jungfer and Schottlaender, 1881–1883.

Kanarfogel, Ephraim. *"Peering through the Lattices": Mystical, Magical and Pietistic Dimensions in the Tosafist Period*. Detroit: Wayne State University Press, 2000.

Kellner, Menachem. *Maimonides' Confrontation with Mysticism*. Oxford: The Littman Library of Jewish Civilisation, 2006.

Klar, Benjamin, ed. *Megillat Ahimaaz: The Chronicle of Ahimaaz* [Hebrew]. Jerusalem: Tarshish, 1944 Reprint, Jerusalem: Tarshish, 1973.

Klein-Braslavy, Sara. "The Concept of Magic in R. Solomon ben Abraham Adret (Rashba) and R. Nissim Gerondi (Ran)." In *Encuentros and Desencuentros: Spanish Jewish Cultural Interaction throughout History*, edited by Carlos Carrete Parrondo, Marcelo Dascal, Francisco Márques Villanueva, and Angel Sáenz Badillos, 105–129. Tel Aviv: Tel Aviv University, 2000.

Lamoreaux, John C. *The Early Muslim Tradition of Dream Interpretation*. Albany: State University of New York Press, 2002.

Leicht, Reimund. "The Legend of St. Eustachius (Eustathius) as Found in the Cairo Genizah." In *Jewish Studies between the Disciplines / Judaistik zwischen den Disziplinen: Papers in Honor of Peter Schäfer on the Occasion of His 60th Birthday*, edited by Klaus Herrmann, Margarete Schlüter, and Giuseppe Veltri, 325–330. Leiden: Brill, 2003.

"Some Observations on the Diffusion of Jewish Magical Texts from Late Antiquity and the Early Middle Ages in Manuscripts from the Cairo Genizah and Ashkenaz." In *Officina Magica: Essays on the Practice of Magic in Antiquity*, edited by Shaul Shaked, 213–231. IJS Studies in Judaica 4. Leiden: Brill, 2005.

Astrologumena Judaica: Untersuchungen zur Geschichte der astrologischen Literatur der Juden. Texts and Studies in Medieval and Early Modern Judaism 21. Tübingen: Mohr Siebeck, 2006.

"Le chapitre II,12 du *Picatrix* latin et les versions hébraïques du *De duodecim imaginibus*." In *Images et magie: Picatrix entre Orient et Occident*, edited by Jean-Patrice Boudet, Anna Caiozzo, and Nicolas Weill-Parot, 295–330. Sciences, techniques et civilisations du Moyen Âge à l'aube des Lumières 13. Paris: Honoré Champion, 2011.

"Nahmanides on Necromancy." In *Studies in the History of Culture and Science: A Tribute to Gad Freudenthal*, edited by Reimund Leicht, Giuseppe Veltri, and Resianne Fontaine, 251–264. Studies in Jewish History and Culture 30. Leiden: Brill, 2011.

Levene, Dan. *Curse or Blessing, What's in the Magical Bowl?* Parkes Institute Pamphlet 2. The Ian Karten Lecture, University of Southampton, 2002, http://www.parkes.soton.ac.uk/articles/levene.pdf

Levene, Dan, and Gideon Bohak. "Divorcing Lilith: From the Babylonian Incantation Bowls to the Cairo Genizah." *Journal of Jewish Studies* 63 (2012): 197–217.

Lewis, H. S. "Maimonides on Superstition." *Jewish Quarterly Review* 17 (1905): 475–488.

Loewe, Raphael. "A Mediaeval Latin-German Magical Text in Hebrew Characters." In *Jewish History: Essays in Honour of Chimen Abramsky*, edited by Ada Rapoport-Albert and Steven J. Zipperstein, 345–368. London: Peter Halban, 1988.

Mann, Jacob. *Texts and Studies in Jewish History and Literature*. 2 vols. Cincinnati: Hebrew Union College Press; Philadelphia: Jewish Publication Society, 1931–1935. Reprint, New York: Ktav, 1972.

Margalioth, Mordechai. *Sepher ha-Razim: A Newly Recovered Book of Magic from the Talmudic Period* [Hebrew]. Tel Aviv: Yediot Acharonot, 1966.

Mesler, Katelyn. "The Medieval Lapidary of Techel/Azareus on Engraved Stones and Its Jewish Appropriations." *Aleph: Historical Studies in Science and Judaism* 14 (2014): 75–143.

"The Three Magi and Other Christian Motifs in Medieval Hebrew Medical Incantations: A Study in the Limits of Faithful Translation." In *Latin-into-Hebrew – Studies and Texts*, vol. 1, *Studies*, edited by Resianne Fontaine and Gad Freudenthal 161–218. *Studies in Jewish History and Culture*, 39–40. Leiden: Brill (2013).

Michelini Tocci, Franco. "Note e documenti di letterature religiosa e parareligiosa giudaica." *Annali dell'Istituto Universitario Orientale di Napoli* 46 (1986): 101–108.

Morgan, Michael A. *Sepher ha-Razim: The Book of the Mysteries*. Chico, CA: Scholars Press, 1983.

Patai, Raphael. "The Love Factor in a Hebrew-Arabic Conjuration." *Jewish Quarterly Review* 70 (1980): 239–253.

Ravitzky, Aviezer. "'The Ravings of Amulet Writers': Maimonides and His Disciples on Language, Nature and Magic." In *Between Rashi and Maimonides: Themes in Medieval Jewish Thought, Literature and Exegesis*, edited by Ephraim Kanarfogel and Moshe Sokolow, 93–130. New York: Yeshiva University Press, 2010.

Rebiger, Bill. "Bildung magischer Namen im *Sefer Shimmush Tehillim*." *Frankfurter Judaistische Beiträge* 26 (1999): 7–24.

——— *Sefer Shimmush Tehillim – Buch vom magischen Gebrauch der Psalmen: Edition, Übersetzung und Kommentar.* Texte und Studien zum antiken Judentum 137. Tübingen: Mohr Siebeck, 2010.

Rebiger Bill, and Peter Schäfer. *Sefer ha-Razim I und II – Das Buch der Geheimnisse I und II.* 2 vols. Texte und Studien zum antiken Judentum 125, 132. Tübingen: Mohr Siebeck, 2009.

Rustow, Marina, and Robert Chazan. *The Cambridge History of Judaism*, vol. 5, *Jews and Judaism in the Islamic World, Seventh through Fifteenth Centuries.* Cambridge: Cambridge University Press (forthcoming).

Saar, Ortal-Paz. "Success, Protection and Grace: Three Fragments of a Personalized Magical Handbook." *Ginzei Qedem* 3 (2007): 101–135.

——— "Jewish Love Magic: From Late Antiquity to the Middle Ages." [Hebrew.] PhD diss., Tel Aviv University, 2008.

——— "A Genizah Magical Fragment and Its European Parallels." *Journal of Jewish Studies* 55 (2014): 237–262.

Schäfer, Peter. "Jewish Magic Literature in Late Antiquity and the Early Middle Ages." *Journal of Jewish Studies* 41 (1990): 75–91.

——— "Jewish Liturgy and Magic." In *Geschichte-Tradition-Reflexion: Festschrift für Martin Hengel zum 70. Geburtstag*, edited by Hubert Cancik, Herman Lichtenberger, and Peter Schäfer, vol. 1, 541–556. Tübingen: Mohr Siebeck, 1996.

Schäfer, Peter, and Shaul Shaked. *Magische Texte aus der Kairoer Geniza.* 3 vols. Texte und Studien zum Antiken Judentum 42, 64, 72. Tübingen: Mohr Siebeck, 1994–1999.

Schibby Johnsson, John William. "Les 'Experimenta duodecim Johannes Paulini.'" *Bulletin de la Société Française d'Histoire de la Médecine et de ses filiales* 12 (1913): 257–267.

Scholem, Gershom. "Bilar the King of Devils." [Hebrew.] *Jewish Studies* 1 (1926): 112–127. Reprint, with addenda, in *Devils, Demons and Souls: Essays on Demonology by Gershom Scholem* [Hebrew], edited by Esther Liebes, 9–53. Jerusalem: Ben-Zvi, 2004.

——— "The Star of David: History of a Symbol." [Hebrew.] *Haaretz Almanac* (1948–1949), 148–163. Reprint, with addenda, as Gershom G. Scholem, *The Star of David: History of a Symbol* [Hebrew], edited by Galit Hasan Rokem. Ein Harod: Mishkan le-Omanut, 2008.

——— "Has a Legacy Been Discovered of Mystic Writings Left by Abu Aaron of Baghdad?" [Hebrew.] *Tarbiz* 32 (1963): 252–265.

——— "Some Sources of Jewish-Arabic Demonology." *Journal of Jewish Studies* 16 (1965): 1–13. Reprint, with addenda, in *Devils, Demons and Souls: Essays on Demonology by Gershom Scholem* [Hebrew], edited by Esther Liebes, 103–115. Jerusalem: Ben-Zvi, 2004.

"The Star of David: History of a Symbol." in *The Messianic Idea in Judaism*, 257–281. New York: Schocken, 1972.

Kabbalah. Jerusalem: Keter, 1974.

"Havdala de-Rabbi Aqiva – A Source for the Tradition of Jewish Magic during the Geonic Period." [Hebrew.] *Tarbiz* 50 (1980–1981): 243–281. Reprint, with addenda, in *Devils, Demons and Souls: Essays on Demonology by Gershom Scholem* [Hebrew], edited by Esther Liebes, 145–182. Jerusalem: Ben-Zvi, 2004.

Schwab, M. "Mots hébreux dans les mystères du Moyen Âge." *Revue des Études Juives* 46 (1903): 148–151.

Schwartz, Dov. *Astral Magic in Medieval Jewish Thought* [Hebrew]. Ramat Gan: Bar-Ilan University Press, 1999.

Amulets, Properties and Rationalism in Medieval Jewish Thought [Hebrew]. Ramat Gan: Bar-Ilan University Press, 2004.

Studies on Astral Magic in Medieval Jewish Thought. Translated by David Louvish and Batya Stein. The Brill Reference Library of Judaism 20. Leiden: Brill, 2005.

Schwartz, Yossef. "Magic, Philosophy and Kabbalah: The Mystical and Magical Interpretation of Maimonides in the Later Middle Ages." [Hebrew.] In *Maimonides and Mysticism: Presented to Moshe Hallamish on the Occasion of His Retirement*, edited by A. Elqayam and D. Schwartz, 99–132. Daat 64–66: Special Volume Dedicated to Thirty Years of DAAT and Its Editor. Ramat-Gan: Bar-Ilan University Press, 2009.

Shaked, Shaul. "Between Judaism and Islam: Some Issues in Popular Religion." [Hebrew.] *Pe'amim* 60 (1994): 4–19.

"Medieval Jewish Magic in Relation to Islam: Theoretical Attitudes and Genres." In *Judaism and Islam: Boundaries, Communication and Interaction (Essays in Honor of William M. Brinner)*, edited by B. H. Hary, J. L. Hayes and F. Astern, 97–109. Leiden: Brill, 2000.

Shatzmiller, Joseph. "In Search of the 'Book of Figures': Medicine and Astrology in Montpellier at the Turn of the Fourteenth Century." *AJS Review* 7–8 (1982–1983): 383–407.

"The Forms of the Twelve Constellations: A 14th Century Controversy." [Hebrew.] In "Shlomo Pines Jubilee Volume 2," special issue, *Jerusalem Studies in Jewish Thought* 9 (1990): 397–408.

Shoham-Steiner, Ephraim. "'This Should Not Be Shown to a Gentile': Medico-Magical Texts in Medieval Franco-German Jewish Rabbinic Manuscripts." In *Bodies of Knowledge: Cultural Interpretations of Illness and Medicine in Medieval Europe*, edited by Sally Crawford and Christina Lee, 53–59. Studies in Early Medicine 1. Oxford: Archaeopress, 2010.

Sirat, Colette. "Should We Stop Teaching Maimonides?" In *Paradigms in Jewish Philosophy*, edited by Raphael Jospe, 136–144. London: Associated University Presses, 1997.

Stern, Gregg. "Philosophy in Southern France: Controversy over Philosophic Study and the Influence of Averroes upon Jewish Thought." In *The Cambridge Companion to Medieval Jewish Philosophy*, edited by Daniel H. Frank and Oliver Leaman, 281–303. Cambridge Companions to Philosophy. Cambridge: Cambridge University Press, 2003.

Stroumsa, Sarah. "Sabéens de Harrân et Sabéens de Maïmonide." In *Maïmonide, philosophe et savant (1138–1204)*, edited by Tony Lévy and Roshdi Rashed, 335–352. Leuven: Peeters, 2004.

Swartz, Michael D. "Jewish Magic in Late Antiquity." In *The Cambridge History of Judaism*, vol. IV, *The Late Roman-Rabbinic Period*, edited by Steven T. Katz, 699–720. Cambridge: Cambridge University Press, 2006.

Symonds, J. Addington, trans. *The Autobiography of Benvenuto Cellini*. New York: Walter J. Black, 1927.

Tambiah, Stanley J. "The Magical Power of Words." *Man*, n.s., 3 (1968): 175–208. Reprint in Stanley J. Tambiah, *Culture, Thought, and Social Action*, 17–59. Cambridge, MA: Harvard University Press, 1985.

Thorndike, Lynn. *A History of Magic and Experimental Science*. 8 vols. New York: Columbia University Press, 1923–1958.

Trachtenberg, Joshua. *Jewish Magic and Superstition: A Study in Folk Religion*. New York: Behrman's Jewish Book House, 1939. Reprint, with an introduction by Moshe Idel, Philadelphia: University of Pennsylvania Press, 2004.

The Devil and the Jews: The Medieval Conception of the Jew and Its Relation to Modern Anti-Semitism. New Haven: Yale University Press, 1943. Reprint, with a preface by Marc Saperstein, Philadelphia: Jewish Publication Society, 1983.

Vajda, Georges. "La magie en Israël." In *Le monde du sorcier*, 127–153. Sources Orientales VII. Paris: Éditions du Seuil, 1966.

Veltri, Giuseppe. "*'Inyan Sota*: Halakhische Voraussetzungen für einen magischen Akt nach einer theoretischen Abhandlung aus der Kairoer Geniza." *Frankfurter Judaistische Beiträge* 20 (1993): 23–48.

"'Watermarks' in the MS Munich, Hebr. 95: Magical Recipes in Historical Contexts." In *Officina Magica: Essays on the Practice of Magic in Antiquity*, edited by Shaul Shaked, 255–268. IJS Studies in Judaica 4. Leiden: Brill, 2005.

Véronèse, Julien, and Benoît Grévin. "Les 'caractères' magiques au Moyen Âge (XIIe–XIVe siècle)." *Bibliothèque de l'École des Chartes* 162 (2004): 305–379.

Versnel, H. S. "The Poetics of the Magical Charm: An Essay in the Power of Words." In *Magic and Ritual in the Ancient World*, edited by Paul Mirecki and Marvin Meyer, 105–158. Religions in the Graeco-Roman World 141. Leiden: Brill, 2002.

Villuendas Sabaté, Blanca. "La geomancia judía: Edición, traducción, y estudio de los manuscritos Judeo-Árabes de la Gueniza del Cairo." MA thesis, Universidad Complutense de Madrid, 2012.

Vukosavović, Filip, ed. *Angels and Demons: Jewish Magic through the Ages*. Jerusalem: Bible Lands Museum, 2010.

Wandrey, Irina. "*Das Buch des Gewandes*" und "*Das Buch des Aufrechten*": *Dokumente eines magischen spätantiken Rituals, ediert, kommentiert und übersetzt*. Texte und Studien zum antiken Judentum 96. Tübingen: Mohr Siebeck, 2004.

Wasserstrom, Steven M. *Between Muslim and Jew: The Problem of Symbiosis under Early Islam*. Princeton: Princeton University Press, 1995.

Weill-Parot, Nicolas. *Les "images astrologiques" au Moyen Âge et à la Renaissance: Spéculations intellectuelles et pratiques magiques, XIIe–XVe siècle*. Sciences, techniques et civilisations du Moyen Âge à l'aube des Lumières 6. Paris: Honoré Champion, 2002.

Weinstock, Israel. "Discovered Legacy of Mystic Writings Left by Abu Aaron of Baghdad." [Hebrew.] *Tarbiz* 32 (1963): 153–159.

"The Alphabet of Metatron and Its Interpretation." In *Temirin* [Hebrew], edited by Israel Weinstock, vol. 2, 51–76. Jerusalem: Kook, 1981.

Zimmels, H. J. *Magicians, Theologians and Doctors: Studies in Folk-Medicine and Folk-Lore as Reflected in the Rabbinical Responsa (12th–19th Centuries).* London: Edward Goldston & Son, 1952. Reprint, Northvale, NJ: Jason Aronson, 1997.

Zonta, Mauro. "Medieval Hebrew Translations of Philosophical and Scientific Texts: A Chronological Table." in *Science in Medieval Jewish Culture*, edited by Gad Freudenthal, 17–73. Cambridge: Cambridge University Press, 2011.

Zoran, Yair. "Magic, Theurgy and the Knowledge of Letters in Islam and Their Parallels in Jewish Literature." [Hebrew.] *Jerusalem Studies in Jewish Folklore* 18 (1996): 19–62.

10 Common Magic (by Catherine Rider)

Primary Sources

Augustine. *De doctrina Christiana.* Edited and translated by R. P. H. Green. Oxford: Clarendon Press, 1995.

Burchard of Worms. *Decretum libri viginti.* Patrologiae Cursus Completus Series Latina 140, edited by J.-P. Migne, cols. 537–1058. Paris: Garnier Fratres, 1880.

Charm, Norfolk Record Office, C/S 3, box 41a.

Fasciculus Morum: A Fourteenth-Century Preacher's Handbook. Edited and translated by Siegfried Wenzel. University Park: Penn State University Press, 1989.

Franz, Adolph. "Des Frater Rudolfus Buch 'De officio cherubyn.'" *Theologische Quartalschrift* 88 (1906): 411–436.

Gratian. *Decretum.* In *Corpus iuris canonici*, edited by Emil Friedberg, vol. 1. Leipzig: Tauchnitz, 1879. Reprint, Graz: Akademische Druck- und Verlaganstalt, 1959.

Hale, William. *A Series of Precedents and Proceedings in Criminal Causes Extending from the Year 1475 to 1640; Extracted from the Act-Books of Ecclesiastical Courts in the Diocese of London.* London: F. & J. Rivington, 1847. Reprint, Edinburgh: Bratton, 1973.

John of Salisbury. *Policraticus.* Translated by Joseph B. Pike as *Frivolities of Courtiers and Footprints of Philosophers.* New York: Octagon Books, 1972.

Kramer, Heinrich, and Jakob Sprenger. *The Hammer of Witches.* Translated by Christopher S. Mackay. Cambridge: Cambridge University Press, 2009.

Lecoy de la Marche, A. ed. *Anecdotes historiques, légendes et apologues tirés du recueil inédit d'Etienne de Bourbon.* Paris: Nogent-le-Rotrou, 1877.

Petrus Hispanus. *Thesaurus pauperum.* Edited by Maria Helena da Rocha Pereira as *Obras Médicas de Pedro Hispano.* Coimbra: University of Coimbra, 1973.

Robert Mannyng of Brunne. *Handlyng Synne.* Edited by Idelle Sullens. Binghamton: Center for Medieval and Early Renaissance Studies, State University of New York at Binghamton, 1983.

Shinners, John. *Medieval Popular Religion 1000–1500: A Reader.* Peterborough, Ontario: Broadview Press, 1997.

Thomas of Chobham. *Summa confessorum.* Edited by F. Bloomfield. Louvain: Editions Nauwelaerts, 1968.

Secondary Sources

Arnold, John. *Belief and Unbelief in Medieval Europe*. London: Hodder Arnold, 2005.

Bailey, Michael D. "The Disenchantment of Magic: Spells, Charms, and Superstition in Early European Witchcraft Literature." *American Historical Review* III (2006): 383–404.

"Concern over Superstition in Late Medieval Europe." *Past and Present*, supplement, 3 (2008): 115–133.

Bailey, Michael, Stuart Clark, Richard Jenkins, Rita Voltmer, Willem de Blécourt, Jesper Sørenson, and Edward Bever. "Forum: Contending Realities: Reactions to Edward Bever." *Magic, Ritual and Witchcraft* 5 (2010): 81–121.

Barry, Jonathan, and Owen Davies. *Palgrave Advances in Witchcraft Historiography*. Basingstoke: Palgrave Macmillan, 2007.

Behar, Ruth. "Sexual Witchcraft, Colonialism, and Women's Powers: Views from the Mexican Inquisition." In *Sexuality and Marriage in Colonial Latin America*, edited by Asunción Lavrin, 178–206. Lincoln and London: University of Nebraska Press, 1989. Reprint in *New Perspectives on Witchcraft, Magic and Demonology*, edited by Brian P. Levack, vol. 4. London and New York: Routledge, 2001.

'Behringer, Wolfgang' here: both *Witchcraft Persecutions in Bavaria* and *Shaman of Oberstdorf* are by him.

Witchcraft Persecutions in Bavaria: Popular Magic, Religious Zealotry and Reason of State in Early Modern Europe. Translated by J. C. Grayson and David Lederer. Cambridge: Cambridge University Press, 1997.

Behringer, Wolfgang. *Shaman of Oberstdorf: Chonrad Stoeckhlin and the Phantoms of the Night*. Translated by H. C. Erik Midelfort. Charlottesville: University of Virginia Press, 1998.

Bever, Edward. *The Realities of Witchcraft and Popular Magic in Early Modern Europe: Culture, Cognition and Everyday Life*. Basingstoke: Palgrave Macmillan, 2008.

Biller, Peter. "Popular Religion in the Central and Later Middle Ages." In *Companion to Historiography*, edited by Michael Bentley, 221–246. London and New York: Routledge, 1997.

de Blécourt, Willem. "Witch Doctors, Soothsayers and Priests: On Cunning Folk in European Historiography and Tradition." *Social History* 19 (1994): 285–303.

Boudet, Jean-Patrice. *Entre science et nigromance: Astrologie, divination et magie dans l'Occident médiéval (XIIe–XVe siècle)*. Histoire ancienne et médiévale 83. Paris: Publications de la Sorbonne, 2006.

Briggs, Robin. *Witches and Neighbors: The Social and Cultural Context of European Witchcraft*. 2nd ed. Oxford: Blackwell, 2002.

The Witches of Lorraine. Oxford: Oxford University Press, 2007.

Brucker, Gene A. "Sorcery in Early Renaissance Florence." *Studies in the Renaissance* 10 (1963): 7–24.

Cameron, Euan. *Enchanted Europe: Superstition, Reason and Religion 1250–1750*. Oxford: Oxford University Press, 2010.

Campagne, Fabián Alejandro. "Charismatic Healers on Iberian Soil: An Autopsy of a Mythical Complex of Early Modern Spain." *Folklore* 118 (2007): 44–64.

Cheape, Hugh. "Charms against Witchcraft: Magic and Mischief in Museum Collections." In *Witchcraft in Early Modern Scotland*, edited by Julian Goodare, Lauren Martin, and Joyce Miller, 227–248. Basingstoke: Palgrave Macmillan, 2008.

Clark, Stuart. "Demons and Disease: The Disenchantment of the Sick (1500–1700)." In *Illness and Healing Alternatives in Western Europe*, edited by Marijke Gijswijt-Hofstra, Hilary Marland, and Hans de Waardt, 38–58. Studies in the Social History of Medicine. London and New York: Routledge, 1997.

"Popular Magic." In *Witchcraft and Magic in Europe*, vol. 4, *The Period of the Witch Trials*, edited by Bengt Ankarloo and Stuart Clark, 99–121. London: The Athlone Press, 2002.

Davies, Owen. *Cunning-Folk: Popular Magic in English History*. London: Hambledon Continuum, 2003.

"Angels in Elite and Popular Magic, 1650–1790." In *Angels in the Early Modern World*, edited by Peter Marshall and Alexandra Walsham, 297–320. Cambridge: Cambridge University Press, 2006.

Dillinger, Johannes. *"Evil People": A Comparative Study of Witch Hunts in Swabian Austria and the Electorate of Trier*. Translated by Laura Stokes. Charlottesville: University of Virginia Press, 2009.

Duffy, Eamon. *The Stripping of the Altars: Traditional Religion in England c. 1400–c. 1580*. New Haven and London: Yale University Press, 1992.

Marking the Hours: English People and Their Prayers 1240–1570. New Haven and London: Yale University Press, 2006.

Gentilcore, David. *From Bishop to Witch: The System of the Sacred in Early Modern Terra d'Otranto*. Manchester: Manchester University Press, 1992.

"Was There a 'Popular Medicine' in Early Modern Europe?" *Folklore* 115 (2004): 151–166.

von Germeten, Nicole. "Sexuality, Witchcraft and Honor in Colonial Spanish America." *History Compass* 9, no. 5 (2011): 374–383.

Gilchrist, Roberta. "Magic for the Dead? The Archaeology of Magic in Later Medieval Burials." *Medieval Archaeology* 52 (2008): 119–159.

Ginzburg, Carlo. *The Night Battles: Witchcraft and Agrarian Cults in the Sixteenth and Seventeenth Centuries*. Translated by John Tedeschi and Anne Tedeschi. London: Routledge and Kegan Paul, 1983.

Goodich, Michael. "Sexuality, Family and the Supernatural in the Fourteenth Century." *Journal of the History of Sexuality* 4 (1994): 493–516.

Harley, David. "Mental Illness, Magical Medicine and the Devil in Northern England 1650–1700." In *The Medical Revolution of the Seventeenth Century*, edited by Roger French and Andrew Wear, 114–144. Cambridge: Cambridge University Press, 1989.

Jolly, Karen Louise. *Popular Religion in Late Saxon England: Elf Charms in Context*. Chapel Hill and London: University of North Carolina Press, 1996.

Kieckhefer, Richard. *European Witch Trials: Their Foundations in Popular and Learned Culture 1300–1500*. London: Routledge and Kegan Paul, 1976.

Magic in the Middle Ages. Cambridge: Cambridge University Press, 1989.

"Erotic Magic in Medieval Europe." In *Sex in the Middle Ages: A Book of Essays*, edited by Joyce E. Salisbury, 30–55. New York: Garland Publishing, 1991.

Le Roy Ladurie, Emmanuel. *Montaillou: Cathars and Catholics in a French Village 1294–1324*. Translated by Barbara Bray. London: Penguin Books, 1980.

Macfarlane, Alan. *Witchcraft in Tudor and Stuart England*. London: Routledge and Kegan Paul, 1970.

Martin, Ruth. *Witchcraft and the Inquisition in Venice 1550–1650*. Oxford: Basil Blackwell, 1989.

Merrifield, Ralph. *The Archaeology of Ritual and Magic*. London: B. T. Batsford, 1987.

Murdoch, Brian. "But Did They Work? Interpreting the Old High German Merseburg Charms in Their Medieval Context." *Neuphilologische Mitteilungen* 89 (1988): 358–69.

Nenonen, Marko. "Culture Wars: State, Religion and Popular Culture in Europe, 1400–1800." In *Palgrave Advances in Witchcraft Historiography*, edited by Jonathan Barry and Owen Davies, 108–124. Basingstoke: Palgrave Macmillan, 2007.

Olsan, Lea. "Charms and Prayers in Medieval Medical Theory and Practice." *Social History of Medicine* 16 (2003): 343–366.

——— "The Corpus of Charms in the Middle English Leechcraft Remedy Books." In *Charms, Charmers and Charming: International Research on Verbal Magic*, edited by Jonathan Roper, 214–237. Basingstoke: Palgrave Macmillan, 2009.

Park, Katharine. "Medicine and Magic: The Healing Arts." In *Gender and Society in Renaissance Italy*, edited by Judith C. Brown and Robert C. Davis, 129–149. London: Longman, 1998.

Pócs, Éva. *Between the Living and the Dead: A Perspective on Witches and Seers in the Early Modern Age*. Translated by Szilvia Rédey and Michael Webb. Budapest: Central European University Press, 1999.

Purkiss, Diane. *Troublesome Things: A History of Fairies and Fairy Stories*. London: Penguin Books, 2000.

Rankin, Alisha. "Duchess, Heal Thyself: Elizabeth of Rochlitz and the Patient's Perspective in Early Modern Germany." *Bulletin of the History of Medicine* 82 (2008): 109–144.

Rider, Catherine. *Magic and Impotence in the Middle Ages*. Oxford: Oxford University Press, 2006.

——— "Medical Magic and the Church in Thirteenth-Century England." *Social History of Medicine* 24 (April 2011): 92–107.

Robbins, Kevin C. "Magical Emasculation, Popular Anticlericalism, and the Limits of the Reformation in France circa 1590." *Journal of Social History* 31 (1997): 61–83.

Roper, Jonathan. *English Verbal Charms*. Helsinki: Suomalainan Tiedeakatemia, 2005.

Roper, Lyndal. "Stealing Manhood: Capitalism and Magic in Early Modern Germany." *Gender and History* 3 (1991): 4–22. Reprint in *Oedipus and the Devil: Witchcraft, Sexuality and Religion in Early Modern Europe*, edited by Lyndal Roper, 126–145. London and New York: Routledge, 1994.

——— "Witchcraft and Fantasy in Early Modern Germany." *History Workshop Journal* (Autumn 1991): 19–43. Reprint in *Oedipus and the Devil: Witchcraft, Sexuality and Religion in Early Modern Europe*, edited by Lyndal Roper, 199–225. London and New York: Routledge, 1994.

Ruggiero, Guido. *Binding Passions: Tales of Magic, Marriage and Power at the End of the Renaissance*. New York and Oxford: Oxford University Press, 1993.

Schulte, Rolf. *Man as Witch: Male Witches in Central Europe*. Translated by Linda Froome-Döring. Basingstoke: Palgrave Macmillan, 2009.

Scribner, Bob. "Is a History of Popular Culture Possible?" *History of European Ideas* 10 (1989): 175–191.

Sharpe, James. *Instruments of Darkness: Witchcraft in England 1550–1750*. London: Hamish Hamilton, 1996.

Skemer, Don C. *Binding Words: Textual Amulets in the Middle Ages*. University Park: Penn State University Press, 2006.

Spencer, Brian. *Pilgrim Souvenirs and Secular Badges*. 2nd ed. Woodbridge: Boydell Press, 2010.

Strobino, Sandrine. *Françoise sauvée des flammes? Une valaisanne accusée de sorcellerie au XVe siècle*. Lausanne: Université de Lausanne, 1996.

Thomas, Keith. *Religion and the Decline of Magic*. London: Weidenfeld and Nicolson, 1971.

Valletta, Frederick. *Magic, Witchcraft and Superstition in England 1640–70*. Aldershot: Ashgate, 2000.

Walsham, Alexandra. "The Reformation and 'The Disenchantment of the World' Reassessed." *Historical Journal* 51 (2008): 497–528.

Wilson, Stephen. *The Magical Universe: Everyday Ritual and Magic in Pre-Modern Europe*. London and New York: Hambledon and London, 2000.

11 Learned Magic (by David J. Collins, S.J.)

Agrippa von Nettesheim, Heinrich Cornelius. "Ars notoria." In *Opera omnia – Agrippa von Nettesheim*, vol. 2, 603–660. Lyon: Beringos Fratres, 1620.

Albertus Magnus. *The Book of Minerals*. Translated by Dorothy Wyckoff. Oxford: Clarendon Press, 1967.

    Le liber de virtutibus herbarum, lapidum et animalium (Liber aggregationis): Un texte à succès attribué à Albert le Grand. Edited by Isabelle Draelants. Micrologus' Library. Florence: SISMEL, 2007.

    Questions Concerning Aristotle's "On animals". Edited by Irven Michael Resnick and Kenneth Kitchell. Fathers of the Church: Mediaeval Continuation. Washington, DC: Catholic University of America Press, 2008.

Albertus Magnus (Pseudo-). *Libellus de alchimia*. Edited by Virginia Heines. Berkeley: University of California Press, 1958.

Armstrong, Arthur Hilary, ed. *The Cambridge History of Later Greek and Early Medieval Philosophy*. London: Cambridge University Press, 1967.

Arnold, Klaus. *Johannes Trithemius (1462–1516)*. Edited by Klaus Wittstadt. Quellen und Forschungen zur Geschichte des Bistums und Hochstifts Würzburg. Würzburg: Kommissionsverlag Ferdinand Schöningh, 1991.

Bailey, Michael D. "The Disenchantment of Magic: Spells, Charms, and Superstition in Early European Witchcraft Literature." *American Historical Review* 111 (2006): 383–404.

    Magic and Superstition in Europe: A Concise History from Antiquity to the Present. Critical Issues in History, edited by Donald T. Critchlow. Lanham, MD: Rowman & Littlefield Publishers, 2007.

Barbierato, Federico. "Magical Literature and the Venice Inquisition from the Sixteenth to the Eighteenth Centuries." In *Magic, Alchemy and Science, 15th–18th Centuries: The Influence of Hermes Trismegistus*, edited by Carlos Gilly and Cis van Heertum, vol. 1, 159–175. Florence: Centro Di, 2002.

Beierwaltes, Werner. *Denken des Einen: Studien zur neuplatonischen Philosophie und ihrer Wirkungsgeschichte*. Frankfurt am Main: V. Klostermann, 1985.

de Blécourt, Willem, and Cornelie Usborne, eds. *Cultural Approaches to the History of Medicine: Mediating Medicine in Early Modern and Modern Europe.* Hampshire: Palgrave Macmillan, 2004.

Boudet, Jean-Patrice. *Entre science et nigromance: Astrologie, divination et magie dans l'Occident médiéval (XIIe–XVe siècle).* Histoire ancienne et médiévale 83. Paris: Publications de la Sorbonne, 2006.

"A 'College of Astrology and Medicine'? Charles V, Gervais Chrétien, and the Scientific Manuscripts of Maître Gervais's College." *Studies in History and Philosophy of Science* 41C (2010): 99–108.

Boudet, Jean-Patrice, Anna Caiozzo, and Nicolas Weill-Parot, eds. *Images et magie: Picatrix entre Orient et Occident.* Sciences, techniques et civilisations du Moyen Âge à l'aube des Lumières 13. Paris: Honoré Champion, 2011.

Brann, Noel L. *Trithemius and Magical Theology: A Chapter in the Controversy over Occult Studies in Early Modern Europe.* Western Esoteric Traditions. Albany: State University of New York Press, 1999.

Burnett, Charles. "Arabic, Greek, and Latin Works on Astrological Magic Attributed to Aristotle." In *Pseudo-Aristotle in the Middle Ages,* edited by Jill Kraye, Charles B. Schmitt, and W. F. Ryan, 84–96. London: The Warburg Institute, 1987.

"The Translating Activity in Medieval Spain." In *Handbuch der Orientalistik: The Legacy of Muslim Spain,* edited by S. K. Jayyusi, vol. 12, 1036–1058. Leiden: Brill, 1992.

"Talismans: Magic as Science? Necromancy among the Seven Liberal Arts." In *Magic and Divination in the Middle Ages,* vol. I, 1–15. Aldershot: Variorum, 1994.

Magic and Divination in the Middle Ages: Texts and Techniques in the Islamic and Christian Worlds. Variorum Collected Studies Series 557. Aldershot: Variorum, 1996.

"Scapulimancy." In *Magic and Divination in the Middle Ages,* edited by Charles Burnett, vol. XII, 1–14. Aldershot: Variorum, 1996.

Burnett, Charles, and W. F. Ryan, eds. *Magic and the Classical Tradition.* Warburg Institute Colloquia 7. London and Turin: Warburg Institute and Nino Aragno, 2006.

Campanella, Tommaso. *Del senso delle cose e della magia a cura di Germana Ernst.* Edited by Germana Ernst. Biblioteca filosofica Laterza. Rome: Laterza, 2007.

Carey, Hilary M. "What is the Folded Almanac?: The Form and Function of a Key Manuscript Source for Astro-Medical Practice in Later Medieval England." *Social History of Medicine* 16 (2003): 481–509.

"Judicial Astrology in Theory and Practice in Later Medieval Europe." *Studies in History and Philosophy of Science,* part C, *Studies in History and Philosophy of Biological and Biomedical Sciences* 41 (2010): 90–98.

Carmody, Francis James. *Arabic Astronomical and Astrological Sciences in Latin Translation.* Berkeley: University of California Press, 1956.

Charmasson, Thérèse. *Recherches sur une technique divinatoire: La géomancie dans l'Occident médiéval.* Centre de recherches d'histoire et de philologie de la IVe section de l'École pratique des hautes études. Geneva: Droz, 1980.

Clark, Stuart. *Thinking with Demons: The Idea of Witchcraft in Early Modern Europe.* Oxford: Clarendon Press, 1997.

Clulee, Nicholas H. "At the Crossroads of Magic and Science: John Dee's Archemastrie." In *Occult and Scientific Mentalities in the Renaissance,* edited by Brian Vickers, 57–71. Cambridge: Cambridge University Press, 1984.

Colish, Marcia L. *Medieval Foundations of the Western Intellectual Tradition, 400–1400.* Yale Intellectual History of the West. New Haven: Yale University Press, 1997.

Compagni, Vittoria Perrone. "'Dispersa Intentio': Alchemy, Magic, and Scepticism in Agrippa." *Early Science and Medicine* 5 (2000): 160–177.

——. "I testi magici di Ermete." In *Hermetism from Late Antiquity to Humanism / La tradizione ermetica dal mondo tardo-antico all'umanesimo,* edited by Paolo Lucentini, Ilaria Parri, and Vittoria Perrone Compagni, 505–534. Instrumenta Patristica et Mediaevalia 40. Turnhout: Brepols, 2003.

Copenhaver, Brian P. "Hermes Trismegistus, Proclus, and the Question of a Philosophy of Magic in the Renaissance." In *Hermeticism and the Renaissance,* edited by Ingrid Merkel and Allen G. Debus, 79–110. Washington, DC: The Folger Shakespeare Library, 1988.

——, ed. *Hermetica: The Greek "Corpus Hermeticum" and the Latin "Asclepius" in a New English Translation with Notes and Introduction.* Cambridge: Cambridge University Press, 1992.

——. "Magic." In *The Cambridge History of Science: Early Modern Science,* edited by Katharine Park and Lorraine Daston, 518–540. Cambridge: Cambridge University Press, 2006.

Crisciani, Chiara. "La *quaestio de alchimia* fra Duecento e Trecento." *Medioevo* 2 (1976): 119–168.

Dasen, Véronique, and Jean-Michel Spieser, eds. *Les savoirs magiques et leur transmission de l'antiquité à la Renaissance.* Edited by Agostino Paravicini Bagliani. Micrologus' Library 60. Florence: SISMEL Edizioni del Galluzzo, 2014.

Davies, Owen. *Grimoires: A History of Magic Books.* Oxford: Oxford University Press, 2009.

Debus, Allen G., ed. *Alchemy and Early Modern Chemistry: Papers from Ambix.* Huddersfield, England: Jeremy Mills Publishing, 2004.

Delatte, Armand. *La catoptromancie grecque et ses dérivés.* Liège: H. Vaillant-Carmanne, 1932.

DeVun, Leah. *Prophecy, Alchemy, and the End of Time: John of Rupescissa in the Late Middle Ages.* New York: Columbia University Press, 2009.

Diderot, Denis, and Jean le Rond d'Alembert, eds. *Encyclopédie, ou dictionnaire raisonné des sciences, des arts et des métiers, etc.* Spring 2013 ed., edited by Robert Morrissey. University of Chicago: ARTFL Encyclopédie Project, 2013. http://encyclopedie.uchicago.edu/.

Dobbs, Betty Jo Teeter. *The Foundations of Newton's Alchemy, or "The Hunting of the Greene Lyon".* Cambridge: Cambridge University Press, 1975.

Donahue, William. "Astronomy." In *The Cambridge History of Science: Early Modern Science,* edited by Katharine Park and Lorraine Daston, 562–595. Cambridge: Cambridge University Press, 2006.

Draelants, Isabelle. "Expérience et autorités dans la philosophie naturelle d'Albert le Grand." In *Expertus sum,* edited by Thomas Bénatouïl and Isabelle Draelants, 89–122. Florence: SISMEL, 2011.

Draelants, Isabelle, and M. Paulmier-Foucart. "Échanges dans la societas des naturalistes au milieu du XIIIe siècle: Arnold de Saxe, Vincent de Beauvais et Albert le Grand." In *Par les mots et les textes ... Mélange de langue, de littérature et d'histoire des science médiévales offerts à Claude Thomasset,* edited by D. James-Raoul and O. Soutet, 219–238. Paris: Presses de la Sorbonne, 2005.

Draelants, Isabelle, and Antonella Sannino. "Albertinisme et hermétisme dans une anthologie en faveur de la magie, le *Liber aggregationis*: Prospective." In *Mélanges offerts à Hossam Elkhadem par ses amis et ses élèves,* edited by Frank Daelemans, Jean-Marie

Duvosquel, Robert Halleux, and David Juste, 223–255. Brussels: Archives et bibliothéques de Belgique, 2007.

Driscoll, Daniel J., ed. *The Sworn Book of Honourius the Magician*. Gillette, NJ: Heptangle Books, 1977.

Eamon, William. "Alchemy in Popular Culture: Leonardo Fioravanti and the Search for the Philosopher's Stone." *Early Science and Medicine* 5 (2000): 196–213.

———. "Magic and the Occult." In *The History of Science and Religion in the Western Tradition: An Encyclopedia*, edited by Gary B. Ferngren, 608–617. New York: Garland Publishing, Inc., 2000.

Ebeling, Florian. *The Secret History of Hermes Trismegistus: Hermeticism from Ancient to Modern Times*. Translated by David Lorton. Ithaca: Cornell University Press, 2007.

Fanger, Claire, ed. *Invoking Angels: Theurgic Ideas and Practices, Thirteenth to Sixteenth Centuries*. The Magic in History Series. University Park: Pennsylvania State University Press, 2012.

Faivre, Antoine. *The Eternal Hermes: From Greek God to Alchemical Magus*. Grand Rapids: Phanes Press, 1995.

Foerster, Richard. *Scriptores physiognomonici graeci et latini*. Leipzig: B. G. Teubner, 1893.

French, Roger Kenneth. *Medicine before Science: The Rational and Learned Doctor from the Middle Ages to the Enlightenment*. Cambridge and New York: Cambridge University Press, 2003.

Fürbeth, Frank. *Johannes Hartlieb: Untersuchungen zu Leben und Werk*. Hermaea: Edited by Hans Fromm and Hans-Joachim Mähl. Germanistische Forschungen, n.s. Tübingen: Max Niemeyer Verlag, 1992.

———. "Das Johannes Hartlieb zugeschriebene 'Buch von der Hand' im Kontext der Chiromantie des Mittelalters." *Zeitschrift für deutsches Altertum und deutsche Literatur* 136 (2007): 449–479.

Geber (Pseudo-). *The "Summa perfectionis" of Pseudo-Geber: A Critical Edition, Translation, and Study*. Translated and edited by William Royall Newman. Collection de travaux de l'Académie internationale d'histoire des sciences. Leiden: Brill, 1991.

Gijswijt-Hofstra, Marijke, Hilary Marland, and Hans de Waardt, eds. *Illness and Healing Alternatives in Western Europe*. Studies in the Social History of Medicine. London: Routledge, 1997.

Gilly, Carlos. "Hermes oder Luther: Der philosophische Hintergrund von Johann Arndts Frühschrift 'De antiqua philosophia et divina veterum Magorum Sapientia recuperanda.'" In *Frömmigkeit oder Theologie*, edited by Hans Otte and Hans Schneider, 163–200. Göttingen: V & R Unipress, 2007.

Gilly, Carlos, and Cis van Heertum, eds. *Magic, Alchemy and Science, 15th–18th Centuries: The Influence of Hermes Trismegistus*. 2 vols. Florence: Centro Di, 2002.

Grant, Edward. *Planets, Stars, and Orbs: The Medieval Cosmos, 1200–1687*. Cambridge: Cambridge University Press, 1994.

———. *A History of Natural Philosophy: From the Ancient World to the Nineteenth Century*. New York: Cambridge University Press, 2007.

Green, Jeffrey E. "Two Meanings of Disenchantment: Sociological Condition vs. Philosophical Act – Reassessing Max Weber's Thesis of the Disenchantment of the World." *Philosophy and Theology* 17 (2005): 51–84.

Hackett, Jeremiah. "Albert the Great and the *Speculum astronomiae*: The State of the Research at the Beginning of the Twenty-First Century." In *A Companion to Albert the Great*, edited by Irven Michael Resnick, 437–449. Leiden: Brill, 2012.

Hadot, Pierre. "Neoplatonism." In *The New Catholic Encyclopedia*, 2nd ed., vol. 10, 240–242. Detroit: Gale, 2003.

Hammond, Mitchell. "Paracelsus and the Boundaries of Medicine in Early Modern Augsburg." In *Paracelsian Moments: Science, Medicine, and Astrology in Early Modern Europe*, edited by Gerhild Scholz Williams and Charles D. Gunnoe, 19–33. Kirksville, MO: Truman State University Press, 2002.

Hanegraaff, Wouter J. "Beyond the Yates Paradigm: The Study of Western Esotericism between Counterculture." *Aries* 1 (2001): 5–37.

"How Magic Survived the Disenchantment of the World." *Religion* 33 (2003): 357–380.

Hardman, Lizabeth. *The History of Medicine*. World History. Detroit: Lucent Books, 2012.

Harkness, Deborah E. *John Dee's Conversations with Angels: Cabala, Alchemy, and the End of Nature*. Cambridge: Cambridge University Press, 1999.

Hartlieb, Johannes. *Das Buch der verbotenen Künste: Aberglaube und Zauberei des Mittelalters*. Translated by Falk Eisermann. Edited by Falk Eisermann and Eckhard Graf. Diederichs gelbe Reihe. Munich: Diederichs, 1998.

Haskins, Charles Homer. *The Renaissance of the Twelfth Century*. New York: Meridian Books, 1957.

Hayton, Darin. "Instruments and Demonstrations in the Astrological Curriculum: Evidence from the University of Vienna, 1500–1530." *Studies in History and Philosophy of Science*, part C, *Studies in History and Philosophy of Biological and Biomedical Sciences* 41 (2010): 125–134.

Headley, John M. *Tommaso Campanella and the Transformation of the World*. Princeton: Princeton University Press, 1997.

Hedegård, Gösta, ed. *Liber iuratus Honorii: A Critical Edition of the Latin Version of the Sworn Book of Honorius*. Acta Universitatis Stockholmiensis, Studia Latina Stockholmiensia. Stockholm: Almovist & Wiksell International, 2002.

Heinz, Schott. "Die Natur als Magierin: Zum paracelsischen Erbe neuzeitlicher Medizin." *Acta historica leopoldina* 55 (2010): 39–50.

Henrichs, Norbert. "Scientia Magica." In *Aufsätze zu Goethes "Faust I"*, edited by Werner Keller, 607–624. Darmstadt: Wissenschaftliche Buchgesellschaft, 1974.

Henry, John. "The Fragmentation of Renaissance Occultism and the Decline of Magic." *History of Science* 46 (2008): 1–48.

Herzig, Tamar. "The Demons and the Friars: Illicit Magic and Mendicant Rivalry in Renaissance Bologna." *Renaissance Quarterly* 64 (Winter 2011): 1025–1058.

Hugh of St. Victor. *The "Didascalicon" of Hugh of St. Victor: A Medieval Guide to the Arts*. Edited by Jerome Taylor. Records of Western Civilization. New York: Columbia University Press, 1991.

Hunter, Michael. "The Royal Society and the Decline of Magic." *Notes and Records of the Royal Society* 65 (2011): 103–119.

Ibn Hayyan, Jabir. *Names, Natures, and Things: The Alchemist Jabir ibn Hayyan and His Kitab al-Ahjar*. Edited by Syed Nomanul Haq. Dordrecht: Kluwer Academic Publishers, 1994.

Idel, Moshe. "Hermeticism and Kabbalah." In *Hermetism from Late Antiquity to Humanism /
La tradizione ermetica dal mondo tardo-antico all'umanesimo,* edited by Paolo Lucentini,
Ilaria Parri, and Vittoria Perrone Compagni, 389–408. Instrumenta Patristica et
Mediaevalia 40. Turnhout: Brepols, 2003.

Isidore of Seville. *Etymologies.* Cambridge: Cambridge University Press, 2006.

Jacquart, Danielle. "Médecine et alchimie chez Michel Savonarole (1385–1466)." In *Alchimie
et philosophie à la Renaissance,* edited by Jean-Claude Margolin, 109–122. Paris: Librairie
philosophique J. Vrin, 1993.

Jenkins, Richard. "Disenchantment, Enchantment and Re-Enchantment: Max Weber at the
Millennium." *Max Weber Studies* 1 (2000): 11–32.

Kassell, Lauren. "Stars, Spirits, Signs: Towards a History of Astrology, 1100–1800." *Studies
in History and Philosophy of Science,* part C, *Studies in History and Philosophy of Biological
and Biomedical Sciences* 41 (2010): 67–69.

Kibre, Pearl. "Alchemical Writings Ascribed to Albertus Magnus." *Speculum* 17 (1942):
499–518.

"An Alchemical Tract Attributed to Albertus Magnus." *Isis* 35 (1944): 303–316.

"The *Alkimia minor* Ascribed to Albertus Magnus." *Isis* 32 (1949): 267–300.

"Albertus Magnus on Alchemy." In *Albertus Magnus and the Sciences,* edited by James A.
Weisheipl, 187–202. Toronto: Pontifical Institute of Mediaeval Studies, 1980.

Kieckhefer, Richard. "The Specific Rationality of Medieval Magic." *American Historical
Review* 99 (1994): 813–836.

Forbidden Rites: A Necromancer's Manual of the Fifteenth Century. University Park: Penn
State University Press, 1998.

Magic in the Middle Ages. Cambridge: Cambridge University Press, 2000.

Klaassen, Frank. "English Manuscripts of Magic, 1300–1500." In *Conjuring Spirits: Texts and
Traditions of Medieval Ritual Magic,* edited by Claire Fanger, 3–31. University Park: Penn
State University Press, 1998.

Transformations of Magic: Illicit Learned Magic in the Later Middle Ages and Renaissance.
Magic in History. University Park: Penn State University Press, 2013.

Kühlmann, Wilhelm, and Joachim Telle, eds. *Corpus Paracelsisticum: Dokumente frühneuzeitli-
cher Naturphilosophie in Deutschland.* Frühe Neuzeit. Tübingen: Niemeyer, 2001.

Láng, Benedek. *Unlocked Books: Manuscripts of Learned Magic in the Medieval Libraries of
Central Europe.* Magic in History. University Park: Penn State University Press, 2008.

Lindberg, David C. *The Beginnings of Western Science: The European Scientific Tradition
in Philosophical, Religious, and Institutional Context, 600 B.C. to A.D. 1450.* Chicago:
University of Chicago Press, 2008.

Lindemann, Mary. *Medicine and Society in Early Modern Europe.* New Approaches to European
History. Cambridge: Cambridge University Press, 2010.

Lucentini, Paolo, Ilaria Parri, and Vittoria Perrone Compagni, eds. *Hermetism from Late
Antiquity to Humanism / La tradizione ermetica dal mondo tardo-antico all'umanesimo.*
Instrumenta Patristica et Mediaevalia 40. Turnhout: Brepols, 2003.

van der Lugt, M. "'Abominable Mixtures': The *Liber vaccae* in the Medieval, West, or the
Dangers and Attractions of Natural Magic." *Traditio* 64 (2009): 229–277.

Luscombe, David. "Thought and Learning." In *The New Cambridge Medieval History IV:
c. 1024–c. 1198,* edited by David Luscombe and Jonathan Riley-Smith, vol. 1, 461–498,
835–842. Cambridge: Cambridge University Press, 2004.

Luther, Martin. *D. Martin Luthers Werke: Kritische Gesamtausgabe (Weimarer Ausgabe)*, Tischreden, 6 vols. Weimar: Böhlau, 1912–1921.

al-Majriti, Maslama. *Picatrix: The Latin Version of the Ghāyat al-hakīm*. Edited by David Edwin Pingree. Studies of the Warburg Institute. London: Warburg Institute, 1986.

  Picatrix: Un traité de magie médiéval. Edited by Béatrice Bakhouche, Frédéric Fauquieret, and Brigitte Pérez-Jean. Miroir du Moyen Âge. Turnhout: Brepols, 2003.

Mathiesen, Robert. "A Thirteenth-Century Ritual to Attain the Beatific Vision from the *Sworn Book* of Honorius of Thebes." In *Conjuring Spirits: Texts and Traditions of Medieval Ritual Magic*, edited by Claire Fanger, 143–162. University Park: Penn State University Press, 1998.

de Mayo, Thomas B. *The Demonology of William of Auvergne: By Fire and Sword*. Lewiston, NY: Edwin Mellen Press, 2007.

Meier, Pirmin. *Paracelsus: Arzt und Prophet, Annäherungen an Theophrastus von Hohenheim*. Zurich: Ammann, 1993.

Melchior-Bonnet, Sabine. *The Mirror: A History*. New York: Routledge, 2001.

Moran, Bruce T. *Distilling Knowledge: Alchemy, Chemistry, and the Scientific Revolution*. New Histories of Science, Technology, and Medicine. Cambridge, MA: Harvard University Press, 2005.

Moreschini, Claudio. *Storia dell'ermetismo cristiano*. Letteratura cristiana antica studi. Brescia: Morcelliana, 2000.

Moureau, Sébastien. *"Elixir atque fermentum*: New Investigations about the Link between Pseudo-Avicenna's Alchemical *De anima* and Roger Bacon: Alchemical and Medical Doctrines." *Traditio* 68 (2013): 277–325.

Newman, William Royall. "Technology and Alchemical Debate in the Late Middle Ages." *Isis* 80 (September 1989): 423–445.

  "An Overview of Roger Bacon's Alchemy." In *Roger Bacon and the Sciences*, edited by Jeremiah Hackett, 317–336. Leiden: Brill, 1997.

  Promethean Ambitions: Alchemy and the Quest to Perfect Nature. Chicago: University of Chicago Press, 2004.

  "What Have We Learned from the Recent Historiography of Alchemy?" *Isis* 102 (2011): 313–321.

Newman, William R., and Lawrence M. Principe. *Alchemy Tried in the Fire Starkey, Boyle, and the Fate of Helmontian Chymistry*. Chicago: University of Chicago Press, 2010.

Page, Sophie. *Magic in Medieval Manuscripts*. Toronto: University of Toronto Press, 2004.

  Magic in the Cloister: Pious Motives, Illicit Interests, and Occult Approaches to the Medieval Universe. The Magic in History Series. University Park: The Pennsylvania State University Press, 2013.

Pagel, Walter. *Paracelsus: An Introduction to Philosophical Medicine in the Era of the Renaissance*. Basel: Karger, 1982.

Paravicini Bagliani, Agostino, and Francesco Santi, eds. *The Regulation of Evil: Social and Cultural Attitudes to Epidemics in the Late Middle Ages*. Micrologus' Library 2. Florence: SISMEL, 1998.

Parry, Glyn. "John Dee and the Elizabethan British Empire in Its European Context." *Historical Journal* 49 (2006): 643–675.

  The Arch-Conjuror of England: John Dee. New Haven: Yale University Press, 2011.

Pereira, Michela. "Heavens on Earth: From the *Tabula smaragdina* to the Alchemical Fifth Essence." *Early Science and Medicine* 5 (2000): 131–144.

Pico della Mirandola, Giovanni. *Oration on the Dignity of Man*. Translated by A. Robert Caponigri. Washington, DC: Regnery Publishing, Inc., 1998.

    Syncretism in the West: Pico's 900 Theses (1486). Edited by S. A. Farmer. Medieval and Renaissance Texts and Studies. Tempe: Medieval and Renaissance Texts and Studies, 1998.

Pomponazzi, Pietro. *De incantationibus*. Edited by V. Perrone Compagni. Lessico intellettuale europeo. Florence: Olschki, 2011.

Principe, Lawrence M. *Chymists and Chymistry: Studies in the History of Alchemy and Early Modern Chemistry*. Sagamore Beach, MA: Science History Publications, 2007.

    "Alchemy Restored." *Isis* 102 (2011): 305–312.

Ptolemy. *Tetrabiblos*. Edited by Frank Egleston Robbins. Loeb Classical Library. Cambridge, MA: Harvard University Press, 1980.

Rabin, Sheila. "Unholy Astrology: Did Pico Always View It That Way?" In *Paracelsian Moments: Science, Medicine, and Astrology in Early Modern Europe*, edited by Gerhild Scholz Williams and Charles D. Gunnoe, 151–162. Kirksville, MO: Truman State University Press, 2002.

Randles, W. G. L. *The Unmaking of the Medieval Christian Cosmos, 1500–1760: From Solid Heavens to Boundless Aether*. Aldershot: Ashgate, 1999.

Resnick, Irven Michael. *Marks of Distinction: Christian Perceptions of Jews in the High Middle Ages*. Washington, DC: Catholic University of America Press, 2012.

Rider, Catherine. "Medical Magic and the Church in Thirteenth-Century England." *Social History of Medicine* 24 (April 2011): 92–107.

Rigo, Antonio. "From Constantinople to the Library of Venice: The Hermetic Books of Late Byzantine Doctors, Astrologers and Magicians." In *Magic, Alchemy and Science*, edited by Carlos Gilly and Cis van Heertum, vol. 1, 77–84. Florence: Centro Di, 2002.

Rouse, Richard H., and Mary A. Rouse. *Manuscripts and Their Makers: Commercial Book Producers in Medieval Paris, 1200–1500*. Turnhout: H. Miller, 2000.

Ruickbie, Leo. *Faustus: The Life and Times of a Renaissance Magician*. Stroud: History Press, 2009.

Rutkin, H. Darrel. "Astrology, Natural Philosophy and the History of Science, c. 1250–1700: Studies toward an Interpretation of Giovanni Pico della Mirandola's *Disputationes adversus astrologiam divinatricem*." PhD diss., Indiana University, 2002.

    "Various Uses of Horoscopes: Astrological Practices in Early Modern Europe." In *Horoscopes and Public Spheres*, edited by Günther Oestmann, H. Darrel Rutkin, and Kocku von Stuckrad, 167–182. Berlin: Walter de Gruyter, 2005.

    "Astrology." In *The Cambridge History of Science: Early Modern Science*, edited by Katharine Park and Lorraine Daston, 541–562. Cambridge: Cambridge University Press, 2006.

Schaffer, Simon. "The Astrological Roots of Mesmerism." *Studies in History and Philosophy of Science*, part C, *Studies in History and Philosophy of Biological and Biomedical Sciences* 41 (June 2010): 158–168.

Schnell, Bernhard. "Neues zur Biographie Johannes Hartliebs." *Zeitschrift für deutsches Altertum und deutsche Literatur* 136 (2007): 444–448.

Scribner, Robert W. "Incombustible Luther: The Image of the Reformer in Early Modern Germany." *Past and Present* 110 (1986): 38–68.

"Magie und Aberglaube: Zur volkstümlichen sakramentalischen Denkart in Deutschland am Ausgang des Mittelalters." In *Volksreligion im hohen und späten Mittelalter*, edited by Peter Dinzelbacher and Dieter R. Bauer, 253–274. Paderborn: Ferdinand Schöningh, 1990.

"The Reformation, Popular Magic, and the 'Disenchantment of the World.'" *Journal of Interdisciplinary History* 23 (Winter 1993): 475–494.

"Reformation and Desacralisation: Reflections Concerning Late Medieval Female Sainthood." In *Problems in the Historical Anthropology of Early Modern Europe*, edited by R. Po-chia Hsia and Robert W. Scribner, 49–74. Wiesbaden: Harrassowitz, 1997.

Sherry, Patrick. "Disenchantment, Re-enchantment, and Enchantment." *Modern Theology* 25 (2009): 369–386.

Siraisi, Nancy G. *Medieval and Early Renaissance Medicine: An Introduction to Knowledge and Practice*. Chicago: University of Chicago Press, 1990.

History, Medicine, and the Traditions of Renaissance Learning. Cultures of Knowledge in the Early Modern World. Ann Arbor: University of Michigan Press, 2008.

Stannard, Jerry, Richard Kay, and Katherine E. Stannard, eds. *Herbs and Herbalism in the Middle Ages and Renaissance*. Variorum collected Studies Series CS650. Aldershot: Ashgate Variorum, 1999.

Stark, Ryan J. *Rhetoric, Science, and Magic in Seventeenth-Century England*. Washington, DC: Catholic University of America Press, 2009.

Sturlese, Loris. *Storia della filosofia tedesca nel Medioevo*. Florence: L. S. Olschki, 1990.

Thābit ibn Qurrah, al-Ḥarrānī. *The Astronomical Works of Thabit b. Qurra*. Edited by Francis J. Carmody. Berkeley: University of California Press, 1960.

Thorndike, Lynn. *A History of Magic and Experimental Science*. 8 vols. New York: Columbia University Press, 1923–1958.

Trithemius, Johannes. *Annales Hirsaugienses*. St. Gallen: J. G. Schlegel, 1690.

Opera historica. Edited by Marquard Hunibald Freher. Frankfurt am Main: Minerva, 1966.

Verger, Jacques. "Patterns." In *Universities in the Middle Ages*, edited by Hilde de Ridder-Symoens, 35–75. Cambridge: Cambridge University Press, 1992.

Walker, Daniel P. *Spiritual and Demonic Magic from Ficino to Campanella*. Studies in Magic. University Park: Penn State University Press, 2000.

Walsham, Alexandra. "The Reformation and 'The Disenchantment of the World' Reassessed." *Historical Journal* 51 (2008): 497–528.

Watt, Jeffrey R. "Calvin's Geneva Confronts Magic and Witchcraft: The Evidence from the Consistory." *Journal of Early Modern History* 17 (2013): 215–244.

Weber, Max. "Scholarship as Profession." In *From Max Weber: Essays in Sociology*, edited by Hans Heinrich Gerth and Charles Wright Mills, 129–156. New York, 1948.

Webster, Charles. "Paracelsus Confronts the Saints: Miracles, Healing and the Secularization of Magic." *Social History of Medicine* 8 (1995): 403–421.

"Paracelsus, Paracelsianism, and the Secularization of the Worldview." *Science in Context* 15 (March 2002): 9–27.

Paracelsus: Medicine, Magic and Mission at the End of Time. New Haven: Yale University Press, 2008.

Weill-Parot, Nicolas. *Les "images astrologiques" au Moyen Âge et à la Renaissance: Spéculations intellectuelles et pratiques magiques, XIIe–XVe siècle*. Sciences, techniques et civilisations du Moyen Âge à l'aube des Lumières 6. Paris: Honoré Champion, 2002.

"Astrology, Astral Influences, and Occult Properties in the Thirteenth and Fourteenth Centuries." *Traditio* 65 (2010): 201–230.

Westman, Robert S. *The Copernican Question: Prognostication, Skepticism, and Celestial Order.* Berkeley: University of California Press, 2011.

White, Nelson H., and Anne White. *Index to the Spirits Given in 'Honourius'.* Pasadena: Technology Group, 1983.

Williams, Gerhild Scholz, and Charles D. Gunnoe, eds. *Paracelsian Moments: Science, Medicine, and Astrology in Early Modern Europe.* Kirksville, MO: Truman State University Press, 2002.

Wirszubski, Chaim. *Pico della Mirandola's Encounter with Jewish Mysticism.* Cambridge, MA: Harvard University Press, 1989.

Zambelli, Paola. *The "Speculum astronomiae" and Its Enigma: Astrology, Theology, and Science in Albertus Magnus and His Contemporaries.* Edited by Robert S. Cohen. Boston Studies in the Philosophy of Science. Dordrecht: Kluwer Academic Publishers, 1992.

12 Diabolic Magic (by Michael D. Bailey)

Primary Sources

Aquinas, Thomas. *Summa contra gentiles.* In *Opera omnia iussu Leonis XIII P. M. edita*, vols. 13–15. Rome: Typis Riccardi Garroni, 1918–1930.

Summa theologiae: Latin Text and English Translation. 60 vols. New York: Blackfriars and McGraw-Hill, 1964–1981.

Augustine. *De civitate Dei.* Edited by Bernard Dombart and Alphonse Kalb. 2 vols. Corpus Christianorum Series Latina 47–48. Turnhout: Brepols, 1955.

De divinatione daemonum. Edited by Iosephus Zycha. Corpus Scriptorum Ecclesiasticorum Latinorum 41. Vienna: Tempsky, 1900.

De doctrina Christiana. Edited by Joseph Martin. Corpus Christianorum Series Latina 32. Turnhout: Brepols, 1962.

Boureau, Alain, ed. *Le pape et les sorciers: Une consultation de Jean XXII sur la magie en 1320 (Manuscrit B.A.V. Borghese 348).* Sources et documents d'histoire de Moyen Âge 6. Rome: École française de Rome, 2004.

Burchard of Worms. *Decretorum libri viginti.* Patrologiae Cursus Completus Series Latina 140, edited by J.-P. Migne, cols. 537–1058. Paris: Garnier Fratres, 1880.

Eymerich, Nicolau. *Directorium inquisitorum.* Edited by F. Peña. Rome: G. Ferrari, 1587.

Friedberg, Emil, ed. *Corpus iuris canonici.* 2 vols. Leipzig: Tauchnitz, 1879–1881. Reprint, Graz: Akademische Druck- und Verlagsanstalt, 1959.

Gui, Bernard. *Practica inquisitionis heretice pravitatis.* Edited by C. Douais. Paris: A. Picard, 1886.

Hansen, Bert, ed. *Nicole Oresme and the Marvels of Nature: A Study of His De causis mirabilium with Critical Edition, Translation, and Commentary.* Texts and Studies 68. Toronto: Pontifical Institute of Medieval Studies, 1985.

Hansen, Joseph, ed. *Quellen und Untersuchungen zur Geschichte des Hexenwahns und der Hexenverfolgung im Mittelalter.* Bonn: Carl Georgi, 1901. Reprint, Hildesheim: Georg Olms, 1963.

Isidore of Seville. *Etymologiarum sive originum libri XX.* Edited by W. M. Lindsay. 2 vols. Oxford: Clarendon Press, 1911. Reprint, Oxford: Clarendon Press, 1971.

Jacquier, Nicolas. *Flagellum hereticorum fascinariorum*. Frankfurt am Main: N. Basseus, 1581.

John of Salisbury. *Policraticus I–IV*. Edited by K. S. B. Keats-Rohan. Corpus Christianorum Continuatio Mediaevalis 118. Turnhout: Brepols, 1993.

Kors, Alan C., and Edward Peters, eds. *Witchcraft in Europe 400–1700: A Documentary History*. 2nd ed. Philadelphia: University of Pennsylvania Press, 2001.

Kramer, Heinrich. *Malleus maleficarum*. Edited and translated by Christopher S. Mackay. 2 vols. Cambridge: Cambridge University Press, 2006.

al-Majriti, Maslama. *Picatrix: The Latin Version of the* Ghāyat al-hakīm. Edited by David Edwin Pingree. Studies of the Warburg Institute. London: Warburg Institute, 1986.

Nider, Johannes. *Formicarius*. Edited by G. Colvener. Douai: Baltazar Bellerus, 1602.

Ostorero, Martine, Agostino Paravicini Bagliani, and Kathrin Utz Tremp, eds., with Catherine Chène. *L'imaginaire du sabbat: Édition critique des textes les plus anciens (1430 c.–1440 c.)*. Cahiers Lausannois d'Histoire Médiévale 26. Lausanne: Université de Lausanne, 1999.

Piché, David, ed. *La condamnation parisienne de 1277: Nouvelle édition du texte latin, traduction, introduction et commentaire*. Paris: Vrin, 1999.

Spee, Friedrich. *Cautio criminalis, or a Book on Witch Trials*. Translated by Marcus Hellyer. Charlottesville: University of Virginia Press, 2003.

Weyer, Johann. *On Witchcraft: An Abridged Translation of Johann Weyer's* De praestigiis daemonum. Edited by Benjamin G. Kohl and H. C. Erik Midelfort. Asheville, NC: Pegasus Press, 1998.

———. *Witches, Devils, and Doctors in the Renaissance: Johann Weyer*, De praestigiis daemonum. Edited by George Mora and Benjamin Kohl, with H. C. Erik Midelfort and Helen Bacon. Translated by John Shea. Binghampton: Medieval and Renaissance Texts and Studies, 1991.

William of Auvergne. *Opera omnia*. Venice: Damian Zenaro, 1591.

Secondary Sources

Anglo, Sydney. "Reginald Scot's *Discoverie of Witchcraft*: Scepticism and Sadduceeism." In *The Damned Art: Essays in the Literature of Witchcraft*, edited by Sydney Anglo, 106–139. London: Routledge and Kegan Paul, 1977.

Ankarloo, Bengt. "Witch Trials in Northern Europe 1450–1700." In *Magic and Witchcraft in Europe: The Period of the Witch Trials*, edited by Bengt Ankarloo and Stuart Clark, 53–95. Philadelphia: University of Pennsylvania Press, 2002.

Apps, Laura, and Andrew Gow. *Male Witches in Early Modern Europe*. Manchester: Manchester University Press, 2003.

Bailey, Michael D. "From Sorcery to Witchcraft: Clerical Conceptions of Magic in the Late Middle Ages." *Speculum* 76 (2001): 960–990.

———. "The Feminization of Magic and the Emerging Idea of the Female Witch in the Late Middle Ages." *Essays in Medieval Studies* 19 (2002): 120–134.

———. *Battling Demons: Witchcraft, Heresy, and Reform in the Late Middle Ages*. University Park: Penn State University Press, 2003.

———. *Magic and Superstition in Europe: A Concise History from Antiquity to the Present*. Critical Issues in History, edited by Donald T. Critchlow. Lanham, MD: Rowman & Littlefield Publishers, 2007.

Bibliography

Bailey, Michael D., Ronald Hutton, Gábor Klaniczay, William Monter, Rune Blix Hagen, and Fumiaki Nakanishi. "Shamanism and Witchcraft." *Magic, Ritual, and Witchcraft* 1 (2006): 207–241.

Baron, Frank. *Doctor Faustus: From History to Legend*. Munich: Fink, 1978.

Behringer, Wolfgang. *Witches and Witch-Hunts: A Global History*. Cambridge: Polity Press, 2004.

"How Waldensians Became Witches: Heretics and Their Journey to the Other World." In *Communicating with the Spirits*, edited by Gábor Klaniczay and Éva Pócs, in collaboration with Eszter Csonka-Takács, 155–192. Demons, Spirits, Witches 1. Budapest and New York: Central European University Press, 2005.

Bostridge, Ian. *Witchcraft and Its Transformations, c. 1650–1750*. Oxford: Clarendon Press, 1997.

Boudet, Jean-Patrice. *Entre science et nigromance: Astrologie, divination et magie dans l'Occident médiéval (XIIe–XVe siècle)*. Histoire ancienne et médiévale 83. Paris: Publications de la Sorbonne, 2006.

Boureau, Alain. *Satan the Heretic: The Birth of Demonology in the Medieval West*. Translated by Teresa Lavender Fagan. Chicago: University of Chicago Press, 2006.

Briggs, Robin. *Witches and Neighbors: The Social and Cultural Context of European Witchcraft*. New York: Viking, 1996.

Broedel, Hans Peter. *The Malleus maleficarum and the Construction of Witchcraft: Theology and Popular Belief*. Manchester: Manchester University Press, 2003.

Chène, Catherine, and Martine Ostorero. "Démonologie et misogynie: L'émergence d'un discours spécifique sur les femmes dans l'élaboration doctrinale du sabbat au XVe siècle." In *Les femmes dans la société européenne / Die Frauen in der europäischen Gesellschaft: 8e Congrès des Historiennes suisses / 8. Schweizerische Historikerinnentagung*, edited by Anne-Lisa Head-König and Liliane Mottu-Weber, 171–196. Geneva: Droz, 2000.

Clark, Stuart. "The 'Gendering' of Witchcraft in French Demonology: Misogyny or Polarity?" *French History* 5 (1991): 426–437.

Thinking with Demons: The Idea of Witchcraft in Early Modern Europe. Oxford: Clarendon Press, 1997.

Cohn, Norman. *Europe's Inner Demons: The Demonization of Christians in Medieval Christendom*. 2nd ed. Chicago: University of Chicago Press, 2000.

Decker, Rainer. *Witchcraft and the Papacy: An Account Drawing from the Formerly Secret Records of the Roman Inquisition*. Translated by H. C. Erik Midelfort. Charlottesville: University of Virginia Press, 2008.

Duni, Matteo. *Under the Devil's Spell: Witches, Sorcerers, and the Inquisition in Renaissance Italy*. The Villa Rossa Series: Intercultural Perspectives on Italy and Europe 2. Florence: Syracuse University in Florence, 2007.

Estes, Leland L. "Reginald Scot and His *Discoverie of Witchcraft*: Religion and Science in Opposition to the European Witch Craze." *Church History* 52 (1983): 444–456.

Fanger, Claire. "Introduction." In *Conjuring Spirits: Texts and Traditions of Medieval Ritual Magic*, edited by Claire Fanger, vii–xviii. University Park: Penn State University Press, 1998.

Fix, Andrew C. *Balthasar Bekker, Spirit Belief, and Confessionalism in the Seventeenth Century Dutch Republic*. Archives internationales d'histoire des idées 165. Dordrecht: Kluwer Academic Publishers, 1999.

Ginzburg, Carlo. *Ecstasies: Deciphering the Witches' Sabbath*. Translated by Raymond Rosenthal. New York: Pantheon, 1991.

Hansen, Joseph. *Zauberwahn, Inquisition, und Hexenprozesse im Mittelalter und die Entstehung der grossen Hexenverfolgung*. Munich: Oldenbourg, 1900.

Hersperger, Patrick. *Kirche, Magie, und "Aberglaube"*: Superstitio *in der Kanonistik des 12. und 13. Jahrhunderts*. Cologne: Böhlau, 2010.

Herzig, Tamar. "Witches, Saints, and Heretics: Heinrich Kramer's Ties with Italian Women Mystics." *Magic, Ritual, and Witchcraft* 1 (2006): 24–55.

——. "Flies, Heretics, and the Gendering of Witchcraft." *Magic, Ritual, and Witchcraft* 5 (2010): 51–80.

Iribarren, Isabel. "From Black Magic to Heresy: A Doctrinal Leap in the Pontificate of John XXII." *Church History* 76 (2007): 32–60.

Karlsen, Carol F. *The Devil in the Shape of a Woman: Witchcraft in Colonial New England*. Rev. ed. New York: Norton, 1998.

Kieckhefer, Richard. *Early European Witch Trials: Their Foundations in Popular and Learned Culture*. Berkeley and Los Angeles: University of California Press, 1976.

——. *Magic in the Middle Ages*. Cambridge: Cambridge University Press, 1989.

——. "The Specific Rationality of Medieval Magic." *American Historical Review* 99 (1994): 813–836.

——. "Avenging the Blood of Children: Anxiety over Child Victims and the Origins of the European Witch Trials." In *The Devil, Heresy and Witchcraft in the Middle Ages: Essays in Honour of Jeffrey B. Russell*, edited by Alberto Ferreiro, 91–110. Cultures, Beliefs, and Traditions 6. Leiden: Brill, 1998.

——. *Forbidden Rites: A Necromancer's Manual of the Fifteenth Century*. University Park: Penn State University Press, 1998.

——. "Did Magic Have a Renaissance? An Historiographic Question Revisited." In *Magic and the Classical Tradition*, edited by Charles Burnett and W. F. Ryan, 199–212. Warburg Institute Colloquia 7. London and Turin: Warburg Institute and Nino Aragno, 2006.

——. "Magic at Innsbruck: The Case of 1485 Reexamined." In *Religion und Magie in Ostmitteleuropa: Spielräume theologischer Normierungsprozesse in Spätmittelalter und Früher Neuzeit*, edited by Thomas Wünsch, 11–29. Religions- und Kulturgeschichte in Ostmittel- und Südosteuropa 8. Münster: LIT Verlag, 2006.

——. "Mythologies of Witchcraft in the Fifteenth Century." *Magic, Ritual, and Witchcraft* 1 (2006): 79–108.

Kivelson, Valerie A. "Lethal Convictions: The Power of a Satanic Paradigm in Russian and European Witch Trials." *Magic, Ritual, and Witchcraft* 6 (2011): 34–61.

Klaassen, Frank. "Medieval Ritual Magic in the Renaissance." *Aries* 3 (2003): 166–199.

Lea, Henry Charles. *A History of the Inquisition of the Middle Ages*. 3 vols. New York: Macmillan, 1888.

Lehrich, Christopher I. *The Language of Demons and Angels: Cornelius Agrippa's Occult Philosophy*. Leiden: Brill, 2003.

Levack, Brian P. "The Decline and End of Witchcraft Prosecutions." In *Witchcraft and Magic in Europe*, vol. 5, *The Eighteenth and Nineteenth Centuries*, edited by Bengt Ankarloo and Stuart Clark, 1–93. Philadelphia: University of Pennsylvania Press, 1999.

——. *The Witch-Hunt in Early Modern Europe*. 3rd ed. London: Pearson Longman, 2006.

Linsenmann, Thomas. *Die Magie bei Thomas von Aquin.* Veröffentlichungen des Grabbmann-Institutes zur Erforschung der mittelalterlichen Theologie und Philosophie 44. Berlin: Akademie Verlag, 2000.

Manitius, Karl. "Magie und Rhetorik bei Anselm von Besate." *Deutsches Archiv für Erforschung des Mittelalters* 12 (1956): 52–72.

de Mayo, Thomas B. *The Demonology of William of Auvergne: By Fire and Sword.* Lewiston, NY: Edwin Mellen Press, 2007.

Midelfort, H. C. Erik. "Witch Craze? Beyond the Legends of Panic." *Magic, Ritual, and Witchcraft* 6 (2011): 11–33.

Moeller, Katrin. *Dass Willkür über Recht ginge: Hexenverfolgung in Mecklenburg im 16. und 17. Jahrhundert.* Hexenforschung 10. Bielefeld: Verlag für Regionalgeschichte, 2007.

Monter, E. William. *Frontiers of Heresy: The Spanish Inquisition from the Basque Lands to Sicily.* Cambridge: Cambridge University Press, 1990.

———. "Witch Trials in Continental Europe 1560–1660." In *Magic and Witchcraft in Europe: The Period of the Witch Trials,* edited by Bengt Ankarloo and Stuart Clark, 1–52. Philadelphia: University of Pennsylvania Press, 2002.

Ostorero, Martine. *Le diable au sabbat: Littérature démonologique et sorcellerie (1440–1460).* Micrologus' Library 38. Florence: SISMEL, 2011.

Peters, Edward. *The Magician, the Witch, and the Law.* Philadelphia: University of Pennsylvania Press, 1978.

Roper, Lyndal. *Witch Craze: Terror and Fantasy in Baroque Germany.* New Haven: Yale University Press, 2004.

Rowlands, Alison, ed. *Witchcraft and Masculinities in Early Modern Europe.* New York: Palgrave Macmillan, 2009.

Russell, Jeffrey Burton. *Witchcraft in the Middle Ages.* Ithaca: Cornell University Press, 1972.

Schulte, Rolf. *Hexenmeister: Die Verfolgung von Männern im Rahmen der Hexenverfolgung von 1530–1730 im Alten Reich.* Frankfurt am Main: Peter Lang, 2000.

Stephens, Walter. *Demon Lovers: Witchcraft, Sex, and the Crisis of Belief.* Chicago: University of Chicago Press, 2002.

Tschacher, Werner. "Der Flug durch die Luft zwischen Illusionstheorie und Realitätsbeweis: Studien zum sog. Kanon Episcopi und zum Hexenflug." *Zeitschrift der Savigny-Stiftung für Rechtsgeschichte* 116, Kanonistische Abteilung 85 (1999): 225–276.

Utz Tremp, Kathrin. *Von der Häresie zur Hexerei: "Wirkliche" und imaginäre Sekten im Spätmittelalter.* Monumenta Germaniae Historica Schriften 59. Hannover: Hahnsche Buchhandlung, 2008.

———. "Witches' Brooms and Magic Ointments: Twenty Years of Witchcraft Research at the University of Lausanne (1989–2009)." *Magic, Ritual, and Witchcraft* 5 (2010): 173–187.

Veenstra, Jan R. "Venerating and Conjuring Angels: Eiximenis's *Book of the Holy Angels* and the *Holy Almandal:* Two Case Studies." In *Magic and the Classical Tradition,* edited by Charles Burnett and W. F. Ryan, 119–134. Warburg Institute Colloquia 7. London and Turin: Warburg Institute and Nino Aragno, 2006.

Véronèse, Julien. *L'Ars notoria au Moyen Âge: Introduction et édition critique.* Micrologus' Library 21, Salomon Latinus 1. Florence: SISMEL, 2007.

Walker, Daniel P. *Spiritual and Demonic Magic from Ficino to Campanella.* University Park: Penn State University Press, 2000.

Willis, Deborah. *Malevolent Nurture: Witch-Hunting and Maternal Power in Early Modern England*. Ithaca: Cornell University Press, 1995.

13 Magic and Priestcraft: Reformers and Reformation (by Helen Parish)

Primary Sources

Anon. *Here begynneth a booke called the fal of the Romish church wyth all the abhominations, wherby euery man may know and perceiue the diuersity of it, betwene the prymatiue church, of the which our souerayne Lorde and king is the supreme head, and the malignant church asunder*. London: W. Copland?, ca. 1550.

Augustine, *The City of God against the Pagans*, edited and translated by R. W. Dyson, Cambridge Texts in the History of Political Thought (Cambridge: Cambridge University Press, 1998), Book 10, chapter 9.

Aquinas, Thomas. *Summa contra gentiles*. Translated by the Fathers of the English Dominican Province. 4 vols. Einsiedeln: Benziger Brothers, 1928.

Summa theologiae. Translated by the Fathers of the English Dominican Province. 3 vols. Einsiedeln: Benziger Brothers, 1947.

Bale, John. *The vocacyon of Ioha[n] Bale to the bishiprick of Ossorie in Irela[n]de his persecucio[n]s in ye same, & finall delyueraunce*. Rome, i.e., Wesel: J. Lambrecht, 1553.

A mysterye of inyquyte contayned within the heretycall genealogye of Ponce Pantolabus, is here both dysclosed & confuted by Iohan Bale. Geneva, i.e., Antwerp: A. Goinus, 1545.

The lattre examinacyon of Anne Askewe latelye martyred in Smythfelde, by the wycked Synagoge of Antichrist, with the Elucydacyon of Iohan Bale. Marpurg, i.e., Wesel: D. van der Straten, 1547.

The apology of Iohan Bale agaynste a ranke papyst anuswering both hym and hys doctours, that neyther their vowes nor yet their priesthode areof the Gospell, but of Antichrist. Anno Do. M.CCCCC.L. A brefe exposycyon also upo[n] the .xxx chaptre of Numerii, which was the first occasion of thys present varyaunce. London: John Day, 1550.

The Image of Both Churches after the moste wonderful and heauenly Reuelacion of Sainct John. London: William Seres, 1550.

The First Two Partes of the Actes or unchast examples of the Englysh Votaryes. London: John Day, 1551.

Acta Romanorvm Pontificum a dispersione discipulorum Christi. Basel: Ioannis Oporini, 1558.

The Pageant of Popes. Translated by J. Studely. London: Thomas Marsh, 1574.

Actes of the English Votaries. London: Abraham Vele, 1551

Barnes, Robert. *A Supplicacion vnto the most gracious prynce H. the viij*. London: John Byddell, 1534.

Becon, Thomas. *Displaying of the Popish Masse in Prayers and Other Pieces*. Edited by J. Ayre. Cambridge: Parker Society, 1844.

Bede. *Vita Sancti Cuthberti*. Edited by B. Colgrave. Cambridge: Cambridge University Press, 1940.

de Besançon, Etienne. *Alphabet of Tales: An English 15th Century Translation of the Alphabetum narrationum of Etienne de Besançon, from Additional MS. 25,719 of the British Museum*. Ann Arbor: University of Michigan Humanities Text Initiative, 1997.

Bradford, John. *Two Notable Sermons ... the one of repentance, the other of the Lordes Supper.* London: Iohn Awdely and Iohn Wyght, 1581.

Calvin, J. *Institutes of the Christian Religion.* Edited by J. T. McNeill. Westminster: John Knox Press, 1973.

Corrie, G. E., ed. *Sermons and Remains of Hugh Latimer, Sometime Bishop of Winchester.* Cambridge: Parker Society, 1845.

Cranmer, Thomas. *A defence of the true and catholike doctrine of the sacrament of the body and bloud of our sauiour Christ with a confutacion of sundry errors concernyng the same, grounded and stablished vpon Goddes holy woorde, [and] approued by ye consent of the moste auncient doctors of the Churche.* London: R. Wolfe, 1550.

Crowley, Robert. *The confutation of the mishapen aunswer to the misnamed, wicked ballade, called the Abuse of ye blessed sacrame[n]t of the aultare Wherin, thou haste (gentele reader) the ryghte vnderstandynge of al the places of scripture that Myles Hoggard (wyth his learned counsail) hath wrested to make for the transubstantiation of the bread and wyne.* London: John Day and William Seres, 1548.

Dorman, Thomas. *A Proufe of Certeyne Articles in Religion Denied by M. Iuell.* Antwerp: Iohn Latius, 1564.

Dupuy, Pierre. *Histoire du differend d'entre le pape Boniface VIII et Philippe le Bel, Roy de France.* Paris: Cramoisy, 1655.

E. P. *A Confutation of Unwritten Verities ... made up by Thomas Cranmer.* Wesel?: J. Lambrecht?, 1556.

Erbe, T., ed. *Mirk's Festial: A Collection of Homilies.* London: Early English Texts Society, 1905.

Flacius, M., M. Judex, and J. Wigand, *Ecclesiastica historia.* Basel: I. Oporinum, 1559–1574.

Foxe, John. *The first volume of the Ecclesiasticall History conteyning the actes and monuments of thynges passed.* London: John Day, 1570.

Furnivall, F. J., ed. *Robert of Brunne's Handlynge Synne.* Early English Texts Society OS 119. London: Early English Texts Society, 1901.

Gregory the Great. "Life of St Benedict." In *Dialogues*, translated by O. Zimmerman, 75–77. Washington, DC: Catholic University of America Press, 1959.

Gualther, R. *Antichrist, that is to say A true reporte that Antichriste is come.* Southwark, i.e., Emden: Egidius van der Erve, 1556.

Hilarie, H. *The resurreccion of the masse, with the wonderful vertues of the same.* Strasbourg, i.e., Wesel: J. Lambrecht? for H. Singleton, 1554.

I. M. *A Briefe Recantation of Maystres Missa.* London: R.Wyer?, 1548.

Jewel, John. *Apology of the Church of England, 1562.* Edited by John Everitt Booty. Ithaca, NY: Cornell University Press, 1963.

John of Salisbury. *Policraticus.* Translated by C. Nederman. Cambridge: Cambridge University Press, 1990.

Lydgate, John. *Merita Missa.* In *The Lay Folks Mass Book*, edited by T. F. Simmons, appendix V, 148–154. Early English Texts Society OS 71. London: Early English Texts Society, 1879.

MacLure, M. *Register of Sermons preached at Paul's Cross.* London: Centre for Reformation and Renaissance Studies, 1989.

Marcourt, A. *A declaration of the masse the fruite thereof, the cause and the meane, wherefore and howe it ought to be maynteyned. Newly perused and augmented by the first author therof. Maister Anthony Marcort at Geneue. Tra[n]slated newly out of French into Englishe.* H. Lufte, i.e., London: John Day, 1547.

Mirk, John. *Instructions for Parish Priests*. Edited by E. Peacock. Early English Texts Society OS 31. London: Early English Texts Society, 1868.

Moone, P. *A short treatyse of certayne thinges abused in the Popysh Church longe vsed: but now abolyshed, to our consolation, and Gods word auaunced, the lyght of our saluation*. London: W. Copland, 1548.

Napier, J. *A Plaine discovery of the whole revelation of St John*. London: John Norton, 1611.

Punt, William. *A New Dialogue called the Endightment Agaynste Mother Masse*. London: William Hill and William Seres, 1548.

Ramsey, John. *A Plaister for a Galled Horse*. London: Thomas Raynalde, 1548.

Scot, R. *The Discoverie of Witchcraft*. London: William Brome, 1584.

Sheldon, R. *Survey of the Miracles of the Church of Rome*. London: Edward Griffin for Nathaniel Butter, 1616.

Shepherd, Luke. *Doctour Dubble Ale*. London: A. Scoloker?, 1548.

The Vpchering of the Messe. London: John Day and William Seres, 1548.

Smith, R. *The assertion and defence of the sacramente of the aulter. Compyled and made by mayster Richard Smythe doctour of diuinitie, and reader of the Kynges maiesties lesson in his graces vniuersitie of Oxforde, dedicate vnto his hyghnes, beynge the excellent and moost worthy defendour of Christes faythe*. London: John Hereford, 1546.

Stubbs, William. "Introduction." In *De gestis regum Anglorum*, edited by William Stubbs. London: H. M. S. O., 1887.

Swinnerton, T. *A Mustre of Scismatyke bysshopes of Rome otherwise naming them selues popes*. London: Johan Byddell, 1534.

Turner, W. *A New Dialogue Wherin is Conteyned the Examination of the Masse*. London: W. Hill, 1548.

The Huntyng of the Romishe Vvolfe. Emden: Egidius van der Erve, 1555.

Tyndale, William. *An Answer to Sir Thomas More's Dialogue*. Edited by H. Walter. Cambridge: Parker Society, 1850.

Veron, J. *The godly saiyngs of the old auncient faithful fathers vpon the Sacrament of the bodye and bloude of Chryste. Newlye compyled and translated oute of Latin intoo English. By Ihon Veron Senonoys*. Worcester: John Oswen, 1550.

de Voraigne, Iacobus. *The Golden Legend*. Translated by William Caxton. London: William Caxton, 1483.

William of Malmesbury. *Gesta Romanorum Pontificum*. Edited by David. Preest. Woodbridge: The Boydell Press, 2002.

Wycliffe, John. *Dialogus Sive Speculum Ecclesie Militantis*. Edited by A. W. Pollard. London: Wiclif Society, 1886.

Tractatus de Potestate Pape. Edited by Johann Loserth. London: Wiclif Society, 1907.

Secondary Sources

Bietenholz, P. *Historia and Fabula. Myths and Legends in Historical Thought from Antiquity to the Middle Ages*. Leiden: Brill, 1994.

Boase, Thomas S. R. *Boniface VIII*. London: Constable & Company, Limited, 1933.

Bossy, John. "The Mass as a Social Institution." *Past and Present* 100, no. 1 (1983): 29–61.

Bowd, Stephen. *Venice's Most Loyal City: Civic Identity in Renaissance Brescia*. Cambridge, MA: Harvard University Press, 2010.

Brigden, Susan. *London and the Reformation*. Oxford: Clarendon Press, 1991.

Brooke, C. N. J. "Religious Sentiment and Church Design in the Later Middle Ages." In *Medieval Church and Society. Collected Essays*, 162–182. London: Sidgwick and Jackson, 1971.

Brown, Peter. "Sorcery, Demons and the Rise of Christianity: From Late Antiquity in the Middle Ages." In *Witchcraft: Confessions and Accusations*, edited by Mary Douglas, 17–45. London: Tavistock, 1970.

Cameron, E. "For Reasoned Faith and Embattled Creed. Religion for the People in Early Modern Europe." *Transactions of the Royal Historical Society*, 6th series, 8 (1998): 165–187.

Clark, Stuart. *Thinking with Demons: The Idea of Witchcraft in Early Modern Europe*. Oxford: Oxford University Press, 1997.

 Vision in Early Modern European Culture. Oxford: Oxford University Press, 2007.

Delehaye, H. *The Legends of the Saints: An Introduction to Hagiography. From the French of Père Hippolyte. Delehaye, S. J., Bollandist.* Translated by V. M. Crawford. South Bend: University of Notre Dame Press, 1961.

Dinzelbacher, Peter. "Heilige oder Hexen." In *Religiöse Devianz: Untersuchungen zu sozialen, rechtlichen und theologischen Reaktionen auf religiöse Abweichung im westlichen und östlichen Mittelalter*, edited by D. Simon, 41–60. Frankfurt am Main: Peter Lang, 1990.

Donaldson, E. T. *Speaking of Chaucer*. London: The Athlone Press, 1970.

Duffy, Eamon. *The Stripping of the Altars: Traditional Religion in England c. 1400–c. 1580*. New Haven: Yale University Press, 1992.

Dugmore, C. *The Mass and the English Reformers*. London: St. Martin's Press, 1958.

Gairdner, James, ed. *The Historical Collections of a Citizen of London in the Fifteenth Century*. Camden Society New Series 17. Westminster: Camden Society, 1876.

Geertz, Hildred. "An Anthropology of Religion and Magic, I." *Journal of Interdisciplinary History* 6 (1975): 71–89.

Gentilcore, David. *From Bishop to Witch: The System of the Sacred in Early Modern Terra d'Otranto*. Manchester: Manchester University Press, 1992.

 Healers and Healing in Early Modern Italy. Manchester: Manchester University Press, 1998.

Grant, G. G. "The Elevation of the Host. A Reaction to the Twelfth Century Heresy." *Theological Studies* 1 (1940): 228–250.

Gurevich, A. *Medieval Popular Culture, Problems of Belief and Perception*. Cambridge: Cambridge University Press, 1988.

Harmening, Dieter. *Superstitio. Überlieferungs- und theoriegeschichtliche Untersuchungen zur kritisch-theologischen Aberglaubensliteratur des Mittelalters*. Berlin: E. Schmidt, 1979.

Harvey, M. "Papal Witchcraft: The Charges against Benedict XIII." *Studies in Church History* 10 (1973): 109–116.

Herzog, R. *Die Wunderheilungen von Epidauros*. Leipzig: Dieterich, 1931.

Hill, Joyce, and Swan, Mary, eds. *The Community, the Family and the Saint: Patterns of Power in Early Medieval Europe. Selected Proceedings of the International Medieval Congress, University of Leeds, 4–7 July 1994, 10–13 July 1995*. Turnhout: Brepols, 1998.

Huizinga, John. *The Waning of the Middle Ages*. London: Penguin Books, 1965.

Iliffe, R. "Lying Wonders and Juggling Tricks. Religion, Nature, and Imposture in Early Modern England." In *Everything Connects. In Conference with Richard H. Popkin. Essays in His Honour*, edited by J. E. Force and D. S. Katz, 185–209. Leiden: Brill, 1999.

Jolly, K., C. Raudvere, and E. Peters, eds. *Witchcraft and Magic in Europe*, vol. 3, *The Middle Ages*. London: The Athlone Press, 2002.

Kamerick, Kathleen. *Popular Piety and Art in the Late Middle Ages: Image Worship and Idolatry in England 1350–1500*. Basingstoke: Palgrave Macmillan, 2002.

Kee, Howard Clark. *Miracle in the Early Christian World. A Study in Sociohistorical Method*. New Haven: Yale University Press, 1983.

Kieckhefer, Richard. "The Holy and the Unholy. Sainthood, Witchcraft and Magic in Late Medieval Europe." *Journal of Medieval and Renaissance Studies* 24 (1994): 355–385.

   Magic in the Middle Ages. Cambridge: Cambridge University Press, 2000.

King, John. *English Reformation Literature. The Tudor Origins of the Protestant Tradition*. Princeton: Princeton University Press, 1986.

Klaniczay, Gabor. *The Uses of Supernatural Power: The Transformation of Popular Religion in Medieval and Early-Modern Europe*. Translated by S. Singerman. Princeton: Princeton University Press, 1990.

MacCulloch, D. *The Reign of Henry VIII: Politics, Policy and Piety*. New York: St. Martin's Press, 1995.

MacNeill, J. T., and H. M. Gamer. *Medieval Handbooks of Penance*. New York: Columbia University Press, 1990.

Malinowski, Bronislaw. *Magic, Science and Religion and Other Essays*. New York: Macmillan, 1925.

Marshall, Peter. *The Catholic Priesthood and the English Reformation*. Oxford: Clarendon Press, 1994.

   "Forgery and Miracles in the Reign of Henry VIII." *Past and Present* 178 (2003): 39–73.

Messenger, Ernst. *The Reformation, the Mass and the Priesthood. A Documented History with Special Reference to the Questions of Anglican Orders*. London: Longmans, Green & Co., 1936.

Milner, M. *The Senses and the English Reformation*. Burlington, VT: Ashgate, 2011.

Mommsen, T. M., and K. F. Morrison, eds. *Imperial Lives and Letters of the Eleventh Century*. New York: Columbia University Press, 1962.

Murray, Alexander C. "Missionaries and Magic in Dark-Age Europe." *Past and Present* 136 (1992): 186–205.

Oldoni, M. "Gerberto a la sua storia." *Studi medievali*, 3rd series, 18 (1977): 629–704.

Parish, Helen. "Impudent and Abominable Fictions: Rewriting Saints' Lives in the English Reformation." *Sixteenth Century Journal* 32 (2001): 45–65.

   Monks, Miracles and Magic: Reformation Representations of the Medieval Church. London: Routledge, 2005.

Remus, H. *Pagan Christian Conflict in the Second Century*. Cambridge, MA: Harvard University Press, 1983.

Rigault, Abel. *Le procès de Guichard, évêque de Troyes (1308–1313)*. Paris: A. Picard et fils, 1896.

Rollo, D. *Glamorous Sorcery. Magic and Literacy in the High Middle Ages*. Minneapolis: University of Minnesota Press, 2000.

Rubin, Miri. *Corpus Christi. The Eucharist in Late Medieval Culture*. Cambridge: Cambridge University Press, 1991.

Scribner, R. W. *Popular Culture and Popular Movements in Reformation Germany*. London–Ronceverte: Hambledon Press 1987.

Stacey, R. C. "From Ritual Crucifixion to Host Desecration: Jews and the Body of Christ." *Jewish History* 12, no. 1 (Spring 1998): 11–28.

Steinmeyer, Jim. *Hiding the Elephant: How Magicians Invented the Impossible and Learned to Disappear*. New York: Carroll and Graf, 2003.

Talbot, C. H. *The Anglo- Saxon Missionaries in Germany, Being the Lives of SS. Willibrord, Boniface, Sturm, Leoba, and Lebuin, Together with the Hodoeporicon of St. Willibald and a Selection from the Correspondence of St. Boniface*. London: Sheed and Ward, 1954.

Teter, Magda. *Sinners on Trial: Jews and Sacrilege after the Reformation*. Cambridge, MA, Harvard University Press, 2011.

Thomas, Keith. "An Anthropology of Religion and Magic, II." *Journal of Interdisciplinary History* 6 (1975): 91–109.

Religion and the Decline of Magic. London: Penguin Books, 1991.

Thorndike, Lynn. *A History of Magic and Experimental Science*. Vol. 2. New York: Columbia University Press, 1929.

Valois, N. *La France et le grand schisme d'Occident*. Paris: Picard et fils, 1902. Reprint, Hildesheim: G. Ohms, 1967.

Veenstra, Jan R. *Magic and Divination at the Courts of Burgundy and France: Text and Context of Laurens Pignon's "Contre les devineurs" (1411)*. Brill's Studies in Intellectual History, edited by Arie Johan Vanderjagt. Leiden: Brill, 1998.

Vincke, J. "Acta concilii Pisani." *Romische Quartalschrift* 46 (1938): 213–294.

Walker, D. P. "The Cessation of Miracles." In *Hermeticism and the Renaissance. Intellectual History and the Occult in Early Modern Europe*, edited by I. Merkel and A. G. Debus, 110–124. Washington, DC: Folger Shakespeare Library, 1988.

Walsham, Alexandra. *Providence in Early Modern England*. Oxford: Oxford University Press, 1999.

14 Spain and Mexico (by Louise M. Burkhart)

Aguirre Beltrán, Gonzalo. *Medicina y magia: El proceso de aculturación en la estructura colonial*. Mexico: Instituto Nacional Indigenista, 1963.

Baudot, Georges. *Utopia and History in Mexico: The First Chronicles of Mexican Civilization, 1520–1569*. Translated by Bernard R. Ortiz de Montellano and Thelma Ortiz de Montellano. Niwot: University Press of Colorado, 1995.

Behar, Ruth. "Sex and Sin: Witchcraft and the Devil in Late-Colonial Mexico." *American Ethnologist* 14 (1987): 34–54.

"Sexual Witchcraft, Colonialism, and Women's Powers: Views from the Mexican Inquisition." In *Sexuality and Marriage in Colonial Latin America*, edited by Asunción Lavrin, 178–206. Lincoln and London: University of Nebraska Press, 1989.

Behringer, Wolfgang. *Witches and Witch-Hunts: A Global History*. Cambridge: Polity Press, 2004.

Bricker, Victoria Reifler. *The Indian Christ, the Indian King: The Historical Substrate of Maya Myth and Ritual*. Austin: University of Texas Press, 1981.

Bristol, Joan. *Christians, Blasphemers, and Witches: Afro-Mexican Ritual Practice in the Seventeenth Century*. Albuquerque: University of New Mexico Press, 2007.

Burkhart, Louise M. *The Slippery Earth: Nahua-Christian Moral Dialogue in Sixteenth-Century Mexico*. Tucson: University of Arizona Press, 1989.

"The Cult of the Virgin of Guadalupe in Mexico." In *World Spirituality: An Encyclopedic History of the Religious Quest*, vol. 4, *South and Meso-American Native Spirituality*, edited by Gary H. Gossen and Miguel León-Portilla, 198–227. New York: Crossroad Press, 1993.

"Pious Performances: Christian Pageantry and Native Identity in Early Colonial Mexico." In *Native Traditions in the Postconquest World*, edited by Elizabeth Hill Boone and Tom Cummins, 361–381. Washington, DC: Dumbarton Oaks, 1998.

Before Guadalupe: The Virgin Mary in Early Colonial Nahuatl Literature. Albany: Institute for Mesoamerican Studies, State University of New York at Albany, 2001.

de Castañega, Martín. *Tratado de las supersticiones y hechicerías*. Edited by Fabián Alejandro Campagne. Buenos Aires: Universidad de Buenos Aires, 1997.

Cervantes, Fernando. *The Devil in the New World: The Impact of Diabolism in New Spain*. New Haven: Yale University Press, 1994.

Chimalpahin Quauhtlehuanitzin, Domingo de San Antón Muñón. *Codex Chimalpahin*. Vol. 1. Edited and translated by Arthur J. O. Anderson and Susan Schroeder. Norman: University of Oklahoma Press, 1997.

Annals of His Time. Edited and translated by James Lockhart, Susan Schroeder, and Doris Namala. Stanford: Stanford University Press, 2006.

Christian, William A. *Apparitions in Late Medieval and Renaissance Spain*. Princeton: Princeton University Press, 1981.

Local Religion in Sixteenth-Century Spain. Princeton: Princeton University Press, 1981.

Clendinnen, Inga. *Ambivalent Conquests: Maya and Spaniard in Yucatan, 1517–1570*. Cambridge: Cambridge University Press, 1987.

"Ways to the Sacred: Reconstructing 'Religion' in Sixteenth-Century Mexico." *Anthropology and History* 5 (1990): 105–141.

Aztecs: An Interpretation. Cambridge: Cambridge University Press, 1991.

de la Cruz, Martín. *The Badianus Manuscript (Codex Barberini, Latin 241)*. Edited and translated by Emily Emmart. Baltimore: Johns Hopkins University Press, 1940.

Durán, Diego. *Book of the Gods and Rites and the Ancient Calendar*. Edited and translated by Fernando Horcasitas and Doris Heyden. Norman: University of Oklahoma Press, 1971.

Farriss, Nancy. *Maya Society under Colonial Rule*. Princeton: Princeton University Press, 1984.

Few, Martha. *Women Who Live Evil Lives: Gender, Religion, and the Politics of Power in Colonial Guatemala*. Austin: University of Texas Press, 2002.

Foster, George E. "Nagualism in Mexico and Guatemala." *Acta Americana* 2 (1944): 85–103.

Frazer, James. *The Golden Bough: A Study in Magic and Religion*. Project Gutenberg eBook. http://www.gutenberg.org/dirs/etext03/bough11h.htm.

Furst, Jill Leslie McKeever. *The Natural History of the Soul in Ancient Mexico*. New Haven: Yale University Press, 1995.

Gosner, Kevin. *Soldiers of the Virgin: The Moral Economy of a Colonial Maya Rebellion*. Tucson: University of Arizona Press, 1992.

Greenleaf, Richard E. *Zumárraga and the Mexican Inquisition 1536–1543*. Washington, DC: Academy of American Franciscan History, 1961.

Hughes, Jennifer Scheper. *Biography of a Mexican Crucifix: Lived Religion and Local Faith from the Conquest to the Present*. Oxford: Oxford University Press, 2010.

Jaffary, Nora E. *False Mystics: Deviant Orthodoxy in Colonial Mexico*. Lincoln and London: University of Nebraska Press, 2004.

Kamen, Henry. *The Spanish Inquisition: An Historical Revision*. London: Weidenfeld & Nicolson, 1997.

Keen, Benjamin. *The Aztec Image in Western Thought*. New Brunswick: Rutgers University Press, 1971.

Klor de Alva, J. Jorge. "Colonizing Souls: The Failure of the Indian Inquisition and the Rise of Penitential Discipline." In *Cultural Encounters: The Impact of the Inquisition in Spain and the New World*, edited by Mary Elizabeth Perry and Anne J. Cruz, 3–22. Berkeley: University of California Press, 1991.

Knab, Timothy J. *The Dialogue of Earth and Sky: Dreams, Souls, Curing, and the Modern Aztec Underworld*. Tucson: University of Arizona Press, 2004.

de León, Martín. *Camino del cielo en lengua mexicana*. Mexico City: Diego López Dávalos, 1611.

Lewis, Laura A. *Hall of Mirrors: Power, Witchcraft, and Caste in Colonial Mexico*. Durham and London: Duke University Press, 2003.

Lockhart, James. *The Nahuas after the Conquest: A Social and Cultural History of the Indians of Central Mexico, Sixteenth through Eighteenth Centuries*. Stanford: Stanford University Press, 1992.

Lopes Don, Patricia. "Franciscans, Indian Sorcerers, and the Inquisition in New Spain, 1536–1543." *Journal of World History* 17 (2006): 27–49.

López Austin, Alfredo. "Los temacpalitotique. Brujos, profanadores, ladrones y violadores." *Estudios de cultura náhuatl* 6 (1966): 97–118.

"Cuarenta clases de magos del mundo náhuatl." *Estudios de cultura náhuatl* 7 (1967): 87–117.

Cuerpo humano e ideología: Las concepciones de los antiguos nahuas. 2 vols. Mexico City: Universidad Nacional Autónoma de México, 1984.

Lorenzana, Francisco Antonio. *Concilios provinciales primero y segundo celebrados en la muy noble, y muy leal ciudad de México*. Mexico City: Imprenta del Superior Gobierno, 1768.

Malinowski, Bronislaw. "Magic, Science and Religion." In *Magic, Science and Religion and Other Essays*, 17–92. Garden City, NY: Doubleday Anchor Books, 1954.

Mauss, Marcel. *A General Theory of Magic*. Translated by Robert Brain. New York: W. W. Norton, 1972.

de Molina, Alonso. *Vocabulario en lengua castellana y mexicano y mexicano y castellano*. Edited by Miguel León-Portilla. Facsimile of 1571 ed. Mexico City: Editorial Porrúa, 1970.

Moreno de los Arcos, Roberto. "New Spain's Inquisition for Indians from the Sixteenth to the Nineteenth Century." In *Cultural Encounters: The Impact of the Inquisition in Spain and the New World*, edited by Mary Elizabeth Perry and Anne J. Cruz, 23–36. Berkeley: University of California Press, 1991.

Motolinia (Toribio de Benavente). *Historia de los indios de la Nueva España*. Edited by Edmundo O'Gorman. Mexico City: Editorial Porrúa, 1979.

de Olmos, Andrés. *Advertencias para los confesores de los naturales*. Mexico City: Melchor Ocharte, 1600.

Tratado de hechicerías y sortilegios. Edited and translated by Georges Baudot. Mexico City: Universidad Nacional Autónoma de México, 1990.

Ortiz de Montellano, Bernard R. *Aztec Medicine, Health, and Nutrition.* New Brunswick: Rutgers University Press, 1990.

Osowski, Edward W. *Indigenous Miracles: Nahua Authority in Colonial Mexico.* Tucson: University of Arizona Press, 2010.

Phelan, John Leddy. *The Millennial Kingdom of the Franciscans in the New World.* Berkeley and Los Angeles: University of California Press, 1970.

"Las representaciones teatrales de la pasión." *Boletín del Archivo General de la Nación* 5 (1934): 353.

Reyes Valerio, Constantino. *Tepalcingo.* Mexico City: Instituto Nacional de Antropología e Historia, 1960.

Ricard, Robert. *The Spiritual Conquest of Mexico.* Translated by Lesley Byrd Simpson. Berkeley: University of California Press, 1966.

Ruiz de Alarcón, Hernando. *Aztec Sorcerers in Seventeenth-Century Mexico: The Treatise on Superstitions by Hernando Ruiz de Alarcón.* Edited and translated by Michael D. Coe and Gordon Whittaker. Albany: Institute for Mesoamerican Studies, State University of New York at Albany, 1982.

de Sahagún, Bernardino. *Florentine Codex, General History of the Things of New Spain.* Edited and translated by Arthur J. O. Anderson and Charles E. Dibble. 12 vols. Santa Fe: School of American Research and University of Utah, 1950–1982.

———. *Historia general de las cosas de Nueva España, Códice florentino.* Facsimile of the *Codex Florentinus* of the Biblioteca Medicea Laurenziana. 3 vols. Mexico City: Archivo General de la Nación, 1979.

Sell, Barry D., and John Frederick Schwaller, eds. and trans., with Lu Ann Homza. *Don Bartolomé de Alva, Guide to Confession Large and Small in the Mexican Language. Critical edition of the 1634 edition.* Norman: University of Oklahoma Press, 1999.

de la Serna, Jacinto. "Manual de los ministros de indios para el conocimiento de sus idolatrías, y extirpación de ellas." In *Tratado de las supersticiones, dioses, ritos, hechicerías y otras costumbres gentílicas de las razas aborígenes de México*, edited by Francisco del Paso y Troncoso, 39–368. Mexico City: Ediciones Fuente Cultural, 1953.

Sousa, Lisa. "The Devil and Deviance in Native Criminal Narratives from Early Mexico." *The Americas* 59 (2002): 161–179.

Summers, Montague, ed. and trans. *The Malleus maleficarum of Heinrich Kramer and Joseph Sprenger.* New York: Dover, 1971.

Tavárez, David. *The Invisible War: Indigenous Devotions, Discipline, and Dissent in Colonial Mexico.* Stanford: Stanford University Press, 2011.

Tedlock, Barbara. *Time and the Highland Maya.* Albuquerque: University of New Mexico Press, 1982.

Villa-Flores, Javier. "Talking through the Chest: Divination and Ventriloquism among African Slave Women in Seventeenth-Century Mexico." *Colonial Latin American Review* 14 (2005): 299–321.

Wake, Eleanor. *Framing the Sacred: The Indian Churches of Early Colonial Mexico.* Norman: University of Oklahoma Press, 2009.

Weckmann, Luis. *La herencia medieval de México.* 2 vols. Mexico City: Colegio de México, 1984.

Wood, Stephanie. "Adopted Saints: Christian Images in Nahua Testaments of Late Colonial Toluca." *The Americas* 47 (1991): 259–293.

15 Folk Magic in British North America (by Richard Godbeer)

Primary Sources

Boyer, Paul, and Stephen Nissenbaum, eds. *Salem-Village Witchcraft: A Documentary Record of Local Conflict in Colonial New England*. Belmont, CA: Wadsworth Pub. Co., 1972. Reprint, Boston: Northeastern University Press, 1993.

Cooper, James F., Jr., and Kenneth P. Minkema, eds. *The Sermon Notebook of Samuel Parris, 1689–1694*. Boston: Colonial Society of Massachusetts, 1993.

Danforth, Samuel. *An Astronomical Description of the Late Comet or Blazing Star*. Cambridge: Samuel Green, 1665.

Dexter, Franklin Bowditch, ed. *The Literary Diary of Ezra Stiles*. 3 vols. New York: Charles Scribner's Sons, 1901.

Ellison and Mulligan Receipt Book. Hutson Family Papers, 34/570. South Carolina Historical Society, Charleston, SC.

Garrett, Margaret. Testimony, June 17, 1665. Willys Papers: Records of Trials for Witchcraft in Connecticut, W-4. Brown University Library, Providence.

Hale, John. *A Modest Enquiry into the Nature of Witchcraft*. Boston: B. Green, and J. Allen, 1702.

Hall, David D., ed. *Witch-Hunting in Seventeenth-Century New England: A Documentary History, 1658–1693*. 2nd ed. Boston: Northeastern University Press, 1999.

Hoadly, Charles J., ed. *Records of the Colony or Jurisdiction of New Haven*. 2 vols. New Haven: Lockwood and Company, 1857–1858.

Lawson, Deodat. *A Brief and True Narrative of Some Remarkable Passages Relating to Sundry Persons Afflicted by Witchcraft at Salem Village*. Boston: Benjamin Harris, 1692.

———. *Christ's Fidelity the Only Shield against Satan's Malignity*. Boston: Benjamin Harris, 1692.

Lawson, John. *A New Voyage to Virginia*. Edited by Hugh Talmage Lefler. Chapel Hill: University of North Carolina Press, 1967.

LeBreton, Edward, and Thomas Bandmill. Depositions, April 11, 1671. Northumberland County Record Book, 1666–1672. Library of Virginia, Richmond. Reprint in "The Good Luck Horseshoe." *William and Mary Quarterly*, 1st series, 17, no. 4 (April 1909): 247–248.

Mather, Cotton. "A Brand Pluck't Out of the Burning." In *Narratives of the Witchcraft Cases, 1648–1706*, edited by George Lincoln Burr, 89–143. New York: Charles Scribner's Sons, 1914.

———. *A Discourse on Witchcraft*. Boston, 1689.

———. "Paper on Witchcraft." *Proceedings of Massachusetts Historical Society* 47 (1914): 265–266.

———. *Wonders of the Invisible World*. Boston, 1692.

Mather, Increase. *Heaven's Alarm to the World*. Boston, 1682.

———. *Kometographia*. Boston: Brabazon Aylmer, 1683.

———. *An Essay for the Recording of Illustrious Providences*. Boston: Samuel Green, 1684.

Mathews, Maurice. Letter, Charleston, May 18, 1680. South Caroliniana Library, Columbia, SC. Reprint in "A Contemporary View of Carolina in 1680." *South Carolina Historical Magazine* 55, no. 3 (July 1954): 153–159.

McGiffert, Michael, ed. *God's Plot: The Paradoxes of Puritan Piety, Being the Autobiography and Journal of Thomas Shepard*. Amherst: University of Massachusetts Press, 1972.

McIlwaine, H. R., ed. *Minutes of the Council and General Court of Colonial Virginia, 1622–1632, 1670–1676.* Richmond: Colonial Press, 1924.

Morton, Charles. "Compendium Physicae." *Collections of the Colonial Society of Massachusetts* 33 (1940): 29.

Middlesex Court Files, fol. 25, no. 4. Massachusetts State Archives, Columbia Point, MA.

Noyes, Nicholas. *New England's Duty and Interest.* Boston: Benjamin Harris, and John Allen, 1698.

Rosenthal, Bernard, ed. *Records of the Salem Witch Hunt.* New York: Cambridge University Press, 2008.

Turrell, Ebenezer. "Detection of Witchcraft." *Collections of the Massachusetts Historical Society,* 2nd series, 10 (1823): 19–20.

Wallett, Francis, ed. *The Diary of Ebenezer Parkman, 1703–1782.* Worcester, MA: American Antiquarian Society, 1974.

Willard, Samuel. *The Danger of Taking God's Name in Vain.* Boston: Benjamin Harris, and John Allen, 1691.

The Christian's Exercise by Satan's Temptations. Boston: B. Green, and J. Allen, 1701.

Secondary Sources

Bonomi, Patricia U. *Under the Cope of Heaven: Religion, Society, and Politics in Colonial America.* 2nd ed. New York: Oxford University Press, 2003.

Boyer, Paul, and Stephen Nissenbaum. *Salem Possessed: The Social Origins of Witchcraft.* Cambridge, MA: Harvard University Press, 1976.

Butler, Jon. *Awash in a Sea of Faith: Christianizing the American People.* Cambridge, MA: Harvard University Press, 1990.

Delbanco, Andrew. *The Puritan Ordeal.* Cambridge, MA: Harvard University Press, 1989.

Demos, John Putnam. *Entertaining Satan: Witchcraft and the Culture of Early New England.* New York: Oxford University Press, 1982.

Drake, Samuel. *Annals of Witchcraft in New England.* Boston: W. Elliot Woodward, 1869. Reprint, New York: Burt Franklin, 1972.

Games, Alison. *Witchcraft in Early North America.* American Controversies Series. Lanham, MD: Rowman & Littlefield Publishers, 2010.

Godbeer, Richard. *The Devil's Dominion: Magic and Religion in Early New England.* New York: Cambridge University Press, 1992.

Flint, Valerie I. J. *The Rise of Magic in Early Medieval Europe.* Princeton: Princeton University Press, 1991.

Galvin, Mary L. "Decoctions for Carolinians: The Creation of a Creole Medicine Chest in Colonial South Carolina." In *Creolization in the Americas,* edited by David Buisseret and Steven G. Reinhardt. College Station, TX: Texas A&M University Press, 2000.

Hall, David D. *Worlds of Wonder, Days of Judgment: Popular Religious Belief in Early New England.* New York: Knopf, 1989.

Hambrick-Stowe, Charles. *The Practice of Piety: Puritan Devotional Disciplines in Seventeenth-Century New England.* Chapel Hill: University of North Carolina Press, 1982.

Hansen, Chadwick. *Witchcraft at Salem.* New York: Braziller, 1969.

Karlsen, Carol F. *The Devil in the Shape of a Woman: Witchcraft in Colonial New England.* New York: Norton, 1987.

Kieckhefer, Richard. *Magic in the Middle Ages.* New York: Cambridge University Press, 1990.

Kittredge, George L. *Witchcraft in Old and New England*. Cambridge, MA: Harvard University Press, 1929. Reprint, New York: Russell and Russell, 1956.

Klaniczay, Gabor. *The Uses of Supernatural Power: The Transformation of Popular Religion in Medieval and Early-Modern Europe*. Translated by S. Singerman. Princeton: Princeton University Press, 1990.

Laing, Annette. "All Things to All Men: Popular Religious Culture and the Anglican Mission in Colonial America, 1701–1750." PhD diss., University of California at Riverside, 1995.

"A Very Immoral and Offensive Man: Religious Culture, Gentility, and the Strange Case of Brian Hunt, 1727." *South Carolina Historical Magazine* 103 (2002): 6–29.

Leventhal, Herbert. *In the Shadow of the Enlightenment: Occultism and Renaissance Science in Eighteenth-Century America*. New York: New York University Press, 1976.

Morgan, Philip D. *Slave Counterpoint: Black Culture in the Eighteenth-Century Chesapeake and Lowcountry*. Chapel Hill: University of North Carolina Press, 1998.

Norton, Mary Beth. *In the Devil's Snare: The Salem Witchcraft Crisis of 1692*. New York: Knopf, 2002.

Pettit, Norman. *The Heart Prepared: Grace and Conversion in Puritan Spiritual Life*. New Haven: Yale University Press, 1966.

Reis, Elizabeth. *Damned Women: Sinners and Witches in Puritan New England*. Ithaca: Cornell University Press, 1997.

Sobel, Mechal. *The World They Made Together: Black and White Values in Eighteenth-Century Virginia*. Princeton: Princeton University Press, 1987.

Taylor, Alan. "The Early Republic's Supernatural Economy: Treasure-Seeking in the American North-East, 1780–1830." *American Quarterly* 38 (1986): 6–34.

Thomas, Keith. *Religion and the Decline of Magic*. New York: Charles Scribner's Sons, 1971.

Weisman, Richard. *Witchcraft, Magic, and Religion in Seventeenth-Century Massachusetts*. Amherst: University of Massachusetts Press, 1984.

Woodward, Walter W. *Prospero's America: John Winthrop, Jr., Alchemy, and the Creation of New England Culture*. Chapel Hill: University of North Carolina Press, 2009.

16 Colonial Magic: The Dutch East Indies
(by Margaret J. Wiener)

Ankarloo, Bengt, and Stuart Clark, eds. *Witchcraft and Magic in Europe*, vol. 5, *The Eighteenth and Nineteenth Centuries*. Philadelphia: University of Pennsylvania, 1999.

Witchcraft and Magic in Europe, vol. 6, *The Twentieth Century*. Philadelphia: University of Pennsylvania, 1999.

Bekker, Balthasar. *The World Bewitch'd, or, An Examination of the Common Opinions Concerning Spirits*. London: R. Baldwin in Warwick Lane, 1695.

Berg, C. C. "Verfijnde Vormen van Tooverij in de Hindoe-Javaansche Maatschappij . [Refined Forms of Magic in Hindu-Javanese Society]." In *Hekserij in de missielanden. Nederlandsche Verslagen der XIVe Missiologische Week van Leuven*, edited by Z. E. P. van Reeth, 67–108. Brussels: Boekhandel-Uitgeverij Universum, N.V., 1936.

De Blécourt, Willem. "The Witch, Her Victim, the Unwitcher and the Researcher: The Continued Existence of Traditional Witchcraft." In *Witchcraft and Magic in Europe*, vol. 6, *The Twentieth Century*, edited by Bengt Ankarloo and Stuart Clark, 141–219. Philadelphia: University of Pennsylvania, 1999.

"Boiling Chickens and Burning Cats: Witchcraft in the Western Netherlands, 1850–1925." In *Witchcraft Continued: Popular Magic in Modern Europe*, edited by Willem de Blécourt and Owen Davies, 89–106. Manchester and New York: Manchester University Press, 2004.

De Blécourt, Willem, and Owen Davies, eds. *Witchcraft Continued: Popular Magic in Modern Europe*. Manchester and New York: Manchester University Press, 2004.

Blussé, Leonard. *Strange Company: Chinese Settlers, Mestizo Women, and the Dutch in VOC Batavia*. Dordrecht: Foris, 1986.

Burns, Peter. *The Leiden Legacy: Concepts of Law in Indonesia*. Leiden: KITLV Press, 2004.

Davies, Owen, and Willem de Blécourt. *Beyond the Witch Trials: Witchcraft and Magic in Enlightenment Europe*. Manchester: Manchester University Press, 2004.

During, Simon. *Modern Enchantments: The Cultural Power of Secular Magic*. Cambridge, MA: Harvard University Press, 2004.

Fasseur, Cees. *De weg naar het paradijs en andere Indische geschiedenissen*. Amsterdam: Bert Bakker, 1995.

Favret Saada, Jeanne. *Deadly Words: Witchcraft in the Bocage*. Cambridge: Cambridge University Press, 1981.

Fields, Karen, E. "Political Contingencies of Witchcraft in Colonial Central Africa: Culture and the State in Marxist Theory." *Canadian Journal of African Studies* 16, no. 3 (1982): 567–593.

Frijhoff, Willem. "Witchcraft and Its Changing Representation in Eastern Gelderland from the Sixteenth to Twentieth Centuries." In *Witchcraft in the Netherlands: From the Fourteenth to the Twentieth Century*, edited by Marijke Gijswijt-Hofstra and Willem Frijhoff, 167–181. Rotterdam: Universitaire Pers, 1991.

Gijswijt-Hofstra, Marijke. "Six Centuries of Witchcraft in the Netherlands: Themes, Outlines, and Interpretations." In *Witchcraft in the Netherlands: From the Fourteenth to the Twentieth Century*, edited by Marijke Gijswijt-Hofstra and Willem Frijhoff, 1–36. Rotterdam: Universitaire Pers, 1991.

"Witchcraft after the Witch-Trials." In *Witchcraft and Magic in Europe*, vol. 5, *The Eighteenth and Nineteenth Centuries*, edited by Bengt Ankarloo and Stuart Clark, 95–190. Philadelphia: University of Pennsylvania Press, 1999.

Gijswijt-Hofstra, Marijke, and Willem Frijhoff, eds. *Witchcraft in the Netherlands: From the Fourteenth to the Twentieth Century*. Rotterdam: Universitaire Pers, 1991.

Gluckman, Max. "The Magic of Despair." In *Order and Rebellion in Tribal Africa*, 137–145. London: Cohen & West, 1963.

Guha, Ranajit. *Dominance without Hegemony: History and Power in Colonial India*. Cambridge, MA: Harvard University Press, 1998.

Hegel, Georg W. F. *The Philosophy of History*. Translated by J. Sibree. 1837. Reprint, Buffalo: Prometheus Press, 1991.

Hekmeijer, F. C. *Wetboek van Strafrecht voor Nederlandsche Indië*. 2nd ed. Weltevreden and Batavia: G. Kolff, 1918.

Hobsbawm, E., and T. Ranger, eds. *The Invention of Tradition*. Cambridge: Cambridge University Press, 1992.

Hoekendijk, C. J. *De Toovenaar der Soendalanden.* Hoenderloo: Drukkerij Stichting Hoenderloo, 1941.

Holleman, J. F., ed. *Van Vollenhoven on Indonesian Adat Law.* The Hague: Martinus Nijhoff, 1981.

De Kat Angelino, P. "De Léak op Bali." *Tijdschrift voor Indische Taal-, Land-, en Volkenkunde van het Koninklijk Bataviaasch Genootschap van Kunsten en Wetenschappen* 60, no. 1 (1921): 1–44.

Der Kinderen, T. H. "Bijgeloof in de Preanger Regentschappen." *Het Regt in Nederlands-Indië* 9, no. 17 (1859): 299–302.

Lesquillier, Nicolaas Willem. *Het Adatdelictenrecht in de Magische Wereldbeschouwing.* Leiden: N. V. Boek- en Steendrukkerij Eduward Ijdo, 1934.

Levack, Brian P. "The Decline and End of Witchcraft Prosecutions." In *Witchcraft and Magic in Europe,* vol. 5, *The Eighteenth and Nineteenth Centuries,* edited by Bengt Ankarloo and Stuart Clark, 1–93. Philadelphia: University of Pennsylvania Press, 1999.

Lévi-Strauss, Claude. "The Sorcerer and His Magic." In *Structural Anthropology,* vol. 1, 167–185. New York: Basic Books, 1963.

Luongo, Katherine. *Witchcraft and Colonial Rule in Kenya, 1900–1955.* Cambridge: Cambridge University Press, 2011.

Mazee, G. W. "Over Heksen-Moord en de Berechting Daarvan." *Tijdschrift voor het Binnenlandsch Bestuur* 41 (1911): 396–401.

Mesaki, Simeon. "Witchcraft and the Law in Tanzania." *International Journal of Sociology and Anthropology* 1, no. 8 (2009): 132–138.

Pels, Peter. "The Magic of Africa: Reflections on a Western Commonplace." *African Studies Review* 41, no. 3 (1998): 193–209.

Pietz, William. "The Problem of the Fetish, I." *Res* 9 (1985): 5–17.

"The Problem of the Fetish, II: The Origin of the Fetish." *Res* 13 (1987): 23–45.

"The Problem of the Fetish, IIIa: Bosman's Guinea and the Enlightenment Theory of Fetishism." *Res* 16 (1988): 105–124.

Porter, Roy. "Witchcraft and Magic in Enlightenment, Romantic, and Liberal Thought." In *Witchcraft and Magic in Europe,* vol. 5, *The Eighteenth and Nineteenth Centuries,* edited by Bengt Ankarloo and Stuart Clark, 191–282. Philadelphia: University of Pennsylvania Press, 1999.

Van Reeth, Z. E. P., et al, ed. *Hekserij in de Missielanden. Nederlandsche Verslagen der XIVe Missiologische Week van Leuven.* Brussels: Boekhandel-Uitgeverij Universum, N.V., 1936.

De Roo, L. W. G. "Een Tovenaar in Batavia Verbrand." *Het Regt in Nederlandsch-Indië* 22 (1866): 13–14.

Siegel, James. *Naming the Witch.* Stanford: Stanford University Press, 2006.

Silverblatt, Irene. *Modern Inquisitions: Peru and the Colonial Origins of the Civilized World.* Durham: Duke University Press, 2004.

Sonius, H. W. J. "Introduction." In *Van Vollenhoven on Indonesian Adat Law,* edited by J. F. Holleman, xxix–lxvii. The Hague: Martinus Nijhoff, 1981.

Strathern, Marilyn. *Partial Connections.* 1991. Walnut Creek, CA: AltaMira, 2004.

Stronks, G. J. "The Significance of Balthasar Bekker's *The Enchanted World.*" In *Witchcraft in the Netherlands: From the Fourteenth to the Twentieth Century,* edited by Marijke Gijswijt-Hofstra and Willem Frijhoff, 149–156. Rotterdam: Universitaire Pers, 1991.

Taylor, Jean Gelman. *The Social World of Batavia: European and Eurasian in Dutch Asia*. Madison: University of Wisconsin Press, 1983.

Tsing, Anna Lowenhaupt. *Friction: An Ethnography of Global Connection*. Princeton: Princeton University Press, 2004.

Watson, C. W., and Roy Ellen. eds. *Understanding Witchcraft and Sorcery in Southeast Asia*. Honolulu: University of Hawaii Press, 1993.

Wiener, Margaret. *Visible and Invisible Realms: Power, Magic, and Colonial Conquest in Bali*. Chicago: University of Chicago Press, 1995.

———. "Hidden Forces: Colonialism and the Politics of Magic in the Netherlands Indies." In *Magic and Modernity: Interfaces of Revelation and Concealment*, edited by Birgit Meyer and Peter Pels, 129–158. Stanford: Stanford University Press, 2003.

———. "Dangerous Liaisons and Other Tales from the Twilight Zone: Sex, Race, and Sorcery in Colonial Java." *Comparative Studies in Society and History* 49, no. 3 (2007): 495–526.

———. "The Magical Life of Things." In *Colonial Collections Revisited*, edited by P. ter Keurs, 45–70. Leiden: CNWS, 2007.

———. "Magic, (Colonial) Science, and Science Studies." *Social Anthropology* 29, no. 4 (2013): 492–509.

———. "Magic in Translation: Ontology and Politics in Colonial Indonesia." Unpublished manuscript.

17 Magic in Common and Legal Perspectives
(by Owen Davies)

Allen, Richard C. "Wizards or Charlatans – Doctors or Herbalists? An Appraisal of the 'Cunning-Men' of Cwrt Y Cadno, Carmarthenshire." *North American Journal of Welsh Studies*, 1, no. 2 (2001): 68–84.

Beaune, Henri. *Les sorciers de Lyon: Épisode judiciaire du XVIIIe siècle*. Dijon: J.-E. Rabutot, 1868.

Behringer, Wolfgang. *Witchcraft Persecutions in Bavaria: Popular Magic, Religious Zealotry and Reason of State in Early Modern Europe*. Translated by J. C. Grayson and David Lederer. Cambridge: Cambridge University Press, 1997.

Bell, Karl. "Breaking Modernity's Spell – Magic and Modern History." *Cultural & Social History* 4 (2007): 115–123.

———. *The Magical Imagination: Magic and Modernity in Urban England, 1780–1914*. Cambridge: Cambridge University Press, 2012.

Benes, Peter. "Fortunetellers, Wise Men, and Magical Healers in New England, 1644–1850." In *Wonders of the Invisible World: 1600–1900*, edited by Peter Benes, 127–149. Boston: Boston University Press, 1992.

Bever, Edward. "Witchcraft Prosecutions and the Decline of Magic." *Journal of Interdisciplinary History* 40 (2009): 263–293.

de Blécourt, Willem. "Witch Doctors, Soothsayers and Priests: On Cunning Folk in European Historiography and Tradition." *Social History* 19 (1994): 285–303.

———. "The Witch, Her Victim, the Unwitcher and the Researcher: The Continued Existence of Traditional Witchcraft." In *Witchcraft and Magic in Europe*, vol. 6, *The Twentieth Century*, edited by Bengt Ankarloo and Stuart Clark, 141–220. London: The Athlone Press, 1999.

"On the Continuation of Witchcraft." In *Witchcraft in Early Modern Europe*, edited by Jonathan Barry, Marianne Hester, and Gareth Roberts, 335–352. Cambridge: Cambridge University Press, 2000.

"'Evil People': A Late Eighteenth-Century Dutch Witch Doctor and His Clients." In *Beyond the Witch Trials: Witchcraft and Magic in Enlightenment Europe*, edited by Owen Davies and Willem de Blécourt, 144–167. Manchester: Manchester University Press, 2004.

de Blécourt, Willem, and Owen Davies, eds. *Witchcraft Continued: Popular Magic in Modern Europe*. Manchester: Manchester University Press, 2004.

de Blécourt, Willem, and Frank Pereboom. "Insult and Admonition: Witchcraft in the Land of Vollenhove, Seventeenth Century." In *Witchcraft in the Netherlands: From the Fourteenth to the Twentieth Century*, edited by Marijke Gijswijt-Hofstra and Willem Frijhoff, 119–132. Rotterdam: Universitaire Pers, 1991.

Bourke, Angela. *The Burning of Bridget Cleary*. London: Viking, 1999.

Brittain, John N. "Hugh Bourne and the Magic Methodists." *Methodist History* 46 (2008): 132–140.

Burton, Richard D. E. *Holy Tears, Holy Blood: Women, Catholicism, and the Culture of Suffering in France, 1840–1970*. Ithaca: Cornell University Press, 2004.

"Methodism, the Clergy, and the Popular Belief in Witchcraft and Magic." *History* 82 (1997): 252–265.

Davies, Owen. "Cunning-Folk in the Medical Market-Place during the Nineteenth Century." *Medical History* 43 (1999): 55–73.

A People Bewitched: Witchcraft and Magic in Nineteenth-Century Somerset. Bruton, 1999.

Witchcraft, Magic and Culture, 1736–1951. Manchester: Manchester University Press, 1999.

Cunning-Folk: Popular Magic in English History. London: Hambledon Continuum, 2003.

"Decriminalising the Witch: The Origin of and Response to the 1736 Witchcraft Act." In *Witchcraft and the Act of 1604*, edited by John Newton and Jo Bath, 207–232. Leiden: Brill, 2008.

"European Folk Medicine." In *Traditional Medicine: A Global Perspective*, edited by Stephen B. Kayne, 25–44. London: Pharmaceutical Press, 2009.

Grimoires: A History of Magic Books. Oxford: Oxford University Press, 2009.

Magic: A Very Short Introduction. Oxford: Oxford University Press, 2012.

America Bewitched: The Story of Witchcraft after Salem. Oxford: Oxford University Press, 2013.

Davies, Owen, and Willem de Blécourt, eds. *Beyond the Witch Trials: Witchcraft and Magic in Enlightenment Europe*. Manchester: Manchester University Press, 2004.

Devlin, Judith. *The Superstition Mind: French Peasants and the Supernatural in the Nineteenth Century*. New Haven: Yale University Press, 1987.

Dillinger, Johannes. *"Evil People": A Comparative Study of Witch Hunts in Swabian Austria and the Electorate of Trier*. Translated by Laura Stokes. Charlottesville: University of Virginia Press, 2009.

Magical Treasure Hunting in Europe and North America: A History. Basingstoke: Palgrave Macmillan, 2012.

Dillinger, Johannes, and Petra Feld. "Treasure-Hunting: A Magical Motif in Law, Folklore, and Mentality, Württemberg, 1606–1770." *German History* 20 (2002): 161–184.

Bibliography

Doering-Manteuffel, Sabine. *Okkultismus: Geheimlehren, Geisterglaube, Magische Praktiken.* Munich: Beck, 2011.

Evans, E. P. "Modern Instances of Demoniacal Possession." *The Popular Science Monthly* (December 1892): 159–168.

Fiume, Giovanna. "The Old Vinegar Lady, or the Judicial Modernization of the Crime of Witchcraft." In *History from Crime: Selections from Quaderni storici*, edited by E. Muir and G. Ruggiero, 65–87. Baltimore: Johns Hopkins University Press, 1994.

Frazer, Persifor. "A Recent Chapter in the Modernist Controversy." *The American Journal of Theology* 13 (1909): 258.

Freeman, Craig, and Stephen Banning. "Rogues, Vagabonds, and Lunatics: How the Right to Listen Cleared the Future for Fortunetellers." In *Law and Magic: A Collection of Essays*, edited by Christine A. Corcos, 31–43. Durham: Carolina Academic Press, 2010.

Freytag, Nils. "Witchcraft, Witch Doctors and the Fight against 'Superstition'" in Nineteenth-Century Germany." In *Witchcraft Continued: Popular Magic in Modern Europe*, edited by Willem de Blécourt and Owen Davies, 29–46. Manchester: Manchester University Press, 2004.

Freytag, Nils, and Diethard Sawicki, eds. *Wunderwelten: Religiöse Ekstase und Magie in der Moderne.* Munich: Beck, 2006.

Van Gent, Jacqueline. *Magic, Body, and the Self in Eighteenth-Century Sweden.* Leiden: Brill, 2009.

Gentilcore, David. *From Bishop to Witch: The System of the Sacred in Early Modern Terra d'Otranto.* Manchester: Manchester University Press, 1992.

Gestrich, Andreas. "Pietismus und Aberglaube. Zum Zusammenhang von popularem Pietismus und dem Ende der Hexenverfolgung im 18. Jahrhundert." In *Das Ende der Hexenverfolgung*, edited by Sönke Lorenz and Dieter Bauer, 269–286. Stuttgart: F. Steiner, 1995.

Gijswijt-Hofstra, Marijke. "Witchcraft before Zeeland Magistrates and Church Courts, Sixteenth to Twentieth Centuries." In *Witchcraft in the Netherlands: From the Fourteenth to the Twentieth Century*, edited by Marijke Gijswijt-Hofstra and Willem Frijhoff, 103–118. Rotterdam: Universitaire Pers, 1991.

———. "Witchcraft after the Witch-Trials." In *Witchcraft and Magic in Europe*, vol. 5, *The Eighteenth and Nineteenth Centuries*, edited by Bengt Ankarloo and Stuart Clark, 95–191. London: The Athlone Press, 1999.

Goldberg, Ann. *Honor, Politics and the Law in Imperial Germany, 1871–1914.* Cambridge: Cambridge University Press, 2010.

Hanegraaff, Wouter J. "How Magic Survived the Disenchantment of the World." *Religion* 33 (2003): 357–380.

Harris, Ruth. "Possession on the Borders: The 'Mal de Morzine' in Nineteenth-Century France." *Journal of Modern History* 69 (1997): 451–478.

Hauser, Walter. *Der Justizmord an Anna Göldi: Neue Recherchen zum letzten Hexenprozess in Europa.* Zurich: Limmat, 2007.

Henke, M. "Observations on Some of the Forms of Monomania." *Medico-Chirurgical Review* 29 (1836): 216–223.

Henningsen, Gustav. "Witch Persecution after the Era of the Witch Trials." *ARV Scandinavian Yearbook of Folklore* 44 (1988): 103–153.

Hoff, Joan, and Marian Yeates. *The Cooper's Wife is Missing: The Trials of Bridget Cleary.* New York: Basic Books, 2000.

Hunter, Michael. "The Royal Society and the Decline of Magic." *Notes and Records of the Royal Society* 65 (2011): 103–119.

———. "The Decline of Magic: Challenge and Response in Early Enlightenment England." *Historical Journal* 55, no. 2 (2012): 399–423.

Kern, Edmund M. "An End to Witchcraft Trials in Austria: Reconsidering the Enlightened State." *Austrian History Yearbook* 30 (1999): 159–185.

Klaniczay, Gábor. "The Decline of Witches and the Rise of Vampires under the Eighteenth-Century Habsburg Monarchy." *Ethnologia Europaea* 17 (1987): 168–188.

———. *The Uses of Supernatural Power: The Transformation of Popular Religion in Medieval and Early-Modern Europe*. Translated by S. Singerman. Princeton: Princeton University Press, 1990.

Kord, Susanne. *Murderesses in German Writing, 1720–1860: Heroines of Horror*. Cambridge: Cambridge University Press, 2009.

Krampl, Ulrike. *Les secrets des faux sorciers: Police, magie et escroquerie à Paris au XVIIIe siècle*. Paris: L'École des hautes études en sciences sociales, 2011.

Levack, Brian P. "The Decline and End of Witchcraft Prosecutions." In *Witchcraft and Magic in Europe*, vol. 5, *The Eighteenth and Nineteenth Centuries*, edited by Bengt Ankarloo and Stuart Clark, 1–93. Philadelphia: University of Pennsylvania Press, 1999.

Leventhal, Herbert. *In the Shadow of the Enlightenment: Occultism and Renaissance Science in Eighteenth-Century America*. New York: New York University Press, 1976.

Marin-Courtoud, Benoît. "Les process de sorcellerie pendant la IIIe République." In *Le défi magique*, edited by Jean-Baptiste Martin, vol. 2, 161–173. Lyon: Presses Universitaires, 1994.

Marshall, Peter. "Disenchantment and Re-Enchantment in Europe, 1250–1920." *Historical Journal* 54, no. 2 (2011): 599–606.

Maxwell-Stuart, Peter. "Witchcraft and Magic in Eighteenth-Century Scotland." In *Beyond the Witch Trials: Witchcraft and Magic in Enlightenment Europe*, edited by Owen Davies and Willem de Blécourt, 88–91. Manchester: Manchester University Press, 2004.

McManners, John. *Church and Society in Eighteenth-Century France*. Oxford: Oxford University Press, 1998.

Meyer, Birgit. *Translating the Devil: Religion and Modernity among the Ewe in Ghana*. Trenton: Africa World Press, 1999.

Meyer, Birgit, and Peter Pels, eds. *Magic and Modernity: Interfaces of Revelation and Concealment*. Stanford: Stanford University Press, 2003.

Midelfort, H. C. Eric. *Exorcism and Enlightenment: Johann Joseph Gassner and the Demons of Eighteenth-Century Germany*. New Haven: Yale University Press, 2005.

Molero, Valérie. *Magie et sorcellerie en Espagne au siècle des Lumières 1700–1820*. Paris: l'Harmattan, 2006.

———. "Heterodoxia y herejía: La última hoguera de la inquisición española." *Nuevomundo* (February 2009), http://nuevomundo.revues.org/56542

Mozzani, Eloïse. *Magie et superstitions de la fin de l'Ancien Régime à la Restauration*. Paris: R. Laffont, 1988.

Oja, Linda. "The Superstitious Other." In *Beyond the Witch Trials: Witchcraft and Magic in Enlightenment Europe*, edited by Owen Davies and Willem de Blécourt, 69–81. Manchester: Manchester University Press, 2004.

Olli, Soili-Maria. "The Devil's Pact: A Male Strategy." In *Beyond the Witch Trials: Witchcraft and Magic in Enlightenment Europe*, edited by Owen Davies and Willem de Blécourt, 100–117. Manchester: Manchester University Press, 2004.

"Blasphemy in Early Modern Sweden – An Untold Story." *Journal of Religious History* 32, no. 4 (2008): 457–470.

Ostling, Michael. *Between the Devil and the Host: Imagining Witchcraft in Early Modern Poland*. Oxford: Oxford University Press, 2011.

Perdiguero, Enrique. "Magical Healing in Spain (1875–1936): Medical Pluralism and the Search for Hegemony." In *Witchcraft Continued: Popular Magic in Modern Europe*, edited by Willem de Blécourt and Owen Davies, 133–151. Manchester: Manchester University Press, 2004.

Perkins, Maureen. *The Reform of Time: Magic and Modernity*. Sterling, VA: Pluto Press, 2001.

Quinn, D. Michael. *Early Mormonism and the Magic World View*. Salt Lake City: Signature Books, 1998.

Ramsey, Matthew. *Professional and Popular Medicine in France, 1770–1830: The Social World of Medical Practice*. Cambridge: Cambridge University Press, 1988.

"Magical Healing, Witchcraft and Elite Discourse in Eighteenth- and Nineteenth-Century France." In *Illness and Healing Alternatives in Western Europe*, edited by Marijke Gijswijt-Hofstra, Hilary Marland, and Hans de Waardt, 14–38. Studies in the Social History of Medicine. London: Routledge, 1997.

Roper, Lyndal. *Witch Craze: Terror and Fantasy in Baroque Germany*. New Haven: Yale University Press, 2004.

Ruff, Julius R. *Crime, Justice and Public Order in Old Regime France*. London: Croom Helm, 1984.

Schiffmann, Aldona. "The Witch and the Crime: The Persecution of Witches in Twentieth-Century Poland." *ARV Scandinavian Yearbook of Folklore* 43 (1987): 147–165.

Sharpe, James. "Witchcraft in the Early Modern Isle of Man." *Cultural and Social History* 4, no. 1 (2007): 11–28.

Sörlin, Per. *Wicked Arts: Witchcraft and Magic Trials in Southern Sweden, 1635–1754*. Leiden: Brill, 1999.

Starkie, Thomas. *A Treatise of the Law of Slander, Libel, Scandalum Magnatum, and False Rumours*. London: W. Clarke, 1813.

Tallis, Lisa. "The Conjuror, the Fairy, the Devil and the Preacher: Witchcraft, Popular Magic, and Religion in Wales 1700–1905." PhD thesis, University of Swansea, 2007.

Tangherlini, Timothy R. "'How Do You Know She's a Witch?': Witches, Cunning Folk and Competition in Denmark." *Western Folklore* 59 (2000): 279–303.

Traimond, Bernard. *Le pouvoir de la maladie. Magie et politique dans les Landes de Gascogne, 1750–1826*. Bordeaux: Presses universitaires de Bordeaux, 1988.

Tschaikner, Manfred. *Schatzgräberei in Voralberg und Liechtenstein*. Bludenz: Geschichtsverein Region Bludenz, 2006.

Walker, Ronald W. "The Persistent Idea of American Treasure Hunting." *BYU Studies* 24 (1984): 429–459.

Walker, Timothy Dale. *Doctors, Folk Medicine and the Inquisition: The Repression of Magical Healing in Portugal during the Enlightenment*. Leiden: Brill, 2005.

Walsham, Alexandra. "The Reformation and 'The Disenchantment of the World' Reassessed." *Historical Journal* 51 (2008): 497–528.

Waters, Thomas. "Belief in Witchcraft in Oxfordshire and Warwickshire, c. 1860–1900: The Evidence of the Newspaper Archive." *Midland History* 34 (2009): 98–116.

Zahl, Simeon. *Pneumatology and Theology of the Cross in the Preaching of Christoph Friedrich Blumhardt.* London: T & T Clark, 2010.

18 Elite Magic in the Nineteenth Century
(by David Allen Harvey)

Andrews, Naomi Judith. *Socialism's Muse: Gender in the Intellectual Landscape of French Romantic Socialism.* New York: Lexington Books, 2006.

Blackbourn, David. *Marpingen: Appearances of the Virgin Mary in Bismarckian Germany.* Oxford: Clarendon Press, 1995.

Blavatsky, Helena Petrovna. *An Abridgement of the Secret Doctrine.* London: Theosophical Publishing House, 1966.

Bricaud, Joany. *L'Abbé Boullan (Docteur Johannes de Là-Bas): Sa vie, sa doctrine, et ses pratiques magiques.* Paris: Chacornac, 1927.

Brower, M. Brady. *Unruly Spirits: The Science of Psychic Phenomena in Modern France.* Urbana: University of Illinois Press, 2010.

Curran, Brian. *The Egyptian Renaissance: The Afterlife of Ancient Egypt in Early Modern Italy.* Chicago: University of Chicago Press, 2007.

Darnton, Robert. *Mesmerism and the End of the Enlightenment in France.* Cambridge, MA: Harvard University Press, 1968.

Decker, Ronald, Thierry Depaulis, and Michael Dummett. *A Wicked Pack of Cards: The Origins of the Occult Tarot.* New York: St. Martin's Press, 1996.

Divoire, Fernand. *Faut-il devenir mage?* Paris: Bibliothèque des Entretiens Idéalistes, 1909.

Dixon, Joy. *Divine Feminine: Theosophy and Feminism in England.* Baltimore: Johns Hopkins University Press, 2001.

Edelman, Nicole. *Voyantes, guérisseuses et visionnaires en France, 1785–1914.* Paris: Albin Michel, 1995.

Eliade, Mircea. *Occultism, Witchcraft, and Cultural Fashions: Essays in Comparative Religion.* Chicago: University of Chicago Press, 1976.

Faivre, Antoine. *Access to Western Esotericism.* Albany: State University of New York Press, 1994.

  Theosophy, Imagination, Tradition: Studies in Western Esotericism. Albany: State University of New York Press, 2000.

Le Forestier, René. *La franc-maçonnerie templière et occultiste au XVIIIe et XIXe siècles.* Paris: Aubier-Montaigne, 1970.

Godwin, Joscelyn. *The Theosophical Enlightenment.* Albany: State University of New York Press, 1994.

Goodrick-Clarke, Nicholas. *The Occult Roots of Nazism.* New York: New York University Press, 1992.

de Guaita, Stanislas. *La clef de la magie noire.* 1890. Reprint, Paris: Guy Tredaniel, 1994.

de Guaita, Stanislas. *Le temple de Satan.* Paris: Librairie du Merveilleux, 1891.

Harper, George Mills. *Yeats's Golden Dawn.* London: Macmillan, 1974.

Harvey, David Allen. *Beyond Enlightenment: Occultism and Politics in Modern France.* DeKalb: Northern Illinois University Press, 2005.

Howe, Ellic. *The Magicians of the Golden Dawn: A Documentary History of a Magical Order, 1887–1923*. London: Routledge and Kegan Paul, 1972.

Israel, Jonathan. *Radical Enlightenment: Philosophy and the Making of Modernity, 1650–1750*. Oxford and New York: Oxford University Press, 2001.

Iversen, Erik. *The Myth of Egypt and Its Hieroglyphs in European Tradition*. Copenhagen: Gec Gad, 1961. Reprint, Princeton: Princeton University Press, 1993.

Jacob, Margaret. *Living the Enlightenment: Freemasonry and Politics in Eighteenth-Century Europe*. Oxford and New York: Oxford University Press, 1991.

Jonas, Raymond A. *France and the Cult of the Sacred Heart: An Epic Tale for Modern Times*. Berkeley: University of California Press, 2000.

Kselman, Thomas A. *Miracles and Prophecies in Nineteenth Century France*. New Brunswick: Rutgers University Press, 1983.

Lachapelle, Sofie. *Investigating the Supernatural: From Spiritism and Occultism to Psychical Research and Metapsychics in France, 1853–1931*. Baltimore: Johns Hopkins University Press, 2011.

Laver, James. *The First Decadent, Being the Strange Life of J. K. Huysmans*. London: Faber and Faber, 1954.

McIntosh, Christopher. *Eliphas Levi and the French Occult Revival*. London: Rider, 1972.

Michelet, Victor-Emile. *Les compagnons de la hiérophanie: Souvenirs du mouvement hermétiste à la fin du XIXe siècle*. Paris: Dorbon ainé, n.d.

Monroe, John Warne. "Evidence of Things Not Seen: Spiritualism, Occultism, and the Search for a Modern Faith in France, 1853–1925." PhD diss., Yale University, 2002.

———. *Laboratories of Faith: Mesmerism, Spiritism, and Occultism in Modern France*. Ithaca: Cornell University Press, 2008.

Nye, Robert A. *Masculinity and Male Codes of Honor in Modern France*. Berkeley: University of California Press, 1993.

Owen, Alex. *The Place of Enchantment: British Occultism and the Culture of the Modern*. Chicago: University of Chicago Press, 2004.

Papus (Gérard Encausse). *Le tarot des bohémiens: Clef absolue de la science occulte, le plus ancien livre du monde*. Paris: Édition Dangles, 1911.

Peladan, Josephin. *Comment on devient mage*. Paris: Robert Dumas, 1975.

von Rijnberk, Gérard. *Un thaumaturge au XVIIIe siècle: Martinès de Pasqually, sa vie, ses oeuvres, son ordre*. Paris: Librairie Félix Alcan, 1935.

Schuré, Edouard. *The Great Initiates: Sketch of the Secret History of Religions*. Translated by Fred Rothwell. London: William Rider & Son, Ltd., 1912. Reprint, Philadelphia: David McKay Company, 1922.

Sharp, Lynn L. "Rational Religion, Irrational Science: Men, Women, and Belief in French Spiritism, 1853–1914." PhD diss., University of California at Irvine, 1996.

———. *Secular Spirituality: Reincarnation and Spiritism in Nineteenth-Century France*. Lanham, MD: Lexington Books, 2006.

Stevenson, David. *The Origins of Freemasonry*. Cambridge: Cambridge University Press, 1988.

Styers, Randall. *Making Magic: Religion, Magic, and Science in the Modern World*. New York and Oxford: Oxford University Press, 2004.

Thomas, Keith. *Religion and the Decline of Magic*. New York: Charles Scribner's Sons, 1971.

Treitel, Corinna. *A Science for the Soul: Occultism and the Genesis of the German Modern*. Baltimore: Johns Hopkins University Press, 2004.

Walker, D. P. *The Ancient Theology: Studies in Christian Platonism from the Fifteenth to the Eighteenth Century*. Ithaca: Cornell University Press, 1972.

Webb, James. *The Occult Underground*. La Salle, IL: Open Court Publishing Co., 1974.

Weber, Eugen. *Peasants into Frenchmen: The Modernization of Rural France, 1870–1914*. Stanford: Stanford University Press, 1976.

Wirth, Oswald. *Stanislas de Guaita, l'occultisme vécu: Souvenirs de son secrétaire*. Paris: Éditions du symbolisme, 1935.

Yates, Frances A. *The Rosicrucian Enlightenment*. London: Routledge and Kegan Paul, 1972.

19 Magic in the Postcolonial Americas (by Raquel Romberg)

Abimbola, Wande. 1996. Lecture, Haverford College, Haverford, PA.

Agosto Cintrón, Nélida. 1996. *Religión y cambio social en Puerto Rico, 1898–1940*. Río Piedras: Ediciones Huracán.

Alegría, Ricardo E. 1956. "The Fiesta of Santiago Apóstol (St. James the Apostle) in Loíza, Puerto Rico." *Journal of American Folklore* 69 (272): 123–134.

——— 1995. Conversation with the author. Centro de Estudios Avanzados de Puerto Rico y del Caribe, San Juan.

Alegría-Pons, José Francisco. 1988. "Aspectos de la religiosidad popular en Puerto Rico." San Juan: Centro de Estudios Avanzados de Puerto Rico y el Caribe. Exhibition catalog. Reprint in *La revista del Centro de Estudios Avanzados de Puerto Rico y el Caribe* 7: 105–109.

Álvarez, Lizette. 1997. "After Years of Secrecy, Santeria is Suddenly Much More Popular and Public." *The New York Times*, January 27.

Amorim, Deolindo. 1994. *Africanismo y espiritismo*. Translated by Pura Argelich Minguella. Venezuela: Ediciones Cima.

Apter, Andrew. 1991. "Herskovits's Heritage: Rethinking Syncretism in the African Diaspora." *Diaspora* 1, no. 3: 235–260.

Asad, Talal. 1983. "Anthropological Conceptions of Religion: Reflections on Geertz." *Man* 18, no. 2: 237–259.

——— 1988. "Towards a Genealogy of the Concept of Ritual." In *Vernacular Christianity, Essays in the Social Anthropology of Religion Presented to Godfrey Lienhardt*, edited Wendy James and Douglas H. Johnson, 73–87. Oxford: IASO.

——— 1993. *Genealogies of Religion: Discipline and Reasons of Power in Christianity and Islam*. Baltimore: Johns Hopkins University Press.

——— 2003. *Formations of the Secular: Christianity, Islam, Modernity*. Stanford: Stanford University Press.

Augé, Marc. 1999. *The War of Dreams: Studies in Ethno Fiction*. London: Pluto Press.

Bacigalupo, Ana Mariella. 2007. *Shamans of the Foye Tree: Gender, Power, and Healing among Chilean Mapuche*. Austin: University of Texas Press.

Barnes, Linda L., and Susan Starr Sered, eds. 2004. *Religion and Healing in America*. Oxford: Oxford University Press.

Bastide, Roger. 1978. *The African Religions of Brazil: Toward a Sociology of the Interpenetration of Civilizations*. Translated by Helen Sebba. Baltimore: Johns Hopkins University Press.

Behar, Ruth. 1987. "Sex and Sin: Witchcraft and the Devil in Late-Colonial Mexico." *American Ethnologist* 14: 34–54.

Beltran, Maria Helena Roxo. 2000. *Imagens de magia e di ciência: Entre o simbolismo e os diagramas da razão*. São Paulo: EDUC.

Benito y Cantero, Juan José. 1886. *La magia disfrazada, o sea el espiritismo*. Madrid: R. Velasco.

Berger, Helen, ed. 2005. *Witchcraft and Magic: Contemporary North America*. Philadelphia: University of Pennsylvania Press.

Berger, Peter L. 2001. "Reflections on the Sociology of Religion Today." In "Religion and Globalization at the Turn of the Millennium," special issue, *Sociology of Religion* 62, no. 4: 443–454.

———. 2006. "Religion in a Globalizing World: Pluralism, Not Secularism Is the Dominant Trend in an 'Age of Explosive, Pervasive Religiosity.'" *Pew Research Center Publications*. http://pewresearch.org/pubs/share.php

Beyer, Peter F. 1990. "Privatization and the Public Influence of Religion in Global Society." *Theory Culture Society* 7, no. 2: 373–395.

———. 1994. *Religion and Globalization*. London: Sage.

Blanco, Celia. 1988. *Manual esotérico*. Caracas: Representaciones Loga Coprensa.

Blázquez Miguel, Juan. 1994. "Brujas e inquisidores en la América." *Espacio, Tiempo y Forma*, series IV, *Historia Moderna* 7: 71–98.

Borges, Dain. 2001. "Healing and Mischief in Brazilian Law and Literature, 1890–1922." In *Crime and Punishment in Latin America: Law and Society since Late Colonial Times*, edited by D. Salvatore Ricardo and Carlos Aguirre, 181–210. Durham: Duke University Press.

Bourdieu, Pierre. 1990 [1980]. *The Logic of Practice*. Translated by Richard Nice. Stanford: Stanford University Press.

Boutrosa, Alexandra. 2011. "Gods on the Move: The Mediatisation of Vodou. In "The Mediatization of Religion," special issue, *Culture and Religion* 12, no. 2: 185–201.

Bram, Joseph. 1957. "Spirits, Mediums, and Believers in Contemporary Puerto Rico." *Transactions of the New York Academy of Sciences* 20: 340–347.

Brandon, George. 1993. *Santería from Africa to the New World: The Dead Sell Memories*. Bloomington: Indiana University Press.

Bronfman, Alejandra. 2004. *Measures of Equality: Social Science, Citizenship, and Race in Cuba, 1902–1940*. Chapel Hill: University of North Carolina Press.

Brown, David H. 1999. "Altared Spaces: Afro-Cuban Religions and the Urban Landscape in Cuba and the U.S." In *Gods of the City: Religion and the American Urban Landscape*, edited by Robert A. Orsi, 155–230. Bloomington: Indiana University Press.

———. 2003a. *The Light Inside: Abakuá Society Arts and Cuban Cultural History*. Washington, DC: Smithsonian Institution Press.

———. 2003b. *Santeria Enthroned: Art, Ritual, and Innovation in an Afro-Cuban Religion*. Chicago: University of Chicago Press.

Brown, Karen M. 1991. *Mama Lola: A Vodou Priestess in Brooklyn*. Berkeley: University of California Press.

———. 1995a. "The Altar Room: A Dialogue." In *Sacred Arts of Haitian Vodou*, edited by Donald J. Consentino, 226–239. Los Angeles: UCLA Fowler Museum of Cultural History. Exhibition catalog.

———. 1995b. "Serving the Spirits: The Ritual Economy of Haitian Vodou." In *Sacred Arts of Haitian Vodou*, edited by Donald J. Consentino, 205–225. Los Angeles: UCLA Fowler Museum of Cultural History. Exhibition catalog.

1999. "Staying Grounded in a High Rise Building: Ecological Dissonance and Ritual Accommodation in Haitian Vodou." In *Gods of the City: Religion and the American Urban Landscape*, edited by Robert A. Orsi, 79–102. Bloomington: Indiana University Press.

Cabrera, Lydia. 1958. *La sociedad secreta abakuá: Narrada por viejos adeptos*. Havana: Ediciones C & R.

1975. *El Monte*. Miami: Ediciones Universal.

1979. *Reglas de Congo, Palo Monte, Mayombe*. Miami: Colección del Chichereku en el Exilio.

Capone, Stefania. 2005. *Les Yoruba du Nouveau Monde: Religion, ethnicité et nationalisme noir aux États-Unis*. Paris: Karthala.

2010 [1999]. *Searching for Africa in Brazil: Power and Tradition in Candomblé*. Translated by Lucy Lyall Grant. Durham: Duke University Press.

Cara, Ana, and Robert Baron, eds. 2011. *Creolization: Cultural Creativity in Process*. Jackson: University Press of Mississippi.

Casanova, José. 1994. *Public Religions in the Modern World*. Chicago: University of Chicago Press.

2001. "Religion, the New Millennium, and Globalization." *Sociology of Religion* 62, no. 4: 415–441.

Castellanos, Israel. 1916. *La brujería y el ñáñiguismo en Cuba desde el punto de vista médico-legal*. Havana: Lloredo.

de Certeau, Michel. 1984. *The Practice of Everyday Life*. Translated by Steven Rendall. Berkeley: University of California Press.

1990 [1970]. *The Possession at Loudun*. Translated by Michael B. Smith. Foreword by Stephen Greenblatt. Chicago: University of Chicago Press.

Club Amor y Ciencia Arecibo, P. R. 1913. *Tesoros espirituales: Dictados de ultratumba obtenidos en Arecibo*. Arecibo: n.p.

Consentino, Donald J., ed. 1995. *Sacred Arts of Haitian Vodou*. Los Angeles: UCLA Fowler Museum of Cultural History. Exhibition catalog.

Cornelius, S. 1992. "Drumming for the Orishas: The Reconstruction of Tradition in New York City." In *Essays on Cuban Music*, edited by P. Manuel, 137–155. New York: University Press of America.

Craig, Timothy Charles. 2007. "Folk-Religious Belief and Practice in Central Mexico: Re-Constructing of Tradition and the Dynamics of Folk-Religious Plasticity." PhD diss., University of Colorado, Boulder.

Cruz Monclova, Lidio. 1957. *Historia de Puerto Rico, siglo XIX*. Río Piedras: Editorial Universitaria, Universidad de Puerto Rico.

1958. *Historia de Puerto Rico, siglo XIX*. Río Piedras: Editorial Universitaria, Universidad de Puerto Rico.

Csordas, Thomas J. 1990. "Embodiment as a Paradigm for Anthropology." *Ethos* 18, no. 1: 5–47.

1993. "Somatic Modes of Attention." *Cultural Anthropology* 8, no. 2: 135–156.

ed. 2009. *Transnational Transcendence: Essays on Religion and Globalization*. Berkeley: University of California Press.

Curbelo de Díaz, Irene. 1986. *El arte de los santeros Puertorriqueños / The Art of the Puerto Rican Santeros*. San Juan: Instituto de Cultura Puertorriqueña, Sociedad de Amigos del Museo de Santos.

Dávila, Arlene. 1997. *Sponsored Identities: Cultural Politics in Puerto Rico*. Philadelphia: Temple University Press.

Dayan, Joan. 1995. *Haiti, History and the Gods*. Berkeley: University of California Press.

———. 1997. "Vodoun, or the Voice of the Gods." In *Sacred Possessions, Vodou, Santería, Obeah and the Caribbean*, edited by Margarite Fernández-Olmos and Lizabeth Paravisini-Gebert, 13–36. New Brunswick: Rutgers University Press.

Delgado, Monica, and Michael Van Wagenen. 1997. *Spirit Doctors*. New York: Filmakers Library.

Departamento de Instrucción. 1951. *La ciencia contra la superstición*. San Juan: División de Educación de la Comunidad.

Deren, Maya. 1985. *Divine Horsemen: The Living Gods of Haiti*, independent film. Filmed 1947–1951. Narrated by Cherel Ito. Maya Deren Collection at Boston University's Howard Gotlieb Archival Research Center.

Desmangles, Leslie G. 1992. *The Faces of the Gods: Vodou and Roman Catholicism in Haiti*. Chapel Hill: University of North Carolina Press.

Díaz-Quiñones, Arcadio. 1996. "On Magic." Paper presented at the meeting of the Puerto Rican Studies Association, San Juan.

Díaz Soler, Luis M. 1974. *Historia de la esclavitud negra en Puerto Rico*. 4th ed. Río Piedras: Editorial Universitaria, Universidad de Puerto Rico.

Droogers, André. 1989. "Syncretism: The Problem of Definition, the Definition of the Problem." In *Dialogue and Syncretism: An Interdisciplinary Approach*, edited by Jerald Gort, Hendrik Vroom, Rein Fernhout, and Anton Wessels, 7–25. Grand Rapids: Eerdmans and Rodopi.

Drummond, Lee. 1980. "The Cultural Continuum: A Theory of Intersystems." *Man* 15: 352–374.

Duany, Jorge. 1998. "La religiosidad popular en Puerto Rico: Una perspectiva antropológica." In *Vírgenes, magos y escapularios: Imaginería, etnicidad y religiosidad popular en Puerto Rico*, edited by Ángel Quintero Rivera, 175–192. San Juán: Centro de Investigaciones Sociales de la Universidad de Puerto Rico.

Dunham, Katherine. 1969. *Island Possessed*. Garden City, NY: Doubleday & Co.

Exhibition Program Guide. 1994. *Face of the Gods: Art and Altars of Africa and the African Americas*. Berkeley: University of California, Berkeley.

Federação Espírita Brasileira (Brazilian Spiritist Federation) (FEB). http://www.febnet.org.br/site.

Ferguson, James, and Akhil Gupta. 1992. "Space, Identity, and the Politics of Difference." Special issue, *Cultural Anthropology* 7, no. 1: 3–120.

Fernández Méndez, Eugenio. 1976. *Crónicas de Puerto Rico, desde la conquista hasta nuestros días (1493–1955)*. Río Piedras: Editorial Universitaria, Universidad de Puerto Rico.

Fernández Olmos, Margarite, and Lizabeth Paravisini-Gebert, eds. 1996. *Sacred Possessions: Vodou, Santeria, Obeah and the Caribbean*. New Brunswick: Rutgers University Press.

———. eds. 2001. *Healing Cultures: Art and Religion as Curative Practices in the Caribbean and Its Diaspora*. New York: Palgrave.

———. eds. 2003. *Creole Religions of the Caribbean: An Introduction from Vodou and Santería to Obeah and Espiritismo*. New York: New York University Press.

Finkler, Kaja. 1985. *Spiritualist Healers in Mexico: Successes and Failures of Alternative Therapeutics*. Foreword by Arthur Kleinman. New York: Praeger.

Flaherty, Gloria. 1992. *Shamanism and the Eighteenth Century*. Princeton: Princeton University Press.

Flores-Peña, Ysamur, and Roberta J. Evanchuk. 1994. *Speaking without a Voice: Santería Garments and Altars*. Jackson: University of Mississippi Press.

Frigerio, Alejandro. 2004. "Re-Africanization in Secondary Religious Diasporas: Constructing a World Religion." *Civilisations* 51: 39–60. http://civilisations.revues.org/index656.html.

de la Fuente, Alejandro. 1998. "Race, National Discourse, and Politics in Cuba." *Latin American Perspectives* 25, no. 3: 43–69.

Garrison, Vivian. 1977. "The Puerto Rican Syndrome in Psychiatry and Espiritismo." In *Case Studies in Spirit Possession*, edited by Vincent Crapanzano and Vivian Garrison, 383–449. New York: John Wiley.

Gay, Peter. 1977 [1966]. *The Enlightenment: The Rise of Modern Paganism*. New York: W. W. Norton.

Giesler, Patrick. 2002. "Selling 'Africa' in Brazil: The Commodification of 'Africa' in the Tourist Industry, the Candomblés, and the Cafundó." Paper presented at the meeting of the Latin American Studies Association, Miami, March 16–18, 2000.

Gillespie, Michael Allen. 2009. *The Theological Origins of Modernity*. Chicago: University of Chicago Press.

Glazier, Stephen. 1996. "New World African Ritual: Genuine or Spurious." *Journal for the Scientific Study of Religion* 35, no. 4: 420–431.

Greenfield, Sydney M. 1987. "The Return of Dr Fritz: Spiritist Healing and Patronage Networks in Urban, Industrial Brazil." *Social Science and Medicine* 24, no. 12: 1095–1108.

Grosfoguel, Ramón. 1997. "The Divorce of Nationalist Discourses from the Puerto Rican People: A Sociohistorical Perspective." In *Puerto Rican Jam: Essays on Culture and Politics*, edited by F. Negrón-Muntaner and R. Grosfoguel, 55–76. Minneapolis: University of Minnesota Press.

———. 2003. *Colonial Subjects: Puerto Ricans in a Global Perspective*. Berkeley: University of California Press.

Guerra, Lilian. 1998. "Elite Appropriations of the Jíbaro." In *Popular Expression and National Identity in Puerto Rico: The Struggle for Self, Community and Nation*. Gainesville: University Press of Florida.

Habermas, Jürgen. 2008. "Secularism's Crisis of Faith: Notes on Post-Secular Society." *New Perspectives Quarterly* 25: 17–29.

Hagedorn, Katherine J. 2001. *Divine Utterances: The Performance of Afro-Cuban Santería*. Washington, DC: Smithsonian Institution Press.

Hajosy Benedetti, María Dolores. 1991. *Hasta los baños te curan! Remedios caseros y mucho más de Puerto Rico*. Saline, MI: Editorial Cultural.

Hall, Stuart. 1992. "Race, Culture, and Communications: Looking Backward and Forward at Cultural Studies." *Rethinking Marxism* 5, no. 1: 10–18.

Harding, Rachel E. 2000. *A Refuge in Thunder: Candomblé and Alternative Spaces of Blackness*. Bloomington: Indiana University Press.

Harwood, Allan. 1987. *RX: Spiritist as Needed, a Study of a Puerto Rican Community Mental Health Resource*. Ithaca: Cornell University Press.

Hazen, Craig James. 2000. *The Village Enlightenment in America: Popular Religion and Science in the Nineteenth Century*. Urbana: University of Illinois Press.

Hegerfeldt, Anne C. 2005. *Lies that Tell the Truth: Magic Realism Seen through Contemporary Fiction from Britain*. New York: Rodopi.

Herskovits, Melville J. 1937. "African Gods and Catholic Saints in New World Negro Belief." *American Anthropologist* 39, no. 4, pt. 1: 635–643.

——— 1938. *Acculturation: The Study of Culture Contact*. New York: J. J. Augustin.

Hess, David J. 1991. *Spirits and Scientists: Ideology, Spiritism and Brazilian Culture*. University Park: Penn State University Press.

Howard, Philip A. 1998. *Changing History: Afro-Cuban Cabildos and Societies of Color in the Nineteenth Century*. Baton Rouge: Louisiana State University Press.

Hurbon, Laënnec. 1995. "American Fantasy and Haitian Vodou." In *Sacred Arts of Haitian Vodou*, edited by Donald J. Consentino, 181–197. California: UCLA Fowler Museum of Cultural History. Exhibition catalog.

Jensen, Tina Gudrun. 2001. "Discursos sobre as religiões afro-brasileiras: Da desafricanização para a reafricanização." *Revista de Estudos da Religião* 1: 1–21.

Johnson, Paul Christopher. 2006. "Secretism and the Apotheosis of Duvalier." *Journal of the American Academy of Religion* 74, no. 2: 420–445.

Klein, Herbert S. 1967. *Slavery in the Americas: A Comparative Study of Virginia and Cuba*. Chicago: University of Chicago Press.

Koss, Joan. 1992. *Women as Healers, Women as Patients: Mental Health Care and Traditional Healing in Puerto Rico*. Boulder: Westview Press.

Kramer, Karen, dir. 1985. *Legacy of the Spirits*, documentary film. Watertown, MA: Documental Educational Resources. Videocassette (VHS), 52 min.

Laguerre, Michel L. 1987. *Afro-Caribbean Folk Medicine*. South Hadley, MA: Bergin and Garvey.

——— 1989. *Voodoo and Politics*. New York: St. Martin's Press.

Landy, Joshua, and Michael Saler, eds. 2009. *The Re-Enchantment of the World: Secular Magic in a Rational Age*. Stanford: Stanford University Press.

Latour, Bruno. 1993. *We Have Never Been Modern*. Translated by Catherine Porter. Cambridge, MA: Harvard University Press.

Long, Carolyn M. 2001. *Spiritual Merchants: Religion, Magic, and Commerce*. Knoxville: University of Tennessee Press.

López Cantos, Ángel. 1992. *La religiosidad popular en Puerto Rico (siglo XVIII)*. San Juan: Centro de Estudios Avanzados de Puerto Rico y el Caribe.

López Valdés, Rafael L. 1985. *Componentes africanos en el etnos cubano*. La Habana: Editorial de Ciencias Sociales.

——— 1994. *African Gods: Cuba and the Diaspora: The Adventures of Elgwa-Eshu and His Companions by Land, Sea, and Air*. Center for Latin American Studies. Rockefeller Humanities Fellowship Program on Afro-American Identity and Cultural Diversity. Gainesville: University of Florida.

——— 1995. Conversation with the author. San Juan, Puerto Rico.

Machuca, Julio. 1982. *¿Qué es el espiritismo?* San Juan: Casa de las Almas.

Macklin, Barbara June, and N. Ross Crumrine. 1973. "Three North Mexican Folk Saint Movements." *Comparative Studies in Society and History* 15, no. 1: 89–105.

Maduro, Renaldo. 1983. "Curanderismo and Latino Views of Disease and Curing." *Western Journal of Medicine* 139, no. 6: 868–874.

Marx, Karl. 1983 [1867]. "Commodities (Capital vol. 1)." In *The Portable Karl Marx*, edited by Eugene Kameka, 437–461. New York: Penguin Books.

Masquelier, Adeline. 2004. "The Return of Magic." *Social Anthropology* 12, no. 1: 95–102.

Matibag, Eugenio. 1996. *Afro-Cuban Religious Experience: Cultural Reflections in Narrative.* Gainesville: University Press of Florida.

Matory, J. L. 2005. *Black Atlantic Religion: Tradition, Transnationalism, and Matriarchy in the Afro-Brazilian Candomblé.* Princeton: Princeton University Press.

Menéndez Vázquez, Lázara. 1995. "¡¿Un cake para Obatalá?!" *Temas* 4: 38–51.

Mesa Redonda Espírita de Puerto Rico. 1969. *¿Qué es el espiritismo científico?* San Juan: Mesa Redonda Espírita de Puerto Rico.

Meyer, Birgit. 2010. "'There Is a Spirit in that Image': Mass-Produced Jesus Pictures and Protestant-Pentecostal Animation in Ghana." *Comparative Studies in Society and History* 52: 100–130.

Meyer, Birgit, and Peter Pels, eds. 2003. *Magic and Modernity: Interfaces of Revelation and Concealment.* Stanford: Stanford University Press.

Mintz, Sidney W. 1974. *Caribbean Transformations.* New York: Columbia University Press.

Moore, Robin. 1994. "Representations of Afrocuban Expressive Culture in the Writings of Fernando Ortiz." *Latin American Music Review / Revista de Música Latinoamericana* 15, no. 1: 32–54.

———. 1997. *Nationalizing Blackness: Afrocubanismo and Artistic Revolution in Havana, 1920–1940.* Pittsburgh: University of Pittsburgh Press.

Moreno de los Arcos, Roberto. 1991. "New Spain's Inquisition for Indians from the Sixteenth to the Nineteenth Century." In *Cultural Encounters: The Impact of the Inquisition in Spain and the New World*, edited by Mary Elizabeth Perry and Anne J. Cruz, 23–36. Berkeley: University of California Press.

Motta, Roberto. 1994. "Ethnicité, nationalité et syncrétisme dans les religions populaires Brésiliennes." *Social Compass* 41, no. 1: 67–78.

Mudimbe, V. Y. 1988. *The Invention of Africa.* Bloomington: Indiana University Press.

———. 1994. *The Idea of Africa.* Bloomington: Indiana University Press.

Murga, Vicente, and Álvaro Huerga, eds. 1989. *Episcopologio de Puerto Rico III de Francisco de Cabrera a Francisco de Padilla (1611–1695).* Ponce, Puerto Rico: Universidad Católica de Puerto Rico.

Murphy, Joseph M. 1988. *Santeria: An African Religion in America.* Boston: Beacon Press.

———. 1994. *Working the Spirit: Ceremonies of the African Diaspora.* Boston: Beacon Press.

———. 2010. "Objects that Speak Creole: Juxtapositions of Shrine Devotions at Botánicas in Washington, DC." *Material Religion* 6, no. 1: 86–109.

Núñez Meléndez, E. 1982. *Plantas medicinales de Puerto Rico, folklore y fundamentos scientíficos.* Río Piedras: Editorial de la Universidad de Puerto Rico.

Núñez Molina, Mario A. 1990. "Therapeutic and Preventive Functions of Puerto Rican Espiritismo." *Homines: Revista Latinoamericana de Ciencias Sociales* 14, no. 1: 267–276.

Ochoa, Todd Ramón. 2010a. "Prendas-Ngangas-Enquisos: Turbulence and the Influence of the Dead in Cuban-Kongo Material Culture." *Cultural Anthropology* 25: 387–420.

———. 2010b. *Society of the Dead: Quita Manaquita and Palo Praise in Cuba.* Berkeley: University of California Press.

Ortiz, Fernando. 1906. *La hampa Afrocubana: Los negros brujos*. Madrid: La Librería de Fernando Fé.

— 1995 [1940]. *Cuban Counterpoint: Tobacco and Sugar*. Translated by Harriet de Onis. Introduction by Bronislaw Malinowski. Prologue by Herminio Portell Vila. New York: Alfred A. Knopf.

Ortiz Aponte, Sally. 1977. *La esotería en la narrativa hispanoamericana*. Río Piedras: Editorial Universitaria, Universidad de Puerto Rico.

Otero, Solimar. 2010. *Afro-Cuban Diasporas in the Atlantic World*. Rochester, NY: University of Rochester Press.

Padilla, Anna María. 2003. "Rezadoras y animadoras: Women, Faith, and Community in Northern New Mexico and Southern Colorado." In "Recovering the U.S. Hispanic Catholic Heritage, Part Two: Parishes, Organizations, and Latina Leadership," special issue, *U.S. Catholic Historian* 21, no. 1: 73–81.

Palmer, Craig T., Lyle B. Steadman, Chris Cassidy, and Kathryn Coe. 2010. "The Importance of Magic to Social Relationships." *Zygon* 45, no. 2: 317–327.

Palmié, Stephan. 1995. "Against Syncretism: Africanizing and Cubanizing Discourses in North American Òrìsà-Worship." In *Counterworks: Managing Diverse Knowledge*, edited by Richard Fardon, 73–104. London: Routledge.

— 2002. *Wizards and Scientists: Explorations in Afro-Cuban Modernity and Tradition*. Durham: Duke University Press.

— 2004. "Fascinans or Tremendum? Permutations of the State, the Body, and the Divine in Late-Twentieth Century Havana." *New West Indian Guide* 78, no. 3/4: 229–268.

— 2006. "Thinking with Ngangas: Reflections on Embodiment and the Limits of 'Objectively Necessary Appearances.'" *Comparative Studies in Society and History* 48, no. 4: 852–886.

— 2008. "On Predications of Africanity." In *Africas of the Americas: Beyond the Search for Origins in the Study of Afro-Atlantic Religions*, edited by Stephan Palmié, 1–37. Leiden: Brill.

Paravisini-Gebert, Lizabeth. 1996. "Eroticism and Exoticism in the Representation of Woman as Zombie." In *Sacred Possessions, Vodou, Santería, Obeah and the Caribbean*, edited by Margarite Fernández-Olmos and Lizabeth Paravisini-Gebert, 37–58. New Brunswick: Rutgers University Press.

Pels, Peter. 2003. "Spirits of Modernity: Alfred Wallace, Edward Tylor, and the Visual Politics of Fact." In *Magic and Modernity: Interfaces of Revelation and Concealment*, edited by Birgit Meyer and Peter Pels, 241–271. Stanford: Stanford University Press.

Pollak-Eltz, Angelina. 1994. *Black Culture and Society in Venezuela*. Caracas: Public Affairs Department of Lagoven.

— 2003. "Imagination in the Creation of New Spiritual Cults in Latin America." In *Imagination in Religion and Social Life*, edited by George F. McLean and John K. White, 79–88. Washington, DC: The Council for Research in Values and Philosophy.

Quezada, Noemí. 1991. "The Inquisition's Repression of Curanderos." In *Cultural Encounters: The Impact of the Inquisition in Spain and the New World*, edited by Mary Elizabeth Perry and Anne J. Cruz, 37–57. Berkeley: University of California Press.

Quintero Rivera, Ángel. 1995. Conversation with the author. Universidad de Puerto Rico, Río Piedras.

Reiff, Marian, Bonnie O'Connor, Fredi Kronenberg, and Michael Balick. 2003. "Ethnomedicine in the Urban Environment: Dominican Healers in New York City." *Human Organization* 62, no. 1: 12–27.

Rey, Terry. 2007. Review of *Les Yoruba du Nouveau Monde: Religion, ethnicité et nationalisme noir aux États-Unis*, by Stefania Capone. *Archives de sciences sociales des religions* 140. Doc. 140-14, http://assr.revues.org/10283

Rodríguez Escudero, Néstor A. 1991. *Historia del espiritismo en Puerto Rico*. 2nd ed. Aguadilla.

Román, Reinaldo L. 2007. "Governing Spirits: Religion, Miracles, and Spectacles in Cuba and Puerto Rico, 1898–1956." Chapel Hill: University of North Carolina Press.

Romberg, Raquel. 1998. "Whose Spirits Are They? The Political Economy of Syncretism and Authenticity." *Journal of Folklore Research* 35, no. 1: 69–82.

———. 2003a. "From Charlatans to Saviors: *Espiritistas*, *Curanderos*, and *Brujos* Inscribed in Discourses of Progress and Heritage." *Centro Journal* 15, no. 2: 146–173.

———. 2003b. *Witchcraft and Welfare: Spiritual Capital and the Business of Magic in Modern Puerto Rico*. Austin: University of Texas Press.

———. 2005a. "Global Spirituality: Consumerism and Heritage in an Afro-Caribbean Folk Religion." In *Caribbean Societies and Globalization*, edited by Franklin W. Knight and Teresita Martínez-Vergne, 131–156. Chapel Hill: University of North Carolina Press.

———. 2005b. "Ritual Piracy: Or Creolization with an Attitude?" *New West Indian Guide* 79, nos. 3–4): 175–218.

———. 2007. "Today, Changó is Changó: Or How Africanness Becomes a Ritual Commodity in Puerto Rico." *Western Folklore* 66, nos. 1–2: 75–106.

———. 2009. *Healing Dramas: Divination and Magic in Modern Puerto Rico*. Austin: University of Texas Press.

———. 2011a. "Flying Witches, Embodied Memories, and the Wanderings of an Anthropologist." In *Serendipity in Anthropological Research: The Nomadic Turn*, edited by Haim Haza and Esther Herzog, 157–174. Burlington, VT: Ashgate Press.

———. 2011b. "Spiritual Capital: On the Materiality and Immateriality of Blessings in Puerto Rican Brujería." In *The Economics of Religion: Anthropological Approaches*, edited by Lionel Obadia and Donald C. Wood, 123–156. Research in Economic Anthropology 31. Bradford, England: Emerald Group Publishing Limited.

———. 2011c. "Creolization or Ritual Piracy? In *Creolization: Cultural Creativity in Process*, edited by Ana Cara and Robert Baron, 109–136. Jackson: University Press of Mississippi.

———. 2012a. "The Moral Economy of Brujería under the Modern Colony: A Pirated Modernity?" In *Obeah and Other Powers: The Politics of Caribbean Religion and Healing*, edited by D. Paton, and Maarit Forde, 288–315. Durham: Duke University Press.

———. 2012b. "Sensing the Spirits: The Healing Dramas and Poetics of Brujería Rituals." In "Good Spirit, Good Medicine: Foundations of Healing in Caribbean Religions," edited by George Brandon, special issue, *Anthropologica* 54, no. 2: 211–225.

Routon, Kenneth. 2010. *Hidden Powers of State in the Cuban Imagination*. Gainesville: University Press of Florida.

Sansi Roca, Roger. 2007. "'Dinheiro Vivo': Money and Religion in Brazil." *Critique of Anthropology* 27, no. 3: 319–339.

Santo, Diana Espirito. 2010. "'Who Else Is in the Drawer?' Trauma, Personhood and Prophylaxis among Cuban Scientific Spiritists." *Anthropology and Medicine* 17, no. 3: 249–259.

Scheper-Hughes, Nancy, and David Stewart. 1983. "Curanderismo in Taos County, New Mexico: A Possible Case of Anthropological Romanticism?" *The Western Journal of Medicine* 139, no. 6: 875–884.

Scott, David, and Charles Hirschkind, eds. 2006. *Powers of the Secular Modern: Talal Asad and His Interlocutors*. Stanford: Stanford University Press.

Sharot, Stephen. 2001. *A Comparative Sociology of World Religions: Virtuosos, Priests, and Popular Religion*. New York: New York University Press.

Sharp, Lynn L. 2006. *Secular Spirituality: Reincarnation and Spiritism in Nineteenth-Century France*. Lanham, MD: Lexington Books.

Shefferman, David Adam. 2006. "Displacing Magic: Afro-Cuban Studies and the Production of Santeria, 1933–1956: Fernando Ortiz, Alejo Carpentier, R. Lachatañere, Nicolás Guillén." PhD diss., University of North Carolina at Chapel Hill.

Sheller, Mimi. 2003. *Consuming the Caribbean: From Arawaks to Zombies*. London: Routledge.

Sowell, David. 2001. *The Tale of Healer Miguel Perdomo Neira: Medicine, Ideologies, and Power in the Nineteenth-Century Andes*. Rowman & Littlefield Publishers.

——— 2003. "Contending Medical Ideologies and State Formation: The Nineteenth-Century Origins of Medical Pluralism in Contemporary Colombia." *Bulletin of the History of Medicine* 77, no. 4: 900–926.

Stewart, Charles. 1995. "Relocating Syncretism in Social Science Discourse." In *Syncretism and the Commerce of Symbols*, edited by Göran Aijmer, 13–37. Goteborg, Sweden: IASA.

——— ed. 2005. *Creolization: History, Ethnography, Theory*. Walnut Creek, CA: Left Coast Press.

Stewart, Charles, and Rosalind Shaw, eds. 1994. *Syncretism/Anti-Syncretism. The Politics of Religious Synthesis*. London and New York: Routledge.

Stoller, Paul. 1995. *Embodying Colonial Memories: Spirit Possession, Power, and the Hauka in West Africa*. New York: Routledge.

——— 1997. *Sensuous Scholarship*. Philadelphia: Pennsylvania University Press.

Styers, Randall. 2004. *Making Magic: Religion, Magic, and Science in the Modern World*. New York and Oxford: Oxford University Press.

Tambiah, Stanley J. 1990. *Magic, Science, Religion, and the Scope of Rationality*. Cambridge: Cambridge University Press.

Taussig, Michael. 1980. *The Devil and Commodity Fetishism in South America*. Chapel Hill: University of North Carolina Press.

——— 1987. *Shamanism, Colonialism, and the Wild Man: A Study of Terror and Healing*. Chicago: University of Chicago Press.

——— 1993. *Mimesis and Alterity: A Particular History of the Senses*. New York: Routledge.

——— 1997. *Magic of the State*. New York: Routledge.

Taylor, Charles. 1994 [1992]. *Multiculturalism, Examining the Politics of Recognition*. Edited by Amy Gutmann. Princeton: Princeton University Press.

——— 2007. *A Secular Age*. Cambridge, MA: Belknap Press of Harvard University Press.

Taylor, Mark C. 2007. *After God*. Chicago: University of Chicago Press.

Thompson, Robert Farris. 1983. *Flash of the Spirit: African and Afro-American Art and Philosophy*. New York: Random House.

1993. *Face of the Gods: Art and Altars of Africa and the African Americas.* New York: Museum for African Art. Exhibition catalog.

Trotter, Robert T. 1997. *Curanderismo, Mexican American Folk Healing.* Athens, GA: University of Georgia Press.

Tsing, Anna Lowenhaupt. 1994. "From the Margins." *Cultural Anthropology* 9, no. 3: 279–297.

Vidal, Jaime R. 1994. Citizens yet Strangers: The Puerto Rican Experience." In *Puerto Rican and Cuban Catholics in the U.S. 1900–1965,* edited by Jay P. Dolan and Jaime R. Vidal, 10–143. Notre Dame: University of Notre Dame Press.

Warnes, Christopher. 2005. "Naturalizing the Supernatural: Faith, Irreverence and Magical Realism." *Literature Compass* 2, no. 1: 1–16.

Weber, Max. 1958 [1930]. *The Protestant Ethic and the Spirit of Capitalism.* Translated by Talcott Parsons. New York: Charles Scribner's Sons.

——— 1960. "Gods, Magicians and Priests." In *From the Sociology of Religion,* edited by Roland Robertson, 407–418. New York: Penguin Books.

Wedel, Johan. 2004. *Santería Healing: A Journey into the Afro-Cuban World of Divinities, Spirits, and Sorcery.* Gainesville: University Press of Florida.

Wexler, Philip. 2007. *The Mystical Society: An Emerging Social Vision* [Hebrew]. Jerusalem: Carmel.

Williams, Raymond. 1980. "Base and Superstructure in Marxist Theory." In *Problems in Materialism: Selected Readings,* 31–49. London: Verso.

Yañez, Teresa Vda. de Otero. 1963. *El espiritismo en Puerto Rico.* San Juan: Cooperativas de Artes Gráficas Romualdo Real.

Yelvington, Kevin A. 2001. "The Anthropology of Afro-Latin America and the Caribbean: Diasporic Dimensions." *Annual Review of Anthropology* 30: 227–260.

——— 2006a. "Introduction." In *Afro-Atlantic Dialogues: Anthropology in the Diaspora,* edited by Kevin A. Yelvington, 3–32. Santa Fe: School of American Research.

——— 2006b. "The Invention of Africa in Latin America and the Caribbean: Political Discourse and Anthropological Praxis, 1920–1940." In *Afro-Atlantic Dialogues: Anthropology in the Diaspora,* edited by Kevin A. Yelvington, 35–82. Santa Fe: School of American Research.

Zenón Cruz, I. 1974. *Narciso descubre su trasero: El negro en la cultura Puertorriqueña.* Vol. 1. Humacao: Editorial Furidi.

20 New Age and Neopagan Magic (by Sabina Magliocco)

Adler, Margot. *Drawing down the Moon.* Boston: Beacon Press, 1979.

Asad, Talal. "Anthropological Conceptions of Religion: Reflections on Geertz." *Man* 18, no. 2 (1983): 237–259.

Bender, Courtney. *The New Metaphysicals: Spirituality and the American Religious Imagination.* Chicago: University of Chicago Press, 2010.

Berger, Helen. "Fifteen Years of Continuity and Change within the American Pagan Community." Paper presented at the meeting of the American Academy of Religion, San Francisco, November 2011.

Blain, Jenny. *Nine Worlds of Seid-Magic: Ecstasy and Neo-Shamanism in North European Paganism.* London: Routledge, 2002.

Bonewits, P. E. Isaac. *Real Magic*. New York: Coward, McCann & Geoghegan, 1971. Reprint, New York, Weiser, 1989.

Brown, Michael F. *The Channeling Zone: American Spirituality in an Anxious Age*. Cambridge, MA: Harvard University Press, 1997.

Burnett, Charles, and W. F. Ryan, eds. *Magic and the Classical Tradition*. Warburg Institute Colloquia 7. London and Turin: Warburg Institute and Nino Aragno, 2006.

Casteneda, Carlos. *The Teachings of Don Juan: A Yaqui Way of Knowledge*. Berkeley: University of California Press, 1968.

Cusack, Carole M. *Invented Religions: Imagination, Fiction and Faith*. Burlington, VT: Ashgate, 2010.

Drury, Nevill. *Stealing Fire from Heaven: The Rise of Modern Western Magic*. Oxford and New York: Oxford University Press, 2011.

Durkheim, Émile. *The Elementary Forms of the Religious Life*. New York: Free Press, 1965.

Evans-Pritchard, E. E. *Witchcraft, Oracles and Magic among the Azande*. Oxford: Oxford University Press, 1976.

Faivre, Antoine. *The Eternal Hermes: From Greek God to Alchemical Magus*. Grand Rapids: Phanes Press, 1995.

Geertz, Clifford. "Religion as a Cultural System." In *The Interpretation of Cultures*, 87–125. New York: Basic Books, 1973.

Goffman, Erving. *Frame Analysis: An Essay on the Organization of Experience*. New York: Harper and Row, 1974.

Greenwood, Susan. *The Nature of Magic: An Anthropology of Consciousness*. Oxford: Berg, 2009.

Hale, Amy. "John Michell, Radical Traditionalism and the Emerging Politics of the Pagan New Right." *The Pomegranate* 13, no. 1 (2011): 77–97.

Hanegraaff, Wouter J. *New Age Religion and Western Culture*. Albany: State University of New York Press, 1998.

  "Beyond the Yates Paradigm: The Study of Western Esotericism between Counterculture." *Aries* 1 (2001): 5–37.

Harner, Michael. *The Jivaro: People of the Sacred Waterfalls*. Berkeley: University of California Press, 1972.

Heelas, Paul. *Spiritualities of Life: New Age Romanticism and Consumptive Capitalism*. Hoboken: Wiley-Blackwell, 2008.

Heselton, Philip. *Witchfather: A Life of Gerald Gardner*. Vol. 1, *Into the Witch Cult*. Loughborough, Leicestershire: Thoth Publications, 2012.

Hess, David J. *Science and the New Age: The Paranormal, Its Defenders and Debunkers, and American Culture*. Madison: University of Wisconsin Press, 1993.

Hutton, Ronald. *Triumph of the Moon: A History of Modern Pagan Witchcraft*. Oxford: Oxford University Press, 1999.

  "The New Old Paganism." In *Witches, Druids and King Arthur*, edited by Ronald Hutton, 87–135. London: Hambledon and London, 2003.

  The Druids. London: Hambledon, 2007.

  "Modern Pagan Festivals." *Folklore* 119 (2008): 251–273.

Lesiv, Maria. *The Return of Ancestral Gods: Modern Ukrainian Paganism as an Alternative Vision for a Nation*. Montreal: McGill University Press, 2013.

Lewis, James R., and J. Gordon Melton. *Perspectives on the New Age*. Albany: State University of New York Press, 1992.

Lewis James R., and M. Pizza, eds. *Handbook of Contemporary Paganism*. Leiden: Brill, 2009.

Lucentini, Paolo, Ilaria Parri, and Vittoria Perrone Compagni, eds. *Hermetism from Late Antiquity to Humanism / La tradizione ermetica dal mondo tardo-antico all'umanesimo*. Instrumenta Patristica et Mediaevalia 40. Turnhout: Brepols, 2003.

Luhrmann, T. M. *Persuasions of the Witches' Craft*. Cambridge, MA: Harvard University Press, 1979.

Magliocco, Sabina. *Witching Culture: Folklore and Neopaganism in America*. Philadelphia: University of Pennsylvania Press, 2004.

McLaughlin, Corrine. *Spiritual Politics*. New York: Ballantine Books, 1994.

Melton, J. Gordon, J. Clark, and A. Kelly, eds. *The New Age Encyclopedia*. Detroit and New York: Gale Research, 1990.

Pike, Sarah. *New Age and Neopagan Religion in America*. New York: Columbia University Press, 2004.

Roszak, Theodore. *Person/Planet: The Creative Disintegration of an Industrial Society*. New York: Doubleday, 1978.

Satin, Mark. *New Age Politics: Healing Self and Society*. New York: Dell Publishing Company, 1979.

Strmiska, Michael. *Modern Paganism in World Cultures*. Santa Barbara: ABC-CLIO, 2006.

Styers, Randall. *Making Magic: Religion, Magic, and Science in the Modern World*. New York and Oxford: Oxford University Press, 2004.

Sutcliffe, Stephen. *Children of the New Age: A History of Spiritual Practices*. New York and London: Routledge, 2002.

Sutcliffe Stephen J., and Ingvild S. Gilhus. *New Age Spirituality: Rethinking Religion*. New York and London: Routledge, 2014.

Tambiah, Stanley J. *Magic, Science, Religion, and the Scope of Rationality*. Cambridge: Cambridge University Press, 1990.

Wax, Murray, and Rosalie Wax. "The Notion of Magic." *Current Anthropology* 4 (1963): 495–518.

Wood, Matthew. *Possession, Power and the New Age: Ambiguities of Authority in Neoliberal Societies*. Burlington, VT: Ashgate, 2007.

York, Michael. *The Emerging Network: A Sociology of the New Age and Neo-Pagan Movements*. London: Rowman & Littlefield, 1995.

"Invented Culture / Invented Religion: The Fictional Origins of Contemporary Paganism." *Nova Religio* 3, no. 1 (1999): 135–146.

Index